T0224131

Communications in
Computer and Information Science 562

Commenced Publication in 2007
Founding and Former Series Editors:
Alfredo Cuzzocrea, Dominik Ślęzak, and Xiaokang Yang

Editorial Board

Simone Diniz Junqueira Barbosa
Pontifical Catholic University of Rio de Janeiro (PUC-Rio),
Rio de Janeiro, Brazil
Phoebe Chen
La Trobe University, Melbourne, Australia
Xiaoyong Du
Renmin University of China, Beijing, China
Joaquim Filipe
Polytechnic Institute of Setúbal, Setúbal, Portugal
Orhun Kara
TÜBİTAK BİLGEM and Middle East Technical University, Ankara, Turkey
Igor Kotenko
St. Petersburg Institute for Informatics and Automation of the Russian
Academy of Sciences, St. Petersburg, Russia
Ting Liu
Harbin Institute of Technology (HIT), Harbin, China
Krishna M. Sivalingam
Indian Institute of Technology Madras, Chennai, India
Takashi Washio
Osaka University, Osaka, Japan

More information about this series at http://www.springer.com/series/7899

Maoguo Gong · Linqiang Pan · Tao Song
Ke Tang · Xingyi Zhang (Eds.)

Bio-Inspired Computing – Theories and Applications

10th International Conference, BIC-TA 2015
Hefei, China, September 25–28, 2015
Proceedings

Springer

Editors

Maoguo Gong
Xidian University
Xi'an
China

Linqiang Pan
Huazhong University of Science
  and Technology
Wuhan
China

Tao Song
University of Petroleum
Qingdao
China

Ke Tang
University of Science and Technology
  of China
Hefei
China

Xingyi Zhang
Anhui University
Hefei
China

ISSN 1865-0929   ISSN 1865-0937 (electronic)
Communications in Computer and Information Science
ISBN 978-3-662-49013-6   ISBN 978-3-662-49014-3 (eBook)
DOI 10.1007/978-3-662-49014-3

Library of Congress Control Number: 2015956129

© Springer-Verlag Berlin Heidelberg 2015
This work is subject to copyright. All rights are reserved by the Publisher, whether the whole or part of the material is concerned, specifically the rights of translation, reprinting, reuse of illustrations, recitation, broadcasting, reproduction on microfilms or in any other physical way, and transmission or information storage and retrieval, electronic adaptation, computer software, or by similar or dissimilar methodology now known or hereafter developed.
The use of general descriptive names, registered names, trademarks, service marks, etc. in this publication does not imply, even in the absence of a specific statement, that such names are exempt from the relevant protective laws and regulations and therefore free for general use.
The publisher, the authors and the editors are safe to assume that the advice and information in this book are believed to be true and accurate at the date of publication. Neither the publisher nor the authors or the editors give a warranty, express or implied, with respect to the material contained herein or for any errors or omissions that may have been made.

Printed on acid-free paper

This Springer imprint is published by SpringerNature
The registered company is Springer-Verlag GmbH Berlin Heidelberg

Preface

Bio-inspired computing is a field of study that abstracts computing ideas from living phenomena or biological systems. The ideas provide abundant inspiration for constructing high-performance computing models and intelligent algorithms, which relies heavily on the inter-discipline of biology, computer science, and mathematics.

Bio-Inspired Computing: Theories and Applications (BIC-TA) is a series of conferences that aims to bring together researchers working in the main areas of natural computing inspired from biology, for presenting their recent results, exchanging ideas, and cooperating in a friendly framework. The four main topics are evolutionary computing, neural computing, DNA computing, and membrane computing.

Since 2006, the conference has taken place at Wuhan (China, 2006), Zhengzhou (China, 2007), Adelaide (Australia, 2008), Beijing (China, 2009), Liverpool (UK, 2010) and Changsha (China, 2010), Penang (Malaysia, 2011), Gwalior (India, 2012), Huangshan (China, 2013), and Wuhan (China, 2014). Following the success of previous editions, the 10th International Conference on Bio-Inspired Computing: Theories and Applications (BIC-TA 2015) was organized by the University of Science and Technology of China, Huazhong University of Science and Technology, Anhui University, National University of Defense Technology, and the Special Committee of Information System and Management Science (System Engineering and Management Society of Hunan Province) in Hefei, China, during September 25–28, 2015.

BIC-TA 2015 attracted a wide spectrum of interesting research papers on various aspects of bio-inspired computing with a diverse range of theories and applications. We received 182 submissions and 63 papers were selected for this volume of *Communications in Computer and Information Science*.

We gratefully acknowledge the financial support of the National Natural Science Foundation of China. We thank the organizers and co-organizers for extensive assistance in organizing the conference. We also thank all other volunteers, whose efforts ensured a smooth running of the conference.

The editors warmly thank the Program Committee members for their prompt and efficient support in reviewing the papers, and the authors of the submitted papers for their interesting papers. Special thanks are due to Springer for the efficient cooperation in the timely production of this volume.

September 2015

Maoguo Gong
Linqiang Pan
Tao Song
Ke Tang
Xingyi Zhang

Organization

Steering Committee

Guangzhao Cui	Zhengzhou University of Light Industry, China
Kalyanmoy Deb	Indian Institute of Technology Kanpur, India
Miki Hirabayashi	National Institute of Information and Communications Technology (NICT), Japan
Joshua Knowles	University of Manchester, UK
Thom LaBean	North Carolina State University, USA
Jiuyong Li	University of South Australia, Australia
Kenli Li	University of Hunan, China
Giancarlo Mauri	Università di Milano-Bicocca, Italy
Yongli Mi	Hong Kong University of Science and Technology, Hong Kong, SAR China
Atulya K. Nagar	Liverpool Hope University, UK
Linqiang Pan	Huazhong University of Science and Technology, China
Gheorghe Păun	Romanian Academy, Bucharest, Romania
Mario J. Pérez-Jiménez	University of Seville, Spain
K.G. Subramanian	Universiti Sains Malaysia, Malaysia
Robinson Thamburaj	Madras Christian College, India
Jin Xu	Peking University, China
Hao Yan	Arizona State University, USA

Program Committee Chairs

Maoguo Gong	Xidian University, China
Linqiang Pan	Huazhong University of Science and Technology, China
Ke Tang	University of Science and Technology of China, China

Local Organizing Chair

Xingyi Zhang	Anhui University, China

Registration Chair

Tingfang Wu	Huazhong University of Science and Technology, China

Publication Chairs

Zhihua Cui	Taiyuan University of Science and Technology, China
Tao Song	China University of Petroleum (Huadong), China

Program Committee

Rosni Abdullah	Universiti Sains Malaysia, Malaysia
Muhammad Abulaish	King Saud University, Saudi Arabia
Chang Wook Ahn	Sungkyunkwan University, South Korea
Adel AlJumaily	Uinversity of Technology Sydney, Australia
Bahareh Asadi	Islamic Azad University Tabriz Branch, Iran
Eduard Babulak	EU CORDIS, Europe
Mehdi Bahrami	Rafsanjan University of Medical Sciences, Iran
Soumya Banerjee	Birla Institute of Technology Mesra, India
Jagdish Chand Bansal	ABV Indian Institute of Information Technology and Managemment, India
Debnath Bhattacharyya	Heritage Institute of Technology, India
Monowar H. Bhuyan	Tezpur University, India
Kavita Burse	Truba Institute of Engineering and Information Technology, India
Xinye Cai	Nanjing University of Aeronautics and Astronautics, China
Michael Chen	University of Jinan, China
Zhihua Chen	Huazhong University of Science and Technology, China
Ran Cheng	University of Surrey, UK
Tsung Che Chiang	National Taiwan Normal University, Taiwan
Raymond Chiong	University of Newcastle, Australia
Sung-Bae Cho	Yonsei University, South Korea
Joseph Chrol Cannon	University of Surrey, UK
Carlos A. Coello Coello	Cinvestavipn, Mexico
Zhihua Cui	Taiyuan University of Science and Technology, China
Kadian Davis	University College of the Caribbean, Jamaica
Sumithra Devi K.A.	RV College of Engineering, India
Ciprian Dobre	University Politehnica of Bucharest, Romania
Amit Dutta	Barkatullah University, India
Eugene Eberbach	Rensselaer Polytechnic Institute, USA
Michael Emmerich	Leiden University, The Netherlands
Andries Engelbrecht	University of Pretoria, South Africa
Zhun Fan	Shantou University, China
Carlos Fernandez-Llatas	Universidad Politecnica de Valencia, Spain
Pierluigi Frisco	Heriot Watt University, UK
Marian Gheorghe	University of Bradford, UK
Wenyin Gong	China University of Geosciences, China
Shan He	University of Birmingham, UK
Jer Lang Hong	Taylors University, Malaysia
Tzung Pei Hong	National University of Kaohsiung, Taiwan
Wei Chiang Hong	Oriental Institute of Science and Technology, Taiwan
Han Huang	South China University of Technology, China
Florentin Eugen Ipate	University of Bucharest, Romania

Sriman Narayana Iyengar	VIT University, India
Antonio J. Jara	University of Murcia, Spain
Sunil Kumar Jha	Banaras Hindu University, India
Guoli Ji	Xiamen University, China
He Jiang	Dalian University of Technology, China
Licheng Jiao	Xidian University, China
Mohamed Rawidean Mohd Kassim	National R&D Centre in ICT, Malaysia
Liangjun Ke	Xi'an Jiaotong University, China
M. Ayoub Khan	Centre for Development of Advanced Computing, India
Razib Hayat Khan	Norwegian University of Science and Technology, Norway
Joanna Kolodziej	University of Bielsko-Biala, Poland
Per KristianLehre	University of Nottingham, UK
Ashwani Kush	Kurukshetra University, India
Shyam Lal	Moradabad Institute of Technology, India
Stephen C.H. Leung	City University of Hong Kong, SAR China
Lenka Lhotska	Czech Technical University, Czech
Kenli Li	Hunan University, China
Ke Li	Michigan State University, USA
Miqing Li	Brunel University London, UK
Xiaodong Li	RMIT University, Australia
Jing Liang	Zhengzhou University, China
Chun Wei Lin	National University of Kaohsiung, Taiwan
Xiangrong Liu	University of Illinois at Urbana-Champaign, USA
Jose Antonio Lozano	University of the Basque Country, Spain
Wenjian Luo	University of Science and Technology of China, China
Chaomin Luo	University of Detroit Mercy, USA
Wanli Ma	University of Canberra, Australia
Mahdi Mahfouf	University of Sheffield, UK
Vittorio Maniezzo	University of Bologna, Italy
Francesco Marcelloni	University of Pisa, Italy
Efrn Mezura Montes	University of Veracruz, Mexico
Hongwei Mo	Harbin Engineering University, China
Hasimah Mohamed	Universiti Sains Malaysia, Malaysia
Chilukuri K. Mohan	Syracuse University, USA
Abdulqader Mohsen	University of Science Malaysia, Malaysia
Daniel Molina	Universidad de Cadiz, Spain
Holger Morgenstern	Albstadt-Sigmaringen University, Germany
Andres Munoz	Universidad de Murcia, Spain
G.R.S. Murthy	Madhav Institute of Technology and Science, India
Akila Muthuramalingam	CSI College of Engineering, India
Jonathan Mwaura	University of Pretoria, South Africa
Atulya Nagar	Liverpool Hope University, UK
Kaname Narukawa	Honda R&D, Japan

Asoke Nath	St. Xavier's College, India
Shinya Nishizaki	Tokyo Institute of Technology, Japan
Yusuke Nojima	Osaka Prefecture University, Japan
Mrutyunjaya Panda	Gandhi Institute for Technological Advancement, India
Manjaree Pandit	MITS Gwalior, India
Andrei Paun	Louisiana Tech University, USA
Gheorghe Paun	Institute of Mathematics of the Romanian Academy, Romania
Yoseba Penya	University of Deusto, Spain
James F. Peters	University of Manitoba, Canada
Ninan Sajeeth Philip	St. Thomas College, India
Hugo Proenca	University of Beira Interior, Portugal
Balwinder Raj	NIT Jalandhar, India
Balasubramanian Raman	Indian Institute of Technology Roorkee, India
NurAini Abdul Rashid	Universiti Sains Malaysia, Malaysia
Mehul Raval	Ahmedabad University, India
Rawya Rizk	Port Said University, Egypt
Thamburaj Robinson	Madras Christian College, India
Alfonso Rodriguez Paton	Universidad Politecnica de Madrid, Spain
Samrat Sabat	University of Hyderabad, India
S.M. Sameer	National Institute of Technology Calicut, India
Rajesh Sanghvi	G.H. Patel College of Engineering and Technology, India
Aradhana Saxena	Indian Institute of Information Technology and Management, India
Sonia Schulenburg	Level E Capital Limited, UK
G. Shivaprasad	Manipal Institute of Technology, India
K.K. Shukla	Indian Institute of Technology, India
Madhusudan Singh	Dongseo University, South Korea
Pramod Kumar Singh	ABV-Indian Institute of Information Technology and Management Gwalior, India
Ravindra Singh	Motilal Nehru National Institute of Technology, India
Sanjeev Singh	Sant Longowal Institute of Engineering and Technology, India
Satvir Singh	SBS College of Engineering and Technology, India
Georgios C. Sirakoulis	Democritus University of Thrace, Greece
Don Sofge	Naval Research Laboratory, USA
Tao Song	China University of Petroleum (Huadong), China
Kumbakonam Govindarajan Subramanian	University Sains Malaysia, Malaysia
Ponnuthurai Suganthan	Nanyang Technological University, Singapore
S.R. Thangiah	Slippery Rock University, USA
D.G. Thomas	Madras Christian College, India
Chuan Kang Ting	National Chung Cheng University, Taiwan
Christos Tjortjis	International Hellenic University, Greece

Ravi Sankar Vadali	Gandhi Institute of Technology and Management, India
Ibrahim Venkat	Universiti Sains Malaysia, Malaysia
Jun Wang	Xihua University, China
Yong Wang	Central South University, China
Ling Wang	Tsinghua University, China
Jiahai Wang	Sun Yat-Sen University, China
Sudhir Warier	Reliance Communications Limited, India
Thomas Weise	University of Science and Technology of China, China
Slawomir Wierzchon	Polish Academy of Sciences, Poland
Kelvin Wong	University of Western Australia, Australia
Lining Xing	National University of Defense Technology, China
Ram Yadav	M.A. National Institute of Technology, USA
Yingjie Yang	De Montfort University, UK
Bosuk Yang	Pukyong National University, South Korea
Shengxiang Yang	De Montfort University, UK
Belgacem Ben Youssef	King Saud University, Saudi Arabia
Yang Yu	Nanjing University, China
Umi Kalsom Yusof	University Sains Malaysia, Malaysia
Xiangxiang Zeng	Xiamen University, China
Xingyi Zhang	Anhui University, China
Jie Zhang	Newcastle University, UK
Gexiang Zhang	Southwest Jiaotong University, China
Pan Zheng	Swinburne University of Technology Sarawak Campus, Malaysia
Shangming Zhou	University of Essex, UK
Aimin Zhou	East China Normal University, China
Zexuan Zhu	Shenzhen University, China
Sotirios Ziavras	New Jersey Institute of Technology, USA

Sponsors

National Natural Science Foundation of China
University of Science and Technology of China
Huazhong University of Science and Technology
Anhui University
National University of Defense Technology
Special Committee of Information System and Management Science
System Engineering and Management Society of Hunan Province

Contents

PSO Optimized Multipurpose Image Watermarking Using SVD and Chaotic Sequence

Irshad Ahmad Ansari[1], Millie Pant[1], Chang Wook Ahn[2(✉)],
and Jaehun Jeong[2]

[1] Department of ASE, Indian Institute of Technology, Roorkee, India
01.irshad@gmail.com, millifpt@iitr.ac.in
[2] Department of CSE, Sungkyunkwan University, Suwon, Republic of Korea
{cwan,a12gjang}@skku.edu

Abstract. This study proposes a novel method for multipurpose image watermarking for both ownership verification and tampered region localization. Two watermarks (robust and fragile) are inserted into the host image. Robust watermark insertion is done by PSO (particle swarm optimization) optimized scaling of the singular values; utilizing the singular value decomposition (SVD). Doing so, leads to reduction in visibility changes (better imperceptibility) of host image as well as enhanced performance of watermarked image towards attacks (better robustness). Fragile watermark insertion is done by making use of SVD and chaotic sequence (block feature's dependent). The image is first divided into non overlapped blocks and block based Arnold transformed is performed. Then after, block grouping is done of scrambled blocks to breakdown their independence in order to sustain the vector quantization and collage attacks. The proposed scheme is tested against various signal processing attacks and results shows a good performance.

Keywords: Ownership claim · Multipurpose image watermarking · Tamper localization · Singular value decomposition · Chaotic sequence · Particle swarm optimization

1 Introduction

The development in computer based communication makes the image sharing very easy among people but the same technological enhancement creates a threat to image security and integrity. Today, many powerful images processing tools are available that can be used to manipulate the data in a harmful way [1,2]. This makes the copyright infringement very common along with the tampering of images to create false claims/financial loss of others. There are two widely used approaches to deal with these problems. One is cryptography based techniques [3] and other one is image watermarking [4]. Cryptography encrypts the image with a secret key and so it restricts image visibility to users, who have the key. Also, cryptography can only be used to check the ownership and not able

© Springer-Verlag Berlin Heidelberg 2015
M. Gong et al. (Eds.): BIC-TA 2015, CCIS 562, pp. 1–17, 2015.
DOI: 10.1007/978-3-662-49014-3_1

to locate the tampered region in host image. On the other hand, watermarking does not restrict the host image visibility, provides ownership information (robust watermarking) and also able to locate the tampered region (fragile watermarking) in host. So the image watermarking is gaining quite popularity these days as a security tool for image.

The image watermarking can be classified into visible/invisible domain based on the watermark type (visible/invisible). The watermarking can also be divided into robust [5], fragile [6] and semi fragile [7] domain. Robust watermarking hides the information (watermark) in such a way that it affected very less/remains intact even after attacks. In contrast, fragile watermark gets destroy as soon as there is any tampering in host image and this provides fragile watermark, ability to locate the tampered region. Semi fragile watermarking is a combination of fragile and robust watermarking and it provides ability to sustain certain attacks along with some tampering localization. A dual watermark insertion is a special case of semi fragile watermarking, where two watermarks are inserted into host image to provide both watermarking (robust and fragile) features to host image.

In literature, three type of dual watermarking is available. First one [8,9] is shown in Fig. 1, in which robust and fragile watermark are inserted one after other. This is called sequential dual watermarking. In this type as the watermarking, the insertion of watermarks should be done in such a way that it affects each other minimally otherwise the dual nature of watermark will get destroyed.

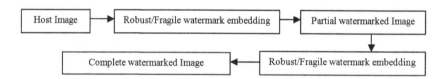

Fig. 1. Sequential dual watermark embedding.

In Second type of watermarking, robust and fragile watermark is combined in a hybrid watermark and this watermark is embedded like a normal watermarking scheme. The scheme is shown in Fig. 2 and related literature can be seen from [10,11]. This strategy is also used for dual nature of tampering localization and recovery [12,13].

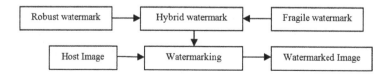

Fig. 2. Hybrid dual watermark embedding.

In third type of watermarking [14–16], the host image is divided into two parts (Fig. 3): robust region and fragile region. The watermarks are embedded into different parts. So that robust and fragile watermark doesn't affect each other. This scheme is also used by many researchers for tamper localization and recovery [17]. Fragile watermark is used for localization, whereas recovery information is saved as robust watermark.

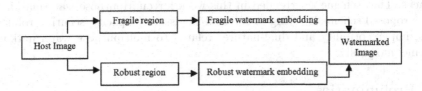

Fig. 3. Region based dual watermark embedding.

Proposed scheme is making use of sequential dual watermarking approach to verify the ownership of host image (using robust watermark) as well locate the tampered area (using fragile watermark) in host image.

Section two is describing the literature review of multipurpose image watermarking and proposed improvements. Section three is giving a glance of basic theories/methods used in this study. Watermarking scheme is describe in section four. Section five is providing a detailed discussion on the results and section six is ending the study with final remarks.

2 Related Work

There is plenty of research work available in the robust and fragile watermarking domains but comparatively less focus is given on the semi fragile watermarking, particularity multipurpose/dual watermarking. Dual watermarking is used to solve two purposes; image authentication and tamper localization. Chemak et al. [8] used sequential insertion of watermarks i.e. first robust watermark gets inserted in wavelet domain and then fragile watermark gets inserted in the LSB2 (second least significant bit) using spatial domain. The scheme generates the robust and fragile watermarks from the same signature. The scheme shows a poor PSNR (peak signal to noise ratio) of watermarked image and fragile watermark was unable to deal with vector quantization and collage attacks. Habib [18] suggest a watermarking scheme based on DCT (Discrete Cosine Transformation), in which the transformed host image is divided into two parts (integer and decimal) and robust and fragile watermarks get inserted into different regions. This scheme is make use of only first place of decimal value and this lead to some data loss; so it affect the quality of watermarked image. This scheme also not provides a way to deal with vector quantization and collage attacks. Based on these schemes, many other variants are proposed in literature. The schemes [9,14,15] also propose a dual watermarking approach but they all suffers with a low watermark data embedding. The security issue is not touched in watermarking scheme [16], which becomes a big drawback of this scheme.

Some watermarking schemes are only able to provide the copyright protection [3–5] whereas some are only able to provide data verification/tampering localization [6, 19]. Even, few schemes can provide both features [8–11, 14–16] but they all suffer with some sort of drawbacks as discussed earlier. Reference [6] proposed a fragile watermarking scheme for tamper localization to deal with complex attacks. That scheme is extended in this work for multipurpose watermarking. The proposed scheme is trying to solve all the issues (capacity, security, robustness, imperceptibility and dual-nature) related to multipurpose watermarking scheme maximally.

3   Preliminaries

3.1   Singular Value Decomposition (SVD)

SVD is a technique of linear Algebra and is used to diagonalize the symmetric matrix. SVD is used to find out the left singular matrix U, right singular matrix V and Singular matrix S of any given matrix A such that

$$A = USV^T \tag{1}$$

The matrix S is a rectangular diagonal matrix and the diagonal contains the elements in a descending order. These values are known as singular values. If A is the matrix of the order of nn then matrix S can have maximum n diagonal elements. These elements are basically tried to pack the energy of matrix A into them. If lesser elements of matrix S are being used in regeneration of matrix A then the quality of A will get affected.

The matrix U and V holds the property $UU^T = I_n$ and $VV^T = I_n$. The diagonal values of diagonal matrix S have the property that

$$d_1 \geq d_2...d_r \geq d_{r+1} \geq d_{r+2}... \geq d_n = 0 \tag{2}$$

Where $(r \leq n)$ is the rank of the matrix S and $d_1, d_2...d_n$ are diagonal elements of matrix S. An image is also a matrix of non-negative scalars.

3.2   Chaotic Maps

In recent years, chaotic system and permutation transform have been used for digital watermarking, in order to reinforce the security [20]. Use the logistic map is done to increase the security and performance of our scheme.

(1) Logistic Map: Logistic map is one of the simplest and most transparent systems exhibiting order to chaos transition. Mathematically it is defined as:

$$x_{n+1} = \mu x_n(1 - x_n), n \in Z, u \in [0, 4], x_n \in (0, 1) \tag{3}$$

The here is a positive constant sometimes known as the biotic potential, when $3.5699456 < \mu < 4$ the map is in the region of fully developed chaos [21]. That is, at this point, the sequence x_k; k = 0, 1, 2, 3 . . . generated by Eq. (3) is non-periodic, non-convergent and sensitive to the initial value.

3.3   Arnold Transform

In order to provide security to the watermark from unauthorized access its pixels
needs to been randomized in such a way that it can be reversed only by the unique
key/code. Arnold transform is a powerful tool for providing iterative movement
to the elements of any given array [22]. A 2D Arnold transform can be defined
as follows

$$\begin{bmatrix} x_i \\ y_i \end{bmatrix} = \begin{bmatrix} 1 & m \\ n & mn+1 \end{bmatrix} \begin{bmatrix} x_{i-1} \\ y_{i-1} \end{bmatrix} mod(h) \tag{4}$$

Here m and n are positive integers. h is the height of the image (considering
a square image). x_i and y_i represents the transformed value of x and y pixels
after i^{th} iterations. This complete process is periodic in nature. This means if
x and y keep on transforming and then after a fixed numbers of iterations T
the elements x and y returns to their original value. The value of this time
period T is dependent on m, n and i. so these values can be used as a key
for the randomization. Suppose that i transforms have been done during the
randomization. Then to get back the original image, further (T-i) transforms
needs to be performed on this randomized image.

3.4   Particle Swarm Optimization (PSO)

Soft computing techniques (ANN, GA, PSO etc.) are used in many fields for
efficient problem solving [23,24]. PSO is an optimization technique proposed by
Kennedy et al. [25] in 1995. It is inspired by the swarm behavior of animals like
bird flocking, animal herding and fish schooling etc. Each member in the group
learns from its own best performance as well as from the best performance of
other members. This kind of property helps it to reach global optimum value in
an efficient manner. PSO is a powerful tool for complex and multidimensional
search [26,27]. The very first step is the bounded initialization of swarm particles
in the search space. Let each particle Pi have an initial position and velocity of
$x_i(t)$ and $y_i(t)$ respectively at the time t. These positions assume to be the local
best for the first iteration. PSO algorithm follows these steps:

1. Initialize the particles number (i), position $x_i(t)$ and velocity $y_i(t)$
2. Compute the value of fitness function for each position
3. Compute the local best position i.e. each particle's best position in all the
   iterations
4. Compute the global best position i.e. best particle's position in current iteration
5. Update the velocity $y_i(t)$ and position $x_i(t)$ of each particle using Eqs. (5)
   and (6)

$$v_i(t+1) = w \times v_i(t) + c1 \times rand(l_{best} - x_i(t)) + c2 \times rand(g_{best} - x_i(t)) \tag{5}$$

$$x_i(t+1) = x_i(t) + v_i(t) \tag{6}$$

Here w is inertia weight, used to determine the step size for every iteration. c1 and c2 are the learning factors, which determines the effectiveness of local and global learning and rand function is used to generate a number between (0, 1).
6. Repeat the steps (2) to (5) till stopping creation reached.

The stopping criterion used in this study is the maximum number of iterations. But it can also be fitness function change below a certain threshold level etc.

4   Watermarking Scheme

In the proposed scheme, the watermarking is divided into two parts; first is robust watermark insertion and second is fragile watermark insertion. In order to insert the robust watermark, the host image is decomposed using singular value decomposition after setting the LSB as zero and scrambled watermark is inserted into the singular values. After performing Inverse SVD, the image is divided into small blocks of size 4×4 and block wise arnold transformed is applied on them. In order to sustain vector quantization and collage attacks, block grouping is per-formed. Two codes (block verification code and group verification code) are generated for each block. The fragile watermark is inserted by replacing the LSB of all the pixels using chaotic sequences, block verification code (BVC) and group verification code (GVC).

4.1   Embedding Process

The embedding scheme is shown in the Fig. 4 and explained in the following steps.

1. The first step is to set least significant bit of all pixels as zero and then perform the singular value decomposition on the host image using Eq. (7).

$$A = USV^T \tag{7}$$

2. Embed the robust watermark W with the help of scaling factor K into matrix S and form a new matrix S_1 using Eq. (8).

$$S_1 = S + KW \tag{8}$$

3. Perform the SVD of matrix S_1 to compute matrix U_{rw}, matrix V_{rw} and matrix S_{rw} using Eq. (9).

$$S_1 = U_{rw} S_{rw} V_{rw}^T \tag{9}$$

4. Compute the robust watermarked image A_{rw} using Eq. (10).

$$A_{rw} = US_{rw}V^T \tag{10}$$

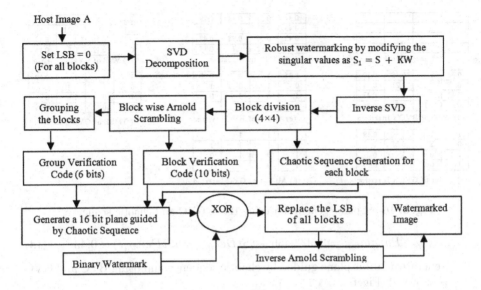

Host Image A

Fig. 4. Block diagram of embedding process.

5. Divide the robust watermarked image A_rw into small blocks of size 4×4 and then, perform a block wise arnold scrambling.
6. Perform SVD on these blocks as per Eq. (7) and calculate the traces.
7. Mapped the traces in the range of $[0, 1023]$ and they serve as block verification code (BVC).
8. Group the five consecutive blocks (Fig. 5) and average them using Eq. (11).

$$Average = \sum_{1}^{5} BVC/5 \qquad (11)$$

		...			
		...	a1	a2	a3
a4	a5	...			
		...			
		...			
		...			

a3		...			
		...			a4
		...			
a5		...		a2	
		...			
	a1	...			

Fig. 5. Group bits in the scrambled image (left most) and original image (right image).

9. Mapped the average values in the range of $[0, 63]$ and they serve as group verification code (GVC).
10. Generate a chaotic sequence of length-16, whose initial and parameter values are generated using statistical information of that group such as average intensity and standard deviation as shown is Eqs. (12) and (13).

$$Initial_{mn} = (Average_{mn} + 1)/257 \qquad (12)$$

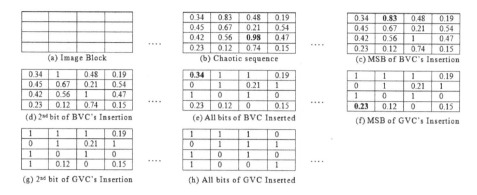

Fig. 6. 16-bit plane generation using BVC, GVC and chaotic sequence.

$$Param_{mn} = 3.5699456 + (StDev_{mn} - bStDev_{mn}c) \times 0.43 \qquad (13)$$

11. Generate a 16-bit plane guided by chaotic sequence and using BVC and GVC as shown in Fig. 6.
12. Divide the binary fragile watermark into 4×4 block size.
13. Perform XOR operation between the fragile watermark block W_i and 16-bit plane. Then, replace the LSB of host block pixels (as obtained in step (6)) with the result.
14. Perform Arnold scrambling (T-i) times to obtain the complete (robust and fragile) watermarked image. Where T is the period of Transform and i is the secret key.

4.2 Extraction Process

The extraction process is quite similar to that of embedding process as shown in the Fig. 7. First Fragile watermark is extracted from the LSB plane and then the robust watermark from singular values. The extraction process contain following steps:

1. The watermarked image is first divided into block size of 4×4 and block based arnold transformed is performed with the same secret key as used in embedding.
2. The LSB is separated and XOR operation is performed with original watermark to get back the 16-bit planes (BVC and GVC).
3. The generated LSB (16-bit planes) replaced the watermarked image LSB.
4. Chaotic sequence, BVC and GVC is generated as per step (6) to step (11) of Sect. 4.1.
5. This chaotic sequence is used to separate the original BVCorig and GVCorig obtained from step (2).
6. The BVC and BVCorig obtained from step (4) and step (5) is compared in order to obtain the authentic blocks (same BVC means authentic block).

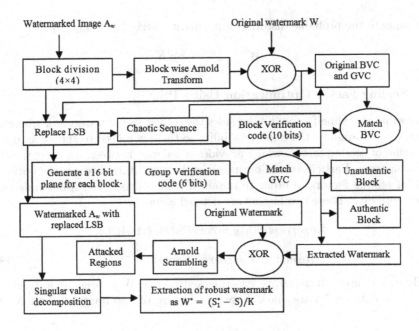

Fig. 7. Block diagram of extraction process.

7. Authentic blocks are assigned original watermark bits whereas unauthentic are assigned opposite bits.

8. The grouped blocks (five consecutive blocks) should have same GVCorig but if they dont have (due to attacks) then find out the most frequent GVCorig among them.

9. Most frequent GVCorig and GVC obtained in step (4) are compared in order to obtain the authentic group blocks (same GVC means authentic group blocks).

10. Authentic group blocks are assigned original watermark bits whereas unauthentic are assigned opposite bits.

11. Perform XOR between the generated and original watermark. It provides the difference image.

12. In order to locate the attacked region, apply the Arnold scrambling (T-i) times on this difference image. Where T is the period of Transform and i is the secret key.

13. To find out the robust watermark, Perform the SVD of watermarked image matrix A_{rw}^* (as obtained in step (3)) to compute matrix U^*, matrix V^* and matrix S_{rw}^* using Eq. (14).

$$U^* S_{rw}^* V^{*T} = A_{rw}^* \tag{14}$$

14. Compute the probable distorted S_1^* using Eq. (15).

$$S_1^* = U_{rw} S_{rw}^* V_{rw}^T \tag{15}$$

15. Compute the probable distorted watermark matrix W^* using Eq. (16).

$$W^* = (S_1^* - S)/K. \tag{16}$$

4.3   Scaling Factor Optimization Using PSO

A low value of scaling factor (K) degrades the robustness of watermark where as a high value minimizes the imperceptibility so there is a need to choose an optimal value of scaling factor, which provides a balance between imperceptibility and robustness. Particle swarm optimization is been utilized to get the optimal value of scaling factors in order to obtain a trade off between robustness and imperceptibility. These two factors are defined as below:

$$Imperceptibility = correlation(A, A_w) \tag{17}$$

$$Robustness = correlation(W, W^*) \tag{18}$$

Here A is host image, A_w is watermarked image, W is original watermark and W* is extracted watermark. Suppose the size of two images X and X^* is

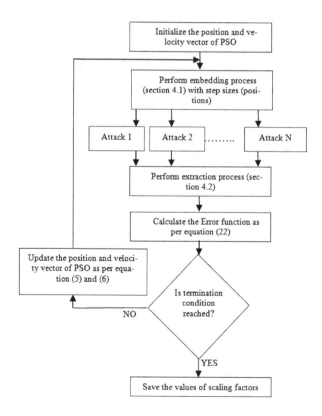

Fig. 8. Block diagram of scaling factor optimization.

$n \times n$ and they can attain a maximum pixel value as X_{max}. Then PSNR and normalized cross correlation can be defines as:

$$PSNR = 10log_{10}(\frac{((n \times n \times (X_{max})^2)}{\sum_{i=1}^{n} \sum_{i=1}^{n}(X(i,j) - X^*(i,j))^2}) \qquad (19)$$

$$correlation(X, X^*) = \frac{\sum_{i=1}^{n} x \sum_{i=1}^{n}(\overline{X_{(i,j)} \oplus X_{(i,j)}^*})}{(n \times n)} \qquad (20)$$

Suppose that N type of attacks has been considered then the combined inverse robustness can be written as

$$Inverse - robustness = \frac{N}{\sum_{i=1}^{N} correlation(W, W_i^*)} \qquad (21)$$

As the objective is to maximize both Imperceptibility and robustness, the following objective function is created for minimization:

$$Error = \frac{N}{\sum_{i=1}^{N} correlation(W, W_i^*)} - correlation(A, A_w) \qquad (22)$$

The error function serves as a multidimensional search of optimal value of K, which can't be visualize graphically and needs special tool like PSO for optimal value search of scaling factors [K]. A bounded initialization of population size of 5 and 50 generations. The value of PSO's step size with other parameters has been kept $w = 0.1$, $c1 = 0.8$, $c2 = 0.12$ though out the search. The block diagram of optimization process is shown in Fig. 8.

5 Results and Discussions

Figure 9 is showing the host images used in this study along with the logo that is used as watermark. All the host images are of size 512×512. The robust watermark is gray with a size of 256×256 and fragile watermark is binary with a size of 512×512, which means that the capacity of proposed scheme is quite high. The use of Arnold scrambling and chaotic sequences provide a very high security to proposed scheme. PSNR (Peak signal to noise ratio) and NCC (normalized cross correlation) are used to compare the quality of generated watermarked images and extracted watermarks.

The logo (watermark) shown is Fig. 9 is used as both watermarks i.e. robust watermark (gray scale) and fragile watermark (binary version). The PSNR of watermarked images with different scaling factors are shown in Table 1. The NCC of watermarked images (Host (W)) and extracted robust watermarks (without any attack) are shown in the Table 2 with different scaling factors (K).

From the Table 2, It can be seen clearly that the increase of scaling factor decrease the imperceptibility whereas decrease in scaling factor causes decrease the robustness. So to obtain a good trade off between imperceptibility and robustness, PSO is been used to find out the optimal scaling factors and the same is been utilized in this study further. Table 3 is showing the NCC of watermarked images and extracted watermarks (without any attack) with PSO optimized scaling factors (K).

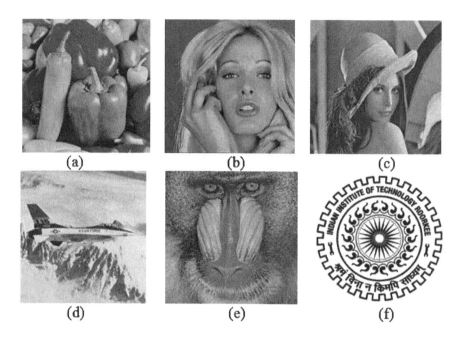

Fig. 9. Host images (a) Pepper (b) Girl (c) Lena (d) Plane (e) Baboon and watermark (f) Logo.

Table 1. PSNR of watermarked image with different scaling factors

Host image	PSNR (dB)		
	K = 0.01	K = 0.05	K = 0.25
Pepper	46.8642	44.3576	39.6354
Girl	44.2576	42.4864	37.4264
Lena	45.1823	43.5017	38.6354
Plane	45.2535	43.4863	38.6587
Baboon	44.2563	42.2636	37.4276

Table 2. NCC of watermarked image and extracted watermark with different scaling factors

Host image	NCC					
	K = 0.01		K = 0.05		K = 0.25	
	Host (W)	Watermark	Host (W)	Watermark	Host (W)	Watermark
Pepper	0.9912	0.9444	0.9752	0.9824	0.9243	0.9999
Girl	0.9921	0.9534	0.9775	0.9812	0.9376	0.9999
Lena	0.9934	0.9454	0.9874	0.9853	0.9265	1.0000
Plane	0.9865	0.9543	0.9645	0.9843	0.9163	0.9999
Baboon	0.9921	0.9664	0.9785	0.9854	0.9247	0.9999

Table 3. NCC of watermarked image and extracted watermark with optimized scaling factors

Host image	NCC	
	Watermarked image	Watermark
Pepper	0.9842	0.9962
Girl	0.9854	0.9902
Lena	0.9904	0.9931
Plane	0.9713	0.9956
Baboon	0.9886	0.9974

Table 4. NCC of extracted robust watermark of hosts under different attacks

Attack	NCC (Normalized Cross Correlation)				
	Pepper	Girl	Lena	Plane	Baboon
Average filtering [3×3]	0.8245	0.8334	0.8352	0.8337	0.8344
Resize (50 % and 200 %)	0.9942	0.9834	0.9923	0.9947	0.9832
Median filter [3×3]	0.8932	0.8936	0.8835	0.8844	0.8936
Histrogram equalization	0.9279	0.9478	0.9326	0.9342	0.9342
JPEG compression (Q = 80)	0.9832	0.9745	0.9747	0.9622	0.9722
JPEG compression (Q = 60)	0.8923	0.8947	0.8852	0.8824	0.8932
JPEG compression (Q = 40)	0.8523	0.8345	0.8647	0.8742	0.8345
Wiener filtering [2×2]	0.9473	0.9462	0.9443	0.9454	0.9446
Crop 20 pixels each side	0.9737	0.9637	0.9736	0.9733	0.9637
Rotation (20°)	0.9835	0.9834	0.9843	0.9901	0.9842
Gaussian Noise (4 %)	0.9823	0.9734	0.9773	0.9742	0.9746
Gaussian Noise (10 %)	0.8537	0.8669	0.8623	0.8642	0.8712

5.1 Attacks on Robust Watermark

There are two types of attacks that are performed on this watermarked image. First type of attack (filtering, cropping etc.) is tried to destroy the ownership information and second type of attack (copy-paste, text addition, content removal etc.) is tried to change the content without changing the watermark information. Table 4 is showing the NCC (normalized cross correlation) of robust watermark for different host images after different attacks and Fig. 10 is showing the robust extracted watermarks from host Lena after different attacks.

5.2 Attacks on Fragile Watermark

The attacks used in this study on the fragile watermark are copy paste attacks, text addition, content removal, vector quantization and collage attack. The results of all these attacks are shown in Figs. 11 and 12. In order to check the

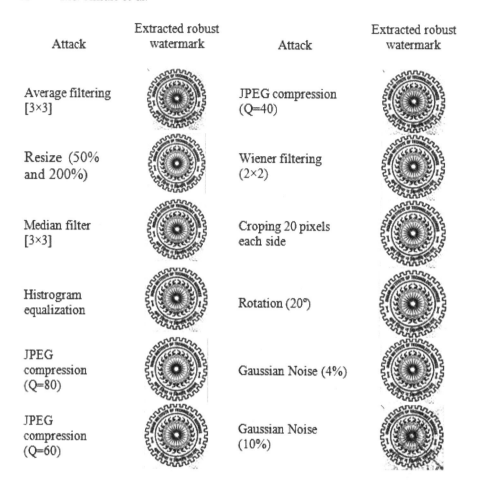

Attack	Extracted robust watermark	Attack	Extracted robust watermark
Average filtering [3×3]		JPEG compression (Q=40)	
Resize (50% and 200%)		Wiener filtering (2×2)	
Median filter [3×3]		Croping 20 pixels each side	
Histrogram equalization		Rotation (20°)	
JPEG compression (Q=80)		Gaussian Noise (4%)	
JPEG compression (Q=60)		Gaussian Noise (10%)	

Fig. 10. Extracted robust watermark from the host Lena after different attacks

scheme ability to with stand with VQ attack, a counterfeit image is being generated by cumulating the portions of multiple watermarked images. During this formation, the relative spatial locations of watermarked images remain intact i.e. spatial location remains same as that in original watermarked images. Two new host images (Tiger and Filed) are used in this experiment as shown in Fig. 12 with a size of 512×512. The counterfeit image is being generated by copying the tiger into the field without changing the spatial location. The result of VQ attack is shown Fig. 12.

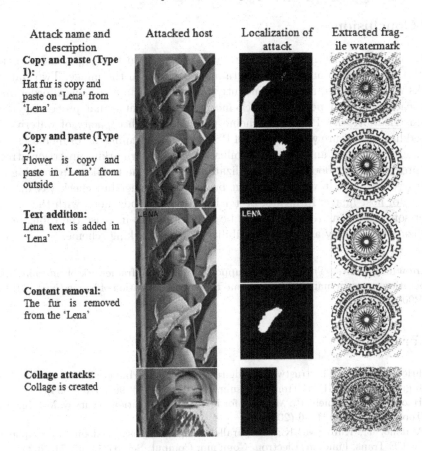

Fig. 11. Host image tampering and corresponding tamper localization

Fig. 12. Result of VQ attack: (a) Watermarked tiger (b) Watermarked field (c) Vector quantized image (d) Localization of attack (e) Fragile watermark (f) Robust watermark

6   Conclusion

A multipurpose watermarking scheme was proposed in this paper in order to verify the ownership and locate the tampered region in the image. Two watermarks were inserted quite independently to each other in a sequential order and this lead to a good perforce of scheme under different signal processing and geo-metrical attacks. Proposed scheme provided a high capacity of watermark embedding in a secure way. The use of PSO optimized scaling factor increases the scheme's robustness and imperceptibility. Fragile watermarking insertion strategy provided very good tamper localization. Even if the fragile watermark gets destroyed the robust watermark can be used for ownership check (as in VQ attack) of host image. In future, better insertion methods along with the use of other soft computing techniques will be investigated to increase the robustness, localization, capacity and imperceptibility of watermarking scheme.

Acknowledgments. This work was supported under the framework of international cooperation program managed by National Research Foundation of Korea (NRF-2013K 2A1B9066056).

References

1. Friedman, G.L.: The trustworthy digital camera: restoring credibility to the photographic image. IEEE Trans. Consum. Electron. **39**(4), 905–910 (1993)
2. Haouzia, A., Noumeir, R.: Methods for image authentication: a survey. Multimedia Tools Appl. **39**(1), 1–46 (2008)
3. Matsuo, T., Kurosawa, K.: On parallel hash functions based on block-ciphers. IEICE Trans. Fundam. Electron. Commun. Comput. Sci. **87**(1), 67–74 (2004)
4. Ansari, I.A., Pant, M., Neri, F.: Analysis of gray scale watermark in RGB host using SVD and PSO. In: IEEE Symposium on Computational Intelligence for Multimedia, Signal and Vision Processing (CIMSIVP), pp. 1–7 (2014)
5. Ansari, I.A., Pant, M.: SVD watermarking: particle swarm optimization of scaling factors to increase the quality of watermark. In: Proceedings of Fourth International Conference on Soft Computing for Problem Solving, pp. 205–214. Springer, India (2015)
6. Kang, Q., Li, K., Chen, H.: An SVD-based fragile watermarking scheme with grouped blocks. In: IEEE 2nd International Conference on Information Technology and Electronic Commerce (ICITEC), pp. 172–179 (2014)
7. Qi, X., Xin, X.: A quantization-based semi-fragile watermarking scheme for image content authentication. J. Vis. Commun. Image Represent. **22**(2), 187–200 (2011)
8. Chemak, C., Bouhlel, M.S., Lapayre, J.C.: A new scheme of robust image watermarking: the double watermarking algorithm. In: Proceedings of the Summer Computer Simulation Conference, pp. 1201–1208 (2007)
9. Niu, S.Z., Shu, N.F.: A digital image double watermarking algorithm based on DCT domain. J. Comput. Res. Dev. **46**(4), 6–10 (2009)
10. Sharkas, M., ElShafie, D., Hamdy, N.: A dual digital-image watermarking technique. In: Proceedings of International Conference on World Academy of Science, Engineering and Technology, pp. 136–139 (2005)

11. Wu, K., Yan, W., Du, J.: A robust dual digital-image watermarking technique. In: IEEE International Conference on Computational Intelligence and Security Workshops, pp. 668–671 (2007)
12. Chen, F., He, H.J., Wang, H.X.: Variable-payload self-recovery watermarking scheme for digital image authentication. Chin. J. Comput. **35**(1), 154–162 (2012)
13. Lee, T.Y., Lin, S.D.: Dual watermark for image tamper detection and recovery. Pattern Recogn. **41**(11), 3497–C3506 (2008)
14. Chamlawi, R., Khan, A., Usman, I.: Authentication and recovery of images using multiple watermarks. Comput. Electr. Eng. **36**(3), 578C–584 (2010)
15. Shen, H., Chen, B.: From single watermark to dual watermark: a new approach for image watermarking. Comput. Electr. Eng. **38**, 1310C–1324 (2012)
16. Song, C.L., Sudirman, S., Merabti, M.: A robust region-adaptive dual image watermarking technique. J. Vis. Commun. Image Represent. **23**(3), 549–568 (2012)
17. Li, C., Wang, Y., Ma, B., et al.: Tamper detection and self-recovery of biometric images using salient region-based authentication watermarking scheme. Comput. Stand. Interfaces. **34**(4), 367C–379 (2012)
18. Habib, M., Sarhan, S., Rajab, L.: A robust-fragile dual watermarking system in the DCT domain. In: Proceedings of the 9th International Conference on Knowledge-Based Intelligent Information and Engineering Systems, pp. 548–553 (2005)
19. Phadikar, A., Maity, S.P., Mandal, M.: Novel wavelet-based QIM data hiding technique for tamper detection and correction of digital images. J. Vis. Commun. Image Represent. **23**(3), 454C–466 (2012)
20. Rawat, S., Raman, B.: A chaotic system based fragile watermarking scheme for image tamper detection. AEU Int. J. Electron. Commun. **65**, 840–847 (2011)
21. Mooney, A., Keating, J.G., Heffernan, D.M.: Performance analysis of chaotic and white watermarks in the presence of common watermark attacks. Chaos Solutions Fractals. **42**, 560–570 (2009)
22. Wu, L., Zhang, J., Deng, W., He, D.: Arnold transformation algorithm and anti-arnold transformation algorithm. In: 1st IEEE International Conference on Information Science and Engineering, pp. 1164–1167 (2009)
23. Ansari, I.A., Singla, R., Singh, M.: SSVEP and ANN based optimal speller design for brain computer interface. Comput. Sci. Tech. **2**(2), 338–349 (2015)
24. Kant, S., Ansari, I.A.: An improved K means clustering with Atkinson index to classify liver patient dataset. Int. J. Syst. Assur. Eng. Manag. 1–7 (2015). doi:10.1007/s13198-015-0365-3
25. Eberhart, R., Kennedy, J.: A new optimizer using particle swarm theory. In: Proceedings of the Sixth International Symposium on Micro Machine and Human Science, pp. 39–43 (1995)
26. Kiranyaz, S., Ince, T., Yildirim, A., Gabbouj, M.: Fractional particle swarm optimization in multidimensional search space. IEEE Trans. Syst. Man Cybern. Part B Cybern. **40**(2), 298–319 (2010)
27. Messerschmidt, L., Engelbrecht, A.P.: Learning to play games using a PSO-based competitive learning approach. IEEE Trans. Evol. Comput. **8**(3), 280–288 (2004)

Cell-Like Fuzzy P System and Its Application of Coordination Control in Micro-grid

Ke Chen[1], Jun Wang[1(✉)], Ming Li[1], Jun Ming[1], and Hong Peng[2]

[1] Sichuan Province Key Laboratory of Power Electronics Energy-saving Technologies and Equipment and School of Electrical Engineering and Electronic Information, Xihua University, Chengdu 610039, Sichuan, China
745257101@qq.com
[2] School of Mathematics and Computer Engineering, Xihua University, Chengdu 610039, Sichuan, China

Abstract. Based on the fuzzy knowledge, this paper presents a cell-like fuzzy P system (CFPS for short). The CFPS is mainly characterized by the introduction of the fuzzy concept and includes the fuzzy catalyst. Afterwards, the definition and the operation process of the CFPS are elaborated. Based on the CFPS, this paper realizes its application in the control of micro-grid. It takes micro-grid system frequency and current work status as inputs. The CFPS gives the decision-making to choice the reasonable working conditions which include the control of the distributed power and the switching of loads in the micro-grid. Firstly, detailed reasoning is presented to prove the rationality and feasibility of the proposed control thoughts. Then, MATLAB simulation verifies the decision made by the CFPS is correct and the application is rationality which is aimed to achieve a stable energy management and control micro-grid system steady. Experimental results show that CFPS can manage micro-grid effectively, and play a role in load shifting by energy management to stabilize the frequency of feeder.

Keywords: Membrane computing · Cell-like fuzzy P system · Micro-grid · Coordination control

1 Introduction

Membrane computing (also called P system) is a theoretical model that simulates the structure and function of the biological tissue and its powerful computing capability can solve many computational problems effectively [1]. There are three main types of membrane computing model currently: cell type, tissue type and neuronal membrane system. Cell type membrane system which was first proposed has been extensively studied [2]. At present, many foreign scholars have involved in the study of membrane systems and their applications. Reference [3] proposed a fuzzy P system, which introduce the fuzzy data and a fuzzy set multiple rewrite rules. In [4], a fuzzy reasoning SN P system (FRSN P systems)

© Springer-Verlag Berlin Heidelberg 2015
M. Gong et al. (Eds.): BIC-TA 2015, CCIS 562, pp. 18–32, 2015.
DOI: 10.1007/978-3-662-49014-3_2

was applied in fault diagnosis. FRSN P systems were extended from SN P systems. Its main character is that FRSN P systems can handle fuzzy information and express fuzzy knowledge. A generalization of various communication models based on the P system paradigm where two objects synchronously move across components was considered in [5]. Nevertheless, the applied research of P systems is still very weak compared to the theoretical study. How to use P system to solve a variety of practical engineering problems has been an important issue in the field of membrane computing [14,15].

Micro-grid is a single control unit which composes of multiple distributed generation units [6], load, the storage devices, the corresponding control devices and other components. It can provide the appropriate quality and reliability of power supply according to user needs [7]. Many scholars have devoted to the research of micro-grid. For example, Ref. [8] proposed a distributed multi-micro-grid inverter cooperative control system for the energy management system of the micro-grid master layer. In [9], it described a micro-grid for energy management systems, and made a specific introduction to the economic operation which used the proposed method as a planning tool in the micro-grid. A fuzzy cognitive map and petri nets constructed applies to independent multi-generation micro-grid energy management system in [10]. An improved particle swarm algorithm was proposed and its application was realized in the economic operation optimization micro-grid in [11]. Reference [12] presented a micro-grid framework based on multi-agent system. It established micro-grid control agents, local control agents, distributed energy agency and workload agent which composed of multi-agent control system, and analyzed the specific functions of the various agents in detail. Thus, there are a lot of control thoughts of the micro-grid control has been proposed, such as the master-slave control, and peer-to-peer control and hierarchical control. Nevertheless, there are few advanced decision algorithms as micro-grid control strategies to be used effectively to manage a micro-grid. It demonstrates that it needs a lot of researches in the control of micro-grid.

In this paper, a cell-like fuzzy P system (CFPS) is proposed based on the fuzzy knowledge. The CFPS is mainly characterized by the introduction of a fuzzy concept and includes the fuzzy catalyst. Afterwards, the definition and the work process of the CFPS are elaborated. Based on the CFPS, this paper realizes the application in the control of micro-grid. It takes micro-grid system frequency and current work status as inputs, and the CFPS gives the decision-making to choice the reasonable working conditions which include the control of the distributed power and the switching of loads in the micro-grid. Firstly, detailed reasoning is presented to prove the rationality and feasibility of the proposed control thoughts. Then, the MATLAB simulation verifies the decision made by the CFPS is correct and the application is rationality which is aimed to achieve a stable energy management and control micro-grid system steady. Experimental results show that CFPS can manage micro-grid effectively, and play a role in load shifting by energy management to stabilize the frequency of AC feeder.

The structure of the paper is organized as follow. The definition and the work process of the CFPS are elaborated in Sect. 2. In Sect. 3, the application of the coordination control in micro-grid using the proposed is elaborated, and the reasoning of the method is developed detailed. In Sect. 4, simulation and analysis are given. Finally, a summary of our approach and future work are given in Sect. 5.

2   Cell-Like P System Fuzzy Logic System

2.1   CFPS for Language Fuzzy Model

The structure of cell-like P system is shown in Fig. 1(a). The tree is shown in Fig. 1(b). Based on the above preparation knowledge, and combined with membrane computing, we define cell-like fuzzy P system for language fuzzy model (referred to as CFPS) as follow.

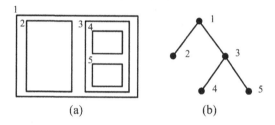

Fig. 1. (a) CFPS, (b) The tree of CFPS.

$$\Pi = (O, \mu, n, \omega_1, \cdots, \omega_m, C_1(u_1), \cdots, C_m(u_m), R_1, \cdots, R_m, i_0) \qquad (1)$$

Where:

(1) $O = \{d_j\}$. O is a fuzzy multi-set [13]. d_j is a object to be used as the input. Operation starts from the compartments which don't contain cells in the next level.

(2) μ indicates that membrane structure is composed by m membranes.

(3) n indicates the levels of the P system. Level contains the input stage, intermediate stage and output stage. Among them, the highest level pattern is output, and the level excluding the lowest level pattern can be used as input. The level which is attached to the next level and the upper level is namely the middle level to do the operation. Intermediate stage can be multiple levels, but the input and output stages is only one. In Fig. 2, for example, the level of the system is 3. There is no next level but the upper level in 2, 4, and 5. They can be used as the input stage. There are the next levels but no upper level in 1, so it used as an output. Membrane 3 includes upper and lower levels, so we can see it as an intermediate layer, not as an input or output.

(4) ω_i, $i = m$. It indicates the fuzzy multi-set exists in the areas $1, 2, \cdots, m$ in the initial state. Here, we define ω_i only exists in the basic structure of the input stage membranes, and other membrane is empty.

(5) $C_m(u_m)$ is catalyst contained in each membrane. The place of the catalyst is unaltered, so that the value of it can be restored, and it let that calculation can be made without having to redefine each catalyst. The values in C_m is between $[0, 1]$. m is the degree of the membrane system. u_m is the reliability of the use of the catalyst, and indicates the intensity of the reliability for the associated rules related to catalyst. The value of u_m is between $[0, 1]$. Where, the catalyst in basic membrane and the membrane which don't include basic membrane is $C[c_1, c_2, \ldots, c_j]$ to act on the j objects, and the value of u_m is 1. The catalyst in the membrane n that in the middle level is $C[c_{n-(n+1)}, c_{n-(n+1)-(n+2)}, \cdots, c_{n-(n+1)-\ldots(k-1)-k}]$, $1 \le n \le k$, $1 \le k \le m$, $U[u_{n-(n+1)}, u_{n-(n+1)-(n+2)}, \cdots, u_{n-(n+1)-\ldots(k-1)-k}] \notin [0, 1]$. $c_{n-(n+1)}, c_{n-(n+1)-(n+2)}, \cdots, c_{n-(n+1)-\ldots(k-1)-k}$ is generated accompanying the cell movement between membrane n and the input level membrane. C is a set of catalysts from membrane n to membrane k through the membranes $n+1, \cdots, k-1$. When the membrane a in the input level meets the excitation conditions, and the relative catalyst exists and meet the conditions, then the objects will be changed by rule R_i from membrane a to membrane b. With this movement, the catalyst $c_{a-b}(u_{a-b})$ is generated. Foot marks a and b express the two membrane that engender related movement.

(6) R_i $(1 \le i \le m)$ is the set of the evolution rules. Rules indicate the form of the movements between the cells, such as transport, exchange and other forms. Here, we have defined the following three categories of fuzzy language model for the evolution rules, in which the input stage and the intermediate stage of the membrane were represented by n, the output stage was represented by m:

(a) In the input level of basic membrane n, a class rule R_A can be used: $d_j c_j \rightarrow (d_j c_j, in_{(n+1)})$; $d_j > c_j(u_j)$. j represents the number of objects and their corresponding catalysts and rules. The rule indicates that when the membrane presence of the catalyst c_j and the object d_j meet excitation conditions $d_j > c_j$, R_A will be activated, and the object d_j will be transported from basic membrane n to the next level membrane $n + 1$.

(b) In the intermediate stage membrane n, a class rule R_B can be used: $d_j c_{n-(n+1)-\ldots(k-1)-k} \rightarrow (p_k c_{n-(n+1)-\ldots(k-1)-k}, in_n)$; $d_j > c_{n-(n+1)-\ldots(k-1)-k}$. j represents the number of objects and their corresponding catalysts and rules. The rule indicates that when the membrane presence of the catalyst $c_{n-(n+1)-\ldots(k-1)-k}$ and the object d_j meet excitation conditions $d_j > c_{n-(n+1)-\ldots(k-1)-k}$, R_B will be activated, and the object d_j will be transformed into p_k and transported from basic membrane m to the next level membrane k through membrane $n + 1$ to $k - 1$.

(c) In the output level membrane n, a class rule R_C can be used: $p_k c_{n-(n+1)-\ldots(k-1)-k} \rightarrow (p_k c_{n-(n+1)-\ldots(k-1)-k}, out)$;

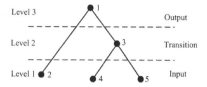

Fig. 2. The levels presentation of cell-like P system.

$p_k > c_{n-(n+1)-\ldots(k-1)-k}$. k represents the number of objects and their corresponding catalysts and rules. The rule indicates that when the membrane presence of the catalyst $c_{n-(n+1)-\ldots(k-1)-k}$ and the object p_k meet excitation conditions $p_k > c_{n-(n+1)-\ldots(k-1)-k}$, R_C will be activated, and the object p_k which is the output of the system will be transported to the environment.

2.2   Operation Process of CFPS

$$\Pi = (O, \mu, n, \omega_1, \cdots, \omega_5, C_1(u_1), \cdots, C_5(u_5), R_1, \cdots, R_5, i_0)$$

Where:

(1) $O = \{d_1, d_2, d_3, d_4, d_5, d_6\}$. $n = 3$. $i_0 = 4, 5$.

(2) $\omega_1 = \omega_3 = \lambda$, $\omega_2 = \{(d_5, 0.3), (d_6, 0.8)\}$, $\omega_4 = \{(d_1, 0.4), (d_2, 0.6)\}$, $\omega_5 = \{(d_3, 0.7), (d_4, 0.3)\}$.

(3) $C_1[c_{4-3-1} = 0.1(0.8), c_{5-3-1} = 0.5(0.7), c_{2-1} = 0.9(0.4)]$, $C_2[c_5 = 0.4(1), c_6 = 0.7(1)]$, $C_3[c_{4-3} = 0.3(0.6), c_{5-3} = 0.8(0.4)]$, $C_4[c_1 = 0.7(1), c_2 = 0.3(1)]$, $C_5[c_3 = 0.1(1), c_4 = 0.8(1)]$.

(4) $R_1 = R_C$, $R_2 = R_3 = R_B$, $R_4 = R_5 = R_A$.

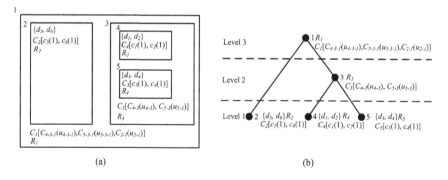

(a)   (b)

Fig. 3. (a) A CFPS as an example, (b) The tree of CFPS as an example.

The structure of CFPS as an example is shown in Fig. 3(a). The tree of it is shown in Fig. 3(b). Operation process is as follows:

Step1. Objects are included in membrane $4, 5, 2$, so the parallel operations start in $4, 5, 2$. In membrane 4, there are $d_1 = 0.4$, $c_1 = 0.7(1)$ and $d_1 < c_1$. Rule R_4 doesn't meet the excitation conditions. There are $d_2 = 0.6$, $c_2 = 0.3(1)$ and $d_2 < c_2$. R_4 meets the excitation conditions, hence d_2 moves into membrane 3. In membrane 5, $d_3 = 0.7$, $c_3 = 0.1(1)$, $d_3 > c_3$. R_5 meets the excitation conditions, hence d_5 moves into membrane 3. $d_4 = 0.3$, $c_4 = 0.8(1)$, $d_4 < c_4$, R_5 doesn't meet the excitation conditions. In membrane 2, $d_5 = 0.3$, $c_5 = 0.4(1)$, $d_5 < c_5$. R_2 doesn't meet the excitation conditions. $d_6 = 0.8$, $c_6 = 0.7(1)$, $d_5 > c_5$. R_2 meets the excitation conditions, hence d_6 moves into membrane 1.

Step2. Membrane 3 gets the objects d_2 and d_3 from membrane 4 and 5. Then, $d_{4-3} = d_2 u_2 = 0.6$, $d_{5-3} = d_3 u_3 = 0.7$. $C_3[c_{4-3} = 0.3(0.6)$, $c_{5-3} = 0.8(0.4)]$. Similarly, $d_{4-3} = d_2 = 0.6$ move into membrane 1.

Step3. Membrane 1 gets the objects d_6 and d_{4-3} from membrane 2 and 3. Thus, $d_{4-3-1} = d_{4-3} u_{4-3} = 0.6 * 0.3 = 0.18$, $d_{2-1} = d_6 u_6 = 0.8$. $C_1[c_{4-3-1} = 0.1(0.8)$, $c_{5-3-1} = 0.5(0.7)$,$c_{2-1} = 0.9(0.4)]$, $d_{4-3-1} > c_{4-3-1}$, R_1 meet the excitation conditions, $d_{out} = d_{4-3-1} u_{4-3-1} = 0.18 * 0.8 = 0.144$. d_{out} which is the output of the system will be transported to the environment. This is the end of operation.

The input objects can be given the appropriate physical sense. When the condition is satisfied, according to the evolution rules, the object will be evolved. Objects generated by the evolution rules also have its corresponding physical sense. The final output of the complete evolution of object called an output target. It is applied to fuzzy probabilistic reasoning and so on.

3 The Application of CFPS in Control of Micro-grid

Here, we use the CPFS with containing intermediate layer of fuzzy P System which also called language fuzzy model (basic model) to achieve its application in micro-grid. In grid-connect mode, system voltage and frequency are supported by the distribution network. In this paper, DGs only run under the islanded mode.

3.1 CFPS of the Control System for Micro-grid

The application object of this paper is a general micro-grid system and its topology structure is shown in Fig. 4. It consists of the photovoltaic generator system (PV), wind turbine generator system (WT), gas turbine generator system (GT), storage systems (Storage1, Storage2), important load (Load1) and general load (Load2). Reasonable control objective is to achieve coordinated control and energy management, maintain the frequency on the bus stability, meet the demands of important load Load1, and extend the service life of the energy storage device. Main control thought is as follow. PV and WT as an important distributed power supply has been accessed the micro-grid to ensure the full use of new energy. Storage1 as main power source responses the instantaneous fluctuation of load in micro-grid to guarantee basic power supply stability and its quality. Load1 is an important load. So the grid shall guarantee basic power supply stability and its quality. Our control objects choose GT, Storage2 and Load2. Their removal and access are not cause energy waste, and control reasonably. Reasons are as follows. The GT can be regarded as constant power source, and its power fluctuation is small. Its power is more smoothly than PV and WT. It is necessary to control fuel gas bubbled into or blocking to control its access or disconnect which reduces the waste of energy, achieves the rational use of fuel gas, and saves energy.

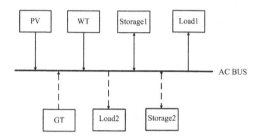

Fig. 4. Topology structure.

Control block diagram is shown in Fig. 5. We use CFPS to control the controllable GT, Storage2 and Load2. CFPS controller has four inputs that are the frequency on AC bus, current operating state of GT, Storage2 and Load2, the charge state of Storage2, and SOC respectively. Using three CFPS control unit to determine the correct state of GT, Storage2 and Load2 in the next moment.

3.2   Fuzzification of the Inputs in CFPS

Here, the values of inputs are in $[0, 1]$ to represent the degree. When f is in $[49, 51]$, micro-grid is working normally and all devices keep the original state. When f is in $[51, +\infty]$, it expresses the frequency is high. Corresponding measure is needed to be taken to regulate f to recover to the normal region. When f is in $[-\infty, 49]$, it expresses the frequency is low. Corresponding measure is needed, too. We will take 50 as the origin of coordinates to converted to zero, the value of f is mapped to $[0, 1]$. The size of the value is said the departure degree to the standard frequency. Polarity is expressed in plus or minus. "+" means the value is larger than standard value and "−" means the value is smaller than standard value. It is not mathematical in the sense of positive and negative. Here, we define "+" can be omitted, and "−" cannot be omitted. Catalyst also has a polarity. The corresponding catalyst also be with "+" or "−". The state of charge (SOC for short) is on behalf of the charge state of battery. SOC= Q_c/Q_0. Q_c is the remaining power. Q_0 is the capacity that battery discharges at a constant current I. SOC $= 1$ represents the full charged state. Here, we define when SOC

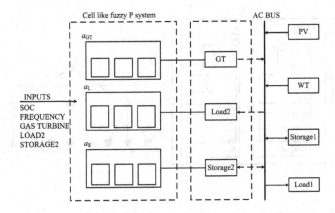

Fig. 5. Micro-grid control structure modeled by CFPS.

is greater than 0.8, storage should be disconnected to prevent the overcharge. When SOC is less than 0.2, it should be timely disconnected to prevent the excessive discharge which is damage to the battery life. There are three states of GT, Load, and Storage: on state, off state and maintaining state. Polarity "−" means disconnect and "+" means access. "±0" means maintain. More than or less than 0 indicates that access or disconnect the length of time $t = X * t$. Revising t to achieve precise control by continuous calculation. Deviation degree of the input f and each DG's control state will affect the switch state of the control objects. For example, GT$= -0.6$ means GT is in an off state, and the judge the turn-off time is $t = 0.6 * t$.

3.3   CFPS Model

Below we set input $f = +0.8$, $soc = 0.8$, $s = -0.4$, $gt = 0.8$ and $l = 0.8$ as an example to reason in detail as follow. Here, we only introduce CFPS model for GT. Using same method, CFPS model for Load2 and CFPS model for Storage2 CFPS model a_{GT} for GT can be expressed using (1). The structure of CFPS for GT is shown in Fig. 6(a). The tree is shown in Fig. 6(b). The operation process of a_{GT} is as follows. Object f exists in a_{GT4}, a_{GT7} and a_{GT10} respectively. $f = +0.8$ meets the excitation condition $f > +0.5$ of rule R_{GT4} in a_{GT4}. Thus, f accesses a_{GT1}. There is no f in a_{GT7} and a_{GT10} so that rules can't be used. a_{GT0} get effective objects from a_{GT1}. The work statement in a_{GT2} and a_{GT3} is needless to be discussed. In a_{GT5}, $soc = 0.8$, $s = 0.4$, $c_{5s} = 0$, $soc = 0.8$. It meets the excitation condition $s < c_{5s}\&soc = c_{5soc}$ of rule R_{GT5}. Then soc accesses a_{GT1}. In a_{GT6}, $gt = 0.8$, $l = 0.8$, $c_{6gt} = 0$, $c_{6l} = 0$. It meets the excitation condition $gt > c_{6gt}\&l > c_{6l}$ of rule R_{GT6}. Then gt and l access a_{GT1}. There are f, s, l and gt in a_{GT1} so that rule R_{GT1} can be used. Therefore, $Output = 0.8 * 0.25 + 0.8 * 0.25 + 0.8 * 0.25 + 0.8 * 0.25 = -0.8$. Similarly, CFPS model for Load2 expressed as a_L and model for Storage2 expressed a_s as can be built using Eq. 1.

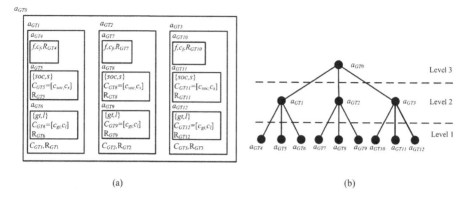

Fig. 6. (a) CFPS model for GT, (b) The tree of CFPS model for GT.

3.4 Result Analysis of Reasoning

Using multiple sets of data reasoning, the computation situation is as follows in Tables 1, 2 and 3. Where, t_{0n} represents the present state. t_{1n} shows the state the next time. $n = 1, 2, 3, 4$. The data in Tables 1, 2 and 3 shows that it obtains a more accurate result by using a cell-type fuzzy inference P system. When micro-grid is under different operating conditions, the change of the operating status of GT, Load2 and Storage2 are more reasonable to achieve effective energy management, maintain a frequency stability of the AC bus, and meet the energy demands of important load Load1. What's more, it extends the device life of the energy storage.

Table 1. f is larger than standard value.

T	t_{01}	t_{11}	t_{02}	t_{12}	t_{03}	t_{13}	t_{04}	t_{14}
f	0.8		0.6		0.7		0.8	
GT	0.8	-0.8	0.8	0.8	0.6	0.6	0.5	0.5
LOAD2	0.8	0.79	-0.2	-0.2	-0.2	0.46	-0.2	-0.2
STORAGE2	-0.4	-0.4	-0.4	0.5	0.5	0.5	-0.4	0.6
SOC	0.8		0.4		0.6		0.1	

4   Simulation

Based on the micro-grid systems given above and CFPS of it, we use MATLAB to verify the feasibility of the ideas. The parameters of DGs and loads are shown in the following Table 4.

Table 2. f is moderation.

T	t_{01}	t_{11}	t_{02}	t_{12}	t_{03}	t_{13}	t_{04}	t_{14}
f	0.3		0.4		−0.3		0.4	
GT	0.4	0.35	−0.4	−0.4	−0.4	−0.4	0.4	0.4
LOAD2	0.5	0.4	−0.5	−0.5	−0.5	−0.5	0.6	0.6
STORAGE2	0.6	0.45	−0.2	−0.2	0.2	−0.25	−0.6	0.5
SOC	0.3		0.8		0.8		0.2	

Table 3. f is smaller than standard value.

T	t_{01}	t_{11}	t_{02}	t_{12}	t_{03}	t_{13}	t_{04}	t_{14}
f	−0.6		−0.7		−0.8		−0.9	
GT	0.8	0.8	−0.2	0.45	0.6	0.6	−0.6	0.5
LOAD2	0.8	0.8	−0.2	0.45	0.6	0.6	−0.6	0.5
STORAGE2	−0.4	0.5	−0.2	0.45	−0.5	−0.65	0.4	0.6
SOC	0.5		0.7		0.2		0.6	

The changes of active power lead to the changes of frequency in Micro-grid. Therefore, we simulate the change of frequency by observing the change of active power. Two cases that are before or after control were compared. Data in 24 h are as example to simulate. The normal output power and power consumption of PV, WT and important load are shown in Fig. 7. The Fig. 8 shows that, when there were only the photovoltaic systems and wind power generation system as important load power supplied in micro-grid system, the system operated in an abnormal state most of the time. Output power appeared excessive in 0–18.2 h and shortage in 18.2–22.4 h, it made a serious impact on quality of power supply and causes AC feeder frequency fluctuations. It was not conducive to the normal operation of important loads. Consequently, accessing part of DGs to mitigate the serious distortion of power quality is essential.

4.1 Original Micro-grid System

In order to ease energy fluctuation, the GT, general load and two storage systems are connected to the above system. Photovoltaic power generation systems and wind power generation system access micro-grid with maximum power tracking control mode to improve the energy utilization. Two storage systems use droop

Table 4. The parameters of DGs and loads

PV/kW	WT/kW	GT/kW	Storage 1/kW	Storage 2/kW	Load 1/kVA	Load 2/kVA
20	15	5	20	10	20	5

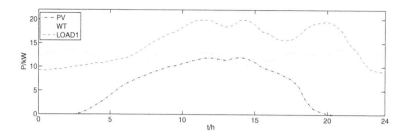

Fig. 7. Power of PV, WT and Load1.

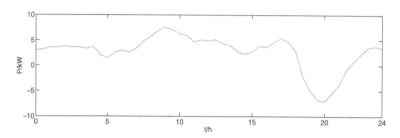

Fig. 8. Power difference curve.

control method. The initial states of charge are SOC1=0.23 and SOC2=0.4. GT operates with rated power shown in Table 1. Two storage systems can absorb the excess power or supplement insufficient power to bring down the energy fluctuation and guarantee the frequency stability in a period of time. The charge states of two storage systems in 24 h are shown in Fig. 9(a). PV, WT, Load1, Storage1 and Storage2 power changes are shown in Fig. 9(b). Figure 9(a)–(c) show that there was excess power at 0–12. Under the consumptive role of storage system Storage1 and Storage2, it achieved the balance of power. Storage1 had reached maximum storage charged state until 12, and cannot continue to absorb the extra power. In 14, Storage2 has reached the maximum charged state and unable to absorb excess power. So in the output power in 13.5 to 18.5 was high. It increased the feeder frequency of the system directly. The discharge of the storage systems in 18–21.3 and the charging of the storage system in 21.3–24 balanced the energy and power stably. The power curve of the whole system is shown in Fig. 9(c). Feeder frequency is shown in Fig. 9(d).

4.2   Micro-grid Using CFPS

We use ON/OFF control to GT, Load2 and Storage2 in the original system. CFPS is used to reasoning the control thought. Experimental results are as follows. The charge states of Storage1 and Storage2 are shown in Fig. 10(a). PV, WT, Load1, Storage1 and Storage2 power changes are shown in Fig. 10(b). The power of GT and Load2 changes are shown in Fig. 10(c) and Fig. 10(d). The figure shows that

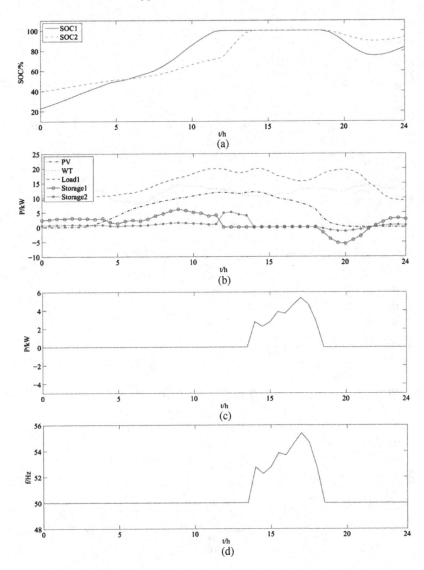

Fig. 9. (a) SOC of the original system, (b) DGs' power distribution of the original system, (c) The power difference curve of the original system, (d) AC frequency curve of the original system.

the surplus energy which can result a high frequency makes Storage1 and Storage2 charged in 0–8.5 h. In 8.5 h, the GT was disconnected and Load2 kept accessing. In 11, Load2 was disconnected and Storage1 and Storage2 stopped charging. Storage1 and Storage2 began to discharge in 12.5–14. In 15, Load2 accessed, Storage1 and Storage2 discharged, and GT kept disconnected. In 16, load2 was disconnected, Storage1 and Storage2 discharged, and GT was disconnected. In 17–18,

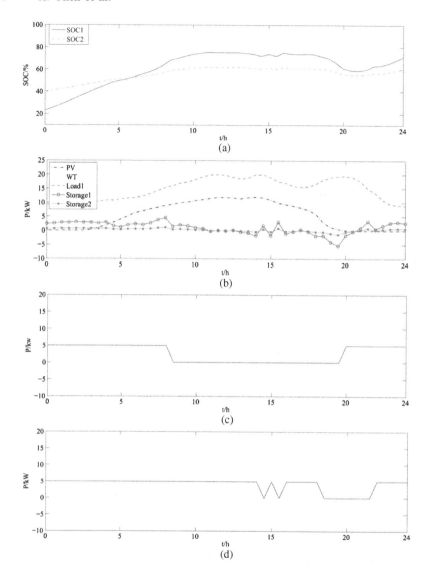

Fig. 10. (a) SOC, (b) Power distribution of DGs, (c) Power of GT, (d) Power of Load2.

Load2 kept accessing, Storage1 and Storage2 discharged, and GT kept being disconnected. Load2 kept disconnecting, Storage1 and Storage2 discharged, and GT was disconnected in 18 to 20. In 20.5–20.5, Load2 was disconnected, GT accessed, Storage1 and Storage2 charged. In 21.5–24, Load2 accessed GT accessed, Storage1 and Storage2 charged to regulate the energy balance and maintain frequency. Power curve after adjusted is shown in Fig. 11(a). It is known that its value is close to 0. It maintains the communication frequency stability of the feeder. The frequency of the AC feeder is shown in Fig. 11(b).

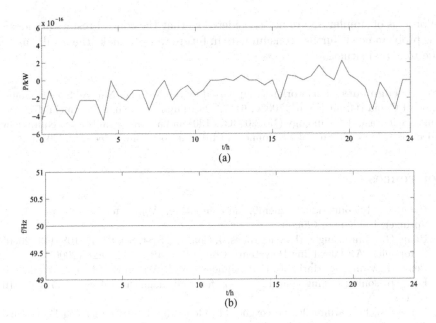

Fig. 11. (a) Power difference curve, (b) AC frequency curve.

4.3 Result Analysis

Simulation results show that it appears power imbalance (13.5-18.5 h) in the process of automatic control system for the micro-grid. The storage system achieves full state. Feeder frequency is higher than the standard. It reduces the utilization rate of DGs. Nevertheless, CFPS is adopted to improve the decision-making control system can better complete the decision making reasoning process in Tables 1, 2 and 3 in Sect. 4. Compared two kinds of control modes, CFPS control mode can maintain 24 h power balance in micro-grid, maintains the system frequency stability, realizes stable control effect and improves the utilization efficiency of DGs to verify the rationality of mind control.

5 Conclusion

This paper presents a cell-like fuzzy P system (CFPS for short) which based on the fuzzy knowledge. Based on the CFPS, this paper realizes the application in the control of micro-grid. Detailed reasoning is presented to prove the rationality and feasibility of the proposed control thoughts. The MATLAB simulation verifies the decision made by the CFPS is correct and the application is rationality which is aimed to achieve a stable energy management and control micro-grid system steady. Experimental results show that CFPS can manage micro-grid effectively, and play a role in load shifting by energy management to stabilize the frequency of AC feeder. Nonetheless, the hardware features of the system in the process of simulation are not considered so that the control results are ideal. This problem needs further consummate in future work to make the results more close to actual situation.

Acknowledgments. This work was supported by the National Natural Science Foundation of China (Grant No. 61170030, 61472328), Fund of Sichuan Provincial Department of Science and Technology (No. 2013GZ0130) and a grant from the key equipment project of Sichuan Provincial Economic and Information Committee (No. [2014]128).

References

1. Păun, G.: Introduction to membrane computing. Appl. Membr. Comput. 1–42. Springer, Heidelberg (2006)
2. Păun, G.: Computing with membranes. J. Comput. Syst. Sci. **61**(1), 108–143 (2000)
3. Syropoulos, A.: Fuzzifying P systems. Comput. J. **49**(5), 619–628 (2006)
4. Peng, H., Wang, J., Mario, J., Pérez-Jiménez, M.J., Wang, H., Shao, J., Wang, T.: Fuzzy reasoning spiking neural P system for fault diagnosis. Inf. Sci. **235**, 106–116 (2012)
5. Verlan, S., Bernardini, F., Gheorghe, M.: Generalized communicating P systems. Theor. Comput. Sci. **404**(1), 170–184 (2008)
6. Lasseter, R.H.: Microgrids. In: 2002 Power Engineering Society Winter Meeting, pp. 305–308 (2002)
7. Lu, X.Z., Wang, C.X., Min, Y.: Overview on micro-grid research. Autom. Electr. Power Syst. **31**(19), 100–107 (2007)
8. Prodanovic, M., Green, T.C.: High-quality power generation through distributed control of a power park microgrid. IEEE Trans. Ind. Electron. **53**(5), 1471–1482 (2006)
9. Muller, H., Rudolf, A., Aumayr, G.: Studies of distributed energy supply systems using an innovance energy management system. In: 2001 IEEE Power Engineering Society Meeting: Institute of Electrical and Electronics Engineers, CPP, pp. 87–90 (2001)
10. Kyriakarakos, G., Dounis, A.I., Arvanitis, K.G.: A fuzzy cognitive maps-petri nets energy management system for autonomous polygeneration microgrids. Appl. Soft Comput. **12**(12), 3785–3797 (2012)
11. Liu, T., Wang, J., Sun, Z.: An improved particle swarm optimization and its application for micro-grid economic operation optimization. In: Pan, L., Păun, G., Pérez-Jiménez, M.J., Song, T. (eds.) Bio-Inspired Computing-Theories and Applications, pp. 276–280. Springer, Heidelberg (2014)
12. Wu, Z., Gu, W.: Active power and frequency control of islanded micro-grid based on multi-agent technology. Electr. Power Autom. Equip. **29**(11), 57–61 (2009)
13. Miyamoto, S.: Multisets and fuzzy multisets. Soft Comput. Human-Centered Mach. 9–33. Springer, Japan (2000)
14. Song, T., Pan, L.: Spiking neural P systems with rules on synapses working in maximum spikes consumption strategy. IEEE Trans. NanoBiosci. **14**(1), 38–44 (2015)
15. Song, T., Pan, L.: Spiking neural P systems with rules on synapses working in maximum spiking strateg. IEEE Trans. NanoBiosci. **14**(4), 465–477 (2015)

Resource Allocation Algorithm Based on Fuzzy Cluster Grouping for Device-to-Device Communication

Puyan Chen[1], Jianbin Xue[1,2]([✉]), Yiming Chen[1], Supan Wei[1], and Yu Ji[1]

[1] College of Computer and Communication, Lanzhou University of Technology,
Lanzhou 730050, China
cpychen@126.com
[2] National Mobile Communications Research Laboratory, Southeast University,
Nanjing 210096, China
317124704@qq.com

Abstract. In order to solve the problem of spectrum scarcity in the mobile communication system, considering more than one D2D pair reuse the same uplink channel resource occupied by cellular user in TD-LTE systems, this research proposes an algorithm of resource allocation based on fuzzy cluster grouping. This algorithm not only determines the group number of D2D pairs based on fuzzy cluster but also able to find a suitable cellular user for each group to reuse its channel resource based on minimizing outage probability. Finally, stimulation results show that the proposed algorithm can admit more D2D pairs, improve the system throughput and meet the target of quality of service.

Keywords: Resource allocation · Fuzzy cluster · Outage probability · Quality of service

1 Introduction

With the increasing number of the mobile users and the improving requirements on communication quality, the traditional LTE system clearly cannot satisfy the communication needs of the users. D2D (device - to - device) communication is a direct communication technology based on point-to-point underlay the cellular system [1]. D2D communication technology can establish the direct communications between two users in short distance. Meanwhile, it also has huge advantages in many aspects, such as saving the power and increasing the spectrum utilization and providing local data service. Therefore, it received extensive attention, research and discussion in recent years [2–4]. The D2D communication technology has been introduced to the traditional LTE cellular system and formed the heterogeneous hybrid network communication system due to its large number of advantages [5–7]. Introducing the D2D communication technology to the LTE system can resolve the shortage of spectrum resource and the problem of huge local data transmission. However, because of the D2D pairs reuse the

© Springer-Verlag Berlin Heidelberg 2015
M. Gong et al. (Eds.): BIC-TA 2015, CCIS 562, pp. 33–44, 2015.
DOI: 10.1007/978-3-662-49014-3_3

radio resources of cellular users for data transmission, co-channel interference is inevitable caused by the resource sharing between D2D pairs and cellular users. And normal communication might be disrupted if the interference is serious enough. As a result, the radio resources allocation of the D2D communication is particularly important.

In [8], the author studied the D2D resource allocation method that one D2D pair reuse the radio resources of one cellular user. But this method is a very simple way of resource allocation and will not be able to accept the communication requests of D2D pairs in the system as much as possible. In [9], the author studied the allocation algorithm that one D2D pair reuses multiple the radio resource of cellular users. But the algorithm only considered the scenario that only one D2D pair exists in the system. The author also studied the algorithm that one D2D pair reuses multiple radio resource [10–12], but the resource allocation algorithms proposed in the two articles are not able to guarantee all D2D pairs can obtain the resources of multiple cellular users, and also have high computational complexity.

To resolve the above problems, this paper proposes a D2D resource allocation algorithm based on fuzzy cluster grouping. This algorithm groups all D2D pairs in the system by fuzzy cluster grouping, which makes each D2D pair in the same group differentiated from others. Then considering the Qos requests of cellular user, assigns optimized radio resources of cellular user to each D2D group. Finally, the simulation results show that this algorithm can quickly allocate resources to D2D pairs and maximize the system throughput. And at the same time, it can meet the Qos requirement of the D2D pairs as well as permit large number of communication requests from D2D pairs.

The rest of this paper is organized as follows. Part II describes the system model of the grouping D2D case, gives corresponding analysis of the interference. Part III proposes a D2D resource allocation method based on fuzzy cluster grouping, which assigns reusable cellular user resources on the basis of minimum interruption possibility. Part IV gives the numerical simulation based on fuzzy cluster grouped D2D communication resource allocation scheme, and analyzes the simulation results. Finally, the summary is in part V.

2 System Model

Compared with the traditional resource allocation scenario that one D2D pair can only reuse a RB for short distance data transmission, this paper allows multiple D2D pairs reuse the uplink RB of one cellular user under certain circumstances in order to maximum the use of the spectrum resources. And all the D2D pairs which can reuse the same RB are called as a D2D group. Because this paper introduced the resources reusing in the cellular systems, the communication users who used the same RB might have interference caused by the same frequency. The normal communication of users might be disrupted if the interference is serious enough. Therefore, when reusing the resources, the communication quality of the user needs to be taken into account.

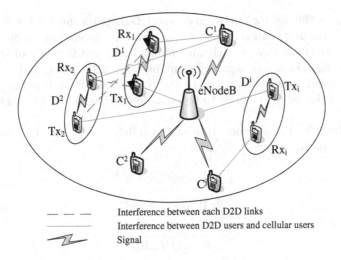

Fig. 1. System model of D2D communication underlaying cellular networks

As showed in Fig. 1, without loss of generality, assume that the single cell contains K cellular users and N D2D pairs and named respectively as set $C = \{C^j | j = 1, 2, \cdots, K\}$ $D = \{D^i | i = 1, 2, \cdots, N\}$, which, $\sqrt{N} < K < N$; The sender of a D2D pair is Tx, and the receiver is Rx. Before D2D resource allocation, eNodeB effectively allocated the resource block(RB) for K cellular users by using PF algorithm. For the convenience of analysis, assuming that all cellular users and D2D pairs need to obey uniform distribution within the cell.

Based on the system model established above, as D2D pairs reuse the uplink RB for short distance direct communication, eNodeB will suffer the interference from T_{X_i} of D2D pairs. At the same time, when multiple D2D pairs reusing the same RB, R_{X_i} of D2D pairs also will be interfered by cellular users, as well as the $T_{X_j}(j \neq i)$ of D2D pairs. If all the D2D pairs who reuse RB of the same cellular users C^l formed a group $G_i = \{D^j | j \in \{1, 2, \cdots, N\}\}(1 \leq i \leq K)$, then the SINR on the eNodeB is:

$$\gamma_L^B = \frac{P_C |h_{c2b}|^2 r_l^{-\partial}}{\sum\limits_{D^j \in G_i} P_D |h_{d2b}|^2 D_j^{-\partial} + N_0} \tag{1}$$

R_{X_j} of D2D pairs received SINR will be:

$$\gamma_L^D = \frac{P_D |h_{d2d}|^2 d_j^{-\partial}}{\sum\limits_{D^i \in G_i - D^j} P_D |h_{d2d}|^2 d_{i,j}^{-\partial} + P_C |h_{c2d}|^2 L_{l,j}^{-\partial} + N_0} \tag{2}$$

Among which, the P_C is the power of cellular users, and P_D is the power of D2D users; r is the distance between cellular users and eNodeB; D is distance between D2D pairs and eNodeB; d_j is the distance between D2D channel T_X

and R_X; $d_{i,j}$ is the distance between different D2D pairs and L_{lj} is the distance between cellular users and D2D pairs; h_{c2b} is the channel fading coefficient from cellular user to eNodeB; h_{d2b} is channel fading coefficient from T_X of D2D pairs to eNodeB; h_{d2d} is the fading coefficient between D2D pairs, and h_{c2b} is the fading coefficient from cellular user to the Rx of D2D pairs. ∂ is the path loss factor; N_0 is the average equals to 0; variance of σ^2 is White Gaussian Noises power.

Then the data transmission rate of the cellular user and D2D pair which reuses the same RB respectively are:

$$r_L^B = W log_2(1 + \kappa \gamma_L^B) \tag{3}$$

$$r_L^D = W log_2(1 + \kappa \gamma_L^D) \tag{4}$$

$$\kappa = \frac{1.5}{ln(0.2/BER_{tar})} \tag{5}$$

Among which, BER_{tar} is target bit error rate; W is a RB occupied channel bandwidth; γ_L^B and γ_L^D are respective SINR of eNodeB and R_x of D2D pairs. Through the above analysis, the total number of uplink transmission rate is as follows:

$$R = \sum_{L=1}^{K} r_L^B + \sum_{L=1}^{N} r_L^D \tag{6}$$

In addition, in order to ensure that the introduction of the D2D communication does not affect the communication quality in traditional cellular users demand, the SINR of eNodeB should meet formula (7). The system will not allow the communication requests of D2D users if do not meet formulas (8).

$$s.t. \quad \gamma_L^B \geq \gamma_1 \tag{7}$$

$$s.t. \quad \gamma_L^D \geq \gamma_2 \tag{8}$$

Among which, γ_1, γ_2 are the threshold of SINR.

3   Channel Resource Allocation

According to the analysis of the above model, compared with the common resources allocation algorithm, this paper studied the D2D resource allocation algorithm not only can maximize the acceptance of D2D communication request but also can ensure the Qos demand from D2D users and cellular users.

3.1   Fuzzy Cluster Grouping for the D2D Pairs

The purpose of grouping for D2D pairs is to divide N D2D pairs into C D2D groups, and name them as $G = \{G_i | i = 1, 2, \cdots, C\}$. At the same time, the D2D pairs in each D2D group G_i has great differences between each other.

The D2D pair attributes set which need to be considered are the location of user, speed requirement, bit error rate requirement and SINR requirement.

Therefore, there are totally N pairs of D2D users in the cell, considering each D2D pair has M(M=4) attributes, using matrix X to represent all the relevant attributes of D2D user is as follows:

$$X = \begin{bmatrix} x_{11} & x_{12} & \cdots & x_{1M} \\ x_{21} & x_{22} & \cdots & x_{2M} \\ \vdots & \vdots & \ddots & \vdots \\ x_{N1} & x_{N2} & \cdots & x_{NM} \end{bmatrix}_{N \times M} \tag{9}$$

Among them $X = [X_1, X_2, \cdots, X_N]^T$, $X_i = [x_{i1}, x_{i2}, \cdots, x_{iM}]$. X_i is the i-th row vector in X matrix, which represents the i-th D2D pair.X_{ij} is the j-th attribute value of the i-th D2D pair, each attribute value is determined based on the actual statistical data values.

The traditional fuzzy clustering grouping is to group the objects with the same or similar attributes to the same group. However, in this paper groups the D2D pairs with big differences to the same set. After theoretical analysis, when the distance between two D2D pairs is relatively far, and wherein the QoS requirements of a D2D pair is high, while the QoS requirements of the other D2D pair is relatively low. In this case, these D2D pairs are able to reuse the same RB for short distance communication.

The clustering group should also meet the following two conditions: (1) each D2D group contains at least one D2D pair; (2) each D2D pair belongs to and only belongs to one D2D group.

Firstly, set the minimum distance threshold value between D2D groups is ε, and define the distance between any two D2D pairs is:

$$(d_{ij})^2 = ||X_i - X_j|| = (X_i - X_j)^T (X_i - X_j) \tag{10}$$

And determine the D2D group C according to the proposed initial clustering center determination method in [12].

Secondly, the introduction of membership function $u_{ik} = u_{G_i}(X_k)$ to represent the membership degree of X_k to D2D group G_i, $u_{ik} \in [0,1]$, the greater the u_{ik}, the higher membership degree of X_k belongs to G_i. In order to get u_{ik}, this paper defines a value function:

$$J(U,P) = \sum_{k=1}^{N} \sum_{i=1}^{C} \frac{1}{(u_{ik})^m (d_{ik})^2}, m \in [1, \infty) \tag{11}$$

$$s.t. \quad \sum_{i=1}^{C} u_{ik} = 1 \tag{12}$$

Among which, $U = [u_{ik}]_{C \times N}$, $P = [p_i | i = 1, 2, \cdots, C]$ is the clustering center, and m is the smoothing parameter.

Then, D2D pair grouping criteria is to obtain the minimum J(U,P), i.e., the $min\{J(U,P)\}$. Using the Lagrange multiplier method to construct a Lagrange objective function:

$$G(U,P,\lambda) = \sum_{i=1}^{C} \frac{1}{(u_{ik})^m (d_{ik})^2} + \lambda(\sum_{i=1}^{C} u_{ik} - 1) \tag{13}$$

The necessary condition to obtain the optimal solution is the first order partial derivative in the above formula equals zero.

$$\frac{\partial G}{\partial \lambda} = \sum_{i=1}^{C} u_{ik} - 1 = 0 \tag{14}$$

$$\frac{\partial G}{\partial u_{ik}} = \sum_{i=1}^{C} \frac{1}{(d_{ik})^2}(-m)(u_{ik})^{-m-1} + \sum_{i=1}^{C} \lambda = 0 \tag{15}$$

According to the formula (12), (14) and (15):

$$u_{ik} = \frac{1}{\sum_{j=1}^{C} (\frac{d_{ik}}{d_{jk}})^{\frac{2}{m+1}}} \tag{16}$$

Similarly, when obtain the minimum value of J(U,P):

$$\frac{\partial J(U,P)}{\partial p_i} = 0 \tag{17}$$

According to the formula above, we can get:

$$p_i = \frac{1}{\sum_{i=1}^{C}(u_{ik})^{-m}(d_{ik})^{-3}} \sum_{i=1}^{C}(u_{ik})^{-m}(d_{ik})^{-3}X_k \tag{18}$$

Finally, as proposed in [12], there are certain relationship between the maximum number of clustering and the research objective, which is:

$$C \leq C_{max}(C_{max} = \sqrt{N}) \tag{19}$$

Based on the above analysis, the algorithm of fuzzy clustering the N pairs of D2D users in the cell into group C is as follows:

Step 1: Initialize the parameters such as ε, m, C_{max}.
Step 2: According to the initial clustering center determination method to determine C numbers of clustering centers $P = [p_1, p_2, \cdots, p_C]$.
Step 3: Use the formula (16) and (18) to iterative update the ownership degree matrix U and the clustering center p_i.

Step 4: If the clustering center converged then use the formula (11) to calculate the current value function which caused by C numbers of clustering group, and names as J_C.

Step 5: Repeat step2 to step4 until the C= C_{max}.

Step 6: Compare the results J_C from different cluster grouping numbers, when J_C reaches the minimum, the corresponding cluster grouping number C is the final determined D2D group numbers.

Step 7: The finally determined D2D group number is generated from the corresponding ownership degree matrix of the ultimate determined D2D grouping C.

3.2   The Outage Probability Analysis

When the D2D pair D^i and the cellular user C^j use the same uplink RB, the SINR of eNodeB is as follows:

$$SINR_{c,j} = \frac{P_C|h_{c2b}|^2 r_j^{-\partial}}{P_D|h_{d2b}|^2 D_i^{-\partial}} + N_0 \tag{20}$$

In order to satisfy the Qos requirements of cellular users, pre-define the SINR threshold value of cellular users is γ_1. Then the outage probability of cellular user C^j will be:

$$P_{c,j}^{out} = P\{SINR_{c,j} \leq \gamma_1\} \tag{21}$$

Among which, α is the path loss index, $N_0 = \eta W$, η is the gaussian white noise spectral density of the receiver. W is the channel bandwidth, h obeys the exponential distribution whose average is $2\delta^2$, its probability density function is as follows:

$$f(h) = \begin{cases} \frac{1}{2\sigma^2}e^{-h/2\sigma^2}, & h > 0 \\ 0, & h \leq 0 \end{cases} \tag{22}$$

Make $x = P_C|h_{c2b}|^2 r_j^{-\partial}$, $y = P_D|h_{d2b}|^2 D_i^{-\partial} + N_0$ then combine (20), (21), (22) can get the following formula:

$$\begin{aligned} P_{c,j}^{out} &= P\{\tfrac{x}{y} \leq \gamma_1\} \\ &= \int_0^{+\infty} \int_0^{y\cdot\gamma_1} \frac{1}{2\sigma^2 P_C r_j^{-\alpha}} exp(-x/2\sigma^2 P_C r_j^{-\alpha}) \\ &\quad \times \frac{1}{2\sigma^2 P_D D_i^{-\alpha}} exp[-(y - N_0)/2\sigma^2 P_D D_i^{-\alpha}] dxdy \end{aligned} \tag{23}$$

Make $a = 2\sigma^2 P_C r_j^{-\alpha}$, $b = 2\sigma^2 P_D D_i^{-\alpha}$ then the above formula can be further converted to:

$$\begin{aligned} P_{c,j}^{out} &= \int_0^{+\infty} \int_0^{y\cdot\gamma_1} \tfrac{1}{a}e^{-x/a}\tfrac{1}{b}e^{-(y-N_0)/b} dxdy \\ &= -\tfrac{1}{b} \int_0^{+\infty} e^{\frac{-y\cdot\gamma_1}{a} - \frac{y-N_0}{b}} dy + \tfrac{1}{b} \int_0^{+\infty} e^{-\frac{y-N_0}{b}} dy \\ &= 1 - \frac{ae^{\frac{N_0}{b}}}{a+b\gamma_1}. \end{aligned} \tag{24}$$

3.3 Resource Allocation Algorithm Analysis

According to the fuzzy cluster grouping method specified in section A, after dividing N D2D pairs to C D2D groups, and then finds the most appropriate cellular user for each D2D group G_i to reuse the uplink RB for short distance communication. In order to meet the communication quality requirements of cellular users, it is necessary to consider the outage probability of cellular users caused by all D2D pairs in D2D group G_i.

Calculating the sum of the outage probability $P^{out}_{G_i,C^j}$ of Cellular user C^j caused by all D2D users in G^i:

$$P^{out}_{G_i,C^j} = \sum_{D_m \in G_i} P^{out}_{c,j} \tag{25}$$

Among which, it represented that when all the D2D pairs reuse the RB of cellular user C^j, the smaller the $P^{out}_{G_i,C^j}$ the smaller the accumulated interference to the cellular user.

Thus, build an outage probability matrix P^{out} and a resource assignment matrix A are as follows:

$$P^{out} = [P^{out}_1 P^{out}_2 \cdots P^{out}_C]^T = [P^{out}_{ij}]_{C \times K} \tag{26}$$

$$A = [a_{ij}]_{C \times K} \tag{27}$$

In which, $P^{out}_1 = [P^{out}_{11} P^{out}_{12} \cdots P^{out}_{1K}]^T$, the P^{out}_{ij} shows the outage probability caused by D2D group G_i when reuse the RB of cellular user C^j. $a_{ij} = 1$ means allow the D2D pairs in G_i to reuse the RB of C^j otherwise, not allowed to reuse the RB.

Therefore, the problem of allocating resources for all D2D pairs in G_i is converted to find the condition of $a_{ij} = 1 (j = 1, 2, \cdots, K)$. Considering the introduction of the D2D communication cannot cause too much interference on the communication quality of cellular users, then the necessary and sufficient condition for $a_{ij} = 1$ is:

$$\begin{cases} P^{out}_{ij} = minP^{out}_i = min(P^{out}_{i1}, P^{out}_{i2}, \cdots, P^{out}_{iK}) \\ \sum_{i=1}^{j} a_{ij} = 0. \end{cases} \tag{28}$$

4 System Simulation

This section select a radius of 500 m single cell as the simulation scenario of LTE. Please refer to Table 1 for the rest of the simulation parameters. Through the performance comparing of the grouping resource allocation algorithm (FCM-GA) proposed in this paper with Random resource allocation algorithm (Random-RA) and the common Greed grouping resource allocation algorithm (Greed C GA), to analyze the system performance index of system throughput and the numbers of D2D pairs.

Table 1. The simulation parameters set

Name of parameter	Value
Cell radius/m	500
Inner distance of D2D pair/m	$10 \sim 50$
System bandwidth/MHz	5
Cellular users/Sector	5
BS Tx power/dBm	46
D2D Tx power/dBm	24
Path loss index	3
Noise densitydB/Hz	-174

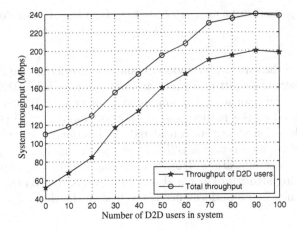

Fig. 2. The impact of different number of D2D pairs on system throughput

As showed on Fig. 2, with the increasing of D2D pair numbers in the system, the throughput of D2D pairs and the total throughput of system also increases. But when D2D pair number increased to a certain level, the throughput of D2D pairs and the total throughput of systems began to become smooth and no longer significantly increased. This means that the introduction of certain quantity of D2D pairs to the LTE cellular system can increase the system throughput. However, due to the resource reuse, when there is too many D2D pairs, interference might occurs not only between each D2D links but also between D2D link and cellular link. When SINR value lower than the threshold values, the communication request of D2D pairs might be rejected, thus resulting in a smooth curve in the later stage.

The Fig. 3 shows the acceptable D2D pair number change of the system from the grouping algorithm proposed by this paper comparing with the other two algorithms. As showed on the graph,the random resource allocation algorithm did not considered the co-channel interference generated by different D2D

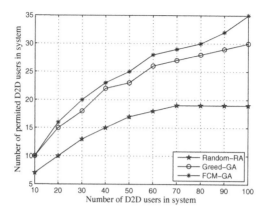

Fig. 3. The comparison of the number of admitted D2D pairs by using different algorithms

links which reuse the same radio resources, and the interference to D2D receiver when cellular users transmitting signals, and as the increasing in D2D pair numbers, such algorithm can accept a minimum number of D2D communication requests.Compared to the random distribution of resources, the Greed grouping resource allocation algorithm considered the interference of cellular link to D2D link, therefore, its acceptable D2D pair number is significantly greater than the random resource allocation algorithm. Among which, this paper proposed the fuzzy grouping algorithm, which also conducted analysis on the interference between D2D links, so its performance is the best in the three algorithms.

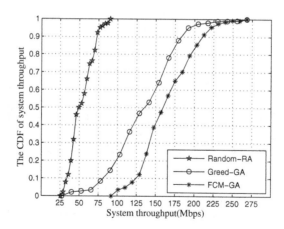

Fig. 4. The comparison of throughputs with different algorithms

Figure 4 compared the throughput CDF curve of the system by using the three resource allocation algorithm. The analysis of this simulation graph obviously shows that the lowest system throughput appears in random resource allocation. Therefore, in this algorithm, the co-channel interference in the system has not been effectively treated and avoided. When using the Greed grouping resource allocation algorithm, the throughput of system was increased greatly due to it effectively coordinated the interference between different communication links. The Fuzzy Grouping resource allocation algorithm proposed in this paper is based on the Greed grouping algorithm and is more stringent in handing interference. It also considered the interference between each D2D channel link, therefore, this algorithm has the highest system throughput and the system performance is significant upgraded.

5 Summary

Based on fuzzy clustering concept, this paper presents a resource allocation algorithm by grouping D2D pairs. This algorithm is applicable to a single cell when the number of D2D pairs is greater than the cellular user numbers. And this algorithm can access more D2D pairs and can greatly improve the throughput simultaneously of system. However, the current study was carried out based on fixed D2D user transmission power and it does not involve multi-cell scenarios. The follow-up study will further combine D2D power control and multi-cell scenarios.

Acknowledgment. This work was supported by the Open Research Found of National Mobile Communication Research Laboratory, Southeast University (No.2014D13) and Gansu Province Natural Science Foundation (No.1310RJZA003).

References

1. Yu, C.H., Tirkkonen, O., Doppler, K., et al.:Power optimization of device-to-device communication underlaying cellular communication, pp. 1–5 (2009)
2. Osseiran, A., Monserrar, J.F., Mohr, W.: Mobile and Wireless Communications for Imt-Advanced and Beyond, Chap. 9. Wiley, UK (2011)
3. Cheng, P., Deng, L., Yu, H., et al.: Resource allocation for cognitive networks with D2D communication: an evolutionary approach. In: Proceedings of Wireless Communications and Networking Conference, pp. 2671–2676 (2012)
4. Song, T., Pan, L.: Spiking neural P systems with rules on synapses working inmaximum spiking strateg. IEEE Trans. NanoBiosci. **14**(4), 465–477 (2015)
5. Sartori, P., Bagheri, H., Desai, V., et al.: Design of a D2D overlay for next generation LTE. In: Proceedings of the 8th Vehicular Technology Conference, pp. 1–5 (2014)
6. Doppler, K., Rinne, M., Wijting, C., et al.: Device-to-device communication as an underlay to LTE-advanced networks. IEEE Commun. Mag. **47**(12), 42–49 (2009)
7. Song, T., Pan, L., Jiang, K., et al.: Normal forms for some classes of sequential-spiking neural P systems. IEEE Trans. NanoBiosci. **12**(3), 255–264 (2013)
8. Zhu, D., Wang, J., Swindlehurst, A.L., et al.: Downlink resource reuse for device-to-device communications underlaying cellular networks. Sig. Process. Lett. **21**(5), 531–534 (2014)

9. Wang, B., Chen, L., Chen, H., et al.: Resource allocation optimization for device-to-device communication underlaying cellular networks. In: Vehicular Technology Conference, pp. 1–6 (2011)

10. Wang, F., Xu, C., Song, L., Zhao, Q., et al.: Energy-aware resource allocation for device-to-device underlay communication. In: Proceedings of International Conference on Communications, Budapest, pp. 6076–6080 (2013)

11. Xu, C., Song, L.Y., Han, Z., et al.: Interference-aware resource allocation for device-to-device communications as an underlay using sequential second price auction. In: Proceedings of 2012 IEEE International Conference on Communications, Ottawa, pp. 445–449 (2012)

12. Zhang, H., Wang, J.: Improved fuzzy C means clustering algorithm based on selecting initial clustering centers. Comput. Sci. **36**(6), 206–209 (2009)

Non-time Synchronization and Localization Based on Seawater Movement

Yiming Chen[1], Jianbin Xue[1,2]([✉]), Puyan Chen[1], Yu Ji[1], and Supan Wei[1]

[1] College of Computer and Communication, Lanzhou University of Technology,
Lanzhou 730050, China
brethless@yeah.net, 523527378@qq.com
[2] National Mobile Communications Research Laboratory, Southeast University,
Nanjing 210096, China

Abstract. For the problem of node position accuracy in underwater wireless sensor network (UWSN), we analyze the effects of node mobility and time synchronization on distance estimation in range-based localization algorithm. This paper proposes a non-time synchronization and localization algorithm based on the semi-periodical property of seawater movement. Firstly, through tracking the trajectory of movement node, this algorithm determines the location where node sends packets to. Secondly, with the help of the nature of underwater acoustic channel broadcast packets, we finish estimating the distance which based on the non-time synchronization algorithm. Finally, we estimate the position of the node by Second-Order Cone Programming algorithm. The simulation results show that the algorithm performs well on the comprehensive achievements of the positioning accuracy and energy consumption.

Keywords: Underwater sensor network · Non-time synchronization · Localization · Second-order cone programming

1 Introduction

Underwater sensor network serves as an important development of the terrestrial wireless sensor network (TWSN), and it aims to be able to meet diverse requirements of applications in underwater environment. However, with respect to the long propagation delay and high error rate of underwater communication channel, the UWSN have to face many challenges [1]. Time synchronization and localization play a key role in many applications, but the existing algorithm does not take fully a number of practical problems into account, such as signal propagation delay, the channel access delay and node mobility [2], while it would render the position accuracy decline in localization algorithm determined by distance. TSHL [3] (Time Synchronization for High Latency Acoustic Networks) is a synchronization algorithm which is designed for high latency and static networks. This algorithm achieves accuracy, although it assumes that all nodes in the stationary state does not fit the real situation. So MU-Sync [4] provides

© Springer-Verlag Berlin Heidelberg 2015
M. Gong et al. (Eds.): BIC-TA 2015, CCIS 562, pp. 45–55, 2015.
DOI: 10.1007/978-3-662-49014-3_4

time synchronization in mobile scenario. Consequently, adopting in improved timestamp of MU-Sync perform better than TSHL. But during the node moves constantly in the process of information exchange which reduces the performance of the algorithm, mainly because half of the round trip time in the algorithm as a transmission extension.

George Washington University X. Cheng and other scholars proposed UPS (Underwater Positioning Schema) [5], which is the silent positioning algorithm. The UPS detects signal arrival time and then converted to distance difference, finally through the trilateral positioning algorithm to calculate the location of unknown node. While the algorithm does not consider the case of the unknown node is outside the communication range of the four reference nodes. Hwee-Pink Tan have proposed wide coverage localization algorithm WPS in [6]. This algorithm solves the major limitations of feasible region of space in UPS. In university of California, B. Liu et al. [7] proposed asymmetrical round trip based synchronization-free location (ARTL). In algorithm the reference nodes can receive their own packets to locate the unknown node. It does not require a complex calculation, since the positioning process without time synchronization. Therefore the algorithm has performed smoothly. As a result the reference nodes need to exchange data packets for many times, it costs much of the energy and takes a long time for positioning. Zhong zhou et al. suggest SLMP which localizes the nodes with two main phases, that is, mobility prediction and localization, based on node mobility patterns demonstrated as a semi-periodical property [8]. The characteristics of the mobile node are the main reasons for the prediction accuracy of the localization algorithm.

In order to solve the above problems, we apply the non-time synchronization range and SOCP [9] into underwater sensor network. This paper mainly displays in two aspects: reducing energy consumption in ranging phase and improving the positioning accuracy. Firstly, this algorithm determines the sending point where node sends packets to according to the semi-periodical property of seawater movement, and it will eliminate the error of location because of the mobile beacon node. Then, we complete estimating the distance based on the non-time synchronization algorithm and get the position of the node through SOCP. The algorithm performs well on the comprehensive achievements of the positioning accuracy and energy consumption.

The rest of paper is organized as follows. Firstly, describe the basic system model and a brief study of the error analysis for time synchronization and positioning algorithm. Then the paper introduces the non-time synchronization and localization based on seawater movement. Finally, give the numerical simulation, the simulation results and analysis.

2   System Model

There are mainly three kinds of nodes in UWSN: the base stations, beacon nodes and unknown nodes. As shown in Fig. 1, the base stations which equipped with global position system (GPS) deployed on the sea surface. Beacon nodes and

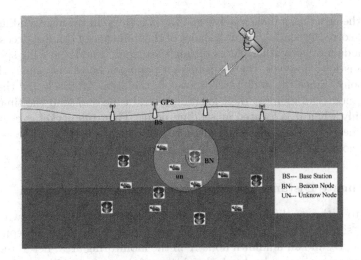

Fig. 1. System description

unknown nodes are randomly tossed to the monitoring area. Due to factors such as the limit of communication bandwidth and energy consumption, unknown nodes can not directly communicate with base stations. However, beacon nodes can get the real-time and location information from the base stations. With the rapid development of microelectronics mechanical systems, we assume that the sensor nodes are equipped with the gyroscope, accelerometer and the depth of the sensor, the sensors are equal to the inertial navigation system (INS) record real-time trajectory of the nodes.

3 Proposed Method

3.1 Protocol Overview

According to marine hydrodynamics and actual experimental tests, we found that ocean current impose periodic force on floater. The node in the sea is not randomly flow but has a semi-periodical flow characteristic, so we think that all nodes have the semi-periodical movement pattern. The algorithm is mainly divided into three parts: select sending point, distance estimation and positioning. Sending point is the only site where the target node sends a timestamp. It makes the target nodes stationary even though the nodes constantly flowing in underwater, which also reduces the error caused by node mobility in localization. In order to extract the sending point from the trajectory of the node. We should firstly divide the monitoring area into several small ocean cubes. Then record the number of nodes occurrence in each small cube. The highest hit ratio represents that the node has arrived at the location frequently and it will reach the cube in the future periodically. If the node founds several points with the same hit ratio, a cube with smallest moving speed of the node is selected as sending point. This is due to the fact that a node maybe sends a timestamp in the near sending point instead of correctly sending point because of the influence of channel access delay and the node moves to other places during that time. If nodes moving speed per unit time is low, however, the transmission point is almost the same with the sending point. Since the node rarely moves in the area. After selected the sending point, node can monitor their location in real time and send the timestamp packets only when it is located at sending point. Then the packet exchange for several times, it can estimate the distance between the beacon nodes and the unknown nodes. And finally complete the node positioning.

3.2 Estimate Distance Based on Non-time Synchronization

In order to estimate distance between the beacon nodes and unknown nodes, we use a similar TOA ranging method for range. Suppose S beacon nodes $B_1, B_2, \cdots, B_s$ and an unknown node X in the monitoring area. Let T represent a global accurate time and t_i be the local time of the node ith. Beacon nodes are able to receive their own packet messages, however the unknown node can only accept messages from the beacon nodes. Entire ranging procedure is described as follows: firstly we initialize a beacon node B_m and broadcast a ranging group message at T_{Bm1} which contains the timestamp t_{Bm1}. Then, the unknown node X, B_m and other beacon nodes B_i $(i \neq m)$ at time T_{X1}, T_{Bm2}, T_{Bi1} will receive the packet message with the timestamp t_{X1}, t_{Bm2}, t_{Bi1}. In order to prevent the potential collisions at X_m, after an arbitrary span, X broadcasts an acknowledgement including timestamps t_{X1}, t_{X2} and t_{Bm1}. Then B_m and other beacon nodes $B_i(i = \{1, \cdots, s\} \backslash \{m\})$ receive it at time T_{Bm3} and T_{Bi2} with timestamp t_{Bm3} and t_{Bi2}. Base on the above description, the following set of equations can be easily derived:

$$D_{BmX} = c(T_{X1} - T_{Bm1}) \tag{1}$$

$$D = c(T_{Bm2} - T_{Bm1}) \tag{2}$$

$$D_{BmX} = c(T_{Bm3} - T_{X2}) \tag{3}$$

$$D_{BmBi} = c(T_{Bi1} - T_{Bm1})(i \neq m) \tag{4}$$

$$D_{BiX} = c(T_{Bi2} - T_{X2})(i \neq m) \tag{5}$$

Where T_i represents the global time when the event occurred, and D denote the distance between the receiver and the transmitter of beacon nodes. But due to the D value is very small, we ignore its influence on ranging. D_{ab} represents the distance between the node a and b. c indicates the propagation velocity.

From Eqs. (1) and (3), we have

$$D_{BmX} = \frac{c}{2} \left[(T_{Bm3} - T_{Bm1}) - (T_{X2} - T_{X1}) \right] \tag{6}$$

From Eqs. (2) and (3), we have

$$D_{BmX} = c\left[(T_{Bm3} - T_{Bm2}) - (T_{X2} - T_{Bm1})\right] + D \tag{7}$$

From Eqs. (4) and (5), we have

$$D_{BiX} = c\left[(T_{Bi2} - T_{Bi1}) - (T_{X2} - T_{Bm1})\right] + D_{BmBi}(i \neq m) \tag{8}$$

From Eqs. (7) and (8), we have

$$D_{BiX} = D_{BmX} + D_{BmBi} - D + c\left[(T_{Bi2} - T_{Bi1}) - (T_{Bm3} - T_{Bm2})\right] (i \neq m) \tag{9}$$

From Eqs. (6) and (9), it follows that $(T_{Bm3}\text{-}T_{Bm1})$ and $(T_{X2}$ - $T_{X1})$ are the elapsed time between the two broadcasts at receivers B_m and X, respectively, while $(T_{Bi2}\text{-}T_{Bi1})$ and $(T_{Bm3}\text{-}T_{Bm2})$ are the elapsed time at X_i and X_m. Therefore these global moment can be expressed by the node local timestamp. Thus the formula (6) and (9) can be expressed as

$$D_{BmX} = \frac{c}{2}\left[(t_{Bm3} - t_{Bm1}) - (t_{X2} - t_{X1}) - \frac{2l}{r}\right] \tag{10}$$

$$D_{BiX} = D_{BmX} + D_{BmBi} - D + c\left[(t_{Bi2} - t_{Bi1}) - (t_{Bm3} - t_{Bm2})\right] (i \neq m) \tag{11}$$

Where l is the packet length and r is the transmission rate of the acoustic modem. Since the position of the beacon nodes are known, it can be directly calculate D_{BmBi}. The distance of D_{BmX} can be obtained from Eq. (10) and the distance D_{BiX} can be also obtained by Eq. (11). When calculating the distance between nodes do not need the global precise time, it only associated with the local time of node, so the algorithm do not have time synchronization.

3.3   Localization

Second-order cone programming (SOCP) is the intersection of a finite number of cones cartesian product of affine subspace to get the minimization of a linear function. As an important branch in the convex optimization theory, it covers the linear programming problem and the quadratic programming problem. So we adopt the SOCP to solve problem of the localization.

Given the previous section, we can get the distance between the beacon nodes and the unknown nodes, i.e. $D_{BiX}(i = 1, \cdots, s)$, and the depth information of the node can be obtained from the depth sensor. Therefore, we can project the beacon nodes into the plane of unknown node using the mathematical knowledge, as shown in Fig. 2.

To convert the three-dimensional positioning into two-dimensional, the beacon nodes and unknown nodes get depth information by depth sensor respectively H_i and H_x. Then the projection of D_{BiX} is $D'_{BiX} = \sqrt{D^2_{BiX} - (H_i - H_X)^2}$. Use the vector $\mathbf{p_i} = [\mathbf{x_i}, \mathbf{y_i}]^{\mathrm{T}}$ represents the projection point of beacon node and the vector $\mathbf{u} = [\mathbf{x}, \mathbf{y}]^{\mathrm{T}}$ represents the position of unknown node. So beacon node B_1 as a reference node, the corresponding measurement equation:

$$\hat{d}_{i1} = d_{i1} + e_{i1}, i = 2, 3, \cdots, s \tag{12}$$

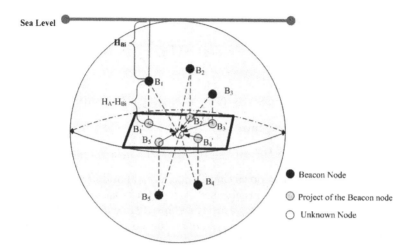

Fig. 2. Three-dimensional positioning into two-dimensional localization

Where $\hat{d}_{i1} = D'_{BiX} - D'_{B1X} (i = 2, 3, \cdots, s)$ represents the distance differences with noise, and $\mathbf{d_{i1}} = ||\mathbf{p_i} - \mathbf{u}|| - ||\mathbf{p_1} - \mathbf{u}||$, $\mathbf{e_{i1}}$ as measurement noise. Then the formula (12) is converted into a vector form,

$$\hat{\mathbf{d}} = \mathbf{d} + \mathbf{e} \tag{13}$$

Where in formula (13) $\hat{\mathbf{d}} = \left[\hat{\mathbf{d}}_{\mathbf{21}}, \hat{\mathbf{d}}_{\mathbf{31}}, \cdots, \hat{\mathbf{d}}_{\mathbf{s1}}\right]^{\mathbf{T}}$, $\mathbf{d} = [\mathbf{d_{21}}, \mathbf{d_{31}}, \cdots, \mathbf{d_{s1}}]^{\mathbf{T}}$ and $\mathbf{e} = [\mathbf{e_{21}}, \mathbf{e_{31}}, \cdots, \mathbf{e_{s1}}]^{\mathbf{T}}$. In order to make full use of observation values, assuming that quantitative measuring noise $\mathbf{e}$ obey the mean to 0, covariance matrix φ for a Gaussian distribution. Therefore, the likelihood function of vector $\hat{\mathbf{d}}$ can be used formula (14).

$$lnf(\hat{\mathbf{d}}/\mathbf{u}) = C - (\hat{\mathbf{d}} - \mathbf{d})^T \varphi^{-1}(\hat{\mathbf{d}} - \mathbf{d}) \tag{14}$$

Where c is a constant, in order to solve the position of the unknown node u, we need to make the likelihood function of formula (14) maximum. Therefore, the solution of process is optimized for formula (15).

$$\min_u (\hat{\mathbf{d}} - \mathbf{d})^T \varphi^{-1}(\hat{\mathbf{d}} - \mathbf{d}) \tag{15}$$

Because of the formula (15) is a nonlinear convex optimization problem, we need to introduce variable $\delta_i = ||p_i - u||$. Then the formula (15) can be converted to (16).

$$\begin{cases} \min\limits_{u,\delta}(\hat{\mathbf{d}} - \mathbf{H}\delta)^T \varphi^{-1}(\hat{\mathbf{d}} - \mathbf{H}\delta) \\ s.t. \quad \delta_{\mathbf{i}} = ||\mathbf{p_i} - \mathbf{u}||, i = 1, 2, \cdots, s \end{cases} \tag{16}$$

In formula (16), where $\delta = [\delta_1, \delta_2, \cdots, \delta_s]^{\mathbf{T}}$ and $\mathbf{H} = [-\mathbf{1}, \mathbf{I}]$, $\mathbf{1}$ is the $(s-1) \times 1$ vector of all 1 and $\mathbf{I}$ is the unit matrix. In order to convert it to SOCP in optimization problem. We will relax equation constraints as the inequality constraints, namely $\delta_i \geq ||\mathbf{p_i} - \mathbf{u}||$. To further limit the relaxed constraint conditions, we introduce the penalty factor $\rho \delta^T \delta$, where ρ is a small non-negative constant. The optimization problem for relaxation is show in formula (17),

$$\begin{cases} \min_{u,\delta}(\hat{\mathbf{d}} - \mathbf{H}\delta)^T \varphi^{-1}(\hat{\mathbf{d}} - \mathbf{H}\delta) + \rho \delta^T \delta \\ s.t. \quad \delta_i \geq ||\mathbf{p_i} - \mathbf{u}||, i = 1, 2, \cdots, s \end{cases} \quad (17)$$

We know the equation

$$(\hat{\mathbf{d}} - \mathbf{H}\delta)^T \varphi^{-1}(\hat{\mathbf{d}} - \mathbf{H}\delta) + \rho \delta^T \delta = ||A_0^{\frac{1}{2}}\delta - A_0^{-\frac{1}{2}}B_0||^2 - B_0^T A_0^{-1} B_0 + C_0 \quad (18)$$

where $A_0 = \mathbf{H^T}\varphi^{-1}\mathbf{H} + \rho \mathbf{I}$, $B_0 = \hat{\mathbf{d}}^T \varphi^{-1}\mathbf{H}$, $C_0 = \hat{\mathbf{d}}^T \varphi \hat{\mathbf{d}}$. In order to transform into SOCP form, we introduce another variable.

$$\begin{cases} \min_{u,\delta,\theta} \theta \\ s.t. \quad \delta_i \geq ||\mathbf{p_i} - \mathbf{u}||, i = 1, 2, \cdots, s \\ \quad\quad \theta \geq ||A_0^{\frac{1}{2}}\delta - A_0^{-\frac{1}{2}}B_0|| \end{cases} \quad (19)$$

Thus Eqs. (17) and (19) are completely equivalent problem, we can through the interior point algorithm to find the global optimal solution. Eventually $\mu^* = (u^*, \delta^*, \theta^*)$ is a global optimal solution, and u^* is the position of the unknown node.

4   Simulation

We set the simulation experiments in the 200 m*200 m*200 m underwater space, other related parameters are shown in the following Table 1.

Table 1. Simulation parameters

Location area	200 m*200 m*200 m
Communication radius	150 m
Beacon node number	3–10
Unknown node number	300
Upper bound of clock skew	1 ppm
Upper bound of clock offset	1 ms
Speed of sound	1500 m/s

In this paper, we compare the proposed method with the two existing algorithms: SeaWeb Navigation (SWN) and time synchronization and localization using seawater movement pattern(SLSMP) respectively from both energy consumption and position accuracy to analyze.

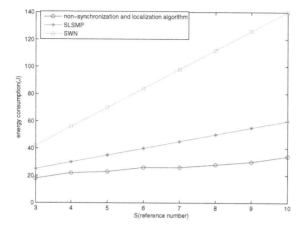

Fig. 3. Energy consumption under different beacon node number

Figure 3 depicts the energy consumption of the node when there is a change
in the beacon nodes in three algorithms. As can be seen from the figure, with
the increasing number of beacon nodes, the energy consumption has increased in
three algorithms, but the non-time synchronization and localization using seawater movement was significantly less than the other two algorithms. In this paper,
only a pair of packet-switched message occurs in ranging process of the algorithm,
one of them occurs in the initial beacon node, another occurs in the unknown
node, and other beacon nodes only listen to the radio. Therefore, we proposed
the method reduce a lot of energy costs in ranging phase. SWN is a symmetrical
round trip schema using the broadcast property of the medium. It requires each
beacon node to broadcast a ranging request to all the unknown nodes, and then
every unknown node to send several packets to reply to all the beacon nodes,
so the energy consumption is very large. For SLSMP its energy consumption
involving both time synchronization and ranging, because the optimization of
the algorithm, its energy consumption between the other two algorithms.

For the analysis of the position accuracy, we should consider the clock offset,
clock skew and the number of beacon nodes. We define the energy-error prod-
uct(EEP) to indicate the overall performance when talking both energy consumption and position accuracy. We fix the clock offset to 1 ms and the clock skew
to 1ppm. $EEP = E * average\_error$. In Figs. 4 and 5, due to the SLSMP complete the time synchronization periodically, it will compensate the offset, so the
change of skew will affect the algorithm. When the smaller the deviation value is,
the better the algorithm of positioning performance will be, and as the deviation
value increasing, the algorithm of positioning performance decrease. The proposed
method and SWN do not need time synchronization, so the change of skew does
not have influence on the performance of algorithms. But SWN will not be able to
reduce communication overhead at the same time, therefore we proposed method
have a good performance on both accuracy and energy consumption.

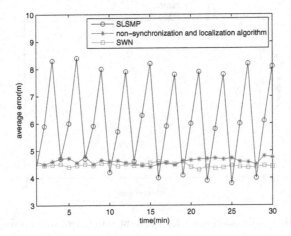

Fig. 4. Skew upper bound is 1 ppm

In Fig. 6, when the growing number of beacon nodes, the positioning precision of the three algorithms have greatly improved. However, with the increase in the number of beacon nodes, nodes will have large energy consumption of the packet switching costs. It can be seen in Fig. 7 when the beacon nodes is 5, the algorithm of positioning accuracy and energy consumption can reach a good compromise.

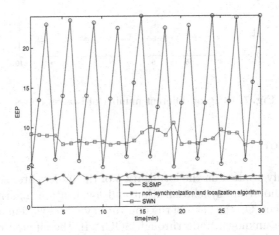

Fig. 5. EEP with 1 ppm skew upper bound

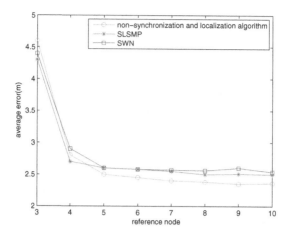

Fig. 6. Localization error for different number of beacon nodes

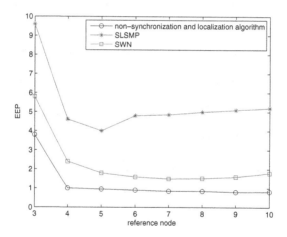

Fig. 7. EEP for different number of beacon nodes

5   Conclusion

This paper mainly studied on the localization of the underwater sensor network. We proposed a non-time synchronization and localization algorithm based on seawater movement. On the basis of the non-time synchronization of ranging, and then localize the unknown node through SOCP. In the simulation experiment we analyze the clock offset, skew and the number of beacon nodes that have influence on positioning accuracy and energy consumption. The results show that the proposed algorithm is not optimal in location accuracy compared with SWN and SLSMP, but have good performance on both accuracy and energy consumption. Therefore in the future work we will focus on range-based location algorithm and introduce relevant mathematical model to reduce the error and improve the positioning accuracy of the node.

Acknowledgment. This work was supported by the Open Research Found of National Mobile Communication Research Laboratory, Southeast University (No.2014D13) and Gansu Province Natural Science Foundation (No. 1310RJZA003)

References

1. Wu, Z., Li, X.: An improved underwater acoustic network localization algorithm. J. Commun. **12**(3), 77–83 (2015)
2. Liu, J., Zhou, Z., Peng, Z., et al.: Mobi-Sync: efficient time synchronization for mobile underwater sensor networks. J. Parallel Distrib. Syst. **24**(2), 406–416 (2013)
3. Syed, A.A., Heidemann, J.S.: Time synchronization for high latency acoustic networks. In: Conference on Infocom (2006)
4. Chirdchoo, N., Soh, W., Chua, K.C.: MU-Sync: a time cynchronization protocol for underwater mobile networks. In: Proceedings of the 3rd ACM International Workshop on Underwater Networks, pp. 35–42 (2008)
5. Cheng, X., Shu, H., Liang, Q., et al.: Silent positioning in underwater acoustic sensor networks. J. Veh. Technol. **57**(3), 1756–1766 (2008)
6. Tan, H.P., Gabor, A.F., Eu Z.A., et al.: A wide coverage positioning system (wps) for underwater localization. In: Proceedings of 2010 IEEE International Conference on Communications, pp. 1–5 (2010)
7. Liu, B., Chen, H., Zhong, Z., et al.: Asymmetrical round trip based synchronization-free localization in large-scale underwater sensor networks. J. Wirel. Commun. **9**(11), 3532–3542 (2010)
8. Song, T., Pan, L., Păun, G.: Asynchronous spiking neural P systems with local synchronization. Inf. Sci. **219**, 197–207 (2013)
9. Zhou, Z., Peng, Z., Cui, J.H., et al.: Scalable localization with mobility prediction for underwater sensor networks. J. Mob. Comput. **10**(3), 335–348 (2011)

Ant Colony Optimization with Different Crossover Schemes for Continuous Optimization

Zhiqiang Chen[1]([✉]), Yun Jiang[1], and Ronglong Wang[2]

[1] Chongqing Engineering Laboratory for Detection Control and Integrated System, Chongqing Technology and Business University, Chongqing 400067, China
`chen@hotmail.com`
[2] Graduate School of Engineering, University of Fukui, Fukui-shi 910-8507, Japan

Abstract. In this paper we present three ant colony optimization (ACO_R) with different crossover operations to solve the continuous optimization problems. Crossover operations in the genetic algorithm are employed to generate some new probability density function set (PDFs) of ACO_R in the promising space, which is aimed at improving the global exploration ability of ACO_R, and avoiding falling into the local minima and exploiting the correlation information among the design variables. The proposed algorithm is evaluated on some benchmark functions and the simulation results show that the proposed algorithm performs quite well and outperforms other algorithms.

Keywords: ACO · Continuous optimization · Crossover operator

1 Introduction

Metaheuristics are a family of optimization techniques that have seen increasingly rapid development and have been applied to continuous optimization problems (CnOPs) over the past few years [1,2]. Among them is ant colony optimization (ACO) [3]. The ant colony optimization was extended to the continuous domains by Socha [4], called ACO_R. The fundamental idea underlying ACO for the continuous domains is the shift of a probability density functions (PDFs), which is from using a discrete probability distribution to using a continuous one. It uses a solution archive as a form of pheromone model for the derivation of a probability distribution over the search space. However, ACO_R concentrates mainly on the small-scale continuous optimization problems, and for the larger CnOPs or multi-modal CnOPs, the results obtained by ACO_R are far from being competitive with the results obtained by the other algorithm.

In order to avoid the local stagnation, a proper trade-off mechanism between diversification and intensification is necessary. In this paper, to solve the CnOPs efficiently, several variants of ant colony optimization (ACO_R) based algorithm with crossover operations are suggested. In the proposed algorithm, the operation similar to the crossover in the GA is introduced to balance the diversification and intensification. The crossover operation is performed to generate some new PDF

© Springer-Verlag Berlin Heidelberg 2015
M. Gong et al. (Eds.): BIC-TA 2015, CCIS 562, pp. 56–62, 2015.
DOI: 10.1007/978-3-662-49014-3_5

set in the promising space. The new generated PDFs enhance the diversification of the algorithm. As a result, the pheromone information is enhanced in the promising space, and the global optima can be found efficiently. Additionally, the crossover operation helps the ant colony exploit the correlation information among the design variables. The proposed algorithms are evaluated by some test functions and are compared the results with other continuous optimization methods in the literature.

2   ACO with Crossover Operators for Continuous Optimization

The first algorithm that can be classified as an ACO algorithm for continuous domains is ACO_R [4]. In ACO_R, the discrete probability distributions used in the solution construction by ACO algorithms for combinatorial optimization are substituted by probability density functions (PDFs). ACO_R uses a solution archive [4] for the derivation of these PDFs over the search space. Additionally, ACO_R uses sums of weighted Gaussian functions to generate multimodal PDFs. For the ACO_R, the better the solution, the higher are the chances of choosing it. Once a guiding solution S_{guide} is chosen, the algorithm samples the neighborhood of the i-th real-valued component of the guiding solution S_{guide}^j using a Gaussian PDF with $S_{guide}^j = \mu_{guide}^j$, and σ_{guide}^j equal to

$$\sigma_{guide}^j = \xi \sum_{r=1}^{k} \frac{|S_r^i - S_{guide}^i|}{k-1} \tag{1}$$

which is the average distance between the value of the i-th component of S_{guide}^j and the values of the i-th components of the other solutions in the archive, multiplied by a parameter ξ [5]. The process of choosing a guiding solution and generating a candidate solution is repeated a total of N_a times (corresponding to the number of "ants") per iteration. Before the next iteration, the algorithm updates the solution archive keeping only the best k of the $k + N_a$ solutions that are available after the solution construction process.

Establishing a balance between exploration and exploitation for global search algorithm is important. For this reason, Crossover behavior is introduced into the ant colony optimization. The ant colony searches the solutions based on the pheromone of the ant colony, which is represented by the PDF set. Figure 1 presents the outline of ACO_R with crossover operator ($COACO_R$). As shown in Fig. 1, some of PDFs are generated by the crossover operations, and some of the other is from the original way of ACO_R. In the proposed algorithm, the crossover operation in genetic algorithm is employed to improve the search ability of the ant colony by enhancing the pheromone distribution in the promising searching space and strengthen the relation among the PDFs. A parameter n_{co}, which is the number of the crossover operations, denotes the degree of the crossover operation. As a result, the set of the PDFs become more diversiform and effective, and the ants could find the good solutions efficiently under the improved PDF set.

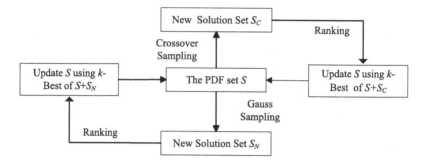

Fig. 1. Updating procedure of ACO with crossover operators

```
Algorithm:
    Input Parameters : k, m, n_co, D, ξ, ···
    Initialize PDFs: S = S_1,S_2,···,S_k)
        L = (x_max-x_min)/(2*(m+k);
        for j = 1 : k
            for i =1 : D
                S_j^i= normrnd(x_min +2*i*L ), L);
            end
        end
    while (termination criterion is not satisfied)
        //Generate m new solutions P = (P_1,P_2,···,P_m)
        for j=1 : m
            for i =1 : D
                Select guiding solution S_guide^i according to weights;
                P_j^i = Gaussian Sampling Based on Eq.(1);
            end
            Store and evaluate newly generated solution P_j;
        end
        Update PDFs S with the best k solutions of S+P .
        // Generate 2n_co solutions Z = (Z_1,Z_2,..., Z_2nco)
        for co=1: n_co
            Crossovers are performed among selected PDFs
        end
        Update PDFs S using  Z replace the worst 2n_co solutions of S;
    end
```

Fig. 2. Outline of the COACO_R

As for the procedure of the COACO_R, initially, the PDF set of the ant colony is filled with randomly generated Gaussian functions. The algorithm iteratively updates the PDF set. The iteration includes two phases, in the first phase, the solutions are constructed according to the PDFs, and in the second phase, the PDF set is updated. In the proposed algorithm, the PDF set consists of not only the PDFs generated by the solutions but also the PDFs generated by the crossover operation. Firstly, m new solutions are built based on the PDF set by each ant independently. Secondly, k PDF vectors are generated by the best

k solutions directly. Meanwhile, new $2n_{co}$ PDF vectors are generated by the crossover operations on the newly generated PDFs. After both the two kinds of PDFs were built, the updating of the PDF set is accomplished by adding the new $2n_{co}$ PDF vectors to the PDF set and removing the same number of worst PDF vectors. The outline of the proposed algorithm is shown in Fig. 2.

As mentioned above, Crossover operator plays an important role to improve the performance of ACO_R. Three crossover methods (BLX-α [6], UNDX [5] and PNX [7]) are employed for $COACO_R$, which are usually used in genetic algorithm.

3   Simulation

We use the 21 test functions reported in the literature [9] to verify the effectiveness of the proposed algorithm. The dimensionality is set to 30 for all test functions.

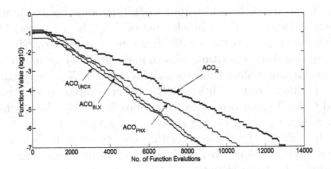

Fig. 3. The convergence process on the sphere f_1

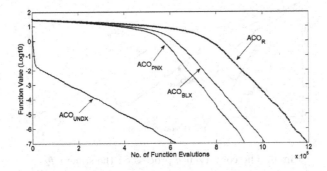

Fig. 4. The convergence process on the sphere f_4

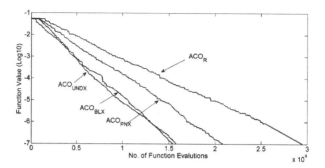

Fig. 5. The convergence process on the sphere f_{11}

Firstly, the convergence properties of the three $COACO_R$ are analyzed as Figs. 3, 4, 5 and 6, which based on four basic functions: Sphere function (f_1); the non-separable function: Rosenbrock function (f_4); the multimodal functions: the Ackley function (f_{11}) and the Schaffer function (f_{20}). As shown in Figs. 3, 4, 5 and 6, the proposed three algorithms all can find the global optimum faster than the ACO_R. Evolutionary algorithms such as MGG+UNDX [8], rc-CGA+FPDD-LX [9] and the differential evolution (DE) [10] are employed to compare with the proposed $COACO_R$ on benchmark functions ($f_1 \sim f_{21}$). We performed 100 independent runs using the stopping criterions $|f(s) - f(s^*)| < 10^{-7}$. The mean numbers of the FEs for the above algorithm are recorded in Table 1. From the result, we can see that the number of the function evaluations (FEs) of the proposed algorithm is far fewer than those of other algorithm for the test functions.

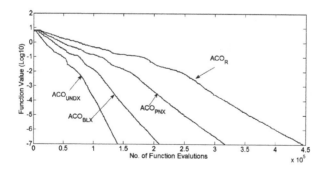

Fig. 6. The convergence process on the sphere f_{20}

Table 1. Comparing with other algorithms on 21 benchmark functions, D = 30

Fun	ACO$_{BLX}$	ACO$_{UNDX}$	ACO$_{PNX}$	ACO$_R$	CGA$_R$ [2]	DE	UNDX-MMG
f_1	8.50E+3	8.15E+3	1.10E+4	1.84E+4	1.26E+4	4.39E+4	8.03E+4
f_2	1.35E+4	2.46E+4*	1.74E+4	2.89E+4	3.75E+4	–	–
f_3	1.22E+4	2.27E+4*	1.54E+4	2.73E+4	4.18E+4	–	–
f_4	3.96E+5	3.85E+5*	3.94E+5	–	3.40E+5	–	–
f_5	1.58E+4	1.76E+4	2.08E+4	3.77E+4	4.86E+4	7.39E+4	–
f_6	2.10E+5	1.37E+5	2.28E+5	3.36E+5	2.50E+5	3.75E+5	1.32E+6
f_7	1.09E+4	1.14E+4	1.24E+4	1.82E+4	1.99E+4	1.13E+5*	3.09E+5
f_8	7.57E+4	4.78E+4	9.58E+4	1.89E+5	1.47E+5	–	2.56E+5
f_9	6.54E+3	6.21E+3	8.35E+3	1.30E+4	1.08E+4	3.54E+4	6.11E+4
f_{10}	1.37E+4	1.34E+4	1.64E+4	2.72E+4	2.52E+4	–	1.12E+5
f_{11}	1.96E+4	2.25E+4*	2.51E+4	3.98E+4	7.46E+4	8.40E+4	3.63E+5
f_{12}	2.97E+4	2.24E+4	8.10E+4	6.18E+4	2.35E+4	4.18E+4	1.58E+5
f_{13}	4.40E+4	8.53E+3*	9.50E+4	9.50E+4	4.34E+4	5.32E+4	1.04E+6
f_{14}	6.80E+3	7.66E+3	8.60E+3	1.39E+4	1.08E+4	3.24E+4	4.45E+5
f_{15}	2.94E+4	3.37E+4	3.86E+4	6.64E+4	2.54E+4	4.48E+4	3.58E+5
f_{16}	1.31E+4	1.36E+4	1.56E+4	2.54E+5	7.43E+5	5.0E+5	–
f_{17}	6.65E+3	7.57E+3	9.15E+3	1.29E+4	1.92E+4	4.40E+4	9.84E+4
f_{18}	7.70E+3	8.84E+3	9.65E+3	1.67E+4	7.67E+4	4.50E+4	1.95E+5
f_{19}	3.77E+4	2.84E+4	5.38E+4	7.85E+4	3.97E+4	4.93E+4	2.41E+6
f_{20}	2.48E+5	1.86E+5*	3.72E+5	6.21E+5	5.90E+5	1.93E+5	–
f_{21}	4.59E+4	3.66E+4	8.54E+4	–	2.40E+5	8.43E+4	4.23E+6

4   Conclusions

In this paper, we proposed three ant colony optimization algorithms with different crossover operations for continuous domains. Simulation results show ACO$_R$ with crossover operations is far well the typical ACO$_R$. So we can draw a conclusion that crossover operators can effectively improve the global exploration ability of ACO$_R$, and avoid falling into the local minima and exploit the correlation information among the design variables. In this way, we can generate new ACO algorithms from the available algorithmic components that have not been considered or tested before.

Acknowledgments. This work was supported by Natural Science Foundation Project of CQ CSTC (No. cstc2012jjA40041, No. cstc201-jjA40059) and Science Research Fund of Chongqing Technology and Business University (No. 1153005).

References

1. Zhang, X., Tian, Y., Jin, Y.: A knee point driven evolutionary algorithm for many-objective optimization. IEEE Trans. Evol. Comput. (2014). doi:10.1109/TEVC.2014.2378512

2. Zhang, X., Tian, Y., Cheng, R., Jin, Y.: An efficient approach to non-dominated sorting for evolutionary multi-objective optimization. IEEE Trans. Evol. Comput. **19**(2), 201–213 (2015)

3. Dorigo, M., Maniezzo, V., Colorni, A.: Ant system: optimization by a colony of cooperating agents. IEEE Trans. Syst. Man Cybern. Part B **26**(1), 29–41 (1996)

4. Hu, X., Zhang, J., Li, Y.: Orthogonal methods based ant colony search for solving continuous optimization problems. J. Comput. Sci. Technol. **23**, 2–18 (2008)

5. Liao, T., Stutzle, T.: A unified ant colony optimization algorithm for continuous optimization. Eur. J. Oper. Res. **234**, 597–609 (2014)

6. Eshelman, L., Schaffer, J.: Real-coded genetic algorithms and interval schemata. In: Whitley, D.L. (ed.) Foundation of Genetic Algorithms II, pp. 187–202. Morgan Kaufmann, San Mateo (1993)

7. Ono, I., Kobayashi, S.: A real-coded genetic algorithm for function optimization using unimodal normal distribution crossover. In: Proceedings of the Seventh International Conference on Genetic Algorithms, pp. 246–253. Morgan Kaufmann, San Mateo (1997)

8. Ballester, P.J., Carter, J.N.: An effective real-parameter genetic algorithm with parent centric normal crossover for multimodal optimisation. In: Deb, K., Tari, Z. (eds.) GECCO 2004. LNCS, vol. 3102, pp. 901–913. Springer, Heidelberg (2004)

9. Chen, Z., Wang, R.: A new framework with fdpp-lx crossover for real-coded genetic algorithm. IEICE Trans. Fundam. Electron. Commun. Comput. Sci. **E94.A**(6), 1417–1425 (2011)

10. Price, K., Storn, R., Lampinen, J.: Differential Evolution: A Practical Approach to Global Optimization. Springer, Heidelberg (2005)

Multi-objective Optimal Operation of Cascaded Hydropower Stations Based on MOPSO with Bacteria Quorum Sensing Inspired Turbulence Mechanism

Shan Cheng[1,2]([✉]), Xiaoyu Jiang[2], and Wei Chen[2]

[1] Hubei Key Laboratory of Cascaded Hydropower Stations Operation and Control, China Three Gorges University, Yichang 443002, Hubei, China
hpucquyzu@ctgu.edu.cn
[2] College of Electrical Engineering and New Energy, China Three Gorges University, Yichang 443002, Hubei, China
{420862691,109614395}@qq.com

Abstract. Operation optimization of the cascaded hydropower stations is of great significance to utilization efficiency of water, safety and stability of the grid, and comprehensive benefits of the reservoirs. In this study, a multi-objective operation optimization model of cascaded hydropower stations is established, and a novel multi-objective particle swarm optimization (MOPSO) algorithm is proposed to deal with the optimization problem of multi-objective, multi-constraint, high-dimension, and strong-coupling. A turbulence mechanism and a circular elimination strategy, are presented to strengthen the performance of MOPSO algorithm. The result of a case study indicates that, with the proposed techniques, the pro-posed algorithm performs well on both convergence and diversity of Pareto solutions, which implies that the proposed MOPSO algorithm can be used as an effective optimization tool to handle the multi-objective operation optimization of the cascaded hydropower stations.

Keywords: Bacteria quorum sensing · Cascaded hydropower stations · Multi-objective optimization · Particle swarm optimization

1 Introduction

Development of hydropower industry and improvement of water utilization efficiency optimize the power energy structure and promote the diversification of electronic power development which consequently plays an important role in saving energy, reducing emissions, and realizing sustainable development of electronic power industry [1,2]. Consequently, optimal operation and management of hydropower reservoirs is a key problem in the economic and stable operation of hydropower & electronic power system [1,3].

© Springer-Verlag Berlin Heidelberg 2015
M. Gong et al. (Eds.): BIC-TA 2015, CCIS 562, pp. 63–74, 2015.
DOI: 10.1007/978-3-662-49014-3_6

With the increasing hydropower stations and reservoirs, the main issues in the optimal operation of cascade hydropower stations [4–9] include: (1) the complexity of the optimal operation of reservoirs is proportional to the number of reservoirs. Therefore, the optimal dispatching model of the cascaded hydropower stations and reservoirs is very complex and difficult to solve, to establish a multi-reservoirs joint dispatching model is necessary, and to find a new way to solve the optimal dispatching model of the hydropower group which provides a good trade-off between the computational time and the computational accuracy should be also taken into consideration. (2) With the operation mechanism of separation of plant and network, the implementation of bidding, as the main former of the joint interest, the cascaded hydropower stations no longer pursue the largest generating capacity of the individual power plant, the generation efficiency and capacity efficiency of the whole cascaded hydropower station is a real pursuit. (3) The joint dispatching of reservoir group not only considers the reservoir water level, storage, output and other basic constraints, but also considers the hydraulic and electric contact between each reservoir, the compensation and coordination ability between reservoirs, which makes the constraints to optimal dispatching of reservoir group more complex.

Traditional optimal dispatching of the reservoir group mainly focus on single objective optimization problem, but the reservoir group is often responsible for power generation, flood control, water supply, shipping and other tasks, the mutual influence and restrictions between each task itself and the different targets in each task exist, therefore, the optimal dispatching of cascaded reservoirs is essentially a complex constrained multi-objective optimization problem. Since the 80 s of last century, many experts and scholars studied the multi-objective optimization problem of the hydroelectric energy, the early research using constraint method [10,11], weight method [12], membership degree function method [13–15] to convert the multi-objective optimization problem into single objective problem, then the intelligent optimization algorithm such as ant colony optimization algorithm, particle swarm optimization algorithm, genetic algorithm was used to solve the problem. These methods are easy to implement but difficult to describe the non-inferior solution of the multi-objective problem accurately. In recent years, with the constructing method of Pareto optimal solution set spreads, NSGA-II [16] and SPEA2 [17] which are represented by multi-objective evolutionary algorithms in hydroelectric energy optimization problems have been successfully applied, the greatest advantage of these methods is that non-dominated frontier of the multi-objective problem including non-inferior solutions can be acquired with only one operation compared to the traditional multi-objective method. Chang [18] sets up a model to minimize the water shortage rate of the two reservoirs, and the NSGA-II algorithm is applied to solve the model.

Based on the aforementioned comments, this study hereby applies an improved multi-objective PSO (MOPSO) algorithm to multi-objective operation optimization model of cascaded hydropower stations. The contributions and characteristics of the study are: (1) Multi-objective optimization model for optimally operating cascaded hydropower stations is constructed, which takes into account the annual power generation and firm power of cascade hydropower stations. In addition, various constraints have been considered in the model. (2) An enhanced MOPSO (named BC-MOPSO) algorithm is applied to solve the multi-objective problem with non-linear constraints and objectives. Special techniques, including a turbulence mechanism and a circular elimination strategy, are presented to strengthen the performance of MOPSO algorithm.

2   Multi-objective Optimization Model

2.1   Objective Functions

Enhancement of firm power is the basic requirement for the stable operation of power system, and increasing annual power generation gurantees the generation companys benefits. Consequently, the main index considered for the optimal operation of cascaded hydropower stations are annual power generation and firm power of cascaded hydropower stations [19]. The optimization objectives considered to establish the operation optimization model are maximization of the annual power generation and maximization of the firm power of cascaded hydropower stations.

The mathematical formulation for maximizing the annual power generation of cascaded hydropower stations can be expressed as follows:

$$f_1 = \max\{\sum_{i=1}^{n_s} \sum_{t=1}^{T} P_i^t \Delta t\} \tag{1}$$

where N_s represents the total number of cascaded hydropower stations, T denotes the number of scheduling intervals, Δt is the length of the tth interval. P_i^t indicates the output of ith station at t, which can be formulated by the following equation.

$$P_i^t = 9.81\eta_i Q_i^t H_i^t \tag{2}$$

where η_i indicates the comprehensive efficiency coefficient of the ith station, Q_i^t denotes the water discharge for generation, and H_i^t represents the mean water head.

The mathematical formulation for maximizing the firm power of cascaded hydropower stations can be expressed as follows:

$$f_2 = max\{min(P_i^t)\}. \tag{3}$$

2.2   Constraints

The main constraint for optimally operating cascaded hydropower stations includes water balance constraints, station level constraints, discharge volume constraints and cascaded hydropower station conservancy relation constraints.

(1) Level (capacity) constraints

$$C^t_{i\,\min} \leq C^t_i \leq C^t_{i\,\max} \tag{4}$$

where $C^t_{i\,\min}$ and $C^t_{i\,\max}$ denote the lower and upper limits for the ith station level at the tth interval, respectively. The value takes scheduling rules in Level (capacity), and the intersection of its own water level (capacity) upper and lower limit.

(2) Output power constraints

$$P^t_{i\,\min} \leq P^t_i \leq P^t_{i\,\max} \tag{5}$$

where $P^t_i \min$ and $P^t_i \max$ are upper and lower limits for the time t i_{th} station output power constraints, respectively. The value takes its own output power constraints, expected output power constraints and the scheduling in the intersection of output constraint part.

(3) Volume constraints

$$Q^t_{i\,\min} \leq Q^t_{iX} \leq Q^t_{i\,\max} \tag{6}$$

where: $Q^t_{i\,\min}$, $Q^t_{i\,\max}$ are respectively upper and lower limits for the time t i^{th} station volume constraints, The value takes its own discharge capacity constraints and the scheduling in the intersection of discharge volume constraints.

(4) Water balance constraints

$$V_{it+1} = V_{it} + (I_{it} - Q^X_{it})t \tag{7}$$

where: V_{it}, V_{it+1} are respectively the capacity of i-th power plant in this period and the next period; I_{it} is the incoming water of the i-th station in period t.

(5) Cascaded hydropower station conservancy relation constraints

$$I_{G,t} = Q^X_{S,t-\tau} + q_t \tag{8}$$

where: τ is the time of water arrival; $I_{G,t}$ is the incoming water of Gezhouba Station in period t, the value takes the discharge volume $Q^X_{S,t-\tau}$ of Three Gorges Power Station in period $(t-\tau)$ and the sum of the inflow from Three Gorges Station to the Gezhouba Station in period t.

3   BC-MOPSO Algorithm and Its Performance

Multi-objective optimization (MOO) has been extensively studied and widely applied to MOPs to provide more information for supporting decision making tasks [20]. Because of advantages such as fast convergence, fewer parameters to adjust, robust adaptability, and relative simplicity of implementation, particle swarm optimization (PSO) has been extended for multi-objective PSO (MOPSO), and such MOPSO has achieved universal application to MOPs [21].

However, such convergence speed may be harmful in the context of MOO, because a PSO based algorithm may converge to a false Pareto front [22]. Thus, when extending PSO to MOPSO, for strengthening convergence, means to maintain the swarm diversity is an important issue to avoid convergence to a single solution and avoid premature convergence [23]. Besides, another two issues [23] have to be considered: (1) how to construct Pareto-optimal solutions; (2) how to make the distribution of identified solutions as smooth and uniform as possible. Non-dominated sorting technique, which was proposed by Deb et al. [24], is a popularly used method to construct the Pareto-optimal solutions. However, this method ignores the effect on the CD(s) of the selected particles caused by the nearby eliminated particle(s), which results in too sparse solutions, and decreases the spread of the solutions.

3.1 BC-MOPSO Algorithm

(a) Initialization. Set population size N and maximum iteration M_t. Initialize each particle with its velocity $v_i = [v_{i1}, v_{i2}, \cdots, v_{iD}]^T$ and position $x_i = [x_{i1}, x_{i2}, \cdots, x_{iD}]^T$, where D stands for the dimensions of the solution space.
Set personal best position $p_i = x$.
Set $t = 0$.

(b) Selection of leader particles.

$$t = t + 1.$$

Identify the non-dominated solutions from the current population P. For each article, evaluate each non-dominated solution according to Eq. (9) and the non-dominated solution with the maximum QuVa value is selected as leader $p_g = [p_{g1}, p_{g2}, \cdots, p_{gD}]^T$.

$$fitness = 1/\sum_{i=1}^{M} w_i f_i, w_i = \lambda_i/\sum_{i=1}^{M} \lambda_i, \lambda_i = U(0,1) \tag{9}$$

where M is the number of objectives, and f_i is the i-th objective. The function $U(0,1)$ generates a uniformly distributed random number within the interval [0,1].
Update p_i.

(c) Generation of new particles. Using Eqs. (10) and (11), generate a new population P' based on the current $V = [v_1, v_2, \cdots, v_i, \cdots, v_N]$ and $X = [x_1, x_2, \cdots, x_i, \cdots, x_N]$ respectively. Combine P and P' together and store them in R.

$$v_{id}(t + 1) = wv_{id}(t) + c(r_1(p_{id} - x_{id}(t))) + r_2(p_{gd} - x_{id}(t)) \tag{10}$$

$$x_{id}(t + 1) = x_{id}(t) + v_{id}(t + 1) \tag{11}$$

where t is the current iteration, w and c are inertia weight and acceleration coefficient, respectively. w and c change dynamically via Eqs. (12) and (13), respectively.

$$w(t) = w_0 + r_3^*(1 - w_0), w_0 \in [0, 0.5] \tag{12}$$

$$c = c_0 + t/Mt \tag{13}$$

where r_3 is a random number uniformly distributed in $[0, 1]$, w_0 is a constant value inside the range of $[0, 0.5]$ [14]. Mt indicates the number of iterations; c_0 is a constant and the suggested range is $[0.5, 1]$

(d) Identification of non-dominated solutions. Identify the non-dominated solutions of the first non-dominated front from R and store them in a matrix ND, while the dominated ones are stored in the matrix D.

(e) Selection of particles for next iteration according to the method stated in Sect. 3.2.

(f) Turbulence operation. If all $|v_i(t)| < V_{limit}$, execute the turbulence operation and replacement according to Sect. 3.3.

(g) Return to (b) until M_t is met.

(h) Store the non-dominated particles as the final Pareto solutions.

3.2 Circular Elimination Strategy and Its Application to Selecting Particles for Next Iteration

Combine P and P$'$ to generate a new population R, the non-dominated solutions are identified according to non-domination. If some non-dominated solutions needs to be selected from the set which these solutions belong to, the CD based non-dominated sorting technique is usually employed to get good spread of the selected non-dominated solutions. However, this approach ignores the effect on the CD(s) of the selected particles caused by the nearby eliminated solution(s), which makes the finally selected solutions too sparse and isn't good for the spread of the final Pareto-optimal solutions.

Instead of direct selection, we realize the selection via circular elimination strategy. Let the selected particles for next iteration be stored in NewP. Firstly, compute the crowing distances of the non-dominated solutions. Then eliminate the non-dominated one with the least crowding distance. Thirdly, re-compute the crowing distances of the rest non-dominated solutions and also eliminate the one with the least crowding distance. Repeat the operation until N non-dominated solutions remain and store them in NewP for next iteration. In case of N > NND, first of all, copy all individuals in ND to NewP. Then identify the non-nominated solutions from the dominated solutions and then do the similar operation. Compared with NSGA-II crowding sorting based sequential selection, circular elimination strategy is more effective for diversity.

Non-dominated solutions of different non-dominated front can be identified from the population R. Particles for next iteration are selected from these non-dominated solutions according to Fig. 1.

3.3 Bacteria-quorum-sensing- Behavior Inspired Turbulence Mechanism

It has long been appreciated that certain groups of bacteria exhibit coopera-tive behavioral patterns. It seems that intercellular communication likewise can

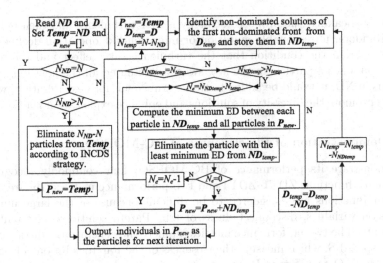

Fig. 1. Scheme for selection of the particles for next iteration

account for such behaviors and the communication was called quorum-sensing (QS) by Fuqua [25].

As Eqs. (10) and (11) show, when the velocities of the particles in the swarm are almost zero, it becomes unable to create new solutions which might lead the swarm out of this stagnating state. Because the leader (pg) guide the flight of each particle, if turbulence exerts to the swarm and some new leader(s) generates, it is possible to lead the swarm away from a current location. Turbulence and generation of new leader(s) potentially facilitate to escape from local optima and to strengthen the exploratory capabilities of PSO. Inspired by the QS phenomenon, QS mechanism is introduced into MPSO. Once the velocities of the whole swarm are less than a threshold Vlimit, generate a new swarm TurP with population size N according to Eq. (7). Then identify the non-dominated particles and store them in a matrix TurND. Thirdly, let the non-dominated particles in TurND compete with the non-nominated solutions stored in ND. If each objective-function value of a non-dominated particles in TurND is less than the corresponding objective-function value of all non-nominated solutions in ND, the non-dominated particles is a candidate to replace one particle in NewP and store such non-nominated particles in WinND. Fourthly, randomly select 20 % particles in NewP and replace them with the particles in WinND.

$$TurX = X_{new} + \beta V_{max}^* sign(2(rand(1, N) - 0.5)) \tag{14}$$

where TurX represents the positions of newly generated swarm, and it is a DN matrix; X_{new} is also a matrix which indicates the positions of population NewP; is the turbulence degree and its value is between 0 and 1; V_{max} is a D1 matrix represents the max velocity values in each dimension; sign is the sign function; rand is the random operator.

Simply speaking, the proposed strategy is first turbulence and then replacement. Random, unreasonable mutation or mutation-like operation declines the evolution. From the condition that the turbulence takes effect and the above description, once a particle in the new swarm dominated all the non-nominated solutions in ND, it would be added to the swarm NewP for next iteration, which possibly promote the diversity of solutions and enhance exploitation via Eq. (14).

3.4   Demonstration of Effectiveness of BC-MOPSO

To demonstrate its performance of BC-MOPSO, four commonly recognized bench-mark functions ZDT1–ZDT4 and two performance metrics [16] are used. The four functions are considered to be difficult because of the large number of decision variables, disconnectedness of true Pareto solutions, and multiple local fronts. The two performance metrics, namely the generational distance GD and the spread S, which measure the closeness of the Pareto solutions identified by BC-MOPSO to the true Pareto solutions in the objective space and diversity of Pareto solutions along the Pareto front, respectively. Figure 2 depicts the Pareto fronts identified by BC-MOPSO. As observed from Fig. 2, BC-MOPSO is capable of attaining the true Pareto front. Techniques adopted to maintain swarm diversity and to enhance global search ability have resulted in the better convergence performance.

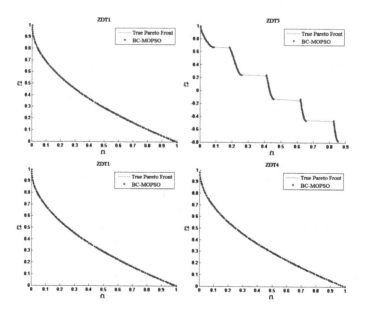

Fig. 2. Pareto fronts identified by BC-MOPSO

4   Simulation Results and Analysis

In order to study the multi-objective optimization of the long-term dispatching, take the optimal operation of the Three Gorges cascade hydropower stations as a case study. The Three Gorges cascaded hydropower station is composed of Three Gorges and Gezhouba power station. Its total installed capacity is 20915000 kw, the guaranteed output of Three Gorges power station is 4990000 kw, while Gezhouba is 946000 kw, the average generated energy of the cascaded is 98.6 billion kwh (designed value). The Three Gorges reservoir has seasonal adjustment ability, Gezhouba is a runoff type power station, does not has the medium and long-term adjustment ability.

The BC-MOPSO is used to determine the optimal dispatching solutions. The Prato optimal solutions and their corresponding objective-values are shown in Fig. 3. And the Its clear that BC-MOPSO can identify a set of well-distributed solutions. Each solution is a possible solution for optimal operation of the cascaded hydropower stations, and each solution has different firm power and annual power generation. Some solutions have a high firm power value, but a low annual power generation value, and vice versa. That's mean the function of firm power conflicts with the function of annual power generation.

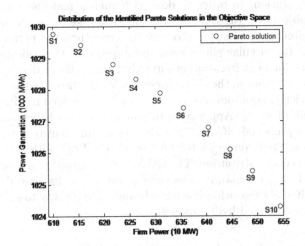

Fig. 3. Pareto optimal solutions in the objective space

The values of firm water, annual power generation and surplus water corresponding to each solution are demonstrated in Fig. 4. Investigation from the figure, we can find that the values of firm power decrease with the increasing annual power generation, while the value of firm power increases with the value of annual power generation. Such relationships result from the seasonal regulation of the Three Gorges station and the non-regulation capability of Gezhouba.

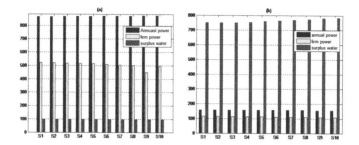

Fig. 4. The values of firm water, annual power generation and surplus water corresponding to each solution. Firm water, annual power generation and surplus water are in 10 MW, 100 M m3, and 100 MWh, respectively. (a) Three Gorges station, (b) Gezhouba Station.

5 Conclusion

In this study, a BC-MOPSO algorithm was presented and employed for determining the optimal operation solution of the cascaded hydropower stations. The study mainly aims to determine the optimal firm power and annual power generation of each station. In order to deal with such a non-linear problem with incompatible objectives, the BC-MOPSO algorithm adopts a turbulence mechanism and a circular elimination strategy to strengthen the performance. The introduction of the circular elimination technique and its application to selection of particles for next iteration ensures that the uniform distribution of the Pareto-optimal solutions in the objective space. While the turbulence mechanism derived from bacteria quorum sensing behavior is introduced to MOPSO to preserve the swarm diversity. Application to four well-known benchmark functions shows that the proposed BC-MOPSO algorithm can identify a set of Pareto-optimal solutions that converges to the true Pareto front with a high accuracy while keeping a good distribution. The BC-MOPSO algorithm has been also successfully tested on a case study. The corresponding results have demonstrated that the BC-MOPSO algorithm is a feasible and effective way to solve the MOO of operating the cascaded hydropower stations.

Acknowledgement. This work was supported by Hubei Key Laboratory of Cascaded Hydropower Stations Operation & Control (China Three Gorges University) through grant number 2013KJX01 and 2015 Scientific Research Innovation Foundation for Postgraduate of CTGU via the Grant Number 2015CX068.

References

1. Wu, X.Y., Wang, Y.Q., Cheng, C.T., Guo, Y.A., Li, H.G.: Optimal operation model for hydropower reservoirs considering probability of non-failure and failure extent. Water Resour. Res. **2**(3), 165–170 (2013)

2. Xie, R.C., Ji, C.M., Wang, C.C., Zhang, Y.K., Yu, S.: Energy storage operation charts of hydropower station reservoir group based on improved discriminate coefficient method. Water Power **39**(5), 62–64 (2012)
3. Ji, C.M., Jiang, Z.Q., Sun, Q., Wu, H., Yu, S.: Optimization of cascade total output dispatching figure based on the optimal output distribution. Oper. Res. Manag. Sci. **23**(4), 184–191 (2014)
4. Zhang, S.H.: The Theory and Practice of Cascade Reservoirs Power Generation Optimized Operation. Xian University of Technology (2007)
5. Duan, W.H., Mei, Y.D., Chen, L.H., Bao, Z.F., Qu, L.N.: Long term optimal operation of cascade hydropower plants on jinshajiang river. Hydropower Autom. Dam Monit. **31**(1), 17–20 (2007)
6. Ji, C.M., Li, K.F., Zhang, Y.K., Zhao, B.K.: Stochastic multi-objective decision-making model of the reservoir operation based on chance-constrained programming. Power Syst. Prot. Control **40**(19), 36–40 (2012)
7. Ding, S.H., Dong, Z.C., Wang, D.Z., Li, Q.H.: MOP of feeding reservoir group optimal operation based on SPEA. Adv. Water Sci. **19**(5), 679–684 (2008)
8. Xu, J.J., Chen, J., Yin, Z.J.: Key issues in the joint operation of large cascade reservoirs in Yangtze river basin. J. Yangtze river Sci. Res. Inst. **28**(12), 48–52 (2011)
9. Ai, X.S., Ran, B.Y.: FS DDDP method and its application to optimal operation of groups of reservoirs. Hydropower Autom. Dam Monit. **31**(1), 13–16 (2007)
10. Nagesh-Kumar, D., Janga-Reddy, M.: Ant colony optimization for multi-purpose reservoir operation. Water Resour. Manag. **20**(6), 879–898 (2006)
11. Janga-Reddy, M., Nagesh-Kumar, D.: Evolving strategies for crop planning and operation of irrigation reservoir system using multi-objective differential evolution. Irrig. Sci. **26**(2), 177–190 (2008)
12. Foued, B.A., Sameh, M.: Application of goal programming in a multi-objective reservoir operation model in Tunisia. Eur. J. Oper. Res. **133**(2), 352–361 (2001)
13. Basu, M.: An interactive fuzzy satisfying method based on evolutionary programming technique for multiobjective short-term hydrothermal scheduling. Electr. Power Syst. Res. **69**(2–3), 277–285 (2004)
14. Hu, G.Q., He, R.M.: Model and algorithm of multi-objective fuzzy optimal scheduling for cascaded hydroelectric power plant. Trans. China Electrotechnical Soc. **22**(1), 154–158 (2007)
15. Hu, G.Q., He, R.M.: Long-term multi-objective fuzzy optimization scheduling model of cascaded hydroelectric station. Electr. Power Autom. Equipment **27**(4), 23–27 (2007)
16. Deb, K., Pratap, A., Agarwa, S., Meyarivan, T.: A fast and elitist multiobjective genetic algorithm: NSGA-II. IEEE Trans. Evol. Comput. **6**(2), 182–197 (2002)
17. Zitzler, E., Laumanns, M., Thiele, L.: SPEA2: improving the strength Pareto evolutionary algorithm. Technical report 103, Computer Engineering and Networks Laboratory (TIK), Swiss Federal Institute of Technology (ETH) Zurich, Gloriastrasse 35, CH-8092 Zurich, Switzerland (2001)
18. Chang, L.C., Chang, F.J.: Multi-objective evolutionary algorithm for operating parallel reservoir system. J. Hydrol. **377**(1–2), 12–20 (2009)
19. Chen, X.B., Wang, X.J., Feng, S.Y.: A multi-objective optimization method considering power output and firm power for reservoir dispatching. Syst. Eng. Theor. Pract. **4**(4), 95–101 (1998)
20. Li, M., Lin, D., Kou, J.: A hybrid niching PSO enhanced with Recombination-replacement crowding strategy for multimodal function optimization. Softw. Comput. **12**(3), 975–987 (2012)

21. Hu, W., Yen, G.G., Zhang, X.: Multiobjective particle swarm optimization based on Pareto entropy. Software **25**(5), 1025–1050 (2014)
22. Coello, A.C., Pulido, G.T., Lechuga, M.S.: Handling multiple objectives with particle swarm optimization. IEEE Trans. Evol. Comput. **8**(3), 256–279 (2004)
23. Reyes-Sierra, M., Coello, A.C.: Multi-objective particle swarm optimizers: a survey of the state-of-the-art. Int. J. Comput. Intell. Res. **2**(3), 287–308 (2006)
24. Deb, K., Pratap, A., Agarwal, S., Meyarivan, T.: A fast and elitist multiobjective genetic algorithm: NSGA-II. IEEE Trans. Evol. Comput. **6**(2), 182–197 (2002)
25. Fuqua, W.C., Winans, W.C., Greenberg, E.P.: Quorum sensing in bacteria: the LuxR LuxI family of cell density responsive transcriptional regulators. J. Bacteriol. **176**(2), 269–275 (1994)

Versatile Archimedean Tilings Self-Assembled from Combined Symmetric DNA Motifs

Guangzhao Cui, Wanli Zheng, Xuncai Zhang[✉], and Yanfeng Wang

College of Electrical and Information Engineering,
Henan Key Lab of Information-based Electrical Appliances,
Zhengzhou University of Light Industry, Zhengzhou 450002, Henan, China
cgzh@zzuli.edu.cn, zhangxuncai@163.com

Abstract. Tilings formed with convex regular polygons are known as k-uniform tilings if there are precisely k different kinds of vertices in the tiling. Archimedes tilings with one kind of vertex are known as 1-uniform tilings. Here we propose a strategy that combines two types of symmetric DNA junction tiles to create two kinds of Archimedean tilings (3,3,3,3,6 and 3,6,3,6) respectively, where there are many influence factors, such as the arm length ratios and stick-ends interactions between two motifs, sequences in arms and stick-ends, the mole concentration ratios between the internal and external of motifs. Archimedean tilings show periodic polygonal tessellations which have fine geometrical symmetry, so we can locate AuNPs, fluoresceins and other biomarkers to different sites in planar structures. These biomarkers assist in revealing various observations under the microscope. Besides, it is expected to produce conductivity, fluorescence and Raman Effect in different levels with the help of biomarkers. In addition, these self-assembly Archimedean Tilings have potential to form quasi-crystals.

Keywords: Self-assembly · Archimedean tiling · Symmetry · DNA motifs

1 Introduction

DNA self-assembly technology has produced many classic versatile assembly components since 1993, such as DX tile [1], TX tile [3], 4 × 4 tile [4], n-point-star tile [5,6,8], sub-tile [9] and so on (Fig. 1). DNA tile self-assembly has good features on predictability, programmability and design flexibility. There are many various two-dimensional lattices [10–12], nanotubes [16–19] and diversified polyhedras [21,22,30] built with simplex tiles or compound tiles. These products present regular polygon with triangular, square or hexagonal cavities. If we put regular polygons edge-to-edge around a vertex to fill the plane, making the orders that polygons embrace every vertex are same, then sets of periodic polygonal tessellations including only one type of vertex appear, and corresponding tiling with strict symmetric are called Regular tilings or Regular Tessellations [24].

Given one type of regular polygon to fill the plane, and there are only three regular tessellations composed by the hexagons, squares, and triangles, respectively (Fig. 2).

© Springer-Verlag Berlin Heidelberg 2015
M. Gong et al. (Eds.): BIC-TA 2015, CCIS 562, pp. 75–83, 2015.
DOI: 10.1007/978-3-662-49014-3_7

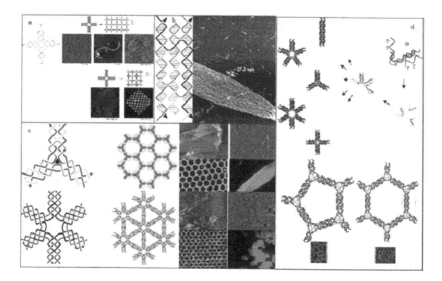

Fig. 1. Classic versatile assembly components. (a) structures formed by 44 tile with two strategies; (b) stable TX tile; (c) n-point-star tile with three- and six-point-star motif; (d) hierarchical sub-tile assembly.

They are the only ways to tessellate the plane with a single regular polygon. Well, we can symbolize these three regular tessellations as $(3,3,3,3,3,3)$, $(4,4,4,4)$ and $(6,6,6)$, where each symbol denotes one of the polygons at each vertex. The digit indicates number of polygon edges around one vertex.

Regular Tessellation has characteristics as follows: there is only one type of vertex and tile in the tiling, and every tile shares one vertex and one edge each other. The resulting patterns with translational symmetry and rotational symmetry are also known as the edge-to-edge tilings. Whether it is finite or infinite self-assembly, a mass of two-dimensional arrays with properties of regular tessellation will be constructed. In the plane, the configurations of tiles vertex have only 21 kinds [26] (Fig. 3), besides above three regular tilings which have one kind of vertex, there are other tessellations tilings with combination of polygons, and they also have one type of vertex like regular tilings.

Regular tessellations filled by two or more convex regular polygons are called semiregular tessellations, or sometimes Archimedean tessellations [27,28]. These compound polygons arrange in the plane in this way that the same polygons in the same order surround each polygon vertex. There are eight such tessellations (Table 1) and the only possible combinations are illustrated in (Fig. 4).

The Archimedean tilings have similar characteristics with the regular tessellations above though they contain more than one type of regular polygons. They are still symmetric with translational symmetry but rotational symmetry. Apart from these eleven 1-uniform tilings, where 1-uniform means that they have one type of vertex can fill the plane, other sets of regular polygons (Fig. 3) will also fit around a single vertex, for example (5,5,10,) but they can't be extended to fill the plane completely.

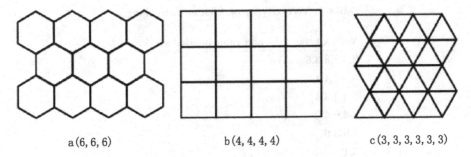

a (6, 6, 6)   b (4, 4, 4, 4)   c (3, 3, 3, 3, 3, 3)

Fig. 2. Three kinds of regular tessellations.

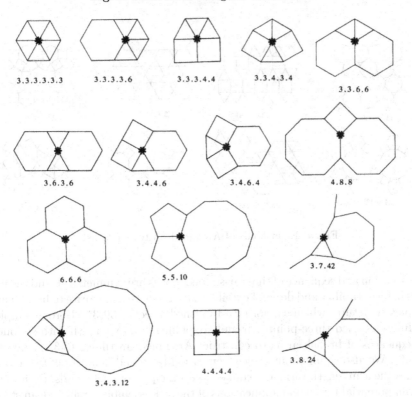

Fig. 3. Possible 21 types of vertex.

Yan [29] was the first to use three-arm and four-arm tiles to build two complex Archimedean tilings (3,3,3,4,4 and 3,3,4,3,4). They designed different arm length ratio and the matching rules of the sticky ends as prerequisites of successful experiments. In their research, they considered that in order to prevent aggregation of single tiles, it was necessary to make branch arms asymmetric even for case when the sticky-ends were identical, as a result the sequences of motifs in their research adopt unsymmetrical and increased the difficulty of sequences design. By contrast, both

Table 1. Vertex types of Archimedean tiling.

Vertex type	left- and right-handed versions
3,3,3,3,3,6	Yes
3,3,3,4,4	No
3,3,4,3,4	Yes
3,4,6,4	No
3,6,3,6	No
3,12,3,12	No
4,6,12	No
4,8,8	No

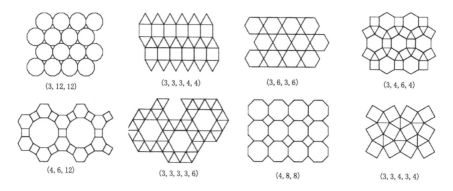

(3, 12, 12)   (3, 3, 3, 4, 4)   (3, 6, 3, 6)   (3, 4, 6, 4)

(4, 6, 12)   (3, 3, 3, 3, 6)   (4, 8, 8)   (3, 3, 4, 3, 4)

Fig. 4. Eight kinds of Archimedean tessellations.

conformation and sequence of the star-shaped motifs are symmetrical, and the features in nice stability and design flexibility have made them favorite to build many complex structures which cannot be established directly [30,31]. Here we employ carefully-designed three-point-star and six-point-star DNA motif with symmetric sequences of branch arms to construct Archimedean tilings (3,3,3,3,3,6 and 3,6,3,6). We also think about the concentration ratio and quantity of two motifs besides the arm length ratio and connection principles of sticky-ends. Besides we explain potential functional applications of the self-assembly Archimedean structures, provide reference information for the construction of quasi-crystals, and verify the versatility of symmetric combined tiles.

2 Design and Modeling

2.1 The Rational Length of Arms

Rational design for the DNA motifs is crucial in order to keep the coexistence and stable assembly of different tiles in the process. Two significant factors should be considered: three-dimensional configurations of DNA double helix; expected geometrical characteristics and space scale of self-assembly Archimedes structures. By the characteristics of DNA double helix we can know that DNA exhibits 10.5 base pairs per helical turn when it stretches in solution. Previous studies [4] indicated that it is the distance of neighboring junctions that play an important role on the accumulation or elimination of curvature when all tiles face-up or alternating face-up and face-down in two-dimensional lattices. In addition, the tessellations Archimedes tiling here are built with three- and six-point-star DNA motifs and they can be symbolized by equilateral triangle and hexagon in blocks shown as (Fig. 4)(upper line), in which polygons connect to each other edge-to-edge. The geometric characteristics restrict the triangular and the hexagonal equal edge length, and the length of inscribed circle radius in polygons are the corresponding arm length. Obviously the ratio of arm length of two motifs is 1:3 (three-point-star: six-point-star). This ratio is the best based on the geometric properties which it can make tiles assembled in such a way that there are neither overlap nor gaps between the adjacent arms. It also satisfies the rigidity and flexibility of tiles as well as guaranteeing that any compression or stretching of the DNA double helices is minimized. On the other hand, taking into account the resolution of atomic force microscope subsequently, we choose the length as 1.5: 4.5 (odd multiples of half spiral) and 2: 6 (even multiples of half spiral). The distance of adjacent tiles are six and eight helical turns which theoretically make it as a guarantee to observe Archimedes Tessellations grids. Apart from two aspects above, the sequences of two tiles are symmetrical respectively that it reduces the complexity of sequence design.

2.2 Matching Rules of the Sticky-Ends

Matching rules of the sticky-ends have an important significance on creating final results. The processes of denatured and annealing are a slow procedure of energy conversion in the corresponding temperature after mixing DNA single strands. The connection between tiles relies on complementary sticky-ends which determine the configuration of self-assembly structures. Archimedean tilings have translational periodicity based on unit cells. We can employ wireframe blocks corresponding to the desired patterns to represent the unit cells intuitively as shown in (Fig. 5)b, e. By considering the symmetry in conformation and sequences of the unit cells, we specify the similar strands with symmetrical arms and unique sticky-ends to reduce the difficulty of sequence design as well as minimize the number of DNA strands. In (Fig. 5), tiles cover the whole plane without overlaps or gaps through translation or rotation that we can get the extended structures like middle (c, f), and structures in (d, g) show the details of cavities in 2D lattices. According to the structure schematics, different connection rules have been designed, but consider the simplicity of designing sequences, one set of unique six-point-star motif and three-point-star motif will meet the requirements of assembly respectively.

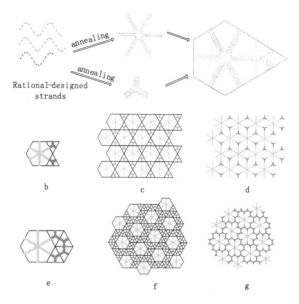

Fig. 5. Design and modeling. (a) shows the rational length of arms, and the ratio is 3:1; (b–d) shows the schematics of (3.6.3.6); (e–g) shows the schematics of (3.3.3.3.6).

2.3   The Molar Concentration of Tiles

The molar concentration is a factor worth careful consideration during the experiment for the formation of self-assembly products. Phenomenon of aggregation is serious when molar concentration is too high while assembly structures are not complete due to the lack of structural unit when molar concentration is too low [29]. Neither case is conducive to form the final products, besides there is a poor view under the atomic force microscope. Therefore, a reasonable allocation of concentration is required. According to the unit cell schematics in (Fig. 5), the molar concentration ratio for six-point- star motif and three-point-star motif are 1:2 (3,6,3,6) and 1:4 (3,3,3,3,6) theoretically. Taking into account the impacts of the final molar concentration on the structures, its necessary to configure appropriate molar concentration.

3   Application and Prospect

There is a (3,3,3,4,4) Archimedean-like tiling structure as the intermediate between a crystal and a quasi-crystal which was observed by researchers in [32]. Later, a joint between Archimedean tilings and quasi-crystals was established when the self-assembly of binary nanoparticles resulted in the formation of quasi-crystalline superlattices with a (3,3,3,4,4). Besides two Archimedes tilings which contain only one type of vertex as show above, there are also many k-uniform tilings which include k kinds of vertexes (2-uniform tilings are shown

in (Fig. 6) [33]. They are all formed with convex polygons, have corresponding symmetry in structure, and can be constructed by appropriate combined
DNA motifs theoretically. It is predictable that the successful hybridization of
combined DNA motifs to construct Archimedean tiling structures will further
increase the complexity and diversity of DNA nanostructures and provide the
ability to form quasi-crystals based on DNA tiling, which are the further research
contents of us. Furthermore, DNA-directed assembly of quasi-crystalline arrays
may generate especial nanostructures with novel properties through function-
alization of the DNA tile motifs with other nanomaterials. For example, with
excellent symmetry in the structures, the vertexes of k-uniform tilings may be
neat molecular anchor for AuNPs, fluoresceins, etc. These molecules can give
rich features for structures, even help to present good vision in atomic force
microscope imaging. So studies on structural and functional DNA self-assembly
are still important areas for future research.

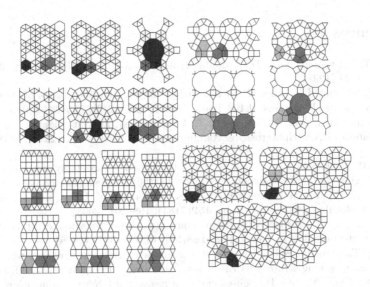

Fig. 6. Twenty kinds of 2-uniform tilings

4   Conclusion

This article has proposed a strategy that using combined tiles to build self-
assembled nanostructures. On the one hand, on the mechanism, we adopt the
combination of the classic tiles instead of single tile, and then discuss the parameters that affecting the results of the self-assembly. We will carry out the
experiments on this basis. On the other hand, benefit from geometric studies
and DNA self-assembly, these two Archimedean tiling structures exist perfect

geometric features theoretically. Besides the complexity of DNA self-assembly will be increased, they will have possibilities to compound quasi-crystals.

In biocomputing, there is another important candidate, named membrane computing [34]. In [20], Shi et al. made up some neural-like logic gates with spiking neural P systems [7,13] and DNA displacement strategy. It deservers further research using self-assembled strategy based on DNA motifs to make up some variants of spiking neural P systems [2,14,15,25].

Acknowledgement. This work was supported by the National Natural Science Foundation of China (No. 61472371,61472372), Basic and Frontier Technology Research Program of Henan Province (Grant Nos. 142300413214), Program for Science and Technology Innovation Talents in Universities of Henan Province (No. 15HASTIT019), and Young Backbone Teachers Project of Henan province (Grant No. 2013GGJS-106), and Innovation Scientists and Technicians Troop Construction Projects of Henan Province (154200510012).

References

1. Fu, T.J., Seeman, N.C.: DNA double-crossover molecules. Biochemistry **32**(13), 3211–3220 (1993)
2. Song, T., Pan, L., Jiang, K., et al.: Normal forms for some classes of sequential spiking neural P systems. IEEE Trans. NanoBiosci. **12**(3), 255–264 (2013)
3. LaBean, T.H., Yan, H., Kopatsch, J.: Construction, analysis, ligation, and self-assembly of DNA triple crossover complexes. J. Am. Chem. Soc. **122**(9), 1848–1860 (2000)
4. Yan, H., Park, S.H., Finkelstein, G.: DNA-templated self-assembly of protein arrays and highly conductive nanowires. Science **301**(5641), 1882–1884 (2003)
5. He, Y., Ye, T., Su, M.: Hierarchical self-assembly of DNA into symemetric supramolecular polyhedra. Nature **452**(7184), 198–201 (2008)
6. He, Y., Tian, Y., Ribbe, A.E.: Highly connected two-dimensional crystals of DNA six-Point-Stars. J. Am. Chem. Soc. **128**(50), 15978–15979 (2006)
7. Song, T., Pan, L.: Spiking neural P systems with rules on synapses working in maximum spiking strategy. IEEE Trans. NanoBiosci. **14**(4), 465–477 (2015)
8. He, Y., Chen, Y., Liu, H.: Self-assembly of hexagonal DNA two-dimensional (2D) arrays. J. Am. Chem. Soc. **127**(35), 12202–12203 (2005)
9. Shi, X.L., Lu, W., Wang, Z.: Programmable DNA tile self-assembly using a hierarchical sub-tile strategy. Nanotechnology **25**(7), 075602 (2014)
10. Park, S.H., Pistol, C., Ahn, S.J.: Finite-size, fully addressable DNA tile lattices formed by hierarchical assembly procedures. Angew. Chem. **45**(5), 735–749 (2006)
11. Liu, Y., Ke, Y., Yan, H.: Self-assembly of symmetric finite-size DNA nanoarrays. J. Am. Chem. Soc. **127**(49), 17140–17141 (2005)
12. Park, S.H., Finkelstein, G., LaBean, T.H.: Stepwise self-assembly of DNA tile lattices using dsDNA bridges. J. Am. Chem. Soc. **130**(1), 40–41 (2008)
13. Song, T., Pan, L.: Spiking neural P systems with rules on synapses working in maximum spikes consumption strategy. IEEE Trans. NanoBiosci. **14**(1), 38–44 (2015)
14. Song, T., Pan, L., Păun, G.: Asynchronous spiking neural P systems with local synchronization. Inf. Sci. **219**, 197–207 (2013)

15. Zhang, X., Pan, L., Paun, A.: On the universality of axon P systems. IEEE Trans. Neural Netw. Learn. Syst. **26**, 2816–2829 (2015). doi:10.1109/tnnls.2015.2396940

16. Mathieu, F., Liao, S.P., Kopatsch, J.: Six-helix bundles designed from DNA. Nano Lett. **5**(4), 661–665 (2005)

17. Ke, Y., Liu, Y., Zhang, J., Yan, H.: A study of DNA tube formation mechanisms using 4-, 8-, and 12-helix DNA nanostructures. J. Am. Chem. Soc. **128**(13), 4414–4421 (2006)

18. Wilner, O.I., Orbach, R., Henning, A.: Self-assembly of DNA nanotubes with controllable diameters. Nat. Commun. **2**, 540 (2011)

19. Qian, H., Tian, C., Yu, J.W.: Self-assembly of DNA nanotubes with defined diameters and lengths. Small **10**(5), 855–858 (2014)

20. Shi, X., Wang, Z., Deng, C., Song, T., Pan, L., Chen, Z.: A novel bio-sensor based on DNA strand displacement. PLoS One **9**, e108856 (2014)

21. Zhang, C., Ko, S.H., Su, M., et al.: Symmetry controls the face geometry of DNA polyhedra. J. Am. Chem. Soc. **131**(4), 1413–1415 (2009)

22. Zhang, C., Su, M., He, Y.: Conformational flexibility facilitates self-assembly of complex DNA nanostructures. PNAS **105**(31), 10665–10669 (2008)

23. Li, Y.L., Liu, Z.Y., Yu, G.M.: Self-assembly of molecule-like nanoparticle clusters directed by DNA nanocages. J. Am. Chem. Soc. **135**(20), 7458–7461 (2013)

24. Woo, M., Neider, J., Davis, T.: OpenGL Architecture Review Board, OpenGL Programming Guide: The Official Guide to Learning OpenGL, 3rd edn. Addison-Wesley, Reading (1999). Version 1.2

25. Song, T., Pan, L., Wang, J., et al.: Normal forms of spiking neural P systems with anti-spikes. IEEE Trans. NanoBiosci. **11**(4), 352–359 (2012)

26. Ball, W.W.R., Coxeter, H.S.M.: Mathematical Recreations and Essays. Dover, New York (1987). pp. 127–128

27. Ghyka, M.: The Geometry of Art and Life. Dover, New York (1977)

28. Wells, D.: The Penguin Dictionary of Curious and Interesting Geometry. Penguin, London (1991). pp. 57–58

29. Zhang, F., Liu, Y., Yan, H.: Complex Archimedean tiling self-assembled from DNA nanostructures. J. Am. Chem. Soc. **135**(20), 7458–7461 (2013)

30. Li, Y.L., Tian, C., Liu, Z.Y.: Structural transformation: assembly of an otherwise inaccessible DNA nanocage. Angew. Chem. **54**(20), 5990–5993 (2015)

31. Tian, C., Li, X., Liu, Z.Y.: Directed self-assembly of DNA tiles into complex nanocages. Angew. Chem. **53**(31), 8179–8182 (2014)

32. Mikhael, J., Roth, J., Helden, L.: Archimedean-like tiling on decagonal quasicrystalline surfaces. Nature **454**, 501–504 (2008)

33. Williams, R.: The Geometrical Foundation of Natural Structure: A Source Book of Design. Dover, New York (1979). pp. 35–43

34. Păun, G.: Membrane Computing: An Introduction. Springer, Heidelberg (2002)

A Parallel Version of Differential Evolution Based on Resilient Distributed Datasets Model

Changshou Deng$^{(\boxtimes)}$, Xujie Tan, Xiaogang Dong, and Yucheng Tan

School of Information Science and Technology, JiuJiang University,
Jiujiang 332005, Jiangxi, China
{csdeng,txj2010,xx_dongxiaogang,yctan}@jju.edu.cn

Abstract. MapReduce is a popular cloud computing platform which has been widely applied in large-scale data-intensive fields. However, when dealing with computation extensive tasks, particularly, iterative computation, frequent loading Map and Reduce processes will lead to overhead. Resilient distributed datasets model which has been implemented in Spark, is an in-memory clustering computing which can overcome this shortcoming efficiently. In this paper, we attempt to use resilient distributed datasets model to parallelize Differential Evolution algorithm. A wide range of benchmark problems have been adopted to conduct numerical experiment, and the speedup of PDE due to use of resilient distributed datasets model is demonstrated. The results show us that resilient distributed datasets model is a potential way to parallelize evolutionary algorithm.

Keywords: Parallel differential evolution · Spark · Resilient distributed datasets · Transformation operation · Action operation

1 Introduction

Evolutionary algorithms (EAs) have been successfully applied in solving numerous optimization problems in diverse fields. Among them, Differential evolution (DE) algorithm is a simple powerful population-based stochastic search technique, which is an efficient and effective global optimizer in the continuous field [1]. Comparing with classical EAs such as Genetic Algorithm (GA), Evolutionary Strategy (ES), and the Swarm Intelligence Optimization algorithm i.e. particle swarm optimization (PSO), it has been claimed that DE exhibited an overall excellent performance for a wide range of benchmark problems [2]. Since its inception, DE has been applied to many real-world problems successfully [3,4].

Inspired by the great success of the classic DE, numerous variants of DE have been developed for solving different types of optimization problems such as noisy, constrained, and dynamic optimization problems. Recently, several enhanced DE has been proposed to improve the performance of DE [5–7]. However, in many engineering applications, each evaluation of the quality of solution is very time consuming. The use of parallel computing is a remedy in reducing the computing

© Springer-Verlag Berlin Heidelberg 2015
M. Gong et al. (Eds.): BIC-TA 2015, CCIS 562, pp. 84–93, 2015.
DOI: 10.1007/978-3-662-49014-3_8

time required for complex problems. Due to DE maintaining a lot of individuals in the population, DE has an implicit parallel and distributed nature. Therefore, several parallelization techniques of EAs have been reported [8]. Actually, a parallel implementation of multi-population DE has been proposed with parallel virtual machine [9]. Recently, Graphics Processing Unit (GPU) was used to implement parallel DE [10,11]. MapReduce is a programming model which was originally designed to simplify the development of distributed application for large scale data processing by Google [12]. There have been several attempts at using MapReduce model to parallelize EAs [13–16]. However, EAs are iterative algorithms working in loops, with output of each iteration being input for next iteration. By contrary, MapReduce is designed to run only once and produce final outputs immediately. Thus, parallelizing EAs with MapReduce leads to restart a MapReduce process during each generation of EAs. Frequent calling MapReduce process will increase much overhead. Previous works have proved that overhead decreased performance gaining from adding new nodes [16].

In this paper, a parallel implementation of DE based on resilient distributed datasets (RDD) [17] model is proposed. RDD is a distributed memory abstraction that allows programmers to perform in-memory computations on large clusters while retaining the fault tolerance of data flow models as MapReduce [19]. RDD supports iterative operations and interactive data mining. To overcome the shortcoming of parallelized DE with MapReduce, we parallelize DE using RDD.

The remainder of the paper is organized as follows. Section 2 describes the conventional DE. Resilient distributed datasets (RDD) model is presented in Sect. 3. With RDD model, the parallel implementation of DE (PDE) is proposed in Sect. 4. Comparing with DE, the performance of PDE is evaluated through numerical experiment in Sect. 5. Finally, Sect. 6 concludes this paper.

2   Differential Evolution

DE is a heuristic approach for minimizing continuous optimization problem which is possibly nonlinear and non-differentiable. DE maintains a population of D-dimensional vectors and requires few control variables. It is robust, easy to use and lends itself very well to parallel computation. The four operations, namely initialization, mutation, crossover and selection, in classical DE [1], are given as follows. Initialization in DE is according to Eq. (1).

$$x_{ij}(G) = x_j^l + rand_j(0,1)(x_j^u - x_j^l).\qquad(1)$$

Where $G = 0, i = 1, 2, ..., NP, j = 1, 2, ..., D, x_j^u$ denotes the upper constraints, and x_j^l denotes the lower constraints.

After being initialized, for each target vector $X_{i,G}, i = 1, 2, ..., NP$, a mutant vector is produced according to Eq. (2)

$$v_{i,G+1} = x_{r1,G} + F(x_{r2,G} - x_{r3,G}).\qquad(2)$$

where $i, r1, r2, r3 \in \{1, 2, ..., NP\}$ are randomly chosen and have to be mutually exclusive. And F is the scaling factor for the difference between the individual x_{r2} and x_{r3}.

In order to increase the diversity of population, DE introduces the crossover operation to generate a trial vector which is the mixture of the target vector and the mutation vector. In traditional DE, the uniform crossover is defined as follows:

$$u_{i,G+1} = \begin{cases} v_{i,G+1} & if \ rand \leq CR \ or \ j = rand(i) \\ x_{i,G} & otherwise \end{cases} \tag{3}$$

where $i = 1, 2, ..., NP, j = 1, 2, ..., D, CR \in [0, 1]$ is the crossover probability and $rand(i) \in (0, 1, 2, ..., D)$ is the randomly selected number which ensures that the trial vector $(u_{i,G+1})$ gets at least one element from the mutation vector $(v_{i,G})$.

To decide which one will survive in the next generation, the target vector $(x_{i,G})$ is compared with the trial vector $(u_{i,G+1})$ in terms of objective value according to

$$x_{i,G+1} = \begin{cases} u_{i,G+1}, & if \ f(u_{i,G+1}) < f(x_{i,G}) \\ x_{i,G} & otherwise. \end{cases} \tag{4}$$

3   Resilient Distributed Datasets (RDD)

Cloud computing represents a pool of virtual resources for information processing. High level cloud computing models like MapReduce [12] and Dryad [18] have been widely used to process the growing big data. These computing cluster systems are based on an acyclic data flow model which does not support for working set. Thus the applications based on an acyclic data flow model have to write data to disk and reload it on each iteration operation with current systems, leading to significant overhead. RDD allow programmers to explicitly cache working sets in memory across iteration operation, leading to substantial speedups on future use.

3.1   RDD Abstraction

RDD provides an abstraction that supports applications with working set. RDD not only supports data flow models, but also be capable of efficiently expressing computations with working sets. During operation on a working set, RDD only supports coarse-grained transformations, where a single operation can be applied to many records. Formally, an RDD is a collection of elements partitioned across the nodes of the cluster that can be operated on in parallel. RDDs can be created only through two ways: (1) either by starting with an existing file in stable storage, or (2) by an existing Scala collection in the driver program and transforming it.

3.2   Programming Model in Spark

Spark is the first system allowing an efficient, general purpose programming language to be used interactively to analyze datasets on clusters [17]. In Spark, RDDs are represented by objects, and transformations are invoked using methods on these objects. After defining one or more RDDs, transformation operations are used to transform these RDDs. Then action operations are used to return value to driver program or export data to disk storage. The programming model is presented in Fig. 1.

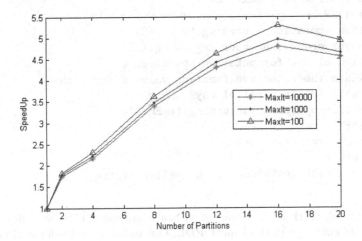

Fig. 1. RDD model in spark

3.3   RDD Operations in Spark

RDD includes mainly three types of operations: transformation operations, control operations and action operations. Transformations create a new dataset from an existing one, and control operations can persist an RDD in memory with cache method, in such case Spark will keep the elements around on the cluster for much faster access the next time you query it. Action operations return a value to the driver program after running a computation on the dataset.

4   Parallel DE

4.1   Procedure of PDE

RDD is a fault-tolerant abstraction for in-memory cluster computing. With the transformations available in Spark, a parallel version of DE is proposed. For many optimization problems, the evaluation of their objective function is costly.

Thus, in our proposed PDE, we only use cluster computing to compute the fitness values of the individuals. The Steps of the PDE is depicted as follows.

Algorithm. PDE

```
Input: NP; F; CR; MaxIt(Maximum number of iterations); 1: Randomly
initialize population P with NP individuals 2: Creation of RDD 3:
Evaluate the objective function value f for each individuals
 in parallel way
4: gengeration=0
5: while generation < MaxIt do
6: for i=1:NP
7: Mutation operation according to Eq.(2)
8: Crossover operation according to Eq.(3)
9: Creation of RDD for mutation operation U
10: Evaluate the objective function value f for each
 individuals (U) in parallel way
11: Selection operation according to Eq.(4)
12:end for
13:generation=generation+1
14: end while
Output: the best individual with smallest fitness
```

The core of Spark is implemented in Scala language. Thus we follow Spark to use Scala language to implement PDE. Our example codes for evaluate the objective function in parallel way are as follows:

val point = sc.parallelize(pop,numSlices).cache()
var popf = points.map(
p = >(p.x,getFitness(p.y,ifun+1),p.y)).collect()

In the codes, the first line is the process of creation of RDD from population individuals denoted by *pop*, and the second line is the demonstration of map transformation and collect action to conduct the evaluation of objective function in parallel way.

4.2 Inspection of PDE

First of all, EAs spend the majority of the computational time for evaluating the objective function values when applied to real-world applications. With RDD, the proposed PDE distributes the objective function evaluation to predefined partitions. Then, all individuals in PDE can be evaluated in parallel way. Consequently, the proposed PDE can be regarded as an efficient program. Comparing DE with PDE, there is no significant difference in the procedure. Therefore, PDE can be regarded as an efficient algorithm. Furthermore, the steps of PDE can be implemented by Scala, Java, or Python programming language. Therefore, the proposed PDE is portable.

5   Numerical Experiment

5.1   Benchmark Problems

In order to evaluate the performance of PDE, the benchmark problems used in this paper are listed in Table 1. Functions f_1 and f_2 are unimodal, while functions f_3, f_4, f_5 and f_6 are multimodal. In our experiment, all the benchmark problems have $D = 30$ dimensional real-parameters.

Table 1. Benchmark problems

Name	Expression	Value Range
Sphere function	$f_1 = \sum_{i=1}^{D} x_j^2$	[-100,100]
Schwefel's Ridge function	$f_2 = \sum_{i=1}^{D}(\sum_{k=1}^{j} x_k)^2$	[-100,100]
Rosenbrock function	$f_3 = \sum_{j=1}^{D-1}(100(x_{j+1} - x_j^2)^2 + (x_j - 1)^2)$	[-30,30]
Rastrigin function	$f_4 = \sum_{j=1}^{D}(x_j^2 - 10cos(2\pi x_j) + 10)$	[-5.12,5.12]
Ackley function	$f_5 = -20\exp(-0.2\sqrt{\frac{1}{D}\sum_{j=0}^{D} x_j^2}$ $- \exp(\frac{1}{D}\sum_{j=1}^{D}\cos(2\pi x_j))$	[-32,32]
Griewank function	$f_6 = \frac{1}{4000}\sum_{j=1}^{D} x_j^2 - \prod_{j=1}^{D}\cos(\frac{x_j}{\sqrt{j}}) + 1$	[-600,600]

5.2   Experimental Results

PDE and DE are applied to the six benchmark problems. The setting of parameters used in PDE and DE are $NP = 10 * D, F = 0.5, CR = 0.9$ and $MaxIT = 10000$. Twenty independent runs are carried out for the two algorithms in each function. In our experiment, Dell computers with 3.4 Ghz Intel Core i7-3770 CPU and 8G of RAM are used to construct the computing cluster. Spark1.2.0 is adopted as experimental platform. In PDE, we choose four different numbers of partition of RDD, namely, 2, 4, 8, and 15. Table 2 shows the objective function values of the best solutions obtained by PDE with different partition number, and DE.

In order to evaluate the speedup of the proposed PDE effectively, we add some delay in each objective function. The speedup metric mentioned in [19] was used in this paper. The speedup of PDE is defined as follows:

$$S_m(N_p) = \frac{T_m(1)}{T_m(N_p)} \tag{5}$$

In Eq. (5) $T_m(1)$ denotes the execution time of DE averaged over m times with one partition, while $T_m(N_p)$ denotes the averaged execution time of the proposed PDE achieved with N_p partitions in RDD. In this paper, $m = 5$.

The speedup curves achieved by the proposed PDE for the six benchmark problems are plotted in from Figs. 2, 3, 4, 5, 6 and 7 respectively.

Table 2. Objective function value

Function	PDE				DE
	(2)	(4)	(8)	(15)	
f_1	7.80E − 073	4.30E − 073	1.55E − 072	3.98E − 073	1.80E − 071
f_2	6.48E − 014	5.92E − 014	5.36E − 014	6.61E − 014	8.43E − 012
f_3	0.00E + 000	0.00E + 000	0.00E + 000	0.00E + 000	0.00E + 000
f_4	9.74E + 001	1.16E + 002	1.26E + 002	1.08E + 002	1.43E + 002
f_5	4.00E − 015	4.00E − 015	4.00E − 015	4.00E − 015	4.44E − 015
f_6	0.00E + 000	0.00E + 000	0.00E + 000	0.00E + 000	0.00E + 000

5.3 Discussion of Experimental Results

From Table 2, there is not a significant difference between PDE, and DE in the quality of solutions for functions f_3 and f_6. For the remainder two functions f_1, f_2, f_4 and f_5, the results of PDE are slightly better than those of DE.

From the speedup carves shown in Figs. 2, 3, 4, 5, 6 and 7, we can confirm that the speedup is larger than one in every instance. Therefore, the proposed PDE reduces the computational time with different numbers of partitions. The speedup achieved by PDE increases as the number of partitions increases steady

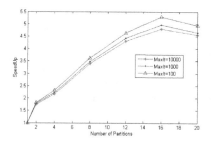

Fig. 2. Speedup by PDE on function: f_1

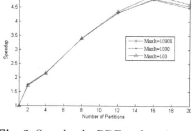

Fig. 3. Speedup by PDE on function: f_2

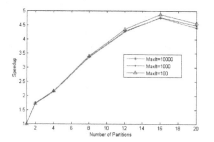

Fig. 4. Speedup by PDE on function: f_3

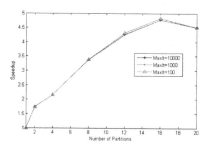

Fig. 5. Speedup by PDE on function: f_4

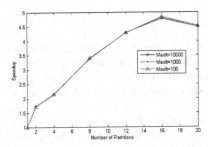 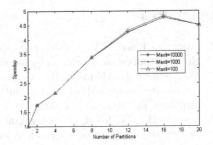

Fig. 6. Speedup by PDE on function: f_5 **Fig. 7.** Speedup by PDE on function: f_6

until $N_p = 16$ in all benchmark problems. The speedup will decrease when the number of partitions is larger than 16. Spark runs one task for each partition of the cluster. When more partitions are involved, the communication cost between nodes will decrease the speedup. There is no significant difference in speedup between the three maximum iterations(MaxIt) for each instance. The speedup of PDE actually depends on the cost of evaluate the objective function. We can expect that the proposed PDE is useful specially for solving the real-world applications that spend the majority of the computational time for evaluating their objective function values.

6   Conclusion

In order to utilize the cloud computing platform to parallelize DE, Spark, an open source cloud computing platform which supports iterative computation, was adopted. The proposed PDE was based on resilient distributed datasets model. In our PDE, the computation of objective function was parallelized. Therefore, we could expect the computational time was reduced by using the proposed PDE on Spark. From the numerical experiment conducted on a variety of benchmark problems, it was confirmed that the speedup achieved by PDE generally increased as the number of computing partitions increased under certain range.

In our future work, we need to parallelize the three operators, i.e., mutation, crossover, and selection and the evaluation of objective function together. Besides, we would like to utilize PDE with more partitions to solve expensive problems such as CEC 2010 large scale benchmark problems [20] which need more than two hundred hours to finish the optimization task with single computer. And parallelizing other EAs with RDD is also very interesting work.

Acknowledgments. This work is partially supported by Natural Science Foundation of China under grant No. 61364025, State Key Laboratory of Software Engineering Foundation under grant No. SKLSE2012-09-39 and the Science and Technology Foundation of Jiangxi Province, China under grant No. GJJ13729 and No. GJJ14742.

References

1. Store, R., Price, K.V.: Differential evolution CA simple and efficient heuristic for global optimization over continuous spaces. J. Glob. Optim. **11**(4), 341–359 (1997)
2. Vesterstrom, J., Thomsen, R.: A comparative study of differential evolution, particle swarm optimization, and evolutionary algorithms on numerical benchmark problems, pp. 1980–1987 (2007)
3. Yousefi, H., Handroos, H., Soleymani, A.: Application of differential evolution in system identification of a servo-hydraulic system with a flexible load. Mechatron. **18**(9), 513–528 (2008)
4. Rocca, P., Oliveri, G., Massa, A.: Differential evolution as applied to electromagnetics. Antennas Propag. Mag. **53**(1), 38–49 (2011)
5. Wang, Y., Li, H.X., Huang, T.: Differential evolution based on covariance matrix learning and bimodal distribution parameter setting. Appl. Softw. Comput. **18**, 232–247 (2014)
6. Wang, Y., Cai, Z., Zhang, Q.: Enhancing the search ability of differential evolution through orthogonal crossover. Inf. Sci. **185**(1), 153–177 (2012)
7. Wang, Y., Cai, Z., Zhang, Q.: Differential evolution with composite trial vector generation strategies and control parameters. IEEE Trans. Evol. Comput. **15**(1), 55–66 (2011)
8. Alba, E., Tomassini, M.: Parallelism and evolutionary algorithms. IEEE Trans. Evol. Comput. **6**(5), 443–462 (2002)
9. Zaharie, D., Petcu, D.: Parallel implementation of multi-population differential evolution. Concurrent Inf. Process. Comput. **48**, 223–232 (2005)
10. Wang, H., Rahnamayan, S., Wu, Z.: Parallel differential evolution with self-adapting control parameters and generalized opposition-based learning for solving high-dimensional optimization problems. J. Parallel Distrib. Comput. **73**(1), 62–73 (2013)
11. Fabris, F., Krohling, R.A.: A co-evolutionary differential evolution algorithm for solving minCmax optimization problems implemented on GPU using C-CUDA. Expert Syst. Appl. **39**(12), 10324–10333 (2012)
12. Dean, J., Ghemawat, S.: MapReduce: Simplified data processing on large clusters. Commun. ACM. **51**(1), 107–113 (2008)
13. Zhou, C.: Fast parallelization of differential evolution algorithm using MapReduce. In: Proceedings of the 12th Annual Conference on Genetic and Evolutionary Computation, pp. 1113–1114, Dubin, Ireland (2011)
14. Pavlech, M.: Framework for development of distributed evolutionary algorithms based on MapReduce. In: Proceedings of the 22nd International DAAAM Symposium on Intelligent Manufacturing and Automation: Power of Knowledge and Creativity, pp. 1475–1476, Vienna (2011)
15. McNabb, A.W., Monson, C.K., Seppi, K.D.: Parallel PSO using mapreduce. In: Proceedings of IEEE Congress on Evolutionary Computation, pp. 7–14. IEEE, Singapore (2007)
16. Verma, A., Llora, X., Goldberg, D.E.: Scaling genetic algorithms using mapreduce. In: Proceedings of the Ninth International Conference on Intelligent Systems Design and Applications, pp. 13–18. IEEE, Pisa (2009)
17. Zaharia, M., Chowdhury, M., Das, T.: Resilient distributed datasets: a fault-tolerant abstraction for in-memory cluster computing. In: The 9th USENIX Conference on Networked Systems Design and Implementation, 2012, pp. 1–16. USENIX Association, Berkeley (2012)

18. Isard, M., Budiu, M., Yu, Y., et al.: Dryad: distributed data-parallel programs from sequential building blocks. ACM SIGOPS Operating Syst. Rev. **41**(3), 59–72 (2007)
19. Kiyouharu, T., Takashi, I.: Concurrent differential evolution based on MapReduce. Int. J. Comput. **4**(4), 161–168 (2010)
20. Tang, K., Li, X., Suganthan, K.: Benchmark Functions for the CEC'2010 Special Session and Competition on Large Scale Global Optimization. Technical report, IEEE (2009)

MOEA/D for Energy-Aware Scheduling on Heterogeneous Computing Systems

Gaoshan Deng[1], Ziming Li[2(✉)], Yuming Zhao[3], and Xiangxiang Zeng[2]

[1] Software School, Xiamen University, Xiamen 361005, China
gaoshan.deng@foxmail.com
[2] Department of Computer Science, Xiamen University, Xiamen 361005, China
xmulzm@163.com, xzeng@xmu.edu.cn
[3] Information and Computer Engineering College, Northeast Forestry University,
Harbin 150001, Heilongjiang, China
zymyoyo@hotmail.com

Abstract. Heterogeneous Computing Systems (HCSs) often consist of a set of heterogeneous processors, and finding a scheduling for a workflow becomes a problem worth considering. The Dynamic Voltage Scaling (DVS) technique, which allows processors to operate at lower voltage to reduce the energy consumption, is widely used on HCSs. However, the technique also cause the loss of executing speed, and it makes the resource allocation a core component of the HCSs. In this paper, those two minimization objectives, the makespan and energy consumption, are considered together. As the heuristic methods have been widely applied in similar field, we adopt a multi-objective evolutionary algorithm based on decomposition (MOEA/D) to solve this scheduling problem. In our experiments, the algorithm shows higher performance in benchmark and the real-world applications than other state-of-art evolutionary algorithms do.

Keywords: Energy efficiency · Heterogeneous computing systems · Evolutionary algorithms · MOEA/D

1 Introduction

In recent years, the increasing use of computer systems leads to a huge amount of energy consumed. The report [10] shows that the world data center's electricity use doubled from 2000 to 2005, which increased social awareness towards the green information technologies (GreenIT) and the rate of electricity consumption growth slowed significantly from 2005 to 2010. It has been estimated that the annual data center's energy consumption in 2011 in the United States is over 100 billion kWh and at a cost of $7.4 billion [2], which may cause environmental and economic burden globally.

Traditional IT only emphasizes the minimization of an application's execution time. Nowadays, the energy consumption has received extensive attention

© Springer-Verlag Berlin Heidelberg 2015
M. Gong et al. (Eds.): BIC-TA 2015, CCIS 562, pp. 94–106, 2015.
DOI: 10.1007/978-3-662-49014-3_9

in the IT field. Therefore, we are supposed to minimize the completion time and take energy consumption into consideration at the same time.

Dynamic Voltage Frequency Scaling (DVFS) is a technology promising to improve the energy-efficiency of chip-multiprocessors (CMPs), which emerged as a widespread way for designers to exploit growing transistor budget. [8,18] shows that DVFS can be highly effective in improving the energy-efficiency of CMPs running multi-threaded commercial and scientific workloads. DVFS enables processors to dynamically adjust the supply voltage and frequency to reduce the energy consumed.

Slack reclamation, [12], is a state-of-art technique using DVFS. It can be used during the execution of the processors, leading to less energy consumption without the loss of makespan.

However, the key issue is how to apply those two methods properly, especially when tackling problem with precedence constraints, heterogeneous processors, communication costs, and energy consumption. This problem can be proved an NP-hard problem in [5].

Traditional deterministic scheduling methods cannot achieve a sound scheduling result. In order to find an optimal scheduling scheme, scholars proposed many new algorithms (see Sect. 'Related Work'). However, those algorithms face a problem- the final solutions of those algorithms have low diversity and convergence, especially when solving the large scale task for large distribution system with a mount of processors.

Our study adopts a multi-objective evolutionary algorithm based on decomposition (MOEA/D), which proposed by [30], is an effective algorithm to solve multi-objective problem. MOEA/D showed its advantages and won the CEC2009 [31] competition. The algorithm also has a good performance in solving the multi-objective 0–1 Knapsack problem for discrete problem than any other evolutionary algorithms. Our result shows MOEA/D also has good performance in solving scheduling problem. Our main contributions include the following aspects:

1. We propose a scheduling algorithm based on MOEA/D framework to solve the heterogeneous multiprocessor multi-objective scheduling problem, and compare it to another two state-of-art evolutionary algorithms, NSGA-II and SPEA2. The experimental results indicate that MOEA/D has a huge improvement in the result's diversity, and it also guarantees convergence.
2. We apply the newest Multi-parent Crossover Operator (MPCO) and compared MPCO with the grouping crossover operator, which can be proved better than traditional single or double crossover in [6].

    The rest of the paper is organized as follows: The next section 'Description' describes the definition of energy-aware scheduling on Heterogeneous Computing Systems. 'Related Work' describes the background and the related works. 'Algorithms Description' proposes the detail of targeted MOEA/D algorithm for scheduling problem. 'Experimentation' shows the results of experiment and analyses. Finally, the paper is concluded in 'Conclusions'.

2   Problem Description

2.1   Definition

A distributed computing system, which aims to finish a parallel application, consists of a set of heterogeneous processors. Each processor can operate with a set of DVFS pairs.

A parallel application executed by distributed system can be described as a Directed Acyclic Graph (DAG):

$$G \equiv (T, E, P_{i_l}, C_{i_j})$$

where T represents a set of nodes in the DAG. Each node represents a non-divisible computing task. P_{i_l} denotes the computation time of $task_i$ on processor r_l. E is the set of edges, which represents the precedence constraints. C_{ij} refers to the communication cost between $task_i$ and $task_j$. $\Phi(i)$ is a set of all the precedence constrains of i, the task which has no precedence constrains is called entry task. Moreover, $\Psi(i)$ is a set of all successors of i, the task that does not have any successors is a sink task.

Figure 1 shows an example of the DAG, which has 8 tasks and 10 edges with the communication cost of each task. The entry task is $task_0$, and the sink task is $task_7$. And Table 1 shows the different computation costs of three giving heterogeneous processors.

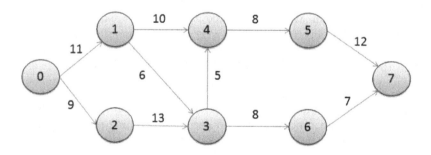

Fig. 1. A example DAG

In DVFS technology, each heterogeneous processor can be divided into different levels with different voltage and frequency. Table 2 gives a set of available DVFS pairs of three heterogeneous processors. Since a gene scheme for problem solving is needed for evolutionary algorithm, we use two vectors to represent a scheduling schema with one vector contains the choosing processors index for the task, the other stores the associated DVFS pairs of the task executing.

Table 1. Computation cost and task priorities

Task	r_0	r_1	r_2	$b - level$
0	6	8	10	112.0
1	10	12	13	92.0
2	7	9	8	95.0
3	11	13	15	74.0
4	12	17	15	56.0
5	6	13	9	33.3
6	11	10	15	31.0
7	9	12	15	12.0

Table 2. Sample of DVFS pairs of processors

Level	Type 1		Type 2		Type 3	
	V_k	$RS_s(\%)$	V_k	$RS_s(\%)$	V_k	$RS_s(\%)$
0	2.20	100	1.50	100	1.75	100
1	1.90	85	1.40	90	1.40	80
2	1.60	65	1.30	80	1.20	60
3	1.30	50	1.20	70	0.9	40
4	1.00	35	1.10	60		
5			1.00	50		
6			0.90	40		

2.2 Time Model

The start time S_i can be determined as:

$$S_i = \begin{cases} 0, & \text{if } i \text{ is entry task} \\ \max\{C_{ij} + F_j | j \in \Phi_i\}, \text{else} \end{cases}$$

C_{ij} is the communication cost between $task_i$ and $task_j$. And the completion time F_i of $task_i$ can be determined as:

$$F_i = S_i + E_i$$

Where E_i is the actual execution time of the $task_i$ on its corresponding processor. The sets EST (Earliest Start Time) and EFT ((Earliest Finish Time)) are defined respectively as:

$$EST \equiv \{S_i | i \in n\}$$

$$EFT \equiv \{F_i | i \in n\}$$

Finally, the make span can be calculated by:

$$makespan = \max\{F_i | i \in EFT\}.$$

2.3 Energy Model

The energy model is derived from power consumption model in complementary metal-oxide semiconductor (CMOS) logic circuits from [13]. The direct energy consumption is defined as:

$$P = ACV^2f$$

Where A is the number of switches per clock cycle, C is the total capacitance load, V is the supply voltage, and f is the clock frequency. We can simplify them to single coefficient α as A and C is constant only for machine, the value of α is often set to 1 in scheduling problem. The frequency f is proportional to the related speed. Finally the total energy consumption can be defined as:

$$E_i = \sum_{i=0}^{n} ACV_i^2 f w_i^* = \sum_{i=0}^{n} \alpha V_i^2 w_i^*$$

Where V_i is the supply voltage of the processor on which task n_i is executed, and w_i is the computation cost of task n_i (the amount of time taken for n_i's execution) on the scheduled processor.

As we mentioned above, a slack reclamation was used in order to reduce the energy consumption, which can be applied during the free time of the processors. Therefore, when the processors are free, they are set to their lowest available DVFS pairs for saving energy.

The goal is to determine a scheduling, which assigns each task a processor and an available DVFS pair during the task executed, and minimize both the total execution time and energy consumed simultaneously.

3 Related Work

Biological systems are rich sources of ideas for designing computing devices. In fact, they have inspired numerous classical computing devices, such as automatons and Turing machines. In recent years, computing devices inspired by cells (or molecules inside cells, such as DNA) have been thoroughly investigated. Most cell-inspired computing systems have been proved to be universal and computationally efficient ([20,28,29]).

Efficiency becomes an emerging research issue this year. [7] has made several important new observations regarding fine-grained dynamic *voltage/frequency* scaling for chip-multi-processors. It shows that DVFS can be highly effective in improving the energy-efficiency of CMPs running multi-threaded commercial and scientific workloads, with the best scheme they evaluated achieving an *energy/throughput²* reduction of 38.2 %.

Genetic algorithms (GAs) has been used in solving the scheduling problems. Recently years, a large number of MOEAs have been proposed to find local regions or points of interest in the Pareto optimal front, [32,34]. In [9], they develop two genetic algorithms with elitist and struggle replacement mechanisms as energy-aware schedulers. [19] proposes a new hybrid genetic algorithm approach composed of a case library (CL) and a multi-objective genetic algorithm to find the set of Pareto-front solutions, hence called CLPS-GA. In [6], three well-known evolutionary algorithms (NSGA-II, IBEA, MOCell) are proved to be effective on problem solving.

Decomposition methods are popular to solve the multi-object problem. For example, in [15], they have presented a new genetic algorithm for scheduling tasks through clustering based on the graph decomposition. MOEA/D [30] is a recent decomposition based algorithm. One of the major advantages of MOEA/D is that it is very easy to use well-developed single optimization local search within it. [16] shows MOEA/D without local search outperforms NSGA-II in the multi-objective Traveling Salesman Problem.

4   Algorithms Description

4.1   Algorithm Framework

MOEA/D decomposes a multi-objective optimization problem into a number of scalar optimization subproblems. The neighborhood relations among these subproblems are defined based on the distances between their aggregation coefficient vectors. MOEA/D Framework is defined as follows:

Algorithm 1. MOEA/D Framework

Require: N for population size
Ensure: A population with non-dominated solution EP
1: Initialize the population $P\{x_1, x_2, ..., x_n\}$ and a set of weight vectors $W\{w_1, w_2, ..., w_n\}$, and ideal point Z^*.
2: **for** each $i \in [0, N]$ **do**
3:    $B(i) = \{i_1, i_2, ..., i_T\}$ as the T closest weight vectors to w_i;
4: **end for**
5: set $EP = \emptyset$
6: **while** ! StopCondition() **do**
7:    **for** each $i \in [0, N]$ **do**
8:       parents = matingSelection($B(i)$);
9:       offspring = crossover(parents);
10:      mutation(offspring);
11:      evaluate(offspring);
12:      updateProblem(offspring);
13:   **end for**
14: **end while**
15: return EP;

4.2   Multi-parents Crossover Operation

Traditional genetic algorithms often use two-parent crossover operator or grouping crossover for discrete problem. Our study considers a Multi-parent Crossover Operator (MPCO) proposed by [19]. Different from two-parent crossover, MPCO randomly selects M parents from the neighbor population and creates an index vector $V(1, N) : v(1, i) = Random\{0, 1, ..., M\}$. Accordingly, the corresponding gene in each new individual's chromosome is determined by the index vector.

Figure 2 shows an example of MPCO when $M = 3$.

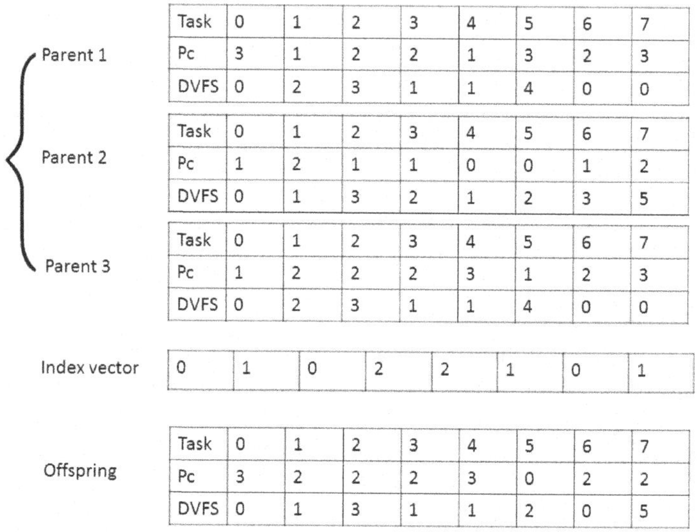

Parent 1

Task	0	1	2	3	4	5	6	7
Pc	3	1	2	2	1	3	2	3
DVFS	0	2	3	1	1	4	0	0

Parent 2

Task	0	1	2	3	4	5	6	7
Pc	1	2	1	1	0	0	1	2
DVFS	0	1	3	2	1	2	3	5

Parent 3

Task	0	1	2	3	4	5	6	7
Pc	1	2	2	2	3	1	2	3
DVFS	0	2	3	1	1	4	0	0

Index vector

0	1	0	2	2	1	0	1

Offspring

Task	0	1	2	3	4	5	6	7
Pc	3	2	2	2	3	0	2	2
DVFS	0	1	3	1	1	2	0	5

Fig. 2. Multi-parent Crossover Operator (MPCO)

4.3   Mutation

There are two types of mutation operators. In the first type, both processor and DVFS pair assignments are changed. In the second type, only DVFS pair changes to another available one, which only impact the DVFS pair or each solution. These two types of mutation are independent and can occur with the same probability in our study.

4.4   Evaluation

Evaluating both makespan and energy consumption for each solution is needed in every generation, and its performance has a critical impact on the whole efficiency.

To improve the efficiency, a greedy list heuristic is proposed by [1], in which a bottom level (*b-level*) is allocated to each task to determine its priority.

5   Experimentation

The behavior of MOEA/D is compared to other two algorithms, NSGA-II [4] and
SPEA2 [35]. Both of them include some classical strategies to maintain diversity
and convergence. Such as a crowded-comparison operator, fitness assignment
strategy, nearest neighbor density estimation technique and an enhanced archive
truncation method and so on.

5.1   Test Instance

A wide range of instances are used in our work to present a variety of real-world
applications. All of them can be described by using the following metrics:

1. Communication to Computation Ratio (CCR) [3]. It is the average communication cost for all tasks.
2. Heterogeneity. It can reflect the volatile of different processors.

Table 3 lists a set of random test instance which are created according to
different metrics for different types of situation.

Table 3. Instance metrics in our study

Type	The value set
Task number	$\{50, 100, 300, 500\}$
CCR	$\{0.1, 0.5, 1, 5, 10\}$
Number of processor	$\{3, 5, 8, 10, 20\}$
Heterogeneity	$\{0.25, 0.5, 0.75, 1\}$

Also, some real-world application problems are used for simulation. Those
problems contain the robot control application, a sparse matrix solver and fpppp
problem. All of them come from www.kasahara.elec.waseda.ac.jp/schedule.

5.2   Performance Metrics

The Inverted Generational Distance (IGD) metric in [14] shows how close are
the points in the approximated set to the closest point of Pareto front.

A Pareto front is required as it is unknown for us, so we replace it with
a pseudo-optimal Pareto front, which consists of all the best non-dominated
solutions for all the test instance.

5.3   Experiments and Result

In this section, we will make a comparison between MOEA/D, NSGA-II and
SPEA2 in the different instance metrics.

Table 4. Comparison between two crossover operators (IGD)

Task number	MOEA/D		NSGA-II		SPEA2	
	MPCO	GCO	MPCO	GCO	MPCO	GCO
50	0.02333	0.077004	0.177005	0.247156	0.07143	0.184032
100	0.080564	0.223734	0.179195	0.393298	0.157082	0.264864
300	0.155258	0.462336	0.441121	0.435443	0.388061	0.461158
500	0.171179	0.691859	0.557510	0.757908	0.321148	0.497952

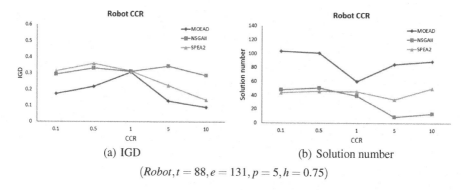

(a) IGD   (b) Solution number

$(Robot, t = 88, e = 131, p = 5, h = 0.75)$

Fig. 3. CCR test

Parameter Setting. In our experiments, we adopt the parameter setting from [6], which can be proved effective. In the parameter setting, the population size is set to 100, and the rate of crossover and mutation is set as: $r_{crossover} = 0.9$, $r_{mutation} = 1/t$.

To make the experiment more valid, each instance will be run 30 times and the average results will be calculated. Every instance stopped when it arrived 100,000 evaluations.

Crossover Test. There are two crossover operators, Grouping Crossover Operator (GCO) and the Multi-parents Crossover Operator (MPCO), in the test.

Processor Number, CCR and Heterogeneity Test. In this test, we compare three real-world applications. There are some parameter related to describe each application: t for task number, e for edge number, p for processor number, h for heterogeneity. And we verify those algorithms' performances in different conditions (Figs. 3, 4 and 5).

5.4 Analysis of the Results

All of the algorithms are able to get a set of Pareto-front solutions. Comparing the attained result in Table 4, the performance of MPCO are better than GCO

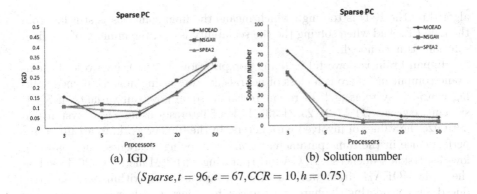

(a) IGD   (b) Solution number

$(Sparse, t = 96, e = 67, CCR = 10, h = 0.75)$

Fig. 4. PC test result

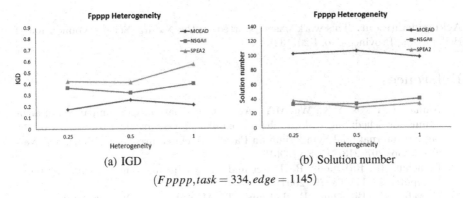

(a) IGD   (b) Solution number

$(Fpppp, task = 334, edge = 1145)$

Fig. 5. Heterogeneity test result

for almost all the algorithms. And the most improved algorithm using MPCO is MOEA/D.

In the following CCR, PC and Heterogeneity tests, it is interesting to see that MOEA/D outperforms other methods in diversity tests. And the solution number founded by MOEA/D is a huge improvement than NSGA-II and SPEA2. SPEA2 has the most stable performance in different giving instances.

6   Conclusions

In this work, a decomposition based evolutionary algorithm method (MOEA/D) is proposed. And it successfully tackles energy-aware scheduling on Heterogeneous Computing Systems. The newest crossover strategy, Multi-Parent Crossover Operator (MPCO), is used. Experimental results have shown its high performances solving the benchmarks in terms of convergence, stability and solutions' diversity. Compared with two state-of-art algorithms, NSGA-II and SPEA2, MOEA/D won almost all of the tests, which proved its effectiveness on improving the quality of solutions. But there are also some limitation in our algorithm: the IGD is too high which means the final solutions is still far from the true PF. And when solving the the scalability issues, the number of the final solutions is not enough.

Human brain is powerful in doing computation. In the framework of membrane computing, there is a class of neural-like computing models, named spiking neural P systems [22]. In recent research, some powerful variants of SN P systems, e.g. see [11,17,21,23,24,33]. It is of interests using SN P systems to optimize the values of involved parameters. In the further work, to attain better performance in the same parameters, some improving strategies, such as using low-dispersion sequences [27], GA incorporating with EM methods [26] based on the basic MOEA/D framework or other evolutionary algorithms can be introduced. Or considering the harder instances, for a larger scale systems, or taking more new objectives into consideration.

Acknowledgment. This work was supported by the Natural Science Foundation of Heilongjiang Province (No. F201132).

References

1. Ahmad, I., Kwok, Y.K., Wu, M.Y.: Analysis, evaluation, and comparison of algorithms for scheduling task graphs on parallel processors. In: Proceedings of the Second International Symposium on Parallel Architectures, Algorithms, and Networks, pp. 207–213. IEEE (1996)
2. Bianchini, R., Rajamony, R.: Power and energy management for server systems. Computer **37**(11), 68–76 (2004)
3. Crovella, M., Bianchini, R., LeBlanc, T., Markatos, E., Wisniewski, R.: Using communication-to-computation ratio in parallel program design and performance prediction. In: Proceedings of the Fourth IEEE Symposium on Parallel and Distributed Processing, pp. 238–245. IEEE (1992)
4. Deb, K., Pratap, A., Agarwal, S., Meyarivan, T.: A fast and elitist multiobjective genetic algorithm: NSGA-II. IEEE Trans. Evol. Comput. **6**(2), 182–197 (2002)
5. Garey, M.R., Johnson, D.S.: Computers and Intractability: A Guide to the Theory of NP-Completeness. Freeman, San Francisco (1979)
6. Guzek, M., Pecero, J.E., Dorronsoro, B., Bouvry, P.: Multi-objective evolutionary algorithms for energy-aware scheduling on distributed computing systems. Appl. Soft Comput. **24**, 432–446 (2014)
7. Herbert, S., Marculescu, D.: Analysis of dynamic voltage/frequency scaling in chip-multiprocessors. In: 2007 ACM/IEEE International Symposium on Low Power Electronics and Design (ISLPED), pp. 38–43. IEEE (2007)
8. Huang, Q., Su, S., Li, J., Xu, P., Shuang, K., Huang, X.: Enhanced energy-efficient scheduling for parallel applications in cloud. In: Proceedings of the 2012 12th IEEE/ACM International Symposium on Cluster, Cloud and Grid Computing (CCGrid 2012), pp. 781–786. IEEE Computer Society (2012)
9. Kolodziej, J., Khan, S.U., Xhafa, F.: Genetic algorithms for energy-aware scheduling in computational grids. In: 2011 International Conference on P2P, Parallel, Grid, Cloud and Internet Computing (3PGCIC), pp. 17–24. IEEE (2011)
10. Koomey, J.: Growth in Data Center Electricity use 2005 to 2010. A report by Analytical Press, completed at the request of The New York Times (2011)

11. Song, T., Pan, L., Jiang, K., et al.: Normal forms for some classes of sequential spiking neural P systems. IEEE Trans. NanoBiosci. **12**(3), 255–264 (2013)

12. Lee, Y.C., Zomaya, A.Y.: On effective slack reclamation in task scheduling for energy reduction. JIPS **5**(4), 175–186 (2009)

13. Lee, Y.C., Zomaya, A.Y.: Energy conscious scheduling for distributed computing systems under different operating conditions. IEEE Trans. Parallel Distrib. Syst. **22**(8), 1374–1381 (2011)

14. Li, H., Zhang, Q.: Multiobjective optimization problems with complicated pareto sets, MOEA/D and NSGA-II. IEEE Trans. Evol. Comput. **13**(2), 284–302 (2009)

15. Pecero, J.E., Trystram, D., Zomaya, A.Y.: A new genetic algorithm for scheduling for large communication delays. In: Sips, H., Epema, D., Lin, H.-X. (eds.) Euro-Par 2009. LNCS, vol. 5704, pp. 241–252. Springer, Heidelberg (2009)

16. Peng, W., Zhang, Q., Li, H.: Comparison between MOEA/D and NSGA-II on the multi-objective travelling salesman problem. In: Goh, C.-K., Ong, Y.-S., Tan, K.C. (eds.) Multi-objective Memetic Algorithms, vol. 171, pp. 309–324. Springer, Heidelberg (2009)

17. Song, T., Pan, L., Wang, J., et al.: Normal forms of spiking neural P systems with anti-spikes. IEEE Trans. NanoBiosci. **11**(4), 352–359 (2012)

18. Semeraro, G., Magklis, G., Balasubramonian, R., Albonesi, D.H., Dwarkadas, S., Scott, M.L.: Energy-efficient processor design using multiple clock domains with dynamic voltage and frequency scaling. In: Proceedings of the Eighth International Symposium High-Performance Computer Architecture, pp. 29–40. IEEE (2002)

19. Tao, F., Feng, Y., Zhang, L., Liao, T.: CLPS-GA: a case library and pareto solution-based hybrid genetic algorithm for energy-aware cloud service scheduling. Appl. Soft Comput. **19**, 264–279 (2014)

20. Zeng, X., Xu, L., Liu, X., Pan, L.: On languages generated by spiking neural P systems with weights. Inf. Sci. **278**, 423–433 (2014)

21. Song, T., Pan, L.: Spiking neural P systems with rules on synapses working in maximum spikes consumption strategy. IEEE Trans. NanoBiosci. **14**(1), 38–44 (2015)

22. Ionescu, M., Păun, G., Yokomori, T.: Spiking neural P systems. Fundamenta Informaticae **71**(2), 279–308 (2006)

23. Song, T., Pan, L., Păun, G.: Asynchronous spiking neural P systems with local synchronization. Inf. Sci. **219**, 197–207 (2013)

24. Zhang, X., Pan, L., Paun, A.: On the universality of axon P systems. IEEE Trans. Neural Netw. Learn. Syst. **26**(11), 2816–2829 (2015). doi:10.1109/TNNLS.2015. 2396940

25. Shi, X., Wang, Z., Deng, C., Song, T., Pan, L., Chen, Z.: A novel bio-sensor based on DNA strand displacement. e108856 (2014)

26. Wang, X., Miao, Y., Cheng, M.: Finding motifs in DNA sequences using low-dispersion sequences. J. Comput. Biol. **21**(4), 320–329 (2014)

27. Wang, X., Miao, Y.: GAEM: a hybrid algorithm incorporating GA with EM for planted edited motif finding problem. Curr. Bioinf. **9**(5), 463–469 (2014)

28. Zeng, X., Zhang, X., Song, T., Pan, L.: Spiking neural P systems with thresholds. Neural Comput. **26**(7), 1340–1361 (2014)

29. Zeng, X., Zhang, X., Zou, Q.: Integrative approaches for predicting microrna function and prioritizing disease-related microRNA using biological interaction networks. Brief. Bioinf. bbv033 (2015)

30. Zhang, Q., Li, H.: MOEA/D: a multiobjective evolutionary algorithm based on decomposition. IEEE Trans. Evol. Comput. **11**(6), 712–731 (2007)

31. Zhang, Q., Liu, W., Li, H.: The performance of a new version of MOEA/D on CEC09 unconstrained MOP test instances. IEEE Congr. Evol. Comput. **1**, 203–208 (2009)
32. Zhang, X., Tian, Y., Jin, Y.: A knee point driven evolutionary algorithm for many-objective optimization. IEEE Trans. Evol. Comput. **PP**(99), 1 (2014)
33. Song, T., Pan, L.: Spiking neural P systems with rules on synapses working in maximum spiking strategy. IEEE Trans. NanoBiosci. **14**(4), 465–477 (2015)
34. Zhang, X., Tian, Y., Cheng, R., Jin, Y.: An efficient approach to nondominated sorting for evolutionary multiobjective optimization. IEEE Trans. Evol. Comput. **19**(2), 201–213 (2015)
35. Zitzler, E., Laumanns, M., Thiele, L.: SPEA2: Improving the strength pareto evolutionary algorithm (2001)

Parameter Identification for Area-Specific Resistance of Direct Methanol Fuel Cell Using Cuckoo Search Algorithm

Jiajun Ding[1], Xiongxiong He[1($\boxtimes$)], Bo Jiang[2], and Yiming Wu[1]

[1] College of Information Engineering, Zhejiang Unviersity of Technology, Hangzhou 310023, China
dingjiajun19901004@163.com, hxx@zjut.edu.cn, yimgwu@hotmail.com
[2] College of Educational Science and Technology, Zhejiang Unviersity of Technology, Hangzhou 310023, China
bjiang@zjut.edu.cn

Abstract. In order to improve the accuracy of the area-specific resistance model for direct methanol fuel cell, a heuristic algorithm named cuckoo search is employed. In this work, the optimal modeling strategy is designed to identify the parameters of the area-specific resistance model and minimize the error between the simulation and real experimental data. In experimental evaluation, the proposed algorithm is compared with four heuristic algorithms. The experimental results show the model based on cuckoo search offering better approximation effect and stronger robustness comparing with four other heuristic algorithms.

Keywords: Cuckoo search algorithm · Parameter identification · Area specific resistance

1 Introduction

In recent years, direct methanol fuel cell (DMFC) has attracted a lot of attention because of its high energy density of methanol and low power requirements of the portable electronic devices [1]. Direct methanol fuel cell directly using methanol as fuel has good potentialities since it eliminate the requirement of a complex reformer unit in the system [2]. In addition, the complex humidification and thermal management are avoided by feeding with water.

The area-specific resistance of direct methanol fuel cell which affects the voltage loss due to ohmic polarization is a very important parameter of direct methanol fuel cell [3]. The area-specific resistance of direct methanol fuel cell is not a constant, its value is influenced by ambient temperature [4]. A semi-empirical model of area-specific resistance which was developed by Q. Yang can estimate the area-specific resistance value accurately [5]. However, Different direct methanol fuel cell has different parameters of the semi-empirical model. In order to understand and control different direct methanol fuel cell, a highly

© Springer-Verlag Berlin Heidelberg 2015
M. Gong et al. (Eds.): BIC-TA 2015, CCIS 562, pp. 107–112, 2015.
DOI: 10.1007/978-3-662-49014-3_10

efficient and accurate calculation method for the semi-empirical model of area-specific resistance is necessary.

Heuristic algorithms have been employed to solve the problems of parameter identification. Genetic algorithm was adopted by Ohenoja and Leiviska to optimize a proper mathematical model of a fuel cell [6]. An adaptive RNA genetic algorithm proposed by Zhang and Wang was applied to estimate the proton exchange membrane fuel cell model parameters [7]. Bo Jiang used cooperative barebone particle swarm optimization with hybrid learning to identity the parameters of solid oxide fuel cells [8]. However, these heuristic algorithms have high computation complexity.

In this paper, a new heuristic algorithm named cuckoo search algorithm [9] is employed to identity the parameters of a semi-empirical model based on the real experimental data. The results illustrate a better performance of cuckoo search algorithm comparing with four other heuristic algorithms.

2   Cuckoo Search Algorithm

Cuckoo search algorithm which developed by Yang and Deb imitates the laying eggs and searching nests behaviors of the cuckoo and the levy flight. Cuckoo search algorithm is simple and efficient [10]. It has been widely used to solve the optimization problems [11].

In the process of cuckoo search algorithm, n randomly chosen nests come into being, and the ith nest is set $nest_i = (x_{i1}, x_{i2}, \cdots x_{id})$, where d is the dimension of the problem. The fitness of each nest can be got according to their own location information. The nests are updated according to Eq. (1)

$$nest_i^{t+1} = nest_i^t + \alpha \oplus Levy(\lambda), \qquad 1 \leq i \leq n \tag{1}$$

Where α is the step size according to the scale of problem. $\alpha = O(1)$ in most cases. The produce $\oplus$ is entry-wise multiplications. $Levy(\lambda)$ is Levy distribution function:

$$Levy(\lambda) \sim u = t^{-\lambda}, (1 < \lambda \leq 3) \tag{2}$$

which has an infinite variance with an infinite mean.

Each nest have a certain probability (P_a) to be abandoned. If a nest is abandoned, new nest will come into being according to Eq. (3)

$$nest_i^{t+1} = nest_i^t + r(nest_j^t - nest_k^t) \tag{3}$$

Where r is scale factor which distributes uniformly between 0 and 1; $nest_j^t$ and $nest_k^t$ is other nests which are randomly selected in tth generation.

3   Problem Description

3.1   Resistance Model

The direct methanol fuel cell consists of three parts: open circuit voltage, overpotential due to ohmic polarization and overpotential due to activation and concentration polarizations at both the anode and cathode. The ohmic overpotential η_R is calculated by:

$$\eta_R = R_e j. \tag{4}$$

Where $R_e(\Omega\ cm^2)$ is the area-specific resistance of direct methanol fuel cell, and $j(A\ cm^{-2})$ is the current density of the fuel cell. Therefore, if the value of area-specific resistance is got, the ohmic overpotential can be calculated.

According to experiments of reference [4], the area-specific resistance R_e is insensitive to methanol solution concentration. Which affects the value of area-specific resistance R_e is the absolute temperature $T(K)$ as expected from known correlations. Temperature will decrease the resistance. The expression of area-specific resistance is [4]:

$$R_e = R_0 \exp(\frac{B}{T} - \frac{B}{T_0}). \tag{5}$$

Where T_0 and R_0 are the known temperature and area-specific resistance, and B is a constant based on experimental data. In order to determine the value of area-specific resistance accurately in any temperature, a semi-empirical model is developed [5]:

$$R_e = a_1 e^{(a_2/T - a_3)}. \tag{6}$$

where T is the absolute temperature in Kelvin, and a_1, a_2, a_3 are the parameters based on experimental data.

3.2   Objective Function

Experimental data based on a DMFCkit, TekStak^{TM}, manufactured by Parker Hannifin Energy Systems at different temperatures are shown in Table 1. Other operating parameters were methanol concentration (0.5 M), air flow rate (81.2 ccm), methanol flow rate (3.5 ccm) [5].

Table 1. Experimental data

No.	1	2	3	4	5
Temperature $T(K)$	298	313	323	333	343
Resistance $R_e(\Omega\ cm^2)$	1.42	1.39	1.11	1.02	0.98

The model in Eq. (6) describes the area-specific resistance of a DMFC. To reflect the resistance of a real DMFC, the three unknown parameters should be identified. In this paper, these parameters are determined by optimization algorithms which are employed to minimize the error between the simulated area-specific resistance and the real experimental data. The average absolute error (AAE) function is defined as follows.

$$\text{AAE} = \frac{1}{5} \sum_{n=1}^{5} \left| a_1 e^{(a_2/T_n - a_3)} - R_n^{real} \right|. \tag{7}$$

Where n is the serial number of experimental data.

4   Algorithmic Comparison

In this section, cuckoo search algorithm (CS) [9] is employed to identity the parameters by minimizing the error between the simulated area-specific resistance and the real experimental data. The search ranges of three unknown parameters are 0 to 2000 ($a_1, a_2, a_3 \in [0, 2000]$). The performance of CS is compared with four optimization algorithms and the parameters from reference [5].

4.1   Algorithmic Setup

Four optimization algorithms are used: particle swarm optimization (PSO) [12], bat algorithm (BA) [13], firefly algorithm (FA) [14], artificial bee colony algorithm (ABC) [15]. Parameter Settings of algorithms are showed in Table 2.

Table 2. Parameter settings

CS	$p_a = 0.25$		
PSO	$w=0.729$	$c_1=1.49445$	$c_2 = 1.49445$
BA	$A = 0.25$	$r = 0.5$	$Q \in [0, 2]$
FA	$\gamma = 1$	$\beta = 0.2$	$\alpha = 0.5$
ABC	$limit = 15$		

For a fair comparison, the population size of all algorithms is 10, and the maximum iteration of algorithms is 400. All the algorithms run 30 times, the best (*Best*), median (*Median*), worst (*Worst*) AAE values and Runtime(s) of the five algorithms in the 30 runs are listed in Table 3. The parameters of each best fitness are listed in Table 4. To be more intuitively, the best convergence progress of 30 runs is plotted in Fig. 1.

Table 3. The performance of algorithms

	CS	PSO	BA	FA	ABC	Reference [5]
Best	**0.0424**	**0.0424**	0.0425	0.0428	0.0442	0.0515
Median	**0.0425**	0.5412	0.2380	1.0027	0.0810	–
Worst	**0.0429**	1.1840	1.1838	1.1840	0.2364	–
Runtime(s)	5.419	4.491	**1.400**	3.707	4.178	–

4.2   Experimental Evaluation

All five heuristic algorithms (CS, PSO, BA, FA, ABC) are able to get better performance than reference [5] according to the best AAE values in Table 4. In term of *Best*, CS can get the best AAE values as good as PSO. Additionally, CS outperformed all the other algorithms in terms of the *Median* and *Worst*. In

Table 4. The parameters of each best fitness

	CS	PSO	BA	FA	ABC	Reference [5]
a_1	1736.7755	1026.9410	0.0653	1235.6846	1483.1735	6.9897
a_2	938.0325	938.0351	927.5992	889.2174	856.7686	916.91
a_3	10.2569	9.7315	0.0330	9.7527	9.8303	4.6392

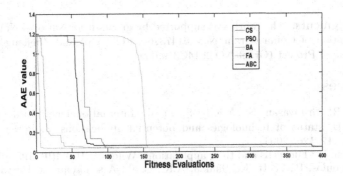

Fig. 1. Convergence progress of the five algorithms on model

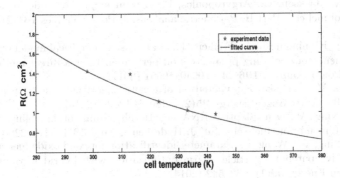

Fig. 2. Influence of temperature on area-specific resistance

Table 4, The *Median* and *Worst* of CS are very close to the *Best* of CS, which means the area-specific resistance model of direct methanol fuel cell based on CS can get better approximation effect and stronger robustness. This property is very important in real-world applications, because we hope the algorithm can provide a solution better than reference [5] even in the worst case. In term of Runtime(s), CS spent most of the time to search, but there is no significant difference between CS and PSO, FA and ABC. BA ranked first in runtime. To be more clearly, the best solution provided by CS in Table 4 is compared with the experiment data in Fig. 2. From Fig. 2, we can easily observe that the experiment data is fitted precisely by the generated curve.

5   Conclusions

In this paper, a new heuristic algorithm named cuckoo search algorithm has been used to identify parameters of DMFC area-specific resistance model. Compared with four other algorithms, the experimental results demonstrated the high effectiveness of CS. It has been shown that the model based on CS performs is more precise and robust than the other models.

Acknowledgments. This work was supported by grants from National Natural Science Foundation of China (Grant Nos. 61473262, 61503340) and Zhejiang Province Public Research Project (Grant NO.2014C31097).

References

1. Dillon, R., Srinivasan, S., Aric, A.S., et al.: International activities in DMFC R and D: status of technologies and potential applications. J. Power Sources. **127**(1), 112–126 (2004)
2. Kordesch, K.: Fuel cells and their applications. Wiley-VCH. **94**(9), 193–199 (1996)
3. Argyropoulos, P., Scott, K., Shukla, A.K., et al.: A semi-empirical model of the direct methanol fuel cell performance: part I. Model development and verification. J. Power Sources **123**(3), 190–199 (2003)
4. Scott, K., Jackson, C., Argyropoulos, P.: A semi empirical model of the direct methanol fuel cell. Part II. Parametric analysis. J. Power Sources **161**(2), 885–892 (2006)
5. Yang, Q., Kianimanesh, A., Freiheit, T., et al.: A semi-empirical model considering the influence of operating parameters on performance for a direct methanol fuel cell. J. Power Sources. **196**(24), 10640–10651 (2011)
6. Ohenoja, M., Leiviska, K.: Validation of genetic algorithm results in a fuel cell model. Int. J. Hydrogen Energy **35**(22), 12618–12625 (2010)
7. Li, Z., Ning, W.: An adaptive RNA genetic algorithm for modeling of proton exchange membrane fuel cells. Int. J. Hydrogen Energy **38**(1), 219–228 (2013)
8. Bo, J., Ning, W., Wang, L.: Parameter identification for solid oxide fuel cells using cooperative barebone particle swarm optimization with hybrid learning. Int. J. Hydrogen Energy **39**(1), 532–542 (2014)
9. Yang, X., Deb, S.: Cuckoo search via levy flights. In: IEEE World Congress on Nature and Biologically Inspired Computing, pp. 210–214 (2009)
10. Yang, X., Deb, S.: Cuckoo search.: recent advances and applications. Neural Comput. Appl. **24**(1), 169–174 (2014)
11. Yang, X.S., Deb, S.: Engineering optimisation by cuckoo search. Int. J. Math. Model. Numer. Optimisation **1**(4), 330–343 (2010)
12. Clerc, M., Kennedy, J.: The particle swarm-explosion, stability, and convergence in a multidimensional complex space. IEEE Trans. Evol. Comput. **6**(1), 58–73 (2002)
13. Yang, S.: A new metaheuristic bat-inspired algorithm. In: González, J.R., Pelta, D.A., Cruz, C., Terrazas, G., Krasnogor, N. (eds.) Nature Inspired Cooperative Strategies for Optimization (NICSO 2010), pp. 65–74. Springer, Heidelberg (2010)
14. Yang, X.: Firefly algorithm, levy flights and global optimization. In: Bramer, M., Ellis, R., Petridis, M. (eds.) Research and Development in Intelligent Systems XXVI, pp. 209–218. Springer, London (2010)
15. Karaboga, D., Basturk, B.: A powerful and efficient algorithm for numerical function optimization: artificial bee colony (ABC) algorithm. J. Global Optim. **39**(3), 459–471 (2007)

SAMD: A System for Abnormal Messages Detection Oriented Microblog Message Stream

Guozhong Dong[1], Bo Wang[2], Wu Yang[1(✉)], Wei Wang[1], and Rui Sun[3]

[1] Information Security Research Center, Harbin Engineering University,
Harbin, China
{dongguozhong,yangwu,w_wei}@hrbeu.edu.cn
[2] National Computer Network Emergency Response Technical Team/Coordination
Center, Beijing, China
wbxyz@163.com
[3] Daqing Lvyuan Wind Power Generation CO., LTD, Daqing, China
leafsun1224@163.com

Abstract. Microblog has been an important medium for providing the rapid communications of public opinion and can quickly publicize a burst topic for discussion when unexpected incidents happen. Abnormal messages are usually the source of burst topics and are important for the diffusion of burst topics. It is necessary to detect abnormal messages from microblog real-time message stream. In this paper, we propose SAMD, a System for Abnormal Messages Detection. In SAMD, sliding time window model is applied to divide the microblog data stream into different shards. Only that the participation of messages exceed initial threshold can be indexed and stored in two-level hash table. An efficient abnormal messages detection model is used to detect abnormal messages in a given time window. The case study on the collected data set can show that SAMD is effective to detect and demonstrate abnormal messages from large-scale microblog message stream.

Keywords: Sina microblog · Sliding time window · Two-level hash table · Abnormal messages detection model

1 Introduction

Along with the rapid development of social media, microblog has been an important medium for providing the rapid communications of public opinion due to its wide range of users and diffusion speed. Different from traditional news media, microblog can allow users to broadcast short textual messages that express users opinions using web-based or mobile-based platforms. Microblog plays an important part in guidance and impetus when kinds of emergencies broke out. How to complete effective management and the control on network popular feelings of microblog has become one of the most compelling causes. In particular, people can post short messages about emergency to be shared with the microblog users using mobile services. When emergency broke out, some malicious messages will

© Springer-Verlag Berlin Heidelberg 2015
M. Gong et al. (Eds.): BIC-TA 2015, CCIS 562, pp. 113–124, 2015.
DOI: 10.1007/978-3-662-49014-3_11

be burst messages or hot messages due to large number of people participating in conversation and discussions. Considering millions of messages produced every day and large number of malicious users, some burst or hot messages that contain fake information may be posted and spread widely. In this paper, we investigate the problem of detecting burst messages, which can be defined as abnormal messages in this paper. The participation of messages has a significant increase during a certain time interval. However, some major challenges arise: the large number of messages and the real-time nature of microblog. It is necessary to detect and analyze abnormal messages from microblog data stream in real-time by monitoring messages. To solve the challenging problems, a system for abnormal messages detection (SAMD) is proposed. In SAMD, we construct a sliding time window model to divide real-time messages stream into different shards according to the size of time window. An efficient data structure called two-level hash table is proposed to store potential abnormal messages for each time window. Message influence of potential abnormal messages in each time window is computed and stored in hash table. Abnormal messages are determined based on message influence series and abnormal messages detection model. Once abnormal messages are detected, SAMD can demonstrate message propagation tree and key users of abnormal messages.

To summarize, the contributions of our work are listed as follows:

- A two-level hash table is proposed to process message stream according to original message ID quickly and efficiently which can reduce the possibility of a hash collision.
- Effective abnormal messages detection model and system are designed to detect abnormal messages in real- time microblog stream. The case study on the collected data set can show that SAMD is effective to detect and demonstrate abnormal messages from large-scale microblog message stream.

The rest of the paper is organized as follows. We first review the related work in Sect. 2. Section 3 presents the overview of SAMD. The methods used in SAMD are described in Sect. 4. Section 5 shows the case study and finally concludes this paper.

2   Related Work

Our work is broadly related to several areas: anomaly detection, social network analysis [1–3] and so on.

Anomaly detection has been an active research topic for the last few years. The impact of anomaly detection in microblog has been explored in many aspects. For example, Link anomaly was used to detect emerging topics in social streams [4]. A statistical analysis of language was used to detect malicious tweets in trending topics [5]. In our previous work, we proposed a microblog burst keywords detection approach based on social trust and dynamics model to detect burst keywords [6]. Also, an effective approach based on novel features is used to detect bots in follower markets [7]. It is important to detect anomaly for online application. Some researchers designed application systems to detect anomaly, such as burst keywords, tags and events. Sakaki, Okazaki et al. [8] conducted an earthquake reporting system to detect an earthquake by monitoring tweets. Alvanaki, Sebastian et al. [9] presented the en Blogue system for emergent topic detection. Li, Sun et al. [10] proposed Twevent system to detect events in twitter stream which can distinguish the realistic events from the noisy ones. Lee, Lakshmanan et al. [11] applied density-based clustering on evolving post network to identify the events. Wang, Liu et al. [12] proposed a system called SEA to detect events and conduct panoramic analysis on Weibo events from various aspects. Xie, Zhu et al. [13] presented a real-time system to provide burst event detection, popularity prediction, event summarization. However, previous works could not design an overall system to detect abnormal messages microblog message stream. Our work presents an efficient framework to detect and analyze abnormal messages in microblog message stream.

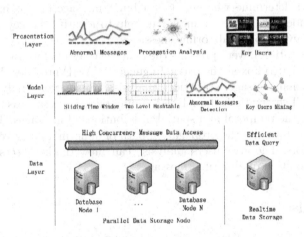

Fig. 1. The framework of SAMD.

3   System Overview

The framework of SAMD is presented in this section. As shown in Fig. 1. It contains three functional layers, namely Data Layer, Model Layer and Presentation Layer.

The "Data Layer" is designed to handle the massive streams of microblog messages. SAMD provides two main functions for data manipulation: high concurrency message data access and efficient data query. The first one is to extract microblog messages from distributed crawler, transform to structured raw messages, and store to database cluster using a paralleled ETL module. As real-time messages keep coming in, the database cluster can add database node online and enable the future expansion of SAMD to the distributed environment. The second one is to retrieve microblog messages from real-time messages storage node, construct message stream to model layer for further processing. Data query is transparent for users and it can speed up the information retrieval via efficient index structure. Due to the page limit, we omit the technical details of the data layer.

The "Model Layer" utilizes several important models to detect and present abnormal messages. In SAMD, sliding time window model is used to divide and filter the message stream, only that the participation of messages exceed initial threshold are indexed in two-level hash table, which can decrease the computing complexity of abnormal messages detection. In order to decrease the worst-case probability, two-level hash table algorithm based on bloom filter counter algorithm is proposed. The algorithm we proposed can not only decrease the worst-case probability, but also reduce the number of memory access in the worst case. Abnormal messages detection model compute each messages influence series in hash table and determine whether it is a burst message or hot message in a given time window. Key users mining can help to identify the key users in the formation and evolution of abnormal messages.

The "Presentation Layer" presents the analytical results for model layer with a user-friendly search box as the entry. In general, SAMD provides three aspects for each abnormal message: statistical analysis, propagation analysis and key users analysis. The "statistical analysis" summarizes a message using statistics in two aspects: the temporal and spatial distributions of messages. The "propagation analysis" provides the propagation path of abnormal messages according to user behaviors. The "key users analysis" can show the key users in the formation and evolution of abnormal messages.

4   Methods

In this section, some key models implemented by SAMD are introduced in detail.

4.1   Sliding Time Window

In order to better describe sliding time window model, the formal descriptions of microblog messages and message stream are introduced before defining sliding time window.

Based on the transformation and storage of crawled microblog messages, microblog message can be formalized as nine tuples. The description of each tuple is shown in Table 1.

A microblog message stream consist of microblog messages according to post time of messages which can be define as:

$$M = [m_1, m_2, ..., m_i, ..., m_N] \tag{1}$$

If $i < j$ and $i, j \in 1, 2, ..., N$, the post time of m_i is smaller than m_j.

Table 1. The Description of each tuple in microblog message

Description of each tuple	Formal representation
Message ID	mid
Original message ID	$root\_mid$
User ID	uid
Comment number of original message	com_num
Retweet number of original message	ret_num
Post time of message	$post\_time$
Post time of original message	$root\_time$
Content of message	$content$

The microblog message stream M can be divided into different time windows according to the post time of microblog message and time window size. Based on the concept of time window, the microblog message stream M can be formalized as:

$$M = [W_1, W_2, ...W_j, ..., W_L] \tag{2}$$

where W_j represents the message set of jth time window and $\sum_{j=1}^{L} |W_j| = M$. If W_L is current time window and K is the size of sliding window, sliding time window SW can be formalized as:

$$SW = [W_{L-L+1}, ..., W_L] \tag{3}$$

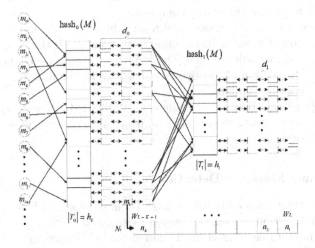

Fig. 2. The structure of two-level hash table.

4.2   Two-Level Hash Table

The two-level hash table is a kind of level hash tables. The brief structure of our proposed two-level hash table is shown in Fig. 2. It has two child hash tables T_0 and T_1 and each of them has corresponding hash function $hash_0(M)$ and $hash_1(M)$. These two functions are chosen from two global hash classes.

If $|T_0| = h_0$, $|T_1| = h_1$, $h_1 = h_0 \times r(0 < r < 1)$, $slot_{i,j}$ is the jth slot position in child hash table T_j and $slot_{i,j} = T_{i,j}$, $i \in \{0,1\}$, $j \in [0, h_i]$. The two child hash tables handle hash collision with separate chaining. $slot_{i,j}.list$ is the collision chain of $slot_{i,j}$. The length of collision chain in child hash table T_0 is limited and the maximum length is set as d_0. The child hash table T_1 is a collision buffer of the child hash table T_0.

Furthermore, each slot in T_0 has a *ofbuffer* which store the node information that the length of collision chain in child hash table T_0 is larger than d_0. Each message node in $slot_{i,j}.list$ can be formalized as:

$$node = (m, N, pw) \tag{4}$$

where m is the microblog information stored in the node, pw is the number of past time windows, N is the message influence series in sliding time window. Message influence in current time window W_L can be computed as

$$n_1 = comment\_num + retweet\_num \tag{5}$$

where $comment\_num$ is the number of comment in time window W_L, $retweet\_num$ is the number of retweet in time window W_L.

When we search the message m_i, we can use the Bloom Filter Counter algorithm to judge the message whether in T_1. If message m_i is not in T_1, we can search it in T_0 to reduce the search complexity.

If the message m_i is not in two-level hash table, we firstly use $hash_0(m_i)$ to locate the position of message in the child hash table T_0. If the length of linked list is more than d_0, we will use $hash_1(m_i)$ to map the message to the child hash table T_1. If the message m_i is in two-level hash table, the message information and influence series are updated.

Microblog message stream processing algorithm based on two-level hash table (Algorithm 1) can generate the message influence series of each message node in two-level hash table.

4.3   Abnormal Messages Detection

When current time window is full, a hash table copy signal is sent to abnormal messages detection thread. Abnormal messages detection algorithm based on two-level hash table (Algorithm 2) can detect abnormal messages in each time window. The algorithm uses the dynamic threshold adjustment strategy to set burst threshold, which can adjust burst threshold according to the message influence series.

Algorithm 1. Microblog message stream processing algorithm

Input:

    M is microblog message stream, W_L is current time window, H is two-level hash table, $curr\_time$ is current time, $delay\_time$ is aging time

Output:

    Message influence series in sliding time window.

 1: **for** each $m_i \in M$ **do**
 2:    **if** m_i divided into W_L **then**
 3:      **if** m_i is not in H **then**
 4:        insert m_i into H
 5:      **else**
 6:        **if** $curr\_time$ - $m_i.root\_time > delay\_time$ **then**
 7:          update the node information of m_i in H
 8:        **else**
 9:          delete m_i from H
10:        **end if**
11:      **end if**
12:    **else**
13:      compute and store the influence series of m_i
14:    **end if**
15: **end for**

Algorithm 2. Abnormal messages detection algorithm

Input:

    $N_i = (n_k, ..., n_2, n_1)$ is message influence series, HT is the threshold for hot messages, K is the size of sliding window

Output:

    M_h is the set of hot messages, M_b is the set of burst messages

 1: **if** each $node$ in two-level hash table **then**
 2:    **if** $node.pw < K$ **then**
 3:      **if** $node.m.com\_num + node.m.ret\_num > HT$ **then**
 4:        add $node$ to M_h and M_b
 5:      **end if**
 6:    **else**
 7:      **if** $node.m.com\_num + node.m.ret\_num > HT$ **then**
 8:        add $node$ to M_h
 9:      **else**
10:        compute the Moving Average MA_k of $node.N$
11:        compute burst threshold BT, $BT = mean(MA_k) + 2 * std(MA_k)$
12:        **if** $node.m.n_1 > BT$ **then**
13:          add $node$ to M_b
14:        **end if**
15:      **end if**
16:    **end if**
17: **end if**

4.4   Key Users Mining

Key users can deliver contents to a larger audience than a normal user and have a key role in message propagation process. User graph is conducted by the information propagation. Nodes in user graph represent users in message propagation process. Edges represent repost relation between nodes and the arrow go opposite to the information flow. We leverage link topological ranking by means of PageRank algorithm to detect key users in message propagation process. The PageRank of the node is the sum of contributions from its incoming edges. Damping factor was set to be 0.85. The top N users of ranking result of PageRank algorithm are key users in message propagation process.

5   Case Study

In this section, we show the case study of SAMD. Sina microblog allows third-party developers to create applications for its openness as the largest microblog platform in China. We selected Sina microblog as observation platform to detect and analyze abnormal messages. Considering the characteristic of real-time and huge data, we developed distributed web crawler to collect microblog data. The collected data set covered the period from March 14 to March 20 in 2015 which contains nearly over 467 million messages. The flow statistic of collected data can be seen in Fig. 3.

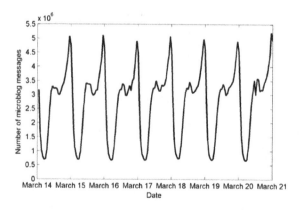

Fig. 3. The flow statistic of microblog messages.

Here, we present the functional interface of SAMD from aspects: abnormal messages detection, statistical analysis, propagation analysis and key users analysis.

Abnormal Messages Detection. By using the abnormal messages detection method introduced in Sect. 4.3, we find 1244528 abnormal messages. Most of abnormal messages are posted by famous users or organizations. Search interface for message retrieval are provided and users can retrieve abnormal messages according to the post time of messages and keywords. The sample abnormal messages search by a query on keywords can be seen in Fig. 4.

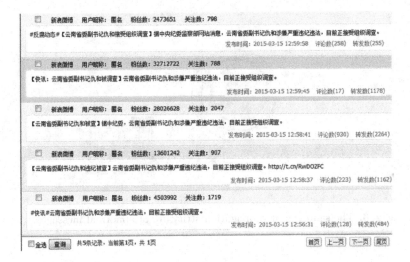

Fig. 4. The sample of abnormal messages detected by SAMD.

Statistical Analysis. The statistical analysis of abnormal messages consists of two aspects: the temporal trend and the spatial distribution. SAMD can collect and analyze the comment and retweet messages set of each abnormal message. The sample message trend of different time windows can be seen in Fig. 5(a). The sample spatial distribution and ranking result of comment and retweet messages set of abnormal message are shown in Fig. 5(b).

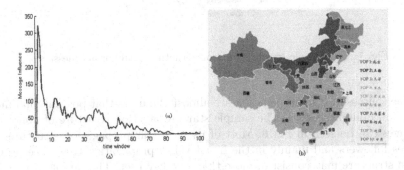

Fig. 5. The Sample statistical analysis of abnormal messages.

Propagation Analysis. Through the analysis of abnormal messages, the propagation topology of forwarding tree can be divided into two categories based on the number of key users: star propagation and tree propagation. "Peking University Weibo Visual Analytic System" [14] is used to visualize the propagation topology of forwarding tree.

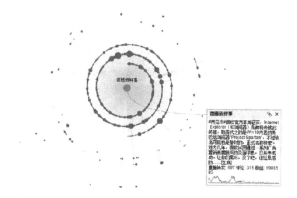

Fig. 6. The sample star propagation structure of abnormal messages.

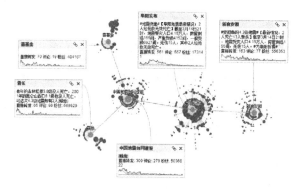

Fig. 7. The sample tree propagation structure of abnormal messages.

The sources of star propagation are almost the users that post original messages and opinion leaders. The sample star propagation structure of abnormal messages can be seen in Fig. 6. Most of users in star propagation structure are sources followers and mainly in the first level of propagation tree. Tree propagation structure may consist of more than one key user. The sample tree propagation structure of abnormal messages can be seen in Fig. 7. Each propagation structure of key user can be seen as star propagation. Based on the analysis of the propagation topology, the width and depth of message propagation were measured. We found that the depth of forwarding tree is small and almost all of messagesdepths are below 6. However, the widths of popular messages are large, especially compared with the depths.

Keyusers mining. By using the key users mining method introduced in Sect. 4.4, we extracted the user graph of abnormal messages and presented the key users. Figure 8 shows the key users of abnormal message about earthquake in Fuyang. Most of the key users about earthquake in Fuyang are organizations which can attract much attention and play an important role in the formation of abnormal messages.

Fig. 8. The key users of abnormal messages about earthquake in Fuyang.

6   Conclusions

In this paper, we propose SAMD to detect and analyze abnormal messages. It contains three functional layers, namely Data Layer, Model Layer and Presentation Layer. SAMD provides three aspects for each abnormal message: statistical analysis, propagation analysis and key users analysis. The case study on the collected data set can show that SAMD is effective to detect and demonstrate abnormal messages from large-scale microblog message stream.

Acknowledgment. The authors would like to thank the reviewers for suggesting many ways to improve the paper. This work was partially supported by the National High Technology Research and Development Program of China (No. 2012AA012802), the Fundamental Research Funds for the Central Universities (No. HEUCF100605) and the National Natural Science Foundation of China (No. 61170242, 60633020, and 61300206).

References

1. Babu, K.S., Hota, J., Jena, S.K.: Privacy preserving social networking. Int. J. Comput. Sci. Eng. **9**(3), 165–176 (2014)
2. Caviglione, L., Coccoli, M., Merlo, A.: A taxonomy-based model of security and privacy in online social networks. Int. J. Comput. Sci. Eng. **9**(4), 325–338 (2014)
3. Wang, T., Zhou, Z., Zhu, T., Wei, Y.: Mood disorder patients language features on their microblogs. Int. J. Embed. Syst. **7**(1), 34–42 (2015)
4. Takahashi, T., Tomioka, R., Yamanishi, K.: Discovering emerging topics in social streams via link anomaly detection. In: Proceedings of IEEE 11th International Conference on Data Mining, Vancouver, pp. 1230–1235 (2011)
5. Martinez-Romo, J., Araujo, L.: Detecting malicious tweets in trending topics using a statistical analysis of language. Expert Syst. Appl. **40**(8), 2992–3000 (2013)
6. Dong, G., Li, R., Yang, W., Wang, W., Gong, L., Shen, G., Yu, M., Lv, J.: Microblog burst keywords detection based on social trust and dynamics model. Chin. J. Electron. **23**(4), 695–700 (2014)
7. Yang, W., Dong, G., Wang, W., Shen, G., Gong, L., Yu, M., Lv, J., Hu, Y.: Detecting bots in follower markets. In: Pan, L., Păun, G., Pérez-Jiménez, M.J., Song, T. (eds.) Bio-Inspired Computing-Theories and Applications, pp. 525–553. Springer, Heidelberg (2014). vol. 472
8. Sakaki, T., Okazaki, M., Matsuo, Y.: Earthquake shakes Twitter users: real-time event detection by social sensors. In: Proceedings of the 19th International Conference on World Wide Web, pp. 851–860 (2010)
9. Alvanaki, F., Michel S., Ramamritham, K., Weikum, G.: EnBlogue: emergent topic detection in web 2.0 streams. In: Proceedings of the 2011 ACM SIGMOD International Conference on Management of data, pp. 1271–1274 (2011)
10. Li, C., Sun, A., Datta, A.: Twevent: segment-based event detection from tweets. In: Proceedings of the 21st ACM International Conference on Information and Knowledge Management, pp. 155–164 (2012)
11. Lee, P., Lakshmanan, L.V.S., Milios, E.: KeySee: supporting keyword search on evolving events in social streams. In: Proceedings of the 19th ACM SIGKDD International Conference on Knowledge Discovery and Data Mining, pp. 1478–1481 (2013)
12. Wang, Y., Liu, H., Lin, H., Wu, J., Wu, Z., Cao, J.: SEA: a system for event analysis on chinese tweets. In: Proceedings of the 19th ACM SIGKDD International Conference on Knowledge Discovery and Data Mining, pp. 1498–1501 (2013)
13. Xie, R., Zhu, F., Ma, H., Xie, W., Lin, C.: CLEar: a real-time online observatory for bursty and viral events. Proc. VLDB Endowment **7**(13), 1–4 (2014)
14. Ren, D., Zhang, X., Wang, Z.H., Li, J., Yuan, X.: WeiboEvents: a crowd sourcing Weibo visual analytic system. In: Proceedings of IEEE Pacific Visualization Symposium, pp. 330–334 (2014)

Adaptive Neighborhood Search's DGSO Applied to Travelling Saleman Problem

Wenbo Dong, Kang Zhou[✉], Qinhong Fu, and Yingying Duan

School of Math and Computer, Wuhan Polytechnic University,
Wuhan 430023, Hubei, China
zhoukang_wh@163.com, 1623572531@qq.com

Abstract. In order to further study the effectiveness and applicability of the glowworm swarm optimization algorithm, this paper proposed a discrete glowworm swarm optimization algorithm with an adaptive neighborhood search, and used it to solve traveling salesman problem (TSP). Based on the analysis and optimization of the different genetic operations, a new adaptive DGSO algorithm is presented (ADGSO), which is effective for both local search and global search. And we defined a new kind of glowworm, which can adjust the flight length of particles by self-adapting. By solving the different instances of TSP, experimental results indicate that ADGSO has a remarkable quality of the global convergence reliability and convergence velocity. It solved the problems of traditional DGSO algorithm "premature". Unlike existing TSP approaches that often aggregate multiple criteria and constraints into a compromise function, the proposed ADGSO optimizes all routing constraints and objectives simultaneously, which improves the routing solutions in many aspects, such as lower routing cost, wider scattering area and better convergence trace. The ADGSO is applied to solve the TSP, which yields solutions better than or competitive as compared to the best solutions published in literature.

Keywords: ADGSO · Local optimization operator · Adaptive · TSP

1 Introduction

Many combinatorial optimization problems of both practical and theoretical importance are known to be NP-hard. Since exact algorithms are not feasible in such cases, these algorithms have the problem of "combinatorial explosion" [1]. Heuristics are the main approach to tackle these problems. The TSP is one of the most well-known combinatorial optimization tasks, and one of the most important reason why TSP remains an interesting subject for research is that the problem is easy to understand and many results and standard benchmark instances with known optima are available, so it makes the problem ideal for testing new approaches [3]. Nature has provided rich intelligence in constructing powerful computing models [2,5,10,15–17] and algorithms [18–20].

© Springer-Verlag Berlin Heidelberg 2015
M. Gong et al. (Eds.): BIC-TA 2015, CCIS 562, pp. 125–137, 2015.
DOI: 10.1007/978-3-662-49014-3_12

Glowworm swarm optimization algorithm is a new type of intelligent bionic swarm optimization algorithm [7], which was put forward by Indian scholar Ghose and Krishnanand in 2005. The algorithm was inspired by natural phenomenon: glowworm in nature attract partner move to his position to achieve the purpose of courtship or foraging. At present, the GSO algorithm has been successfully applied to the complicated multi-objective function optimization, the signal source localization, sensor noise processing, etc., and shows good performance [4].

This paper proposed a discrete glowworm swarm optimization algorithm with an adaptive neighborhood search, which enhance the performance of the DGSO algorithm [6], parallel and distributed experimentation. Different from DGSO algorithm and other algorithms, we designed a new adaptive local search algorithm, and the algorithm and DGSO combined to form a new algorithm called the ADGSO algorithm, which is effective for both local search and global search. And we also introduced a bulletin board to record the optimal solution in the process of iteration. In order to gain a deeper insight into the behavior of an algorithm, a very large amount of work is necessary, both for measurement and evaluation. We then use TSP instances to compare the performance of several artificial intelligence algorithms, such as Ant Colony Optimization Algorithm (ACO) [9], Genetic Algorithm (GA) [8] and Particle Swarm Optimization Algorithm (PSO) [12], Simulated Annealing Algorithm (SA) [11], etc. The experimental results show that our algorithm can compete with the best existing algorithms for the TSP in terms of both solution quality and running time. ADGSO algorithm are more likely to jump out of local optimum, and has the characteristics of fast convergence speed and high precision, and its calculation results are better than the best results published in other literature, has a good application prospect.

2 Knowledge Preparation

In this section, we briefly describe the GSO metaheuristic and the DGSO algorithm. We refer the reader to [4] for a more detailed presentation.

GSO is a population-based method. An individual of the GSO population is a virtual glowworm, which can attract partner move to his position to achieve the purpose of courtship or foraging. As a glowworm, a virtual glowworm constructs at each iteration a solution to the problem. In GSO algorithm, firstly, the glowworms randomly distributed in the solution space, then the glowworm selects neighbor sets in its decision-making domain, after that choose a glowworm from neighbor sets as moving objects according to the luminous intensity. Overall, GSO algorithm mainly includes the glowworm deployment, updating of the fluorescein, glowworm movement and decision-making domain update these four stages. Discrete glowworm swarm optimization algorithm to solve TSP, we can refer to the literature [4].

3   The Adgso Metaheuristic and Its Application to TSP

A heuristic should keep a balance between the exploration of new regions in the search space and the exploitation of promising regions already found. The ADGSO incorporates the local search heuristics in order to exploit local routing solutions in parallel with global evolutionary optimization. In ADGSO, the adaptive strategy allows to abandon regions of the search space that are no longer promising and to start exploring new regions. In this section, after describing the ADGSO algorithm, we present its formalization as a metaheuristic and analyze its operation.

3.1   Adaptive Neighborhood Search

The goal of a metaheuristic is to guide the solution search toward promising regions of the search space, where high-quality solutions are expected to be found. The ADGSO algorithm uses a sophisticated local improvement strategy that combines many local search heuristics. In DGSO algorithm, glowworms adapt roulette method to move to a new position, but this kind of method retain existing populations of glowworm encoding information too much, it is not conducive to expanding the scope of the search, and it is easy to cause algorithm falls into local optimum. To avoid algorithm trapping in local optimum, and expanding scope of the search, this paper introduced the mutation operator of genetic algorithm, and extend to four local optimization operators. The four types of mutation operator are exchange mutation, insertion mutation, inversion mutation and locus mutation. The implementation of mutation operator is as follows:

(1) Exchange mutation operator. Firstly, we have two different integers which generate randomly, and then exchange codes which these two numbers correspond. The mathematical model of the operator as follows: For $X = (x_1, x_2, \cdots, x_n)$, u and v $(1 \leq u < v \leq n)$,

$$f(X, u, v) = (x_1, x_2, \cdots, x_{u-1}, x_v, x_{u+1}, \cdots, x_{v-1}, x_u, x_{v+1}, \cdots, x_n) \quad (1)$$

where X is the path encoding, u and v are two numbers which generated randomly($u < v$). After exchange mutation operator operation, $f(X, u, v)$ is the new path encoding.

For example: We assume that there are two random numbers $u = 2$ and $v = 5$, the old path encoding is:

$$X = 3 \quad 2 \quad 1 \quad 9 \quad 4 \quad 8 \quad 7 \quad 6 \quad 5$$

After operation, the new path encoding is:

$$X = 3 \quad 4 \quad 1 \quad 9 \quad 2 \quad 8 \quad 7 \quad 6 \quad 5.$$

(2) Insertion mutation operator. There are two different random numbers. Insert one number before another. The mathematical model of the operator as follows: For $X = (x_1, x_2, \cdots, x_n)$, u and v $(1 \le u < v \le n)$,

$$f(X, u, v) = (x_1, x_2, \cdots, x_{u-1}, x_v, x_u, \cdots, x_{v-1}, x_{v+1}, \cdots, x_n) \qquad (2)$$

where X is the path encoding, u and v are two different random numbers $(u < v)$. After insertion mutation operator operation, $f(X, u, v)$ is the new path encoding.

For example: Assuming that there are two random numbers $u = 2$ and $v = 5$, the old path encoding is:

$$X = 3 \quad 2 \quad 1 \quad 9 \quad 4 \quad 8 \quad 7 \quad 6 \quad 5$$

After operation, the new path encoding is:

$$X = 3 \quad 4 \quad 2 \quad 1 \quad 9 \quad 8 \quad 7 \quad 6 \quad 5.$$

(3) Inversion mutation operator. There are two different random numbers. Reverse the encoding between the two numbers. The mathematical model of the operator as follows: For $X = (x_1, x_2, \cdots, x_n)$, u and v $(1 \le u < v \le n)$,

$$f(X, u, v) = (x_1, x_2, \cdots, x_{u-1}, x_v, x_{v-1}, \cdots, x_{u+1}, x_u, x_{v+1}, \cdots, x_n) \qquad (3)$$

where X is the path encoding, u and v are two different random numbers $(u < v)$. After inversion mutation operator operation, $f(X, u, v)$ is the new path encoding.

For example: Assuming that there are two random numbers $u = 2$ and $v = 7$, the old path encoding is:

$$X = 3 \quad 2 \quad 1 \quad 9 \quad 4 \quad 8 \quad 7 \quad 6 \quad 5$$

After operation, the new path encoding is:

$$X = 3 \quad 7 \quad 8 \quad 4 \quad 9 \quad 1 \quad 2 \quad 6 \quad 5.$$

(4) Locus mutation operator. There is a random number, exchange code the number represent with another code in front of it. The mathematical model of the operator as follows: For $X = (x_1, x_2, \cdots, x_n)$, $(1 \le u \le n)$,

$$f(X, u) = (x_1, x_2, \cdots, x_u, x_{u-1}, x_{u+1}, \cdots, x_n) \qquad (4)$$

where X is the path encoding, u is a random number. After locus mutation operator operation, $f(X, u)$ is the new path encoding.

For example: Assuming that there is a random numbers $u = 3$, the old path encoding is:

$$X = 3 \quad 2 \quad 1 \quad 9 \quad 4 \quad 8 \quad 7 \quad 6 \quad 5$$

After operation, the new path encoding is:

$$X = 3 \quad 1 \quad 2 \quad 9 \quad 4 \quad 8 \quad 7 \quad 6 \quad 5.$$

3.2 Other Improvements

(1) **The Import of the Bulletin Board.** In DGSO algorithm, best solution generated in process of iteration may not appear again in the later iterations, which caused the deterioration of the algorithm. In order to overcome these defects, this paper introduced a bulletin board to record the best state.

   The bulletin board in the program was achieved with a function whose function is to compare the status of the incoming glowworm and the optimal individual recorded in the bulletin board. If the former is better, replace the bulletin board, else remains the same to guarantee that the record in the bulletin board is always the optimal value of the iterative process.

(2) **Confirm the Departure City.** When encoding, there may be a problem, for example: the path 1-2-4-3-5-8-7-6-9 and 7-6-9-7-6-9-3-5-8 are different paths in form, but actually, they represent the same. They all can be expressed as a loop that means starting from the city 1, and then through the city 2, 4, 3, 5, 8, 7, 6, 9 one time. Finally back to the city 1. In order to avoid this problem, here, we set the city 1 as starting city, i.e., fix the position of the starting city. Because the starting city is fixed, so this kind of coding is unique, i.e., the path 1-2-4-3-5-8-7-6-9 and 3-5-8-7-6-9-1-2-4 are the identical.

(3) **The Establishment of the Initial Population.** First of all, for the sequence of (1, 2, 3, ..., n), disrupt its order, random arrangement, get a random arrangement from 1 to n, repeat M times (M is the size of population). The population we get in this way not only can be ensured all the solutions are feasible, but also increase the diversity of the population.

(4) **Repair Unfeasible Code.** After coding is updated, there may be duplicate code or code beyond $[1, n]$. In this case, we should repair unfeasible code. If the code less than 1, the code is set to 1; Otherwise, set the code into n and find out the duplicate code, finally, replace duplicate coding with city coding which does not appear before.

3.3 ADGSO Algorithm Steps

According to the improvement ideas, the algorithm steps of the ADGSO algorithm can be implemented as follows:

Step 1. Initialize the glowworm populations. According to Sect. 3.2(4) build the glowworm populations. Set the following parameters: gsonum(size of the population), iter_max(maximum iterations), $l_i(0)$(value of initial fluorescein), $r_d^i(0)$(decision domain radius), r_s (maximum radius), γ (fluorescein update rate), ρ (fluorescein volatile coefficient), n_t (neighborhood threshold), β (radius update rate), p_1 and p_2 (parameters for choose update formula).

Step 2. For a glowworms individual i, calculate the objective function value, and then transform objective function value into fluorescein value.

Step 3. Calculate the distance between the firefly i and other fireflies, and then in its decision domain radius($r_d^i(t)$), choose glowworms whose fluorescein value is higher than its compose the neighbor set($N_i(t)$).

Step 4. Calculate the probability that glowworm i move to the glowworm $j(j \in N_i(t))$, and than according to the roulette wheel select the moving object; If the neighbor set $(N_i(t))$ are empty, the results show clearly that glowworm i is a local optimal value, go to step 6.

Step 5. Generate a random sequence r, $r = (r_1, \cdots, r_k, \cdots, r_n)$, where $r_i \in [0, 1]$. According to the size of each dimension, update the glowworm's code.

Step 6. We should randomly select a formula from the formula (1)–(4) to perform neighborhood search.

Step 7. Adjust the glowworm's decision domain radius.

Step 8. Judge whether the current number of iterations reach the max iterations or algorithm end conditions, if not, go to step 2, $i = i + 1$, continue to execute step by step; Otherwise, end the execution of program and output the global optimal solution and the global optimal path.

4   Simulation Results and Comparisons

4.1   Parameter Analysis and Setting

The most well-known benchmark dataset for the TSP is the TSPLIB. This library contains 110 instances of symmetric TSPs with scales n ranging from 14 to 85900. For each instance, the globally optimal tour is known.

ADGSO algorithm is simple and easy to implement without adjusting too many parameters, only a few parameters directly affect the performance and convergence of the algorithm. By reading a large number of references, a summary of a number of targeted measures is made to solve such problems. In GSO algorithm, ρ, γ, β, l_0 and n_t do not need to set different values for different problems, that is to say, these parameters can be set to a fixed value in solving different problems. Only population size N and r_s need to be set to different values according to the different problems. In ADGSO algorithm, there are p_1, p_2 and c need to be tuned.

In ADGSO algorithm, the fixed parameters can be set as follows (Table 1):

Table 1. Parameter settings

ρ	γ	β	n_t	l_0
0.4	0.6	0.08	5	5

In algorithm, there are several parameters need to be changed according to the different problems, they are N, r_s, p_1, p_2 and constant c. Here is a TSP

Table 2. gsonum = 500, r_s = 10.0, c = 30, iter_max = 300, p_2 = 0.90

p_1	Average	Best results	Optimal value
0.80	6143.208409	6112.745359	6110
0.85	6198.440920	6149.134894	

instance, ch130, where we want to tune parameters(p_1) using a certain type of methodology. Experimental analysis as shown in Table 2.

The data in Table 2 show that when p_1 = 0.80 the stability of the algorithm is better than p_1 = 0.85. So in this paper p_1 = 0.80.

Finally, the variable parameters we set can be seen in Table 3.

Table 3. Variable parameter settings

r_s	c	p_1	p_2	gsonum	iter_max
10.0	20	0.80	0.90	200	300

4.2 Comparisons and Analysis

DGSO Algorithm and ADGSO Algorithm. In order to check the efficiency of the proposed improvements, we provide the results of computational experiments in Table 4.

Note: "TSPLIB" item is calculated according to the optimal path; "Optimal solution" item is recorded in TSPLIB; "-" item means that this paper have not provide the date.

Table 4. DGSO algorithm vs ADGSO algorithm

TSP case	Optimal solution (TSPLIB)	Algorithm		Error rate		Iteration	
		DGSO	ADGSO	DGSO	ADGSO	DGSO	ADGSO
Bays29	9074.15(9291.35)	9074.15	9074.15	0.00	0.00	200	10
Att48	33523(33523.71)	33523.71	33523.71	0.00	0.00	200	10
Pr76	108159(108159.44)	108159.44	108159.44	0.00	0.00	200	20
Krob100	22141(-)	22139.07	22139.07	0.00	0.00	200	110
Ch130	6110(6110.86)	6125.07	6112.75	0.25	0.03	200	140
Krob150	26130(-)	26206.69	26186.00	0.29	0.21	200	160
Krob200	29437(-)	29605.13	29575.88	0.57	0.47	200	200

Results analysis: As we can see from Table 4, when the city scale is less than 100, DGSO algorithm and ADGSO algorithm can find the optimal solution, but

Table 5. ADGSO algorithm vs TS, PSO, ACO, GA

TSP case	TS [13]	PSO [12]	ACO [9]	GA [8]	ADGSO	Optimal solution (TSPLIB)
Berlin52	9614.11	22769.96	7748.44	9449.60	7544.37	7542(7544.37)
Pr76	167369.47	451346.7	108329	157604.32	108159.44	108159(108159.44)
Bier127	204970.83	542558.0	128147.20	196275.98	119285.17	118282(-)
Ch130	13076.03	39010.87	6732.87	12667.41	6112.75	6110(6110.86)
A280	9653.61	29045.81	3070.60	9671.67	2652.00	2579(2586.77)

experiments demonstrate that ADGSO algorithm is effective, moreover, it can converge to the global optimal solution within short epochs. While the city scale is larger, ADGSO algorithm's accuracy is better than DGSO algorithm, and ADGSO algorithm spend less time than DGSO algorithm.

Based on the above analysis, we can draw the following conclusions: ADGSO algorithm in convergence speed and accuracy has excellent performance, at the same time, the local search ability of the algorithm has been enhanced, which can jump out of local optimum easily, it should be continued to search in the solution space until the global optimal solution is found.

ADGSO Algorithm and Other Algorithms. In this section, the results obtained from ADGSO are compared with the best-known routing solutions obtained from different heuristics published in the literature according to the authors' best knowledge. Table 5 shows the comparison results between ADGSO and the best-known results in literature, for which instances with significant results or improvements are bolded.

This paper select multiple examples from TSPLIB, we contrast ADGSO algorithm with some classical artificial intelligence algorithms, the proposed algorithms is proved to be feasible and effective by comparative experiments. Details are shown in Table 5.

It should be noted that all the routing costs have been normalized to their mean values for easy comparisons among different test cases. In addition, Table 5 lists the means and standard deviations for the various simulation results as a supplement to the Fig. 1.

Table 5 compares the routing performance between several popular heuristics and ADGSO based on the average cost of routing in each category.

Results analysis: As we can see from Table 5, in Berlin52 and Pr76, ADGSO algorithm compared with other four kinds of algorithms can find the optimal solution; With the urban expansion, these algorithms are unable to find the optimal solution, only can find a near optimal solution, but ADGSO algorithm has good converging speed and local searching ability of local methods, the solution found by ADGSO has higher accuracy than other algorithms.

Based on the above analysis, we can draw the conclusions as follows: ADGSO algorithm characterizes with global search ability, efficiency in search and

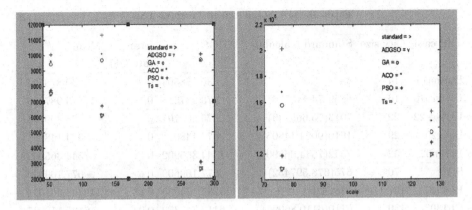

Fig. 1. ADGSO vs TS, PSO, ACO, GA

avoiding premature phenomena which often occurs in traditional GSO. When the city scale is small and medium-sized, ADGSO must be able to find the global solution, with the urban expansion, it can find the approximately optimal solution in a short time. Compared with other algorithms mentioned in this paper, ADGSO algorithm has higher accuracy and global search ability.

5 Update Tsplib with Adgso Algorithm

5.1 ADGSO Algorithm Compare with TSPLIB

In order to make a deeper understanding of ADGSO algorithm proposed in this paper, we used the multiple TSP benchmark instances to test algorithm. You could see the test results in Table 6.

To study the consistency and reliability of the results obtained by ADGSO, 13 different but repeated simulations with randomly generated initial populations have been performed for TSP.

Results analysis: From Table 6 we can see that when the city scale is small, ADGSO algorithm could find the optimal solution recorded in TSPLIB, some solutions even better than optimal solution recorded in TSPLIB; when the city scale is larger, ADGSO algorithm does not always find the optimal solution, but the error is under 1 %. With the urban expansion, the error is become larger, but the comparison results show that the discrepancy is within the acceptable range. In addition, we can see from average, ADGSO algorithm has a good stability, i.e., ADGSO algorithm has good robustness. Although error rate increases as the size of the problem, but when the city size reached a thousand, the error rate is still below 10 %.

5.2 TSPLIB Update

In this paper, many experiments based on the data of TSPLIB show the improved algorithm has better ability to find global optimal solution in TSP. We did what

Table 6. ADGSO algorithm to solve TSP

TSP case	City size	Standard (calculate)	ADGSO	Error rate (%)	Mean
Burma14	14	3323(-)	30.878504	0	30.878504
Ulysses16	16	6859(74.118736)	73.987618	0	73.987618
Ulysses22	22	7013(75.665149)	75.309701	0	75.309701
Bayg29	29	1610(9074.14805)	9074.14805	0	9074.14805
Berlin52	52	7542(7544.36590)	7544.365902	0	7544.365902
St70	70	675(678.597452)	677.109609	0	677.109609
Bier127	127	118282(-)	119285.171035	0.85	119463.861031
Ch130	130	6110(6110.86095)	6112.745359	0.03	6190.112035
Tsp225	225	3916(3859.00000)	3966.941918	1.30	3981.883854
A280	280	2579(2586.76965)	2652.001009	2.52	2673.446418
Rat575	575	6773(-)	7338.218609	(-)	7348.901786
Rat783	783	8806(-)	9740.883231	(-)	9784.577838
Pr1002	1002	259066.663053(-)	288156.009170	(-)	289345.718176

we were supposed to do and we found something which we like much more than before. Our solutions are better than the records in the TSPLIB. The comparison results of each instances, we can see from Fig. 2.

For burma14, TSPLIB did not provide the optimal path, only provided the optimal solution: 3323. This paper provides the optimal path is: (13 12 14 1 2 3 4 5 6 7 8 9 10 11), the optimal path value is: 30.878504.

For ulysses16, the optimal path recorded in TSPLIB is: (1 14 13 12 7 6 15 5 11 9 10 16 3 2 4 8), the optimal path value is: 74.108736. This paper provides the optimal path is: (1 3 2 4 8 15 5 11 9 10 7 6 14 13 12 16), the optimal path value is: 73.987618.

For ulysses22, the optimal path recorded in TSPLIB is: (1 14 13 12 7 6 15 5 11 9 10 19 20 21 16 3 2 17 22 4 18 8), the optimal path value is: 75.665149. This paper provides the optimal path is: (1 14 13 12 7 6 15 5 11 9 10 19 20 21 16 3 2 17 4 18 22 8), the optimal path value is: 75.309701.

For eil51, the optimal path recorded in TSPLIB is: (1 22 8 26 31 28 3 36 35 20 2 29 21 16 50 34 30 9 49 10 39 33 45 15 44 42 40 19 41 13 25 14 24 43 7 23 48 6 27 51 46 12 47 18 4 17 37 5 38 11 32), the optimal path value is: 429.983312. This paper provides the optimal path is: (1 32 11 38 5 49 10 39 33 45 15 37 17 44 42 19 40 41 13 25 14 18 4 47 12 46 51 27 6 48 23 24 43 7 26 8 31 28 3 36 35 20 29 21 34 30 9 50 16 2 22), the optimal path value is: 428.871756.

For st70, the optimal path recorded in TSPLIB is: (1 36 29 13 70 35 31 69 38 59 22 66 63 57 15 24 19 7 2 4 18 42 32 3 8 26 55 49 28 14 20 30 44 68 27 46 25 45 39 61 40 9 17 43 41 6 53 5 10 52 60 12 34 21 33 62 54 48 67 11 64 65 56 51 50 58 37 47 16 23), the optimal path value is: 678.597452. This paper provides

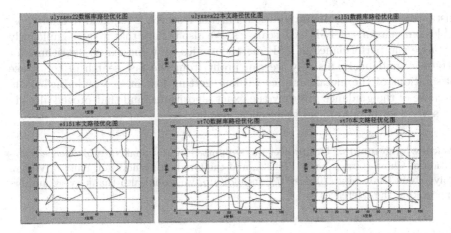

Fig. 2. Roadmap

the optimal path is: (1 16 47 37 58 50 51 56 65 64 11 67 48 54 62 33 34 21 12 60 52 10 5 53 6 41 43 17 9 40 61 39 25 45 46 27 68 44 30 20 14 28 49 55 26 8 3 32 42 18 4 2 7 19 24 15 57 63 66 22 59 38 31 69 35 70 29 13 23 36), the optimal path value is: 677.109609.

6   Conclusions

This paper has made some contributions to the research on Glowworm swarm optimization algorithm. A adaptive DGSO algorithm(ADGSO) has been proposed in this paper, which incorporates various heuristics for local exploitation in the evolutionary search. The proposed ADGSO has been featured with specialized genetic operators to accommodate the sequence-oriented optimization in TSP. Unlike most other artificial intelligence algorithms, this paper proposed a bulletin board to record the optimal solution in the process of iteration and fixed traveling salesman's departure city to expand the diversity of the glowworm population, moreover, the paper defined a new kind of glowworm, which can adjust the flight length of particles by self-adapting. From the above experimental data and analysis, we can get the following conclusions: ADGSO algorithm to solve TSP has very good effect and has excellent performance in the global and local search, convergence speed and precision. And it can induce the iteration times enormously. Some solutions we calculated are even better than the optimal solutions recorded in TSPLIB. We believe that ADGSO algorithm is more effective and has stronger ability to get the optimum solution compared with other artificial intelligence algorithms.

The analysis offers promising perspectives for further research. A generalization of the results to other instance sizes should be addressed as well as a systematic comparison to other local and global search. However, it has to be kept in mind that the computational effort intensely increase with increasing instance size as the optimum solution. Further research is required to study possible combinations of TSP local searches. We also believe that it can significantly improve the performance of TSP metaheuristics by using exact algorithms for strategic guidance. This way we can profit from the fast search of the space of solutions of the metaheuristics without getting lost in a "wandering" path, because of the guidance given by the exact algorithms, and that proved already by several authors can lead to excellent results.

Acknowledgements. This project was supported by National Natural Science Foundation of China (Grant No. 61179032), and the Graduate Innovation Fund of Wuhan Polytechnic University (2014cx007). In addition, we would also thank every authors appeared in the references.

References

1. Zhou, K., Chen, J.: Simulation DNA algorithm of set covering problem. Appl. Math. Inf. Sci. **8**, 139–144 (2014)
2. Song, T., Pan, L., Wang, J., et al.: Normal forms of spiking neural P systems with anti-spikes. IEEE Trans. Nanobiosci. **11**(4), 352–359 (2012)
3. Zhou, K., Fan, L.L., Shao, K.: Simulation DNA algorithm model of satisfiability problem. J. Comput. Theor. Nanosci. **12**, 1220–1227 (2015)
4. Zhou, K., Tong, X.J., Xu, J.: Closed circle DNA algorithm of change positive-weighted hamilton circuit problem. J. Syst. Eng. Electron. **20**, 636–642 (2009)
5. Song, T., Pan, L., Păun, G.: Asynchronous spiking neural P systems with local synchronization. Inf. Sci. **219**, 197–207 (2013)
6. Zhou, Y.Q., Huang, Z.X., Liu, H.X.: Discrete glowworm swarm optimization algorithm for TSP problems. Acta Electronica Sin. **40**, 1164–1170 (2012)
7. Krishnand, K.N., Ghose, D.: Glowworm swarm optimisation: a new method for optimising multi-modal functions. Int. J. Comput. Intell. Stud. **1**, 93–119 (2009)
8. Li, H.Z., Yang, J.H.: Application in TSP based on genetic algorithm. Comput. Knowl. Technol. **6**(3), 672–673 (2010)
9. Dorigo, M., Birattari, M., Stutzle, T.: Ant colony optimization. IEEE Comput. Intell. Mag. **1**(4), 28–39 (2006)
10. Song, T., Pan, L., Jiang, K., et al.: Normal forms for some classes of sequential spiking neural P systems. IEEE Trans. Nanobiosci. **12**(3), 255–264 (2013)
11. Yao, M.H., Wang, N., Zhao, L.P.: Improved simulated annealing algorithm and genetic algorithm for TSP. Comput. Eng. Appl. **49**(14), 60–65 (2013)
12. Zhong, Y.W., Yang, J.G., Ning, Z.Y.: Discrete particle swarm optimization algorithm for TSP problem. Syst. Eng. Theory Pract. **26**(6), 88–94 (2006)
13. He, Y., Liu, G.Y.: Research on solving TSP in tabu search algorithm. J. Southwest China Normal Univ. **27**(3), 341–345 (2002)
14. TSPLIB. http://www.iwr.uni-heidelberg.de/groups/comopt/software/TSPLIB95/tsp/?C=D;O=A
15. Song, T., Pan, L.: Spiking neural P systems with rules on synapses working in maximum spikes consumption strategy. IEEE Trans. Nanobiosci. **14**(1), 38–44 (2015)
16. Song, T., Pan, L.: Spiking neural P systems with rules on synapses working in maximum spiking strateg. IEEE Trans. Nanobiosci. **14**(4), 465–477 (2015)

17. Zhang, X., Pan, L., Paun, A.: On the universality of axon P systems. IEEE Trans. Neural Networks Learn. Syst. (2015). doi:10.1109/TNNLS.2015.2396940
18. Shi, X., Wang, Z., Deng, C., Song, T., Pan, L., Chen, Z.: A novel bio-sensor based on DNA strand displacement. Plos One **9**, e108856 (2014)
19. Wang, X., Miao, Y., Cheng, M.: Finding motifs in DNA sequences using low-dispersion sequences. J. Comput. Biol. **21**(4), 320–329 (2014)
20. Wang, X., Miao, Y.: GAEM: a hybrid algorithm incorporating GA with EM for planted edited motif finding problem. Curr. Bioinform. **9**(5), 463–469 (2014)

Improved Genetic Algorithm to Optimization Pattern in Traffic Network Layout Problem

Yingying Duan, Kang Zhou$^{(\boxtimes)}$, Wenbo Dong, and Qinhong Fu

School of Math and Computer, Wuhan Polytechnic University, Wuhan, China
{767503653,1623572531,996477540}@qq.com, zhoukang_wh@163.com

Abstract. The main core problem in optimization filed is to apply the optimization method devised by adopting a meta-heuristic algorithm to large-scale traffic network layout problem based on contribution center (TNLOSP). Improved Genetic Algorithm (IGA) is proposed to deal with this problem instead of traditional one. Two improvements are added to previous algorithm: Prim Stochastic Algorithm (PSA) and a fair competition strategy. In tuning phase, such core parameters in crossover rate, fairness coefficient p_0, and the like as are synchronously optimized; In comparative analysis phrase, in large part as a consequence of comparison, the thesis focuses on a great deal of experimental analysis on determining more accurately some advantages of the algorithm. Showing though the experiment that improved algorithm has more advantages in efficiency and precision of solutions than traditional one by testing different scale populations. Therefore, proving that these improvements are of feasibility.

Keywords: Traffic network layout problem · Prim stochastic algorithm · Repairing operator · Fair competition strategy

1 Introduction

Traffic network problem based on distribution center is the most critical problem of the layout and planning of distribution center which is about the logistics industry [2]. This optimization problem is considered as a hot point to develop in this research field. For solving this hot problem, many scholars have proposed a amount of methods to dispose of it. For instance, Reference [5,7,8] applied genetic algorithm to solve this problem; Reference [1,9,10] aimed to Simulation DNA Algorithm Model of Satisfiability and Set Covering Problem; and Closed circle DNA algorithm of change positive-weighted Hamilton circuit problem have been developed to efficiently solve this problem in reference [12,13]; The research of route optimization of expressing distribution based on the harmony search algorithm is put forward to solve it in reference [17]. And P systems are also natural-inspired computing devices, which are a rich framework for handling many problems related to computing. Many of the P systems have been proved to be universal as number computing devices [6,11,14–16,18]. All of the

© Springer-Verlag Berlin Heidelberg 2015
M. Gong et al. (Eds.): BIC-TA 2015, CCIS 562, pp. 138–149, 2015.
DOI: 10.1007/978-3-662-49014-3_13

above references enrich the solved methods for that problem and push on the application of this problem in these research filed.

However, we found two deficiencies with the expansion of population scales when we are performing experiments in GA [17]:

(1) As the expansion of population scales, the operational efficiency of traditional algorithm is constantly getting worse. Especially, several feasible chromosomes can not be obtained with limited iterations when the population reaches a certain scale;

(2) As our own studies have advanced, we have increasingly observed the differentiation cracking of accuracy of solutions, which is evaluated by computing the fitness value of each chromosome, between the current value and the optimal value and less so with the optimization effect that could constitute such a solution further closed to the optimal solution value.

The above analysis show that some improvements to improve the efficiency of the algorithm will need to be proposed in the paper as follows:

(1) In order to really improve the essence of producing initial population, we may think of a new method restructured by this algorithm as a technology to instead of the method that blind random generation of initial population, one that tends to make current population became feasible after being structured.

(2) It has thus generally been by the way of the emphasis on the equity that the fairness coefficient, whose value plays a decisive role in the selection of chromosomes, is designed the powerful and decisive parameter that characterized the secondary status of improved algorithm.

The broad experiments of the paper strongly suggests that improved genetic algorithm is proposing to solve the above two questions for improving the performance of the algorithm, which is developed by treating each parameter as a coefficient of an optimization. The experiment is evaluated by using the ones that need stability, a better result to prove the effectiveness of the proposed algorithm in paper during the question-solving process, according to these criteria, good results have been achieved, which proves that IGA is very fruitful.

2   Traffic Network Layout Problem Based on Distribution Center and Improved Genetic Algorithm

2.1   Traffic Network Layout Problem Based on Distribution Center

Traffic network layout problem based on distribution center [17] is described as follows: In a certain city traffic network, the initial point v1 is allotted as the distribution center in logistics enterprises, $v_i(i = 2, 3, \cdots, m)$ represents customer served every day by logistics enterprises. Set $V(G) = \{v_i : i = 1, 2, \cdots, m\}$ and $E(G) = \{e_i : i = 1, 2, \cdots, n\}$ respectively stand for crunode set and edge set on traffic network graph and set $W(G) = \{w_i : i = 1, 2, \cdots, n\}$ stores the shortest route between customer nodes. In a city network, layout problem is converted into the shortest route optimization problem, which model is $G = (V(G), E(G), W(G))$.

2.2   Two Improved Technologies for Traditional Algorithm

(1) **The Application of PSA in Initial Population Stage.** The design method [17] is as follows: firstly, some chromosomes are created randomly; Secondly, each of them should be checked for satisfying the length constraint. if meet, it is added to initial population; if not, a new one need to be reproduced randomly. Known that this way exists purposelessness, thus leading to increase massive difficulties to chase for feasible chromosomes; Especially when this scale reaches a certain level, the algorithm could not get a feasible chromosome. Therefore, it is necessary to find a new improved method to ensure its viability, These improved methods are described as follows:

a. The new algorithm, fully considering the length constraint problem when computing in the cut-set U compared with the original, should be marked all of these points adjacent to the current access node, and then put the edge into the cut-set U and determine whether to meet the length constraint, the formula is as follows: For $\forall a_{ij}(a_{ij} \in U)$,

$$p_i + w_{ij} \le p_0 \tag{1}$$

where if meet this condition, it is put into set W which stores some edges satisfied the length constraint.

b. Improved prim algorithm (PSA) is a new method, which every edge is randomly selected by adopting to roulette method according to the size of edge weights in the cut-set instead of getting a certain minimum weight edge, the set of the probability which value computed according to some elements in set W, according to the principle that the weight is smaller and easier to be selected, this formula is devised as follows:

$$P_i = (1/w_i)/(\sum_{a_i \in W} 1/w_i) \tag{2}$$

(2) **The Application of FCS in Selection Operator Phrase.** The reference [17] revealed that the precision of solutions will be getting worse and the search for seeking to the optimization is easy to fall into local optimum. Analyzing that the different degree between two chromosomes is not obvious; Therefore known that the selected ratio of a chromosome is highly related to its fitness value. Thereby the fairness competition strategy (FCS) is put forward to solving these two defects in the phase.

An attenuation coefficient p_0 which is supposed to be in the range of 0.9 to 1.00 can make the selected probability decreased when a chromosome is again kept constantly active after selected in the last generation, so as to ensure a chromosome is selected fairly, its formula is as follows:

$$P_{i*} = P_i \times p_0 \tag{3}$$

In three operations, fitness values P_i of each chromosome which is randomly selected from parent population will be become p_0 times of their original one when their are again put into parent population, resulting in that sum of the probability values in parent population is less than 1 and break the fair to again choice chromosomes from parent population.

The following operation, therefore in order to maintain probability fairness that each chromosome is selected from parents, is mainly to change the probability distribution of the random selection of parent population, only when previous operation is crossover action that associate Case 1 within the process and when it is mutation motion or replication action that associate Case 2 within these following solutions may the entire algorithm properly be modified again the probability distribution of parent population, These two status are stated as follows:

Case 1:
   Input: $P_1, P_2, ..., P_S, i, j (1 \leq i < j \leq S)$
   Let $P_i = P_i \times p_0$, $P_j = P_j \times p_0$
   For $1 \leq k \leq S$
      $P_k = P_k / (\sum_{l=1}^{S} P_l)$
   End
   Output: $P_1, P_2, ..., P_S$

Case 2:
   Input: $P_1, P_2, ..., P_S, i (1 \leq i \leq S)$
   Let $P_i = P_i \times p_0$
   For $1 \leq k \leq S$
      $P_k = P_k / (\sum_{l=1}^{S} P_l)$
   End
Output: $P_1, P_2, ..., P_S$

Known from the above analysis that in these cases, that is, in the crossover phrase, in the mutation and replication phrase, of each chromosome which is applied to do some interchange operations, the fitness value of a selected chromosome is recorded and replaced into parent population instead of original fitness value and update the population distribution, for mutation and replication, respectively, of PM percent and $1.0/S$ percent of transformation production and update fitness value distribution of contemporary population until the next iterations is entered.

2.3   IGA is Applied to Traffic Network Layout Problem

The new algorithm are on much firmer large-scale ground when it attempt to acquire the optimum under satisfying the constraint condition than when it undertake to do the same thing that exist in a small-scale population composed of few points. That improving the method of Step 1 and Step 2 in the traditional algorithm [17] is necessary to be made for solving the complex traffic problem.

In Step 1, the paper attempt to discard the traditional way and establish a new method of such initial forms as prim stochastic algorithm and to explore the internal performance of the improved algorithm. This new situation is partly ameliorated in the paper as follows:

Step 1. For initial population, all the routes can be initialized randomly by applying this new method.

  (a) S routes that any route of which composes of n customer nodes are randomly produced by introducing PSA. The way of producing these routes is described as follows:

   (1) Intialization collection $S = \{v_1\}$, $T = V - S$, $Z = \varnothing$, $P_1 = 0$.

   (2) Compute set $U = \{a_{ij} : v_i \in S \wedge v_j \in T\}$.

   (3) Compute set $W = \{a_{ij} : p_i + w_{ij} \leq p_0 \wedge a_{ij} \in U\}$.

   (4) If $W = \varnothing$, then no solution, end; else, randomly get a_{ij} ($a_{ij} \in W$); and set $p_j = p_i + w_{ij}$.

   (5) $Z = Z \cap \{a_{ij}\}$, $S = S \cap \{v_j\}$, $T = T - \{v_j\}$.

   (6) If $T = \varnothing$, then end; else, return (2).

  (b) Determine the probability of changing customer nodes between two routes and adjusting its own position in selected route, so as to calculate the customer number of the required changes.

Step 2. According to the distribution of fitness value of a chromosome, it is randomly selected by using the roulette method, which fitness value will be remedied when he was once again put back to the parent population at a certain probability after this.

3   Simulation Experiment

3.1   Simulation Experimental Environment Configuration

The simulation experiment platform is configured as: in the aspect of hardware, we carried out all programs based on a cluster of Intel(R) Core(TM)i3-2350M with 4.00 GB RAM, CPU 2.3 GHz under Windows7 System; in software: we develop a series of simulation programs on such the Visual C++ 6.0 platform.

3.2   Experiment Analysis

With regard to the validation of this experiment, the initial network composed of the 22 nodes and 92 edges as the initial conditions and two experiments have been certainly selected to verify the core performance of improved algorithm.

(a) Parameter Tuning Module Experiment
(1) The idea of an autonomous combination parameter PC and PM is to determine the number of some major operations on such pursuits as precision and

Table 1. Changes in the different values of PC and PM

PC	PM	Min	Expected	Variance	Time
0.80	0.15	85	099.500000	090.516667	392735
0.70	0.25	89	103.400000	127.906681	406234
0.65	0.30	83	102.800000	088.826652	427968
0.55	0.40	84	101.933333	105.728890	545671
0.30	0.65	92	106.566667	108.512207	412265
0.25	0.70	94	108.733333	104.928898	372719

efficiency turn out to be the optimal combination. The process of parameter tuning is described in Table 1 as follow:

(2) The fairness coefficient p_0 that the paper devises to make low probability chromosomes selected in current phrase come into being to preserve an parameter that algorithm perceives as essential, based this, the results is shown in Table 2 as follows:

Table 2. Different values of P_0 on effect of the performance

P_0	Min	Expected	Variance	Time
0.90	101	122.966667	151.165560	198250
0.95	085	109.833333	144.472233	265546
0.97	091	109.133333	122.648885	297734
0.98	086	104.066667	133.395573	319187
0.99	082	100.233333	071.445557	391546
1.00	087	099.700000	053.343327	471390

(3) These two parameters S and D, are based primarily on a series of population scales and iterations directly related to the performance of the algorithm, they can find an optimal solution through fully iterations. The tuning processes are shown in Table 3 below:

(4) The parameter R is used for running to test the stability of improved algorithm, the trail will select values of expected value and variance as indicators by multiple(R) running programs. The experimental data is shown in Table 4 as follows:

In experiment, some graph regarded as a useful description for clearly describing tends of performances of the algorithm is used to express the experiment results in Fig. 1 as follows: where Exp represents Expected Value, Var is Variance.

Table 3. The influence of parameters S and D on optimal solutions

S	D	Opti	Expected	Variance	Time
250	0050	91	119.133333	115.582210	0059922
250	0300	90	105.200000	079.693335	0235421
250	0500	84	103.833333	111.138883	0366187
250	0750	85	099.033333	109.698877	0517375
250	1000	81	098.366667	079.498893	0679000
100	0500	90	106.433333	074.312231	0135937
350	0500	83	097.066667	061.662223	0509125
750	0500	81	098.266667	086.462215	1004468
1000	0500	86	098.933333	079.928898	1323406

Table 4. Parameter R impact on the stability of algorithm

R	Opti	Exp	Var	Time	OptRat
Rt-0030	83	097.066667	61.662223	00509125	0.633
Rt-0070	86	100.342857	71.825293	01218359	0.514
Rt-0100	82	100.910000	81.941895	01691625	0.481
Rt-0250	81	099.556000	72.838844	04267750	0.540
Rt-0500	83	100.024000	75.099469	08426086	0.508
Rt-1000	80	100.291000	71.566695	16800578	s 0.496

All of these diagrams from Fig. 1.(a) to (d) to mean and stability, as is known, reflect the fluctuations of the performance at the oscillation of these parameters. In Fig. 1.(a) explains that they are basically showing a downward trend, where the algorithm apparently reaches the convergence and the operational efficiency gets the good peak after being labeled as 0.80, and Fig. 1.(b) represents the same meaning curves, yet they are the curves of parameter P_0, for the former, there will give many more equitable opportunities to chromosomes not chosen when $P0$ is 0.99. Two curves in Fig. 1.(c) are viewed that the upper solid line behaves as a decreased tread when iterations D is increasing in each phrase and the lower dotted line continued decline before 350, contrarily, it is on the increase after this. Inferred that the algorithm has reached the convergence in 350 and the solutions are the near-optimal value at the same time; In Fig. 1.(d), two curves indicate that fitness value and stability are greatly fluctuating in the frequency in the interval (30, 250], after that, the optimum has basically reached a steady state in each run. Consequently, the datum point 250 is accord with the requirement of satisfying the stability.

(b) Comparing Performance with Traditional Algorithm. The evaluation of the performance is based primarily on a series of experimental comparison with other algorithms. The paper also choose some core values, such as the con-

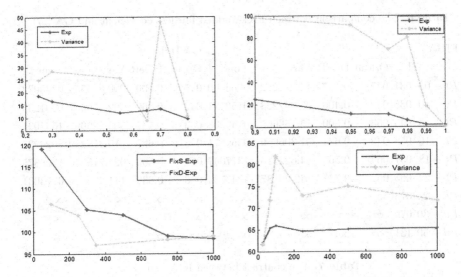

Fig. 1. In the case of parameter values chance, performance trends distribution figure

vergence and success rate, that can well reflect the performance as the evaluated conditions. Experimental results are shown in Tables 5, 6, 7 and 8 as follows:

Where "∞" indicates that the program which fell into an infinite loop can not find a optimal route when population scales reach a certain level.

Table 5. The parameter tuning value

Pa-name	S	D	PC	PM	P_0
$Pa-value$	350	500	0.80	0.15	0.99

Comprehensive analysis for the results of Tables 6, 7 and 8, the reason that the algorithm of introducing this coefficient showed for its results in Table 6 has broadened a search rang of populations to other filed of algorithm, for while this value can change the ratio of the optimum selected into the next generation, it also increases the selected probability of each chromosome. As we can see from Table 7, only in the case of PSA do this algorithm can run large-scale populations that general described it as a complex network owned more than 22 nodes, this is because this improved method is directly random search to produce a minimum spanning tree, thus greatly improving the efficiency of the algorithm. Known from Table 8, The simultaneous introduction of two improved methods make this algorithm more powerful search mechanism than the separate use of each improved algorithm. In summary, the new improvement is effective.

(c) Using Graph to Describe the Trend of these Curve. The paper will select a more intuitive graph form to allege advantages of IGA in order to more

Table 6. The comparison between FIGA added fairness coefficient and GA [17]

FIGA						GA [17]			
	LC	Optim	DiveR	Var	Time	Optim	DiveR	Var	Time
$Pt-09$	031	047	0.167	10.912222	0006000	047	0.100	000.845556	0335093
$Pt-10$	035	042	0.400	07.232223	0152171	042	0.300	002.556667	0291235
$Pt-15$	045	053	0.500	15.156665	0943203	053	0.467	003.826667	1534031
$Pt-16$	053	048	0.634	51.306669	0369671	048	0.667	019.378889	2624237
$Pt-18$	057	064	0.567	54.622225	1377047	061	0.500	024.715556	1308375
$Pt-22$	065	092	0.734	149.298877	4247734	086	0.633	141.498889	6773031
$Pd-25$	073	∞	∞	∞	∞	∞	∞	∞	∞
$Pd-30$	079	∞	∞	∞	∞	∞	∞	∞	∞
$Pd-50$	131	∞	∞	∞	∞	∞	∞	∞	∞

Table 7. The contrast between IGA and GA

PIGA						GA [17]		
	Edges	LC	Optim	Expt	Time	Optim	Expet	Time
$Pt-09$	030	031	047	051.440000	0010703	47	047.766667	0335093
$Pt-10$	040	035	042	047.880000	0057468	42	043.900000	0291235
$Pt-15$	052	045	053	070.220000	0150265	53	054.200000	1534031
$Pt-16$	060	053	050	078.660000	0127656	48	054.233333	2624237
$Pt-18$	072	057	065	076.700000	0215546	61	070.466667	1308375
$Pt-22$	092	061	089	110.880000	0229296	86	110.633333	6773031
$Pd-25$	106	073	104	138.140000	0273937	∞	∞	∞
$Pd-30$	138	079	134	177.100000	1025375	∞	∞	∞
$Pd-50$	216	131	613	642.600000	2326609	∞	∞	∞

Table 8. The comparison of the comprehensive index between PFIGA and PIGA

PFIGA					PIGA			
	Min	Expected	Variance	Time	Min	Expected	Variance	Time
$Pt-09$	047	048.866667	004.248889	0029437	047	051.440000	016.606401	010703
$Pt-10$	042	044.233333	005.312222	0092421	042	047.880000	007.505599	057468
$Pt-15$	053	058.266667	021.462220	0079500	053	070.220000	128.571572	0150265
$Pt-16$	048	057.666667	040.088888	0205062	050	078.660000	253.304375	0127656
$Pt-18$	060	070.066667	048.395557	0359953	065	076.700000	067.730000	0215546
$Pt-22$	085	103.566667	084.512231	0365625	089	110.880000	114.625605	0229296
$Pd-25$	097	115.033333	101.898885	0341140	104	138.140000	296.640410	0273937
$Pd-30$	133	164.100000	302.823275	0580437	134	177.100000	315.369980	1025375
$Pd-50$	600	621.000000	096.000000	1945765	613	642.600000	201.506657	2326609

clearly show the evolution process. Adopting respectively 10 nodes, 16 nodes, 18 nodes, 22 nodes, 25 nodes, 30 nodes and 50 nodes as a comparison of data, curves of improved algorithm are described in Fig. 2 as follows

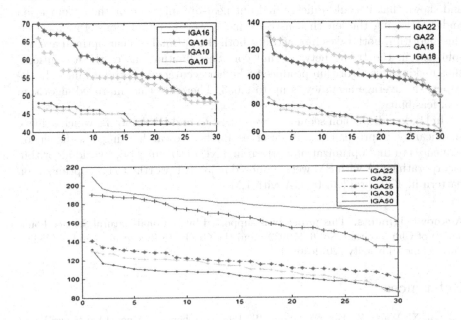

Fig. 2. The comparison of algorithm performance between IGA and GA

In Fig. 2., (a) and (b) describe respectively the change trend of the minimum value of fitness. It can be seen that the mean of 10 nodes is greater than those of GA, and IGA begins to converge in range the 15 to 17 range and GA in the 22 to 25, after this, two algorithms have reached convergence status. This phenomenon indicates that the convergence rate of the improved algorithm is better than previous one; In Fig. 2.(b), with the increase of network scales, the solutions improve gradually and far to small direction deviates from the value of the solution of GA. Proving that the elitism of solutions gets promoted at some extent and the performance become more and more stable. Therefore, this improvement is effective; As shown in Fig. 2.(c), there is only one curve contained 22 nodes in GA, that is because when this scale expands constantly, the algorithm can not find an optimal result. However, due to IGA introduce PSA and a fairness coefficient, therefore, this algorithm can be used for testing large-lot populations. More importantly, its expectations and variance both reach better results than those of original one. Based on comprehensive condition, IGA has made certain improvement in these fields.

4   Conclusion

The paper studies that different parameters have an effect on the performance and makes a comparison. IGA is applied to the layout optimization problem, and shows that it could quickly find out near-optimization or the optimization under satisfying the length constraint in large-scale populations. Proving that this algorithm both takes into account both the optimal or near-optimal average solutions in the traffic network and considers fluctuations of these solutions, thus making this algorithm produced a higher accuracy in optimal values. In the paper, the average accuracy is up to 0.633. Therefore this improved algorithm is of feasibility.

In [4], low-dispersion sequences were used to find DNA motifs, which achieve significantly improvements. It deserves further research using low-dispersion sequences to find optimization pattern in TNL problem. Also, hybrid algorithm incorporating GA with EM were proposed in [3]. It is worthy to find optimization pattern in TNL problem by GA with EM.

Acknowledgments. This project was supported by National Natural Science Foundation of China (Grant No. 61179032), and the Graduate Innovation Fund of Wuhan Polytechnic University (2014cx007).

References

1. Shi, X., Wang, Z., Deng, C., Song, T., Pan, L., Chen, Z.: A novel bio-sensor based on DNA strand displacement. PLoS ONE **9**, e108856 (2014)
2. Xiang, T., Zhou, Q., Li, F.P.: Research on niche genetic algorithm for reactive power optimization. Proc. Chin. Soc. Electr. Eng. **25**, 48–51 (2005)
3. Wang, X., Miao, Y., Cheng, M.: Finding motifs in DNA sequences using low-dispersion sequences. J. Comput. Biol. **21**(4), 320–329 (2014)
4. Wang, X., Miao, Y.: GAEM: a hybrid algorithm incorporating GA with EM for planted edited motif finding problem. Curr. Bioinform. **9**(5), 463–469 (2014)
5. Sun, Y., Jiang, L.: Route optimizing method of loaded car flow with capacity limit in railway network. Railway Transport Econ. **27**, 82–84 (2005)
6. Song, T., Pan, L.: Spiking neural P systems with rules on synapses working in maximum spikes consumption strategy. IEEE Trans. NanoBiosci. **14**(1), 38–44 (2015)
7. Tran, D.A., Raghavendra, H.: Congestion adaptive routing in mobile ad hoc networks. IEEE Trans. Parallel Distrib. Syst. **17**, 1294–1305 (2006)
8. Wu, Y.C.: Study on optimization of logistics distribution route based on AMPSO. J. Lanzhou Jiaotong Univ. **31**, 1–4 (2012)
9. Zhou, K., Fan, L.L., Shao, K.: Simulation DNA algorithm model of satisfiability problem. J. Comput. Theor. Nanosci. **27**, 1220–1227 (2015)
10. Zhou, K., Chen, J.: Simulation DNA algorithm of set covering problem. Appl. Math. Inf. Sci. **8**, 139–144 (2014)
11. Song, T., Pan, L.: Spiking neural P systems with rules on synapses working in maximum spiking strateg. IEEE Trans. NanoBiosci. **14**(4), 465–477 (2015)
12. Zhou, K., Tong, X., Liu, W.: Closed circle DNA algorithm of shortest route problem. Syst. Eng. Electr. **30**, 556–560 (2008)

13. Zhou, K., Tong, X., Xu, J.: Closed circle DNA algorithm of change positive-weighted Hamilton circuit problem. J. Syst. Eng. Electr. **20**, 636–642 (2009)
14. Song, T., Pan, L., Păun, G.: Asynchronous spiking neural P systems with local synchronization. Inf. Sci. **219**, 197–207 (2013)
15. Song, T., Pan, L., Wang, J., et al.: Normal forms of spiking neural P systems with anti-spikes. IEEE Trans. NanoBiosci. **11**(4), 352–359 (2012)
16. Zhang, X., Pan, L., Paun, A.: On the Universality of Axon P Systems. IEEE Trans. Neural Netw. Learn. Syst. (2015). doi:10.1109/TNNLS.2015.2396940
17. Xu W., Shen R.J., Wu G.F., Zhou K.: Traffic network distribution based on distribution center problem and genetic algorithm. In: IEEE International Conference on Information Science and Technology Wuhan, pp. 219–223, 23 March 2012
18. Song, T., Pan, L., Jiang, K., et al.: Normal forms for some classes of sequential spiking neural P systems. IEEE Trans. NanoBiosci. **12**(3), 255–264 (2013)
19. Zhang, X., Liu, Y., Luo, B., Pan, L.: Computational power of tissue P systems for generating control languages. Inf. Sci. **278**, 285–297 (2014)

An Algorithm for Finding Non-dominated Set Based on Two-Dimension Sorting

Yuzhen Fu[1]([⊠]), Han Huang[2], Shujin Ye[2], Liang Lv[2], Hui Zhang[2], and Longqiu Shao[3]

[1] Department of Computer Engineering, MaoMing Polytechnic,
MaoMing 525000, China
123075258@qq.com
[2] College of Software Engineering, South China University of Technology,
Guangzhou 510006, China
[3] Guangdong Provincial Key Laboratory of Petrochemical Equipment Fault
Diagnosis, Guangdong University of Petrochemical Technology,
Maoming 525000, China

Abstract. The complexity of multi-objective evolutionary algorithms based on the non-dominated principles mainly depends on finding non-dominated fronts. In order to reduce complexity and improve construction efficiency, this paper introduces a non-dominated set construction algorithm based on Two Dimensional Sequence (TSNS). When the non-dominated set closes to the Pareto optimal front, it always maintains one dimension by ascending order while the other dimension by descending order. In order to verify the effectiveness of the proposed algorithm, we integrate the algorithm into GA, DE, PSO, then we tested and compared it with classical benchmark functions. The experimental results indicate that the proposed algorithm performs better than NSGA-II in terms of the quality of solutions and the speed of convergence.

Keywords: Multi-objective optimization · Non-dominated set · Evolutionary algorithm

1 Introduction

Multi-objective optimization problems (MOPS) are common in areas such as engineering, biological and economic [1,2]. Since the conflict happens among multiple objectives, the MOPS does not exist an optimal solution. That is to say, no single solution can be found as the global optimal solution. The optimal solution of MOPS is a set of optimal solutions, known as the non-dominated set, also known as Pareto optimal solution set. In traditional methods, the simplest and the most commonly used method is transformed multi-objective problems into single objective problems, which is usually very time-consuming. There are also a kind of methods which choose one objective to optimize, then deal with the rest of the objectives as constraints. There are also some other hybrid algorithms that were proposed to improve the ability to approach the real optimal solution, but many of them did not show any advantages on computation

© Springer-Verlag Berlin Heidelberg 2015
M. Gong et al. (Eds.): BIC-TA 2015, CCIS 562, pp. 150–160, 2015.
DOI: 10.1007/978-3-662-49014-3_14

time. Over the last twenty years, many researchers showed great interests in applying evolutionary algorithms to MOPS [3–5], therefore many evolutionary algorithms have been proposed. The typical algorithms of Multi-objective evolutionary algorithms (MOEA) are the NSGA-II [6], SPEA2 [7], PESA2 [8], etc. As an important research content of MOEA, the approximation and the distribution of the non-dominated set have attracted many scholars' interests. Zhou Caochen made a systematic review of multi-objective reduction algorithms and comparative analysis of the effectiveness of various algorithms [9]. Li Miqing proposed a boundary solution set based spread indicator without the information of the Pareto optimal front [10]. For the MOEA based on non-dominated sorting mechanism, the running time is consumed mainly on construction of the non-dominated solution set. How to improve the efficiency of the construction of the non-dominated set is very worthy research, at the same time the approximation and distribution of the non-dominated set should be guaranteed. Liu Min proposed a fast bi-objective non-dominated sorting algorithm [11]. Several non-dominated set built methods based on Pareto are discussed including algorithm complexity [12]. In this paper,we proposed a non-dominated set construction method based on two-dimensional sorting, and this method is simple, low complexity and easy integrated into evolutionary algorithms.

The outline of the paper is as follows: in Sect. 2, we described the two dimensional sorting non-dominated set construction algorithm in detail; Sect. 3 experiment results of TSNS and compares it with NSGA-II were presents; Sect. 4 offered the conclusion.

2 Two Dimensional Sorting Non-dominated Set Construction Algorithm

2.1 Motivation

How to construct non-dominated set for MOPS actually is to study how to construct non-dominated set for evolution population. Evolutionary algorithms need to reconstruct the non-dominated set in each generation, thus the efficiency of constructing the non-dominated set directly influences the run-time efficiency of MOEAs. Drozdik, M. [13] found that 98 % of the total computational cost was attributed to non-dominated sorting and crowding distance, while less than 1 % to the objective function, and the reset were recombination and system activities. So there exist many studies on how to reduce the cost of constructing the non-dominated set, such as NSGA-II proposed by Deb [6], an efficient method of non-dominated structure were used by Jensen [14] which reduce the complexity of the NSGA-II from the $O\left(GMN^2\right)$ down to $O\left(GNlog_{M-1}N\right)$, Deb [15,16] proposed a method for calculating the nearest neighbor distance to make the solution set have better diversity and reduce the time cost, so a simple and effective method to solve the construction of the non-dominated set is very meaningful.

2.2 Basic Concepts and Terminology

To facilitate the discussion, the related concepts can be formally defined as follows:

Definition 1 (MOPS): The general Multi-Objective Optimization Problem (MOOP) may be stated as finding the value for a set of n decision variables which must satisfy some constraints (J inequalities and K equalities) such that the M objective functions are optimized and can be modeled as follows:

$$MOPS = \begin{cases} Minimize f_m(x_i) & m = 1, 2, ...M; \\ s.t. g_j(x_i) \leq 0 & j = 1, 2, ...J; \\ h_k(x_i) & k = 1, 2, ...K; \end{cases} \tag{1}$$

where x_i is the vector of decision variables, $f_m(X)$ is the objective functions.

Definition 2 (Pareto Dominance): Given the vector of objective functions $f_m = (f_1, \cdots, f_M)$ is said that candidate x^1 dominates x^2 (for minimizing)

$$f_m(x^1) \leq f(x^2), \forall 1 \leq m \leq M \ \ and \ \ \exists 1 \leq m \leq M : f_m(x^1) \leq f(x^2) \tag{2}$$

It said that x^1 dominate x^2, denoted as $x^1 \preceq x^2$.

Definition 3 (Pareto Optimal Set): For a MOP, the Pareto Optimal Set (P^*) is defined as

$$P^* = \{x \in \Omega \| \neg \exists x^* \in \Omega : F(x^*) \preceq F(x)\} \tag{3}$$

Definition 4 (Pareto Front): For a MOP and Pareto Optimal Set (P^*), the Pareto Front (pf^*)

$$pf^* = \{f_m(x) = (f_1(x), f_2(x), \cdots, f_m(x)) | x \in P^*\}. \tag{4}$$

2.3 The Construction Process of TSNS

The most important feature of the proposed algorithm is always maintaining an ordered sequence to reduce the computational complexity. Assuming the set of non-dominated solutions is NDSet, the construction process is as follows: when the $|NDSet| = \varnothing$, the individual u directly insert into NDSet; when the $|NDSet| = 1$, the individual u have four situations:

(a) Insert into the tail of NDSet;
(b) Insert into the header of NDSet;
(c) Dominated by the NDSet, cannot be insert into the NDSet;
(d) Dominate the solution of NDSet, delete the solution and insert the individual u into NDSet.

All of the situations can be shown in Formula 5:

$$NDSet = \begin{cases} (x_1, u) & if \ f_1(x_1) < f_1(u) \ and \ f_2(x_1) > f_2(u) \\ (u, x_1) & if \ f_1(x_1) > f_1(u) \ and \ f_2(x_1) < f_2(u) \\ (x_1) & if \ f_1(x_1) < f_1(u) \ and \ f_2(x_1) < f_2(u) \\ (u) & if \ f_1(x_1) > f_1(u) \ and \ f_2(x_1) > f_2(u) \end{cases} \tag{5}$$

While $|NDSet| = n$, the situations of the individual u as follows:

(a) Insert into the tail of NDSet;
(b) Insert into the header of NDset, and some solutions need to be deleted whose the value of the second dimension is greater than the second dimension of the individual u, then the individual u and the remainder solutions together constitute the new NDSet;
(c) Dominated by the NDSet, cannot be insert into the NDSet;
(d) The individual u insert into the middle of the NDSet. In this situation, the NDSet consists of three parts: solutions whose the value of the first dimension is less than the first dimension of individual u, the individual u, and solutions whose the value of the second dimension is smaller than the second dimension of individual u. As shown in Formula 6.

$$NDSet = \begin{cases} (x_1, x_2, \cdots x_i, \cdots, x_n, u), & if \ f_1(x_n) < f_1(u) \ and \ f_2(x_n) > f_2(u) \\ (u, x_m, x_{m+1}, \cdots, x_{m+i}, \cdots, x_n), & if \ f_1(x_1) < f_1(u) \ and \ f_2(x_1) > f_2(u) \\ (x_1, x_2, \cdots, x_i, \cdots, x_n), & if \ f_1(x_i) < f_1(u) \ and \ f_2(x_i) > f_2(u) \\ (x_1, x_2, \cdots x_i, u, x_m, \cdots, x_n), & if \ f_1(x_i) < f_1(u) \ and \ f_2(x_i) > f_2(u) \end{cases} \quad (6)$$

If $j \in [m, n]$, x_j must meet the condition: $f_1(u) < f_1(x_j)$ and $(f)_2(u) > f_2(x_j)$. Figure 1 shows the position of individual u insert into the NDSet.NDSet consist of two parts:NDset1 and NDSet2. There are two special situations: one is that the individual u is inserted before the header of NDSet, then the NDSet1 is empty; another is that the individual u is inserted after the end of the NDSet, then the NDSet2 is empty.

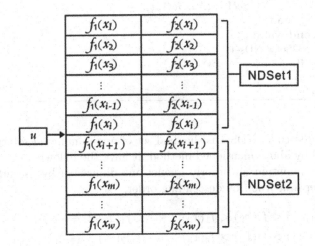

Fig. 1. The insert position of u individual.

2.4   The Pseudo-Code of the Algorithm

The pseudo-code of the algorithm is described below:

Algorithm 1. TSNS

Input: population $P = \{u_1, u_2, u_3, \cdots, u_i, \cdots, u_n\}$
Output: $NDSet = \{x_1, x_2, x_3, \cdots, x_i, \cdots, x_n\}$
 1: Initialization $NDSet = \varnothing$
 2: i=1
 3: **while** $i \leq n$ **do**
 4:     **if** $NDSet = \varnothing$ **then**
 5:         $NDSet = (u)$
 6:     **end if**
 7:     **if** $u(1) > x_w(1)$ (x_w is the tail individual of the NDSet) **then**
 8:         **if** $u(2) < x_w(2)$ **then**
 9:             $NDSet = (NDSet, u)$
10:         **end if**
11:     **else**
12:         **if** $u(1) < x_1(1)$ **then**
13:             $NDSet1 = \varnothing$,NDSet2=NDSet
14:         **else**
15:             NDSet1=$\{x_1, x_2, x_3, \cdots, x_{k-1}\}$
16:             NDSet2=$\{x_k, x_{k+1}, x_{k+2}, x_{i+3}, \cdots, x_w\}$. $(x_{k-1}(1) < u_i(1) < x_k(1))$
17:             j=k
18:             **while** $(j \leq w)$ **do**
19:                 **if** $x_j(2) > u(2)$ **then**
20:                     $NDSet1 = (NDSet1, x_j)$
21:                 **end if**
22:             **end while**
23:             NDSet= NDset1
24:         **end if**
25:     **end if**
26: **end while**

In the pseudo-code, NDSet is the final set of non-dominated solutions which is constructed by above mentioned method, it have the following characteristics that is always maintain an orderly queue: one dimension by ascending order, while the other dimension by descending order.

$$f_1(x_1) < f_1(x_2) < f_1(x_3) < \cdots < f_1(x_i) < \cdots < f_1(x_n)$$
$$f_2(x_1) > f_2(x_2) > f_2(x_3) > \cdots > f_2(x_i) > \cdots > f_2(x_n)$$

According to the definition of non-dominated set, the set belongs to non-dominated set.

2.5 The Strategy of Diversity Preservation

The crowded-comparison approach is used to maintain the diversity of the population. However, due to the set of non-dominated solutions has the characteristic of ordering, the individual does not need to find the nearest neighbor of it, the nearest neighbor of it just arranged in the front of it and behind of it, $d_u = d(u - 1, u) + d(u, u + 1), 1 < u < n, d(u - 1, u)$ is the Euclidean distance between individual u and the individual $u-1$. When the number of set reach up to the population size, the minimum distance of individual is chose to delete. Since the small distance between two individuals will has a huge effect of the population diversity, so the individual who has the smallest distance will be selected to delete. The strategy is simple but can make individual maintain a good spread throughout the Pareto domain to ensure the good diversity of the population.

2.6 Complexity Analysis

A. When the number of non-dominated set less than the number of population members, the complexity of algorithm mainly constructed the set of non-dominated solutions. The construction process mainly composed of two parts, one is to find the position that the individual u insert into, the second part is to remove the solutions in NDSet2 which dominated by individual u. It can be seen from the process, the numbers of non-donimated set is dynamic, the worst complexity is less than $O(lgN)$, while the best complexity is O (1), so the total complexity is less than $O(NlgN)$ even in the worst case.

B. When the number of non-dominated set have reached up to the number of population members, the complexity of TSNS is to find the individual inserting position and maintain the good diversity of the set. The biggest complexity of inserting an individual is $O(lgN)$, once the number of set is greater than the number of population members, the strategy of diversity preservation will be used. Compare the crowding of current insertion individual with the biggest population of set, the more crowded one will be delete, the complexity is $O(1)$.

Based on the above analysis, the algorithm complexity is always no more than $NlogN$. When the size of population is large, TSNS will has a greater advantage in reducing complexity and improving the efficiency of construction, since the orderly charactee of non-dominated set, whether an individual belongs to NDSet or not, only a certain dimension of some individuals needs to be compared (Table 1).

3 Experimental Studies

3.1 Experiment Conditions

In this section, in order to demonstrate the effectiveness of TSNS. Experiments have been carried out on Intel Core i7-4790 (TM) k @ 4.0 GHZ and 4.0 GHZ CPU processor. The parameter of population number is 100. The evaluation number is 50000 times in our experiment. Zitzler et al. [18] suggested six test problems, we choose five of those six problems here and call them ZDT1, ZDT2, ZDT3, ZDT4, and ZDT6, Fonseca and Flemings study (FON) [19], so test problems used in our experiments were ZDT1-ZDT4, ZDT6, FON. Tests repeated 25 times and mean & variance values were reported in Tables 2, 3 and 4. Since NSGA-II recognized as an effective evolutionary multi-objective optimization algorithm, we compared TSNS with NSGA-II on three indicators: errors, diversity and run-time, where in the errors and diversity indicators, the first row represent mean, the second row represent variance.

Table 1. Parameter settings for evolutionary algorithm

Algorithm	Parameter settings
GA	CR = 0.9 mutation = 0.001
DE	W = 0.5 mutation = 0.9
PSO	W = 0.4 + rand*0.3
	$C1 = 1 - FEs/Max_FEs * 0.1$
	$C2 = 2 - FEs/Max_FEs * 0.1$

Table 2. Mean (first rows) and variance (second rows) of the errors metric

Algorithm	ZDT1	ZDT2	ZDT3	ZDT4	ZDT6	FON
NSGA-II	0.0324	0.0461	0.0518	34.9689	0.0789	1.0001
	5.1259e-004	5.5045e-04	5.2959e-04	68.8379	0.0118	1.1196e-10
TSNS-GA	5.4270e-04	0.0024	0.0010	5.7105e-04	0.0011	0.0339
	1.3090e-06	1.4831e-006	4.5205e-06	1.44936e-06	4.9600e-06	0.0051
TSNS-DE	0.0052	0.0016	0.0012	8.5739	0.0205	0.0785
	1.2143e-04	1.1089e-05	6.0742e-06	326.7209	0.0019	0.0274
TSNS-PSO	0.0021	0.0022	0.0043	13.2443	0.0047	0.3151
	63.6948e-008	1.6028e-008	0	0	0	0

3.2 Experimental Results and Analysis

Comparing to other algorithms, NSGA-II has the better convergence [12]. So we integrated TSNS into the GA algorithm and compared it with the NSGA-II. It can be seen from Fig. 2, for two target ZDT series of test functions, NSGA-II cannot close to Pareto optimal front, while TSNS-GA does not have any difficulty in finding a wide spread of solutions over the Pareto optimal front, it

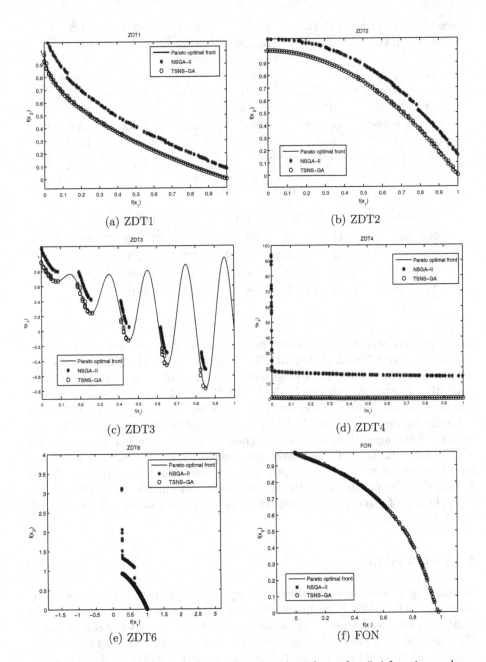

Fig. 2. Optimal PF* obtained by the comparing algorithms after 5e4 function evaluations

Table 3. Mean (first rows) and variance (second rows) of the diversity metric

Algorithm	ZDT1	ZDT2	ZDT3	ZDT4	ZDT6	FON
NSGA-II	0.4360	0.4497	70.7836	0.6826	1.1210	0.9872
	0.0011	0.0018	3.0709e-004	0.0059	0.0332	0
TSNS-GA	0.2353	0.2802	0.9985	0.2079	0.6717	1.0000
	8.0928e-4	6.6088e-04	0.0023	21.7232e-4	4.9993e-04	2.3380e-26
TSNS-DE	0.4121	0.5505	1.0109	0.9112	0.8246	1.0000
	0.0068	0.0068	0.0033	0.0024	0.0029	4.3507e-27
TSNS-PSO	0.3150	0.3325	0.9078	0.9342	0.6645	1.0000
	6.8947e-004	9.8217e-004	0	0	0	0

Table 4. Runtime

Algorithm	ZDT1	ZDT2	ZDT3	ZDT4	ZDT6	FON
NSGA-II	67.0411	69.9425	70.7836	69.5553	74.7192	67.2001
TSNS-GA	28.5412	22.0236067	17.8771	20.2754	15.9226	15.4526
TSNS-DE	7.1044	5.6332	8.8189	2.1419	4.9502	3.192634
TSNS-PSO	41.0183	31.6052	28.1177	37.3904	24.9112	20.9979

almost entirely access to the Pareto optimal front and the convergence precision completely above NSGA-II. For ZDT6, Although NSGA-II also very closes to the Pareto optimal front, there exist many scatter points even after 50000 times evaluation. For testing function FON, NSGA-II has better convergence accuracy, but poor in distribution. From the point of view of running time, TSNS-GA is totally superior than NSGA-II. To further confirm the generalizability and validity of the algorithm, we have integrated the algorithm into the algorithm of PSO and DE. The set which were constructed by TSNS-PSO and TSNS-DE are highly closed to the Pareto optimal front exception ZDT4. Tables 2, 3 and 4 show that the proposed algorithm has better performance than NSGA-II on the indicator of error, diversity and run-time which can be seen from Tables 2, 3 and 4.

4   Conclusion

In this paper, we have introduced a new algorithm to construct the non-dominated set), which is by maintaining an orderly non-dominated set, TSNS greatly improves construction efficiency by reducing the number of comparisons. The proposed TSNS was able to maintain a better spread of solutions and convergence in the obtained non-dominated front compared to NSGA-II. The proposed algorithm can be easily integrated into other evolutionary algorithms. Although we didn't considered more than two objectives at the moment, we believed that extensions of these test problems for more than two objectives can also be done by TSNS, so our further work is focused on expanding the TSNS to three or more objective problems.

Acknowledgments. This work is partially supported by Guangdong Provincial Key Laboratory of Petrochemical Equipment Fault Diagnosis, Guangdong University of Petrochemical Technology.

References

1. Ansgar, K., Dieter, H.: Multi-objective ant colony optimisation-based routing in WSNs. Int. J. Bio-Inspired Comput. (IJBIC) **6**(5), 322–332 (2014)
2. Saeideh, S., Mathias, S., Drechsler, R.: Multi-objective BDD optimization with evolutionary algorithms. In: Proceedings of the 2015 on Genetic and Evolutionary Computation Conference, pp. 751–758. ACM, New York (2015)
3. Giagkiozis, I., Fleming, P.J.: Methods for multi-objective optimization: an analysis. Inf. Sci. **293**, 338–350 (2015)
4. von Lucken, C., Barán, B., Brizuela, C.: A survey on multi-objective evolutionary algorithms for many-objective problems. Comput. Optim. Appl. **58**(3), 707–756 (2014)
5. Zeng, S., Zhou, D., Li, H.: Non-dominated sorting genetic algorithm with decomposition to solve constrained optimisation problems. Int. J. Bio-Inspired Comput. **5**(3), 150–163 (2013)
6. Deb, K., Pratap, A., Agarwal, S., et al.: A fast and elitist multi-objective genetic algorithm: NSGA-II. IEEE Trans. Evol. Comput. **6**(2), 182–197 (2002)
7. Zitzler, E., Laumanns, M., Thiele, L.: Improving the strength pareto evolutionary algorithm for multiobjective optimization, optimization and control with applications to industrial problems, pp. 95–100 (2002)
8. Knowles, J, Corne, D: The pareto archived evolution strategy: a new baseline algorithm for pareto multiobjective optimization. In: Proceedings of the Congress on Evolutionary Computation, pp. 98–105. IEEE Press, Washington (1999)
9. Zhou, C., Chen, Z., He, Z.: Survey of many-objective optimization algorithms. Comput. Sci. **41**(z1), 57–60 (2014)
10. Li, M., Zhang, J.: An indicator for assessing the spread of solutions in muti-objective evolution. Chin. J. Comput. **34**(4), 647–664 (2011)
11. Liu, M., Zeng, W., Zhao, J.: A fast Bi-objective non-dominated sorting algorithm. Pattern Recog. Artif. Intell. **24**(4), 538–547 (2011)
12. Li, Z., Lin, X.: Research advance of multi-objective optimization non-dominated set construction methods. Comput. Eng. Appl. **49**(19), 31–35 (2013)
13. Drozdik, M., Aguirre, H., Tanaka, K.: Attempt to reduce the computational complexity in multi-objective differential evolution algorithms. In: Proceedings of the 15th Annual Conference on Genetic and Evolutionary Computation, pp. 599–606. ACM, New York (2013)
14. Jensen, M.T.: Reducing the run-time complexity of multiobjective EAs: the NSGA-II and other algorithms. IEEE Trans. Evol. Comput. **7**(5), 503–515 (2003)
15. Kukkonen, S, Deb, K: Improved pruning of non-dominated solutions based on crowding distance for Bi-objective optimization problems. In: Proceedings of the World Congress on Computational Intelligence, pp. 1179–1186 (2006)

16. Kukkonen, S., Deb, K.: A fast and effective method for pruning of non-dominated solutions in many-objective problems. In: Runarsson, T.P., Beyer, H.-G., Burke, E.K., Merelo-Guervós, J.J., Whitley, L.D., Yao, X. (eds.) PPSN 2006. LNCS, vol. 4193, pp. 553–562. Springer, Heidelberg (2006)
17. Qi, Y., Liu, F., Chang, W., Ma, X., Jiao, L.: Memetic immune algorithm for multiobjective optimization. J. Softw. **24**(7), 1529–1544 (2013)
18. Zitzler, E., Deb, K., Thiele, L.: Comparison of multiobjective evolutionary algorithms: empirical results. Evol. Comput. **8**(2), 173–195 (2000)
19. Fonseca, C.M., Fleming, P.J.: Multiobjective optimization and multiple constraint handling with evolutionary algorithms. Part II: application example. Trans. Syst. Man Cybern. Part A: Syst. Hum. **28**, 38–47 (1998)

Cloud Avoidance Scheduling Algorithm for Agile Optical Satellites

Lei He[1], Xiaolu Liu[1,2], Lining Xing[1(✉)], and Yingwu Chen[1]

[1] College of Information System and Management,
National University of Defense Technology,
Changsha 410073, People's Republic of China
`xing2999@qq.com`
[2] Canada Research Chair in Distribution Management, HEC Montréal,
3000 Chemin de la Côte-Sainte-Catherine, Montréal H3T 2A7, Canada

Abstract. The existence of cloud seriously influences the imaging quality and efficiency of traditional optical satellites, which can be overcome thanks to the enhancement of the mobility of the new generation of agile satellites. The problem of agile optical satellite scheduling considering real-time cloud information is therefore investigated. A two-phased scheduling framework, containing off-line scheduling on the ground and on-line rescheduling onboard, is proposed. An algorithm based on the ant colony algorithm is designed to solve this problem. An on-line re-scheduling algorithm based on confliction sliding strategy is proposed. A series of experiments are carried out to testify the effectiveness of the algorithm. The results show that almost 50 % of the satellite observation capacity is saved with consideration of real-time cloud information.

Keywords: Agile satellite scheduling · Cloud avoidance · Off-line scheduling · Ant colony algorithm · On-line re-scheduling

1 Introduction

The existence of cloud seriously influences the efficiency of traditional optical earth observing satellites (EOS) [1]. The traditional EOS (non-agile satellite), can image only when it is flying right above the target and the image process can easily fail due to the cloud coverage. New agile optical satellites own more flexible maneuver abilities in both cross-track (roll) and along-track (pitch) direction [2], resulting in prolonged available time windows (ATW) for targets. An ATW is the window of opportunity [3], which refers to the specified time period during which the satellite can observe ground targets. By pitching, an agile satellite can image before or after it flies above the targets [4] (see Fig. 1). The paper investigates the problem of agile optical satellite scheduling under the consideration of real-time cloud information and finally generate a cloud-free schedule.

To get rid of or relive the influence of cloud, much work has been done. Image recognition technology was developed to realize automatic and accurate cloud

© Springer-Verlag Berlin Heidelberg 2015
M. Gong et al. (Eds.): BIC-TA 2015, CCIS 562, pp. 161–172, 2015.
DOI: 10.1007/978-3-662-49014-3_15

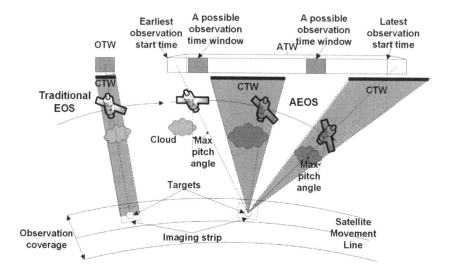

Fig. 1. Comparison of non-agile satellite and agile satellite

detection [5,6], prediction [7,8] as well as real-time cloud detector [9]. Besides, cloud removal technology [10,11] was commonly used. But as an afterthought, it can only improve the lightly contaminated images. A better way is to avoid clouds when imaging. Wang et al. [12] modeled the cloud as a stochastic event for each ATW. The ATWs covered by cloud was discarded directly. However, for an AEOS, whose ATW is much longer, a better way is to assign the cloud-covered parts a punishment according to different cloudiness level. And the concept of Cloud-obscuring Time Window (CTW) was proposed, which referred to the time section during when the target is obscured by clouds [13,14].

Due to the uncertainty of clouds, the traditional off-line scheduling is not enough. Onboard autonomous scheduling focuses on the uncertainties occurs in the work process of the satellite, such as new arrival of requests and influence of cloud [15]. Cloud screening methods [16,17] were used to store and download only the uncontaminated images, saving the satellite resources. Efforts to reduce the on-line re-scheduling calculation complexity were also made, such as using modular computing [18] to relax constraints and using orthogonal design [19] to enhance the searching efficiency of new plans. Although most of the works were based on the non-agile EOS, they provided a great of inspirations to our work.

In above, the problem of agile optical satellite scheduling problem with the consideration of real-time cloud information is investigated. A two phased scheduling framework is presented. A series of experiments prove the validity of the proposed algorithms.

2   Problem Formulation

Input Tasks: Let T be the set of tasks, $T = \{t_1, t_2, \cdots, t_{N_T}\}$, where N_T is the number of tasks. Let P_i be the priority of the task t_i, which shows the benefit brought by the task. And S_i^r is the least image quality for task t_i, which is proposed by the user. The time duration that the imaging process should last to ensure the integrity of task t_i is defined as $t_i^{observe}$.

Clouds: The off-line cloud information is defined by weather forecast and the real-time (on-line) information is informed by the detector onboard. Assume that the detector can obtain the cloud information in a range of 5 min. And the change of clouds in these 5 min can be neglected. For each cloud, it is characterized by the cloudiness level c^{level} [20] as well as its position. Cloudiness level is a weighing factor that maps the cloud influence into several levels according to its thickness and density.

Output Solution: A sequence of time windows with a specified look angle.

Decision Variables. The decision variable x_{ik} is a binary variable. If $x_{ik} = 1$, it means that the kth ATW is selected to observe task t_i. Otherwise, it means that the kth ATW of task t_i is not selected.

Objective Functions. Since both cloud and the timing of photographing affect the quality of satellite images, two measurements p_{ik}^t and p_{ik}^c are defined to quantify the influence. We divide the image quality into ten levels.

Formula (1) shows how the selection of observation start time influences the image quality, and t_{ik}^{mid} is the midpoint time of the kth ATW of task t_i. Apparently, when imaging at t_{ik}^{mid}, imaging quality is the best.

$$p_{ik}^t = \left\lfloor 10 - \frac{9 \left| t - t_{ik}^{mid} \right|}{t_{ik}^{mid} - t_{ik}^0} \right\rfloor \tag{1}$$

Formula (2) presents the impacts of cloud coverage for each ATW, where t_j^{cover} is the length of the jth CTW, $t_i^{observe}$ is the length of the time needed to image task t_i and m is the number of CTWs related to current time window. According to Formula (2), the image quality would be best with a score of 10 when there is no cloud during photographing. Otherwise the quality decreases gradually with increasing number of clouds.

$$p_{ik}^c = 10 - \sum_{j=1}^{m} \frac{c^{level} \times t_j^{cover}}{t_i^{observe}} \tag{2}$$

To combine the two factors together, a new merit called image score noted by S_{ik} is given out, which is shown in Formula (3). It is square root of product of p_{ik}^t and p_{ik}^c. Based on S_{ik}, the real benefit of each imaged target is defined in Formula (4). It is easy to get that, when S_{ik} is 10, the image score is largest, obtaining the whole task priority P_i. On the contrary, if S_{ik} cannot reach user's least image quality requirement, it would be a waste of satellite resources, a negative benefit is obtained to show punishment.

$$S_{ik} = \sqrt{p_{ik}^c p_{ik}^t} \tag{3}$$

$$g_i = \begin{cases} \frac{P_i S_{ik}}{10} & S_{ik} > S_i^r \\ -1 & S_{ik} < S_i^r \end{cases} \tag{4}$$

Therefore, the mathematical formulation of the problem is shown as follow. Its objective function is defined in Formula (5), maximizing the total benefits of the satellite. And N_i is the number of ATWs of task t_i.

$$\max \sum_{i=1}^{N_T} \sum_{k=1}^{N_i} x_{ik} g_i \tag{5}$$

s.t.

$$\sum_{k=1}^{N_i} x_{ik} \leq 1, \forall t_i \in T, \tag{6}$$

$$x_{ik} = 1, to_{ik}^0 \leq to_i^0 < to_i^{end} \leq t_{ik}^{end} \tag{7}$$

$$to_i^{end} + t_{ij}^{trans} \leq to_j^0 \tag{8}$$

$$to_i^{end} - to_i^0 = d_i \tag{9}$$

Constraint (6) is a uniqueness constraint, meaning each task can be observed at most once. Constraint (7) defines the time period of imaging must locate within some ATW. Constraint (8) is the transition time between two successive tasks, where t_{ij}^{trans} is the needed time for satellite to adjust its camera from a previous gesture to the current gesture. Constraint (9) confines the time duration for each task, which means the imaging process must last a time of d_i to ensure the integrity of acquired pictures.

3   Proposed Algorithm

3.1   Algorithm Framework

In this paper, we develope a two-phased scheduling framework based on the assumptions that the satellite owns somewhat onboard calculation capability.

According to Fig. 2, an initial schedule is generated on the ground. All the constraints rising from satellites, users and environment are considered. Then the initial schedule is uploaded and the satellite operates the schedule based on it. At the same time, the cloud detector provides real-time cloud information. Once the scheduled task is obscured by the cloud, an online rescheduling will be started to avoid cloud coverage or to get rid of the task.

3.2   Off-Line Scheduling on the Ground

Offline scheduling for agile satellite is a NP-Hard combination optimization problem [2]. Ant colony optimization (ACO) algorithm is applied to solve the offline scheduling problem of agile satellite. Real ants are capable of finding the shortest path from a food source to their nest without using any visual cue. Instead, they communicate information about the food source via depositing a chemical

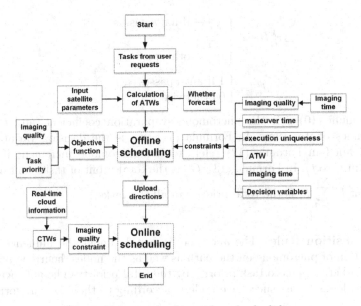

Fig. 2. Framework of two-phased scheduling

substance, called pheromone, on the paths. The following ants are attracted by the pheromone. Since the shorter paths have higher traffic densities, these paths can accumulate higher proportion of pheromone. Hence, the probability of ants following these shorter paths would be higher [21]. ACO has been successfully applied to a series of combinatorial optimization problem, such as the traveling salesman problem and the vehicle routing problem, and has been proved to be very competitive to other metaheuristics for this problem [22]. For the offline scheduling part of this problem, the precision is important and there are usually hundreds of tasks.

In order to use ACO, tasks are regarded as nodes on the ants' paths and the proportion of the task priority by the total priority are regarded as the heuristic information of the nodes.

Pheromone Definition and Update Rule. The pheromone on a path shows the value of the profit of this path, which can influence the ants' choice of nodes.

Let τ_{ij} be the pheromone from node t_i to node t_s. Initialize $\tau_{ij} = \tau_0$. Set the number of ants to be m. When ant k traverses all the task nodes, the pheromone on the path this ant passes is updated according to Formula (10).

$$\tau_{ij}(t + N_T) = (1 - \rho)\tau_{ij}(t) + \Delta\tau_{ij}(t) \tag{10}$$

$$\Delta\tau_{ij}(t) = \begin{cases} \dfrac{\sum\limits_{k=1}^{m} \Delta\tau_{ij}^k(t)}{\sum\limits_{k=1}^{m} d_{ij}^k} & \text{if } \sum\limits_{k=1}^{m} d_{ij}^k > 0 \\ 0 & \text{otherwise} \end{cases} \tag{11}$$

$$\Delta \tau_{ij}^k(t) = \begin{cases} \dfrac{G_k}{\sum\limits_{i=1}^{N_T} P_i} & \text{if ant } k \text{ passes } (i,j) \\ 0 & \text{otherwise} \end{cases} \tag{12}$$

$$d_{ij}^k = \begin{cases} 1 \text{ if ant } k \text{ passes } (i,j) \\ 0 \text{ otherwise} \end{cases} \tag{13}$$

In Formula (10) ρ is the pheromone evaporation coefficient, and t is the current times of iterations. In Formula (11), d_{ij} is the decision variable and $\Delta \tau_{ij}^k(t)$ defined in Formula (12) refers to the pheromone increment if ant k passes from t_i to t_j. In Formula (13), G_k is the total profit of tasks contained in path of ant k. $\sum\limits_{i=1}^{N_T} P_i$ is the total priority of all the tasks.

State Transition Rule. The ant chooses a node under the influence of the concentration of pheromone on the path as well as the nodes' heuristic information, which here equals to task priority by the total priority. The ant located at the node t_i looks for its successive node t_j according to the following formula:

$$j = \begin{cases} \arg \max\limits_{s \in allowed_k} \{\tau_{is}^\alpha \eta_s^\beta\} & q > q_0 \\ \phi & q < q_0 \end{cases} \tag{14}$$

$$\eta_s = \frac{P_s}{\sum_{i=1}^{N_T} P_i}$$

where, $q_0 \in [0,1]$ is a selection parameter and q is a randomly generated number which values in $[0,1]$, $allowed_k^i$ is a reachable node set from task t_i for the kth ant, containing only tasks that is not observed and with ATWs after t_i, τ_{ij} is the pheromone from node t_i to node t_s and η_s is the heuristic information of node s, α is the pheromone importance factor, β is the heuristic information importance factor. When $q > q_0$, φ chooses its successive nodes according to the following formula:

$$p_{ij}(t) = \begin{cases} \dfrac{\tau_{ij}^\alpha \eta_j^\beta}{\sum\limits_{s \in allowed_k} \tau_{is}^\alpha \eta_s^\beta} & j \in allowed_k \\ 0 & \text{otherwise} \end{cases} \tag{15}$$

After the ants traverse all these nodes, a complete task scheduling path is constructed. To evaluate this path, a detailed schedule which produces an observation window for each target, constructing the complete task imaging sequence should be made.

ATW Selection Rules. When a task has multiple ATWs, we need to choose one to arrange the observation. To maximize the number of tasks that can be observed and image quality for each observed task, two heuristic rules are proposed.

- Preferentially select the ATW with the smallest overlapping degree, which refers to the number of time windows conflicting with current time window. The conflicting time window must be from the same satellite and share a common time period with current time window.
- When multiple windows have the same overlapping degree, choose the window with the highest imaging quality according to Formula (3).

3.3 Onboard On-line Scheduling

In contrast to scheduling on the ground, online scheduling is a rescheduling process applied to adjust the initial schedule to meet the changes of both requests and work circumstances of the satellite. Due to cloud uncertainty, the scheduled tasks might be covered when imaging. To avoid clouds, a rescheduling process is triggered to adjust the observation window of the task.

The workflow of the on-board rescheduling process is shown in Fig. 3. The computer onboard judges the feasibility of the current schedule according to the work status of the satellite and changes of its workload. Once any inconsistency is detected, the online scheduling is triggered.

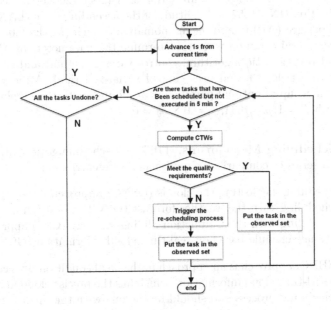

Fig. 3. Workflow of re-scheduling process

Confliction Sliding Strategy. The on-line re-scheduling algorithm is based on confliction sliding strategy (CSS), which means that if confliction is detected, the scheduler will try to slide the observation time window with its ATW and make it meet the quality constraints. If the trail succeed, the imaging process will be executed, otherwise the task will be removed and other tasks will be tested whether they can be imaged in the time window former task occupies.

4   Experiments Results

4.1   Design of Experiments

The algorithm was coded in $C\#$, and the experiments were conducted using Inter (R) Core (TM) i5-3317U CPU 1.70 GHz under Windows 8 with 4 G RAM. The configurations of different scenarios are shown as follows.

Twenty different scenarios are designed. The number of targets contained in the scenario changing evenly from 20 to 200, with an increment step of 20. For each target number, two target distribution modes were designed. The first is sparse distribution, under which targets were randomly generated worldwide. The second is dense distribution, which means targets were distributed in a specified area; here the area was defined by the region of 3°N~53°N and 74°E~133°E.

The time horizon of the scheduling is 24 h. The initial orbital parameters for the satellites are as follows: semi-major axis (SA) 7200000.0, eccentricity (EC) 0, inclination (IN) 96.5760, longitude of the ascending node (LAN) 175.72, argument of perigee (AP) 0, and mean anomaly at epoch (MAE) 0.0750.

There are several common ways to determine the parameters of ACO, such as orthogonal test, genetic algorithm, control variate method and so on. This paper refers to article [23] and uses control variate method. After a series of experiments, a group of optimal parameters are found, with the number of ants $= 100$, $\alpha = 1.5, \beta = 1, \rho = 0.34, q_0 = 0.8, \eta_0 = 0.01$.

Different Scheduling Mechanisms. 4 different scheduling mechanisms were applied and a series of comparison experiments were carried out.

- Off-line scheduling neglecting the clouds (OSNC) approach.
- Off-line scheduling with the weather forecast (OSWF) approach.
- On-line scheduling with the Confliction Sliding strategy (CSS) approach.
- Global optimal schedule based on real-time cloud information (GOSBRCI).

The GOSBRCI approach is an approach in the ideal condition. It is calculated based on the real-time cloud information, which has the precise cloud information before the scheduling process and should be the one with the highest profit.

4.2   Result and Analysis

Comparison of Benefits. Figure 4(a) represents the differences between expected profit and real profit for two offline algorithms. From the comparison above, the effective profit of the OSNC algorithm is quite low. Therefore, it was a great waste of the satellite resource. In contrast, the OSWF has a lower expected profit, but a much higher real profit ratio, indicating that the algorithm considering the cloud information is beneficial.

Figure 4(b) shows the comparison of offline and online scheduling algorithms. It is clear that, the online scheduling algorithms worked much better than offline algorithms because of the consideration of real-time cloud information. Although the online algorithm is based on only some simple heuristics without too much iteration due to the limits of onboard computation, it performs well because though the offline scheduling took no considerations of real-time cloud, it provided online scheduling with a solution, generated by ACO, which is of very good and effective global view.

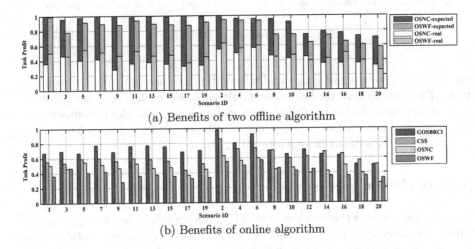

(a) Benefits of two offline algorithm

(b) Benefits of online algorithm

Fig. 4. Comparison of benefits

Comparison of CPU Time. The results of scheduling CPU time are shown in Fig. 5. An apparent result could be drawn is that the CPU time increases with the increasing number of tasks. Figure 5(a) compares two offline scheduling methods. Generally, it takes less time for the algorithm to get an optimal solution when the tasks are sparsely distributed. This is because fewer conflicts exist and fewer iterations are needed when generating an observation schedule. At the same time, the cloud coverage contributed a lot to the runtime. As we have to compute CTWs for each ATW to find a proper start time so that the image quality is qualified. Figure 5(b) shows the runtime of online algorithm based on CSS. It can complete the re-scheduling task within 1 s. This is quite important because the calculation must be confined in a short time, or the online scheduling is impossible. The bottom line for the calculation time is that the new schedule must be generated before the satellite flying to the nearest cloud detected.

To sum up, schedules with consideration of real-time cloud information increases the profit gained by satellites. To improve the efficiency of agile satellites,

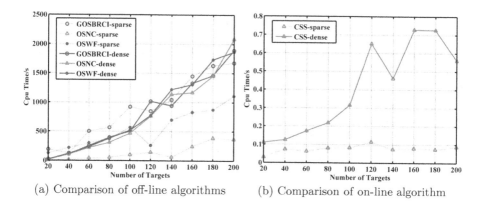

(a) Comparison of off-line algorithms   (b) Comparison of on-line algorithm

Fig. 5. Comparison of CPU time

the best way is to take real-time cloud information into account. And the required task CPU running time of the online algorithm is acceptable. Another point we want to emphasize is that the distribution of the tasks affects a lot the efficiency of the satellite. When the tasks are not urgent, it is better to separate tasks that are geographically close into different scheduling horizon.

5 Conclusion

We have investigated the problem of cloud avoidance scheduling for agile optical satellite is investigated in the paper. Real-time cloud information is taken into account through two-staged scheduling framework, and the generated schedule is able to avoid clouds, thus producing images without cloud contamination. An objective function which takes image quality into consideration was defined. Our results show that almost 50 % of the satellite observation capacity can be saved, which allows more requests to be satisfied and save significant data processing work when producing images on the ground. The work presented in this paper represents a major importance to the current scheduling mechanism, since satellites are still an oversubscribed resource. Since capability of onboard computation is limited and expensive we need to improve the efficiency of on-line scheduling and also investigate the application on the hardware onboard.

Acknowledgments. This research is supported by the National Natural Science Foundation of China (No. 71331008 and 71101150), the Program for New Century Excellent Talents in University, Foundation for the Author of National Excellent Doctoral Dissertation of PR China (201492), the Youth Training Program for Innovation and Entrepreneurship Platform of Science and Technology at Hunan Province, the Outstanding Youth Fund Project of Hunan Provincial Natural Science Foundation.

References

1. Gasch, J., Kenneth, A.: Cloud cover avoidance in space-based remote sensing acquisition. Algorithms Multispectral Hyperspectral Ultraspectral Imagery VI **4049**, 335–347 (2000)
2. Lemaitre, M., Verfaillie, G., Jouhaud, F., Lachiver, J., Bataille, N.: Selecting and scheduling observations of agile satellites. Aerosp. Sci. Technol. **6**(5), 367–381 (2002)
3. Wolfe, W., Sorensen, S.: Three scheduling algorithms applied to the earth observing systems domain. Manag. Sci. **46**(1), 148–166 (2000)
4. Lian, Z., Tan, Y., Yan, Z.: Temporal reasoning technology for AEOS scheduling. Syst. Eng. Electr. **35**(6), 1206–1211 (2013)
5. Ismaya, H., Rahayu, M., Adiningsih, E.: New automated cloud and cloud-shadow detection using landsat imagery. Int. J. Remote Sens. Earth Sci. **9**(2), 100–111 (2014)
6. Hughes, M., Hayes, D.: Automated detection of cloud and cloud shadow in single-date landsat imagery using neural networks and spatial post-processing. Remote Sens. **6**(6), 4907–4926 (2014)
7. Avgoustoglou, E., Tzeferi, T.: The effect of a sub-grid statistical cloud-cover scheme applied to the COSMO local numerical weather prediction model over the wider geographical domain of Greece. Atmos. Res. **152**, 69–73 (2015)
8. Morf, H.: Sunshine and cloud cover prediction based on markov processes. Solar Energ. **110**, 615–626 (2014)
9. Algra, T.: Real-time cloud sensing for efficiency improvement of optical high-resolution satellite remote sensing. In: Proceedings of Geoscience and Remote Sensing Symposium, pp. 4311–4313. IEEE Press, New York (2003)
10. Tang, W., Liang, D., Hu, G.: The algorithm for removing thick clouds in remote sensing image based on support vector machine. Remote Sens. Technol. Appl. **26**(1), 111–116 (2011)
11. Lin, C., Tsai, P., Lai, K., Chen, J.: Cloud removal from multitemporal satellite images using information cloning. IEEE Trans. Geosci. Remote Sens. **51**(1), 232–241 (2013)
12. Wang, J., Demeulemeester, E., Qiu, D.: A pure proactive scheduling algorithm for multiple earth observation satellites under uncertainties of clouds (2014). SSRN 2495339
13. Lin, W., Liao, D., Liu, C., Lee, Y.: Daily imaging scheduling of an earth observation satellite. IEEE Trans. Syst. Man Cybern. Part A: Syst. Hum. **35**(2), 213–223 (2005)
14. He, M., He, R.: Research on agile imaging satellites scheduling techniques with the consideration of cloud cover. Sci. Technol. Eng. **13**(28), 8373–8379 (2013)
15. Chien, S., Muscettola, N., Rajan, K.: Automated planning and scheduling for goal-based autonomous spacecraft. Intell. Syst. Appl. **13**(5), 50–55 (1998)
16. Algra, T.: On the effectiveness of cloud cover avoidance methods in support of the super-spectral mission for land applications. In: Proceedings of Geoscience and Remote Sensing Symposium, pp. 982–985. IEEE Press, New York (2002)
17. Thompson, D., Green, R., Keymeulen, D., Lundeen, S., Mouradi, Y., Nunes, D., Chien, S.: Rapid spectral cloud screening onboard aircraft and spacecraft. IEEE Trans. Geosci. Remote Sens. **52**(11), 6779–6792 (2014)
18. Aldinger, J., Lohr, J.: Planning for agile earth observation satellites. In: Proceedings of International Conference on Automated Planning and Scheduling-2013 Workshop on Planning in Continuous Domains (2013)

19. Fukushima, Y., Mita, M.: A new approach to onboard planning and scheduling for autonomous remote systems. In: Proceedings of IEEE International Conference on Mechatronics, pp. 439–444. IEEE Press, New York (2011)
20. Baek, S., Han, S., Cho, K., Lee, D., Yang, J., Bainum, P., Kim, H.: Development of a scheduling algorithm and GUI for autonomous satellite missions. Acta Astronaut. **68**(7), 1396–1402 (2011)
21. Dorigo, M., Gambardella, L.M.: Ant colony system: a cooperative learning approach to the traveling salesman problem. IEEE Trans. Evol. Comput. **1**(1), 53–66 (1996)
22. Cai, G.Y., Dong, E.Q.: Comparison and analysis of generation algorithm and ant colony optimization on TSP. Comput. Eng. Appl. **43**(10), 96–98 (2007)
23. Ye, Z.W., Zheng, Z.B.: Configuration of parameters α, β, ρ in ant algorithm. Geomatics Inf. Sci. Wuhan Univerisity **29**(7), 597–601 (2004)

Design Swapping Encryption System for Video Streaming with Brain Storm Optimization

Jun S. Huang, Qiong Wu[✉], and Qi Chen

Suqian College, 399 South Huanghe, Suqian 223800, People's Republic of China
414243114@qq.com

Abstract. The basic concept of wireless video streaming system, the main requirements from the law enforcement communities and related encryption algorithm of the wireless system are described. The major challenge in this research area is providing a low computation algorithm that runs easily on an embedded Java application, within pre-optimized key space. The key space is optimized under the object of minimizing the standard deviation of the spectrum of the key. Due to the large space of the key, the brain storm optimization is used to rule out the likely weak key set.

Keywords: Video · Swap · Encryption · Optimization

1 Introduction

Finding the optimization solutions is the way to deal with the practical applications and engineering problems. A simple optimization can be based on a single goal. Different optimization problems correspond to different solution space, including feasible solution and infeasible solution. Thus the optimization is divided into the optimization problem with constraints and optimization problem without constraints. In real life solution space can be huge, and can not be exhausted with limited computation, as such, recent years, different population based heuristic optimal algorithms were studied and applied, especially swarm intelligence. The traditional optimal algorithms become less effective while facing the complex optimization problems. Swarm intelligence includes Particle Swarm Optimization (PSO), ant colony algorithm, fire flies optimization algorithm [5], which is a set of optimal algorithm inspired by simple self-designed synergy.

Most swarm intelligence algorithms are inspired by simple self-designed synergy. For example, PSO is inspired by synergistic effect by birds, ant colony algorithm is inspired by synergistic effect by ants and fire flies optimization algorithm is inspired by synergistic effect by fire flies. However, human beings are the most intelligent individual in nature. So the Optimization algorithms inspired by synergistic effect by us may be better [8].

Now network security measures can be divided into two categories, physical way and mathematical way. In the first way, fiber optic replaces cable in order to prevent electromagnetic radiation being monitored. The second way, wireless

© Springer-Verlag Berlin Heidelberg 2015
M. Gong et al. (Eds.): BIC-TA 2015, CCIS 562, pp. 173–180, 2015.
DOI: 10.1007/978-3-662-49014-3_16

signal is transformed into unknown signal by encryption. In the computer field, Advanced Encryption System (AES) algorithm is the popular encryption algorithm, which has wide application and many software or hardware can be used. But the disadvantage is that it consuming more power, which is not suitable for portable wireless usage. Although the Data Encryption System (DES) algorithm is relative simple, the key is too short to be secure.

From mathematical point of view, the encryption algorithm is divided into confusion and diffusion. The principle of confusion algorithm is that the cipher text can be obtained by adding up the password with the original text. On the contrary is decryption process. The principle of diffusion algorithm is that the cipher text can be obtained by moving or exchanging the original information bits according to the value of the key (derived from password). On the contrary is decryption process. In the computer field, the shifting of information bits is equivalent to multiplication and division. Swapping bits randomly is a combination of multiplication/division and addition, which is actually a nonlinear operation.

Thus our Swapping Encryption System (SES) algorithm is not a linear mapping, even it is simple. In case of a hacker attacks, it has to calculate factorial number of times, the time needed to decode increases faster than exponential with respect to key length. This diffusion algorithm is a nonlinear mapping. Changing the swapping pattern we will get different mapping. The mappings are not equal, to prevent a hacker attack, diffusion algorithm has to go through pre-optimization, which doesn't increase the online decode or encode time.

The principle of the easier diffusion algorithm is that the original text is stored into the matrix memory by rows, then which will be read out by columns. On the contrary is decryption process. But the principle of the complex diffusion algorithm is that the random number generator decides the storage sequence, rather than simply read out by rows or columns. During the decryption process, we follow the same sequence, which is the key value. The random number generator may be a pseudo-random electronic circuit, a true random quantum circuit or a true random chaos circuit.

Although diffusion algorithm has high strength and consumes less power, but the transposition rules will directly affect the effect of encryption. For example, the cyclic shift won't lead to a strong nonlinear mapping, which will happen only when nearly half of the non-contiguous transposition occurs. Then when all information bits are moved, they may be go back to the original, the nonlinear property disappearing, the results may have little difference with the original. In a word, transposition algorithms must adjust dynamically, according to the cipher text. In another word, choosing the optimal transposition consequence for the different data types is necessary. We can combine confusion algorithm with diffusion algorithm in the practical application, to avoid the situation of running into a weak key.

In order to retain the nonlinear strength, the major work is to improve the SES algorithm. The data can be divided into categories and sub-categories. Then apply brainstorming algorithm to select the rules for each categories. The goal is to make the statistics of cipher text approaching white noise. The rest paper is organized below: Sect. 2 is the concept for the swapping encryption method for video signals, Sect. 3 explains the details of transcendental number that is iterated over Fibonacci polynomial, with video time stamp and user pass phrase, Sect. 4 is the simulation and experiment report, and Sect. 5 is the summary.

2   System and Solution

There are video streaming solutions used for law enforcement community for many years. Analog video monitoring system is the first generation of video surveillance system, it is used for light weight drones. Digital Video Recorder is the second generation of such system; it is used for average weight drones. The third generation video monitoring and control system is based on Internet Protocol (IP), in which the video and audio are encoded/compressed using FLV format. The IP packets are then transmitted through WiFi, it is used in heavy weight drones. Here we focus on the end-to-end encryption aspect of the latest system.

In the law enforcement application, with third generation solution, greater numbers of problematic sites can be monitored in less bandwidth than can be covered with conventional video techniques. In the event of a major occurrence police can fly small, low-bandwidth drone(s) with cameras to provide the command post with real time video of the event scene.

The typical network configuration for wireless camera is shown in Fig. 1. The first block is the video capture end, which is called transmitter (Tx). It transmits encrypted video to the receiver, and at the same time it can also receive commands from the laptop or even handheld device like BlackBerry through the cloud. The transmitter is mounted on the drone.

The second block is the receiver (Rx), inside the Blackberry. The link between transmitter is 2.4 GHz WiFi radio. The transmitter transmits the video signal from a remote site to the APP on the Blackberry. APP transmits commands back to the drone camera, such as turn on hazard flashing light etc. The next block LTE network and handheld devices such as iPhone. When the network cloud is a private system, the existing encryption might be sufficient; however when the network cloud includes public network, and when the drone has the limited power supple, a better encryption becomes necessary. Maintaining several passwords across a number of wireless networks can be cumbersome. An end-to-end pass phrase and time-stamp based encryption in this case is highly desirable for most end users. The next section will detail this scheme and its optimization.

3   Encryption Scheme and Optimization

3.1   Mathematics Background

In order to explain the key swapping based encryption schemes, we need to establish some basic mathematics here. A Fibonacci polynomial [3] is defined as

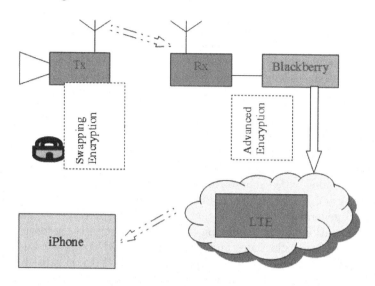

Fig. 1. Sample streaming network csonfiguration

the next number in the sequence being made from the weighted summation of previous two numbers,

$$F_{n+1}(x, y) = xF_n(x, y) + yF_{n-1}(x, y) \tag{1}$$

If the very first two weights x = y = 1, then it is called original Fibonacci sequence.

For the Fibonacci sequence, we have following known properties,

$$F_{2n}(x, y) = F_{n+1}^2 - F_{n-1}^2 = F_n(2F_{n+1} - F_n) \tag{2}$$

To ensure the whitening property of the scrambling method, the other seed is picked from a transcendental number like e^π. Above formulas can be used to speed up the embedded calculations.

There are a number of particular pretty algebraic identities involving the Fibonacci primes [1] and e^π, including $e^\pi = i^{-2i}$ is transcendental number. The proof of this statement can be seen in [2]. $e^\pi = \pi + 20$ can be used to simplify the calculation as well.

3.2   Swapping Encryption Scheme

There are two types of encryption, symmetrical or asymmetrical. We focus on the former one. Since the same key is used, it is important to safe guard that key. The recommended method for exchanging the key is through a secured near field communication system. In this paper we focus on generating the good symmetrical key. Where the key is optimized by using brain storm optimization [6], in the sense that the spectrum of the key is white enough, once applied to the video frame, it will alter the spectrum of the frame, and make it also white.

There are two main encryption algorithms on the market. They are DES (Data Encryption Standard) and AES (Advanced Encryption Standard). We are not using anyone of them on the drone due to the computation burden. The method we used is explained by following pseudo code.

```
Initialize the code
Select the reference key such as eᵖⁱ, pi=3.1415926......
Select the seed key such as 123456789
Select the key space index and a prime number
Obtain hint key by module index against the prime number
Swapping the bit of the seed key according to the hint key
Obtain the user pass phrase
Obtain the video time stamp
Mix them with Fibonacci polynomial formula:
Key(n+1) = Key(n)*passPhrase + Key(n-1)*timeStamp
Compute the spectrum and its standard deviation (std) against
the reference key
Using brain storm optimization obtain the key strength
distribution against the index
If std is small enough to white out the frame, stop, otherwise
go back to step 4.
```

3.3 Brain Storm Optimization

There are many types of optimization algorithm. We focus on the brain storm one, because the key space is huge. The Fig. 4 shows the flow diagram of the basic Brain Storm Optimization (BSO) algorithm [7–11]. The details can be found in the reference, will not be repeated here.

4 Simulation and Experiments

We have done a number of trials for Security companies related to delivery business like Suning and Alibaba partnership. The distance ranges from 200 m to 400 m depends on the obstruction level. The typical FLV files are captured from the field and simulated in Matlab. Following figure shows the actual picture and the spectrum for before/after the convolution with the key, as well as the spectrum of the key itself.

From Fig. 3 we can see that the FLV format has more high frequency component, it requires us to obtain a white enough key, to balance out the peaks after the encryption. From Fig. 4 we can see the keys associated with lower key space index are weak, as the fitness value is high, the smaller value means better fit. In another word, these keys should be avoided (Fig. 2).

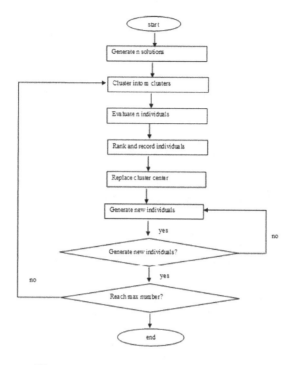

Fig. 2. Flow chat of brain storm algorithm

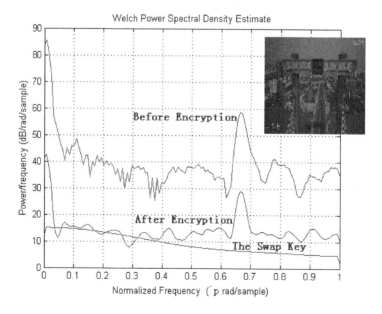

Fig. 3. FLV frame and its spectrum with the swap key

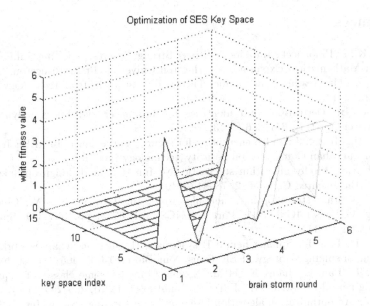

Fig. 4. Solution space and its object space for the key

5   Summary and Future Work

In conclusion, the encryption for live video dedicated to the security communities has its own specific requirements and needs a special attention. We believe that Fibonacci polynomial based on transcendental number swapping key generation algorithm fits for such design. Its spectrum based brain storm optimized key has advantage over a regular fixed permutation and substitution algorithm. It will offer merits such as low power consumption, low latency and high security [4]. The main information we offered here is that the transcendental number in general will provide very white base spectrum that is needed to cover up the video information. The best number we have found so far is e^pi, the next good number is brain storm optimized swapped number. As such, we mixed the two numbers to generate the Fibonacci polynomial, using pass phrase and the time stamp as the variables. This way, we inherit the white spectrum from the previous iteration, mean while using brain storm optimization to find the key space, not just one key or two, which match with the streaming video type.

Finally our encryption algorithm applies to wireless sensor networks, based on swarm intelligence hierarchical learning brainstorming algorithm. The future work is to apply developmental brainstorming algorithm to the wireless sensor network data security, in particular on multimedia encryption.

Acknowledgments. This research was financially supported by GenieView subsidiary HaiQin Technology 2015.4.17.4.20.66. Project and the Suqian Excellence Expert Allowance 2013.18.14.5.9.2. Thanks go to Prof. Yuhui Shi, and Prof. Qihong Yu for discussions.

References

1. Ball, K.M.: Fibonacci's Rabbits Revisited, Strange Curves, Counting Rabbits, and Other Mathematical Explorations. Princeton University Press, Princeton (2003)
2. Qing, Z.: The Aesthetics in Number Theory. Harbin Institute of Technology Press, Harbin (2014)
3. Leonid, B.: Derivations and identities for Fibonacci and Lucas polynomials. Fibonacci Q. **51**(4), 351–366 (2013)
4. Qian, H., Huang, J.: Video encryption for security surveillance. In: IEEE International Carnahan Conference on Security Technology (2007)
5. Yang, X.S.: Firefly algorithm stochastic test functions and design optimization. Int. J. Bio-Inspired Comput. **2**, 78–84 (2010)
6. Shi, Y.: Brain storm optimization algorithm. In: Tan, Y., Shi, Y., Chai, Y., Wang, G. (eds.) ICSI 2011, Part I. LNCS, vol. 6728, pp. 303–309. Springer, Heidelberg (2011)
7. Song, T., Pan, L.: Spiking neural P systems with rules on synapses working in maximum spiking strategy. IEEE Trans. NanoBiosci. **14**(4), 465–477 (2015)
8. Song, T., Pan, L., Jiang, K., et al.: Normal forms for some classes of sequential spiking neural P systems. IEEE Trans. NanoBiosci. **12**(3), 255–264 (2013)
9. Shi, Y.: An optimization algorithm based on brainstorming process. Int. J. Swarm Intell. Res. **2**(4), 35–62 (2011)
10. Schachner, E.: How has the human brain evolved. Sci. Am. Mind, 24(3) (2013). http://www.scientificamerican.com/article/how-has-human-brain-evolved/
11. Wang, X., Miao, Y., Cheng, M.: Finding motifs in DNA sequences using low-dispersion sequences. J. Comput. Biol. **21**(4), 320–329 (2014)

An Evolutionary Approach to Generate Rhythm and Melody Based on Repertories

Jae Hun Jeong and Chang Wook Ahn[✉]

Department of Computer Engineering, Sungkyunkwan University (SKKU),
2066 Seobu-Ro, Suwon 440-746, Republic of Korea
{a12gjang,cwan}@skku.edu

Abstract. This paper presents a new evolutionary approach for automatic composition of a melody. The proposed system consists of three steps. In the first step, we obtain a music template as a repertory from the existing music. Next, rhythm is automatically composed based on the selected template. Lastly, based on the generated rhythm, pitch sequences is rendered on the generated rhythm based on a multi-objective genetic algorithm. The fitness functions are designed based on harmony theory and music template. A set of melodies that encompass two aspects which are stability and tension are obtained from the proposed system. They can cover a very broad range of a user's preferences.

Keywords: Evolutionary music · Multi-objective · Generative music · Automatic music composition

1 Introduction

There have been many attempts to compose music automatically for centuries by musicians and researchers. Before the invention of a computer, simple methods based on mathematic such as Fibonacci sequence, gold ratio, random number and so on are used to compose music [1]. For example, Mozart used dice to randomly arrange music pieces which are pre-composed. After the invention of a computer, various computer algorithms are introduced to make a music [2]. Especially, Markov chain is a one of the eldest and popular techniques.

Recently, the automatic music composition systems have grown with a development of artificial intelligent techniques such as artificial neural network, knowledge-based system, and genetic algorithm [2]. Among them, genetic algorithm has become the most popular technique for music composition, due to the great advantages to handling a creative and artistic domain than the other metaheuristic algorithm [3]. Thus, it has established a new field known as an Evolutionary Music Composition. Evolutionary music composition is a field of composing music using evolutionary process. According to an approach for evaluating music, there are two categories in the evolutionary music composition. The first is an interactive music composition that human users evaluate generated music after listening. Aesthetic preferences to a music differ from individual to

© Springer-Verlag Berlin Heidelberg 2015
M. Gong et al. (Eds.): BIC-TA 2015, CCIS 562, pp. 181–199, 2015.
DOI: 10.1007/978-3-662-49014-3_17

individual. Also, to formalize mathematical model of music is too difficult. The interactive evaluation approach avoids these problems by using human evaluation itself in the fitness evaluation step [4]. For example, GenJam [5] and GP-Music [6] are the representative research in this group. GenJam is an improvisation system for trading fours in real-time based on the interactive genetic algorithm [5]. GP-Music is also the interactive system, but it used a genetic programming and autonomous measure together for melody composition [6].

However, the human evaluator inevitably suffers from a time-consuming and daunting task. This phenomenon is called fitness bottleneck [1]. Most of the performance time of the system is spent by waiting the decision of the human evaluator. In addition, he or she can easily lose a consistency. Especially music systems based on the interactive approach suffer from this phenomenon more than the others, because of the characteristics of time art of a music [1].

Another category of the evolutionary music composition is an automatic evaluation approach. It can produce a lot of desirable music without fitness bottleneck by using automated evaluation. There has been a lot of research based on a machine Learning, rule-based expert system, a rule of thumb and so on [1]. They have tried to automate music evaluation using given music, data or music composition theory, even though it is still hard to capture complete musical model. Contrary to the interactive approach, it has the disadvantage to reflect a users preference to generated music.

In this paper, we suggest an automatic music composition system based on a multi-objective genetic algorithm. The proposed system consists of three steps which are extracting structural music template from a target music, automatic rhythm composition and melody composition. This system can produce a set of melodies that cover two aspects of the music which are stability and tension. We could obtain a set of compositions that are well optimized to the two aspects. In addition, the set of compositions could cover a very broad range of a user's preferences.

This paper consists of five sections including this introductory section. Section 2 begins by explaining a related work and background of this research brief. Section 3 explains the automatic music composition system in detail. Section 4 presents the experimental results. Finally, Sect. 5 concludes with a summary.

2   Related Works

2.1   Multi-objective Optimization

The general multi-objective optimization problem is defined as follows:

$$Minimize_{\mathbf{x}} F(\mathbf{x}) = [f_1(\mathbf{x}), ..., f_k(\mathbf{x})]^T$$
$$subject\,to\,g_i(\mathbf{x}) \leq 0, \ i = \{1, ..., m\} \ and \ h_j(\mathbf{x}) = 0, \ j = \{1, ..., p\} \tag{1}$$

The $\mathbf{x}$ is a n-dimensional decision variable vector $\mathbf{x} = [x_1, x_2, \cdots, x_n]^T$. The $\mathbf{F}(\mathbf{x})$ is a vector of the objectives that have to be optimized. $\mathbf{F}(\mathbf{x})$ assigns $\mathbf{x}$ from the decision variable space to a objective space that can be represented by $\mathbf{F}(\mathbf{x}) = (f_1(\mathbf{x}), \cdots, f_k(\mathbf{x}))$. k is a number of objective functions. $g_i(\mathbf{x}) \leq 0$ and $h_j(\mathbf{x}) = 0$ are constraint conditions that have to be satisfied, while optimizing $\mathbf{F}(\mathbf{x})$. m is a number of inequality constraints and p is a number of equality constraints. The minimization problem can be converted to maximization problems easily by multiplying negative value to the all objective functions.

To solve the multi-objective problem, Pareto dominance concept is introduced. Vector $u = (u_1, \cdots, u_k)$ is said to dominate vector $v = (v_1, \cdots, v_k)$ if and only if $\forall\, i \in \{1, \cdots, k\}$, $u_i \leq v_i \land \exists i \in \{1, \cdots, k\} : u_i < v_i$. A solution $\mathbf{x}$ is said to Pareto optimal if and only if there does not exist another solution $\mathbf{x}'$ that $\mathbf{F}(\mathbf{x})$ is dominated $\mathbf{F}(\mathbf{x}')$. All Pareto optimal for a given multi-objective optimization problem are called the Pareto optimal set (P^*). Solutions in P^* projected into the objective space are called Pareto front.

2.2   Genetic Algorithm

A Genetic Algorithms (GAs) is an algorithm inspired by the process of natural evolution for searching massive solution space [7]. A conventional GAs begin with a population which is generated randomly. After initializing population, a first evaluation is conducted for assigning a fitness value to each individual. Genetic operators such as selection, crossover and mutation are used to produce a new population. At the selection stage, the superior individual survives to the next generation by comparing two individuals which are selected randomly. During crossover, two survivors shuffle their subparts each other. Small parts of the individual are changed randomly by the mutation operator. After then, fitness values are assigned to the new population. These processes continue until satisfying predefined stop criteria.

To solve the multi-objective optimization problem, at the selection stage, Pareto ranking is used instead of fitness value itself [8]. In this paper, the conventional genetic algorithm is used to produce a rhythm automatically. And the multi-objective genetic algorithm is used to produce a set of melodies that encompass stability and tension in a music.

2.3   Music Background

A computational approach to a music is very difficult because music belongs to a field of art. However, for centuries, Harmony theory that guarantees a good sound of simultaneous pitches had been established from the 18th century. It can be a solid foundation for automatic composition.

Tonal music means that music has musical relation based on a specific pitch or chord. Tonality is a phenomenon which is emerging from a progress of music that has a dominant pitch or chord. The concept of the tonality appeared in the early 19th century as an extended concept of a key. Chord means that different two or more pitches sound simultaneously. In the tonal music, a purpose of chord progression makes a tonality based on key, root, or tonic chord. This concept is

Fig. 1. C major diatonic scale member

frequently used in Western music. In addition, most of the pop music is composed based on the tonality (Figs. 1, 2 and 3).

Fig. 2. C major diatonic triad chords

Fig. 3. C major diatonic seventh chords

A scale is a set of notes ordered by fundamental pitch. For example, C major scale consists of 7 notes which are C, D, E, F, G, A and B. We can obtain diatonic chords by stacking three pitches with third intervals. If a third note from a root is a major third interval, the chord is a major. If a third note from a root is a minor third interval, the chord is a minor. Also, we can make seventh diatonic chords by stacking one more note on the top with a third interval (Fig. 4).

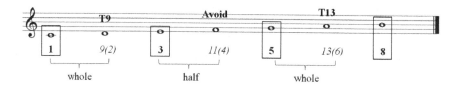

Fig. 4. Chord tones and non-chord tones in the C major scale

Chord tone that belongs to the chord members makes a consonance with the chord sound. On the other hand, a non-chord tone that does not belong to the chord members makes dissonance with the chord. Among the non-chord tone, the note which is different from below the chord tone as much as a whole tone is called tension note. Although they are dissonance, it is acceptable as a tension. On the other hand, the note which is different from below the chord tone as much as a semitone, it is called avoid note. Because they make too much dissonance sound, it cannot be used on the beat. For example, based on the C major seventh chord, 1, 3, 5, 7th notes from root note are chord tone that is consonant with the chord. 9th (or 2nd) note is tension note and 11th (or 4th) note is an avoid note. In the music, through a proper combination of the consonance and dissonance, interesting and sophisticated music could be composed. In this paper, we suggest a method that generates various melodies, according to the relation between chord tone and non-chord tone based on multi-objective optimization.

3   Automatic Melody Composition

We propose a new melody composition system to obtain a set of melodies encompassing two aspects which are stability and tension. The compositions set can cover a very broad range of a user's preferences. Users can select a most favorite composition among them (Fig. 5).

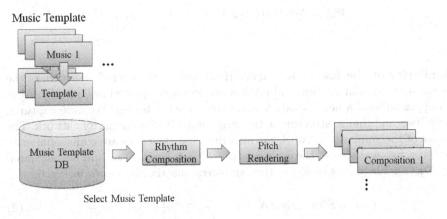

Fig. 5. Overall structure of the proposed automatic music composition system

Our system consists of three steps. In the first step, music template which is related to structural music information is extracted from a target music. On the second step, rhythm whose length is equal to the target is produced automatically based on the conventional genetic algorithm. Then, at the third step, based on the multi-objective genetic algorithm, set of melodies that optimized with regard to stability and tension aspects are produced by rendering pitches to the rhythm composition.

3.1   Music Template

In a lot of research about automatic evolutionary music composition, a similarity with a target music have been used as a fitness value for generating new music [9]. This is a very simple and useful method to obtain an acceptable music result. However, the obtained music from this process is too much similar to the target as a result. It has limited a diversity and creativity of the generated music.

We propose a use of a new music template that consists of a set of metrics that capture an organizing method of the target music. It contains a similarity network, rhythm density, distribution of rhythm duration, and a degree of syncopation.

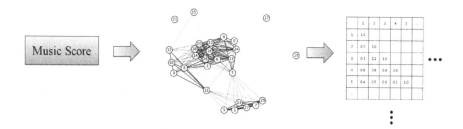

Fig. 6. Similarity matrix from a target score

Similarity of the Each Measures. If we look to the overall structure of the music score, similar rhythm and pitch sequences are repeated periodically. Also, an appearance of a new melody is necessary to avoid boring. We have captured repetition and change structure of the target music to the similarity network. The nodes of the similarity network are measures and the edges are cosine similarity between two melodies of the each measure. Cosine similarity could be calculated by Eq. (2). Then, it is stored in the symmetric matrix like shown in Fig. 6.

$$CosineSimilarity(\mathbf{A}, \mathbf{B}) = \frac{\sum_{i=1}^{n} A_i \times B_i}{\sum_{i=1}^{n}(A_i^2) \times \sum_{i=1}^{n}(B_i^2)}. \tag{2}$$

Rhythm Density. There exist melody parts and break corners in every music. At the measure that gives a feeling of a break, the rhythm density is very low. On the other hand, at the measure that shows the main melody, the rhythm density is relatively high. A vector of the rhythm density values could capture this structural information of the target music. The rhythm density vector could be obtained by the Eq. (3). The $rd(x)$ means a rhythm density value of the x-th measure. Rhythm density can be calculated by dividing the number of notes by the length of the measure. We will use the rhythm density vector to distribute notes properly at the step of rhythm generation.

$$\mathbf{R} = \langle rd(1), rd(2), \cdots, rd(N) \rangle. \tag{3}$$

Distribution of Note Durations. The distribution of note durations vector is obtained to make up a consistent rhythm. A randomly generated rhythm is easy to be unstable, because of lack of consistency of use of note durations. Thus, we resolve the problem by using the distribution of the note durations from the target music. If the users want to high frequency of the specific rhythm duration, it can be modified easily by their preferences. The distribution of the rhythm durations can be represented by a vector whose length is a number of the rhythm duration types. Usually, the length of the vector is a 16 which means a whole note. The vector is calculated by Eq. (4). The $count(x)$ means a number of x-th notes in the target music.

$$\mathbf{D} = \frac{\langle count(1), count(2), \cdots, count(16) \rangle}{number\ of\ notes}. \tag{4}$$

Degree of Syncopation. Syncopation is an effect that changes an accent position of weak and strong beats. It could be calculated by Eq. (5). The R is a rest note or holding part by tie preceding N which is a note. The value of the R and N refers to the Table 1. When the R value is bigger than the value of the N, the syncopation occurs. The degree of the syncopation could be calculated by summing all $R - N$ when the syncopation occurs [10]. We make a vector of the degree of the syncopation every four measures.

$$Degree\ of\ Syncopation = \sum (R - N) \times u(R - N). \tag{5}$$

Table 1. Accent degrees at each position of a measure

Strong				Weak				Medium				Weak			
S	W	M	w	S	W	M	w	S	W	M	w	S	W	M	w
0	−4	−3	−4	−2	−4	−3	−4	−1	−4	−3	−4	−2	−4	−3	−4

3.2 Automatic Rhythm Generation

Our goal of the rhythm generation part is to produce creative rhythm based on the target rhythm structure. Figure 7 shows a rhythm generation process. This process is based on the genetic algorithm. At the first stage, we extracted music template that contains structural information from the target music. Then randomly generated rhythms are evaluated by rhythm fitness functions which are proposed in this paper. The new population of the rhythms is produced through the genetic operators such as selection, crossover, and mutation. This process is repeated until satisfying stop criteria. The best solution is selected as a rhythm template for a next step.

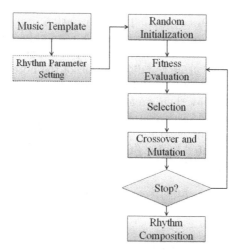

Fig. 7. Flowchart of the proposed automatic rhythm composition system

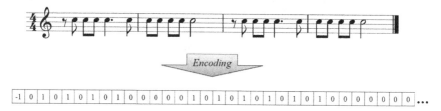

Fig. 8. Encoding rhythm to a chromosome

Rhythm Representation. Rhythm can be encoded to the linear chromosome as shown in Fig. 8. A single element of chromosome means a duration of sixteenth notes. Zero means the holding of the left side note. In other words, the number of the successive zeros which are the right side of the note means the duration of the note as described in Table 2. For example, the duration of the note that does not neighbor with zero on the right is a sixteenth note. If the three successive zeros adjoin at the right side of the note, the duration of the note is a quarter note. The rest note is represented by negative integer values. A length of the rest is represented by the same way.

Genetic Operators for Rhythm. The genetic operator plays an important role to produce new rhythms from parents rhythms. Figure 9 shows the genetic operators for rhythm generation. A one-point crossover is used to shuffle part of the rhythm. Two or three points crossover also can be useful. But the uniform crossover is not suitable because music rhythm has a high dependency with neighboring notes. Mutation operator switches the randomly selected value to 1, 0 or −1.

Table 2. Note duration according to the rhythm representation

Representation	Note duration
1	Sixteenth note
10	Eighteenth note
100	Dotted eighteenth note
1000	Quarter note
100000	Dotted quarter note
10000000	Half note
100000000000	Dotted half note
1000000000000000	Whole note

Rhythm Fitness Functions. We use four metrics for evaluating a generated rhythm. Our evaluating method is based on the similarity with the target music. Instead of rhythm itself, we use structural information which was extracted in the first step. It allows this system to automatically generate various and creative rhythms.

$$Fitness_{rhythm}(x) = \alpha SM + \beta RD + \gamma DD + \delta DS \qquad (6)$$

SM is a cosine similarity of the similarity matrix of the target and generated rhythm. The way of obtaining a similarity matrix from music was described in the Sect. 3. This is considered as a most important measure because it determines the overall procedure of the generated rhythm. Thus, α which is the weight of the similarity matrix is assigned 5 as the best value.

RD is a cosine similarity between the rhythm density vector of the target and generated rhythm. Due to this metric, the generated rhythm has a rest part at proper positions by imitating the density of the target. The β which is a weight of the rhythm density is assigned 4 as a second best.

DD is a cosine similarity of the distribution of note durations vector between the target and generated rhythm. By imitating the distribution of the length of the notes which are units of the rhythm, it drives the generated rhythm to the most stable rhythm that has a consistency. The γ which is a weight value of the DD is assigned 2.

DS is a cosine similarity of a degree of syncopation vector between the target and generated rhythm. It is a metric for making rhythm whose degree of syncopation is equal to the target music. The δ which is a weight value of the DS is 1.

We used a genetic algorithm to get the rhythm composition by optimizing Eq. (6). A 2-size tournament selection, crossover and mutation operators that we described in the previous part, are applied.

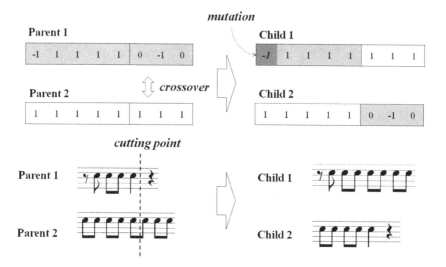

Fig. 9. Genetic operators of rhythm composition

3.3   Automatic Melody Composition

Our final goal is to automatically compose a set of melodies that encompass various preferences with respect to a stability and tension. The overall process of the proposed automatic melody composition system based on the multi-objective genetic algorithm is described in Fig. 10. Based on the rhythm which was produced in the previous step, pitches are rendered randomly to the all population. The population is evaluated in terms of stability and tension considering chord

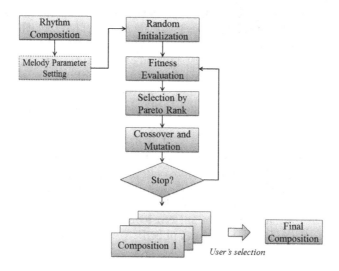

Fig. 10. Flowchart of the proposed automatic melody composition system

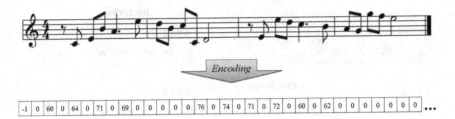

| -1 | 0 | 60 | 0 | 64 | 0 | 71 | 0 | 69 | 0 | 0 | 0 | 0 | 0 | 76 | 0 | 74 | 0 | 71 | 0 | 72 | 0 | 60 | 0 | 62 | 0 | 0 | 0 | 0 | 0 | 0 | 0 | 0 | ··· |

Fig. 11. Encoding melody to a chromosome

progression. Then, Pareto rank is assigned. Selection is conducted based on the Pareto rank. Crossover and mutation produce a new population. These processes are iterated until satisfying stop criteria. Finally, we can obtain a set of solutions that encompass the two aspects simultaneously (Fig. 11).

Melody Representation. Melody consists of the sequences of the notes consist of durations and pitches. Melody would be composed by rendering a pitch sequence on the rhythm from the result of the previous step. It can be done by alternating positive integer of the rhythm representation to the pitch values of Table 3.

Table 3. Mapping table of pitch and rest

Note	Rest	···	B3	C4	C#4	D4	D#4	E4	F4	F#	···
Value	−1	···	59	60	61	62	63	64	65	66	···

Genetic Operators for Melody Composition. Genetic operators for producing new melodies from two parents melodies are described in Fig. 12. One-point crossover shuffles part of the melody. Then randomly selected pitch is modified to another pitch in a valid range. Only pitch changes in the melody mutation operators, not rhythmic elements. For example, in Fig. 12, the crossover point is selected on the 5th position of the parents melodies. The rear parts of the melodies change their position by the crossover. The first pitch of the child 1 is modified from 69 to 65 by mutation operator.

Multi-objective Fitness Functions. In this step, using the rhythm composition which is obtained in the previous step as a template, pitch sequence are rendered considering given chord progression. We designed two fitness functions for melody evaluation that contain trade-off relations which are stability and tension.

Chord tone members can be used as a most important elements to make a melody which is very stable and well harmonized with the chord sound. Thus, in terms of stability, chord tone becomes the most important key factor.

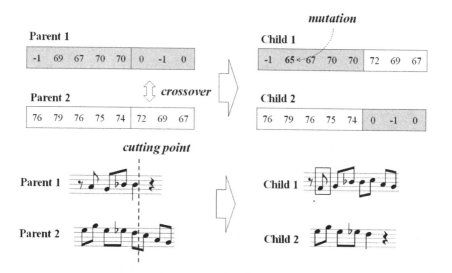

Fig. 12. Genetic operators of melody composition

$$fitness_s(x) = \alpha CT(x) + \beta ST(x) + \gamma ML(x) + \delta SM(x) - Penalty \quad (7)$$

$$CT(x) = \frac{\sum_{i=1}^{n} c(x_i) \times (z(x_i) + 1)}{total\ length} \quad (8)$$

$$c(k) = \begin{cases} 1 & if\ note\ k\ is\ a\ chord\ tone \\ 0 & else \end{cases} \quad (9)$$

The first fitness function that evaluates melody in terms of stability is designed this background as shown in the Eq. (7). $CT(x)$ measures a degree of chord tones in the melody x as shown in Eq. (9). The $c(x_i)$ return 1 if i-th note is a chord tone. Otherwise, it returns 0. The $z(x_i)$ return a number of successive zeros which is the right side of the i-th note.

$$ST(x) = \frac{\sum_{i=1}^{n} s(x_i) \times (z(x_i + 1))}{total\ length} \quad (10)$$

$$s(k) = \begin{cases} 1 & if\ note\ k\ is\ a\ scale\ tone \\ 0 & else \end{cases} \quad (11)$$

$$ML1(x) = \sum_{i=1}^{n-2} \{\alpha step(x_i, x_{i+1}, x_{i+2}) + \beta leap(x_i, x_{i+1}, x_{i+2})\} \quad (12)$$

$$step(x, y, z) = \begin{cases} 1 & if\ |x - y| \le 2\ and\ |y - z| \le 2 \\ 0 & otherwise \end{cases} \quad (13)$$

$$leap(x, y, z) = \begin{cases} 1 & if \ |x - y| \le 2 \ and \ |y - z| > 2 \\ 1 & if \ |x - y| > 2 \ and \ |y - z| \le 2 \\ 0 & otherwise \end{cases} \quad (14)$$

In the same way, the $ST(x)$ measures a degree of scale tone in the melody x as described in the Eq. (10). The $ML1(x)$ measures a melody line. The *step* (x_i, x_{i+1}, x_{i+2}) returns 1 if the successive three notes are connected as step motion. Otherwise, it returns 0. The $leap(x_i, x_{i+1}, x_{i+2})$ returns 1 if the successive three notes are connected as combination of step and leap motion. Otherwise, it returns 0.

Definitely undesirable elements are penalized for eliminating them. First, too much big intervals which are over an octave are penalized. Even though these big intervals sometimes might make good a melody in a very specific condition, usually it sounds unpleasant. Second, a successive same direction interval which is over an octave is also penalized. This is an indirect case of the first penalty. Third, unpleasant dissonance is penalized. An avoid note which is on the strong beats or long duration, has to be avoided, because it sounds very offensively. Fourth, too many leaping motions that are more than step motion is penalized. A melody which contains too many leaping motions is prone to be distracted. A possibility of generating failed melody is reduced noticeably by eliminating these undesirable features in the melody.

A melody that only consists of the chord tone easily can be boring. Thus, tension elements could be added to make melody interesting and sophisticated. A tension which appears on the strong beat has to be solved by following chord tone as a step motion. If this tension and resolve motion fails, the tension sounds unpleasant. Thus, in terms of tension, tension and resolve motion is a key factor.

$$fitness_t(x) = \alpha TR(x) + \beta SN(x) + \gamma ML(x) + \delta SM(x) - Penalty \quad (15)$$

$$TR(x) = \frac{t(x_i)c(x_{i+1})u(z(x_{i+1}) - z(x_i))}{total \ length - 1} \quad (16)$$

$$t(k) = \begin{cases} 1 & if \ note \ k \ is \ a \ tension \ note \\ 0 & else \end{cases} \quad (17)$$

Equation (15) describes the second fitness that evaluates melody in terms of a tension. $TR(x)$ measures the tension and resolve motion. $t(x_i)$ returns 1 if x_i is a tension note, otherwise it returns 0. $c(x_{i+1})$ returns 1 if x_{i+1} is a chord tone, otherwise it returns 0. $u(x)$ is a unit step function that returns 1 when the $x \ge 0$ (Fig. 13).

Also, non-chord tone embellishes the melody in various ways. They are described as follows:

- Passing tone: Passing tone is a non-chord tone that connect the two chord tones as a step motion in the same direction. If the passing tone is accented, it creates tension and resolve motion.

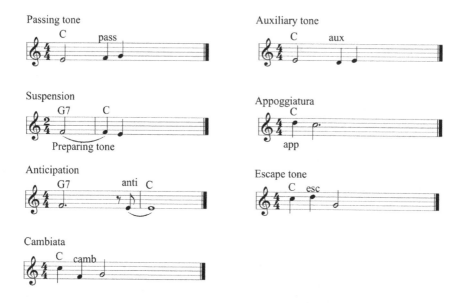

Fig. 13. Non-chord tones that embellish the melody line

- Neighbor tone: Neighbor tone or auxiliary note is a non-chord tone that connect the two chord tones as a step motion in the different direction. Thus, it shows up-down or down-up melody line.
- Suspension: Suspension is a chord tone which is changed to non-chord tone suspending sound to the next chord. And then it is resolved by chord tone as a step motion.
- Appoggiatura: An appoggiatura is a non-chord tone that appears on the strong beat. It processes chord tone by step motion.
- Anticipation: Anticipation is a non-chord tone which is prepared by chord tone as a step motion and then followed by chord tone which is a same pitch changing chords.
- Escape tone: Escape tone or eschappee is a non-chord tone which is prepared by chord tone as a step motion and then followed by chord tone as a leap motion in a different direction.
- Cambiata: Cambiata is a non-chord tone on the weak beat that follows the chord tone by leap motion. And it goes to the chord tone by step motion.

$$ML2(x) = \sum c(x_i)n(x_{i+1})c(x_{i+2}) \left\{ \alpha step(x_i, x_{i+1}, x_{i+2}) + \beta leap(x_i, x_{i+1}, x_{i+2}) \right\} \tag{18}$$

$$n(k) = \begin{cases} 1 & if \ note \ k \ is \ a \ nonchord \ tone \\ 0 & else \end{cases} \tag{19}$$

The $ML2(x)$ measures melody lines considering non-chord tone. The $c(x_i)$ $n(x_{i+1})c(x_{i+2})$ means that non-chord tone which is between chord tone. *step*

(x_i, x_{i+1}, x_{i+2}) returns 1, when the successive three notes are connected as a step motion. Otherwise, it returns 0. It awards the passing tone and neighboring tone. The $leap(x_i, x_{i+1}, x_{i+2})$ return 1 when the successive three notes are connected as a combination of step and leap motion. Otherwise, it returns 0. It awards the other non-chord tones which embellish the melody line. The α which is the weight value of the *step* is assigned a higher value than β which is a weight value of the *leap*. Because encouraging step motion is good to make a smooth melody line. The $SM(x)$ evaluates a cosine similarity between the similarity matrix of the target and generated melody x.

The two fitness functions evaluate melody with their point of view. They have trade-off relation. Thus, it is impossible to find the best single solution. The multi-objective genetic algorithm can give a set of solutions that are optimized at the two aspects simultaneously. At the next section, we will explain the optimizing process of the two fitness functions for generating melody using multi-objecitve optimization algorithm.

Optimizing Melody Fitness Functions. If we already know information about music that the user wants to exactly, we can generate the one best solution. However, when we have to generate music without that information, generation of the music set that can cover a broad range of the user's preferences can be a good alternative. Thus, we proposed the multi-objective approach to generate set of melodies that encompass two fitness functions in the trade-off relation. We used a NSGA-II (Non-dominated Sorting Genetic Algorithm II) to optimize the two fitness functions simultaneously. NSGA-II has been widely used in various fields because of the fast convergence speed and the ability to find good spread solutions. The process of the optimization of the two fitness functions is described as follows:

First, N-size P_0 is randomly created and assigned Pareto rank based on the nondomination. Then new population Q_0 whose size is same with P_0 is created by operating binary tournament selection, crossover and mutation to P_0.

1. Emerging P_t and Q_t to R_t.
2. Evaluate R_t and sort them in descending order according to the Pareto rank.
3. P_{t+1} is created by selecting upper 50 % of R_t (If the Pareto ranks is same, individual which has a higher crowding distance is selected) [8].
4. Q_{t+1} is created from P_{t+1} by applying binary tournament selection, crossover and mutation operators.
5. $t = t + 1$.

This process is repeated until satisfying stop criteria. At the last iteration, the group whose Pareto rank is 1, is selected as a solution set. The melodies in the set of solutions can cover a very broad range of a user's preferences.

4   Composition Results

Automatic melody generation using the proposed system is described in this section. We chose a lyrical music of an A major scale. From the target music, we

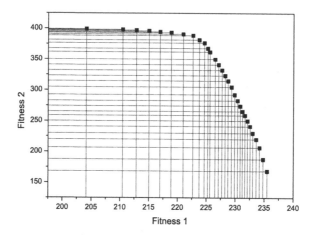

Fig. 14. Pareto front of the generated compositions

Fig. 15. Composition which is optimized in terms of stability

Fig. 16. Composition which is optimized in terms of tension

extracted similarity matrix, rhythm density vector, distribution of note duration vector, and syncopation vector. We could obtain the 400 different melodies which are well spread in the multi-objective space as shown in Fig. 14.

We analyzed two melodies which are the extreme cases for the validating ability of melody composition of the proposed system. Figure 14 shows a Pareto front of the final results. Fitness 1 evaluates the melody with respect to stability. Fitness 2 evaluates the melody in terms of tension. Thus, the solution which is on the right side edge is the best solution in terms of stability. On the other hand, the solution which is on the left side edge is the best solution with respect to a tension.

Figure 15 shows the composition which is optimized in terms of stability. If we look to the first four bar melodies, it consists of only chord tones. This melody sounds very stable with the chord sound. It may sound like a children's song because of the lack of the non-chord tone. On the other hand, Fig. 16 shows the most sophisticated melody. The box on the music score means a non-chord tone. The first four bar melody contains many non-chord tones in contrast with the Fig. 15. All non-chord tone are resolved by following chord tone as a step motion. We have uploaded our composition results on the http://seal.skku.edu/EvolutionaryMusic/.

5   Conclusion

We proposed new automatic melody composition system based on the multi-objective genetic algorithm. We could get a set of melodies that are optimized with respect to stability and tension. Thus, the proposed system could cover very broad preferences of users by one execution. Also, the proposed system could generate always new melodies which are very different from the target music. Only structural information is similar to the target. The melody is composed by the evolutionary process whose the fitness functions based on a harmony theory and abstract level music information of the target music.

Non-musician who has no expert knowledge of music composition could compose full-length music not just a musical piece using the proposed system. Therefore, our technique can be developed to a new software for supporting non-musicians. Also, it can be a useful tool for musicians because it can provide an infinite musical idea for the user.

We did not deal with a way of generating chord progression. Because we focused on an automatic melody composition in this paper. By combining the chord generation system, the creativity of this system could be extended. We remain it as a future work.

The proposed system has succeeded to compose melodies of an ordinary level. But, the automatic composition of a music that can move people is very difficult. It could be possible by an integrated research of computational aesthetic evaluation with a cognitive science of music.

Acknowledgement. This work was supported under the framework of international cooperation program managed by National Research Foundation of Korea (NRF-2013 K2A1B9066056).

References

1. Dostál, M.: Evolutionary music composition. In: Zelinka, I., Snasel, V., Abraham, A. (eds.) Handbook of Optimization. ISRL, vol. 38, pp. 935–964. Springer, Heidelberg (2013)
2. Miranda, E.R., Biles, J.A.: Evolutionary Computer Music. Springer, London (2007)
3. Gartland-Jones, A., Copley, P.: The suitability of genetic algorithms for musical composition. Contemp. Music Rev. **22**(3), 43–55 (2003)
4. Tokui, N., Iba, H.: Music composition with interactive evolutionary computation. In: Proceedings of the 3rd International Conference on Generative Art, vol. 17(2) (2000)
5. Biles, J.A.: GenJam: evolution of a jazz improviser. In: Creative Evolutionary Systems, vol. 168 (2002)

6. Johanson, B., Poli, R.: GP-music: an interactive genetic programming system for music generation with automated fitness raters. University of Birmingham, Cognitive Science Research Centre (1998)
7. Marques, M., et al.: Music composition using genetic evolutionary algorithms, pp. 714–719 (2000)
8. Deb, K., et al.: A fast and elitist multiobjective genetic algorithm: NSGA-II. IEEE Trans. Evol. Comput. **6**(2), 182–197 (2002)
9. Jensen, J.H.: Evolutionary music composition: a quantitative approach (2011)
10. Fitch, W.T., Rosenfeld, A.J.: Perception and production of syncopated rhythms. Interdisc. J. **25**(1), 43–58 (2007)

Parallel Implementation of P Systems for Data Clustering on GPU

Jie Jin[1], Hui Liu[1], Fengjuan Wang[1], Hong Peng[1(⊠)], and Jun Wang[2]

[1] School of Computer and Software Engineering,
Center for Radio Administration and Technology Development, Xihua University,
Chengdu 610039, China
ph.xhu@hotmail.com
[2] School of Electrical and Information Engineering, Xihua University,
Chengdu 610039, Sichuan, China

Abstract. Membrane clustering algorithm is a novel membrane computing-inspired clustering algorithm, whose key component is a P system. Although P systems are distributed and parallel computing models, the membrane clustering algorithm was only realized in a serial algorithm because of serial architecture of current computer. Therefore, the membrane clustering algorithm was not able to exhibit the parallel computing characteristic of P systems. This paper focuses on parallel implementation of membrane clustering algorithm and proposes a GPU-based parallel computing framework and parallel version of the membrane clustering algorithm. In the parallel implementation, the blocks are used to represent the cells, while threads are used to realize the evolution-communication mechanism of objects. The comparison results on several artificial and real-life data sets demonstrate that the proposed parallel version not only ensures the clustering quality of the membrane clustering algorithm but also evidently reduce its computing time.

Keywords: Membrane computing · P systems · Data clustering · GPU

1 Introduction

As a branch of natural computing, membrane computing aims to abstract the computing models from the structure and functioning of living cells as well as interaction of living cells in tissues and organs [1]. Membrane computing is a class of distributed parallel computing models, also known as P systems or membrane systems. In past years, a various of P systems and variants have been proposed, and most of them are universal and effective [2–5, 15, 21, 25–27]. Distributed parallel computing is an important characteristic of P systems, however, the parallel computing characteristic can not be realized in current computers due to its serial architecture. Thus, the parallel implementation of a variety of P systems has become a hot topic in membrane computing area in recent years. Fortunately, general parallel computing devices such as GPU and GPGPU provide a effective way to realize the parallel computing characteristic of P systems. In recent years,

© Springer-Verlag Berlin Heidelberg 2015
M. Gong et al. (Eds.): BIC-TA 2015, CCIS 562, pp. 200–211, 2015.
DOI: 10.1007/978-3-662-49014-3_18

a variety of P systems and variants have been simulated or realized in GPU [6–8,12], for example, spiking neural P systems, cell-like P systems, tissue-like P systems, P systems with active membranes.

Recently, application of membrane computing in real-world problems has received a great deal of attention. P systems have been used to solve a lot of real-world problems, such as DNA motif finding [9–11], optimization problems [13], fuzzy reasoning [14], fault diagnosis [16], image processing [17] and signal processing [18]. In order to apply the idea of membrane computing to process data clustering problem, Huang et al. [19] proposed a novel clustering algorithm, PSO-MC, which used the velocity-location model and the object's communication mechanism to determine the cluster centers. By using differential evolution mechanism in stead of velocity-location model, Peng et al. [20] presented a clustering algorithm, called DE-MC. Jiang et al. [22] reported a membrane clustering method of using genetic operations as evolution rules. In Peng et al. [23], a membrane clustering algorithm with hybrid evolutionary mechanisms was discussed. In addition, Peng et al. [24] used membrane systems to solve fuzzy clustering problem. From the realization point of view, however, the membrane computing-inspired clustering algorithms are still serial algorithms rather than parallel algorithms, so they are not able to reflect the parallel computing advantage of P systems. The motivation behind this work is how to realize the membrane computing-inspired clustering algorithm on GPU. The main contribution stays in proposing a realization framework of membrane clustering algorithm and developing a parallel version of PSO-MC algorithm. In the realization framework, "blocks" and "threads" in GPU architecture simulate the cells and objects in P systems respectively, which can run in maximum parallel way.

The rest of paper is organized as follows. The proposed PSO-MC algorithm is discussed in detail in Sect. 2. Section 3 presents experimental results to illustrate the efficiency of the algorithm. Finally, Sect. 4 includes the conclusion.

2   Preliminary

2.1   Membrane Computing-Inspired Clustering Algorithms

This section reviews a membrane computing-inspired clustering algorithm, PSO-MC [19], which integrates the velocity-location model in particle swarm optimization (PSO) as its evolution rules of objects. PSO-MC uses a tissue-like P system as its computing framework, which is used to determine the optimal cluster centers for a data clustering problem. The tissue-like P system can be formally described as follows:

A tissue-like P system of degree q is defined as

$$\Pi = (O, w_1, w_2, \ldots, w_q, R_1, R_2, \ldots, R_q, R', i_o) \tag{1}$$

where

(1) O is a set of all objects.
(2) w_i is initial multiset of objects in ith cell, $1 \leq i \leq q$.
(3) R_i is finite set of evolution rules in ith cell, which are described by the following velocity-location model, $1 \leq i \leq q$:

$$\begin{cases} V_j^i = w \cdot V_j^i + c_1 r_1 (P_{best}^i - Z_j^i) + c_2 r_2 (G_{best} - Z_j^i) \\ Z_j^i = Z_j^i + V_j^i \end{cases} \tag{2}$$

where w is the inertia weight, c_1 and c_2 are two constants, r_1 and r_2 are two random number in $[0,1]$; Z_j^i is jth object in ith cell and V_j^i is the corresponding velocity vector; P_{best}^i is the best object in ith cell, while G_{best} is the best object in the whole system.
(4) R' is finite set of communication rules of the form: $< i, Z/Z', 0 >$, where Z and Z' are two objects, $i = 1, 2, \ldots, q$.
(5) i_o indicates the output region.

Figure 1 shows the tissue-like P system, which consists of the q cells labeled by $1, 2, \ldots, q$. The outer region of the q cells is called the environment, and it is labeled by 0. Each cell contains some objects, and its number is denoted by m. The objects in cells are evolved, and then some of them are communicated between two cells or between cells and the environment.

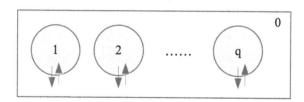

Fig. 1. The membrane structure of the designed cell-like P system

Suppose that in a d-dimensional space, the clustering problem is considered to partition data set $D = \{X_1, X_2, \ldots, X_n\}$ into k clusters, $C_1, C_2, \ldots, C_k$, where $z_1, z_2, \ldots, z_k$ are the corresponding cluster centers. In order to process the clustering problem, the objects in the system are designed as a $k \times d$-dimensional vector, shown in Fig. 2,

$$Z = (z_1, z_2, \ldots, z_k) = (z_{11}, z_{12}, \ldots, z_{1d}, \ldots, z_{k1}, z_{k2}, \ldots, z_{kd}) \tag{3}$$

where $z_i = (z_{i1}, z_{i2}, \ldots, z_{id})$ is ith cluster center.

In order to evaluate each object in cells, the following measure is used as its fitness function:

$$f(Z) = M(C_1, C_2, \ldots, C_k) = \sum_{i=1}^{k} \sum_{X_j \in C_i} d(X_j, z_i) \tag{4}$$

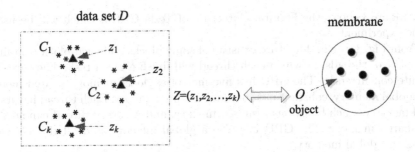

Fig. 2. The representation of objects in cells

where $d(X_j, z_i)$ denotes the distance of data point X_j to ith cluster center z_i. Generally, the smaller the f value, the better the object, and vice versa.

Based on the tissue-like P system, PSO-MC algorithm can be described as follows:

Step 1. Loading data: give input parameters, q, m, k, c_1, c_2 as well as data set $D = \{X_1, X_2, \ldots, X_n\}$;

Step 2. Initialization: generate m initial objects for each of the q cells respectively;

Step 3. For each object in the q cells, execute the following evolution and communication operations
   (a) Object evolution: evolve the object by Eq. (2);
   (b) Object evaluation: compute the fitness value of the object by Eq. (4);
   (c) Object communication: transport the object to update the global best object G_{best};

Step 4. Halting judgment: if maximum iteration number is reached, the system halts and export the global best object G_{best}; otherwise, go to Step 3.

As usual in P systems, the q cells as computing units work in parallel. However, the q cells are executed one by one and objects in them are processed in serial because of the serial architecture of current computers. So, the algorithm described above is essentially a serial version of PSO-MC. From the serial version, it can be observed that the time complexity of PSO-MC mainly stays on the object's evolution, evaluation and communication operations. Let T denote the maximum iteration number of the algorithm. Thus, the time complexity of PSO-MC is $O(qmT)$. So, the parallel computing advantage of PSO-MC can not be really reflected. In this work, the parallel implementation of PSO-MC on GPU will be developed.

2.2 GPU

Compute unified device architecture (CUDA) is a programming model proposed by NVIDIA corporation in 2007, which can effectively apply its powerful processing ability and larger memory bandwidth to complete the general computation task. Figure 3 shows the Fermi architecture of Tesla C2075, which will be used in the experiment.

From Fig. 3, the architecture consists of some blocks and each block contains a number of threads, in which each thread will finish a given task. The threads execute concurrently. The GPU has five memories: local memory, shared memory, global memory, constant memory and texture memory. Each thread has its a local memory. Each block has a shared memory and its every thread can access the shared memory. The GPU has also a global memory, and all threads can access the global memory.

In the architecture, a computation task can be realized by using the HOST+ GPU way. Usually, some non-parallel components, such as data loading and initialization, are accomplished in a host, while parallel components should be realized in GPU.

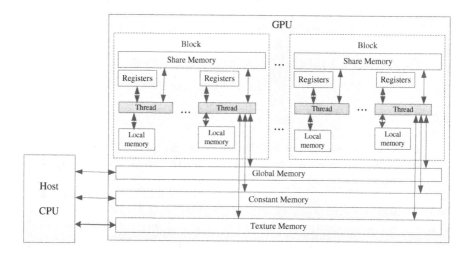

Fig. 3. Fermi architecture of Tesla C2075 (GPU)

3   Parallel Implementation of PSO-MC on GPU

As described above, the serial version of PSO-MC includes six main steps: loading data/parameters, initialization, object evolution, object evaluation, object communication and halting judgment. The P system used consists of q cells and each cell has m objects. In the content of P systems, the q cells as computing units run in parallel. In this work, the P system is considered to work in maximum parallel way by applying the GPU's parallel computing advantage, that is, objects in the cells execute the evolution, evaluation and communication operations. In order to synchronize the object's evolution-communication operation, a synchronization operation is introduced into the parallel version. Figure 4 gives the proposed parallel framework of PSO-MC algorithm.

In the parallel framework, several main computing steps will be realized in CPU and GPU respectively. According to the principle of P systems, cells work in parallel and the object's evolution-communications are executed concurrently. Therefore, the evolution, evaluation and communication steps will be realized in GPU, also including synchronization operation and halting judgment. However, loading data, initialization and output result are achieved in CPU. The detail realizations are described as follows.

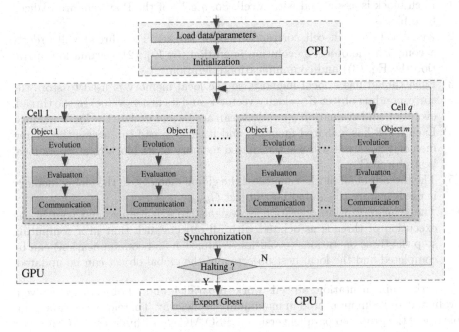

Fig. 4. The parallel computing framework of PSO-MC algorithm

3.1 CPU Realization

The three steps of PSO-MC, such as loading data, initialization and output result, are usually realized in CPU. The three steps can be described as follows:

(1) Loading data. Read data set, $D = \{X_1, X_2, \ldots, X_n\}$, and give the parameters, q, m, k, c_1, c_2.
(2) Initialization. Generate m initial objects for each of the q cells randomly, which is same to serial version of PSO-MC.
(3) Output result. Transport the global best object G_{best} from GPU to CPU and export it as the computing result.

3.2 GPU Realization

The architecture in Fig. 3 shows that a GPU has some blocks and each block also contains a number of threads. Moreover, the GPU has five kinds of memories: shared memory, local memory, global memory, constant memory and texture memory. The first three memories are used to store the objects, local best objects P_{best}^i, and global best object G_{best}, respectively.

According to the architecture in Fig. 3, the GPU components of PSO-MC algorithm can be described as follows.

(1) Each block is associated with a cell. So, q cells of the P system are realized by q blocks.
(2) An object in each cell corresponds to a thread. The thread will orderly accomplish the object's evolution operation (by Eq. (2)), evaluation operation (by Eq. (3)) and communication operation.
(3) Each thread has a local memory, so the local memory is used to store the corresponding object Z, velocity vector V and its fitness value. In the thread, evolution and evaluation operations can access and update the local memory.
(4) Each block has a shared memory, and it each thread can access the shared memory. So, a cell will use the shared memory of its block to store its local best object P_{best}^i.
(5) The threads of all blocks can access the global memory, so the global memory is used to store the global best object G_{best}.
(6) The synchronization operation is designed to synchronize and control the execution of threads associated with all objects such that in a computing step the three operations (evolution, evaluation and communication) can be completed and the local best objects and the global object can be updated.

In the implementation, all cells work in parallel, and all objects are evolved, evaluated and communicated in maximum parallel way. Therefore, the time complexity of the proposed parallel version of PSO-MC algorithm is $O(T)$. Compared with its serial version, the proposed parallel version can really exhibit the parallel computing advantage of P systems.

4   Experiment Results and Analysis

In order to evaluate the performance of the proposed parallel version of PSO-MC, five artificial data sets and four real-life data sets are chosen to compare it and the corresponding serial version, which are AD_5_2, $data\_9\_2$, $data7$, $square4$, sym_3_22, $LungCancer$, $LiveDisorder$, $Glass$ and $Iris$. The detail information of the data sets is provided in Table 1. The comparison includes two aspects: clustering performance and computing time. The M value defined in Eq. (4) will be used to measure the clustering qualities of the different clustering algorithms.

Table 1. The used artificial and four real-life data sets.

Data se	No. of data	Dimension	No. of clusters	Description
AD_5_2	250	2	5	artificial
data_9_2	1800	2	9	artificial
Sym_3_32	600	2	3	artificial
data_7	1200	2	4	artificial
square4	1000	2	4	artificial
NewThyroid	215	5	3	real-life
Live Disorder	345	6	2	real-life
Iris	150	4	3	real-life

Table 2. The average computing times of the parallel and serial versions of PSO-MC algorithm on the different data sets (second).

Data set	Version	The number of cells						
		4	8	16	32	64	128	256
AD_5_2	Parallel	36.63	39.76	86.76	159.56	363.32	707.56	1338.76
	Serial	79.21	253.10	477.32	638.71	1666.20	2340.26	16338.87
data_9_2	Parallel	127.02	234.94	400.52	762.53	1443.86	2321.54	4038.47
	Serial	620.81	1293.68	2221.54	5057.93	10146.87	25719.74	38923.72
Sym_3_32	Parallel	42.35	62.74	112.30	208.85	338.92	625.10	1101.86
	Serial	119.21	302.16	599.85	1129.38	2222.03	3906.88	9509.30
data_7	Parallel	31.24	31.61	32.12	50.21	73.20	130.41	252.36
	Serial	35.39	55.99	111.70	230.02	445.33	895.61	1767.49
square4	Parallel	63.82	109.32	203.68	397.98	502.24	1251.58	2839.61
	Serial	230.82	451.76	903.57	1809.12	3911.23	8343.87	23993.82
NewThyroid	Parallel	20.55	20.08	21.36	40.55	61.58	106.89	224.94
	Serial	18.66	35.32	71.38	140.73	283.79	572.96	1134.00
Live disorder	Parallel	23.32	25.00	50.71	88.51	149.32	209.32	386.71
	Serial	33.42	65.55	131.28	248.91	509.58	1098.71	2245.51
Iris	Parallel	20.86	22.35	73.36	89.95	112.55	138.62	303.73
	Serial	49.90	59.70	100.55	196.76	400.36	799.79	1618.68

The computing time can evaluate the improvement extent of the proposed parallel version of PSO-MC by comparing the parallel version and the corresponding serial version.

In the experiment, the used GPU is Tesla's C2075. The parameters of PSO-MC are: $c_1 = c_2 = 1.2$, $m = 1024$. In order to test the effect of the number of cells, q is chosen to be 4, 8, 16, 32, 64, 128 and 256, respectively.

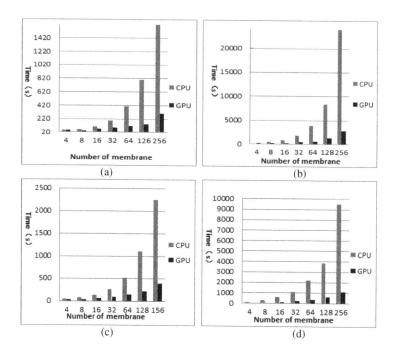

Fig. 5. The comparison of the parallel and serial versions of PSO-MC algorithm in terms of computing times: (a) Iris; (b) Square4; (c) Live disorder; (d) Newthyroid.

Table 2 shows the average computing times of the parallel and serial versions of PSO-MC algorithm on the different data sets, where the results of $q = 4, 8, 16, 32, 64, 128, 256$ are provided respectively. It can be found from Table 2 that for all of data sets the computing times of parallel version of PSO-MC algorithm are lower than that of its serial version. We can also observe that With the increase of q the computing times of the parallel version are reduced significantly. Figure 5 shows the comparison of the computing times of the parallel and serial versions of PSO-MC algorithm on four data sets, Iris, Square4, Live disorder and Newthyroid. The comparison results illustrate the advantage of the parallel version in term of computing time.

Table 3 provides the comparison results of clustering performances of the parallel and serial versions of PSO-MC algorithm on the nine data sets, which are corresponding to the results of $q = 4, 8, 16, 32, 64, 128, 256$ respectively. Table 3 clear shows that the parallel and serial versions of PSO-MC algorithm have approximately equal clustering performances on each of the nine data sets.

In summary, the proposed parallel version can more significantly reduce the computing time of PSO-MC algorithm without causing degradation in performance.

Table 3. The comparison results of clustering performances for the parallel and serial versions of PSO-MC algorithm on the different data sets (M value).

Data set	Version	The number of cells						
		4	8	16	32	64	128	256
AD_5_2	Parallel	362.56	346.12	348.32	330.49	331.27	327.29	327.56
	Serial	361.27	366.12	350.18	341.49	340.60	336.70	327.40
data_9_2	Parallel	833.20	829.68	800.91	800.34	805.61	790.71	795.32
	Serial	833.25	819.99	801.65	815.82	808.30	796.73	796.18
Sym_3_32	Parallel	1383.26	1357.21	1260.62	1292.26	1325.35	1248.21	1246.48
	Serial	1380.11	1347.77	1264.01	1312.62	1315.55	1250.88	1250.31
data_7	Parallel	818.01	800.38	804.04	799.71	786.31	769.35	758.49
	Serial	819.06	804.24	806.17	796.35	790.14	788.31	759.35
square4	Parallel	2608.95	2539.74	2550.09	2456.86	2388.87	2341.20	2250.61
	Serial	2609.30	2528.41	2551.65	2384.53	2410.87	2342.92	2249.24
NewThyroid	Parallel	2081.84	1981.03	1972.04	2000.96	1978.14	1988.27	1980.66
	Serial	2181.84	1991.04	1972.04	2000.32	1963.25	1991.21	1973.66
Live disorder	Parallel	10042.89	10101.70	9987.24	9980.20	9901.33	9903.35	9879.02
	Serial	10068.20	10026.60	10000.01	9852.96	9869.62	9855.36	9853.20
Iris	Parallel	101.01	99.12	99.66	100.31	98.01	97.85	97.01
	Serial	101.32	100.12	97.68	98.56	97.32	96.86	96.69

5   Conclusion

To take full advantage of P systems, this paper presented a parallel realization framework of membrane clustering algorithm and a parallel version of PSO-MC algorithm. The components of GPU architecture were used to simulate the mechanisms of the used tissue-like P system. In experiment, five artificial data sets and four real-life data sets were chosen to evaluate the performance of the proposed parallel version of PSO-MC and compare it with the corresponding serial version. The comparison results indicated that the proposed parallel version not only guarantee the clustering performance of PSO-MC algorithm but also can more significantly reduce its computing time.

Acknowledgements. This work was partially supported by the National Natural Science Foundation of China (Grant Nos. 61170030 and 61472328), and Research Fund of Sichuan Science and Technology Project (No. 2015HH0057), China.

References

1. Păun, G.: Computing with membranes. J. Comput. Syst. Sci. **61**(1), 108–143 (2000)
2. Păun, G., Pérez-Jiménez, M.J.: Membrane computing: brief introduction, recent results and applications. BioSystem **85**, 11–22 (2006)

3. Păun, G., Rozenberg, G., Salomaa, A.: The Oxford Handbook of Membrance Computing. Oxford University Press, New York (2010)
4. Pan, L., Zeng, X.: Small universal spiking neural P systems working in exhaustive mode. IEEE Trans. NanBiosci. **10**(2), 99–105 (2011)
5. Zhang, X., Liu, Y., Luo, B., Pan, L.: Computational power of tissue P systems for generating control languages. Inf. Sci. **278**(10), 285–297 (2014)
6. Cabarle, F., Adorna, H., Martínez-del-Amor, M.A., Pérez-Jiménez, M.J.: Improving GPU simulations of spiking neural P systems. Rom. J. Inf. Sci. Technol. **15**(1), 5–20 (2012)
7. Cecilia, J.M., Garca, J.M., Guerrero, G.D., Martínez-del-Amor, M.A., Pérez-Jiménez, M.J., Ujaldón, M.: The GPU on the simulation of cellular computing models. Soft Comput. **16**(2), 231–246 (2012)
8. Martínez-del-Amor, M.A., Pérez-Carrasco, J., Pérez-Jiménez, M.J.: Characterizing the parallel simulation of P systems on the GPU. Int. J. Unconventional Comput. **9**(5–6), 405–424 (2013)
9. Shi, X., Wang, Z., Deng, C., Song, T., Pan, L., Chen, Z.: A novel bio-sensor based on DNA strand displacement. PLoS ONE **9**(10), e108856 (2014)
10. Wang, X., Miao, Y., Cheng, M.: Finding motifs in DNA sequences using low-dispersion sequences. J. Comput. Biol. **21**(4), 320–329 (2014)
11. Wang, X., Miao, Y.: GAEM: a hybrid algorithm incorporating GA with EM for planted edited motif finding problem. Curr. Bioinf. **9**(5), 463–469 (2014)
12. Martínez-del-Amor, M.A., et al.: DCBA: simulating population dynamics P systems with proportional object distribution. In: Csuhaj-Varjú, E., Gheorghe, M., Rozenberg, G., Salomaa, A., Vaszil, G. (eds.) CMC 2012. LNCS, vol. 7762, pp. 257–276. Springer, Heidelberg (2013)
13. Zhang, G.X., Cheng, J.X., Gheorghe, M., Meng, Q.: A hybrid approach based on differential evolution and tissue membrane systems for solving constrained manufacturing parameter optimization problems. Appl. Soft Comput. **13**(3), 1528–1542 (2013)
14. Wang, J., Shi, P., Peng, H., Pérez-Jiménez, M.J., Wang, T.: Weighted fuzzy spiking neural P systems. IEEE Trans. Fuzzy Syst. **21**(2), 209–220 (2013)
15. Song, T., Pan, L.: Normal forms for some classes of sequential spiking neural P systems. IEEE Trans. NanoBiosci. **12**(3), 255–264 (2013)
16. Peng, H., Wang, J., Pérez-Jiménez, M.J., Wang, H., Shao, J., Wang, T.: Fuzzy reasoning spiking neural P system for fault diagnosis. Inf. Sci. **235**, 106–116 (2013)
17. Peng, H., Wang, J., Pérez-Jiménez, M.J., Shi, P.: A novel image thresholding method based on membrane computing and fuzzy entropy. J. Intell. Fuzzy Syst. **24**(2), 29–237 (2013)
18. Peng, H., Wang, J., Pérez-Jiménez, M.J., Riscos-Núñez, A.: The framework of P systems applied to solve optimal watermarking problem. Sig. Process. **101**, 256–265 (2014)
19. Huang, X., Peng, H., Jiang, Y., Zhang, J., Wang, J.: PSO-MC: a novel PSO-based membrane clustering algorithm. ICIC Express Lett. **8**(2), 497–503 (2014)
20. Peng, H., Zhang, J., Jiang, Y., Huang, X., Wang, J.: DE-MC: a membrane clustering algorithm based on differential evolution mechanism. Rom. J. Inf. Sci. Technol. **17**(1), 76–88 (2014)
21. Song, T., Pan, L.: Spiking neural P systems with rules on synapses working in maximum spikes consumption strategy. IEEE Trans. NanoBiosci. **14**(1), 38–44 (2015)
22. Jiang, Y., Peng, H., Huang, X., Zhang, J., Shi, P.: A novel clustering algorithm based on P systems. Int. J. Innovative Comput. Inf. Control **10**(2), 753–765 (2014)

23. Peng, H., Jiang, Y., Wang, J., Pérez-Jiménez, M.J.: Membrne clustering algorithm with hybrid evolutionary mechanisms. J. Softw. **26**(5), 1001–1012 (2015) (in Chinese)
24. Peng, H., Wang, J., Pérez-Jiménez, M.J., Riscos-Núñez, A.: An unsupervised learning algorithm for membrane computing. Inf. Sci. **304**, 80–91 (2015)
25. Song, T., Pan, L.: Spiking neural P systems with rules on synapses working in maximum spiking strategy. IEEE Trans. NanoBiosci. **14**(4), 465–477 (2015)
26. Song, T., Pan, L., Păun, G.: Asynchronous spiking neural P systems with local synchronization. Inf. Sci. **219**, 197–207 (2013)
27. Zhang, X., Pan, L., Paun, A.: On the universality of axon P systems. IEEE Trans. Neural Netw. Learn. Syst. **26**(11), 2816–2829 (2015). doi:10.1109/TNNLS.2015.2396940

A New BN Structure Learning Mechanism Based on Decomposability of Scoring Functions

Guoliang Li, Lining Xing$^{(\boxtimes)}$, and Yingwu Chen

College of Information System and Management,
National University of Defense Technology, Changsha 410073, China
xing2999@qq.com

Abstract. Bayesian networks are a powerful approach for representing and reasoning under conditions of uncertainty. Many researchers aim to find good algorithms for learning Bayesian networks from data. And the bio-inspired search algorithm is one of the most effective algorithms. We proposed a hybrid algorithm called MIC-BPSO (Maximal Information Coefficient – Binary Particle Swarm Optimization). This algorithm firstly applies network construction method based on Maximal Information Coefficient to improve the quality of initial particles, and then uses the decomposability of scoring function to modify BPSO algorithm. Experiment results show that, without a given node ordering, this algorithm outperforms MI-BPSO, I-BN-PSO, MWST-HC and K2 algorithm.

Keywords: Bayesian network · Structure learning · Maximal information coefficient · Decomposability · Binary particle swarm optimization

1 Introduction

A Bayesian network (BN) is a directed graph that represents the joint probability distribution among a large number of variables and allows for performing probabilistic inference with these variables. A BN consists of two important components: a directed acyclic graph (DAG) representing the dependency structure among the variables in the network and a conditional probability table (CPT) for each variable in the network given its parent set. Learning the structure of these networks from data is one of the most challenging problems. Though there are numerous algorithms in the literature for structure learning, all of them fall under the three principle approaches: a score and search approach through the space of Bayesian network structures; a constraint-based approach that uses conditional independencies identified in the data; a hybrid approach that combines advantages of the above two approaches. The third approach has drawn a lot of attention from various areas of science in recent years, especially these hybrid algorithms based on genetic algorithm [1], ant colony algorithm [2] and other intelligent algorithms.

Pinto et al. introduced a hybrid algorithm max-min ant colony optimization (MMACO), based on the local discovery algorithm max-min parents and

© Springer-Verlag Berlin Heidelberg 2015
M. Gong et al. (Eds.): BIC-TA 2015, CCIS 562, pp. 212–224, 2015.
DOI: 10.1007/978-3-662-49014-3_19

children (MMPC) and ACO to learn the structure of a BN [3]; Li et al. combined mutual information and binary PSO algorithm to propose a hybrid algorithm mutual information binary particle swarm optimization (MI-BPSO). The MI-BPSO algorithm firstly uses MI and conditional independence test to prune the search space, then calls BPSO algorithm to search the constrained space [4]; Ji et al. presented a hybrid method combining dependency analysis, ant colony optimization (ACO), and the simulated annealing strategy [5]; Hu proposed a new algorithm I-BN-PSO for learning DBNs structure. First, the mutual information obtained in independence tests phase is used as heuristic knowledge to initialize the particle swarm. And then, a new particle positions subtraction operator is designed based on the increase of MDL score. At last, a disturbed strategy is applied to accelerate the particles to overstep the local extremum [6]; Barrire et al. presented a cooperative-coevolution-Parisian trend-algorithm, IMPEA (Independence Model based Parisian EA) [7].

For the application of bio-inspired algorithms in Bayesian network structure learning, Cowie et al. discussed the potential of Particle Swarm Optimization (PSO) for inducing BNs and detailed two algorithms CONAR and REST. The two algorithms are similar in that they both use PSO as the search algorithm, and the K2 metric to score the resulting network [8]; Tonda et al. presented a Memetic Algorithm for Bayesian network structure learning, that combines the exploratory power of an Evolutionary Algorithm with the speed of local search, and used The Akaike information criterion as fitness function [9]; Ji et al. developed the artificial bee colony algorithm as search algorithm, and used K2 metric as scoring function [10]; all bio-inspired algorithms above only use one operator to select high-score individual by scoring whole network structure, while ignoring the decomposability in scoring function.

The remainder of this paper is organized as follows. We begin with some preliminaries about Bayesian Network and Binary Particle Swarm Optimization in Sect. 2. In Sect. 3, we describe the initial network construction method based on Maximal Information Coefficient. Then, Sect. 4 proposes the new mechanism of updating personal best particle and global best particle in BPSO algorithm. We show a new hybrid optimization algorithm MIC-BPSO in Sect. 5. Section 6 presents the experimental results of several benchmark datasets with known structures. Finally, in Sect. 7 we present our final conclusions and outline future research.

2 Preliminaries

2.1 Bayesian Network

Let B_P be a discrete joint probability distribution of the random variables in some set U and $B_S = <U, E>$ be a Directed Acyclic Graph. We call $<B_S, B_P>$ a Bayesian network if $<B_S, B_P>$ satisfies the Markov Condition: every variable is independent of any subset of its non-descendant variables conditioned on its parents. In definition, B_S represents the network structure, and $U = X_1, X_2, \cdots, X_n$ is a set of nodes. E is a set of directed edges, and each edge shows a dependency relationship between two nodes. When each node is discrete, $B_P = P(X_i|\pi(X_i)) : X_i \in U$ is a collection of conditional probability tables. $\pi(X_i)$ includes all parent nodes of X_i, and $P(X_i|\pi(X_i))$ means conditional probability distribution under the parent nodes in an objective combination of state. If the network structure of Bayesian network meets the following set of conditional independence assumptions:

$$P(X_i|X_1, X_2, \cdots, X_{i-1}) = P(X_i|\pi(X_i)) \quad i = 1, 2, \cdots, n \tag{1}$$

The joint probability distribution of can be decomposed into:

$$P(U) = \prod_{i=1}^{n} P(X_i|\pi(X_i)). \tag{2}$$

2.2 Binary Particle Swarm Optimization

Currently, When PSO algorithm is applied in Bayesian network structure learning, the position of particle represents Bayesian network structure, and the structure is represented by a binary coded square matrix, so the search algorithm need to be BPSO(Binary Particle Swarm Optimization) [11]. Since the original BPSO algorithm is proposed by Kennedy and Eberhart, this paper refers it as KEBPSO algorithm.

When the position of a particle is represented by matrix $G(n, n)$, and n is the number of nodes in one network, the matrix element G_{ij} is defined as follows:

$$G(i, j) = \begin{cases} 1, & \text{if i is the j's father node} \\ 0, & \text{otherwise} \end{cases} \tag{3}$$

Different from the real-coded method in basic PSO algorithm, each particles position is binary-coded in KEBPSO. BPSO uses the concept of velocity as a probability that a bit (position) takes on one or zero.

The velocity and position updating equation for the particle are stated as follows:

$$v_i^{k+1} = \omega \cdot v_i^k + c_1 \cdot rand() \cdot (p_{best_i} - x_i^k) + c_2 \cdot rand() \cdot (g_{best^k} - x_i^k) \tag{4}$$

$$(x_i^{k+1})_{jl} = \begin{cases} 1, & S((v_i^{k+1})_{jl}) > rand(); \\ 0, & S((v_i^{k+1})_{jl}) < rand(). \end{cases} \quad j = 1, \cdots, n; \quad l = 1, \cdots, n \tag{5}$$

Where $S(\cdot)$ is a sigmoid function for transforming the velocity to the probability constrained to the interval $[0.0, 1.0]$, and $rand()$ is a quasirandom number selected from a uniform distribution in $[0.0, 1.0]$.

The specific form of sigmoid function [12] is stated as follows:

$$S((v_i^{k+1})_{jl}) = \frac{1}{1 + \exp^{-(v_i^{k+1})_{jl}}} \tag{6}$$

In common sense, the maximum velocity value V_{max} is used to limit the particle value $(v_i^{k+1})_{jl}$, shown as $(v_i^{k+1})_{jl} \in [-V_{max}, +V_{max}]$. Here it is taken as 4.

In KEBPSO, The pseudo code for updating i_{th} personal best particle in k_{th} iteration is described as follows [13,14]:

if $F(X_i^k) > F(P_i^k)$ **then**
    for $j = 1 \rightarrow n$ **do**
        for $l = 1 \rightarrow n$ **do**
            $(p_i^k)_{jl} = (x_i^k)_{jl};$ ▷ Update personal best particle p_{best}
        end for
    end for
end if

Meanwhile, the pseudo code for updating global best particle after updating i_{th} personal best particle in k_{th} iteration is described as follows:

$g = i;$
for $m = 1 \rightarrow N_p$ **do**   ▷ Update global best particle g_{best}
    if $F(P_m^k) > F(P_g^k)$ **then**
        $g = m;$
    end if
end for

3 The Initial Network Construction Method Based on MIC

Maximal Information Coefficient (MIC) is firstly introduced to BN structure learning problem in [15]. It measures correlation of two variables and captures a larger wide association than Mutual Information (MI) [16].

Let us define $I_{|X|,|Y|}^*(X;Y) = max_G I(X;Y)$, where the maximum is over all the possible grids G of size $|X| \times |Y|$ imposed on the bi-variate data. MIC is then defined as:

$$MIC(X;Y|D) = \max_{|X||Y|<B(N)} \left\{ \frac{I_{|X|,|Y|}^*(X;Y|D)}{\log \min |X|, |Y|} \right\} \tag{7}$$

Here N is the data set size, and $B(N)$ is a maximum value for the grid size, which Reshef et al. suggest to be $B(N) = N^{0.6}$ [17]. Since MI tends to increase as the number of quantization levels increases, they used a normalized version of the MI, which is adjusted for the grid size. The core idea of MIC is to test every possible grid of size up to $B(N)$ and find the highest normalized MI.

From the above equations, it is obvious that the Maximum Information Coefficient between two random variables X and Y is symmetric in nature, that is to say: $MIC(X;Y|D) = MIC(Y;X|D)$.

The initial network construction method based on Maximal Information Coefficient includes three phases:

Phase 1: Constructing undirected graph based on maximal information coefficient, and ensuring complete connectivity;

Phase 2: Using the d-separation rule and the condition independence criterion to eliminate one triangular loop every time;

Phase 3: Orienting the edge by use of conditional independence test on three nodes in one chain.

4   BPSO Algorithm Based on Decomposability of Scoring Function

In KEBPSO algorithm, whether updating personal best value for each individual particle or updating global best value for the particle swarm, the algorithm mechanism to update personal best particles or global best particle is to select the particle scoring highest fitness value on the whole network structure. Obviously, the updating mechanism is on the whole network level.

However, the whole network structure can be decomposed into a family set. A particle failing to score highest on the whole network structure tends to have some highest sub-scores on family level in reality, and the current algorithms ignores this feature. According to the decomposability of scoring functions, this paper updates personal best particles and global best particle on the family level, more accurate than on the whole network level.

4.1   The Decomposability of Scoring Functions

To illustrate the decomposability of scoring functions, we take the Bayesian Information Criterion (BIC) scoring function as an example. BIC scoring function as follows:

$$Score_{LL}(G|D) = \ln \prod_{i=1}^{n} \prod_{j=1}^{q_i} \prod_{k=1}^{r_i} (\widehat{\theta_{ijk}})^{N_{ijk}} - \frac{1}{2} \ln m \cdot \sum_{i=1}^{n} q_i(r_i - 1) \qquad (8)$$

In view of the decomposability, BIC scoring function can be decomposed into the sum of the scores on family level:

$$Score_{LL}(G|D) = \sum_{i=1}^{n} Score\_family(i) = \sum_{i=1}^{n} \{\ln \prod_{j=1}^{q_i} \prod_{k=1}^{r_i} (\widehat{\theta_{ijk}})^{N_{ijk}} - \frac{1}{2} \ln m \cdot q_i(r_i - 1)\}$$

$$(9)$$

where $U = X_1, X_2, \cdots, X_n$ is the variable set, $r_1, r_2, \cdots, r_n$ is the number of corresponding possible values, $D = D_1, D_2, \cdots, D_m$ is the sample dataset, $\pi(X_i)$ is the parent set of node X_i in structure S, the corresponding values are $\pi^1(X_i), \pi^2(X_i), \cdots, \pi^{q_i}(X_i)$. $\theta_{ijk} = P(X_i = x_{ik}|\pi(X_i) = \pi^j(X_i))$ is the conditional probability of X_i taking the k_{th} value when $\pi(X_i)$ taking the j_{th} value. N_{ijk} is the number of samples that X_1 taking x_{ik} and $\pi(X_i)$ taking $\pi^j(X_i)$.

4.2   The New Updating Mechanism of Personal Best Particle

The new updating mechanism of personal best particle is as follows:

When updating the i_{th} particle in the k_{th} iteration, we first obtain a score vector $score(x_{i,new}^{k+1}, Pa(x_{i,new}^{k+1}))$ on family set from the decomposition of $score(X_{i,new}^{k+1})$, and then compare it with the vector $score(x_i^k, Pa(x_i^k))$ in the $(k-1)_{th}$ iteration. In this comparison, a score element in vector corresponds to a family structure, so selecting the higher score element means to select the corresponding family structure. We can get a renewed network structure by assembling all selected family structure. However, the renewed structure may be illegal, so we find and repair illegal structure to get a validated Bayesian network structure $X_{i,renew}^{k+1}$. So far, we obtain three scores about personal best particle, including $score(X_i^k)$ for the $(k-1)_{th}$ iteration, $score(X_{i,new}^{k+1})$ for the $(k)_{th}$ iteration and $score(X_{i,renew}^{k+1})$ for the validated structure $X_{i,renew}^{k+1}$. Finally, we select the highest score from these three and assign it to $score(X_i^{k+1})$, the corresponding network structure is assigned to X_i^{k+1}.

The pseudo code for updating every particles best value in k_{th} iteration is described as follows:

Begin Procedure
for $i = 1 \rightarrow N_p$ **do**
    Update particle X_i^k's velocity and position;
    Get the next iteration's position $X_{i,new}^{k+1}$;
    Find and repair illegal structure in $X_{i,new}^{k+1}$;
    Score the family set in $X_{i,new}^{k+1}$;
    Get $score(X_{i,renew}^{k+1})$ and $score(x_{i,new}^{k+1}, Pa(x_{i,new}^{k+1}))$;
    Mark=0;
    $X_{i,renew}^{k+1} = X_{i,new}^{k+1}$;
    for $j = 1 \rightarrow N$ **do**   ▷ Assemble the higher-scored family structures
        if $score(x_{i,j,new}^{k+1}, Pa(x_{i,j,new}^{k+1})) < score(x_{i,j}^k, Pa(x_{i,j}^k))$ **then**
            Update $X_{i,renew}^{k+1}$ with X_i^k;
            Mark=Mark+1;
        end if
    end for
    if Mark>0 **then**
        Find and repair illegal structure in $X_{i,renew}^{k+1}$;
        Get $score(X_{i,renew}^{k+1})$ and $score(x_{i,renew}^{k+1}, Pa(x_{i,renew}^{k+1}))$;
        Update X_i^{k+1},$score(x_i^{k+1}, Pa(x_i^{k+1}))$ and $score(X_i^{k+1})$ from the comparison among $score(X_{i,renew}^{k+1})$,$score(X_i^k)$ and $score(X_{i,new}^{k+1})$;
    else
        Update X_i^{k+1},$score(x_i^{k+1}, Pa(x_i^{k+1}))$ and $score(X_i^{k+1})$ from the comparison between $score(X_i^k)$ and $score(X_{i,new}^{k+1})$;
    end if
    Update global best particle $X_{g,i}^{k+1}$;

end for
return X^{k+1},$score(X^{k+1})$ and $score(x^{k+1}, Pa(x^{k+1}))$;
End procedure

4.3   The New Updating Mechanism of Global Best Particle

The new updating mechanism of global best particle is as follows:

In each iteration, for each particle in turn, we combine the family structures of every personal best particle and the family structures of newly updated global best particle together by selecting the higher family score between these two particles. However the renewed network structure may be illegal, so we validate it and then score it. So far, we obtain three scores about global best particle, including $score(X_{g,i}^{k})$ for the newly updated global best particle, $score(X_{i}^{k+1})$ for the i_{th} personal best particle and $score(X_{g,i+1,new}^{k})$ for the validated structure $X_{i,renew}^{k+1}$. Finally, we select the highest score from these three and assign it to $score(X_{g,i+1}^{k})$, and the corresponding network structure is assigned to $X_{g,i+1}^{k}$.

The pseudo code for updating global best value for i_{th} particle in k_{th} iteration is described as follows:

Begin Procedure
Update particle X_i^k's velocity and position;
Update the i_{th} particle's best position X^{k+1},$score(X^{k+1})$ and $score(x^{k+1}, Pa(x^{k+1}))$;
Mark=0;
$X_{g,i+1,new}^{k} = X_i^{k+1}$;
for $j = 1 \rightarrow N$ **do**   ▷ Assemble the higher-scored family structures
    if $score(x_{i,j}^{k+1}, Pa(x_{i,j}^{k+1})) < score(x_{g,i,j}^{k}, Pa(x_{g,i,j}^{k}))$ **then**
        Update $X_{g,i+1,new}^{k}$ with $X_{g,i}^{k}$;
        Mark=Mark+1;
    end if
end for
if Mark>0 **then**
    Find and repair illegal structure in $X_{g,i+1,new}^{k}$;
    Get $score(X_{g,i+1,new}^{k})$ and $score(x_{g,i+1,new}^{k}, Pa(x_{g,i+1,new}^{k}))$;
    Update $X_{g,i+1}^{k}$,$score(x_{g,i+1}^{k}, Pa(x_{g,i+1}^{k}))$ and $score(X_{g,i+1}^{k})$ from the comparison among $score(X_{g,i+1,new}^{k})$,$score(X_i^{k+1})$ and $score(X_{g,i}^{k})$;
else
    Update $X_{g,i+1}^{k}$,$score(x_{g,i+1}^{k}, Pa(x_{g,i+1}^{k}))$ and $score(X_{g,i+1}^{k})$ from the comparison between $score(X_i^{k+1})$ and $score(X_{g,i}^{k})$;
end if
return $X_{g,i+1}^{k}$,$score(X_{g,i+1}^{k})$ and $score(x_{g,i+1}^{k}, Pa(x_{g,i+1}^{k}))$;
End procedure

When the score of global best particle G_{best} no longer increases as iteration goes on, we introduce the mutation mechanism of evolutionary computation [18]:

for $i = 1 \rightarrow n$ do
   if $rand() < r_{mu}$ then
      $(X_{g,i}^{k+1})_{j_r l_r} = -(X_{g,i}^{k+1})_{j_r l_r};$
   end if
end for

5 MIC-BPSO Algorithm

Algorithm MIC-BPSO includes three phases:

Phase 1: Initial-BN Construction based on Maximal Information Coefficient. We make use of the network construction method based on maximal information coefficient to obtain the initial network;

Phase 2: We orient undirected edge in the initial network by scoring, and use chaotic mapping to do edge-add, delete and reverse operation, so we get the beginning particles for BPSO;

Phase 3: We apply BPSO algorithm based on the decomposability of scoring function to search the optimal network structure and score.

The pseudo code for MIC-BPSO algorithm is described as follows:

Algorithm 1. MIC-BPSO

Require: V-variable set; D-dataset; $F(\cdot)$-scoring function; N_p-the number of particles; $MaxStep$-the number of iteration times; r_{mu}-mutation probability;
Ensure: G_{best}-best network structure
 1: Begin Procedure
 2:   ▷ Phase 1. Initial-BN Construction based on Maximal Information Coefficient
 3: Building an Undirected Network based on MIC;
 4: Elimination of triangular loops;
 5: CI test on three nodes in one chain;
 6:   ▷ Phase 2. Initialize particles based on scoring orientation and kent mapping
 7: Orient the left undirected edges base on score function;
 8: Initialize particles using Kent mapping;
 9:   ▷ Phase 3. Algorithm BPSO based on the decomposability of scoring function
10: Initialize the parameters in algorithm;
11: Search for the best BN structure during iterations;
12: Update particles velocity and position;
13: Find and repair illegal structure;
14: Update personal best particle on family level;
15: Update global best particle on family level;
16: **return** graph G_{best};
17: End procedure

---

6 Experimental Evaluation

To evaluate MIC-BPSO algorithm, static Asia network and Alarm network are selected as the BN benchmarks used in the experiments. We compare it with

MI-BPSO, I-BN-PSO, K2 and MWST-HC algorithm in terms of structure learning accuracy and efficiency. MI-BPSO algorithm and I-BN-PSO algorithm are described in Sect. 1.

Given the node order and the maximum number of parent nodes, K2 algorithm uses greedy search method to select the parent nodes getting the highest score for every node except the first node, and thus build up the network structure [19]. The researchers use K2 algorithm as the classical BN structure learning algorithm to evaluate the performance of the other proposed algorithms.

MWST-HC algorithm is a hybrid algorithm combining the MWST algorithm and hill-climbing algorithm (HC). The algorithm firstly calculates the mutual information between each node to return an undirected maximum weight tree, then initializes each individual by a tree directed from a randomly-chosen root, finally uses hill-climbing algorithm to search for the optimal network structure [20].

We adopt two performance indicators in our research. The BIC score is a widely metric of reconstruction quality in learning BNs. In addition, we introduce F-score to offer a comprehensive reflection on precision and recall of structure learning algorithm [21].

All programs are developed on BNT toolkit by K. Murphy. The experimental platform is a PC with Pentium (R) 4 3.20 GHz CPU, 1 GB RAM, and Windows XP, and the algorithm is implemented by Matlab. All BN benchmarks (structure and probability tables) were downloaded from the bnlearn repository (http://www.bnlearn.com/bnrepository).

All experiments are repeated 10 times for each sample size and each BN. We generate 10 random datasets for the two benchmark BNs respectively. For each sampled dataset, we learned five Bayesian networks using each of the five algorithms.

The experiment result from 1000 Asia samples and 1000 Alarm samples is presented in Figs. 1, 2, 3 and 4. The result shows that all iterative algorithms tend to converge in about 30 iterations, and we use the algorithm results in

Sample size	Algorithm	Metric	Iteration number (Population size is 10)		
			10	30	50
1000	MIC-BPSO	Mean BIC Score(+Time/s)	-570.20 (+6.89)	-566.60 (+21.08)	-566.02 (+35.65)
		Standard Deviation	3.6	2.1	0.9
	MI-BPSO	Mean BIC Score(+Time/s)	-570.87 (+6.39)	-568.38 (+19.34)	-566.04 (+32.65)
		Standard Deviation	4.3	2.6	1.7
	I-BN-PSO	Mean BIC Score(+Time/s)	-572.72 (+6.67)	-569.06 (+20.46)	-568.40 (+34.58)
		Standard Deviation	6.2	4.1	2.3
	MWST-HC	Mean BIC Score(+Time/s)	-566.85(+8.12)		
	K2	Mean BIC Score(+Time/s)	-565.95(+2.26)		

Fig. 1. The statistical result on Asia network structure learning.

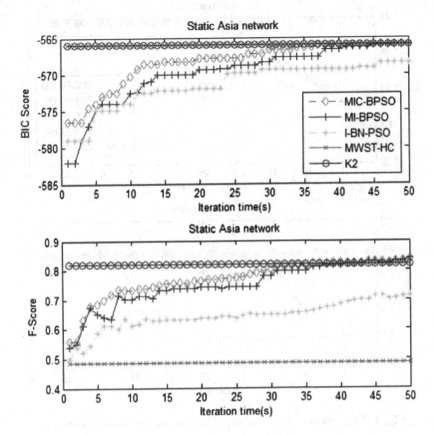

Fig. 2. BIC scores and F-scores on Asia network structure learning.

Sample size	Algorithm	Metric	Iteration number (Population size is 10)		
			10	*30*	*50*
1000	MIC-BPSO	*Mean BIC Score(+Time/s)*	-12588.29 (+18.43)	- 12435.77 (+59.46)	-12429.65 (+101.12)
		Standard Deviation	36.4	21.1	10.2
	MI-BPSO	*Mean BIC Score(+Time/s)*	-12725.89 (+18.10)	-12500.78 (+58.91)	-12485.04 (+98.86)
		Standard Deviation	57.3	39.8	25.8
	I-BN-PSO	*Mean BIC Score(+Time/s)*	-12775.50 (+25.23)	-12538.06 (+76.48)	-12515.46 (+126.60)
		Standard Deviation	83.7	62.1	44.9
	MWST-HC	*Mean BIC Score(+Time/s)*	-12445. 59(+18.62)		
	K2	*Mean Score(+Time/s)*	-12419.95(+2.25)		

Fig. 3. The statistical result on Alarm network structure learning.

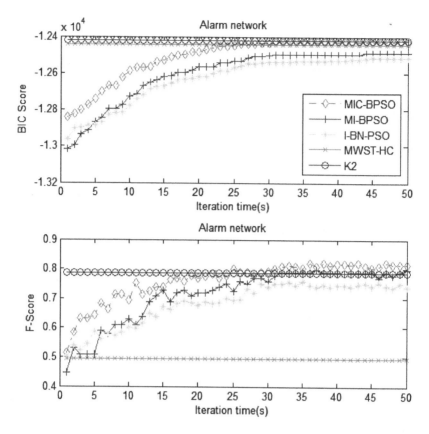

Fig. 4. BIC scores and F-scores on Alarm network structure learning.

30th iteration for the next evaluation. These figures show that initial particle swarm in MIC-BPSO algorithm scores higher than MI-BPSO and I-BN-PSO. The experimental result illustrates that the initial network construction based on MIC method is better than MI method, and MIC can better mine the association between two variables. The network structure learned by MIC-BPSO algorithm has the higher quality than MI-BPSO and I-BN-PSO, indicating that the updating mechanism on family level obtains better performance than on whole network level.

7   Conclusion

This paper proposes a new algorithm mechanism applied in Bayesian network structure learning, and takes BPSO algorithm as an example. The mechanism to update personal best particle and global best particle is down to the family level by the decomposability of scoring function. The hybrid algorithm MIC-BPSO combines the initial network construction method based on maximal information coefficient and modified BPSO algorithm. The experimental results show that, without a given node ordering, this algorithm outperforms MI-BPSO, I-BN-PSO, MWST-HC and K2 algorithm. The proposed mechanism can be applied to other bio-inspired algorithms, including genetic algorithms, ant colony algorithm et al. When the iteration goes on, the algorithm achieve better performance by comparing, selecting and renewing individuals on family level instead of only selecting the better individual on the network level, and these added operators do not increase the computational complexity of algorithm. The future work is to apply this new mechanism in more algorithms.

References

1. Larranaga, P., Karshenas, H., Bielza, C., Santana, R.: A review on evolutionary algorithms in Bayesian network learning and inference tasks. Inf. Sci. **233**, 109–125 (2013)
2. Wu, Y., McCall, J., Corne, D.: Two novel Ant Colony Optimization approaches for Bayesian network structure learning. In: IEEE Congress on Evolutionary Computation, pp. 1–7 (2010)
3. Pinto, P.C., Nagele, A., Dejori, M., Runkler, T.A., Sousa, J.: Using a local discovery ant algorithm for bayesian network structure learning. IEEE Trans. Evol. Comput. **13**(4), 767–779 (2009)
4. Li, G., Gao, X., Di, R.: DBN structure learning based on MI-BPSO algorithm. In: Proceedings of 13th IEEE/ACIS International Conference on Computer and Information Science, pp. 245–250 (2014)
5. Ji, J., Hu, R., Zhang, H., Liu, C.: A hybrid method for learning bayesian networks based on ant colony optimization. Appl. Soft Comput. **11**, 3373–3384 (2011)
6. Hu, R.: The Research on Structure Learning of Dynamic Bayesian Network. Beijing University of technology, Beijing (2009)
7. Barriere, O., Lutton, E., Wuillemin, P.H.: Bayesian network structure learning using cooperative coevolution. In: 11th Annual Conference on Genetic and Evolutionary Computation, pp. 755–762 (2009)
8. Cowie, J., Oteniya, L., Coles, R.: Particle Swarm Optimization for learning Bayesian Networks. Technical Report (2007)
9. Tonda, A., Lutton, E., Squillero, G., Wuillemin, P.-H.: A memetic approach to bayesian network structure learning. In: Esparcia-Alcázar, A.I. (ed.) EvoApplications 2013. LNCS, vol. 7835, pp. 102–111. Springer, Heidelberg (2013)
10. Ji, J., Hu, R., Zhang, H., Liu, C.: An artificial bee colony algorithm for learning Bayesian networks. Soft. Comput. **17**, 983–994 (2013)
11. Kennedy, J., Eberhart, R.: A discrete binary version of the particle swarm algorithm. In: Proceedings of the World Multi-conference on Systemics, Cybernetics and Informatics, pp. 4104–4109 (1997)
12. Lee, C., Chaotang, T., Pin, L.: A discrete version of particle swarm optimization for flowshop scheduling problems. Comput. Oper. Res. **34**, 3099–3111 (2007)
13. Kennedy, J., Eberhart, R., Shi, Y.: Swarm Intelligence. Morgan Kaufmann, San Francisco (2001)
14. Guo, Q., Yu, H., Xu, A.: A hybrid PSO-GD based intelligent method for machine diagnosis. Digit. Sig. Proc. **16**(4), 402–418 (2006)

15. Zhang, Y., Zhang, W.: A novel Bayesian network structure learning algorithm based on maximal information coefficient. In: Proceedings of the Fifth International Conference on Advanced Computational Intelligence, pp. 862–867 (2012)
16. Zhang, Y., Zhang, W., Xie, Y.: Improved heuristic equivalent search algorithm based on maximal information coefficient for Bayesian network structure learning. Neurocomputing **117**, 186–195 (2013)
17. Reshef, D.N.: Detecting novel associations in large data sets. Science **334**(6062), 1518–1524 (2011)
18. Wei, B., Peng, Q., Zhao, J., Chen, X.: A binary particle swarm optimization algorithm inspired by multi-level organizational learning behavior. Eur. J. Oper. Res. **219**, 224–233 (2012)
19. Cooper, G., Herskovits, E.: A Bayesian method for the induction of probabilistic networks from data. Mach. Learn. **9**(4), 309–347 (1992)
20. Brouard, T., Delaplace, A., Cardot, H.: Evolutionary methods for learning bayesian network structures. In: Advances in Evolutionary Algorithms, pp. 335–360 (2008)
21. Patrick, E., Kevin, K., Frederic, L.: Information-theoretic inference of large transcriptional regulatory networks. EURASIP J. Bioinform. Syst. Biol. **2007**, 8 (2007)

A Half-Subtracter Calculation Model Based on Stand Displacement Technology

Minghui Li[1], Fangfang Liu[2], Ming Song[2],
Xiangxiang Chen[2], and Yafei Dong[1,2(✉)]

[1] College of Computer Sciences, Shannxi Normal University, Xi'an 710119, China
{liminghui,dongyf}@snnu.edu.cn
[2] College of Life Sciences, Shannxi Normal University, Xi'an 710119, China

Abstract. In this work, we construct a half-subtracter calculation model with the principle of complementary base pairs and the technology of fluorescence labeling through the combination of INH and XOR calculation model. We implement the calculation process of a half-subtracter utilizing the strand displacement technology that two DNA signal strands as the input signal and the intensity of fluorescence as the output signal. The sequence of strands used in the experiment is designed by NUPACK. The simulation experiment is constructed with Visual DSD which is convenient to analyze the experiment results. The results show that the model performs well with high stability and feasibility and decreases the complexity of calculation.

Keywords: Logic gates · Molecular computing · Half-subtracter · DNA strand displacement · Fluorescence beacon

1 Introduction

With the development of science and technology, the field of bio-molecular computing has attracted more and more attention in the scientific community. The properties of biological molecules–such as DNA specificity, parallelism and so on–make DNA molecules become one of most important tools in the field of molecular computation. DNA strand displacement [1] is one of the basic DNA molecular computing technologies by virtue of its own energy level cause, specificity, sensitivity and accuracy to achieve chain release and combination. Since Adleman [2] showed a solution to the Hamiltonian path problem in 1994 through DNA strand displacement, demonstrating that an algorithm can be encoded in DNA, research works using DNA strand displacement concept has been proposed theoretically and/or proved by experiments to demonstrate the possibility that designed DNA sequences can achieve elementary computing devices [3–9]. In logic circuit and Boolean logic operation process, DNA strand displacement is one of the main techniques that is used to perform a wide range of information processing process. In addition, fluorescence technique [10] with a main detection method is easy to observe and detect advantage by the research on the calculation

© Springer-Verlag Berlin Heidelberg 2015
M. Gong et al. (Eds.): BIC-TA 2015, CCIS 562, pp. 225–231, 2015.
DOI: 10.1007/978-3-662-49014-3_20

model used as molecular. In 2003, Saghatelian [11] established a DNA logic gate for the first time by using the characteristics of DNA molecules and fluorescent technology. DNA logic operations with fluorescence detection method accepted by scientists favor [12–17]. The DNA strand displacement and fluorescent labeling technology are utilized to design the more complex structure, coming to widely used in the field of electronic calculation, such as half-subtracter.

Half-subtracter [19,20,23,24] is composed of an XOR gate and an INH gate to produce a difference (D) output and a borrow (B) output, respectively. In Boolean operations, there are two binary inputs and four input states are: $(0,0),(0,1),(1,0),(1,1)$. The output of $D = I1 \oplus I2 = (I1') \cdot (I2) + (I1) \cdot (I2')$, $B = (I1) \cdot (I2')$. After a logic operation, for instance, the input is $(0,0)$, related to $D = 0 \oplus 0 = 0$, $B = 0 \cdot 0' = 0$, the output is $(0,0)$; the input is $(0,1)$, related to $D = 1 \oplus 0 = 1$, $B = 1 \cdot 0' = 1$, the output is $(1,1)$; the input is $(1,0)$, related to $D = 0 \oplus 1 = 1$, $B = 0 \cdot 1' = 0$, the output is $(0,1)$; the input is $(1,1)$, related to $D = 1 \oplus 1 = 0$, $B = 1 \cdot 1' = 0$, the output is $(0,0)$.

Herein, a half subtracter logic component is proposed using the strand displacement technology that two DNA strands are regarded as the input signal and the intensity of fluorescence is regarded as the output signal. Based on the principle of Watson-Crick complementary base pairing formation of DNA double chain structure and the fluorescence labeling technique, a half-subtracter logic component is constructed. The components are respectively introduced two input chain, achieve the half calculation process is the use of principle and fluorescent strand displacement detection technology. The model is simple and stable making it easy to operate. More complex logic components of the molecular "circuit" will be the next step for smaller or larger molecular circuit provides important support.

2   Design and Construction of Half-Subtracter Model

2.1   Materials and Analysis

Herein, We designed five DNA single strands (a, b, c, d, e), and these strands were obtained by NUPACK simulation (see Table 1). In the process of sequence design, we adjusted the sequence relying on the principle of complementary base pairing. The half-subtracter model is composed of three segments: c(4*3*1*), d(2*), e(5213), and they are 34nts, 20nts and 56nts long, respectively. c is modified with HEX at the 3end. d is respectively modified with black hole quencher(BHQ) at the 5and 3end. e is modified with FAM between segments 5 and 2. DNA single strands c and d are hybridized with e, forming the calculator structure (Fig. 1(A)). Sequences b(52*134) and a(4*3*1*2*5*) with 60nts long, almost completely complementary were regarded as the input1 and input2, respectively.

2.2   Principle of the Proposed Method

For the half-subtracter model, we defined the fluorescence HEX (red fluorescent) as the difference (D) and FAM (green fluorescent) as the borrow (B).

Table 1. The sequences of the strands used in the half-subtracter model.

Note	Sequence(5'-3')
a	5'-ACAG CGCCAATACG TAAGCATCGTACTGCGGCGC CGCCGCGAGTTGCACGGGGC TGAGGT-3'
b	5'-TCCTCA CGCCGCGAGTTGCACGGGGC GCGCCGCA GTACGATGCTTA CGTATTGGCG CTGT-3'
c	5'-ACAG CGCCAATACG TAAGC?ATCGTACTGCGGCGC-3'
d	5'CCGCGAGTTGCACGGGGC-3'
e	5'-TCCTCA GCCCCGTGCAACTCGCGGCG GCGCCGCAG TACGATGCTTA CGTATTGGCG -3'

$$D = I1 \oplus I2 = (I1') \cdot (I2) + (I1) \cdot (I2'), B = (I1) \cdot (I2').$$

Figure 1(A) illustrates the half-subtracter operations.

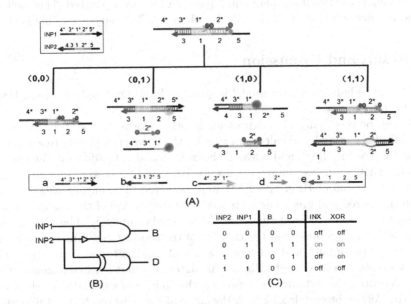

Fig. 1. (A) Schematic representation of the half-subtracter structure. INH operation with the reading channel set to green fluorophore emission. XOR operation with the reading channel set to red fluorophore emission. (B) Symbolic representation of the half-subtracter. B and D represent INH and XOR operation, respectively. (C) Truth table for INH and XOR operations (Color figure online).

- In the $(0,0)$ state that $D = I1 \oplus I2 = 0 \oplus 0 = 0$, $B = (I1) \cdot (I2') = 0 \cdot 0' = 0$, neither I1 nor I2 is present and the output reading is $(0,0)$.
- In the $(0,1)$ state that $D = I1 \oplus I2 = 1 \oplus 0 = 0' \cdot 1 + 0 \cdot 1' = 1$, $B = (I1) \cdot (I2') = 1 \cdot 0' = 1$, only I1 is present, input1 and calculator occurred replacement reaction, input1 and e of calculator hybridized complementary to form a double strands structure, and the strands d and c were released. The strand d quencher BHQ with two fluorescent groups HEX and FAM were separated, and fluorescence signal of HEX and FAM was observed. Thus, the output reading is $(1,1)$.
- In the $(1,0)$ state that $D = I1 \oplus I2 = 0 \oplus 1 = 0' \cdot 1 + 0 \cdot 1' = 1$, $B = (I1) \cdot (I2') = 0 \cdot 1' = 0$, only I2 is present, input2 and calculator occurred replacement reaction, input2 and c of calculator hybridized complementary to form a double strands structure, and released the structure of d and e composition. The quencher and fluorescent groups HEX separate, but the fluorescence groups FAM and quenching agent without separate. Hence only fluorescence signal HEX is observed. The output reading is $(0,1)$.
- In the $(1,1)$ state that $D = I1 \oplus I2 = 1 \oplus 1 = 0' \cdot 1 + 0 \cdot 1' = 0$, $B = (I1) \cdot (I2') = 1 \cdot 1' = 0$. When I1 and I2 are added simultaneously, a duplex of I1/I2 is formed as shown in Fig. 1(A), while calculator is not involved in the reaction, so the two fluorophore and quencher are not separated. Thus neither fluorescence signal of HEX nor FAM is observed. The output reading is $(0,0)$.

3   Result and Discussion

Moreover, the half-subtracter model is simulated and analyzed by Visual DSD. (See Figs. 2 and 3)

As can be seen, only I1 was present, in other words, in the $(0,1)$ state and the ratio of the input1 and calculator was 11, the I1 was completely reacted with calculator (see Fig. 2(a)), and released the chain d and c. In addition, the chain d quencher BHQ with two fluorescent groups HEX and FAM were separated, and fluorescence signal of HEX and FAM were observed. The output was $(1,1)$. In Fig. 2(a), the red and green curves represented the change of the calculator and I1, respectively. The red and green curves coincided completely. The blue, orange and yellow curves represented the changes of the product (see Fig. 1(A)). While the ratio of the input1 and calculator was $3:2$, that is to say, excessive input chain was completely reacted with the calculator. When it reached a steady state in the reaction, the red curve is represent the change of calculator as shown in Fig. 2(b). As can be seen from Fig. 2, the curve of Fig. 2(b) reached a stable value faster and converged better than that of Fig. 2(a). Calculator is fully reacted, so the curve tends to 0, finally.

Only I2 was present, in other words, in the $(1,0)$ state and the ratio of the input2 and calculator was 11, the I2 is completely reacted with calculator (see Fig. 3(a)). The chain b and c of calculator hybridized to complementary form a double chain structure and the structure of d and e composition were released. The quencher was separated, fluorescent groups HEX were separated, but the

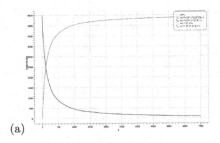
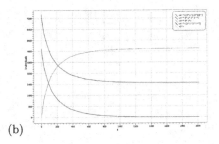

(a)   (b)

Fig. 2. The kinetic characterization of the half-subtracter model when input I2. (a) the ratio of the input2 and calculator is 11. (b) the ratio of the input2 and calculator is 32. The vertical axis represents the concentration of the reactants, the unit is mmol, the abscissa represents the reaction time, the unit is second (Color figure online).

fluorescence groups FAM and quenching agent were not separated. Hence, only fluorescence signal of HEX was observed. The output reading was (0,1). In Fig. 3(a), the red and green curves represented the changes of the calculator and I2, respectively. The red and green curves coincided completely. The blue and yellow curves represented the changes of the product (see Fig. 1(A)). While the ratio of the input2 and calculator was 3 : 2, that is to say, excessive input chain was completely reacted with the calculator. When it reached a steady state in the reaction, the red curve represented the change of calculator as shown in Fig. 3(b). As can be seen from Fig. 3(b). The curve of Fig. 3(b) reached a stable value faster and converged better than that of Fig. 3(a). Calculator was fully reacted, so the curve tended to 0, finally.

Both I1 and I2 were presented, in other words, in the (1,1) state. The chain a and b hybridization formed a double chain structure as shown in Fig. 1(A). While calculator was not involved in the reaction, the two fluorophore and quencher were not separated. Thus neither fluorescence signal of HEX nor FAM was observed. The output reading was (0,0). Here, I1 and I2 were almost completely complementary pairing, and they directly reacted with each other, so the simulation results didnt have curve diagram.

4   Conclusions

The calculation model was established with complementary base pairing in which two almost complementary DNA strands were regarded as inputs and fluorescent agent HEX and FAM were regarded as the detection signals. The half-subtracter structure was formed by the strand displacement and fluorescent technology. From the simulation experiment, we found that:

(1) When the ratio of input strand and calculator quantity was change, the reaction time and rate were affected. The curves trend is shown in Figs. 2 and 3. When the input strand was excessive, the reaction speed more quickly and the process reached more steady state.

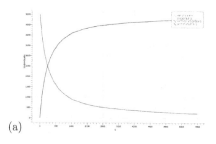 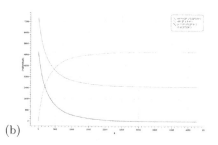

(a)   (b)

Fig. 3. The kinetic characterization of the half-subtracter model when input I2. (a) the ratio of the input2 and calculator is 11. (b) the ratio of the input2 and calculator is 32. The vertical axis represents the concentration of the reactants, the unit is mmol, the abscissa represents the reaction time, the unit is second (Color figure online).

(2) In the processing of experiment, the ratio of a/b and calculator was $1:1$, calculator and a/b almost completely participated in the strand displacement reaction; and the ratio of a/b and calculator was $3:2$, calculator fully participated in the reaction. The amount of detected fluorescence showed no difference with the initial design.

In summary, the half-subtracter calculation model was constructed with DNA strand displacement and fluorescence labeling technique to form a DNA double strand structure. Some special sites in the model are modified with two different colors of fluorescence (see Fig. 1). The simple, stable and low consumptive structure with low experimental complexity can be observed easily. We use the Visual DSD for simulation and the results are in agreement with that in Fig. 1, demonstrating the feasibility of our design purpose. However, in the actual biological experiment, there are still some uncontrollable factors. We will verify the feasibility of the model by biological experiments in the research of future.

Some neural-like bio-computing models, called spiking neural membrane systems, have been proposed in [18,21,22]. It deserves to use stand displacement technology to make up a neural-like membrane system, although neural-like logic gates based on stand displacement has been developed in [25].

Acknowledgments. This research is supported by National Natural Science Foundation of China(Grant Nos. 61272246, 61173113) and Innovation Funds of Graduate Programs Fund of Shaanxi Normal University. The authors acknowledge the anonymous referees suggestion to this paper.

References

1. Ma, L.: Research on application of strand displacement technology in DNA self assembly model. ShannXi: College of life sciences, Shannxi Normal university (2012)
2. Adleman, L.: Molecular computation of solutions to combinatorial problems. Science **266**, 1021–1024 (1994)

3. Soloveichik, D.G., Winfree, E.: DNA as a universal substrate for chemical kinetics. Proc. Natl. Acad. Sci. USA **107**(12), 5393–5398 (2000)
4. Qian, L., Winfree, E.: Scaling up digital circuit computation with DNA strand displacement cascades. Science **332**(6034), 1196–1201 (2011)
5. Qian, L., Winfree, E., Bruck, J.: Neural network computation with DNA strand displacement cascades. Nature **475**(7356), 368–372 (2011)
6. Li, W., Yang, Y., Yan, H.: Three-input majority logic gate and multiple input logic circuit based on DNA strand displacement. Nano Lett. **13**, 2980–2988 (2013)
7. Zhang, C., Ma, J., Yang, J.: Control of gold nanoparticles based on circular DNA strand displacement. J. Colloid Interface Sci. **418**, 31–36 (2014)
8. Huang, S., Hu, J.: Sensitive detection of point mutation using exponential strand displacement amplification-based surface enhanced Raman spectroscopy. Biosens. Bioelectron. **65**, 191–197 (2015)
9. Xu, Y., Zhou, W.: Toehold strand displacement-driven assembly of G-quadruplex DNA for enzyme-free and non-label sensitive fluorescent detection of thrombin. Biosens. Bioelectron. **64**, 306–310 (2015)
10. Zhang, C., Yang, J., Wang, S.: Development and application of fluorescence technologyin DNA computing. Chin. J. Comput. **12**, 2300–2310 (2009)
11. Saghatelian, A., Volcker, N.H., Guckian, K.M.: DNA-Based Photonic Logic Gates: AND, NAND, and INHIBIT. J. Am. Chem. Soc. **125**, 346–347 (2003)
12. Zhang, D., Seelig, G.: Dynamic DNA nanotechnology using strand-displacement reactions. Nat. Chem. **3**(2), 103–113 (2011)
13. Alex, P., James, H., Alexander, D.: DNA compitation: a photochemically controlled AND gate. J. Am. Chem. Soc. **134**, 3810–3815 (2012)
14. Yang, J., Shen, L., Ma, J.: Fluorescent nanoparticle beacon for logic gate operation regulated by strand displacement. ACS Appl. Mater Interfaces **5**, 5392–5396 (2013)
15. Yang, J., Chen, D.: Logic nanoparticle beacon triggered by the binding-induced effect of multiple inputs. ACS Appl. Mater Interfaces **6**, 14486–14492 (2014)
16. Song, W., Zhang, Q.: Fluorescence aptameric sensor for isothermal circular strand-displacement polymerization amplification detection of adenosine triphosphate. Biosens. Bioelectron. **61**, 51–56 (2014)
17. Feng, C., Dai, S., Wang, L.: Optical aptasensors for quantitative detection of small biomolecules: a review. Biosens. Bioelectron. **59**, 64–74 (2014)
18. Song, T., Pan, L., Wang, J., et al.: Normal forms of spiking neural P systems with anti-spikes. IEEE Trans. NanoBiosci. **11**(4), 352–359 (2012)
19. Yang, C., Hsu, C., Chuang, Y.: Molecular beacon-based half-adder and half-subtractor. Chem. Commun. **48**(1), 112–114 (2012)
20. Yang, C., Chen, Y., Lin, H.: An optical deoxyribonucleic acid-based half-subtractor. Chem. Commun. **49**, 8860–8862 (2013)
21. Song, T., Pan, L., Păun, G.: Asynchronous spiking neural P systems with local synchronization. Inf. Sci. **219**, 197–207 (2013)
22. Zhang, X., Pan, L., Păun, A.: On the universality of axon P systems. IEEE Trans. Neural Netw. Learn. Syst. (2015). doi:10.1109/TNNLS.2015.2396940
23. Xu, S., Li, H.: Implementation of half adder and half subtractor with a simple and universal DNA-based platform. NPG Asia Mater. **5**, e76 (2013)
24. Kamin, F.: Calculation model based on nucleic acid logic gate. ShannXi: College of life sciences, Shannxi Normal university (2013)
25. Shi, X., Wang, Z., Deng, C., Song, T., Pan, L., Chen, Z.: A novel bio-sensor based on DNA strand displacement. PLoS One **9**, e108856 (2014)

Identification of Remote Sensing Image of Adverse Geological Body Based on Classification

Xiang Li[1] and Hao Zhang[2(✉)]

[1] School of Computer Science, China University of Geosciences,
Wuhan 430074, China
[2] School of Engineering, China University of Geosciences, Wuhan 430074, China
1165028771@qq.com

Abstract. Identification of interested landmark is a hot topic in the field of remote sensing. Taking QuickBird as an example, this paper focuses on the typical adverse geological phenomenon, such as desert, saltmarsh, gobi, lakes, etc., in Yuli Rob Village of Xinjiang Province. Three classification methods, i.e., extreme learning machine, SVM algorithm, and K-means algorithm, are used for classification and recognition of remote sensing image. The image recognition rate and accuracy are analyzed. Experimental results and comparison analysis indicate that extreme learning machine algorithm, SVM algorithm and K-means algorithm in general is not significant. The SVM algorithm for image continuity provides better results. The extreme learning machine obtains classification results, yet it is easy to fall into local optimum.

Keywords: Remote sensing image · Adverse geological · Classification · Image recognition

1 Introduction

Recently the technology of remote sensing is developing rapidly used in many fields such as medical, mapping, meteorology and geology, and now becomes an important technical mean for many research areas. During the construction, adverse geology often an adverse effects on geological research, in order to avoid unnecessary economic losses, the classification and recognition for the construction of adverse geology are needed. Nowadays there are a number of remote sensing image processing softwares, such as American ENVI, ERDAS, Canadian PCI Geomatica etc. The image processing softwares play a crucial role in the promotion the application of remote sensing data. The sample data used in this paper is the high-definition remote sensing image shot by American QuickBird satellite. In data processing, Li proposed an optimum index factor method improve the image spatial information and maintain the spectral feature of multi-spectral images [1], then he used the improved differential evolution algorithm for hyperspectral data dimensionality reduction model not only obtains the optimal band combination, but also greatly improves the classification accuracy [2].

© Springer-Verlag Berlin Heidelberg 2015
M. Gong et al. (Eds.): BIC-TA 2015, CCIS 562, pp. 232–241, 2015.
DOI: 10.1007/978-3-662-49014-3_21

However, the commonly used remote sensing image processing softwares have a poor performance facing the problem of comprehensive observations of different scale satellite, which needs the help of computer technology, physics, biology to achieve comprehensive analysis and implementation. Commonly used artificial intelligence approaches include Bayes Network Classifier [3], the vector machines classification and neural network classification, etc., which have been already widely applied in related fields.

Extreme learning machine algorithm (ELM) belongs to artificial intelligence approaches which is proposed by Huang et al. [4] in 2006. This algorithm is a supervised learning method for feed forward neural networks [5] containing a single hidden nodes. Extreme learning machine was proposed for efficiently training single-hidden-layer feed forward neural networks (SLFNs). It was much faster than the traditional gradient-descent-based learning algorithms due to the analytical determination of output weights with the random choice of input weights and hidden layer biases [6]. In ELM, the input weights (linking the input layer to the hidden layer) and hidden biases are randomly chosen, and the output weights (linking the hidden layer to the output layer) are analytically determined by using MooreCPenrose (MP) generalized inverse [7]. ELM uses non-differentiable or even discontinuous functions as an activation function [8].

In practice, data collection is often a process of continuous renewal, on account that the complete sample can not be obtained at one time, which makes algorithm design very complex, Huang et al. proposed ELM online timing algorithm [9] on the basis of existing algorithms, this algorithm effectively seamlessly connected the training of the new and old sample, which not only avoided reiterative training on the raw data, but also dynamically updated and improved the algorithm, afterwards, Huang on this basis made further improvements and optimization measures, such as the FOS-ELM algorithm, to reduce the effect of the failure data on network parameters training, it added the forgotten mechanism on the basis of the original algorithm and ensured that in the training of network, the online data can be updated in time, and harmful effect of old data on the network training process are to be avoided.

This paper focuses on the QuickBird images of adverse geology, such as desert, saltmarsh, gobi, lakes, etc., in Yuli Rob Village of Xinjiang Province, and proposes the use of extreme learning method for classification and recognition of remote sensing image, then discusses and analyzes the image recognition rate and recognition accuracy.

2 Brief Introduction of Extreme Learning Machine

The main idea of the Extreme Learning Machine algorithm put forward by Huang et al. [4] in 2006 is that only weights between input layer and the hidden layer, and a bias vector parameter over hidden layer are needed, unlike other gradient algorithms, there is no need to repeatedly refresh and adjust parameters through iteration, solving ways are straightforward, least squares problems of the minimum norm are ultimately classified into solving generalized inverse matrix.

The core of the ELM algorithm is that parameter values of hidden nodes can be randomly selected and determined, so the original single hidden layer feedforward network before (SLFN) becomes a linear system whose output can be analyzed and then determined by inverse matrix of output matrix of generalized hidden layer nodes.

2.1 Single Layer Feedforward Neural Network of Random Hidden Nodes

Feedforward neural network specific functions containing L implicit nodes can be expressed as follows [10]:

$$f_L = \sum_{i=1}^{L} \beta_i g_i(x) = \sum_{i=1}^{L} \beta_i G(w_i, b_i, x), x \in R^D, \beta^i \in R^m \qquad (1)$$

It represents the output function value of the its hidden node, set the activation function as g, the increased node of activation function are as follows:

$$g_i = G(w_i, b_i, x) = g(w_i.x + b_i), w_i \in R \qquad (2)$$

For the radial basis function hidden nodes, Functions are defined as follows:

$$g_i = G(w_i, b_i, x) = g(b_i||x - w_i||), w_i \in R^d, b_i \in R^+ \qquad (3)$$

For N arbitrary determined different samples, among them, the standard single hidden layer feedforward neural network (SLFNs) contains L hidden nodes, and is expressed in mathematical model as follows [11]:

$$\sum_{i=1}^{L} \beta_i g_i(x_j) = \sum_{i=1}^{L} \beta_i G(w_i, b_i, x_j) =$$

$$\sum_{i=1}^{L} \beta_i g(w_i.x + b_i) = o_j, j = 1, 2, \cdots, N. \qquad (4)$$

When $L \geq N$, SLENs can be approaching to N samples with zero error, namely the error equals 0, that is to say, there exists sum making it possible [12].

$$\sum_{i=1}^{L} \beta_i G(w_i, b_i, x_j) = \sum_{i=1}^{L} \beta_i g(w_i.x_j + b_i)$$

$$= t_j, j = 1, 2, \cdots, N. \qquad (5)$$

For the convenience of calculation and understanding, the above equation can be simply described as: $H\beta = T$, H is the output matrix of the neural network hidden nodes, among which, the ith column is the output of hidden layer nodes of the its hidden node.

2.2 Principle of Extreme Learning Machine

From the above analysis, it can be found that when $L > N$, H has more than one solution of zero error; When $L < N$, based on SLENs if we want to find a solution, making $||H\beta - T|| <$, that means to need to find a certain value to meet the conditions of cases and meanwhile in lowest cost.

Here the concept of a minimum cost function [13] is put forward, the concrete representations are as follows:

$$C = \sum_{j=1}^{N}(\sum_{i=1}^{L} \beta_i G(w_i, b_i, x_j) - t_j)^2 \tag{6}$$

The essence of minimizing the cost function is hoping to find a set of specific data, so that

$$||H(\hat{w}_1, \cdots, \hat{w}_L, \hat{b}_1, \cdots, \hat{b}_L)\beta - T|| =$$
$$min_{w_i, b_i, \beta}||H(\hat{w}_1, \cdots, \hat{w}_L, \hat{b}_1, \cdots, \hat{b}_L)\beta - T|| \tag{7}$$

Almost all classification algorithms expect that the error is as small as possible and that a high data matching ability of the sample in order to obtain more accurate and precise classification results. As previously mentioned formula, extreme learning algorithm is not like traditional classification algorithms that need to constantly adjust the input values and the related parameters, in the process of extreme learning algorithm, parameter between input and hidden layer is randomly determined, algorithm implementation process does not have to refresh the two types of parameters, only the activation function [14] is constantly changing.

2.3 Inverse Matrix

On the whole, the goal of the algorithm is to get inverse matrix of H, there are many methods of solving the inverse matrix, such as elementary transformation, full set decomposition method [15], orthogonal projection method [16], and singular value decomposition method.

According to the analysis above, ELM algorithm can be divided into three steps, the second step is using two nested loop to realize the calculation the input matrix H of the hidden layer. Because in the MATLAB environment loop execution requires more time, the corresponding matrix is considered to replace the cyclic process.

The output of the ELM function can be replaced with the following formula:

$$f_x = h(x).\beta \tag{8}$$

Among them $h(x) = [G(w_1, b_1, x), \cdots, G(W_L, B_L, x)]$.

3 Classification of Adverse Geologic Body Image Based on Limit Learning

3.1 Adverse Geologic Body and Remote Sensing Image Processing

In this paper, we use remote sensing image data of Yuli County, Xinjiang, which is in the northwest of our country, from the view of the relationship between land and sea, it is located in the hinterland of the Eurasian continent, Its special natural conditions determines the characteristics of the natural development, and also has a profound impact on the characteristics of land. However, the common poor geological body in Xinjiang includes saline soil and desert soil.

Saline soil and desert soil are adverse geological bodies, which will seriously affect the construction plans in geological engineering construction process, the construction in under these adverse geological conditions first of all calls for scientific and reasonable research and analysis to avoid unnecessary economic losses.

Remote sensing images are usually reflected from the ground, and they are obtained after the analysis and interpretation of electromagnetic waves received by the sensor, at present, the remote sensing sensor mainly adopts the digital form to record the electromagnetic wave, that is, the remote sensing information is recorded by the digital image.

3.2 Classification Algorithm and Evaluation Based on ELM

Algorithm Steps of ELM. ELM algorithm is mainly composed of basic parameters settings, initialization of hidden node parameters, computing the hidden layer output matrix and output weight vector, the specific algorithm is as follows:

(1) Basic parameters are given
   - The given a training sample set
     $x = (x_i, t_i)|x_i \in R^D, t_i \in R, i = 1, \cdots, N$;
   - Give the activation function $G(w_i, b_i, x)$;
   - Given the number of hidden nodes L.
(2) Randomly initialize the hidden node parameter values (w_i, b_i), where $i = 1, 2, \cdots, L$;
(3) Calculate the output matrix of the hidden layer H;
(4) Calculate and output the weight vector.

4 Experimental Results and Analysis

This experiment applies ENVI software platform for processing and separating of the original data, which is made of TIF files and TSW files, only the separated TIF files can be applied into MATLAB software for image identification and classification. Then using the limitation of machine learning algorithms to training sample data, finally the classification result is obtained. The original

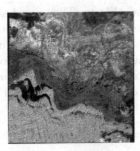

Fig. 1. The original data image

Fig. 2. ELM image classification results

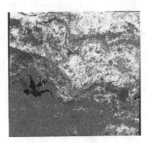

Fig. 3. K-means algorithm classification results

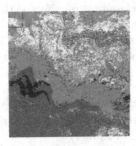

Fig. 4. SVM algorithm classification results

data has four types of ground objects. They are desert, Gobi, lakes and saline soil. The Fig. 2 shows the specific classification results.

Figure 3 is the image classification results by use of k-means algorithm. Figure 4 is the image classification results by use of k-Means algorithm [17]. Analysis of the recognition results of ELM algorithm, K-Means algorithm and SVM algorithm through the confusion matrix (Fig. 1).

Table 1. The confusion matrix of QB image and SVM classification (%)

Classification criterion	Desert	Lake	Saltmarsh	Gobi	User accuracy
Desert	94.56	0.65	3.88	0.52	99.04
Lake	1.88	85.66	5.78	7.73	80.88
Saltmarsh	2.27	2.38	87.42	17.89	86.29
Gobi	1.29	11.31	2.92	73.86	79.84
Precision of production	94.56	85.66	87.42	73.86	88.45
Total accuracy of classification = 88.45 %					

Table 2. The confusion matrix of QB image and K-means classification (%)

Classification criterion	Desert	Lake	Saltmarsh	Gobi	User accuracy
Desert	98.23	1.98	7.85	0.45	95.83
Lake	1.13	84.87	3.67	8.86	88.25
Saltmarsh	0.47	4.78	83.66	9.37	82.18
Gobi	0.17	8.37	4.82	81.22	80.04
Precision of production	98.23	84.87	83.66	81.22	85.77
Total accuracy of classification = 85.77 %					

Comparing and observing the tables above, it can be found that in the aspect of overall accuracy, the best classification effect is the SVM algorithm, followed by ELM algorithm; the effect of k-means algorithm is poorer. According to the classification of image effect, the SVM classification algorithm is virtually block distribution, and classification of regional continuity is better. However ELM algorithm and k-means algorithm classified area basically dotted, classification of areas with poor continuity. Viewing from the classified categories, the classification of accuracy of desert and lakes is less effective than other algorithms; however, the classification precision of soil type and Gobi class is better than other algorithms through ELM (Table 1).

ELM algorithm has a better identifier for Gobi on the whole, desert, lake and saline soil. The recognition effect is more ideal, so it has a practical reference value.

Table 3. The confusion matrix of QB image and ELM classification (%)

Classification criterion	Desert	Lake	Saltmarsh	Gobi	User accuracy
Desert	95.19	0.29	0.47	20.06	77.00
Lake	1.16	99.56	0.36	50.9	67.76
Saltmarsh	0.00	0.00	94.09	1.43	96.89
Gobi	95.19	99.56	94.09	73.42	85.81
Precision of production	98.23	84.87	83.66	81.22	85.77
Total accuracy of classification = 85.81 %					

But when compared with SVM algorithm and K-Means algorithm, the overall effect of ELM algorithm is slightly worse, the identify to part of the category features is not good, but the recognition effect is particularly good to another part of the category features, which means ELM algorithm is easily falling into local optimal classification process (Table 2).

Another experiment is carried out to test whether ELM algorithm does is easy to fall into local optimum. The data is from a mountain area in Urumqi. Figures 5 and 6 respectively represents the original image and the classification image after using ELM algorithm. In Fig. 6, Yellow areas represent the clouds and the red areas represent the mountains, green areas are representative of the bottom. The Fig. 6 shows specific classification results (Table 3).

Fig. 5. The original image in Urumqi

Analysis of the classification results in Table 4, it is can be found that the effect of classification of Fig. 5 is better than the classification in Fig. 2 on the whole, may be this is related to the complexity of the image itself. In addition, the characteristics of local optimum in Table 4 is not obvious, but it can be concluded that the classification accuracy of statistics is close to 100 % of clouds, while the classification accuracy of statistics of the bottom and mountains is slightly difference, which is embodies the characteristics of local optimum.

In short, on the same remote sensing images, the SVM algorithm is a general classification effect is best, k-means algorithm and ELM algorithm slightly bad,

Fig. 6. Classification image after using ELM algorithm (Color figure online)

Table 4. The confusion matrix of QB image and ELM classification in Urumqi (%)

Classification criterion	Valley bottom	Valley bottom	Clouds	User accuracy
Valley bottom	97.82	1.81	0.00	97.81
Clouds	2.11	98.19	0.00	98.25
Clouds	0.07	98019	10.00	98.65
Precision of production	97.82	98.19	100.00	98.65
Total accuracy of classification = 98.65 %				

the accuracy is higher when limit learning algorithm classified in some category features, but the classification accuracy is poorer in the other category feature, ELM algorithm in classification are easy to fall into a problem such as local optimum. Then the conclusion is verified by further experiments.

5   Conclusions

This article train and classify the remote sensing image of adverse geological bodies of Xinjiang region by using Extreme Learning Machine. The selected area is divided into four categories-deserts, Gobi, saline soil and lakes. The method of confusion matrix is used to count and calculate the classification accuracy of the results that have being classified. After comparing with the classification results of SVM algorithm and K-means algorithm, it is can be found that the effect of extreme learning machine classification algorithm is better, while classification rate is as same as other algorithms. However, the shortage of Extreme Learning Machine algorithm is that it easily falls into local optimum phenomenon in the classification process. A part of classification accuracy of the category features is particularly high, while the effect of another part is little than other algorithms. So, it is necessary to explore and improve constantly in the future.

References

1. Li, X., Wang, L.: On the study of fusion techniques for bad geological remote sensing image. J. Ambient Intell. Humanized Comput. **6**(1), 141–149 (2015)
2. Li, X., Wang, G.: Optimal band selection for hyperspectral data with improved differential evolution. J. Ambient Intell. Humanized Comput. **6**, 1–14 (2015)
3. Wang, Q., Guo, L., Li, X.: Remote sensing image classification by bayesian network classifier based on causality. Sens. Transducers **168**(4), 23–29 (2014)
4. Huang, G., Chen, L., Siew, C.K.: Universal approximation using incremental constructive feedforward networks with random hidden nodes. IEEE Trans. Neural Netw. **17**(4), 879–892 (2006)
5. Liang, H., Huang, G., Saratchandran, P., Sundararajan, N.: A fast and accurate online sequential learning algorithm for feedforward networks. IEEE Trans. Neural Netw. **17**(6), 1411–1423 (2006)
6. Huynh, H.T., Won, Y., Kim, J.J.: An improvement of extreme learning machine for compact single-hidden-layer feedforward neural networks. Int. J. Neural Syst. **18**(5), 433–441 (2008)
7. Sun, Z., Au, K., Choi, T.M.: A neuro-fuzzy inference system through integration of fuzzy logic and extreme learning machines. IEEE Trans. Syst. Man Cybern. Part B-Cybern. **37**(5), 1321–1331 (2007)
8. Suresh, S., Saraswathi, S., Sundararajan, N.: Performance enhancement of extreme learning machine for multi-category sparse data classification problems. Eng. Appl. Artif. Intell. **23**(7), 1149–1157 (2010)
9. Huang, G., Chen, L.: Convex incremental extreme learning machine. Neurocomputing **70**(16–18), 3056–3062 (2007)
10. Mohammed, A., Minhas, R., Wu, J., Sid-Ahmed, M.: Human face recognition based on multidimensional PCA and extreme learning machine. Pattern Recogn. **44**(10–11, SI), 2588–2597 (2011)
11. Minhas, R., Baradarani, A., Seifzadeh, S., Wu, Q.: Human action recognition using extreme learning machine based on visual vocabularies. Neurocomputing **73**(10–12, SI), 1906–1917 (2010)
12. Miche, Y., Sorjamaa, A., Bas, P., Simula, O., Jutten, C., Lendasse, A.: OP-ELM: optimally pruned extreme learning machine. IEEE Trans. Neural Netw. **21**(1), 158–162 (2010)
13. Liao, S.Z., Chang, F.: Meta-ELM: ELM with ELM hidden nodes. Neurocomputing **128**, 81–87 (2014)
14. Qing, H., Xin, J., Chang, Y.D.: Clustering in extreme learning machine feature space. NeuroComputing **128**, 88–95 (2014)
15. Luo, C.-L.: A way to work out generalized inverse matrix. J. Sci. Teachers' Coll. Univ. **27**(3), 12–13 (2007)
16. Bo, L.: Image classification algorithm based elm. Hangzhou: China Institute of Metrology Master Thesis (2012)
17. Wang, Q., Li, X., Wang, L.: Adverse geological classification recognition based on research and analysis. Geol. Sci. Technol. Inf. **33**(6), 203–209 (2014)

The Study on Dynamic Conditional Correlation-GARCH Model and its Application

Ziyu Li[1(✉)] and Atsuyuki Naka[2]

[1] College of Economics and Management,
Shanghai Maritime University, Shanghai 201306, China
ziyuli0767@163.com
[2] College of Business Administration,
University of New Orleans, New Orleans, LA 70148, USA

Abstract. This paper studies the Dynamic Conditional Correlation-GARCH model with asymmetries in volatilities and applies the model to estimate the time-varying conditional correlations of stock market returns between Greece and other 8 European countries from January 1st, 2001 through October 31st, 2012. The results show that the cross-market correlations have varied over time and there exist asymmetries in volatilities.

Keywords: DCC-GARCH model · Asymmetries in volatilities · Application

1 Introduction

DCC-GARCH (Dynamic Conditional Correlation - GARCH) model is proposed by Engle [1]. The DCC-GARCH model is estimated in two steps from the univariate GARCH equations and is widely used to estimate the dynamic conditional correlations of different variables. Many researchers have applied DCC-GARCH model to estimate conditional correlations of stock market returns, such as Chiang, Jeon, Li [2], Yiu, Ho, Choi [3], and Brooks, Faff, Hiller [4]. The DCC-GARCH model has mainly three advantages over other techniques. First, the DCC-GARCH model estimates correlations based on standardized residuals and thus it can overcome the problem of heteroskedasticity. Second, we can use multivariate DCC-GARCH model to examine multiple stock market returns and the number of estimated parameters can be substantially reduced, which provides us with convenience of computation. Third, we can apply DCC-GARCH model to obtain the time series of correlations of different stock market returns and study whether and how the correlations vary over time.

Some researchers have found that the stock market correlations estimated from DCC-GARCH model are significantly time-varying, such as Narayan, Sriananthakumar, Islam [5], Ahmad, Sehgal, Bhanumurthy [6], and Syllignakis, Kouretas [7]. For example, Narayan, Sriananthakumar, in [5], Islam used DCC-GARCH model to examine the patterns and causes of stock market integration

© Springer-Verlag Berlin Heidelberg 2015
M. Gong et al. (Eds.): BIC-TA 2015, CCIS 562, pp. 242–248, 2015.
DOI: 10.1007/978-3-662-49014-3_22

of selected emerging Asian nations from 2001 to 2012. They found that the conditional correlations vary over time and were strongest during 2007–2009 global financial crisis period. DCC-GARCH model assumes that both negative and positive news have symmetric effects on variance and conditional correlations. However, Cappiello, Engle, Sheppard in [8] find the presence of asymmetric responses in conditional variances to negative stock returns. Thus how to incorporate asymmetries in volatilities in DCC-GARCH model has become an important research topic. In this paper, we study the DCC-GARCH model with asymmetries in volatilities and apply the model to estimate the conditional stock market correlations of selected European countries from 2001 to 2012. Since little research has been done on examining how the dynamic stock market correlations react to sovereign rating changes. We also explore the impact of sovereign rating changes on the selected European stock market correlations during the sample period. This paper is organized as follows: first, the specification of DCC-GARCH model with asymmetries in volatilities; second, the application of the asymmetric DCC-GARCH model; third, the empirical results and the conclusion.

2   Model Specification

In DCC-GARCH models, the conditional covariance matrix M_t can be decomposed as:

$$M_t = F_t R_t F_t \tag{1}$$

Where $F_t = diag\{\sqrt{m_{it}}\}$ is the $n \times n$ diagonal matrix of time-varying standard deviations from the univariate GARCH models, and R_t is the $n \times n$ time-varying conditional correlation matrix.

The DCC-GARCH model uses a two-stage estimation of M_t. In the first stage, univariate GARCH models are estimated for each variable and estimates of $\sqrt{m_{it}}$ are obtained. The mean equation is specified as

$$x_t = \gamma_0 + \gamma_1 x_{t-1} + \varepsilon_t$$

$$\varepsilon_t / \xi_{t-1} \sim N(0, M_t) \tag{2}$$

Where x_t is an $n \times 1$ vector, and ξ_{t-1} is the information set at time $t - 1$. The AR(1) term is used to take into acount the autocorrelation of variables.

In the second stage, the transformed residuals u_{it} to estimate the dynamic conditional correlation parameters. The evolution of the conditional correlations in DCC-GARCH model is given by

$$P_t = (1 - a - b)\overline{P} + a u_{t-1} u_{t-1} + b P_{t-1} \tag{3}$$

$$R_t = P_t^{*-1} P_t P_t^{*-1} \tag{4}$$

Where $P_t = [p_{ij,t}]$ is the $n \times n$ time-varying covariance matrix of u_t, $\overline{P} = E[u_t u_t']$ is the $n \times n$ unconditional variance matrix of u_t, a and b are scalars which satisfy $(a + b) < 1$. $P_t^* = [p_{ii,t}^*] = [\sqrt{p_{ii,t}}]$ is a diagonal matrix with the square root of the ith diagonal element of P_t. If P_t is positive definite, we can obtain the correlation matrix R_t whose diagonal element are ones. And the absolute values of other elements of R_t are less than 1.

Following research from [1] we can use a two-stage method to maximize the log-likelihood function in DCC-GARCH model. Let the parameters F be denoted by λ and the parameters in R be denoted by η. The log likelihood function can be written as the sum of a volatility part $L_v(\lambda)$ and a correlation part $L_C(\lambda, \eta)$:

$$L(\lambda, \eta) = L_v(\lambda) + L_C(\lambda, \eta)$$
$$= [-\frac{1}{2}\sum_t (n log(2\pi) + log|F_t|^2 + \varepsilon_t' F_t^{-2} \varepsilon_t)]$$
$$+ [-\frac{1}{2}\sum_t (log|R_t| + u_t' R_t^{-1} u_t - u_t' u_t)] \tag{5}$$

The volatility part of the likelihood is the sum of individual GARCH likelihoods. First, the volatility part of the likelihood is maximized as follows,

$$\widetilde{\lambda} = argmax[L_v(\lambda)] \tag{6}$$

Second, take the value above to maximize the correlation part of the likelihood,

$$\max_\eta [L_C(\widetilde{\lambda}, \eta)] \tag{7}$$

Cappiello, Engle, Sheppard in [8] extend the previous DCC-GARCH model by permitting asymmetries in correlation dynamics. As suggested by Cappiello, Engle, Sheppard in [8], we can use asymmetric GJR (1,1) as the variance equation in DCC-GARCH model to incorporate the asymmetries in volatilities.

The variance equation is specified as the asymmetric GJR (1,1),

$$m_{ii,t} = c + (\alpha + \theta I_t[\varepsilon_{t-1} < 0])\varepsilon_{ii,t-1}^2 + \beta m_{ii,t-1} \tag{8}$$

Where $I_t = 1$, if $\varepsilon_{t-1} < 0$; $I_t = 0$, if $\varepsilon_{t-1} \geq 0$.

The DCC-GJR-GARCH process extends previous specifications by permitting conditional asymmetries in volatilities. The DCC-GJR-GARCH specification is well suited to examine correlation dynamics among different variables and investigate the presence of asymmetric responses in conditional variance to negative shocks.

3   Model Application

Next, we applies DCC-GJR-GARCH process model to estimate conditional stock market correlations between Greece and other 8 European countries and examine the response of stock market correlations to Greek sovereign rating downgrades.

The data used in this study are daily stock-price indices from January 1, 2001 through October 31, 2012 for nine European countries. The dataset consists of the stock market indices of Greece (ATHEX 20 Index), Germany (DAX

Index), Spain (IBEX35 Index), Netherlands (AEX Index), Austria (ATX Index), Belgium (BEL20 Index), Ireland (ISEQ-OVERALL Index), France (CAC40 Index), UK (FTSE100 Index). Stock-index returns are calculated as the first difference of the natural log of each stock-price index.

Table 1. Results of statistical tests

	Q(10)	P-value	ADF	P-value	ARCH(5)	P-value
Austria	20.4840	(0.0250)	−50.0680	(0.0001)	1134.7000	(0.0000)
Belgium	33.3490	(0.0000)	−48.5908	(0.0001)	1551.3000	(0.0000)
France	28.7370	(0.0010)	−54.4959	(0.0001)	1172.1000	(0.0000)
Germany	25.3350	(0.0050)	−53.0730	(0.0001)	1488.6000	(0.0000)
Greece	25.2470	(0.0050)	−50.5050	(0.0001)	850.3700	(0.0000)
Ireland	26.6240	(0.0030)	−50.2200	(0.0001)	1911.5000	(0.0000)
Netherlands	33.7060	(0.0000)	−53.0360	(0.0001)	1859.1000	(0.0000)
Spain	17.8490	(0.0580)	−52.5710	(0.0001)	938.9500	(0.0000)
UK	31.4960	(0.0000)	−54.8120	(0.0001)	1754.0000	(0.0000)

Table 1 presents the results of statistical tests of the nine stock-index return series, P-values of tests of significance are in parenthesis. Q(10) is the Ljung-Box statistics with up to 10-day lags. All of the stock-index return series are found to have fist-order autocorrelation at different significance level. According to the results of ADF tests, all the stock-index return series are stationary. ARCH(5) refers to the Q-statistics of ARCH tests with up to 5-day lags. All the stock-index return series have significant ARCH effects.

4 Main Results

We estimate the dynamic correlations of European stock market returns using DCC-GJR-GARCH model. Table 2 reports the estimation results, P-values of tests of significance are in parenthesis.

In Panel A of Table 2, the AR(1) term is significantly positive for Greece, Austria and Ireland while it is significantly negative for France, Netherlands, Germany and UK. In Panel B, θ is significant and positive for all countries, implying that the conditional variance of stock market returns is affected more significantly by negative shocks than by positive shock. In Panel C, the significant a and b indicate that conditional correlations of the selected stock market are highly dynamic and time-varying.

We obtain eight time series of conditional correlations from DCC-GJR-GARCH model. In order to analyze the impact of Greek sovereign rating downgrade announcements on stock market correlations, we apply the following regression:

$$\rho_{Gi,t} = \varphi_0 + \varphi_1 \rho_{Gi,t-1} + d_{1,Gi} DM_{G,t} + d_{2,Gi} DM_{i,t} + e_{Gi,t}, \qquad (9)$$

Table 2. Estimation results of DCC-GJR-GARCH model

Panel A: Mean equation

	γ_0	P-value	γ_1	P-value
Greece	0.0288	(0.3186)	0.0581	(0.0000)
France	0.0251	(0.1855)	−0.0365	(0.0000)
Austria	0.0708	(0.0010)	0.0525	(0.0000)
Belgium	0.0398	(0.0247)	0.0091	(0.2575)
Netherlands	0.0190	(0.2915)	−0.0141	(0.0537)
Spain	0.0417	(0.0317)	−0.0131	(0.1592)
Germany	0.0457	(0.0191)	−0.0246	(0.0022)
Ireland	0.0411	(0.0520)	0.0252	(0.0357)
UK	0.0208	(0.1962)	−0.0571	(0.0000)

Panel B: Variance equation

	c	P-value	α	P-value
Greece	0.0108	(0.0101)	0.0368	(0.0000)
France	0.0140	(0.0000)	−0.0139	(0.0013)
Austria	0.0179	(0.0000)	0.0262	(0.0000)
Belgium	0.0148	(0.0000)	0.0216	(0.0001)
Netherlands	0.0109	(0.0000)	−0.0105	(0.0218)
Spain	0.0131	(0.0000)	−0.0172	(0.0000)
Germany	0.0127	(0.0000)	−0.0076	(0.1170)
Ireland	0.0209	(0.0000)	0.0491	(0.0000)
UK	0.0094	(0.0000)	−0.0038	(0.3968)

	β	P-value	θ	P-value
Greece	0.9444	(0.0000)	0.0383	(0.0000)
France	0.9510	(0.0000)	−0.0582	(0.0000)
Austria	0.9424	(0.0000)	0.0448	(0.0000)
Belgium	0.9410	(0.0000)	0.0583	(0.0000)
Netherlands	0.9510	(0.0000)	−0.0662	(0.0000)
Spain	0.9463	(0.0000)	−0.0617	(0.0000)
Germany	0.9527	(0.0000)	−0.0651	(0.0000)
Ireland	0.9288	(0.0000)	0.0293	(0.0035)
UK	0.9524	(0.0000)	−0.0719	(0.0000)

Panel C: DCC estimators

	Coefficient	P-value
a	0.0143	(0.0000)
b	0.9824	(0.0000)

where $\rho_{Gi,t}$ is the conditional correlation between Greece and country i. $DM_{G,t}$ equals 1 if sovereign rating downgrade announcements of Greece occurs. $DM_{i,t}$ equals 1 if sovereign rating downgrade announcements of country i occurs.

Table 3 presents the results of the tests of the impact of Greek sovereign rating downgrades on the stock market correlations, P-values of tests of significance are in parenthesis.

Table 3. Tests of the impact of sovereign rating changes on stock market correlations

	ϕ_1	ϕ_2	d_1	d_2
Spain	0.0015	0.9965	0.0073	−0.0032
	(0.0350)	(0.0000)	(0.0190)	(0.3920)
France	0.0015	0.9967	0.0066	−0.0026
	(0.0420)	(0.0000)	(0.0300)	(0.8380)
Austria	0.0012	0.9973	0.0018	−0.0002
	(0.0830)	(0.0000)	(0.5510)	(0.9880)
Belgium	0.0013	0.9970	0.0043	0.0004
	(0.0600)	(0.0000)	(0.1600)	(0.9520)
Ireland	0.0018	0.9954	0.0078	0.0016
	(0.0290)	(0.0000)	(0.0190)	(0.7930)
Netherlands	0.0015	0.9966	0.0060	0.0200
	(0.0480)	(0.0000)	(0.0420)	(0.0200)
Germany	0.0017	0.9961	0.0053	0.0242
	(0.0210)	(0.0000)	(0.0900)	(0.0080)
UK	0.0016	0.9962	−0.0034	−0.0047
	(0.0360)	(0.0000)	(0.2110)	(0.5500)

In Table 3, d_2 is significantly positive for only two countries, including Netherlands and Germany. d_1 is significantly positive for five countries. The correlations of stock index returns between Greece and four countries, including Spain, France, Ireland, and Netherlands are positively affected by Greek sovereign rating downgrade announcements, at 5 % significance level. And the stock market correlation between Greece and Germany is positively affected by Greek rating downgrades, at 10 % significance level. The results imply that the negative rating news on Greece seem to badly influence investors' perception of the financial stance of other countries, and lead to a significant increase in the cross-market correlations.

5   Conclusion

In this paper, we study the DCC-GARCH model with asymmetries in volatilities and applies the model to estimate the time-varying conditional correlations of stock market returns between Greece and other 8 European countries from January 1st, 2001 through October 31st, 2012. We find that the cross-market correlations have varied over time and there exist asymmetries in volatilities. The correlations of stock index returns between Greece and other 5 countries, including Spain, France, Ireland, Netherlands, and Germany are significantly increased by Greek sovereign rating downgrades.

References

1. Engle, R.F.: Dynamic conditional correlation: a simple class of multivariate generalized autoregressive conditional heteroskedasticity models. J. Bus. Econ. Stat. **20**(3), 339–350 (2002)
2. Chiang, T.C., Jeon, B.N., Li, H.: Dynamic correlation analysis of financial contagion: evidence from Asian markets. J. Int. Money Finan. **26**, 1206–1228 (2007)
3. Yiu, M.S., Ho, W.A., Choi, D.F.: Dynamic correlation analysis of financial contagion in Asian markets in global financial turmoil. Appl. Fin. Econ. **20**, 345–354 (2010)
4. Brooks, R., Faff, R.W., Hillier, D., Hillier, J.: The national market impact of sovereign rating changes. J. Bank. Finance. **28**, 233–250 (2004)
5. Narayan, S., Sriananthakumar, S., Islam, S.Z.: Stock market integration of emerging Asian economies: patterns and causes. Econ. Model. **39**, 19–31 (2014)
6. Ahmad, W., Sehgal, S., Bhanumurthy, N.R.: Eurozone crisis and BRIICKS stock markets: contagion or market interdependence? Econ. Model. **33**, 209–225 (2013)
7. Syllignakis, M.N., Kouretas, G.P.: Dynamic correlation analysis of financial contagion: evidence from the central and eastern European markets. Int. Rev. Econ. Finance. **20**, 717–732 (2011)
8. Cappiello, L., Engle, R.F., Sheppard, K.: Asymmetric dynamics in the correlations of global equity and bond returns. J. Financ. Econometrics. **4**(4), 537–572 (2006)

Protein Function Prediction Using Multi-label Learning and ISOMAP Embedding

Huadong Liang, Dengdi Sun[✉], Zhuanlian Ding, and Meiling Ge

School of Computer Science and Technology, Anhui University,
Hefei 230039, People's Republic of China
sundengdi@163.com

Abstract. As more and more high-throughput proteome data are collected, automated annotation of protein function has been one of the most challenging problems of the post-genomic era. To address this challenge, we propose a novel functional annotation framework incorporating manifold embedding and multi-label classification to predict protein function on protein-protein interaction (PPI) network. Unlike the existing approaches that depend on the original network, our method weights it by edge betweenness, and embeds simultaneously the annotated and unannotated proteins into an Euclidean metric space via isometric feature mapping (ISOMAP). Then, with these low-dimensional coordinates, the protein expressions are quantified and the functional assignment is transformed into a multi-label classification problem. The approach results in a set of feasible functional labels for each unannotated protein. We conduct extensive experiments on yeast PPI database to evaluate the performance of different multi-label learning methods. The results demonstrate that the proposed method is an effective tool for protein function prediction.

Keywords: Protein function prediction · ISOMAP · Protein-protein interaction network · Multi-label learning

1 Introduction

The accurate annotation of protein function is key to understanding life at the molecular level and has great biomedical and pharmaceutical implications. Nowadays, with the development of novel high-throughput experimental techniques, more and more protein data have been collected for various organisms. However, there is a continually widening gap between the large scale protein data and the limited functional annotation, even the best-studied organisms also contain a large number of proteins whose functions are currently unknown. Therefore, the determination of protein functions at the proteomics scale has been one of the most challenging problems in post-genomic era. Because of the inherent difficulty and huge expense of function assignment using traditional experimental techniques, the computational annotation of protein function via the vast amount of accumulated data has therefore emerged as a feasible idea,

© Springer-Verlag Berlin Heidelberg 2015
M. Gong et al. (Eds.): BIC-TA 2015, CCIS 562, pp. 249–259, 2015.
DOI: 10.1007/978-3-662-49014-3_23

which make it possible to automatically predict protein functions to guide laboratory experiments and speed up the annotation process.

In molecular biology, genes are basic functioning units containing genetic information, and can be used as templates for protein transcriptions [1,2], which is critical for protein functions, so traditional methods for assigning protein function automatically are mainly based on genomic sequences homologous [3,4]. For example, ConFunc [5] first assigns the proteins found via PSI-BLAST to groups so that all members of a group share a particular gene sequence term. Looking at the alignments in each group, the method then identifies conserved functional residues, scores them and only outputs the groups above a certain combined score. GOSLING [6] first derives various features of the gene terms found in the BLAST result (e.g. GO evidence code, E-Value and bit score). Using many decision trees, the prediction is then flagged as either correct or incorrect. Following this idea, GOstruct [7] takes the idea of co-occurrence to the next level and builds a sophisticated SVM machinery around "structured output spaces". This refers to the extension of the input space (E-Values, asf.) with all experimentally observed GO-subgraphs. Nevertheless, closely related proteins do not always share the same function. For example, the yeast Gal1 and Gal3 proteins are paralogs that have evolved very different functions with Gal1 being a galactokinase and Gal3 being a transcriptional inducer. Obviously, the error rates of prediction is also increased gradually as the discrepancies and corruptions of gene expression and sequence.

In recent years, a wealth of researches concentrated on the protein-protein interactions [8], which have unequivocally demonstrated that these interactions play an essential role in cellular function, such as cellular signal transduction, metabolism, cell propagation, and so on. Based on the results, and recent availability of protein interaction networks for many genomic species have stimulated several prediction-related researches to built on the framework of a protein-protein interaction (PPI) network for protein function prediction [9]. Typically, the PPI network is first modeled as a graph, each node corresponds to one protein, and each detected interaction between pairwise proteins is represented by one edge, then a network based statistical learning method is used to infer putative protein functions. Consequently, the most straightforward method using network to predict protein function determines the putative functions of a protein from the known functions of its neighboring proteins on a PPI network [10], which only leverages the local information of a network. Lately, several researchers used the global optimization approaches to improve the protein function predictions by taking into account the full topology of PPI networks [11]. However, this idea is relied on the global topological structure of PPI network, which is time-consuming and difficult to obtain the unique optimal solution. In fact, according to the principle of manifold learning, the structure of PPI network should be usually a low-dimensional manifold, that embed in a high-dimensional space. If the low-dimension representation of PPI network can be discovered, it may be effectively to analysis. A plenty of recent literatures on function annotation follow this way. For example, You et al. [12] utilizes isometric feature mapping (ISOMAP) to embed the PPI network in low-dimension, then to access pairwise similarity between proteins. Sun et al. [13] applies locally linear embedding (LLE) to reconstruct the PPI network into low-dimensional subspace, then predict function of unannotated proteins. Moreover, Huang et al. [14] proposes an Extended Link Clustering method (ELC) for overlapping community detection. This method provides the capability to analyze overlapping of the various structural functional units in PPI networks.

Furthermore, in related database, each protein is described by the concatenation of micro-array expression data and phylogenetic profile, and is associated with a set of feasible functional classes not just one function. It means that the prediction of protein functions is a typical multi-label learning problem, i.e., each sample (protein) can belong to a set of labels (functions). Therefore, many researchers integrate the topological properties of PPI with multi-label methods. These approaches can be divided roughly into three categories: SVM based model, neural network based model and data distribution based model. For the SVM based model, A. Elisseeff et al. [15] improves the traditional SVM approach by incorporating a large margin ranking system to minimize generalization error. For neural network based model, Zhang et al. [16] proposed a BP-MLL method where a neural network is associated to the characteristics of multi-label learning and responsible for the predictions in that level iteratively. For data distribution based model, Zhang et al. [17] utilized the K-nearest-neighbors to determine the label set for the unannotated protein.

In this paper, we first study on the topological of the PPI network, and then embedding the whole weighted PPI network into a low dimensional Euclidean metric space in Sect. 2. Moreover, we apply multi-label learning techniques to classify unannotated proteins in Sect. 3. Finally, we evaluate the performance of prediction among the different multi-label classification algorithms via a large number of comparison experiments in Sect. 4.

2   Embedding the Protein-Protein Interaction Network into Low-Dimension

Manifolding learning is a novel class of nonlinear dimensionality reduction techniques proposed in recent years. According to this approach, the PPI network is considered to lie actually on a low-dimensional manifold within the higher-dimensional space. Once high dimensional protein data points are closely interact with their close neighbors, the intrinsic dimensionality of protein data can be uncovered by manifold embedding. If the manifold is actually low enough dimension, the data can be visualized in the low-dimensional space and computed more efficiently. So find a well-fitting representation for PPI networks could provide insights into the interplay between network structure and biological function [18]. Here, we use the classic ISOMAP [19] to embed PPI network. This embedding technique can reveal the intrinsic nonlinear dimension, embed the PPI network into a metric space uniformly and preserve the global topological structure faithfully at the same time. It's worth noting that although the real-world PPI networks are generally non-fully connected, there is one largest connected sub-network, which contains most of the nodes and edges. So, only the largest connected component is embedded by ISOMAP. The processes are as follows.

(1) Firstly, a PPI network can be simplified as a graph $G(V, E)$, the set of n proteins can be represented like $V = \{x_1, \ldots, x_N\}$, and each interaction between proteins x_i and x_j can be denoted as $e_{ij} \in E$. Then we construct the adjacent matrix $W = \{w_{ij}\}_{N \times N}$, where $w_{ij} = 1$ denote that there is an edge between node x_i and x_j, otherwise $w_{ij} = 0$. The $\{0, 1\}$ adjacent matrix can indicate the connectivity information of PPI network. However, the truth interaction strength between any proteins may different (i.e. if two proteins share more function classes, the edge between them tend to have a larger value of weight and the corresponding points are close enough in the metric space; otherwise the lower value, the lower interaction strength). Therefore, the new weight adjacent matrix $W^B = \{w_{ij}^B\}$ is defined by edge betweenness as $w_{ij}^B = \sum_{s \neq t \in V} \delta_{st}(e_{ij}) = \sum_{s \neq t} \frac{\sigma_{st}(e_{ij})}{\sigma_{st}}$, where σ_{st} indicates the number of all shortest path between protein x_s and x_t, and $\sigma_{st}(e_{ij})$ computes the number of these paths through the edge e_{ij}. It is reasonable to take advantage of the edge betweenness to weight network, since the edges passed frequently tend to have a high credibility and interactivity in the real PPI network.

(2) Moreover, although many of proteins are not neighbors each other, they also could be connected by a series of neighbor links. According to it, the geodesic distance d_{ij}^G is utilized to describe the hidden true relationship between two proteins x_i and x_j in the manifold approximately. Here, the geodesic distance is defined by the shortest path distances between all pairwise vertices in the weight adjacent matrix W^B, which can be computed through the Dijkstra algorithm.

(3) Finally, the weight matrix of graph distance $D^G = \{d_{ij}^G\}$ is embedded into a d-dimensional subspace Y with Multidimensional Scaling (MDS). The embedding coordinate vectors y_i for protein x_i in PPI are optimized to minimize the cost function: $E = \|\tau(D^G) - \tau(D^Y)\|$, where $D^Y = \{d_{ij}^Y\}$ denotes the matrix of Euclidean distances in d-dimensional subspace Y, which $d_{ij}^Y = \|y_i - y_j\|$; $\tau(D^G) = -\frac{H(D^G)^2 H}{2}$ and $\tau(D^Y) = -\frac{H(D^Y)^2 H}{2}$ are the centered matrix of squared graph distances D^G and squared embedding Euclidean distances D^Y respectively, and $H = I_N - 11^T/N$ is the centering matrix. The optimal solution is given by the $v_1, \cdots, v_d$ with corresponding to the largest eigenvalues, $\lambda_1 > \cdots > \lambda_d$ of $\tau(D^G)$, that is the d-dimensional vector y_i equal to $\sqrt{\lambda_d} v_d^i$, so that the estimated intrinsic geometry of the manifold is preserved accurately.

3   Predicting Protein Functions with Multi-label Learning

Recent availability of PPI network for many genomic species has encouraged researchers to improve the methods to predict the protein functions.

Generally, traditional methods train the binary classification models and predict each functional category independently in the feature space. However, in these methods, each protein is assigned to only one functional category. It is incompetent to fit well, as one protein is natural observed to play several functional roles in different biological processes within an organism. Lately, several researchers have shown that such process can be seamlessly mapped to the multi-label learning framework.

Multi-label learning deals with objects having multiple labels simultaneously, which widely exist in real-world applications. Let $\mathcal{X}$ be the input space and $\mathcal{Y} = \{1, \cdots, L\}$ be the label space with L possible labels. In protein function prediction, we denote by $\{(x_1, y_1), \cdots, (x_n, y_n)\}$ the training data that consist of n annotated proteins, where each protein $x_i = [x_{i1}, \cdots, x_{id}]$ is a vector of d dimensions and $y_i = [y_{i1}, \cdots, y_{iL}]$ is the functional label vector of protein x_i, y_{il} is $+1$ if x_i has the l-th function and -1 otherwise. The goal is to learn a map $f : \mathcal{X} \rightarrow \mathcal{Y}$ which can predict the functional label vectors for unannotated proteins. In this paper, three categories of multi-label classification algorithms, i.e. SVM based methods, neural network based methods and data distribution based methods, are applied to predict the protein functions.

- Firstly, the methods based on SVM model decompose ordinarily the multi-label classification into many two-class problems. Here, the **RankSvm** [15] based on a large margin ranking system is chosen to minimize generalization error of functional prediction. Then, we also utilize the **ML-LOC** [20], which allows label correlations to be exploited locally to enhance the feature representation of each protein. Then the global discrimination fitting and local correlation sensitivity are incorporated into a unified framework to predict the possible set of labels associated with one protein.
- Moreover, the neural network are also a considerable category of multi-label Learning approaches, such as BP strategy. The **BP-MLL** [16] is derived from the popular Backpropagation algorithm through employing a novel error function capturing the characteristics of multi-label learning, i.e. the labels belonging to an protein should be ranked higher than those not. Recently, a new approach named **ML-RBF** [21] is proposed, which derived from the traditional radial basis function (RBF) methods. Briefly, the first layer of an ML-RBF neural network is formed by conducting clustering analysis on proteins of each function class, where the centroid of each clustered groups is regarded as the prototype vector of a radial basis function. Both of the two models are applied in the prediction of protein function in this paper.
- Finally, there are also a plenty of multi-label methods relied on the data distribution in ordinary space or subspace after feature selection, such as ML-KNN [17], ML-NB [22], and LIFT [23]. **ML-KNN** is derived from the traditional k-Nearest Neighbor (kNN) algorithm, which based on the number of neighboring proteins belonging to each possible class, maximum a posteriori (MAP) principle is utilized to determine the label set for the unannotated protein. Analogously, **ML-NB** adapts the conventional naive Bayes classifiers to deal with multi-label proteins. In addition, **LIFT** constructs the input

features of proteins specific to each label by conducting clustering analysis on its positive and negative instances, then use a common classifier and performs training and testing by querying the clustering results.

4   Experiments and Results

4.1   Data Sets

In this paper, we exploit the Functional annotations database compiled by Munich Information Centre for Protein Sequences (MIPS) and the Gene Ontology (GO) project. The functional classification is obtained from the MIPS scheme, which contains 24 functional categories in the coarse-grained level, except for two categories for proteins with no assigned function: "Classification not yet clear-cut" and "Unclassified proteins". To validate the proposed method, the yeast Saccharomyces cerevisiae PPI network is analyzed in this section, which contains 4594 proteins annotated by the MIPS scheme with 110440 PPIs, as well as 983 unannotated proteins.

4.2   Evaluation Metrics

Each protein in multi-label learning is associated with multiple function labels simultaneously, so it is much more complicated than conventional single-label learning. After embedding the PPI network into low-dimensional space, a multi-label data set $D = \{(x_i, Y_i)|1 \leq i \leq n\}$ is obtained, and a series of metrics are used to evaluated the different multi-label learning methods $f(\cdot)$ as follow.

- **hamming loss:**

$$hloss_D(f) = \frac{1}{n} \sum_{i=1}^{n} \frac{1}{L} |f(x_i) \triangle Y_i|. \tag{1}$$

where $\triangle$ stands for the symmetric difference between two sets. The hamming loss evaluates the fraction of misclassified instance-label pairs, i.e. a relevant label is missed or an irrelevant is predicted;

- **one-error:**

$$one\text{-}error_D(f) = \frac{1}{n} \sum_{i=1}^{n} |[max_{y \in \mathcal{Y}} f(x_i, y)] \notin Y_i|. \tag{2}$$

where $|\pi|$ equals to 1 if π holds and 0 otherwise. The one-error evaluates how many times the top-ranked label is not in the set of proper labels of the protein;

- **coverage:**

$$coverage_D(f) = \frac{1}{n} \sum_{i=1}^{n} max_{y \in Y_i} rank_f(x_i, y) - 1. \tag{3}$$

The coverage evaluates how many steps are average need to move down the label list in order to cover all the proper labels of the protein;

- **ranking loss:**

$$rloss_D(f) = \frac{1}{n}\sum_{i=1}^{n}\frac{1}{|Y_i||\bar{Y}_i|}|\{(y_1,y_2)|f(x_i,y_1) < f(x_i,y_2)\}|. \qquad (4)$$

where $\forall y_1 \in Y_i$, $\forall y_2 \notin Y_i$, $(y_1,y_2) \in Y_i \times \bar{Y}_i$, and $\bar{Y}_i$ is the complementary set of Y_i. The ranking loss evaluates the fraction of reversely ordered label pairs;

- **average precision:**

$$avgprec_D(f) = \frac{1}{n}\sum_{i=1}^{n}\frac{1}{|Y_i|}\cdot\frac{|\{y'|rank_f(x_i,y') \leq rank_f(x_i,y), y' \in Y_i\}|}{rank_f(x_i,y)}. \qquad (5)$$

The average precision evaluates the average fraction of labels ranked above a particular label $y \in Y_i$ which actually are in Y.

In our experiment, for hamming loss, one-error, coverage and ranking loss, the smaller the metric value, the better the performance with optimal value of $\frac{1}{n}\sum_{i=1}^{n}|y_i|-1$ for coverage and 0 for one-error and ranking loss. For the average precision, the larger the metric value, the better the performance.

4.3 Experimental Results

In this section, both of weighted and unweighted PPI network are embedded into low-dimensional space and then several multi-label classification methods are compared and evaluated.

Embedding and Low-Dimensional Representation for PPI Network. Firstly, we compare the embedding data representation result for weighted PPI network with that for original PPI data. Previous researches attempt to adopt only the binary connection information to compute the shortest paths. Here the edge betweenness weight matrix W^B is utilized to compute the shortest path between any two proteins, then both of them are embedded to obtain the expression of proteins in low-dimensionality. We compute the corresponding residual of data representation for the unweighted and weighted PPI network. The experiment results are shown in Fig. 1. Obviously, residual variance declines sharply at first, and then the intrinsic dimension of the PPI data can be estimated by looking for the "elbow" where this curve ceases to decrease significantly with added dimensions. It is worth noting that the residual error for embedding binary adjacent matrix are consistently larger within the whole dimensional interval as shown in Fig. 1(a), in contrast to the one utilizes the edge betweenness weight matrix. The results demonstrate that the edge betweenness is more efficient in preserving the structure of PPI network. In our experiments, the intrinsic dimension is set at 174 based on Fig. 1(a).

Using ISOMAP methods, the data points are projected in to a low-dimensional metric space so that the topological structure of a PPI network can be faithfully preserved. Figure 1 also vividly exhibits an example for local

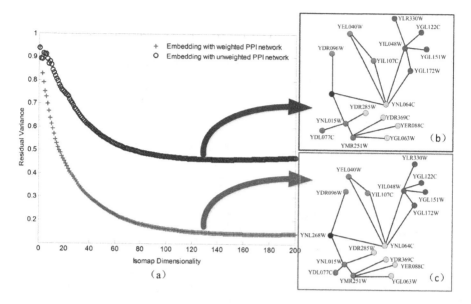

Fig. 1. Embedding and distribution information about two different weighted PPI network

low-dimensional distribution and connection of PPI network. As shown in Fig. 1, the low-dimensional distribution of proteins shared common functional class in weighted PPI (see Fig. 1(c)) is significantly closer than in the binary PPI network as shown in Fig. 1(b).

Comparison and Evaluation for Different Multi-label Approaches. In this paper, several state-of-the-art multi-label classification methods are used predict the protein functions as introduced above. To evaluate the prediction precision of multi-label learning methods based on weight ISOMAP, we measured the performance of each method by an 10-fold cross-validation, i.e., the yeast proteome was divided into 10 groups, and each group, in turn, was separated randomly from the original data set and used for testing; and then the remaining data is trained. The goal of the method is to predict the annotations of the proteins in the test set using the functional annotations of the remaining proteins. The training-test procedure is repeated 10 times. Table 1 summarizes the experimental results of the comparing algorithms, and the mean value of each algorithm is recorded. In Table 1, for each evaluation criterion, "↓" indicates "the smaller the better", while "↑" indicates "the larger the better". Furthermore, the best performance among the seven comparing algorithms is highlighted in bold-face.

As shown in Table 1, ML-KNN performs consistently better than the other methods, merely inferior to LIFT in terms of *hamming loss*. In fact, there are so many overlaps among different functional proteins that the linear classifier

Table 1. Experimental results of each comparing algorithm

Category	Algorithm	Evaluation metrics				
		Avgprec ↑	Coverage ↓	Hloss ↓	One-error ↓	Rloss ↓
SVM model	ML-LOC	0.5485	10.2217	0.1674	0.4761	0.1979
	RANK-SVM	0.5076	11.7174	0.1754	0.5304	0.2433
Neural network	BP-MLL	0.5545	9.9217	0.1801	0.4609	0.1871
	ML-RBF	0.5607	10.9109	0.1563	0.4739	0.2061
	ML-KNN	**0.5696**	**9.4326**	0.1592	**0.4358**	**0.1750**
Data distribution	ML-NB	0.5402	10.1000	0.1635	0.4826	0.1994
	LIFT	0.5406	9.9109	**0.1561**	0.4717	0.1887

based approaches cannot discriminate them preciously. In contrast, ML-KNN utilizes the maximum a posteriori (MAP) principle to determine the label set for unannotated protein under the framework of traditional KNN. That's the reason why ML-KNN has performed better than others in most of the evaluation metrics. In addition, LIFT is actually a kind of feature selection method. However, the entire low-dimensional features are abstracted from the PPI network, which have no specific physical meanings. So, the LIFT cannot improve the prediction accuracies significantly. ML-NB also incorporates the feature subset extracted by genetic algorithms. In Table 1, compared with LIFT, ML-NB gets a better performance in terms of *hamming loss*, but fails in other criterions, that reveals each feature selection method has its own merits and shortage for prediction of protein functions.

Furthermore, for neural network based methods, ML-RBF outperform the BP-MLL in terms of the evaluation criteria *average precision* and *hamming loss*. These results demonstrate that the complex global error function used by ML-RBF really works better than the intuitive error of BP-MLL.

Finally, it is also worth noting that the prediction performances of RankSVM are inferior to the other multi-label classification algorithms consistently. Therefore, the generalization error function of RankSVM is not suitable to learn the Yeast data set. In fact, the correlation among different classes is also a significant factor to multi-label learning. Follow this principle, ML-LOC incorporates the label correlations matrix into the framework of SVM. So, it's apparent that the accuracies of ML-LOC are higher than RankSVM. Besides, we also notice that k-means clustering is used in both of ML-LOC and LIFT. Due to the positive and negative proteins instances are clustered simultaneously in LIFT, LIFT performs better than ML-LOC in all metrics except *average precision*.

5   Conclusions

In this article, we introduced a prediction algorithm for protein functions based on ISOMAP and multi-label learning. Firstly, the protein-protein interaction network is weighted with edge betweenness, which could lead to more accurate low-dimensional represents. Moreover, prediction of protein function can be seamlessly mapped to the multi-label learning framework, so several state-of-the-art multi-label methods are applied to the task of functional prediction. Through evaluating these approaches in different criterions, the experiments demonstrated that the proposed method is an effective approach for prediction of protein function.

Acknowledgments. This work is supported by the National Natural Science Foundation of China (No. 61402002), the National Science Foundation of Anhui Province (No. 1408085QF120), and the Key Foundation of Natural Science Research for Institution of Higher Education of Anhui province (No. KJ2013A007).

References

1. Wang, X., Miao, Y., Cheng, M.: Finding motifs in DNA sequences using low-dispersion sequences. J. Comput. Biol. **21**(4), 320–329 (2014)
2. Wang, X., Miao, Y.: GAEM: a hybrid algorithm incorporating GA with EM for planted edited motif finding problem. Curr. Bioinform. **9**(5), 463–469 (2014)
3. Hamp, T., et al.: Homology-based inference sets the bar high for protein function prediction. BMC Bioinform. **14**(3), 327–346 (2013)
4. Radivojac, P., et al.: A large-scale evaluation of computational protein function prediction. Nat. Methods **10**(3), 221–227 (2013)
5. Wass, M.N., Sternberg, M.J.: ConFunc–functional annotation in the twilight zone. Bioinformatics **24**, 798–806 (2008)
6. Jones, C.E., Schwerdt, J., Bretag, T.A., Baumann, U., Brown, A.L.: GOSLING: a rulebased protein annotator using BLAST and GO. Bioinformatics **24**, 2628–2629 (2008)
7. Sokolov, A., Ben-Hur, A.: Hierarchical classification of gene ontology terms using the GOstruct method. J. Bioinf. Comput. Biol. **8**, 357–376 (2010)
8. Piovesan, D., et al.: Protein function prediction using guilty by association from interaction networks. Amino Acids **7**, 1–10 (2015)
9. Vazquez, A., Flammini, A., Maritan, A., Vespignani, A.: Global protein function function prediction from protein-protein interaction networks. Nat. Biotechnol. **21**(6), 697–700 (2003)
10. Chua, H., Sung, W., Wong, L.: Exploiting indirect neighbours and topological weighted to predict protein function from protein-protein inteactions. Bioinformatics **22**(13), 1623–1630 (2006)
11. Nabieva, E., Jim, K., Agarwal, A., Chazelle, B., Singh, M.: Whole-proteome prediction of protein function via graph-theoretic analysis of interaction maps. Bioinformatics **21**, 302–310 (2005)
12. You, Z.H., Lei, Y.K., Huang, D.S., Zhou, X.B.: Using mainfold embedding for asessing and predicting protein interactions from high-throughput experimental data. Bioinformatics **26**(21), 2744–2751 (2010)
13. Zhao, H.F., Sun, D.D., Wang, R.F., Luo, B.: A network-based approach for protein functions prediction using locally linear embedding. In: 4th International Conference on Bioinformatics and Biomedical Engineering, pp. 1–4. IEEE Press, Chengdu (2010)
14. Huang, L., et al.: Link clustering with extended link similarity and EQ evaluation division. PLoS One **8**(6), e66005 (2013)

15. Elisseeff, A., Weston, J., Becker, S.: A kernel method for multi-labbelled classification. In: Dietterich, T.G., Ghahramani, Z. (eds.) Advances in Neural Information Processing Systems 14, pp. 681–687. MIT Press, Cambridge (2002)
16. Zhang, M.L., Zhou, Z.H.: Multi-label neural networks with applications to functional genomics and text categorization. IEEE Transl. Knowl. Data Eng. **18**(10), 1338–1351 (2006)
17. Zhang, M.L., Zhou, Z.H.: ML-kNN: a lazy learning approach to multi-label learning. Pattern Recogn. **40**(7), 2038–2048 (2007)
18. Desmond, J.: Higham,: fitting a geometric graph to a protein-protein interaction network. Bioinformatics **24**, 1093–1099 (2008)
19. Tenenbaum, J.B.: A global geometric framework for nonlinear dimensionality reduction. Science **290**, 2319 (2000)
20. Zhang, M.L., Zhang, K.: Multi-label learning by exploiting label dependency. In: Proceedings of the 16th ACM SIGKDD Conference on Knowledge Discovery and Data Mining, pp. 999–1007. Washington (2010)
21. Zhang, M.L.: ML-RBF: RBF neural networks for multi-label learning. Neural Process. Lett. **29**(2), 61–74 (2009)
22. Zhang, M.L., Peña, J.M., Robles, V.: Feature selection for multi-label naive bayes classification. Inf. Sci. **179**(19), 3218–3229 (2009)
23. Zhang, M.L.: LIFT: Multi-label learning with label-specific features. In: Proceedings of the 22nd International Joint Conference on Artificial Intelligence, pp. 1609–1614. Barcelona, Spain (2011)

Logic Gates Based on Circular DNA Strand Displacement and a Fluorescent Agent

Fangfang Liu[1], Yanchai Wang[2], Minghui Li[2], Xiangxiang Chen[2], and Yafei Dong[1(✉)]

[1] Department of Life Science, Shaanxi Normal University, Xi'an 710119, China
dongyf@snnu.edu.cn
[2] Department of Computer Science, Shaanxi Normal University, Xi'an 710119, China

Abstract. We constructed a three-input OR logic gate based on a single-strand DNA circle and a two-input AND logic gate measuring fluorescence signals produced by strand displacement to detect the outputs. The simple, cost effective OR and AND logic gates produced the expected results, demonstrating their feasibility for future use in DNA computing. Fluorescently labeled DNA oligonucleotide inputs were initially hybridized with a quencher strand, which was displaced when the input strands hybridized to circular DNA.

Keywords: Circular DNA · DNA self-assembly · DNA strand displacement · Fluorescent agent · Logic gate

1 Introduction

Bio-inspired computing models are a hot research topic in natural computing, wherein many parallel computing models, such as DNA computing [2,4,5], membrane computing [3,7,10], have been proposed. Logic gates are core components in conventional silicon-based computers and are also applied to information processing in DNA (molecular) computing. Recently, a fluorescent agent [1] and DNA/gold nanoparticles (DNA/AuNP) [4,5] book have been used in DNA computing. Adleman [6] first reported the use of molecular biology to solve a seven-vertices Hamiltonian path problem. Then, Saghatelian et al. [8] proposed the DNA-based photonic logic gates: AND, NAND, and INHIBIT. Subsequently, DNA computing has attracted the attention of many researchers and various molecular models have been proposed. In particular, Zhang et al. [9] established a circular DNA molecule for the maximum clique problem and constructed circular DNA logic gates based on DNA three-way branch migration [12]. Cheng et al. [13] proposed a logic model for gene detection of the influenza H1N1 virus. Li et al. [14] built a circular DNA strand model with three unique domains that are identical joint sequences. Later, Zhang et al. [15] developed DNA strand displacement based on circular DNA that controlled the aggregation of AuNPs.

© Springer-Verlag Berlin Heidelberg 2015
M. Gong et al. (Eds.): BIC-TA 2015, CCIS 562, pp. 260–267, 2015.
DOI: 10.1007/978-3-662-49014-3_24

Here, we established a three-input OR logic gate and a two-input AND logic gate depending on a single-strand DNA circle, demonstrated assembly realization via a fluorescence signal, and recorded the emergence and quenching of the fluorescence signal by strand displacement.

2 Materials and Methods

2.1 Logic Calculation Models

A simple logic gate consists of a transistor and a combination of transistors can implement two signals, high or low. High-and low-level signals can represent the logical "true" and "false" values or the binary numbers 1 and 0, so as to realize logic operations.

2.2 And Logic Gate and or Logic Gate

The AND logic gate is the most common gate [16,17], which outputs a "true" value only when all the input values are "true", otherwise the output is "false". The OR logic gate [18,21] outputs a "true" value if one or more of the inputs are "true", only when all the inputs are "false" the output is "false". The AND and OR logic gates are the core of the common DNA logic gates, which act like doors in the DNA (Table 1).

Table 1. Simple interpretation of AND logic gate and OR logic gate

Type	Simple interpretation	Logic functions
X	Y	Output
AND	AND gate: When all inputs are "true" the output is true. Otherwise the output is "false"	X*Y
0	0	0
0	1	0
1	0	0
1	1	1
OR	When all inputs are "false", the output is "false". Otherwise, "true". the output is "false". Otherwise the output is "true"	X+Y
0	0	0
0	1	1
1	0	1
1	1	1

2.3   Fluorescent Agents and DNA Strand Displacement

Fluorescent agents can absorb certain wavelengths of incident light, which excites the electrons in the molecules to a higher energy level causing them to emit light. DNA fluorescence techniques have been used extensively in many areas of biology, including DNA fluorescence labeling, real-time detection technologies, and molecular marker technology [19,22]. DNA marked with a fluorescent signal can be detected in real time with high sensitivity, which makes it highly suited for application in DNA computing.

DNA strand displacement technology has been used to join an input strand to form an intact DNA duplex based on a single-strand DNA molecule [2]. The characteristics of this technology are spontaneity, sensitivity, and accuracy [23]. This technology also is applicable to logic operations such as the construction of the basic logic gates (e.g., AND gate and OR gate).

3   Results

3.1   Circularization of Strand T

To build the DNA fluorescence system, we first generated a DNA circular structure (Fig. 1). Strand T hybridized with TP (the red region in the TP strand was complementary with the two ends of strand T), which brought the two ends of T into close proximity. The gap was then ligated by T4 ligase to produce a circular strand via DNA displacement. Strand displacement can effectively translate the strand so that a DNA circle can be obtained conveniently. To construct a three-input OR gate, we made a circular DNA strand (T) composed of three distinct domains that could hybridize with linear DNA strand (Fig. 1 shows an example).

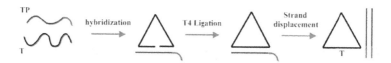

Fig. 1. Generation of a single-strand DNA circle T. Strand T hybridized with TP to bring the two ends of the T strand together. The red region of the TP strand is complementary with the two ends of strand T. T4 ligase was used to ligate the two ends. The blue region of the TP strand is the foothold for strand displacement. TP* can form a double strand with TP by strand displacement, leaving behind the DNA circle T (Color figure online).

We constructed the logic gates by the sequences of listed in Table 2, the oligonucleotides sequences were designed by NUPACK.

Table 2. DNA sequences

No.	Sequence (from 5' to 3')
T	5'-Phosphorylated-TGACCATAGAATTGCCGTTAGTGGTTATTGATGA-GTAACAGGATAGTCGTATGCCTAAGCAGG-3'
TP	5'-TATGGTCACCTGCTTAGGGTAGTGC-3'
TP	5'-GCACTACCCTAAGCAGGTGACCATA-3'
X_1	5'-TTTTTTTTTCTATGGTCACCTGCTTAGGTTG TAGTGCTAATGTT-GTTTTTTTTTTTTTTTT-3' 3'-AAAAAAAAAGCTACCA-5'
X_2	5'-TTTTTTTTTTATCAATAACCACTAACGGCAAT GCAGTATGTAGAT-CCTTTTTTTTTTTTTTTTT-3' 3'-AAAAAAAAAATAGTTAT-5'
X_3	5'-TTTTTTTTTTCATACGACTATC CTGTTACTCTTGACAGCTCAGGT-AGATTTTTTTTTTTTTTTTT-3' 3'-AAAAAAAAAAGTATGCT-5'
Y_1	5'-AAAAAAAAAAAAAAAAAACAAC ATTAGCACTACAACCTAAGCAGG TGACCATAGAAAAAAAAA-3'
Y_2	5'-AAAAAAAAAAAAAAAA AGGATCTACATACTGCATTGCC GTTAGTGGTTATTGATAAAAAAAAAA-3'

3.2 OR Logic Gate with DNA Circle

The DNA circle T was used as the reaction substrate and partial double strands X_1, X_2, and X_3 with the same lengths but different sequences were used as inputs (Fig. 2A). The 3 ends of the longer strands were marked with fluorescent agents; X_1 and X_2 were marked with green fluorescent agent, and X_3 was marked with a red fluorescent agent. The 5 ends of the shorter strands were marked with the corresponding quenching agent.

For the major three-input OR logic system, the three input sequences had the same preference to hybridize with the DNA circle T. In an OR logic system, adding one or more of the three input strands that bind to circle T will make the output true (Fig. 2B).

Step 1. When the X_1 or X_2 partial double strand was input (Fig. 2B), the longer single-strand a or b was captured by the circle T, a green fluorescence signal was produced and the shorter linear single-strand a or b was released. When the X_3 partial double strand was input, the c strand was captured, a red fluorescence signal was produced and the shorter c strand was released. Thus, as expected, the output was true.

Step 2. Next, we used two different, partial double strands as inputs to observe whether the system still worked (Fig. 2B). First, when X_1 and X_2 were added

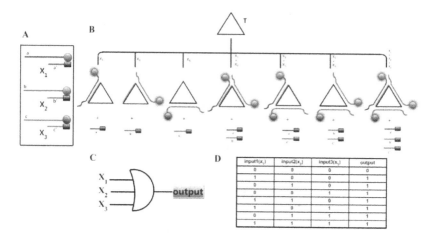

Fig. 2. Representation of a three-input OR logic system (A) Three types of partial double strands $X_{1,\,2}$, and X_3 used as inputs. The red circles represent the red fluorescence agent, the green circles represent the green fluorescence agent, and the black rectangles represent the corresponding quenching agent. (B) Schematic of the design of the OR logic gate. Different input combinations produce different outputs, all of which are true. (C) Logic element of the OR logic gate. (D) Truth table of the three-input OR logic system (Color figure online).

together, a and b were captured by circle T and a and b were released. We observed only a green fluorescence signal that was higher in intensity than the fluorescence intensity observed in step 1. When X_1 and X_3 or X_2 and X_3 were input into the system, because a and c or b and c were captured by the circle T, a and c or b and c were released, and both red and green fluorescence signals were observed. Thus, as expected, the output was true.

Step 3. When we used all three of the partial double strands, a, b, and c were captured by circle T simultaneously, a, b, and c were released and we observed red and green fluorescence signals that were high in intensity (Fig. 2B). Thus, as expected, the output was true.

3.3   And Logic Gate with a Product-Supermolecule Assembly

In this experiment, we used the former experimental product-supermolecule assembly when the a, b and c were captured by T simultaneously as the reaction substratesas the reaction substrate, with the same a, b, and c single strands this time with complete complementary strands of only a and b, here called Y_1 and Y_2 respectively, as inputs (Fig. 3A). The 3 ends of Y_1 and Y_2 were marked with the corresponding quenching agent. In the AND logic system, only when both input values are true, the output result is true. The AND gate can be proved by distinguishing the different colors of the fluorescence signal; in this example,

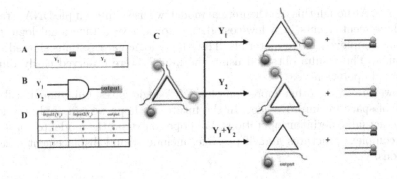

Fig. 3. Representation of a two-input AND logic system (A) Two linear single-strand DNAs, Y_1 and Y_2, which were complete complementary strands of only a and b, are used as inputs. The black rectangles represent the corresponding quenching agent. (B) Logic element of the AND logic gate. (C) Schematic of the design of the AND logic gate. The output is true only when Y_1 and Y_2 are added at the same time. The red circles represent the red fluorescence agent, and the green circles represent the green fluorescence agent. (D) Truth table of the two-input AND logic system (Color figure online).

when the circular polymer is marked only with the red fluorescence signal, the result is true.

Step 1. The addition of strand Y_1 displaced only strand a, leaving strands b and c bounded to the DNA circle (Fig. 3C). Double-strand aY_1 was produced and a green fluorescence signal was observed; no red fluorescence signal was quenched. Moreover, if strand Y_2 was added alone, only double-strand bY_2 was produced and a green fluorescence signal can be observed. Again no red fluorescence signal quenched (Fig. 3C). Therefore, when either Y_1 or Y_2 were added, as expected, the output was false.

Step 2. When strands Y_1 and Y_2 were both added together (Fig. 3C), a and b were both displaced from the circular scaffold and two types of double-strand DNA were produced, leaving only the linear single-strand c with the red fluorescent agent on the DNA circle (Fig. 3C). As expected, the output was true. This result indicates that complex displacements of this type can be handled in the circular, DNA logic gate system.

4 Discussion

We have constructed a three-input OR logic gate based on a single-strand DNA circle, and demonstrated its application using fluorescence signals. We also used the former experimental product-supermolecule assembly and strand displacement to distinguish different colors of the fluorescence signal to detect an AND logic gate. Although this is a theoretical model, we used only simple DNA strands and fluorescent agents in a low-cost design to achieve a functional logic gate without complex reactive materials. The simple logic gate systems showed high feasibility. The results obtained using the models were observed easily during the actual operation.

However, unlike other more complex DNA logic gates, this model still has plenty of space for improvement. In the future, we hope we can apply the logic gate to actual experiment operations. We hope to extend the model to construct more complex structures and, if possible, include strand displacement cascade reactions.

Acknowledgments. This research is supported by National Natural Science Foundation of China (Grant Nos. 61272246) and National Natural Science Foundation of China (Grant Nos. 61173113) and Innovation Funds of Graduate Programs Fund of Shaanxi Normal University. The authors acknowledge the anonymous referees suggestion to this paper.

References

1. Zhang, C., Yang, J., Wang, S.: Development and application of fluorescence technology in DNA computing. Chin. J. Comput. **32**, 2300–2310 (2009)
2. Shi, X., Wang, Z., Deng, C., Song, T., Pan, L., Chen, Z.: A novel bio-sensor based on DNA strand displacement. PLoS One **9**, e108856 (2014)
3. Song, T., Pan, L.: Spiking neural P systems with rules on synapses working in maximum spikes consumption strategy. IEEE Trans. NanoBiosci. **14**(1), 38–44 (2015)
4. Dong, Y., Wang, Y., Ma, J., Jia, L.: The application of DNA nanoparticle conjugates on the graph's connectivity problem. Adv. Intell. Syst. Comput. **212**, 257–265 (2013)
5. Herman, A.: Tip-based nanofabrication as a rapid prototyping tool for quantum science and technology. Rev. Theor. Sci. **1**, 3–33 (2013)
6. Adleman, L.M.: Molecular computation of solutions to combinatorial problems. Science **266**, 1021 (1994)
7. Song, T., Pan, L.: Spiking neural P systems with rules on synapses working in maximum spiking strategy. IEEE Trans. NanoBiosci. **14**(4), 465–477 (2015)
8. Saghatelian, A., Volcker, N.H., Guckian, K.M., et al.: DNA-based photonic logic gates: AND, NAND, and INHIBIT. J. Am. Chem. Soc. **125**, 346–347 (2003)
9. Yang, J., Zhang, C., Xu, J., Liu, X.R., Qiang, X.L.: A novel computing model of the maximum clique problem based on circular DNA. Sci. Chin. Inf. Sci. **53**, 1409 (2010)
10. Song, T., Pan, L., Jiang, K., et al.: Normal forms for some classes of sequential spiking neural P systems. IEEE Trans. NanoBiosci. **12**(3), 255–264 (2013)
11. Song, T., Pan, L., Păun, G.: Asynchronous spiking neural P systems with local synchronization. Inf. Sci. **219**, 197–207 (2013)
12. Zhang, C., Yang, J., Xu, J.: Circular DNA logic gates with strand displacement. Langmuir **26**, 1416 (2010)
13. Cheng, Z., Jing, Y., Jin, X.: Molecular logic computing model based on self-assembly of DNA nanoparticles. Chin. Sci. Bull. **33**, 3566 (2011)

14. Li, W., Yang, Y., Yan, H., Liu, Y.: Three-input majority logic gate and multiple input logic circuitbased on DNA strand displacement. Am. Chem. Soc. **13**, 2980–2988 (2013)
15. Zhang, C., Ma, J.J., Yang, J., Dong, Y.F., Xu, J.: Control of gold nanoparticles based on circular DNA strand displacement. J. Colloid Interface Sci. **418**, 31–36 (2014)
16. Frezza, B.M., Cockroft, S.L., Ghadiri, M.R.: Modular multi-level circuits from immobilized DNA-based logic gates. J. Am. Chem. Soc. **129**, 14875–14879 (2007)
17. Ogasawara, S., Ami, T., Fujimoto, K.: Autonomous DNA computing machine based on photochemical gate transition. J. Am. Chem. Soc. **130**, 10050–10051 (2008)
18. Miyoshi, D., Inoue, M., Sugimoto, N.: DNA logic gates based on structural polymorphism of telomere DNA molecules responding to chemical input signals. Angew. Chem. Int. Ed. **45**, 7716–7719 (2006)
19. Song, T., Pan, L., Wang, J., et al.: Normal forms of spiking neural P systems with anti-spikes. IEEE Trans. NanoBiosci. **11**(4), 352–359 (2012)
20. Zhang, X., Pan, L., Păun, A.: On the universality of axon P systems. IEEE Trans. Neural Netw. Learn. Syst. (2015). doi:10.1109/TNNLS.2015.2396940
21. Voelcker, N.H., Guckian, K.M., Saghatelian, A., Ghadiri, M.R.: Sequence-addressable DNA logic. Small **4**, 427–431 (2008)
22. Jonathan, B., Turberfield, A.J.: DNA nanomachines. Nat. Nanotechnol. **2**, 275–284 (2007)
23. Wang, X., Song, T.: MRPGA: motif detecting by modified random projection strategy and genetic algorithm. J. Comput. Theor. Nanosci. **10**, 1209–1214 (2013)

Hybrid Ejection Chain Methods
for the Traveling Salesman Problem

Weichen Liu[1], Thomas Weise[1]([✉]), Yuezhong Wu[1], and Raymond Chiong[2]

[1] Joint USTC-Birmingham Research Institute in Intelligent Computation
and Its Applications (UBRI), School of Computer Science and Technology,
University of Science and Technology of China, Hefei 230027, Anhui, China
tweise@ustc.edu.cn, {lwc,yuezhong}@mail.ustc.edu.cn
[2] School of Design, Communication and IT, Faculty of Science and IT,
The University of Newcastle, Callaghan NSW 2308, Australia
Raymond.Chiong@newcastle.edu.au

Abstract. Local search such as Ejection Chain Methods (ECMs) based
on the stem-and-cycle (S&C) reference structure, Lin-Kernighan (LK)
heuristics, as well as the recently proposed Multi-Neighborhood Search
(MNS), are among the most competitive algorithms for the Traveling
Salesman Problem (TSP). In this paper, we carry out a large-scale experiment with all 110 symmetric instances from the *TSPLib* to investigate
the performances of these algorithms. Our study is different from previous work along this line of research in that we consider the entire runtime behavior of the algorithms, not just their end results. This leads to
one of the most comprehensive comparisons of these algorithms to date.
We introduce a new, improved S&C-ECM that can outperform LK and
MNS. We then develop new hybrid versions of our ECM implementations
by combining them with Evolutionary Algorithms and Population-based
Ant Colony Optimization (PACO). We compare them to similar hybrids
of LK and MNS. Our results show that hybrid PACO-S&C, PACO-LK
and PACO-MNS are all very efficient. We also find that the full runtime
behavior comparison provides deeper and clearer insights, while focusing
on end results only would have led to a misleading conclusion.

Keywords: Traveling salesman problem · Ejection chain methods ·
Lin-Kernighan heuristic · Multi-neighborhood search · Hybrid
algorithms

1 Introduction

The Traveling Salesman Problem (TSP) [1,14,22] is a well-known $\mathcal{NP}$-hard
problem in the field of combinatorial optimization. The problem can be stated
as follows: Given n cities (named from 1 to n) and the distances $D_{i,j}$ (with
$i,j \in 1,2,\dots n$) between them, a salesman starts from one city, visits each of
the cities once, and then returns to the original city. The assignment is to find
the order in which the salesman should visit the cities with the shortest overall

© Springer-Verlag Berlin Heidelberg 2015
M. Gong et al. (Eds.): BIC-TA 2015, CCIS 562, pp. 268–282, 2015.
DOI: 10.1007/978-3-662-49014-3_25

travel distance. A tour, i.e., a candidate solution to the TSP, can be defined as permutation $t = (t_1, t_2, \ldots, t_n)$ of the cities to visit. The task is to find a t that minimizes the sum $D_{t[1],t[2]} + D_{t[2],t[3]} + \cdots + D_{t[n],t[1]}$. We focus on symmetric TSP instances in which $D_{i,j} = D_{j,i}$ holds.

The TSP is $\mathcal{NP}$-hard, therefore any existing exact TSP algorithms have exponential worst-case runtime complexity. To get good approximate solutions within acceptable time, many approaches have been introduced, including Local Search (LS) algorithms, Evolutionary Algorithms (EAs) [3,5,29], and Ant Colony Optimization (ACO) [6,7,9]. The state-of-the-art algorithms are two LS families: The more well-known is the Lin-Kernighan (LK) heuristic [23], while the other is the Ejection Chain Method (ECM) based on a stem-and-cycle (S&C) structure. ECMs are reported to provide better results than (pure) LK in several studies [25–27], but at the cost of more runtime. Recently, another competitive LS algorithm, the Multi-Neighborhood Search (MNS) [30], was introduced and found to be particularly suitable for hybridization [32].

In this paper, we introduce a new, improved ECM working on the S&C structure. We compare it with two existing S&C-ECMs and show that it significantly outperforms them. An in-depth and statistically sound comparison of all three S&C-ECMs with LK and MNS is then carried out, and the results show that our improved ECM outperforms both LK and MNS in terms of results and speed. We also hybridize S&C-ECMs with EAs and PACO, and compare them to similar hybrids based on LK and MNS. We conduct a large-scale experimental study and apply advanced, runtime-behavior based statistics that provide much more performance information of these algorithms than simple end-result comparisons. We confirm that PACO-based hybrids are much better than EA-based ones (i.e., Memetic Algorithms) and pure LS approaches. Interestingly, hybrid MNS is shown to be the most suitable LS for hybridization in our experiments, although it is outperformed by both LK and ECMs in its pure form. This study provides more precise, comprehensive, and statistically sound evaluations than any other previous work on this topic.

The remainder of this paper is organized as follows. First, we present the investigated S&C-ECMs, LK heuristic and MNS, as well as their new hybrid versions in Sect. 2. Since LK, ECMs based on the S&C structure and MNS mark the state-of-the-art in terms of LS for the TSP, this section indirectly also describes the related work. In Sect. 3, we discuss our experimental study and analyze its results. The paper ends with conclusions and plans for future work in Sect. 4.

2   Investigated Algorithms

Today, the best known algorithms for the TSP are LS methods and in this paper, we consider three of them. An LS algorithm maintains and iteratively tries to improve a single candidate solution. The initial solution is often randomly generated or stemmed from a simple heuristic. In each step, the LS explores the neighborhood of the solution, which is spanned by possible applications of a search operator. If it contains a better solution, then this solution is accepted as the basis for the next iteration. If no better solution is found, the LS either terminates or restarts. In the latter case, either a new, random solution is used or the current solution is randomly modified in a way that is beyond what the search operation could achieve. Restarts are necessary, because the neighborhoods spanned by search operators are much smaller than the search space. As a result, local optima, i.e., solutions that are not optimal but whose neighborhoods only contain inferior solutions, exist.

In the TSP, the most common search operations are k-opt moves, which delete k edges in a tour and replace them with k other edges [30]. A 2-opt move, replacing two edges, corresponds to the reversal of a part of the tour [18,21]. Rotating a part of the tour one step to the left or right corresponds to a 3-opt move [8,21]. Swapping two cities is a 4-opt move [21,24].

2.1 ECMs

The ECM was introduced by Glover in 1992 [11]. ECMs provide k-opt moves for discrete optimization problems. The basic component of an ECM is the data structure it processes with its search operations. This structure can be different from simple path or adjacency list representations.

We investigate the S&C reference structure, which consists of a path (called stem) attached to a cycle of nodes, as illustrated in Fig. 1a. The common node of S&C is called root r and its two adjacent nodes on the cycle are called sub-roots (s_1 and s_2). The root r marks one end of the stem. The other end is the tip t.

Only if the stem is degenerated to become a single node (i.e., $r = t$), the S&C structure is a tour. Otherwise, the S&C structure can be transformed to two candidate tours by removing the edge between one of the sub-roots si and the root r, and then re-connecting si to the tip t. The better one of these two trial solutions can be chosen.

The search does not take place in the space of possible tours, but directly on the S&C structures, which are iteratively refined according to a set of rules.

2.2 Fundamental S&C Approaches

The Fundamental S&C (FSC) algorithm proposed by Rego [26] defines a complete LS procedure including tabu criteria and concepts of limiting the search depth to improve performance. The core of FSC is Glover's two rules [12] for updating the S&C, i.e., the search operations of FSC:

1. Choose a node j on the cycle. Let the two nodes adjacent to it be q_1 and q_2. Select one of them and refer to it as q. Delete any edge adjacent to j and then add edge (t, j).
2. Choose a node j on the stem. Let the node adjacent to j and farther away from r than the other adjacent node be called q. Connect t to j and delete edge (j, q).

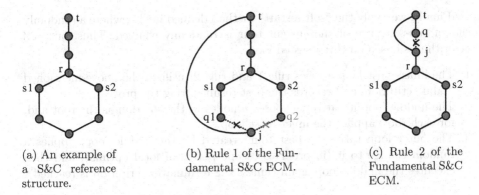

(a) An example of a S&C reference structure.

(b) Rule 1 of the Fundamental S&C ECM.

(c) Rule 2 of the Fundamental S&C ECM.

Fig. 1. Examples of a S&C reference structure and the two rules of the Fundamental S&C ECM.

In both cases, q becomes the new tip t (see Fig. 1b, c). Each of their applications *ejects* a sequence of edges from a tour and replaces them. Based on these two rules, a S&C structure can be transformed to another one.

What Glover [10] did not specify, however, is how to choose j and how to iterate the rule application. Rego [26] therefore defined the equation $e = D_{add} - D_{delete}$, where D_{add} is the length of the edges to be added and D_{delete} the length of the deleted ones. FSC iterates over all the available j nodes in the S&C and applies both rules 1 and 2. From these choices, it identifies the move with the smallest corresponding value of e. By applying this move, a solution is changed to another one.

It is worth noting that both rules never change the root node r. The LS is iteratively applied to different roots. This is achieved by starting with a set R containing all n nodes, randomly choosing one to be the root, and removing it from R. Then, the search for minimal e values starts at "level 0". Whenever the solution is changed, the level increases. Glover [11] and Rego [26] found that stopping the search at a relatively low level leads to better performance. After that, another node from R is randomly extracted to be the root for the next iteration.

Glover [11] and Rego [26] defined a "tabu" criterion to prevent generating the same trial solutions repetitively, i.e., no deleted edge should be added back to a S&C structure. This led to the algorithm defined by Rego as P_SEC in [26]. Here, we refer to it as FSM and improve it in several ways.

First, we propose a new criterion for permitting more moves in order to increase the searchable neighborhood: no previously *deleted* edge can be deleted again (after being re-inserted). This method is denoted as FSM*. We will show that it can produce much better performance not only in terms of speed but also in the quality of the end results. Second, in algorithm version FSM**, we reduce the number of redundant moves by more aggressively limiting the maximum level to $0.45n$ and testing only 15 % of the nodes in R as the root node to restart.

Finally, we apply the "soft restart" method defined in [30], where a randomly chosen sub-sequence of the current tour is randomly shuffled. Thus, our FSM algorithm is based on three nested loops:

1. The inner-most loop applies rule 1 and rule 2, utilizes the above-mentioned "tabu" criterion, and records the best result during the process.
2. The middle loop iteratively chooses n nodes in the solution as the root and, for each root, applies the inner-most loop.
3. The outer loop takes the best tour created by the middle loop, applies a random change to it (in order to escape potential local optima), and then executes the middle loop again (unless the termination criterion is reached).

2.3 LK Heuristics

Today, the domain of TSP solvers is "ruled" by derivatives of the LK heuristic [23], which can either be considered as a variable k-op heuristic [2,16,17] or as an ECM based on a detached stem reference structure [26]. The former perspective is obviously more common.

For ascending values of k, the LK heuristic tries to obtain a shorter tour by replacing k edges. It therefore proceeds as follows to improve a given tour T. Step by step, the algorithm builds two sets: $X = \{X_1, \ldots, X_k\}$ of edges to be deleted from T, and $Y = \{Y_1, \ldots, Y_k\}$ the set of edges to be added to T. Each edge X_i is chosen such that its start node is the end node of edge Y_{i-1}, while the start node of edge Y_{i+1} is the end node of X_i. By additionally ensuring that the end of Y_k is the start node of X_1, deleting the edges X from T and inserting those from Y will always yield a valid tour. This constitutes a k-opt move, of which the result is accepted if it is shorter than T.

The standard LK heuristic tries all possible choices of X and Y only for $i \leq 2$. While for larger i, no backtracking is allowed. We compare our ECMs with the LK heuristic from [32], where the first improved tour is accepted instead of searching the whole neighborhood, following the suggestion in [16]. This implementation also applies the restart method from [30] used in our FSM.

2.4 MNS

While FSM and LK both investigate potentially very large neighborhoods, the recently proposed MNS applies traditional fixed-k-opt moves. In each iteration, MNS performs a $\mathcal{O}(n^2)$ scan, which investigates all possible 2-opt and a subset of the possible 3- and 4-opt moves at once. It therefore tests all indexes i and j as potential indexes for cities to swap or start and end indexes of sub-sequence rotations and reversals. For each operation and pair $\{i, j\}$, the gain is computed and all discovered improving moves enter a queue. The access to distance matrix D is minimized by remembering (and updating) the lengths of all n edges in the current tour and avoiding checking redundant moves (swapping the cities at indexes i and $i + 1$ is equivalent to a reversal of the sub-sequence from i to $i + 1$, for instance). After the scan, the best discovered move is carried out.

This may invalidate other moves in the queue, e.g., if a sub-sequence reversal that overlaps with a potential sub-sequence left rotation was performed. After pruning all invalidated moves from the queue, the remaining best move is carried out, if any. If the queue becomes empty, another scan of the current solution is performed, as new moves may have become possible. During this scan, only moves that at least intersect with the previously modified sub-sequence(s) of the current best solution need to be considered for additional speed-up. If no improving moves can be found anymore, the same "soft restart" method as discussed before is applied [30].

2.5 MAs

EAs are global optimization algorithms inspired by the natural processes of selection and reproduction. They start with a set of λ (usually random) solutions. Among them, the best $\mu \leq \lambda$ solutions are chosen as "parents" of the second generation, which is generated by applying a (unary) mutation or a (binary) crossover operator to the "parents". From then on, the parents are the μ best individuals from the joined set of parents and offspring $[(\mu + \lambda)\text{-EA}]$.

MAs are EAs hybridized with LS. In our MAs, the LS algorithm is applied to every solution generated by crossover. We use Edge Crossover [31] at a crossover rate of 100 %. Edge Crossover is one of the best crossover operators for the TSP. It generates a new solution by picking edges belonging to either of its two parents.

We introduce three different MAs, namely hMA$(\mu + \lambda)$ECM, hMA$(\mu + \lambda)$LK and hMA$(\mu + \lambda)$MNS. The little h at the beginning of the name means that the initialization of these MAs is generated by the Edge-Greedy, Double Minimum Spanning Tree, Savings, Double-Ended Nearest Neighbor and Nearest Neighbor heuristics, as in [30].

2.6 Memetic ACO

The ACO algorithm is inspired by the way ants find and enhance short paths during foraging by using pheromones for communication [6]. PACO [13] is considerably the best-performing ACO variant. Different from standard ACO, which requires storing a pheromone matrix of size in $\mathcal{O}(n^2)$, PACO has linear memory requirements. PACO(k,m) maintains a population of k solutions and the amount of pheromone on an edge of the TSP is proportional to how many solutions this edge has. For every algorithm iteration, m solutions are created and the "oldest" solution in the entire population is replaced by the best solution in the new generation. Similar to our MAs, our hybrid PACO algorithms are defined in a way that each new solution generated is used as the starting point of a LS procedure whose output then competes to join the population. Such hybrids have performed the best in [30]. Like in our MAs as well as our algorithms from [30], we initialize the first population heuristically.

3   Experiments and Results

3.1   Experimentation with Anytime Algorithms

Most metaheuristics, including EAs, MAs, ACO, as well as all LS methods, are anytime algorithms [4]. Anytime algorithms can provide a best guess of what the optimal solution of a problem could be at *any time during* their run. Experiments for analyzing the behavior of an algorithm over runtime are therefore essential, but are rarely done due to the amount of data they generate and the amount of work required in evaluating the data.

Our *TSP Suite* [30] focuses on investigation of TSP solvers, where data is automatically collected during the evaluation of candidate solutions. Reports showing results based on the data can be automatically generated and freely configured. They contain in-depth descriptions of the experimental procedure and provide several different statistical analyses such as statistical tests comparing the measured runtimes and end results, automated comparisons of the estimated running time (ERT) [15] curves over goal objective values or problem scales, and automated comparisons of empirical cumulative distribution functions (ECDFs) [15,19,28]. All of the information is aggregated into human-readable conclusions about the algorithm performance in the form of global rankings.

The *TSP Suite* is the very first framework addressing the issue of measuring runtime. Measuring runtime in CPU seconds produces machine-dependent results. Even if normalized runtimes (NT) are calculated based on machine performance factors, they remain problem specific and may not represent the utility of black-box metaheuristics in general. Counting the number of generated solutions (i.e., objective function evaluations or *FEs* in short) is the most-often used alternative in benchmarking. To provide a balanced overview of algorithm performance, the *TSP Suite* evaluates runtime using four different measures: CPU time, normalized CPU time, FEs, and the number DE of accesses to the distance matrix D of a TSP.

3.2   Experimental Setup

We conducted our experiments using the symmetric *TSPLib* benchmark cases, for which all optima are known. We can therefore define the quality of a solution as relative error f, the factor by which a solution (tour) is longer than the optimum. Here, $f = 0$ stands for the optimal solution, and $f = 1$ indicates one that is twice as long. We performed 30 independent runs for each setup on all of the 110 symmetric instances in the *TSPLib* to deal with different hard and easy instances [20], with scales n ranging from 14 to above 85900.

Related work usually focuses on fewer and smaller instances. Rego [26], for example, reported results only for 66 instances with n up to 7397. In [25], 8 instances with n from 48 to 666 were used.

We compared the following algorithms: *(1)* FSM, *(2)* FSM*, *(3)* FSM**, *(4)* LK, and *(5)* MNS. For each algorithm, seven setups were built: The original (pure) algorithm, three hybrids with PACO and three MAs.

3.3 Pure Algorithm Performance

Let us first explore the performance of the three pure versions of FSM (FSM, FSM*, FSM**) and compare them with pure LK and the pure MNS methods. According to the automated ranking provided by the *TSP Suite*, FSM** has the best performance among these algorithms.

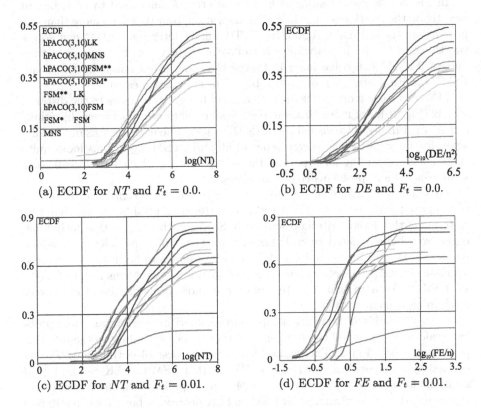

(a) ECDF for NT and $F_t = 0.0$.

(b) ECDF for DE and $F_t = 0.0$.

(c) ECDF for NT and $F_t = 0.01$.

(d) ECDF for FE and $F_t = 0.01$.

Fig. 2. ECDF diagrams for different (log-scaled) runtime measures and goal errors.

In Fig. 2, we plot the ECDF for different goal errors F_t and runtime measures. The ECDF illustrates the fraction of runs that have discovered a (best) solution with $F_b \leq F_t$ up to a given amount of runtime. Hence, an algorithm is good if its ECDF comes as close to 1 as possible in as soon a manner as possible.

The ECDF of FSM** in Fig. 2a, based on the normalized CPU runtime measure NT, increases quickly and approaches 0.4 for $F_t = 0$. In other words, a global optimum can be reached in about 40 % (of the runs) of all benchmark cases under the given computational budget. Although this does not seem to be very good, FSM** is faster in solving the problems among all pure algorithm settings, as its ECDF curve is always higher than the others. We can further-more see that the ECDF of FSM* increases a little faster than the one of LK at the beginning, but is eventually overtaken by LK. The performance of FSM is similar to that of FSM* at the beginning, but needs more and more time to solve harder problems. The ECDF of MNS increases slightly faster than the one of FSM** in the beginning, but later slows down and finally reaches a little more than 0.1. For small time budgets, MNS solves more problems than the other methods.

In Fig. 2c, we show results with the goal error F_t increased to 0.01, i.e., to investigate the fraction of runs in finding a solution/tour that is no more than 1% longer than the optimum. Again, the ECDF curves intersect. FSM** now solves two thirds of the problems while LK can solve slightly less. For any given time budget, FSM** can solve more instances than any other non-hybrid method. FSM* and FSM are again overtaken by LK as the time goes on.

MNS can solve more problems with a small budget of accesses to the distance matrix (Fig. 2b). For more *DE*s, we see the same relationship between algorithms as per *NT*. Finally, if we visualize the ECDF under time measure *FE*s in Fig. 2d – again for $F_t = 0.01$ – the performance of all three FSM algorithms looks quite similar, except for the later part in the search, during which FSM** can solve significantly more problems than the others.

We thereby conclude that FSM** can solve more problems than the other tested pure LS algorithm and that FSM* is better than FSM but worse than LK. In terms of the design criteria discussed in Sect. 2.2, this means that forbidding edges from being deleted twice is better than forbidding the deletion of added edges (FSM* vs. FSM). Limiting the number of nodes to be tested as the root aggressively further increases the chance of solving the problems faster (FSM** vs. FSM*). We note that a better solution is more probably found at a lower level, in agreement with [12, 26].

Next, we analyzed the relationship between algorithm performance and problem scale n. We grouped the problems by their scales according to the different powers of two in Fig. 3. This figure illustrates the best objective value F_b discovered by an algorithm over runtime. We see that FSM and LK can find good solutions for instances with n below 1024 quite rapidly. With the increasing of instance scale, the performance of FSM and LK decreases, but they can still find approximate solutions with $F_t \leq 0.05$ for $n < 32768$.

In Fig. 3c, we can see that FSM** is always better than LK when $n < 4096$. For a higher scale, LK is better at the beginning but eventually overtaken. FSM* behaves similar to FSM** at the beginning, but is overtaken by both LK and FSM**. FSM is worse than FSM*. Compared to FSM and LK, MNS performs better on small instances but worse for moderate and large-sized ones.

In Fig. 4, we plot the ERT in terms of *NT* (y-axis) for a given solution quality threshold F_t (x-axis), i.e., the expected normalized runtime it will take for an algorithm to reach F_t. Obviously, the smaller F_t, the higher the expected time. In terms of the ERT measured by counting accesses to the distance matrix as time unit (*DE*s, not illustrated), FSM** is always better than any other pure algorithm in the test. FSM* (FSM) is only faster than LK when an F_t of more than 10% (20%) is acceptable. In terms of *NT*, the situation changes again

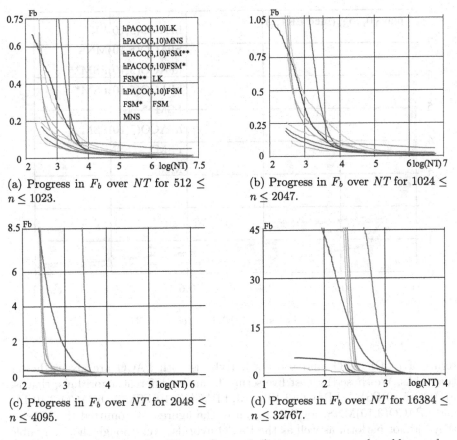

(a) Progress in F_b over NT for $512 \leq n \leq 1023$.

(b) Progress in F_b over NT for $1024 \leq n \leq 2047$.

(c) Progress in F_b over NT for $2048 \leq n \leq 4095$.

(d) Progress in F_b over NT for $16384 \leq n \leq 32767$.

Fig. 3. Progress diagrams for different (log-scaled) time measures and problem scales.

and there are two intersections of the ERT curves: MNS performs better for $0.1 \leq F_t \leq 0.5$ while the FSM and LK methods are faster otherwise (but goal errors of 10 % and above are of no practical relevance anyway). Thus, if different time measures were used, different observations could be found.

From all the above, we conclude that FSM** is the best LS in our experiments. When the acceptable F_t is big enough, even FSM* and FSM might outperform LK, while pure MNS is the worst.

3.4 Hybrid Algorithm Performance

We also investigated our newly proposed hybridized versions of FSM with EAs (i.e., MAs) and PACO and compared them to similar hybrids of LK and MNS. From the complete ranking generated by the *TSP Suite* over all setups, it can be seen that the different setups of the same corresponding algorithms have relatively similar behaviors, no matter what kind of measure is considered (e.g., hPACO(3,10)MNS and hPACO(5,10)MNS have similar behaviors in

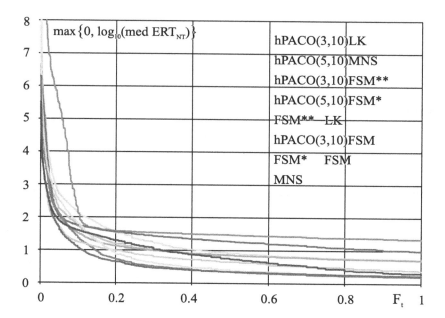

Fig. 4. (Log-scaled) ERT in terms of *DE*.

terms of ECDF, ERT and progress). Hybrids with PACO are always better than MAs. We chose the best five setups from the different algorithms, that is, hPACO(5,10)FSM*, hPACO(3,10)FSM, hPACO(3,10)FSM**, hPACO(3,10)LK and hPACO(3,10)MNS, for illustration in the figures. We omitted the MAs as they did not perform as well as the PACO hybrids, even though they were able to outperform the pure algorithms.

From the ECDF curves in Fig. 2, we can see some significant improvement of FSM and LK after being hybridized with PACO. hPACO(5,10)FSM*, hPACO(3,10)FSM, hPACO(3,10)FSM** and hPACO(3,10)LK outperform the pure algorithms in terms of both the number of problems they can solve as well as the time they need to solve them. Same observations are made with the MNS hybrids: hPACO(3,10)MNS solves 52 % of the problems, which is five times as many as the pure MNS.

hPACO(3,10)MNS is much faster than any other tested algorithms at the beginning, but hPACO(3,10)LK can solve more problems in the end. hPACO(3,10)FSM** is faster than hPACO(3,10)LK at the beginning but eventually overtaken by the latter. Its ECDF is always lower than the one of hPACO(3,10)MNS. hPACO(5,10)FSM* is better than hPACO(3,10)FSM but worse than the other algorithms.

When we set $F_t = 0.01$ (Fig. 2c), the hybrid algorithms again outperform the pure ones. Their ECDF curves increase earlier, more rapidly, and finally reach higher end points. hPACO(3,10)FSM** is as fast as hPACO(3,10)MNS and even better at some point, but is finally overtaken as hPACO(3,10)MNS can reach solutions that are one percent longer than the optimum more often. hPACO(3,10)FSM** and hPACO(3,10)MNS are always better than hPACO(3,10)LK. hPACO(5,10)FSM* and hPACO(3,10)FSM can solve more problems than hPACO(3,10)LK early on, but later hPACO(3,10)LK discovers more solutions.

The ERT diagrams in terms of DEs for a given F_t share similar trends with those in Fig. 4. When F_t is over 0.05, hPACO(3,10)FSM* can be as good as hPACO(3,10)FSM**. For better target tour lengths, hPACO(3,10)FSM** takes over hPACO(3,10)FSM*, and only hPACO(3,10)MNS and hPACO(3,10)LK perform as well as hPACO(3,10)FSM**.

From Fig. 3, we again confirm that the FSM hybrids are initially faster than the hybrid LK algorithms but slower than MNS hybrids, although these of LK later on find better-quality solutions.

Regardless of what runtime is available, we confirm that hybrid algorithms are better than pure LS. A more interesting observation, however, is that hybrid MNS methods tend to outperform both hybrid FSM and LK approaches, although pure MNS is clearly much worse than pure FSM (which in turn is better than pure LK). While an almost "additive" effect of hybridization was observed in [30], i.e., a better LS algorithm hybridized with a better global search method leads to a better hybrid approach, here we have a contrasting observation. Although hybrid FSM and LK can find better solutions on the long run, the efficient main loop of MNS, which can be implemented in a compact way, makes use of a (linear sized) cache and can discover several improvements at once, therefore provides faster convergence. LK and FSM have been the two *best known* LS approaches for the TSP, with decades of research behind them. Our results, however, make MNS the *best* candidate for hybridization today.

The aggregated algorithm ranking provided by the *TSP Suite* when comparing all setups regarding ECDF, ERT, final results, expected runtime to the optimum, and progress according to different runtime measures is:

hPACO(5,10)MNS, hPACO(3,10)MNS, hPACO(3,25)MNS,
hPACO(3,10)FSM**, hPACO(3,25)FSM**, hPACO(5,10)FSM**,
hMA(2+4)FSM**, hMA(16+64)FSM**, hMA(16+64)MNS, hMA(2+4)MNS,
hMA(2+8)FSM**, hPACO(5,10)LK, hPACO(3,25)LK, hMA(2+8)MNS,
hPACO(3,10)LK, hPACO(5,10)FSM*, hPACO(3,25)FSM*,
hPACO(3,10)FSM*, hMA(16+64)FSM*, hMA(16+64)LK, hMA(2+8)LK,
hMA(2+4)LK, hMA(2+4)FSM*, hMA(2+8)FSM*, hPACO(3,10)FSM,
FSM**, hPACO(5,10)FSM, hMA(16+64)FSM, hPACO(3,25)FSM,
hMA(2+8)FSM, hMA(2+4)FSM, LK, FSM*, FSM, MNS.

This ranking also reveals that PACO appears to be a better method to hybridize with than an EA. This is exactly the same observation already made in [30].

4   Conclusions and Future Work

In this work, we have introduced a new and improved FSM (FSM**), which can outperform the state-of-the-art of this algorithm family (FSM*) as well as the state-of-the-art in LS for the TSP in general (LK). We also introduced new hybrid versions of these algorithms with both EAs and PACO. We compared these hybrids with similar hybrids of LK and the best hybrid algorithms in our *TSP Suite*, hybrid MNS. We conducted a large-scale experiment based on all 110 symmetric instances from the *TSPLib*, performing 30 runs per setting, each limited to 1 h of runtime. Our experiments have led us to four major conclusions:

1. The new, pure FSM** algorithm works well on both small and large TSP instances and outperforms LK and MNS.
2. The restriction that no edge may be deleted twice from a solution is better than the criterion that deleted edges cannot be added again as used in [12,26].
3. Another measure to improve performance is restricting the number of levels of the search, as pointed out by Glover [12] and Rego [26]. We additional find that testing fewer root nodes also improves the performance.
4. Based on the same LS algorithm, the best setup of hybrid PACO is always better than any setup of hybrid EAs (MAs). The hybrids of FSM with PACO are the best variants among other FSM-based algorithms.
5. Although pure FSM and LK is better than MNS, hybrid MNS outperforms hybrid FSM and LK.

The last point is especially interesting and deserves more exploration. We will investigate hybrid EC-LK/FSM/MNS methods, which can use either FSM, LK or MNS as LS. Before refining a solution, we could randomly select which LS algorithm to apply. The random distribution could change over time, starting mainly with MNS and later switching more regularly to FSM and LK. This could utilize the initial high speed of MNS hybrids while also leverage the better end result quality provided by FSM and LK hybrids. At present, we are also investigating several Tabu Search variants and comparing them with the algorithms presented here.

Acknowledgements. We acknowledge support from the Fundamental Research Funds for the Central Universities, the National Natural Science Foundation of China No. 61150110488, Special Financial Grant 201104329 from the China Postdoctoral Science Foundation, the Chinese Academy of Sciences (CAS) Fellowship for Young International Scientists 2011Y1GB01, and the European Union 7th Framework Program under Grant 247619. The experiments reported in this paper were executed on the supercomputing system in the Supercomputing Center of University of Science and Technology of China.

References

1. Applegate, D.L., Bixby, R.E., Chvátal, V., Cook, W.J.: The Traveling Salesman Problem: A Computational Study. Princeton University Press, Princeton (2007)
2. Applegate, D.L., Cook, W.J., Rohe, A.: Chained lin-kernighan for large traveling salesman problems. INFORMS J. Comput. **15**(1), 82–92 (2003)
3. Bäck, T., Fogel, D.B., Michalewicz, Z. (eds.): Handbook of Evolutionary Computation. Oxford University Press, New York (1997)

4. Boddy, M.S., Dean, T.L.: Solving time-dependent planning problems. Technical report CS-89-03, Brown University, RI, USA (1989)
5. De Jong, K.A.: Evolutionary Computation: A Unified Approach. MIT Press, Cambridge (2006)
6. Dorigo, M.: Optimization, learning and natural algorithms. Ph.D. thesis, Dipartimento di Elettronica, Politecnico di Milano, Milano, Italy (1992)
7. Dorigo, M., Birattari, M., Stützle, T.: Ant colony optimization - artificial ants as a computational intelligence technique. IEEE Comput. Intell. Mag. 1(4), 28–39 (2006)
8. Fogel, D.B.: An evolutionary approach to the traveling salesman problem. Biol. Cybern. 60(2), 139–144 (1988)
9. Gambardella, L.M., Dorigo, M.: Solving symmetric and asymmetric TSPs by ant colonies. In: Proceedings of IEEE International Conference on Evolutionary Computation, pp. 622–627. IEEE, Los Alamitos, CA, USA, Symposium and Toyoda Auditorium, Nagoya, Aichi, Japan (1996)
10. Glover, F.: Ejection chains with combinatorial leverage for the traveling salesman problems. University of Colorado-Boulder, Technical report (1992)
11. Glover, F.: New ejection chain and alternating path methods for traveling salesman problems. Comput. Sci. Oper. Res. 1992, 449–509 (1992)
12. Glover, F.: Ejection chains, reference structures and alternating path methods for traveling salesman problems. Discrete Appl. Math. 65(1), 223–253 (1996)
13. Guntsch, M., Middendorf, M.: Applying population based ACO to dynamic optimization problems. In: Dorigo, M., Di Caro, G., Sampels, M. (eds.) Ant Algorithms 2002. LNCS, vol. 2463, pp. 111–122. Springer, Heidelberg (2002)
14. Gutin, G.Z., Punnen, A.P. (eds.): The Traveling Salesman Problem and its Variations. Kluwer Academic Publishers, Norwell (2002)
15. Hansen, N., Auger, A., Finck, S., Ros, R.: Real-parameter black-box optimization benchmarking: experimental setup. Technical report, Université Paris Sud, INRIA Futurs, TAO, Orsay, France (2012)
16. Helsgaun, K.: An effective implementation of the lin-kernighan traveling salesman heuristic. Technical report, Roskilde University, Denmark (1998)
17. Helsgaun, K.: General k-opt submoves for the Lin-Kernighan TSP heuristic. Math. Program. Comput. 1(2–3), 119–163 (2009)
18. Holland, J.H.: Adaptation in Natural and Artificial Systems: An Introductory Analysis with Applications to Biology, Control, and Artificial Intelligence. University of Michigan Press, Ann Arbor (1975)
19. Hoos, H.H., Stützle, T.: Evaluating Las Vegas Algorithms - pitfalls and remedies. In: Proceedings of the 14th Conference on Uncertainty in Artificial Intelligence (UAI 1998), pp. 238–245. Morgan Kaufmann, San Francisco (1998)
20. Jiang, H., Sun, W., Ren, Z., Lai, X., Piao, Y.: Evolving hard and easy traveling salesman problem instances: a multi-objective approach. In: Dick, G., et al. (eds.) SEAL 2014. LNCS, vol. 8886, pp. 216–227. Springer, Heidelberg (2014)
21. Larrañaga, P., Kuijpers, C.M.H., Murga, R.H., Inza, I., Dizdarevic, S.: Genetic algorithms for the travelling salesman problem: a review of representations and operators. J. Artif. Intell. Res. 13(2), 129–170 (1999)
22. Lawler, E.L.G., Lenstra, J.K., Rinnooy Kan, A.H.G., Shmoys, D.B.: The Traveling Salesman Problem: A Guided Tour of Combinatorial Optimization. Wiley, Chichester (1985)
23. Lin, S., Kernighan, B.W.: An effective heuristic algorithm for the traveling-salesman problem. Oper. Res. 21(2), 498–516 (1973)

24. Michalewicz, Z.: Genetic Algorithms + Data Structures = Evolution Programs. Springer, Berlin (1996)
25. Pesch, E., Glover, F.: TSP ejection chains. Discrete Appl. Math. **76**(1), 165–181 (1997)
26. Rego, C.: Relaxed tours and path ejections for the traveling salesman problem. Eur. J. Oper. Res. **106**(2), 522–538 (1998)
27. Rego, C., Gamboa, D., Glover, F., Osterman, C.: Traveling salesman problem heuristics: leading methods, implementations and latest advances. Eur. J. Oper. Res. **211**(3), 427–441 (2011)
28. Tompkins, D.A.D., Hoos, H.H.: UBCSAT: an implementation and experimentation environment for SLS algorithms for SAT and MAX-SAT. In: Hoos, H.H., Mitchell, D.G. (eds.) SAT 2004. LNCS, vol. 3542, pp. 306–320. Springer, Heidelberg (2005)
29. Weise, T.: Global Optimization Algorithms - Theory and Application. it-weise.de (self-published), Germany (2009)
30. Weise, T., Chiong, R., Tang, K., Lässig, J., Tsutsui, S., Chen, W., Michalewicz, Z., Yao, X.: Benchmarking optimization algorithms: an open source framework for the traveling salesman problem. IEEE Comput. Intell. Mag. **9**(3), 40–52 (2014)
31. Whitley, L.D., Starkweather, T., Fuquay, D.: Scheduling problems and traveling salesman: the genetic edge recombination operator. In: Proceedings of the 3rd International Conference on Genetic Algorithms, pp. 133–140. Morgan Kaufmann, San Francisco (1989)
32. Wu, Y., Weise, T., Chiong, R.: Local search for the traveling salesman problem: a comparative study. In: Proceedings of 14th IEEE Conference on Cognitive Informatics and Cognitive Computing, pp. 213–220 (2015)

Remote Sensing Image Fusion Based on Shearlet and Genetic Algorithm

Qiguang Miao$^{(\boxtimes)}$, Ruyi Liu, Yiding Wang, Jianfeng Song, Yining Quan, and Yunan Li

School of Computer and Technology, Xidian University, Xi'an, China
qgmiao@gmail.com, xdfzliyunan@163.com,
{jfsong,ynquan}@mail.xidian.edu.cn, {qgmiao,ruyi198901210121}@126.com

Abstract. Image fusion is a technology which can effectively enhance the utilization ratio of image information, the accuracy of target recognition and the interpretation ability of image. However, traditional fusion methods may lead to the information loss and image distortion. Hence a novel remote sensing image fusion method is proposed in this paper. As one of the multi-scale geometric analysis tools, Shearlet has been widely used in image processing. In this paper, Shearlet is used to decompose the image. Genetic Algorithm, a intelligent optimization algorithm, is also applied to image fusion and it aims to optimize the weighted factors in order to improve the quality of fusion. Experimental results prove the superiority and feasibility of this method.

Keywords: Image fusion · Shearlet · Genetic algorithm · Fitness function

1 Introduction

With the development of image processing technologies, image fusion has been widely applied to each area. Remote sensing image fusion is a kind of technology which aims at fusing the image data of the same region obtained by multi-sensor platforms into a more comprehensive, accurate and informative image. Both higher spatial resolution and hyper-spectral information are reserved in fused image.

Remote sensing image has a wide application range, such as military, geological prospecting, mapping, environment and agriculture. In recent years, there are some common fusion methods, such as linear weighting method [1], HSI transform method [1], PCA [1], pyramid-based fusion method [2], and Discrete Wavelet Transform [3]. However, it is difficult for these traditional fusion methods to get a satisfactory result.

As one of the multi-scale geometric analysis tools, Shearlet overcomes the deficiency of information loss when Wavelet Transform is applied into image fusion. Besides, compared with Contourlet [4], the limitation of the number of directions has been successfully eliminated by Shearlet. Moreover, as a new

© Springer-Verlag Berlin Heidelberg 2015
M. Gong et al. (Eds.): BIC-TA 2015, CCIS 562, pp. 283–294, 2015.
DOI: 10.1007/978-3-662-49014-3_26

optimal tool, intelligent optimization algorithms play a vital role in solving optimization problems. Among them, Genetic Algorithm [5] is now getting more attention for its powerful searching ability.

In this paper, a novel image fusion method based on Shearlet [6–13] and Genetic Algorithm is discussed. It mainly focuses on the application of Genetic Algorithm into image fusion. The experimental results prove the effectiveness of the proposed method. This paper is organized as follows. The basic theory of Shearlet is introduced in Sect. 2. In Sect. 3, Genetic Algorithm is described. The novel algorithm is presented in Sect. 4 and experimental results are shown in Sect. 5. Finally, this paper is concluded in Sect. 6.

2   Shearlet

K. Guo et al. had proposed the wavelet theory [14,15].

In dimension $n = 2$, the affine system with composite dilations can be described as $\{\psi_{AB}(\psi)\}$, where $\psi \in L^2(R^2)$. A, B are 2×2 invertible matrices with $|\det B| = 1$. Its specific expression is shown as follows:

$$\psi_{AB}(\psi) = \{\psi_{j,k,l}(x) = |\det A|^{j/2}\psi(B^l A^j x - k) : j,l \in Z, k \in Z^2\} \qquad (1)$$

The element in $\psi_{AB}(\psi)$, are defined as composite wavelet if $\psi_{AB}(\psi)$ forms a tight frame.

Shearlet is a special example of affine systems with composite wavelets in $L^2(R^2)$. Shearlet can be described as Eq. (1) if $A = A_0$, $B = B_0$. A_0 and B_0 are defined as follows: $A_0 = \begin{pmatrix} 4 & 0 \\ 0 & 2 \end{pmatrix}$, $B_0 = \begin{pmatrix} 1 & 1 \\ 0 & 1 \end{pmatrix}$.

For $\xi = (\xi_1, \xi_2) \in \hat{R}^2, \xi_1 \neq 0$, let $\psi^{(0)}$ be given by

$$\hat{\psi}^{(0)}(\xi) = \hat{\psi}^{(0)}(\xi_1, \xi_2) = \hat{\psi}_1(\xi_1)\hat{\psi}_2(\xi_2/\xi_1) \qquad (2)$$

where $\hat{\psi}_1, \hat{\psi}_2 \in C^\infty(\hat{R})$, $\mathrm{supp}\hat{\psi}_1 \subset [-1/2, -1/16] \bigcup [1/16, 1/2]$, and $\mathrm{supp}\hat{\psi}_2 \subset [-1,1]$. It can be proved that $\hat{\psi}^{(0)}$ is C^∞ and compactly supported with supp $\hat{\psi}^{(0)} \subset [-1/2, 1/2]^2$.

$$\sum_{j\geq 0} |\hat{\psi}_1(2^{-2j}\omega)|^2 = 1, |\omega| \geq 1/8 \qquad (3)$$

Then for $j \geq 0$,

$$\sum_{l=-2^j}^{2^j-1} |\hat{\psi}_2(2^j\omega - l)|^2 = 1, |\omega| \leq 1 \qquad (4)$$

The support set of $\psi_{j,k,l}$ in frequency domain is obtained as follows:

$$\{(\xi_1, \xi_2) : \xi_1 \in [-2^{2j-1}, -2^{2j-4}] \bigcup [2^{2j-4}, 2^{2j-1}], |\frac{\xi_2}{\xi_1} + l2^{-j}| \leq 2^{-j}\} \qquad (5)$$

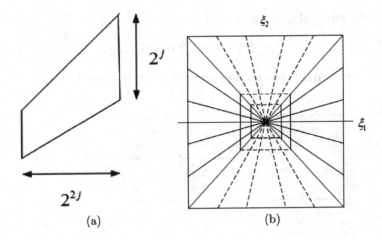

Fig. 1. (a) A single frequency support of Shearlet; (b) The tiling of the frequency using Shearlet.

This support set is shown in Fig. 1(a). It can be seen that each element $\hat{\psi}_{j,k,l}$ is supported on a pair of trapezoids, approximate size $2^{2j} \times 2^j$, oriented along lines of slope $l2^{-j}$.

According to Eqs. (3) and (4), the compact support of D_0 is formed by $\{\hat{\psi}^{(0)}(\xi A_0^{-j} B_0^{-l})\}$, where $D_0 = \{(\xi_1, \xi_2) \in \hat{R}{}^2 : |\xi_1| \geq 1/8, |\xi_2/\xi_1| \leq 1\}$.

For $(\xi_1, \xi_2) \in D_0$,

$$\sum_{j \geq 0} \sum_{l=-2^j}^{2^j-1} |\hat{\psi}^{(0)}(\xi A_0^{-j} B_0^{-l})|^2 = \sum_{j \geq 0} \sum_{l=-2^j}^{2^j-1} |\hat{\psi}_1(2^{-2j}\xi_1)|^2 |\hat{\psi}_2(2^j \xi_2/\xi_1 - l)|^2 = 1$$

(6)

The tiling of frequency using Shearlet transform is shown in Fig. 1(b). A Parseval frame for $L^2(D_0)^\vee$ can be defined as follows:

$$\{\psi_{j,k,l}^{(0)}(x) = 2^{3j/2} \psi^{(0)}(B_0^l A_0^j x - k) : j \geq 0, -2^j \leq l \leq 2^j - 1, k \in Z^2\} \quad (7)$$

where $L^2(D_0)^\vee$ is the set of function $f \in L^2(R^2)$, and the support set of $\hat{\psi}^{(0)}$ is included in $[-1/2, 1/2]^2$. Similarly we can construct a Parseval frame for $L^2(D_1)^\vee$, where D_1 is the vertical cone $D_1 = \{(\xi_1, \xi_2) \in \hat{R}{}^2 : |\xi_2| \geq 1/8, |\xi_1/\xi_2| \leq 1\}$. Let

$$A_1 = \begin{pmatrix} 2 & 0 \\ 0 & 4 \end{pmatrix}, B_1 = \begin{pmatrix} 1 & 0 \\ 1 & 1 \end{pmatrix} \quad (8)$$

$$\hat{\psi}^{(1)}(\xi) = \hat{\psi}^{(1)}(\xi_1, \xi_2) = \hat{\psi}_1(\xi_2)\hat{\psi}_2(\xi_1/\xi_2) \quad (9)$$

Then the Parseval frame is defined as

$$\{\psi_{j,k,l}^{(1)}(x) = 2^{3j/2}\, \psi^{(1)}(B_1^l A_1^j x - k) : j \geq 0, -2^j \leq l \leq 2^j - 1, k \in Z^2\} \quad (10)$$

The decomposition process of discrete Shearlet is shown in Fig. 2.

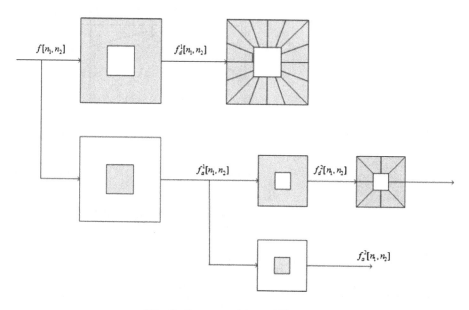

Fig. 2. Decomposition of Shearlet

3 Genetic Algorithm

Genetic Algorithm (GA) [16,17] was proposed by John Holland in 1975. It is an evolutionary computational method based on evolutionism. Starting with a group of random solutions, GA optimizes the solutions through selection, crossover, and mutation. These initial solutions are called initial population. Every individual called chromosome in this group is a solution of the question. Chromosomes are all coded based on some certain rules according to the requirements of the question. Selections are mainly based on the values of fitness function, which means that the individual with a higher fitness will be selected in the subsequent genetic process. Finally, when the algorithm converges to one certain fitness, the corresponding individual is the optimal chromosome. And the decoded chromosome is the optimum solution of the question.

The flow diagram for GA is shown in Fig. 3.

The detail of the steps in Genetic Algorithm is given below.

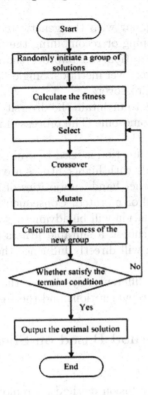

Fig. 3. Flow diagram of GA

1. Coding. There are several coding schemes such as binary coding, gray coding, large character set coding, real coding and multi-parameter cascade coding. Among them, we perform binary coding to express the solution of the question as the genotype string structure data. Coding plays a vital role in genetic research because the quality of coding directly influences the results obtained by the subsequent genetic iterations.

2. Selection. As one of the most important steps in GA, selection determines the convergence of the population. Meanwhile, it aims to improve the convergence and heighten the optimization efficiency. A common method for selection is roulette wheel selection.

   It is defined as follows:

$$P_i = \frac{f_i}{\sum\limits_{j=1}^{N} f_j} \tag{11}$$

where N is the size of the population, f_i is the fitness of the individual i. The probability P_i reflects the proportion of the individual fitness in the whole population. Therefore, it can be seen that the higher the individual fitness is, the greater the probability for selection is.

3. Crossover. Crossover, similar with the genetic recombination, can generate new individuals by swapping or recombining the fragments of a pair of parent individuals. This operation can improve the searching ability and efficiency. There are three crossover methods: Single Point Crossover, Multipoint Crossover and Uniform Crossover.

4. Mutation. Mutation aims to maintain the diversity of the population by randomly disturbing the chromosome. The process of mutation is determined by the mutation probability P_m.

5. Fitness function. Fitness function is used to evaluate the quality of individuals. In general, individuals with higher fitness are more likely to be selected and generated. On the other hands, majorities of individuals with lower fitness are either eliminated or mutated. Consequently, the average fitness and performance of the population will be advanced gradually. It is undoubtedly that it is significant to choose a suitable fitness function for the question since the fitness function will directly influence the rate of convergence and the optimizing results.

6. Termination. There are different ways to set the terminal conditions. For instance, fix the number of generations and the step size in search.

4   Image Fusion Method Based on Shearlet and Genetic Algorithm

In this section, a novel image fusion method for remote sensing image based on Shearlet and Genetic Algorithm is presented. Genetic Algorithm is mainly used to optimize the weight factors among the fusion strategy of the high frequency coefficients. In this algorithm, the fitness function is constructed by using specific objective evaluation index. The following evaluation indexes are applied to this paper.

4.1   Evaluation Criteria

1. Entropy (EN). EN is used to measure the amount of the information in the fused image because it reflects the ability to preserve detail information. EN is defined as follows:

$$EN = -\sum_{i=0}^{i-1} P_i ln P_i \tag{12}$$

where P_i is the probability of gray level i on each pixel. The larger the EN is, the higher the quality of fusion is.

2. Mean Cross Entropy (MCE). CE is the cross entropy of images and given below.

$$\begin{cases} CE_{(f_A,f)} = \sum_{i=0}^{255} P_{f_A}(i) log|\frac{P_{f_A}(i)}{P_f(i)}| \\ CE_{(f_B,f)} = \sum_{i=0}^{255} P_{f_B}(i) log|\frac{P_{f_B}(i)}{P_f(i)}| \end{cases} \tag{13}$$

where f_A, f_B are the original images, and f is the fused image. Then MCE can be described as follows:

$$MCE = \frac{CE_{(f_A,f)} + CE_{(f_B,f)}}{2} \qquad (14)$$

The smaller the MCE is, the less the difference between the original images and fused image is.

3. Average Grads (AG). AG can reflect the blurring level of images and the expressing ability of minor details. The calculation formula of AG is given as follows:

$$AG = \frac{1}{M \times N} \sum_{i=1}^{M-1} \sum_{j=1}^{N-1} \sqrt{\frac{(F(i,j) - F(i+1,j))^2 + F(i,j) - F(i,j+1))^2}{2}} \qquad (15)$$

where $F(i,j)$ is the pixel value of image in row i, column j. M, N are the total row and total column. The larger the AG is, the clearer the fused image is.

4. Standard Deviation (STD). STD indicates the dispersion degree of comparison between the pixel value and the average pixel value of the image.

$$STD = \sqrt{\frac{\sum\limits_{i=0}^{N-1} \sum\limits_{j=0}^{M-1} [(x,y) - \mu]^2}{M \times N}} \qquad (16)$$

The larger the STD is, the worse the fusion result is.

5. Structure Similarity (Qw). Given the original image X (X can be f_A, f_B), the fusion image is f. The size of each image is $M \times N$.

$$\sigma_X^2 = \frac{1}{MN-1} \sum_{m=1}^{M} \sum_{n=1}^{N} (X(m,n) - \overline{X}^2) \qquad (17)$$

$$\sigma_{Xf} = \frac{1}{MN-1} \sum_{m=1}^{M} \sum_{n=1}^{N} (X(m,n) - \overline{X})(f(m,n) - \overline{f}) \qquad (18)$$

where $X = \{x_i | i = 1, 2, ..., N\}, f = \{f_i | i = 1, 2, ..., N\}$. The mean value of X and f are $\overline{X}$ and $\overline{f}$, respectively.

Define Q as the following formula.

$$Q = \frac{4\sigma_{Xf}\overline{X}\overline{f}}{\overline{X}^2 + \overline{f}^2} = \frac{\sigma_{Xf}}{\sigma_X \sigma_f} \cdot \frac{2\overline{X}\overline{f}}{\overline{X}^2 + \overline{f}^2} \cdot \frac{2\sigma_X \sigma_f}{\sigma_X^2 + \sigma_f^2} \qquad (19)$$

In image processing, sliding window is usually used to calculate the value of Q in the local region so that we could synthesis an overall index. The overall index can be described as follows:

$$Q = \frac{1}{M} \sum_{i=1}^{M} Q_i(X, f|\lambda) \qquad (20)$$

where λ is the size of the sliding window, and M is the calculation times. Then Qw is constructed.

$$Qw = \lambda_A Q(f_A, f) + \lambda_B Q(f_B, f) \qquad (21)$$

where $\lambda_A = \frac{\sigma_{f_A}^2}{\sigma_{f_A}^2 + \sigma_{f_B}^2}, \lambda_B = 1 - \lambda_A$.

Qw is used to measure the level of similarity between two original images and the fused image. Its value belongs to $[0, 1]$. The larger the value of Qw is, the better the fusion result is.

6. Degree of Distortion (DD). DD reflects the degree of spectral distortion and the differences of spectral information between the original image and fused image. The smaller the value of DD is, the better the preservation of spectral information is.

$$\begin{cases} DD_{f_A, f} = \frac{1}{M \times N} \sum\limits_{i=1}^{M} \sum\limits_{j=1}^{N} |f(i,j) - f_A(i,j)| \\ DD_{f_B, f} = \frac{1}{M \times N} \sum\limits_{i=1}^{M} \sum\limits_{j=1}^{N} |f(i,j) - f_B(i,j)| \end{cases} \qquad (22)$$

7. Correlation Coefficient (CC). The degree of correlation between the original image and the fused image can be described by CC. It can reflect the preserving ability of spectral information by comparing the correlation coefficients.

$$CC_{X, f} = \frac{\sum\limits_{i=1}^{M} \sum\limits_{j=1}^{N} [f(i,j) - \mu_f][X(i,j) - \mu_X]}{\sqrt{\sum\limits_{i=1}^{M} \sum\limits_{j=1}^{N} [f(i,j) - \mu_f]^2 [X(i,j) - \mu_X]^2}} \qquad (23)$$

μ_f, μ_X are the gray average value of the fused image X and the original image X. The larger the CC is, the better the quality of the fused image is.

4.2 Image Fusion Algorithm

According to the requirements and the data characteristics of remote sensing image, GA and Shearlet are applied into image fusion.

The basic steps of our proposed method are as follows:

Step 1: Image Decomposition. Decompose the original image in multi-scale and multi-direction by Shearlet. The high frequency coefficients and low frequency coefficients are obtained through this step. The window function of shear filter used in this step is formed by Meyer wavelet.

Step 2: Process the coefficients. The coefficients are processed based on some certain fusion rules.

Step 3: Image reconstruction. The fused image is obtained using inverse Shearlet transform.

The fusion framework of the proposed method is shown in Fig. 4. In Step 2, the low frequency coefficients are fused based on the rule given below.

$$f_{low} = 0.5f_{A-low} + 0.5f_{B-low} \tag{24}$$

The most important part of image fusion is to determine the fusion rule for the high frequency coefficients. In the proposed method, we choose weighting method to fuse the high frequency coefficients. Its formula is shown as follows:

$$f = \alpha f_A + (1 - \alpha f_B) \tag{25}$$

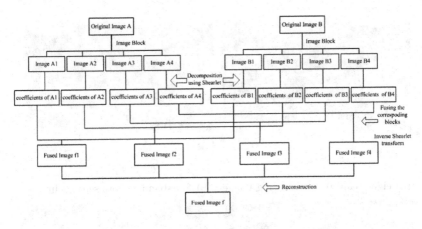

Fig. 4. Image fusion framework based on Shearlet and GA

The weighted factor is optimized by GA. In order to get the high performance of algorithm, the population of GA cannot be oversize. However, the limitation of the number of the population will easily result in the local optimum and influence the quality of fusion. Therefore, the original images are cut into blocks before decomposition. Then the blocks are decomposed and the corresponding coefficients are fused. Finally, all of the blocks are reconstructed by inverse Shearlet transform.

Fitness function is an important part of GA. On the basis of the data features of remote sensing image, it can be seen that the fused image is required to contain rich spectral information and high resolution information. Hence the evaluation criteria CC, DD, EN and AG are applied to construct the fitness function. It is defined as follows:

$$fit = \frac{CC - \beta DD}{\gamma} + EN + \eta AG \tag{26}$$

where β, γ, η are parameters. We set $\beta = 10, \gamma = \eta = 100$.

5 Experiments and Analysis

In our experiment, the size of the original images is 512×512. Many different methods, including averaging method, Laplacian pyramid, Wavelet-GA, Contourlet-PCNN, Shearlet-PCNN, are used to compare with our proposed approach. The parameters in GA are set as follows.

1. The length of individual strings: $bn = 22$;
2. The number of initial population: $inn = 50$;
3. Maximum iterations: $gnmax = 15$;
4. The probability of crossover and mutation: $pc = 0.75, pm = 0.05$;
5. Step size in search: 0.001.

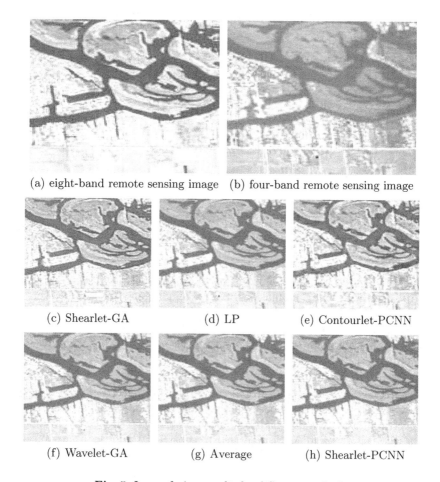

(a) eight-band remote sensing image   (b) four-band remote sensing image

(c) Shearlet-GA   (d) LP   (e) Contourlet-PCNN

(f) Wavelet-GA   (g) Average   (h) Shearlet-PCNN

Fig. 5. Image fusion results by different methods

The original image, Fig. 5(a), (b), are the multi-band remote sensing images. From Fig. 5(c) to (h) are the fusion results using different methods. Figure 5 indicates that the proposed method gets a better performance in image fusion than any other methods. The information of rivers and roads obtained by our method are clear in the fused image. For example, Fig. 5(f), (g) show that the information of rivers, cities and roads are blurring.

The values of evaluation criteria are shown in Table 1. We choose seven evaluation criteria to assess the quality of fusion results. From Table 1 we can see that most evaluation index values using by proposed method are better than other methods do.

Table 1. The value of evaluation criteria

Fusion method	Qw	EN(μm)	MCE	STD	AG	CC	DD
Average	0.7581	6.1975	2.9600	46.1587	0.0236	308.2206	23.4156
LP	0.7530	6.9594	3.3738	49.2283	0.0399	311.1215	21.9003
C-PCNN	0.7516	7.3332	3.0628	54.3504	0.0390	311.2017	23.0147
S-PCNN	0.7775	7.0900	2.9046	56.5274	0.0385	311.6649	21.9768
Wavelet-GA	0.7511	6.8412	3.2246	57.0124	0.0334	322.6384	22.0031
Shearlet-GA	0.7445	7.2996	**3.3963**	**45.5746**	0.0397	**328.3706**	**20.1492**

6   Conclusion

The theory of Shearlet and GA is introduced in this paper, and a new algorithm of image fusion based on them is proposed. As a multi-scale geometric analysis tool, Shearlet is equipped with a rich mathematical structure similar to wavelet and can capture the information in any direction. We take full advantage of multi-direction of Shearlet to fuse image. Moreover, GA is used to get a better performance in image fusion by the process of selection, crossover and mutation. The experimental results illustrate the effectiveness and feasibility of the proposed method, and improve the quality of the fusion.

References

1. Rockinger, O.: Image Fusion Toolbox [EB/OL]. http://www.metapix.de
2. Burt, P.J., Adelson, E.H.: The laplacian pyramid as a compact image code. IEEE Trans. Commun. **31**(4), 432–540 (1983)
3. Amolins, K., Zhang, Y., Dare, P.: Wavelet based image fusion techniques-an introduction, review and comparison. Photogram. Remote Sens. **62**, 249–263 (2007)
4. Yang, X., Jiao, L.: Fusion algorithm for remote sensing images based on nonsubsampled contourlet transform. Acta Autom. Sinica **34**, 274–281 (2008)
5. Kotenko, I., Saenko, I.: Improved genetic algorithms for solving the optimisation tasks for design of access control schemes in computer networks. Int. J. Bio-Inspired Comput. **7**(2), 98–110 (2015)

6. Miao, Q., Shi, C., Xu, P., Yang, M., Shi, Y.: Multi-focus image fusion algorithm based on shearlets. Chin. Opt. Lett. **9**(4), 041001 (2011). 1–5
7. Miao, Q., Shi, C., Xu, P., Yang, M., Shi, Y.: A novel algorithm of image fusion using shearlets. Opt. Commun. **284**(6), 1540–1547 (2011)
8. Miao, Q., Shi, C., Xu, P., Yang, M., Shi, Y.: A Novel Algorithm of Image Fusion based on Shearlet and PCNN, Neurocomputing (2012)
9. Shearlet webpage. http://www.shearlet.org
10. Easley, G.R., Demetrio, L., Wang, Q.: Optimally sparse image representations using shearlets. Sig. Syst. Comput. **11**, 974–978 (2006)
11. Mallat, S.G.: Theory for multiresolution signal decomposition: the wavelet representation. IEEE Trans. Pattern Anal. Mach. Intell. **11**(7), 674–693 (1989)
12. Guo, K., Labate, D., Lim, W.: Edge analysis and identification using the continuous shearlet transform. Appl. Comput. Harmonic Anal. **30**(2), 24–46 (2009)
13. Easley, G., Labate, D., Lim, W.: Sparse directional image representations using the discrete shearlet transform. Appl. Comput. Harmonic Anal. **25**(1), 25–46 (2008)
14. Guo, K., Lim, W., Labate, D., Weiss, G., Wilson, E.: Wavelets with composite dilations and their MRA properties. Appl. Comput. Harmonic Anal. **99**, 231–249 (2006)
15. Guo, K., Lim, W., Labate, D., Weiss, G., Wilson, E.: The theory of wavelets with composite dilations. Harmonic Anal. Appl. **4**, 231–249 (2006)
16. Erkanli, S., Rahman, Z.: Entropy-based image fusion with continuous genetic algorithm. In: Proceedings of IEEE 10th International Conference on Intelligent Systems Design and Applications, pp. 278–283 (2010)
17. Hong, L., He, Z., Xiang, J., Li, S.: Fusion of infrared and visible image based on genetic algorithm and data assimilation. In: Intelligent Systems and Applications, pp. 1–5 (2009)

Direct Torque Control of PMSM with Torque Ripple Reduction Based on Fuzzy Logic Control

Bowen Ning, Shanmei Cheng$^{(\boxtimes)}$, and Yi Qin

Key Laboratory of Education Ministry for Image Processing and Intelligent Control
School of Automation, Huazhong University of Science and Technology,
Wuhan 430074, China
{ningbowen,chengsm}@hust.edu.cn, hustqin@163.com

Abstract. This paper is presented to examine and improve the performance of the torque ripple suppression for direct torque controlled permanent magnet synchronous motor by using fuzzy control method. On the basis of analyzing the torque ripple of the direct torque control in details, the fuzzy controllers are designed for two parts. Since the errors of the torque and flux could not assess accurately in hysteresis structure, the hysteresis controllers of the conventional DTC method are replaced by the fuzzy controller which could select the optimal voltage vector by judging the deviation degree of the torque and flux errors according to the fuzzy logic inference. Then the action time of the selected optimal voltage vector is determined by using the fuzzy duty ratio control method, the ripples of torque and flux can be attenuated effectively. The comprehensive simulation experiment is exhibited to reveal the excellent response performance of the system and verify the feasibility of the proposed fuzzy control scheme.

Keywords: Permanent magnet synchronous motor (PMSM) · Direct torque control (DTC) · Torque ripple · Fuzzy control

1 Introduction

The direct torque control (DTC) and field oriented control (FOC) which have made the outstanding contributions to the electric drive development are the most commonly used control method in motor control as we know nowadays [1]. DTC is firstly applied to induction motor and then is extended to PMSM which has high motion performance and the simple structure [2,3].

Unlike field oriented control, the direct torque control is based on stationary frame and focuses on controlling torque and flux directly. Therefore some parts like the transformation of coordinate, current regulation and pulse width modulator are eliminated. In this way the DTC presents some merits as fast torque dynamic response with the simple control structure. Meanwhile the concept of space voltage vector is applied in the DTC. In practical application, the applied voltage vector is obtained according to the outputs of the hysteresis controllers and the location of the stator flux. However the fixed hysteresis width could

© Springer-Verlag Berlin Heidelberg 2015
M. Gong et al. (Eds.): BIC-TA 2015, CCIS 562, pp. 295–305, 2015.
DOI: 10.1007/978-3-662-49014-3_27

not assess the actual error values accurately, in addition usually only one-state voltage vector is fed by voltage-source inverter (VSI) in a sampling period, the actual controlled torque and flux often exceed the set values of the hysteresis controllers. It thus that DTC has some weakness include large flux and torque ripples, high current distortions [4].

In recent years, many researchers have paid much attention to improve the above shortcomings to utilize the DTC more widely. Some useful methods have proposed, among which the multilevel method and the DTC combined with space vector modulation (SVM-DTC) methods are effective to perfect the DTC performance [5–8]. However multilevel method may increase the complexity of the system on the hardware and the control design, and some SVM-DTC methods may weaken the control simplicity and robustness. In addition the duty ratio method which is similar to SVM method to some extent is also used to attenuate the ripple of the torque [9–13]. The basic concept of duty ratio is that in every sampling time the active vector is only chosen to work a part time of the period and the rest time a zero vector is chosen. The duty ratio method uses the concept of combining vectors and it is easier to implement than the SVM method. Several kinds of schemes have been proposed according to the different optimized targets of minimizing the torque ripple to determine the duty ratio. These schemes have shown the better performance to weaken the torque ripple significantly compared with conventional DTC scheme. However they often depend on the motor parameters and need a series of complicated computations [11–13].

Fuzzy control which is also known as fuzzy logic control is a kind of intelligent control technology. The most major feature of fuzzy control is that it designs the rules based on imitating the human experience to control the system. Fuzzy control does not depend on the exact object model and it can deal with nonlinear problems. Fuzzy control has been applied to control DTC systems to handle the different problems [14–18]. In [14], the fuzzy control method is used to design the outer speed loop of DTC system to obtain the excellent dynamic and steady state performance and improve the robustness of the system when external disturbance and the parameter variations are encountered. The authors in [15] focus on implementing the fuzzy controller of the DTC on FPGA by using the VHDL language. In [16], the widths of hysteresis controllers are adjusted on-line based on fuzzy control, the torque ripple is decreased as well as the dynamic response is improved.

In this paper, the fuzzy control is applied to DTC PMSM system to decrease the ripple of torque and improve the system performance. The fuzzy controller is designed for two parts. First of all, the conventional hysteresis controllers are replaced by the fuzzy controller, and the optimal voltage vector could be selected by judging the deviation degree of the torque and flux errors. Since the actual system is controlled discretely by sampling time, the controlled torque and flux may exceed the command values even though the optimal voltage vector is selected. Then after the optimal voltage vector is obtained, the action time of the selected voltage vector is taken into account by drawing on the experience of duty ratio method. The fuzzy control is also used to determining the duty ratio. At last, the comprehensive simulation experiment is carried out to show the proposed system has the less torque ripple than the conventional DTC method, the test results verify the feasibility of the proposed scheme.

2   The Principle of PMSM DTC

To simplify the analysis, take the typical surface mounted PMSM for example. The stator flux equation of PMSM could be described by complex vector form as

$$\boldsymbol{\psi_s} = \int (\boldsymbol{u_s} - R_s\boldsymbol{i_s})dt \tag{1}$$

where $\boldsymbol{\psi_s}$ is the stator flux vector, $\boldsymbol{u_s}$ is the stator voltage vector, R_s is the stator resistance, $\boldsymbol{i_s}$ is the stator current vector. If the stator resistance is neglected, the stator flux is mainly affected by the applied voltage vector. The change direction of the stator flux is as same as the direction of the voltage vector, thus the voltage vector could change the amplitude of the stator flux.

The electromagnetic torque expression is described as follows

$$T_e = \frac{3n_p}{2L_s}\psi_f\,|\boldsymbol{\psi_s}|\sin\delta \tag{2}$$

where T_e is electromagnetic torque, n_p is the number of pole pairs, L_s is the stator inductance, ψ_f is the permanent magnet flux, δ is the torque angle.

In above torque equation, the number of pole pairs, stator inductance and permanent magnet flux are regarded as the constant values. The torque is only affected by the torque angle if the amplitude of the stator flux is remained unchanged. It thus the torque could be controlled when the torque angle is changed by applying the different voltage vectors.

In DTC method, the six non-zero voltage vectors (V_1-V_6) and two zero voltage vectors (V_0, V_7) are generated by the VSI with the help of voltage space vector concept. Meanwhile the stationary $\alpha - \beta$ plan is divided into six sectors (S_1-S_6) according to the location of stator flux. All voltage vectors and sectors are presented as Fig. 1 The appropriate vector is selected to output by VSI on the basis of the signs of the torque and flux errors and the sector of the stator flux. As Fig. 1 shows, when the stator flux is located at sector $S_k(k = 1, ..., 6)$, the controlled torque will be increased if vector V_{k+1} or V_{k+2} is applied, whereas the controlled torque will be decreased if vector V_{k-1} or V_{k-2} is applied. The amplitude of stator flux will be increased if vector V_{k+1} or V_{k-1} is selected, and the amplitude of stator flux will be decreased if vector V_{k+2} or V_{k-2} is selected. In this way, the appropriate vector is selected to control the torque and stator flux every sector when the signs of hysteresis controllers are determined.

In hysteresis controllers, only the signs of torque and flux errors are considered rather than the amplitudes of their errors. It thus the current vector is changed only if the amplitudes of the torque and flux exceed the boundary of the hysteresis. And the same vector will be applied no matter the errors are large

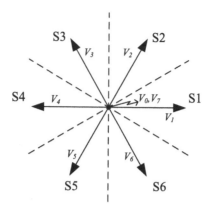

Fig. 1. Voltage vector and sector distribution

or small due to the two digital value outputs of the hysteresis controllers when the signs of errors are not changed. Moreover the control process is discrete by sampling time rather than continuous, the ripples of torque and flux are higher than the limit of the hysteresis. The conventional DTC presents the large torque and flux ripples due to these reasons.

3   The Analysis of Torque Ripple

The electromagnetic torque equation is rewritten in rotor $d - q$ frame as

$$T_e = \frac{3}{2}n_p\psi_f i_q \tag{3}$$

Since n_p and ψ_f are constant values, the variation of the torque is described as

$$\frac{dT_e}{dt} = \frac{3}{2}n_p\psi_f \frac{di_q}{dt} \tag{4}$$

For the typical surface mounted PMSM, the variation of the q-axis current is given as

$$\frac{di_q}{dt} = -\frac{R_s}{L_s}i_q - \frac{\omega_{re}(L_s i_d + \psi_f)}{L_s} + \frac{u_q}{L_s} \tag{5}$$

Where ω_{re} is rotor electrical angular velocity, u_q is the q-axis voltage, i_d and i_q are d-axis and q-axis current respectively. Then the following expression is obtained

$$\frac{dT_e}{dt} = -\frac{3}{2}n_p\psi_f \frac{R_s}{L_s}i_q - \frac{3}{2}n_p\psi_f \frac{\omega_{re}(L_s i_d + \psi_f)}{L_s} + \frac{3}{2}n_p\psi_f \frac{u_q}{L_s} \tag{6}$$

It can be seen that the change of torque is consisted of three parts from the above expressions. Since the motor is only controlled by the voltage vector fed by VSI, the voltage vector will directly affect the torque. When the zero vector is selected, the change of torque is different from the ones when active vector is selected. In the real discrete control application, using one active vector in whole period could make the torque change bigger and fail to fulfill the desired requirement of the system. If the combination of the active vector and zero vector is used in every sampling period, the ripple of torque could be decreased significantly.

4   Fuzzy Control of PMSM DTC

In this part, the fuzzy controllers are designed for two parts. As discussed above, the fuzzy controller will be designed firstly to replace the hysteresis controllers which could not distinguish the amplitudes of the torque and flux errors. The errors of the torque and flux could be differentiated in fuzzy method, so the optimal vector is selected by assessing the deviation degrees of the errors. Then after the optimal vector is obtained by fuzzy control method, using one vector during the whole period may cause the larger torque ripple in the discrete control process, the fuzzy duty ratio control is designed.

4.1   Fuzzy Controller Designer of Vector Selection

As is well known, the fuzzy controller generally consists of four parts: fuzzification, knowledge base, fuzzy inference, defuzzification. The torque error E_T, flux error E_ψ and stator flux angle θ_s are chosen as the fuzzy input variables of controller, and the controller output variable V is the voltage vector generated by the VSI. The flux angle in the whole plan could be mapped to the range of $(-\pi/6, \pi/6)$ by the following expression since the symmetry of the sector.

$$\theta_s^* = \theta_s - \frac{\pi}{3} \left\lceil \frac{\theta_s - \pi/6}{\pi/3} \right\rceil \tag{7}$$

Where θ_s is the actual flux angle, and θ_s^* is the flux angle input of the fuzzy controller after mapping. The operator $\lceil \ \rceil$ is on the behalf of rounding to the nearest bigger integer. The design process is simpler as the decreased fuzzy rules through this step. The fuzzy set of the flux angle is defined as NS, ZO, PS in view of controlling the vector accurately, and the membership function is shown as Fig. 2a. The fuzzy sets of the torque and flux errors are both included four components as NB, NS, PS, PB due to the reason that it could distinguish the variation accurately, the membership functions are shown as Fig. 2b and Fig. 2c. The above elements NB, NS, ZO, PS, PB represent negative big, negative small, zero, positive small, positive big respectively. The fuzzy set of the output variable is the singleton set in order to obtain the voltage vector, as shown in Fig. 2d. The fuzzy rules which are acquired by analysis and trial are designed as the Table 1.

The fuzzy inference operator is based on Mamdani method by using above fuzzy rules, and the maximum criterion is adopted to obtain the exact voltage vector. Finally, the output voltage vector of the controller needs to be converted to the whole plan due to the above mapping process.

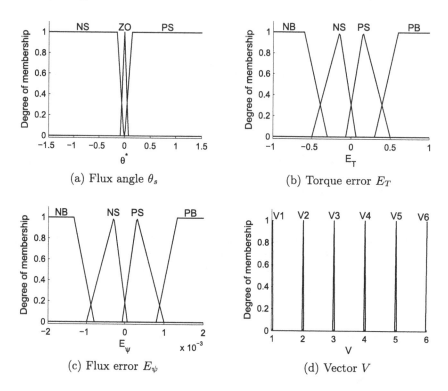

Fig. 2. The membership function of three input variables and the output variable

4.2   Fuzzy Controller Designer of Duty Ratio

The fuzzy controller of duty ratio is designed as single input single output structure. Since the torque variation is affected by duty ratio, the input variable of the controller is torque error which is represented as ΔT here. The controller output variable is the duty ratio represented as Δd. The fuzzy sets of them both have five language sets as NB, NS, ZO, PS, PB. The membership function is presented as Fig. 3. The fuzzy rules are designed as the following IF-THEN expressions according to the analysis and trial.

Table 1. Fuzzy control rules

θ_s^*		NS				ZO				PS			
		E_ψ				E_ψ				E_ψ			
		NB	NS	PS	PB	NB	NS	PS	PB	NB	NS	PS	PB
E_T	NB	V_4	V_5	V_5	V_6	V_5	V_5	V_6	V_6	V_5	V_5	V_6	V_6
	NS	V_4	V_5	V_6	V_6	V_5	V_5	V_6	V_6	V_4	V_5	V_1	V_1
	PS	V_3	V_2	V_1	V_1	V_3	V_3	V_2	V_2	V_4	V_3	V_2	V_2
	PB	V_3	V_2	V_2	V_1	V_3	V_3	V_2	V_2	V_3	V_3	V_2	V_2

Rule1: If ΔT is NB, then Δd is NB;
Rule2: If ΔT is NS, then Δd is NS;
Rule3: If ΔT is ZO, then Δd is ZO;
Rule4: If ΔT is PS, then Δd is PS;
Rule5: If ΔT is PB, then Δd is PB;

The Mamdani method is applied in the fuzzy inference process by using above fuzzy rules and the exact duty ratio is obtained by the gravity method in defuzzification process. Based on above two fuzzy controllers, the active vector and the zero vector are alternatively output by VSI to control the PMSM.

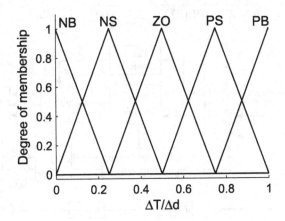

Fig. 3. The membership function of the variables ΔT and Δd

5   Simulation Results

To verify the validity of the proposed fuzzy DTC control method, the comprehensive simulation tests are carried out in the Matlab/Simulink environment. The block diagram of simulation is shown as Fig. 4, where two fuzzy controllers are used to choose the appropriate vector and determine the duty ratio respectively. The hysteresis controllers and lookup table in the conventional DTC are eliminated, and the action times of the active vector and zero vector are allocated through the duty ratio. The parameters of the PMSM for simulation are shown in Table 2. The fixed sample time of the simulation is set as 50 μs for the two control methods.

The various responses of the conventional DTC method and the proposed fuzzy DTC method, included the speed, torque, stator flux and the current performances, are shown and compared as Figs. 5, 6, 7 and 8, respectively. The motor starts up with rated load of 4 Nm, and the load decreases to 50 % rated value at 0.2 s. The simulation tests of the two methods are both under the same situation. The speed responses of the two methods are compared as Fig. 5, the interesting

Table 2. PMSM parameters

Parameter	Value	Unit
Mechanical inertia(J)	0.000828	kg·m^2
Magnet flux linkage(ψ_f)	0.09428	Wb
Stator resistance(R_s)	0.779	Ω
Stator inductance(L_s)	0.003026	H
Number of pole pairs(n_p)	4	-
Rated torque(T_N)	4	N·m
Rated voltage(U_N)	220	V
Rated speed(n_N)	3000	r/min

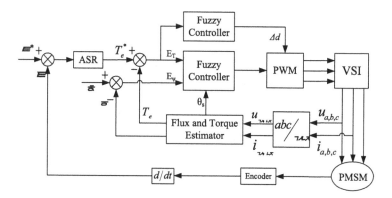

Fig. 4. Control schematic diagram of the proposed fuzzy PMSM DTC system

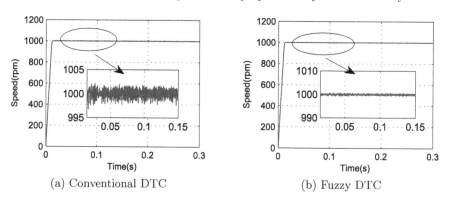

(a) Conventional DTC   (b) Fuzzy DTC

Fig. 5. The simulation results of the speed response

details of the steady state response are partial enlarged clearly. The proposed fuzzy DTC method also show the excellent dynamic response as the conventional one, and its steady state speed ripple is smaller compared to the conventional

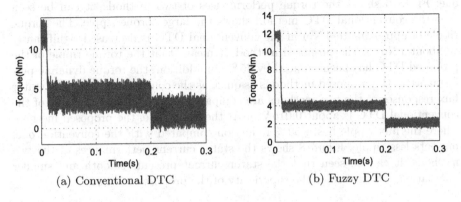

Fig. 6. The simulation results of the torque response

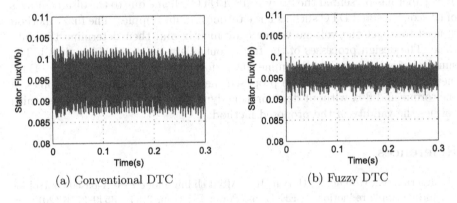

Fig. 7. The simulation results of the flux response

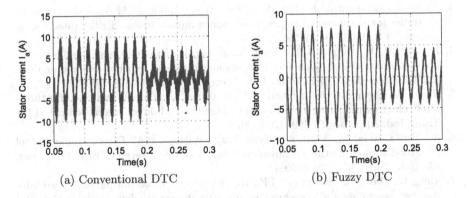

Fig. 8. The simulation results of the stator current response

one. Figure 6 shows the torque performances of two methods, it can be seen that the conventional DTC method shows the large torque ripple. The torque ripple of approximate 4 Nm in the conventional DTC is decreased significantly to about 1 Nm in the proposed method, it means that the torque ripple of the proposed DTC has been reduced by 75 %. In addition, the torque dynamic performance of the proposed method is as quick as the conventional one. The stator flux responses of the two methods are compared as Fig. 7, the flux ripple of the conventional DTC is about 0.015 Wb. At the same time, the proposed method, where the flux ripple has a 50 % reduction compared with the convention one, presents less ripple. Figure 8 shows the stator current performances of the two methods, it can be seen that the stator current presents smooth and smaller fluctuation, which verifies the superiority of the proposed method.

6   Conclusion

This paper has presented the fuzzy PMSM DTC scheme due to the disadvantages of the conventional DTC such as large torque and flux ripples. The fuzzy method is used to select the voltage vector conveniently and then determine the duty ratio. The design processes of the fuzzy controllers are discussed in detail. The simulation is carried out to examine the performance of the proposed fuzzy DTC method, tests results show the proposed method could decrease the ripples of the torque and flux without deteriorating dynamic response of the torque, which verifies the validity of the proposed method.

References

1. Jezernik, K., Korelic, J., Horvat, R.: PMSM sliding mode FPGA-based control for torque ripple reduction. IEEE Trans. Power Electron. **28**(7), 3549–3556 (2013)
2. Rahman, M.F., Zhong, L., Lim, K.W.: A direct torque-controlled interior permanent magnet synchronous motor drive incorporating field weakening. IEEE Trans. Ind. Appl. **34**(6), 1246–1253 (1998)
3. Zhong, L., Rahman, M.F., Hu, W.Y., Lim, K.W., Rahman, M.A.: A direct torque controller for permanent magnet synchronous motor drives. IEEE Trans. Energ. Convers. **14**(3), 637–642 (1999)
4. Rahman, M.F., Haque, M.E., Tang, L., Zhong, L.: Problems associated with the direct torque control of an interior permanent-magnet synchronous motor drive and their remedies. IEEE Trans. Ind. Electron. **51**(4), 799–809 (2004)
5. Sapin, A., Steimer, P.K., Simond, J.J.: Modeling, simulation, and test of a three-level voltage-source inverter with output LC filter and direct torque control. IEEE Trans. Ind. Appl. **43**(2), 469–475 (2007)
6. del Toro Garcia, X., Arias, A., Jayne, M.G., Witting, P.A.: Direct torque control of induction motors utilizing three-level voltage source inverters. IEEE Trans. Ind. Electron. **55**(2), 956–958 (2008)
7. Tang, L., Zhong, L., Rahman, M.F., Hu, Y.: A novel direct torque controlled interior permanent magnet synchronous machine drive with low ripple in flux and torque and fixed switching frequency. IEEE Trans. Power Electron. **19**(2), 346–354 (2004)

8. Inoue, Y., Morimoto, S., Sanada, M.: A novel control scheme for maximum power operation of synchronous reluctance motors including maximum torque per flux control. IEEE Trans. Ind. Appl. **47**(1), 115–121 (2011)
9. Kang, J.K., Sul, S.K.: New direct torque control of induction motor for minimum torque ripple and constant switching frequency. IEEE Trans. Ind. Appl. **35**(5), 1076–1082 (1999)
10. Abad, G., Rodrguez, M.A., Poza, J.: Two-level VSC based predictive direct torque control of the doubly fed induction machine with reduced torque and flux ripples at low constant switching frequency. IEEE Trans. Power Electron. **23**(3), 1050–1061 (2008)
11. Liu, X., Wang, W.: DSVM and duty ratio control combined direct torque control for bearingless induction motor. In: 2010 Chinese Control and Decision Conference, pp. 2025–2030 (2010)
12. Zhang, Y., Wang, Q., Liu, W.: Direct torque control strategy of induction motors based on predictive control and synthetic vector duty ratio control. In: 2010 International Conference on Artificial Intelligence and Computational Intelligence, pp. 96–101 (2010)
13. Tang, X., Yang, X., Zhao, S.: New direct torque control method considering voltage vector duty ratio used in PMSM drive. In: 2013 International Conference on Electrical Machines and Systems, pp. 1189–1193 (2013)
14. Zhang, Y., Zhu, J., Zhao, Z., Xu, W., Dorrell, D.G.: An improved direct torque control for three-level inverter-fed induction motor sensorless drive. IEEE Trans. Power Electron. **27**(3), 1502–1513 (2012)
15. Shi, X., Wang, Z., Deng, C., Song, T., Pan, L., Chen, Z.: A novel bio-sensor based on DNA strand displacement. PLoS One **9**, e108856 (2014)
16. Uddin, M.N., Hafeez, M.: FLC-based DTC scheme to improve the dynamic performance of an IM drive. IEEE Trans. Ind. Appl. **48**(2), 823–831 (2012)
17. Sun, D., He, Y., Zhu, J.G.: Fuzzy logic direct torque control for permanent magnet synchronous motors. In: Fifth World Congress on Intelligent Control and Automation, pp. 4401–4405 (2004)
18. Wei, X., Chen, D., Zhao, C.: Minimization of torque ripple of direct-torque controlled induction machines by improved discrete space vector modulation. Electr. power Syst. Res. **72**(2), 103–112 (2004)

A Uniform Solution for Vertex Cover Problem by Using Time-Free Tissue P Systems

Yunyun Niu[1], Zhigao Wang[2], and Jianhua Xiao[3]([⊠])

[1] School of Information Engineering, China University of Geosciences in Beijing,
Beijing 100083, China
niuyunyun1003@163.com
[2] Basic Department, China Institute of Industrial Relations, Beijing 100048, China
zgwang_ciir@163.com
[3] The Research Center of Logistics, Nankai University, Tianjin 300071, China
jhxiao@nankai.edu.cn

Abstract. This work focuses on the computational efficiency of timed tissue P system. A rule in traditional P systems is usually executed in one time unit. We investigate the timed tissue P systems by removing the restriction. It is constructed by adding a time mapping to the rules to specify the execution time for each rule. A uniform and time-free solution to vertex cover problem is proposed, where the execution time of the computational processes involved can vary arbitrarily and the output produced is always the same.

Keywords: Membrane computing · Tissue P system · Computation efficiency · Vertex cover problem

1 Introduction

Membrane computing is a branch of natural computing [18]. It is inspired by the structure and the functioning of living cells as well as the organization of cells in tissues, organs and other higher order structures. The computing models investigated in the framework of membrane computing are called P systems, which are a class of bio-inspired computing models. There are three types of P systems: cell-like P systems [9,18], tissue P systems [10,31] and spiking neural P systems [11,14]. P systems provide distributed and parallel computing models, which were proved to be a rich framework for handling many problems related to computing [25,26]. Most of the variants of P systems are computationally universal as number computing devices [28–30,32], language generators [27,33], and can solve presumably intractable problems in polynomial time or even in linear time [13,15,31]. Especially, it is proved that some PSPACE-complete problems can be solved in polynomial time in the framework of membrane computing [1,12]. Rules for cell division, cell separation and cell creation, are usually used to generate an exponential workspace in linear time. For the motivations, definitions and applications of various P system models we refer to [4,19,21].

© Springer-Verlag Berlin Heidelberg 2015
M. Gong et al. (Eds.): BIC-TA 2015, CCIS 562, pp. 306–314, 2015.
DOI: 10.1007/978-3-662-49014-3_28

Tissue P system is an abstraction of communicating and cooperating cells in tissues [10]. Membranes in tissue P systems are placed in the nodes of a graph [16]. However, alive tissues are not static networks of cells, since new cells are generated by membrane fission in a natural way. Tissue P systems with cell division were introduced in [20] based on the biological inspiration. Cell division rules can be used to generate exponential workspace in linear time. Thus, tissue P systems with cell division can solve NP-complete problems in polynomial time (even linear time), e.g., the subset sum problem [6], the 3-coloring problem [7], and the partition problem [8].

In traditional P systems, a global clock exists to synchronize the execution of different parallel processes [19]. Each rule has the same execution time. From a biological point of view, the time of execution of certain biological processes could vary because of external uncontrollable conditions. Therefore, it is natural to investigate P systems without the constraint on the execution time of rules [2,3,5,17]. Recently, several types of P systems have been considered by adding a time mapping to specify the execution time of each rule [22,23]. If for an arbitrary time mapping, a system always generates the same results, we say that it is time-free. It is independent of the time mapping assignment, and has captured the attention of researchers. A time-free spiking neural P system has been introduced in [17] with the investigation of its universality. Finding time-free solutions to hard computational problems has been discussed in [2] from a theoretical point of view. In [22], a family of time-free P systems with d division is constructed in a uniform way to solve Hamiltonian Path Problem (HPP). In [23], the computational efficiency of timed P systems with active membrane was investigated, and a time-free solution to SAT problem was proposed. In [24], the timed and time-free SN P systems are considered to solve subset sum problem. In this work, we propose a uniform solution for the vertex cover problem by a family of time-free recognizer tissue P systems. For an arbitrary time mapping of the rules, the system always generates the same results.

2   Tissue P Systems with Cell Division

Formally, a *tissue P system with cell division* of degree $q \geq 1$ is defined as follows [20]

$$\Pi = (\Gamma, \Omega, w_1, \dots, w_q, \mathcal{R}, i_{out}),$$

where:

1. $q \geq 1$ (the initial degree of the system; the system contains q cells, labeled with $1, 2, \cdots, q$; we use 0 to refer to the environment);
2. Γ is the *alphabet* of *objects*;
3. $w_1, \dots, w_q$ are strings over Γ, describing the multisets of objects placed in the cells of the system at the beginning of the computation;
4. $\Omega \subseteq \Gamma$ is the set of objects in the environment, each with an arbitrarily many copies;
5. $\mathcal{R}$ is a finite set of rules of the following forms:

(a) *Communication rules:* $(i, u/v, j)$, for $i, j \in \{0, 1, 2, \ldots, q\}, i \neq j, u, v \in \Gamma^*$ ($|u| + |v|$ is called the length of the communication rule $(i, u/v, j)$).

(b) *Division rules:* $[a]_i \rightarrow [b]_i[c]_i$, where $i \in \{1, 2, \ldots, q\}$, $a \in \Gamma$ and $b, c \in \Gamma \cup \{\lambda\}$.

6. $i_{out} \in \{0, 1, 2, \ldots, q\}$ is the output cell if $i_{out} \neq 0$ or the environment if $i_{out} = 0$.

The rules of a system as above are used in the non-deterministic maximally parallel manner. In each step, all cells which can evolve must evolve in a maximally parallel way (in each step the system applies a multiset of rules which is maximal, no further rule can be added). This way of applying rules has only one restriction: when a cell is divided, the division rule is the only one which is applied for that cell in that step; the objects inside that cell do not evolve by means of communication rules. The labels of membranes precisely identify the rules which can be applied to them.

When applying the division rules $[a]_i \rightarrow [b]_i[c]_i$, all the objects in the original cells are replicated and copies of them are placed in each of the new cells, with the exception of the object a, which is replaced by $b \in \Gamma \cup \{\lambda\}$ in the first new cell and by $c \in \Gamma \cup \{\lambda\}$ in the second one.

A configuration of Π at an instant t is described by the multisets of objects over Γ associated with all the cells present in the system at that moment, and the multiset over Ω associated with the environment at the instant t. All computations start from the initial configuration $(w_1, \ldots, w_q, \emptyset)$ and proceed as defined above; only halting computations give a result, and the result is encoded by the objects present in the output cell or the environment i_{out} in the halting configuration.

3   Timed Tissue P Systems with Cell Division

A timed tissue P system $\Pi(e) = (\Gamma, \Omega, w_1, \ldots, w_q, \mathcal{R}, i_{out}, e)$ can be constructed by adding to the tissue P system Π a mapping $e : \mathcal{R} \rightarrow \mathbb{N} \setminus \{0\}$, which specifies the execution time of each rule of the system. We denote by $e(r)$ the time for which rule r lasts. When a rule is started, the occurrences of objects subject to this rule cannot be subject to other rules until the implementation of the rule completes.

By adding different time mappings we can obtain a family of timed tissue P systems. The systems in the same family may produce different computation results for having different time mapping. A timed tissue P system $\Pi(e)$ is said to be time-free if and only if for any time mapping e, the system $\Pi(e)$ produces the same computation result (if any), i.e., the execution time of the rules has no influence on the computation results of such systems.

3.1   A Timed Recognizer Tissue P System

A timed recognizer tissue P system with cell division of degree $q \geq 1$ is a construct

$$\Pi(e) = (\Gamma, \Sigma, \Omega, w_1, \ldots, w_q, \mathcal{R}, i_{in}, i_{out}, e)$$

where:

- $(\Gamma, \Omega, w_1, \ldots, w_q, \mathcal{R}, i_{out}, e)$ is a timed tissue P system with cell division of degree $q \geq 1$ (as defined in the previous section).
- The working alphabet Γ has two distinguished objects **yes** and **no**, at least one copy of them present in some initial multisets $w_1, \ldots, w_q$, but are not present in Ω.
- Σ is an input alphabet strictly contained in Γ.
- $i_{in} \in \{1, \ldots, q\}$ is the input cell.
- The output region i_{out} is the environment.
- All computations halt.
- If $\mathcal{C}$ is a computation of Π, then either the object **yes** or the object **no** (but not both) must exist in the environment when the computation halts.

The rules of a system as above are used in the non-deterministic maximally parallel manner. The execution time of rules is determined by the time mapping e, thus it is possible that there exist one rule whose execution time is inherently exponential steps. The step is called a *RS-step* (rule starting step), if at this step at least one rule of system $\Pi(e)$ starts its execution [23]. The *RS-steps* can be used to characterize how fast to solve a decision problem by using timed tissue P systems. So in the timed P systems, we count the *RS-steps*, and denote the computation time as the total of the *RS-steps*.

The computations of the system Π with input multiset $w \in \Gamma^*$ start from an initial configuration of the form $(w_1, w_2, \ldots, w_{in}w, \ldots, w_q, \emptyset)$, that is, after adding the multiset w to the contents of the input cell i_{in}. A computation $\mathcal{C}$ is called an accepting computation (respectively, rejecting computation) if the object **yes** (respectively, **no**) appears in the environment associated to the corresponding halting configuration of $\mathcal{C}$, and only in the last step of the computation.

With the previous definitions we define the concepts of *timed soundness*, *timed completeness* and *timed polynomially bounding* for recognizer timed tissue P systems. Let $\mathbf{\Pi} = \{\Pi(n, e) | n \in \mathbb{N}\}$ be a family of timed recognizer tissue P systems. There is a pair of polynomial computable functions (cod, s) over the problem X such that:

- for each instance $u \in I_X$, $cod(u)$ is the input of the system $\Pi(s(u), e)$ and $s(u) \in \mathbb{N}$;
- the family $\mathbf{\Pi}$ is *timed sound* with respect to X, cod, s, that is, for each instance of the problem $u \in I_x$ and a given time mapping e, if there exists an accepting computation of $\Pi(s(u), e)$ with input $cod(u)$, then we have $\Theta_X(u) = 1$;
- the family $\mathbf{\Pi}$ is *timed complete* with respect to X, cod, s, that is, for each instance of the problem $u \in I_x$ and a given time mapping e, if $\Theta_X(u) = 1$, every computation of $\Pi(s(u), e)$ is an accepting computation;
- the family $\mathbf{\Pi}$ is *timed polynomial bounded* if there exists a polynomial function p such that, for each $u \in I_X$ and a given time mapping e, computations in $\Pi(s(u), e)$ halt in at most $p(|u|)$ *RS-steps*.

Furtherly, we can define the concepts of *time-free soundness*, *time-free completeness* and *time-free polynomially bounding* for timed recognizer tissue P systems. Let $\mathbf{\Pi} = \{\Pi(n,e)|n \in \mathbb{N}\}$ be a family of timed recognizer tissue P systems. There is a pair of polynomial computable functions (cod, s) over the problem X such that:

- for each instance $u \in I_X$, $cod(u)$ is the input of the system $\Pi(s(u), e)$ and $s(u) \in \mathbb{N}$;
- the family $\mathbf{\Pi}$ is *time-free sound* with respect to X, cod, s, that is, for each instance of the problem $u \in I_x$ and any time mapping e, if there exists an accepting computation of $\Pi(s(u), e)$ with input $cod(u)$, then we have $\Theta_X(u) = 1$;
- the family $\mathbf{\Pi}$ is *time-free complete* with respect to X, cod, s, that is, for each instance of the problem $u \in I_x$ and any time mapping e, if $\Theta_X(u) = 1$, every computation of $\Pi(s(u), e)$ is an accepting computation;
- the family $\mathbf{\Pi}$ is *time-free polynomial bounded* if there exists a polynomial function p such that, for each $u \in I_X$ and any time mapping e, computations in $\Pi(s(u), e)$ halt in at most $p(|u|)$ *RS-steps*.

Let $X = (I_X, \theta_X)$ be a decision problem. A family $\mathbf{\Pi} = \{\Pi(s(u), e) \mid u \in I_x\}$ of timed recognizer tissue P systems is a uniform solution to decision problem X if the following holds:

- The family $\mathbf{\Pi}$ is *polynomially uniform* by Turing machines, that is, there exists a deterministic Turing machine which constructs the system $\Pi(n, e)$ for $n \in \mathbb{N}$ in polynomial time.
- The family $\mathbf{\Pi}$ is time-free polynomially bounded, time-free sound and time-free complete.

4   An Uniform Solution for Vertex Cover Problem

We consider the decision version of the vertex cover problem. It can be defined as follows: given an undirected graph, $\gamma = (V, E)$, and a natural number $k \leq |V|$, determine if there exists a subset $V' \subseteq V$, such that for each edge of the graph at least one of its endpoints belongs to V' and $|V'| \leq k$.

Let us consider an undirected graph $\gamma = (V, E)$, where $V = \{v_1, v_2, \ldots, v_n\}$ is the set of vertices and E is the set of edges. The input of instant γ can be defined as $cod(\gamma) = \{e_{i,j} \mid \{v_i, v_j\} \in E$ and $i < j\}$ and $s(\gamma) = n$. We construct a family of timed recognizer tissue P system of degree 2

$$\Pi(n, e) = (\Gamma, \Sigma, \Omega, w_1, w_2, \mathcal{R}, i_{in}, i_{out}, e),$$

where:

- $\Gamma = \Sigma \cup \{\{A_i, T_i, F_i, T'_i, F'_i, t_i, t'_i, t''_i \mid 1 \leq i \leq n\}\} \cup \{\{b_i \mid 1 \leq i \leq k\}\} \cup \{\{a_0, g, d, d', yes, no\}\}$;
- $\Sigma = \{\{e_{i,j} \mid 1 \leq i < j \leq n\}\}$;

- $\Omega = \Gamma - \{\{yes, no\}\}$;
- $w_1 = \{\{yes, no\}\}$, $w_2 = \{\{A_1, d, b_1, \ldots, b_k\}\}$;
- $i_{in} = 2$ is the input cell;
- The output region i_{out} is the environment;
- $e : R \to \mathbb{N}$ is the time mapping from R to natural numbers, and the execution time of the division rule is set to a constant;
- R is the set of rules:
  - $r_{1,i} \equiv [A_i]_2 \to [T_i]_2[F_i]_2$, for $1 \le i \le n$;
  - $r_2 \equiv (1, no/\lambda, 0)$;
  - $r_{3,i} \equiv (2, T_i/a_0 T_i' t_i t_i', 0)$, for $1 \le i \le n$;
  - $r_{4,i} \equiv (2, F_i/a_0 F_i', 0)$, for $1 \le i \le n$;
  - $r_{5,i} \equiv (2, T_i'/\lambda, 1)$, for $1 \le i \le n$;
  - $r_{6,i} \equiv (2, F_i'/\lambda, 1)$, for $1 \le i \le n$;
  - $r_{7,i,j} \equiv (2, t_i b_j/\lambda, 0)$, for $1 \le i \le n, 1 \le j \le k$;
  - $r_{8,i} \equiv (2, t_i'/(t_i'')^{(n-1)} g^2, 0)$, for $1 \le i \le n$;
  - $r_{9,i} \equiv (1, T_i' F_i'/A_{i+1}^2, 0)$, for $1 \le i \le n$;
  - $r_{10,i} \equiv (1, A_{i+1}/ga_0, 2)$, for $1 \le i \le n - 1$;
  - $r_{11} \equiv (1, A_{n+1} d/gda_0, 2)$;
  - $r_{12,i,j} \equiv (2, t_i'' e_{i,j}/\lambda, 0)$, for $1 \le i < j \le n$;
  - $r_{13,i,j} \equiv (2, t_j'' e_{i,j}/\lambda, 0)$, for $1 \le i < j \le n$;
  - $r_{14,i} \equiv (2, A_{n+1} b_i/\lambda, 0)$, for $1 \le i \le k$;
  - $r_{15,i} \equiv (2, A_{n+1} e_{i,j}/\lambda, 0)$, for $1 \le i < j \le n$;
  - $r_{16} \equiv (1, d/d', 0)$;
  - $r_{17} \equiv (2, A_{n+1}/d', 1)$;
  - $r_{18} \equiv (2, d'/yes, 1)$;
  - $r_{19} \equiv (2, yes/no, 0)$.

Now let's briefly describe how the system $\Pi(n, e)$ works. At the first step, rules $r_{1,1}$ and r_2 must be started at the same time. They need one *RS-step*. After $e(r_2)$ steps, the object *no* will arrive at the environment. By using rules of $r_{1,1}$, the system generates two membranes labeled by 2 after $e(r_{1,1})$ time units. Rules $r_{3,1}$ and $r_{4,1}$ must be started at the same time, so they need one *RS-step*. And then rules $r_{5,1}$, $r_{6,1}$, $r_{7,1,j}$ and $r_{8,1}$ must be started at the same time, so they need also one *RS-step*. When both of the object T_1' and the object F_1' reach to the membrane with label 1, rule $r_{9,1}$ must be started at the next step. Then rule $r_{10,1}$ will be used to send the object A_2 to membrane with label 2. It takes at most 5 *RS-steps* to obtain the object A_2 in membrane with label 2. In the same way, after $5n$ *RS-steps* 2^n kinds of subsets are generated and respected by different object sets in membrane labeled by 2. The generation stage needs $5n$ *RS-steps*.

Rules $r_{12,i,j}$ and $r_{13,i,j}$ must be started at the same time as rule $r_{10,i}$ or rule r_{11}. They check if there exists a subset for each edge of the graph at least one of its endpoints belongs to it. Rules $r_{7,i,j}$ are used to check if the size of the subset is more than k. After the generation stage, object A_{n+1} appears in cells with label 2, and objects a_0, d and g appear in cell with label 1. If there exists object b_i or $e_{i,j}$ in membrane 2 at that time, rules $r_{14,i}$, $r_{15,i}$ and r_{16} will be started at the same time, and object A_{n+1} will disappear. Otherwise, only rule r_{16} is started, and object A_{n+1} remains unchanged in membranes with label 2. This process need at most one *RS-steps*. When object d in the membrane with label 1 is replaced by object d', if object A_{n+1} is still in membrane with label 2, rule r_{17} must be started. It also takes one *RS-steps*.

Rule r_{18} and rule r_{19} are used to send the right answer to the environment. According to the above analysis, if at least one copy of the object d' appears in a membrane labeled by 2, the object *yes* will be sent to the environment to exchange for object *no*. The process needs two *RS-steps*. The system halts with object *yes* in the environment, which means that the answer to the decision problem is positive. If the object *yes* remains in membrane labeled by 1, it will not be sent to the environment. In that case, the object *no* will exist in the environment when the computation halts, which means that the answer to the decision problem is negative. According to the above analysis, at most $5n + 4$ *RS-steps* are needed to complete the whole computation process. That is to say, our algorithm can solve the vertex cover problem in polynomial *RS-steps*.

5   Informal Verification

It is easy to check that the rules of system $\Pi(n, e)$ can be built in polynomial time with respect to n. Furthermore, the necessary resources to build an element of the system are of a polynomial order, as shown below:

- Size of the alphabet: $0.5n^2 + 7.5n + k + 6 \in \Theta(n^2)$;
- Initial number of cells: $2 \in \Theta(1)$;
- Initial number of objects: $k + 4 \in \Theta(1)$;
- Number of rules: $0.5n^2 + (9.5 + k)n + k + 5 \in \Theta(n^2)$;
- Maximal length of a rule: $n + 2 \in \Theta(n)$.

Therefore, there exists a deterministic Turing machine working in polynomial time which constructs the system with respect to n. That is to say, the family $\Pi(n, e)$ is polynomial uniform by deterministic Turing machines.

It is clear that the family of timed tissue P systems constructed above is time-free sound, time-free complete, and time-free polynomial bounded. According to the definition of uniform time-free solution at the end of Sect. 3, the family of time-free tissue P systems $\Pi(n, e)$ is a uniform solution to vertex cover problem. For any time mapping e, the correctness of the solution does not depend on the execution time of the rules.

6   Conclusion

In this study, a time-free solution to a famous NP-complete problem, vertex cover problem was obtained. The computation result was independent of the time mapping assignment. The output of the time-free tissue P system did not vary no matter how the execution time changed. It was also a uniform version.

Although other NP-complete problems can be reduced to vertex cover problem in polynomial time, it still remains open how one can compute the reduction of an NP-complete problem to another NP-complete problem by P systems. In the future work, we will give direct time-free solutions to other NP-complete problems or even PSPACE-complete problems.

Acknowledgment. This work was supported by the Fundamental Research Funds for the Central Universities (2652015340) and the National Natural Science Foundation of China (No.61502012, No.61373066).

References

1. Alhazov, A., Martin-Vide, C., Pan, L.: Solving a PSPACE-complete problem by recognizing P systems with restricted active membranes. Fundamenta Informaticae **58**(2), 66–77 (2003)
2. Cavaliere, M.: Time-free solution to hard computational problems. Proc. Tenth Brainstorming Week Membr. Comput. **1**, 204–210 (2012)
3. Cavaliere, M., Deufemia, V.: Further results on time-free P systems. Int. J. Found. Comput. Sci. **17**(1), 69–89 (2006)
4. Ciobanu, G., Pérez-Jiménez, M.J., Păun, G.: Applications of Membrane Computing. Springer, Berlin (2006)
5. Cavaliere, M., Sburlan, D.: Time–independent P systems. In: Mauri, G., Păun, G., Pérez-Jímenez, M., Rozenberg, G., Salomaa, A. (eds.) WMC 2004. LNCS, vol. 3365, pp. 239–258. Springer, Heidelberg (2005)
6. Wang, X., Miao, Y., Cheng, M.: Finding motifs in DNA sequences using low-dispersion sequences. J. Comput. Biol. **21**(4), 320–329 (2014)
7. Díaz-Pernil, D., Gutiérrez-Naranjo, M.A., Pérez-Jiménez, M.J., Riscos-Núñez, A.: A linear-time tissue P system based solution for the 3-coloring problem. Electr. Notes Theor. Comput. Sci. **171**, 81–93 (2007)
8. Shi, X., Wang, Z., Deng, C., Song, T., Pan, L., Chen, Z.: A novel bio-sensor based on DNA strand displacement. PLoS One **9**(10), e108856 (2014)
9. Gutiérrez–Naranjo, M.A., Pérez–Jiménez, M.J., Riscos–Núñez, A., Romero–Campero, F.J.: On the power of dissolution in P systems with active membranes. In: Freund, R., Păun, G., Rozenberg, G., Salomaa, A. (eds.) WMC 2005. LNCS, vol. 3850, pp. 224–240. Springer, Heidelberg (2006)
10. Martín-Vide, C., Păun, G., Pazos, J., Rodríguez Patón, A.: Tissue P Systems. Theor. Comput. Sci. **296**, 295–326 (2003)
11. Ionescu, M., Păun, G., Yokomori, T.: Spiking neural P systems. Fundamenta Informaticae **71**, 279–308 (2006)
12. Ishdorj, T., Leporati, A., Pan, L., Zeng, X., Zhang, X.: Deterministic solutions to QSAT and Q3SAT by spiking neural P systems with pre-computed resources. Theor. Comput. Sci. **411**, 2345–2358 (2010)
13. Pan, L., Daniel, D.P., Pérez-Jiménez, M.J.: Computation of ramsey numbers by P system with active membranes. Int. J. Found. Comput. Sci. **22**, 29–38 (2011)
14. Pan, L., Păun, G.: Spiking neural P systems: an improved normal form. Theor. Comput. Sci. **411**, 906–918 (2010)
15. Pan, L., Păun, G., Pérez-Jiménez, M.J.: Spiking neural P systems with neuron division and budding. Sci. China Inf. Sci. **54**(8), 1596–1607 (2011)

16. Pan, L., Pérez-Jiménez, M.J.: Computational complexity of tissue-like P systems. J. Complex. **26**(3), 296–315 (2010)
17. Pan, L., Zeng, X., Zhang, X.: Time-free spiking neural P systems. Neural Comput. **23**, 1320–1342 (2011)
18. Păun, G.: Computing with membranes. J. Comput. Syst. Sci. **61**(1), 108–143 (2000)
19. Păun, G.: Membrane Computing. An Introduction. Springer, Berlin (2002)
20. Song, T., Pan, L., Jiang, K., et al.: Normal forms for some classes of sequential spiking neural P systems. IEEE Trans. NanoBiosci. **12**(3), 255–264 (2013)
21. Păun, G., Rozenberg, G., Salomaa, A.: Handbook of Membrane Computing. Oxford University Press, Oxford (2009)
22. Song, T., Zheng, H., He, J., Zhang, L.: Time-free solution to hamilton path problems using P systems with d-Division. J. Appl. Math. Article ID 975798, p. 7 (2013), doi:10.1155/2013/975798. ISSN 1110–757X
23. Song, T., Macías-Ramos, L.F.M., Pan, L., Pérez-Jiménez, M.J.: Time-free solution to SAT problem using P systmes with active membranes. Theor. Comput. Sci. **529**, 61–68 (2014)
24. Song, T., Luo, L., He, J., Chen, Z., Zhang, K.: Solving subset sum problems by time-free spiking neural P systems. Appl. Math. Inf. Sci. **8**(1), 327–332 (2014)
25. Zhang, G., Cheng, J., Gheorghe, M., Meng, Q.: A hybrid approach based on differential evolution and tissue membrane systems for solving constrained manufacturing parameter optimization problems. Appl. Soft Comput. **13**(3), 1528–1542 (2013)
26. Zhang, G., Gheorghe, M., Li, Y.: A membrane algorithm with quantum-inspired subalgorithms and its application to image processing. Natural Comput. **11**(4), 701–717 (2012)
27. Zhang, X., Liu, Y., Luo, B., Pan, L.: Computational power of tissue P systems for generating control languages. Inf. Sci. **278**(10), 285–297 (2014)
28. Song, T., Pan, L., Păun, G.: Asynchronous spiking neural P systems with local synchronization. Inf. Sci. **219**, 197–207 (2013)
29. Zhang, X., Pan, L., Păun, A.: On universality of axon P systems. IEEE Trans. Neural Netw. Learn. Syst. (2015). doi:10.1109/TNNLS.2015.2396940
30. Zhang, X., Wang, B., Pan, L.: Spiking neural P systems with a generalized use of rules. Neural Comput. **26**(12), 2925–2943 (2014)
31. Song, T., Pan, L.: Spiking neural P systems with rules on synapses working in maximum spiking strateg. IEEE Trans. NanoBiosci. **14**(4), 465–477 (2015)
32. Zhang, X., Zeng, X., Luo, B., Pan, L.: On some classes of sequential spiking neural P systems. Neural Comput. **26**(5), 974–997 (2014)
33. Song, T., Pan, L., Wang, J., et al.: Normal forms of spiking neural P systems with anti-spikes. IEEE Trans. NanoBiosci. **11**(4), 352–359 (2012)

A Multi-objective Simulated Annealing for Bus Driver Rostering

Kunkun Peng[1,2], Yindong Shen[1,2(✉)], and Jingpeng Li[3]

[1] School of Automation, Huazhong University of Science and Technology,
Wuhan 430074, Hubei, China
pengkunkun@126.com, yindong@hust.edu.cn
[2] Key Laboratory of Image Processing and Intelligent Control (Huazhong University
of Science and Technology), Ministry of Education, Wuhan 430074, Hubei, China
[3] Division of Computer Science and Mathematics, University of Stirling,
Stirling FK9 4LA, UK
jli@cs.stir.ac.uk

Abstract. This paper presents a Multi-Objective Simulated Annealing
(MOSA) approach for noncyclic bus driver rostering. A heuristic is first
devised to construct an initial solution. Next, a SA-based feasibility
repairing algorithm is designed to make the solution feasible. Finally,
a SA-based non-dominated solution generating algorithm is devised to
find the Pareto front based on the feasible solution. Differing from previous work on the problem, the MOSA provides two options to handle
user preferences: one with a weighted-sum evaluation function encouraging moves towards users' predefined preferences, and another with a
domination-based evaluation function encouraging moves towards a more
diversified Pareto set. Moreover, the MOSA employs three strategies, i.e.
incremental evaluation, neighbourhood pruning and biased elite solution
restart strategy, to make the search more efficient and effective. Experiments show that the MOSA can produce a large number of solutions
that reconcile contradictory objectives rapidly, and the strategies can
enhance the computational efficiency and search capability.

Keywords: Public transit · Bus driver rostering · Multi-objective
optimization · Simulated annealing

1 Introduction

Driver rostering is an important component of public transit operations planning process [1,2]. Different from driver scheduling concerned with partitioning
the vehicle work into a set of legal driver duties, driver rostering is concerned
with assigning the duties to drivers [3]. Moreover, bus driver rostering has not
attracted as much attention as bus driver scheduling [4–7], this may be because
it is less standardized among bus transit companies [4].

In the bus driver rostering, many labour union contracts, institutional and
legal requirements have to be satisfied, e.g. drivers must not work more than a

© Springer-Verlag Berlin Heidelberg 2015
M. Gong et al. (Eds.): BIC-TA 2015, CCIS 562, pp. 315–330, 2015.
DOI: 10.1007/978-3-662-49014-3_29

certain number of consecutive days. Therefore, the problem is very complex and NP-hard [5,6]. The early attempts on the problem were presented in [8]. Subsequent researches have mainly concentrated on cyclic rostering [9–11], where drivers are obliged to cycle from week to week within a set of pre-defined work schedules over the planning period [4]. This can easily balance the workload among drivers. However, it is too restrictive and does not allow personal preferences to be addressed [4]. Noncyclic driver rostering can cope with the situation. Apart from saving salary costs, it also increases flexibility which may match drivers preferences and may be better tailored to cover irregular demand [6]. In recent years, there has been an increasing level of interest in the study of noncyclic driver rostering. In essence, the available approaches range from mathematical programming methods to heuristics [4–7,12–15].

The bus driver rostering problem generally considers the interests of both bus drivers and company's administration, therefore, it is a multi-objective optimization problem. To the best of our knowledge, until now there has been limited work on the application of multi-objective techniques to noncyclic driver rostering [4–7,12,14,16]. The approaches are either based on weighted sum or domination. [5,7] solved the problem using commercial solvers (i.e. CPLEX and Gurobi). [4] presented two evolutionary algorithms, i.e. utopic genetic heuristic and adapted improved strength Pareto evolutionary algorithm, which is probably the first attempt to address the problem in terms of Pareto-based optimization. [6,12] found the two algorithms present complementary properties, based on which, they further proposed memetic algorithms. [14] introduced a multi-objective Simulated Annealing (SA) based on a weighted-sum evaluation function.

In this paper, we present a new Multi-Objective Simulated Annealing (MOSA) approach for noncyclic bus driver rostering, aiming to develop more flexible systems that are capable of addressing the real-world problem. Unlike the multi-objective SA in [14], our proposed MOSA provides two options to address user preferences in a flexible way: one weighted-sum evaluation function encouraging moves towards users' predefined preferences, and another domination-based evaluation function encouraging moves towards a more diversified Pareto set. Moreover, two strategies (i.e. neighbourhood pruning and biased elite solution restart strategy) are applied to enhance the performance of the MOSA.

Specifically, in the MOSA, a heuristic is first designed to quickly construct an initial solution. Due to the highly-constrained nature of the problem, the resulting solution maybe infeasible. To make it feasible, a SA-based feasibility repairing algorithm is then devised. To find the Pareto front based on the feasible solution, a SA-based non-dominated solutions generating algorithm with two choices is devised to deal with the objectives in flexible ways. Moreover, based on the domain knowledge, three strategies, i.e. incremental evaluation, neighbourhood pruning and biased elite solution restart strategy, are devised to enhance the computational efficiency and search power.

The rest of this paper is organized as follows. The bus driver rostering problem is introduced in Sect. 2. The details of the MOSA are described in Sect. 3. Experimental results are presented in Sect. 4. The conclusions are given in Sect. 5.

2   The Bus Driver Rostering Problem

Bus driver rostering involves creating a sequence of duties and days off for each driver to operate a company's vehicles within a planning period (say, α weeks). Therefore, the solution of this problem is a set of sequences of duties and days off [4–6,15].

The objectives and constraints of the problem can be illustrated as follows [4]:

O_1: minimize the total overtime of the driver with the maximum total overtime during the planning period;

O_2: minimize the number of drivers who has been assigned to several duties (say, n duties) in the rostering period satisfying $0 < n < q$, where q is the contractual number of duties of the planning period.

C_1: each duty must be assigned to one and only one driver;

C_2: each driver must be assigned one and only one duty or day off on each day;

C_3: some drivers must be granted specific days off due to planned absences (e.g. holidays), or all weekends off, in view of seniority;

C_4: each driver must enjoy a minimum rest period between consecutive duties, which defines compatible consecutive duties per driver;

C_5: drivers must not work more than a certain number of consecutive days;

C_6: drivers must have at least a certain number of days off a week;

C_7: drivers must have at least a certain number of Sundays off in each rostering period;

C_8: drivers must work no more than a certain number of hours per week and a certain number of hours per rostering period.

The corresponding mathematical model of the problem can be illustrated as follows [4].

Indices.

$i = 1, \ldots, |I|$ driver index

$j = 1, \ldots, 7\alpha$ day index of the rostering period

$k = 1, \ldots, |L^j|, |L^j| + 1$ duty (or day off) index on day j

$h = 7\alpha + 1 - g, \ldots, 7\alpha$ day index of the previous rostering period

$m = 1, \ldots, |T^h|, |T^h| + 1$ duty (or day off) index on day h

$l = 1, \ldots, \alpha$ week index

Parameters.

$I = \{1, \ldots, |I|\}$ set of drivers

$J = \{1, \ldots, 7\alpha\}$ set of days in the rostering period

$H = \{7\alpha + 1 - g, \ldots, 7\alpha\}$ set of the last g days in the previous rostering period

$L^j = \{1, \ldots, |L^j|\}$ set of duties of day $j, j \in J$

$T^h = \{1, \ldots, |T^h|\}$ set of duties of day $h, h \in H$

$|L^j| + 1$ the day off for day $j, j \in J$

$|T^h| + 1$ the day off for day $h, h \in H$

L^j_{ik} set of duties (and day off) that can be assigned to driver i on day j according to C_4, given that he/she performs duty (or day off) k on day $j - 1, i \in I$, $j = 2, \ldots, 7\alpha, k \in L^{j-1} \bigcup \{|L^{j-1}| + 1\}$

L_{im}^1 set of duties (and day off) that can be assigned to driver i on day 1 according to C_4, given that he/she performs duty (or day off) m on the previous day (i.e. day 7α in the previous rostering period) $i \in I, m \in T^{7\alpha} \bigcup \{|T^{7\alpha}| + 1\}$

$$e_{ihm} = \begin{cases} 1, \text{if driver } i \text{ was assigned to duty } m \text{ on day } h \text{ in the previous} \\ \quad \text{rostering period}, i \in I, h \in H, m \in T^h \\ 0, \text{otherwise} \end{cases}$$

t_{jk} spread of duty k on day $j, j \in J, k \in L^j$
D_i set of days off for driver i during the rostering period, $i \in I$
q contractual number of duties of the rostering period
t_c contractual daily working time of a driver
g maximum number of consecutive days per driver can work
α number of weeks within the rostering period
n_1 minimum number of days off per week per driver
n_2 minimum number of Sundays off per rostering period per driver
t_1 maximum total work time per week per driver
t_2 maximum total work time per rostering period per driver

Decision Variables.
$$x_{ijk} = \begin{cases} 1, \text{if driver } i \text{ is assigned to duty (or day off) } k \text{ on day } j \text{ in the} \\ \quad \text{rostering period}, i \in I, j \in J, k \in L^j \bigcup \{|L^j| + 1\} \\ 0, \text{otherwise} \end{cases}$$

Objective Function.

$$Minimize \ F(x) = [f_1(x), f_2(x)]^T \tag{1}$$

where

$$f_1(x) = \max_{i \in I} \sum_{j \in J} \sum_{k \in L^j} x_{ijk} \max\{t_{jk} - t_c, 0\} \tag{2}$$

$$f_2(x) = \sum_{i \in I} z_i(x) \tag{3}$$

Subject to:

$$\sum_{i \in I} x_{ijk} = 1, \forall j \in J, k \in L^j \tag{4}$$

$$\sum_{k \in L^j \bigcup \{|L^j|+1\}} x_{ijk} = 1, \forall i \in I, j \in J \tag{5}$$

$$\sum_{i \in I} \sum_{j \in D_i} \sum_{k \in L^j} x_{ijk} = 0 \tag{6}$$

$$e_{i,7\alpha,m} + \sum_{w \in (L^1 \bigcup \{|L^1|+1\}) \setminus L_{im}^1} \leqslant 1, \forall i \in I, m \in T^{7\alpha} \bigcup \{|T^{7\alpha}| + 1\} \tag{7}$$

$$x_{i,j-1,k} + \sum_{w \in (L^j \bigcup \{|L^j|+1\}) \setminus L_{ik}^j} \leqslant 1, \tag{8}$$

$$\forall i \in I, j = 2, ..., 7\alpha, k \in L^{j-1} \bigcup \{|L^{j-1}| + 1\}$$

$$\sum_{t=h}^{7\alpha} \sum_{m \in T^t} e_{itm} + \sum_{t=1}^{h-7\alpha+g} \sum_{k \in L^t} x_{itk} \le g, \forall i \in I, h \in H \tag{9}$$

$$\sum_{t=0}^{g} \sum_{k \in L^{j+t}} x_{i,j+t,k} \le g, \forall i \in I, j = 1, ..., 7\alpha - g \tag{10}$$

$$\sum_{j=7(l-1)+1}^{7l} x_{i,j,|L^j|+1} \ge n_1, \forall i \in I, l = 1, ..., \alpha \tag{11}$$

$$\sum_{l=1}^{\alpha} x_{i,7l,|L^{7l}|+1} \ge n_2, \forall i \in I \tag{12}$$

$$\sum_{j=7(l-1)+1}^{7l} \sum_{k \in L^j} t_{jk} x_{ijk} \le t_1, \forall i \in I, l = 1, ..., \alpha \tag{13}$$

$$\sum_{j \in J} \sum_{k \in L^j} t_{jk} x_{ijk} \le t_2, \forall i \in I \tag{14}$$

$$x_{ijk} \in \{0, 1\}, \forall i \in I, j \in J, k \in L^j \bigcup \{|L^j| + 1\} \tag{15}$$

$$z_i(x) \in \{0, 1\}, \forall i \in I \tag{16}$$

where $z_i(x) = \begin{cases} 1, \text{if } 0 < \sum_{j \in J} \sum_{k \in L^j} x_{ijk} < q \\ 0, \text{otherwise} \end{cases}$, Formulas (2) and (3) correspond to objective O_1 and O_2 respectively, Formulas (4), (5) and (6) correspond to constraint C_1, C_2 and C_3 respectively, Formulas (7) and (8) correspond to C_4, Formulas (9) and (10) correspond to C_5, Formulas (11) and (12) correspond to C_6 and C_7 respectively, and Formulas (13) and (14) correspond to C_8.

3   A Multi-objective Simulated Annealing Approach for Bus Driver Rostering

In this section, the components of the proposed MOSA, i.e. a heuristic for constructing an initial solution, a SA-based feasibility repairing algorithm, and a SA-based non-dominated solutions generating algorithm, are sequentially described.

3.1   A Heuristic for Constructing an Initial Solution

In this section, we devise a heuristic to create an initial solution with a small number of constraint violations. It first assigns days off to each driver to satisfy two constraints C_3 and C_6, and then assigns duties and days off to satisfy the other two constraints C_1 and C_2. In more detail, the steps are as follows:

Step 1 Assign days off to each driver on the days specified in C_3, and then check whether C_6 has been satisfied for all drivers: if not satisfied, assign days off to the drivers to satisfy C_6.

Step 2 Assign duties randomly to each driver on the days that duties and days off have not been assigned. Note that the duties on some day can only be assigned on that day.

Step 3 If C_1 has not been satisfied, i.e. there are some duties have not been assigned to any drivers on some day, cancel the duties and days off assigned to all drivers, and go to Step 1.

Step 4 If C_2 has not been satisfied, assign the driver a day off on that day.

Step 5 Output the generated solution.

3.2   A SA-Based Feasibility Repairing Algorithm

Due to high complexity of the problem [4,6], solutions generated by the above heuristic are rarely feasible. A SA-based Feasibility Repairing (SAFR) algorithm is devised to eliminate the infeasibility. SA is a stochastic local search algorithm which has been applied successfully to address a large number of combinatorial optimization problems due to its efficiency and effectiveness [17,18].

In SA, the neighbourhood should first be defined. In this paper, inspired by the neighbourhood for nurse rostering [19], we use the neighbourhoods of swapping consecutive duties and days off between any two drivers, where the length of consecutive days ranges from one to the length of the rostering period minus one. Swaps are only allowed vertically, since the duties on a specific day can only be fulfilled on the day. To clarify the neighbourhoods, we use Fig. 1 to show the neighbourhoods between two drivers (say, driver 1 and driver 4), where only 4 days of the rostering period is illustrated. The number denotes the duty number assigned to the driver on the day, D denotes a day off, and the arrow denotes a possible move.

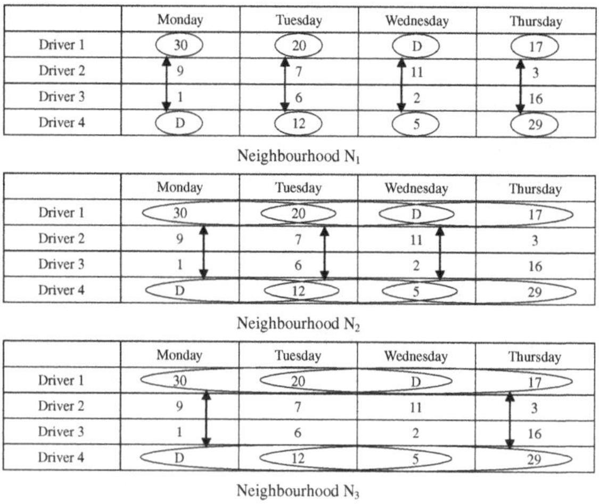

Fig. 1. Illustration of neighbourhoods between two drivers.

Based on the neighbourhoods, neighbouring solutions are generated. Then they would be evaluated, for a solution x, its evaluation function $v(x)$ is defined as the sum of all driver's degree of constraint violations, i.e.

$$v(x) = \sum_{i \in I} v_i(x) \tag{17}$$

where $v_i(x)$ measures the degree of constraint violations of driver i in x.

An incremental evaluation technique is applied to evaluate a solution efficiently. Assume y is a neighbouring solution of x, instead of calculating $v(y)$ completely from scratch, we only evaluate the difference between $v(x)$ and $v(y)$, denoted by $\triangle v(y, x)$, since x and y differ only in two drivers (say, driver j and driver k) for the assignment of several duties and days off. Specifically, $\triangle v(y, x)$ can be obtained as follows,

$$\triangle v(y, x) = v(y) - v(x) = v_j(y) + v_k(y) - v_j(x) - v_k(x) \tag{18}$$

Given initial temperature T_0, maximum number of iterations in outer and inner loops N and M, the pseudo-code of the SAFR is presented in Algorithm 1, where n and m denote the number of iterations in outer and inner loop respectively, and T_n denotes the temperature at the nth iteration.

Algorithm 1. The pseudo-code of the SAFR

1: Let x and $v(x)$ be the initial solution and corresponding evaluation function respectively;
2: $n = 0, T(n) = T_0$;
3: **while** stopping condition not met (e.g. $n < N$) **do**
4:    $m = 0$;
5:    **while** stopping condition not met (e.g. $m < M$) **do**
6:       Generate a neighbouring solution y of x by a random move in a randomly selected neighbourhood N_t between two randomly selected drivers;
7:       Replace x by y with probability $p = min(1, exp(-\triangle v(y, x)/T_n))$;
8:       **if** $v(x) == 0$ **then**
9:          return x;
10:       **else**
11:          $m = m + 1$;
12:       **end if**
13:    **end while**
14:    $n = n + 1; T_n = \alpha T_{n-1}$;
15: **end while**

3.3 A SA-based Non-dominated Solutions Generating Algorithm

After obtaining a feasible solution, to obtain the Pareto front based on it, we devise a SA-based Non-Dominated Solutions Generating (SANDSG) algorithm, since SA has been applied successfully to solve several multi-objective personnel rostering problems, e.g. nurse rostering and aircrew rostering [19,20].

In the SANDSG, the neighbourhoods in the Sect. 3.2 are also employed, and only feasible moves are allowed. The size of the neighbourhoods (i.e. the number of neighbouring solutions) is as large as $O(|I|^2(7\alpha)^2)$. Neighbourhood pruning is a technique that considers the tradeoff between the benefits of using large neighbourhoods and the associated time complexity, by using large neighbourhoods but reducing their size by never examining neighbouring solutions that are unlikely to (or provably cannot) yield any improvements [21]. We apply neighbourhood pruning in the SANDSG to generate the neighbouring solutions: for any two drivers, if only one (or none) of their workloads is smaller than q duties, meanwhile, both (or none of) their total overtimes are the maximum among all the drivers, then the two drivers are not considered for swapping, since the resulting solutions will provably not lead to any improvements. Note that neighbourhood pruning only make a portion of non-improving moves are not considered for implementing, and the remaining still have probability to be accepted, since SA can accept some worsen moves. Hence, the SANDSG has the ability to escape from local minima.

When the neighbouring solutions are generated, incremental evaluation is applied to evaluate the objective O_2. Let x and y be the current solution and its neighbouring solution respectively, and they differ only in two drivers (say, driver j and driver k). We evaluate only the difference between x and y on O_2 (say, $\triangle f_2(y,x)$) rather than calculate $f_2(y)$ completely from scratch,

$$\triangle f_2(y,x) = f_2(y) - f_2(x) = z_j(y) + z_k(y) - z_j(x) - z_k(x) \qquad (19)$$

After obtaining the objective function values of a neighbouring solution, it is judged whether it can be accepted as the current solution, where two evaluation functions can be used: (1) weighted-sum evaluation function encouraging moves towards users' predefined preferences, (2) domination-based evaluation function encouraging moves towards more non-dominated solutions which spread well in the Pareto set, which is inspired by the multi-objective SA for nurse rostering [19] but different from the previous work on the bus driver rostering. Moreover, if the solution is a non-dominated solution, it would be stored in a set (say P) as follows: store the solution in a FIFO queue corresponding to the same objective function values, and the queue size is a given number; when the queue is below its size, the solution is incorporated, otherwise, discard its top element and push the solution to the end; and P is the union of all the queues.

When the SANDSG encounters consecutive non-improving iterations, we devise a biased elite solution restart strategy based on the work of [22] to restart the search. It can be described as follows: select randomly one of the following three sets, i.e. P, the FIFO queue with the lowest value of objective O_1, and the FIFO queue with the lowest value of O_2, then select randomly a solution from the set to restart the search. Note that once a solution is selected, it will be marked as explored and will not be selected again to avoid repeated searches.

Given initial temperature T_0, maximum number of iterations in outer and inner loops N and M, and maximum number of consecutive non-improving iterations K, the pseudo-code of the SANDSG is presented in Algorithm 2, where n and m denote the number of iterations in outer and inner loop respectively, T_n denotes the temperature at the nth iteration, and k denotes the number of consecutive non-improving iterations.

Algorithm 2. The pseudo-code of the SANDSG

1: Let x be the obtained feasible initial solution, and y be a neighbouring solution of x generated by employing neighbourhood pruning;

2: Choose a option as the solution acceptance criteria: 0 or 1 for a weighted-sum or domination-based evaluation function respectively;

3: $n = 0, k = 0, P = \{x\}$;

4: **while** stopping condition not met (e.g. $n < N$) **do**

5:     $m = 0$;

6:     **while** stopping condition not met (e.g. $m < M$) **do**

7:         Generate y and calculate $\triangle v(y,x)$ by incremental evaluation;

8:         **while** $\triangle v(y,x)! = 0$ **do**

9:             Generate y;

10:         **end while**

11:         **if** option==0 **then**

12:             $\triangle f(y,x) = \sum_{i=1}^{2} w_i(f_i(y) - f_i(x))$, where w_i is weight of the ith objective;

13:         **else**

14:             $\triangle f(y,x) = N_y - N_x$, where N_y and N_x denote the number of solutions in P dominating y and x respectively;

15:         **end if**

16:         Replace x by y with probability $p = min(1, exp(-\triangle f(y,x)/T_n))$;

17:         **if** y is not dominated by the solutions in P and does not exist in P **then**

18:             Add y to P; Remove the dominated solutions from P if any;

19:         **end if**

20:         **if** y is not dominated by the solutions in P and its objective function values are different from those of the solutions in P **then**

21:             $k = 0$;

22:         **else**

23:             $k = k + 1$;

24:             **if** $k == K$ **then**

25:                 $k = 0$; Perform biased elite solution restart strategy;

26:             **end if**

27:         **end if**

28:         $m = m + 1$;

29:     **end while**

30:     $n = n + 1$; $T_n = \alpha T_{n-1}$;

31: **end while**

32: return P;

---

4   Computational Results

The main concern about using heuristics is the quality of the obtained solutions. However, one does not know whether the solutions obtained are indeed efficient ones, nor does one know the distance from the approximate Pareto front to the exact front, since the difficulty in reaching optimality for bus driver rostering instances have been shown in [4,6]. In this paper we employ the metrics used in [4,6] to assess the performance of our proposed MOSA.

The MOSA has been tested on ten instances. For each instance, the sets of duties are equally established for weekdays or weekends, thus, the total number of duties for the rostering period is $5\alpha|T_1^w|+2\alpha|T_6^w|$, where T_1^w and T_6^w denote the set of duties for Monday and Saturday respectively. Moreover, we set the values of the following parameters to be the same as in [4]: $q = 20$ duties, $t_c = 8$ h, $g = 6$ days, $\alpha = 4$ weeks, $n_1 = 2$ days, $n_2 = 1$ day, $t_1=48$ h, and $t_2=176$ h. Meanwhile, $D_i = \emptyset, i \in I$, as in [5]. For the weighted-sum evaluation function, we use the weight values in [5], i.e. $w_1 = 0.04, w_2 = 0.96$.

The MOSA is coded in C++ and implemented on a 2.60 GHz PC with 992M RAM under Windows XP. We set the initial temperature to be 100, the cooling rate to be 0.99, the maximum number of iterations in outer and inner loops of the SANDSG to be 3000 and 300 respectively, and the size of the FIFO queue and maximum number of consecutive non-improving iterations to be both 100. Note that all the parameters used in our experiments are the same for all instances, although it is possible that better solutions would be found by using a set of instance-dependent parameters. Experiments are firstly carried out on the MOSA, and then on the effects of three embedded strategies, where each instance is independently run ten times.

4.1   Results of the MOSA Approach

Table 1 lists the average results of ten runs performed for each instance under weighted-sum evaluation function and dominance-based evaluation function. Column 1 identifies the instance, and column 2 reports the total number of duties for the rostering period. Columns 3–5 and 6–8 give the results for MOSA under the two evaluation functions respectively, according to three criteria, i.e. (1) the number of candidate efficient solutions (i.e. number of archived non-dominated solutions); (2) the approximate Pareto front size (i.e. number of non-dominated points in the objective space); (3) the elapsed time. The last column presents the relative difference between the values of f_2 obtained by MOSA under weighted-sum and domination-based evaluation functions (say, f_2^w and f_2^d), denoted by $\triangle f_2 = \frac{f_2^w - f_2^d}{f_2^d} \times 100\%$. Moreover, the last row Avg. indicates the algorithm's average performance.

Table 1 shows that, on average, the MOSA under dominance-based evaluation function produced front of a larger size, 8.5 against 2.1 of the MOSA under weighted-sum evaluation function. Meanwhile, the set of the candidates for non-dominated solutions was, on average, larger for MOSA under dominance-based

Table 1. Average results of 10 runs for the MOSA

Data	Number of duties	Weighted-sum evaluation function			Domination-based evaluation function			$\triangle f_2$ (%)
		Candidate efficient solutions	Approximate Pareto front size	Elapsed time (sec.)	Candidate efficient solutions	Approximate Pareto front size	Elapsed time (sec.)	
P1	624	210.0	2.1	77.1	650.0	8.7	95.1	3.13
P2	896	207.2	2.1	122.9	521.4	6.1	148.0	0.31
P3	1260	336.7	3.5	197.3	1399.3	18.3	264.7	−4.90
P4	1652	100.0	1.0	183.4	168.0	1.7	211.6	6.16
P5	1736	256.4	2.6	234.3	959.4	11.0	312.8	−3.64
P6	1792	120.0	1.2	171.3	186.4	2.0	225.1	2.46
P7	1904	146.4	1.5	179.0	279.6	3.4	245.8	−3.32
P8	1960	108.2	1.1	205.0	193.7	2.0	250.6	1.52
P9	2408	262.4	2.7	328.8	1491.9	17.6	431.8	−10.99
P10	2408	252.0	2.8	344.4	1149.1	13.9	488.4	−6.51
Avg.	1664	199.9	2.1	204.4	699.9	8.5	267.4	−1.58

evaluation function, i.e. 699.9 against 199.9 for MOSA under weighted-sum evaluation function. This also reveals that the MOSA can provide users with up to hundreds choices in decision making.

Furthermore, the non-dominated solutions obtained by MOSA under weighted-sum evaluation function is 1.58 % less in terms of the value of f_2 than that under dominance-based evaluation function on average, which reveals that weighted-sum evaluation function can make MOSA produce a Pareto front more towards users' predefined preferences. Moreover, the results are obtained at low computing times, i.e. 204.4 and 267.4 s, under the two evaluation functions on average.

4.2 Discussion and Analysis

We now turn our attention to discussing and analyzing the incremental evaluation, neighbourhood pruning and biased elite solution restart strategy.

The Significance of Incremental Evaluation. In the Sects. 3.2 and 3.3, we employ incremental evaluation to assess the feasibility and objective O_2 of neighbouring solutions. To demonstrate its significance, we conduct an additional experiment to compare the MOSA with its variant, i.e. the MOSA without incremental evaluation, denoted by MOSA-I, on instance P10. We keep other ingredients in the two algorithms same, and they are both independently run for ten times. The connection between the average elapsed time and the number of outer loop iterations, under the weighted-sum and dominance-based evaluation function, are shown in Fig. 2(a) and (b) respectively.

It can be seen from Fig. 2(a) and (b) that the MOSA is much faster than MOSA-I (about 12.4 and 9.9 times faster on average). Similar results can be

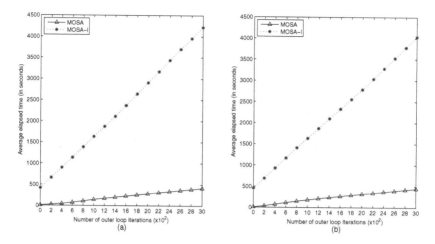

Fig. 2. Performance comparison of MOSA and MOSA-I for P10 under weighted-sum and domination-based evaluation functions respectively.

observed on other instances, although the actual values may differ among various instances. This experiment confirms the importance of incremental evaluation.

The Impact of Neighbourhood Pruning. In the Sect. 3.3, we utilize neighbourhood pruning to enhance the performance of the MOSA. To make sure that it does make a meaningful contribution, we carry out another experiment to compare the MOSA with its variant, i.e. MOSA without neighbourhood pruning, denoted by MOSA-II. The comparative results are displayed in Table 2.

In Table 2, columns 2, 3 (6, 7) display the percentage of points in the final Pareto front obtained by one algorithm that are not dominated by or are equal to that obtained by another, under weighted-sum evaluation function (domination-based evaluation function), where the final Pareto front is obtained by merging the approximations obtained by ten runs of a algorithm and eliminating the dominated points. The four columns reveal that the MOSA performs better than the MOSA-II. Specifically, for the weighted-sum evaluation function, on average 81 % of the MOSA's points are non-dominated by those of the MOSA-II, while 57 % of MOSA-II's points are not dominated by the MOSA's. As for domination-based evaluation function, the behaviour is similar. Columns 4, 5, 8 and 9 display another metric: the contribution of each algorithm to the best approximation of the Pareto front, which was obtained by merging the final Pareto fronts from the two algorithms and eliminating the dominated points. Note that in some instances, the summation of the values in Columns 4 and 5 (8 and 9) may be larger than 1, since some points in the best approximation were attained by both algorithms. The four columns show that, on average the MOSA contributes with a larger percentage of points to the best approximation, i.e. 68 % against 35 % under weighted-sum evaluation function while 64 % against 36 % under domination-based evaluation function. This demonstrates that the MOSA

Table 2. Comparative results of MOSA and MOSA-II

Data	Weighted-sum evaluation function				Domination-based evaluation function			
	Potential non-dominated points		Contribution to the best front		Potential non-dominated points		Contribution to the best front	
	MOSA	MOSA-II	MOSA	MOSA-II	MOSA	MOSA-II	MOSA	MOSA-II
P1	0.83	1.00	0.50	0.60	0.09	0.89	0.11	0.89
P2	0.71	1.00	0.56	0.67	0.33	0.70	0.30	0.70
P3	0.50	0.89	0.43	0.57	0.15	0.94	0.21	0.79
P4	1.00	0.00	1.00	0.00	1.00	0.00	1.00	0.00
P5	0.56	1.00	0.31	0.69	0.87	0.45	0.57	0.43
P6	1.00	0.00	1.00	0.00	1.00	0.00	1.00	0.00
P7	1.00	0.00	1.00	0.00	1.00	0.00	1.00	0.00
P8	1.00	0.00	1.00	0.00	1.00	0.00	1.00	0.00
P9	0.75	0.92	0.45	0.55	0.88	0.32	0.73	0.27
P10	0.73	0.89	0.58	0.42	0.57	0.60	0.46	0.54
Avg.	0.81	0.57	0.68	0.35	0.69	0.39	0.64	0.36

clearly outperforms the MOSA-II. Moreover, one can easily observe that the MOSA performs better than the MOSA-II for 5 instances (i.e. instances P4, P6, P7, P8 and P10) and 6 instances (i.e. P4, P5, P6, P7, P8 and P9) under weighted-sum and domination-based evaluation function, respectively. Furthermore, for 4 larger instances, i.e. P4, P6, P7 and P8, the MOSA totally filled the best front, revealing that the MOSA was able to explore the regions of objective space unexplored by the MOSA-II. Therefore, this experiment shows the advantage of neighbourhood pruning in enhancing the search power of the MOSA.

The Importance of Biased Elite Solution Restart Strategy. We study now the biased elite solution restart strategy. In order to evaluate its significance, we also perform another experiment to compare MOSA with its two variants without using it, i.e. (1) MOSA with restart strategy commonly used in classical multi-objective SA [23] (denoted by MOSA-III), i.e. the solution for restart is randomly selected from the archived non-dominated solutions; (2) MOSA without restart (denoted by MOSA-IV). The comparative results between MOSA and MOSA-III, MOSA and MOSA-IV are displayed in Tables 3 and 4 respectively.

Tables 3 and 4 show that under weighted-sum and domination-based evaluation functions, MOSA can totally fill the best front obtained by MOSA and the MOSA-III for both 3 instances, meanwhile, it can totally fill that obtained by MOSA and MOSA-IV for 6 and 3 instances. Moreover, as the contribution to the best front, MOSA contributes with a larger percentage than MOSA-III

Table 3. Comparative results of MOSA and MOSA-III

| Data | Weighted-sum evaluation function | | | | Domination-based evaluation function | | | |
| | Potential non-dominated points | | Contribution to the best front | | Potential non-dominated points | | Contribution to the best front | |
	MOSA	MOSA-III	MOSA	MOSA-III	MOSA	MOSA-III	MOSA	MOSA-III
P1	0.50	0.71	0.43	0.71	0.73	0.31	0.67	0.33
P2	0.71	0.83	0.56	0.56	0.78	0.30	0.70	0.30
P3	0.67	0.83	0.44	0.56	0.44	0.73	0.43	0.57
P4	1.00	0.00	1.00	0.00	1.00	0.67	0.67	0.67
P5	1.00	0.57	0.53	0.47	0.67	0.68	0.40	0.60
P6	1.00	0.00	1.00	0.00	1.00	0.00	1.00	0.00
P7	1.00	0.00	1.00	0.00	1.00	0.00	1.00	0.00
P8	1.00	1.00	0.50	1.00	1.00	0.00	1.00	0.00
P9	0.83	0.67	0.60	0.30	0.67	0.70	0.58	0.42
P10	0.73	0.62	0.58	0.42	0.70	0.67	0.50	0.50
Avg.	0.84	0.52	0.67	0.41	0.80	0.41	0.70	0.34

Table 4. Comparative results of MOSA and MOSA-IV

| Data | Weighted-sum evaluation function | | | | Domination-based evaluation function | | | |
| | Potential non-dominated points | | Contribution to the best front | | Potential non-dominated points | | Contribution to the best front | |
	MOSA	MOSA-IV	MOSA	MOSA-IV	MOSA	MOSA-IV	MOSA	MOSA-IV
P1	1.00	0.00	1.00	0.00	1.00	0.08	0.92	0.08
P2	1.00	0.00	1.00	0.00	1.00	0.50	0.64	0.36
P3	0.92	0.44	0.73	0.27	1.00	0.22	0.82	0.18
P4	1.00	0.00	1.00	0.00	1.00	0.13	0.50	0.50
P5	1.00	0.43	0.75	0.25	1.00	0.25	0.71	0.29
P6	1.00	0.00	1.00	0.00	1.00	0.00	1.00	0.00
P7	1.00	0.00	1.00	0.00	1.00	0.00	1.00	0.00
P8	1.00	0.00	1.00	0.00	1.00	0.00	1.00	0.00
P9	1.00	0.29	0.86	0.14	1.00	0.15	0.89	0.11
P10	1.00	0.13	0.94	0.06	1.00	0.21	0.79	0.21
Avg.	0.99	0.13	0.93	0.07	1.00	0.15	0.83	0.17

(on average 67 % against 41 % under weighted-sum evaluation function, while 70 % against 34 % under domination-based evaluation function, where some points were attained by both of the algorithms). Meanwhile, MOSA significantly performs better than MOSA-IV for 10 and 9 instances under the two evaluation functions respectively. Therefore, MOSA is more stable in reaching the best front. Furthermore, when it comes to the potential non-dominated points, MOSA is no worse than MOSA-III for 7 instances while performs better than MOSA-IV for 10 instances under both evaluation functions. This experiment clearly demonstrates the significance of the proposed strategy.

5   Conclusions

This paper proposes a MOSA approach for noncyclic bus driver rostering. Unlike previous work on bus driver rostering, the MOSA provides both weighted-sum and domination-based evaluation functions to address user preferences, meanwhile, three strategies are embedded to make the MOSA more efficient and more effective. Experiments have demonstrated the approach can produce many non-dominated solutions at low computing times. Moreover, the computational results have confirmed that the effectiveness of the strategies. The MOSA is currently presented in terms of bus driver rostering. As the future work, we will demonstrate whether it can be applied to other problems.

Acknowledgments. The work was supported by the National Natural Science Foundation of China (Grant No. 70971044 and 71171087) and the Major Program of National Social Science Foundation of China (Grant No. 13&ZD175).

References

1. Shen, Y., Xia, J.: Integrated bus transit scheduling for the Beijing bus group based on a unified mode of operation. Int. Trans. Oper. Res. **16**(2), 227–242 (2009)
2. Shen, Y., Xu, J., Zeng, Z.: Public transit planning and scheduling based on AVL data in China. Int. Trans. Oper. Res., 1–23 (2015). doi:10.1111/itor.12164
3. Shen, Y., Peng, K., Chen, K., Li, J.: Evolutionary crew scheduling with adaptive chromosomes. Transp. Res. Part B **56**, 174–185 (2013)
4. Moz, M., Respício, A., Pato, M.V.: Bi-objective evolutionary heuristics for bus driver rostering. Public Transp. **1**(3), 189–210 (2009)
5. Mesquita, M., Moz, M., Paias, A., Paixão, J., Pato, M., Respício, A.: A new model for the integrated vehicle-crew-rostering problem and a computational study on rosters. J. Sched. **14**(4), 319–334 (2011)
6. Respício, A., Moz, M., Margarida, V.P.: Enhanced genetic algorithms for a bi-objective bus driver rostering problem: a computational study. Int. Trans. Oper. Res. **20**(4), 443–470 (2013)
7. Xie, L., Suhl, L.: Cyclic and non-cyclic crew rostering problems in public bus transit. OR Spectrum **37**(1), 99–136 (2015)
8. Odoni, A., Rousseau, J., Wilson, N.: Models in urban and air transportation. In: Pollock, S., Rothkopf, M., Barnett, A. (eds.) Handbooks in Operations Research and Management Science, pp. 107–150. North-Holland, Amsterdam (1994)

9. Emden-Weinert, T., Kotas, H., Speer, U.: DISSY - a driver rostering system for public transport. DISSY project of programme ESPRIT, pp. 1–30 (2001)
10. Pedrosa, D., Constantino, M.: Days-off scheduling in public transport companies. In: Voss, S., Daduna, J. (eds.) Computer-Aided Scheduling of Public Transport. Lecture Notes in Economics and Mathematical Systems, vol. 505, pp. 215–232. Springer, Heidelberg (2001)
11. Xie, L., Kliewer, N., Suhl, L.: Integrated driver rostering problem in public bus transit. Procedia-Soc. Behav. Sci. **54**, 656–665 (2012)
12. Respício, A., Moz, M., Margarida, P.V.: A memetic algorithm for a bi-objective bus driver rostering problem. Centro de Investigação Operacional, Universidade de Lisboa, Working paper 13, pp. 1–25 (2007)
13. Nurmi, K., Kyngäs, J., Post, G.: Driver rostering for bus transit companies. Eng. Lett. **19**(2), 125–132 (2011)
14. Xie, L.: Metaheuristics approach for solving multi-objective crew rostering problem in public transit. Decision Support & Operations Research Lab, University of Paderborn, Working paper, WP1306, pp. 1–23 (2013)
15. Mesquita, M., Moz, M., Paias, A., Pato, M.: A decomposition approach for the integrated vehicle-crew-roster problem with days-off pattern. Eur. J. Oper. Res. **229**(2), 318–331 (2013)
16. Catanas, F., Paixão, J.M.P.: A new approach for the crew rostering problem. In: Daduna, J.R., Branco, I., Paixão, J.M.P. (eds.) Computer-Aided Transit Scheduling. Lecture Notes in Economics and Mathematical Systems, vol. 430, pp. 267–277. Springer, Heidelberg (1995)
17. Torres-Jimenez, J., Izquierdo-Marquez, I., Garcia-Robledo, A., Gonzalez-Gomez, A., Bernal, J., Kacker, R.N.: A dual representation simulated annealing algorithm for the bandwidth minimization problem on graphs. Inf. Sci. **303**, 33–49 (2015)
18. Yu, V.F., Lin, S.: A simulated annealing heuristic for the open location-routing problem. Comput. Oper. Res. **62**, 184–196 (2015)
19. Burke, E.K., Li, J., Qu, R.: A Pareto-based search methodology for multi-objective nurse scheduling. Ann. Oper. Res. **196**(1), 91–109 (2012)
20. Lučić, P., Teodorović, D.: Metaheuristics approach to the aircrew rostering problem. Ann. Oper. Res. **155**(1), 311–338 (2007)
21. Hoos, H.H., Stützle, T.: Stochastic Local Search: Foundations and Applications. Morgan Kaufmann, San Francisco (2004)
22. Liang, Y., Lo, M.: Multi-objective redundancy allocation optimization using a variable neighborhood search algorithm. J. Heuristics **16**(3), 511–535 (2010)
23. Suman, B., Hoda, N., Jha, S.: Orthogonal simulated annealing for multiobjective optimization. Comput. Chem. Eng. **34**(10), 1618–1631 (2010)

Generating Diophantine Sets by Virus Machines

Álvaro Romero-Jiménez, Luis Valencia-Cabrera,
and Mario J. Pérez-Jiménez(✉)

Research Group on Natural Computing Department of Computer Science
and Artificial Intelligence, University of Seville,
Avda. Reina Mercedes s/n, 41012 Seville, Spain
{romero.alvaro,lvalencia,marper}@us.es

Abstract. Virus Machines are a computational paradigm inspired by the manner in which viruses replicate and transmit from one host cell to another. This paradigm provides non-deterministic sequential devices. Non-restricted virus machines are unbounded virus machines, in the sense that no restriction on the number of hosts, the number of instructions and the number of viruses contained in any host along any computation is placed on them. The computational completeness of these machines has been obtained by simulating register machines. In this paper, virus machines as set generating devices are considered. Then, the universality of non-restricted virus machines is proved by showing that they can compute all diophantine sets, which the MRDP theorem proves that coincide with the recursively enumerable sets.

Keywords: Virus machines · Computational completeness · Diophantine sets · MRDP theorem

1 Introduction

A new computational paradigm inspired by the replications and transmissions of viruses was introduced in [1]. The computational devices in this paradigm are called *Virus Machines* and they consist of several processing units, called *hosts*, connected to each other by *transmission channels*. A host can be viewed as a group of cells (being part of a colony, organism, system, organ or tissue). Each cell in the group will contain at most one virus, but we will not take into account the number of cells in the group, we will only focus on the number of viruses that are present in some of the cells of that group (not every cell in the group does necessarily hold a virus). Only one type of viruses is considered. Channels allow viruses to be transmitted from one host to another or to the environment of the system. Each channel has a natural number (the *weight* of the channel) associated with it, indicating the number of copies of the virus that will be generated and transmitted from an original one (i.e., one virus may replicate, generating a number of copies to be transmitted to the target host group of cells). Each transmission channel is closed by default and it can be opened by

© Springer-Verlag Berlin Heidelberg 2015
M. Gong et al. (Eds.): BIC-TA 2015, CCIS 562, pp. 331–341, 2015.
DOI: 10.1007/978-3-662-49014-3_30

a control instruction unit. Specifically, there is an *instruction-channel control network* that allows opening a channel by means of an activated instruction. In that moment, the opened channel allows a virus (only one virus) to replicate and transmit through it. Instructions are activated individually according to a protocol given by an *instruction transfer network*, so that only one instruction is enabled in each computation step. That is, an instruction activation signal is transferred to the network to activate instructions in sequence.

In this work, new virus machines as set generating devices are introduced. The universality of non-restricted virus machines working in this mode is proved by showing that they can generate all diophantine sets. The celebrated MRDP theorem assures that these sets are exactly the same as the recursively enumerable sets [4].

This paper is structured as follows. First, the computing model of virus machines is formally defined. Then, in Sect. 3 the computational completeness of non-restricted virus machines is stated. Finally, in Sect. 4 the main conclusions of this work are summarized and some suggestions for possible lines of future research are outlined.

2   Virus Machines

In what follows we formally define the syntax of the Virus Machines (see [1] for more details).

An *undirected graph* G is a pair (V, E), where V is a finite set and E is a subset of $\{\{x, y\} \mid x \in V, y \in V, x \neq y\}$. The set V is called the *vertex set* of G, and its elements are called *vertices*. The set E is called the *edge set* of G, and its elements are called *edges*. If $e = \{x, y\} \in E$ is an edge of G, then we say that edge e is incident on vertices x and y. In an undirected graph, the *degree* of a vertex x is the number of edges incident on it. A *bipartite graph* G is an undirected graph (V, E) in which V can be partitioned into two sets V_1, V_2 such that $\{u, v\} \in E$ implies either $u \in V_1$ and $v \in V_2$ or $u \in V_2$ and $v \in V_1$; that is, all edges are arranged between the two sets V_1 and V_2 (see [2] for details).

A *directed graph* G is a pair (V, E), where V is a finite set and E is a subset of $V \times V$. The set V is called the vertex set of G, and its elements are called vertices. The set E is called the *arc set* of G, and its elements are called *arcs*. In a directed graph, the *out-degree* of a vertex is the number of arcs leaving it, and the *in-degree* of a vertex is the number of arcs entering it.

Definition 1. *A Virus Machine Π of degree (p, q), with $p \geq 1, q \geq 1$, is a tuple $(\Gamma, H, I, D_H, D_I, G_C, n_1, \ldots, n_p, i_1, h_{\text{out}})$, where:*

- *$\Gamma = \{v\}$ is the singleton alphabet;*
- *$H = \{h_1, \ldots, h_p\}$ and $I = \{i_1, \ldots, i_q\}$ are ordered sets such that $v \notin H \cup I$ and $H \cap I = \emptyset$;*
- *$D_H = (H \cup \{h_{\text{out}}\}, E_H, w_H)$ is a weighted directed graph, verifying that $E_H \subseteq H \times (H \cup \{h_{\text{out}}\})$, $(h, h) \notin E_H$ for each $h \in H$, out-degree(h_{out}) = 0, and w_H is a mapping from E_H to $\mathbb{Z}_{>0}$;*

- $D_I = (I, E_I, w_I)$ *is a weighted directed graph, where* $E_I \subseteq I \times I$, w_I *is a mapping from* E_I *to* $\mathbb{Z}_{>0}$ *and, for each vertex* $i_j \in I$, *the out-degree of* i_j *is less than or equal to 2;*
- $G_C = (V_C, E_C)$ *is an undirected bipartite graph, where* $V_C = I \cup E_H$, *being* $\{I, E_H\}$ *the partition associated with it (i.e., all edges go between the two sets* I *and* E_H*). In addition, for each vertex* $i_j \in I$, *the degree of* i_j *in* G_C *is less than or equal to 1;*
- $n_j \in \mathbb{N}$ *($1 \le j \le p$) and* $i_1 \in I$;
- $h_{\text{out}} \notin I \cup \{v\}$ *and* h_{out} *is denoted by* h_0 *in the case that* $h_{\text{out}} \notin H$.

A Virus Machine $\Pi = (\Gamma, H, I, D_H, D_I, G_C, n_1, \ldots, n_p, i_1, h_{\text{out}})$ of degree (p, q) can be viewed as an ordered set of p *hosts* labelled with $h_1, \ldots, h_p$ (where each host h_j, $1 \le j \le p$, initially contains exactly n_j *viruses* –copies of the symbol v–), and an ordered set of q *control instruction units* labelled with $i_1, \ldots, i_q$. The symbol h_{out} represents the *output region* of the system (we use the term *region* to refer to host h_{out} in the case that $h_{\text{out}} \in H$ and to refer to the environment in the case that $h_{\text{out}} = h_0$). Arcs $(h_s, h_{s'})$ from D_H represent *transmission channels* through which viruses can travel from host h_s to $h_{s'}$.

Each channel is *closed* by default, and so it remains until it is opened by a control instruction (which is attached to the channel by means of an edge in graph G_C) when that instruction is *activated*. Furthermore, each channel $(h_s, h_{s'})$ is assigned with a positive integer weight, denoted by $w_{s,s'}$, which indicates the number of viruses that will be transmitted/replicated to the receiving host of the channel.

Arcs $(i_j, i_{j'})$ from D_I represent *instruction transfer paths*, and they have a weight, denoted by $w_{j,j'}$, associated with it. Finally, the undirected bipartite graph G_C represents the *instruction-channel network* by which an edge $\{i_j, (h_s, h_{s'})\}$ indicates a control relationship between instruction i_j and channel $(h_s, h_{s'})$: when instruction i_j is activated, the channel $(h_s, h_{s'})$ is opened.

A *configuration* $\mathcal{C}_t$ of a virus machine at an instant t is described by a tuple $(a_{1,t}, \ldots, a_{p,t}, u_t, e_t)$, where $a_{1,t}, \ldots, a_{p,t}$ and e_t are non-negative integers and $u_t \in I \cup \{\#\}$, with $\# \notin H \cup \{h_0\} \cup I$. The meaning is the following: at instant t the host h_s of the system contains exactly $a_{s,t}$ viruses, the output region h_{out} contains exactly e_t viruses and, if $u_t \in I$, then the control instruction unit u_t will be activated at step $t+1$. Otherwise, if $u_t = \#$, then no further instruction will be activated. The *initial configuration* of the system is $\mathcal{C}_0 = (n_1, \ldots, n_p, i_1, 0)$.

A configuration $\mathcal{C}_t = (a_{1,t}, \ldots, a_{p,t}, u_t, e_t)$ is a *halting configuration* if and only if u_t is the object $\#$. A non-halting configuration $\mathcal{C}_t = (a_{1,t}, \ldots, a_{p,t}, u_t, e_t)$ yields configuration $\mathcal{C}_{t+1} = (a_{1,t+1}, \ldots, a_{p,t+1}, u_{t+1}, e_{t+1})$ in one *transition step*, denoted by $\mathcal{C}_t \Rightarrow_\Pi \mathcal{C}_{t+1}$, if we can pass from $\mathcal{C}_t$ to $\mathcal{C}_{t+1}$ as follows:

1. First, given that $\mathcal{C}_t$ is a non-halting configuration, we have $u_t \in I$. So the control instruction unit u_t is activated.
2. Let us assume that instruction u_t is attached to channel $(h_s, h_{s'})$. Then this channel will be opened and:

- If $a_{s,t} \geq 1$, then a virus (only one virus) is consumed from host h_s and $w_{s,s'}$ copies of v are produced in host $h_{s'}$ (if $s' \neq out$) or in the output region h_{out}.
- If $a_{s,t} = 0$, then there is no transmission of virus.

3. Let us assume that instruction u_t is not attached to any channel $(h_s, h_{s'})$. Then there is no transmission of virus.

4. Object $u_{t+1} \in I \cup \{\#\}$ is obtained as follows:
   - Let us suppose that out-degree$(u_t) = 2$, that is, there are two different instructions $u_{t'}$ and $u_{t''}$ such that $(u_t, u_{t'}) \in E_I$ and $(u_t, u_{t''}) \in E_I$.
     - If instruction u_t is attached to a channel $(h_s, h_{s'})$ and $a_{s,t} \geq 1$ then u_{t+1} is the instruction corresponding to the *highest* weight path.
     - If instruction u_t is attached to a channel $(h_s, h_{s'})$ and $a_{s,t} = 0$ then u_{t+1} is the instruction corresponding to the *lowest* weight path.
     - If both weights are equal or if instruction u_t is not attached to a channel, then the next instruction u_{t+1} is either $u_{t'}$ or $u_{t''}$, selected in a non-deterministic way.
   - If out-degree$(u_t) = 1$ then the system behaves deterministically and u_{t+1} is the instruction that verifies $(u_t, u_{t+1}) \in E_I$.
   - If out-degree$(u_t) = 0$ then u_{t+1} is object $\#$ and configuration C_{t+1} is a halting configuration.

A *computation* of a virus machine Π is a (finite or infinite) sequence of configurations such that: (a) the first element is the initial configuration C_0 of the system; (b) for each $n \geq 1$, the n-th element of the sequence is obtained from the previous element in one transition step; and (c) if the sequence is finite (called *halting computation*) then the last element is a halting configuration. All the computations start from the initial configuration and proceed as stated above; only halting computations give a result, which is encoded in the contents of the output region for the halting configuration.

In this paper we consider virus machines working in the *generating mode*. That is, we think of the result of a computation of a virus machine Π as the total number n of viruses sent to the output region during the computation. We say that $A \subseteq \mathbb{N}$ is the set *generated* by Π if it is verified that $n \in A$ if and only if there exists a halting computation of Π that outputs n.

3 The Universality of Non-Restricted Virus Machines

A *non-restricted Virus Machine* is a virus machine for which there is no restriction on the number of hosts, the number of instructions and the number of viruses contained in any host along any computation.

For each $p, q, n \geq 1$, we denote by $NVM(p, q, n)$ the family of all subsets of $\mathbb{N}$ generated by virus machines with at most p hosts, q instructions, and all hosts having at most n viruses at any instant of each computation. If one of the parameters p, q, n is not bounded, then it is replaced with $*$. In particular, $NVM(*, *, *)$ denotes the family of all subsets of natural numbers generated by non-restricted virus machines.

3.1   Generating Diophantine Sets by Virus Machines

In this section, the computational completeness of non-restricted virus machines working in the generating mode is established. Specifically, we prove that they can generate all diophantine sets of natural numbers. Indeed, we will design non-restricted virus machines that, given a polynomial $P(x, y_1, \ldots, y_k)$ with integer coefficients:

1. Generate, in a non-deterministic manner, any tuple $(x, y_1, \ldots, y_k)$ of natural numbers.
2. Compute the value of P over the tuple $(x, y_1, \ldots, y_k)$.
3. If the computed value is zero, then halt and output x.
4. If the computed value is non-zero, then do not halt.

3.2   Modules

In order to ease the design of the virus machines generating any diophantine set, the construction of such virus machines will be made in a modular manner. A *module* can be seen as a virus machine without output host, with the initial instruction marked as the *in* instruction and with at least one instruction marked as an *out* instruction. The *out* instructions must have out-degree less than two, so that they can still be connected to another instruction. In this way, a module m_1 can be plugged in before another module m_2 or virus machine instruction i by simply connecting the *out* instructions of m_1 with the *in* instruction of m_2 or with the instruction i.

The layout of a module must be carefully done to avoid conflicts with other modules and to allow the module to be executed any number of times. To achieve the first condition, we will consider that all the hosts (with the only exception of the parameters of the module) and instructions of a module are individualized for that module, being distinct from the ones of any other module or virus machine. There are several ways to meet the second condition: for example, we can ensure that, after the execution of the module, all its hosts except its parameters contain the same number of viruses as before the execution.

In this paper we consider two types of modules: action modules and predicate modules. For the action modules we require all of its *out* instructions to be connected to the *in* instruction of the following module, or to the following instruction of the virus machine. For the predicate modules we consider its *out* instructions to be divided in two subsets: the *out* instructions representing a *yes* answer and the *out* instructions representing a *no* answer of the predicate. For each of these subsets, all of its instructions have to be connected to the same module *in* instruction or virus machine instruction.

The library of modules used in this paper consists of the following modules (we name the action modules as verbs and the predicate modules as questions):

- EMPTY(h): action module that sets to zero the number of viruses in host h. To implement this module we only need to introduce an internal host h', initially with zero viruses, and associate with the channel from h to h' an action that transfers all the viruses from h. Note that host h' may end with a nonzero number of viruses, but this does not prevent the module to be reused, because h' plays a passive role.

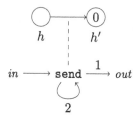

- ADD(h_1, h_2): action module that adds to host h_2 the number of viruses in host h_1, without modifying the number of viruses in h_1.
  This module is implemented as follows:

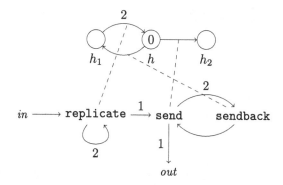

This way, the module starts by transferring one by one all the viruses from h_1 to h, duplicating them along the way. Then it sends, again and again, one virus from h to h_2 and another one from h to h_1, until there are no more viruses left. It is clear then that when the module ends, the host h_1 retains its initial number of viruses, the host h is empty (thus allowing the module to be reused), and the host h_2 has a number of viruses equal to the sum of the initial number of viruses in h_1 and h_2.
- COPY(h_1, h_2): action module that sets the number of viruses in h_2 the same as in h_1, without modifying the number of viruses in h_1.
  This module is implemented by the following concatenation of modules:

$$in \rightarrow \text{EMPTY}(h_2) \rightarrow \text{ADD}(h_1, h_2) \rightarrow out$$

That is, we first get rid of all the viruses from h_2, and then add the viruses from h_1, so h_2 ends with the same number of viruses as h_1. Also observe that the module ADD(h_1, h_2) does not modify the number of viruses in h_1, what will be important later.
- SET(h, n): action module that sets to n the number of viruses in host h.
  This module is implemented simply by introducing an internal host h' with initial number of viruses n and using the module COPY(h', h).

– AREEQUAL?(h_1, h_2): predicate module that checks if the number of viruses in hosts h_1 and h_2 coincides.
This module is implemented as follows, where h_1', h_2' and h are new internal hosts:

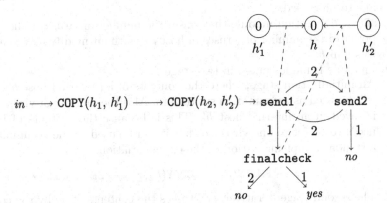

We first copy the contents of h_1 and h_2 into the internal hosts h_1' and h_2', so that they do not get modified. Then, in turns, we send one virus from h_1' to h and then another one from h_2' to h. If the latter can not be done, this is because the contents of h_1 were greater than the contents of h_2 and the answer is no. If the former can not be done, we must try once more to send a virus from h_2' to h to determine if the contents were or not equal.
Notice that the contents of h_1', h_2' and h get modified, but this does not prevent the module to be reused, because the first two get initialized by the first two COPY modules and the latter plays a passive role.

– MULTIPLY(h_1, h_2): action module that multiplies the number of viruses in host h_2 by the number of viruses in host h_1, without modifying the number of viruses in h_1.

This module is implemented in two stages:

1. An initialization stage, where the contents of an internal host h_1', which will be used as a counter, is set to zero. Also the number of viruses in h_2 is saved in an internal host h_2'. This is because host h_2 needs to be emptied, so that it can be used as the accumulator in a standard implementation of the multiplication.

$$in \to \text{EMPTY}(h_1') \to \text{COPY}(h_2, h_2') \to \text{EMPTY}(h_2) \to$$

2. The second stage iteratively adds the contents of h_2' to h_2, until the counter h_1' reaches the number of viruses in h_1. The counter is incremented in each step by adding to it the contents of an internal host h_{one} that has only one virus within.

$$\to \text{AREEQUAL}?(h_1, h_1') \overset{no}{\to} \text{ADD}(h_2', h_2) \to \text{ADD}(h_{one}, h_1') \to \text{back to stage 2}$$

$\downarrow yes$

out

It is clear that when the module ends, the host h_1 retains its initial number of viruses and the host h_2 has a number of viruses equal to the product of the initial number of viruses in h_1 and h_2. The internal host h_{one} is never modified and both internal hosts h_1' and h_2' are initialized in stage 1, what allows the module to be reused.

- RAISE(h_1, h_2): action module that raises the number of viruses in host h_2 to the power of the number of viruses in host h_1, without modifying the number of viruses in h_1.

This module is implemented in two stages:

1. An initialization stage, where the contents of an internal host h_1', which will be used as a counter, is set to zero. Also the number of viruses in h_2 is saved in an internal host h_2'. This is because the contents of host h_2 needs to be set to one virus, so that it can be used as the accumulator in a standard implementation of the exponentiation.

$$in \rightarrow \texttt{EMPTY}(h_1') \rightarrow \texttt{COPY}(h_2, h_2') \rightarrow \texttt{SET}(h_2, 1) \rightarrow$$

2. The second stage iteratively multiplies the contents of h_2 by the contents of h_2', until the counter h_1' reaches the number of viruses in h_1. The counter is incremented in each step by adding to it the contents of an internal host h_{one} that has only one virus within.

$$\rightarrow \texttt{AREEQUAL?}(h_1, h_1') \overset{no}{\rightarrow} \texttt{MULTIPLY}(h_2', h_2) \rightarrow \texttt{ADD}(h_{one}, h_1') \rightarrow \quad \begin{array}{l} \text{back to} \\ \text{stage 2} \end{array}$$

$\downarrow yes$

out

It is clear that when the module ends, the host h_1 retains its initial number of viruses and the host h_2 has a number of viruses equal to the initial number of viruses in h_2 raised to the initial number of viruses in h_1. The internal host h_{one} is never modified and both internal hosts h_1' and h_2' are initialized in stage 1, what allows the module to be reused.

- EXPT(h, n): action module that raises the number of viruses in h to the power of n.

This module is implemented simply by introducing an internal host h' with initial number of viruses n and using the module RAISE(h', h).

3.3 Generation of a Diophantine Set

In what follows we show how to design, given a polynomial $P(x, y_1, \ldots y_k)$ with integer coefficients, a virus machine Π_P that generates the diophantine set characterized by that polynomial.

- The hosts are

$$H = \{h_x, h_x', h_{y_1}, h_{y_1}', \ldots, h_{y_k}, h_{y_k}', h_+, h_-, h_{one}, h_{out}\} \cup$$
$$\{h_c \mid c > 0 \text{ and there exists } \alpha, \beta_1, \ldots, \beta_k \in \mathbb{N} \text{ such that}$$
$$c\, x^\alpha y_1^{\beta_1} \cdots y_k^{\beta_k} \text{ or } -c\, x^\alpha y_1^{\beta_1} \cdots y_k^{\beta_k} \text{ is a monomial of } P\}$$

together with the internal hosts of the modules.
- The initial contents of h_{one} is 1, and of h_c is c. The initial contents of the rest of hosts is 0, except for the internal hosts of the modules, which have their specific initial contents.
- The output host is h_{out}.
- The instructions are

$$I = \{\text{increment } x, \text{increment } y_1, \ldots, \text{increment } y_k,$$
$$\text{halt, infinite loop}\}$$

together with the individualized instructions of the modules.
- The initial instruction is $\text{increment } x$.
- The functioning of the virus machine is given by the following sequence of concatenated instructions and modules, which determines the graphs D_H, D_I and G_C:
1. First a value for x is generated, in a non-deterministic manner.

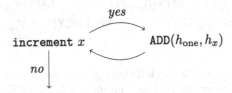

The instruction transfer paths labelled by yes and no are set to have the same weight (for example, weight 1) so, according to the semantics of the model, it is non-deterministically chosen to add or not the contents of h_{one}, one virus, to h_x. In the former case, the machine comes back to instruction increment x to make the choice again. In the latter case, it has finished generating a value for x.
2. Analogously, a value for each of y_1 to y_k is generated in a non-deterministic manner.

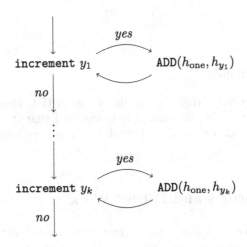

3. For each monomial $c x^\alpha y_1^{\beta_1} \cdots y_k^{\beta_k}$ of P, with $c > 0$, its value over the arguments $x, y_1, \ldots, y_k$ previously generated is computed and accumulated in h_+.

$$\to \text{COPY}(h_x, h'_x) \to \text{COPY}(h_{y_1}, h'_{y_1}) \to \cdots \to \text{COPY}(h_{y_k}, h'_{y_k}) \to$$
$$\text{EXPT}(h'_x, \alpha) \to \text{EXPT}(h'_{y_1}, \beta_1) \to \cdots \to \text{EXPT}(h'_{y_k}, \beta_k) \to$$
$$\text{MULTIPLY}(h'_{y_1}, h'_x) \to \cdots \to \text{MULTIPLY}(h'_{y_k}, h'_x) \to \text{MULTIPLY}(h_c, h'_x) \to$$
$$\text{ADD}(h'_x, h_+) \to$$

4. For each monomial $c x^\alpha y_1^{\beta_1} \cdots y_k^{\beta_k}$ of P, with $c < 0$, its absolute value over the arguments $x, y_1, \ldots, y_k$ previously generated is computed and accumulated in h_-.

$$\to \text{COPY}(h_x, h'_x) \to \text{COPY}(h_{y_1}, h'_{y_1}) \to \cdots \to \text{COPY}(h_{y_k}, h'_{y_k}) \to$$
$$\text{EXPT}(h'_x, \alpha) \to \text{EXPT}(h'_{y_1}, \beta_1) \to \cdots \to \text{EXPT}(h'_{y_k}, \beta_k) \to$$
$$\text{MULTIPLY}(h'_{y_1}, h'_x) \to \cdots \to \text{MULTIPLY}(h'_{y_k}, h'_x) \to \text{MULTIPLY}(h_{|c|}, h'_x) \to$$
$$\text{ADD}(h'_x, h_-) \to$$

5. Finally, in order to check if the arguments $x, y_1, \ldots, y_k$ constitute a solution of the polynomial P, the contents of h_+ and h_- are compared. If they are equal, the value of the argument x is copied from h_x to h_{out} and the computation halts. Otherwise, an infinite loop is started to make the computation non-halting.

$$\text{AREEQUAL?}(h_+, h_-) \xrightarrow{\ yes\ } \text{COPY}(h_x, h_{\text{out}}) \longrightarrow \text{halt}$$

$$\Bigg\downarrow {\scriptstyle no}$$

$$\text{infinite loop} \quad \circlearrowleft$$

3.4   Main Result

Taking into account that, by virtue of the MRDP theorem every recursively enumerable set is diophantine, it is guaranteed that it is possible to construct virus machines that compute any such set. Then, we have the following result.

Theorem 1. *NVM(*, *, *) = NRE.*

4   Conclusions and Future Work

Virus machines are a bio-inspired computational paradigm based on the transmissions and replications of viruses [1]. The computational completeness of virus machines having no restriction on the number of hosts, the number of instructions and the number of viruses contained in any host along any computation has been established by simulating register machines. However, when an upper bound on the number of viruses present in any host during a computation is set, the computational power of these systems decreases; in fact, a characterization of semi-linear sets of numbers is obtained [1].

The semantics of the model makes it easy to construct specific virus machines by assembling small components that carry out a part of the task to be solved. It is then convenient to develop a library of modules solving common problems such as comparisons or arithmetic operations between contents of hosts.

In this paper, a new variant of virus machines able to generate sets of natural numbers is introduced. The universality of non-restricted virus machines is then proved by showing that they can generate all diophantine sets.

Being shown the computational completeness of virus machines (in the unrestricted form) working in several modes, we can turn our attention to their computational efficiency. A computational complexity theory for these devices is therefore required, so that the resources needed to solve (hard) problems can be rigorously measured.

To this respect, it is convenient to point out that, according to the formalization given in this paper, virus machines are inherently sequential devices. To increase their efficiency it could be interesting to consider variants of the model where the instructions are activated in parallel.

Acknowledgments. This work was supported by Project TIN2012-37434 of the Ministerio de Economía y Competitividad of Spain, cofinanced by FEDER funds.

References

1. Chen, X., Valencia-Cabrera, L., Pérez-Jiménez, M.J., Wang, B., Zeng X.: Computing with Viruses. International Journal of Bioinspired Computation, submitted, **7**(3) 176-182 (Submitted 2015)
2. Cormen, T.H., Leiserson, C.E., Rivest, R.L.: An Introduction to Algorithms. MIT Press, Cambridge (1994)
3. Dimmock, N.J., Easton, A.J., Leppard, K.: Introduction to Modern Virology, 6th edn. Blackwell Publishing, Malden (2007)
4. Matijasevich, Y.: Hilbert's Tenth Problem. MIT Press, Cambridge (1993)
5. Rozenberg, G., Bäck, T., Kok, J.N.: Handbook of Natural Computing. Springer, Heidelberg (2012)

A Verified Algorithm for the Centrosymmetric Solution of Sylvester Matrix Equations

Haifeng Sang[1], Ziyu Li[2], Ying Cui[1], and Qingchun Li[1 (✉)]

[1] College of Mathematics and Statistics, Beihua University, Jilin 132013, China
liqingchun01@163.com
[2] College of Economics and Management, Shanghai Maritime University,
Shanghai 201306, China

Abstract. We study the verification for a centrosymmetric solution of Sylvester matrix equations by the interval theory. Propose an algorithm which outputs an approximate centrosymmetric solution and its error bounds with the property that the exact solution exists within this verified interval solution.

Keywords: Verified error bounds · Sylvester matrix equation · Centrosymmetric solution · INTLAB

1 Introduction

In many important fields such as biomathematics, mechanics, physics and control theory [1–3], some problems can be come down to compute a solution of the Sylvester matrix equation

$$AX + XB = C. \tag{1}$$

In this paper, the accuracy of numerically computed solutions in the Sylvester Eq. (1) is concerned. We investigate the methods for computing enclosing intervals for all entries of the approximate centrosymmetric solution X of the matrix equation, where A, B and C are real matrices of size $m \times m, n \times n$ and $m \times n$, respectively.

Generally speaking, classical mathematical proofs is build by pencil and paper, but there are many problems can be computed in computers [4]. In 1980, Rump [5] proposed the standard methods for verification, and discuss how they can assist in achieving a mathematically rigorous result by floating-point arithmetic. In other words, determing the error bounds of an approximate solution, there is an exact solution within this verified interval. The purpose of verification methods is ambitious. For a given problem, it is proved that there exists a solution of a problem within computed bounds by the computer. The application of verification is very wildly, such as some finite-dimensional problems (sparse linear systems, systems of nonlinear equations, semi-definite programming) and infinite-dimensional problems (two-point boundary value problems, semilinear elliptic boundary value problems) [6,7]. The purpose of this paper is to obtain

© Springer-Verlag Berlin Heidelberg 2015
M. Gong et al. (Eds.): BIC-TA 2015, CCIS 562, pp. 342–349, 2015.
DOI: 10.1007/978-3-662-49014-3_31

the error bounds for the approximate centrosymmetric solution of (1). We base
the construction of our algorithm on that of Frommer [8] and Liu [9]. This algorithm outputs an approximate centrosymmetric solution $\widetilde{X}$ and its error bounds
$\widetilde{V}$ with the property that the exact centrosymmetric solution exists within this
computed bound $\widetilde{X} + \widetilde{V}$.

This paper is organized as follows. In Sect. 2 we introduce the preliminary
definitions and notation we shall use. The main result, the algorithm for verifying the centrosymmetric solution of Sylvester matrix equations, is presented in
Sect. 3. In Sect. 4 we provide some examples for demonstrating the performance
of our algorithm.

2   Notation and Preliminaries

We denote by $\mathbb{IR}$, $\mathbb{IR}^n$ and $\mathbb{IR}^{n \times n}$ the set of real interval, the set of n real
interval vectors and the set of $m \times n$ real interval matrices, respectively. We
use $\langle X, Y \rangle = tr(X^T, Y)$, $M(X)$ and $\|X\|$ to stand for the inner product of
$\langle X, Y \rangle$, the function about a matrix X and the Frobenius norm of a matrix X,
respectively.

Definition 1.   [10] *The matrix $A \in \mathbb{R}^{n \times n}$ is centrosymmetric if*

$$a_{ij} = a_{n+1-i,n+1-j}, \ i, j = 1, 2, \ldots, n.$$

Lemma 1.   [4] *Let $A, T \in \mathbb{R}^{n \times n}$, $b \in \mathbb{R}^n$ and $x \in \mathbb{IR}^n$ be given. Assume*

$$Tb + (I - TA)x \subseteq int(x).$$

Then the matrices A, T are non-singular and $A^{-1}b \in Tb + (I - TA)x$.

Lemma 2.   [8] *Let $\mathcal{Z}$ be convex and compact with non-empty interior and
assume that*

$$\mathcal{K}(\widetilde{x}, \mathcal{Z}) = \{-T(A\widetilde{x} - b) + (I - TA)z : z \in \mathcal{Z} \subset int(\mathcal{Z})\}.$$

*Then the matrix A is non-singular and there exists a vector $\widehat{x} \in \widetilde{x} + \mathcal{Z}$ such that
$A\widehat{x} = b$.*

The practical implementation **verifylss** in INTLAB [11] can verify solutions
of dense systems of linear equations. If its coefficient matrix is an interval matrix,
verifylss can output the interval vector which contains all solutions of this
system of linear equations. And **verifylss** is also suitable for systems of linear
matrix equations.

Lemma 3.   [12,13] *Let interval matrices $\boldsymbol{A}$, $\boldsymbol{B} \in \mathbb{IR}^{n \times n}$ be given. If **veri-
fylss($\boldsymbol{A}$,$\boldsymbol{B}$)** successfully returns the interval matrix $\boldsymbol{X} \subset \mathbb{IR}^{n \times n}$, then*

$$\Sigma(\boldsymbol{A}, \boldsymbol{B}) = \{X \in \mathbb{R}^{n \times n} : AX = B, A \in \boldsymbol{A}, B \in \boldsymbol{B}\} \subseteq \boldsymbol{X}.$$

The matrix Eq. (1) can be written as a system of linear equations as follow

$$Px = c, \tag{2}$$

where $P = I_n \otimes A + B^T \otimes I_m$, $x = vec(X)$ and $c = vec(C)$. Here, $\otimes$ represents the Kronecker product, and vec is the operation of stacking the columns of a matrix in order to obtain one long vector. So P is the matrix of size $mn \times mn$, and $vec(X)$ and $vec(C)$ are vector of length mn [10].

Therefore, we can obtain a verified solution of the matrix Eq. (1) by verifying a solution of the linear system (2). Unexpectly, the complexity of this method above is very high. In order to reduce the verification time and improve computing efficiency, we propose an algorithm which outputs an approximate centrosymmetric solution and its error bounds with the property that the exact solution exists within this verified interval solution.

3   Main Results

Throughout this paper we assume that A and B are both diagonalizable. Then there are the spectral decompositions

$$A = V_1 D_1 W_1, \text{with} V_1, D_1, W_1 \in \mathbb{C}^{m \times m}, \ D_1 = \texttt{diag}(\lambda_1, \ldots, \lambda_m),$$
$$B = V_2 D_2 W_2, \ \text{with} V_2, D_2, W_2 \in \mathbb{C}^{n \times n}, \ D_2 = \texttt{diag}(\mu_1, \ldots, \mu_n).$$

Let

$$P = \left((V_2^{-1})^T \otimes W_1^{-1} \right) [I_n \otimes (W_1 A W_1^{-1}) + (V_2^{-1} B V_2)^T \otimes I_m](V_2^T \otimes W_1).$$

For the sake of clearness, define

$$Q = I_n \otimes (W_1 A W_1^{-1}) + (V_2^{-1} B V_2)^T \otimes I_m,$$
$$y = (V_2^T \otimes W_1)x,$$
$$f = (V_2^T \otimes W_1)c.$$

Further, we can reformulate the linear system (2) as

$$Qy = f. \tag{3}$$

Because we cannot obtain the exact inverses W_1^{-1} and V_2^{-1} by a numerical computation, we use interval algorithms to obtain interval matrices $\boldsymbol{W}_1^{-1}$ and $\boldsymbol{V}_2^{-1}$, such that $W_1^{-1} \in \boldsymbol{W}_1^{-1}$ and $V_2^{-1} \in \boldsymbol{V}_2^{-1}$. Denote

$$\boldsymbol{S}_1 = (W_1 A)\boldsymbol{W}_1, \ \boldsymbol{S}_2 = \boldsymbol{V}_2(B V_2).$$

Similarly, $W_1^{-1} A W_1$ as well as $V_2^{-1} B V_2$ will not be exactly diagonal by numerical computation, but we expect them to be very close to D_1 and D_2, respectively. Defining

$$\Delta = I_n \otimes D_1 + D_2^T \otimes I_m,$$

then the diagonal matrix Δ is a good approximation for Q and Δ^{-1} is a good approximate for Q^{-1}.

The next theorem is the main theoretical result of the paper and gives the theoretical foundations to the algorithm presented in the following.

Theorem 1. *Let $\widetilde{X} \in \mathbb{R}^{m \times n}$ be an approximate centrosymmetric solution of the matrix equation $AX + XB = C$, and let $\mathbf{Z} \in \mathbb{IR}^{m \times n}$ with $z = vec(\mathbf{Z})$. Define*

$$T = W_1 \cdot (A\widetilde{X} + \widetilde{X}B - C) \cdot V_2,$$
$$\mathbf{M} = (D_1 - \mathbf{S}_1)\mathbf{Z},$$
$$\mathbf{N} = \mathbf{Z}(D_2 - \mathbf{S}_2),$$
$$\mathbf{U} = (-T + \mathbf{M} + \mathbf{N})./D,$$
$$\widetilde{y} = (V_2^T \otimes W_1)\widetilde{x},$$

where $D \in \mathbb{R}^{m \times n}$ satisfies $vec(D) = diag(\Delta)$. If $\mathbf{U} \subset int(\mathbf{Z})$, then the system $Qy = f$ has a unique solution $\widehat{y} \in \widetilde{y} + vec(\mathbf{U})$.

Proof. Let $\widetilde{Y}$ satisfy $vec(\widetilde{Y}) = \widetilde{y}$ and let $\widetilde{x} = vec(\widetilde{X})$. Then

$$\begin{aligned}
vec(T) &= vec(W_1(A\widetilde{X} + \widetilde{X}B - C)V_2) \\
&= (V_2^T \otimes W_1)vec(A\widetilde{X} + \widetilde{X}B - C) \\
&= (V_2^T \otimes W_1)((I_n \otimes A)\widetilde{x} + (B^T \otimes I_m)\widetilde{x} - C) \\
&= (V_2^T \otimes W_1)(I_n \otimes A + B^T \otimes I_m)(V_2^{-T} \otimes W_1^{-1})(\widetilde{y} - f) \\
&= Q(\widetilde{y} - f).
\end{aligned}$$

By the property of Kronecker products and the vec operator [10],

$$vec(\mathbf{M}) = vec((D_1 - \mathbf{S}_1)\mathbf{Z}) \supset \{(I_n \otimes (D_1 - \mathbf{S}_1)z, z \in \mathbf{z}, \mathbf{S}_1 \in \mathbf{S}_1\} \text{ and}$$
$$vec(\mathbf{N}) = vec(\mathbf{Z}(D_2 - \mathbf{S}_2)) \supset \{(D_2 - \mathbf{S}_2)^T \otimes I_m)z, z \in \mathbf{Z}, \mathbf{S}_2 \in \mathbf{S}_2\}.$$

Since

$$\Delta - Q = I_n \otimes (D_1 - W_1 A W_1^{-1}) + (D_2 - V_2^{-1}BV_2)^T \otimes I_m)$$

and

$$W_1 A W_1^{-1} \in \mathbf{S}_1, \quad V_2^{-1}BV_2 \in \mathbf{S}_2,$$

we have

$$\{(\Delta - Q)z, z \in \mathbf{z}\} \subset vec(\mathbf{M}) + vec(\mathbf{N}).$$

Further

$$\{-\Delta^{-1}(Q\widetilde{y} - f) + (I_{mn} - \Delta^{-1}Q)z : z \in \mathbf{z}\} \subseteq vec(\mathbf{U}).$$

Based on Lemma 2, we obtain that $Qy = f$ has a unique solution $\widehat{y} \in \widetilde{y} + vec(\mathbf{U})$. $\qquad\square$

Remark 1. Define $\widetilde{V} = W_1 U V_2$. Based on Proposition 1, we can conclude that if $U \subset \text{int}(Z)$, then there is a unique matrix $\widehat{X} \in \widetilde{X} + \widetilde{V}$ such that $A\widehat{X} + \widehat{X}B = C$.

Based on the above theory, we design the algorithm as follow.

Algorithm 1.

Input: 1. $AX + XB = C$: the Sylvester matrix equation.
        2. X_1: the initial centrosymmetric matrix.
        3. N: the maximum number of iterations.
        4. ε: the numerical tolerance.

Output: 1. The approximate centrosymmetric solution $\widetilde{X}$ and its verified error bounds $\widetilde{V}$.
          2. Or "Failure".

(1) Matrix $A \in R^{m \times m}$, $B \in R^{n \times n}$, $C \in R^{m \times n}$, $X_1 \in CSR^{m \times n}$.
(2) Compute $R_1 = C - AX_1 - X_1 B$; $P_1 = G - M(X_1)$; $Q_1 = M(P_1)$; $k = 1$.
(3) If $R_k = 0$ or $k > N$, return "Failure" and stop. Otherwise $k := k + 1$.
(4) Compute

$$X_{k+1} = X_k + \frac{\|P_k\|^2}{\langle Q_k, M(P_k) \rangle} Q_k;$$

$$R_{k+1} = C - AX_{k+1} - X_{k+1}B;$$

$$P_{k+1} = P_k - \frac{\|P_k\|^2}{\langle Q_k, M(P_k) \rangle} M(Q_k);$$

$$Q_{k+1} = P_{k+1} - \frac{\langle P_{k+1}, M(Q_k) \rangle}{\langle Q_k, M(Q_k) \rangle} Q_k.$$

If $\|R_{k+1}\| \leq \varepsilon$, then return $\widetilde{X} = X_{k+1}$ and go to Step 5. Otherwise go to Step 3.
(5) If A and B are diagonalizable, then compute spectral decompositions:

$$A = V_1 D_1 W_1, \quad B = V_2 D_2 W_2.$$

Otherwise, return "Failure" and stop.
(6) Denote

$$D = \begin{pmatrix} \lambda_1 + \mu_1 & \lambda_1 + \mu_2 & \cdots & \lambda_1 + \mu_n \\ \lambda_2 + \mu_1 & \lambda_2 + \mu_2 & \cdots & \lambda_2 + \mu_n \\ & \cdots & & \\ \lambda_m + \mu_1 & \lambda_m + \mu_2 & \cdots & \lambda_m + \mu_n \end{pmatrix}.$$

(7) Using **verifylss** function in INTLAB, compute interval matrices W_1, W_2 such that $W_1 \in \boldsymbol{W_1}$, $W_2 \in \boldsymbol{W_2}$.
(8) Compute interval matrices

$$T = W_1(A\widetilde{X} + \widetilde{X}B - C)V_2, S_1 = (W_1 A)\boldsymbol{W_1}, S_2 = \boldsymbol{W_2}(BV_2), U = -T./D.$$

(9) Set iter=0.

(9.1) If iter ≤ 15, then go to Step 9.2. Otherwise, return "Failure" and stop.

(9.2) Set iter=iter+1, and

$$Z = \texttt{hull}(U \cdot \texttt{infsup}(0.9, 1.1) + e^{-20} \cdot \texttt{infsup}(-1, 1), 0).$$

(9.3) Compute

$$M = (D_1 - S_1) \cdot Z, \ N = Z \cdot (D_2 - S_2), \ U = (-T + M + N)./D.$$

(9.4) If $U \subseteq \texttt{int}(Z)$, return $\widetilde{V} = W_1 U W_2$ and stop. Otherwise, go to Step 9.1.

Algorithm 1 stops after finitely many steps and computes verified error bounds for the approximate centrosymmetric solution, since the strategy to construct $\widetilde{V} = W_1 U W_2$ is the same as in the algorithm of [8].

We can obtain the proposition as follow by Theorem 1.

Proposition 1. *Given the Sylvester matrix equation $AX + XB = C$ and a approximate centrosymmetric solution $\widetilde{X}$, if Algorithm 1 successfully returns the verified error bounds $\widetilde{V}$, then there is the unique matrix $\widehat{X}$ in the interval matrix $V = \widetilde{X} + \widetilde{V}$, such that $\widehat{X}$ is the exact solution of $AX + XB = C$.*

4   Numerical Experiments

The following experiments are done in Matlab R2011a(INTLAB V6) under Windows 7.

In the following examples, we apply Algorithm 1 to compute the centrosymmetric solution $\widetilde{X}$, the error bounds $\widetilde{V}$ and the verified centrosymmetric solution $V = \widetilde{X} + \widetilde{V}$ of the Sylvester matrix equation $AX + XB = C$.

Example 1. Consider the verified centrosymmetric solution of Sylvester matrix equations $AX + XB = C$, where

$$A = \begin{pmatrix} 4.4745 & 7.2934 & 8.1464 \\ 1.6546 & 0.6131 & 4.6152 \\ 2.5658 & 1.1328 & 9.0879 \end{pmatrix}, B = \begin{pmatrix} 8.9632 & 2.3729 & 4.2658 \\ 2.0698 & 6.8430 & 1.7417 \\ 8.7409 & 9.6012 & 3.9737 \end{pmatrix},$$

$$C = \begin{pmatrix} 201.8086 & 198.0669 & 160.7922 \\ 127.7478 & 129.9399 & 88.7680 \\ 162.0806 & 183.2784 & 129.0815 \end{pmatrix}.$$

It can be verified that the matrix equation $AX + XB = C$ is consistent and has a unique exact centrosymmetric solution

$$X = \begin{pmatrix} 6.7093 & 5.6352 & 3.8259 \\ 4.8506 & 4.8989 & 4.8506 \\ 3.8259 & 5.6352 & 6.7093 \end{pmatrix}.$$

Input: $X_1 = \begin{pmatrix} 0\,0\,0 \\ 0\,0\,0 \\ 0\,0\,0 \end{pmatrix}, N = 100, \varepsilon = 10^{-5}.$

Output: $\widetilde{X} = \begin{pmatrix} 6.7092\ 5.6352\ 3.8259 \\ 4.8506\ 4.8989\ 4.8506 \\ 3.8259\ 5.6352\ 6.7092 \end{pmatrix},$

$\widetilde{V} = 1.0e - 009 * \begin{pmatrix} [-0.0787, -0.0786] & [0.0678, 0.0679] & [0.0473, 0.0474] \\ [0.0342, 0.0343] & [-0.1940, -0.1939] & [0.0342, 0.0343] \\ [0.0473, 0.0474] & [0.0678, 0.0679] & [-0.0788, -0.0787] \end{pmatrix},$

$V = \begin{pmatrix} [6.7092, 6.7093]\ [5.6352, 5.6353]\ [3.8259, 3.8260] \\ [4.8506, 4.8507]\ [4.8988, 4.8989]\ [4.8506, 4.8507] \\ [3.8259, 3.8260]\ [5.6352, 5.6353]\ [6.7092, 6.7093] \end{pmatrix}.$

Example 2. Given 3 matrices

$$A = \begin{pmatrix} 9.3424\ 8.7286\ 9.6689 \\ 2.6445\ 2.3788\ 6.6493 \\ 1.6030\ 6.4583\ 8.7038 \end{pmatrix}, B = \begin{pmatrix} 0.0993\ 4.3017\ 6.8732 \\ 1.3701\ 8.9032\ 3.4611 \\ 8.1876\ 7.3491\ 1.6603 \end{pmatrix},$$

$$C = \begin{pmatrix} 118.5369\ 319.4746\ 118.5305 \\ 59.3063\ 157.1301\ 59.3423 \\ 76.4947\ 225.7040\ 93.9047 \end{pmatrix},$$

consider the verified centrosymmetric solution of Sylvester matrix equations $AX + XB = C$.

It can be verified that the matrix equation $AX + XB = C$ is consistent and has a unique exact centrosymmetric solution

$$X = \begin{pmatrix} 1.5561\ 8.5598\ 4.2245 \\ 1.9112\ 4.9025\ 1.9112 \\ 4.2245\ 8.5598\ 1.5561 \end{pmatrix}.$$

Input: $\overline{X} = \begin{pmatrix} 0\,0\,0 \\ 0\,0\,0 \\ 0\,0\,0 \end{pmatrix}, N = 100, \varepsilon = 10^{-5}.$

Output: $\widetilde{X} = \begin{pmatrix} 1.5561\ 8.5599\ 4.2245 \\ 1.9112\ 4.9025\ 1.9112 \\ 4.2245\ 8.5599\ 1.5561 \end{pmatrix},$

$\widetilde{V} = 1.0e - 009 * \begin{pmatrix} [-0.1118, -0.1117] & [0.1510, 0.1511] & [-0.0461, -0.0460] \\ [0.1841, 0.1842] & [-0.3488, -0.3487] & [0.1841, 0.1842] \\ [-0.0461, -0.0460] & [0.1510, 0.1511] & [-0.1118, -0.1117] \end{pmatrix},$

$V = \begin{pmatrix} [1.5561, 1.5562]\ [8.5598, 8.5599]\ [4.2244, 4.2245] \\ [1.9111, 1.9112]\ [4.9025, 4.9026]\ [1.9111, 1.9112] \\ [4.2245, 4.2246]\ [8.5598, 8.5599]\ [1.5561, 1.5562] \end{pmatrix}.$

Acknowledgments. We thank the reviewers for their valuable comments and suggestions on this paper. This work is supported by Jilin Province Department of Education Science and Technology Research Project under Grants 2014213, 2015131 and 2015156.

References

1. Datta, B.: Numerical Methods for Linear Control Systems. Elsevier Academic Press, Amsterdam (2004)
2. Antoulas, A.: Approximation of Large-Scale Dynamical Systems, Advances in Design and Control. SIAM, Philadelphia (2005)
3. Sorensen, D.C., Antoulas, A.C.: The Sylvester equation and approximate balanced reduction. Linear Algebra Appl. **351**, 671–700 (2002)
4. Rump, S.M.: Verification methods: rigorous results using floating-point arithmetic. Acta Numerica **19**, 287–449 (2010)
5. Rump, S.M.: Kleine Fehlerschranken bei Matrixproblemen. Universitat Karlsruhe, Karlsruhe (1980)
6. Tucker, W.: The Lorenz attractor exists. C. R. de l'Acadmie des Sci. Ser. I Math. **328**(12), 1197–1202 (1999)
7. Tawarmalani, M., Sahinidis, N.V.: A polyhedral branch-and-cut approach to global optimization. Math. Program. **103**(2), 225–249 (2005)
8. Frommer, A., Hashemi, B.: Verified error bounds for solutions of Sylvester matrix equations. Linear Algebra Appl. **436**(2), 405–420 (2002)
9. Liu, D., Zhou, H., Yuan, D.: An iterative algorithm for the centrosymmetric solutions and optimal approximation of $AXB+CXD = F$. J. Yangzhou Univ. (Natural Science Edition) **11**(3), 9–13 (2008)
10. Horn, R.A., Johnson, C.R.: Topics in Matrix Analysis. Cambridge University Press, Cambridge (1994)
11. Rump, S.M.: INTLABinterval Laboratory Developments in Reliable Computing, pp. 77–104. Kluwer Academic Publishers, Dordrecht (1999)
12. Sang, H., Li, M., Liu, P., Li, Q.: Verified algorithm for a solution of matrix operator equation. J. Beihua Univ. (Natural Science) **16**(4), 411–414 (2015)
13. Rump, S.M.: Verification methods: rigorous results using floating-point arithmetic. Acta Numerica **19**, 287–449 (2010)

Maximal Synchronization of Feeder Buses to Metro Using Particle Swarm Optimization

Yindong Shen[1,2](✉) and Siqi Wang[1,2]

[1] School of Automation, Huazhong University of Science and Technology,
Wuhan 430074, Hubei, China
yindong@hust.edu.cn, wasq1801@163.com
[2] Key Laboratory of Image Processing and Intelligent Control (Huazhong University
of Science and Technology), Ministry of Education, Wuhan 430074, Hubei, China

Abstract. In public transport, transfer optimization aims either to minimize the passengers' waiting times or to maximize the number of synchronization arrivals at transfer points. Under the objective of maximal synchronization, much research is carried out based on a single transit mode independently. This paper proposes a new model for the maximal synchronization between two most popular transit modes (i.e. bus and metro), which is helpful to increase the ridership of metro systems and enhance the service level of an entire public transport system. Based on the model, a maximal synchronization approach based on particle swarm optimization is devised. Experiments on benchmark instances and a case study on a real-world problem show the proposed approach is feasible and efficient.

Keywords: Public transport · Transfer optimization · Maximal synchronization · Metro

1 Introduction

Large capacity and fast speed are the outstanding features of the metro system, which has been one of the most important transit systems in many, especially metropolitan cities [1,2]. Therefore, due to the high cost of construction, metro has usually a lower level of access than conventional public transit (e.g. bus). To fully perform its function, it needs to keep seamless connection with conventional public transit to achieve a smooth transfer [3]. Bus and metro are normally two most important modes in urban public transport, mutually effective transfer between them can improve the efficiency of urban public transport and keep it sustainable [4]. Thus, the transfer optimization problem of feeder buses to metro has drawn great attention of researchers. The transfer optimization problem can be roughly classified into two types according to their objective functions. One is to minimize passengers transfer waiting times [5–8]; another is to maximize the number of synchronization arrivals at transfer points [9–12]. It is hard to say which problem model is more efficient, since both lead to the same goal of

© Springer-Verlag Berlin Heidelberg 2015
M. Gong et al. (Eds.): BIC-TA 2015, CCIS 562, pp. 350–361, 2015.
DOI: 10.1007/978-3-662-49014-3_32

reducing the total passengers transfer time and improving the service level of public transit.

Under the objective of maximal synchronization, much research is carried out based on a single transit mode independently and mainly focuses on bus transit system. For example, the synchronization is defined by Ceder et al. [9] as two trips on different bus lines arrive simultaneously at a transfer point, in which a constructive heuristic procedure is designed to generate timetables based on the selection of points. Later, an improvement is made by Eranki [12], in which the synchronization is defined as the arrival times of two trips at a transfer point fall in a time window, meanwhile, the Ceder's algorithm [9] is adapted to solve the problem model. To reduce bus bunching and maximize passengers' transfer, Rojas and Solis [10] build a new model, in which the synchronization arrival times at a transfer point must be larger than zero and an multi-start iterated local search algorithm is employed. In general, due to the complexity of the transfer optimization problem models, the existing solution methods are mainly heuristic, many of which produce a timetable for each transfer point of a line in sequence. The simultaneous arrivals of the remaining points may gradually become less since they are affected by their previously selected points. Therefore, there are rooms for improvement and a brand-new approach is to be proposed in this paper.

Instead of based on a single transit mode, this paper focuses on the transfer optimization problem between bus and metro and amongst the feeder buses. The objective is to create maximal synchronization arrivals to achieve efficient transfer. A mathematical model of the maximal synchronization problem of feeder buses to metro is first built and a brand-new approach is then devised based on particle swarm optimization (PSO). Experiments on benchmark instances and a case study on a real-world problem are shown before conclusion, remarks are given at the end.

2   Definition of Synchronization

The maximal synchronization problem of feeder buses to metro in this paper aims to maximize the total number of simultaneous arrivals between the train trips passing by a given metro station and the bus trips passing the nearby transfer points, and between the bus trips on the different bus lines. This section is to define the simultaneous arrival, which is essential to the problem formulation.

2.1   Synchronization at a Transfer Point

Synchronization is the temporal coordination of trips from different lines at the same transfer points. Simultaneous arrivals can help on saving the transfer (waiting) times and reducing the total travel times of passengers. Studies have shown that more simultaneous arrivals may increase ridership of public transit systems [4].

A *simultaneous arrival* is normally defined if any two trips on different lines arrive at the same transfer point simultaneously as shown in Fig. 1(a), where the single black spot represents the synchronization time at the transfer point k.

In practice, it can be regarded as a *simultaneous arrival* if two trips on different lines arrive simultaneously or in succession within a short time range (say between 0 to 3 min), which is defined as a *synchronization time window*. For example, in Fig. 1(b), the two trips on lines 1 and 2 are simultaneous because the difference of their arrival times at the transfer point k lies in the synchronization time window $[0, \mu_k]$, denoted by the line between two adjacent black spots.

When the *synchronization* amongst bus trips is considered, bunching (i.e. buses arrive simultaneously at a bus stop) often occurs, which may cause the bus stop in disorder. Therefore, to avoid bus bunching at the transfer point k, the following restrictions can be enforced on the definition of a *simultaneous arrival*.

(1) The headway (i.e. the interval between two consecutive trips on the same line) of each line must lie within the range $[h_l, H_l]$, where $h_l > 0$ and $H_l > h_l$ denote the minimum and maximum headway of the line l respectively.
(2) The synchronization time window for two trips on the different lines at the transfer point k is defined as the range $[\varepsilon_k, \mu_k]$, where $\varepsilon_k > 0$ and $\mu_k > \varepsilon_k$.

Figure 1(c) illustrates a *synchronization time window* avoiding bunching, which is presented by the line between two adjacent black spots.

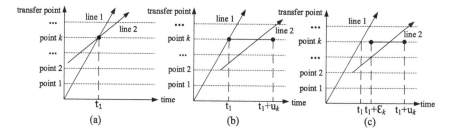

Fig. 1. Different definitions of synchronization at a transfer point k

2.2 Synchronization Considering Walking Time

Walking time is usually ignored when a transfer occurs between different bus lines at the same bus stop. However, it is obviously necessary for passengers when the transfer is taken between a metro station and a bus stop.

Suppose the walking time between a metro station and any transfer point k nearby is determined and denoted as ω_k, the *synchronization time window* can be defined as $[\omega_k, \omega_k + \mu_k]$ instead of $[0, \mu_k]$ demonstrated in Fig. 1(b), where t_1 denotes the time when line 1 arrives at point k.

To keep consistency in the definition of the *synchronization time window* $[0, \mu_k]$, the walking time ω_k can be considered by redefining t_1 in Fig. 1(b) as the sum of t_1 (i.e. the arrival time of line 1) and ω_k, i.e. replacing t_1 by $t_1' = t_1 + \omega_k$.

3   Formulation of Maximal Synchronization Problem

Given a certain metro station, suppose a sequence of train trips $R = (1, 2, \ldots, f)$ pass the metro station during the planning horizon T (e.g. peak period or an entire day), where f denotes the total number of train trips, and t_r^{Metro} denotes the arrival time of any trip $r \in R$. Around the metro station, there are a set of bus lines $L = \{1, 2, \ldots, m\}$ and a set of transfer points $K = \{1, 2, \ldots, n\}$. At any point $k \in K$, a set of bus lines $L_k = \{1, 2, \ldots, m_k\}$ pass by, where $L_k \in L = \bigcup_{k=1}^{n} L_k$. On each line $l \in L$, there is a sequence of trips $I_l = (1, 2, \ldots, f_l)$, where any $i \in I_l$ denotes the ith trip and f_l denotes the total number of trips on the line l. Let t_{lk} denote the travel time from the terminal of line $l \in L_k$ to the transfer point $k \in K$, ω_k denotes the time duration for passengers walking between the metro station and the transfer point $k \in K$, and h_l and H_l denote the minimum and maximum headways of the line l during the planning horizon T respectively.

The maximal synchronization problem of feeder buses to metro is concerned with the determination of the departure time of each bus trip on all the bus lines L. The objective is to maximize the total number of simultaneous arrivals. Therefore, two types of decision variables can be defined as follows: one is denoted as y_i^l to represent the departure time of the ith trip from the terminal of the line l; another is to identify the existence of a synchronization arrival, which contains the following three 0–1 variables.

$x_{r,il}^k = 1$, if this is a $train - to - bus\, synchronization\, arrival$, i.e. the sum of the arrival time t_r^{Metro} of the train trip r and the walking time ω_k is earlier than the arrival time of the ith trip on bus line l, and their time difference falls into a synchronization time window $[0, \mu_k]$ at the transfer point k; otherwise, $x_{r,il}^k = 0$.

$x_{il,r}^k = 1$, if this is a $train - to - bus\, synchronization\, arrival$, i.e. the sum of the arrival time of the ith trip on bus line l and the walking time ω_k is earlier than the arrival time t_r^{Metro}, and their time difference falls into a synchronization time window $[0, \mu_k]$ at the metro station; otherwise, $x_{il,r}^k = 0$.

$x_{il,js}^k = 1$, if this a $bus - to - bus\, synchronization\, arrival$, i.e. the bus trip i on line l arrives earlier than the bus trip j on line $s(l \neq s)$ and both fall into a synchronization time window $[\varepsilon_k, \mu_k]$ at the transfer point k; otherwise, $x_{il,js}^k = 0$.

The maximal synchronization problem of feeder buses to metro can be modeled as follows.

$$max(\sum_{k \in K} \sum_{r \in R} \sum_{l \in L_k} \sum_{i \in I_l} x_{r,il}^k + \sum_{k \in K} \sum_{r \in R} \sum_{l \in L_k} \sum_{i \in I_l} x_{il,r}^k + \sum_{k \in K} \sum_{l \in L_k} \sum_{i \in I_l} \sum_{s \in L_k} \sum_{j \in I_s} x_{il,js}^k)$$

(1)

subject to

$$y_1^l \leq H_l, \forall l \in L \tag{2}$$

$$y_{f_l}^l \leq T, \forall l \in L \tag{3}$$

$$h_l \leq y_{i+1}^l - y_i^l \leq H_l, \forall l \in L, i = 1, 2, \ldots, f_l - 1 \tag{4}$$

$$(y_i^l + t_{lk}) - t_r^{Metro} - \omega_k \geqslant M(x_{r,il}^k - 1), \forall k \in K, r \in R, l \in L_k, i \in I_l \tag{5}$$

$$(y_i^l + t_{lk}) - t_r^{Metro} - \omega_k \leq \mu_k - M(x_{r,il}^k - 1), \forall k \in K, r \in R, l \in L_k, i \in I_l \tag{6}$$

$$t_r^{Metro} - (y_i^l + t_{lk}) - \omega_k \geqslant M(x_{il,r}^k - 1), \forall k \in K, r \in R, l \in L_k, i \in I_l \tag{7}$$

$$t_r^{Metro} - (y_i^l + t_{lk}) - \omega_k \leq \mu_k - M(x_{il,r}^k - 1), \forall k \in K, r \in R, l \in L_k, i \in I_l \tag{8}$$

$$(y_j^s + t_{sk}) - (y_i^l + t_{lk}) \geqslant \varepsilon_k + M(x_{il,js}^k - 1), \tag{9}$$
$$\forall k \in K, l \in L_k, i \in I_l, s \in L_k, j \in I_s \text{ and } l \neq s$$

$$(y_j^s + t_{sk}) - (y_i^l + t_{lk}) \leq \mu_k - M(x_{il,js}^k - 1), \tag{10}$$
$$\forall k \in K, l \in L_k, i \in I_l, s \in L_k, j \in I_s \text{ and } l \neq s$$

$$y_i^l \in \{0, 1, ..., T\}, \forall l \in L, i = 1, 2, ..., f_l - 1 \tag{11}$$

$$x_{r,il}^k, x_{il,r}^k \in \{0, 1\}, \forall k \in K, r \in R, l \in L_k, i \in I_l \tag{12}$$

$$x_{il,js}^k \in \{0, 1\}, \forall k \in K, l \in L_k, i \in I_l, s \in L_k, j \in I_s \tag{13}$$

where M is a large enough constant to ensure the inequalities (5–10) hold when their associated variable $x_{r,il}^k, x_{il,r}^k$ or $x_{il,js}^k$ is equal to 0.

Formula (1) represents the objective of maximizing the total number of simultaneous arrivals. Constrains (2) to (4) ensure the departure time of each trip is between 0 and the planning horizon T, i.e. any $y_l^i \in [0, T]$. For any line l, the first trip cannot depart later than the maximum headway H_l, the last trip cannot depart later than T, and each headway (i.e. the difference of the departure times between two consecutive trips on the same line) must lie within the given range $[h_l, H_l]$. Constrains (5) to (6) ensure $x_{r,il}^k = 1$ if it is a *train − to − bus synchronization arrival*. Constrains for the decision variables related to the existence of a synchronization arrival. Constrains (7) to (8) ensure $x_{il,r}^k = 1$, if it is a *bus − to − train synchronization arrival*. Constrains (9) to (10) ensure $x_{il,js}^k = 1$, if it is a *bus − to − bus synchronization arrival*. Formulae (11) to (13) present the constrains on the decision variables.

4   Particle Swarm Optimization for Maximal Synchronization Problem

Particle swarm optimization (PSO) is a population based stochastic optimization technique developed by Eberhart and Kennedy [13], inspired by social behavior of bird flocking or fish schooling. The potential solutions, called *particles*, fly through the problem space by following the current optimum particles. Each *particle* keeps track of its coordinates in the problem space. The PSO, at each time step, is to change the velocity of each particle toward its *pbest* and *gbest* locations. The *pbest* location is the best solution that the particle has achieved so far, whilst the *gbest* location is the best solution of the entire swarm. Based on this PSO technique, various approaches have been developed to solve real-world optimization problems [14, 15].

4.1   Representation of a Particle

To solve the maximal synchronization problem, a *particle* (i.e. solution) can be represented as in Fig. 2, where the location of the particle is decided by a d-dimensional coordinate ($d = \sum_{l=1}^{m} f_l$), and $y_{li}(l \in L, i \in I_l)$ denotes the location of the particle on one axis of the d-dimensional coordinate. The value of y_{li} is a real number and equals to the departure time of the ith trip on line l, which corresponds to the variable y_i^l in our proposed model. $\mu = \sum_{j=1}^{l-1} f_j + i$, $\mu \in \{1, 2, ..., d\}$ is a serial number, which denotes a position (coordinate axis or direction) of y_i^l in the particle.

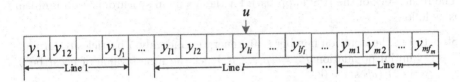

Fig. 2. Representation of a particle

4.2   Location and Velocity of a Particle

The location and velocity of a particle on each axis of the d-dimension coordinates are the essential elements in PSO [16].

For any particle i, at the current step (i.e. generation) t, we can define y_{iu}^t and v_{iu}^t as its location and velocity, respectively, on the uth coordinate axis at the generation t. The location y_{iu}^{t+1} and velocity v_{iu}^{t+1} at the next generation $t+1$ can be calculated by formulae (14) and (15) respectively.

$$v_{iu}^{t+1} = \omega * v_{iu}^t + \gamma_1 * c_1 * (y_{iu}^{pbest} - y_{iu}^t) + \gamma_2 * c_2 * (y_u^{gbest} - y_{iu}^t) \quad (14)$$

$$y_{iu}^{t+1} = y_{iu}^t + v_{iu}^{t+1} \quad (15)$$

where y_{iu}^{pbest} and y_u^{gbest} are the best locations of the particle i and the entire swarm, that have been achieved up to the tth generation on the uth coordinate axis, respectively; ω is the inertia weight that provides a balance between global and local exploration and exploitation; c_1 and c_2 weighting the stochastic acceleration terms that pull each particle toward *pbest* and *gbest* positions; γ_1 and γ_2 are random numbers between 0 and 1.

It should be noticed that there is a constrained search space in the PSO for the maximal synchronization problem. A particle is feasible if its location satisfies the constraints (2)(3)(4); infeasible otherwise.

4.3   Enhancement of PSO by Using Backup Library

To avoid the PSO algorithm getting into early local convergence, an improved PSO approach for the maximal synchronization problem (IPSO for short) is developed, in which an elite strategy is designed using backup library. The basic idea is to employ a backup library to store the *pbest* locations of all the elite particles, while an elite particle is defined as the particle with *pbest* lying at the top percentile (e.g. 10 %). Once the *gbest* cannot be improved for certain iterations, a particle is to be selected randomly from the backup library using a standard roulette wheel method. The selected elite particle will play the role of the particle with *gbest* at the next generation.

4.4 Framework of the Maximal Synchronization Approach Based on PSO

The framework of the IPSO approach for the maximal synchronization problem is as follows.

Step 1: Let the iteration number $t=0$, generate randomly n particles to form an initial population $P^t = \{p_1^t, ..., p_n^t\}$, let the fitness value of *gbest* be 0, i.e. $F(gbest) = 0$;

Step 2: Calculate the fitness value $F(p_i^t)$ of each particle $p_i^t \in P^t$ using Formula (1), let $P_{best}^t = \{pbest_1^t, ..., pbest_n^t\}$, $gbest^t = max\{pbest_i^t | i = 1, ..., n\}$. If $F(gbest^t) > F(gbest)$, then let $gbest = gbest^t$. If the *gbest* cannot be improved for certain iterations, go to Step 3; otherwise go to Step 4;

Step 3: Use standard roulette wheel method to select a particle from the top 10 % of P_{best}^t to form a new $gbest^t$;

Step 4: Update the location and velocity of each particle according to Formulae (14) (15) based on P_{best}^t and $gbest^t$, while keeping the particle feasible;

Step 5: If the termination condition is satisfied, then stop; otherwise $t = t + 1$ and go to step 2.

5 Computational Results

The PSO, as an evolutionary computing approach, is still of the heuristic family. The major concern about using heuristics is the quality of the produced solution. In this study, to verify the efficiency of our proposed PSO approach, experiments on the 11 benchmark instances presented in [12] were first carried out, before a case study was implemented.

5.1 Experiments on Algorithm Verification

The proposed IPSO approach and a PSO (without backup library) for the maximal synchronization problem has been implemented using C++. The values of the IPSO and PSO parameters are both set as follows: the population size is 40, $\omega = 0.9$, $c_1 = c_2 = 0.5$, $\gamma_1 = \gamma_2 = 1$, the maximum generation is 500, and the backup library in IPSO is employed after the *gbest* cannot be improved for 30 iterations.

A Genetic Algorithm (GA) for the maximal synchronization problem has also been developed for comparison purpose, in which the representation of a chromosome is defined as same as the representation of a particle shown in Fig. 2 and the one-point crossover and multi-point mutation operations of GA are employed. Based on experiences, the values of the GA parameters are set as follows: the population size is 100, the values of crossover rate and mutation rate are set as 0.75 and 0.05 respectively.

The benchmark experimental results by the heuristic approach reported in [12] and the GA, PSO are shown in Fig. 3 in comparison with the IPSO results.

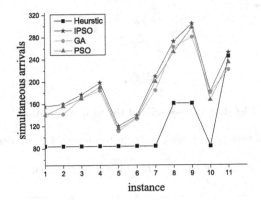

Fig. 3. Experimental results of three algorithms

It can be seen from Fig. 3 that the GA, PSO and IPSO approaches perform considerably better than the heuristic algorithm for the first ten instances. For the last instance, the solutions produced by the heuristic, GA, PSO and IPSO are 245, 221, 234 and 252 respectively. The average relative percentage deviation of the GA, PSO and IPSO solutions over the heuristic solutions are 73.8 %, 77.5 % and 87 % respectively.

5.2 A Case Study

Demonstrated the efficiency, the proposed IPSO approach was applied to a real-world instance derived from the metro line No. 2 in the city of Wuhan, China. The Guanggu Square (GS) station, which is one of the stations with largest passenger flow volumes. There are about 50 lines passing through the 5 transfer points (P1-P5) round the GS metro station. 24 of the 50 lines are selected into our test problem. According to whether they pass through the same transfer points, the 24 lines are classified into 7 groups, labeled as ① − ⑦ in Fig. 4, where only one direction (inbound or outbound) of each line is considered and the arrows denote the directions.

Considering the morning peak between 6:40am-8:30am, the planning horizon $T = 110$ (minutes) and the headway of the metro line is 4 min. The frequency f_l, minimum headway h_l, maximum headway H_l of any line l in a group are given in Table 1, where the RT (1st to 2nd) denotes the running time from the

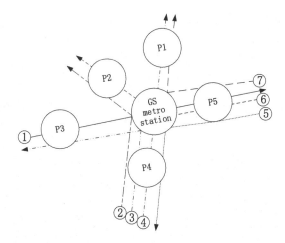

Fig. 4. Bus lines related to the metro station

Table 1. Headways and running times of bus lines by group and frequency

Group	Point		Run time	f_l	h_l	H_l	Line (RT, terminal to 1st)				
#	1st	2nd	(1^{st}to2^{nd})								
①	P3	P5	3	8	8	15	1(31)				
②	P4	P2	2	12	5	8	2(13)	3(28)			
③	P4	P3	3	9	7	10	4(12)	5(21)			
④	P4	P1	2	8	8	12	6(21)	7(18)	8(18)		
⑤	P5	P4	2	5	12	18	9(42)	10(20)			
⑥	P5	P2	2	15	3	6	11(21)	12(28)	13(8)	14(15)	15(22)
⑥	P5	P2	2	6	8	15	16(15)	17(10)			
⑦	P5	P1	2	9	7	10	18(52)	19(28)	20(62)		
⑦	P5	P1	2	5	10	20	21(54)	22(20)	23(41)	24(68)	

RT (1st to the 2nd transfer points, the RT (terminal to 1st) denotes the running time from the terminal of the line to the 1st transfer point.

The walking times between the GS metro station and the transfer point k and the synchronization time windows at transfer points are listed in Table 2.

The parameters in the IPSO approach are as follow: the population size is 120, $\omega = 1.1$, $c_1 = c_2 = 2$, $\gamma_1 = \gamma_2 = 1$, the maximum generation is 500, and the backup library is employed after the gbest cannot be improved for 30 iterations. The PSO (without backup library) whose values of the parameters are same as the IPSO is also applied. The computational results at each iteration are listed in Fig. 5 in comparison with results of GA whose parameters are same as the GA used in Sect. 5.1.

Table 2. Walking times and synchronization time windows at transfer points

	P1	P2	P3	P4	P5
ω_k	7	5	4	5	8
ε_k	1	1	1	1	1
μ_k	3	3	3	3	3

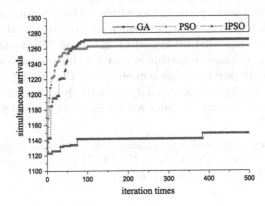

Fig. 5. Convergence trend of the algorithms

Table 3. Part of the timetables produced by the IPSO

Line	Departure time											
1	6:40	6:55	7:07	7:15	7:30	7:45	7:54	8:09				
2	6:40	6:48	6:56	7:04	7:09	7:14	7:19	7:26	7:31	7:39	7:44	7:52
3	6:46	6:51	6:59	7:07	7:15	7:23	7:31	7:36	7:44	7:52	7:57	8:02
4	6:40	6:50	7:00	7:07	7:14	7:21	7:31	7:41	7:48			
5	6:42	6:49	6:50	7:06	7:16	7:26	7:34	7:41	7:48			
6	6:40	6:52	7:04	7:16	7:24	7:32	7:40	7:48				
7	6:52	7:02	7:10	7:18	7:29	7:37	7:45	7:53				
...	...											

A convergence trend can be clearly seen from Fig. 5 for the IPSO, PSO and GA. Based on experiments, the PSO and IPSO often converges at about the 100th iteration and the IPSO preforms better among the three algorithms. The timetables of all the lines produced by the IPSO approach are displayed partly in Table 3, which contain 1271 simultaneous arrivals and all the constraints are satisfied.

6 Conclusions

Different from based on a single transit mode, this paper has presented a study on the maximal synchronization problem between the two most popular urban transit modes: bus and metro. A mathematical model of the maximal synchronization problem of feeder buses to a metro station has been built, in which three types of synchronization time windows and the transfer walking times between a metro station and a transfer point are considered. The objective is to create maximal synchronization arrivals to achieve efficient transfer. Based on the model, a brand-new approach has been developed by using the PSO technique, in which an elite strategy is devised. Experiments on benchmark instances and a case study on a real-world problem have demonstrated the feasibility and efficiency of the approach. The further research may consider the maximal synchronization amongst the metro lines and bus lines within the same service corridor.

Acknowledgements. The work was supported by the Major Program of National Social Science Foundation of China (Grant No. 13&ZD175) and National Natural Science Foundation of China (Grant No. 71171087).

References

1. Yang, X., Chen, A., Li, X., Ning, B., Tang, T.: An energy-efficient scheduling approach to improve the utilization of regenerative energy for metro systems. Transp. Res. Part C **57**, 13–29 (2015)
2. Shen, Y.D., Xu, J., Zeng, Z.Y.: Public transit planning and scheduling based on AVL data in China. Int. Trans. Oper. Res. **1**, 1–23 (2015)
3. Guo, Z., Wilson, N.H.M.: Assessing the cost of transfer inconvenience in public transport systems: a case study of the London Underground. Transp. Res. Part A **45**(2), 91–104 (2011)
4. Poorjafari, V., Yue, W.L.: Synchronisation of public transport services: comparison of Methods. In: Preceedings of the 10th International Conference of Eastern Asia Society for Transportation Studies. EASTS Press, Taiwan (2013)
5. Shrivastava, P., Dhingra, S.L.: Development of coordinated schedules using genetic algorithms. J. Transp. Eng. **128**(1), 89–96 (2002)
6. Chang, S.K.J., Hsu, C.L.: Modeling passenger waiting time for intermodal transit stations. Transp. Res. Rec. **1753**(9), 69–75 (2007)
7. Li, Z.C., William, H.K., Wong, S.C., Sumalee, A.: An activity-based approach for scheduling multimodal transit services. Transportation **37**(5), 751–774 (2010)
8. Kim, M.E., Schonfeld, P.: Integration of conventional and flexible bus services with timed transfers. Transp. Res. Part B **68**, 76–97 (2014)
9. Ceder, A., Golany, B., Tal, O.: Creating bus timetables with maximal synchronization. Transp. Res. Part A **35**(10), 913–928 (2001)
10. Ibarra-Rojas, O.J., Rios-Solis, R.S.: Synchronization of bus timetablings. Transp. Res. B **46**(5), 599–614 (2012)
11. Nesheli, M.M., Ceder, A.: Optimal combinations of selected tactics for public-transport transfer synchronization. Transp. Res. Part C **48**, 491–504 (2014)
12. Eranki, A.: A model to create bus timetables to attain maximum synchronization considering waiting times at transfer stops. Masters thesis, Department of Industrial and Management Systems Engineering, University of South Florida (2004)

13. Eberhart, R.C., Kennedy, J.: A new optimizer using particle swarm theory. In: Proceedings of the Sixth International Symposium on Micromachine and Human Science, pp. 39–43. IEEE Press, Nagoya (1995)
14. Pradeep, K., Asheesh, K.S., Anurag, K.S.: A novel optimal capacitor placement algorithm using Nelder-Mead PSO. Int. J. Bio-Inspired Comput. **6**(4), 290–302 (2014)
15. Gopi, R., Durbadal, M., Rajib, K., Sakti, P.G.: Optimal design of non-uniform circular antenna arrays using PSO with wavelet mutation. Int. J. Bio-Inspired Comput. **6**(4), 424–433 (2014)
16. Eberhart, R.C., Shi, Y.H.: Particle swarm optimization: developments, applications and resources. In: Proceedings of IEEE International Conference on Evolutionary Computation, pp. 81–86. IEEE Press, Seoul (2001)

A Fast Differential Evolution for Constrained Optimization Problems in Engineering Design

Aili Shen and Jinlong Li[✉]

School of Computer Science and Technology,
University of Science and Technology of China, Hefei 230027, China
jlli@ustc.edu.cn

Abstract. A fast differential evolution (FDE) approach to solve several constrained engineering design optimization problems is proposed. In this approach, a new mutation strategy "DE/current-to-*pp*best/bin" is proposed to get a balance between exploration and exploitation of the population. What's more, a ranking based selection mechanism selects the promising individuals from the combination of parents and offspring to update the population. Experimental results on 5 instances extracted from engineering design show that FDE can acquire quite competitive performance. FDE is comparable to other state-of-the-art approaches in terms of solution quality. As for convergence speed, FDE is more fast, or at least comparable to, other state-of-the-art approaches. When the number of function evaluation is limited or the cost of function evaluation is expensive, FDE is a good choice.

Keywords: Differential evolution · Constrained optimization problems · Engineering design

1 Introduction

In real world engineering applications, lots of optimization problems are subject to various kinds of constraints. Without of loss generality, the minimization of constrained optimization problems (COPs) is considered in this paper. The COPs can be formulated as follows:

$$\min \ f(\boldsymbol{x}) \quad \boldsymbol{x} = (x_1, \ldots, x_n) \in S, \tag{1}$$

S is the decision space bounded by lower and upper parametric constraints:

$$L_i \leq x_i \leq U_i, 1 \leq i \leq n. \tag{2}$$

where n is the number of decision variables. The objective function $f(\boldsymbol{x})$ is subject to numbers of inequality constraints and equality constraints:

$$g_j(\boldsymbol{x}) \leq 0, j = 1, \ldots, q \tag{3}$$

$$h_j(\boldsymbol{x}) = 0, j = q + 1, \ldots, m. \tag{4}$$

© Springer-Verlag Berlin Heidelberg 2015
M. Gong et al. (Eds.): BIC-TA 2015, CCIS 562, pp. 362–377, 2015.
DOI: 10.1007/978-3-662-49014-3_33

There are q inequality constraints and $m - q$ equality constraints. The region that meets the above constraints is defined as feasible region $F \subseteq S$.

The degree of constraint violation is often computed as

$$G(\boldsymbol{x}) = \sum_{j=1}^{m} G_j(\boldsymbol{x}) \tag{5}$$

where $G_j(\boldsymbol{x})$ is the degree of constraint violation of individual $\boldsymbol{x}$ at the jth constraint. The degree of constraint violation at the jth constraint is defined as.

$$G_j(\boldsymbol{x}) = \begin{cases} \max\{0, g_j(\boldsymbol{x})\}, 1 \le j \le q, \\ \max\{0, |h_j(\boldsymbol{x})| - \epsilon\}, q + 1 \le j \le m. \end{cases} \tag{6}$$

Evolutionary algorithms (EAs) can tackle various kinds of COPs by incorporating a constraint handling mechanism. In the literature, different kinds of EAs are used as the search engine to solve various kinds of optimization problems, such as genetic algorithm (GA), particle swarm optimization (PSO) and differential evolution (DE).

In this paper, we propose a fast DE, named FDE. A new mutation strategy "DE/current-to-ppbest/bin", which is a generalization of mutation strategy "DE/current-to-$p$best/bin", is proposed to get a balance between exploration and exploitation of the population. A sorting based selection mechanism selects the promising individuals from the combination of parents and offspring to update the population. Experimental results on 5 instances extracted from engineering design show that FDE can acquire quite competitive performance. FDE is comparable to other state-of-the-art approaches in terms of solution quality on 5 real world benchmarks. As for convergence speed on 5 real world applications, FDE is better than, or at least comparable to, other state-of-the-art approaches.

The remainder of this paper is organized as follows. Section 2 briefly reviews the related work of solving constrained optimization problems via EAs. Section 3 presents our proposed approach in detail. Section 4 shows the experimental results on 5 COPs in engineering design. Comparisons with some state-of-the-art approaches are presented in Sect. 5. Section 6 discusses the effectiveness of some mechanisms proposed in this paper. In Sect. 7 a conclusion of this paper and a few remarks are given.

2   Related Work

Penalty function has received lots of attention from the community of constrained optimization evolutionary algorithms. The main motivation of penalty function is to punish infeasible individuals in order to direct the population into the feasible space. However, the penalty term is often instance dependent, the setting of penalty value is a hard problem itself. To avoid the trivial setting of penalty term, Deb [5] proposed a criterion for pair wise comparison: (1) any feasible individual is superior to any infeasible individual; (2) among two feasible individuals, the one having smaller objective value is superior; (3) among two infeasible individuals, the one having smaller constraint violation value is preferred. Deb's criterion rule can avoid using the penalty term. However, it always prefers feasible individuals over infeasible individuals. The population may get stuck in local optima.

Without using of penalty value, Runarsson and Yao [14] proposed a stochastic ranking method, shortly called SR. SR can get a balance of exploration and exploitation of the population by introducing a probability parameter p_f. When two adjacent individuals are compared, the following rules are used: (1) if both two individuals are feasible, the one having smaller objective value is preferred; (2) otherwise, a uniformly generated value is compared with the probability parameter p_f, if the uniformly generated value is smaller than p_f, then the one having a smaller objective value is superior; otherwise, the one having a smaller constraint violation value is preferred. SR can achieve competitive results on 13 well-known benchmarks. Later Li et al. [10] proposed a new constraint handling mechanism for evolutionary strategy named RPCH, which shows competitive performance on 24 benchmark instances.

There are also some approaches solving COPs using multiobjective techniques. The constrained optimization problems are firstly converted into unconstrained optimization problems. Then techniques used in multiobjective optimization can be applied to solve the converted unconstrained optimization problem. Cai and Wang [17–19] proposed a multiobjective optimization based evolutionary algorithm for constrained optimization, which acquired competitive performance on 24 well-known benchmark instances.

Takahama and Sakai [16] proposed the ε constrained differential evolution, εDEg, which combines gradient-based mutation and feasible elites. In εDEg, the target individual and trial individual are compared according to the ε level comparison, which is defined by a lexicographic order. In lexicographic order, the degree of constraint violation precedes minimizing the objective value. To deal with COPs with many equality constraints, the ε infeasible individual is repaired by using the gradient information of constraint with a probability. With the differential evolution as the search engine, their approach can acquire quite competitive performance on 24 benchmark instances. Inspired by the gradient based mutation, Bu et al. [3] proposed a species-based repair strategy (SRS) to select representative infeasible individuals instead of randomly selecting infeasible individuals to execute gradient based mutation. By applying SRS to εDEag, approach SRS-εDEag was proposed. Experimental results show that SRS-εDEag outperforms εDEag in most benchmarks.

To solve COPs emerged from engineering design field, a lot of algorithms were proposed. Youyun Ao and Hongqin Chi [2] proposed an adaptive DE (ADE) to solve several COPs extracted from engineering design field. A novel mutation operator, which can generate multiple trial vectors, is employed in ADE to improve the probability of generating better offspring; A new adaptive mechanism is used to control crossover rate parameter. Min Zhang et al. [21] proposed a dynamic stochastic selection mechanism within the framework of multimember

DE, DSS-MDE. In DSS-MDE, one parent can generate multiple offspring, and the dynamic stochastic selection mechanism is applied to choose the best individual from the multiple offspring and parent. DSS-MDE achieved quite competitive performance on both test instances and engineering design problems. Ray and Liew [13] proposed a society and civilization model based algorithm to solve engineering design problems. Hedar and Fukushima [7] proposed a simulated annealing based method, which is called Filter Simulated Annealing (FSA). Coello [4] proposed a GA based technique that uses co-evolution to adjust the penalty coefficients automatically. And it can work effectively on several test problems with a comparatively large FES. Montes et al. [11] proposed a modified version of DE. In this approach, each parent is allowed to generate more than one offspring to increase the probability of generating a better offspring. Akhtar [1] solved single objective constrained optimization problems by using a socio-behavioral simulation model.

3   Proposed Approach

Differential evolution (DE) is a population based evolutionary algorithm, which was first proposed by Storn and Price [15] in 1995. Due to its simplicity and efficiency, a lot of DE based algorithms have been developed to solve kinds of COPs. DE starts with an initial population consisting of λ individuals, which is randomly generated within the whole search space. Then three operators of DE: mutation, crossover and selection are used in succession to update the population. The three operators are executed in a loop until a stopping criterion is reached. The three operators used in our DE will be explained in detail after the framework of our proposed approach is described.

3.1   Framework of FDE

The framework of FDE is shown in Algorithm 1. It works as follows. Initially, λ individuals are randomly generated within the decision space, which forms the initial population P. Subsequently, λ individuals generate λ offspring O by using the "DE/current-to-ppbest/1" mutation strategy and binomial crossover. After evaluation of offspring O, the objective value and degree of constraint violation of parent individuals P and that of offspring individuals O are combined. Then the ranking based selection model is applied to the combined population C, the top λ individuals in C are selected to replace P, so the population P can evolve to optima or near optima. This process is repeated until current FES exceeds the maximum FES. Mutation strategy "DE/current-to-ppbest/1", the crossover operator and the ranking based selection model will be explained in detail in following section.

3.2   Mutation Operator

In mutation operation, k number of difference vectors are scaled by a scaling factor F. Then the k scaled difference vectors are added to the base vector, which

---

Algorithm 1. Framework of FDE

Input: λ: the size of population

     Max_FES: maximum of FES.

Output: x^*:the best solution found in the evolution process and its

     corresponding optimum value $f(x^*)$

1 randomly generate an initial population (P) size of λ;

2 evaluate the objective value and the degree of constraint violation of the initial population P;

3 $FES = \lambda$;

4 **while** $FES \leq Max\_FES$ **do**

5   generate λ offspring (O) by using the mutation and crossover operation, which will be explained in the following section;

6   evaluate the objective value and the degree of constraint violation of O;

7     $FES = FES + \lambda$;

8   combine the objective value and degree of constraint violation of P and O, which forms C;

9   execute ranking based selection model and select the top λ individuals from C to replace P;

10 **end**

---

forms the mutant vector. In this paper, the number of difference vector k is 2. Jingqiao Zhang and Arthur C. Sanderson [20] proposed a new mutation strategy "DE/current-to-$p$best/1" to solve unconstrained optimization problems, which can be formed as follows.

$$v_i = x_i + F \times (x_{best}^p - x_i) + F \times (x_{r1} - x_{r2}) \tag{7}$$

where r_1, r_2 are mutually different integers randomly selected from $[1, NP]$, satisfying $r_1 \neq r_2 \neq i$. v_i is the generated mutant vector, x_i is the ith individuals of all individuals participated in DE operation, and x_{best}^p is one of top p individuals in current population, and F is a scaling factor ranging from $(0, 1]$. In the "DE/current-to-$p$best/1" mutation strategy, the top p best individuals are selected randomly with the same probability. However, to make the approach converge to optima fast, the better individuals among the top p individuals are more likely to be selected to direct the population converge to optima. Therefore, we propose a generalized "DE/current-to-$p$best/1", which is "DE/current-to-ppbest/1".

$$v_i = x_i + F \times (x_{best}^{pp} - x_i) + F \times (x_{r1} - x_{r2}) \tag{8}$$

The first p refers to the top p individuals of the population, the second p refers to different probabilities of being selected from the top p. When the first p is 1, then mutation "DE/current-to-$p$best/1" and "DE/current-to-ppbest/1" becomes "DE/current-to-best/1". By using "DE/current-to-ppbest/1" mutation strategy, population can get a balance between exploration and exploitation. The best individual in the whole population has the biggest probability to be selected as the direct vector. The second best individual in the whole population has the second biggest probability to be selected. The probability of top p individuals are selected as direction vector can be computed as:

$$P_{DE/current-to-ppbest/1} = \frac{p+1-i}{\sum_{j=1}^{p} j} \quad 1 \le i \le n, \quad i \in Z. \tag{9}$$

While the probability of top p individuals in the "DE/current-to-$p$best/1" mutation strategy can be computed as:

$$P_{DE/current-to-pbest/1} = \frac{1}{p} \tag{10}$$

Therefore, "DE/current-to-$p$best/1" is a specialization of "DE/current-to-ppbest/1" that all top p individuals have the same probability to be selected as best individual.

Some components in mutant vector v_i may violate the boundary constraints after mutation. Then the violated elements in the individuals are repaired by reflecting the component back from the violated boundary. This can be formed as follows:

$$v_{i,j} = \begin{cases} 2L_j - v_{i,j} & v_{i,j} < L_j, \\ 2U_j - v_{i,j} & v_{i,j} > U_j, \\ v_{i,j} & \text{otherwise.} \end{cases} \tag{11}$$

3.3   Crossover Operator

There are two mostly used crossover operator used in DE: binomial crossover and exponential crossover. In this paper, only binomial crossover is used. So only the binomial crossover is discussed in this paper. Binomial crossover can be formed as:

$$v_{i,j} = \begin{cases} v_{i,j} & \text{if } rand \le CR \ \text{ or } \ j = j_{rand} \\ x_{i,j} & \text{otherwise.} \end{cases} \tag{12}$$

where $rand$ is a uniformly distributed value in the interval $[0, 1)$, CR is the rate of crossover. j_{rand} is an integer number randomly chosen within the range $[1, n]$. The condition of $j = j_{rand}$ is to guarantee that there is at least one component inherited from the mutant vector in the trial vector.

3.4   Selection Operator

In the traditional DE selection operation, the target vector and trial vector are compared against each other after evaluation. The one having better objective value will survive into next generation.

$$v_i = \begin{cases} v_i & \text{if } f(v_i) \le f(x_i) \\ x_i & \text{otherwise.} \end{cases} \tag{13}$$

Algorithm 2. Ranking based selection model

Input: C: the 2λ individuals of C
$\qquad$ $fitC$: the objective value of C
$\qquad$ GC: the degree of constraint violation of C
Output: $Q^{'}$:the best λ individuals from C
$\qquad$ $fitQ^{'}$: the objective value of $Q^{'}$
$\qquad$ $GQ^{'}$: the degree of constraint violation of $Q^{'}$

1 $size = 2\lambda$;
2 **for** $i = 1 : size$ **do**
3 $\quad$ $ranked[i] = 0$;
4 $\quad$ **for** $j = 1 : size$ **do**
5 $\quad\quad$ **if** $GC_i < GC_j$ **then**
6 $\quad\quad\quad$ $ranked[i] = ranked[i] + 1$;
7 $\quad\quad$ **end**
8 $\quad\quad$ **else if** $GC_i == GC_j$ **then**
9 $\quad\quad\quad$ **if** $fitC_i \leq fitC_j$ **then**
10 $\quad\quad\quad\quad$ $ranked[i] = ranked[i] + 1$;
11 $\quad\quad\quad$ **end**
12 $\quad\quad$ **end**
13 $\quad$ **end**
14 $\quad$ sort the values of ranked in descending order;
15 $\quad$ the first λ individuals are selected as $Q^{'}$;
16 **end**

However, the pairwise selection is not adopted in this paper. We develop a ranking based selection model, which select the better individuals from the combination of λ parents and λ offspring.

Algorithm 2 describes the ranking based selection model. Initially, all the ranked value of 2λ individuals in C are set to zero. Then every individual in C are compared with the other $2\lambda - 1$ individuals using Deb's feasibility rule. After the inner loop completes, the ith individual can get its ranked value. The ranked value means that this individual is superior to the number of individuals in C according to Deb's feasibility rule. The bigger the ranked value, the more superior of this individual to other individuals. All the individuals in C can get their corresponding ranked values after the outer loop finishes. Then the ranked value are sorted in descending order, the first λ better individuals are selected as $Q^{'}$. In this way, the ranking based selection model can update the population.

4   Experimental Setup

In this section, instances to demonstrate the capacity of FDE are introduced first, then the parameter settings are given, and the general performance of FDE and the convergence are presented.

4.1   Benchmark Instances

To demonstrate the capacity of FDE, 5 benchmark instances from real world are employed. They are welded beam design, spring design, speed reducer design, three-bar truss design, and himmelblaus nonlinear optimization problem, respectively. The details of these test instances are described in Table 1, where n is the number of decision variables, LI is the number of linear inequality constraints, NI is the number of nonlinear inequality constraints, LE is the number of linear equality constraints, NE is the number of nonlinear equality constraints, and $f(x^*)$ is the objective function value of the best known solution.

Table 1. Details of 5 test instances

Prob.	n	Type of function	LI	NI	LE	NE	$f(x^*)$
Welded beam design	4	Cubic	2	5	0	0	2.380956580
Spring design	3	Polynomial	1	3	0	0	0.0126652328
Speed reducer design	7	Polynomial	0	11	0	0	2994.47106615
Three-bar truss design	2	Linear	0	3	0	0	263.89584338
Himmelblau's nonlinear optimization	5	Quadratic	0	6	0	0	−31025.56024

4.2   Parameter Settings

There are five parameters in FDE: the population size (λ), the scaling factor (F), the crossover factor (CR), and the number of individuals in the whole population denoted as best individuals (p). The number of population λ are usually given in accordance with the number of decision variables in COPs. J. Lampinen and R. Storn [9], Gmperle [6] suggested $\lambda \in [3n, 10n]$. The value of F usually ranges from 0 to 1. Values of F within the range of $[0, 1]$ can achieve good performance as reported in [6, 9]. CR is also chosen from the interval $[0, 1]$. However, high values as 0.9 or 1.0 can achieve good results for most benchmark instances. High value of CR means that more components of mutant vector are adopted, thus more new information can get incorporated into the population. p is chosen from the interval $[1, NP]$. A small p can improve the convergence speed, while the population may get stuck to local optima due to a lack of diversity in top p best individuals. A big p can improve the diversity of top p best individuals, while the exploitation of top p best individuals can be reduced. Thus the convergence speed may be slowed down. To make a tradeoff between exploration and exploitation, a suitable value of p need to be determined. Actual parameter values used in this paper are set as follows: λ is set as 50, $F = 0.7$, $CR = 0.9$, and $p = 5$.

4.3   General Performance of FDE

The optimal value, best, median, mean, worst and FES needed by FDE are listed in Table 2. It can be clearly seen that FDE can achieve the optima over 30 runs under 6,000 FES for three-bar truss design problem, FDE can achieve the optima over 30 runs under 14,500 FES for welded beam design and himmelblaus nonlinear optimization problem, FDE can achieve the optima over 30 runs under 16,000 FES for speed reducer problem. However, for the spring design problem, the best, median achieved by FDE can reach optima under 40,000 FES, the mean and worst value can't reach optima under 40,000 FES. This may be because FDE need more FES to solve spring design problem.

Table 2. Results on 5 real world application design problems 30 runs

Instance	Optimal	Best	Mean	Worst	Std	FES
Welded beam	2.380956580	**2.380956580**	**2.380956580**	**2.380956580**	0	14,392
Spring	0.0126652328	**0.0126652328**	0.0126652430	0.0126653838	2.94e-08	38,837
Speed reducer	2994.47106615	**2994.47106615**	**2994.47106615**	**2994.47106615**	1.85e-12	15,870
Three-bar truss	263.89584338	**263.89584338**	**263.89584338**	**263.89584338**	0	5,587
Himmelblau's	−31025.56024	**−31025.56024**	**−31025.56024**	**−31025.56024**	1.35e-12	13,252

[a] The results achieved by FDE reaching the optima are highlighted in boldface.

4.4   Convergence Graph

The convergence graph of these 5 well studied application design problems is plotted in Fig. 1. From Fig. 1, it can be clearly seen that FDE can converge to the optimal in 1.0×10^4 FES.

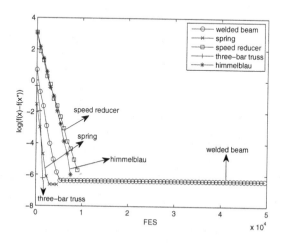

Fig. 1. Convergence graph for welded beam design, spring design, speed reducer design, three-bar truss design and himmelblau's problem.

5 Comparisons with Some Other State-of-the-art Approaches

In this section, comparisons with other approaches on welded beam design, spring design, speed reducer design, three-bar truss design, and himmelblaus nonlinear optimization problem are presented. The results of other approaches are taken directly from their original papers respectively. 30 independent runs are executed for each instance in this paper, and the best, median, mean, worst and standard deviation of values obtained by different approaches are presented. The best solutions achieved by different algorithms are also presented. Then the experimental results on welded beam design, spring design, speed reducer design, three-bar truss design, and himmelblaus nonlinear optimization problem are presented in Tables 3, 4, 5, 6 and 7.

5.1 Comparison with Other Algorithms on Welded Beam Design

For welded beam design problem, the experimental results are provided with Table 3. According to Table 3, FDE is competitive with DSS-MDE [21] in terms of the best, median, mean and worst value achieved, and FDE has a smaller standard deviation and a smaller FES. The best, median value achieved by FDE is competitive with ADE [2], however, ADE [2] can't achieve the best solution for all runs, even with a larger FES. And the best, median, mean and worst achieved by FDE are much better than those obtained by Ray and Liew [13], FSA [7] and Deb [5], even FDE execute with a much smaller FES. The solution value obtained by Deb [5] is not provided in their original paper, so we don't list their corresponding value. From the comparisons, it is obvious that FDE is superior to ADE [2], Ray and Liew [13], FSA [7] and Deb [5], and is competitive with DSS-MDE [21]. When a smaller FES is demanded, FDE can achieve better results than that achieved by DSS-MDE [21].

Table 3. Comparison with other algorithms on welded beam design over 30 runs

Algorithms	Best	Median	Mean	Worst	Std	FES
ADE [2]	**2.380956580**	**2.380956580**	2.380956585	2.3809708	2.35e-08	75,000
DSS-MDE [21]	**2.38095658**	**2.38095658**	**2.38095658**	**2.38095658**	3.19e-10	24,000
Ray and Liew [13]	2.3854347	3.2551371	3.0025883	6.3996785	0.959078	33,095
FSA [7]	2.381065	NA	2.404166	2.488967	NA	56,243
Deb [5]	2.38119	2.39289	NA	2.64583	NA	40,080
FDE	**2.380956580**	**2.380956580**	**2.380956580**	**2.380956580**	0	**14,392**

[a] NA denotes that the results are not available from their corresponding papers.
[b] The best results among all the algorithms are highlighted in boldface.

5.2 Comparison with Other Algorithms on Spring Design

For spring design problem, the experimental results are provided with Table 4. According to Table 4, FDE, ADE [2] and DSS-MDE [21] can find out the best value when compared with respect to Ray and Liew [13], FSA [7] and Coello [4]. The median value obtained by FDE is the best value and better than those obtained by other methods. Although FDE is worse than FSA [7] in terms of the mean, worst and standard deviation, it is better than FSA [7] in terms of the best and median value. What's more, the mean, worst and standard deviation obtained by FDE is better than those obtained by ADE [2], DSS-MDE [21], Ray and Liew [13] and Coello [4].

Table 4. Comparison with other algorithms on spring design over 30 runs

Algorithms	Best	Median	Mean	Worst	Std	FES
ADE [2]	**0.0126652328**	0.0126652458	0.0129336018	0.02064372078	1.46e-03	60,000
DSS-MDE [21]	**0.012665233**	0.012665304	0.012669366	0.012738262	1.25e-05	**24,000**
Ray and Liew [13]	0.01266924934	0.012922669	0.012922669	0.016717272	5.92e-04	25,167
FSA [7]	0.012665285	NA	0.012665299	**0.012665338**	**2.2e-08**	49,531
Coello [4]	0.01270478	0.01275576	0.01276920	0.01282208	NA	900,000
FDE	**0.0126652328**	**0.0126652328**	**0.0126652430**	0.0126653838	2.94e-08	38,837

[a] NA denotes that the results are not available from their corresponding papers.
[b] The best results among all the algorithms are highlighted in boldface.

5.3 Comparison with Other Algorithms on Speed Reducer Design

For speed reducer design problem, the experimental results are provided with Table 5. According to Table 5, the results obtained by FDE, ADE [2] and DSS-MDE [21] are much better than those obtained by Ray and Liew [13], Montes et al. [11], Akhtar et al. [1]. FDE is competitive with ADE [2] and DSS-MDE [21] in terms of the solution quality with different FES. From Table 5, it is clear that our approach need much less FES to achieve the optima. In other words, when FES is limited or the cost of function evaluation is expensive, FDE is a good choice to solve the speed reducer design problem.

Table 5. Comparison with other algorithms on speed reducer design over 30 runs

Algorithms	Best	Median	Mean	Worst	Std	FES
ADE [2]	**2994.4710662**	2994.4710662	2994.4710662	2994.4710662	1.85e-12	120,000
DSS-MDE [21]	**2994.471066**	2994.471066	2994.471066	2994.471066	3.58e-12	30,000
Ray and Liew [13]	2994.744241	3001.758264	3001.758264	3009.964736	4.0091423	54,456
Montes [11]	2996.356689	NA	2996.367220	NA	8.2e-03	24,000
Akhtar [1]	3008.08	NA	3012.12	3028	NA	19,154
FDE	**2994.47106615**	**2994.47106615**	**2994.47106615**	**2994.47106615**	**1.85e-12**	**15,870**

[a] NA denotes that the results are not available from their corresponding papers.
[b] The best results among all the algorithms are highlighted in boldface.

5.4   Comparison with Other Algorithms on Three-Bar Truss Design

For three-bar truss design problem, the experimental results are provided with Table 6. According to Table 6, the solution quality achieved by ADE [2], DSS-MDE [21] and FDE is much better than that achieved by Ray and Liew [13]. The best, median value achieved by DSS-MDE [21] is competitive with those achieved by ADE [2] and FDE, but mean and worst value acquired by DSS-MDE [21] is worse than that achieved by ADE [2] and FDE. FDE is competitive with ADE [2] in terms of solution quality. However, FDE need much less number of FES to reach optima than that need by ADE [2].

Table 6. Comparison with other algorithms on three-bar truss design over 30 runs

Algorithms	Best	Median	Mean	Worst	Std	FES
ADE [2]	**263.89584338**	**263.89584338**	**263.89584338**	**263.89584338**	4.72e-014	45,000
DSS-MDE [21]	**263.8958434**	**263.8958434**	263.8958436	263.8958498	9.72e-07	15,000
Ray and Liew [13]	263.8958466	263.8989	263.9033	263.96975	1.26e-02	17,610
FDE	**263.89584338**	**263.89584338**	**263.89584338**	**263.89584338**	0	**5,587**

a The best results among all the algorithms are highlighted in boldface.

5.5   Comparison with Other Algorithms on Himmelblaus Nonlinear Optimization Problem

For himmelblaus nonlinear optimization problem, the experimental results are provided with Table 7. According to Table 7, the solution quality achieved by ADE [2], COPSO [12] and FDE is much better than that achieved by HU-PSO [8]. COPSO [12] can not find feasible solution for all 30 runs. FDE is competitive with ADE [2] in terms of solution quality. ADE [2] need 90,000 FES to reach the optima, while FDE only need 13,500 FES. In other words, when FES is limited or the cost of function evaluation is expensive, FDE is a good choice to solve the himmelblaus nonlinear optimization problem.

Table 7. Comparison with other algorithms on himmelblaus nonlinear optimization problem over 30 runs

Algorithms	Best	Median	Mean	Worst	Std	FES
ADE [2]	**−31025.56024**	**−31025.56024**	**−31025.56024**	**−31025.56024**	5.91e-010	90,000
COPSO [12]	**−31025.56024**	NA	**−31025.56024**	NA	0	200,000
HU-PSO [8]	−31025.56142	NA	−31025.56142	NA	0	200,000
FDE	**−31025.56024**	**−31025.56024**	**−31025.56024**	**−31025.56024**	1.35e-12	**13,252**

a NA denotes that the results are not available from their corresponding papers.
b The best results among all the algorithms are highlighted in boldface.

In sum, it can be seen that FDE can acquire quite competitive performance on the 5 well studied engineering design applications under fewer function evaluations when compared with several state-of-the-art algorithms. It is clearly shown that FDE is feasible and effective to solve constrained optimization problems in engineering design. Especially, when the cost of function evaluation is expensive, FDE is quite a good choice to solve constrained optimization problems in real world design.

6 Discussion

In this section, the effectiveness of some mechanisms proposed in this paper on the performance of FDE will be discussed.

6.1 Effect of "DE/current-to-ppbest/1" Mutation Strategy

In order to confirm whether making use of the top p best individuals with different probabilities exhibits better performance than making use of the top p best individuals with the same probability, we performed three computational trials. The algorithm using all the individuals in the population as the best individuals with the same probability is denoted as FDE-1; the algorithm using the "DE/current-to-$p$best/1" mutation strategy is denoted as FDE-2. Tables 8 and 9 provides the experimental results of FDE-1, FDE-2 and FDE.

From Table 8, it can be concluded that FDE-1 and FDE can reach the optima over 30 runs on welded beam design, speed reducer design and himmelblau nonlinear optimization problem, and FDE need much less FES to reach the optima. However, the worst solution quality of FDE on spring design is worse than that of FDE-1, it may be because FDE-1 uses all the individuals in the population as the best individuals that the diversity of FDE-1 is maintained. The worst solution quality of FDE on three-bar truss can reach the optima within 6, 000 FES while the worst solution quality of FDE-1 can't reach the optima. It may be because the individuals in the population of FDE-1 are too diverse that FDE-1 can't converge to the optima in the limited FES. As shown in Table 9, both FDE-2 and FDE can reach optima on welded beam design, speed reducer design, treebar truss design and himmelblau nonlinear optimization problem over 30 runs, nevertheless, FDE uses less FES to reach optima. As for the spring design problem, the worst solution quality achieved by FDE-2 is better than that of FDE, however, FDE uses less FES than FDE-2. It may be because the FDE-2 use the top p individuals with the same probability that individuals in FDE-2 are more diverse.

From the results of Tables 8 and 9, we can conclude that "DE/current-to-ppbest/1" mutation strategy can speed the converge speed of FDE.

6.2 Effect of Ranking Based Selection Model

In order to ascertain whether the ranking based selection model shows better performance than the pairwise selection operator in traditional DE, one additional experiments was executed. The algorithm using the pairwise selection operator is denoted as FDE-3. The experimental result was presented in Table 10.

Table 8. Comparison results of FDE with FDE-1

Instance	FDE-1			FDE		
	Best	Worst	FES	Best	Worst	FES
Welded beam	2.380956580*	2.380956580*	32,325	2.380956580*	2.380956580*	**14,392**
Spring	0.0126652328*	0.0126652328*	40,801	0.0126652328*	0.0126653838	**38,837**
Speed reducer	2994.47106615*	2994.47106615*	36,312	2994.47106615*	2994.47106615*	**15,870**
Three-bar truss	263.89584338*	263.89680975	50,000	263.89584338*	263.89584338*	**5,587**
Himmelblau's	−31025.56024*	−31025.56024*	38,242	−31025.56024*	−31025.56024*	**13,252**

[a] The results reaching optima are denoted by using *.
[b] The results achieved by using maximum FES are highlighted in boldface.

Table 9. Comparison results of FDE with FDE-2

Instance	FDE-2			FDE		
	Best	Worst	FES	Best	Worst	FES
Welded beam	2.380956580*	2.380956580*	15165	2.380956580*	2.380956580*	**14,392**
Spring	0.0126652328*	0.0126653091	46,248	0.0126652328*	0.0126653838	**38,837**
Speed reducer	2994.47106615*	2994.47106615*	17,125	2994.47106615*	2994.47106615*	**15,870**
Three-bar truss	263.89584338*	263.89584338*	7,987	263.89584338*	263.89584338*	**5,587**
Himmelblau's	−31025.56024*	−31025.56024*	15,367	−31025.56024*	−31025.56024*	**13,252**

[a] The results reaching optima are denoted by using *.
[b] The results achieved by using maximum FES are highlighted in boldface.

As shown in Table 10, both FDE-3 and FDE can reach optima on welded beam design, speed reducer design, three-bar truss design and himmelblau non-linear optimization problem over 30 runs, however, FDE can reach the optima with less FES. As for the spring design problem, both the worst solution quality of FDE-3 and FDE can't reach the optima, but the worst solution quality of FDE is better than that of FDE-3.

It can be concluded that the ranking based selection model can improve the convergence speed than the pairwise selection without loss of solution quality.

Table 10. Comparison results of FDE with FDE-3

Instance	FDE-3			FDE		
	Best	Worst	FES	Best	Worst	FES
Welded beam	2.380956580*	2.380956580*	20,435	2.380956580*	2.380956580*	**14,392**
Spring	0.0126652328*	0.0126797111	43,105	0.0126652328*	0.0126653838	**38,837**
Speed reducer	2994.47106615*	2994.47106615*	19,028	2994.47106615*	2994.47106615*	**15,870**
Three-bar truss	263.89584338*	263.89584338*	9,357	263.89584338*	263.89584338*	**5,587**
Himmelblau's	−31025.56024*	−31025.56024*	15,075	−31025.56024*	−31025.56024*	**13,252**

[a] The results reaching optima are denoted by using *.
[b] The results achieved by using minimum FES are highlighted in boldface.

7   Conclusion and Future Work

By combining a new improved mutation strategy "DE/current-to-ppbest/1" with a ranking based selection model, a fast method FDE was proposed. The information of top p best individuals can be exploited more wisely, while the diversity of best individuals can be maintained. With different probabilities of using the top p best individuals, the population can make more use of the relatively better individuals, thus an improvement of convergence speed can be attained. The ranking based selection mechanism can eliminate unpromising individuals from the population more severely compared with the pairwise selection in DE.

Experimental results on 5 well studied engineering applications show that our FDE can acquire quite competitive performance in terms of solution quality. Meanwhile, FDE can converge to optima in relatively smaller number of FES compared with other state-of-the-art approaches in 5 real world engineering design instances. Therefore, FDE should be considered first when the cost of FES is expensive.

In the future, the mutation strategy "DE/current-to-ppbest/1" will be applied to unconstrained optimization problems or boundary constrained optimization problems. The effectiveness of ranking based selection model will be tested on unconstrained optimization problems or boundary constrained optimization problems. The effectiveness of ranking based selection model will be verified on other EAs for COPs. Also, we intend to test FDE on more instances from real world.

References

1. Akhtar, S., Tai, K., Ray, T.: A socio-behavioural simulation model for engineering design optimization. Eng. Optim. **34**(4), 341–354 (2002)
2. Ao, Y.Y., Chi, H.Q., et al.: An adaptive differential evolution algorithm to solve constrained optimization problems in engineering design. Engineering **2**(01), 65 (2010)
3. Bu, C., Luo, W., Zhu, T.: Differential evolution with a species-based repair strategy for constrained optimization. In: 2014 IEEE Congress on Evolutionary Computation (CEC), pp. 967–974. IEEE (2014)
4. Coello, C.A.C.: Self-adaptive penalties for ga-based optimization. In: Proceedings of the 1999 Congress on Evolutionary Computation, CEC 99, vol. 1. IEEE (1999)
5. Deb, K.: An efficient constraint handling method for genetic algorithms. Comput. Methods Appl. Mech. Eng. **186**(2), 311–338 (2000)
6. Gämperle, R., Müller, S.D., Koumoutsakos, P.: A parameter study for differential evolution. Adv. Intell. Syst. Fuzzy Syst. Evol. Comput. **10**, 293–298 (2002)
7. Hedar, A.R., Fukushima, M.: Derivative-free filter simulated annealing method for constrained continuous global optimization. J. Global Optim. **35**(4), 521–549 (2006)
8. Hu, X., Eberhart, R.C., Shi, Y.: Engineering optimization with particle swarm. In: Swarm Intelligence Symposium, SIS 2003. Proceedings of the 2003 IEEE, pp. 53–57. IEEE (2003)
9. Lampinen, J., Storn, R.: Differential Evolution. Springer, Heidelberg (2004)
10. Li, J., Shen, A., Lu, G.: Reference point based constraint handling method for evolutionary algorithm. In: Tan, Y., Shi, Y., Buarque, F., Gelbukh, A., Das, S., Engelbrecht, A. (eds.) ICSI-CCI 2015. LNCS, vol. 9140, pp. 294–301. Springer, Heidelberg (2015)

11. Mezura-Montes, E., Coello, C.A.C., Velázquez-Reyes, J.: Increasing successful off-spring and diversity in differential evolution for engineering design. In: Proceedings of the Seventh International Conference on Adaptive Computing in Design and Manufacture (ACDM 2006), pp. 131–139 (2006)
12. Muñoz Zavala, A.E., Hernández Aguirre, A., Villa Diharce, E.R., Botello Rionda, S.: Constrained optimization with an improved particle swarm optimization algorithm. Int. J. Intell. Comput. Cybern. 1(3), 425–453 (2008)
13. Ray, T., Liew, K.M.: Society and civilization: an optimization algorithm based on the simulation of social behavior. IEEE Trans. Evol. Comput. 7(4), 386–396 (2003)
14. Runarsson, T.P., Yao, X.: Stochastic ranking for constrained evolutionary optimization. IEEE Trans. Evol. Comput. 4(3), 284–294 (2000)
15. Storn, R., Price, K.: Differential evolution-a simple and efficient adaptive scheme for global optimization over continuous spaces, vol. 3. ICSI Berkeley (1995)
16. Takahama, T., Sakai, S.: Constrained optimization by the ε constrained differential evolution with gradient-based mutation and feasible elites. In: IEEE Congress on Evolutionary Computation, CEC 2006, pp. 1–8. IEEE (2006)
17. Wang, Y., Cai, Z.: Constrained evolutionary optimization by means of $(\mu\mu + \lambda\lambda)$-differential evolution and improved adaptive trade-off model. Evol. Comput. 19(2), 249–285 (2011)
18. Wang, Y., Cai, Z.: Combining multiobjective optimization with differential evolution to solve constrained optimization problems. IEEE Trans. Evol. Comput. 16(1), 117–134 (2012)
19. Wang, Y., Cai, Z.: A dynamic hybrid framework for constrained evolutionary optimization. IEEE Trans. Syst. Man Cybern. Part B Cybern. 42(1), 203–217 (2012)
20. Zhang, J., Sanderson, A.C.: Jade: adaptive differential evolution with optional external archive. IEEE Trans. Evol. Comput. 13(5), 945–958 (2009)
21. Zhang, M., Luo, W., Wang, X.: Differential evolution with dynamic stochastic selection for constrained optimization. Inf. Sci. 178(15), 3043–3074 (2008)

A Picture Array Generating Model Based on Flat Splicing Operation

K.G. Subramanian[1], Atulya K. Nagar[1], and Linqiang Pan[2]($\boxtimes$)

[1] Department of Mathematics and Computer Science, Faculty of Science,
Liverpool Hope University, Liverpool L16 9JD, UK
`kgsmani1948@gmail.com, nagara@hope.ac.uk`
[2] Key Laboratory of Image Information Processing and Intelligent Control,
School of Automation, Huazhong University of Science and Technology,
Wuhan 430074, Hubei, China
`lqpan@mail.hust.edu.cn`

Abstract. The bio-inspired operations of linear and circular splicing respectively on linear and circular strings of symbols have been extensively investigated by many researchers for their theoretical properties. Recently, another kind of splicing of two words, referred to as flat splicing on strings, has been considered. We here extend this operation to flat splicing on picture arrays, thus defining a new model of picture generation, which we call as array flat splicing system (AFS) and obtain some results on the generative power of AFS in comparison with certain well-known picture array defining models.

Keywords: Splicing on words · Flat splicing · Picture array · Picture language

1 Introduction

In modelling the recombinant behaviour of DNA molecules, Head defined an operation on strings of symbols, called splicing [5]. Subsequently, several theoretical studies on the power of this operation in terms of language theoretic results have been established [7,8]. Recently, a specific kind of splicing on circular words has been suitably adapted to linear words, resulting in a splicing operation, referred to as flat splicing [1]. While the usual splicing on two words involves the idea of "cutting" and "pasting" according to a splicing rule [7], the flat splicing on a pair of words (u, v) involves "cutting" u and "inserting" v into it, as dictated by a flat splicing rule.

Motivated by problems in image analysis and picture processing, several two-dimensional picture array generating models have been proposed and investigated, e.g., [4,15]. One such study is done in [3], by extending the operation of splicing on words [7] to arrays. The generative power of the resulting splicing system, called H array splicing system, is examined in [3].

We here extend the operation of flat splicing on linear words considered in [1] to picture arrays and define a system called array flat splicing system (AFS).

© Springer-Verlag Berlin Heidelberg 2015
M. Gong et al. (Eds.): BIC-TA 2015, CCIS 562, pp. 378–386, 2015.
DOI: 10.1007/978-3-662-49014-3_34

The extension we have defined is more close to the alphabetic case of flat splicing on words considered in [1]. We then make a theoretical investigation of (AFS) by comparing the family of picture languages generated by these systems with the families of picture languages of certain well-known two-dimensional picture generating models.

2   Preliminaries

We refer to [4,9] for concepts and results related to formal languages, array grammars and two-dimensional languages.

Given a finite alphabet Σ, a linear word or simply, a word (also called a string) α is a finite sequence $a_1 a_2 \cdots a_n$ of letters a_i, $1 \leq i \leq n$, in Σ. The set of all words over Σ, including the empty word λ with no symbols, is denoted by Σ^*. The length of a word α is the number of letters in the word, denoted by $|\alpha|$. For any word $\alpha = a_1 a_2 \ldots a_n$ $(n \geq 1)$, we denote by ${}^t\alpha$ the word α written vertically. For example, if $\alpha = bab$ over $\{a, b\}$, then

$$ {}^t\alpha = \begin{matrix} b \\ a \\ b \end{matrix} . $$

An $p \times q$ picture array (also called an array or a picture) X over an alphabet Σ is a rectangular array with p rows and q columns and is of the form

$$ X = \begin{matrix} a_{11} & \cdots & a_{1q} \\ \vdots & \ddots & \vdots \\ a_{p1} & \cdots & a_{pq} \end{matrix} $$

where each symbol $a_{ij} \in \Sigma, 1 \leq i \leq p, 1 \leq j \leq q$. For the sake of convenience, we may write $X = [a_{ij}]_{p,q}$. We denote the number of rows and the number of columns of X, respectively, by $|X|_r$ and $|X|_c$. The set of all rectangular arrays over Σ is denoted by Σ^{**}, which contains the empty array λ with no symbols. $\Sigma^{++} = V^{**} - \{\lambda\}$. A picture language is a subset of V^{**}.

Let $X = [a_{ij}]_{p,q}$ and $Y = [b_{ij}]_{r,s}$ be two non-empty arrays over an alphabet Σ. The operation of column concatenation of arrays X and Y, denoted by $X \circ Y$, is defined only when $p = r$ and is given by

$$ X \circ Y = \begin{matrix} a_{11} & \cdots & a_{1q} & b_{11} & \cdots & b_{1s} \\ \cdots & \cdots & \cdots & \cdots & \cdots & \cdots \\ a_{p1} & \cdots & a_{pq} & b_{p1} & \cdots & b_{ps} \end{matrix} $$

Likewise, the operation of row concatenation of X and Y, denoted by $X \diamond Y$, is defined only when $q = s$ and is given by

$$X \diamond Y = \begin{matrix} a_{11} \cdots a_{1q} \\ \cdots \cdots \cdots \\ a_{p1} \cdots a_{pq} \\ b_{11} \cdots b_{1q} \\ \cdots \cdots \cdots \\ b_{r1} \cdots b_{rq} \end{matrix}$$

Furthermore, $X \circ \lambda = \lambda \circ X = X \diamond \lambda = \lambda \diamond W = W$, for every array W.

We now recall an operation, called flat splicing on linear words, considered by Berstel et al. [1]. Given an alphabet Σ, a flat splicing rule r is of the form $(\alpha|\gamma - \delta|\beta)$, where $\alpha, \beta, \gamma, \delta$ are words over the alphabet Σ. Given two words $u = x\alpha\beta y$, $v = \gamma z\delta$, an application of the flat splicing rule $r = (\alpha|\gamma - \delta|\beta)$ to the pair (u, v) yields the word $w = x\alpha\gamma z\delta\beta y$. In other words, the second word v is inserted between α and β in the first word u as a result of applying the rule r.

3   Array Flat Splicing Systems

We extend the notion of flat splicing on words [1] to arrays. In fact we introduce two kinds of flat splicing rules, namely, column flat splicing rule and row flat splicing rule. We then define their application on a pair of arrays and thus introduce a new model of picture generation, namely, array flat splicing system.

Definition 1. *Let V be an alphabet.*

(i) *A column flat splicing rule is of the form $(^t(a_1 a_2)|^t(x_1 x_2) - {}^t(y_1 y_2)|^t(b_1 b_2))$ where $a_1, a_2, b_1, b_2 \in \Sigma \cup \{\lambda\}$ with $|a_1| = |a_2|$ and $|b_1| = |b_2|$, $x_1, x_2, y_1, y_2 \in \Sigma \cup \{\lambda\}$ with $|x_1| = |x_2|$ and $|y_1| = |y_2|$.*

(ii) *A row flat splicing rule is of the form $(c_1 c_2 | u_1 u_2 - v_1 v_2 | d_1 d_2)$ where $c_1, c_2, d_1, d_2 \in \Sigma \cup \{\lambda\}$ with $|c_1| = |c_2|$ and $|d_1| = |d_2|$, $u_1, u_2, v_1, v_2 \in \Sigma \cup \{\lambda\}$ with $|u_1| = |u_2|$ and $|v_1| = |v_2|$.*

(iii) *Let $r_1, r_2, \cdots, r_{m-1}$ be a sequence of $(m - 1)$ column flat splicing rules given by*

$$r_i = (^t(\alpha_i \alpha_{i+1})|^t(\gamma_i \gamma_{i+1}) - {}^t(\delta_i \delta_{i+1})|^t(\beta_i \beta_{i+1})),$$

for $1 \leq i \leq (m - 1)$. Let X, Y be two picture arrays, each with m rows, for some $m \geq 1$, and given by

$$X = X_1 \circ {}^t(\alpha_1 \alpha_2 \cdots \alpha_m) \circ {}^t(\beta_1 \beta_2 \cdots \beta_m) \circ X_2,$$

$$Y = {}^t(\gamma_1 \gamma_2 \cdots \gamma_m) \circ Y' \circ {}^t(\delta_1 \delta_2 \cdots \delta_m),$$

where X_1, X_2, Y' are arrays over Σ with m rows, $\alpha_i, \beta_i, \in \Sigma \cup \{\lambda\}$ $(1 \leq i \leq m)$, with $|\alpha_1| = |\alpha_2| = \cdots = |\alpha_m|$, $|\beta_1| = |\beta_2| = \cdots = |\beta_m|$, $\gamma_i, \delta_i, (1 \leq i \leq m)$, $\in \Sigma \cup \{\lambda\}$ with $|\gamma_1| = |\gamma_2| = \cdots = |\gamma_m|$, $|\delta_1| = |\delta_2| = \cdots = |\delta_m|$.

An application of the column flat splicing rules $r_1, r_2, \cdots, r_{m-1}$ *to the pair of arrays* (X, Y) *yields the array* Z

$$= X_1 \circ^t (\alpha_1 \alpha_2 \cdots \alpha_m) \circ^t (\gamma_1 \gamma_2 \cdots \gamma_m) \circ Y' \circ^t (\delta_1 \delta_2 \cdots \delta_m) \circ^t (\beta_1 \beta_2 \cdots \beta_m) \circ X_2.$$

The pair (X, Y) *yielding* Z *is then denoted by* $(X, Y) \vdash_c Z$.

(iv) *Let* $s_1, s_2, \cdots, s_{n-1}$ *be a sequence of* $(n-1)$ *row flat splicing rules given by*

$$s_j = (\eta_j \eta_{j+1} | (\mu_j \mu_{j+1}) - (\nu_j \nu_{j+1}) | \theta_j \theta_{j+1}),$$

for $1 \le j \le (n-1)$. *Let* U, V *be two picture arrays, each with* n *columns, for some* $n \ge 1$, *and given by*

$$U = U_1 \diamond (\eta_1 \eta_2 \cdots \eta_n) \diamond (\theta_1 \theta_2 \cdots \theta_n) \diamond U_2,$$

$$V = (\mu_1 \mu_2 \cdots \mu_n) \diamond V' \diamond (\delta_1 \delta_2 \cdots \delta_n)$$

where U_1, U_2, V' *are arrays over* Σ *with* n *columns,* η_j, θ_j, $(1 \le j \le n)$, $\in \Sigma \cup \{\lambda\}$ *with* $|\eta_1| = |\eta_2| = \cdots = |\eta_n|$, $|\theta_1| = |\theta_2| = \cdots = |\theta_n|$, μ_j, ν_j, $(1 \le j \le n)$, $\in \Sigma \cup \{\lambda\}$ *with* $|\mu_1| = |\mu_2| = \cdots = |\mu_n|$, $|\nu_1| = |\nu_2| = \cdots = |\nu_n|$. *An application of the row flat splicing rules* $s_1, s_2, \cdots, s_{n-1}$ *to the pair of arrays* (U, V) *yields the array* W

$$= U_1 \diamond (\eta_1 \eta_2 \cdots \eta_n) \diamond (\mu_1 \mu_2 \cdots \mu_n) \diamond V' \diamond (\delta_1 \delta_2 \cdots \delta_n) \diamond (\theta_1 \theta_2 \cdots \theta_n) \diamond U_2.$$

The pair (U, V) *yielding* W *is then denoted by* $(U, V) \vdash_r W$.

(v) *An array flat splicing rule is either a column flat splicing rule or a row flat splicing rule. The notation* $\vdash$ *denotes either* $\vdash_c$ *or* $\vdash_r$.

(vi) *For a picture language* $L \subseteq \Sigma^{**}$ *and a set* R *of array flat splicing rules, we define*

$$f(L) = \{M \in \Sigma^{**} \mid (X, Y) \vdash M, for X, Y \in L, and\ some\ rule\ in\ R\}.$$

Definition 2. *An array flat splicing system* (AFS) *is* $\mathcal{A} = (\Sigma, M, R_c, R_r)$ *where* Σ *is an alphabet,* M *is a finite set of arrays over* Σ, *called initial set,* R_c *is a finite set of column flat splicing rules and* R_r *is a finite set of row flat splicing rules.*

The picture language $L(\mathcal{A})$ *generated by* $\mathcal{A}$ *is iteratively defined as follows:*

$$f^0(M) = M; For\ i \ge 0, f^{i+1}(M) = f^i(M) \cup f(f^i(M));$$

$$L(\mathcal{A}) = f^*(M) = \cup_{i \ge 0} f^i(M).$$

The family of picture languages generated by array flat splicing systems is denoted by $L(AFS)$.

We illustrate the definitions and the working of array flat splicing systems with an example.

Example 1. Consider the array flat splicing system $\mathcal{A}_C$ with alphabet $\{a, b\}$ and the initial set $M = \{\begin{smallmatrix} a\,b \\ b\,a \end{smallmatrix}, \begin{smallmatrix} b\,a \\ a\,b \end{smallmatrix}\}$. The column flat splicing rules are c_1, c_2 where $c_1 = (\begin{smallmatrix} a \\ b \end{smallmatrix}|\begin{smallmatrix} b \\ a \end{smallmatrix} - \begin{smallmatrix} a \\ b \end{smallmatrix}|\begin{smallmatrix} b \\ a \end{smallmatrix}), c_2 = (\begin{smallmatrix} b \\ a \end{smallmatrix}|\begin{smallmatrix} a \\ b \end{smallmatrix} - \begin{smallmatrix} b \\ a \end{smallmatrix}|\begin{smallmatrix} a \\ b \end{smallmatrix})$. The row flat splicing rules are r_1, r_2 where $r_1 = (ab|ba - ab|ba), r_2 = (ba|ab - ba|ab)$.

We illustrate the working of the array flat splicing system $\mathcal{A}_C$. The column flat splicing rule c_1 is applicable to the pair $(\begin{smallmatrix} a\,b \\ b\,a \end{smallmatrix}, \begin{smallmatrix} b\,a \\ a\,b \end{smallmatrix})$ since both the arrays have equal number of rows and the second array in the pair begins with the column $\begin{smallmatrix} b \\ a \end{smallmatrix}$ and ends with the column $\begin{smallmatrix} a \\ b \end{smallmatrix}$, as required in the rule c_1. The first array is "cut" between the columns $\begin{smallmatrix} a \\ b \end{smallmatrix}$ and $\begin{smallmatrix} b \\ a \end{smallmatrix}$ while the second array is "inserted" between them, yielding the array $\begin{smallmatrix} a\,b\,a\,b \\ b\,a\,b\,a \end{smallmatrix}$. Likewise, the application of rule c_2 to the pair $(\begin{smallmatrix} b\,a\ a\,b \\ a\,b\ b\,a \end{smallmatrix})$ yields the array $(\begin{smallmatrix} b\,a\,b\,a \\ a\,b\,a\,b \end{smallmatrix})$. If we now apply this rule c_1 to the pair $(\begin{smallmatrix} a\,b\,a\,b\ b\,a \\ b\,a\,b\,a\ a\,b \end{smallmatrix})$, it will expand the "chess board pattern" columnwise. On the other hand, the row flat splicing rules r_1, r_2 can be used to expand the "chess board pattern" rowwise. For example, the sequence of rules r_1, r_2, r_1 could be applied to the pair of arrays $(\begin{smallmatrix} a\,b\,a\,b\ b\,a\,b\,a \\ b\,a\,b\,a\ a\,b\,a\,b \end{smallmatrix})$ since both the arrays have the same number of columns. In fact, the first array is "cut" between the first row $a\,b\,a\,b$ and the second row $b\,a\,b\,a$. The second array satisfies the requirements of the sequence of rules r_1, r_2, r_1. The second array therefore can be "inserted" into the first array to yield the array $\begin{smallmatrix} a\,b\,a\,b \\ b\,a\,b\,a \\ a\,b\,a\,b \\ b\,a\,b\,a \end{smallmatrix}$. Proceeding like this, we compute the successive terms $f^0(M), f^1(M), \cdots$. In fact

$$f^0(M) = M = \{\begin{smallmatrix} a\,b \\ b\,a \end{smallmatrix}, \begin{smallmatrix} b\,a \\ a\,b \end{smallmatrix}\},$$

$$f^1(M) = M \cup f(M) = \{\begin{smallmatrix} a\,b \\ b\,a \end{smallmatrix}, \begin{smallmatrix} b\,a \\ a\,b \end{smallmatrix}, \begin{smallmatrix} a\,b\,a\,b \\ b\,a\,b\,a \end{smallmatrix}, \begin{smallmatrix} b\,a\,b\,a \\ a\,b\,a\,b \end{smallmatrix}, \begin{smallmatrix} b\,a \\ a\,b \\ b\,a \end{smallmatrix}, \begin{smallmatrix} a\,b \\ b\,a \\ a\,b \end{smallmatrix}\}, \cdots.$$

Thus the picture language $L(\mathcal{A}_C) = f^*(M)$ consists of rectangular "chess board" patterns of even side length over the symbols a, b with a standing for a white unit square and b for a black unit square. One such "chess board" pattern is shown in Fig. 1.

Fig. 1. A Chess Board pattern

In what follows, we obtain some properties on the generative power of array flat splicing system by comparing this with certain well-known picture array generative models. We first informally recall here the two-dimensional right-linear grammar (2RLG) [4] (originally introduced in [10]). There are two sets of rules in a 2RLG grammar: horizontal and vertical rules that correspond to Chomsky regular grammars. This model operates in two phases with the first phase generating a (horizontal) string over intermediate symbols using the horizontal rules and then the vertical rules are applied in parallel generating the columns of a rectangular array made of terminal symbols. We denote the family of array languages generated by two-dimensional right-linear grammars by $L(2RLG)$. We now show that there is a picture language generated by an array flat splicing system while no two-dimensional right-linear grammar can generate it.

Theorem 1. $L(AFS) \setminus L(2RLG) \neq \emptyset$.

Proof. We consider the picture language L_1 consisting of picture arrays with even sides, of the form $M_1 \diamond M_2$, where M_1 is a $m \times p$ rectangular array over the symbol a while M_2 is a $n \times q$ rectangular array over the symbol b, where $m, n \geq 1$ and $p, q \geq 2$. A member of L_1 is shown in Fig. 2. The language L_1 is generated by the AFS S_1 with alphabet $\{a\}$, initial array $\begin{smallmatrix} a & a \\ b & b \end{smallmatrix}$, column flat splicing rules $\left(\begin{smallmatrix} a \\ b \end{smallmatrix}\middle|\begin{smallmatrix} a \\ b \end{smallmatrix} - \begin{smallmatrix} a \\ b \end{smallmatrix}\middle|\begin{smallmatrix} a \\ b \end{smallmatrix}\right), \left(\begin{smallmatrix} a \\ a \end{smallmatrix}\middle|\begin{smallmatrix} a \\ a \end{smallmatrix} - \begin{smallmatrix} a \\ a \end{smallmatrix}\middle|\begin{smallmatrix} a \\ a \end{smallmatrix}\right), \left(\begin{smallmatrix} b \\ b \end{smallmatrix}\middle|\begin{smallmatrix} b \\ b \end{smallmatrix} - \begin{smallmatrix} b \\ b \end{smallmatrix}\middle|\begin{smallmatrix} b \\ b \end{smallmatrix}\right)$, and row flat splicing rules $(\,aa\,|\,aa - bb\,|\,bb\,)$. It can be seen that the column flat splicing rules and the row flat splicing rule can respectively be used to expand an array columnwise and rowwise, starting with the initial array $\begin{smallmatrix} a & a \\ b & b \end{smallmatrix}$. But the language L_1 cannot

```
a a a a a a
a a a a a a
b b b b b b
b b b b b b
```

Fig. 2. A member of the language L_1

be generated by any $2RLG$ since in the vertical derivation, there is no control which will synchronize the application of regular rules in order to generate a row of b's in passing from generation of a's to generation of b's in the columns. This proves the result. □

We now informally recall the notion of a local picture language [4]. Extending the notion of local string language, local picture language L is defined in terms of "tiles" that are square arrays of side length two. In fact a local picture language L contains all picture arrays M such that M contains only the 2×2 tiles that are allowed in defining the picture language L. The family of local picture languages is denoted by LOC. We now show that there is a picture language which is not in LOC but which can be generated by an array flat splicing system.

Theorem 2. $L(AFS) \setminus LOC \neq \emptyset$.

Proof. We consider the picture language L_2 consisting of picture arrays over the symbol a, with each of these arrays having three columns and an even number of rows. A member of L_2 is shown in Fig. 3. This language is generated by the AFS S_2 with alphabet $\{a\}$, initial array $\begin{smallmatrix} a & a & a \\ a & a & a \end{smallmatrix}$ and a row splicing rule $r = (aa|aa - aa|aa)$. On the other hand, L_2 is not a local picture language. Suppose it is, then L_2 will be defined by a set of tiles which will include a tile $\begin{smallmatrix} a & a \\ a & a \end{smallmatrix}$ besides the corner tiles and border tiles. But this will mean that L_2 can contain picture arrays over a having more than three columns. □

```
a a a
a a a
a a a
a a a
```

Fig. 3. A member of the language L_2

The notion of splicing on strings originally introduced by Head [5] has been extensively investigated theoretically [7]. Extending this notion, the operation of splicing applied to picture arrays (also called images) has been introduced in [3] and the generative power and other properties of an array splicing system, called H array splicing system, have been investigated in [3]. The family of picture languages generated by H array splicing systems is denoted by $L(HASL)$. The concept of array flat splicing considered here is different from the splicing notion studied in [3]. Yet we find the two families $L(HASL)$ and $L(AFS)$ have nonempty intersection.

4 Conclusion and Discussion

The concept of flat splicing introduced in [1], especially, the alphabetic case, is extended to arrays here and a new model of picture array generation, called array flat splicing system is introduced. The place of the family $L(AFS)$ with respect to Chomsky-like hierarchies of array families, comparison with other kinds of picture generating models (for example, models in [11]), closure properties of the family $L(AFS)$ remain to be investigated. Moreover, the flat splicing is a particular case of context-dependent insertion operation, much investigated in formal language theory and in DNA computing and so comparison of the flat splicing with the insertion operation can be examined both for strings and arrays. Although the study here has been theoretical, possible application to generation of patterns such as "floor designs" using AFS can also be examined.

Human brain is powerful in recognizing pictures. In the framework of membrane computing, there is a class of neural-like computing models, named spiking neural P systems [16]. In recent research, some powerful variants of SN P systems were proposed, e.g. see [2,6,12–14,17]. It is of interests using SN P systems to generate and recognize picture arrays and picture languages.

Acknowledgments. The authors are grateful to the reviewers for their very useful comments. This work was supported by National Natural Science Foundation of China (61033003 and 61320106005), Ph.D. Programs Foundation of Ministry of Education of China (20120142130008).

References

1. Berstel, J., Boasson, L., Fagnot, I.: Splicing systems and the Chomsky hierarchy. Theoret. Comput. Sci. **436**, 2–22 (2012)
2. Song, T., Pan, L., Păun, G.: Asynchronous spiking neural P systems with local synchronization. Inf. Sci. **219**, 197–207 (2013)
3. Chandra, P.H., Subramanian, K.G., Thomas, D.G.: Parallel splicing on images. Int. J. Pattern Recogn. **18**(6), 1071–1091 (2004)
4. Giammarresi, D., Restivo, A.: Two-dimensional Languages. In: [7], vol. 3, pp. 215–267 (1997)
5. Head, T.: Formal language theory and DNA: an analysis of the generative capacity of specific recombinant behaviours. Bull. Math. Biol. **49**, 735–759 (1987)

6. Song, T., Pan, L.: Spiking neural P systems with rules on synapses working in maximum spikes consumption strategy. IEEE Trans. NanoBiosci. **14**(1), 38–44 (2015)

7. Wang, X., Miao, Y., Cheng, M.: Finding motifs in DNA sequences using low-dispersion sequences. J. Comput. Biol. **21**(4), 320–329 (2014)

8. Păun, G., Rozenberg, G., Salomaa, A.: Computing by splicing. Theoret. Comput. Sci. **168**, 321–336 (1996)

9. Rozenberg, G., Salomaa, A. (eds.): Handbook of Formal Languages, vol. 1–3. Springer, Berlin (1997)

10. Siromoney, G., Siromoney, R., Krithivasan, K.: Abstract families of matrices and picture languages. Comput. Graph. Imag. Process. **1**, 284–307 (1972)

11. Subramanian, K.G., Ali, R.M., Geethalakshmi, M., Nagar, A.K.: Pure 2D picture grammars and languages. Discrete Appl. Math. **157**, 3401–3411 (2009)

12. Song, T., Pan, L.: Spiking neural P systems with rules on synapses working in maximum spiking strateg. IEEE Trans. NanoBiosci. **14**(4), 465–477 (2015)

13. Song, T., Pan, L., Wang, J., et al.: Normal forms of spiking neural P systems with anti-spikes. IEEE Trans. NanoBiosci. **11**(4), 352–359 (2012)

14. Zhang, X., Pan, L., Paun, A.: On the universality of axon P systems. IEEE Trans. Neural Netw. Learn. Syst. (2015). doi:10.1109/TNNLS.2015.2396940

15. Subramanian, K.G., Rangarajan, K., Mukund, M.: Formal Models, Languages and Applications. Machine Perception and Artificial Intelligence, vol. 66. World Scientific Publishing, Singapore (2006)

16. Ionescu, M., Pun, G., Yokomori, T.: Spiking neural P systems. Fundamenta Informaticae **71**(2), 279–308 (2006)

17. Song, T., Pan, L., Jiang, K., et al.: Normal forms for some classes of sequential spiking neural P systems. IEEE Trans. NanoBiosci. **12**(3), 255–264 (2013)

Connections of Multi Memristors

Junwei Sun[1,2], Yanfeng Wang[1,2], and Guangzhao Cui[1,2](✉)

[1] School of Electric and Information Engineering,
Zhengzhou University of Light Industry, Zhengzhou 450002, China
[2] Henan Key Lab of Information-Based Electrical Appliances,
Zhengzhou University of Light Industry, Zhengzhou 450002, China
cgzh@zzuli.edu.cn

Abstract. After the successful solid state implementation of the memristor, the memristor based on circuit has gained an increasing attention as next generation electronic passive devices. In this work, multi memristors in series and parallel connection are considered as different subsystems. First, these subsystems are driven by a voltage source, respectively. The inter-dependence relation among voltage, current, charge, flux and the normalized width of the doped region are taken into consideration to a complete mathematical model for each memristor. Then, we use these connected subsystems of multi memristors to replace Chua's diode. The combinations of memristors in circuits can give rise to rich enough dynamical behavior that it wouldn't produce further complications of adding in other circuit elements. Multi memristors in series and parallel are given to illustrate an important step towards real world memristor system applications.

Keywords: Memristor · Series · Parallel

1 Introduction

The memristor is considered as the missing fourth fundamental circuit element which has been postulated to exist from symmetry arguments in 1971 [1]. It is a two terminal passive circuit element, which is stateful and the internal state is related to past history of the circuit element. Because of the memristor's ability, it has been learned that the memristor could be a choice to neuromorphic or brain-like hardware. As the achievement of memristor is widely anticipated, it is applied in not just computing, but science and even society. In 2008, Stan Williams and other reseachers in this field [2] have constructed a solid state implementation of the memristor and thereby have cemented its place as the fourth basic circuit element. Potential applications of such memristors span distinct fields ranging from nonvolatile memories on the nano-scale [2] to neural network model [3] have been exploited. Since a memristor is a novel fundamental circuit element, circuit applications of memristors are also the active and interesting topics of research [3].

© Springer-Verlag Berlin Heidelberg 2015
M. Gong et al. (Eds.): BIC-TA 2015, CCIS 562, pp. 387–399, 2015.
DOI: 10.1007/978-3-662-49014-3_35

Chua's circuit is the simplest electronic circuit that can exhibit enough chaotic behaviour [4]. This circuit can be obtained by one inductor, one resistor, two capacitors and a component called Chua's diode which is a non-linear circuit element usually fabricated from several other circuit components including op amps. Due to the nonlinearity of memristor element, the memristor based on circuits has been exploited as fundamental block for the definition of new nonlinear circuits which can easily generate a chaotic signal. Itoh and Chua [5] have derived several oscillators from Chua's oscillators by replacing Chua's diodes with memristors characterized by monotone-increasing and piece-wise linear function.

Several of chaotic oscillator circuits by replacing Chua's diode with an flux-controlled active memristor have been designed to produce many interesting oscillation properties and rich nonlinear dynamics behaviour as a new perspective (eg. [6,9–11,14–18,21–25]), but all these simulations used Chua's equations for the perfect theoretical memristor model and the electronic experiments with a circuit equivalent, presumably due to the trouble in obtaining an actual memristor to apply. A step forward in the direction of real world functionality is Buscarino's research [21] where Chua's diode in Chua's circuit has been replaced with a pair of memristors modelled by using Strukov et al.'s phenomenological model [2] which is depended on real world measurables. The resulting simulation has produced enough chaotic behavior, which has made use of a pair of Strukov memristors connected in anti-parallel to give a symmetrical $I - V$ curve as a replacement for Chua's diode. They also have used a voltage frequency that put the memristors up to their limits to introduce asymmetry and richer behavior. It may be doubted whether the chaotic behavior they have produced in the simulation process arose from the memristors or from the interaction of the errors in the model, which (even with window functions) is weakest at the edges of the memristor. Despite this, paper [22] demonstrated an important step towards real world memristor system applications. Memristive behavior of two Floating MR emulators connected in serial and parallel are experimentally investigated, where only the connections with identical polarity directions are taken into account [23]. By exploring the threshold-dependent resistance switching behavior of single MR and connection compositions, memristor computational methods and reconfigurable structures are designed in [24]. The resulting new pulse behavior, set and reset operation may be useful for the future applications in neural networks and logic circuits.

In our paper, the realistic model of the Hewlett-Packard memristor is introduced [2]. The HP model is a physical model based on the ionic drift of the oxygen vacancies in the titanium dioxide layer. Taking into account assumptions suitable for existing real devices poses several problems, the HP memristor is a passive non-symmetrical element having a nonlinear window function different from that more frequently investigated (often cubic or piece-wise linear), which will be discussed in the paper. Multi memristors in series and parallel connection are considered as different subsystems. First, those subsystems are driven by a voltage source. Some important constitutive relations for each memristor are gained such as voltage, current, charge, flux and the normalized width of the doped region. Then, we use those connected subsystems of multi memristors to give a symmetrical $I - V$ curve as a replacement for Chua's diode. The combination of memristors in circuits can give rise to rich enough dynamical behavior that we wouldn't need further complications of adding in other circuit elements. The development of reliable nonlinear circuits will enable the construction of more complex time domain signals, which may result in applications for secure communications and encryption.

This paper is organized as follows: we begin by discussing the fundamental theory behind memristors in Sect. 2. Next, multi memristors in series and parallel connection are driven by a voltage source in Sects. 3 and 4, respectively. Then, we use those connected subsystems of multi memristors to replace Chua's diode for obtaining rich enough behavior. Finally, we will conclude in Sect. 5 with a brief summary.

2   Model of the HP Memristor

The physical model of the memristor from [2], shown in Fig. 1(a), consists of a layer thin film of TiO_2 of thickness D, sandwiched between platinum contacts. One of the layers is doped with oxygen vacancies and thus it behaves as a semiconductor. As a result of complex material processes, the width of the doped region is modulated due to the amount of electric charge passing across the memristor. With electric current passing in a given order, the boundary between the two regions is moving in the same order.

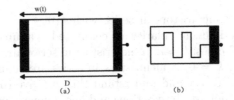

Fig. 1. (a) Schematic representation of the TiO_2 memristor. (b) Electrical symbol.

The width $w(t)$ of the doped region changes as a function of an external bias $i(t)$ injected in the device. The relationship between voltage and current of the memristor (whose electrical symbol is given in Fig. 1(b)) is described by the following equation:

$$v(t) = (R_{on}\frac{w(t)}{D} + R_{off}(1 - \frac{w(t)}{D}))i(t), \tag{1}$$

where $w(t)$ is the width of the doped region, D is the whole length of the TiO_2 thin layer, R_{off} and R_{on} are the limit values of the memristor resistance for $w(t) = 0$ and $w(t) = D$. The variable $w(t)$ is limited to values between zero and D, which is linked to the charge q by

$$\dot{w}(t) = \varphi \frac{\mu_v R_{on}}{D} i(t),\tag{2}$$

where the parameter φ characterizes the polarity of the memristor, $\varphi = 1$ if the doped region in memristor is expanding, $\varphi = -1$ otherwise. It is commonly referred to as the linear drift model. As mentioned in [2], in nanoscale devices, a few small voltages can yield a large electric field, which can secondarily produce significant nonlinearities in ionic-drift transport. These nonlinearities manifest themselves particularly at the thin film edges, where the speed of the boundary between the doped and undoped regions gradually decreases to zero. This phenomenon, called nonlinear dopant drift, can be modeled by the so-called window function $f(x)$ on the right side of (3),

$$\dot{w}(t) = \varphi \frac{\mu_v R_{on}}{D} F(\frac{w(t)}{D}) i(t).\tag{3}$$

The paper [26] has proposed the window function as the following form:

$$F(x) = 1 - (2x - 1)^{2p},\tag{4}$$

where p is a positive integer which controls the nonlinearity, and $x = \frac{w(t)}{D} \in (0,1)$. The form of function (4) can make sure zero speed of the x-coordinate when approaching boundary, which becomes more evident at the boundaries. Moreover, the differences between the models with linear and nonlinear drift disappear when p increases.

3   Multi Memristors in Series Connection

In this section, multi memristors in series with $k(0 \le k \le n)$ same polarity interactions and $n-k$ diffenent polarity are connected as a subsystem in Fig. 2(a). There are two special cases, $k = n$, n memristors in series are connected in same polarity interactions; $k = 0$, n memristors in series are connected in opposite polarity interactions. To try and understand this, we give three memristors in series with two same polarity interactions and one diffenent polarity interaction as an example in Fig. 2(b). It has been thought that the memristors would change with the change of voltage and this would cause a change in resistance within a single memristor, this set-up circuit would lead to a voltage change across the other memristors and the other circuit elements.

Let us apply a sinusoidal voltage source $V(t) = 1.2sin2\pi t$ across the subsystem of three memristors in series as Fig. 2(b), the total current across the two-terminal subsystem is defined as I. Two mathematical variables of the flux ϕ and the charge q are represented by the time integral of the element's voltage V and current I, respectively. Applying the Kirchoff Voltage Law (KVL), the voltage is the sum of the voltage of each memristor $V = V_1 + V_2 + V_3$ in Fig. 3(a), thus the flux is the sum of the flux of each memristor $\phi = \int_0^t V(\tau)d\tau = \int_0^t V_1(\tau)d\tau + \int_0^t V_2(\tau)d\tau + \int_0^t V_3(\tau)d\tau = \phi_1 + \phi_2 + \phi_3$ in Fig. 3(b). Applying Kirchoff Current Law (KCL), the current across each memristor is equal to the current across the two-terminal subsystem $I = I_1 = I_2 = I_3$ in Fig. 3(c), thus the

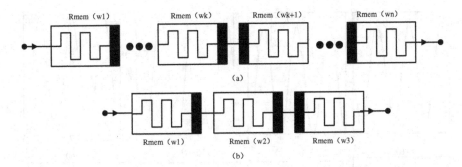

Rmem (w1)   Rmem (wk)   Rmem (wk+1)   Rmem (wn)

(a)

Rmem (w1)   Rmem (w2)   Rmem (w3)

(b)

Fig. 2. (a) Multi memristors in series connection with $k(0 \leq k \leq n)$ same polarity interactions and $n - k$ different polarity. (b) Three memristors in series connection with two same polarity interactions and one different polarity.

charge across each memristor is equal to the charge across the two-terminal subsystem $q = q_1 = q_2 = q_3$ in Fig. 3(d), where $q = \int_0^t I(\tau)d\tau$, $q_1 = \int_0^t I_1(\tau)d\tau$, $q_2 = \int_0^t I_2(\tau)d\tau$, $q_3 = \int_0^t I_3(\tau)d\tau$. The normalized width of the doped region is switched between the low and high levels near the limiting values of 0 and 1 in Fig. 3(e), which would change with the change of current and this would cause a change of the resistance value within a single memristor. It follows that only the memristors $q - \phi$ curve in the first quadrant is visited during every period of $i(t)$ in Fig. 3(f). The memristors work in a regime such that the boundary between the doped and undoped layers does not approach the edges with dominant nonlinear effects. Due to the change of the normalized width in the doped region, it easily leads to a change of the resistance value within each memristor as Fig. 3(g), the memristors $R_{mem} - x$ diagram is hyperbola in Fig. 3(g), which implies this nonlinearity more evident at the boundaries. The $I - V$ behavior can be observed in terms of pinched hysteresis, as shown in Fig. 3(h). The hysteresis occurs because the maxima and minima of the sinusoidal current across each memristor in Fig. 3(c) do not occur at the same time as the corresponding memristor voltage in Fig. 3(a). The pinching at the origin in Fig. 3(h) occurs because both current and voltage for each memristor become zero at the same time.

Remark: A sinusoidal voltage source $V(t) = 1.2sin2\pi t$ is applied to the subsystem of three memristors $R_{mem}(w_1)$, $R_{mem}(w_2)$ and $R_{mem}(w_3)$. Some variables are defined as the voltage V_1, the flux ϕ_1, the current I_1, the charge q_1 and the normalized width of the doped region x_1 for the memristor $R_{mem}(w_1)$; other variables are also defined as the voltage V_2, the flux ϕ_2, the current I_2, the charge q_2 and the normalized width of the doped region x_2 for the memristor $R_{mem}(w_2)$, and still other variables are also defined as the voltage V_3, the flux ϕ_3, the current I_3, the charge q_3 and the normalized width of the doped region x_3 for the memristor $R_{mem}(w_3)$. Although the following connection methods are different from three memristors in series, the definitions of the variables remain the same as three memristors in series. The following sections will no longer repeat these definitions of the variables.

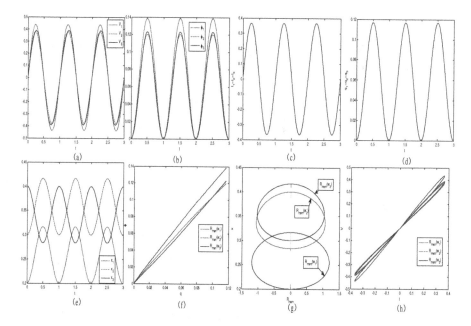

Fig. 3. Memristors in series connection with parameters $R_{on} = 100\,\Omega$, $R_{off} = 16\,k\Omega$, $p = 10$, driven by a voltage source $V(t) = 1.2\sin 2\pi t$.

The behavior of the three memristors in series connection is now exploited to design a circuit. It is based on the topology of the canonical Chua's oscillator [4] with the Chua's diode substituted by three memristors in series connection with two same polarity interactions and one different polarity as Fig. 2(b). In other words, the subsystem of three memristors as Fig. 2(b) is connected to the subcircuit as Fig. 4. The circuit consists of two capacitors, an inductor, and three memristors in series connection. Applying to the circuit introduced above the Kirchhoff's circuit laws and the constitutive relationships of the memristor (Eqs. (1) and (4)), we obtain the following set of differential equations:

$$
\begin{cases}
\frac{du_1}{dt} = \frac{1}{C_1}\left(i - \frac{u_1}{R_{mem}(w_1)+R_{mem}(w_2)+R_{mem}(w_3)}\right), \\
\frac{di}{dt} = \frac{1}{KL_1}(u_1 - u_2), \\
\frac{u_2}{dt} = \frac{K}{C_2}i, \\
\frac{dw_1}{dt} = \varphi_1 \frac{\mu_v R_{ON}}{D} F\left(\frac{w_1}{D}\right) \frac{u_1}{R_{mem}(w_1)+R_{mem}(w_2)+R_{mem}(w_3)}, \\
\frac{dw_2}{dt} = \varphi_2 \frac{\mu_v R_{ON}}{D} F\left(\frac{w_2}{D}\right) \frac{u_1}{R_{mem}(w_1)+R_{mem}(w_2)+R_{mem}(w_3)}, \\
\frac{dw_3}{dt} = \varphi_3 \frac{\mu_v R_{ON}}{D} F\left(\frac{w_3}{D}\right) \frac{u_1}{R_{mem}(w_1)+R_{mem}(w_2)+R_{mem}(w_3)},
\end{cases}
\tag{5}
$$

where

$$
R_{mem}(w_i) = R_{ON}\frac{w_i}{D} + R_{OFF}\left(1 - \frac{w_i}{D}\right), \varphi_1 = \varphi_2 = -\varphi_3 = 1.
\tag{6}
$$

Assume $\tilde{R}_{mem}(W_i) = W_i + \frac{R_{OFF}}{R_{ON}}(1 - W_i)$, $X = u_1/u_0$, $Y = i/i_0$, $Z = u_2/u_0$, $W_1 = w_1/D$, $W_2 = w_2/D$, $W_3 = w_3/D$, $\tau = t/t_0$, $u_0 = 1v$, $i_0 = u_0/R_{ON}$,

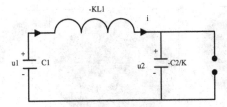

Fig. 4. Subcircuit of three elements.

$t_0 = D^2/\mu_v u_0$, $C_0 = D^2/\mu_v u_0 R_{ON}$, and $L_0 = D^2 R_{ON}/\mu_v u_0$, it is easy to see that the following equation should be obtained as follows:

$$
\begin{cases}
\frac{X}{d\tau} = \frac{C_0}{C_1}\left(Y - \frac{X}{\tilde{R}_{mem}(W_1)+\tilde{R}_{mem}(W_2)+\tilde{R}_{mem}(W_3)}\right), \\
\frac{Y}{d\tau} = \frac{L_0}{KL_1}(Z - X), \\
\frac{Z}{d\tau} = \frac{KC_0}{C_2}Y, \\
\frac{dW_1}{d\tau} = \varphi_1 F(\frac{W_1}{D})\frac{X}{\tilde{R}_{mem}(W_1)+\tilde{R}_{mem}(W_2)+\tilde{R}_{mem}(W_3)}, \\
\frac{dW_2}{d\tau} = \varphi_2 F(\frac{W_2}{D})\frac{X}{\tilde{R}_{mem}(W_1)+\tilde{R}_{mem}(W_2)+\tilde{R}_{mem}(W_3)}, \\
\frac{dW_3}{d\tau} = \varphi_3 F(\frac{W_3}{D})\frac{X}{\tilde{R}_{mem}(W_1)+\tilde{R}_{mem}(W_2)+\tilde{R}_{mem}(W_3)}.
\end{cases} \tag{7}
$$

Typical values of the memristor parameters are $R_{on} = 100\,\Omega$, $R_{off} = 16\,k\Omega$, $p = 10$, $D = 10\,nm$, $\mu_v = 10^{-14}m^2s^{-1}v^{-1}$, $\frac{C_0}{C_1} = 3 \times 10^{-8}$, $\frac{L_0}{KL_1} = 0.08$, and $\frac{KC_0}{C_2} = 4 \times 10^{-9}$. The circuit dynamics has been studied by numerical integration of (7), obtained by adopting a standard 4th order Runge-Kutta algorithm. An example of dynamical behavior is shown in Fig. 5. Figure 5(a)–(d) show the transient nonlinear behavior. Figure 5(e) shows the trajectories of state variables X, Y, Z of system (5) with the time evolution. Figure 5(f) shows the trajectories of state variables W_1, W_2, W_3 of system (5) with the time evolution. Time-domain waveforms in Fig. 5(e) and (f) are nonperodic. A kind of seeming random chance or irregular movement appears in phase portrait and time-domain waveform of Fig. 5.

4   Multi Memristors in Parallel Connection

In this section, multi memristors in parallel with $k(0 \leq k \leq n)$ same polarity interactions and $n - k$ different polarity are connected as subsystem in Fig. 6(a). Three memristors in parallel connection with two same polarity interactions and one different polarity interaction are given as an example in Fig. 6(b).

Let us apply a sinusoidal voltage source $V(t) = 1.2sin2\pi t$ across the subsystem of three memristors in parallel as Fig. 6(b), the total current across the two-terminal subsystem is also defined as I. Two mathematical variables of the flux ϕ and the charge q are also represented by the time integral of the element's voltage V and current I, respectively. In such configuration, applying the Kirchoff Voltage Law (KVL), the voltage of each memristor is equal to

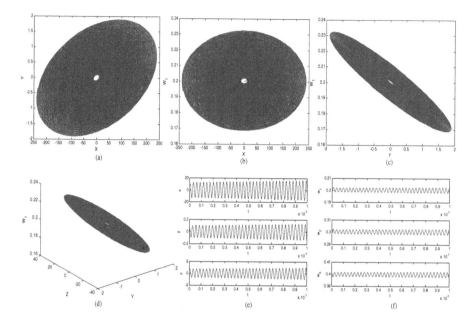

Fig. 5. For initial conditions $(1,0.1,-0.3,0.2,0.3,0.4)$. (a) Phase portrait $X - Y$. (b) Phase portrait $X - W_1$. (c) Phase portrait $Y - W_1$. (d) Phase portrait $Y - Z - W_1$. (e) Time-domain waveforms of variables X, Y, Z in the time interval $[0\,\text{s}, 0.001\,\text{s}]$. (f) Time-domain waveforms of variables W_1, W_2, W_3 in the time interval $[0\,\text{s}, 0.001\,\text{s}]$

the voltage of the two-terminal subsystem in Fig. 7(a), $V = V_1 = V_2 = V_3$, thus the flux of each memristor is equal to the flux of the two-terminal subsystem $\phi = \phi_1 = \phi_2 = \phi_3$ in Fig. 7(b), where $\phi = \int_0^t V(\tau)d\tau$, $\phi_1 = \int_0^t V_1(\tau)d\tau$, $\phi_2 = \int_0^t V_2(\tau)d\tau$, $\phi_3 = \int_0^t V_3(\tau)d\tau$. Applying Kirchoff Current Law (KCL), the current is the sum of the current across each memristor $I = I_1 + I_2 + I_3$ in Fig. 7(c), thus the charge is the sum of the charge across each memristor $q = \int_0^t I(\tau)d\tau = \int_0^t I_1(\tau)d\tau + \int_0^t I_2(\tau)d\tau + \int_0^t I_3(\tau)d\tau = q_1 + q_2 + q_3$ in Fig. 7(d). The normalized width of the doped region is also switched between the low and high levels near the limiting values of 0 and 1 in Fig. 7(e), which would change with the change of current and this would cause a change of the resistance value within a single memristor. It follows that only the memristors $q - \phi$ curve in the first quadrant is also visited during every period of $i(t)$ in Fig. 7(f). The memristors work in a regime such that the boundary between the doped and undoped layers does not approach the edges with dominant nonlinear effects. With the change of the normalized width in the doped region, it easily leads to a change of the resistance value within each memristor as Fig. 7(g), the memristors $R_{mem} - x$ diagram is hyperbola in Fig. 7(g), which implies this nonlinearity more evident at the boundaries. The same behavior can be observed in terms of pinched hysteresis, as shown in Fig. 7(h). The hysteresis occurs because the maxima and minima of the sinusoidal current across each memristor in Fig. 7(c) do

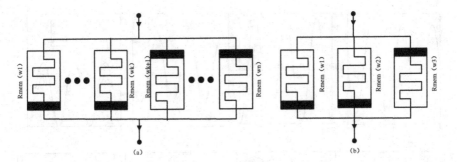

Fig. 6. (a) Multi memristors in parallel connection with $k(0 \leq k \leq n)$ same polarity interactions and $n - k$ different polarity. (b) Three memristors in parallel connection with two same polarity interactions and one different polarity.

not occur at the same time as the corresponding memristor voltage in Fig. 7(a). The pinching at the origin in Fig. 7(h) occurs because both current and voltage for each memristor become zero at the same time.

The behavior of the three memristors in parallel connection is now exploited to design a dynamical circuit. Three memristors in parallel connection with two same polarity interactions and one different polarity as Fig. 6 are connected to the subcircuit as Fig. 4. The circuit consists of two capacitors, an inductor, and three memristors in parallel connection. Applying to the circuit introduced above the Kirchhoff's circuit laws and the constitutive relationships of the memristor (Eqs. (1) and (4)), we get the following set of differential equations:

$$
\begin{cases}
\frac{du_1}{dt} = \frac{1}{C_1}\left(i - \frac{u_1}{R_{mem}(w_1)} - \frac{u_1}{R_{mem}(w_2)} - \frac{u_1}{R_{mem}(w_3)}\right), \\
\frac{di}{dt} = \frac{1}{KL_1}(u_1 - u_2), \\
\frac{u_2}{dt} = \frac{K}{C_2}i, \\
\frac{dw_1}{dt} = \varphi_1 \frac{\mu_v R_{ON}}{D} F\left(\frac{w_1}{D}\right)\frac{u_1}{R_{mem}(w_1)}, \\
\frac{dw_2}{dt} = \varphi_2 \frac{\mu_v R_{ON}}{D} F\left(\frac{w_2}{D}\right)\frac{u_1}{R_{mem}(w_2)}, \\
\frac{dw_3}{dt} = \varphi_3 \frac{\mu_v R_{ON}}{D} F\left(\frac{w_3}{D}\right)\frac{u_1}{R_{mem}(w_3)},
\end{cases}
\tag{8}
$$

where

$$
R_{mem}(w_i) = R_{ON}\frac{w_i}{D} + R_{OFF}\left(1 - \frac{w_i}{D}\right), \varphi_1 = \varphi_2 = -\varphi_3 = 1. \tag{9}
$$

Assume $\tilde{R}_{mem}(W_i) = W_i + \frac{R_{OFF}}{R_{ON}}(1 - W_i)$, $X = u_1/u_0$, $Y = i/i_0$, $Z = u_2/u_0$, $W_1 = w_1/D$, $W_2 = w_2/D$, $W_3 = w_3/D$, $\tau = t/t_0$, $u_0 = 1v$, $i_0 = u_0/R_{ON}$, $t_0 = D^2/\mu_v u_0$, $C_0 = D^2/\mu_v u_0 R_{ON}$, and $L_0 = D^2 R_{ON}/\mu_v u_0$, it is easy to see that the following equation should be obtained as follows:

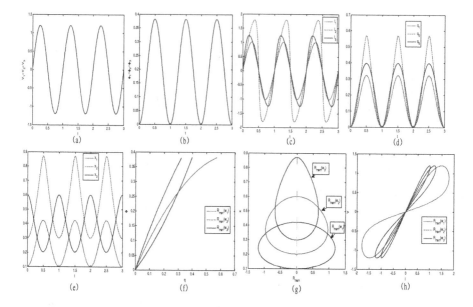

Fig. 7. Memristors in parallel connection with parameters $R_{on} = 100\,\Omega$, $R_{off} = 16\,\mathrm{k}\Omega$, $p = 10$, driven by a voltage source $V(t) = 1.2sin2\pi t$.

$$
\begin{cases}
\frac{X}{d\tau} = \frac{C_0}{C_1}(Y - \frac{X}{R_{mem}(W_1)} - \frac{X}{R_{mem}(W_2)} - \frac{X}{R_{mem}(W_3)}), \\
\frac{Y}{d\tau} = \frac{L_0}{KL_1}(Z - X), \\
\frac{Z}{d\tau} = \frac{KC_0}{C_2}Y, \\
\frac{dW_1}{d\tau} = \varphi_1 F(\frac{W_1}{D})\frac{X}{R_{mem}(W_1)}, \\
\frac{dW_2}{d\tau} = \varphi_2 F(\frac{W_2}{D})\frac{X}{R_{mem}(W_2)}, \\
\frac{dW_3}{d\tau} = \varphi_3 F(\frac{W_3}{D})\frac{X}{R_{mem}(W_3)}.
\end{cases}
\tag{10}
$$

Typical values of the memristor parameters are chosen by $R_{on} = 100\,\Omega$, $R_{off} = 16\,\mathrm{k}\Omega$, $p = 10$, $D = 10\,\mathrm{nm}$, $\mu_v = 10^{-14}m^2s^{-1}v^{-1}$, $\frac{C_0}{C_1} = 3 \times 10^{-8}$, $\frac{L_0}{KL_1} = 0.08$, and $\frac{KC_0}{C_2} = 4 \times 10^{-9}$. The circuit dynamics has been studied by numerical integration of (10), obtained by adopting a standard 4th order Runge-Kutta algorithm. An example of nonlinear behavior is shown in Fig. 8. Figure 8 (a)–(d) show the transient nonlinear behavior. Figure 8(e) shows the trajectories of state variables X, Y, Z of system (10) with the time evolution. Figure 8(f) shows the trajectories of state variables W_1, W_2, W_3 of system (10) with the time evolution. Time-domain waveforms in Fig. 8(e) and (f) are also nonperodic. A kind of seeming random chance or irregular movement also appears in phase portrait and time-domain waveform of Fig. 8.

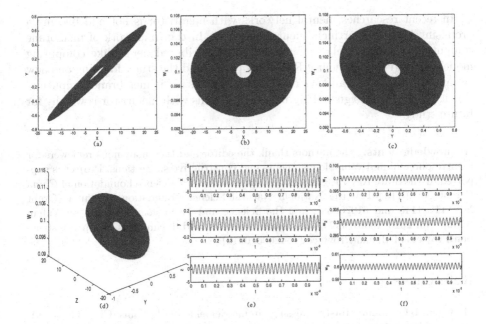

Fig. 8. For initial conditions $(1,0.1,-0.3,0.1,0.3,0.6)$. (a) Phase portrait $X - Y$. (b) Phase portrait $X - W_1$. (c) Phase portrait $Y - W_1$. (d) Phase portrait $Y - Z - W_1$. (e) Time-domain waveforms of variables X, Y, Z in the time interval $[0\,\text{s},\ 0.001\,\text{s}]$. (f) Time-domain waveforms of variables W_1, W_2, W_3 in the time interval $[0\,\text{s},\ 0.001\,\text{s}]$.

5 Conclusion

Many memristor-based circuits and nonlinear oscillators have been recently introduced by assuming theoretical flux-charge constitutive relation for the memristive component. Different choices for this nonlinear functions are often cubic or piece-wise linear functions. However, a fundamental model (for instance, to describe the behavior of the first memristor manufactured in the HP laboratories) has been considered the memristor as a device with a memristance $R(w)$ depending on the width of the doped region (which in turns is function of the quantity of charge passed through the device). First, we connect multi memristors in series and parallel as different subsystems. Second, those subsystems are driven by a voltage source to get important constitutive relations among voltage, current, charge, flux and the width of the doped region, respectively. Finally, we apply those connected subsystems of multi memristors to replace Chua's diode. The combination of memristors in circuits can give rise to rich enough behavior that we wouldn't need further complications of adding in other circuit elements. Multi memristors in series and parallel connection are given to illustrate an important step towards real world memristor system applications, in which to fully exploit the memory effect of real memristors is still an open and challenging problem with interesting potential applications in the design of chaotic circuits with a certain number of components.

In recent researches, neural networks with memristor is hot and become a promising branch in artificial neural networks. In the framework of membrane computing, there is a class of parallel and distributed neural-like computing models, named spiking neural P systems [7,27], and the study focusing one new variants of spiking neural P systems [12,13,19,20] is hot in membrane computing. If is it possible to design spiking neural P systems with memristor is worthy for future study.

Acknowledgments. The authors thank the editor and the anonymous reviewers for their resourceful and valuable comments and constructive suggestions. Project is supported by the State Key Program of the National Natural Science Foundation of China (Grant No. 61134012), the National Natural Science Foundation of China (Grant Nos. 11271146 and 61070238), and the Science and Technology Program of Wuhan (Grant No. 20130105010117), Innovation Scientists and Technicians Troop Construction Projects of Henan Province (154200510012).

References

1. Chua, L.O.: Memristor-the missing circuit element. IEEE Trans. Circ. Theor. **34**, 507–519 (1971)
2. Strukov, D.B., Snider, G.S., Stewart, D.R., Williams, R.S.: The missing memristor found. Nature **4**, 80–83 (2008)
3. Persin, Y.V., Ventra, M.D.: Practical approach to programmable analog circuits with memristors. IEEE Trans. Circ. Syst. I-Regul. Pap. **57**, 1857–1864 (2009)
4. Madan, R.N.: Chua's Circuit: A Paradigm for Chaos. World Scientific, Singapore (1993)
5. Itoh, M., Chua, L.O.: Memristor oscillators. Int. J. Bifurcat. Chaos **18**, 3183–3206 (2008)
6. Wang, X., Miao, Y., Cheng, M.: Finding motifs in DNA sequences using low-dispersion sequences. J. Comput. Biol. **21**(4), 320–329 (2014)
7. Song, T., Pan, L.: Spiking neural P systems with rules on synapses working in maximum spiking strateg. IEEE Trans. NanoBiosci. **14**(4), 465–477 (2015)
8. Shi, X., Wang, Z., Deng, C., Song, T., Pan, L., Chen, Z.: A novel bio-sensor based on DNA strand displacement. PLoS One **9**, e108856 (2014)
9. Muthuswamy, B.: Implementing memristor based chaotic circuits. Int. J. Bifurcat. Chaos **20**, 1335–1350 (2010)
10. Bao, B.C., Liu, Z., Xu, J.P.: Hopf bifurcation from lines of equilibria without parameters in memristor oscillators. Electron. Lett. **20**, 237–238 (2010)
11. Bao, B.C., Ma, Z.H., Xu, J.P., Liu, Z., Xu, Q.: A simple memristor chaotic circuit with complex dynamics. Int. J. Bifurcat. Chaos **21**, 2629–2645 (2011)
12. Song, T., Pan, L., Wang, J., et al.: Normal forms of spiking neural P systems with anti-spikes. IEEE Trans. NanoBiosci. **11**(4), 352–359 (2012)
13. Zhang, X., Pan, L., Pun, A.: On the universality of axon P systems. IEEE Trans. Neural Netw. Learn. Syst. (2015). doi:10.1109/TNNLS.2015.2396940
14. Sun, J.W., Shen, Y., Zhang, G.: Transmission projective synchronization of multi-systems with non-delayed and delayed coupling via impulsive control. Chaos **22**, 043107–043116 (2012)

15. Song, T., Pan, L., Jiang, K., Song, B., Chen, W.: Normal forms for some classes of sequential spiking neural P systems. IEEE Trans. NanoBiosci. **12**(3), 255–264 (2013)
16. Sun, J.W., Yin, Q., Shen, Y.: Compound synchronization for four chaotic systems of integer order and fractional order. Europhys. Lett. **106**(4), 40005 (2014)
17. Sun, J.W., Shen, Y.: Quasi-ideal memory system. IEEE Trans. Cybern. **45**(7), 1353–1362 (2015)
18. Song, B., Pérez-Jiménez, M.J., Pan, L.: Efficient solutions to hard computational problems by P systems with symport/antiport rules and membrane division. Biosystems **130**, 51–58 (2015)
19. Song, T., Pan, L., Jiang, K., et al.: Normal forms for some classes of sequential spiking neural P systems. IEEE Trans. NanoBiosci. **12**(3), 255–264 (2013)
20. Song, T., Pan, L., Păun, G.: Asynchronous spiking neural P systems with local synchronization. Inf. Sci. **219**, 197–207 (2013)
21. Buscarino, A., Fortuna, M., Frasca, M., Gambuzza, L.V.: Memristor oscillators. Chaos **22**, 023136 (2012)
22. Buscarino, A., Fortuna, L., Frasca, M., Gambuzza, L.V., Sciuto, G.: Memristive chaotic circuits based on cellular nonlinear networks. Int. J. Bifurcat. Chaos **22**, 1250070 (2012)
23. Wang, X., Miao, Y.: GAEM: a hybrid algorithm incorporating GA with EM for planted edited motif finding problem. Curr. Bioinform. **9**(5), 463–469 (2014)
24. Papandroulidakis, G., Vourkas, I., Vasileiadis, N., Sirakoulis, G.C.: Boolean logic operations and computing circuits based on memristors. IEEE Trans. Cir. Syst. II Exp. Briefs **61**, 972–976 (2014)
25. Wen, S.P., Zeng, Z.G., Huang, T.W.: Adaptive synchronization of memristor-based Chua's circuits. Phys. Lett. A **376**, 2775–2780 (2012)
26. Joglekar, Y.N., Wolf, S.J.: The elusive memristor: properties of basic electrical circuits. Eur. J. Phys. **30**, 661–675 (2009)
27. Song, T., Pan, L.: Spiking neural P systems with rules on synapses working in maximum spikes consumption strategy. IEEE Trans. NanoBiosci. **14**(1), 38–44 (2015)
28. Muthuswamy, B., Chua, L.O.: Simplest chaotic circuit. Int. J. Bifurcat. Chaos **20**, 1567–1580 (2010)

Self-adaptive Multiple Evolution Algorithms for Image Segmentation Using Multilevel Thresholding

Liling Sun[1,2], Jingtao Hu[1], Na Lin[3], Qiaocui Zhang[4], and Hanning Chen[5(✉)]

[1] Department of Information Service and Intelligent Control,
Shenyang Institute of Automation, Chinese Academy of Sciences,
Shenyang 110016, China
[2] University of Chinese Academy of Sciences, Beijing 100049, China
[3] Beijing Shenzhou Aerospace Software Technology Co. Ltd., Beijing, China
[4] China Huanqiu Contracting and Engineering Corporation Liaoning Company,
Fushun 113006, China
[5] School of Computer Science and Software, Tianjin Polytechnic University,
Tianjin 300387, China
perfect_chn@hotmail.com

Abstract. Multilevel thresholding based on Otsu method is one of the most popular image segmentation techniques. However, when the number of thresholds increases, the consumption of CPU time grows exponentially. Although the evolution algorithms are helpful to solve this problem, for the high-dimensional problems, the Otsu methods based on the classical evolution algorithms may get trapped into local optimal or be instability due to the inefficiency of local search. To overcome such drawback, this paper employs the self-adaptive multiple evolution algorithms (MEAs), which automatically protrudes the core position of the excellent algorithm among the selected algorithms. The tests against 10 benchmark functions demonstrate that this multi-algorithms is fit for most problems. Then, this optimizer is applied to image multilevel segmentation problems. Experimental results on a variety of images provided by the Berkeley Segmentation Database show that the proposed algorithm can accurately and stably solve this kind of problems.

Keywords: Multiple evolution algorithms · Multilevel threshold · Image segmentation

1 Introduction

The target of image segmentation is to extract meaningful objects from the input image. Segmentation is having major importance and elementary place in image processing for interpretation of any image. It is useful in discriminating an object from some objects or background which has distinct gray levels. In recent years, various methods for image segmentation have been developed. Typically, image segmentation based on fuzzy C-means proposed by Bexdek [1], mean shift

© Springer-Verlag Berlin Heidelberg 2015
M. Gong et al. (Eds.): BIC-TA 2015, CCIS 562, pp. 400–410, 2015.
DOI: 10.1007/978-3-662-49014-3_36

filters in-vented by Comaniciu [2] and nonlinear diffusion exploited by Perona [3] have become the widely adopted methods in image processing. It was found that the thresholding technique is the most popular technique out of all the existing approaches used for segmentation of various types of images [4].

In general, the Otsu method has been proved as one of the powerful and famous thresholding techniques for uniformity and shape measures, due to its simplicity, robustness and accuracy [5,6]. However, with the increase of the number of thresholds, the computation time grows exponentially, which would limit the multilevel thresholding applications. Nowadays evolutionary computational algorithms are most extensively used due to optimum solution properties for finding the best threshold values with a high computational efficiency [7]. However, the evolution algorithms all fail to conquer "the Curse of Dimensionality", which results in trapping into local optimum without stability and consistency.

This paper applies the self-adaptive Multiple Evolution Algorithms (MEAs) [8] to solve this problem. The MEAs with the self-adaptive mechanism and the elitism search strategy can automatically protrude the core position of the excellent algorithm among the selected algorithms, which well overcomes the problem that different fitness landscapes require different search approaches, which approved in No Free Lunch Theorem [9].

The rest of this paper is organized as follows: Sect. 2 gives a brief explanation of the self-adaptive multiple evolution algorithms in detail. In Sect. 3, the performance of this method based multilevel thresholding for image segmentation is evaluated. Finally, Sect. 4 concludes the paper.

2   Self-adaptive Multiple Evolution Algorithms

2.1   Sub-populations and Multiple Evolution Algorithms

The algorithm is initiated using a random initial population P_{size} within the predefined search spaces. Then, the initial population is divided into q sub-populations, where q is equal to the number of selected algorithms. It should be noted that the whole population of size N is not equipartitioned. Before the population division process, the numbers of individuals in q sub-populations are set as $G = g_1, g_2, \cdots, g_i, \cdots, g_q$, where $g_1 \geq g_2 \geq \cdots \geq g_i \geq \cdots \geq g_q$ and $N = g_1 + g_2 + \cdots + g_i + \cdots + g_q$. Each evolution algorithm is stochastically assigned to a number of individuals. The goal of asymmetrical division is that the excellent algorithm occupies the sub-population with the larger number of individuals in the later evolution period as far as possible. Oppositely, the algorithms with poor performance obtain small amounts of resources. In the evolution process, each algorithm with a specific evolution strategy searches its optima independently. After an iteration of evolution, the fitness value of each individual will be calculated according to the predefined objective function. Finally, the self-adaptive mechanism will protrude the core position of the excellent algorithm.

2.2   Self-adaptive Mechanism and Information Exchange Mechanism

In order to implement the self-adaptive selection of the most suitable algorithm for the target problem, the fitness values $\{FBest_1^t, FBest_2^t, \cdots, FBest_i^t, \cdots, FBest_q^t\}$ of the best individuals $\{PBest_1^t, PBest_2^t, \cdots, PBest_i^t, \cdots, PBest_q^t\}$ of sub-populations are regarded as the evaluation criterion of selecting the excellent algorithm, where t denotes generation number. Given a maximization problem, if the fitness value of the ith sub-population is larger than the one of the jth sub-population ($FBest_i^t > FBest_j^t$), it means the mth algorithm assigned to ith sub-population may be more excellent than the nth algorithm assigned to the jth sub-population. Therefore, in the next iteration, the mth algorithm may own more resources (larger number of individuals of sub-population) than the nth algorithm. Roulette Wheel method is employed to decide the relationship between sub-populations and the selected algorithms:

$$P_m = \frac{FBest_m}{\sum_{i=1}^{q} FBest_i} \tag{1}$$

The self-adaptive multiple evolution algorithms employ the elitism search strategy to accelerate the convergence rate of searching the global optimum. Before each time of evolution, the parent population Pt of size N and their fitness values $\{Fit_1^t, Fit_2^t, \cdots, Fit_i^t, \cdots, Fit_q^t\}$ are recorded in Elites Container. After evolution, the offspring population P_{t+1} is generated and their fitness values $\{Fit_1^{t+1}, Fit_2^{t+1}, \cdots, Fit_i^{t+1}, \cdots, Fit_q^{t+1}\}$ are calculated, and then both are recorded into Elites Container ($EC = P_t \cup P_{t+1}$). The population of the next iteration is chosen from Elites Container. The individuals with larger fitness values in Elites Set containing both parent and offspring populations have larger probability to be selected as elites.

In order to enhance the information exchange between the sub-populations, the crossover operation is applied. As the same as the crossover operation of the genetic algorithm, the two new individuals are created by arithmetic crossover on stochastically selected individuals in different sub-populations, as following:

$$\begin{cases} ind_i^{t+1} = a \cdot ind_i^t + (1-a) \cdot ind_j^t \\ ind_j^{t+1} = a \cdot ind_j^t + (1-a) \cdot ind_i^t \end{cases} \tag{2}$$

where a is a random number in the range of $[0,1]$.

2.3   Framework of Multiple Evolution Algorithms

The flowchart of self-adaptive multiple evolution algorithms is listed in Fig. 1.

For illustrative purposes, only the most popular and commonly used, general-purpose, evolutionary optimization algorithms are adopted. These methods are: (1) particle swarm optimization (PSO) [10]; (2) artificial bee colony optimizer (ABC) [11]; (3) ge-netic algorithm (GA) [12]; (4) differential evolution (DE) [13]; (5) the covariance matrix adaptation (CMA) evolution strategy [14]. The specific parameters of the selected algorithms are given in Table 1.

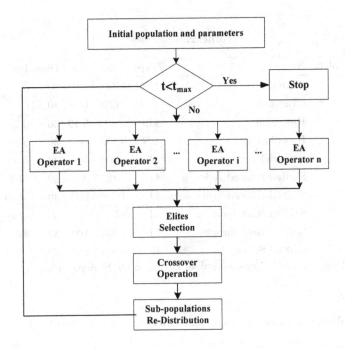

Fig. 1. The flowchart of self-adaptive multiple evolution algorithms

2.4 Benchmark Test

The benchmark test suite includes ten 30-D benchmark functions, which are commonly used in intelligent computation literatures [15,16] to show solution quality and convergence rate of new developed evolutionary and swarm intelligence optimizers. The involved benchmark functions can be classified as classical benchmarks (F1–F5) and CEC05 benchmarks (F6–F10) [17]. The detailed setting of these test functions are listed in Table 2.

Table 1. Parameters setting

Algorithm	Parameters
PSO	$c_1 = 2.05, c_2 = 2.05$
ABC	$Limit = 20$
GA	$P_{cross} = 0.8, P_{mut} = 0.1$
DE	$F = 0.9, CR = 0.9$
CMA-ES	$\sigma_F = 0.2, \lambda = 10, \mu = 5$

Table 3 shows the basic statistical results (i.e., the mean and standard deviations of the function values found in 20 runs) of the 30D benchmark test functions F1–F10. Due to the relatively low difficulty of the basic benchmark test

Table 2. Test suite

Problem	Name	Type	Low	Up	Dim	Bia
F1	Ackley	MN	−32	32	30	0
F2	Griewank	MN	−600	600	30	0
F3	Rastrigrin	MS	−5.12	5.12	30	0
F4	Rosenbrock	UN	−30	30	30	0
F5	Schewfel	MS	−500	500	30	0
F6	Shifted rotated Ackleys	M	−32	32	30	−140
F7	Shifted rotated Griewanks	M	0	600	30	−180
F8	Shifted Rastrigins	M	−5	5	30	-330
F9	Shifted Rosenbrocks	M	−100	100	30	390
F10	Shifted Schwefel	U	−100	100	30	−450

M: Multimodal, N:Non-Separable, U:Unimodal, S: Separable

Table 3. Performance of all algorithms on test functions F1–F10

Problem		MEAs	PSO	ABC	GA	DE	CMA-ES
F1	Mean	3.5527E-18	3.5532E-15	3.9068E-14	19.0812	3.0426	3.5527E-15
	Std	0	0	1.5642E-18	0.3643	0.5813	0
F2	Mean	0.0020	0.021	0.002	0.020	0.0200	0.002
	Std	0	0	1.5640E-18	2.7622E-15	4.2481E-11	0
F3	Mean	0	0	4.4410E-17	457.6520	1.1471	0
	Std	0	0	6.0810E-17	24.045	6.8968E-3	0
F4	Mean	−9.6992	−9.18455	−9.6750	−8.5342	−9.6263	−9.6942
	Std	2.7532E-5	0.6533	2.1739E-6	0.1602	0.04234	0
F5	Mean	0	**0**	0	157.221	1.5379	0
	Std	0	**0**	0	6.8924	0.4279	0
F6	Mean	−1.1999E2	−1.1996E2	−1.1990E2	−1.1889E2	−1.1909E2	−1.1993E2
	Std	9.4719E-3	0.17489	0.08614	3.3141E-2	0.02876	0.5001
F7	Mean	−1.7998E2	1.0958E4	1.6102E3	4.8137E3	4.5163E3	−1.8001E2
	Std	0	3.7149E3	2.3913E2	70.6580	0	0
F8	Mean	−3.3001E2	−1.9910E2	−3.301E2	−3.2890E2	−330	−3.2842E2
	Std	0	17.2850	0	0.2106	0	0.8899
F9	Mean	4.0923E2	4.1737E2	3.9453E2	7.1915E3	4.1646E2	2.2110E3
	Std	3.1392	39.9079	5.6006	7.9795E3	1.1103	4.0483E3
F10	Mean	−4.4999E2	−2.3889E2	3.5116E3	7.6600E3	1.2945E3	−4.4996E2
	Std	0	73.8832	1.5146E3	2.6765E3	3.6259E2	3.9186E-9

functions, the basic statistical results obtained by multiple evolution algorithms are very similar to the ones obtained by other evolution algorithms (EAs). With the increase of solving difficulty, the differentiation of the statistical results of CEC2005 obtained by these EAs can be observed. Generally, the multiple evolution algorithms surpass the other single algorithms because the self-adaptive mechanism keeps the excellent algorithm with more individuals and the elitism search strategy strengthens the local search ability around the global optima.

3   Multilevel Threshold for Image Segmentation

3.1   Image Segmentation Based on Between-Class Variance

The Otsu multi-threshold measure [5] proposed by Otsu has been popularly employed in determining whether the optimal threshold method can provide image segmentation by maximizing the variance of the various classes. The traditional Otsu method can be described as follows.

Let the gray levels of a given image with N pixels range over $[0, L-1]$ and $h(i)$ denotes the number of the ith gray level pixel. $P(i)$ is the probability of i.

$$N = \sum_{i=0}^{L-1} h(i), P(i) = h(i)/N \quad for \quad 0 \leq i \leq L - 1 \tag{3}$$

$$Maximize \quad f(t) = w_0 w_1 (u_0 - u_1)^2 \tag{4}$$

where

$$w_0 = \sum_{i=0}^{t-1} P_i; u_0 = \sum_{i=0}^{t-1} i \times P_i/w_0 \tag{5}$$

$$w_1 = \sum_{i=t}^{L-1} P_i; u_1 = \sum_{i=t}^{L-1} i \times P_i/w_1 \tag{6}$$

Bi-level thresholding based on the between-class variance can be extended to multi-level thresholding. The extended between class variance function is calculated as follows:

$$Maximize \quad f(t) = \sum_{i=0}^{M} \delta_i \tag{7}$$

where M is the number of thresholds. And

$$\delta_0 = w_0 (u_0 - u_T)^2$$
$$\delta_j = w_j (u_j - u_T)^2 \tag{8}$$
$$\delta_M = w_M (u_M - u_T)^2$$

$$u_0 = \sum_{i=0}^{t_1-1} i \times P_i/w_i$$

$$u_j = \sum_{i=t_j}^{t_{j+1}-1} i \times P_i/w_i \tag{9}$$

$$u_M = \sum_{i=t_M}^{L-1} i \times P_i/w_i$$

Equation 7 is used as the objective function which is to be optimized (maximized).

3.2 Experiment Setup

For evaluating the performance of the multiple evolution algorithms (MEAs), we implemented it on a wide variety of images. These images include the popular tested images 41033.jpg, 42049.jpg, and 62096.jpg provided by the Berkeley Segmentation Database (BSDS) (Available at http://www.eecs.berkeley.edu/Research/Projects/CS/vision/bsds/BSDS300/html/dataset/images.html). The sizes of 41033.jpg, 42049.jpg, and 62096.jpg are 321×481. Each image has a unique grey-level histogram. Most of the images are difficult to segment due to multimodality of the histograms. Figure 2 presents nine original images and their histograms.

3.3 Experimental Results of Multilevel Threshold

We employ Eq. (7) as the fitness function to provide a comparison of performances. Since the classical Otsu method is an exhaustive searching algorithm, we regarded its results as the "standard." Table 4 shows the fitness function values (with $M = 2, 3, 4$) attained by Otsu methods. For $M > 4$, owning to the unbearable consumption of CPU time, we don't list the correlative values in our experiment.

It is well known that, the EA-based Otsu method for multilevel thresholding segmentation can only accelerate the computation velocity. The mean fitness function values and their standard deviations obtained by the test algorithms (with $M = 2, 3, 4, 5, 7, 9$) are shown in Table 5. According to the mean CPU times shown in Table 6, there is no obvious difference between the EA-based Otsu methods. Compared with traditional Otsu method, all of them effectively shorten the computation time.

From the test results listed in Table 5, the results obtained by MEAs are equal to or close to the ones obtained the traditional Otsu method when $M = 2, 3, 4$. Moreover, the standard deviations obtained by MEAs are considerably small among the results obtained by the EA-based Otsu methods. With the growth in dimension, there are statistically significant gap between experiments using these EA-based Otsu methods for image segmentation, in the term of both efficiency (fitness values) and stability (standard deviation). Benefiting from self-adaptive

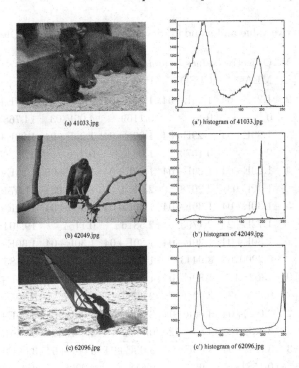

Fig. 2. Test images and their histograms

mechanism and elitism search strategy, MEAs owns the best performance and stability on high-dimension problems for image segmentation with Otsu method. As demonstrated in Table 5, the self-adaptive multiple evolution algorithms is suitable for the multilevel thresholding problem based on Otsu method.

Table 4. Objective values and thresholds by the OTSU method

Image	M=2		M=3		M=4	
	Objective values	Optimal thresholds	Objective value	Optimal thresholds	Objective values	Optima thresholds
41033	1.2753E4	64,131	1.2885E4	57,107,165	1.2945E4	49,79,122,171
42049	3.0559E4	90,162	3.0629E4	75,133,179	3.0661E4	59,102,146,182
62096	2.7469E4	102,196	2.7585E4	86,156, 218	2.7631E4	71,121,176,225
CPU time	1.4012s		45.0423s		2334.1540s	

Table 5. Objective value and standard deviation by the EA-based Otsu methods

Image	M	Objective values (standard deviation)				
		MEAs	CPSO	PSO	DE	GA
41033	2	1.28E+04	1.28E+04	1.28E+04	12753	1.27E+04
		0	0	0.1169	4.06E-03	14.768
	3	1.29E+04	1.29E+04	1.29E+04	1.29E+04	1.29E+04
		0	0.1079	1.0243	0	42.8287
	4	1.29E+04	1.29E+04	1.29E+04	1.29E+05	1.29E+04
		1.40E-03	2.2078	2.0414	1.32E-03	31.5746
	5	1.30E+04	1.30E+04	1.30E+04	1.30E+04	1.29E+04
		1.72E-02	2.1793	2.5816	0.1151	19.4046
	7	1.30E+04	1.30E+04	1.30E+04	1.30E+04	1.30E+04
		0.220026	3.9443	1.9642	0.1466	12.1857
	9	13021.1	1.30E+04	1.30E+04	1.30E+04	1.30E+04
		0.883857	2.4286	2.4069	1.2077	5.8058
42049	2	3.06E+04	3.06E+04	3.06E+04	3.06E+04	3.05E+04
		3.83E-12	3.83E-12	0.0862	3.83E-12	69.3913
	3	3.06E+04	3.06E+04	3.06E+04	3.06E+04	3.06E+04
		0.1581	0.007	0.618	0.0298	46.4996
	4	3.07E+04	3.07E+04	3.07E+04	3.07E+04	3.06E+04
		0	0.091	0.9848	0.5921	28.104
	5	3.07E+04	3.07E+04	3.07E+04	3.07E+04	3.07E+04
		9.2216	0.7255	1.4903	0.8694	1.7513
	7	3.07E+04	3.07E+04	3.07E+04	3.07E+04	3.07E+04
		9.955	0.7294	1.9956	0.0942	1.7918
	9	3.07E+04	3.07E+04	3.07E+04	3.07E+04	3.07E+04
		6.0562	0.9065	1.7663	0.3772	1.9325
62096	2	2.75E+04	2.75E+04	2.75E+04	2.75E+04	2.75E+04
		0	0	0.1693	3.83E-12	15.246
	3	2.76E+04	2.76E+04	2.76E+04	2.76E+04	2.76E+04
		0.5133	0.1933	0.8584	0	35.4894
	4	2.76E+04	2.76E+04	2.76E+04	2.76E+04	2.76E+04
		0.2255	1.0023	1.1273	1.52E+02	33.2765
	5	2.77E+04	2.77E+04	2.77E+04	2.77E+04	2.77E+04
		3.57E-02	2.2228	1.0799	0.252	5.7383
	7	2.77E+04	2.77E+04	2.77E+04	2.77E+04	2.77E+04
		0.1319	2.1289	1.1261	6.76E-02	5.7592
	9	2.77E+04	2.77E+04	2.77E+04	2.77E+04	2.77E+04
		0.545201	1.1693	1.6069	0.4215	9.1974

Table 6. The mean CPU time of the compared EA-based methods on Otsu algorithm

Dim	Algorithms				
	MEAs	CMA-ES	PSO	GA	DE
2 Dim	0.3108	0.2247	0.1932	0.3255	0.1898
3 Dim	0.3219	0.2317	0.2106	0.3249	0.1888
4 Dim	0.3289	0.2341	0.2126	0.3252	0.2221
5 Dim	0.329	0.2348	0.1998	0.3235	0.2087
7 Dim	0.3281	0.2358	0.212	0.3231	0.2021
9 Dim	0.3294	0.2339	0.218	0.3238	0.2406

4 Conclusion

The No Free Lunch Theorem (NFL) has demonstrated that it is impossible to develop a single search algorithm that is always most efficient on a large range of problems. The self-adaptive multiple evolution algorithms with the self-adaptive mechanism and the elitism search strategy can automatically select the suitable algorithm solving the target problem. We applied this method in solving the multilevel image segmentation problem. This multi-algorithms gets favorable results than the other compared methods.

References

1. Bexdek, J.C.: A convergence theorem for the fuzzy isodara clustering algorithms. IEEE Trans. Pattern Anal. Mach. Intell. **PAMI–2**(1), 1–8 (1980)
2. Comaniciu, D., Meer, P.: Mean shift analysis and applications. In: Proceedings of 7th International Conference on Computer Vision, pp. 1197–1203, Kerkyra (1999)
3. Perona, P., Malik, J.: Scale-space and edge detection using anisotropic diffusion. IEEE Trans. Pattern Anal. Mach. Intell. **12**(7), 629–639 (1990)
4. Agrawal, S., Panda, R., Bhuyan, S., Panigrahi, B.K.: Tsallis: entropy based optimal multi-level thresholding using cuckoo search algorithm. Swarm Evol. Comput. **11**, 16–30 (2013)
5. Sezgin, M., Sankur, B.: Survey over image thresholding techniques and quantitative performance evaluation. J. Electron. Imaging **13**(1), 146–165 (2004)
6. Sahoo, P.K., Soltani, S., Wong, A.K.C.: A survey of thresholding techniques. Comput. Vis. Graph Image Process. **41**(2), 233–260 (1988)
7. Gao, H., Xu, W., Sun, J., Tang, Y.: Multilevel thresholding for image segmentation through an improved quantum-behaved particle swarm algorithm. IEEE T. Instrum. Measur. **59**(4), 290–301 (2010)
8. Vrugt, J.A., Robinson, B.A., Hyman, J.M.: Self-adaptive multimethod search for global optimization in real-parameter spaces. IEEE Trans. Evol. Comput. **13**(2), 243–259 (2009)
9. Wolpert, D.H., Macready, W.G.: No free lunch theorems for optimization. IEEE Trans. Evol. Comput. **1**(1), 67–82 (1997)

10. Kennedy, J.: The particle swarm as collaborative sampling of the search space. Adv. Complex Syst. **10**, 191–213 (2007)

11. Li, W., Zhou, Q., Zhu, Y., Pan, F.: An improved MOPSO with a crowding distance based external archive maintenance strategy. In: Tan, Y., Shi, Y., Ji, Z. (eds.) ICSI 2012, Part I. LNCS, vol. 7331, pp. 74–82. Springer, Heidelberg (2012)

12. Chen, H.N., Zhu, Y.L., Hu, K.Y., Ku, T.: RFID network planning using a multi-swarm optimizer. J. Netw. Comput. Appl. **34**(3), 88–901 (2011)

13. El-Abd, M.: Performance assessment of foraging algorithms vs. evolutionary algorithms. Inf. Sci. **182**(1), 243–263 (2012)

14. Kmpf, J.H., Robinson, D.: A hybrid CMA-ES and HDE optimization algorithm with application to solar energy potential. Appl. Soft Comput. **9**(2), 738–745 (2009)

15. Civicioglu, P., Besdok, E.: A conceptual comparison of the cuckoo-search, particle swarm optimization, differential evolution and artificial bee colony algorithms. Artif. Intell. Rev. **39**(4), 315–346 (2013)

16. Simon, D.: Biogeography-based optimization. IEEE Trans. Evol. Comput. **12**(6), 702–713 (2008)

17. Suganthan, P.N., Hansen, N., Liang, J.J., Deb, K., Chen, Y.P., Auger, A., Tiwari, S.: Problem definitions and evaluation criteria for the CEC 2005 special session on real-parameter optimization. Technical report, Nanyang Technological University, Singapore and Kan-GAL Report Number 2005005 (Kanpur Genetic Algorithms Laboratory, IIT Kanpur), pp. 1–50 (2005)

Clustering Quantum-Behaved Particle Swarm Optimization Algorithm for Solving Dynamic Optimization Problems

Mengmei Wang, Wei Fang$^{(\boxtimes)}$, and Chaofeng Li

Key Laboratory of Advanced Process Control for Light Industry,
Department of Computer Science and Technology, School of IT Engineering,
Jiangnan University, Wuxi, Jiangsu, China
fangwei@jiangnan.edu.cn

Abstract. Solving dynamic optimization problems (DOPs) has become
the research focus in the optimization area in recent years. In view of
the dynamics and complexity of DOPs, quantum-behaved particle swarm
optimization (QPSO) algorithm, which is based on the quantum mechanics and Particle Swarm Optimization (PSO) algorithm, is proposed in
this paper to solve DOPs with the help of the algorithms global search
ability. The hierarchical clustering method is also used in the QPSO
algorithm in order to enhance the relocation ability and improve the
ability of tracking the optimal solution. During the optimization procedure, the convergence check, overcrowding check, and over-lapping check
are appointed to keep the diversity of the swarm. Experimental results
on the standard benchmark functions show that QPSO algorithm with
hierarchical clustering and diversity maintaining has strong ability to
adapt the dynamics and good optimization ability.

Keywords: Dynamic environment · Particle swarm optimization ·
Multimodal optimization · Hierarchical clustering

1 Introduction

Dynamic Optimization Problems (DOPs) are very popular in many real-world
applications and have been widely studied using Evolutionary Algorithms (EAs).
The optimal solution for DOPs [1] timely changes following the objective function, environment parameters and constraint conditions. This requires optimization algorithms not only to find the global optimal solution under a specific
environment, but also to track the trajectory of the changing optima over different dynamic environments.

As a population based stochastic optimization technique, Particle swarm
optimizer (PSO) algorithm [2] can be easily implemented and applied to DOPs.
In the standard PSO, the strong attraction of the global best particle results in
the diversity loss and is difficult to track the changing optima. For DOPs, the loss

© Springer-Verlag Berlin Heidelberg 2015
M. Gong et al. (Eds.): BIC-TA 2015, CCIS 562, pp. 411–421, 2015.
DOI: 10.1007/978-3-662-49014-3_37

of diversity makes a population slowly be responding in an ever-changing environment. Over the years, several approaches have been developed into standard PSO algorithm to address DOPs. In [3], the centers of different clusters of particle are identified by a k-means clustering algorithm in the population, and these clusters are used to replace the personal best or neighborhood best position. Branke et al. in [4] proposed a self-organizing scouts (SOS) in PSO algorithm. In SOS, the population is made up of a parent population searching in the entire search place and child population tracking local optima. Brits et al. in [5] designed an nbest PSO algorithm for locating multiple solutions, which defines the "neighborhood" of a particle as the closest particles in the population. In [6], Wang proposed a new multi-swarm optimization algorithm forking PSO (FPSO). In FPSO, a large main swarm is continuously searching for new peaks, and a number of smaller child swarm, divided form main swarm, are used for tracking the achieved peaks over time. Currently more attentions for DOPs are focused on the treatment of dynamic environment, but the performance improvement on the PSO algorithm to deal with DOPs gets less attention.

In this paper, in view of the dynamics and complexity of DOPs, quantum-behaved particle swarm optimization (QPSO) [7] algorithm, which is based on the quantum mechanics and PSO algorithm, is proposed to solve DOPs with the help of the algorithm's global search ability. The hierarchical clustering method [8] is also used in the QPSO algorithm in order to enhance the relocation ability, and improve the ability of tracking the optimal solution. During the optimization procedure, the convergence check, overcrowding check, and overlapping check are appointed to keep the diversity of the swarm. Experimental results on the standard benchmark functions show that QPSO algorithm with hierarchical clustering and diversity maintaining has strong ability to adapt the dynamics and good optimization ability.

The organization of the paper is as follows. Section 2 introduces the QPSO algorithm. The hierachical clustering method and diversity maintaining approach are presented in Sect. 3. Section 4 shows the experimental results and conclusions are given in Sect. 5.

2   Quantum-Behaved Particle Swarm Optimization

In quantum mechanics [9], it is difficult to determine particles position and velocity at the same time. Instead the particle is characterized by a wave function ψ and $|\psi|^2$ is the probability density function of particle location.

$$\psi \lceil x_{t+1} \rceil = \frac{1}{\sqrt{L_{id}(t))}} exp \left[-\frac{|x_{id}(t+1) - p_{id}(t)|}{L_{id}(t))} \right] \tag{1}$$

where $x_{id}(t+1)$ represents the position in the dth dimension of particle i at $(t+1)th$ iteration. $p_{id}(t)$ represents potential well in the dth dimension of particle i at $(t+1)th$ iteration. $L_{id}(t)$ is the standard deviation of the delta potential well in the dth dimension of particle i at $(t+1)th$ iteration. The probability density function of particles Q is expressed as:

$$Q\left[x_{id}(t+1))\right] = |\psi\left[x_{id}(t+1)\right]|^2 = \frac{1}{L_{id}(t)}exp\left[\frac{-2\,|x_{id}(t+1)-p_{id}(t)|}{L_{id}(t))}\right] \quad (2)$$

The probability distribution function of particles T is donated as following:

$$T\left[x_{id}(t+1))\right] = exp\left[\frac{-2\,|x_{id}(t+1)-p_{id}(t)|}{L_{id}(t))}\right] \quad (3)$$

By employing the Monte Carlo method [10], position of the particle can be updated iteratively as per the following equation:

$$x_{id}(t+1)) = p_{id}(t) \pm \frac{L_{id}(t)}{2}\ln\left[1/u_{id}(t)\right] \quad (4)$$

where $u_{id}(t)$ is a random number uniformly distributed in $(0,1)$. $L_{id}(t)$ is defined as follow:

$$L_{id}(t) = 2\alpha(t)\,|C_d(t) - x_{id}(t)| \quad (5)$$

where $C_d(t)$ is the mean best position of all the particle.

$$C(t) = (C_1(t), C_2(t), \cdots, C_D(t)) = \frac{1}{N}\sum_{i=1}^{N} p_i(t)$$

$$= \left(\frac{1}{N}\sum_{i=1}^{N} p_{i1}(t), \sum_{i=1}^{N} p_{i2}(t), \cdots, \sum_{i=1}^{N} p_{iD}(t)\right) \quad (6)$$

The QPSO Algorithm.

1: Initialize population random x_i

2: Do

3: Find out $C_d(t)$ using Eq. (6)

4 For each particle do

5: If $f\left[x_i(t+1)\right] < f\left[p_i(t)\right]$ then

$p_i(t+1) = x_i(t+1)$

6: $p(t+1) = arg\min\left\{f\left[p_i(t)\right]\right\}, 1 \leqslant i \leqslant N$

7: For each dimension

8: $fl_1 = rand(0,1), fl_2 = rand(0,1)$

9: $p_{id} = (fl_1 * p_{id} + fl_2 * p_{gd})/(fl_1 + fl_2)$

10: $u_{id} = rand(0,1)$

11: If $rand(0,1) > 0.5$ then

12: $x_{id}(t+1)) = p_{id}(t) - \frac{L_{id}(t)}{2}\ln\left[1/u_{id}(t)\right]$

13: Else

14: $x_{id}(t+1)) = p_{id}(t) + \frac{L_{id}(t)}{2}\ln\left[1/u_{id}(t)\right]$

15: Until termination criterion is met

According to the equations of (4) and (5), the update equation of particles position is

$$x_{id}(t+1) = p_{id}(t) \pm \alpha(t) \, |C_{id}(t) - x_{id}(t)| \times ln\,[1/u_{id}(t)] \tag{7}$$

where α is known as the contraction expansion coefficient. The best position of each particle is updated by:

$$p_i(t+1) = \begin{cases} x_i(t+1) & (f\,[x_i(t+1)] < f\,[p_i(t)]) \\ p_i(t) & (f\,[x_i(t+1)] \geqslant f\,[p_i(t)]) \end{cases} \tag{8}$$

$$p_i(t+1) = arg\min\{f\,[p_i(t)]\}, 1 \leq i \leqslant N \tag{9}$$

where $f(.)$ is the fitness function. The PSO with Eq. (7) is called Quantum-behaved Particle swarm optimization (QPSO) [11].

3   The Clustering Quantum-Behaved Particle Swarm Optimization

3.1   The Hierarchical Clustering Method

In this paper, a clustering method [8] is adopted for Moving Peaks Benchmark (MPB) Problem over dynamic environment optimization problems. In MPBs, the fitness of the optima will change when the position of peaks change. The clustering method, which creates several subswarms to check the changes of peaks, can effectively track the optimal solution. The clustering method works as follows. Each particle in the initial swarm is regarded as a cluster. Then according to the distance between two subswarms, a new subswarm will be emerged by two small cluster until the best optima is found. The distance $d(i,j)$ between subswarm r and subswarm s is defined as the following:

$$d(i,j) = \sqrt{\sum_{d=1}^{D}(x_r^d - x_s^d)^2} \tag{10}$$

A convergence metric is used to evaluate the performance of algorithm, which can be formulated as

$$\varepsilon(r,s) = \min d(i,j) \tag{11}$$

Smaller the value of ε, means more converge of the swarm.

3.2   Detecting Environmental Changes

It is important to detect the environment changes for an algorithm to address DOPs efficiently. In this paper, we use an efficient method to detect the environment by setting the monitoring particles in the search space. This method uses the global best particle over all subswarm as the monitoring particle to detect environment changes. Before updating the global best particle, we reevaluate its fitness in each iteration. If its fitness changes, it demonstrates that an environmental change occurs. The evaluation formula of the global best particle in each subswarm is as the following:

$$\phi(t) = |f(x_i(t)) - f(x_i(t-1))| \qquad (12)$$

where t is the current iteration, $f(x_i(t-1))$ represents the monitoring particles fitness in the $(t-1)th$ iteration of particle i. $x_i(t)$ represents the position of the best particle. $f(x_i(t))$ represents the monitoring particles fitness in the tth iteration of particle. If $\phi(t) \leq \sigma$, the environment have no changes or a little change.

3.3 Keeping the Diversity

In this paper, three steps are proposed for keeping the diversity, which are the convergence check, the overlapping check and the overcrowding check. The convergence check means that if the radius of a *subswarm* is less than a small value, which is set to 0.0001 in this paper, the *subswarm* is regarded as converging on a peak. Then the converged *subswarm* is removed. The overlapping check means that two subswarm are combined only when the overlapping ratio between them is greater than a given value, which is 0.7 in this paper. The overcrowding check means that if the number of particles in a subswarm is greater than the predefined value $max_subsize$, the particles with the worst personal best positions are removed one by one until the size of the subswarm is equal to $max_subsize$. According to the analysis above, the proposed algorithm can be described as the following in Table 1.

4 Experimental Results

4.1 Moving Peaks Benchmark (MPB) Problem

Branke [13] proposed the MPB problem which has been utilized as dynamic benchmark problems. In the MPB problem, the optima are composed of the location, height and width of peaks. The problem is defined as follows:

$$F(x,t) = \max \frac{H_i(t)}{i + W_i(t) \sum_{i,j=1}^{D} (x_j(t) - X_{ij}(t))^2} \qquad (13)$$

where $H_i(t)$ and $W_i(t)$ are the height and width of peak i at time t, and $X_{ij}(t)$ is the jth element of the location of peak i at time j. The movement of a single peak can be described as the following:

$$v_i(t) = \frac{s}{|r + v_i(t-1)|}((1-\lambda)r + \lambda v_i(t-1)) \qquad (14)$$

where the shift vector $v_i(t)$ is a linear combination of the previous shift vector $v_i(t-1)$ and a random vector r. The correlated parameter λ is set to 0, which indicates that the peak movements are uncorrelated.

$$H_i(t) = H_i(t-1) + height_severity * \sigma \qquad (15)$$

Table 1. Procedure of the proposed algorithm

1: Generate an initial swarm
2: While stop criteria is not satisfied do
3: Create clusters by clustering method and calculate the distance between all clusters
4: for each particle do
5: $x_{id}(t+1)) = p_{id}(t) \pm \frac{L_{id}(t)}{2} ln\,[1/u_{id}(t)]$
6: End for
7: for each subswarm do
8: calculate the fitness of each paricle
9: evaluate the fitness and choose the best one
10: end for
11: for each subswarm do
12: $\phi(t) = |f(x_i(t)) - f(x_i(t-1))|$
13: If $\phi(t) \leq \sigma$ then jump 3
14: End for
15: for each subswarm do
16: convergence check
17: overlapping check
18: overcrowding check
19: end for
20: end while

$$W_i(t) = w_i(t-1) + width_severity * \sigma \tag{16}$$

$$X_i(t) = X_i(t-1) + v_i(t) \tag{17}$$

where $height_severity$ is the shift length of height and $width_severity$ is the shift length of width. $\sigma \in N(0,1)$ is a normal distributes random number with mean zero and variation of one.

A new offline error, which is one of the performance measures, is defined as the following:

$$\theta = \frac{1}{T} \sum_{i=1}^{T} (\frac{1}{N} \sum_{j=1}^{N} (F_i - fit_i)) \tag{18}$$

where fit_i is the best solution obtained by an algorithm just before the jth environment change, F_i is the optimum value of the ith environment, N is the number of environment changes, T is the number of running.

4.2 Parameter Settings

In QPSO, the compression-expansion coefficient α is an important parameter, which influences the performance of the algorithms. According to [7], when

$\alpha <$ 1.781, QPSO algorithm can guarantee the convergence. In this paper, we propose three strategies to control α. *A Static Strategy.*

For the static strategy, the value of α is a constant throughout the whole evolutionary process. In this paper, we set the value of α to 0.20.40.60.81.01.2 respectively. Consequently, the QPSO with these constant compression-expansion coefficient values is denoted as $R_{0.2} R_{0.4} R_{0.6} R_{0.8} R_{1.0} R_{1.2}$. *B Linearly Decreasing Strategy.*

For the linearly decreasing strategy, the value of the compression-expansion coefficient α (denoted as R^1) is linearly decreased from the beginning of the evolutionary process to the end. This strategy can be formulated as (13).

$$\alpha(t) = (\alpha_0 - \alpha_1)(t_{max} - t)/t_{max} + \alpha_1 \tag{19}$$

where $\alpha_0 = 1.0, \alpha_1 = 0.5$. t_{max} is the maximum iteration. t is the current iteration. *C Non-Linearly Decreasing Strategy.*

For the non-linearly decreasing strategy, the value of the compression-expansion coefficient α (denoted as R^2 and R^3) gets its value according to a parabola function with different shapes. The function can be expressed by (14) and (15).

$$\alpha(t) = (\alpha_0 - \alpha_1)(t/t_{max})^2 + (\alpha_1 - \alpha_0)(2 \cdot t/t_{max}) + \alpha \tag{20}$$

$$\alpha(t) = (\alpha_0 - \alpha_1)(t/t_{max})^2 + \alpha_0 \tag{21}$$

where α_0, α_1, $t\alpha_0$, t, t_{max} share the same meaning with those in (19).

The parameter setting and definition of the benchmark used in the experiments of this paper can be found in Table 1, which are the same as in all the involved algorithms. In Table 1 the term number of peaks (p) means that the number of peaks for QPSO algorithm. The dynamism of changes is described as the following. The height of peaks is shifted randomly in the range H = [30, 37] and the width of peaks is shifted randomly in the range W = [1, 12]. The term change frequency (U) means that environment changes every U fitness evaluations, S denotes the range of allele values, and I denotes the initial height for all peaks.

4.3   Results

(1) In order to test the performance of the algorithm in this paper, eight initial population size (M) of QPSO algorithm, which are 10, 30, 50, 70, 100, 120, 150, and 200, have been used for solving four kinds of MPB problems. These four MPB problems are different by the number of peaks (p), which are 10, 30, 50, and 100.

Figure 1 shows the offline error of QPSO algorithm with different initial population size on the four MPB problems. From Fig. 1, similar results can be obtained on four problems with different number of peaks. On the four MPB problems, when the initial population size M is set to a specific number (e.g., M = 100), the offline error always increases with the value

Table 2. Parameter settings for MPB problem in this paper

Parameter	Value
Number of peaks$p$	10
Change frequency$U$	5000
Height severity	7.0
Width severity	1.0
Peak shape	cone
Shift length$s$	1.0
Number of dimensions$D$	5
Correlation coefficientλ	0
S	$[0, 100]$
H	$[30.0, 70.0]$
W	$[1, 12]$
I	50.0

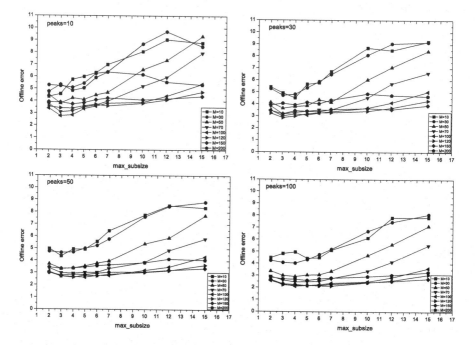

Fig. 1. Offline error of QPSO algorithm with different initial population size on the MPB problems with the peaks 10,30,50 and 100.

of $max_subsize$ (N). In addition, it can be seen from Fig. 1 that the turning point is different for different configurations. For the ten peaks problem, the turning point is N = 3 for M = 100 and N = 7 for M = 200. For the best the performance, it is necessary that QPSO algorithm needs to adjust the value

Table 3. The offline error under nine different with the number of peaks 5,10,15,20,25 and 30

α \ P	5	10	15	20	25	30
$R_{0.2}$	**2.8028**	2.89022	3.32634	**3.0509**	3.04864	3.02142
$R_{0.4}$	**2.43374**	2.95475	**3.00789**	3.23352	3.23352	**2.91833**
$R_{0.6}$	2.55256	3.08418	3.27454	3.35389	2.99567	2.9538
$R_{0.8}$	2.52342	2.91662	3.31207	3.15009	3.12567	3.06766
$R_{1.0}$	2.61719	3.25391	3.27188	3.0862	**2.99636**	3.06689
$R_{1.2}$	2.56145	3.08801	3.31285	3.12352	3.09608	2.97215
R^1	2.56145	3.08801	3.31285	3.12352	3.09608	2.97215
R^2	2.58238	3.16707	3.1386	3.1386	3.1211	2.93425
R^3	2.61719	3.25391	3.27188	3.0862	2.99636	3.06689

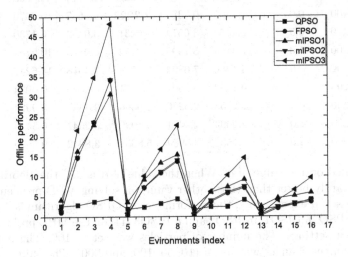

Fig. 2. Compared QPSO with other four algorithms in different environment

of $max_subsize$ to adapt to the environment when the initial population size M is determined. From Fig. 1, the optimal configuration of QPSO is N = 3 for M = 100 on the MPB problems with different number of peaks.

(2) This group of experiments is aimed to test the effect of QPSO algorithm with different compression-expansion coefficients as described in Subsect. 4.2 for solving six kinds of MPB problems. The number of peaks for six MPB problems are 5, 10, 15, 20, 25 and 30.

In Table 2, the offline error is presented for nine parameter settings in ($R_{0.2}R_{0.4}R_{0.6}R_{0.8}R_{1.0}R_{1.2}$). The smaller the offline error is, the better performance will be. For all the six problems, the best results obtained by QPSO algorithm have been shown in bold. From Table 2, it is clearly that in the static strategy for QPSO the performance of the algorithm is greatly

Table 4. Offline error of algorithms on the MPBs with different shift severities and environment changes

Dynamics moving		Moving peaks problem				
change	shift	QPSO	FPSO	mIPSO1	mIPSO2	mIPSO3
10	0.05	2.6604	1.1217	4.1952	1.3352	2.0638
10	0.5	2.9036	14.8033	16.3827	14.8412	21.6552
10	1.0	3.7533	23.6406	22.9140	23.6569	34.8249
10	2.0	4.5919	34.1763	30.6354	34.2043	48.2048
50	0.05	1.9155	0.4157	3.6556	0.7198	0.9137
50	0.5	2.3715	7.2462	9.2199	7.3064	10.1319
50	1.0	3.2789	10.9127	13.4754	11.2296	16.8064
50	2.0	4.3801	13.7850	15.4626	14.0714	22.8009
100	0.05	1.7462	0.2384	**2.2222**	0.5657	0.7070
100	0.5	2.4194	3.6574	6.0231	3.9452	6.1730
100	1.0	2.4194	5.7992	7.3553	6.0863	10.2783
100	2.0	4.1280	7.0894	9.1729	7.4518	14.6242
200	0.05	0.1459	0.1501	2.4971	0.4529	0.6024
200	0.5	2.2753	2.0236	4.5366	2.3487	3.9924
200	1.0	2.9694	2.9481	5.1039	3.2641	6.5513
200	2.0	4.1538	3.5924	5.8657	3.8942	9.5579

depended on the value of α. When the value of α is 0.4, the algorithm will significantly better than those other values in solving MPB problems.

(3) In this set of experiments, the performance of QPSO algorithm is compared with FPSO, mIPSO1, mIPSO2 and mIPSO3 [11] on the MPB problems with different settings. The number of particles was set to 100. The number of environment changes was set in (10, 50, 100, and 200). The shift was set in (0.05, 0.5, 1.0, and 2.0) (Fig. 2).

Form Table 3, it can be seen that the results achieved by QPSO algorithm are much better than the results of the other four algorithms on the MPB problems with different shift severity and environment changes. The performance of all algorithms degrades when the shift length increases, but the performance of all algorithms improves when the environment changes increases. This result shows that the algorithm in this paper is very robust to locate and track multiple optima even in severely changing environments (Table 4).

5   Conclusions

In this paper, quantum-behaved particle swarm optimization (QPSO) algorithm is proposed to solve DOPs and the hierarchical clustering method is used in the QPSO algorithm in order to enhance the relocation ability and improve the ability of tracking the optimal solution. The convergence check, overcrowding check, and overlapping check are appointed to keep the diversity of the swarm. Experimental results on the standard benchmark functions show that QPSO algorithm with hierarchical clustering and diversity maintaining has strong ability to adapt the dynamics and good optimization ability.

Acknowledgments. This work was supported by National Natural Science foundation of China (Nos. 61105128, 61170119, 61373055), the Natural Science Foundation of Jiangsu Province, China (Grant Nos. BK20131106, BK20130161, BK20130160), the Postdoctoral Science Foundation of China (Grant No. 2014M560390), the Fundamental Research Funds for the Central Universities, China (Grant No. JUSRP5141 0B), Six Talent Peaks Project of Jiangsu Province (Grant No. DZXX-025), the PAPD of Jiangsu Higher Education Institutions, China.

References

1. Fu, H.B., Lewis, P.R., Sendhoff, B., Tang, K., Yao, X.: What are dynamic optimization problems. In: Proceedings of 2014 IEEE Congress on Evolutionary Computation, China, pp. 1550–1557 (2014)
2. Kennedy, J., Eberhart, R.: Particle swarm optimization. In: Proceedings of IEEE International Conference on Neural Networks, vol. 4, pp. 1942–1948 (1995)
3. Kennedy, J.: Stereotyping: improving particle swarm performance with cluster analysis. In: Proceedings of IEEE Congress on Evolutionary Compution, Piscataway, pp. 1507–1512 (2000)
4. Breanke, J., Kaussier, T., Smidt, C., Schmeck, H.: A Multi-population approach to dynamic optimization problems. In: Proceedings of the 4th International Conference on Adaptive Computation, pp. 299–308. Springer (2000)
5. Brits, R., Engelbrecht, A.P.: Solving systems of unconstrained equations using particle swarm optimization. In: Proceedings of IEEE International Conference on Systems, Man and Cybernetics, vol. 3, pp. 102–107 (2002)
6. Wang, H.F., Wang, D.W., Huang, M.: Forking PSO algorithm for dynamic optimization problems. J. Syst. Simul. **22**(12), 2895–2899 (2010). (in Chinese)
7. Sun, J.: Particle Swarm Optimization with Particles having Quantum Behavior. Jiangnan University, Doctor Thesis (2009) (in Chinese)
8. Yang, S.X., Li, C.: A clustering particle swarm optimizer for locating and tracking multiple optima in dynamic environments. IEEE Trans. Evol. Comput. **14**(6), 959–973 (2010)
9. Pat, A., Hota, A.R.: An improved quantum-behaved particle swarm optimization using fitness-weighted preferential recombination. In: Proceedings of 2010 Second World Congress on Nature and Biologically Inspired Computing, Kitakyushu, Fukuoka, Japan (2010)
10. Fang, W., Sun, J., Xie, Z.P.: Convergence analysis of quantum-behaved particle swarm optimization algorithm and study on its control parameter. Acta Phys. Sin. **59**(6), 3686–3694 (2010). (in Chinese)
11. Fang, W., Sun, J., Wu, X.: Adaptive web QoS controller based on online system identification using quantum-behaved particle swarm optimization. Soft Comput. **19**(6), 1715–1725 (2014)
12. Breake, J.: Memory enhanced evolutionary algorithms for changing optimization problems. In: Proceedings of Congress of Evolutionary Computation, vol. 3, pp. 1875–1882 (1999)

Analogical China Map Self-assembled from Single-Stranded DNA Tiles

Yanfeng Wang, Xin Ma, Mengmeng Li, and Guangzhao Cui[✉]

Henan Key Lab of Information-based Electrical Appliances,
College of Electrical and Information Engineering, Zhengzhou University
of Light Industry, Zhengzhou 450002, Henan, China
cgzh@zzuli.edu.cn

Abstract. Single-stranded DNA tile (SST) assembly provides a simple, modular and robust framework for constructing nanostructures with prescribed shapes from short synthetic DNA strands. Here we presents a nanoscale DNA structure of analogical China map which is constructed by a number of SSTs. The constructing nanostructure is roughly $98 \, \mathrm{nm} \times 67 \, \mathrm{nm}$ in diameter with a spatial resolution of $3 \, \mathrm{nm} \times 7 \, \mathrm{nm}$. The pattern appeared in atomic force microscopy (AFM) conforms to the pre-designed shape of Chinese map with the approximately expected dimensions, and AFM images of the field selected randomly from the mica give an 11 % assembly yield. Through this research, the capability of constructing complicated two-dimensional shapes by SST and the controllability of the internal array are fully vindicated.

Keywords: DNA self-assembly · Single-stranded DNA tile · DNA Nanostructure

1 Introduction

Bio-inspired computing is a field of study that abstracts computing ideas (data structures, operations with data, ways to control operations, computing models, etc.) from the living phenomena or biological systems such as evolution, cell, tissue, neural network, immune system and ant colony. The obtained computing models are called bio-inspired computing models. There are two main classes of bio-inspired computing models: membrane computing models (also known as P systems, see e.g. [10,12,18,24,25]) and DNA computing [3–5,8].

Over the past three decades, DNA has emerged as a versatile molecular building block for nanoconstruction due to its predictable conformation and programmable intra- and inter-molecular Watson-Crick base-pairing interactions [1]. As the first DNA building blocks, double crossover (DX) molecules [2] contain two Holliday junctions connected by two double helical arms, and have been used to construct one-dimensional (1D) DNA arrays [3], two-dimensional (2D) lattices [4,5], and DNA nanomechanical devices [6,7,22,26]. In 2000, LaBean et al. [8] constructed DNA triple crossover (TX) complex to extend the set of

© Springer-Verlag Berlin Heidelberg 2015
M. Gong et al. (Eds.): BIC-TA 2015, CCIS 562, pp. 422–431, 2015.
DOI: 10.1007/978-3-662-49014-3_38

experimentally characterized building blocks. The TX molecule consists of four oligonucleotides hybridized to form three double-stranded DNA helices lying in a plane and linked by strand exchange at four immobile crossover points, and has been used to perform computation [9] and construct DNA three-dimensional (3D) nanotubes as templates for conductive nanowires [11]. In 2003, Yan et al. [13] constructed a DNA nanostructure consisting of four 4-arm junctions oriented with a square aspect ratio. This programmable self-assembly of 4 × 4 tiles resulted in two distinct lattice morphologies. In 2014, Shi et al. [14] developed a new DNA sub-tile strategy to easily create whole families of programmable tiles, and demonstrated the stability and flexibility of the sub-tile structures by constructing 3-, 4-, and 6-arm DNA tiles that were subsequently assembled into 2D lattices and 3D nanotubes according to a hierarchical design.

An extraordinary breakthrough in the construction of DNA nanostructures occurred in 2006 with the introduction of the DNA origami method proposed by Rothemund [15]. In his study, the long single-stranded DNA strand (scaffold, 7.25 kilobase long) was folded into a desired 2D shape with the help of hundreds of short oligonucleotides, called staple strands. By means of this method, Rothemund has constructed six desired shapes of ∼100 nm in diameter, including square, rectangle, star, disk with three holes, etc., and several patterns including the map of western hemisphere. Inspired by Rothemund's work on DNA origami, Qian et al. [16] designed and constructed a nanoscale structure in the shape of a China map, folded from a long single-stranded DNA virus genome and over 200 synthesized short strands. With the development of DNA origami in two-dimensional plane, Shih et al. [17] extend it to the three-dimensional space. They demonstrated their design and assembly of nanostructures approximating six shapes (monolith, square nut, railed bridge, genie bottle, stacked cross, and slotted cross) with precisely controlled dimensions ranging from 10 to 100 nm. However, lengths of conventional single-stranded scaffolds limit the scales of these uniquely addressable structures, LaBean et al. [19] used a λ/M13 hybrid virus to produce a 51466-nucleotide DNA single-stranded, then successfully assembled into a large-scale DNA origami structure. And they used an inkjet-printing process on a chip embossed with functionalized micropillars to synthesize staple strands, greatly reducing the cost.

In this research, a nanoscale DNA structure of analogical China map is constructed by one-pot annealing of all those strands including 182 internal single-stranded DNA tiles (SSTs) and 72 half-length single-stranded DNA tiles (SSTs) on horizontal boundaries. A SST is abstracted as a brick, the rectangle likes a brick wall or a canvas, and drawing a "China map" pattern on the canvas. The desired shape is then constructed by one-pot annealing of all those strands corresponding to pixels covered by the target shape. We observed a clear map of the structure of China, with an atomic force microscope (AFM). The realization of nanoscale China map shows the SST effectiveness for creating a wide range of complicated two-dimensional DNA crystals, while the controllability of the internal array.

2   Materials and Methods

2.1   Single-Stranded DNA Tile

In 2012, Yin et al. [20] proposed an innovation DNA self-assembly method using single-stranded DNA tiles, SST, for short. With this method, hundreds of complex shapes had been constructed. Each SST, a 42-base (divided into four domain) strand of DNA (Fig. 1(a)), is composed entirely of concatenated sticky ends, and each SST binds to four local neighbors (Fig. 1(b)) during self-assembly. As the sequences of the SST had been designed rigorously, any two SSTs have different sequences to make sure each SST can bind to other four SSTs specifically. Consequently, they will associate with each other into a rectangle serving as a molecular canvas (Fig. 1(d)). Each of the constituent SST on the canvas is folded into a 3 nm × 7 nm tile (Fig. 1(c)) and attached to four neighboring tiles-acting as a pixel.

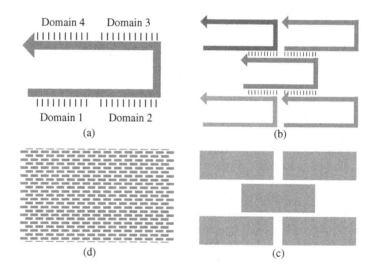

Fig. 1. (a) A SST with 42-bases was divided into four domains (domain 1, domain 2, domain 3 and domain 4). (b) A SST binds to four local neighbors. (c) Five 3 nm-by-7 nm tiles. (d) Molecular canvas.

If a SST could be abstracted as a brick, the rectangle will be like a brick wall or a canvas. When design a pattern, just draw on the canvas. The desired shape is then constructed by one-pot annealing of all those strands corresponding to pixels covered by the target shape. And the remaining strands are absent.

2.2   Design of DNA Sequences

The target structure is self-assembled from hundreds of single-stranded DNA tiles, referring to the map of China. To design a pattern, as the rectangular

SST lattice can be viewed as a "molecular canvas", where each SST serves as a 3 nm × 7 nm "molecular pixel", just drawn on the canvas. Then the pattern will be produced by one-pot annealing of all those strands that correspond to pixels covered by the target pattern; the remaining strands are excluded. People sometimes refer to the map of China as a cock, a complex asymmetrical planar graph, including three parts: Chinese mainland, Hainan Island and Taiwan Island (Fig. 2(a)). We just draw the rough sketch of China map on the canvas and keep the tiles covered by the target shape. Hence the obtained structure to be more reasonable and artistic.

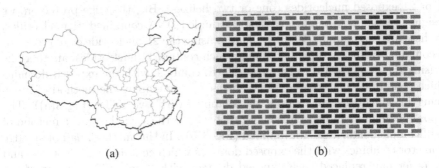

(a)   (b)

Fig. 2. (a) The map of China. (b) The shape designed on the canvas.

There are many difficulties in the construction of the map of china; for instance, Hainan Island and Taiwan Island don't connect to the mainland, and the link between the northeast of China and the mainland is relatively frail. In order to ensure the integrity of the map, we have to join the two islands to the mainland and enhance the fragile parts such as the part of "chicken neck" connecting the Northeast. The result is as shown in Fig. 2(b). After that, one problem emerged. As we can see, although the internal SSTs can self-assemble to be stable double-stranded DNA structures, the SSTs on the boundary of the pattern had exposed single-stranded domains that would result in non-specific interactions between patterns called aggregation. The aggregation resulted in no detectable product band on an agarose gel and unsatisfactory imaging under the AFM. Two ways were designed to eliminate aggregation: one in which exposed domains could be replaced by a poly (T) segment of the same length, and another one in which we could design the "edge protector" with a segment complementary to the exposed domain to assemble with the exposed domain into stable structure, DNA double helix. In this research, "edge protector" is chosen to eliminate aggregation.

In this research, we use a computer-software developed by Mi et al. [21], with graphic interfaces for generating DNA sequence of various DNA motifs for DNA nanotechnology research, to design the sequences of the SSTs. Two main principles should be followed. One is the principle of complementarities, not only the principle of A to T and G to C but also the principle that a certain sequence of one domain must be complementary to another domain, including the length of the helices, etc. The other one is the exclusion of mismatching caused by overlong repeating sequences among all the strands of the motif. In this research, it is permitted that the length of repeating segment is more than eight nucleotides, if the recently generated seven nucleotides of the last SST were in accord with the former, the eighth nucleotide would be chose from A, T, C and G until the repeating-segment requirement is satisfied. Furthermore four consecutive A, C, G or T bases are not allowed.

The edge protector should be designed in accordance with specific conditions of the exposed domains. The SSTs on the boundaries of the pattern usually have 11 or 21 exposed nucleotides (one or two helixes). But the edge protectors we designed in this research are all single-stranded DNA contained 21 nucleotides. So there are two cases to deal with. One is using the 21-nucleotide edge protector to combine with the exposed domains which contain 11 nucleotides; another one is using the 21-nucleotide edge protector to combine with the exposed domains which contain 21 nucleotides. In the first case, we employ the method of inter-lacing in which one edge protector combines with two SSTs (Fig. 3(a)). The exposed domains can be well fixed by this way. In the second one, the method of "half complementarities" was applied (Fig. 3(b)). In this method, half of an edge protector combines with the exposed domains which contain 11 nucleotides, and the other half replaced each exposed domain with a poly (T) segment of the same length.

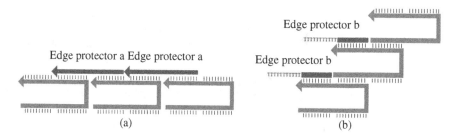

Fig. 3. (a) Edge protector combining with 21 exposed nucleotides. (b) Edge protector combining with 11 exposed nucleotides.

2.3   Experimental Procedures

Dissolution. Custom oligonucleotides were purchased from Sangon Biotech Co., Ltd (http://www.sangon.com) and purified by HAP, then dissolved by the TE/Mg^{2+} buffer (20 mM Tris (PH 7.6–8.0), 2 mM EDTA, 12.5 mM MgCl$_2$). The concentration of each strand was measured using calculated extinction coefficients based on the sequences and the A260 from a NanoDrop UV-vis spectrophotometer. The final concentration was about 100 μM.

Mixing. Take 1 μL of each sample, and then mix them with ultrapure water to reach a final concentration of 100 nM.

Annealing. Oligo mixtures were annealed in PCR instrument from 94°C to 25°C over 20 h. And then kept in a refrigerator at 4°C before being examined by AFM.

AFM Imaging. AFM was performed using scanasyst-fluid mode on a Multimode AFM with a Digital Instruments Nanoscope IIIa controller (Veeco) using oxide-sharpened silicon probes. A 5 μL of sample solution was dropped on a freshly cleaved mica, and left to adsorb on the surface for 2 min.

3   Results

CanDo, a kind of online software, is used in this article to offer designers DNA nanostructures computational predictions of the 3D solution shape and flexibility of single- and multi-layer structures to inform and enhance their design process. Computational feedback is needed to reduce the financial cost and time required to design these structures successfully, which are additionally difficult to assay experimentally due to their nanoscale dimensions. Here we draw the structure (Fig. 4(a)) in Autodesk Maya, which is comprehensive 3D animation software. And then the file is submitted to the website for analysis. From this result (Fig. 4(b) & (c)), the China map is not straight planar, but distorted. The twist angle is about 60 degrees, less than 90 degrees. It shows that the degree of crook is ideal and dose not affect the observation. Therefore the design is reasonable.

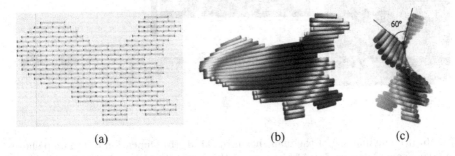

(a)   (b)   (c)

Fig. 4. (a) The structure constructed by Autodesk Maya. (b) and (c) The results shown by CanDo.

AFM images show that the pattern is the expected analogical China map morphology (Fig. 5(a)) with approximately the expected dimensions of ∼98 nm in length, ∼67 nm in width, and 2 nm in height (Fig. 5(b)). The dimension of the map is less than 100 nm, which is according to the concept of nanoscale.

The details such as Shandong Peninsula, Hainan Island and Taiwan Island can be distinguished despite the teeny dimension.

In this research, the ratio between well-formed (defined as those showing no defects with 98 ± 1 nm in length and 67 ± 2 nm in width) patterns and recognizable patterns in an AFM field is called as "AFM yield". AFM images of the field selected randomly from the mica gave an 11 % assembly yield (N = 37; Fig. 5(c)). There are four factors responsible for the low yield. In the first place, native gel electrophoresis is not used to purify the sample in view of the relative fragility of SST maps. So we can see in the Fig. 5(c) that there are nearly 50 % of the ill-formed structures whose dimension is half less than the well-formed structures. In the second place, the fragility of the structure may lead to fracture in particular positions such as the neck of the map and the links of two islands. Once more, the structure, in a manner, would be damaged owing to the crook shown in Fig. 5 when absorbing on the mica. Finally, the probe of AFM may scratch the patterns in case of the improper spacing between the probe and the mica.

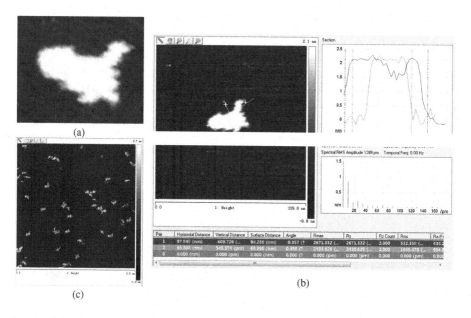

Fig. 5. (a) The imaging of the map shown by AFM. (b) Dimension of the map shown in NanoScope Analysis. (c) AFM image of the map with yield calculation. The maps marked with empty blue circles are 'ill-formed' and the maps marked with empty red circles are 'well-formed'. According to our analysis, the yield of 'well-formed' structures was 11 % (N = 37) (Color figure online).

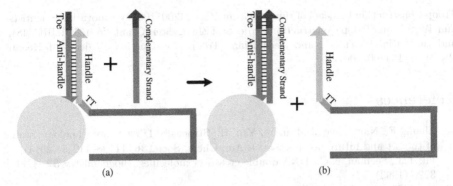

Fig. 6. (a) Streptavidin labeling of the SST and the complementary strand. (b) The displaced biotin and the SST.

4   Discussion

In this paper, a nanoscale China map whose dimension is less than 100 nm is constructed by single-stranded DNA tiles. But the fineness of the map is not very ideal due to the matter of dimension. It is a pity that the streptavidin labeling is unsuccessful. There are two factors responsible for the failure. Firstly, the position to be labeled is around the neck of the map which is one of the most fragile places. The modification of this position may lead to fracture of the map. In the second place, the different buffer system of the streptavidin solution and the sample solution would also result in the failure.

In the following work, we will focus on the marker on the structure, such as streptavidin labeling [23]. To do the marker, firstly we will modify the SSTs at selected locations to ensure that they can bind to biotin labeled strands which specifically bind to steptavidin. Then, after the annealed sample imaged with AFM, streptavidin would add to the sample on the mica surface for an incubation of 2 min before re-imaging. To unload the streptavidin labeling, toehold should be designed. And the DNA strand displacement would accomplish the unloading. A SST to be labeled with streptavidin must be modified firstly, which contains an extra 2nt TT spacer followed by a 15nt "handle" segment to the 3' end of the SST. Then an "anti-handle" strand complementary to the "handle" segment is labeled with biotin at the 3' end and a toehold segment at the 5' end. As a result, the streptavidin would combine with the modified SST via the 3' biotin modified "anti-handle" strand (Fig. 6(a)). When unloading the label of streptavidin, the DNA strand complementary to the "anti-handle" strand should been added into the solution. And the "anti-handle" strand labeled by biotin would been displaced (Fig. 6(b)).

Acknowledgement. Research is supported by the NSFC (Grant Nos. 61472372, 61272022, 61272071, 60773122, 61070238), Basic and Frontier Technology Research Program of Henan (Grant No. 122300413211), Innovation Scientists and Technicians

Troop Construction Projects of Henan (Grant No. 124200510017), Innovation Scientists and Technicians Troop Construction Projects of Zhengzhou (Grant No. 131PLJRC648), and Innovation Scientists and Technicians Troop Construction Projects of Henan Province (154200510012).

References

1. Zhang, F., Nangreave, J., Liu, Y., Yan, H.: Structural DNA nanotechnology: state of the art and future perspective. J. Am. Chem. Soc. **136**, 11198–11211 (2014)
2. Fu, T.J., Seeman, N.C.: DNA double-crossover molecules. Biochemistry **32**, 3211–3220 (1993)
3. Yang, X., Wenzler, L.A., Qi, J., Li, X., Seeman, N.C.: Ligation of DNA triangles containing double crossover molecules. J. Am. Chem. Soc. **120**, 9779–9786 (1998)
4. Winfree, E., Liu, F., Wenzler, L.A., Seeman, N.C.: Design and self-assembly of two-dimensional DNA crystals. Nature **394**, 539–544 (1998)
5. Wang, X., Song, T., Wang, Z., Su, Y., Liu, X.: MRPGA: Motif detecting by modified random projection strategy and genetic algorithm. J. Comput. Theor. Nanosci. **10**, 1209–1214 (2013)
6. Mao, C., Sun, W., Shen, Z., Seeman, N.C.: A nanomechanical device based on the B-Z transition of DNA. Nature **397**, 144–146 (1999)
7. Shi, X., Wang, Z., Deng, C., Pan, L., Chen, Z.: A novel bio-sensor based on DNA strand displacement. PLOS One **9**, e108856 (2014)
8. LaBean, T.H., Yan, H., Kopatsch, J., Liu, F.R., Winfree, E., Reif, J.H., Seeman, N.C.: Construction, analysis, ligation, and self-assembly of DNA triple crossover complexes. J. Am. Chem. Soc. **122**, 1848–1860 (2000)
9. Mao, C., LaBean, T.H., Reif, J.H., Seeman, N.C.: Logical computation using algorithmic self-assembly of DNA triple-crossover molecules. Nature **407**, 493–496 (2000)
10. Song, T., Pan, L.: Spiking neural P systems with rules on synapses working in maximum spiking strateg. IEEE Trans. NanoBiosci. **14**(4), 465–477 (2015)
11. Liu, D., Park, S.H., Reif, J.H., LaBean, T.H.: DNA nanotubes self-assembled from triple-crossover tiles as templates for conductive nanowires. Proc. Natl. Acad. Sci. USA **101**, 717–722 (2004)
12. Song, T., Pan, L., Păun, G.: Asynchronous spiking neural P systems with local synchronization. Inf. Sci. **219**, 197–207 (2013)
13. Yan, H., Park, S.H., Finkelstein, G., Reif, J.H., LaBean, T.H.: DNA-templated self-assembly of protein arrays and highly conductive nanowires. Science **301**, 1882–1884 (2003)
14. Shi, X., Lu, W., Wang, Z., Pan, L., Cui, G., Xu, J., LaBean, T.H.: Programmable DNA tile self-assembly using a hierarchical sub-tile strategy. Nanotechnology **25**, 075602 (2014)
15. Rothemund, P.W.: Folding DNA to create nanoscale shapes and patterns. Nature **440**, 297–302 (2006)
16. Qian, L., Wang, Y., Zhang, Z., Zhao, J., Pan, D., Zhang, Y., Liu, Q., Fan, C., Hu, J., He, L.: Analogic China map constructed by DNA. Chin. Sci. Bull. **51**, 2973–2976 (2006)
17. Douglas, S.M., Dietz, H., Liedl, T., Högberg, B., Graf, F., Shih, W.M.: Self-iassembly of DNA into nanoscale three-dimensional shapes. Nature **459**, 414–418 (2009)

18. Song, T., Pan, L., Jiang, K., et al.: Normal forms for some classes of sequential spiking neural P systems. IEEE Trans. NanoBiosci. **12**(3), 255–264 (2013)
19. Marchi, A.N., Saaem, I., Vogen, B.N., Brown, S., LaBean, T.H.: Toward larger DNA origami. Nano Lett. **14**, 5740–5747 (2014)
20. Wei, B., Dai, M., Yin, P.: Complex shapes self-assembled from single-stranded DNA tiles. Nature **485**, 623–626 (2012)
21. Wei, B., Wang, Z., Mi, Y.: Uniquimer: software of de novo DNA sequence generation for DNA self-assembly–An introduction and the related applications in DNA self-assembly. J. Comput. Theor. Nanosci. **4**, 133–141 (2007)
22. Song, T., Pan, L., Wang, J., et al.: Normal forms of spiking neural P systems with anti-spikes. IEEE Trans. NanoBiosci. **11**(4), 352–359 (2012)
23. Hyre, D.E., Le, T.I., Merritt, E.A., Eccleston, J.F., Green, N.M., Stenkamp, R.E., Stayton, P.S.: Cooperative hydrogen bond interactions in the streptavidin biotin system. Protein Sci. **15**, 459–467 (2006)
24. Păun, G., Rozenberg, G., Salomaa, A.: The Oxford Handbook of Membrane Computing. Oxford University Press, Inc., New York (2010)
25. Song, T., Pan, L.: Spiking neural P systems with rules on synapses working in maximum spikes consumption strategy. IEEE Trans. NanoBiosci. **14**(1), 38–44 (2015)
26. Zhang, X., Pan, L., Păun, A.: On the universality of axon P systems. IEEE Trans. Neural Netw. Learn. Syst. (2015). doi:10.1109/TNNLS.2015.2396940
27. Shi, X., Wang, Z., Deng, C., Song, T., Pan, L., Chen, Z.: A novel bio-sensor based on DNA strand displacement. PLoS One **9**, e108856 (2014)

Bio-inspired Algorithms Applied in Multi-objective Vehicle Routing Problem: Frameworks and Applications

Yuan Wang, Yongming He, Lei He, and Lining Xing[⊠]

College of Information System and Management,
National University of Defense Technology, Changsha 410073, China
`xing2999@qq.com`

Abstract. Multi-objective vehicle routing problem (MOVRP) is developed from vehicle routing problem (VRP). MOVRP is a classic multi-objective optimization problem. During the recent years, the MOVRPs had a progress in problem scales and complex level. As a result, to get better solutions of MOVRPs, Bio-inspired algorithms were introduced into this area. This article first analyses the MOVRP framework, and then reviews the bio-inspired algorithm frameworks that designed to solve MOVRPs. This analysis leads to the identification of bio-inspired algorithms which can get better solutions for MOVPRs and can be applied to real-life cases successfully.

Keywords: Bio-inspired algorithm · Multi-objective · Vehicle routing · Literature review

1 Introduction

For modern industry, it is a practical problem for business owners to deliver their products to their customers from the distribution factories. In operation research (OR) community, these kinds of problems are so called Vehicle Routing Problem (VRP). A typical VRP problem is normally described as followed: A fleet of vehicles departs from a depot and then delivers goods to a set of customers along the routes, then go back to a depot. This question was first described by Dantzig and Ramser [1].

As the VRP is studied, a lot of theoretical subproblems as well as practical cases that were depicted under VRP framework. These subproblems either add some constraints, e.g. time constraints, traveling distance constraints and capacity constraints, or describe VRP under special situations, e.g. multiple depots, pickup and delivery, planning period. These special requirements are generally extracted from real-life cases. Some of the most important VRP subproblems are showed in Fig. 1.

These VRPs and their subproblems which are depicted as rich VRPs are always closely connected to practical production and distribution problems. As the operation research community gets a further understanding of the rich VRPs,

© Springer-Verlag Berlin Heidelberg 2015
M. Gong et al. (Eds.): BIC-TA 2015, CCIS 562, pp. 432–446, 2015.
DOI: 10.1007/978-3-662-49014-3_39

researchers realize that in real-life cases, normally there are several costs associated with a single tour rather than just traveling distance. Moreover, there may be other objectives such as balancing the workloads or minimizing the total environmental impacts. That is to say, naturally, VRPs are mostly multi-objective problems. As a result, in the past decade, VRPs moved from single objective optimization problems to multi-objective ones, widely known as Multi-objective vehicle routing problem (MOVRP).

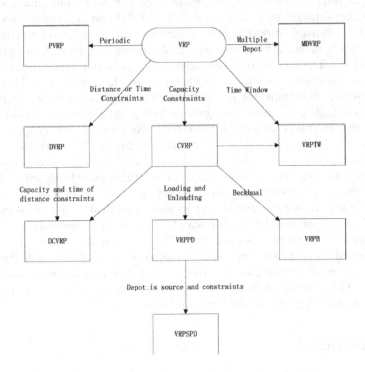

Fig. 1. VRP and its important variants (see as [2]).

Since the MOVRPs emerged, they received many attentions form the OR community. The main reasons are: (a) the VPRs are generally described as a combination of bin packing problem and traveling salesman problem, thus it is obviously a NP-hard problem [3]; (b) the MOVRPs are closely connected with real-life problems, thus have a high practical value; (c) a MOVRP sometimes has conflict optimization objectives which make it also has a high theoretical value.

The methods that were developed to solve MOVRPs are widely applicable. The practical applications of these methods include (but not limit in): supply chain design, hazard wastes collection, mobile health care station routing, green vehicle routing. These practical applications normally have many objectives as well as a huge amount of possible solutions. Wen et al. [4] described a real-life case that included hundreds of nodes of customers and depots, the planning period is longer than 15 days. Govindan et al. [5] described a case which includes more than 40 optimization constraints and more than 5 optimization objectives. This case takes environment impacts into account and gives a permission of opening or closing depots which makes it very different from formal ones. In a word, the practical applications normally includes fuzzy optimization objectives, complex constraints and have large scales. These make them difficult for exact methods such as integer programming or column generation to solve. On the other hand, some of these practical problems do not need an optimum solution but a feasible solution under certain time and CPU cost constraints. For these reasons, the bio-inspired optimization algorithms are introduced into this area.

This article makes a literature review of bio-inspired algorithms applied in the MOVRPs. The aim is to briefly summarize the subproblems, optimization objectives, constraints and methods that link to these problems. Then some future research directions are pointed out. This literature review divides the reviewed methods into three catalogues include genetic algorithm (GA) framework, particle swarm optimization (PSO) framework and ant colony optimization (ACO) framework based on a method oriented technique. The articles that were reviewed in this literature review were selected form four different databases and some important conference proceedings. This articles include algorithm framework design, method design and some important literature reviews in this area. At last, as the MOVRPs mainly aim to solve practical problems, some real-life applications are listed to help researchers figure out important constraints and optimization objectives for future studies. The remained parts of this article are organized as follow: the Sect. 2 illustrates the MOVRPs definition and some important optimization objectives; Sect. 3 describes the most up-to-date bio-inspired algorithms application in MOVRPs; Sect. 4 gives out some practical application; Sect. 5 gives out the final conclusion.

2 Definition

2.1 Problem Description

A MOVRP is most used in three ways: (a) to extend a classic theoretical problem in order to make it fit a certain practical application; (b) to generalize a classic problem; (c) to provide a solution for a real-life case, which its optimization objectives are identified by decision-makers [6]. A typical MOVRP can be described as follow: (a) a graph $G = (V, E)$, which includes a set of node V and a set of edges E; a set of depots $\{d_i \in D | i = 1, 2, 3 \ldots N\}$ which includes locations of depots and number of vehicle of a certain depot and a set of customers $\{c_i \in C | j = 1, 2, 3 \ldots P\}$ which includes the customer location and demand information, these two sets can be separated for the node set V; (b) a set of vehicles $\{v_h \in V | h = 1, 2, 3 \ldots M\}$, which may include the capacity information Ca_i of v_i; (c) a set of edges $\{e_k \in E | k = 1, 2, 3 \ldots K\}$ includes the cost t_k correlated with the edge e_k; (d) an objective set $\{f_l(x) \in O | l = 1, 2, 3 \ldots O\}$. Figure 2 shows a typical MOVRP problem:

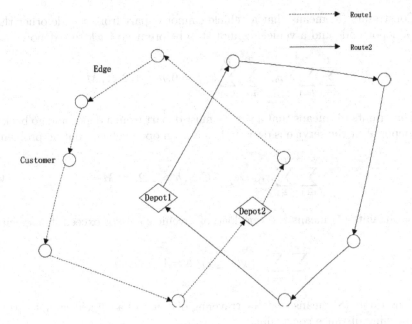

Fig. 2. Multi-objective vehicle routing problem.

The general mathematical definition framework of a MOVRP is:

$$minf(x) = (f_1(x), f_2(x) \ldots f_3(x))$$ (1)

$$s.t. x \in D$$ (2)

In this framework, the $f_1(x)$ to $f_n(x)$ are objectives of the MOVRP, and the constraint set D normally includes (but not limited in):

$$\sum_{j=1}^{N+P} \sum_{k=1}^{K} x_{ijk} = 1, j = 1, 2, \ldots P$$ (3)

$$\sum_{j=1}^{N+P} \sum_{k=1}^{K} x_{ijk} = 1, i = 1, 2, \ldots P$$ (4)

Constraints (3) and (4) together mean that one customer can be severed exactly once by a certain vehicle (in multi-objective periodic vehicle routing problem, once in a period). The x_{ijk} means vehicle k depart from node i to node j.

$$\sum_{i=1}^{P+N} x_{ijh} - \sum_{h=1}^{P+N} x_{jlh} = 0, \begin{matrix} l = 1, 2, \ldots P \\ h = 1, 2, \ldots M \end{matrix}$$ (5)

Constraints (5) means that a vehicle cannot depart from a node other than it is a depot node and a vehicle cannot stop before it go back to a depot.

$$\sum_{i=1}^{P}\sum_{l=1}^{D} x_{lih} - \sum_{i=1}^{P}\sum_{l=1}^{D} x_{lih} = 0, h = 1, 2, \ldots M \tag{6}$$

Constraints (6) means that a vehicle must depart from a depot and go back to this depot after the service is over (unless it is an open vehicle routing problem).

$$\sum_{i=1}^{N+P}\sum_{j=1}^{P} x_{ijk} De_j \leq Ca_k, h = 1, 2, \ldots M \tag{7}$$

Constraints (7) means the workload of a vehicle cannot exceed its capacity.

$$\sum_{i=1}^{N+P}\sum_{j=1}^{P} x_{ijk} t_k \leq T_h, h = 1, 2, \ldots M \tag{8}$$

Constraints (8) means that the traveling distance of a vehicle cannot surpass the traveling distance constraint.

2.2   General Optimization Objectives

Traveling Distance Minimization. This is the classical optimization objective of classic VRPs which aims to minimize the total traveling distance of all vehicles.

Service Satisfaction Maximization. In many real-life cases, especially supply chain design cases, customers requests of product distribution services always include demand and time constraints. These requests can be either fully satisfied or partially satisfied. Some of the MOVRP researches use service satisfaction level to represent these requests. And as a result, service satisfaction maximization becomes an objective of MOVRPs. To our knowledge, the first article that described the service satisfaction maximization MOVRP is Sessomboon et al. [7].

Balancing Workload. In practical problems, sometimes there are limitations of the longest working hours of vehicle drivers, longest traveling distance of a vehicle and numbers of vehicles in a depot. Thus some of the MOVRPs take the workload balance into account. The original article that described the MOVRP with workload balance optimization is Lee et al. [8].

Environmental Impact Minimization. Because of the increasing attention citizens paid to the transportation environmental impact, the transportation cost caused by protecting the environment along the delivery routes increases sharply. Thus decision-makers now consider the environmental impact as an objective of supply chain design. To our knowledge, the first MOVRP that considers environmental impact as an objective is Ageron et al. [9].

2.3 Multi-objective Optimization Technologies

Scalar Techniques. Scalar techniques are one kind of widely used multi-objective optimization methods. These techniques mainly use mathematical transformations to get better solutions. This kind of optimization methods includes weighted linear aggregation, goal programming and constructive heuristic method in which the output of the formal algorithm is the input constraints of the next step, e.g. [10–12].

Pareto Method. Pareto method is also a widely applied multi-objective optimization method which introduce the Pareto dominance into optimization algorithms. This method was first introduced by Goldberg for genetic algorithm in [13]. Some other bio-inspired algorithms using Pareto method to solve MOVRPs can be seen in [14,15].

Hybrid Heuristics. Hybrid heuristics is another method of solving MOVRPs. This kind of methods commonly duels with each of the objectives separately with different heuristic methods, or uses one heuristic rule to find a possible solution and then use another one to improve it. In fact, as a result of the increase of MOVRPs complex level and problem scalars, applications of hybrid-heuristic methods to MOVRPs are more and more common, e.g. [16–18].

2.4 Important Subproblems

Time Window. In real-life cases, the customers may give out of a time window which is correlated with the goods request. The business owners must send their products to the customers just in the time window to get profit. This problem is called a vehicle routing problem with time window (VRPTW) which is first described by Pollen et al. [19,20]. The recent works and methods can also be seen in literature review [21,22]. Heterogeneous fleet. Practically, a fleet of vehicles may deliver many types of goods for different customers. This kind of problems refers to multi-objective vehicle routing problem with heterogeneous fleet (HFMOVRP), which means the customers demands of goods can be delivered by any kind of vehicles but the requests cannot be split. The first article that described this problem is Kirby [23]. And the literature review of the recent works of HFVRP can be seen in [24,25].

Pickup and Delivery. Sometimes the vehicles have to satisfy a set of specific service requests which include the original location, the destination location and the loads to be transferred. This kind of VRPs is called vehicle routing problem with pickup and delivery (VRPPD). The first literature that considers pickup and delivery is [26].

Periodic. Sometimes a VRP repeats several times until the end of it. And the routes and delivery solutions maybe different in different periods. This kind of VPRs is called periodic vehicle routing problem (PVPR). Beltrami and Bodin [27] are the first ones who described PVRP.

Multiple Depots. In real-life cases, a company may not have just one depot. So there maybe multiple depots with different kinds and numbers of vehicles in a case. This kind of VRP is called multi-depot vehicle routing problem (MDVRP). Sometimes this kind of problem can be solved by transferring this kind of problem into single depot VRP by clustering every depot in the depot set and the customers around them. But mostly this kind of problems can be treated as one of the most important subproblems of VRP. The description and recent work of MDVRP can be seen in [28].

Others. VRP includes a lot of subproblems, the problems listed above are just some common ones. Other subproblems of VRP and some method frameworks can be seen in [29,30].

3   Heuristics for MOVRP

3.1   Genetic Algorithm

Genetic algorithm (GA) was first designed by Holland [31] in 1975. It is a widely applicable bio-inspired optimization algorithm framework. This algorithm solves a large scale optimization problem using a search strategy of stimulating the revolutionary process of creatures. In the year 1989, Moscato [32] developed an algorithm called memetic algorithm based on the classic GA which raised the searching efficiency of GA by controlling the revolutionary direction of GA. By now, the GA framework has been applied in many VRP problems and proved to have good performances, e.g. VRPTW, CVRP (capacitated vehicle routing problem), MTVRP [33–36]. As the VRPs changing into MOVRPs, the GA framework that was used to solve VRPs is now applying to MOVRPs either. A classic GA framework is showed in Fig. 3.

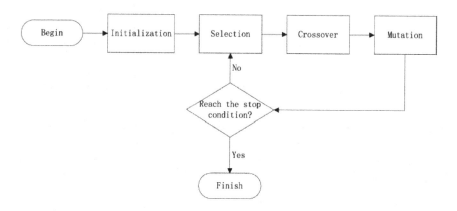

Fig. 3. GA framework.

To our best knowledge, the important applications of GA framework that used to solve MOVRPs from year 2005 are: Nicolas et al. [37] solved vehicle routing problem with route balancing (VRPRB) using a GA based on target aiming Pareto search, the optimization objectives are the total length and balance of the route lengths; Thibaut et al. [38] designed a hybrid genetic algorithm combining GA with neighbor search to solve a VRPTW with four optimization objectives (distance excess duration, load, and time-warp); Chiang and Hsu [39] designed a GA based on Pareto-optimal to solve a MOVRPTW, the optimization objectives include the number of required vehicles and the total travel distance; Yang et al. [40] designed a GA to solve the heterogeneous fleet multi-objective vehicle routing problem (HFMOVRP), the objectives include the total network cost, the customer satisfaction degree and the environmental pollution; Liu and Jiang [41] designed a MA to solve a close and open mixed vehicle routing problem (COMVRP), the optimization objectives are the sum of total transportation fixed costs and variable costs; Ghoseici and Seyed [42] designed a GA based on goal programming to solve VRPTW, the objectives are the total required fleet size and total traveling distance; Ghannadpour et al. [43] used GA to solve Multi-objective dynamic VRP with fuzzy time window (MO-DVRPTW), the objectives include the total required number of vehicles, the total distance traveled, the waiting time imposed on vehicles and the total customers satisfaction for service; Abel [44] used evolutionary algorithm (EA) to improve the solution of classic MOVRP in which the objectives include the number of routes along with the total travel distance; Sherinov et al. [45] designed a EA to solve fuzzy vehicle routing problem (FVRP), the objectives are the loading capacity of vehicles, the distance traveled by vehicles, the waiting time of customers, the satisfaction grade of customers, the delay times of vehicles; Urquhart et al. [46] used EA to solve multi-objective vehicle routing problem with Time Windows (MOVRPTW) which considers CO2 savings, distance and number of vehicles used as optimization objectives.

3.2 Particle Swarm Optimization

Particle Swarm Optimization (PSO) was first designed by Kennedy and Eberhart [47] in year 1995, and it has been proved to have good performance solving sophisticated combination optimization problems. Since the first PSO framework was designed, many frameworks based on classic PSO were developed. The most important ones are Inertia Particle Swarm Optimization, Constriction Particle Swarm Optimization, Cognition-only Particle Swarm Optimization, Social-only Particle Swarm Optimization, Local Neighborhood topology Particle Swarm Optimization [14,17,48,49]. The PSO has also been introduced into VRPs, e.g. CVRP, VRPSPD, VRPTW. The classic PSO framework is showed in Fig. 4.

From the year 2005, PSO that are applied into MOVRP are: Panagiotis et al. [50] designed a PSO to solve Urban Transit Network Design Problem (UTNDP) considering demand unsatisfied, demand satisfied, average travel time, efficiency of the route network; Voratas et al. [51] designed a PSO to solve a multi-depot vehicle routing problem with multiple pickup and delivery (GVRP-MDMPDR), the optimization objectives include total routing cost, the number of vehicle, and the fulfilled demand; Farhang et al. [52] designed a PSO to solve Stochastic

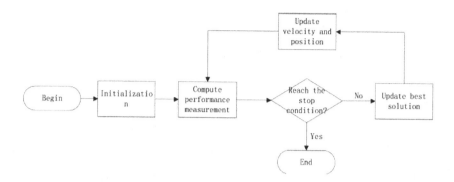

Fig. 4. Particle swarm optimization framework.

Vehicle Routing Problem (SVRP) which considers robustness and cost; Norouzi et al. [53] used PSO to solve a PVRP problem considering the travel cost of routes and the obtained sale; Xu and Yan [54] designed a PSO to solve a vehicle routing problem with soft time windows (VRPSTW) considering the total travel cost of all vehicles and the mean value of the service levels for customers; The and Voratas [55] designed a PSO to solve a vehicle routing problem with simultaneous pickup and delivery (VRPSPD) which considers transportation fixed cost and variable cost; Norouzi et al. [56] designed a PSO to solve an open vehicle routing problem (OVRP) considering the travel cost of routes, the obtained sales and balance the goods of each vehicle.

3.3   Ant Colony Optimization

Ant Colony Optimization (ACO) [57] was first designed be Morigo and Gambardella in the year 1996 inspired by the forging activate of ants. This algorithm has been proved to be efficient in large scale optimization problems. There are also some heuristic algorithm framework based on ACO, e.g. Ant Colony System (ACS) [58] and Max-Min Ant System (MMAS) [59]. ACO framework are applied in many VRPs, e.g. VRPTW, 2-D loading and vehicle routing problem, DVRP [60–62]. The latest review of ACO can be seen in [63]. An ACO framework is showed in Fig. 5.

Because the ACO framework has good performance in VRPs, it was naturally introduced into MOVRPs. Donati et al. [64] designed an ACO to solve VRPTW, the optimization objectives include the number of tours and the total travel time; Tang et al. [65] designed a method based on MMAS to solve a split delivery weighted vehicle routing problem (SDWVRP), the objectives include load quality and travel distance; Huang and Lin [66] designed a method based on modified ant colony optimization algorithm to solve VRP with stochastic demands and multi-items, the objectives include stockout costs and transportation costs; Balseiro et al. [67] designed a method based on ACS to solve a Time Dependent VRP with Time Window, the objectives are number of vehicles used and total travel time of all routes; Gong and Fu [68] designed a method based

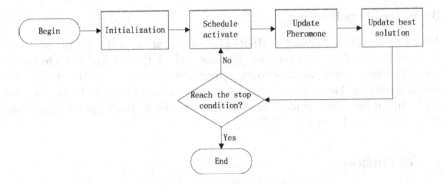

Fig. 5. ACO framework.

on Ant Colony Optimization with ABC customer classification (ABC-ACO) to solve a VRPTW considering fixed vehicle cost, operation cost, shelf life loss and default cost.

4 Important Practical Applications

4.1 Green Vehicle Routing

Green Vehicle Routing Problem (GVRP) is a kind of special VRP. GVRP generally considers energy consumption as well as the classic VRP optimization objectives. The energy consumption includes fuel, electronic energy and, sometimes, CO_2 emission. Other optimization objectives of GVRP include driving speed, gas station location and battery rechargeability. GVRP is studied as a result of the increasing attentions which are paid to the environmental impacts of transportation networks. Because the GVRP has a closely connection with the sustainable development, it received increasing attentions from the OR community and governments during the recent years. Bio-inspired heuristic algorithms that were used in GVRP are little, e.g. [69–71]. The GVRP and some of the optimization methods for GVRP can be seen in [72].

4.2 Supply Chain Design

Supply chain design is meanwhile for modern industry. The aim of supply chain design is to offer high quality or lowest cost services to the customers within the shortest possible time [73]. VRPs applied in supply chain design are always including complex constraints and multiple optimization objectives. And the problem scales are always huge. To solve these practical problems, bio-inspired algorithms are introduced into this area. The bio-inspired algorithms applied in supply chain design are little, e.g. [18,74].

4.3   School Bus Routing

School Bus Routing Problem (SBRP) is a combination optimization problem. It is first described by Newton and Thomas [75]. A typical SBRP includes for phases: bus stop selection, bus route generation, school bell time adjustment, route scheduling. There is no dominant solution construction framework for SBRP, thus it has been studied since it was described. Bio-inspired algorithms used in SBRP are little, e.g. [76,77].

5   Conclusion

MOVRP has received many attentions from OR community since it aims to solve practical large scale optimization problems. During the last decade, as more and more constraints and optimization objectives were extracted from real-life cases and added to MOVRP, the complex level and problem scale of MOVRPs increased rapidly. To get better solutions for new MOVRPs, OR community introduced bio-inspired algorithms to MOVRP area. On the other hand, because the bio-inspired algorithms are convenient when they are combined with other algorithms, they are widely used to solve complex real-life cases, including MOVRPs. This paper briefly summarized the heuristic algorithm used in MOVRP problem in the last decade, then point out some future research areas that need more focus.

References

1. Dantzig, G.B., Ramser, J.H.: The truck dispatching problem. Manag. Sci. **6**(1), 80–91 (1959)
2. Weise, T., Podlich, A., Gorldt, C.: Solving real-world vehicle routing problems with evolutionary algorithms. In: Chiong, R., Dhakal, S. (eds.) Natural Intelligence for Scheduling, Planning and Packing Problems, pp. 29–53. Springer, Heidelberg (2010)
3. Bodin, L., Golden, B.: Classification in vehicle routing and scheduling. Networks **11**, 97–108 (2006)
4. Min, W., Jean-Franois, C., Gilbert, L., Jesper, L.: The dynamic multi-period vehicle routing problem. Comput. Oper. Res. **37**(9), 1615–1623 (2010)
5. Govindan, K., Jafarian, A., Khodaverdi, R., Devika, K.: Two-echelon multiple-vehicle location crouting problem with time windows for optimization of sustainable supply chain network of perishable food. Int. J. Prod. Econ. **152**(2), 9–28 (2014)
6. Jozefowiez, N., Semet, F., Talbi, E.-G.: Multi-objective vehicle routing problems. Eur. J. Oper. Res. **189**(2), 293–309 (2008)
7. Sessomboon, W., Watanabe, K., Irohara, T., Yoshimoto, K.: A study on multi-objective vehicle routing problem considering customer satisfaction with due-time: the creation of Pareto Optimal solutions by hybrid genetic algorithm. Trans. Jpn. Soc. Mech. Eng. **64**, 1108–1115 (1998)
8. Lee, T.-R., Ueng, J.-H.: A study of vehicle routing problem with load balancing. Int. J. Phys. Distrib. Logistics Manag. **29**, 646–648 (1998)

9. Ageron, B., Gunasekaran, A., Spalanzani, A.: Sustainable supply management: an empirical study. Int. J. Prod. Econ. **140**(1), 168–182 (2011)
10. Ghoseiri, K., Ghannadpour, S.F.: Multi-objective vehicle routing problem with time windows using goal programming and genetic algorithm. Appl. Soft Comput. **10**(4), 1096–1107 (2010)
11. Yalcin, G.D., Erginel, N.: Fuzzy multi-objective programming algorithm for vehicle routing problems with backhauls. Expert Syst. Appl. **42**, 5632–5644 (2015)
12. Jozefowiez, N., Semet, F., Talbi, E.-G.: The bi-objective covering tour problem. Comput. Oper. Res. **34**, 1929–1942 (2007)
13. Goldberg, D.E.: Genetic Algorithms in Search, Optimization, and Machine Learning. Addison-Wesley Professional, Boston (1989)
14. Chiang, T.C., Hsu, W.H.: A knowledge-based evolutionary algorithm for the multiobjective vehicle routing problem with time windows. Comput. Oper. Res. **45**(5), 25–37 (2014)
15. Garcia-Najera, A., Bullinaria, J.A.: An evolutionary approach for multi-objective vehicle routing problems with backhauls. Comput. Indus. Eng. **81**, 90–108 (2015)
16. Banos, R., Ortega, J., Gil, C., Marquez, A.L., Toro, F.D.: A hybrid meta-heuristic for multi-objective vehicle routing problems with time windows. Comput. Indus. Eng. **65**(2), 286–296 (2013)
17. Yang, B., Hu, Z.H., Wei, C., Li, S.Q., Zhao, L., Jia, S.: Routing with time-windows for multiple environmental vehicle types. Comput. Indus. Eng. (2015)
18. Balseiro, S.R., Loiseau, I., Ramonet, J.: An ant colony algorithm hybridized with insertion heuristics for the time dependent vehicle routing problem with time windows. Comput. Oper. Res. **38**(6), 954–966 (2011)
19. Pullen, H., Webb, M.: A computer application to a transport scheduling problem. Comput. J. **10**, 10–13 (1967)
20. Knight, K., Hofer, J.: Vehicle scheduling with timed and connected calls: a case study. Oper. Res. Q. **19**, 299–310 (1968)
21. Kallehauge, B.: Formulations and exact algorithms for the vehicle routing problem with time windows. Comput. Oper. Res. **35**(7), 2307–2330 (2008)
22. Gendreau, M., Tarantilis, C.D.: Solving large-scale vehicle routing problems with time windows: the state-of-the-art. Technical report 04, CIRRELT, Montreal, QC, Canada (2010)
23. Kirby, D.: Is your fleet the right size? Oper. Res. Q. **10**, 252–252 (1959)
24. Baldacci, R., Battarra, M., Vigo, D.: Routing a heterogeneous fleet of vehicles. In: Golden, B., Raghavan, S., Wasil, E. (eds.) The Vehicle Routing Problem: Latest Advances and New Challenges, pp. 3–27. Springer (Operation Research/Computer Science Interfaces), New York (2008)
25. Thibaut, V., Teodor, G.C., Michel, G., Christian, P.: Heuristics for multi-attribute vehicle routing problems: a survey and synthesis. Eur. J. Oper. Res. **231**, 1–21 (2013)
26. Sophie, N.P., Karl, F.D., Hartl, R.F.: A survey on pickup and delivery problems. J. für Betriebswirtschaft **58**(2), 81–117 (2008)
27. Beltrami, E.J., Bodin, L.D.: Networks and vehicle routing for municipal waste collection. Networks **4**, 65–94 (1974)
28. Montoya-Torres, J.R., Franco, J.L., Isaza, S.N., Jiménez, H.F., Herazo-Padilla, N.: A literature review on the vehicle routing problem with multiple depots. Comput. Indus. Eng. **79**, 115–129 (2015)
29. Lahyani, R., Khemakhem, M., Semet, F.: Rich vehicle routing problems: from a taxonomy to a definition. Eur. J. Oper. Res. **241**, 1–14 (2015)

30. Derigs, U., Vogel, U.: Experience with a framework for developing heuristics for solving rich vehicle routing problems. J. Heuristics **20**, 75–106 (2014)
31. Holland, J.: Adaptation in Natural and Artificial Systems. University of Michigan Press, Ann Arbor (1975)
32. Mascato, P.: On evolution, search, optimization, genetic algorithms and martial arts: toward memetic algorithms. Technical report Caltech Concurrent Computation Program, California Institute of Technology, Pasadena California, USA (1989)
33. Labadi, N., Prins, C., Reghioui, M.: A memetic algorithm for the vehicle routing problem with time windows. RAIRO - Oper. Res. **42**, 415–431 (2008)
34. Ngueveu, S.U., Prins, C., Wolfler Calvo, R.: An effective memetic algorithm for the cumulative capacitated vehicle routing problem. Comput. Oper. Res. **37**(11), 1877–1885 (2010)
35. Bin, S., Fu, Z.: An improved genetic algorithm for vehicle routing problem with soft time windows. Syst. Eng. **21**(6), 12–15 (2003)
36. Jing, H.M., Zhang, L.J.: Modeling and simulation of multi-type vehicle scheduling problem. Comput. Simul. **23**(4), 261–264 (2006)
37. Jozefowiez, N., Semet, F., Talbi, E.-G.: Target aiming pareto search and its application to the vehicle routing problem with route balancing. J. Heuristics **13**(5), 455–469 (2007)
38. Thibaut, V., Teodor, G.C., Michel, G., Christian, P.: A hybrid genetic algorithm with adaptive diversity management for a large class of vehicle routing problems with time-windows. Comput. Oper. Res. **40**(1), 475–489 (2013)
39. Liu, R., Jiang, Z.: The close-open mixed vehicle routing problem. Eur. J. Oper. Res. **220**(2), 349–360 (2012)
40. Keivan, G., Seyed, F.G.: Multi-objective vehicle routing problem with time windows using goal programming and genetic algorithm. Appl. Soft Comput. **10**(4), 1096–1107 (2010)
41. Ghannadpour, S.F., Noori, S., Tavakkoli-Moghaddam, R.: A multi-objective vehicle routing and scheduling problem with uncertainty in customers request and priority. J. Comb. Optim. **28**(2), 414–446 (2014)
42. Garcia-Najera, A.: Preserving population diversity for the multi-objective vehicle routing problem with time windows. In: Gecco Proceedings of Annual Conference Companion on Genetic and Evolutionary Computation, pp. 2689–2692 (2009)
43. Sherinov, Z., Unveren, A., Acan, A.: An evolutionary multi-objective modeling and solution approach for fuzzy vehicle routing problem. In: 2011 International Symposium on Proceedings of Innovations in Intelligent Systems and Applications (INISTA), pp. 450–454. IEEE (2011)
44. Neil, U., Emma, H., Cathy, S.: Building low CO2 solutions to the vehicle routing problem with time windows using an evolutionary algorithm. In: Proceedings of IEEE Congress on Evolutionary Computation (CEC), pp. 1–6 (2010)
45. Kennedy, J., Eberhart, R.: Particle swarm optimization. In: Proceedings of IEEE International Conference on Neural Networks, vol. 4, pp. 1942–1948 (1995)
46. Shi, Y., Eberhart, R.: A modified particle swarm optimizer. In: Proceedings of 1998 IEEE World Congress on Computational Intelligence, pp. 69–73 (1998)
47. Clerc, M., Kennedy, J.: The particle swarm: explosion, stability and convergence in a multi-dimensional complex space. Proc. IEEE Trans. Evol. Comput. **6**, 58–73 (2002)
48. Engelbrecht, A.P.: Computational Intelligence: An Introduction, 2nd edn. Wiley, England (2007)

49. Kennedy, J.: The particle swarm: social adaptation of knowledge. In: Proceedings of the IEEE International Conference on Evolutionary Computation, pp. 303–308 (1997)

50. Panagiotis, N.K., Grigorios, N.B.: Solving the urban transit routing problem using a particle swarm optimization based algorithm. Appl. Soft Comput. **21**, 654–676 (2014)

51. Voratas, K., Pandhapon, S., Siwaporn, K.: Two solution representations for solving multi-depot vehicle routing problem with multiple pickup and delivery requests via PSO. In: Computers and Industrial Engineering Scheduling Problem. Computer and Industry Engineering (2015)

52. Babak, F.M., Rubn, R., Seyed, J.S.: Vehicle routing problem with uncertain demands: an advanced particle swarm algorithm. Comput. Indus. Eng. **62**, 306–317 (2012)

53. Norouzi, N., Sadegh-Amalnick, M., Alinaghiyan, M.: Evaluating of the particle swarm optimization in a periodic vehicle routing problem. Measurement **62**, 162–169 (2015)

54. Xu, J., Yan, F., Li, S.: Vehicle routing optimization with soft time windows in a fuzzy random environment. Transp. Res. Part E Logistics Transp. Rev. **47**(6), 1075–1091 (2011)

55. The, J.A., Voratas, K.: A particle swarm optimization for the vehicle routing problem with simultaneous pickup and delivery. Comput. Oper. Res. **36**, 1693–1702 (2009)

56. Norouzi, N., Tavakkoli-Moghaddam, R., Ghazanfari, M., Alinaghian, M., Salamatbakhsh, A.: A new multi-objective competitive open vehicle routing problem solved by particle swarm optimization. Netw. Spat. Econ. **12**(4), 609–633 (2012)

57. Dorigo, M., Maniezzo, V., Colorni, A.: Ant system: optimization by a colony of cooperating agents. IEEE Trans. Syst. Man Cybern. Part B **26**(1), 1–13 (1996)

58. Dorigo, M., Gambardella, L.M.: Ant colony system: a cooperative learning approach to the traveling salesman problem. IEEE Trans. Evol. Comput. **1**, 53–66 (1997)

59. Stutzle, T., Hoos, H.H.: MAX-MIN ant system. Future Gener. Comput. Syst. **16**, 889–914 (2000)

60. Tan, X., Zhuo, X., Zhang, J.: Ant colony system for optimizing vehicle routing problem with time windows (VRPTW). In: Huang, D.-S., Li, K., Irwin, G.W. (eds.) ICIC 2006. LNCS (LNBI), vol. 4115, pp. 33–38. Springer, Heidelberg (2006)

61. Fuellerer, G., Doerner, K.F., Hartl, R.F., Iori, M.: Ant colony optimization for the two-dimensional loading vehicle routing problem. Comput. Oper. Res. **36**(3), 655–673 (2009)

62. Mavrovouniotis, M., Yang, S.: Ant colony optimization with memory-based immigrants for the dynamic vehicle routing problem. In: 2012 IEEE Congress on Proceedings of Evolutionary Computation (CEC), vol. 22, pp. 1–8. IEEE (2012)

63. Mullen, R.J., Monekosso, D., Barman, S., Remagnino, P.: A review of ant algorithms. Expert Syst. Appl. **36**(6), 9608–9617 (2009)

64. Donati, A.V., Montemannia, R., Casagrandea, N., Gambardellaa, R.L.M.: Time dependent vehicle routing problem with a multi ant colony system. Eur. J. Oper. Res. **185**(3), 1174–1191 (2008)

65. Tang, J., Ma, Y., Guan, J., Yan, C.: A Max-Min ant system for the split delivery weighted vehicle routing problem. Expert Syst. Appl. **40**(18), 7468–7477 (2013)

66. Huang, S.H., Lin, P.C.: A modified ant colony optimization algorithm for multi-item inventory routing problems with demand uncertainty. Transp. Res. Part E Logistics Transp. Rev. **46**(5), 598–611 (2010)
67. Gong, W., Fu, Z.: ABC-ACO for perishable food vehicle routing problem with time windows. In: Proceedings of 2012 Fourth International Conference on Computational and Information Sciences, pp. 1261–1264. IEEE (2012)
68. Liu, S., Huang, W., Ma, H.: An effective genetic algorithm for the fleet size and mix vehicle routing problems. Transp. Res. Part E: Logistics Transp. Rev. **45**, 434–445 (2009)
69. Vidal, T., Crainic, T.G., Gendreau, M., Lahrichi, N., Rei, W.: A hybrid genetic algorithm for multidepot and periodic vehicle routing problems. Oper. Res. **60**, 611–624 (2012)
70. Yu, B., Yang, Z.Z.: An ant colony optimization model: the period vehicle routing problem with time windows. Transp. Res. Part E: Logistics Transp. Rev. **47**, 166–181 (2011)
71. Lin, C., Choy, K.L., Ho, G.T.S., Chung, S.H., Lam, H.Y.: Survey of green vehicle routing problem: past and future trends. Expert Syst. Appl. **41**(4), 1118–1138 (2014)
72. Zhang, D.Z.: Towards theory building in agile manufacturing strategy: case studies of an agility taxonomy. Int. J. Prod. Econ. **131**(1), 303–312 (2011)
73. Altiparmak, F., Gen, M., Lin, L., Paksoy, T.: A genetic algorithm approach for multi-objective optimization of supply chain networks. Comput. Indus. Eng. **51**, 196–215 (2006)
74. Moncayo-Martnez, L.A., Zhang, D.Z.: Multi-objective ant colony optimization: a meta-heuristic approach to supply chain design. Int. J. Prod. Econ. **131**(1), 407–420 (2011)
75. Savas, E.: On equity in providing public services. Manag. Sci. **24**, 800–808 (1978)
76. Minocha, B., Tripathi, S.: Solving school bus routing problem using hybrid genetic algorithm: a case study. In: Advances in Intelligent Systems and Computing, vol. 236, pp. 93–103 (2014)
77. Huo, L., Yan, G., Fan, B., Wang, H., Gao, W.: School bus routing problem based on ant colony optimization algorithm. In: 2014 IEEE Conference and Expo Transportation Electrification Asia-Pacific (ITEC Asia-Pacific), pp. 1–5. IEEE (2014)

A DNA Code Converter Model for Decimal Numbers Displaying

Zicheng Wang$^{(\boxtimes)}$, Wenwen Zhang, Yanfeng Wang, and Guangzhao Cui

School of Electrical and Information Engineering,
Henan Key Lab of Information-based Electrical Appliances,
Zhengzhou University of Light Industry, Zhengzhou 450002, Henan, China
wzch@zzuli.edu.cn

Abstract. DNA has recently emerged as a powerful and novel material for creating nano-scale electronic architectures and devices. Based on DNA strand displacement (DSD) reactions, sophisticated multilayered DNA molecular circuits have been rationally designed to perform different functions. In this paper, a code converter circuit, which can be used to compute logic states of a seven-segment digital tube, is designed for decimal numbers displaying. In addition, the logic circuit is further translated into its correspondingly dual-rail circuit and seesaw cascade circuit. The simulation results show that our logic circuits are effective and feasible for decimal numbers displaying.

Keywords: DNA strand displacement · Code converter · Dual-rail circuit · Seesaw circuit

1 Introduction

The specificity and predictability of Watson-Crick base pairing enable DNA nanotechnology a reliable and programmable way of constructing dynamic DNA devices that implement digital and analog behaviors [1–3]. Recent attempts toward massive and intricate dynamic devices and circuit mainly relay on DNA strand displacement technology [4–6]. DNA strand displacement is the process of two partly or full complementary DNA strands hybridizing with each other and displacing the former less complementary DNA sequences. It has been demonstrated to be capable of implementing logic computing function at the molecular scale [7,8]. These molecular computing systems can operate because DNA strand displacement reactions can be cascaded, wherein the output signals released from the upper cascade can motivate the next cascade reactions.

In 2011, Qian and Winfree presented an elementary DNA gate architecture suitable for constructing logic AND and OR gates, and they further illustrated how arbitrary feedforward digital logic circuits, arbitrary relay contact circuits, and various analog circuits could be systematically built [9,10]. The largest circuit at that time, which can calculate the square root of numbers up to 15, was built with this approach using 130 DNA strands [7]. In 2013, Hemphill and

© Springer-Verlag Berlin Heidelberg 2015
M. Gong et al. (Eds.): BIC-TA 2015, CCIS 562, pp. 447–455, 2015.
DOI: 10.1007/978-3-662-49014-3_40

Deiters had fabricated oligonucleotide AND gates to detect specific miRNAs in live mammalian cells through DNA computation [11]. Nucleic acid logic gates that are functional in vivo are demonstrated as a stepping stone toward reliable design of biologic systems [11,12].

Based on molecular logic gates implemented by DNA strand displacement, we construct a code converter circuit for decimal numbers displaying. The paper is arranged as follows. A four-input DNA gate architecture based on the "seesaw" gate motif is firstly introduced, together with a logic circuit that computes logic states of a seven-segment nixie tube. Subsequently, the logic circuit is translated into seesaw circuit using the dual-rail implementation. The whole DNA strand displacement reactions that simulate in DSD software afterwards indicate the correctness of the circuit design.

2   Seesaw Motif of Four-Input Or and AND Gates

Logic gates are the basic elements in modern computers, implementing simple mathematical operations based on one or more physical or chemical inputs and a single output [13,14]. Logic circuits have achieved great progress constantly with the development of science and technology in recent years. However, modern electronic circuits are limited by the physical size of elementary components. DNA technology has been demonstrated as a promising method to overcome the miniaturization challenge of circuit components. To perform mathematical logic, this paper proposes constructions for basic DNA gates (AND, OR, and NOT) based on DNA strand displacement [15]. In the reversible DNA strand displacement, the invading single strand $\langle a\ t\ b \rangle$ first binds to the toehold t* and subsequently performs branch migration to displace the former bound one [16]. This progress finally translates input single strand to corresponding output single-stranded signal (Fig. 1(a)). Reactions between each input and gate complexes are similar, input signals X_1, X_2, X_3 and X_4 are summed together at this gate, resulting in the release of single-stranded DNA output signal $\langle c\ t\ b \rangle$ (Fig. 1(b)).

Based on the reversible toehold-mediated strand displacement process [17], we have constructed molecular four-input logic gates implemented with the seesaw DNA motif (Fig. 1(c)(d)). The second layer of seesaw OR gate has a fixed threshold of 0.6, and the second layer of seesaw AND gate has a threshold of 3.2. For the multi-input gate, the original single strand DNA signal carrier can be recognized simply as either ON or OFF according to its average concentration at each stage of computation. Note that the thresholds for the logic gates are calculated based on Qian's research and no threshold is allowed in integrating gates [9].

Digital DNA circuits operate in binary, distinguishing between two values: '0' and '1', represented by low and high concentrations respectively. We consider signal levels as OFF state with range being (0.0-0.1)x and ON state with range being (0.9-1)x, wherein 1x is a standard concentration. Logic gates perform binary operations on more than one input to produce a meaningful output.

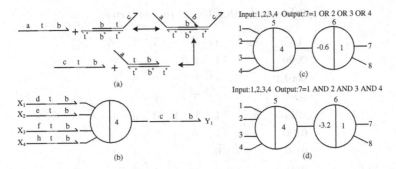

Fig. 1. Digital four-input logic gates implemented with the seesaw DNA motif. (a) The process of a reversible DNA strand displacement. (b) Equivalent seesaw circuit for the general integrating gate. (c) Abstract diagram of a Seesaw circuit that computes four-input OR. (d) A four-input AND gate implemented with the seesaw DNA motif.

In the four-input OR logic gate, the output is ON as long as not less than one input is ON. However, in AND logic, the output is ON only if the whole inputs are ON. Based on the available design of DNA gates, large logic circuits may be constructed synthesized and executed.

3   Logic Circuit of the Code Converter

A seven-segment digital tube is an electronic device composed of seven light-emitting diodes for displaying numerals, and it has ten states in the shapes of numerals 0 to 9 (Fig. 2(a)). To perform this function, a logic circuit is built to control seven segments of the digital tube. We regard four bits of binary 0000-1001 as four independent inputs A_0-A_3, which adopt only two kinds of states: '0' and '1', and the seven segments of the digital tube as seven independent outputs whose states are also '0' and '1'. With possible inputs from 0000 to 1001, seven independent outputs separately turn to the correct ON state or OFF state. According to the truth table for the converter, the logic circuit of the code converter is built from logic OR, AND and NOT gates (Fig. 2(b)). The output will produce a corresponding change while the input varies from 0000 to 1001. For example, when the four-bit binary input is 0000, the outputs Y_0, Y_1, Y_2, Y_3, Y_4 and Y_5 are 1, but Y_6 is 0 (Table 1).

In the so-called dual-rail circuit, wherein logic values ('1' and '0') of each input are represented by the presence of two strands separately, AND and OR by themselves suffice to compute any Boolean function [15]. Each input X_i is replaced by a pair of new inputs X_i^0 and X_i^1, representing logic 'OFF' and logic 'ON' separately; original AND or OR gate is replaced by a pair of AND and OR gates, producing a pair of dual-rail outputs [9]. A NOT gate only needs to reroute wires and swap their labels. This method avoids the difficulty of directly implementing NOT gate, at a cost of twice as many as gates contained. For part of the whole dual-rail circuit that represents Y_0, if Y_0^0 is 1, this indicates that

Table 1. Truth table for the converter.

$A_3A_2A_1A_0$	Y_0	Y_1	Y_2	Y_3	Y_4	Y_5	Y_6
0000	1	1	1	1	1	1	0
0001	0	1	1	0	0	0	0
0010	1	1	0	1	1	0	1
0011	1	1	1	1	0	0	1
0100	0	1	1	0	0	1	1
0101	1	0	1	1	0	1	1
0110	1	0	1	1	1	1	1
0111	1	1	1	0	0	0	0
1000	1	1	1	1	1	1	1
1001	1	1	1	1	0	1	1

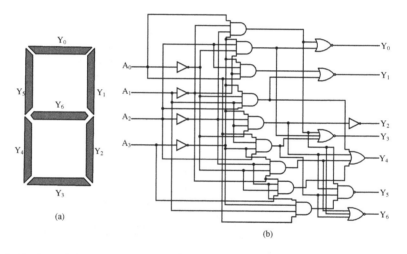

Fig. 2. Design of the code converter. (a) A seven-segment digital tube. (b) A digital logic circuit that implements the conversion.

the logic value of Y_0 is 0; while if Y_0^1 is 1, this indicates that the logic value of Y_0 is 1 (Fig. 3(b)).

Then, any dual-rail circuit can be further transformed into an equivalent seesaw circuit using seesaw gates we described above. Every logic operation of the seesaw circuit includes threshold and catalysis to perform digital signal restoration, enabling reliable function in large circuits. For part of the seesaw circuit that represents Y_0, if the output single strand that represents Y_0^0 has a high concentration, this indicates that the logic value of Y_0 is 0; if Y_0^1 strand has a high concentration, this indicates that the logic value of Y_0 is 1 (Fig. 3(c)).

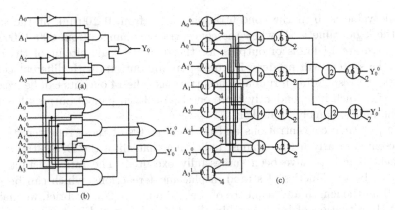

Fig. 3. Implementations of Y_0. (a) Logic circuit of output Y_0. (b) Abstract diagram of the dual-rail circuit for output Y_0. (c) The resulting seesaw circuit using the dual-rail implementation for output Y_0.

4 Simulation with Visual DSD

Visual DSD is a design and analysis tool for DNA strand displacement systems [18,19]. It allows rapid prototyping and analysis of computational devices implemented using DNA strand displacement. Here we simulate the reaction process of the code converter based on DNA strand displacement in DSD. With 10 kinds of combinations inputs we mainly discussed for the converter, the system will produce 10 relevant simulation results. In the deterministic simulation plots,

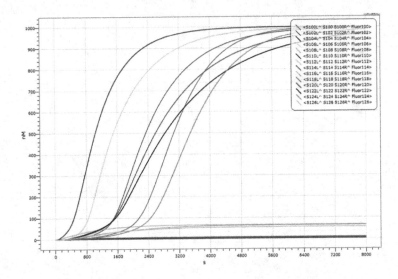

Fig. 4. The simulation result of the code converter corresponding to input combination 0000.

the logic value is '0' if the concentration ranges from 0–100 nm, at the same time, the logic value is '1' when the concentration changes from 900–1000 nm. Since there are 14 kinds of outputs for the dual-rail logic circuit of the converter, the system will produce 14 corresponding outputs with different colors tracing to corresponding terminal concentrations. The 14 outputs can be treated as 7 pairs, which independently represent Y_0-Y_6. Each pair of outputs has two different values, namely '0' and '1'.

The real-time concentrations and terminal states of these reporter strands are presented clearly in the graphs, indicating that all of the DNA strand displacement reactions have been successfully executed. The rate constants are influenced by the kinetics of strand displacement reactions, which can be predicted from the length and sequence of toehold domain [20]. To brief, we mainly discuss the situation of input combination 0000 shown in Fig. 4. The abscissa

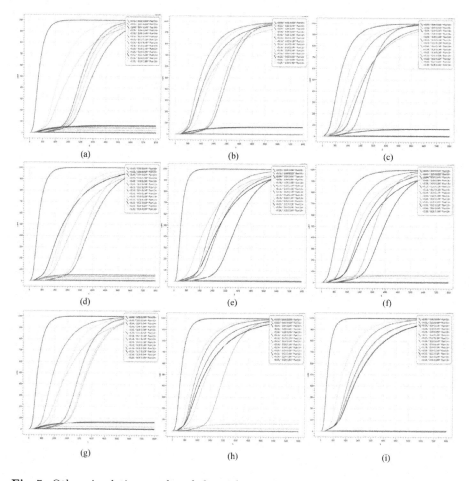

Fig. 5. Other simulation results of the code converter corresponding to inputs from 0001 to 1001.

represents the reaction time, and the ordinate represents the DNA strand concentration. Seven curves gradually rise with different rate constants and successively reach the defined saturation concentration ranging from 900 nm–1000 nm. In the beginning of this period, rate constants approximate to zero, which are limited by the rates of molecular diffusion. As time goes on, molecular collision frequency increases, making the reaction rates gradually accelerate until to the maximum values. Finally influenced by the low species concentrations and reaction temperature, rate constants gradually decrease to zero. These sharply rising curves, whose final concentrations are 900 nm–1000 nm, indicate the logic values of their corresponding Y_i^j are 1. At the same time, the other 7 curves gradually approach X axis with concentrations ranging from 0 nm–100 nm, indicating their corresponding logic values are 0. For instance, the green curve that represents Y_0^1 finally exceeds the concentration of 900 nm, but the red curve that represents Y_0^0 always keeps ranging from 0 nm to 100 nm, which together indicates the logic value of Y_0 is 0. The simulation result in Fig. 4 demonstrates when the input signals $A_3 A_2 A_1 A_0$ is 0000, the values of Y_0-Y_5 are '1' and Y_6 is '0'. Other simulation results of the code converter corresponding to inputs from 0001 to 1001 are similar to input 0000 in the reaction mechanisms, so we will not illustrate them repeatedly (Fig. 5).

5 Conclusion

In this paper, we first illustrate DNA strand displacement in detail, and further construct logic four-input AND and OR gates using DNA seesaw motif. These designed DNA gates are capable of synthesizing arbitrary large-scale logic circuits. Based on the DNA gates designed above, the code converter is constructed to implement the code conversion from binary input 0000-1001. The simulation results in Visual DSD software indicate the code converter is feasible and efficient.

Steady progress has been made towards DNA computing circuits that are reliable and scalable. Compared to traditional circuit components, DNA technology has been demonstrated as a promising method to overcome the miniaturization challenge of circuit components. Logic molecular circuits based on DNA strand displacement provide a perfect way to perform correct logic computations in the nano-scale. Signals from the upper cascade can motivate the following cascade reactions, so massive and intricate molecular circuits can be constructed using DNA strand displacement technology.

Moreover, these multilayer DNA circuits enable fast and reliable digital computing function, on account of a threshold and catalysis within every logic operation. The defined thresholds have a great effect on cleaning up erroneous signals and catalysis is also essential for fast signal propagation in multi-layer circuits. Logic computation based on threshold and catalysis has made solid foundation for implementing more complicated and significant systems and networks.

Spiking neural P systems and their variants (see, e.g. [21–23]) have been proved to be powerful intelligent computing models. It is of interests to consider using spiking neural P systems for decimal numbers displaying.

Acknowledgments. This work is supported by the NSFC (Grant Nos.U1304620, 61472372, 61272022), Innovation Scientists and Technicians Troop Construction Projects of Henan (Grant No. 124200510017), and Innovation Scientists and Technicians Troop Construction Projects of Zhengzhou (Grant No. 131PLJRC648).

References

1. Beaver, D.: Computing with DNA. J. Comput. Biol. **3**, 254–257 (1996)
2. Xu, J., Qiang, X., Yang, Y., Wang, B., Yang, D., Luo, L., Pan, L., Wang, S.: An unenumerative DNA computing model for vertex coloring problem. IEEE Trans. Nanobiosci. **10**(2), 94–98 (2011)
3. Chen, Y.J., Dalchau, N., Srinivas, N., Phillips, A., Cardelli, L., Soloveichik, D., Seelig, G.: Programmable chemical controllers made from DNA. Nat. Nanotechnol. **8**, 755–762 (2013)
4. Jung, C., Ellington, A.D.: Diagnostic applications of nucleic acid circuits. Acc. Chem. Res. **47**(6), 1825–1835 (2014)
5. Qian, L., Winfree, E.: Parallel and scalable computation and spatial dynamics with DNA-based chemical reaction networks on a surface. In: Murata, S., Kobayashi, S. (eds.) DNA 2014. LNCS, vol. 8727, pp. 114–131. Springer, Heidelberg (2014)
6. Zhang, D.Y., Hariadi, R.F., Choi, H.M.T., Winfree, E.: Integrating DNA strand-displacement circuitry with DNA tile self-assembly. Nat. Commun. **4**, 1965 (2013)
7. Shi, X., Wang, Z., Deng, C., Song, T., Pan, L., Chen, Z.: A novel bio-sensor based on DNA strand displacement. PLoS One **9**, e108856 (2014)
8. Zhang, D.Y., Seelig, G.: Dynamic DNA nanotechnology using strand-displacement reactions. Nat. Chem. **3**, 103–113 (2011)
9. Qian, L., Winfree, E.: A simple DNA gate motif for synthesizing large-scale circuits. J. Roy. Soc. Interface **8**, 1281–1297 (2011)
10. Qian, L., Winfree, E., Bruck, J.: Neural network computation with DNA strand displacement cascades. Nature **475**, 368–372 (2011)
11. Wang, X., Miao, Y., Cheng, M.: Finding motifs in DNA sequences using low-dispersion sequences. J. Comput. Biol. **21**(4), 320–329 (2014)
12. Gaber, R., Lebar, T., Majerle, A., Šter, B., Dobnikar, A., Benčina, M., Jerala, R.: Designable DNA-binding domains enable construction of logic circuits in mammalian cells. Nat. Chem. Biol. **10**(3), 203–208 (2014)
13. Stojanovic, M.N., Mitchell, T.E., Stefanovic, D.: Deoxyribozyme-based logic gates. J. Am. Chem. Soc. **124**(14), 3555–3561 (2002)
14. Zeng, X., Song, T., Zhang, X., Pan, L.: Performing four basic arithmetic operations with spiking neural P systems. IEEE Trans. Nanobiosci. **11**(4), 366–374 (2012)
15. Seelig, G., Soloveichik, D., Zhang, D.Y., Winfree, E., Stefanovic, D.: Enzyme-free nucleic acid logic circuits. Science **314**(5805), 1585–1588 (2006)
16. Wang, Y., Tian, G., Hou, H., Ye, M., Cui, G.: Simple logic computation based on the DNA strand displacement. J. Comput. Theor. Nanosci. **11**(9), 1975–1982 (2014)
17. Srinivas, N., Ouldridge, T.E., Šulc, P., Schaeffer, J.M., Yurke, B., Louis, A.A., Doye, J.P.K., Winfree, E.: On the biophysics and kinetics of toehold-mediated DNA strand displacement. Nucleic Acids Res. **41**(22), 10641–10658 (2013)
18. Lakin, M.R., Youssef, S., Polo, F., Emmott, S., Phillips, A.: Visual DSD: a design and analysis tool for DNA strand displacement systems. Bioinformatics **27**(22), 3211–3213 (2011)

19. Lakin, M.R., Petersen, R., Gray, K.E., Phillips, A.: Abstract modelling of tethered DNA circuits. In: Murata, S., Kobayashi, S. (eds.) DNA 2014. LNCS, vol. 8727, pp. 132–147. Springer, Heidelberg (2014)
20. Zhang, D.Y., Winfree, E.: Control of DNA strand displacement kinetics using toehold exchange. J. Am. Chem. Soc. **131**, 17303–17314 (2009)
21. Zhang, X., Pan, L., Păun, A.: On the universality of axon P systems. IEEE Trans. Neural Netw. Learn. Syst. **26**, 2816–2829 (2015). doi:10.1109/TNNLS.2015.2396940
22. Song, T., Pan, L.: Spiking neural P systems with rules on synapses working in maximum spikes consumption strategy. IEEE Trans. NanoBiosci. **14**(1), 38–44 (2015)
23. Song, T., Pan, L.: Spiking neural P systems with rules on synapses working in maximum spiking strategy. IEEE Trans. NanoBiosci. **14**(4), 465–477 (2015)

The Design of Digital Circuit Based on DNA Strand Displacement Reaction

Zicheng Wang, Zijie Cai, Zhonghua Sun, Yanfeng Wang,
and Guangzhao Cui[✉]

Henan Key Lab of Information-based Electrical Appliances, College of Electrical
and Information Engineering, Zhengzhou University of Light Industry,
No. 5 Dongfeng Road, Zhengzhou 450002, China
{wzch,cgzh}@zzuli.edu.cn

Abstract. Because of its outstanding advantages, DNA strand displacement (DSD) reaction has been widely used for signals processing and molecular logic circuit constructing. Two digital logic circuits are constructed in this paper. One is the encoder circuit with four inputs and two outputs, and the other is the decoder circuit with two inputs and four outputs. Finally, the circuits can be programmed and simulated with the software Visual DSD. The simulated results based on DSD show that the molecular circuits constructed in this paper is reliable and effective, which has wide prospects in logical circuits and nano electronics study.

Keywords: DNA strand displacement reaction · Encoder · Decoder · Visual DSD

1 Introduction

With the rapid development of society, it was found that the traditional electronic computing cannot meet people's needs in many areas. Unconventional computing, including membrane computing [1], (particular interests of neural-like membrane computing systems, see, e.g. [2–4], as well as some variants of such spiking neural systems [11,18,25]), quantum computation [5] and biological calculation and DNA computing [35], has attracted researcher's attention. What is noteworthy is that biological calculation has been paid special attention. In particular, DNA computing, which is a relatively new calculation method equips with modern molecular biology techniques. It aims to solve complex computing problem and construct computing devices with DNA strands. As the carrier of biological information, DNA molecules can form double helix structures according to the Watson-Crick base pairing principle, which make the predictability of molecular behavior possible.

DNA, as an excellent engineering material, has been used in the building of synthetic biochemical computing. As early as 1998, Seeman proposed that the DNA molecules can be used to constitute the self-assembly tile structure. Then he took advantage of DX Tile structure to establish a variety of complex

© Springer-Verlag Berlin Heidelberg 2015
M. Gong et al. (Eds.): BIC-TA 2015, CCIS 562, pp. 456–464, 2015.
DOI: 10.1007/978-3-662-49014-3_41

algorithm models [6,7]. In 2000, Mao et al. first built the self-assembled DNA computing model with experiments to solve the cumulative XOR implementation process [8]. The attempts to construct several enzyme-catalyzed [9,10,12] and enzyme-free [13–15] DNA automata systems have been undertaken on the basis of well-developed technology of DNA strand displacement, in which two strands with partial or full complementarity hybridize to each other, displacing one or more pre-hybridized strands in the process [16]. Strand displacement can be initiated at the toehold domain and progresses through the branch migration process to produce the output signal. It is very suitable for use in logic circuits, since both the input and output signals are single-stranded oligonucleotides. In 2011, Qian et al. accomplished a four-bit binary square-root circuit that comprised 130 DNA strands and four interconnected neurons that can play mind-reading game by DNA strand displacement cascades [17,19], which has attracted great attention in the field of information calculation. These excellent works have provided reference for further research and shown the direction of the future research clearly.

Here, we achieved the construction of a encoder circuit and a decoder circuit based on the DNA strand displacement reaction. And the circuits could be simulated with the software Visual DSD. The paper is organized as follows. Section 2 introduces the concept of basic logic gate. Section 3 describes the design of logic circuits and Sect. 4 analyses the simulation results. Finally, Sect. 5 makes conclusion for the design of the circuits.

2   Build of Basic Logic Gate

In this paper, we use the simple DNA gate motif: a "seesaw" gate [20] which makes use of a reversible strand displacement reaction based on the principle of toehold exchange [21,22]. A pair of seesaw gates can perform AND or OR operation using dual-rail logic [15] to realize the universal Boolean function. Whats more, the output of a reaction can be used as the input of a downstream reaction. In the ideal state, reaction will occur according to the certain order by turns, until the final output produce. With the using of these seesaw gates, a digital logic circuit can be built.

The abstract diagram of seesaw gate is shown in Fig. 1(a). There are two kinds of DNA strands. One is single-stranded DNA molecules which we call "signal strands", the other is partially double-stranded DNA molecules which we call "gate:signal complexes" or "threshold complexes". Black numbers indicate identities of nodes or interfaces to those nodes in a network. Red numbers within the nodes or on the wires indicate relative concentration of different initial DNA species. Each species plays a specific role (e.g., input) within a gate and has a unique name (e.g., $W1,3$) within a network. $S1$, $S3$ and $S4$ are long recognition domains corresponding to nodes 1, 3 and 4. T is a short toehold domain; $T*$ is the Watson-Crick complement of T. $s1*$ is the first few nucleotides of $S1*$.

A seesaw network includes two basic reactions: seesawing, thresholding. Firstly, seesawing reaction happens when a free signal (e.g., input) binds to the uncovered toehold of a gate complex, triggering branch migration through the recognition domain and subsequently releasing the signal strand bound to the gate complex. The resulting gate complex will have an exposed toehold on the opposite side, thus it occurs that the released signal strand can bind to the gate complex again, initiating the release of the original signal strand. So the reaction of seesawing is reversible. Here, the introduction of an auxiliary species-the fuel, with a high initial concentration can drive the reaction in a desired direction. Secondly, threshold complex can react with input strands by means of a longer toehold, but the product has no uncovered toehold so that the reaction isnt reversible. Because of the toehold-mediated strand displacement rate exponentially with the increasing of the toeholds length [23, 24], thresholding is faster than seesawing with the threshold complexs extended toehold. As a result, seesawing will occur effectively unless the input concentration exceeds the threshold concentration.

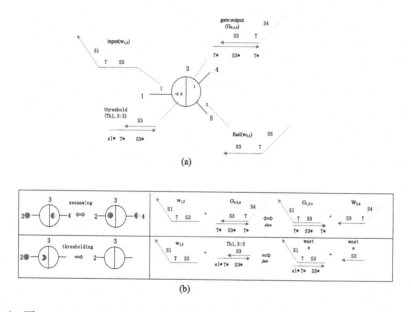

Fig. 1. The seesaw gate motif and its basic reactions. (a) Abstract gate diagram. (b) Two basic reaction mechanisms involved in a seesaw network.

In order to build an ideal digital circuit which can implement Boolean function, we utilize the basic seesaw motif. The abstract seesaw network introduced in Fig. 2 can compute either OR or AND, which depends on the initial concentration of the threshold. The first seesaw gate (e.g., gate 2) has two inputs without threshold and fuel, so the output will be the sum of the two inputs. To ensure all free inputs being transformed into free output, the initial amount of bound output must be at least the maximum sum of all inputs which can possibly arrive. In the second gate (e.g., gate 5), the threshold of the OR gate is set at 0.6, indicating that the output will be 1 as the sum larger than 0.6 and being

0 otherwise. It can also be accomplished by assuming a digital abstraction with 0–0.3 being OFF and 0.7–1 being ON. Thus the output will be ON only when one or all inputs are ON. The threshold of the AND gate is set at 1.2, working in the same way of the OR gate. The output can be ON only when all inputs are ON. In order to efficiently ensure the release of all outputs, the amount of initial free fuel must be twice the sum of all initially bound outputs.

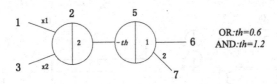

Fig. 2. Abstract diagram of a seesaw circuit.

3 Construction of the Logic Circuits

Based on the construction of basic logic gateseesaw gate, a digital encoder circuit is built which converts four binary numbers I_0, I_1, I_2 and I_3 to the output Y_0 and Y_1. There are four output cases in the circuit: $Y_1Y_0=00$, $Y_1Y_0=01$, $Y_1Y_0=10$, $Y_1Y_0=11$. Four kinds of output corresponding to four kinds of input: $I_0I_1I_2I_3=10000$, $I_0I_1I_2I_3=01000$, $I_0I_1I_2I_3=0010$ and $I_0I_1I_2I_3=0001$. The logic gates of AND, OR and NOT are constructed in circuit, while NOT gates appear to be difficult to implement directly due to they hardly turning OFF after being ON. In addition, NOT gates can produce ON signals in the absence of the inputs, leading to the output false before all inputs are added.

Therefore, to avoid this problem, we use the dual-rail logic. In the new circuit, one AND gate and one OR gate are used to implement each original AND, OR, NAND, or NOR gate; Furthermore, dual-rail logic can effectively solve the problem of NOT gates as no computation will take place before the input signals arrive. Consequently, any circuit including AND, OR, NOT, NAND and NOR gates can be converted to an equivalent dual rail circuit with AND and OR only and finally to its equivalent seesaw circuit, as illustrated in Fig. 3(a), (b) and (c). In the same principle, we further built a decoder circuit with two inputs and four output. We compiled this circuit to seesaw gates (Fig. 4).

4 Simulation with Visual DSD

The Visual DSD is a tool that allows rapid prototyping and analysis of computational devices implemented using DNA strand displacement. It is an implementation of the DSD programming language and compiler described by Lakin et al. [26–28]. This software has three regions: the code region, the setting region and the display region. In the code region, we can code to design the structure

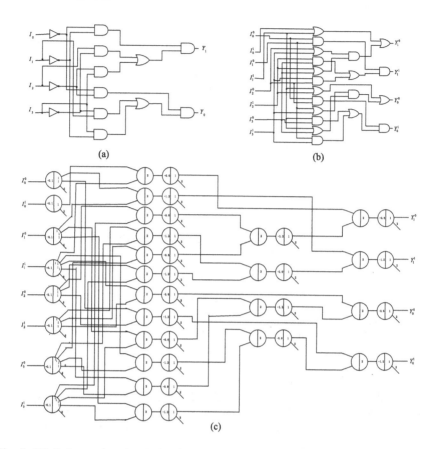

Fig. 3. Digital encoder circuit implemented with the seesaw gate. (a) The diagram of digital encoder logic circuit; (b) Translation into an equivalent dual-rail circuit; (c) Translation into an equivalent seesaw gate circuit.

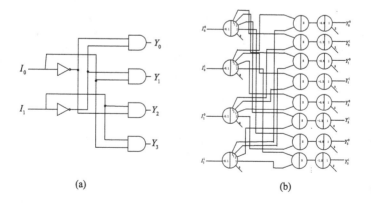

Fig. 4. The decoder circuit implemented with the seesaw gate. (a) The diagram of digital decoder logic circuit; (b) Translation into an equivalent seesaw gate circuit.

of DNA, and set the amount of substance; In the setting region, three semantic models can be selected; We also can select the simulation models as stochastic, deterministic, JIT (just-in-time) simulation. The last is the display region. We can get the simulation data and plot from it.

Here, we first write the program code in the code region. Then compile the code, the DSD automatically produce the DNA species, reaction network and sequences of DNA. Subsequently, after clicking the "Simulation" button, we can get the output plot of reaction. There are four kinds of output plots produced for encoder in the simulation of Visual DSD and all simulation plots accord with the correct computing results. The simulation results of encoder are shown in Fig. 5(a)–(d). In the plot, the red curve represents the value of Y_1^0; the green curve represents the value of Y_1^1; the blue curve represents the value of Y_0^0; the yellow curve represents the value of Y_0^1. If the final concentration of output ranges from 0 to 10 nM, then the value of the corresponding output is logic "0". If the ultimate concentration of output changes between 90 nM and 100 nM, then the value of the corresponding output is logic "1". In the encoder circuit, the input signal is I_0, I_1, I_2 and I_3, the output signal is Y_0 and Y_1. The Fig. 5(a)–(d) indicate four kinds of simulations results. As the reverse circuit of the encoder, the decoder can also get the ideal output results. The Fig. 6(a)–(d) show the simulation results of decoder circuit.

As for plots of Figs. 5 and 6, we can summarize that: first, some curves are closed to overlap, we can infer that the reaction rates in the simulation are approximately equivalent. Second, although some curves that represent logic OFF state are approaching X axis and others fluctuate slightly, the final concentration is still below a certain value. Thus the logic OFF state can be expressed

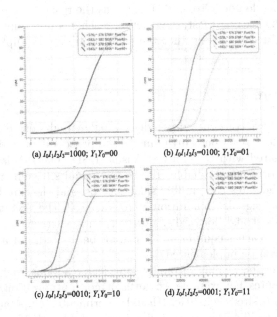

(a) $I_0I_1I_2I_3$=1000; Y_1Y_0=00

(b) $I_0I_1I_2I_3$=0100; Y_1Y_0=01

(c) $I_0I_1I_2I_3$=0010; Y_1Y_0=10

(d) $I_0I_1I_2I_3$=0001; Y_1Y_0=11

Fig. 5. Simulation results of the encoder for all 4 possible inputs (Color figure online).

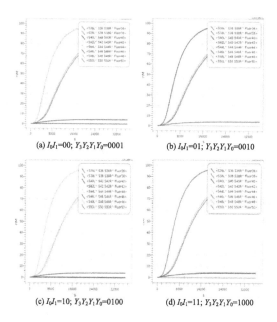

(a) $I_0I_1=00$; $Y_3Y_2Y_1Y_0=0001$

(b) $I_0I_1=01$; $Y_3Y_2Y_1Y_0=0010$

(c) $I_0I_1=10$; $Y_3Y_2Y_1Y_0=0100$

(d) $I_0I_1=11$; $Y_3Y_2Y_1Y_0=1000$

Fig. 6. Simulation results of the decoder for 4 possible inputs.

accurately. Third, at the beginning of simulation, the curve is very gentle, then the curve begin to become very steep. With the deepening of the reaction, the curve begin to become slow again. We can infer that at the beginning of the reaction, reactants do not fully contact. Then as the reaction proceeds, the reactants contact sufficiently. At last, the reaction reaches equilibrium. From all plots of Figs. 5 and 6, it can be seen that the simulation system implements correct results.

5   Conclusion

In summary, we have constructed two digital logic circuits on the basis of DNA strand displacement reaction. Furthermore, the process of strand displacement reaction is simulated with the software Visual DSD. The simulation results of the circuits are correct and reliable. The seesaw circuits have many advantages. In this system, the gates can amplify small signals, and the threshold can clean up upstream leaky signals. In addition, we can compile the circuits into systems of DNA molecules straightforwardly. However, once a seesaw reaction has been implemented and reaches equilibrium, it cannot be re-used, put a limit on what class of circuits can be implemented.

In the experiments, we may encounter some leak reactions, so it can be needed to take some measures. For example, we can use a more optimization DNA sequence design, choosing a desired toehold length and experimental temperature. Although we may meet some difficulties, seesaw circuits based on toehold-mediated strand displacement show great theoretical advances. At present, other DNA and RNA cascade reactions based on toehold-mediated strand displacement have already been applied to the development of cancer drugs and biomedical diagnosis [29–32]. Moreover, there is a structural similarity between seesaw gates motif and miRNAs and siRNAs [33,34], all of which are short duplex nucleic acids with single-stranded overhangs. Therefore, the mechanism of strand displacement circuitry has a great application prospect in the biological systems.

Acknowledgements. This work is supported by the NSFC (No. U1304620, 61472372, 61272022), Innovation Scientists and Technicians Troop Construction Projects of Henan (Grant No. 124200510017), and Innovation Scientists and Techni-cians Troop Construction Projects of Zhengzhou (Grant No. 131PLJRC648), Basic and Frontier technologies Research Program of Henan Province (132300410183), Innovation Scientists and Technicians Troop Construction Projects of Henan Province(154200510 012).

References

1. Păun, G., Rozenberg, G., Salomaa, A.: The Oxford Handbook of Membrane Computing. Oxford University Press Inc., Oxford (2010)
2. Song, T., Pan, L.: Spiking neural P systems with rules on synapses working in maximum spikes consumption strategy. IEEE Trans. NanoBiosci. **14**(1), 38–44 (2015)
3. Zhang, X., Pan, L., Păun, A.: On the universality of axon P systems. IEEE Trans. Neural Netw. Learn. Syst. **26**(11), 2816–2829 (2015). doi:10.1109/TNNLS.2015. 2396940
4. Song, T., Pan, L.: Spiking neural P systems with rules on synapses working in maximum spiking strategy. IEEE Trans. NanoBiosci. **14**(4), 465–477 (2015)
5. Tzn, B., Erko, S.: Structural and electronic properties of unusual carbon nanorods. Quantum Matter **13**, 136–148 (2012)
6. Seeman, N.C.: DNA nanotechnology: novel DNA constructure. Ann. Rev. Biophys. Biomol. Struct. **27**, 225–248 (1998)
7. Mao, C., Sun, W., Seeman, N.C.: Designed two dimensional DNA holliday junction arrays vis-ualized by atomic force microscopy. J. Am. Chem. Soc. **121**(23), 5437–5443 (1999)
8. Mao, C., LaBean, T.H., Reif, J.H.: Logical computation using algorithmic self-assembly of DNA triple-crossover molecules. Nature **407**(6803), 493–496 (2000)
9. Stojanovic, M.N.: A deoxyribozyme-based molecular automaton. Biotechnology **21**, 1069–1074 (2003)
10. Elbaz, J., Lioubashevski, O., Wang, F.: All-DNA finite-state automata with finite memory. Nanotechnology **107**(51), 21996–22001 (2010)
11. Song, T., Pan, L., Păun, G.: Asynchronous spiking neural P systems with local synchronization. Inf. Sci. **219**, 197–207 (2013)
12. Benenson, Y., Gil, B., Ben-Dor, U., Adar, R., Shapiro, E.: An autonomous molecular computer for logical control of gene expression. Nature **429**(6990), 423–429 (2004)
13. Yurke, B., Turberfield, A.J., Mills, A.P., Simmel, F.C.: A DNA-fuelled molecular machine made of DNA. Nature **406**(6796), 605–608 (2000)

14. Turberfield, A.J., Mitchell, J.C., Yurke, B.: DNA fuel for free-running nanomachines. Phys. Rev. Lett. **90**, 118102 (2003)
15. Yurke, B., Mills, A.P.: Using DNA to power nanostructures. Program. Evol. Mach. **4**(2), 111–122 (2003)
16. Zhang, D.Y., Seelig, G.: Dynamic DNA nanotechnology using strand-displacement reactions. Nat. Chem. **3**(2), 103–113 (2011)
17. Qian, L., Winfree, E.: Scaling up digital circuit computation with DNA strand displacement cascades. Science **332**(6034), 1196–1201 (2011)
18. Song, T., Pan, L., Wang, J., et al.: Normal forms of spiking neural P systems with anti-spikes. IEEE Trans. NanoBiosci. **11**(4), 352–359 (2012)
19. Qian, L., Winfree, E., Bruck, J.: Neural network computation with DNA strand displacement cascades. Nature **475**(7356), 368–372 (2011)
20. Qian, L., Winfree, E.: A simple DNA gate motif for synthesizing large-scale circuits. In: Goel, A., Simmel, F.C., Sosík, P. (eds.) DNA Computing. LNCS, vol. 5347, pp. 70–89. Springer, Heidelberg (2009)
21. Zhang, D.Y., Andrew, J., Bernard, Y., Winfree, E.: Engineering entropy-driven reactions and networks catalyzed by DNA. Science **318**(5853), 1121–1125 (2007)
22. Zhang, D.Y., Winfree, E.: Control of DNA strand displacement kinetics using toehold exchange. Am. Chem. Soc. **131**(47), 17303–17314 (2009)
23. Wang, X., Miao, Y., Cheng, M.: Finding motifs in DNA sequences using low-dispersion sequences. J. Comput. Biol. **21**(4), 320–329 (2014)
24. Yurke, B., Mills, A.P.: Using DNA to power nanostructures. Genet. Program. Evol. Mach. **4**(2), 111–122 (2003)
25. Song, T., Pan, L., Jiang, K., et al.: Normal forms for some classes of sequential spiking neural P systems. IEEE Trans. NanoBiosci. **12**(3), 255–264 (2013)
26. Phillips, A., Cardelli, L.: A programming language for composable DNA circuits. Interface **6**(4), 419–436 (2009)
27. Matthew, L., Simon, Y.: Visual DSD: a design and analysis tool for DNA strand displacement systems. Bioinformatics **27**(22), 3211–3213 (2011)
28. Lakin, M.R., Youssef, S., Cardelli, L., Phillips, A.: Abstractions for DNA circuit design. J. Royal Soc. Interface **9**(68), 470–486 (2012)
29. Venkataraman, S., Dirks, R.M., Ueda, C.T., Pierce, N.A.: Selective cell death mediated by small conditional RNAs. PNAS **39**(107), 16777–16782 (2010)
30. Eckhoff, G., Codrea, V., Ellington, A.D., Chen, X.: Beyond allostery: catalytic regulation of a deoxyribozyme through an entropy-driven DNA amplifier. J. Syst. Chem. **1**(1), 1–6 (2010)
31. Su, Y., Pan, L.: Identification of logic relationships between genes and subtypes of non-small cell lung cancer. PLoS One **9**(4), 94664 (2014)
32. Wang, X., Miao, Y.: GAEM: a hybrid algorithm incorporating GA with EM for planted edited motif finding problem. Curr. Bioinf. **9**(5), 463–469 (2014)
33. Kim, V.N.: MicroRNA biogenesis: coordinated cropping and dicing. Nat. Rev. Mol. Cell Biol. **6**(5), 376–385 (2005)
34. Carthew, R.W., Sontheimer, E.J.: Origins and mechanisms of miRNAs and siRNAs. 136(4), 642–655 (2009)
35. Shi, X., Wang, Z., Deng, C., Song, T., Pan, L., Chen, Z.: A novel bio-sensor based on DNA strand displacement. PLoS One **9**(10), e108856 (2014)

The Design of Voting Device Based on DNA Strand Displacement Reaction

Zicheng Wang$^{(\boxtimes)}$, Zhonghua Sun, Zijie Cai, Yanfeng Wang, and Guangzhao Cui

Henan Key Lab of Information-Based Electrical Appliances, College of Electrical and Information Engineering, Zhengzhou University of Light Industry, No. 5 Dongfeng Road, Zhengzhou 450002, China
wzch@zzuli.edu.cn

Abstract. DNA strand displacement reaction (DSDR) has become a significant issue in DNA computing in recent years. The voting device has been playing an important role in some occasions. A 4-people voting device was designed based on DSDR in this paper. The process of DSDR is programmed and simulated in visual DSD. The simulated results demonstrate that the molecular model of voting device is feasible and reliable, which has wide prospects in complicated molecular logic circuits study.

Keywords: DNA strand displacement reaction · 4-people voting device · Visual DSD

1 Introduction

Bio-inspired computing, short for biologically inspired computing, is a field of study that loosely knits together subfields related to the topics of connectionism, social behaviour and emergence. The main candidates in this field is membrane computing [1] (wherein, neural-like membrane computing models and their variants is hot in the field, see e.g. [2,16]) and DNA (molecular) computing [3–5].

DNA computing is a new field that combining computer science and molecular biology subject. It uses DNA as the computing tool and has solved many problems utilizing its promising power of parallelism computation. Such as solving Hamition path, maximal clique problem [3–5]. DNA computing has merged a lot of molecule operation technology, self-assembly [6,7], fluorescence labeling [8–10], strand displacement and Nano-powder [11,12].

DNA strand displacement [13–15] is a new method in the bio-computing in recent years, and has become a common method in DNA self-assembly. It's also a dynamic DNA nanotechnology, which has the spontaneity, sensitivity and veracity. In the past few years, DNA strand displacement technology has reached tremendous development. Through the Strand displacement cascade reaction [18], we have achieved the dynamical connection adjacent logic module [19,20,22] which makes it possible for the researcher to establish large-scale, complicated

© Springer-Verlag Berlin Heidelberg 2015
M. Gong et al. (Eds.): BIC-TA 2015, CCIS 562, pp. 465–474, 2015.
DOI: 10.1007/978-3-662-49014-3_42

logic circuit [23,24]. Moreover, with the advantage of high-capacity information accumulation, high performance parallel computing, programming and simulating, it had acquired an in-depth study in the field of molecular computing, nano-machine, diagnosis and remedy of the disease. DNA strand displacement technology has the gigantic proficiency in solving the maths problem [25–27], managing the nano-machine and discussing the life course. Biochemistry logic circuit is the basis of the DNA strand displacement. So by way of mastering the design procedures to structure the biochemistry logic circuit that based on DNA strand displacement has significant research means.

Voting device is the client-side of voting system. It is a voting device that delegate ballot or voting by a show of hand. So far voting device has been divided into two types, wired and wireless. The wired voting machine had retreated from the market, and the wireless had become the main stream.

We present a logical circuit of implementing 4-people voting device which would be simulated in the programming language software. The paper is arranged as follows. Section 2 introduces the DNA strand displacement. Section 3 depicts the logic circuit of 4-people voting device, and its dual-rail circuit, seesaw cascade circuit. The simulation is exhibited in Sect. 4 and Sect. 5 concluding and raising question of the voting device.

2   DNA Strand Displacement

DNA strand displacement technique originated from DNA self-assembly technique, which multiple DNA single strand come into being the course of orderly multi-dimensional assembly spontaneously on account of base complementary pair rule. DNA strand displacement reaction needs a single-strand and a double-strand. The single-strand is complementary pair with the one strand of the double-strand based on A,G,C,T (A pairs with T,G pairs with C). The one strand of double-strand has a toehold domain, which is an exposed single strand domain in the double-strand. It can react with the part of the signal-strand firstly, and conduct branch migration in the next time, until the one strand of double-strand substituted by the single-strand, forming a new single-strand and a new double-strand. If it generate a new toehold domain in the new double-strand, it occur similar reaction we called reverse reaction. It can reach a dynamic equilibrium. If there is no new toehold domain produce, the reaction finished. It is the two kind of DNA strand displacement reaction (Fig. 1), we usually called the single-strand is input strand and the new single-strand is output strand. DNA strand displacement is implemented at natural temperature, and without enzymes or transcription machinery. We can control the reaction trends toward the state which our hoped only by changing the length and sequence of toehold domain.

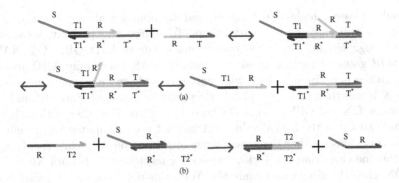

Fig. 1. (a) The reversible reaction of the DNA strand displacement. T* is the toehold domain, T1* is the new toehold domain. R is the branch migration domain. (b) the irreversible reaction of the DNA strand displacement. T2* is the toehold domain, R1 is the branch migration domain.

3 Logic Circuit of 4-people Voting Device

3.1 Digital Logic Circuit

The logic operation adapts two kinds of state-"0" and "1", which the "0" represents "against" and the "1" represents "approval". In digital logic circuit, logic algorithm includes three fundamental logic operation, namely logic AND, logic OR, and logic NOT. In the logic circuit of 4-people voting device which calculates the result of 4 people whether agree the suggestion or not. There are at least 3 people select "1", the result will show "1", otherwise the result will show "0". The logic circuit is shown in Fig. 2.

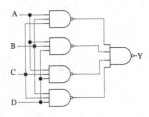

Fig. 2. The logic circuit of the 4-people voting device.

3.2 Dual-Rail Logic Circuit

In the DNA computing, NOT gate is difficult to be implemented directly. It is because that in DNA strand displacement reaction, NOT gate must be operated between a low input signal reacted by an upstream gate, in which condition it should release a high output signal, and an input signal that is low cant be computed, so it cant reaction with others. To address this problem, we use the dual-rail logic circuit. Namely we transform a circuit of AND, OR, NOT, NAND and NOR gates into an identical dual-rail circuit that uses only AND and OR gates. In the new circuit, which will contain roughly twice as many gates, each input X is substitute for X0 and X1. Respectively represent state "0" and "1", we can use ON and OFF command whose input state. If neither of them is ON, this indicates that the logical value of X has not been computed yet; if only X0 is ON, this indicates that the logical value of X must be "0"; while if only X1 is ON, this indicates that the logical value of X must be "1". If both X0 and X1 are ON, then the circuit occur mistake. With this notation, each original AND, OR, NAND gate can be implemented using one AND gate and one OR gate.

In Fig. 3, it appeared the dual-rail circuit, the 4 inputs were transformed into 8 inputs, respectively represent their ON and OFF, and the AND, OR, NOT gate converting 5-pair AND gate and OR gate. Ultimately, the dual-rail circuit come into being output signal Y0 and Y1 represent OFF and ON.

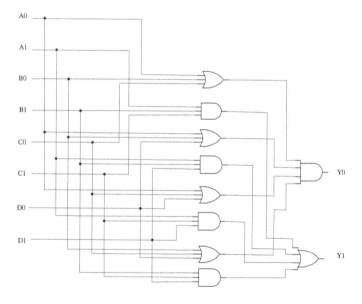

Fig. 3. The dual-rail logic circuit of the 4-people voting device.

3.3   Seesaw Cascade Circuit

In the circuit design based on DNA strand displacement, we present seesaw circuits using a systematic abstraction, the first is amplifying gate it contain three signal strands, "input", "fuel" and "output" which all are the single-stranded

DNA molecules. They will interaction with partially double-stranded DNA molecules we call "gate: signal complexes" and "threshold complexes" based on the underlying mechanism of "toehold-mediated DNA strand displacement" in which a single-stranded DNA molecule displaces another from a double stranded complex with the help of a "short toehold" domain. It used to acquire an original input signal strand.

We can use the amplifying gate as an example, which has the one input and four output (Fig. 4(a)) and one of its reaction mechanism (Fig. 4(c)). The second is the integrate gate, which serving multiply input and one output (Fig. 5(a)). There is no threshold and fuel in integrate gate. Its mechanism is shown in (Fig. 5(b)). Following the integrate gate it is the threshold gate, which divided into two variants, AND gate and OR gate. we can differentiate them with the threshold value. When the input is two, the AND gates threshold value is 1.2, OR gate is 0.6, when the input is three, the AND gates threshold value is 2.4, OR gate is 0.6.The AND gates threshold value is 3.2, OR gate is 0.6. 3 input threshold gate for logic OR and AND is shown in (Fig. 5(c)). The seesaw circuit is shown in (Fig. 6).

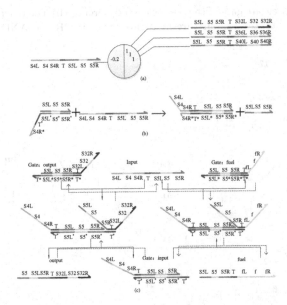

Fig. 4. (a) The amplifying gate of the seesaw cascade circuit. (b) The threshold reaction of the amplifying gate. (c) The reaction mechanism of the amplifying gate. Solid arrow represent forward reaction, dotted arrow represent reverse reaction.

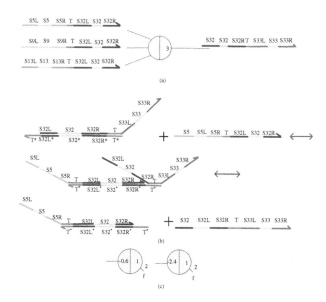

Fig. 5. (a) The integrate gate of the seesaw cascade circuit. (b) The reaction mechanism of the integrate gate. (c) 3 input threshold gate for logic OR and AND.

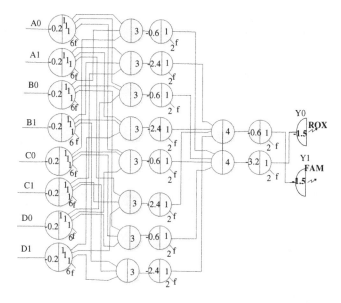

Fig. 6. The seesaw cascade circuit of the 4-people voting device.

4   Simulation with Visual DSD

Visual DSD is an implementation of a programming language for constituent DNA circuits based on DNA strand displacement. The language includes basic

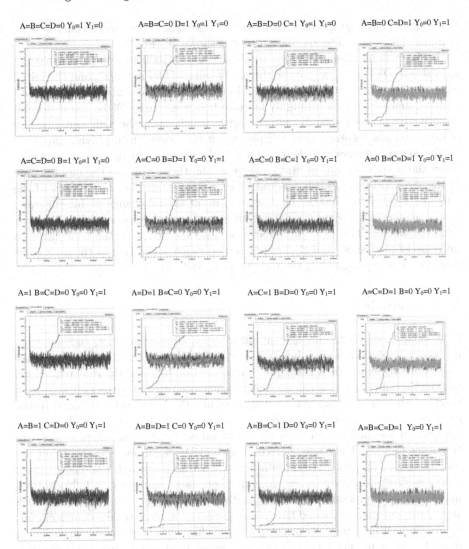

Fig. 7. Simulation results of the 4-people voting device.

elements of sequence domains, toeholds and branch migration. The interface composed of setting area, coding area and display area. In the setting area, it is setting for simulation condition, simulation results and molecular model visual effect. In the coding area, it is usually for devising DNA molecular structure through compiling program, setting parameter. Such as, reaction time, information collecting times, molecular combine and separate time. In the display area, it is usually for preserving the data about simulation platform compile, simulating and analyzing. Including molecular computing simulation of the whole process, the changing curve graph of DNA molecular, the onset state and terminate state of molecular model. The simulation plot is shown in (Fig. 7).

In the 16 simulation plots, the simulation time is 100000 s. We put the threshold value of OFF is "0.1x", so the threshold value of ON is "0.9x", and the initial concentration of the input strand is 90. In the process, the concentration of input strands almost the same. Roughly fall into two stage, in 0–4000 s, the molecular quantitative of input strands reduce sharply, it is because the high concentration of input strands occurred strand displacement reaction with amplifying gate. The output strands generate little, on account of seesaw circuit is cascade reaction, when the output strands of first stage generate, they turn into the input strand of the second stage. On this account, it needs some time for the produce of the output strand. After 4000 s, the density of input strand change undulating, and keeping essentially constant. The output strand growth exponentially, when the time to 40000 s. The reaction velocity will slow down with the concentration decrease of reactants. And the output strand reach saturation in the next time. The grey line represent Y1, the red line represent Y0.

5   Conclusion

In this paper, we reveal the logic circuit of 4-people voting device, and elaborate its seesaw cascade circuit using DNA strand displacement, after that we make corresponding simulation. Basing on the simulation plot and the research before, the simulation results is ideal, our model have some advantages: (1) It has a fast reaction process, and can get a satisfied result. (2) It has litter demand to the condition and environment, so it is economical. (3) It has a broad scope of application for combination logic circuit based on DNA strand displacement. In the other hand, it has some shortcomings: (1) Dual-rail and seesaw circuit are enormous for complex circuits, which leaves to be improved. (2) The reaction is at an idealized condition, we assume there is no unnecessary hybridization happened, it is impossible in reality. With the construct of voting device, DNA strand displacement is proved have a vast potential in large-scale complex circuit.

In [30], DSD is used to construct neural-like logic gate based on DSD. In recently, some powerful neural-like computing models are proposed, see, e.g. [17,21,28,29]. It is worthy to design novel neural-like logic circuits with DSD.

Acknowledgments. The research is supported by the NSFC (Nos. U1304620, 61472372, 61272022), Innovation Scientists and Technicians Troop Construction Projects of Henan (Grant No. 124200510017), and Innovation Scientists and Technicians Troop Construction Projects of Zhengzhou (Grant No. 131PLJRC648), Basic and Frontier technologies Research Program of Henan Province (132300410183), and Innovation Scientists and Technicians Troop Construction Projects of Henan Province (154200510012).

References

1. Păun, G., Rozenberg, G., Salomaa, A.: The Oxford Handbook of Membrane Computing. Oxford University Press Inc., Oxford (2010)
2. Song, T., Pan, L.: Spiking neural P systems with rules on synapses working in maximum spikes consumption strategy. IEEE Trans. NanoBiosci. 14(1), 38–44 (2015)
3. Adleman, L.M.: Molecular computation of solutions to combinatorial problems. Science 226, 1021–1024 (1994)
4. Carlson, R.: The changing economics of DNA synthesis. Nat. Biotechnol. 27, 1091–1094 (2009)
5. Turberfield, A.J., Mitchell, J.C., Yurke, B., Mills Jr, A.P., Blakey, M.I., Simmel, F.C.: DNA fuel for free-running nanomachines. Phys. Rev. Lett. 90, 118102 (2003)
6. Yin, P., Choi, H.M.T., Calvert, C.R., Pierce, N.A.: Programming biomolecular self-assembly pathways. Nature 451, 318–322 (2008)
7. Gothelf, K.V., LaBean, T.H.: DNA-programmed assembly of nanostructures. Org. Biomol. Chem. 3, 4023–4037 (2005)
8. Zhang, D.Y., Turberfield, A.J., Yurke, B., Winfree, E.: Engineering entropy-driven reactions and networks catalyzed by DNA. Science 318, 1121–1125 (2007)
9. Seelig, G., Soloveichik, D., Zhang, D.Y., Winfree, E.: Enzyme-free nucleic acid logic circuits. Science 314, 1585–1588 (2006)
10. Chiniforooshan, E., Doty, D., Kari, L., Seki, S.: Scalable, time-responsive, digital, energy-efficient molecular circuits using DNA strand displacement. In: Sakakibara, Y., Mi, Y. (eds.) DNA 16 2010. LNCS, vol. 6518, pp. 25–36. Springer, Heidelberg (2011)
11. Srinivas, N., Ouldridge, T.E., Sulc, P., Schaeffer, J.M., Yurke, B., Louis, A.A., Doye, J.P.K., Winfree, E.: On the biophysics and kinetics of toehold-mediated DNA strand displacement. Nucleic Acids Res. 41(22), 10641–10658 (2013)
12. Wang, X., Miao, Y., Cheng, M.: Finding motifs in DNA sequences using low-dispersion sequences. J. Comput. Biol. 21(4), 320–329 (2014)
13. Zhang, D.Y., Winfree, E.: J. Am. Chem. Soc. 131, 17303–17314 (2009)
14. Soloveichik, D., Seelig, G., Winfree, E.: Proceedings of the National Academy of Sciences USA, vol. 107, pp. 5393–53989 (2010)
15. Phillips, A., Cardelli, L.: J. Royal Soc. Interface 6, S419–S436 (2009)
16. Song, T., Pan, L.: Spiking neural P systems with rules on synapses working in maximum spiking strateg. IEEE Trans. NanoBiosci. 14(4), 465–477 (2015)
17. Song, T., Pan, L., Jiang, K., et al.: Normal forms for some classes of sequential spiking neural P systems. IEEE Trans. NanoBiosci. 12(3), 255–264 (2013)
18. Eckhoff, G., Codrea, V., Ellington, A.D., Chen, X.: J. Syst. Chem. 1, 13 (2010)
19. Qian, L., Winfree, E.: A simple DNA gate motif for synthesizing large-scale circuits. In: Goel, A., Simmel, F.C., Sosík, P. (eds.) DNA Computing. LNCS, vol. 5347, pp. 70–89. Springer, Heidelberg (2009)
20. Lund, K., Manzo, A.J., Dabby, N., Michelotti, N., Johnson-Buck, A., Nangreave, J., Taylor, J.S., Pei, R., Stojanovic, M.N., Walter, N.G., Winfree, E., Yan, H.: Nature 465, 206–210 (2010)
21. Song, T., Pan, L., Wang, J., et al.: Normal forms of spiking neural P systems with anti-spikes. IEEE Trans. NanoBiosci. 11(4), 352–359 (2012)
22. Qian, L., Soloveichik, D., Winfree, E.: Efficient turing-universal computation with DNA polymers. In: Sakakibara, Y., Mi, Y. (eds.) DNA 16 2010. LNCS, vol. 6518, pp. 123–140. Springer, Heidelberg (2011)

23. Chiniforooshan, E., Doty, D., Kari, L., Seki, S.: Scalable, time-responsive, digital, energy-efficient molecular circuits using DNA strand displacement. In: Sakakibara, Y., Mi, Y. (eds.) DNA 16 2010. LNCS, vol. 6518, pp. 25–36. Springer, Heidelberg (2011)

24. Gaber, R., Lebar, T., Majerle, A., Ster, B., Dobnikar, A., Bencina, M., Jerala, R.: Designable DNA-binding domain enable construction of logic circuit in mammalian cells. Nat. Chem. Biol. **10**(3), 203–208 (2014)

25. Zhang, Z., Li, J., Pan, L., Ye, Y., Zeng, X., Song, T., Zhang, X., Wang, E.: A novel visualization of DNA sequences, reflecting GC-content. Match Commun. Math. Comput. Chem. **72**(2), 533–550 (2014)

26. Zeng, X., Xu, L., Liu, X., Pan, L.: On languages generated by spiking neural P systems with weights. Inf. Sci. **278**, 423–433 (2014)

27. Zhang, X., Liu, Y., Luo, B., Pan, L.: Computational power of tissue P systems for generating control languages. Inf. Sci. **278**, 285–297 (2014)

28. Song, T., Pan, L., Păun, G.: Asynchronous spiking neural P systems with local synchronization. Inf. Sci. **219**, 197–207 (2013)

29. Zhang, X., Pan, L., Păun, A.: On the universality of axon P systems. IEEE Trans. Neural Netw. Learn. Syst. **26**(11), 2816–2829 (2015). doi:10.1109/TNNLS.2015.2396940

30. Shi, X., Wang, Z., Deng, C., Song, T., Pan, L., Chen, Z.: A novel bio-sensor based on DNA strand displacement. PLoS One **9**(10), e108856 (2014)

Improved Niche Genetic Algorithm for Protein Structure Prediction

Xue Wei, Xuedong Zheng, Qiang Zhang[⊠], and Changjun Zhou

Key Laboratory of Advanced Design and Intelligent Computing,
Ministry of Education, Dalian University, Dalian 116622, China
Zhangq26@126.com, zhou-chang231@163.com

Abstract. Due to the complexity and variety of protein structure, the protein structure prediction (PSP) is a challenging problem in the field of bioinformatics. In this paper, we adopt an improved niche genetic algorithm for protein structure prediction, the niche genetic algorithm (NGA) bonds with some improvement strategies, which have a competitive selection, a random crossover and random linear mutation operator. These improvement strategies can maintain the population diversity and avoid the shortcomings of the Niche Genetic algorithm that stagnate evolution and be caught in local optimum. And our experiment gains some better results than other algorithms with the Fibonacci sequence and the real protein sequence. Finally, the experiment results illustrate the efficiency of this algorithm on the Fibonacci sequence and the real protein sequence.

Keywords: Protein structure prediction · Niche genetic algorithm · Fibonacci sequence · Real protein sequence

1 Introduction

With the development of bioscience and the successful completion of the Human Genome Project, bioscience has entered the post-genomic era, and bioinformatics have emerged. At present, there are many different directions of new technology in bioinformatics. For instance, the binary profile method was proposed to identify protein coding domains [1]; QPM-Branching method was used to detect motifs in DNA sequences [2]; HIGEDA was improved to solve the planted edited motif finding problem [3]; the low-dispersion projection algorithm was adopted in motif finding problems [4]. Of course, protein is the manifestation of life activities and also an indispensable part of biological substances [5]. The major function of the protein is determined by its space structure. The study of protein structure prediction is of great significance to medicine. It can give some theoretical help to a lot of misfolding protein diseases such as Dickinson syndrome, mad cow disease and some cancers. So protein structure prediction is one of the most important tasks of study on protein and reveals that the secret of life is significant.

© Springer-Verlag Berlin Heidelberg 2015
M. Gong et al. (Eds.): BIC-TA 2015, CCIS 562, pp. 475–492, 2015.
DOI: 10.1007/978-3-662-49014-3_43

Protein structure prediction is also known as the protein folding problem, a typical NP-hard problem. At present, the protein structure prediction techniques mainly include X-ray diffraction method, nuclear magnetic resonance techniques [6]. Although the protein structure prediction techniques have a more significant progress, experimental method is still very complex process and has a higher price to solve protein structure prediction problem. Therefore, there are many ways to use a computer to predict protein structure [6]. Currently, there is a wide variety of algorithms to solve the problem by computer. For example: the basic genetic algorithm, particle swarm optimization, ant colony algorithm, tabu search algorithm, simulated annealing algorithm artificial bee colony algorithm and so on [8–11,13].

There are many models of protein structure prediction. Two simplified models that are HP lattice model and AB off-lattice model are the most widely used. And they are divided into hydrophobic residues and hydrophilic residues based on hydrophobic amino acids. In the HP lattice model [14], bond angle that is a kind of angle between two bonds, which is a right angle or a straight angle, while in the AB off-lattice model, its folding angle is arbitrary. In other words, any adjacent three residues must be in the same plane in the HP lattice model, while any adjacent three residues are not in the same plane in the AB off-lattice model. And AB off-lattice model not only considers the effect of the interaction of the protein structure between two adjacent monomers, but also considers the impact of non-local effects between non-adjacent monomers [13]. So AB off-lattice model is closer to real protein structures than HP lattice model.

In this paper, we adopt the AB off-lattice model to solve the problem of protein structure prediction. At present, a lot of intelligent algorithms relate to AB off-lattice model on the protein structure prediction at internal and abroad. Zhou et al. [9] adopted an improved genetic-particle swarm and tabu search algorithm (PGATS). The algorithm could combine the best aspects of genetic particle swarm optimization and tabu search algorithm. But it will cost a lot of running time. Zheng et al. [10] proposed a hybrid algorithm (GATS) that combined tabu search algorithm and genetic algorithm to develop an efficient optimization. And the algorithm has some strategies, such as the crossover operator and the mutation operator, variable population size strategy and the ranking selection strategy and so on. So the algorithm can obtain some better results. Li et al. [11] used a balance-evolution artificial bee colony algorithm to solve the problem. And the algorithm (BE-ABC) obtains the good results. However, the result of longer sequences is weak. So it may be more suitable for shorter sequences. Cheng et al. [13] adopted an improved tabu search algorithm (TS) and AB off-lattice model. This algorithm can get better results when the length of protein sequence is little. But when the length of protein sequence is great, the algorithm will be difficult to converge to the global optimum. Zhu et al. [16] used Euclidean particle swarm optimization (EPSO). This algorithm has fast convergence speed and is easy to jump out of the local optimum. Chen et al. [17] proposed an improved particle swarm optimization that is levy flight particle swarm optimization (LPSO). And the algorithm can jump out of the local optimum. But the speed of convergence is slow so that it might spend a lot of running time.

According to research status, we use an improved niche genetic algorithm that combines the niche genetic algorithm with the some improvement strategies that have a competitive selection, a random crossover and random linear mutation operator to solve the problem of protein structure prediction with AB off-lattice model in this paper. So the algorithm inherits the advantages of the basics niche genetic algorithm that can increase the diversity of the population with the Niche elimination algorithm. However, the basics niche genetic algorithm is easy to evolve to stagnation and trap in the local optimum. Thus, we add some improvement strategies to the niche genetic algorithm for making up for the deficiency. For instance, competitive selection algorithm can avoid premature convergence and evolutionary stagnation, and random linear mutation algorithm can increase the local search capability. And the improved niche genetic algorithm is simple and fast convergence, so that it takes little time. Through the comparison of the results with other algorithms, we can see that the algorithm is effective and outperform the other algorithms in most cases.

2   Related Work

2.1   The AB Off-Lattice Model

Stillinger et al. [6,8–11,13] proposed the AB off-lattice model in 1993 [15]. In this model, the amino acid is divided into hydrophobic residue (H) and hydrophilic residue (P) by the strength of the affinity of an amino acid with water [15]. As shown in Fig. 1 [9], hydrophobic residue (H) is represented by a black solid circle and hydrophilic residue (P) is indicated by an open circle in the configuration diagram of AB off-lattice model. And AB off-lattice model includes bond angles (α) that are angle between two bonds within the same surface and torsion angles (β) that are angle between two surfaces in the three-dimensional structure [9,11,13,15]. If the length of a protein structure sequence is n, then the sequence has n−2 bond angles ($\alpha_1, \alpha_2, ..., \alpha_{n-2}$) and n−3 torsion angles ($\beta_1, \beta_2, ..., \beta_{n-3}$). So this protein structure sequence has 2n−5 angles ($\alpha_1, \alpha_2, ..., \alpha_{n-2}, \beta_1, \beta_2, ..., \beta_{n-3} \mid -\pi \le \alpha, \beta \le \pi$) in total.

In this paper, we assign a random number to each angle. The bond angles and torsion angles can determine the coordinates of residues. And the three-dimensional coordinates of residues is as follows [9–11]:

$$(x_i, y_i, z_i) = \begin{cases} (0,0,0) & i = 1 \\ (0,1,0) & i = 2 \\ (\cos \alpha_1, \sin \alpha_1, 0) & i = 3 \\ (x_{i-1} + \cos(\alpha_{i-2}) \cos(\beta_{i-3}), \\ \quad y_{i-1} + \sin(\alpha_{i-2}) \cos(\beta_{i-3}), \\ \quad z_{i-1} + \sin(\beta_{i-3})) & 4 \le i \le n \end{cases} \tag{1}$$

Protein structure prediction problem is also known as protein folding problem [9] which solves the minimum energy (Eq. (2) [9–11,13,15,17]) of protein folding

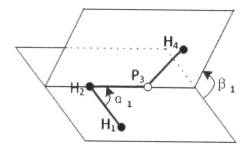

Fig. 1. Configuration diagram of AB off-lattice model.

and has stable protein structure. In the AB off-lattice model, protein folding energy (Eq. (3) [9–11,13,15,17]) is made up bending potential energy (E_1) of the main chain and gravitational potential energy (E_2) that is a kind of energy between non-adjacent residues by the Lennard-Jones form [6].

$$\min_{\alpha_i,\beta_j \in (-\pi,\pi)} E(\alpha_1,\alpha_2,...,\alpha_{n-2},\beta_1,\beta_2,...,\beta_{n-3}) \tag{2}$$

$$E = \sum_{i=2}^{n-1} E_1(\alpha_i) + \sum_{i=1}^{n-2} \sum_{j=i+2}^{n} E_2(r_{ij},\xi_i,\xi_j) \tag{3}$$

$$E_1(\alpha_i) = \frac{1}{4}(1 - \cos\alpha_i) \tag{4}$$

$$E_2(r_{ij},\xi_i,\xi_j) = 4[r_{ij}^{-12} - C(\xi_i,\xi_j)r_{ij}^{-6}] \tag{5}$$

As is shown in Eq. (4) [9–11,13,15,17] and Eq. (5) [9–11,13,15,17], the bending potential energy is closely related to the bond angles (α), the gravitational potential energy is closely related to spacing distance (r) and polarity (C) with any two non-adjacent residues.

$$r_{ij} = \sqrt{(x_i - x_j)^2 + (y_i - y_j)^2 + (z_i - z_j)^2} \tag{6}$$

$$C(\xi_i,\xi_j) = \frac{1}{8}(1 + \xi_i + \xi_j + 5\xi_i\xi_j) = \begin{cases} +1 & \xi_i = 1, \xi_j = 1 \\ +0.5 & \xi_i = -1, \xi_j = -1 \\ -0.5 & \xi_i \neq \xi_j \end{cases} \tag{7}$$

Equation (6) [9–11,13,15,17] is spacing distance with two non-adjacent residues. Equation (7) [9–11,13,15,17] is polarity with two non-adjacent residues. In Eq. (7), $\xi(1 \leq i \leq n)$ is a set of binary variables which represents residues. If the residue is a hydrophobic residue (H), then ξ_i equals 1; if it is a hydrophilic residue (P), then ξ_i equals -1. So when two residues are H, the polarity of residues is a strong gravitation (C$=+1$); when the two residues are P, the polarity of residues is a weaker gravitation (C$=+0.5$); when one residue is H, and the other is P, the polarity of residues is a weak repulsive force (C$=-0.5$). This reflects the actual characteristics of the protein to some extent [18].

2.2   Basics of NGA

The basic idea of niche method is derived from biological niche that refers to creatures always live with their own same species in the process of evolution. So niche refers to a structure under certain circumstances. And in the genetic algorithm, it is to make the individual of genetic algorithm [20] evolutionary in a particular living environment [21].

In the basics of NGA, the main steps have fitness proportional selection algorithm, uniform crossover algorithm, uniform mutation algorithm and niche elimination algorithm.

In the niche elimination algorithm, Euclidean distance between individuals is counted as a shared function to adjust the fitness of each individual in the population. First, we compare Euclidean distance between individuals in the population. If difference in distance is smaller than L that is a pre-known variable, then we compare their fitness. And we add a penalty function to the fitness of the smaller individual to reduce its fitness, so that its fitness will become worse [22]. And the probability of being eliminated will become greater in the evolutionary process [23].

The NGA not only maintains the diversity of population, but also maintains a certain distance between each individual.

2.3   Improved NGA

The basic of NGA protects the diversity of solution, and avoids a lot of duplicate solution in the solution space. However, this algorithm has some shortcomings that are easy evolutionary stagnation and poor local optimum performance [24]. Therefore, we have taken some measures to improve the basic of NGA. Selection strategy adopt competitive selection algorithm to solve the problem of evolutionary stagnation. And mutation strategy adopt random linear mutation algorithm to solve the problem of poor local optimum performance. Although these improvement strategies may be mentioned in the other algorithm, the improved NGA algorithm is proposed for the first time in the protein structure prediction problem. These are described in more detail as follows:

Selection Strategy. In the fitness proportional selection algorithm, the individual probability of being selected depends on the fitness of individual [25].

In this paper, we use competitive selection algorithm. Competitive selection algorithm is called the tournament selection algorithm. Its selection probability is the relative value of the fitness. And the relationship between the selection probability and the numerical size of the fitness is not a direct proportion. So that it can avoid the influence of the super individual. To some extent, it can avoid premature convergence and stagnation behavior [26].

Competitive selection algorithm selects the winners to become individuals of the next generation by competition. In the population of each generation, every time we randomly select k individuals to constitute a small population. And we copy the optimal individual of K individual to the next generation. But the individual returns to the parent population, to participate the next selection. This random selection is repeated M times. And there are M individuals to become the next generation population.

In the competitive selection algorithm, the intensity of selection depends on the size of k. If the value of k is big, then each selected individual has a good fitness. Conversely, if the value of k is small, then each selected individual has a good or bad fitness and randomness is very high.

Mutation Strategy. In this paper, we adopt random linear mutation algorithm, which is known as single-point climbing mutation. And the algorithm increases the local search capability and speeds up the convergence for the NGA. The random linear mutation algorithm uses the Eq. (8) [9].

$$x_i' = x_i + f(r) \times 2\pi \times r^{1-\alpha} \times (1 - fit(h)) \tag{8}$$

Where f(r) and fit(h) are defined as follows [9]:

$$f(r) = \begin{cases} 1 & r \geq 0.5 \\ -1 & r < 0.5 \end{cases} \tag{9}$$

$$fit(h) = \frac{n - i + 1}{n + 1} \tag{10}$$

f(r) is a correlation coefficient and r is a random number between 0 and 1. And fit(h) is a kind of relative fitness of individual h. Where n is the size of population, and i is the index of individual h in the orderly population according to the fitness. The mutation strategy can make many individuals of good fitness get a small mutation probability so that they are protected effectively.

3   To Implement Algorithm

According to the basic of niche genetic algorithm and improvement strategies, we give an improved NGA in this paper. And the flow chart of improved NGA is expressed, as shown in Fig. 2.

And we give the specific steps as follows:

Step 1: Initialization parameters and initialize a population X.
Step 2: According to Eq. (3), we can calculate the fitness of each individual $(F_i, i = 1, 2, ..., 200)$. And according to fitness, population is sorted in ascending order to get a new population X';
Step 3: Set the iteration counter $t = 1$ and iterate;
Step 4: Select the top one hundred individuals to a memory population B for the niche elimination algorithm from the population X';
Step 5: Tournament selection algorithm for population X' and obtain a new population X'';

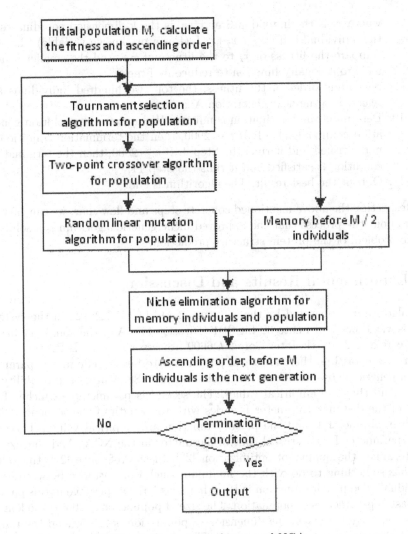

Fig. 2. Flow chart of improved NGA

Step 6: Two-point crossover algorithm for population X'' and obtain a new population X''';

Step 7: Uniform mutation algorithm for population X''', obtain a new population X'''' and calculate the fitness of each individual;

Step 8: Niche elimination algorithm for a new population N (the size of the population is 300) that combines B (in the Step 2) with X''''. For the population, Euclidean distance between x_i and x_j is as follows:

$$d_{ij} = \| x_i - x_j \| = \sqrt{\Sigma(x_{ik} - x_{jk})^2}, i = 1, 2, ..., 300; j = i + 1, ..., 300 \quad (11)$$

where x_i is the individual i and x_{ik} is the k-dimension coordinates of the individual i. If $\| x_i - x_j \| < L$ (L is a pre-known variable), then we compare the fitness of x_i to the fitness of x_j. And the smaller fitness adds to a penalty function to reduce its fitness;

Step 9: Ascending order of the fitness, the top two hundred individuals are selected to the next generation X';

Step 10: Determine the termination condition. We update the evolution generation counter $t = t + 1$. If $t < 2000$, then the termination condition is not satisfied and it runs the Step 4. If $t \geq 2000$, then the termination condition is satisfied and it runs the Step 11;

Step 11: Output the best result. The algorithm is end.

Respecting the above mentioned concrete steps and flow char, we can easy to know about the process that the improved niche genetic algorithm is a solution to the problem of the protein structure prediction.

4 Experimental Results and Discussion

Our algorithm is operated by the software of MATLAB R2012a in the system that is Windows 7 ultimate 32 bit SP1 (DirectX 11). And the computer has a quad-core and 2.40 GHz Inter Core 2 Q6600 processor with 4 GB RAM.

In this algorithm, there are three parameters to be set. The first is parameters of genetic algorithm. Crossover probability is 0.88, Mutation probability is 0.021. And they are empirical values. The second is parameters of niche. The value of the distance parameter L varies with the length of the sequence. The distance parameter L and the penalty function are empirical values. The distance parameter L is a critical control parameter in the NGA. And the size of L determines the quality of optimization [27]. In the reference [27], the value of L has something to do with the minimum Euclidean distance between each individual. The penalty function is 10^{15} that is as large as possible in this paper. The last is parameters of population. The size of population is 200. If the length of the sequence is n, then the dimension of population is 2n−5. And the range of each dimension is between $-\pi$ and π. The iteration is 2000.

In the protein structure prediction, the Fibonacci sequence and the real protein sequences are common protein sequences. We calculate experimental results with the Fibonacci sequence and the real protein sequences. And for convenience, the improved niche genetic algorithm is expressed as NGA below.

4.1 The Fibonacci Sequence

In the protein structure prediction, the Fibonacci sequence is defined in (12) [15]:

$$S_0 = H, S_1 = P, S_{i+1} = S_{i-1} \otimes S_i \tag{12}$$

Where '$\otimes$' is defined as a connection symbol. Such as $S_2 = HP, S_3 = PHP$ and so on, H is a hydrophobic residue and P is a hydrophilic residue.

Table 1. Fibonacci sequence

Length	Fibonacci sequence
5	HPPHP
8	PHPHPPHP
13	HPPHPPHPHPPHP
21	PHPHPPHPHPPHPPHPHPPHP
34	HPPHPPHPHPPHPPHPHPPHPHPPHPPHPHPPHP
55	PHPHPPHPHPPHPPHPHPPHPHPPHPPHPHPPHPHPPHPHPPHPHPP HPHPPHPPHPHPPHP

Table 2. Compare the results of the Fibonacci sequence

Length	Compare the results				
	E(LPSO) [17]	E(EPSO) [16]	E(PGATS) [9]	E(BE-ABC) [11]	E(NGA)
5	−1.0627	−	4.8695	−	4.8695
8	−2.0038	−	−0.4402	−	−0.4310
13	−4.6159	−3.2941	−0.6914	−3.3945	−0.8189
21	−6.6465	−6.1980	−7.2423	−6.9064	9.3263
34	−7.3375	−9.8341	−8.9361	−10.4224	−10.3853
55	−13.0487	−16.4474	−17.4538	−18.8385	−21.6099

As shown in the Table 1, we give six kinds of the length of the Fibonacci sequence by the definition.

Table 2 shows the results of NGA, which better than that of other algorithm, such as levy flight particle swarm optimization (LPSO) [17], Euclidean particle swarm optimization (EPSO) [16], particle swarm optimization-genetic algorithm-tabu search (PGATS) [9], balance-evolution artificial bee colony algorithm (BE-ABC) [11]. Where E(NGA) refers to the minimum free energy value for the protein's sequence based on our algorithm that is an improved niche genetic algorithm.

As is shown in the Table 2, we can notice that when the length of Fibonacci sequence is from 5 to 13, the energy values of LPSO are better than that of NGA. But with the increase of the Fibonacci sequence length, the energy values of NGA obtains the better result. For example, when the length of sequence is 5, the energy values of LPSO is −1.0627, the energy values of NGA is 4.8695, and the difference between them is −5.9322. But when the length of sequence is from 21 to 55, the energy values of NGA are better than that of LPSO. For example, when the length of sequence is 55, the energy values of LPSO is −13.0487, the energy values of NGA is −21.6099, and the difference between them is −8.5612. When the length of sequence is 55, E(BE-ABC) is the least than other algorithm except NGA. But E(NGA) is less than it. There are two

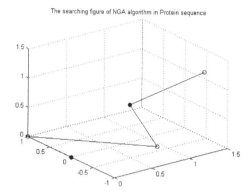

Fig. 3. The best result (Length = 5) represented by three-dimensional diagram.

reasons to cause the results, one is the NGA that can maintain diversity and avoid duplication solution, and the other is improvement strategies that can jump out of local optimum with the NGA.

Figures 3, 4, 5, 6, 7 and 8 show the three-dimensional diagram of Fibonacci sequence with corresponding best results by NGA. Where black dot represents a hydrophobic residue (H) and white dot represents a hydrophilic residue (P).

In the Fig. 3, the best result of encoding is $[-0.3790, 0.2222, -0.0385, 2.0308, 0.2439]$.

In the Fig. 4, the best result of encoding is $[0.3281, 1.4366, -0.3275, -0.0897, -0.4880, -0.0194, 0.0543, -0.6358, -2.2184, 2.6733, -1.8515]$.

In the Fig. 5, the best result of encoding is $[0.8130, 1.9822, 0.2182, 0.8442, 0.6682, -0.4610, -0.8512, 0.0161, -0.3843, -0.5105, 0.1706, -2.8362, 1.1247, 2.6494, -2.0598, 0.0897, -1.8879, -1.4086, -2.9777, 1.8492, -2.6797]$.

In the Fig. 6, the best result of encoding is $[0.1613, 1.6693, 1.1844, -0.4798, 1.4639, 0.3142, 1.2007, 0.0909, 1.8802, 0.3248, -0.1374, -1.010, 0.3257, -2.0191, -0.4497, -0.4020, 0.1419, -0.1778, 0.9958, -0.6997, -2.5939, -2.7059, 0.5698, 2.9494, 0.6806, 3.0248, 2.2936, 0.1760, 2.1219, -2.6469, -0.4467, 1.7577, -0.3950, 0.0699, -1.4802, -2.9655, -0.4790]$.

In the Fig. 7, the best result of encoding is $[-2.8521, -0.6040, -0.1398, -0.079, -0.0434, 1.3494, 0.2348, -0.2908, -0.0344, 0.7595, 0.2669, 1.3698, -0.3452, -0.0591, 0.4657, 0.1458, -0.6381, -0.4541, -1.1187, -1.3482, -0.0350, -0.0837, -2.9367, 2.1010, -0.3402, -0.3281, 0.7428, -0.3742, -0.0208, 0.7230, 0.1071, -0.0075, -0.9172, -2.7705, 2.5553, -2.6642, 0.0549, -2.5121, -1.6390, -1.5329, -2.3993, 2.0910, 1.7708, 0.7467, 2.6193, 0.5346, 2.3619, 1.8473, 0.8237, 0.9426, -0.9814, -1.8218, -1.7057, -2.4857, 2.2844, -0.4332, -2.0579, 0.0279, -2.6346, -1.5463, -3.1177, 1.7504, -2.7332]$.

In the Fig. 8, the best result of encoding is $[2.6500, 1.6598, 0.0666, -0.0482, 0.2587, -1.4238, 0.4445, -0.2478, -0.0308, 0.0972, -0.0050, 0.0988, -0.1307, 0.7975, -0.3306, 0.0332, 0.0930, 0.0857, 0.3024, -0.5601, 0.2273, -0.0349, -0.6036, 0.7681, -0.0695, -0.0102, -0.5568, 1.4182, -0.2464, -0.0955, -0.4483, -0.0486, 0.3259, -0.3205, -0.4676, -1.3889, 0.1626, -0.1722, -0.0959, -0.3442,

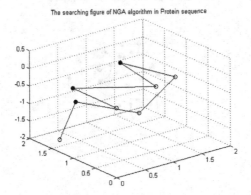

Fig. 4. The best result (Length = 8) represented by three-dimensional diagram.

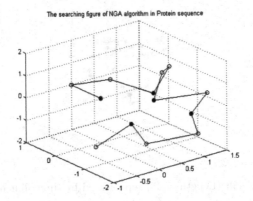

Fig. 5. The best result (Length = 13) represented by three-dimensional diagram.

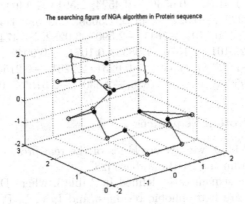

Fig. 6. The best result (Length = 21) represented by three-dimensional diagram.

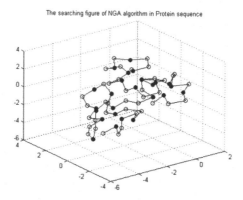

Fig. 7. The best result (Length = 34) represented by three-dimensional diagram.

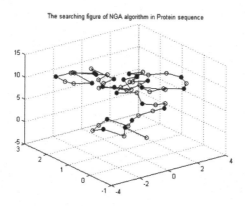

Fig. 8. The best result (Length = 55) represented by three-dimensional diagram.

−2.0600, 0.0142, −0.2783, −0.0317, −0.8934, −0.4279, 1.5674, 0.8145, 0.1234, −0.6829, −0.3235, 1.0161, −0.6536, −0.4524, 2.5913, 1.1464, −0.0948, 0.4236, −0.3150, 1.2231, 0.2222, −0.3228, 1.4919, 2.5059, 2.5086, 0.3944, 3.1106, 1.2679, 0.1519, 1.1985, 2.9751, 0.7191, 2.7611, −2.5907, 3.0282, −0.4746, 0.9746, 2.4353, −3.0481, 3.1072, 2.9101, 2.1570, 1.9833, 0.1071, −0.9949, −0.1406, 1.7314, −0.3087, 2.9067, −1.8278, −0.3599, −0.6251, 2.2201, −0.2154, 1.2742, 2.7766, 0.7053, 0.6310, 2.3056, 2.6024, −1.7830, −2.5301, −2.3155, −0.7698, 0.2318].

4.2 The Real Protein Sequences

As shown in the Table 3, we give six kinds of the real protein sequence. These sequences are got from the PDB database [28].

The real protein sequences is defined in Table 3, where D, E, F, H, K, N, Q, R, S, T, W, Y are hydrophobic residues, and I, V, L, P, C, M, A, G are hydrophilic residues [9,11,17].

Table 3. The real protein sequence

Name	Real protein sequences
2KGU	GYCAEKGIRCDDIHCCTGLKCKCNASGYNCVCRKK
1CRN	TTCCPSIVARSNFNVCRLPGTPEAICATYTGCIIIPGATCPGDYAN
2KAP	KEACDAWLRATGFPQYAQLYEDFLFPIDISLVKREHDFLDRAIEA LCRRLNTLNKCAVMK
1PCH	AKFSAIITDKVGLHARPASVLAKEASKFSSNITIIANEKQGNLKSI MNVMAMAIKTGIEITIQADGNDADQAIQAIKQTMIDTALIQG

Table 4. Compare the results of the real protein sequence

Name	Compare the results				
	Length	E(LPSO) [17]	E(BE-ABC) [11]	E(PGATS) [9]	E(NGA)
2KGU	35	−20.9633	−	−32.2599	−33.1307
1CRN	46	−28.7591	−	−49.6487	−54.9538
2KAP	60	−15.9988	−25.2558	−28.1052	−30.0708
1PCH	88	−46.4964	−	−49.5729	−49.9916

Table 4 shows the results of NGA, which better than that of other algorithm, such as levy flight particle swarm optimization (LPSO) [17], balance-evolution artificial bee colony algorithm (BE-ABC) [11], particle swarm optimization-genetic algorithm-tabu search (PGATS) [9].

As is shown in the Table 4, the result of 2KGU is −32.2599 with PGATS and the result of NGA is −33.1307; the result of 2KAP is −28.1052 with PGATS and the result of NGA is −30.0708; the result of 1PCH with PGATS and the result of NGA is −49.9916. As can be seen from the above data, our algorithm gains the smaller energy value than other algorithm with the several kinds of the real protein sequence. Especially for the protein of 2KAP, the energy value of this algorithm is −30.0708 and 1.9656 smaller than the best result that is −28.1052 in other algorithm except the NGA, and this result achieves an obvious improvement in efficiency. Therefore, the algorithm also obtains good results for the real protein in this paper, and it is confirmed as an effective algorithm to resolve the problem of protein structure prediction.

From the above two tables of comparing results, the improved niche genetic algorithm can get better results with AB off-lattice model for the Fibonacci sequence and the real protein sequences. We can see that the longer the length of protein sequence, the better the result is got with the algorithm in this paper. And the algorithm can add diversity and avoid trapping in local optimum, so we can gain some better results with the algorithm. Finally, Figs. 9, 10, 11 and 12 show the three-dimensional diagram of the real protein sequence with corresponding best results by NGA and the corresponding reference structure from the PDB database [28]. In the left side of the four figures, black dot represents a hydrophobic residue and white dot represents a hydrophilic residue. As can be seen form Fig. 11, on the left side of the figure is somewhat similar to the right side on shape.

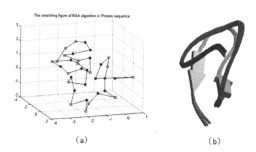

(a)   (b)

Fig. 9. (a) is the best result (Name = 2KGU) with three-dimensional diagram. (b) is the corresponding reference structure from the PDB database [28].

In the Fig. 9, the best result of encoding is $[-1.8776 \ -1.2031 \ 0.2852 \ 2.8131$ $0.11 \ 19 \ -0.2476 \ 0.3366 \ 1.5385 \ 2.2689 \ -0.0585 \ -0.3299 \ 0.9083 \ 2.4524 \ -1.3521$ $2.7274 \ 1.644 \ 8 \ 2.6574 \ 2.1893 \ 0.0970 \ 1.2807 \ 2.3101 \ -0.8230 \ -2.4827 \ -0.8149$ $-0.2023 \ 0.4623 \ -1.3197 \ 0.2396 \ -2.1085 \ 0.0225 \ -2.8903 \ 0.5202 \ -1.2544 \ 1.9241$ $0.7297 \ -2.7236 \ -1.9431 \ -1.8527 \ -0.2495 \ 2.7807 \ -2.6087 \ -2.3130 \ 2.5180$ $-2.71673 \ 1.0846 \ 1.3620 \ -3.0662 \ -0.2787 \ 1.1782 \ 2.4516 \ 3.1410 \ -3.0264 \ -0.5777$ $-2.4174 \ 2.6607 \ -2.6450 \ 1.68 \ 97 \ -2.7535 \ 0.5370 \ 0.3521 \ 2.8370 \ 2.8155 \ -0.1591$ $-2.4641 \ -1.0382].$

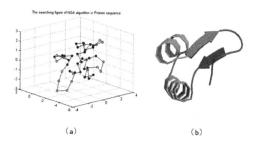

(a)   (b)

Fig. 10. (a) is the best result (Name = 1CRN) with three-dimensional diagram. (b) the corresponding reference structure from the PDB database [28].

In the Fig. 10, the best result of encoding is $[-1.7589, \ -0.0849, \ -0.0645,$ $1.0844, \ -0.1507, \ -0.0241, \ -0.2358, \ 0.1935, \ 0.0956, \ 0.0758, \ -0.6826, \ 0.0691,$ $0.1186, \ 1.3894, \ 0.4416, \ -1.4344, \ -0.0591, \ -1.6080, \ -1.8291, \ -1.0907, \ -1.9105,$ $0.4941, \ 0.3739, \ 2.0412, \ 0.3315, \ -0.4779, \ 0.3705, \ 0.1245, \ 1.8755, \ 0.1340, \ -1.1529,$ $-0.3903, \ 0.0136, \ 0.0720, \ 0.0072, \ -2.1385, \ -1.4704, \ 0.1453, \ 1.6915, \ -0.0721,$ $-0.3873, \ 0.5735, \ 2.3968, \ 0.4923, \ 2.4639, \ -3.1375, \ -2.9921, \ 0.4211, \ -0.1558,$

−2.1549, −2.5571, −2.0459, −1.8082, 0.0502, 0.9181, 1.0064, −0.1248, −0.5485, 0.3752, 1.9249, 0.7702, 0.1603, −1.8060, 0.1672, −1.3253, 0.1394, −0.3649, 0.9683, 0.0091, −0.7221, 1.1484, 0.4785, 3.1415, −2.5886, 2.0351, −0.0099, 1.7644, 3.0233, −0.0564, 0.4772, −0.2042, −0.8031, 0.0794, 0.7740, −0.4846, −0.3769, −0.2021].

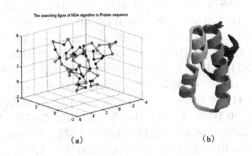

(a)   (b)

Fig. 11. (a) is the best result (Name = 2KAP) represented by three-dimensional diagram. (b) is the corresponding reference structure from the PDB database [28].

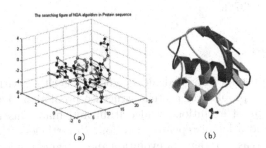

(a)   (b)

Fig. 12. (a) is the best result (Name = 1PCH) represented by three-dimensional diagram.(b) is the corresponding reference structure from the PDB database [28].

In the Fig. 11, the best result of encoding is [−0.2664 1.9665 −1.5072 0.0633 −1.7723 1.5419 1.5154 1.9204 −2.6599 1.1969 −1.2463 0.1814 1.9979 0.4986 −0.1331 0.43 45 −0.4163 2.7675 0.3632 −1.1128 −0.9121 0.9934 2.0606 −1.9489 0.1450 −1.3801 −2.4796 0.2450 −0.3500 −1.3976 −0.2541 2.3429 0.1918 −0.6517 −0.7145 −1.9282 −0.3836 1.2471 2.2988 −1.1105 −2.0592 2.6167 1.9133 −0.6476 1.9752 −1.7618 0.4975 −0.3806 1.2082 −0.6558 0.2389 −1.5959 1.1826 1.1124 −0.5996 −0.0437 −1.7127 −0.8302 −2.8479 0.4869 0.3658 −2.2973 −2.0063 −0.0290 −0.4980 0.6464 0.4127 0.5476 0.7499 0.3149 −3.0409 1.3013 −3.0422 1.3123 2.2361 −0.7381 2.9376 2.4791 −0.6230 1.1447 0.8151 1.1368 −2.6889 2.9181 −1.7901 −2.3252 −2.9212 2.2960 −0.4682 −2.6960 −1.1294 0.5523 −0.2095 2.1577 0.7618 2.8745 −0.1176 0.8800 0.0202 −2.0787 −0.1502 2.1341

0.2508 −2.0910 −2.8341 2.9379 0.5536 2.1847 −3.0593 −0.0319 −0.8973 −1.6937
2.6089 −2.4713 −3.0055].

In the Fig. 12, the best result of encoding is [0.0476, 0.3540, −0.0202, −1.1324,
0.8693, −0.6697, −0.6725, 0.6298, 0.5089, 1.5141, −1.1798, 0.1407, −0.2341,
0.9822, −0.0594, 0.3811, −0.0266, −1.5891, 0.2376, −1.5510, −1.6756, 0.2854,
−1.1245, 0.0106, 0.0438, −1.8850, −0.8389, 0.2314, 0.8417, 0.4081, 1.3188,
−0.1315, 0.1714, −0.8872, −0.0411, 0.1020, −1.1414, 0.4405, 0.2655, 0.0192,
−0.2808, −0.1202, −0.1729, −0.0190, −0.0718, −0.5442, −0.0775, 1.6008, 0.4210,
0.0026, −2.0642, −0.1186, −0.4141, −0.0670, 0.2301, 0.1585, 0.1814, −0.1066,
1.8133, −0.1287, 1.6159, −0.3166, −1.1606, −0.9025, 0.9040, - 0.0053, 0.5475,
0.1435, 0.0678, 0.3031, 0.5694, 2.0133, 0.0530, −0.5590, −0.8209, −1.0286,
−0.8947, −0.0625, 1.0037, −0.0635, −0.3224, 0.5230, −0.0660, 1.2558, −0.0248,
0.4891, 0.6308, 0.6412, 0.0598, −2.8844, −1.3644, −2.8138, 0.1389, 0.5982,
−0.5240, −0.7297, −0.1669, 1.8502, 0.0193, 2.5377, 2.4776, 1.4210, −0.4140,
−0.8249, 0.3249, 0.3392, 2.6556, 3.0244, 0.6678, 0.5759, 0.3688, −1.3321, 0.3729,
−1.414, −0.9769, 0.3140, −2.6143, −2.1908, 0.0643, −1.0757, −1.1127, 3.0165,
−2.8233, −1.7060, 0.1280, −1.8532, −0.0041, 0.9740, 0.1773, 0.9287,−0.0034,
−2.0290, −0.0266, 0.0303, −1.9755, −0.093, 0.5006, −0.3871, −1.2830, −1.1786,
0.6796, 1.6158, 0.8490, 0.0117, 0.2265, −0.2515, 0.0955, 2.0772, 0.1319, 0.5247,
−0.8981, −2.1165, −0.2532, 0.7263, 0.5131, 0.9658, 0.3999, −1.5667, −0.4226,
−1.3372, −0.4903, 1.3495, 2.1242, 0.4530, 0.7776, 0.9595, 0.9971, 1.2531,
−0.4455, 0.0315, 2.0976].

5   Conclusion

In this paper, we use an improved niche genetic algorithm with AB off-lattice
model to settle the problem of protein structure prediction. The niche genetic
algorithm is a type of evolutionary algorithm and maintains the diversity of
population to avoid a lot of repeated solution. Nevertheless, the niche genetic
algorithm could be easy to stagnant evolution and be caught in local optimum. So
we adopt an improved niche genetic algorithm with improvement strategies that
include a competitive selection, a random crossover and random linear mutation
operator. And our experiment can get some better results with the Fibonacci
sequence and the real protein sequence, which clearly signals that the improved
niche genetic algorithm can be superior to other algorithms. And the algorithm
has fast convergence rate and costs a little of time. Hence, the algorithm is an
effective and feasible method for the problem of protein structure prediction.
However, the main shortcoming of this algorithm is poor stability. So in the
future, we will concentrate on increasing stability of this algorithm.

Human brain is powerful in recognizing function patterns, such as motifs,
faces. In the framework of membrane computing, there is a class of neural-like
computing models, named spiking neural P systems. In recent research, some
powerful variants of SN P systems, e.g. see [7,12,19,29–31]. It is of interests
using SN P systems to generate and recognize DNA and molecule motifs.

Acknowledgment. This work is supported by the National Natural Science Foundation of China (No.61425002, 61402066, 61402067, 31370778, 61370005, 31170797), the Program for Changjiang Scholars and Innovative Research Teams in University (Grant No. IRT1109), the Basic Research Program of the Key Lab in Liaoning Province Educational Department (No.LZ2014049), the Project is supported by the Natural Science Foundation of Liaoning Province (No. 2014020132), the Project is sponsored by 'Liaoning BaiQianWan Talents Program' (No. 2013921007), and by the Program for Liaoning Key Lab of Intelligent Information Processing and Network Technology in University.

References

1. Song, T., Su, Y.S.: A novel approach to identify protein coding domains by sampling binary profiles from genome. J. Comput. Theor. Nanos. **11**, 147–152 (2014)
2. Song, T., Zhang, Z.J., Hong, L.: Detecting motifs in DNA sequences by branching from neighbors of qualified potential motifs. J. Comput. Theor. Nanos. **10**, 2201–2206 (2013)
3. Wang, X., Miao, Y.: GAEM: a hybrid algorithm incorporating GA with EM for planted edited motif finding problem. Curr. Bioinform. **9**, 463–469 (2014)
4. Wang, X., Miao, Y., Cheng, M.: Finding motifs in DNA sequences using low-dispersion sequences. J. Comput. Biol. **21**, 320–329 (2014)
5. Chen, H.J.: Protein Results of Model Prediction Based on Differential Evolution Algorithm. Fujian Agriculture and Forestry University, Fuzhou (2012)
6. Li, W.Y., Wang, Y.: Multi-population genetic algorithm for three-dimensional protein structure prediction. Fujian Comput. **28**, 20–24 (2012)
7. Song, T., Pan, L., Wang, J., et al.: Normal forms of spiking neural P systems with anti-spikes. IEEE Trans. NanoBiosci. **11**(4), 352–359 (2012)
8. Shatabda, S., Newton, M.A.H., Rashid, M.A., et al.: An efficient encoding for simplified protein structure prediction using genetic algorithms. IEEE CEC **6**, 1217–1224 (2013)
9. Zhou, C.J., Hou, C.X., Wei, X.P.: Improved hybrid optimization algorithm for 3D protein structure prediction. J. Mol. Model. **20**, 2289–2301 (2014)
10. Zhang, X.L., Wang, T., Luo, H.P., et al.: 3D Protein Structure Prediction with Genetic Tabu Search Algorithm. Wuhan University of Science and Technology, Wuhan (2010)
11. Li, B., Chiong, R., Lin, M.: A balance-evolution artificial bee colony algorithm for protein structure optimization based on a three-dimensional AB off-lattice model. Comput. Biol. Chem. **2**, 1–12 (2015)
12. Song, T., Pan, L., Jiang, K., et al.: Normal forms for some classes of sequential spiking neural P systems. IEEE Trans. NanoBiosci. **12**(3), 255–264 (2013)
13. Cheng, W., Zhang, X.L.: Protein 3D Structure Prediction by Improved Tabu Search. Wuhan University of Science and Technology, Wuhan (2008)
14. Zhou, C.J., Hou, C.X., Zhang, Q.: Enhanced hybrid search algorithm for protein structure prediction using the 3D-HP lattice model. J. Mol. Model. **19**, 3883–3891 (2013)
15. Guo, H., Lan, R., Chen, X., et al.: Tabu search-particle swarm algorithm for protein folding prediction. Comput. Eng. Appl. **47**, 46–50 (2011)
16. Zhu, H.B., Pu, C.D., Lin, X.L., et al.: Protein structure prediction with EPSO in toy model. In: 2th ICINIS 2009, pp. 673–676. ICINIS Press, Wuhan (2009)
17. Chen, X., Lv, M.W., Zhao, L.H., et al.: An improved particle swarm optimization for protein folding prediction. Inf. Eng. Electron. Bus. **2**, 1–8 (2011)

18. Zhu, H.B., Wu, J., Pu, C.D., et al.: Clonal selection algorithm with aging operators for protein structure prediction on AB off-lattice model. In: 2th ICINIS 2009, pp. 685–688. ICINIS Press, Tianjin (2009)

19. Song, T., Pan, L.: Spiking neural P systems with rules on synapses working in maximum spikes consumption strategy. IEEE Trans. NanoBiosci. **14**(1), 38–44 (2015)

20. Kotenko, I., Saenko, I.: Improved genetic algorithms for solving the optimization tasks for design of access control schemes in computer networks. Int. J. Bio-Inspired Comput. **7**, 98–110 (2015)

21. Huang, C.M., Chen, X.X.: Improvements on niche genetic algorithm. Trans. Beijing Inst. Technol. **24**, 675–678 (2004)

22. Xiang, T.Y., Zhou, Q.S., Li, F.P., et al.: Research on niche genetic algorithm for reactive power optimization. Proc. CSEE. **25**, 48–51 (2005)

23. Li, W., Zhang, Z.G., Yan, N.: Pareto multi-objective distribution network reconfiguration based on improved niche genetic algorithm. Power Syst. Prot. Control **39**, 1–5 (2011)

24. Chen, Y.W.: An improved selection operator of genetic algorithm based on niches. Comput. Digit. Eng. **37**, 21–24 (2009)

25. Wu, W.Y., Yue, T.: Genetic algorithm selection operator review. Fujian Comput. **6**, 43–44 (2012)

26. Xia, G.M., Zeng, J.C.: Stochastic particle swarm optimization algorithm based on genetic algorithm of tournament selection. Comput. Eng. Appl. **43**, 51–53 (2007)

27. Yuan, L.H., Li, M., Li, J.H.: Research on evolving control parameters in niche genetic algorithm. Comput. Eng. **32**, 206–208 (2006)

28. The PDB database. http://www.rcsb.org/pdb/home/home.do

29. Song, T., Pan, L.: Spiking neural P systems with rules on synapses working in maximum spiking strateg. IEEE Trans. NanoBiosci. **14**(4), 465–477 (2015)

30. Song, T., Pan, L., Păun, G.: Asynchronous spiking neural P systems with local synchronization. Inf. Sci. **219**, 197–207 (2013)

31. Zhang, X., Pan, L., Păun, A.: On the universality of axon P systems. IEEE Trans. Neural Netw. Learn. Syst. (2015). doi:10.1109/TNNLS.2015.2396940

Optimization of BeiDou Receiver Front-End for High Dynamic Pseudolite Signals

Di Wu[1]([✉]), Jing Ji[2], Jing Li[3], Dongming Zhao[1], and Wei Chen[1]

[1] School of Automation, Wuhan University of Technology, Hubei, China
29649243@qq.com
[2] School of Information Engineering, Wuhan University of Technology, Hubei, China
[3] China Transport Telecommunications and Information Center, Beijing, China

Abstract. Legacy receiver is susceptible to the interference of high dynamic pseudolite signals. The high energy pulses always saturate the widely used 1-bit ADC in the legacy receiver so that useful signals are buried in the noise. Multi-bits ADC indeed improve the quantization resolution, where the useful signals can be distinguished from the pulses. However, the saturation is inevitable in some extreme cases; pulse blanking is required to suppress the pulsing interference. In this paper, an optimized receiver front-end consists of multi-bits ADC and pulse blanker is proposed. An optimal set of parameter settings is determined by evaluating the SNR loss, in which the optimal blanker configuration has been analyzed with respect to ADC quantization levels. Simulation results show that the optimized front-end is able to reduce the SNR loss in the saturation case by 1.3 dB, leading to a 40 % maximum duty cycle tolerance.

Keywords: AGC/ADC · High dynamic pseudolite signals · Pulse blanking · Duty cycle

1 Introduction

The primary benefit of deploying Beidou pseudolites is that it can be used to compliment the BeiDou constellation if there are insufficient observable satellites, such as in an urban canyon or a deep open mine [1]. Moreover, by transmitting differential error corrections, the system is able to provide high accuracy positioning service [2]. On the other hand, another problem called "near-far problem" [3] arises from the implementation of the BPLs. The BPL signal power varies greatly in accordance with the distance from the user whereas the satellite signal power is nearly constant. The dynamic range of the BPL signal power is far beyond the capacity of the legacy receiver. One way to avoid this problem is to pulse the signals [4]. The basic idea of this method is to divide one period signal into several portions, where each portion is transmitted by a high power, low duty cycle pulse which interferes with the satellite signals within merely a small part of the period.

© Springer-Verlag Berlin Heidelberg 2015
M. Gong et al. (Eds.): BIC-TA 2015, CCIS 562, pp. 493–504, 2015.
DOI: 10.1007/978-3-662-49014-3_44

Nevertheless, the legacy receiver with 1-bit ADC always operates in the saturation mode where the ADC produces the maximum and the minimum values of the quantization [5]. Under this condition, the ADC is unable to process the much weaker satellite signals. The other way is to use an ADC greater than 1-bit to improve the dynamic range. Because the multi-bits ADC employs the automatic gain control (AGC) to regulate the amplitudes of the incoming signals. It is possible to process both the strong and weak signals simultaneously within the AGC scaling range. On the other hand, the implementation of the multi-bits ADC is more expensive than the 1-bit ADC. Plus that the saturation is still inevitable if the signal amplitude exceeds the AGC's scaling range. Another technique is also required to maintain the effectiveness of the ADC.

Recently, a simple technique named "pulse blanking" (PB) has been used to suppress the impact of the saturation by outputting the zeros when the saturation is detected [6]. The saturation detection can be performed by analyzing the histograms of the ADC output levels in real-time. Therefore, a careful ADC/AGC implementation is required to guarantee the suppression. In this paper, an extended model consists of the multi-bits ADC and the blanker is presented and the optimal parameter settings are analyzed. The theory developed then used to establish an optimized front-end architecture for high dynamic BeiDou receiver. The remainder of this paper is organized as follows. Section 2 defines the signal and system model adopted in the paper whereas the parameter setting is derived in Sect. 3. Simulation results are provided in Sect. 4. Finally, Sect. 5 concludes the paper.

2   The Extended Front-End Model

The base-band notation of the incoming signal $r(t)$ in a one-path additive Gaussian channel can be expressed as [7]:

$$r(t) = s(t) + \eta(t) = S^{l_s}(t) + S^{l_p}(t) + \eta(t) \tag{1}$$

which is the composition of the signals of L different satellites $S^{l_s}(t)$, signals of L different pseudolites $S^{l_p}(t)$ and the noise term $\eta(t)$. The satellite signal $S^{l_s}(t)$ can be written as:

$$S^{l_s}(t) = \sqrt{2C_l}d_l\left(t - \tau_{0,l}\right)c_l\left(t - \tau_{0,l}\right)\cos\left(2\pi\left(f_{RF} + f_{d,l}\right)t + \varphi_{0,l}\right) \tag{2}$$

where C_l is the power of the lth signal, $d_l(\cdot)$ is the navigation data, $c_l(\cdot)$ is the lth ranging code, $\tau_{0,l}$, $f_{d,l}$, $\varphi_{0,l}$ and f_{RF} are the delay, Doppler frequency, phase distortion and center frequency of the satellite signal. The following pseudolite signal can be denoted as:

$$S^{l_p}(t) = S^{l_s}(t) \cdot P_s[n] \tag{3}$$

where $P_s[n]$ is a series of $\{0,1\}$ denoting the pulsing scheme.

The main functions of the front-end are to down-convert and digitize the incoming radio frequency (RF) signals for later base-band processing [8]. The

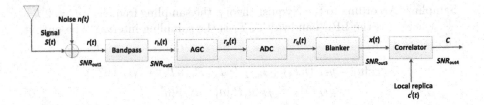

Fig. 1. The extended front-end model.

extended frond-end model is presented in Fig. 1. Compared with the legacy receiver's front-end, it contains a band pass filter (BPF), a multi-bits ADC with a dynamic AGC and a blanker to improve the dynamic range.

BPF: A BPF is a filter that passes signals with a frequency lower than the cut off bandwidth β which is determined by the capacity of the digital components. A well designed BPF is necessary here to prevent the aliasing effects of the pulsed signals. Assuming an ideal brick-wall filter with the bandwidth $\left[-\frac{\beta}{2}, \frac{\beta}{2}\right]$ is employed, the output signal $r_h(t)$ is:

$$
\begin{aligned}
r_h(t) &= r(t) * h(t) = r(t) * s_a(t) \\
&= S^{k_s}(t) * s_a(t) + S^{\sim k_p}(t) * s_a(t) + \eta(t) * s_a(t) \\
&= \sum_{l=0}^{L-1} y_l(t) + i(t) + \eta(t) \\
&= y(t) + i(t)P_s(t) + N(t)
\end{aligned}
\tag{4}
$$

where $S^{k_s}(t)$ denotes the satellite signals whereas $S^{\sim k_p}(t)$ represents the pseudolite signals, $s_a(t)$ is the Sinc function $\frac{\sin(\pi x)}{\pi x}$ [8].

AGC: Input of the ADC component is usually assumed as Gaussian distribution noise. For the multi-bits ADC, the quantization thresholds are normally set as a ladder of "$1\sigma, 2\sigma \ldots$" points in the Gaussian distribution [9]. The actual signal amplitudes corresponding to these points are often distorted by the temperature and the environment. Therefore, an AGC is set to provide a fixed gain $G(t)$ to regulate the signal amplitudes at its output for proper quantization. The signal output after the AGC is:

$$
r_g(t) = G(t) \cdot r_h(t)
\tag{5}
$$

where $G^2(t) = \frac{1}{\frac{1}{RT} \int_0^{RT} r_h^2(t)dt}$ given by [9], $G(t)$ is inversely proportional to the power during the recovery time (RT). The RT can be classified into 3 categories: fast, slow and very slow. In our research, a slow AGC is adopted where the RT equals to the pulse duration.

ADC: The ADC converts the continuous physical quantity into a discrete digital form. The AGC output $r_g(t)$ is then digitized by the ADC, in which contains two steps: sampling and quantization.

– Sampling: According to the Nyquist theory, the sampling frequency $f_s = 2\beta = \frac{1}{T_s}$, where β is the LPF bandwidth., T_s is the sampling interval. The output signal $r_{IF}[n]$ is:

$$r_{IF}[n] = y_{IF}(nT_s) + i_{c,IF}(nT_s) P_s(nT_s) + N_{IF}(nT_s)$$
$$= y_{IF}[n] + i_{c,IF}[n] P_s[n] + N_{IF}[n]. \tag{6}$$

where $y_{IF}[n]$ is sampled satellite signals, $i_{c,IF}[n]P_s[n]$ is sampled pseudolite signals and $N_{IF}[n]$ is sampled noise.

– Quantization: Quantization is the process of mapping continuous signals to discrete symbols. The quantization of signal amplitude is done on a number of levels equal to 2^B where B is the number of bits. The output can be modeled as:

$$r_q[n] = Q_B \left[A_g \left(y_{IF}[n] + i_{c,IF}[n]P_s[n] + N_{IF}[n] \right) \right], \tag{7}$$

where $Q_B[.]$ represents the stair-case function,

$$Q_B[.] = \left\{ -2^B + 1, -2^B + 3, \ldots, -1, 1, \ldots, 2^B - 3, 2^B - 1 \right\}. \tag{8}$$

Depending on the AGC outputs, two quantization operations are involved:
• for small signal mode:

$$r_q[n] = Q_B \left[A_g \left(y_{IF}[n] + N_{IF}[n] + i_{c,IF}[n]P_s[n] \right) \right]$$
$$\approx \frac{a_1}{\sigma^2} \left[y_{IF}[n] + i_{c,IF}[n]P_s[n] \right] + N_q[n], \tag{9}$$

where $a_1 = \sqrt{\frac{2}{\pi}} \left[1 + 2 \sum_{i=1}^{2^B - 1} \exp \left\{ -\frac{i^2}{2A_g^2 \sigma_{IF}^2} \right\} \right]$, given by [10].

• for saturation mode:

$$r_q[n] \approx Q_B[A_g(y_{IF}[n] + N_{IF}[n])](1 - P_s[n]) + A_{\max} sign(i_{c,IF}[n])P_s[n] \tag{10}$$

where $A_{\max} = \pm 2^B - 1$, representing the highest and the lowest output of the ADC.

In this paper, only the saturation mode is considered to test the performance of the pulse blanking.

Blanker: Pulse blanking is a very simple technique to mitigate the interferences of the pulsed signals. It is applied to the signal $r_q[n]$ before the correlation process. The ADC outputs outside the blanking threshold BTH $(0, L)$ are replaced by a set of zeros in order to reject the pulsing interferences. The output of the blanker is expressed as:

$$x(t) = f_B(r_a(t)) = \begin{cases} r_q(t), & \text{if } |r_q(t)| < BTH \\ 0, & \text{else} \end{cases} \tag{11}$$

Correlator: The ranging is achieved by correlation process of the PN codes. The signal $r_q[n]$ is then correlated with the locally generated signal chip by chip to integrate the signal power for useful signal extraction from the noise. The output of the correlator is computed as:

$$C = \frac{1}{N} \sum_{n=0}^{N-1} r_q[n]c\,(nT_s - \tau) \cdot \exp\{-j2\pi\,(f_{IF} + f_d)\,nT_s - j\varphi\}, \quad (12)$$

where N is the chip numbers, T_s is the sampling interval, τ is the delay, f_{IF} is the intermediate frequency, f_d is the Doppler frequency and φ is the phase. Computation of the correlator output C is essential for signal acquisition, tracking and demodulation.

3   Optimization of the Front-End

Quality of the signal is normally measured by its signal-to-noise ratio (SNR). The incoming signal $r(t)$ suffers various SNR degradations due to the front-end configurations. An optimal set of parameters will be analyzed by measuring the SNR degradations.

3.1   SNR Loss After LPN

In signal processing, the brick-wall filter is an idealized filter that removes all frequencies above the two-sided filter bandwidth β without affecting the lower frequencies. The filter's transfer function is specified by $s_a\,(t) = \frac{\sin \beta t}{\beta t}$, where the Fourier transformation form is:

$$\mathcal{F}\,[s_a(t)] = H\,(j\omega) = \begin{cases} 1, & -\beta < \omega < \beta \\ 0, & else. \end{cases} \quad (13)$$

Since the signal power during the integration time T can be derived as:

$$P_y = \frac{1}{T} \int_0^T \left\{ \sqrt{2C_1}d_1(t - \tau_{0,1})c_1(t - \tau_{0,1})\cos[2\pi(f_{RF} + f_{d,1})t + \varphi_{0,1}] * \frac{\sin \beta t}{\beta t} \right\}^2 dt, \quad (14)$$

its Fourier transformation form is:

$$P_y = \mathcal{F}^{-1}\left[\frac{1}{T} \int_0^T \mathcal{F}\left\{\frac{1}{2}[F(\omega + \omega_0) + F(\omega - \omega_0)]e^{-j\omega\tau_0} \cdot [u(\omega) - u(\omega - \frac{\beta}{2})]\right\} dt\right], \quad (15)$$

where $\omega_0 = 2\pi\,(f_{RF} + f_{d,1})$, $\omega_0\tau_0 = \varphi_{0,1}$. SNR after the LPN can be obtained by:

$$SNR_{out2} = \quad (16)$$

$$\frac{\mathcal{F}^{-1}\left[\frac{1}{T}\int_0^T \mathcal{F}\left\{\frac{1}{2}\,[F\,(\omega + \omega_0) + F\,(\omega - \omega_0)]\,e^{-j\omega\tau_0} \cdot \left[u\,(\omega) - u\left(\omega - \frac{\beta}{2}\right)\right]\right\} dt\right]}{\sigma^2},$$

where σ^2 is the noise power. It is clear seen from Fig. 2 that the best normalized low pass filter bandwidth is 0.1, which has the best noise filtering performance without causing the loss of useful signals.

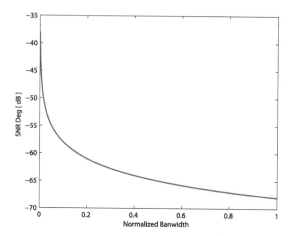

Fig. 2. Signal SNR after the LPF.

3.2   SNR Loss After ADC

Although the multi-bits ADC features higher dynamic tolerance and less quantization loss, the implementation is limited by the hardware complexity. A balance must be made between the quantization level and the complexity according to the quantization losses. In order to evaluate the SNR losses, it is necessary to obtain the expectation and variance of the quantized signal.

The stair-case function $Q_B[.]$ can be further expressed in a set of odd numbers:

$$\{2i+1\}_{i=-2^{B-1},-2^{B-1}+1,\ldots,2^{B-1}-1}, \tag{17}$$

where the probability of any value in the set is $p_{B,2i+1} = P\left(r_q[n] = 2i+1\right)$. By evaluating the probability, the expectation of $r_q[n]$ can be obtained by [8]:

$$
\begin{aligned}
E\left\{r_q[n]\right\} &\approx \frac{\mathrm{sign}\left\{y[n]\right\}}{\sqrt{2\pi\sigma_{\mathrm{IF}}^2}}\left[\sum_{i=-2^{B-1}+1}^{2^{B-1}-1} 2\left|y[n]\right|\exp\left\{-\frac{(i/A_{\mathrm{g}})^2}{2\sigma_{\mathrm{IF}}^2}\right\}\right] \\
&= \frac{2y[n]}{\sqrt{2\pi\sigma_{\mathrm{IF}}^2}}\left[1+2\sum_{i=1}^{2^{B-1}-1}\exp\left\{-\frac{(i/A_{\mathrm{g}})^2}{2\sigma_{\mathrm{IF}}^2}\right\}\right],
\end{aligned}
\tag{18}
$$

where $\mathrm{sign}\left\{y[n]\right\}$ denotes the ADC output values, σ_{IF}^2 is the variance of the noise, A_{g} is the AGC gain. The variance $Var\left\{r_q[n]\right\}$ is given by:

$$Var\left\{r_q[n]\right\} \approx 1+8\sum_{i=1}^{2^{B-1}-1} ierfc\left(\frac{i/A_g}{\sqrt{2}\sigma_{IF}}\right), \tag{19}$$

where $ierfc(\cdot)$ denotes the complementary error function. Therefore, SNR of $r_q[n]$ is given by:

$$\text{SNR} = \frac{E\left\{r_q[n]\right\}^2}{Var\left\{r_q[n]\right\}} = \frac{2}{\pi} \frac{\left[1 + 2\sum_{i=1}^{2^{B-1}-1} \exp\left\{-\frac{(i/A_g)^2}{2\sigma_{IF}^2}\right\}\right]^2}{1 + 8\sum_{i=1}^{2^{B-1}-1} ierfc\left(\frac{i/A_g}{\sqrt{2}\sigma_{IF}}\right)} \frac{A^2 N}{2\sigma_{IF}^2}, \tag{20}$$

which responds to the SNR loss L_B:

$$L_B = \frac{2}{\pi} \frac{\left[1 + 2\sum_{i=1}^{2^{B-1}-1} \exp\left\{-\frac{(i/A_g)^2}{2\sigma_{IF}^2}\right\}\right]^2}{1 + 8\sum_{i=1}^{2^{B-1}-1} ierfc\left(\frac{i/A_g}{\sqrt{2}\sigma_{IF}}\right)}. \tag{21}$$

By computing Eq. (21), $L_B(B = \{2, 3, 4\ldots, 10\})$ are illustrated in Fig. 3. It is assumed that the optimal quantization level is $B = 6$ bits, any greater quantization levels only produce similar losses with higher implementation complexity.

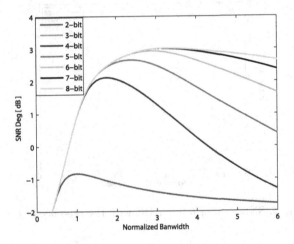

Fig. 3. SNR Loss after multi-bits ADC.

3.3 Signal Loss After Blanker

Since saturation detection is performed by analyzing the histograms of the ADC outputs, the decision threshold can only assume a value belongs to the stair-case function $Q_B[.]$ with two exceptions. The first exception, setting a threshold higher than the maximum ADC output $2^B - 1$ passes all signals and in fact disables pulse blanking. The second one, a threshold lower than 1 leads to the denial of all signals. Therefore, only thresholds in the set $T = \{-2^B + 2, \ldots, -4, -2, 2, 4, \ldots, 2^B - 2\}$ are considered. Assuming all the pulse positions are known to the receiver, the SNR loss after the Blanker is the product of two terms: $L_{\mathrm{pb}} = L_\mathrm{T} \cdot L_{\mathrm{ex}}$. L_T is the ADC loss with the presence of pulse blanking [11]:

$$
L_\mathrm{T} = \frac{2}{\pi} \frac{\left[1 + 2\sum_{i=1}^{K} \exp\left\{-\frac{i^2}{2A_\mathrm{g}^2\sigma_{\mathrm{IF}}^2}\right\} - (2K+1)\exp\left\{-\frac{(K+1)^2}{2A_\mathrm{g}^2\sigma_{\mathrm{IF}}^2}\right\}\right]^2}{1 + 8\sum_{i=1}^{K} ierfc\left(\frac{i}{\sqrt{2}A_\mathrm{g}\sigma_{\mathrm{IF}}}\right) - (2K+1)^2\, ierfc\left(\frac{K+1}{\sqrt{2}A_\mathrm{g}\sigma_{\mathrm{IF}}}\right)},
\tag{22}
$$

where $K = \lfloor\frac{T-1}{2}\rfloor = \lfloor\frac{2^B-3}{2}\rfloor$ represents the positive levels not clipped by the blanker. Because of the symmetry of the stair-case function $Q_B[.]$, only the positive levels are considered to reduce the computational complexity. L_{ex} is the loss caused by the signal removal, which is equivalent to $(1 - p_\mathrm{s}[n])$. Given the ADC level $B = 6$ bits, available thresholds are $T = \{2, 4, \ldots, 32\}$. According to (22) Fig. 4 illustrates that $T = 32$ cause the lowest SNR loss, it is possible to conclude that the optimal threshold for $B = 6$ bits is $T = 32$.

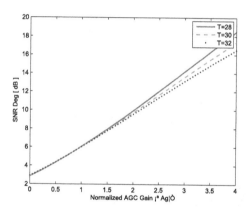

Fig. 4. SNR loss for 6 bits ADC with the presence of PB.

4   Simulation Results

4.1   Simulation Settings

SNR loss of the correlator is computed to assess the performance of the optimized front-end. Each block of the front-end model is emulated and the composite signal is transmitted in the chain, through each component successively.

Parameters settings used in simulation are as follows:

– Front-end:
  • LPF bandwidth: 0.10 normalized bandwidth
  • ADC quantization level: 6 bits
  • Blanker threshold: T = 32

– Signal specification:
  - Noise power: N0 = −107 dBm
  - Satellite signal:
    * Code modulation: QPSK
    * Received power: −133 dBm
    * Carrier frequency: 1561.098 MHz
    * Code period: 1 ms
    * Chip rate: 2.046 Mbit/s
  - Pseudolite signal:
    * Code modulation: QPSK
    * Received power: −45–−5 dBm
    * Carrier frequency: 1561.098 MHz
    * Code period: 1 ms
    * Chip rate: 2.046 Mbit/s
    * Duty cycle: 0–50 %

The generated signal is shown in Fig. 5. The PB effectively removes the pulsed interferences with the amplitudes over the threshold, leaving some margins in the continuous wave.

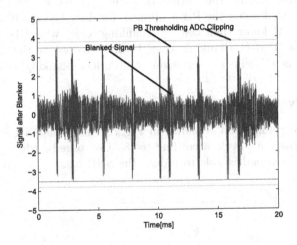

Fig. 5. Signal after the optimized front-end.

4.2 Performance Improvement

Performance improvement is depicted in Fig. 6 where three cases are considered. The 'No Blanking' case refers to the saturation loss developed in [7]. In this case, the ADC is saturated by the pulsed interferences without applying the PB. On the other hand, if the pulsed signals are perfectly removed, the SNR loss equals to ADC loss derived in [10,12–14]. The 'Optimal Threshold' case corresponds to

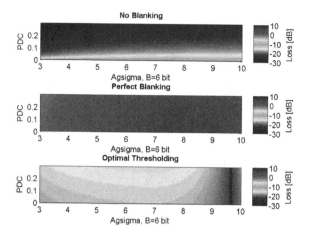

Fig. 6. SNR losses for three cases: 'No Blanking', 'Perfect Blanking' and 'Optimal Threshold'.

the PB threshold $T = 32$. From Fig. 6, it can be seen that the 'No Blanking' case is the worst scenario, while the 'Perfect Blanking' case has the best performance. It is also noted that when the PB is applied, for duty cycle = 0.3, the average SNR loss is 20 dB lower than the 'No Blanking' case, while the loss is 10 dB higher than the 'Perfect Blanking' case. In order to reduce the SNR loss, the optimal $A_g \sigma_{IF}$ is 9.7, which is very close the 'Perfect Blanking' case.

4.3   Duty Cycle Consideration

The duty cycle comparison is shown in Fig. 7, where the SNR is depicted as a function of the duty cycle according to [3]. Compared with legacy receiver, the optimized front-end is able to reduce the SNR loss for nearly 1.3 dB with

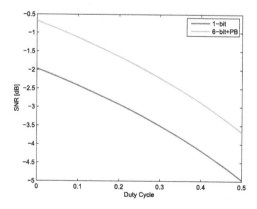

Fig. 7. PDC comparison between the optimized and legacy receivers.

the same duty cycle. Assuming the maximum duty cycle for legacy receiver is 12.68 with SNR $= -2.5\,$dB [3], than the maximum duty cycle for the optimized receiver is 0.4. As expected, the optimized receiver features higher interference tolerance and lower SNR.

5 Conclusion

In order to handle the high dynamic pulsing interference, an optimized Beidou receiver front-end is proposed to process the satellite signals with the presence of pulsed pseudolite signals.

An optimized set of parameter setting has been analyzed based on the SNR loss through each component. For an ideal BPF, the optimal normalized filter bandwidth is 0.1, which has the best noise filtering performance without causing the loss of useful signals. By evaluating the SNR loss, the optimal quantization level is $B = 6\,$bits, higher quantization levels produce similar losses with more implementation complexity. Subsequently, the optimal blanking threshold for $B = 6\,$bits has been determined to $T = 32$. Simulation results prove the effectiveness of the optimization where the SNR loss is very close to the 'Perfect Blanking' case with $A_g\sigma_{IF}$ is 9.7.

Acknowledgment. This work was financially supported by the National Natural Science Foundation of China (61074169), the National High Technology Research and Development Program of China (2013AA122403), and the Self-determined and Innovative Research Funds of WUT (2013-YB-018).

References

1. Wang, H., Zhai, C., Zhan, X., He, Z.: Outdoor navigation system using integrated GPS and pseudolite signals: theoretical analysis and simulation. In: International Conference on Information and Automation, ICIA, 2008. Changsha (2008)
2. Li, T., Wang, J., Huang, J.: Analysis of ambiguity resolution in precise positioning. In: 2012 International Conference on Indoor Positioning and Indoor Navigation (IPIN), Sydney (2012)
3. Edward Alan, L.: Self-calibrating Pseudolite Arrays: Theory and Experiment. Stanford University, California (2002)
4. Thomas, A.S.: RTCM, SC-104 recommended pseudolite signal specification. Navig.: J. Inst. Navig. **33**(1), 42–59 (1986)
5. Borio, D., O'Driscoll, C., Fortuny-Guasch, J.: Pulsed pseudolite signal effects on non-participating GNSS receivers. In: 2011 International Conference on Indoor Positioning and Indoor Navigation (IPIN). Guimaraes (2011)
6. Hegarty, C., Van Dierendonck, A.J., Bobyn, D., Tran, M., Grabowski, J.: Suppression of pulsed interference through blanking. In: Proceedings of the IAIN World Congress and the 56th Annual Meeting of the Institute of Navigation. San Diego (2000)
7. Borio, D., O'Driscoll, C., Fortuny-Guasch, J.: Impact of pseudolite signals on non-participating GNSS receivers. In: 2011 International Conference on Indoor Positioning and Indoor Navigation (IPIN). Guimaraes (2011)

8. Low-pass Filter [EB/OL] (2013). https://en.wikipedia.org/wiki/Low-pass_filter
9. Soualle, F., Cattenoz, M., Giger, K., Zecha, C.: Improved analytical models of SNIR degradation in presence of pulsed signals and impact of code-pulse synchrony. In: Proceedings of the Fifth European Workshop on GNSS Signals and Signal 23 Processing. Institut Aéronautique et Spatial (IAS). Toulouse (2011)
10. Borio, D.: A Statistical Theory for GNSS Signal Acquisition. Politecnico Di Torino, Torino (2008)
11. Borio, D., Cano, E.: Optimal GNSS pulse blanking in the presence of signal quantization. IET Signal Process. **7**(5), 400–410 (2013)
12. Shi, X., Wang, Z., Deng, C., Song, T., Pan, L., Chen, Z.: A novel bio-sensor based on DNA strand displacement. PLoS One **9**(10), e108856 (2014)
13. Wang, X., Miao, Y., Cheng, M.: Finding motifs in DNA sequences using low-dispersion sequences. J. Comput. Biol. **21**(4), 320–329 (2014)
14. Wang, X., Miao, Y.: GAEM: a hybrid algorithm incorporating GA with EM for planted edited motif finding problem. Current Bioinf. **9**(5), 463–469 (2014)

Approximation Performance of the (1+1) Evolutionary Algorithm for the Minimum Degree Spanning Tree Problem

Xiaoyun Xia[1,2] and Yuren Zhou[1,3(✉)]

[1] School of Computer Science and Engineering, South China University
of Technology, Guangzhou 510006, China
scutxxy@gmail.com, yrzhou@scut.edu.cn
[2] School of Information Engineering, Jiangxi University of Science and Technology,
Ganzhou 341000, China
[3] School of Data and Computer Science, Sun Yat-sen University,
Guangzhou 510006, China

Abstract. Evolutionary algorithms (EAs) are stochastic heuristic algorithms which are often successfully used for solving many optimization problems. However, the rigorous theoretical analysis results on the behavior of EAs on combinatorial optimizations are comparatively scarce, especially for NP-hard optimization problems. In this paper, we theoretically investigate the approximation performance of the (1+1) EA, a simple version of EAs on the minimum degree spanning tree (MDST) problem which is a classical NP-hard optimization problem. We show that the (1+1) EA can obtain an approximate solution for the MDST problem with maximum degree at most $O(\Delta_{opt} + \log n)$ in expected polynomial runtime $O(m^2 n^3 + m \log n)$, where Δ_{opt} is the maximal degree of the optimal spanning tree. It implies that EAs can obtain solutions with guaranteed performance on the MDST problem.

Keywords: Minimum degree spanning tree · Evolutionary algorithms · Local search · Approximation performance · Runtime analysis

1 Introduction

Making the maximum degree as small as possible is important and desirable for designing communications networks. Due to that the failure of a single node does not affect the rest part of the network. Such this problems in the design of communication networks can be modeled as the minimum degree spanning tree (MDST) problem. The MDST problem also has other practical applications in fields such as broadcast in dynamic networks and design of power grids. And the MDSY problem is a well known NP-hard problem [1].

For this problem, Fürer and Raghavachari [2] gave the first approximation algorithm, and they achieved a spanning tree of degree $O(\log n\Delta_{opt})$, where Δ_{opt} denotes the minimum possible maximum degree over all spanning trees.

© Springer-Verlag Berlin Heidelberg 2015
M. Gong et al. (Eds.): BIC-TA 2015, CCIS 562, pp. 505–512, 2015.
DOI: 10.1007/978-3-662-49014-3_45

The algorithm is generalized to find approximation minimum indegree rooted spanning tree in directed graphs. Furthermore, they improved their previous work and proposed a local search approximation algorithm which can find a local optimum of $O(\Delta_{opt} + \log n)$, and also achieved spanning trees with maximum degree of $O(\Delta_{opt} + 1)$ in polynomial time which is the best approximation ratio for this problem [3]. Their Local search techniques have been generalized to obtain approximation algorithms for a variety of minimum-degree network design problems in [4]. In the Steiner version of the MDST problem, Fürer and Raghavachari [5] used the iterative approximation algorithms to obtain spanning trees with maximal degree of $O(\Delta_{opt} + 1)$ in polynomial time.

Evolution algorithms (EAs) are class of random algorithms, which are usually considered to be global search methods [6]. A large number of experiments show that EAs are very effective randomized search heuristics for solving real-world problems. The performance of local search algorithms on the MDST problem has been deeply investigated [2,3]. However, we know little about how the performance of EAs on this NP-hard problem.

The theoretical study of EAs on fundamental optimization problems has received much attention from many researchers. A major part of the theoretical study of EAs is the runtime analysis of a simple (1+1) EA to find global optimum for optimization problems. These problems include classical pseudo-Boolean functions [7] and some combinatorial optimization problems [8] which can be solved in polynomially time by exact algorithms.

However, many combinatorial optimization problems are NP-hard, and we cannot expect the algorithms to find the optimal solutions on all instances of such problems in polynomial time. Therefore, the approximate performance analysis of EAs on some NP-hard problems receives much attention, and it becomes a very interesting research field.

Witt [10] analyzed the approximate performance of randomized search heuristics for the general partition problem $(P2\|C_{max})$, and he showed that the (1+1) EA and randomized local search algorithm can obtain a $\frac{4}{3}$-approximation ratio to this problem in expected runtime $O(n^2)$. Yu et al. [11] investigated the approximation performance of an EA framework SEIP, which is a simple evolutionary algorithm with isolated population. They showed that SEIP can achieve a guaranteed approximate solution. And they revealed that SEIP can efficiently achieve a H_k-approximation ratio for the unbounded set cover problem, and also a $H_k - \frac{k-1}{8k^9}$-approximation ratio for the k-set cover problem in expected polynomial times. Recently, Xia et al. [12] analyzed the approximate performance of the (1+1) EA for the maximum leaf spanning tree problem, and they showed that the (1+1) EA can obtain some approximation guarantees for this problem in expected polynomial runtime.

In practice, EAs are often used to obtain satisficing solutions. A natural question arises how the heuristics work on the NP-hard optimization problems or what approximation performance they can achieve. In this paper, we investigate the performance of the (1+1) EA on the MDST problem. We demonstrate that the (1+1) EA can efficiently achieve a approximation solution with maximal degree $O(\Delta^* + \log n)$ in expected polynomial runtime $O(m^2 n^3 + m \log n)$.

The remainder of the paper is organised as follows. The next section introduces some preliminaries including the MLST problem, evolutionary algorithms. Section 3 analyzes the approximation performance of the (1+1) EA on MDST problems. Finally, Sect. 4 presents the conclusions and discussions.

2   The MDST Problem and Algorithms

We begin by stating some definitions and notations that will be used throughout the paper. Given a connected undirected graph $G = (V, E)$, where V are the set of vertices or nodes of a graph G, and E are the set of edges of graph G. Suppose $|V| = n$ and $|E| = m$. A spanning tree T is a subgraph of G that connects all the nodes of G and contains no cycles. Note that a spanning tree always consists of $n - 1$ edges, and a complete graph has n^{n-2} spanning trees. We denote the degree of a node $v \in V$ in a tree T by $\delta_T(v)$. For a spanning tree T, the degree of T is defined as the maximum degree in T of all vertexes, and we denote it by $\Delta(T) = \max_{v \in V} \delta_T(v)$. For simplicity, we write it as Δ. The MDST problem is that of finding a spanning tree whose maximal degree is the smallest among all spanning trees of G. Denote T_{opt} by an optimal spanning tree, whose maximal degree is Δ_{opt}.

The existence of a spanning tree of max degree 2 is equivalent to having a Hamiltonian path in the graph. In fact, the MDST problem is NP-complete to decide for any $k \geq 2$ whether G contains a spanning tree of maximum degree k [1]. We can not expect that there is an algorithm that can solve any MDST instance in polynomial time unless $P = NP$.

We now introduce a local search approximation algorithm proposed by Fürer and Raghavachari [2] for the MDST problem. The procedure starts with a spanning tree and tries to improve it by swapping non-tree edges against tree edges, and we call it a T-swap.

Definition 1 (T-swap neighborhood). *Let T_1 and T_2 be two spanning trees of the MDST problem. Consider a non-tree edge $e_1 = (u, v) \notin T_1$, and let C be the unique cycle generated when e_1 is added to T_1. Suppose there is a vertex w in C with the property that $\delta_T(w) - 1 \geq max(\delta_T(u), \delta_T(v)) + 1$. If T_2 is derived from T_1 by adding the edge e_1 and remove one of the edges in C incident to w, we call this step T-swap operation, also an improvement for that the maximum of $\{\delta_T(u), \delta_T(v), \delta_T(w)\}$ has decreased by at least one, and say that T_2 is in T-swap neighborhood of T_1, denoted by $T_2 \in$ T-swap (T_1).*

The local search with T-swap neighborhood might be easy to get trapped into local optimum. According to Definition 1, for an arbitrary tree, if there are no such edges to produce any improvements, we say the tree is a local optimal tree (LOT).

We consider the (1+1) EA in this paper. The coding of candidate solutions and operators in EAs play an important role which can determine the success

or failure of the algorithm. We use the edge sets encoding which has been investigated intensively by Raidl and Julstrom [13]. The search space $S = \{0,1\}^m$,
we encode a solution as a bit string $x = (x_1, x_2, \cdots, x_m) \in S$, where each bit
$x_i (1 \leq i \leq m)$ corresponds to one edge. If $x_i = 1 (i = 1, 2, \cdots, m)$, then relative
edge is selected, otherwise it is not. We consider the generating subgraph $H(x)$ of
G, where $V(H(x)) = V(G)$, and $E(H(x)) = \{e | x_i = 1\}$. Therefore, a bit string
x represents a subgraph of G, and $|x|$ represents the number of edges included
in $H(x)$.

Consider an exponential potential function ϕ on the vertex set of $H(x)$. If
the degree of a vertex u is d in $H(x)$, the potential $\phi(u)$ is defined to be c^d, for
any constant $c > 2$. The total potential $\Phi(H(x))$ of $H(x)$ is defined to be the
sum of the potential of all the vertices, i.e., $\Phi(H(x)) = \sum\limits_{u \in H} c^{\delta_H(u)}$.

In order to optimize the MDST problem, the (1+1) EA uses the fitness
function to guide the solutions searching. According to the above representation,
we define the fitness function as

$$f(x) = (c(H(x) - 1)) * n^2 + (e(H(x) - (n-1))) * n + \frac{1}{nc^n} \Phi(H(x)) \quad (1)$$

where $c(H(x))$ is the number of connected components in $H(x)$, $e(H(x))$ is the
number of edges in $H(x)$ and $\Phi(H(x))$ is the sum of the potential of all the
vertices in $H(x)$.

The MDST problem is a minimization problem, the lower the value of $f(x)$,
the better the quality of the solution. The first part of the fitness function is to
make sure that $H(x)$ is a connected spanning subgraph, the second part is to
make sure that $H(x)$ is a spanning tree and the last part is to make sure that
the maximal degree of the current tree or the number of maximal degree nodes
is decreased.

The considered (1+1) EA is a very popular algorithm in the theory of evolutionary algorithms, which use one individual and only mutation operation
without recombination. The (1+1) EA flips each bit with probability $1/n$ and
uses elitist selection. We give the definition of the (1+1) EA as follows.

Algorithm 1. (1+1) EA for the MDST problem

01: Begin
02:    Initialize a solution $x \in \{0,1\}^n$ uniformly at random;
03:    while (termination condition does not hold) do
04:        Generate the offspring x' by flipping each bit in x with probability $1/n$;
05:        if $f(x') \leq f(x)$ then $x = x'$;
06:    End while
07: End

The (1+1) EA starts with an arbitrary solution, and obtains an offspring
solution from the current one by using the mutation operator repeatedly. If the

offspring solution is strictly better than the current one, then the (1+1) EA uses it to replace the current solution.

The (1+1) EA is a randomized algorithm, and we focus on the number of fitness function evaluation until the algorithm obtain the optimal solutions or approximation solutions for the first time. In the Algorithm 1, given an arbitrary initial feasible solution T, if the offspring $T' \in T\text{-swap}(T)$, then it is the local search algorithm with the T-swap neighborhood.

3   The Approximation Performance Guarantee of the (1+1) EA for the MDST Problem

The MDST problem considered in the paper is NP-hard, and so we cannot expect the algorithm to find the optimal solutions on all instance of this problem in polynomial time. We are interested in the number of fitness evaluations until the algorithm produce a good approximation optimal solution or relative satisfactory solutions.

Approximation ratio shows the degree of approximation that the approximation algorithm find the solutions of problem, which is the most basic and important indicator to measure the performance of the approximation algorithm. We give the definition of the approximation ratio as follows.

Definition 2 *(r-approximation). Given a search space S, let $f : S \to \mathbb{R}$ be an objective function of an optimization problem P which should be minimized. let $x_A \in S$ be the objective function value of a solution produced by an algorithm A on P, and f_{min} denote the optimal objective function value. We call r the approximation ratio of A on P iff $r = \max\limits_{x_A \in S} \frac{f(x_A)}{f_{min}}$, which implies $f(x_A) \leq r f_{min}$.*

In this section, we attempt to gain deeper insights into the approximability or the limits of EAs when dealing with a NP-hard optimization problem. Especially, we focus on that how well or how badly EAs may perform for the MDST problem. The main idea is that the (1+1) EA can simulate the T-swap local search algorithm to obtain the approximation guarantee for the MDST problem. In order to show that the (1+1) EA can obtain a approximation guarantee on the MDST problem, the fist step is that the (1+1) EA starting from an arbitrary initial solution finds a feasible solution, i.e., a spanning tree, then starting from any spanning tree the (1+1) EA finds near-optimal solutions for the MDST problem.

As shown in the following Lemma, for a given connected undirected graph $G = (V, E)$, the (1+1) EA starting with any initial solution can efficiently find a feasible solution, i.e., a spanning tree [9].

Lemma 1. *Given a connected undirected graph $G = (V, E)$, where $|V| = n$ and $|E| = m$. Then the expected runtime of the (1+1) EA starting from any initial solution constructs a feasible solution (spanning tree) on G is $O(m \log n)$.*

For the local search algorithm around the T-swap neighborhood, Fürer and Raghavachari [3] proved that this algorithm can find a spanning tree with maximal degree of less than $b\Delta_{opt} + \lceil \log_b n \rceil$ for any $b > 1$.

Theorem 1. [3] *For any $b > 1$, the local search algorithm with T-swap neighborhood can find a spanning tree of maximal degree $O(b\Delta_{opt} + \lceil \log_b n \rceil)$ in expected polynomial time for any instance of the MDST problem.*

Indeed, following the local search with T-swap neighborhood, if a spanning tree t is not the local optimum, then there always exists a T-swap operation which can cause an improvement of the fitness value, and produce a new spanning tree t^*. According to [3], we have

$$\Phi(t^*) \le (1 - \frac{c}{n^2})\Phi(t) \tag{2}$$

For the sake of convenience, we partition all feasible solutions into two disjoint sets. One is $S_1 = \{T \in S | \Delta(T) \le b\Delta_{opt} + \lceil \log_b n \rceil\}$, the other is $S_2 = \{T \in S | \Delta(T) > b\Delta_{opt} + \lceil \log_b n \rceil\}$.

Denote the sequence of spanning trees by $t_i(i = 0, 1, 2, \cdots)$ and the total potential of t_i by Φ_i at iteration i. So, if $t_i \in S_2$ at iteration i, then the probability that the $(1+1)$ EA can improve the solutions in each step by performing a T-swap operation is $(\frac{1}{m})^2(1 - \frac{1}{m})^{m-2} \ge \frac{1}{em^2}$. We denote it by $P_m = \Omega(\frac{1}{m^2})$.

Let $E[\Phi_i]$ be the expectation of Φ_i at iteration i. And we need to estimate the expected one-step potential decrease. The detailed statement can be described as follows.

Lemma 2. $E[\Phi_{i+1}|\Phi_i] = O((1 - \frac{c}{m^2n^2})\Phi_i)$, where c is a constant, $c > 2$.

Proof. If the $(1+1)$ EA can improve the solutions by a T-swap operation in each step, we call the step a good step. By the above discussion, we know that the expected potential of current spanning tree consists of two parts: accept case(with good step), and non-accepted case. Hence, we have

$$E[\Phi_{i+1}|\Phi_i] = P_m(1 - \frac{c}{n^2})\Phi_i + (1 - P_m)\Phi_i \text{ (By the definition of expectation)}$$

$$= (P_m - \frac{cP_m}{n^2} + 1 - P_m)\Phi_i$$

$$= (1 - \frac{cP_m}{n^2})\Phi_i$$

$$= O((1 - \frac{c}{m^2n^2})\Phi_i) \text{ } (For \text{ } P_m = \Omega(\frac{1}{m^2}), \text{ c is a constant})$$

Based on the above discussion, the $(1+1)$ EA can improve the fitness value by performing a T-swap operation with probability $\Omega(\frac{1}{m^2})$. So, by Theorem 1, we can analyze the expected time for the $(1+1)$ EA finding a local optimum spanning tree of maximal degree $O(\Delta_{opt} + \log n)$ for the MDST problem by simulating the local search around the T-swap neighborhood. In order to analyze the runtime, we would like to evaluate the best-so-far solutions during the execution $t_0, t_1, t_2, \ldots$ as an infinite stochastic process.

Theorem 2. *Given an undirected and connected graph $G = (V, E)$, and we let $|V| = n$, $|E| = m$. The (1+1) EA can find a spanning tree with maximum degree $O(\Delta_{opt} + \log n)$ in expected polynomial time $O(m^2 n^3 + m \log n)$.*

Proof. If a spanning tree $t_i = t \in S_2$ at iteration i, there must exist a spanning tree $t' \in T$-swap(t) such that $E[\Phi_{i+1}|\Phi_i] \le (1 - \frac{c}{m^2 n^2})\Phi_i$. So, replacing t with t' decreases the potential by an amount with respect to Φ_i. We can estimate the expected time of (1+1) EA starting from any spanning tree for finding a local optimum spanning tree with maximum degree $O(\Delta_{opt} + \log n)$.

$$
\begin{aligned}
E[\Phi_i|t_0, t_1, \cdots, t_{i-1}] &\le (1 - \frac{c}{m^2 n^2})E[\Phi_{i-1}|t_0, t_1, \cdots, t_{i-2}] \text{ (By Lemma 2)} \\
&\le (1 - \frac{c}{m^2 n^2})^2 E[\Phi_{i-2}|t_0, t_1, \cdots, t_{i-3}] \\
&\le \cdots\cdots \\
&\le (1 - \frac{c}{m^2 n^2})^t E[\Phi_0] \text{ (By induction)}
\end{aligned}
$$

Note that, the lowest possible potential is the case of a Hamiltonian path, which has potential $2 \cdot c^1 + (n - 2) \cdot c^2 > n$. So, for a spanning tree T, $n < 2 \cdot c^1 + (n-2) \cdot c^2 \le \Phi_i \le n \cdot c^{n-1} < n \cdot c^n, i = 0, 1, \cdots$. So long as the solutions in the S_1, the algorithm terminates. Let $T = c_1 \cdot m^2 n^3$, c_1 is an appropriate constant. Then, when $t > T$, We have $(1 - \frac{c}{m^2 n^2})^t E[\Phi_0] \le (1 - \frac{c}{m^2 n^2})^t \cdot n \cdot c^n \le n$.

This implies that the (1+1) EA starting from an arbitrary spanning tree can obtain a locally optimal with maximum degree $O(\Delta_{opt} + \log n)$ in expected polynomial time $O(m^2 n^3)$.

Combining Lemma 1 and Theorem 1, this completes the proof.

It should be noted that the Theorem 2 also can be obtained by using the multiplicative drift analysis [17].

4   Conclusion

In this paper, we study the approximation performance of the (1+1) EA on the minimum degree spanning tree problem. The analyses confirms that the (1+) EA can guarantee to obtain some approximation solutions. A very interesting but maybe very challenging work is that whether and how the EAs can improve these obtained approximation ratios. And we need further investigations to know how the crossover operators or different population sizes [16] can affect the approximation performance.

Multiobjectivization is another efficient approach for solving a single objective optimization problem, which can add additional information to guide the search in promising directions. Therefore, it may be another interesting work to analyze the performance of multiobjective EAs [14,15] for the minimum degree spanning tree problem. Gaining a theoretical understanding of EAs on the NP-hard problems is still a challenging topic for future work.

Acknowledgments. This work was supported by National Natural Science Foundation of China (61170081, 61472143), and Natural Science Foundation of Jiangxi Province of China (20151BAB217008).

References

1. Garey, M.R., Johnson, D.S.: Computers and Intractability: A Guide to the Theory of NP-Completeness. Freeman, San Francisco (1979)
2. Fürer, M., Raghavachari, B.: An NC approximation algorithm for the minimum degree spanning tree problem. In: Proceedings of the 28th Annual Allerton Conference on Communication, Control and Computing, pp. 274–281 (1990)
3. Fürer, M., Raghavachari, B.: Approximating the minimum degree spanning tree to within one from the optimal degree. In: Proceedings of the 3rd Annual ACM-SIAM Symposium on Discrete Algorithms, pp. 317–324. ACM, USA (1992)
4. Ravi, R., Raghavachari, B., Klein, P.: Approximation through local optimality: designing networks with small degree. In: Shyamasundar, R.K. (ed.) FSTTCS 1992. LNCS, vol. 652, pp. 279–290. Springer, Heidelberg (1992)
5. Fürer, M., Raghavachari, B.: Approximating the minimum-degree steiner tree to within one of optimal. J. Algorithms **17**, 409–423 (1994)
6. Gallagher, K., Sambridge, M.: Genetic algorithms: a powerful tool for large-scale non-linear optimization problems. Comput. Geosci. **20**(7–8), 1229–1236 (1994)
7. Droste, S., Jansen, T., Wegener, I.: On the analysis of the (1+1) evolutionary algorithm. Theor. Comput. Sci. **276**, 51–81 (2002)
8. Jansen, T.: Analyzing Evolutionary Algorithms - The Computer Science Perspective. Natural Computing Series. Springer, Heidelberg (2013)
9. Neumann, F., Wegener, I.: Randomized local search, evolutionary algorithms, and the minimum spanning tree problem. Theor. Comput. Sci. **378**(1), 32–40 (2007)
10. Witt, C.: Worst-case and average-case approximations by simple randomized search heuristics. In: Diekert, V., Durand, B. (eds.) STACS 2005. LNCS, vol. 3404, pp. 44–56. Springer, Heidelberg (2005)
11. Yu, Y., Yao, X., Zhou, Z.: On the approximation ability of evolutionary optimization with application to minimum set cover. Artif. Intell. **180–181**, 20–33 (2012)
12. Xia, X., Zhou, Y., Lai, X.: On the analysis of the (1+1) evolutionary algorithm for the maximum leaf spanning tree problem. Int. J. Comput. Math. **92**(10), 2023–2035 (2015)
13. Raidl, G.R., Julstrom, B.A.: Edge sets: an effective evolutionary coding of spanning tree. IEEE Trans. Evol. Comput. **7**(3), 225–239 (2003)
14. Zhang, X., Tian, Y., Jin, Y.: A knee point driven evolutionary algorithm for many-objective optimization. IEEE Trans. Evol. Comput. **PP**(99), 1 (2014). doi:10.1109/TEVC.2014.2378512
15. Zhang, X., Tian, Y., Cheng, R., Jin, Y.: An efficient approach to non-dominated sorting for evolutionary multi-objective optimization. IEEE Trans. Evol. Comput. **19**(2), 201–213 (2015)
16. Chen, T., Tang, K., Chen, G., Yao, X.: A large population size can be unhelpful in evolutionary algorithms. Theor. Comput. Sci. **436**, 54–70 (2012)
17. Doerr, B., Johannsen, D., Winzen, C.: Multiplicative drift analysis. Algorithmica **64**, 673–697 (2012)

A Stochastic Local Search Heuristic for the Multidimensional Multiple-choice Knapsack Problem

Youxin Xia, Chao Gao, and JinLong Li$^{(\boxtimes)}$

School of Computer Science and Technology,
University of Science and Technology of China, Hefei, China
xyx1991@mail.ustc.edu.cn, chao.gao.ustc@gmail.com, jlli@ustc.edu.cn

Abstract. The Multidimensional Multiple-choice Knapsack Problem (M MKP) is an NP-hard combinatorial optimization task that appears in various applications. We present a fast stochastic local search heuristic for the MMKP that uses an iterative perturbative search paradigm with penalty weights for dimensions, and an additive weighting scheme is adopted to diversify the search. Our heuristic is tested on the standard benchmark problem instances. Experiments show that it is very competitive in terms of the best solutions found, compared the fast heuristics in the literature. Besides, our heuristic is easy to implement, has no parameter to tune in practice.

Keywords: Combinatorial optimization · Multidimensional multiple-choice knapsack problem · Stochastic local search

1 Introduction

The 0–1 Knapsack Problem (KP) [1] is a classic combinatorial optimization problem that appears in a number of industrial applications. The Multiple Choice Knapsack Problem (MCKP) [2] is an important variant of the 0–1 KP generalized by partitioning the items into different groups and asking to select exact one from each group. The Multidimensional Knapsack Problem (MDKP) [3], on the other hand, extends the resource into multi-dimensions. The Multidimensional Multiple-Choice Knapsack Problem (MMKP) is a combination of MCKP and MDKP, which can be formulated as the 0–1 Integer Linear Programming (ILP) form as below:

As shown above, in MMKP, the items are divided into n groups, and for group i, N_i denotes the set of items in it. Each item is associated with a profit value and a m dimensional resource cost. The total resources available in every dimension is given by $b = \{b^1, b^2, .., b^m\}$. For each group exactly one item should be selected (the choice constraint), and the objective is to maximize the total profit of the selected items, with the constraint that on each dimension the total resource cost is not exceeded the resource available.

© Springer-Verlag Berlin Heidelberg 2015
M. Gong et al. (Eds.): BIC-TA 2015, CCIS 562, pp. 513–522, 2015.
DOI: 10.1007/978-3-662-49014-3_46

$$\max \sum_{i=1}^{n} \sum_{j=1}^{N_i} c_{ij} x_{ij} \qquad (1)$$

$$\text{subject to } \sum_{i=1}^{n} \sum_{j=1}^{N_i} v^k{}_{ij} x_{ij} \leq b^k, \quad k = 1, ..., m, \qquad (2)$$

$$\sum_{j=1}^{N_i} x_{ij} = 1, \quad i = 1, ..., n \qquad (3)$$

$$x_{ij} \in \{0, 1\}, i = 1, \dots n; j = 1, \dots N_i. \qquad (4)$$

The MMKP is often regarded as the most challenging among the knapsack problems, and is NP-hard. It has many practical applications, such as logistics [4], running time resource management [5], global routing of wiring in circuits [6], web service composition [7] and capital budgeting [8], etc [9].

A number of algorithms have been proposed for MMKP in recent years due to its increasing relevance to real-life applications. Exact methods based on Branch and Bound [10–12] are able to guarantee the optimality of the solutions found, however they are not suitable for large scale problem instances because of the very large computing time required.

The first results on the resolution to MMKP are due to Moser et al. [13]. They proposed a heuristic based on Lagrangian Relaxation that starts from building an infeasible solution, then repeatedly permuting to reduce the infeasibility. This method was improved by Akbar et al. [14]. Then Khan et al. [15] proposed a heuristic based on the aggressive resource usage, and the comparative results show that their heuristic performs better than Moser's method. Later, a guided local search and a reactive local search heuristic proposed by Hifi et al. [16,17] were shown to be able to outperform Khan and Moser's heuristics. A column generation method proposed Cherfi and Hifi [18] was considered to be able to obtain better quality solutions on the standard benchmark instances. A hybrid algorithm approach that combines local branching with column generation and a truncated branch-and-bound method was also proposed by Cherfi and Hifi in [19], which was shown to be able to obtain many better results than their former approach. The ant colony optimization approach has also been applied to MMKP [20,21]. Ren and Feng propose to use an efficient operator to repair the infeasible solution during a constructive process. Iqbal et al. [20] integrated a conventional local search to improve the convergence of their algorithm, claiming that their method can find near optimal solution with relative short computation time.

Due to different real-world application requirements, the development of heuristics is progressed into two different directions. The first type stresses on finding feasible solution using small computation cost to meet real-time demands. For example, the methods proposed by Ykman-Couvreur et al. [5] and Shojaei et al. [22] aim to find feasible solution in real time on embedded systems at the sacrifice of some solution qualities. Whereas the second ones try to obtain high quality solutions with relatively larger runtime. Recent solution quality aimed approaches are the iterative relaxation based heuristic introduced by Hanafi et al. [23], a family of iterative semi-continuous relaxation heuristics named ILPH, IMIPH, IIRH and ISCRH proposed by Crévits et al. [24], a hybrid heuristic [25] in which a family of cuts is proposed to define the reduced problem and a reformulation procedure is used to further enhance the performance of the algorithm, a "reduce and solve" approach [26], and a fully parameterized CPH heuristic based on pareto algebra [27].

The solution quality aimed heuristics [23–26] share the idea that the original problem somewhat reduced by proposed (pseudo) cuts, and then by adjusting the cuts, a iterative heuristic is introduced using the MIP solver CPLEX to solve the reduced or redefined subproblem. The sophisticated combination of heuristics and exact solvers push them to be able to obtain very hight solution qualities on the benchmark instances originally from [15, 17], along with computation times up to thousands of seconds on modern PC.

The fast heuristics in the literature [5, 13–17, 20–22, 28] pay more attention on obtaining good results with limited computing resources. In one latest paper [28], Htiouech et al. propose a strategic oscillation approach that explore both feasible and infeasible sides of the current solution by alternating constructive and destructive phrases. The surrogate multipliers are determined by the state of the search and the feasibility of the current solution, which are periodically normalized to strengthen surrogate constraint.

In this paper, we present a new stochastic local search heuristic for the MMKP. Similar to those heuristics that based on surrogate information, we also give multipliers to dimensions as weights. However, unlike the former heuristics, we propose to use a simple additive weighting scheme to adjust the weight (multiplier) on dimensions. Our heuristic is an iterative search procedure that consists of a perturbing phrase and a destructive phrase. Experiments show that our heuristic has the merit of high efficiency, is able to obtain competitive results with the heuristics in the literature.

2   Stochastic Local Search for MMKP

In this section, we present our heuristic for MMKP. We first give description about the weighting strategy, and then present our heuristic step by step, finally we illustrate our algorithm in detail.

2.1   Weights for Dimensions

In our heuristic, each dimension is assigned to a multiplier as the weight on this dimension. This idea is used to deal with the dimension constraint of MMKP which requires the sum of resource consumption on each dimension should not exceed the resource available. Suppose λ is an m dimensional vector for the multiplier, the weights as choice rule for prioritizing variable selection. Whenever choosing an item to add to the candidate solution, we aim to

$$\text{Maximize } \{r_{ij} = \frac{c_{ij}}{s_{ij}} | x_{ij} = 0\} \qquad (5)$$

where $s_{ij} = \sum_{k=1}^{m} v_{ij}\lambda_k$. Since the value of c_{ij} is deterministic for every item in MMKP, the value of r_{ij} is controlled by the multiplier λ. In our heuristic, λ is adjusted as follows:

- Initially, λ is set to all 1, i.e., $\lambda = \{1\}^m$,
- Suppose the set of violated dimensions is noted as τ, in each iteration, for each dimension in τ, the corresponding multiplier is increased by 1.

It is easy to see that initially, this choice rule is equivalent to the traditional aggregate resource usage first proposed in [29]. However, as the search processes, the weights for dimensions are adjusting at the same time, making those discarded items become selectable subsequently. The key aspect of a heuristic is its ability to balance intensification and diversification. We use a greedy-like manner to select r_{ij} to fulfill the intensification purpose, while the weighting increase scheme to achieve the goal of diversification.

2.2   Initialize the Candidate Solution

We note the candidate solution as ρ, for group i, $\rho_i = j$ indicates that in this group the item with index j is selected. We adopt the greedy algorithm for constructing the initial candidate solution. More specifically, as in MMKP, it is restricted that in each group, exact one item should be selected. We initialize ρ by traversing each group, and for group i, suppose j^* is the one with the maximum r_{ij} value, thus $\rho_i = j^*$. The total profit value of the candidate solution is noted by $profit(\rho)$. LB represent the best lower bound found during the search, initially as -1. If the initial ρ is feasible, then $LB = profit(\rho)$.

It is noteworthy that such a candidate solution is usually infeasible. However, the initial feasibility of the candidate does not influence our local search subsequently, because our heuristic mostly work by perturbing a infeasible solution into feasible.

2.3   Perturbing the Candidate Solution

The perturbing phrase is the core component of our heuristic. We suppose τ stores the set of dimensions that the total resources consumption have been violated. Our perturbing phrase consists of the following steps:

- Step 1: Choose a dimension k^* in τ whose violation is the greatest.
- Step 2: Randomly choose a group i^* from ρ with respect to the resource consumption in k^*.

- Step 3: In the selected group i^*, choose an item other than ρ_{i^*}, guaranteed that the exchange with ρ_{i^*} will result $profit(\rho) > LB$ and to maximize r_{ij}. If no such items found in group i^*, go to Step 2.
- Step 4: Increase the weights of the dimensions in τ by 1.

Our perturbing phrases stops when the candidate solution becomes feasible, which leads to the destructive phrase of our heuristic.

2.4 Destructive Phrase

The purpose of the destructive phrase is to break the feasible candidate solution ρ into a "good" infeasible solution for perturbing. This process is actually an enhancement of ρ, because it results to a new ρ' with $profit(\rho') > profit(\rho)$. We describe it as follows:

- For each group i, record each item whose profit value is greater than ρ_i to T.
- Randomly select an item in T.
- Replace the selected item to ρ in the corresponding group.

During this phrase, whenever a better feasible solution is found, the LB and stored best found solution are updated.

2.5 Algorithm in Detail

We give the detailed description of heuristic. It is illustrated as Algorithm 1.

As the description of Algorithm 1. SLS_MMKP is an iterative heuristic which stops when a pre-indicated maximum iteration number is reached. Line 3 to Line 6 corresponds to the initialization of the candidate solution ρ. Line 10 to Line 31 is the local search phrase that aims to find a near-optimal feasible solution with $maxIte$ iterations process. The local search is further partitioned as two phrases. Whenever $\tau = \emptyset$, which means the candidate solution is feasible, then ρ is break into infeasible by the destructive phrase from Line 11 to Line 21.

From Line 22 to Line 29 is the perturbing search of our heuristic in each iteration. First, a dimension is selected from τ, and then regarding to the selected dimension, a group is randomly selected with the biased probability distribution, finally an item is picked according the pseudo utility to replace the old one in the candidate solution ρ. The multipliers for the violated dimensions are updated subsequently. In case that there is no viable items to select in Line 25, the algorithm process into the next iteration.

We now analysis the time complexity of our heuristic. In each iteration, we simplify this analysis by considering only the perturbing phrase of the algorithm, since in practice, the predominant number were spending on perturbing phrase. Line 22 can be done with $O(m)$, Line 23 to 24 is with $O(n)$, while Line 25 to 26 cost $O(lm+m)$ where l is the maximum of $N_i, i = 1, \ldots n$. The weighting increase scheme takes anther $O(m)$. Therefore, we conclude that the time complexity of the perturbing each iteration takes $O(3m + n * l + n)$.

Algorithm 1. SLS_MMKP

Input: An MMKP instance
Output: A MMKP solution $bestSol$

1   Let ρ be candidate solution vector;
2   Let λ be the multiplier in each dimension, for $k = 1, ..., m, \lambda_k = 1$;
3   **for** $i \leftarrow 1$ **to** n **do**
4   $\quad$ $j_* = \text{argmax}\{u_{ij}|j = 1, \ldots, N_i\}$;
    $\quad$; $\qquad\qquad\qquad$ // $u_{ij} = c_{ij}/s_{ij}$ is the penalized utility ratio
5   $\quad$ $\rho_i \leftarrow j_*$;
6   **end**
7   Let τ be the set of dimensions that the resource available violated by ρ;
8   Let LB be the best lower bound, initialized as -1;
9   $iteration \leftarrow 1$;
10 **while** $iteration \leq maxIte$ **do**
11 $\quad$ **while** $\tau = \emptyset$ **do**
12 $\quad\quad$ $LB \leftarrow \sum_{i=1}^{n} c_{i\rho_i}$;
13 $\quad\quad$ $bestSol \leftarrow \rho$;
14 $\quad\quad$ **for** $k \leftarrow 1$ **to** m **do**
15 $\quad\quad\quad$ $\lambda_k \leftarrow 1$; $\qquad\qquad$ // normalize penalty weights
16 $\quad\quad\quad$;
17 $\quad\quad$ **end**
18 $\quad\quad$ Randomly select an (i', j') such that $profit(\rho) - c_{i'\rho_{i'}} + c_{i'j} > LB$;
19 $\quad\quad$ $\rho_{i'} \leftarrow j'$;
20 $\quad\quad$ update τ;
21 $\quad$ **end**
22 $\quad$ $k_* \leftarrow \text{argmax}\{\sum_{i=1}^{n} v_{i\rho_i}{}^k - b^k|k \in \tau\}$;
23 $\quad$ Let $f_i(\rho) \leftarrow \frac{v_{i\rho_i}^{k_*}}{\sum_{i=1}^{n} v_{i\rho_i}^{k_*}}$, $i = 1, \ldots n$;
24 $\quad$ select a group i_* according to probability distribution of $f_i(\rho)$;
25 $\quad$ $j_* \leftarrow \text{argmax}\{u_{i_*j}|j = 1, \ldots N_{i_*} \wedge \sum_{i=1}^{n} c_{i\rho_i} - c_{i_*\rho_{i_*}} + c_{ij} > LB\}$;
26 $\quad$ $\rho_{i_*} \leftarrow j_*$, update τ;
27 $\quad$ **foreach** $k \in \tau$ **do**
28 $\quad\quad$ $\lambda_k \leftarrow \lambda_k + 1$;
    $\quad\quad$; $\qquad\qquad\qquad\qquad$ // additive weighting scheme
29 $\quad$ **end**
30 $\quad$ $iteration \leftarrow iteration + 1$;
31 **end**

---

3   Experimental Results

3.1   Problem Instances

We test our heuristic on a set of instances from the literature. The details of the problems are shown in Table 1. One common character of this set of instances is that the number of items in each group is the same. The number of variables in this 13 instances varies from 25 to 4000.

Table 1. Details of the test problem instances. n is the number of groups, N_i is the group size, m is the number of dimensions. $\bar{v}(P)$ is the best upper bound in the literature, for I01 to I06 $\bar{v}(P)$ is the optimal. $*$ indicates optimal.

Instance	m	N_i	m	$\bar{v}(P)$
I01	5	5	5	173*
I02	10	5	5	364*
I03	15	10	10	1602*
I04	20	10	10	3597*
I05	25	10	10	3905.7*
I06	30	10	10	4799.3*
I07	100	10	10	24604.1
I08	100	10	10	36900.6
I09	100	10	10	49190.6
I10	100	10	10	61483.5
I11	100	10	10	73795.6
I12	100	10	10	86098.8
I13	100	10	10	98446.7

3.2 Solutions from SLS_MMKP

Table 2 gives the computational comparisons between 6 different fast algorithm from the literature and our heuristic. Our algorithm is noted as SLS_MMKP, while the results from HEU [15], CPC [16], FanTabu [30], HIFI [17], Ant [21] and Osc [28] were borrowed from [28]. Our algorithm were written in C, running on an Intel(R) Core(TM) i3-3220 3.30 GHz CPU 4 GB RAM machine with 32bit Linux system. The maximum iteration number for our heuristic is set to 10^7. For each problem instance, 100 independent trials were performed with different random seeds, the results were presented as the *best* solution value found, the average solution value, number of trials finding the *best* as well as average computation time on those trials finding the *best*.

As it is shown from Table 2, for small size instances from I01 to I06, where the optima are known, our heuristic provides better solutions than HEU and CPC. It finds 5 out 6 optimal results using negligible time along with 100 % percent successful rate. For I04, though SLS_MMKP fails to achieve the optimal, its result is still better than the rest algorithms. For large instances from I07 to I13, the solutions provided by our heuristic become unstable, since they all have only one successful run in finding the corresponding *best*, but the *best* for I07, I08 and I09 are better than the rest in the table. Our heuristic obtains inferior results than *Osc* on instances I10, I11, I12 and I13, it seems that the performance of our heuristic decreases with the increase of number of variables in the test problems. It is worth to note that we directly borrow the comparison results before our algorithm from [28], where the computation times were not reported. For *Osc*, it is mentioned their results were obtained from a PC with centrino

Table 2. Solutions obtained by SLS_MMKP.

Instance	HEU	CPC	FanTabu	HIFI	ANT	OSC	SLS_MMKP			
							Best	Average	Time	#best
I01	154	159	169	173	173	173	173*	173.00	0.00	100
I02	354	312	354	364	364	364	364*	364.00	0.00	100
I03	1518	1407	1557	1602	1598	1594	1602*	1602.00	0.77	100
I04	3297	3322	3473	3569	3562	3514	**3592**	3587.70	13.72	16
I05	3894.5	3889.9	3905.7	3905.7	3905.7	3905.7	3905.7*	3905.70	0.00	100
I06	4788.2	4723.1	4799.3	4799.3	4799.3	4799.3	4799.3*	4799.30	0.00	100
I07	-	23237	2369	24159	24170	24162	**24311**	24270.06	16.48	1
I08	-	35403	35684	36401	36211	36405	**36463**	36397.86	13.28	1
I09	-	47154	47202	48367	48204	48567	**48580**	48512.09	39.17	1
I10	-	58990	58964	60475	60258	60858	*60661*	60609.18	23.71	1
I11	-	70685	70555	72558	72240	73022	*72778*	72718.31	35.42	1
I12	-	82754	81833	84707	84282	85284	*84889*	84839.34	55.99	1
I13	-	94465	94168	96834	96343	97545	*97082*	97000.42	72.79	1

1.6 GHz and 512M RAM with Windows XP system. However, Osc was using an $NumIter$ as its stopping criterion, its computation times were not reported by the authors. We further note that in Osc, there are a bunch of parameters need to be set manually, while SLS_MMKP does not have any instance dependent parameters.

4 Conclusion

We have presented a new heuristic for solving the MMKP. Our heuristic explores the idea of iterative perturbing search and a weighting scheme for dimensions. It shares similar idea with the surrogate constraint which summarize the m dimension constrains into one by a multiplier vector. However, properly adjusting the multipliers during the search is a problem itself. In this paper, we adopted a simple additive weighting increase strategy, and the experimental results are encouraging. However, we believe there are still future work could be done to further improve our heuristic, such as tabu strategies that consider the information of frequency and recency of items in the candidate solution, although this may introduce instance dependent parameters to our heuristic while improving the effectiveness of this algorithm.

References

1. Martello, S., Toth, P.: Algorithms for knapsack problems. North-Holland Math. Stud. **132**, 213–257 (1987)
2. Sinha, P., Zoltners, A.A.: The multiple-choice knapsack problem. Oper. Res. **27**(3), 503–515 (1979)

3. Chu, P.C., Beasley, J.E.: A genetic algorithm for the multidimensional knapsack problem. J. Heuristics **4**(1), 63–86 (1998)
4. Basnet, C., Wilson, J.: Heuristics for determining the number of warehouses for storing non-compatible products. Int. Trans. Oper. Res. **12**(5), 527–538 (2005)
5. Ykman-Couvreur, C., Nollet, V., Catthoor, F., Corporaal, H.: Fast multi-dimension multi-choice knapsack heuristic for MP-SoC run-time management. In: International Symposium on System-on-Chip, pp. 1–4. IEEE (2006)
6. Shojaei, H., Wu, T.H., Davoodi, A., Basten, T.: A pareto-algebraic framework for signal power optimization in global routing. In: Proceedings of the 16th ACM/IEEE International Symposium on Low Power Electronics and Design, pp. 407–412. ACM (2010)
7. Yu, T., Zhang, Y., Lin, K.J.: Efficient algorithms for web services selection with end-to-end QoS constraints. ACM Trans. Web (TWEB) **1**(1), 6 (2007)
8. Pisinger, D.: Budgeting with bounded multiple-choice constraints. Eur. J. Oper. Res. **129**(3), 471–480 (2001)
9. Li, V., Curry, G.L., Boyd, E.A.: Towards the real time solution of strike force asset allocation problems. Comput. Oper. Res. **31**(2), 273–291 (2004)
10. Ghasemi, T., Razzazi, M.: Development of core to solve the multidimensional multiple-choice knapsack problem. Comput. Indus. Eng. **60**(2), 349–360 (2011)
11. Khan, S.: Quality adaptation in a multi-session adaptive multimedia system: model and architecture. Ph.D. thesis, Department of Electronical and Computer Engineering, University of Victoria, Canada (1998)
12. Sbihi, A.: A best first search exact algorithm for the multiple-choice multidimensional knapsack problem. J. Comb. Optim. **13**(4), 337–351 (2007)
13. Moser, M., Jokanovic, D.P., Shiratori, N.: An algorithm for the multidimensional multiple-choice knapsack problem. IEICE Trans. Fundam. Electr. Commun. Comput. Sci. **80**(3), 582–589 (1997)
14. Akbar, M.M., Manning, E.G., Shoja, G.C., Khan, S.: Heuristic solutions for the multiple-choice multi-dimension knapsack problem. In: Alexandrov, V.N., Dongarra, J., Juliano, B.A., Renner, R.S., Tan, C.J.K. (eds.) ICCS-ComputSci 2001. LNCS, vol. 2074, pp. 659–668. Springer, Heidelberg (2001)
15. Khan, S., Li, K.F., Manning, E.G., Akbar, M.M.: Solving the knapsack problem for adaptive multimedia systems. Stud. Inform. Univ. **2**(1), 157–178 (2002)
16. Hifi, M., Michrafy, M., Sbihi, A.: Heuristic algorithms for the multiple-choice multidimensional knapsack problem. J. Oper. Res. Soc. **55**(12), 1323–1332 (2004)
17. Hifi, M., Michrafy, M., Sbihi, A.: A reactive local search-based algorithm for the multiple-choice multi-dimensional knapsack problem. Comput. Optim. Appl. **33**(2–3), 271–285 (2006)
18. Cherfi, N., Hifi, M.: A column generation method for the multiple-choice multidimensional knapsack problem. Comput. Optim. Appl. **46**(1), 51–73 (2010)
19. Cherfi, N., Hifi, M.: Hybrid algorithms for the multiple-choice multi-dimensional knapsack problem. Int. J. Oper. Res. **5**(1), 89–109 (2009)
20. Iqbal, S., Bari, M.F., Rahman, M.S.: Solving the multi-dimensional multi-choice knapsack problem with the help of ants. In: Dorigo, M., et al. (eds.) ANTS 2010. LNCS, vol. 6234, pp. 312–323. Springer, Heidelberg (2010)
21. Ren, Z., Feng, Z.: An ant colony optimization approach to the multiple-choice multidimensional knapsack problem. In: Proceedings of the 12th Annual Conference on Genetic and Evolutionary Computation, pp. 281–288. ACM (2010)

22. Shojaei, H., Ghamarian, A., Basten, T., Geilen, M., Stuijk, S., Hoes, R.: A parameterized compositional multi-dimensional multiple-choice knapsack heuristic for cmp run-time management. In: Proceedings of the 46th Annual Design Automation Conference, pp. 917–922. ACM (2009)
23. Hanafi, S., Mansi, R., Wilbaut, C.: Iterative relaxation-based heuristics for the multiple-choice multidimensional knapsack problem. In: Blesa, M.J., Blum, C., Di Gaspero, L., Roli, A., Sampels, M., Schaerf, A. (eds.) HM 2009. LNCS, vol. 5818, pp. 73–83. Springer, Heidelberg (2009)
24. Crévits, I., Hanafi, S., Mansi, R., Wilbaut, C.: Iterative semi-continuous relaxation heuristics for the multiple-choice multidimensional knapsack problem. Comput. Oper. Res. **39**(1), 32–41 (2012)
25. Mansi, R., Alves, C., Valério de Carvalho, J., Hanafi, S.: A hybrid heuristic for the multiple choice multidimensional knapsack problem. Eng. Optim. **45**(8), 983–1004 (2013)
26. Chen, Y., Hao, J.K.: A "reduce and solve" approach for the multiple-choice multidimensional knapsack problem. Eur. J. Oper. Res. **239**(2), 313–322 (2014)
27. Shojaei, H., Basten, T., Geilen, M., Davoodi, A.: A fast and scalable multidimensional multiple-choice knapsack heuristic. ACM Trans. Des. Autom. Electron. Syst. **18**(4), 51:1–51:32 (2013)
28. Htiouech, S., Bouamama, S., Attia, R.: Using surrogate information to solve the multidimensional multi-choice knapsack problem. In: 2013 IEEE Congress on Evolutionary Computation (CEC), pp. 2102–2107. IEEE (2013)
29. Toyoda, Y.: A simplified algorithm for obtaining approximate solutions to zero-one programming problems. Manag. Sci. **21**(12), 1417–1427 (1975)
30. Hiremath, C.S., Hill, R.R.: New greedy heuristics for the multiple-choice multidimensional knapsack problem. Int. J. Oper. Res. **2**(4), 495–512 (2007)

An Investigation of Hybrid Tabu Search for the Traveling Salesman Problem

Dan Xu[1], Thomas Weise[1]([✉]), Yuezhong Wu[1], Jörg Lässig[2],
and Raymond Chiong[3]

[1] Joint USTC-Birmingham Research Institute in Intelligent Computation and Its
Applications (UBRI), School of Computer Science and Technology,
University of Science and Technology of China, Hefei 230027, Anhui, China
{dandy,yuezhong}@mail.ustc.edu.cn, tweise@ustc.edu.cn
[2] Department of Computer Science, Enterprise Application Development Group,
University of Applied Sciences Zittau/Görlitz, 02826 Görlitz, Germany
jlaessig@hszg.de
[3] School of Design, Communication and IT, Faculty of Science and IT,
The University of Newcastle, Callaghan, NSW 2308, Australia
Raymond.Chiong@newcastle.edu.au

Abstract. The Traveling Salesman Problem (TSP) is one of the most
well-known problems in combinatorial optimization. Due to its $\mathcal{NP}$-
hardness, research has focused on approximate methods like metaheuristics. Tabu Search (TS) is a very efficient metaheuristic for combinatorial
problems. We investigate four different versions of TS with different tabu
objects and compare them to the Lin-Kernighan (LK) heuristic as well
as the recently developed Multi-Neighborhood Search (MNS). LK is currently considered to be the best approach for solving the TSP, while
MNS has shown to be highly competitive. We then propose new hybrid
algorithms by hybridizing TS with Evolutionary Algorithms and Ant
Colony Optimization. These hybrids are compared to similar hybrids
based on LK and MNS. This paper presents the first statistically sound
and comprehensive comparison taking the entire optimization processes
of (hybrid) TS, LK, and MNS into consideration based on a large-scale
experimental study. We show that our new hybrid TS algorithms are
highly efficient and comparable to the state-of-the-art algorithms along
this line of research.

Keywords: Traveling Salesman Problem · Tabu Search · Evolutionary
Algorithms · Ant Colony Optimization · Memetic Algorithms

1 Introduction

The Traveling Salesman Problem (TSP) [1–4] is perhaps the most-studied optimization problem. Given n cities, a salesman leaves from a start city, visits each
of the other cities exactly once, and returns back to the start city. The tour
of the salesman thus forms a cyclic path passing through each node in a fully-
connected graph of n nodes exactly once. In the graph, each edge from city i to

© Springer-Verlag Berlin Heidelberg 2015
M. Gong et al. (Eds.): BIC-TA 2015, CCIS 562, pp. 523–537, 2015.
DOI: 10.1007/978-3-662-49014-3_47

city j has a weight $D_{i,j}$, which represents the distance. The task is to find a tour (path) that yields the minimal total weight sum.

The TSP has been researched for decades. The optimization version of it is $\mathcal{NP}$-hard [3], so the worst-case runtime complexity of any exact TSP solver is exponential [5]. As exactly solving the TSP is not generally feasible, many approximate algorithms such as Evolutionary Algorithms (EAs) [6–8] and Ant Colony Optimization (ACO) [9–11] have been introduced to tackle it. The Lin-Kernighan (LK) heuristic [12], a Local Search (LS) method, and its derivatives are considered to be the best performers for the TSP. In [13], an alternative approach known as Multi-Neighborhood Search (MNS) was introduced and found to be a more efficient LS approach for the TSP than, e.g., Variable Neighborhood Search [14] or Hill Climbing. MNS has also been shown to perform better than pure EAs and Population-based ACO (PACO) [15].

Tabu Search (TS) [16,17] is one of the most widely known metaheuristics for combinatorial problems and is able to provide high-quality solutions for many problems. An EA hybridized with TS is shown to outperform pure TS on small-scale TSP instances in [18].

The TSP is an ideal testbed for investigating and comparing new algorithms' performances, since it is easy to understand and standard benchmarks with known solutions (like the *TSPLib*[19]) are available. Additionally, there is a large body of related work involving both the TSP and TS. However, virtually all of them either only focused on small-scale problems, only compared different parameter settings of the same tabu object [20] or did not apply sound statistics to evaluate their results.

With the present work, we make the following contributions:

1. A full in-depth analysis of the performance of a TS algorithm *over runtime* on all 110 of the symmetric *TSPLib* benchmark instances. The analysis is based on both small-scale and large-scale instances, several different performance metrics, and several different ways to measure runtime.
2. The comparison of three different tabu criteria as well as two different ways to search the neighborhood of the current solution in TS.
3. A detailed comparison of TS to state-of-the-art LS algorithms such as LK and MNS.
4. The introduction of two novel hybrid forms of the investigated TS algorithm based on both EAs and ACO.
5. A detailed comparison of these hybrid TS algorithms to hybrid variants of the above-mentioned LS approaches constructed in the same way as those of TS.

The remainder of this paper is organized as follows. We first discuss related work on automated experimentation (Sect. 2.1) and the TSP (Sect. 2.2). We then present our TS approach, the three tabu criteria and new hybrid algorithms in Sect. 3. Our large-scale experimental study is discussed in Sect. 4 and conclusions as well as future work are given in Sect. 5.

2 Related Work

The focus of this paper is not only to introduce new TS algorithms for the TSP, but also on sound experimentation. Before outlining the state-of-the-art TSP algorithms, we discuss the nature of these algorithms and how they influence the experimental approach.

2.1 Related Work on Experimentation

All LS methods and most metaheuristics (e.g., EAs, ACO) are anytime algorithms [21]. Even some exact methods, like Branch and Bound (BB) [22], belong to this category. Anytime algorithms can provide a best guess of what the optimal solution of a problem could be at *any time* during their run. LS methods, for instance, begin with a random solution and iteratively refine it. Given a TSP instance, BB would maintain the best solution discovered so far and investigate a set of other solutions only if the lower bound for their tour length is better than the actual tour length of that best-so-far solution. If an anytime algorithm $\mathcal{A}$ provides a better final solution than another anytime algorithm $\mathcal{B}$, does this make $\mathcal{A}$ better? The traditional answer would be *yes*, but what if the best guess of $\mathcal{A}$ for the solution is much worse than $\mathcal{B}$'s until after a very long (run)time? Due to their nature, anytime algorithms thus cannot be assessed just by a final solution and runtime requirement, but by their entire runtime behavior [13].

In the field of metaheuristic optimization, experimentation is the most important tool to assess and compare the performance of different algorithms. Even though this has been the case for a long time, experimentation approaches adopted in most of the existing studies rely mainly on the most basic statistics, some of which are even flawed [13]. Proper experimentation is a complex, time-demanding and cumbersome process.

The *COmparing Continuous Optimisers* (COCO) [23] system for numerical optimization, used in the Black-Box Optimization Benchmarking workshops, is one of the earliest approaches aiming to reduce the workload of an experimenter by automatizing most of the steps involved in an experimentation process. Its evaluation procedure generates statically structured papers that contain diagrams with runtime behavior information. The necessary data is automatically collected from executed experiments.

UBCSAT [24], an experimental framework for satisfiability problems, is another representative example of work in this area. UBCSAT focuses on a specific family of algorithms: the Stochastic LS [25]. In COCO, the objective function would automatically gather log data before returning its result to the algorithm. In UBCSAT, this would be done through a trigger architecture, which can also compute complex statistics online and provide them to the running algorithm. COCO and UBCSAT both explore algorithm behavior over runtime instead of just comparing end results.

The *TSP Suite* [13] used for running the experiments in our work takes the idea one step further. First, it provides software development support such as unit testing. Second, it takes care of parallelization or distribution of workload on a multi-processor system or cluster. Third, like in COCO, an algorithm performance report can be created automatically. The difference, however, is that it includes an in-depth description of the experimental procedure and presents several different statistical analyses, such as statistical tests comparing the measured runtimes and end results, automated comparisons of the estimated running time (ERT) [23] curves over goal objective values or problem scales, and automated comparisons of empirical cumulative distribution functions (ECDFs) [23,24,26]. All of these statistics result in algorithm rankings, which are later aggregated into a global ranking list. The global ranking provides some insights on the general performance of a TSP solver.

Our *TSP Suite* is the first framework addressing the issue of runtime measures. Traditionally, runtime is either measured in CPU seconds or the number of generated candidate solutions (i.e., objective "function evaluations" or FEs in short). The problem with using CPU time as time measure is that results obtained on different machines are inherently incomparable, while the number of generated candidate solutions gives no information about the actual runtime of an algorithm, since 1 FE may have different computational complexities in different algorithms. For instance, in a LS algorithm or a mutation operator in an EA, a new solution may be obtained from an existing tour of known length by swapping two cities, which has the complexity of $\mathcal{O}(1)$. In ACO, the creation of one new solution has time complexity $\mathcal{O}(n^2)$. In the *TSP Suite*, these shortcomings have been addressed by introducing two new time measures: the normalized runtime (NT) and the number of times the distance matrix D is accessed (distance evaluations, DEs). The NT is the CPU time divided by a specific performance factor based on machine and problem instances, thus rendering (somewhat) machine independent time measure results. The DEs take into account the different complexities of 1 FE in different algorithms. Statistical analyses through the *TSP Suite* are all conducted three times, based on the FE, NT, and DE respectively. The algorithm ranking created therefore represents a more balanced and fair perspective of an algorithm's performance.

2.2   Related Work on the Traveling Salesman Problem

A large body of work on the TSP exists, but the relevant literature focuses mainly on single-algorithm end result comparisons and rarely takes into account algorithms of different families. Notable exceptions for the latter can be found in [27,28], while the runtime behavior of different pure and hybrid metaheuristics as well as LS methods were studied in [13]. BB, LS and Evolutionary Computation (EC) methods were considered in [22], and the state-of-the-art LS methods LK and MNS were compared in [29].

Generally speaking, LS algorithms dominate the research on TSP. They start at a random or heuristically-generated solution. They remember the best solution discovered so far and try to improve it. These improvements usually take place in the form of modifications to the tour. The most prominent examples of such modifications within the TSP domain are m-opt moves [13]: the exchange of two cities in a tour, for instance, corresponds to the deletion and addition of four edges ($m = 4$-opt) [30,31], the rotation of a sub-sequence of cities to the left or right results in the deletion and addition of three edges (3-opt) [30,32], while the reversal of a sub-sequence of a tour requires deleting and adding two edges (2-opt) [30,33]. However, LS is likely to be trapped by local optima.

TS [16,34] is a LS method attempting to avoid this premature convergence problem. In the last 30 years, TS was used to solve the TSP and its variants several times as discussed in the comprehensive survey by Basu [20]. According to Basu's survey, most of the past TS-related studies have focused on just small-scale TSP instances with no comparison of different tabu criteria, and typically used only brittle end-of-run statistics. To fill this gap, we will conduct a large-scale experimental study considering problem instances with more than 1000 nodes. We will also compare different tabu objects and final results with robust statistical tests before applying statistics over the entire optimization processes. In Sect. 3.1, where our algorithm and its components are introduced, we will provide additional references to corresponding related studies on TS for the TSP.

3   Investigated Algorithms

3.1   Tabu Search

In each iteration, a LS algorithm will look for a better solution s' in the neighborhood $N(s)$ of the current (best) solution s. $N(s)$ is spanned by the available search operators. For a very simple LS algorithm that only accepts s' when it is better than s, the algorithm is likely to get trapped in a local optimum, i.e., a solution whose neighborhood does not contain any better solution while itself is not the globally optimal one.

To prevent this, the LS algorithm should be able to accept a move from s to s' even if s' is worse than s – Simulated Annealing [35] is an example of such an algorithm. However, this may lead to a "cycling" effect in the search space, if the move leading out of the local optimum is undone in the next algorithm iteration. TS therefore incorporates a memory structure, called tabu list T, to forbid certain moves that would return to a recently visited solution. Instead of searching the neighborhood $N(s)$ of s, TS investigates $N(s)\backslash T$. For this general procedure, we analyze the performance impact of the following design criteria.

Tabu Object. One design criterion for TS is the data structure that is used to represent prohibited solutions and the tabu list. We investigate three such tabu criteria [36]:

Solutions. The simplest way is to "tabu" solutions that have been accepted in the process of the algorithm. Our implementation does this by forbidding not only a specific solution, such as $(1, 2, 3, 4, 5)$, but also all *equivalent* solutions in the symmetric TSP, such as $(5, 4, 3, 2, 1)$, $(3, 4, 5, 1, 2)$ or $(4, 3, 2, 1, 5)$. T here is implemented as a hash table with $\mathcal{O}(n)$ cost to compute the hash code of a tour. We refer to TS using this method as TSS.

Moves. We also prevent certain *moves*, i.e., applications of search operators, that could lead back to a recently visited solution. Our TS uses three different search operators, namely 2-, 3-, and 4-opt, each of which has a tuple of two node indexes as parameters. We implement this tabu object by storing the nodes corresponding to the indexes in T and preventing using them again for the tabu tenure. If we apply a 2-opt move (sub-tour reversal) at index 2 and 4 to tour $(5, 3, 2, 1, 4)$, we would get $(5, 1, 2, 3, 4)$ and prevent the two nodes 3 and 1 from being the start or end node of subsequent moves. We refer to TS using this method as TSM.

Objective Values. We forbid repetitive objective values, i.e., tour lengths. If a tour with length 783 is discovered, then for the tabu tenure $|T|$, the search must not move to any tour with the same length (regardless of whether this tour is the one previously discovered, equivalent to it, or entirely different). We refer to TS using this method as TSO.

Tabu Tenure. The number of times (algorithm iterations) a certain move or solution is prohibited by the tabu list is called the tabu tenure. It corresponds to the maximum amount of elements in T. This tenure can be either fixed or based on the problem scale. We compare both methods in our study. In the notation of setup names used in our experiments, we append a tuple $(\alpha + \gamma)$ to the algorithm names, e.g., TSO(10 + 10). The tabu tenure then equals $\alpha + \gamma\sqrt{n}$, i.e., α is an absolute value and γ will be multiplied by the square root of the problem scale.

Soft Restarts. If the algorithm cannot improve its best solution any further, it can be restarted. Instead of restarting at a completely random solution, we randomly shuffle a uniformly chosen part of the current best solution. This policy, introduced by us in [13], leads to sufficient randomness while having a chance of preserving some good building blocks. At a restart, the tabu list T will *not* be emptied. This means two restarts that happen to start at the same solution (by chance) will still take different paths in the search space.

Investigating the Neighborhood. In TS, the non-tabu neighborhood $N(s) - T$ of the current solution s is scanned for a better solution s'. If no such solution can be found, our algorithms will immediately perform a soft restart (see above). For all three tabu objects, we search the entire neighborhood for the best possible s'. An alternative way is to search the neighborhood and if an s' better than s is discovered then accept that one immediately. Since this approach is often considered as inferior [29, 37], we only test it for the solution tabu object setups. We refer to it as TSF.

3.2   The Lin-Kernighan Algorithm

The LK heuristic [12] and its derivatives dominate today's TSP research [37–39]. A tour can be considered as β-optimal when it is impossible to improve the tour quality by replacing β edges. LK can be considered as a variable β-opt LS. At each step, the algorithm tests whether replacing β edges may achieve a shorter tour (for increasing values of β). Let s be the current tour. The algorithm will then, in each iteration, construct the sets $X = \{X_1, \ldots, X_\beta\}$ of edges to be deleted from s and $Y = \{Y_1, \ldots, Y_\beta\}$ of edges to be added to s, such that the resulting tour would be valid and shorter. The interchange of these edges is then a β-opt move. In the beginning, X and Y are empty. Pairs of edges are added to X and Y such that the end node of the edge added to X is the start node of the edge added to Y, whose end node will then become the start node of the edge added to X in the next iteration, if any. The LK heuristic we compare our TS to is based on that by Wu et al. [29], which uses the restart policy defined in [13], the same as our TS.

3.3 Multi-neighborhood Search

MNS is another efficient LS method for the TSP. In each iteration, MNS performs an $\mathcal{O}(n^2)$ scan that investigates the same neighborhoods as our TS at once. It therefore tests all indexes i and j as potential indexes of start or end of a search operation. For each pair $\{i, j\}$, the gain of each operation is computed and all discovered improving moves enter a queue. The access to distance matrix D is minimized by remembering (and updating) the lengths of all n edges in the current tour and avoiding the check of redundant moves (swapping the cities at indexes i and $i+1$ is equivalent to a reversal of the sub-sequence from i to $i+1$, for instance).

After the scan, the best discovered move is carried out. Doing this may invalidate some other moves in the queue, e.g., a sub-sequence reversal performed overlaps with a potential sub-sequence left rotation. After pruning all invalidated moves from the queue, the remaining best move is carried out, if any. If the queue becomes empty, another scan of the current solution will be performed, as new moves may have become possible. During this scan, only moves that at least intersect with the previously modified sub-sequence(s) of the current best solution need to be considered in order to speed up the search. If no improving moves can be found anymore, a random sub-sequence of the current tour will be randomly shuffled – the same soft restart method as used in our TS and LK.

MNS scans for all 2-opt and some 3- and 4-opt moves, thus investigates the same neighborhoods as our TS. LK, on the other hand, investigates a larger sub-set of possible m-opt moves.

3.4 Evolutionary Algorithms

EAs are population-based EC methods that start by generating a set of λ random solutions. Out of these, the best $\mu \leq \lambda$ solutions are selected as "parents" of the second generation: λ offspring are created by applying either a unary (mutation) or binary (crossover) operator to the parents. From then on, the μ best individuals are selected from the λ offspring and their μ parents in each generation in the case of a $(\mu + \lambda)$-EA. A (μ, λ)-EA selects only from the μ

offspring. In this paper, we investigate such EAs using the neighborhoods also used by our TS as mutation operators. Edge Crossover [40], which generates a new solution by picking edges belonging to either of its two parents, is applied as the recombination operator at a crossover rate of 1/3.

Hybridization of LS and EAs has a long tradition. Such hybrid algorithms, where the LS algorithm either takes the place of the mutation operator or is applied to each new solution (stemming from mutation or crossover), are called Memetic Algorithms (MAs). Especially in the TSP domain, MAs are considered to perform well. We propose MAs based on our TS, so called hMA($\mu \stackrel{+}{,} \lambda$)TS, and compare them with likewise-structured hybrids using LK and MNS as LS. The little h in the name indicates that the first population of the MAs is not generated randomly, but instead stemmed from the Edge-Greedy, Double Minimum Spanning Tree, Savings, Double-Ended Nearest Neighbor, and Nearest Neighbor Heuristics, as in [13].

3.5 Ant Colony Optimization

ACO is another EC approach first introduced by Dorigo in 1992 [9]. It took inspiration from the way ants find and reinforce short paths during foraging using pheromones for communication. Although such algorithms are able to perform well in many small-scale combinatorial problems, they suffer from quadratic memory requirements as well as quadratic complexity of the process of creating solutions.

In this paper, we investigate a state-of-the-art ACO variant, Population-based ACO (PACO) [15], which has linear memory requirements. The PACO algorithm maintains a population of k solutions. Pheromones are defined by the edges occurring in these solutions. In each algorithm iteration, m solutions are created as in standard ACO and the "oldest" solution in the whole population is replaced by the best of the new generated solutions. Limited hybrid ACO approaches have been applied to the TSP, although it was shown in [13] that they perform particularly well. We therefore propose hybrid hPACO(k, m)TS and similar variants with LK and MNS (which are heuristically initialized in the same way as the hMAs).

4   Experiments and Results

4.1   Experimental Setup

We conducted experiments using the symmetric *TSPLib* benchmark cases, for which all optima are known. We thus can measure the quality of a solution as relative error f, i.e., the factor by which a solution (tour) is longer than the optimum. Here, $f = 0$ stands for the optimal solution, and $f = 1$ indicates one that is twice as long. We obtained results for all 110 problem instances up to 85,900 cities, and we considered all the results in the evaluation.

A total of 45 TS setups were built: 25 pure algorithms, 10 hybrids with PACO, and 10 hybrid MAs. For each type of the tabu objects, we tested seven tabu tenure settings: $(10+0)$, $(100+0)$, $(500+0)$, $(10000+0)$, $(0+10)$, $(0+20)$, and $(0+40)$. For TSF, we only tested four tabu tenure settings: $(10+0)$, $(100+0)$, $(500+0)$, and $(10000+0)$. For the hybrid algorithms, we tested the best known settings from [13], i.e., hPACO(3,10) and hMA(16+64). We hybridized them with all four TSF settings and tabu tenures $(10+10)$ and $(500+0)$ for each of the three tabu criteria.

Additionally, we investigated the pure LK and MNS as well as hybrids of PACO with LK and MNS. Obviously, there are too many setups to present all of them in a single plot. Therefore, we divided our analysis into comparisons of pure and hybrid algorithms. We present only the setups that have performed the best in our experiments each time.

4.2 Pure Algorithm Performance

Let us first explore the performance of the pure TS algorithms. In Fig. 1, we plot the ECDF for different goal errors F_t and runtime measures. The ECDF illustrates the fraction of runs that have discovered a solution with $F_b \leq F_t$ at a given point in time. If the ECDF reaches 1, all runs have found such a solution. In Fig. 2, we plot the best normalized objective value F_b discovered by an algorithm over runtime, where $F_b = 0$ means that the global optimal has been reached and $F_b = 1$ indicates the discovery of a tour twice as long.

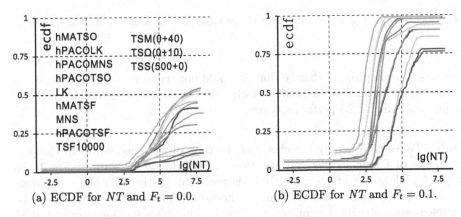

(a) ECDF for NT and $F_t = 0.0$.   (b) ECDF for NT and $F_t = 0.1$.

Fig. 1. ECDF diagrams for different (log-scaled) runtime measures and goal errors.

Tabu Object. We first analyze the three types of tabu criteria introduced in Sect. 3.1. In Fig. 1, whether based on runtime measure NT or FE, the ECDF of TSO increases faster in the beginning and reaches higher end values. TSM and TSS are not distinguishable.

Figure 2 shows the improvement of solution quality over time, As can be seen, all three criteria have very similar performances. A tabu object actually begins to control the search at a relatively late stage, at the point when the algorithm

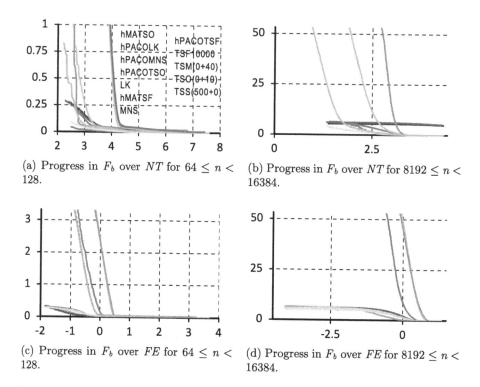

Fig. 2. Progress diagrams for different (log-scaled) time measures and problem scales.

reaches a local optimum (before that, it would not try to visit the same solution twice). It seems that at this point, which is not visible in Fig. 2 (due to the large range of y-axis), TSO performs better.

Tabu Tenure. Not only the choice of the tabu object contributes to the performance of TS algorithms, but also the choice of the tabu tenure. In Fig. 3, the seven ECDF curves of TS using the objective value as the tabu object separate into two groups depending on whether the tabu tenure is fixed or based on the problem scale. In the beginning, the two groups share similar curves, but in the end, the algorithms using the problem-scale based tabu tenure reach higher ECDF values.

However, the impact of tabu tenure strongly depends on the tabu object. In the experiments, we see that the best settings for the three different types of tabu objects are TSM$(0 + 20)$, TSO$(0 + 10)$, and TSS$(500 + 0)$.

Investigating the Neighborhood. The most interesting finding in this set of experiments is that the way our TS algorithms search the neighborhood has a huge impact on the performance. In Fig. 1, TSF has much better performance than the TS algorithms that accept only the best solution in the neighborhood. Its curve rises the fastest in the beginning and reaches the highest ECDF in the end among all the TS algorithms. This proves that it can solve the most benchmark instances.

Comparison with LK and MNS. In Fig. 1, we see that LK always as higher ECDF values than TS and MNS in the end. MNS starts a little faster in the beginning but its ECDF in the end is lower than TS and LK. All in all, we find that the best TS setup is better than MNS and worse than LK. Consequently, the *TSP Suite* ranks the algorithms as follows: LK, TSF, TSO(0 + 10), MNS, TSS(500 + 0), and TSM(0 + 20).

4.3 Hybrid Algorithm Performance

We also investigated our newly proposed hybridized versions of TS with EAs and PACO. Both of the hybrids were tested using two different settings for each of TSS, TSO and TSM, as well as four different settings for TSF. We compared them with the best known settings of the hybrid versions of LK and MNS, namely hPACO(3,10)LK and hPACO(3,10)MNS.

Two of the best hybrid setups for TS accepting only the best solution in the neighborhood in each iteration are hPACO(3, 10)TSO(10+10) and hMA(16+64) TSO(10 + 10). For TSF, the best settings are hPACO(3, 10)TSF(10+0) and hMA(16 + 64)TSF(10+0).

Interestingly, in our experiments, the best tabu tenure for pure TSF is 10000, but for hybrid TSF it is 10. A potential reason for this could be that operators

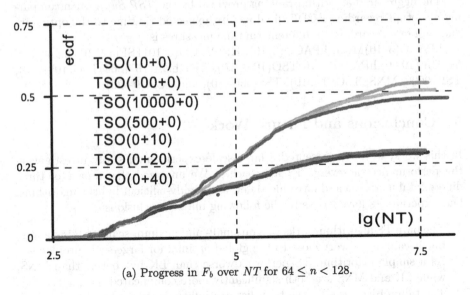

(a) Progress in F_b over NT for $64 \leq n < 128$.

Fig. 3. ECDF diagrams for different (log-scaled) runtime measures and goal errors.

of the EA, such as crossover and selection, already somewhat avoid convergence and a long tabu list would require more runtime for less additional benefits in a hybrid algorithm.

From Fig. 1, we can see significant improvement of TS after being hybridized with EAs and PACO. The hybrids of TS outperform pure TS both in terms of speed and end results: the ECDF curves of the hybrids start slightly earlier, increase more rapidly, and finally reach at higher end points than those of the pure algorithms. The pure TSO is able to solve less than 20 % of the benchmark instances, while hPACO(3, 10)TSO can solve almost 45 % and hMA(2, 4)TSO 41 %, making PACO the better global optimization method to hybridize TS with than an EA.

The same observations can be made with the hybrids of LK and MNS. We see that hPACO(3, 10)LK and hPACO(3, 10)MNS outperform the pure LK and MNS significantly. Besides that, hPACO(3, 10)LK and hPACO(3, 10)MNS perform better than hPACO(3, 10)TS.

When we set $F_t = 0.1$, the hybrid algorithms again outperform the pure ones and can reach ECDF values higher than 0.9. The PACO hybrids of TSO and TSF behave very similarly to the MAs. The hybrids of TSF even start earlier than hPACO(3, 10)LK. If we measure time with FE, the hybrids of TSO start the earliest among the investigated algorithms.

From Fig. 2, we see that the hybrids algorithms always start at a lower F_b, mainly due to their heuristic initialization. For small-scale problems, both the hybrids and pure algorithms can decrease F_b towards 0 quickly, i.e., find the optima quickly. However, in large-scale problems (Fig. 2b), the hybrids of TSO start at a lower F_b and barely decrease it, while pure TSO gets a smaller F_b in the end.

The aggregated algorithm ranking provided by the *TSP Suite* when comparing all setups regarding ECDF, final results, expected runtime to the optimum, and progress according to different runtime measures is:

hPACO(3, 10)MNS, hPACO(3, 10)LK, hPACO(3, 10)TSF(10+0), hEA(16 + 64)TSF(10+0),hPACO(3, 10)TSO(10 + 10), LK, hEA(16 + 64)TSO(10 + 10), TSF10000, MNS, TSO(0 + 10), TSS(500 + 0), and TSM(0+20).

5   Conclusions and Future Work

In this work, we have presented a large-scale experimental study investigating the performance of several TS approaches. We analyzed the impact of three different tabu criteria and introduced new and highly-efficient hybrid algorithms. Our experiments have led us to the following major conclusions:

1. The pure TS algorithm works well on small- and medium-scale TSP instances, but it cannot get very close to the global optimal for large-scale problems.
2. As a simple algorithm, TS performs worse than LK but better than MNS, while LK and MNS are both significantly more complicated.
3. The tabu object used in the tabu list can influence the performance.

4. Using a tabu object that forbids repeating objective values works better than forbidding candidate solutions, even though the relevant literature has focused largely on the latter.
5. Hybridization provides some considerable performance improvement.
6. Hybrid PACO works better than MAs (hybrid EAs), although the relevant literature has focused largely on the latter.

We will continue to investigate TS algorithms on the TSP. We next plan to implement additional tabu criteria mentioned in the literature such as [16]. In addition, we will try more strategies to improve the performance of TS.

Acknowledgments. We acknowledge support from the Fundamental Research Funds for the Central Universities, the National Natural Science Foundation of China under Grant 6115 0110488, Special Financial Grant 201104329 from the China Postdoctoral Science Foundation, the Chinese Academy of Sciences (CAS) Fellowship for Young International Scientists 2011Y1GB01, and the European Union 7th Framework Program under Grant 247619. The experiments reported in this paper were executed on the supercomputing system in the Supercomputing Center of University of Science and Technology of China.

References

1. Applegate, D.L., Bixby, R.E., Chvátal, V., Cook, W.J.: The Traveling Salesman Problem: A Computational Study. Princeton University Press, Princeton (2007)
2. Lawler, E.L., Lenstra, J.K., Rinnooy Kan, A.H.G., Shmoys, D.B.: The Traveling Salesman Problem: A Guided Tour of Combinatorial Optimization. Wiley Interscience, Chichester (1985)
3. Gutin, G.Z., Punnen, A.P. (eds.): The Traveling Salesman Problem and its Variations. Kluwer Academic Publishers, Norwell (2002)
4. Jiang, H., Sun, W., Ren, Z., Lai, X., Piao, Y.: Evolving hard and easy traveling salesman problem instances: a multi-objective approach. In: Dick, G., Browne, W.N., Whigham, P., Zhang, M., Bui, L.T., Ishibuchi, H., Jin, Y., Li, X., Shi, Y., Singh, P., Tan, K.C., Tang, K. (eds.) SEAL 2014. LNCS, vol. 8886, pp. 216–227. Springer, Heidelberg (2014)
5. Woeginger, G.J.: Exact algorithms for np-hard problems: a survey. In: Revised Papers of the 5th International Works on Combinatorial Optimization, pp. 185–207. Springer, Aussois (2001)
6. Weise, T.: Global Optimization Algorithms - Theory and Application. Self-Published, Germany (it-weise.de) (2009)
7. Bäck, T., Fogel, D.B., Michalewicz, Z. (eds.): Handbook of Evolutionary Computation. Oxford University Press, New York (1997)
8. De Jong, K.A.: Evolutionary Computation: A Unified Approach. MIT Press, Cambridge (2006)
9. Dorigo, M.: Optimization, Learning and Natural Algorithms, Ph.D. thesis. Dipartimento di Elettronica, Politecnico di Milano, Milano (1992)
10. Dorigo, M., Birattari, M., Stützle, T.: Ant colony optimization - artificial ants as a computational intelligence technique. IEEE Comput. Intell. Mag. 1(4), 28–39 (2006)

11. Gambardella, L.M., Dorigo, M.: Solving symmetric and asymmetric tsps by ant colonies. In: Proceedings of IEEE International Conference on Evolutionary Computation, pp. 622–627. Nagoya, 20–22 May 1996
12. Lin, S., Kernighan, B.W.: An effective heuristic algorithm for the traveling-salesman problem. Oper. Res. **21**(2), 498–516 (1973)
13. Weise, T., Chiong, R., Tang, K., Lässig, J., Tsutsui, S., Chen, W., Michalewicz, Z., Yao, X.: Benchmarking optimization algorithms: an open source framework for the traveling salesman problem. IEEE Comput. Intell. Mag. **9**(3), 40–52 (2014)
14. Hansen, P., Mladenović, N., Moreno Pérez, J.A.: Variable neighbourhood search: methods and applications. Ann. Oper. Res. **175**(1), 367–407 (2010)
15. Guntsch, M., Middendorf, M.: Applying population based aco to dynamic optimization problems. In: Proceedings of the 3rd International Works on Ant Colony Optimization, pp. 111–122. Brussels (2002)
16. Glover, F.W., Taillard, É.D., de Werra, D.: A user's guide to tabu search. Ann. Oper. Res. **41**(1), 3–28 (1993)
17. Misevičius, A.: Using iterated tabu search for the traveling salesman problem. Inf. Technol. Control **32**(3), 29–40 (2015)
18. Osaba, E., Diaz, F.: Comparison of a memetic algorithm and a tabu search algorithm for the traveling salesman problem. In: 2012 Federated Conference on Computer Science and Information Systems, pp. 131–136 (2012)
19. Reinelt, G.: Tsplib 95. Technical report. Universität Heidelberg, Institut für Mathematik, Heidelberg (1995)
20. Basu, S.: Tabu search implementation on traveling salesman problem and its variations: a literature survey. Am. J. Oper. Res. **2**(2), 163–173 (2012)
21. Boddy, M.S., Dean, T.L.: Solving time-dependent planning problems. Technical report CS-89-03. Brown University, Providence (1989)
22. Jiang, Y., Weise, T., Lässig, J., Chiong, R., Athauda, R.: Comparing a hybrid branch and bound algorithm with evolutionary computation methods, local search and their hybrids on the TSP. In: Proceedings of the IEEE Symposium Series on Computational Intelligence. Orlando, 9–12 Dec 2014
23. Hansen, N., Auger, A., Finck, S., Ros, R.: Real-parameter black-box optimization benchmarking: experimental setup. Technical report, Université Paris Sud, INRIA, Équipe TAO, Orsay (2012)
24. Tompkins, D.A.D., Hoos, H.H.: UBCSAT: an implementation and experimentation environment for SLS algorithms for SAT and MAX-SAT. In: 7th International Conference on Theory and Applications of Satisfiability Testing, pp. 306–320. Springer, Berlin (2004)
25. Hoos, H.H., Stützle, T.: Stochastic Local Search: Foundations and Applications. Morgan Kaufmann, San Francisco (2005)
26. Hoos, H.H., Stützle, T.: Evaluating Las Vegas algorithms - pitfalls and remedies. In: Proceedings of the 14th Conference on Uncertainty in AI, pp. 238–245. Morgan Kaufmann, Madison, 24–26 July 1998
27. Johnson, D.S., McGeoch, L.A.: Experimental analysis of heuristics for the STSP. The Traveling Salesman Problem and its Variations, pp. 369–443. Springer, New York (2002)
28. Johnson, D.S., Gutin, G.Z., McGeoch, L.A., Yeo, A., Zhang, W., Zverovitch, A.: Experimental analysis of heuristics for the ATSP. The Traveling Salesman Problem and its Variations, pp. 445–487. Kluwer, Dordrecht (2002)
29. Wu, Y., Weise, T., Chiong, R.: Local search for the traveling salesman problem: a comparative study. In: Proceedings of 14th IEEE Conference on Cognitive Informatics and Cognitive Computing, pp. 213–220, 6–8 July 2015

30. Larrañaga, P., Kuijpers, C.M.H., Murga, R.H., Inza, I., Dizdarevic, S.: Genetic algorithms for the travelling salesman problem: a review of representations and operators. J. Artif. Intell. Res. **13**(2), 129–170 (1999)
31. Michalewicz, Z.: Genetic Algorithms + Data Structures = Evolution Programs. Springer, Berlin (1996)
32. Fogel, D.B.: An evolutionary approach to the traveling salesman problem. Biol. Cybern. **60**(2), 139–144 (1988)
33. Holland, J.H.: Adaptation in Natural and Artificial Systems: An Introductory Analysis with Applications to Biology, Control, and Artificial Intelligence. University of Michigan Press, Ann Arbor (1975)
34. Glover, F.W.: Future paths for integer programming and links to artificial intelligence. Comput. Oper. Res. **13**(5), 533–549 (1986)
35. Kirkpatrick, S., Gelatt Jr., C.D., Vecchi, M.P.: Optimization by simulated annealing. Sci. Mag. **220**(4598), 671–680 (1983)
36. Wang, D., Wang, J., Wang, H., Zhang, R., Guo, Z.: Intelligent Optimization Methods. Higher Education Press, China (2007)
37. Helsgaun, K.: An effective implementation of the Lin-Kernighan traveling salesman heuristic. Technical report, Roskilde University, Denmark (1998)
38. Applegate, D.L., Cook, W.J., Rohe, A.: Chained Lin-Kernighan for large traveling salesman problems. INFORMS J. Comput. **15**(1), 82–92 (2003)
39. Helsgaun, K.: General k-opt submoves for the Lin-Kernighan TSP heuristic. Math. Program. Comput. **1**(2–3), 119–163 (2009)
40. Whitley, L.D., Starkweather, T., Fuquay, D.: Scheduling problems and traveling salesman: the genetic edge recombination operator. In: Proceedings of the 3rd International Conference on Genetic Algorithms, pp. 133–140 (1989)

A Sorting Based Selection for Evolutionary Multiobjective Optimization

Zhixiang Yang[1], Xinye Cai[1(✉)], and Zhun Fan[2]

[1] College of Computer Science and Technology, Nanjing University of Aeronautics
and Astronautics, Nanjing 210016, Jiangsu, China
xiang052@163.com, xinye@nuaa.edu.cn
[2] Department of Electronic Engineering, Shantou University, Guangdong, China
zfan@stu.edu.cn

Abstract. In this paper, we propose a new solution selection method
to balance the convergence and diversity during the evolutionary process
for evolutionary multiobjective optimization. The method sorts the solutions based on their ensemble convergence performance, then selects
the solutions based on diversity. The selection method is integrated to
the framework of decomposition based multiobjective evolutionary algorithms (MOEAs). In order to demonstrate the performance of the algorithm, it is compared with three classical MOEAs and one state-of-art
MOEA. The results indicate that our proposed algorithm is very competitive.

Keywords: Multiobjective optimization · Association · Decomposition ·
Convergence · Diversity

1 Introduction

A multiobjective optimization problem (MOP) can be defined as follows:

$$\text{minimize } F(x) = (f_1(x), \ldots, f_m(x))^T \tag{1}$$
$$\text{subject to } x \in \Omega$$

where Ω is the decision space, $F : \Omega \to R^m$ consists of m real-valued objective
functions. The attainable objective set is $\{F(x)|x \in \Omega\}$.

Let $u, v \in R^m$, u is said to *dominate* v, denoted by $u \prec v$, if and only if $u_i \leq v_i$
for every $i \in \{1, \ldots, m\}$ and $u_j < v_j$ for at least one index $j \in \{1, \ldots, m\}$[1]. Given
a set S in R^m, a solution $x \in S$ can be called non-dominated in S if no other
solution in S can dominate it. A solution $x^* \in \Omega$ is *Pareto-optimal* if $F(x^*)$ is
non-dominated in the attainable objective set. $F(x^*)$ is then called a *Pareto-
optimal (objective) vector*. In other words, any improvement in one objective
of a Pareto optimal solution is bound to deteriorate at least another objective.

---

[1] In the case of maximization, the inequality signs should be reversed.

© Springer-Verlag Berlin Heidelberg 2015
M. Gong et al. (Eds.): BIC-TA 2015, CCIS 562, pp. 538–549, 2015.
DOI: 10.1007/978-3-662-49014-3_48

The set of all the Pareto-optimal solutions is called the *Pareto set* (*PS*) and the image of (*PS*) on the objective vector space is called the *Pareto front* (*PF*) [11].

Usually, it is desirable to balance between convergence and diversity for obtaining good approximation to the set of Pareto optimal solutions. Over the last two decades, three major evolutionary algorithm paradigms have been developed, i.e., dominance-based MOEAs (e.g., [4,6,18]), indicator-based MOEAs (e.g., [1,2,12,17]) and decomposition-based MOEAs (e.g., [8,14,15]).

Arguably, NSGA-II [6] is the most well-known domination-based MOEA, which uses Pareto dominance relation as the primary selection criterion to promote the convergence and the crowding distance is used as density metric to maintain the diversity.

The indicator based approaches utilize various performance indicators like ϵ-indicator [17], R2 indicator [12] and hypervolume indicator [2] to measure the quality of solutions. Among these indicators, the most commonly used performance indicator is hypervolume, which can measure convergence and diversity simultaneously. However, the hypervolume prefers convex regions to concave ones [1] and its computational complexity is quite huge.

As a representative of the decomposition-based method, the basic idea of MOEA/D [15] is to decompose a MOP into a number of single objective optimization subproblems through aggregation functions and optimizes them simultaneously. The update of solutions is decided by their aggregation function values, and the population diversity is achieved by the wide spread of weight vectors.

Apparently, selection is a major issue in designing MOEAs. In this paper, we propose a sorting-based-selection (SBS) scheme and integrate it into MOEA/D. First, SBS sorts the solutions in the population according to their ensemble convergence performance on all subproblems. Then, the diversity selection is conducted on the sorted population according to each subproblem.

The remainder of this paper is organized as follows. Section 2 provides some background knowledge of this paper. Section 3 explains our motivation of this work. Section 4 details the proposed method, sorting-based-selection. Section 5 mainly describes the proposed MOEA/D-SBS. Experimental settings and performance indicators for MOEAs are detailed in Sect. 6. In Sect. 7, we conduct experiments and present the results of compare our proposed algorithm with three classical MOEAs, NSGA-II, MSOPS-II [7], MOEA/D-DE [9] and one state-of-art MOEA, MOEA/D-STM [10]. Section 8 concludes the paper.

2 Motivation

In this paper, a new solution selection method, SBS, is proposed and used in the framework of MOEA/D to select solutions from the merged population. In SBS, the merged population is sorted based on convergence. The sorting is emphasis on the ensemble performance of each solution on all the subproblems. In order to maintain the diversity, the solutions in the population are associated with the subproblems, first. And then the solutions are selected for each subproblem. Note that the priority relations of the solutions associated with each subproblem are subject to the ensemble convergence. Consequently, a number of solutions that have a good balance between convergence and diversity are selected in MOEA/D-SBS. Different from MOEA/D, where each subproblem is allowed with one solution, MOEA/D-SBS can be associated with any number of solutions.

3   Sorting-Based-Selection

The new solution selection method, SBS, which selects N solutions from the merged population, is detailed in this section. First, the merged population is sorted based on convergence. Then, the solutions in the sorted population are associated with the subproblems. Finally, N solutions are selected based on diversity depending on the sorted and associated results.

The pseudo-code of SBS is presented in Algorithm 1.

3.1   Convergence Based Sorting

For each subproblem s^j, the aggregation function value, $g^{te}(x|\lambda^j, z^*)$, of each solution x^i in population Z is calculated and stored in $\Delta(i,j)$, as shown in Step 2.1a. Each row of Δ represents a solution and each column represents a subproblem, and λ^j denotes the weight vector with regard to the j-th subproblem. In Step 2.1b, each column of matrix Δ, $\Delta(:, j)$, is sorted in an ascending order and the rank values are kept in $R(:, j)$.

In Step 2.2a, each row of matrix R are sorted in an ascending order of rank values. So, the first column of R will hold the best rank achieved for each solution across the N subproblems, and the N-th column of R will hold the worst rank achieved. Thus the matrix R may be used to rank the population. In Step 2.2b, the solutions in the Z are sorted according to the lexicographical order of the corresponding rows in R.

3.2   Association

In **Step 3**, each solution $x \in Z$ needs to associate with a subproblem. Solution x will be associated with the subproblem whose weight vector has the minimum angle with its objective vector. The acute angle between a solution x and the weight vector λ of a subproblem can be computed as follows:

$$\alpha = \arccos(\frac{(F(x) - z^*)^T \lambda}{\|F(x) - z^*\|\|\lambda\|}). \tag{2}$$

where $F(x) = (f_1(x), f_2(x), \ldots, f_m(x))^T$ is the objective vector of the solution x, and z^* is the ideal objective vector.

In **Step 3**, each solution in the sorted solution set Z is associated with a subproblem. Furthermore, solutions associated with each subproblem are ordered by ensemble convergence.

Algorithm 1. SBS(Z, z^*, N)

Input:

1. Z: the solution set;
2. z^*: the ideal objective vector z^*;
3. N: the number of subproblems or the maximum size of P.

Output: the population P, index set I

Step 1 Initialization:

a) Set $I = \emptyset$.
b) Set $P = \emptyset$.
c) Set $M = |Z|$.

Step 2 Sorting:
Step 2.1:
For each $j = 1, \ldots, N$, do:

a) For each solution x^i in Z, evaluate the aggregation function $g^{te}(x^i|\lambda^j, z^*)$, and store it in $\Delta(i, j)$.
b) Sort $\Delta(:, j)$ in an ascending order and keep the rank values in $R(:, j)$.
Step 2.2:

a) For each $i = 1, \ldots, M$, sort $R(i, :)$ in an ascending order.
b) Sort Z according to the lexicographical order of the rows in R.

Step 3 Association:

For each solution x in the sorted solution set Z, associate it with the subproblem whose weight vector has the minimum angle with the objective vector of x, based on (2).

Step 4 Selection:
For each $k = 1, \ldots, M$, do:

a) Set $A = \emptyset$;
b) For each subproblem, if the k-th solution associated with it is exist, then add it to A.
c) If $|P| + |A| \leq N$, then set $P = P \bigcup A$; else, the $N - |P|$ solutions in A are selected and added to P based on the rankings in Z, then break.

Step 5 Termination: Record the indexes of the subproblems in I, which are associated with solutions in P. Then return P and I.

3.3 Diversity Based Selection

In order to keep a good population diversity, the solutions will be selected according the subproblems. In **Step 4**, the best associated solution of each subproblem is selected and added to P, if they are exist. Then, the second best associated solution is selected, and so on. When $|P| + |A|$ is greater than N, the $N - |P|$

solutions in A are selected and added to P, depending on their performance. Here, the selection is based on their rankings in Z, in which solutions has been sorted according to their ensemble convergence performance in **Step 2**.

3.4   Termination

Algorithm 2 is terminated when the size of P reaches N. In **Step 5**, record the indexes of the subproblems in I, which are associated with solutions in P. Then return it and P as outputs.

3.5   Computational Cost of the SBS

In Algorithm 1, the calculation of matrix Δ (Step 2.1a) costs $O(mMN)$ computations, where m is the number of objectives. $O(NMlogM)$ comparisons are used to sort Δ (Step 2.1b). The sorting of matrix R and population Z needs $O(MNlogN)$ and $O(NMlogM)$ comparisons (Step 2.2), respectively. And association (Step 3) requires $O(mMN)$ computations. N solutions are selected from the population Z, so the complexity of selection (Step 4) is $O(N)$. In summary, the computational cost of the SBS is $O(NMlogM)$.

4   Algorithm

In this section, we present the whole algorithm, multiobjective evolutionary algorithm based on decomposition with diversity-based-sorting (MOEA/D-SBS). The pseudo-code of MOEA/D-SBS is demonstrated in Algorithm 2.

At each generation, MOEA/D-SBS maintains:

- a set of N subproblems, $S = \{s^1, \ldots, s^N\}$;
- a population of N solutions, $P = \{x^1, \ldots, x^N\}$;
- objective function values, $FV^1, \ldots, FV^N$, where FV^i is the F-value of x^i;

Let $\lambda^1, \ldots, \lambda^N$ be a set of even spread weight vectors [15] and z^* be the reference point. The MOP of (1) can be decomposed into N scalar optimization subproblems by using Tchebycheff approach. The k-th subproblem is:

$$\text{minimize } g(x|\lambda^k, z^*) = \max_{1 \leq i \leq m} \{|f_i(x) - z_i^*|/\lambda_i^k\}$$

$$\text{subject to } x \in \Omega. \tag{3}$$

In initialization, for each $k = 1, \ldots, N$, let $B(k)$ be the set containing the indices of the T closest weight vectors to λ^k in terms of the Euclidean distance. If $i \in B(k)$, i-th subproblem is called a neighbor of k-th subproblem. I is a set of subproblem indices that each solution x^i belongs to. It is initialized by calling SBS function in Algorithm 1.

New solutions are generated in **Step 2**. In MOEA/D, each new solution is generated according to each subproblem, while in MOEA/D-SBS is according

---

Algorithm 2. MOEA/D-SBS

Input:

1. MOP(1);
2. a stopping criterion;
3. N: the number of subproblems;
4. $\lambda^1, \ldots, \lambda^N$: a set of N weight vectors;
5. T: the size of the neighborhood for each subproblem.

Output: population P

Step 1 Initialization:

a) Compute the Euclidean distances between any two weight vectors and obtain T closest weight vectors to each weight vector. For each $i = 1, \ldots, N$, set $B(i) = \{i_1, \ldots, i_T\}$ where $\lambda^{i_1}, \ldots, \lambda^{i_T}$ are the T closest weight vectors to λ^i.
b) Generate an initial population $P = \{x^1, \ldots, x^N\}$ randomly.
c) Initialize the ideal objective vector z^* by setting $z_i^* = \min\{f_i(x^1), \ldots, f_i(x^N)\}, i = 1, \ldots, m$.
d) Get the set P and I: $[P, I] = \text{SBS}(P, z^*, N)$.

Step 2 New Solution Generation:

For each $i = 1, \ldots, |P|$, do:

a) **Selection of the Mating Solutions:**
   1) Track the index k of the subproblem that x^i is associated with : $k = I(i)$.
   2) If $rand(0, 1) < \delta$, then set D is the set of solutions that are associated with the subproblem in $B(k)$, else, set $D = P$.
b) **Reproduction:** Set $r_1 = i$ and randomly select two indices r_2 and r_3 from D, and then generate a solution $\bar{y}$ from x^{r_1}, x^{r_2} and x^{r_3} by DE, and then perform a mutation operator on $\bar{y}$ with probability p_m to produce a new solution y^i.
c) **Evaluation** y^i : $FV^i = F(y^i)$.
d) **Update of z^* :** For each $j = 1, \ldots, m$, if $z_j^* > f_j(y^i)$, then set $z_j^* = f_j(y^i)$.

Step 3 Sorting-based-selection: $[P, I] = \text{SBS}(P \bigcup Y, z^*, N)$
Step 4 Stopping Criteria: If stopping criteria is satisfied, then stop and output P. Otherwise, go to **Step 2**.

---

to each individual in population. So the number of times that a subproblem is selected to generate offspring is equal to the number of solutions associated with it. In Step 2a, for each individual in population P, the subproblem k is tracked according to the set of subproblem indices I, then all individuals which are associated with the neighborhood of subproblem k in population P are selected as the possible mating range D. In Step 2b, two parent solutions are selected from the D, and then the differential evolution (DE) operator [13] and polynomial mutation [5] are applied to three parent solutions, x^{r_1}, x^{r_2} and x^{r_3}, to generate an offspring y^i.

In DE operator, each element $\bar{y}_j$ in $\bar{y} = (\bar{y}_1, \ldots, \bar{y}_n)^T$ is generated as follows:

$$\bar{y}_j = \begin{cases} x_j^{r_1} + F \times (x_j^{r_2} - x_j^{r_3}), & \text{if } rand \leq CR \text{ or } j = j_{rand} \\ x_j^{r_1}, & \text{otherwise} \end{cases} \tag{4}$$

where $j = 1, \ldots, n$, $rand \in [0, 1]$, $j_{rand} \in [1, n]$ is a random integer, and CR and F are two control parameters.

The mutation operator generates $y = (y_1, \ldots, y_n)^T$ from $\overline{y}$ in the following way:

$$y_j = \begin{cases} \overline{y}_j + \sigma_j \times (b_j - a_j), & \text{with probability } p_m \\ \overline{y}_j, & \text{with probability } 1 - p_m \end{cases} \tag{5}$$

with

$$\sigma_j = \begin{cases} (2 \times rand)^{\frac{1}{\eta+1}} - 1, & \text{if } rand < 0.5 \\ 1 - (2 - 2 \times rand)^{\frac{1}{\eta+1}}, & \text{otherwise} \end{cases} \tag{6}$$

where $rand$ is a uniformly random number from $[0, 1]$; the distribution index η and the mutation rate p_m are two control parameters; and a_j and b_j are the lower and upper bounds of the j-th decision variable, respectively.

The procedure (Step 2a–c) will be repeated N times, so an population $Y = \{y^1, \ldots, y^N\}$ will be got. In **Step 3**, the SBS, detailed in Sect. 4, is adopted to select offsprings from the merged population.

5   Experimental Studies

5.1   Experimental Setting

The UF test suite, which contains ten unconstrained MOP test instances (UF1 to UF10) from the CEC2009 MOEA competition [16], is considered in our experimental studies. For all UF test functions, the number of decision variables is set to 30.

All the algorithms were implemented in Matlab. The parameters of NSGA-II, MSOPS-II, MOEA/D-DE and MOEA/D-STM were set according to the corresponding references [6,7,9,10]. The parameter settings of our proposed MOEA/D-SBS are as follows:

1) Control parameters in DE and polynomial mutation: $CR = 1.0$ and $F = 0.5$ in DE operator; $\eta = 20$ and $p_m = 1/n$ in the polynomial mutation operator.
2) Probability used to select in the neighborhood: $\delta = 0.9$.
3) Population size: $N = 300$ for bi-objective test instances, 595 for the three-objective ones.
4) Neighborhood size: $T = 10$ for bi-objective test instances except for UF3, for which T is set to 20, $T = 595$ for three-objective ones.
5) Number of runs and stopping condition: Each algorithm is run 30 times independently on each test instance. The algorithm stops after 300,000 function evaluations.

It is worth noting that the population size and the number of function evaluations are set same for all compared algorithms.

In our experimental studies, we employ two widely used performance indicators inverted generational distance metric (IGD) [3] and hypervolume metric (I_H) [19]. Both of them can simultaneously measure the convergence and diversity of obtained solutions.

Table 1. Mean and standard deviation values of IGD, obtained by MOEA/D-SBS, MOEA/D-DE, MSOPS-II and NSGA-II on UF instances.

Instance	IGD			
	MOEA/D-SBS	MOEA/D-DE	MSOPS-II	NSGA-II
UF1	**0.0017** (5.67E-05)	0.0024 (4.94E-04)†	0.0743 (5.44E-03)†	0.0839 (1.17E-02)†
UF2	**0.0057** (1.69E-03)	0.0112 (3.21E-03)†	0.0572 (2.10E-02)†	0.0327 (2.32E-03)†
UF3	**0.0037** (1.72E-03)	0.0254 (2.12E-02)†	0.3141 (1.75E-02)†	0.0703 (1.14E-02)†
UF4	**0.0560** (2.67E-03)	0.0677 (2.80E-03)†	0.0567 (4.09E-03)	0.0761 (1.35E-02)†
UF5	**0.2469** (2.46E-02)	0.2901 (4.56E-02)†	0.3437 (9.80E-02)†	0.6793 (9.88E-02)†
UF6	**0.0927** (4.21E-02)	0.1868 (1.34E-01)†	0.2985 (2.29E-01)†	0.3217 (7.60E-02)†
UF7	**0.0023** (2.64E-04)	0.0041 (9.31E-04)†	0.0418 (7.21E-03)†	0.3504 (8.65E-03)†
UF8	**0.0522** (7.66E-03)	0.0658 (7.89E-03)†	0.1916 (4.92E-03)†	0.2693 (5.59E-02)†
UF9	**0.0278** (2.98E-03)	0.0720 (3.96E-02)†	0.2540 (2.29E-02)†	0.2054 (6.92E-02)†
UF10	1.3755 (2.51E-01)	0.4846 (5.52E-02)‡	**0.2147** (4.98E-02)‡	0.6429 (8.84E-02)‡

Wilcoxon's rank sum test at a 0.05 significance level is performed between MOEA/D-SBS and each of the other competing algorithms.
† and ‡ denotes that the performance of the corresponding algorithm is significantly worse than or better than that of MOEA/D-SBS, respectively. The best mean is highlighted in boldface

Table 2. Mean and standard deviation values of I_H, obtained by MOEA/D-SBS, MOEA/D-DE, MSOPS-II and NSGA-II on UF instances.

Instance	I_H			
	MOEA/D-SBS	MOEA/D-DE	MSOPS-II	NSGA-II
UF1	**3.6582** (0.0020)	3.6504 (0.0076)†	3.4418 (0.0918)†	3.3859 (0.0175)†
UF2	**3.6422** (0.0142)	3.6073 (0.0399)†	3.4618 (0.0884)†	3.6090 (0.0076)†
UF3	**3.6598** (0.0027)	3.5493 (0.1092)†	2.5711 (0.0457)†	3.5191 (0.0402)†
UF4	3.1672 (0.0117)	3.1352 (0.0165)†	**3.1876** (0.0064)‡	3.0787 (0.1345)
UF5	**2.8680** (0.0865)	2.5807 (0.1622)†	2.5875 (0.3309)†	1.5901 (0.2338)†
UF6	**3.1558** (0.0932)	2.9058 (0.2428)†	2.6652 (0.4505)†	2.6228 (0.1497)†
UF7	**3.4885** (0.0062)	3.4796 (0.0080)†	3.4029 (0.0627)†	2.5452 (0.0091)†
UF8	**7.3028** (0.0267)	6.9542 (0.2821)†	6.4215 (0.0098)†	6.6184 (0.3498)†
UF9	**7.6812** (0.0419)	6.4168 (0.7147)†	5.7602 (0.2120)†	7.0840 (0.2283)†
UF10	9.615 (4.7472)	16.224 (1.2106)‡	**24.269** (1.0457)‡	14.770 (1.4454)‡

Wilcoxon's rank sum test at a 0.05 significance level is performed between MOEA/D-SBS and each of the other competing algorithms.
† and ‡ denotes that the performance of the corresponding algorithm is significantly worse than or better than that of MOEA/D-SBS, respectively. The best mean is highlighted in boldface

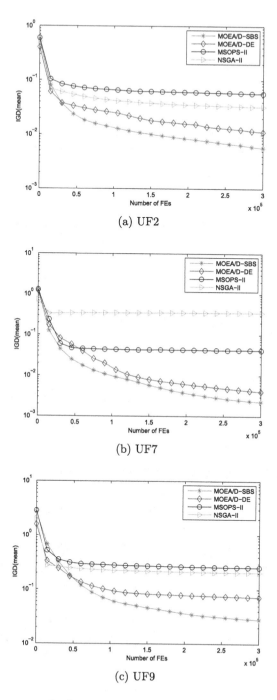

Fig. 1. Convergence graphs in terms of *IGD* (mean) obtained by MOEA/D-DIS, MOEA/D-DE, MSOPS-II and NSGA-II on three UF instances.

5.2 Comparisons with Classical MOEAs

In this section, we compare MOEA/D-SBS with three classical MOEAs, NSGA-II, MSOPS-II and MOEA/D-DE. Each algorithm is run 30 times independently on each test instance. The comparison results of MOEA/D-SBS with the other three MOEAs in terms of IGD metric values are presented in Table 1. From the table, we can find that MOEA/D-SBS has obtained the best mean metric values on all the test problems except UF10. No algorithm can approximate UF10' PF very well, as it has many local PFs. MSOPS-II has best performance among all the compared algorithms on the UF test problem. In Table 1, all comparisons are statistically significant except the comparison of between MOEA/D-SBS with MSOPS-II on UF4. From Table 2, we can find that the comparison results in terms of I_H metric are similar to the ones in terms of IGD.

The evolution of the average IGD values versus the number of function evaluations in the four algorithms on UF test problems are plotted in Fig. 1. It can be observed from these figures that MOEA/D-SBS performs best on both the convergence speed and the quality of the final solution sets.

5.3 Comparison with MOEA/D-STM

In this section, MOEA/D-STM which has a good performance on UF test problems in [10], will be compared with the proposed MOEA/D-SBS. Table 3 presents their comparison results in terms of IGD metric. From the results, we can find that the performance of MOEA/D-SBS is significantly better than that

Table 3. Mean and standard deviation values of IGD, obtained by MOEA/D-SBS and MOEA/D-STM on UF instances.

Instance	IGD		
	MOEA/D-SBS	MOEA/D-STM	p-value
UF1	**0.001711** (5.67E-05)	0.001980 (6.32E-05)	3.69E-11
UF2	**0.005661** (1.69E-03)	0.007074 (1.84E-03)	1.17E-03
UF3	0.003658 (1.72E-03)	0.003721 (2.48E-03)	0.4918
UF4	0.055980 (2.67E-03)	0.056139 (3.75E-03)	0.9705
UF5	0.246915 (2.46E-02)	0.252158 (2.45E-02)	0.1907
UF6	0.092737 (4.21E-02)	0.082018 (3.75E-02)	0.0824
UF7	**0.002276** (2.64E-04)	0.002658 (6.35E-04)	5.61E-05
UF8	**0.052198** (7.66E-03)	0.067490 (1.26E-02)	3.32E-06
UF9	0.027832 (2.98E-03)	0.030200 (2.07E-02)	0.1087
UF10	1.375528 (2.51E-01)	**1.238261** (2.23E-01)	1.63E-02

Wilcoxon's rank sum test at a 0.05 significance level is performed between MOEA/D-SBS and MOEA/D-STM. Boldface denotes that the performance of the corresponding algorithm is significantly better than that of the other of MOEA/D-STM on UF1, UF2, UF7 and UF8, but it is significantly worse on UF10, on the other test problems it is not statistically significant. So, we can claim that the proposed algorithm MOEA/D-SBS is competitive with MOEA/D-STM.

6 Conclusion

This paper proposed a sorting-based-selection (SBS) to select offspring population for MOEA/D. The proposed algorithm, MOEA/D-SBS, was tested on the 10 unconstrained problems for CEC09 algorithm competition. The comparison results with 4 multiobjective evolutionary algorithms (NSGA-II, MSOPS-II, MOEA/D-DE and MOEA/D-STM) show that MOEA/D-SBS outperforms other compared algorithms.

Further work includes investigation of the proposed SBS integrated to other framework of multiobjective evolutionary algorithms. We also intend to extend MOEA/D-SBS to tackle many optimization problems.

Acknowledgments. This work was supported in part by the National Natural Science Foundation of China (NSFC) under grant 61300159, by the Natural Science Foundation of Jiangsu Province under grant BK20130808, by the Research Fund for the Doctoral Program of Higher Education of China under grant 20123218120041.

References

1. Auger, A., Bader, J., Brockhoff, D., Zitzler, E.: Hypervolume-based multiobjective optimization: theoretical foundations and practical implications. Theor. Comput. **425**(2), 75–103 (2011)
2. Bader, J., Zitzler, E.: Hype: an algorithm for fast hypervolume-based many-objective optimization. Evol. Comput. **19**(1), 45–76 (2011). http://dx.doi.org/10.1162/EVCO_a_00009
3. Coello, C.A.C., Cortés, N.C.: Solving multiobjective optimization problems using an artificial immune system. Genet. Program. Evolvable Mach. **6**(2), 163–190 (2005)
4. Deb, K.: Multi-Objective Optimization using Evolutionary Algorithms. Wiley, Chichester (2001)
5. Deb, K., Goyal, M.: A combined genetic adaptive search (geneas) for engineering design. Comput. Sci. Inf. **26**, 30–45 (1996)
6. Deb, K., Pratap, A., Agarwal, S., Meyarivan, T.: A fast and elitist multiobjective genetic algorithm: NSGA-II. IEEE Trans. Evol. Comput. **6**(2), 182–197 (2002)
7. Hughes, E.: MSOPS-II: a general-purpose many-objective optimiser. In: IEEE Congress on Evolutionary Computation, CEC 2007, pp. 3944–3951, September 2007
8. Hughes, E.J.: Multiple single objective pareto sampling. In: Proceedings of the 2003 Congress on Evolutionary Computation (CEC 2003), vol. 4, pp. 2678–2684. IEEE Press, Canberra, December 2003
9. Li, H., Zhang, Q.: Multiobjective optimization problems with complicated pareto sets, MOEA/D and NSGA-II. IEEE Trans. Evol. Comput. **13**(2), 284–302 (2009)

10. Li, K., Zhang, Q., Kwong, S., Li, M., Wang, R.: Stable matching based selection in evolutionary multiobjective optimization. IEEE Trans. Evol. Comput. **18**(6), 909–923 (2014)
11. Miettinen, K.: Nonlinear Multiobjective Optimization. Kluwer Academic Publishers, Boston (1999)
12. Phan, D.H., Suzuki, J.: R2-IBEA: R2 indicator based evolutionary algorithm for multiobjective optimization. In: 2013 IEEE Congress on Evolutionary Computation (CEC), pp. 1836–1845 (2013)
13. Price, K., Storn, R.M., Lampinen, J.A.: Differential Evolution: A Practical Approach to Global Optimization. Natural Computing Series. Springer, Heidelberg (2005)
14. Schaffer, J.D., Grefenstette, J.J.: Multiobjective learning via genetic algorithms. In: Proceedings of the 9th International Joint Conference on Artificial Intelligence (IJCAI-85), pp. 593–595. AAAI, Los Angeles (1985)
15. Zhang, Q., Li, H.: MOEA/D: a multiobjective evolutionary algorithm based on decomposition. IEEE Trans. Evol. Comput. **11**(6), 712–731 (2007)
16. Zhang, Q., Zhou, A., Zhao, S., Suganthan, P.N., Liu, W., Tiwari, S.: Multiobjective optimization test instances for the CEC 2009 special session and competition. University of Essex, Colchester, UK and Nanyang Technological University, Singapore, Special Session on Performance Assessment of Multi-objective Optimization Algorithms, Technical report (2008)
17. Zitzler, E., Künzli, S.: Indicator-based selection in multiobjective search. In: Yao, X., Burke, E.K., Lozano, J.A., Smith, J., Merelo-Guervós, J.J., Bullinaria, J.A., Rowe, J.E., Tiño, P., Kabán, A., Schwefel, H.-P. (eds.) PPSN 2004. LNCS, vol. 3242, pp. 832–842. Springer, Heidelberg (2004)
18. Zitzler, E., Laumanns, M., Thiele, L.: SPEA2: improving the strength pareto evolutionary algorithm. In: Giannakoglou, K., Tsahalis, D., Periaux, J., Papailou, P., Fogarty, T. (eds.) EUROGEN 2001. Evolutionary Methods for Design, Optimization and Control with Applications to Industrial Problems, pp. 95–100, Athens, Greece (2002)
19. Zitzler, E., Thiele, L.: Multiobjective evolutionary algorithms: a comparative case study and the strength pareto approach. IEEE Trans. Evol. Comput. **3**(4), 257–271 (1999)

An Improved Genetic Algorithm for Bi-objective Problem: Locating Mixing Station

Shujin Ye[1], Han Huang[2], Changjian Xu[2(✉)], Liang Lv[2], and Yihui Liang[2]

[1] Hong Kong Baptist University, Hong Kong, China
[2] South China University of Technology, Guangzhou, China
hhan@scut.edu.cn, x.changjian@hotmail.com

Abstract. Locating mixing station (LMS) optimization has a considerable influence on controlling quality and prime cost for the specific construction. As a NP-hard problem, it is more complex than common p-median problem. In this paper, we proposed a hybrid genetic algorithm with special coding scheme, crossover and mutation to solve LMS. In addition, a specified evaluation functions are raised in order to achieve a better optimization solution for the LMS. Moreover, a local search strategy was added into the genetic algorithm (GALS) for improving the stability of the algorithm. On the basis of the experiment results, we can conclude that the proposed algorithm is more stable than the compared algorithm and GALS can be considered as a better solution for the LMS.

Keywords: Locating mixing station · Genetic algorithm · Local search

1 Introduction

Locating mixing station optimization plays a significant role in distribution for construction companies to control their cost and time. The location of mixing stations will influence not only the quality of the concrete but also the schedule of the construction. In many underdevelop countries such as China, the output of the existing mixing station could not satisfy the increasing requirement of the concrete. For example, the concrete requirement of Nanning (a city in China) will rise up to 14 million m^3/year which will need the supplement reach at least 19.5 million m^3/year in 2015. However, the output of mixing stations just provide 13.8 million m^3/year supplement showing that the supplying amount is far less than the requirement. To achieve the new and increasing requirement of urban construction, additional mixing stations which should be located in a suitable location are needed for increasing the supplement.

One-to-many mode, one central site serves many service centers and a service center will build up connection with only one central site, is the key mode of distribution location problems and the location of first-aid center problems. They are considered as the traditional location problems and belong to the integer programming problem. These arise several researchers interest for modeling and developing an algorithm to solve p-median problem [1,3,4,8]. However, LMS is

© Springer-Verlag Berlin Heidelberg 2015
M. Gong et al. (Eds.): BIC-TA 2015, CCIS 562, pp. 550–562, 2015.
DOI: 10.1007/978-3-662-49014-3_49

much different from traditional one because of its many-to-many model. In LMS problem, one central site can serve many service site and at the same time one service site can accept the service from many central sites. The major task of solving LMS problems is determining the proportion from 0 to 1 which reflects the supplement from central site to service site. The solution for the traditional one is not suitable for LMS because it could not satisfy the requirement of LMS.

In addition, the selection of the candidate mixing stations are another essential difficulty for LMS. Especially, while the size of the candidate mixing stations increases, its difficult to enumerate and analyze every station. To solve this problem, many heuristic algorithms such as ant colony algorithm [6], particle swarm optimization [2], genetic algorithm [5] and differential evolution [7] can be used to overcome the task.

In order to solve the LMS, we proposed a local search added into the traditional genetic algorithm which is first provided by John Holland [5].

The rest of this paper is constructed as follow: the problem definitions and formulation will be presented in Sect. 2. In Sect. 3, genetic algorithm with local search will be introduced in details. Whats more the experimental analysis will be discussed in Sect. 4. Finally, the conclusion will be drawn in the last section.

2   Problem Definitions and Formulation

2.1   Problem Analysis

We take the location of mixing station in Nanning as the research object. For shortening the length of supplying transportation, several new mixing station will be built in Nanning. However, as we discuss in the last section, LMS is different with p-median distribution problems and the features of LMS are listed as follow:

(1) Bi-objective Programming. There are two objectives of LMS problem, one for minimizing the total weighed length of the concrete mixing station and the other for minimizing the number of new adding stations. The first objective is similar to the traditional p-median problems goal. If this objective is achieved in LMS problem, a good solution could shorten the length of transporting concrete, relieve the traffic jam and reduce the pollution emitted by vehicles. Not only reserving the land resources, but also avoiding the vicious competition brought by the high-density of concrete stations can be achieved after the realization of the latter goal.

(2) The limits of the transportation length. Due to the specifically chemical feature of concrete, the concrete cannot be sent to a far place. We should set an upper limit for the transporting length.

(3) The limit of the supplying ability. In common p-median problem, there is no limitation for supplying ability while the supplying capability of the concrete station in LMS is limited. Virtually, the actual supplement of each concrete mixing station should not be too large, otherwise it would cause the diseconomy of scale. In addition, a large number of vehicles in and out of the

city can aggravate the traffic jam. As a result, the supplying ability of each concrete mixing station can not be expanded extremely.

(4) The uncertain number of new adding stations. In LMS, the number of new adding stations is uncertain because under the proves that the longest transporting length is limited by the number of new adding stations. Also, it is determined and limited by the demanding supplying gap and the distribution of the original sites, candidate stations as well as the construction group. Namely, we cannot decide the sites of stations only according to the demanding-supplying gap.

(5) The relationship between groups and the concrete mixing stations is many-to-many mode. One group can receive service from many concrete mixing stations and, each mixing station can serve many groups. By this way, the improvement of the efficiency for the mixing station could be achieved. However, it increases the complexity of the modeling process.

(6) The already existing stations must take part in the supplying service. In terms of the requirement that exploits the supplying ability as much as possible, the address of new adding concrete mixing stations should be carefully considered with the original stations.

2.2 Symbol Description

In this subsection, we proposed the definition and description of the sets, parameters and deciding variables.

(i) Set. Let $K = \{1, 2, 3, \ldots, k\}$ be the set of construction group; $I = \{1, 2, 3, \ldots, i\}$ be the set of existing station; $J = \{1, 2, 3, \ldots, j\}$ be the set of candidate stations.

(ii) Parameters. Dem_k denotes the required supplying ability for group k; d_{ik} denotes the distance from ith candidate station to the kth construction group; td denotes the upper bounds of the limited transporting distance (in this paper, $td = 25\,\text{km}$); $news_j$ represents the supplying capability of station j and the supplying ability of all stations is $500000\,\text{m}^3/\text{year}$; $olds_j$ represents the original station js ability to supply concrete; $news_{ik}$ denotes the supply of station i to group k.

(iii) Decision variables. In this model, a variable sel_i is designed for marking the selection of each station. If the ith station is selected, the value of sel_i is 1. Otherwise, the value of it will be 0.

2.3 Modeling

According to the definition of symbols and variables above, the integer programming is as follows:

$$min(Z_1) = \sum_{k \in K} \sum_{i \in I} c_{ik} d_{ik} \tag{1}$$

$$min(Z_2) = \sum_{i_2 \in I_2} \sum_{i \in I} sel_{i_2} \tag{2}$$

$$\sum_{i \in I} c_{ik} \geq dem_k \quad \forall k \in K \tag{3}$$

$$\sum_{k \in K} newq_{ik} \geq news_i \quad \forall i \in I \tag{4}$$

$$\sum_{k \in K} oldq_{jk} \leq olds_j \quad \forall j \in J \tag{5}$$

$$\sum_{k \in K} y_{jk} \geq 1 \quad \forall j \in J \tag{6}$$

$$d_{ik} \leq td \quad \forall i \in I \tag{7}$$

Equations (1) and (2) are the target evaluation functions which require that the solution should find a shortest transportation distance and at the same time require as less as possible for building new station. Here Eqs. (2)–(7) are the constraint conditions. The requirements which are represented by the equations are as follow: Eq. (3) shows that every group should have enough supplying ability; Eqs. (4) and (5) is the limitation of each stations supplying ability. Whats more, Eq. (6) represents that every existing concrete mixing station must take part in supplying process. Finally, Eq. (7) represents that the distance for concrete delivery cannot exceed 25 km.

3   The Improved Genetic Algorithm

Even though the hybrid integer programming model above belongs to p-median problem, the number of newly additional sites is uncertain. Further, every construction group could accept service from several mixing stations and every mixing station could serve several groups at the same time, which makes LMS more difficult than the p-median problems because of its NP-hard feature.

Genetic algorithm [8], a widely adopted method for solving real-world engineer problems, has an adoptable fast convergence speed but the solution accuracy is not good enough for solving LMS problem. To address LMS and improve the accuracy of solution, we add a local search to genetic algorithm so that the quality of solution can be improved and make good use of genetic algorithm feature.

The Fig. 1. shows the flowchart of genetic algorithm with local search (GALS).

3.1   Encoding

In this paper, a matrix, chr, with (N+2) rows and M columns is adopted for one individual where M is the current maximum number of sites and N represented the group number. To overcome the uncertain feature of newly additional sites, two additional rows record the location of sites and the remained count. In the matrix, the supplying amount of each site is recorded in the first N rows element respectively. In addition, each element in row N+1 represents the site location for each column while the one in row N+2 represents the available supplying amount of its relative column.

The Fig. 2 introduce the scheme of encoding.

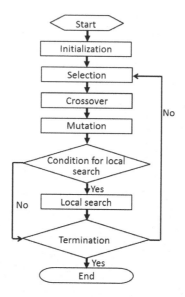

Fig. 1. GALS flowchart

3.2 Initialization for the Population

Each individual in the population is a solution of the LMS problem. Therefore every individual containing the sites should satisfy all the constraint condition. In addition, to maintain the diversity of solutions, a random selection is adopted for selecting the site and the details will be presented as follow:

Step 1: Pick up M sites randomly for each individual. If contains its original sites and the total supplying amount is more than the total requirement. Then execute Step 2 otherwise return Step 1 unlit all individual are served.

Step 2: Check out all distribution amounts for the groups. If there is any groups whose requirement could not be satisfied, then randomly select one of those groups without satisfaction of requirement and allocate one site which is unallocated to it until all requirement has been satisfied. Otherwise, allocation end.

The flowchart of initialization for population is present in the Fig. 3

3.3 Selection

Roulette wheel selection is adopted as the selection operation which reflect the idea of the GALS that the higher fitness the individual holds, the larger probability for existence it has. The target function in this paper is counting the cost of transportation for concrete. The lower cost solution can be considered as a

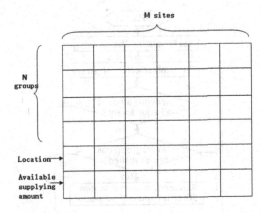

Fig. 2. The encoding of scheme

better solution for the LMS. Equation (8) is the fitness function for evaluating the quality of a solution.

$$fit(i) = (\frac{g_{min} - \beta(g_i - g_{min})}{g_{min}})^2 \tag{8}$$

Where g_i is the fitness value of ith individual while g_{min} is the minimum fitness value among population. Here, α and β are designed to control the convergence speed.

According to the Eq. (8), the smaller g_i is, the larger $fit(i)$ will be, meaning that an individual with higher fitness value holds a higher probability for being selected. However, variable β is designed to control the distance between the g_i and g_{min} because of the uncertain range of g_i. For example, while $g_i - g_{min} = 1000$, β can make the range of $g_{min} - \beta(g_i - g_{min})$ be $(-\infty, 1]$. Whats more, with adjusting the value of β, $g_{min} - \beta(g_i - g_{min})$ can reflect the information of distance on the basis of custom intention.

Further, for better controlling the convergence speed of the GALS, variable α is also added into the fitness function. Obviously, a smaller value of reflecting the diversity of selected individual is better, which can be considered that individual with long distance has a high probability to be selected and the convergence speed of GALS will slow down. In contrast, a high quality solution will be selected while the value of is large enough. That means the probability that individual with long distance will be selected is low and GALS has a fast convergence speed.

3.4 Crossover

Two-point crossover, which will randomly generate two crossover point in two individuals and then exchange all elements between them, is adopted in this paper. After crossover, original individual considered as the parent will produce two offspring. To make sure that the offspring provided by crossover is still a

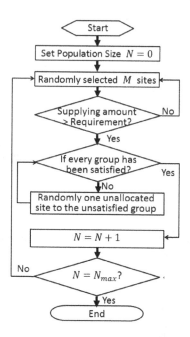

Fig. 3. Flowchart of initialization for population

qualified solution for LMS, an improvement strategy for crossover should be added and its detail will be presented as follow:

Step 1: Randomly generate two crossover points, point A and point B., for executing the crossover process and then generate offspring.
Step 2: Check out whether there is any reduplicated sites and replace them.
Step 3: Check out offspring satisfy the requirement or not. If the supplying amount of the offspring is larger than requirement it needs, adjust the allocation solution so that every group could get an enough supplying for achieving their requirement. Otherwise, there will be no crossover.

The adjustment for the allocation solution details are as follow:

Remark 1. Iterate all the groups. If supplying amount of anyone group is larger than requirement, then the site with longest path will be reallocated until the supplying amount equals to requirement.

Remark 2. Iterate all the groups. If there is any group suffering from the problem that the supplying amount is lower than the requirement, a site with shortest path picked up from the newly allocated sites should be allocated to this group. Repeat the process until its requirement is satisfied.

Assume that the crossover point is a = 2, b = 4, one of the off-spring is shown in Fig. 4.

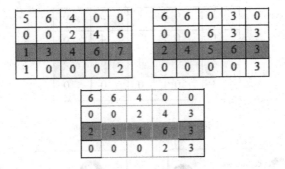

Fig. 4. two points crossover

After crossover, the site 3 is duplicated. Then randomly select the sites among crossover point A and point B and replace one of the duplicate the sites, site 3, with it. Here site 4, site 5 and site 5 are qualified to finish this task. And the Fig. 6 shows the result of the adjustment offspring. In addition, GALS will not change the sites among A to B for maintaining the gene diversity (Fig. 5).

6	6	4	0	0
0	0	2	4	6
2	3	4	6	5
0	0	0	2	0

Fig. 5. Replace the reduplicated sites

If the offspring can not satisfy the requirement, according to the step 3, GALS adjusts the gene. One of the samples in this situation is presented in Fig. 6.

3.5 Mutation

There are two mutation strategies for GASL because of the LMS feature.

Mutation Strategy 1. Replace a randomly selected site of the solution by the site which is not included in the individual solution, as Fig. 7 shown. To make sure that the mutated individual is still the qualified solution for the LMS, a check should be executed for confirming that the requirement of the group is satisfied. Otherwise, no mutation will be executed.

Mutation Strategy 2. Randomly transform the path between group as Fig. 8 shown.

1	6	4	2	0
0	0	2	4	6
2	3	4	6	5
3	0	0	0	0

Fig. 6. Solution adjustment

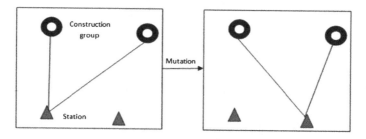

Fig. 7. Mutation Strategy 1

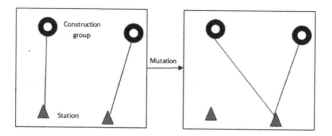

Fig. 8. Mutation Strategy 2

Step 1: Randomly pick two path between site and group, $l_{i,m}$ and $l_{i,n}$, where i and j mean the site of mixing station while n and m mean group. Assume that the distance of $l_{i,n}$ is shorter than $l_{i,m}$.

Step 2: Replace $l_{i,m}$ with $l_{i,n}$ and offer the same supplying amount to them.

Step 3: Add a path $l_{i,n}$, adjust the supply amount of site j to achievement the requirement of all groups.

3.6 Local Search

The local search strategy has the same component of mutation strategy 2. However, if the fitness value is less than the one of original solution after changing the path, the local search will be adopted. Hence, the local search is adopted conditionally.

To decrease the runtime of algorithm and make good use of the convergence ability of genetic algorithm, a threshold is designed for the local search which

Table 1. Parameter setting

Population size	100
Number of iteration	200
Number of local search	10
Threshold for local search	3.56E+05
Crossover rate	0.7
Mutation rate	0.02
α	2
beta	3.5
Max number of sites	35

will allow execution of local search after denoting that after n iterations the so far best solution did not have any improvement.

4   Experimental Analysis

4.1   Parameter Setting

The concrete requirement of Nanning city is adopted as the research object and the experiment is developed to simulate the programming of locating mixing station to meet the concrete demand. For simulation, the parameter setting is

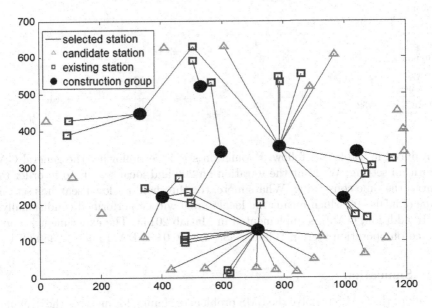

Fig. 9. The distribution diagram of solution

Table 2. Performance comparison between GA and GALS

–	GA	GALS
Best result	3.68E+05	3.46E+05
Average result	3.77E+05	3.52E+05

Table 3. Solution details for allocating amount

	XiNing group	Qinglliang group	Jiangnan group	Central group	City west group	City north group	Qingxiu group	Xianhu group
Huarun xitang				47				
Shengda				76				
Tengning					90			
Jiaqin					50			
Huarun Nanning						47		
Jin Hui Tong						66		
Qing Dian						83		
Jianye							66	
Sheng Dong							74	
Huarun Qinxiu	25					20		
Huohong	32							
Jiarun	55							
Jiada		52						
Hengri			51					
Fuyuda			37					
Tongda Cheng			56					
Dadu	52	24	97					

introduced in Table 1 as follow. Population size is set following the general GA algorithm setting. We limit the iteration on 200 and local search 10 in order to control the time consuming. Whats more, the threshold for local search is set on value of 3.56e+05 which means the local search will be performed conditionally.

In addition, GASL is implemented in Matlab 2014a. The experiment is conducted on operation system Windows 8.1 with 6.0 GB RAM and i5-2350 CPU.

4.2   Simulation

We adopt the GALS to solve the LMS problem of Naning for meeting the demand of concrete in 2015. One of the good enough allocation solution is present in Fig. 9

where a yellow line means supplying amount in this path should be lower than 50 thousand m^3/year. In addition, Table 2 presents the best result and the average result of GALS which outperform the ones of original GA. Furthermore, Table 3 introduces a solution detail presented in Fig. 9 for allocating amount. The results of the solution presented in Fig. 9 is solution of $3.46e+5$ m^3/year.

The result is not invariant because of the random feature of crossover and mutation adopted by GA. However, according to the result, GALS can achieve average solution of $3.52e+05$ m^3/year showing that the GALS has a great stability.

From Table 2, we can find out that the result of original genetic algorithm is higher than GALS. The result shows that with the help of specific encoding scheme, crossover, mutation strategy and local search, the GALS outperforms original GA.

In Table 3, we propose the final result for LMS station, the rows show the site of the mixing station, the columns are the construction group. The number of the Table 3 means the supplement from specific site to construction group.

5   Conclusion

We adopt a new idea to study the LMS problem and provide an improved genetic algorithm with local search for solving the LMS problem in addition finding out a good enough solution to satisfy the requirement for Nanning city in 2015. Furthermore, the GALS overcomes the accuracy problem which the original algorithm suffers from.

For future work, we hope to control the convergence speed of GA algorithm so that the GALS could have a better convergence speed so that it could find out a better solution and prevent itself from losing performance while premature convergence occurs.

Acknowledge. This work is supported by National Training Program of Innovation and Entrepreneurship for Undergraduates (201410561096), National Natural Science Foundation of China (61370102, 61203310, 61202453, 61370185), the Fundamental Research Funds for the Central Universities, SCUT (2014ZG0043), the Ministry of Education C China, Mobile Research Funds (MCM20130331), Project of Department of Education of Guangdong Province (2013KJCX0073) and the Pearl River Science & Technology Star Project (2012J2200007).

References

1. Aerts, J.C., Heuvelink, G.B.: Using simulated annealing for resource allocation. Int. J. Geogr. Inf. Sci. **16**(6), 571–587 (2002)
2. Davis, L.: Handbook of Genetic Algorithms. Van Nostrand Reinhold, New York (1991)
3. Eason, G., Noble, B., Sneddon, I.: On certain integrals of Lipschitz-Hankel type involving products of Bessel functions. Philos. Trans. R. Soc. Lond. A: Math. Phys. Eng. Sci. **247**(935), 529–551 (1955)

4. Espejo, L.G.A., Galvao, R.D., Boffey, B.: Dual-based heuristics for a hierarchical covering location problem. Comput. Oper. Res. **30**(2), 165–180 (2003)
5. Holland, J.H.: Concerning Efficient Adaptive Systems. Self-Organizing Systems, p. 230. Spartan Books, Washington, D.C. (1962)
6. Kennedy, J.: Particle swarm optimization. Encyclopedia of Machine Learning, pp. 760–766. Springer, US (2010)
7. Storn, R., Price, K.: Differential evolution-a simple and efficient heuristic for global optimization over continuous spaces. J. glob. Optim. **11**(4), 341–359 (1997)
8. Wang, N., Lu, J.C., Kvam, P.: Reliability modeling in spatially distributed logistics systems. IEEE Trans. Reliab. **55**(3), 525–534 (2006)

Recognition of Spam Microblog for TV Program Evaluation Under Mircoblog Platform

Fulian Yin, Xinran Wang[✉], Yanyan Wang, and Jianping Chai

Information Engineering School, Communication University of China,
Beijing 100021, China
1149779627@qq.com

Abstract. Aimed at the serious problem of the microblog platform used in the field of evaluating TV program that is badly affected by spam microblog, this paper proposes a recognition method about combination of lexicon match with SVM based on pattern matching and machine learning. At the same time, considering the impact that spam information caused in the public-opinion-trend and topic-attention-degree, it is important to identify the spam microblog correctly. They are various cleaning modes for different spam information. And the results of experiment shows that the total-recognition-rate has already reached 80 %. This method is useful for the following text mining.

Keywords: Microblog platform · Spam microblog · Navy detection · Pattern matching · Machine learning

1 Introduction

The microblog is a social platform for sharing, spreading, and obtaining information by paying attention to another person among microblog-users. It becomes the major activity of Internet users because of its considerable real-time property and interactivity. However, at the same time, the unique mode of fission-communication attracts massive amount of spam information. They exert a great influence on the text analysis. However, the spam information have a variable linguistic for which is very complex, so it's difficult to define their textual features and identify them in a fixed mode. Then, how to precisely identify network navy and the reliability of Internet information in the flood of microblog become a problem, which need to be solved in the microblog platform.

The scholars pay their attention to the spam web and spam recognition at present, and this orientation develops a mature processing method and theoretical system, and the accuracy of recognition also improve as a result. However, the recognition of spam comments is only at an early stage [1]. In recent years, the researchers have gradually kept a watchful eye on spam comments among blog, BBS, etc. By analyzing the characters of comments such as repetitive quantities of meaningless adjectives, having repetitive language in the context, or the authenticity of the comments can be judged [2]. The network navy can

© Springer-Verlag Berlin Heidelberg 2015
M. Gong et al. (Eds.): BIC-TA 2015, CCIS 562, pp. 563–570, 2015.
DOI: 10.1007/978-3-662-49014-3_50

be detected by finding out the different characters between normal users and abnormal users, such as lots of the following users with little fans or posting less [3]. Wang and some other people introduced the complex relationship model for the first time and applied the theory to help building the relationship models among Internet navy, the comments they make, and the target; then analyzed the interaction of nodes to identify all the suspicious reviewers [4]. Song and some other people believed that measuring the distance between users and the tightness of user-contact could help to identify network navy [5].

The work of recognition is mostly based on the deeply understanding of microblog posters. It seems to be particularly important how to eliminate the invalid postings and reserve the meaningful comments without the posters information.

2   The Classification of Spam Microblog of Program Comments

Spam microblog mainly refers to the postings which uses microblog platform for making public topics, promotion of various microblog events or product, and guiding the public opinion to achieve self-profit. With the dramatic increase of the number of users and data, the spam microblogs are constantly increasing, which has already become an important factor affecting the trend of the topics. The paper mainly studies the spam microblog recognition of evaluation in the TV program, and it is mainly classified into two types: advertising microblog and public opinion guiding microblog.

Advertising microblog postings mainly display comments on advertising information, URL, pornographic and violence content. These spam microblog have little or even no relationship, just causing people's attention for the promotion. For example: "Welcome friends to visit and collect my shop, as long as you like clothes in this shop, all of which can be further price reductions, some parts of the products can be free shipping, you will regret if you don't have a look. It is a good choice for your own use or sending to friends and family. In addition, we will send a small gift if you buy something here. http://shop64021208.taobao. com". Moreover, when network users use some applications, they often publishes related links, and the applications would be promoted. For example: "I found great amount of good drama in Letv, The Palace Lock LianCheng TV Version, I Love Male Girlfriends, Bud Girl Heart Sutra, Dad Go Home, let's hurry to chase them, there are message reminding too. http://t.cn/8spMduj"; "Choose to face heart in essence, I am listening to the song of Qu Wanting The courage of love (TV series The Divorce Lawyer theme song) http://t.cn/R7htA4Y (From @QQ music)". This kind of spam microblog has an obvious propaganda motivation, so it is easy to decide the text characteristic, and it is suitable to filtrate by pattern recognition.

Public opinion microblog-oriented is mainly to improve the attention of topics, and increase the topics of high praise. Some programs in the pre-show will post a large number of spam microblogs to improve its program discussion. For example, before the release of TV series I Love Male Girlfriends, the recommended postings of the plot are largely forwarded: "[titles MV, lyrics big run] title song created by Chen Xi and Dong Dongdong, who are the lyric and song writer of the popular song Time Is Where Did You Go. Various beautiful girls come together, and take a look at your side whether your male girlfriends do? If do, @ he to show off to others, if not, still @ he, let him learn from cook Huang". This kind of Spam microblog has a bigger influence on public opinion trend and the attention of topics, however it owns changeable language forms, complex context, obscure text feature, undefined fixed pattern; therefore, these texts are fits to use machine learning method to filtrate.

3 Detection Method of Spam Microblog

Recognition the problem of Spam microblog can be converted to a dichotomy problem [6]. Set W as text content collection about a particular program in microblog: $W = \{w_1, w_2, \ldots, w_i, \ldots, w_{|W|}\}$, among them, wi is one of the microblogs. The identification of the spam microblog is to judge whether postings belong to the spam. Therefore, the objective function can be simplified as $\Phi(w_i) : W \to \{0, 1\}$. This paper uses two different detection methods for two types of spam microblog, and proposes a new identification method to combine pattern matching with machine learning.

3.1 The Filtering Method Based on Rules and Pattern Matching

The filtering based on rules is to analyze the statistic of a large number of spam microblogs to find the obvious characteristics, such setting a few filtering rules as "discounted" "promotion", "share" and other words. Some product advertisement released by few marketing numbers, often contain similar words, so it is suitable to filter by this method.

This paper uses artificial dictionary, to determine the ratio of the words shown in the text and the total number of words in dictionary, then that the one reaches the threshold value is spam microblog. Set dictionary as U, $U = \{u_1, u_2, u_3, \ldots, u_i, \ldots, u_n\}$, then word frequency as:

$$T_i = \frac{\sum_{j=1}^{n} n_{i,j}}{n_u}. \tag{1}$$

Among $n_{i,j}$ shows if there is a word u_j in Dictionary could be find in microblog w_i, if do, record as 1, if not, record as 0. The dictionary contains a total of 350 entries based on statistics of the long-term consolidation, including "buy", "half price", "shop", etc. The threshold is selected from many experiments by the highest correct rate, and this text selects 0.5 % as the threshold. Obviously, the bigger the dictionary, the greater the accuracy.

3.2   Spam Microblog Recognition Based on Text Polarity Analysis

This paper analyzes the text by machine learning which uses the text data as input to extract the characteristics and find the information from it to predict and analyze the new data. Public opinion guide microblog mentioned above is suitable to detect by this method.

At present, there are three main methods of machine learning that are logistic regression, support vector machine (SVM) and random forest [7]. This paper mainly uses the method of SVM to identify the spam microblog, and the basic idea is to construct a super plane as the decision plane, so that there is the largest [8] the gap between positive and negative mode. Figure 1 is a flow chart of Spam microblog detection based on machine learning.

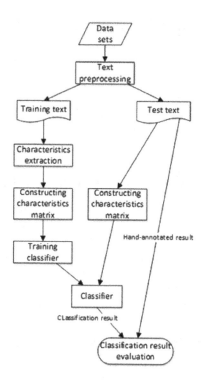

Fig. 1. Spam microblog detection based on machine learning

Associated with television program evaluation, this paper uses content of the microblog as data sets, including spam microblog labeled 1, meaningful microblog of a practical significance labeled −1. Some of the sample data is selected as the training set, and the remaining data is used as the test set, and the model parameters are used to predict the test set. Among them, the feature extraction mainly uses the method based on string matching and graph scanning for word segmentation, then arranging the result statistically, selecting high frequency words as the key, on the basis, establishing document of word frequency matrix as the feature matrix. The training accuracy reaches 97.8 % by using the *kernlab* package of *R* language for machine learning and testing.

3.3 Detection Method Based on Machine Learning and Pattern Matching

Due to the method based on pattern matching is suitable for the advertising microblog detection, and the method based on the text polarity analysis is more suitable for filtering the public opinion microblog-oriented; Therefore, this paper uses detection method of combining pattern matching with machine learning, in order to improve the recall rate of the whole test. The process is shown in Fig. 2. Using two methods of dictionary matching and training of support vector machine (SVM) for testing respectively, and combining them to detect as well as deleting spam microblog, only remaining meaningful comments for later data analysis.

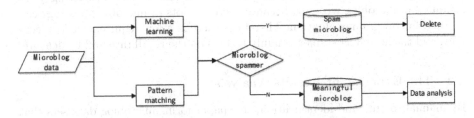

Fig. 2. Spam microblog detection based on pattern matching and machine learning

4 Experiment and Result Analysis

4.1 Evaluation Index of Classification Method

The evaluation of the effect of spam recognition usually uses the accuracy, precision and recall and F-Measure for evaluation. Table 1 is a matrix of two-type problems to conclude the calculation method of various measurements from the confusion [9].

Classified correctly sample is on the main diagonal, so the value should be as big as possible, and the value on the secondary diagonal should be as small as possible. Here are the specific calculating formulas:

The correct classified sample is on the main diagonal,the data should be as big as possible, and the data on the secondary diagonal should be as small as possible. Here are the specific calculating formulas:

$$Accuracy = \frac{TP + TN}{TP + FP + TN + FN},$$

Table 1. Confusion matrix of two type problems

		Predicted class	
		+	−
Actual class	+	Correct normal polarity (TP)	False negative polarity (FN)
	−	False positive polarity (FP)	Correct negative polarity (TN)

$$Precision = \frac{TP}{TP + FP},$$

$$Recall = \frac{TP}{TP + FN},$$

$$F - Measure = \frac{2 * Recall * Precision}{Recall + Precision}.$$

This paper sets the spam microblog as a normal polarity text, and the comments with actual meanings of postings as negative polarity text. It needs to identify spam microblog as much as possible, but effects little if deleting some meaningful microblog wrongly, because there are lots of microblog postings can be used for program evaluation. Therefore, there is a low requirement for accuracy, and the actual assessment mainly focuses on the recall rate and F-Measure.

4.2   The Experiment Results Analysis

By manual sorting and identification, this paper forms microblog data sets that the experiment required. The corpus contains 1038 microblogs, including 436 spam microblogs, and 602 significant ones.

Based on pattern matching combined with machine learning, this paper is tested to pick out spam microblog, selected 838 samples randomly as training ones, the rest for testing. The result contains 80 correct normal polarity corpus, 20 wrong negative polarity corpus, 24 wrong normal polarity corpus, and 76 correct negative polarity corpus. Form 2 shows the comparison of the above test methods and simplex ones. According to the Form 2, the method that

Table 2. Experimental index of the method of the identification of spam microblog

	Accuracy (A) (%)	Precision (F) (%)	Recall (R) (%)	F-Measure (F)
Method based on pattern matching	81.8	81.5	64.2	0.718
Method based on machine learning	65	87.5	35	0.5
Methods for the combination of the two	78	77	80	0.785

unites pattern matching and machine learning owns the highest recall rate and F-Measure (Table 2).

By taking content related to The CCTV News as example, this paper compares before the filtering with after the filtering. The word cloud are displayed in Figs. 3 and 4. The Fig. 3 shows that there are many spam words before the filtering, such as promotion of memorizing software "Word" and advertisement of real estate named "Jellyfish", etc. While after the filtering, the word cloud includes discussion of the program mainly. Therefore, the method in the paper fits the data cleaning of the early text analysis.

Fig. 3. The word cloud before filtering   **Fig. 4.** The word cloud after filtering

5   Conclusion

Aimed at the postings content is severely affected by spam microblog for the evaluation of TV program in the microblog platform, this paper puts forward a recognition method combining the dictionary match with SVM which is based on the principle of pattern matching and machine learning, as well as corresponding cleaning schemes for different types of spam. The experimental result shows the total recognition rate of spam microblog is 80 %, which indicates an effective improvement of the accuracy and recall rate. Compared with other classification methods of spam microblog, the method in this paper achieves a particular applicability through an expansion of dictionary.

References

1. Mo, Q., Yang, K.: Study on network navy recognition. Softw. J. **07**, 1505–1526 (2014)
2. Liu, H., Zhao, Y., Qin, B., Liu, T.: Comment target extraction and sentiment classification. J. Chin. Inf. Process. **24**(1), 84–88 (2010)
3. Jindal, N., Liu, B., Lim, E.P.: Finding Unusual Review Patterns Using Unexpected Rules. ACM Press, New York (2010)
4. Wang, G., Xie, S., Liu, B., Yu, P.S.: Review graph based online store review spammer detection. In: Proceedings of the 2011 IEEE 11th International Conference on Data Mining, pp. 1242–1247 (2011)

5. Song, T., Pan, L., Păun, Gh: Asynchronous spiking neural P systems with local synchronization. Inf. Sci. **219**, 197–207 (2013)
6. Zhang, L., Zhu, J., Yao, T.: An evaluation of statistical spam filtering techniques. Asian Lang. Inf. Process. **3**(4), 243–269 (2004)
7. Cortes, C., Vapnik, V.: Support vector machine. Mach. Learn. **20**(3), 273–297 (1995)
8. Platt, J.: Sequential minimal optimization: a fast algorithm for training support vector or machines. In: Advances in Kernel Methods-Support Vector Learning. MIT Press (1998)
9. Yu, R., Liu, C., Jin, X., Wang, Y., Cheng, X.: Chinese spam filtering based on multi angle of feature fusion. J. Shandong Univ. **11**, 53–58 (2013)

An Algorithm Simulated Sticker Model for MIS

Deyuan Wu, Kang Zhou$^{(\boxtimes)}$, Di Hu, and Shuangqi Ge

School of Math and Computer, Wuhan Polytechnic University, Wuhan 430023, China
{849493516,1623302442,469557084}@qq.com, zhoukang_wh@163.com

Abstract. Through analysis of properties of sticker model and maximum independent set, an algorithm simulated sticker model for maximum independent set problem (MIS) is designed, and order of detecting vertex problem is put forward. Algorithm for order of detecting vertex problem is given to simplify tube matrix. In algorithm simulated sticker model for MIS, first initial tube matrix is set; then tube matrix of all independent set is constructed; finally all maximum independent sets are figured out. The effectiveness and feasibility of algorithm simulated sticker model are explained by a simulated experiment.

Keywords: DNA computing · Sticker model · Maximum independent set problem · Order of detecting vertex problem · Tube matrix

1 Introduction

Maximum Independent Set Problem (MIS) was an important topic of graph theory, which was proved to be a famous NP-complete problem [1]. For simple undirected graph $G = (V, E)$, where vertex set $V(G) = \{v_i | i = 1, 2, \ldots, n\}$ and edge set $E(G) = \{e_i | i = 1, 2, \ldots, m\}$, set k ($k \subseteq V(G)$) is called an independent set of graph G, if arbitrary two vertices in set k are nonadjacent in graph G. Independent set k is maximum independent set of graph G, if there is no independent set k' of graph G satisfying $|k'| > |k|$. MIS is to find a maximum independent set. MIS was widely used [3] in the field of coding theory, the transportation route planning, geographic information system, fault diagnosis, economics, channel allocation, information retrieval and resource allocation. Therefore, research on algorithm of MIS is challengeable and important.

Algorithms of MIS [4] were divided into exact algorithms and heuristic approaches. The research of exact algorithms was mainly aimed at the special graph, and most of them can only be improved in the exponential time [5]. That is to say, the exact algorithm was not suitable for a large scale and general network graph. So large and hard instances of MIS were typically solved by using heuristic approaches, but these algorithms cannot obtain exact solution of MIS. So it was essential to find an exact algorithm to find all maximal independent sets which was more practical and can effectively control calculation time.

In nature, there are rich computing intelligence for constructing computing models, such as neural-like computing models [2,9–11,21] and molecular computing systems [12]. In this work, we consider DNA computing models in solving MIS. DNA motifs and computing model [6,7,13,14] had two characteristics:

© Springer-Verlag Berlin Heidelberg 2015
M. Gong et al. (Eds.): BIC-TA 2015, CCIS 562, pp. 571–582, 2015.
DOI: 10.1007/978-3-662-49014-3_51

highly parallel computing ability and magnanimous information processing ability, which created the conditions to be solve NP-complete problems. And DNA computing had more advantages in a kind of problems which need to figure out all optimal solutions [8,15,16]. So to simulate DNA computing by simulating DNA encoding and biochemistry experiments to solve practical problems was one of the important applications of DNA computing for algorithm research. In 2009, in order to obtain all solutions of eight queens problem, Zhou Kang et al. [17] put forward simulation DNA algorithm for the first time, that was successful attempt. The deep study of simulation DNA computing was necessary, so based on sticker model [18,19], Zhou Kang et al. [20,22] made further research on simulation DNA algorithm and put forward variable length vector and biochemical operators which contain batch separation operator and electrophoresis operator. They also introduced concepts of minimal element, deriving element and less-than relation to simplify batch separation operator set and electrophoresis operator set.

2   Simulating Sticker Model

2.1   Simulating Memory Strand

Memory strand $h_1 h_2 \cdots h_n$ is DNA strand mixing single-stranded and double-stranded; $h_i = b_i$, if h_i is double-stranded; and $h_i = c_i$, if h_i is single-stranded.

Definition 1. Let row vector $a = (a_1, a_2, \ldots, a_n)$, where $a_i \in \{0, 1, -1\}$.

a. Memory strand $h_1 h_2 \cdots h_n$ is denoted by a (**memory strand vector**), if

$$a_i = \begin{cases} 0, & h_i = b_i \\ 1, & h_i = c_i \\ -1, & h_i = c_i \ \text{ or } \ b_i \end{cases}$$

b. Tube S is denoted by matrix S, if S is composed of memory strand vectors corresponding to memory strands in tube S. Matrix S is called **tube matrix**.

c. The jth column vector of tube matrix S is denoted by $S(j^\mathrm{T})$; The ith row memory strand vector of tube matrix S is denoted by $S(i)$.

d. $S - \{i\} = (S(1), \ldots, S(i-1), S(i+1), \ldots, S(p))^\mathrm{T}$, if $S = (S(1), S(2), \ldots, S(p))^\mathrm{T}$.

e. $S = S'$, if $\forall i \exists j (S(i) = S'(j)) \land \forall i \exists j (S'(i) = S(j))$. $\square$

For example, tube $S = \{c_1 b_2 c_3 b_4 b_5 b_6, c_1 b_2 c_3 b_4 c_5 b_6\}$ is denoted by memory strand vector $(1, 0, 1, 0, -1, 0)$. And tube matrix $S = \begin{pmatrix} 1 & 0 & 1 & 0 & -1 & 0 \\ 0 & -1 & 0 & 1 & 1 & 0 \end{pmatrix}$ denotes tube $S = \{c_1 b_2 c_3 b_4 b_5 b_6, c_1 b_2 c_3 b_4 c_5 b_6, b_1 c_2 b_3 c_4 c_5 b_6, b_1 b_2 b_3 c_4 c_5 b_6\}$.

And for $S = \begin{pmatrix} 0 & 1 & -1 & 1 & 0 & 1 \\ 1 & 0 & 1 & 0 & -1 & 0 \\ 0 & -1 & 0 & 1 & 1 & 0 \end{pmatrix}$, $S(4^\mathrm{T}) = \begin{pmatrix} 1 \\ 0 \\ 1 \end{pmatrix}$, $S - \{2\} = \begin{pmatrix} 0 & 1 & -1 & 1 & 0 & 1 \\ 0 & -1 & 0 & 1 & 1 & 0 \end{pmatrix}$.

2.2   Simulating Biochemistry Experiment

Definition 2. a. Tube matrix $S_1 \cup S_2$ is merge matrix of S_1 and S_2, if $\forall i \exists j (S_1 \cup S_2(i) = S_1(j) \vee S_1 \cup S_2(i) = S_2(j))$ and $\forall i \exists j (S_1(i) = S_1 \cup S_2(j) \wedge S_2(i) = S_1 \cup S_2(j))$.

b. The j_0th separation operation of S is $+(S, j_0)$ and $-(S, j_0)$.

Tube matrix $+(S, j_0)$ is composed of all memory strand vectors of tube matrix S, whose the j_0th component is 1 and is -1 instead of 1.

Tube matrix $-(S, j_0)$ is composed of all memory strand vectors of tube matrix S, whose the j_0th component is 0 and is -1 instead of 0.

c. The j_1th, j_2th, ..., j_kth group separation operation of S is tube matrix $-(S, \{j_1, j_2, \ldots, j_k\})$ composed of all memory strand vectors of tube matrix S whose the j_1th, j_2th, ..., j_kth components are 0 or are -1 instead of 0.

d. Electrophoresis operation of $S = (a_{ij})$ is tube matrix $\max(S)$ which is a tube matrix of the longest memory strand vector of S. The length of memory strand vector is the sum of absolute value of its component. □

For example, $S = \begin{pmatrix} 0 & 1 & 1 & 1 & 0 & 0 \\ 0 & -1 & 0 & 1 & 1 & 0 \end{pmatrix} \cup \begin{pmatrix} 1 & 0 & 1 & 0 & -1 & 0 \\ 0 & 1 & 1 & 0 & 0 & 0 \end{pmatrix} = \begin{pmatrix} 1 & 0 & 1 & 0 & -1 & 0 \\ 0 & 1 & 1 & -1 & 0 & 0 \\ 0 & -1 & 0 & 1 & 1 & 0 \end{pmatrix}.$

$$-(S, \{2, 3, 6\}) = \begin{pmatrix} 0 & 0 & 0 & 1 & 1 & 0 \end{pmatrix}.$$

$$+(S, 4) = \begin{pmatrix} 0 & 1 & 1 & 1 & 0 & 0 \\ 0 & -1 & 0 & 1 & 1 & 0 \end{pmatrix},$$

$$-(S, 4) = \begin{pmatrix} 1 & 0 & 1 & 0 & -1 & 0 \\ 0 & 1 & 1 & 0 & 0 & 0 \end{pmatrix}.$$

$$|S| = \begin{pmatrix} 1 & 0 & 1 & 0 & 1 & 0 \\ 0 & 1 & 1 & 1 & 0 & 0 \\ 0 & 1 & 0 & 1 & 1 & 0 \end{pmatrix} \Rightarrow \max(S) = \begin{pmatrix} 1 & 0 & 1 & 0 & 1 & 0 \\ 0 & 1 & 1 & 1 & 0 & 0 \\ 0 & 1 & 0 & 1 & 1 & 0 \end{pmatrix}.$$

3   Algorithm Design of MIS

3.1   Analysis of Detecting Operation of Simulated Sticker Model

Theorem 1. Set k is an independent set $\Leftrightarrow \forall v_i \in k$,

$$\{v_{i_1}, v_{i_2}, \ldots, v_{i_k}\} \cap k = \emptyset \tag{1}$$

where set $\{v_{i_1}, v_{i_2}, \ldots, v_{i_k}\}$ is composed of vertices adjacent to vertex v_i. □

For vertex v_i $(i = 1, 2, \ldots, n)$, if set $\{v_{i_1}, v_{i_2}, \ldots, v_{i_k}\}$ is adjacent to vertex set of vertex v_i, then $(i_1, i_2, \ldots, i_k)$ is its subscript vector, and $i(i_1, i_2, \ldots, i_k)$ is called adjacent labeling of vertex v_i.

By doing various biochemistry operators based on sticker model, algorithm simulated sticker model for MIS can be designed for three parts as follows:

a. Construct tube matrix S_1 representing all vertex subsets of graph G;
b. For vertex v_i $(i = 1, 2, \ldots, n)$, do detecting operation to obtain tube matrix representing all independent sets as follows:

> Let $V = \{v_i | i = 1, 2, \ldots, n\}$
> For $l = 1$ to n
> > Let $S' = +(S_l, i)$ for $v_i \in V$
> > Let $S'' = -(S', \{i_1, i_2, \ldots, i_k\})$ for $v_i : i(i_1, i_2, \ldots, i_k)$
> > Let $S_{l+1} = -(S_l, i) \cup S''$
> > Let $V = V - \{v_i\}$
> End

c. Do electrophoresis operation $S^* = \max(S_{n+1})$, then tube matrix S^* is all maximal independent sets.   □

Definition 3. For tube matrix S_l, adjacent labeling $i(i_1, i_2, \ldots, i_k)$ and vertex subset $k(k \in V(G))$, let memory strand vector $S_l(i) = (a_{i1}, a_{i2}, \ldots, a_{in})$.

a. Calculation formula of detecting operation is as follows:

$$S_{l+1} = -(S_l, i) \cup -(+(S_l, i), \{i_1, i_2, \ldots, i_k\}) \tag{2}$$

b. $k \subseteq S_l(i)$, if for $\forall j(j = 1, 2, \ldots, n)$,

$$a_{ij} = \begin{cases} 0, & v_j \overline{\in} k \\ 1, & v_j \in k \\ -1, & (v_j \in k) \vee (v_j \overline{\in} k) \end{cases}$$

c. $k \subseteq S_l$, if $\exists i(k \subseteq S_l(i))$.   □

Theorem 2. For tube matrix S_{l+1} of formula (2),

a. $\forall k(k \subseteq S_{l+1}), (v_i \in k \wedge \{v_{i_1}, v_{i_2}, \ldots, v_{i_k}\} \cap k = \emptyset) \vee (v_i \overline{\in} k)$
b. $\forall k(k \subseteq S_{l+1} \to k \subseteq S_l)$.

Proof. $-(S_l, i)$ is the tube matrix whose the ith component is 0, namely, $\forall k(k \subseteq -(S_l, i) \to v_i \overline{\in} k)$. $+(S_l, i)$ is the tube matrix whose the ith component is 1, namely, $\forall k(k \subseteq +(S_l, i) \to v_i \in k)$. $-(S', \{i_1, i_2, \ldots, i_k\})$ is the tube matrix whose the i_1th, i_2th, $\ldots$, i_kth components are 0, namely, $\forall k(k \subseteq -(S', \{i_1, i_2, \ldots, i_k\}) \to \{v_{i_1}, v_{i_2}, \ldots, v_{i_k}\} \cap k = \emptyset)$. So $\forall k(k \subseteq -(+(S_l, i), \{i_1, i_2, \ldots, i_k\}) \to v_i \in k \wedge \{v_{i_1}, v_{i_2}, \ldots, v_{i_k}\} \cap k = \emptyset)$.

$\forall k(k \subseteq -(S_l, i) \cup -(+(S_l, i), \{i_1, i_2, \ldots, i_k\}) \to (v_i \in k \wedge \{v_{i_1}, v_{i_2}, \ldots, v_{i_k}\} \cap k = \emptyset) \vee (v_i \overline{\in} k))$. Therefore, conclusion **a** and conclusion **b** is established.   □

Theorem 3. Let initial tube matrix be $S_0 = (-1, -1, \ldots, -1)$, tube matrix S_{l+1} of formula (2) satisfies property as follows:

a. For no detecting column j, $\forall i(S_{l+1}(j^T)(i) \neq 1)$ and $\exists i(S_{l+1}(j^T)(i) = -1)$.
b. For detected column j, $\forall i(S_{l+1}(j^T)(i) \neq -1)$ and $\exists i(S_{l+1}(j^T)(i) = 1)$.
c. For tube matrix S_l, do the ith detecting operation according to two cases to obtain tube matrix S_{l+1}:

(a) For $\forall j$, let $(S_l(j))(i) = 0$, let $S_{l+1} = S_{l+1} \cup S_l(j)$.

(b) For $\forall j((S_l(j))(i) = -1 \wedge \forall q(1 \leq q \leq k \rightarrow (S_l(j))(i_q) \neq 1))$, let $(S_l(j))(i) = 1$, let $(S_l(j))(i_q) = 0$ $(1 \leq q \leq k)$, let $S_{l+1} = S_{l+1} \cup S_l(j)$.

Proof. Based on formula (2), for tube matrix S_l, do the ith detecting operation according to three cases and to obtain tube matrix S_{l+1} as follows:

(a) First for $\forall j((S_l(j))(i) \neq 1)$ let $(S_l(j))(i) = 0$, then $S_{l+1} = S_{l+1} \cup S_l(j)$.

(b) First for $\forall j((S_l(j))(i) = -1 \wedge \forall q(1 \leq q \leq k \rightarrow (S_l(j))(i_q) \neq 1))$ let $(S_l(j))(i) = 1$ and let $(S_l(j))(i_q) = 0$ $(1 \leq q \leq k)$, then $S_{l+1} = S_{l+1} \cup S_l(j)$.

(c) For $\forall j((S_l(j))(i) = -1 \wedge \exists q(1 \leq q \leq k \wedge (S_l(j))(i_q) = 1))$, memory strand vector $S_l(j)$ does not add into tube matrix S_{l+1}.

According to $S_0 = (-1, -1, \ldots, -1)$ and these three cases, for no detecting column j, $\forall i(S_{l+1}(j^{\mathsf{T}})(i) \neq 1)$; and for detected column j, $\forall i(S_{l+1}(j^{\mathsf{T}})(i) \neq -1)$.

When $l = 0$, $S_0 = (-1, -1, \ldots, -1)$, so conclusion **a** is established.

When $l = 1$, according to case (a), there exist memory strand vector $S_1(i)$ whose all no detecting components are -1 (without loss of generality, let the memory strand vector be $S_1(1)$), so for no detecting column j, $\exists i(S_1(j^{\mathsf{T}})(i) = -1)$. According to $S_0 = (-1, -1, \ldots, -1)$ and case (b), for detected column j, $\exists i(S_1(j^{\mathsf{T}})(i) = 1)$. So conclusion **a** and conclusion **b** are established.

Suppose conclusion **a** and conclusion **b** are established for tube matrix S_l, and all no detecting components of $S_l(1)$ are -1. When $l = l + 1$, according to $S_l(1)$ and case (a), all no detecting components of $S_{l+1}(1)$ are also -1, so for no detecting column j, $\exists i(S_{l+1}(j^{\mathsf{T}})(i) = -1)$. According to $S_l(1)$ and case (b), for detected column j, $\exists i(S_{l+1}(j^{\mathsf{T}})(i) = 1)$. So conclusion **a** and conclusion **b** are established.

According to conclusion **a**, for no detecting column i, $\forall j((S_l(j))(i) \neq 1)$, so case (a) of conclusion **c** $\Rightarrow$ case (a).

Case (b) of conclusion **c** $\Leftrightarrow$ case (b).

Case (a) and case (b) of conclusion **c** $\Rightarrow$ case (c).

So conclusion **c** is established. □

3.2   Order of Detecting Vertex Problem

Theorem 4. For adjacent labeling $i(i_1, i_2, \ldots, i_k)$ and adjacent labeling $i_1(i, j_1, j_2, \ldots, j_r)$, and

$$S_l = -(S_{l-1}, i) \cup -(+(S_{l-1}, i), \{i_1, i_2, \ldots, i_k\}),$$

$$S_{l+1} = -(S_l, i_1) \cup -(+(S_l, i_1), \{j_1, j_2, \ldots, j_r\}),$$

then arbitrary vertex subset k of tube matrix S_{l+1} satisfies as follows:

$$(v_{i_1} \in k \wedge \{v_i, v_{j_1}, v_{j_2}, \ldots, v_{j_r}\} \cap k = \emptyset) \vee (v_{i_1} \overline{\in} k).$$

Proof. Arbitrary vertex subset k of tube matrix S_l satisfies as follows:

$$(v_i \in k \wedge \{v_{i_1}, v_{i_2}, \ldots, v_{i_k}\} \cap k = \emptyset) \vee (v_i \overline{\in} k)$$

Namely, for k of tube matrix S_l, $v_{i_1} \overline{\in} k \vee v_i \overline{\in} k$.

Tube matrix S_{l+1} is obtained from tube matrix S_l, so for arbitrary vertex subset k of tube matrix S_{l+1}: $v_{i_1} \overline{\in} k \vee v_i \overline{\in} k$.

Arbitrary vertex subset k of tube matrix S_{l+1} satisfies as follows:

$$(v_{i_1} \in k \wedge \{v_{j_1}, v_{j_2}, \ldots, v_{j_r}\} \cap k = \emptyset) \vee (v_{i_1} \overline{\in} k)$$

So $(v_{i_1} \in k \wedge \{v_i, v_{j_1}, v_{j_2}, \ldots, v_{j_r}\} \cap k = \emptyset) \vee (v_{i_1} \overline{\in} k)$. Therefore, conclusion is established. □

Conclusions are as follows:

a. If vertex v_i is detected in tube matrix S_l, and tube matrix S_{l+1} will detect vertex v_{i_1}, then $i_1(i, j_1, j_2, \ldots, j_r) \Rightarrow i_1(j_1, j_2, \ldots, j_r)$. So adjacent labeling of vertex v_{i_1} can be simplified.

b. If adjacent labeling simplified of vertex v_{i_1} is $i_1\emptyset$, then $S_{l+1} = S_l$. So tube matrix S_{l+1} is not necessary to detect vertex v_{i_1}, and vertex v_{i_1} of $i_1\emptyset$ is called **no labeling vertex**. □

Choosing order of detecting vertex can reduce iteration times of detecting operation and reduce the scale of tube matrix. **Order of detecting vertex problem** is that choosing the optimum order of detecting vertex makes detecting operation reduce the row number of tube matrix on the premise of producing no labeling vertices as much as possible. Let d_i be the number of adjacent labeling of vertex v_i, a method to solve order of detecting vertex problem is as follows:

a. Obtain order C of no detecting vertices according to d_i value from big to small, then obtain subscript set E in set C of the biggest d_i value.

b. Choose vertices adjacent to more no detecting vertices which is low d_i value from set E, and obtain subscript set E' of these vertices.

c. Choose column vector of more 0 value from tube matrix S_l corresponding to set E', the vertex corresponding to the column vector is detecting vertex v_i.

d. Revise adjacent labeling of no detecting vertices. □

3.3   Simplifying Tube Matrix Problem

Theorem 5. $S = S'$, if $\exists i_1 \exists i_2 (i_1 \neq i_2)$, $S_l = (a_{ij})$ and S'_l satisfy as follows:

a. $a_{i_1 j} = a_{i_2 j}, (j \neq j_0 \wedge 1 \leq j \leq n)$;
b. $a_{i_1 j_0} = 0 \wedge a_{i_2 j_0} = 1$;
c. $S'_l = S_l - \{i_1\}$.

Proof. $a_{i_2 j_0} = 1$ represents that the j_0th column of tube matrix S_l has been detected. So $\forall k_1 \exists k_2 (k_1 \subseteq S_l(i_1) \wedge k_2 \subseteq S_l(i_2) \to k_1 \subseteq k_2)$.

So if $k(k \subseteq S_l(i_1))$ is a maximum independent set, then $k \subseteq S_l(i_2)$, and vertex subset k is a maximum independent set.

Therefore, $S_l - \{i_1\}$ and S_l have the same maximum independent set. Namely, tube matrix S'_l and tube matrix S_l is equivalent in detecting operation. □

Definition 4. The rule is $0 \lhd 1$, $0 \lhd -1$. $(a_l, a_2, \ldots, a_n) \subset (a'_l, a'_2, \ldots, a'_n)$, if for $i = 1, 2, \ldots, n$, $a_i \lhd a'_i$. $\qquad\square$

Theorem 6. $S_l = S_l - \{i_1\}$, if $S_l(i_1) \subset S_l(i_2)$. $\qquad\square$

The calculation process of the ith detecting operation of tube matrix S_l is as follows:

a. Let $S_l = S_1 \cup S_2$, where $S_1(i^T) = 0 \wedge S_2(i^T) = -1$. Let $S_{l+1} = S_1$.
b. Let $S_2(i^T) = 0$.
c. Simplify S_2 according to S_1:
  For $\forall j$, if $\exists k(S_2(j) \subset S_1(k))$, then $S_2 = S_2 - \{j\}$.
d. Let $S_{l+1} = S_{l+1} \cup S_2$.
e. For adjacent labeling $i(i_1, i_2, \ldots, i_k)$, let $S_2(i^T) = 1$ and $S_2(i_1^T) = \cdots = S_2(i_k^T) = 0$.
f. Simplify S_2: For $\forall j$, if $\exists k(S_2(j) \subset S_2(k))$, then $S_2 = S_2 - \{j\}$.
g. Simplify S_{l+1}: For $\forall j$, if $\exists k(S_{l+1}(j) \subset S_2(k))$, then $S_{l+1} = S_{l+1} - \{j\}$.
h. Let $S_{l+1} = S_{l+1} \cup S_2$. $\qquad\square$

4   Algorithm Simulated Sticker Model

4.1   Algorithm Simulated Sticker Model

For simple undirected graph $G = (V, E)$, where $V(G) = \{v_i | i = 1, 2, \ldots, n\}$, $E(G) = \{e_i | i = 1, 2, \ldots, m\}$. Algorithm simulated sticker sodel for MIS is as follows:

Step 1. Set initial state.
  a. Compute adjacent labeling of each vertex v_i of graph G: $i(i_1, i_2, \ldots, i_k)$, where $(i_1, i_2, \ldots, i_k)$ is subscript vector of adjacent vertex set $\{v_{i_1}, v_{i_2}, \ldots, v_{i_k}\}$ to vertex v_i.
  b. Obtain order of no detecting vertices according to d_i value from big to small as follows:
    (a) Set no detecting vertex set $H = \{1, 2, \ldots, n\} - \{i | d_i = 0\}$, let $h = |H|$.
    (b) Let matrix $\begin{pmatrix} C \\ D \end{pmatrix} = \begin{pmatrix} c_1 & c_2 & \cdots & c_h \\ d_{c_1} & d_{c_2} & \cdots & d_{c_h} \end{pmatrix}$, where d_i is the subscript number of vector $(i_1, i_2, \ldots, i_k)$ of vertex v_i, and $d_{c_i} \geq d_{c_{i+1}}(1 \leq i \leq h - 1)$, $H = \{c_1, c_2, \ldots, c_h\}$.
  c. Let $1 \times n$ tube matrix representing all vertex subsets be as follows: $S_0 = \{-1, -1, \ldots, -1\}$, let $l = 0$.
Step 2. Choose detecting vertex v_i.
  Let $S_l = (a_{ij})_{p(l) \times n}$, $a_{ij} \in \{0, 1, -1\}$.
    a. Compute model:
$$\max\{d_j | j \in H\}$$

Calculation process is as follows:

Find out submatrix $\begin{pmatrix} C' \\ D' \end{pmatrix} = \begin{pmatrix} c_1 & c_2 & \cdots & c_{h'} \\ d_{c_1} & d_{c_2} & \cdots & d_{c_{h'}} \end{pmatrix}$, where $C' = (c_1, c_2, \ldots, c_{h'})$ is on the left of C and has the biggest d_i value, $d_{c_1} = d_{c_2} = \cdots = d_{c_{h'}}$.
Obtain the optimal solution set $E = \{c_1, c_2, \ldots, c_{h'}\} \subseteq H$.

b. Let adjacent labeling of vertex $v_{c_i}(c_i \in E)$ be $c_i(c_{i1}, c_{i2}, \ldots, c_{iq})$. Compute model:

$$\min\{d_{i1} + d_{i2} + \ldots + d_{iq} | i = 1, 2, \ldots, h'\}$$

Obtain the optimal solution set $E' \subseteq E$ of vertex adjacent to the low d_i value no detecting vertex as much as possible.

c. Compute model:

$$\min\{|S_l(j^T)||j \in E'\}$$

where $|S_l(j^T)| = |a_{1j}| + |a_{2j}| + \cdots + |a_{p(l)j}|$. Obtain detecting vertex v_i corresponding to the biggest 0 component of column vector of tube matrix S_l.

Step 3. Detect vertex v_i whose adjacent labeling is $i(i_1, i_2, \ldots, i_k)$.

a. Compute formula as follows:

$$S_{l+1} = -(S_l, i) \cup -(+(S_l, i), \{i_1, i_2, \ldots, i_k\})$$

Calculation process is as follows:

(a) Divide tube matrix S_l into two parts:

$$S_l = \begin{pmatrix} -S_l^i \\ +S_l^i \end{pmatrix}$$

where $-S_l^i(i^T) = 0$; $+S_l^i(i^T) = -1$.

(b) Obtain matrix S_l^1 and matrix S_l^2 from matrix $+S_l^i$ as follows:
Let $+S_l^i(i^T) = 0$
Let $S_l^1 = +S_l^i$.
Let $+S_l^i(i^T) = 1$
For $j = 1$ to k
  Let $+S_l^i(i_j^T) = 0$
End
Let $S_l^2 = +S_l^i$.

(c) For S_l^1 and $-S_l^i$, if $\exists i_1 \exists i_2(S_l^1(i_2) \subset -S_l^i(i_1))$, then let $S_l^1 = S_l^1 - \{i_2\}$.

(d) For S_l^2, if $\exists i_1 \exists i_2(i_1 \neq i_2 \wedge S_l^2(i_2) \subset S_l^2(i_1))$, then let $S_l^2 = S_l^2 - \{i_2\}$.

(e) For S_l^1 and S_l^2, if $\exists i_1 \exists i_2(S_l^1(i_2) \subset S_l^2(i_1))$, then let $S_l^1 = S_l^1 - \{i_2\}$.

(f) Obtain tube matrix as follows:

$$S_{l+1} = \begin{pmatrix} -S_l^i \\ S_l^1 \\ S_l^2 \end{pmatrix}$$

b. Revise adjacent labeling and d_i value of vertex $v_{i_1}, v_{i_2}, \ldots, v_{i_k}$.

    (a) Delete the ith value in adjacent labeling of vertex $v_{i_1}, v_{i_2}, \ldots, v_{i_k}$.

    (b) Revise d_i value of vertex $v_{i_1}, v_{i_2}, \ldots, v_{i_k}$. Let $d_{i_j} = d_{i_j} - 1$ ($j = 1, 2, \ldots, k$).

c. Compute $H = H - \{i\} - \{i | d_i = 0\}$, let $h = |H|$.

    Adjust renewedly $\begin{pmatrix} C \\ D \end{pmatrix} = \begin{pmatrix} c_1 & c_2 & \cdots & c_h \\ d_{c_1} & d_{c_2} & \cdots & d_{c_h} \end{pmatrix}$ to make

    $d_{c_i} \geq d_{c_{i+1}}$, $(1 \leq i \leq h - 1)$.

Step 4. Select out tube matrix S_t representing all independent sets.

    If $H = \emptyset$, then obtain tube matrix S_t, and return to step 5; otherwise, let $l = l + 1$, return to step 2.

Step 5. Figure out tube matrix representing all maximal independent sets.

    a. Tube matrix $|S_t|$ represents all maximal independent sets.

    b. Tube matrix $\max(S_t)$ represents all maximum independent sets.

    c. End.   □

Note 1. In algorithm simulated sticker model for MIS, each vertex subset represented by tube matrix $|S_t|$ is a maximal independent set, and tube matrix $|S_t|$ contains memory strand vectors representing all maximum independent sets; each vertex subset represented by tube matrix $\max(S_t)$ is a maximum independent set, and tube matrix $\max(S_t)$ contains memory strand vectors representing all maximum independent sets.

Note 2. Let $n = |V|$ in undirected graph $G = (V, E)$, the number of all maximum independent sets is m, the complexity of algorithm simulated sticker model for MIS is $O(n^2(m^2 + n))$.   □

4.2 Simulation Experiment

We do a simulation experiment referring to Fig. 1 to verify effectiveness and feasibility of algorithm simulated sticker model for MIS. For the simple undirected graph $G = (V, E)$ referring to Fig. 1, where $V = \{v_1, v_2, v_3, v_4, v_5, v_6\}$, $E = \{e_1, e_2, e_3, e_4, e_5, e_6\}$. The process and results to compute are as follows.

a. For each vertex v_i to compute adjacent labeling as follows:

$$v_1 : 1(3, 6); v_2 : 2(3, 5, 6); v_3 : 3(1, 2); v_4 : 4(5); v_5 : 5(2, 4); v_6 : 6(1, 2).$$

b. Let tube matrix representing all vertex subsets be as follows:

$$S_0 = (-1, -1, -1, -1, -1, -1);$$

The subscript set of no detecting vertex is as follows: $H = \{1, 2, 3, 4, 5, 6\}$,

$$\begin{pmatrix} C \\ D \end{pmatrix} = \begin{pmatrix} 2 & 1 & 3 & 5 & 6 & 4 \\ 3 & 2 & 2 & 2 & 2 & 1 \end{pmatrix} = \begin{pmatrix} C' \\ D' \end{pmatrix}$$

$\begin{pmatrix} C'' \\ D'' \end{pmatrix} = \begin{pmatrix} 2 \\ 3 \end{pmatrix}$, So vertex v_2 is detecting vertex.

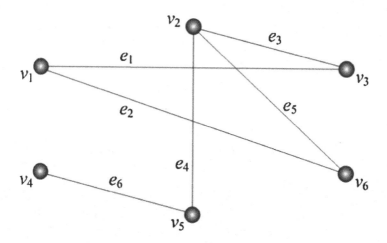

Fig. 1. An example of MIS.

c. To detect vertex v_2 whose adjacent labeling is $2(3, 5, 6)$:

$$S_1 = \begin{pmatrix} -1 & 0 & -1 & -1 & -1 & -1 \\ -1 & 1 & 0 & -1 & 0 & 0 \end{pmatrix}$$

Revise adjacent labeling: v_1: $1(3,6)$; v_3: $3(1)$; v_4: $4(5)$; v_5: $5(4)$; v_6: $6(1)$.
The subscript set of no detecting vertex: $H = \{1, 3, 4, 5, 6\}$;

$$\begin{pmatrix} C \\ D \end{pmatrix} = \begin{pmatrix} 1 & 3 & 5 & 6 & 4 \\ 2 & 1 & 1 & 1 & 1 \end{pmatrix}; \qquad \begin{pmatrix} C' \\ D' \end{pmatrix} = \begin{pmatrix} 1 \\ 2 \end{pmatrix}$$

So vertex v_1 is detecting vertex.

d. Detect vertex v_1 whose adjacent labeling is $1(3, 6)$:

$$S_2 = \begin{pmatrix} 0 & 0 & -1 & -1 & -1 & -1 \\ 0 & 1 & 0 & -1 & 0 & 0 \\ 1 & 0 & 0 & -1 & -1 & 0 \\ 1 & 1 & 0 & -1 & 0 & 0 \end{pmatrix} = \begin{pmatrix} 0 & 0 & -1 & -1 & -1 & -1 \\ 1 & 0 & 0 & -1 & -1 & 0 \\ 1 & 1 & 0 & -1 & 0 & 0 \end{pmatrix}$$

Revise adjacent labeling: v_4: $4(5)$; v_5: $5(4)$
The subscript set of no detecting vertex:

$$H = \{4, 5\}; \qquad \begin{pmatrix} C \\ D \end{pmatrix} = \begin{pmatrix} 5 & 4 \\ 1 & 1 \end{pmatrix} = \begin{pmatrix} C' \\ D' \end{pmatrix}; \qquad E' = \{4, 5\}$$

Vertex of the biggest 0 component of S_2 is vertex v_5.

e. To detect vertex v_5 whose adjacent labeling is $5(4)$:

$$S_3 = \begin{pmatrix} 1 & 1 & 0 & -1 & 0 & 0 \\ 0 & 0 & -1 & -1 & 0 & -1 \\ 1 & 0 & 0 & -1 & 0 & 0 \\ 0 & 0 & -1 & 0 & 1 & -1 \\ 1 & 0 & 0 & 0 & 1 & 0 \end{pmatrix} = \begin{pmatrix} 1 & 1 & 0 & -1 & 0 & 0 \\ 0 & 0 & -1 & -1 & 0 & -1 \\ 0 & 0 & -1 & 0 & 1 & -1 \\ 1 & 0 & 0 & 0 & 1 & 0 \end{pmatrix}; \qquad H = \emptyset$$

f. $|S_3| = \begin{pmatrix} 1 & 1 & 0 & 1 & 0 & 0 \\ 0 & 0 & 1 & 1 & 0 & 1 \\ 0 & 0 & 1 & 0 & 1 & 1 \\ 1 & 0 & 0 & 0 & 1 & 0 \end{pmatrix}$. All maximal independent sets are: $\{v_1, v_2, v_4\}$, $\{v_3, v_4,$

$v_6\}$, $\{v_3, v_5, v_6\}$, $\{v_1, v_5\}$.

$\max(S_3) = \begin{pmatrix} 1 & 1 & 0 & 1 & 0 & 0 \\ 0 & 0 & 1 & 1 & 0 & 1 \\ 0 & 0 & 1 & 0 & 1 & 1 \end{pmatrix}$. All maximum independent sets are: $\{v_1, v_2, v_4\}$,

$\{v_3, v_4, v_6\}$, $\{v_3, v_5, v_6\}$.

5 Conclusion

Material for calculation and biochemistry experiments of sticker model are first simulated with matrix and operations in the paper, and property of the matrix and operations simulating sticker model are discussed and analyzed. Based on these properties, algorithm simulated sticker model for MIS is designed.

Simulation experiment shows that this algorithm simulated sticker model is feasible and effective. Application prospect of simulation sticker model is extensive.

Acknowledgments. The work is supported by the National Natural Science Foundation of China (61179032), and the Graduate Innovation Fund of Wuhan Polytechnic University(2014cx007). In addition, we would also thank every authors appeared in the references.

References

1. Brause, C., Ngoc, C.L., Schiermeyer, I.: The maximum independent set problem in subclasses of subcubic graphs. Discrete Math. **338**, 1766–1778 (2015)
2. Song, T., Pan, L., Păun, G.: Asynchronous spiking neural P systems with local synchronization. Inf. Sci. **219**, 197–207 (2013)
3. Sun, Y.R.: An algorithm for generating all maximum independent sets in an undirected graph. J. Chin. Comput. Syst. **34**, 1862–1865 (2013)
4. Zhang, X.Y., Wang, B.J., Pan, L.Q.: Spiking neural P systems with a generalized use of rules. Neural Comput. **26**, 2925–2943 (2014)
5. Xiao, M., Nagamochi, H.: An exact algorithm for maximum independent set in degree-5 graphs. In: Fellows, M., Tan, X., Zhu, B. (eds.) FAW-AAIM 2013. LNCS, vol. 7924, pp. 72–83. Springer, Heidelberg (2013)
6. Zhou, K., Tong, X.J., Xu, J.: Closed circle DNA algorithm of change positive-weighted Hamilton circuit problem. J. Syst. Eng. Electron. **20**, 636–642 (2009)
7. Song, T., Pan, L.: Spiking neural P systems with rules on synapses working in maximum spiking strateg. IEEE Trans. NanoBiosci. **14**(4), 465–477 (2015)
8. Sakamoto, K., Gouzu, H., Komiya, K.: Molecular computation by DNA hairpin formation. Science **288**, 1223–1226 (2000)
9. Song, T., Pan, L.: Spiking neural P systems with rules on synapses working in maximum spikes consumption strategy. IEEE Trans. NanoBiosci. **14**(1), 38–44 (2015)

10. Song, T., Pan, L., Wang, J., et al.: Normal forms of spiking neural P systems with anti-spikes. IEEE Trans. NanoBiosci. **11**(4), 352–359 (2012)
11. Zhang, X., Pan, L., Paun, A.: On the universality of axon P systems. IEEE Trans. Neural Netw. Learn. Syst. **26**(11), 2816–2829 (2015). doi:10.1109/TNNLS.2015. 2396940
12. Shi, X., Wang, Z., Deng, C., Song, T., Pan, L.: A novel bio-sensor based on DNA strand displacement. PLoS One **9**(10), e108856 (2014)
13. Wang, X., Miao, Y., Cheng, M.: Finding motifs in DNA sequences using low-dispersion sequences. J. Comput. Biol. **21**(4), 320–329 (2014)
14. Wang, X., Miao, Y.: GAEM: a hybrid algorithm incorporating GA with EM for planted edited motif finding problem. Current Bioinf. **9**(5), 463–469 (2014)
15. Zhang, X.Y., Luo, B., Fang, X.Y., Pan, L.Q.: Sequential spiking neural P systems with exhaustive use of rules. Biosystems **108**, 52–62 (2012)
16. Zhang, X.Y., Liu, Y.J., Luo, B., Pan, L.Q.: Computational power of tissue P systems for generating control languages. Inf. Sci. **278**, 285–297 (2014)
17. Zhou, K., Wei, C.J., Liu, S.: Simulation DNA algorithm of all solutions of eight queens problem. J. Huazhong Univ. Sci. Technol. (Nat. Sci. Ed.) **37**(6), 24–27 (2009)
18. Xu, J., Dong, Y.F., Wei, X.P.: Sticker DNA computer model-PartI: theory. Chin. Sci. Bull. **49**, 205–212 (2004)
19. Xu, J., Li, S.P., Dong, Y.F.: Sticker DNA computer model-PartII: application. Chin. Sci. Bull. **49**, 229–307 (2004)
20. Zhou, K., Jin, C.: Simulation DNA algorithm of set covering problem. Appl. Math. Inf. Sci. **8**, 139–144 (2014)
21. Song, T., Pan, L., Jiang, K., et al.: Normal forms for some classes of sequential spiking neural P systems. IEEE Trans. NanoBiosci. **12**(3), 255–264 (2013)
22. Zhou, K., Fan, L.L., Shao, K.: Simulation DNA algorithm model of satisfiability problem. J. Comput. Theor. Nanosci. **12**, 1220–1227 (2015)

A NSGA-II with ADMM Mutation for Solving Multi-objective Robust PCA Problem

Weitao Yuan[1], Na Lin[2], Hanning Chen[1(✉)], Xiaodan Liang[1], and Maowei He[1]

[1] School of Computer Science and Software Engineering,
Tianjin Polytechnic University, Tianjin, People's Republic of China
chenhanning@sia.cn
[2] Beijing Shenzhou Aerospace Software Technology Co. Ltd., Beijing, China

Abstract. Robust Principal Component Analysis is generalized to a multi-objective optimization problem, named as Multi-objective Robust Principal Component Analysis (MRPCA) in this paper. We aim to solve MRPCA via Evolutionary Algorithm. To the best knowledge of authors, this is the first attempt to use evolutionary algorithm to solve MRPCA problem, which is a high dimension convex optimization problem. Specifically, one of the popular evolutionary algorithm, NSGA-II, is tested on MRPCA problem. The curse of dimensionality is observed when the dimension of MRPCA problem increases. Since this problem is convex, which is a friendly structure, we propose a modified NSGA-II by introducing a new mutation method: ADMM (Alternating Direction Method of Multipliers) mutation. Numerical experiments show our modified NSGA-II algorithm converges much faster than the standard one.

Keywords: Proximal operator · NSGA-II · Robust PCA · Multi-objective Robust PCA · ADMM

1 Introduction

Multi-objective optimization problems (MOPs), which involve simultaneous optimization of several competing criteria or objectives, naturally arise in a variety of real-world applications and many fields of disciplines, including engineering, economics and logistics. Instead of one single solution, the fact of optimizing multiple conflicting objectives simultaneously in MOP leads to a set of solutions, which is known as the pareto-optimal solutions set. Without any further information, one of these Pareto-optimal solutions cannot be preferred than the other. Traditional optimization methods convert the MOP into a single-objective optimization problem by the process of scalarization [1], which produces one particular Pareto-optimal solution at a time in some conditions. Therefore in order to solve MOPs, it has to be applied many times, hopefully finding a different solution at each run, which is not a direct and natural approach for solving MOPs. However, over the past two decades, much effort has been made to design multi-objective evolutionary algorithms (MOEAs) for approximating the Pareto

© Springer-Verlag Berlin Heidelberg 2015
M. Gong et al. (Eds.): BIC-TA 2015, CCIS 562, pp. 583–597, 2015.
DOI: 10.1007/978-3-662-49014-3_52

optimal solutions set of MOPs [2–4]. The main reason for this trend is that MOEAs are able to find multiple Pareto-optimal solutions in one single run. Because evolutionary algorithms (EAs) run with a population of agents or individuals, each agent or individual can be designed to approach the Pareto-optimal region of MOPs. This implies that an EA can be easily extended to solve the MOP (multiple Pareto-optimal solutions) in one single simulation run and it has been recognized as a major approach for MOPs.

Principal Component Analysis (PCA) is a widely used major statistical tool for data analysis and dimensionality reduction today. With the coming era of Big Data, pervasive sensors produce massive amounts of information on our every day lives, which causes those real world data to become more and more complex. In fact those unprecedented volumes of data include grossly corrupted observations or gross errors due to corrupted measurements or simply irrelevant to our interests. However, these errors or inaccurate observation will put the validity of PCA in danger. Over several decades, a number of approaches have been developed to robustify PCA. Among those approaches, a recent algorithm in [5] is considered as an idealized version of Robust PCA, which aims to recover a low-rank matrix $L \in \mathbf{R}^{M \times N}$ and a sparse error (or outlier) matrix $S \in \mathbf{R}^{M \times N}$ from highly corrupted observation matrix $I \in \mathbf{R}^{M \times N}$. Specifically, Robust PCA, according to [5], is defined as the following single objective optimization problem where λ is a weighted coefficient for low rank and sparse components:

$$\min_{L,S} \operatorname{rank}(L) + \lambda ||S||_{\ell_0}, \quad \text{s.t.} \quad I = L + S, \tag{1}$$

where $|| \cdot ||_{\ell_0}$ is ℓ_0 norm of a matrix (the number of non-zero entries).

Problem (1) is not convex and its convex version is named as Principal Component Pursuit or relaxed R-PCA, which is defined as followed:

$$\min_{L,S} ||L||_* + \lambda ||S||_{\ell_1}, \quad \text{s.t.} \quad I = L + S, \tag{2}$$

where $|| \cdot ||_*$ is nuclear norm of a matrix (the sum of its singular values) and $|| \cdot ||_{\ell_1}$ is ℓ_1 norm of a matrix ($||L||_{\ell_1} = \sum_{i,j} |L_{ij}|$).

This present paper introduces a novel multi-objective optimization problem, named as Multi-objective Robust PCA (MRPCA), defined as followed:

Definition 1. *Multi-Objective Robust PCA is defined as*

$$\min_{L,S} (\operatorname{rank}(L), ||S||_{\ell_0})^T, \quad s.t. \quad I = L + S, \tag{3}$$

Definition 2. *Multi-Objective Principal Component Pursuit or relaxed Multi-Objective R-PCA is defined as*

$$\min_{L,S} (||L||_*, ||S||_{\ell_1})^T, \quad s.t. \quad I = L + S. \tag{4}$$

In fact MRPCA is a multi-objective optimization version of Robust PCA. The motivation behind these definition is described as followed. Obviously, Robust PCA (problem (1)) and relaxed RPCA (problem (2)) are single objective optimization problems, where weighted coefficient λ controls the balance of two competing criteria (objectives): low rank and sparse. Therefore RPCA (relaxed RPCA) is scalarized version of MRPCA (relaxed MRPCA): one fixed λ of RPCA (relaxed RPCA) nearly means one solution in pareto-optimal solutions set of MRPCA (relaxed MRPCA). Therefore our idea is that, instead of chasing one solution point in pareto-optimal set at a time, we solve the relaxed MRPCA directly in one run by multi-objective evolutionary algorithms (MOEAs).

It is worth noting that much research and theoretical analysis made on Robust PCA have been limited to a focus on the original single-objective optimization problem. To the best knowledge of authors, little or no work and analysis on solving multi-objective version of Robust PCA by evolutionary algorithms have been explicitly considered to date. This paper thus makes an attempt to fill in this gap and to inspire further research in this direction. Specifically we attempt to solve relaxed MRPCA by a popular multi-objective evolutionary algorithm, NSGA-II. Our numerical experiments suggest a rapid deterioration of the performance of NSGA-II algorithm, when we increases the dimension of decisive variable in relaxed MRPCA problem. This curse of dimension phenomenon has not been thoroughly well investigated before. In this study, we use NSGA-II as a representative to investigate the effectiveness of multi-objective evolutionary algorithms in solving high dimension convex optimization problems.

In order to improve the convergence speed, we add a novel mutation method into NSGA-II to take advantage of the convex structure in this high-dimension problem. Surprisingly, the new mutation operator, even not involved in evolutionary computation with high percentage, greatly improves the convergence speed of NSGA-II. In summary, the contributions of this paper are listed:

- Define a new type of high dimension multi-objective optimization problem: Multi-objective Robust PCA.
- It is the first attempt to use Evolutionary Algorithm to solve relaxed MRPCA problem.
- We introduce a modified NSGA-II algorithm with a new mutation method: ADMM (Alternating Direction Method of Multipliers) mutation.
- In numerical experiments of solving relaxed MRPCA problem, our method converges much faster compared with standard NSGA-II.

2   NSGA-II and Performance Measurements

Among MOEAs, NSGA-II has been a well-known popular multiobjective evolutionary algorithm and was introduced in [6]. There are two basic requirements in designing evolutionary multi-objective optimization algorithms: convergence and diversity. NSGA-II uses Pareto dominance relation to promote the convergence and crowding distance to address the diversity.

Algorithm 1. NSGA-II

Input: N
Output: pop
  1: pop = initialize-variables(...);
  2: pop = non-domination-sort(pop);
  3: **for** $i = 1$ to N **do**
  4:     parent-pop = tournament-selection(pop);
  5:     offspring-pop = **genetic-operator**(parent-pop)
  6:     combined-pop = pop $\bigcup$ offspring-pop
  7:     combined-pop = non-domination-sort(combined-pop)
  8:     pop = replace-chromosome(combined-pop)
  9: **end for**
10: **return** pop

2.1 NSGA-II

NSGA-II is described in Algorithm 1. One iteration of NSGA-II algorithm is shortly described as followed:

1. Parents are selected from the current population (suppose the population size is N) by using binary tournament selection based on the rank and crowding distance. (see line 4 in Algorithm 1)
2. The selected population generates offsprings from genetic operator including crossover and mutation operators[1]. (see line 5 in Algorithm 1)
3. Both the current population and current offsprings are unionized (see line 6 in Algorithm 1)
4. The unionized populations are sorted based on non-domination sorting. (see line 7 in Algorithm 1)
5. At last only the best N individuals are selected according to crowded-comparison operator. (see line 8 in Algorithm 1)

2.2 Performance Metrics

A number of quantitative metrics have been proposed to assess the performances of different MOEAs. According to [7], there are six representative metrics, including Generational Distance (GD), ϵ-indicator, Spread, Generalized Spread, Inverted Generational Distance (IGD) and Hypervolume (HV). These metrics of MOEAs performance measurements also are based on those two

---

[1] Real-coded NSGA-II use Simulated Binary Crossover (SBX) [10,11] operator for crossover and polynomial mutation [10,12].

requirements mentioned above: convergence and diversity. Details can be found in [7]. It is pointed out that the first 5 metrics need true pareto-optimal solutions set as parameter, the last metric (HV) need reference point. The relaxed true pareto set is created by choosing uniformly distributed values in $\frac{1}{\sqrt{\max{(M,N)}}}[0,3]$ as λ and solving problem (2) by proximal algorithms [8,9]. Reference points for HV in our numerical tests are summarized in Table 1.

Table 1. Reference point for HV in different dimension problems.

4×4 dimension	10×10 dimension	20×20 dimension
(3,9)	(10,60)	(35,200)

In the following section we use these six metrics to test the performance of NSGA-II on solving relaxed MRPCA.

3 Solving Relaxed MRPCA with Standard NSGA-II

3.1 General Parameter Settings

The NSGA-II algorithm has several parameters summarized as follows:

1. Settings for reproduction operations: The original NSGA-II algorithm uses Simulated Binary Crossover (SBX) and Polynomial mutation. Crossover probability $p_c = 0.9$ and mutation probability is $p_m = \frac{1}{M \times N}$, where $M \times N$ is the number of decision variables. The distribution index for crossover and mutation operators as $\eta_c = 20$ and $\eta_m = 20$ respectively.
2. Population size: The population size N is 50.
3. Number of runs and stopping condition: Each algorithm is run 30 times independently on each test problem. The algorithm stops after 1000 generations.

3.2 Numerical Results

We create matrix data in random for testing in different $M \times N$ dimensions: $4 \times 4 (= 16)$, $10 \times 10 (= 100)$ and $20 \times 20 (= 400)$. Those testing matrices are made of two random created component matrices, where one is low rank and the other is sparse. The range of testing matrix is between 0 and 1.

Figure 1(a), (c) and (e) plot the distributions of non-dominated solutions of NSGA-II with the lowest IGD-metric value found in 30 runs for different dimensions of relaxed MRPCA problem. Tables 2, 3 and 4 include the mean, best, worst and standard deviation of all six performance metric values with NSGA-II for different dimensions of relaxed MRPCA problem in 30 runs. Figures 2, 3, and 4 draw in red line the evolution of the average and standard deviation (in 30 runs) of six metric value with the number of generations (x20) in NSGA-II for different dimensions.

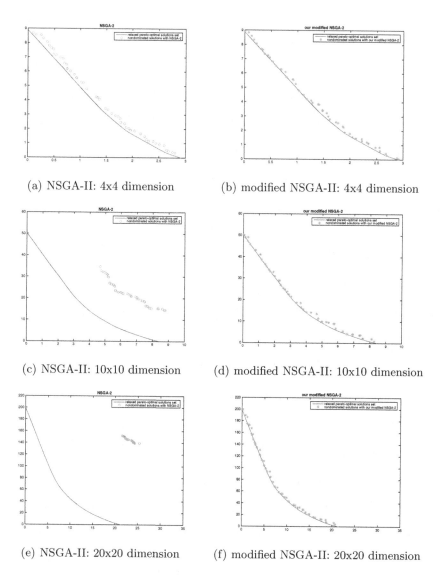

(a) NSGA-II: 4x4 dimension

(b) modified NSGA-II: 4x4 dimension

(c) NSGA-II: 10x10 dimension

(d) modified NSGA-II: 10x10 dimension

(e) NSGA-II: 20x20 dimension

(f) modified NSGA-II: 20x20 dimension

Fig. 1. Plots of the non-dominated solutions with the lowest IGD-metric in 30 runs of NSGA-II and our modified NSGA-II for different dimensions relaxed MRPCA test instances.

Table 2. Performance Comparison in IGD and GD Metrics. Best performance is highlighted with gray background.

Multi-Row	Inverted Generational Distance (IGD)				Generational Distance (GD)			
	mean	best	worst	std	mean	best	worst	std
NSGA-II (4 × 4)	0.002576	0.001770	0.005863	0.000862	0.004974	0.003704	0.006275	0.000542
modified (4 × 4)	0.001592	0.001063	0.002413	0.000345	0.002848	0.002265	0.003762	0.000326
NSGA-II (10 × 10)	0.019178	0.016860	0.023263	0.001564	0.048147	0.040734	0.058501	0.004266
modified (10 × 10)	0.001449	0.001154	0.002267	0.000269	0.003057	0.002651	0.003922	0.000305
NSGA-II (20 × 20)	0.039843	0.034151	0.045318	0.002379	0.120511	0.102944	0.135856	0.006828
modified (20 × 20)	0.002108	0.001048	0.004084	0.000786	0.004640	0.003633	0.005212	0.000350

Table 3. Performance Comparison in Spread and Generalized Spread Metrics. Best performance is highlighted with gray background.

Multi-Row	Spread				Generalized Spread			
	mean	best	worst	std	mean	best	worst	std
NSGA-II (4 × 4)	0.467990	0.352796	0.633229	0.062635	0.562544	0.369172	0.704593	0.075903
modified (4 × 4)	0.401152	0.278414	0.506828	0.052387	0.495660	0.278247	0.634363	0.079661
NSGA-II (10 × 10)	0.763523	0.676438	0.840416	0.040414	0.834479	0.763244	0.899776	0.034092
modified (10 × 10)	0.445890	0.377561	0.508641	0.033829	0.559948	0.419098	0.742376	0.076001
NSGA-II (20 × 20)	0.920265	0.888016	0.984962	0.022083	0.942938	0.919009	0.979710	0.013274
modified (20 × 20)	0.592593	0.429974	0.712528	0.075312	0.592593	0.429974	0.712528	0.075312

Table 4. Performance Comparison in ε-indicator and HV metrics. Best performance is highlighted with gray background.

Multi-Row	ϵ-indicator				Hypervolume (HV)			
	mean	best	worst	std	mean	best	worst	std
NSGA-II (4 × 4)	0.438812	0.212770	1.050784	0.222737	14.663534	13.134261	15.007525	0.357040
modified (4 × 4)	0.257550	0.150341	0.535780	0.118449	15.468007	15.313999	15.592462	0.078543
NSGA-II (10 × 10)	17.150157	12.896635	19.701033	1.733661	209.570664	184.139555	230.137089	13.616935
modified (10 × 10)	1.242926	0.641920	2.197557	0.432413	436.319294	432.608761	438.738039	1.487950
NSGA-II (20 × 20)	139.917657	129.393586	149.460808	5.563144	567.470251	289.840335	799.138570	124.445435
modified (20 × 20)	6.666880	3.542543	10.461330	2.259473	5498.757704	5439.021578	5544.118709	32.248364

From these numerical results, it can be observed that NSGA-II is less likely to converge when the dimension of decision (variable) space increases. Specifically, as can be seen in Fig. 1(a), the non-dominated solutions of NSGA-II are near the relaxed pareto-optimal solutions set with the population size of 50 after 1000 generations iterations in 16 (4×4) dimension relaxed MRPCA problem. However with the increasing dimension of decision (variable) space from 100 (10×10) dimension to 400 (20×20) dimension shown in Figs. 1(c) and (e), the non-dominated solutions of NSGA-II steadily deteriorated. The same convergence difficulty phenomenon can be observed in the first 5 metrics[2]. For example, the mean of ϵ-indicator metric for NSGA-II increased dramatically from 0.438812 in 16 (4×4) dimension to 139.917657 in 400 (20×20) dimension. Besides, when comparing the different evolution behavior of all six median metric values in different dimension problems, as illustrated in Figs. 2, 3 and 4, we can find the convergence of NSGA-II is getting noticeably much slower. For example, as indicated in Fig. 2(a) the IGD metric approaches zero really fast with increasing generation while the convergence is drastically shower in higher dimension of Fig. 4(a). From all these observations in numerical results, we can draw a conclusion that this kind of rapid deterioration of performance of NSGA-II is caused by the *high dimension of decision space*, which will be discussed in the following subsection.

3.3   Curse of Dimensionality

The reason for the numerical results in Sect. 3.2 can be explained with *the curse of dimensionality*. The curse of dimensionality means that in high dimensional decision (variable) space (often with hundreds or thousands of dimensions) the algorithms behavior quite differently compared with the low-dimensional settings. The common reason of these phenomena is that when the dimensionality increases, the volume of the space increases so fast that the available data for algorithms to use become sparse. In order to obtain a reliable result, the amount of data needed to support algorithms to make a sound judgement often grows exponentially with the dimensionality. More specifically, in order to create a new population, NSGA-II uses genetic operator which includes crossover and mutations. Effective crossover relies on the fact that both farther and mother share superior or similar good quality properties to reproduce high quality offsprings. However in high dimensional space all data appear to be sparse and dissimilar in many ways which prevents common data organization strategies like crossover from being efficient. Mutations can result in harmful or beneficial changes (near toward or farther away from pareto-optimal solutions set) in population. Beneficial changes will be selected by the non-dominated sorting of NSGA-II. However in high dimension space, mutation by random is less likely to be beneficial or good quality, that is unlikely to approaching the pareto-optimal solutions set.

---

[2] HV metric is not used for comparing because it has different reference point for different dimensions. Besides, the value of Hypervolume can not be compared for different dimension because of different pareto-optimal solutions set.

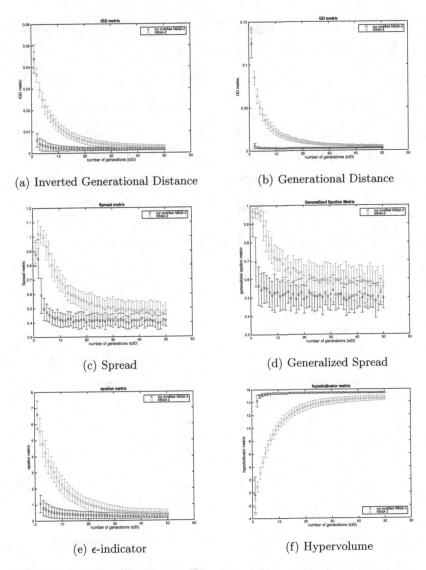

(a) Inverted Generational Distance

(b) Generational Distance

(c) Spread

(d) Generalized Spread

(e) ε-indicator

(f) Hypervolume

Fig. 2. Evolution of the median metric values versus the number of generations (4×4 dimension) (Color figure online).

Therefore genetic operator (crossover and mutations) will work less effectively in high dimension since the same number of population will be very sparse with the increasing dimension decision (variable) space. Therefore in order to improve the convergence performance of genetic operator, we introduce the modified NSGA-II with a new mutation method, ADMM mutation, which will be explained in the next section.

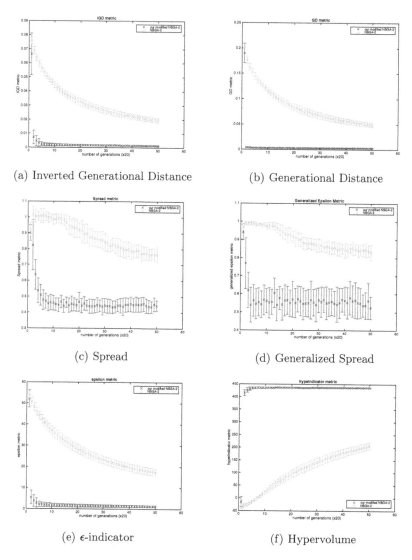

(a) Inverted Generational Distance

(b) Generational Distance

(c) Spread

(d) Generalized Spread

(e) ϵ-indicator

(f) Hypervolume

Fig. 3. Evolution of the median metric values versus the number of generations (10×10 dimension) (Color figure online).

4 Solving Relaxed MRPCA with Modified NSGA-II

4.1 NSGA-II with ADMM Mutation

Based on the above discussion, we introduce a modified NSGA-II, which is named as NSGA-II with the alternating direction method of multipliers (ADMM) mutation. Suppose a convex problem to be solved,

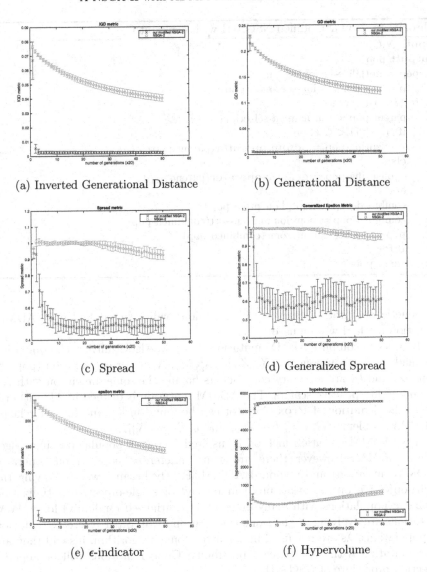

(a) Inverted Generational Distance

(b) Generational Distance

(c) Spread

(d) Generalized Spread

(e) ϵ-indicator

(f) Hypervolume

Fig. 4. Evolution of the median metric values versus the number of generations (20×20 dimension) (Color figure online).

$$\min_{X} f(X) + g(X),$$

The main algorithm is shown in Algorithm 2. The difference with NSGA-II is that for each generation there is C percent possibility that we will not use genetic operator (crossover and mutation) to make new population, instead we will activate a new mutation method: ADMM mutation. When C is less than zero, our modified NSGA-II is standard NSGA-II. When C is larger than 1,

---

Algorithm 2. Our modified NSGA-II with constant C

Input: N,C
Output: pop
 1: pop = initialize-variables(...);
 2: pop = non-domination-sort-mod(pop);
 3: **for** $i = 1$ to N **do**
 4:     parent-pop = tournament-selection(pop);
 5:     **if** rand(1) $< C$ **then**
 6:        offspring-pop = **admm-operator**(parent-pop)
 7:     **else**
 8:        offspring-pop = **genetic-operator**(parent-pop)
 9:     **end if**
10:     combined-pop = pop $\bigcup$ offspring-pop
11:     combined-pop = non-domination-sort(combined-pop)
12:     pop = replace-chromosome(combined-pop)
13: **end for**
14: **return** pop

---

no genetic operator (crossover and mutation) will be used and only ADMM mutation method will be used.

In order to compute ADMM mutation shown in Algorithm 3, each population i is made of five components $(X_i, Z_i, U_i, \lambda_i^1, \lambda_i^2)$, X_i is current solution (population), Z_i and U_i are auxiliary components having the same dimension with X_i, λ_i^1 and λ_i^2 are positive scalars. The ADMM mutation is defined in Algorithm 3, where the definition of **Prox** operator can be found in [8], and for our relaxed MRPCA problem, $f(X) = ||I - X||_{\ell_1}$ and $g(X) = ||X||_*$.

This ADMM mutation method is inspired by one of popular proximal algorithm, ADMM. However there are some differences between our operator (ADMM mutation) and standard ADMM. Firstly because we are solving the multi-objective optimization problem instead of single-objective optimization problem, populations with many different λs (initialized randomly) for ADMM mutations are evolving at the same time. Secondly, in order to create mutation in populations, λs are not fixed in our evolutionary algorithm, instead they are kept mutating with 50 % percent possibility. Good mutations will be kept by selection procedure of NSGA-II.

The motivation for introducing ADMM mutation is that we need to make full use of the high dimension problem structure that we are solving. Specifically, ADMM mutation depends on the first-order information of objective functions. In fact, since relaxed MRPCA problem has a favorite structure: the objective functions are convex or can be approximated by convex function. As in [8], many useful convex functions have proximal operators which can be evaluated sufficiently quickly. Since proximal operator carries the first-order information of problems, it will lead the populations to move to pareto-optimal solutions set faster than pure crossover and mutations. Our modified NSGA-II uses these first-order information by a specific type of popular proximal operator, i.e., ADMM,

---

Algorithm 3. ADMM mutation

Input: parents
Output: offsprings
1: **for** the ith individual population **do**
2: **if** randn(1)> 0.5 **then**
3:   $\lambda_i^1 =$ new random number ; $\lambda_i^2 =$ new random number
4: **end if**
5: $X_i = \mathbf{Prox}_{\lambda_i^1 f}(Z_i - U_i)$
6: $Z_i = \mathbf{Prox}_{\lambda_i^2 g}(X_i + U_i)$
7: $U_i = U_i + X_i - Z_i$
8: **end for**
9: **return** pop

---

to speed the convergence. At the same time, the selection in standard NSGA-II will promise the diversity of the final output solutions.

But we need answer an important question: How does this new mutation operator (ADMM mutation) help relieving the curse of dimensionality phenomenon? The next subsections will try to answer this question in numerical experiments.

4.2 Numerical Results

In order to illustrate the relief of curse of dimensionality, we give numerical simulation results of our modified algorithm ($C = 0.6$) and NSGA-II on solving relaxed MRPCA problems with dimensions of 16, 100 and 400. Figure 1(b), (d) and (f) show all non-dominated solutions, obtained after 1000 generations with our modified NSGA-II, that has the lowest IDG-metric in 30 runs. These figures demonstrate the abilities of our modified NSGA-II in converging to the true front in high dimension and in finding diverse solutions in the front. Specifically, when compared the obtained nondominated solutions of our modified algorithm (Figs. 1(d) and (f)) and NSGA-II (Figs. 1(c) and (e)), we can conclude that in both aspects of convergence and distribution of solutions our modified NSGA-II performed much better than original NSGA-II in this relaxed MRPCA problem.

Tables 2, 3 and 4 include the mean, best, worst and standard deviation of the six performance metric values with our modified NSGA-II for different dimensions. These tables prove that the final means obtained by our modified algorithms are much better than that obtained by NSGA-II, in terms of all six metrics. Taking instance 20×20 dimension as an example, on average, ϵ-indicator metric is 6.666880 for our algorithm while 139.917657 for NSGA-II. Tables 2, 3 and 4 also show that the standard deviations of all six metrics in our modified algorithm are smaller than those in NSGA-II for almost all the instances (except in Spread and Generalized Spread metrics where our algorithm is slightly worse than NSGA-II), which implies that our algorithm is more stable than NSGA-II in solving relaxed MRPCA problem.

Figures 2, 3 and 4 draw in blue line the evolution of the average and standard deviation of six metrics with the number of generations (x20) in 30 runs of our modified NSGA-II. All these figures clearly indicate that for all the test instances of different dimensions, our modified algorithm needs much fewer generations than NSGA-II for minimizing all the six metric values, which suggests that our modified algorithm is more efficient and effective than NSGA-II for the relaxed MRPCA.

5   Conclusion

A new multi-objective optimization problem, Multi-objective RPCA (MPRCA) problem, is introduced. A modified NSGA-II algorithm with ADMM mutation is provided to solve relaxed MRPCA problems. The other convex low rank optimization models besides relaxed MRPCA can also be solved in our algorithm with trivial modifications. Furthermore, our algorithm can be extended by replacing ADMM mutation with any other proximal operators. This present paper, we hope, can inspire further researches on applying evolutionary algorithms in solving high-dimension low-rank modeling multi-objective convex optimization problems.

In our future paper, higher dimension (more than 20×20 dimension) MPRCA numerical experiments will be given. Furthermore, we will compare the multi-objective optimization algorithms with traditional single-objective methods which are used for solving RPCA, which is important to demonstrate the superiority of multi-objective algorithms against single-objective algorithm on RPCA problem. At last, the efficient non-dominated sorting method [13] will be adopted for improving the computational efficiency of our modified NSGA-II.

References

1. Hwang, C.L., Masud, A.S.M.: Multiple Objective Decision Making Methods and Applications. Lecture Notes in Economics and Mathematical Systems, vol. 164. Springer, Berlin (1979)
2. Li, K., Zhang, Q., Kwong, S., Li, M., Wang, R.: Stable matching based selection in evolutionary multiobjective optimization. IEEE Trans. Evol. Comput. **6**(18), 909–923 (2014)
3. Li, K., Fialho, Á., Kwong, S., Zhang, Q.: Adaptive operator selection with bandits for multiobjective evolutionary algorithm based on decomposition. IEEE Trans. Evol. Comput. **1**(18), 114–130 (2014)
4. Li, K., Kwong, S., Zhang, Q., Deb, K.: Interrelationship-based selection for decomposition multiobjective optimization. IEEE Trans. Cybern. **45**, 2076–2088 (2015)
5. Candès, E.J., Li, X., Ma, Y., Wright, J.: Robust principal component analysis? J. ACM **58**(3), 1–37 (2011)
6. Deb, K., Agrawal, S., Pratap, A., Meyarivan, T.: A fast and elitist multiobjective genetic algorithm: NSGA-II. IEEE Trans. Evol. Comput. **6**(2), 182–197 (2002)
7. Jiang, S., Zhang, J., Ong, Y., Feng, L.: Consistencies and contradictions of performance metrics in multiobjective optimization. IEEE Trans. Cybern. **44**, 2391–2404 (2014)

8. Parikh, N., Boyd, S.: Proximal algorithms. Found. Trends Optim. **1**(3), 123–231 (2014)
9. Sboyd, S., Boyd, N., Parikh, E., Chu, B., Eckstein, J.: Distributed optimization and statistical learning via the alternating direction method of multipliers. Found. Trends Optim. **3**(1), 1–122 (2011)
10. Deb, K., Agarwal, R.B.: Simulated binary crossover for continuous search space. Complex Syst. **9**(2), 115–148 (1995)
11. Beyer, H., Deb, K.: On self-adaptive features in real-parameter evolutionary algorithm. IEEE Trans. Evol. Comput. **3**(5), 250–270 (2001)
12. Raghuwanshi, M.M., Kakde, O.G.: Survey on multiobjective evolutionary and real coded genetic algorithms. In: Proceedings of the 8th Asia Pacific Symposium on Intelligent and Evolutionary Systems, pp. 150–161 (2004)
13. Zhang, X., Tian, Y., Cheng, R., Jin, Y.: An efficient approach to non-dominated sorting for evolutionary multi-objective optimization. IEEE Trans. Evol. Comput. **19**(2), 201–213 (2015)

Negative Selection Algorithm Based Unknown Malware Detection Model

Jinquan Zeng[1]([⊠]) and Weiwen Tang[2]

[1] School of Computer Science and Engineering,
University of Electronic Science and Technology of China, Chengdu 610054, China
zengjq@uestc.edu.cn
[2] Sichuan Communication Research Planning and Designing Co., Ltd,
Chengdu 610041, China

Abstract. Nowadays, malwares have become one of the most serious security threats for computer systems and how to detect malwares is a difficult task, especially, unknown malwares. Artificial immune systems (AIS) is spired by biological immune system (BIS) and it is a relatively novel field. AIS is used to detect malwares and gets some exciting results. The most known AIS model is negative selection algorithm (NSA) and it can only use normal samples to train. The traditional NSAs generate detectors in the training phase and then detect anomaly elements in the testing phase. There are some drawbacks in the traditional NSAs. Firstly, the real applications often change, normal can change to anomalous, and vice versa. The traditional NSAs easily produce many of false alarm and false negative in the real applications. Secondly, the traditional NSAs lack continuous learning ability in the testing phase and it is costly to generate enough detectors to cover the total non-self space in the training. In order to overcome the drawbacks of the traditional NSAs, a new scheme with online adaptive learning is introduced to NSA, and it includes that constructing the appropriate profile of the system, generating new detectors cover the holes of the non-self space, deleting these detectors which lie in the self-space decreases false alarms and amending these detectors which cover partly self-space decreases false alarm and increase detecting rate.

Keywords: Artificial immune systems · Negative selection algorithm · Adaptive learning · Malware

1 Introduction

With the development of Internet, more and more computers and mobile smart devices connect to the Internet. People, companies and governments increasingly depend on network-enabled applications, such as office automatic, browsing websites, sending or receiving e-mails, et al. Unfortunately, the growing connectivity of computers and mobile smart devices through the Internet makes an hacker launch attacks easily, and an hacker can download and execute malwares without

© Springer-Verlag Berlin Heidelberg 2015
M. Gong et al. (Eds.): BIC-TA 2015, CCIS 562, pp. 598–608, 2015.
DOI: 10.1007/978-3-662-49014-3_53

human intervention. Nowadays, malwares, or malicious codes, have become the mainly security threat for computer system and mobile smart devices. Indeed, McAfee threats report [1] said that they gathered only 792 mobile threat samples in 2011, but at the first quarter 2013, the number of mobile malware reached 50926 and the number of general malwares was more than 128 million. Symantec 2014 Threat Report [2] said that targeted attacks campaigns increased 91 % and 38 % of mobile users had experienced mobile cybercrime in 2013. A more recent report from McAfee said "malware continues to grow" [3]. In order to defense malwares, many researchers begin to study malwares [4–8], and many of works focus on how to detect malwares [9–13].

Nowadays, more and more researchers have gotten ideas from the biological mechanisms to develop new paradigms for computer intelligence. Biological immune systems (BIS) have many characteristics such as uniqueness, autonomous, recognition of foreigners, distributed detection, and noise tolerance [14]. Inspired by BISs, Artificial Immune Systems (AIS) have become one of the relatively new areas of soft computing [15–18]. Applications of AIS mainly include anomaly detection, fault diagnosis, network security, objective optimization, and etc. [19]. The vast majority of developments within AIS include clonal selection based algorithms, negative selection based algorithms and artificial immune network models. Negative selection algorithm (NSA) is one of the most developed models in AIS [20] and was proposed by Forrest et al. [21]. NSA is inspired by the mechanism of T-cell maturation and self-tolerance in BIS. If a T-cell recognizes any self-cell, it is eliminated, the others are deployed to recognize outside pathogens.

Early data representations of NSA are binary representation (low-level) [21]. Binary representation can hardly process many applications that are natural to be described in real-valued space, and generates a higher false alarm rate when applied to anomaly detection for some data sets [20,22]. Gonzalez et al. introduced a real-valued data representation, called real-valued negative selection (RNS) algorithm [23]. Real-valued representation has some advantages such as increased expressiveness, extracting high-level knowledge and improved scalability [22]. More and more works adopt real-valued representation in NSA. An important variation among RNSs, is V-detector [24], which uses variable-sized detector and terminates training phase when enough coverage is achieved. Gong et al. introduced an improved negative selection algorithm by integrating a novel further training strategy into the training stage, where generating self-detectors cover the self-region, and it can reduce self-samples to reduce computational cost in testing stage [25]. Li et al. proposed a new detector for anomaly detection named interface detector based on the boundary samples, which surround the self space with an appropriate self radius and carry out the learning process during the testing stage to adapt itself to real-time change of self space [26].

NSA mainly includes two phases, training phase and detecting phase. In training phase, detectors are generated at random and the detectors are eliminated which match any training self element. The legal detectors are retained to detect nonself elements in detecting phase. Usually, if more self elements are used to train, it is useful to decrease the false alarm rate. But we cannot get all of self elements, we have to use part of self elements to train detectors. How to use part of self elements to construct self space is a challenging task. Another task is that the traditional NSAs lacks adaptive learning ability and the real applications often change, normal can change to anomalous, and vice versa. This paper tries to address above issues, and the representation of the self space is introduced with variable-sized self radius and a new scheme with online adaptive learning is introduced to NSA.

2 Model Theory

2.1 Constructing Self Space

In BIS, negative selection is a mechanism to protect body against self-reactive lymphocytes and self-reactive T-cells are eliminated by a controlled death. As a result, only self-tolerant T-cells survive the negative selection process and are allowed to leave the thymus. Similarly, the negative selection algorithm generates detector set by eliminating any detector candidate that match elements from a group of self samples. The system state space can be defined by $U \subseteq [0.0, 1.0]^n$, where n denotes the number of dimensions. A state of the system can be represented by a vector of features $x^i = (x_1^i, x_2^i, \ldots x_n^i)$ and each feature is normalized to $[0.0, 1.0]$. The self-space is defined by the set S and the complement space is defined by the set N, satisfied by:

$$S \cup N = U, S \cap N = \phi \tag{1}$$

In real applications, it is difficult to get all of self samples, such as benign files in every computer. In order to construct self-space, we have to use only some of self-sample $S' \subset S$ to build the profile of the system $\hat{S}'$ that reflects self-space. If an element is enough close to a self-sample, it is considered as a self-element. In RNS, the closeness is determined by the self-radius, the self-radius allows other elements to be considered as self-elements which lie close to the self-center and represents the allowed variability of the self-samples. Based on these definitions, the set $\hat{S}'$ can be defined by:

$$\hat{S}' = \left\{ x \, \middle| \, x \in U, \exists s^i \in S, \left\| s^i - x \right\| \le r^i \right\} \tag{2}$$

where r^i is the self-radius of the self-element s^i. Figure 1 show the definitions for NSA. The light gray area is the self-space S and the dark gray area is the constructed self-space $\hat{S}'$. A good profile of the system $\hat{S}'$ is almost equal to S, but it is a difficult task. Figure 1 also show the classification concepts of NSAs, including true positive, false positive, true negative and false negative.

The self-radius of self-sample specifies the capability of its generalization. The bigger the self radius is, the more generalization the self sample is. The traditional RNSs adopt const-sized self-radius showed by Fig. 2. The gray area is self-space, the training samples include a, b, c and d, and the self-radius is r.

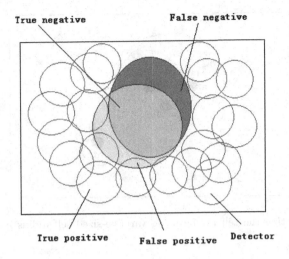

Fig. 1. General definitions for NSA.

Figure 2 shows that the const-sized self-radius cannot construct the appropriate profile of the system $\hat{S}'$ and false alarm rate is high, at the same time detection rate is low. Figure 3 shows that variable self radius can appropriately cover self space and build the profile of the system. In conventional NSAs, the self radius is in constant size, so the appropriate profile of the system is difficult to construct. While our proposed approach adopts variable-sized self radius and the appropriate profile of the system can be built, the appropriate profile of the system can increase the true positive rate and decrease the false positive rate.

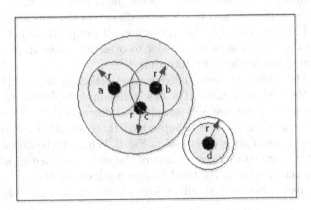

Fig. 2. Constructing the self profile using constant-sized self radius in 2-dimensional space.

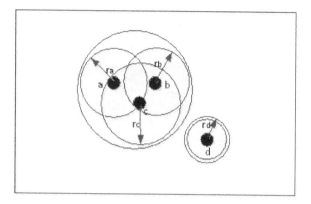

Fig. 3. Constructing the self profile using variable-sized self radius in 2-dimensional space.

2.2 Online Adaptive Learning Mechanism

The traditional NSAs lacks adaptive learning ability and the real applications often change, normal can change to anomalous, and vice versa. There are two phases in NSAs, training and testing phases. In the training phase, some self-samples are chosen to train detectors, and the detectors are used to detect anomaly samples. In Fig. 4, there are five samples, sample 1 is the training self-sample, sample 2 is the testing self-sample, sample 3 is the testing self-sample, sample 4 is the testing nonself-sample and sample 5 is the testing nonself-sample. Figure 5 shows that 4 detectors are generated in the training phase, d1, d2, d3 and d4. The testing process is self-sample 2, self-sample 3, nonself-sample 4 and nonself-sample 5. The detector d1 covers the nonself-sample 4, no detectors cover the nonself-sample 5, and the detector d2 covers the self-sample 3. At last, the detector d2 induces a false alarm, the nonself-sample 5 cannot be detected and decreases the detection rate. In order to overcome these drawbacks, online adaptive learning mechanisms are introduced.

Firstly, in the testing process, the generated detectors are real time adapted according to the testing results. If a new self-sample is found, the generated detectors, which cover the new self-sample, will decrease their detection radius. This is an active mechanism, and it hopes that there are other self-samples near the found self-sample. This is described in Fig. 6. When the testing self-sample 2 is found, only the detector d2 covers part of the new self-space which is decided by the testing self-sample 2. By the learning mechanism, the constructed self-space $\hat{S}'$ adds new self-space, $\hat{S}'$ will enough close to S, and the false alarm will also decrease.

Secondly, the generated detectors covering all of nonself-space is an important task in the training phase. If we generate a large number of detectors, the cost is very expensive and the detection efficiency is very low. So we introduce a new mechanisms, the new detectors are generated in the testing phase. The new mechanism can increase the diversity of the detectors, and increase the covering

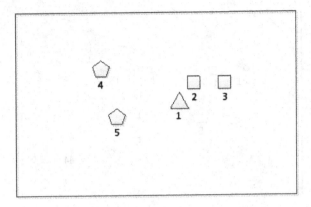

Fig. 4. The training and testing samples.

of nonself-space. Figure 7 shows that the nonself-sample 5 cannot be detected by the detectors which are generated in the training phase. But the new generated detector d5 can cover the nonself-sample 5 in the testing phase, and the new mechanism can increase the detection rate.

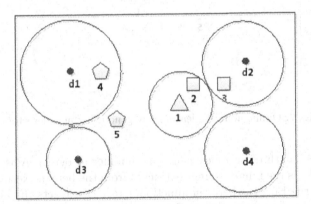

Fig. 5. Generating detectors and testing samples.

3 Model Simulations

3.1 Antibody Gene

Define the binary strings extracted from benign executables as antibody gene, and let Agd_l devote the antibody gene set given by:

$$Agd_l = \{ad \,|\, ad \in D_l, |ad| = l, l \in N \} \tag{3}$$

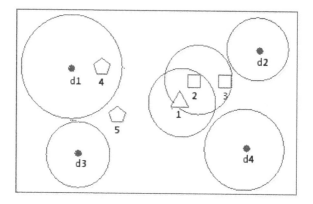

Fig. 6. Online adaptive learning by adapt detectors.

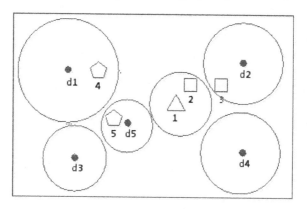

Fig. 7. Online adaptive learning by generating new detectors.

where l is the length of antibody gene (the number of bytes), N is the natural number and D_l is the binary strings extracted from the benign executables. D_l is described by the Eq. (4), where the function $f_e(b, i, l)$ extracts the binary string from the benign executable $b(b \in B)$, i is the extracted position and l is the number of extracted bytes, respectively.

$$D_l = \bigcup_{b \in B} \bigcup_{l \in N, i=0}^{|b|} \{f_e(b, i, l)\} \tag{4}$$

$$ad_g = \frac{ad_g^b / B_g}{ad_g^b / B_g + ad_g^m / M_g} \tag{5}$$

$$ad_f = \frac{ad_f^b / B_f}{ad_f^b / B_f + ad_f^m / M_f} \tag{6}$$

$$\sqrt{ad_g^2 + ad_f^2} \geq \delta \tag{7}$$

In order to select the fit antibody gene, the antibody gene ad has to satisfy the Eq. (7), where ad_g describes its occurrence frequency on gene sequence (described by the Eq. (5), where ad_g^b is the number of ad occurrence count in the benign executable, B_g is the total gene number in the benign executable, ad_g^m is the number of ad occurrence count in the malwares, and M_g is the total gene number in the benign executable, ad_f describes its occurrence frequency on files (described by the Eq. (6), where ad_f^b is the file number of ad occurrence count in the benign executable, B_f is the total file number in the benign executable, ad_f^m is the file number of ad occurrence count in the malwares, and M_f is the total file number in the benign executable, and δ is the threshold value.

Let Agd denote the antibody gene library given by:

$$Agd = Agd_{l_1} \cup Agd_{l_2} \cup, \ldots, \cup Agd_{l_n} \tag{8}$$

where $l_i \in N, i = 1, \ldots, n$ is the length of antibody gene, and N is the natural number. The Eq. (8) shows that the antibody gene library is made up of variable-length antibody gene, and the antibody gene library is used to extract the characteristics of the executables.

3.2 Antigen Presenting

Antigens are defined as the executables, simulating the antigen presenting cells in BIS, and the characteristics of the executables are extracted by the antibody gene library Agd. Let C $(C \subset U)$ devote the set of executable characteristics given by:

$$C = \{c = \langle x_{l_1}, x_{l_2}, \ldots, x_{l_n} \rangle \,|\, 0 \leq x_{l_i} \leq 1, e \in E, \ x_{l_i} = f_c(e, Agd_{l_i}), i = 1, \ldots, n\} \tag{9}$$

where $x_{l_i}, i = 1, \ldots, n$ is the characteristic of the executable e $(e \in E)$ extracted by the antibody gene set Agd_{l_i}, and n is the dimension; the function $f_c(e, Agd_{l_i})$ counts the characteristic of the executable e $(e \in E)$ in the antibody gene set Agd_{l_i} described by the Eq. (10). The Eq. (9) shows that the state vector of the executable is made up of the characteristics extracted from the whole antibody gene set $Agd_{l_i}, i = 1, \ldots, n$.

$$f_c(e, Agd_{l_i}) = \frac{\left| Agd_{l_i} \cap \left\{ \bigcup_{l_i \in N, j=0}^{|e|} \{f_e(e, j, l_i)\} \right\} \right|}{\left| \bigcup_{l_i \in N, j=0}^{|e|} \{f_e(e, j, l_i)\} \right|}. \tag{10}$$

3.3 Self Elements

Let S denote the benign executables set given by:

$$S = \{s = \langle ch, rd \rangle \,|\, ch \in C_b, rd \in R\} \tag{11}$$

where ch is the characteristics of the benign executables, C_b is the set of the characteristics of the benign executables, rd is the self radius of benign executables, and R is the real number, respectively. The self radius of benign executables specifies the capability of its generalization (the elements within the self radius of benign executables are considered as benign executables). The bigger the self radius of benign executables is, the more generalization the benign executables is. The big self radius of benign executables can decrease the number of benign executables used to train detectors and false positive rate. Furthermore, the characteristics extracted from the benign executables are used to build the profile of the benign executables, and then the detectors can be generated to cover the space of the malicious executables.

3.4   Detectors

Let D denote the detector set given by:

$$D = \{d = \langle ch, rd \rangle \,|ch \in U, rd \in R\} \tag{12}$$

where ch is the characteristics of the detectors, rd is the detection radius of the detectors, and R is the real number, respectively. D is subdivided into immature and mature detectors. Immature detectors are newly generated ones given by:

$$I = \{\langle x_{l_1}, x_{l_2}, \ldots, x_{l_n} \rangle \,|0 \le x_{l_i} \le 1, i = 1, \ldots, n\} \tag{13}$$

Mature detectors are the ones that are tolerant to S given by:

$$M = \{x \,|\forall s \in S, f_d(s, x) > s.rd, \exists s' \in S, \forall s'' \in S, \\ f_d(s', x) < f_d(s'', x), x.rd = f_d(s', x) - s'.rd\} \tag{14}$$

The Eq. (14) shows that a detector is tolerant to S if the detector does not lie within S. Furthermore, the detection radius of the detectors is decided by the nearest benign executable in S, and so the detector cannot detect benign executables and decrease the false-positive rate. $f_d(x, y)$ is the Euclidean distance between x and y given by:

$$f_d(x, y) = \sqrt{\sum_{i=1}^{n} (x_i - y_i)^2}. \tag{15}$$

3.5   Immune Surveillance

After the characteristics $c(c \in C)$ of an executable $e(e \in E)$, its characteristics are presented to the detectors for detecting and the detecting process is given by:

$$f_{detect}(c) = \begin{cases} 0, & \text{iff } \forall m \in M \wedge f_d(c, m) > m.ra \\ 1, & \text{iff } \exists m \in M \wedge f_d(c, m) \le m.ra \end{cases} \tag{16}$$

if the executable lies within the detection radius of a detector, the function $f_{detect}(c)$ returns 1 and then the executable is malicious. Otherwise, the function $f_{detect}(c)$ returns 0 and then the executable is benign.

4   Conclusion

The traditional NSAs lack adaptive learning ability and the paper introduce some new adaptive learning mechanisms to NSA. Firstly, in order to construct the appropriate profile of the system, the new found self-samples are added to the constructed self-space $\hat{S}'$, the detectors are checked whether the detectors cover the self-space. Secondly, the new detectors are generated in the testing phase, and it can increase the diversity of the detectors and the covering of nonself-space. These mechanisms can increase adaptive learning ability in NSA, increase detection rate and decrease false alarm rate.

Acknowledgments. This work is supported by 863 High Tech Project of China under Grant No. 2013AA01A213, the Applied Basic Research Plans of Sichuan Province (No. 2014JY0140 and No. 2014JY0066), and special technology development fund for research institutes of the Ministry of Science and Technology of China (No. 2013EG126063).

References

1. McAfee Threats Report: First Quarter (2013). http://www.mcafee.com/au/resources/reports/rp-quarterly-threat-q1-2013.pdf
2. Symantec: Threat Report (2014). www.symantec.com/content/en/us/enterprise/otherresources/b-istr_main_report_v19_21291018.en-us.pdf
3. Mcafee and Lab: 2013 Threats Predictions (2013)
4. Uppal, D., Mehra, V., Verma, V.: Basic survey on malware analysis, tools and techniques. Int. J. Comput. Sci. Appl. 4(1), 103–112 (2014)
5. McGraw, G., Morrisett, G.: Attacking malicious code: a report to the infosec research council. IEEE Softw. 17(5), 33–41 (2000)
6. Ashish, J., Kanak, T., Vivek, K., Dibyahash, B.: Integrating static analysis tools for improving operating system security. Int. J. Comput. Sci. Mob. Comput. 3(4), 1251–1258 (2014)
7. Yin, Z.M., Yu, X., Niu, L.: Malicious code detection based on software fingerprint. In: Proceedings of International Conference on Artificial Intelligence and Software Engineering, pp. 212–216 (2013)
8. Kolter, J., Maloof, M.: Learning to detect and classify malicious executables in the wild. J. Mach. Learn. Res. 7, 2721–2744 (2006)
9. Schulte, B., Andrianakis, H., Sun, K., Stavrou, A.: NetGator: malware detection using program interactive challenges. In: Flegel, U., Markatos, E., Robertson, W. (eds.) DIMVA 2012. LNCS, vol. 7591, pp. 164–183. Springer, Heidelberg (2013)
10. Saeed, I.A., Selamat, A., Abuagoub Ali, M.: A survey on malware and malware detection systems. Int. J. Comput. Appl. 67(16), 25–31 (2013)
11. Lamia, K., Mohammadi, A.K.: A review of malicious code detection techniques for mobile devices. Int. J. Comput. Theory Eng. 4(2), 212–216 (2012)
12. Zahra, B., Hashem, H., Seyed, M.H.F., Ali, H.: A survey on heuristic malware detection techniques. In: Proceedings of the 5th Conference on Information and Knowledge Technology, pp. 113–120 (2013)
13. Fan, W., Lei, X.: Obfuscated malicious code detection with path condition analysis. J. Netw. 9(5), 1208–1214 (2014)

14. Castro, L., Zuben, F.: Artificial immune systems: Part I - basic theory and applications. TR - DCA 01/99 (1999)
15. Dasgupta, D., Yu, S., Majumdar, N.S.: MILA-multilevel immune learning algorithm. In: Cantú-Paz, E., et al. (eds.) GECCO 2003. LNCS, vol. 2723, pp. 183–194. Springer, Heidelberg (2003)
16. Wang, D., Zhang, F., Xi, L.: Evolving boundary detector for anomaly detection. Expert Syst. Appl. **38**, 2412–2420 (2011)
17. Alonso, F.R., Oliveira, D.Q., Zambroni de Souza, A.C.: Artificial immune systems optimization approach for multi objective distribution system reconfiguration. IEEE Trans. Power Syst. **30**(2), 840–847 (2014)
18. Zhang, P., Tan, Y.: Immune cooperation mechanism based learning framework. Neurocomputing **148**(19), 158–166 (2015)
19. Li, T.: Computer Immunology. Publishing House of Electronics Industry, Beijing (2004)
20. Zhou, J., Dasgupta, D.: Revisiting negative selection algorithms. Evol. Comput. **15**(2), 223–251 (2007)
21. Forrest, S., Perelson, A., Allen, L., Cherukuri, R.: Self-nonself discrimination in a computer. In: Proceedings of the 1994 IEEE Symposium on Research in Security and Privacy. IEEE Computer Society Press (1994)
22. Dasgupta, D., Yu, S., Majumdar, N.S.: MILA-multilevel immune learning algorithm. In: Proceedings of the 2003 Genetic and Evolutionary Computation Conference, pp. 183–194 (2003)
23. Dasgupta, D., Gonzalez, F.: An immunity based technique to characterize intrusions in computer network. IEEE Trans. Evol. Comput. **6**, 281–291 (2002)
24. Ji, Z., Dasgupta, D.: Real-valued negative selection algorithm with variable-sized detectors. In: Deb, K., Tari, Z. (eds.) GECCO 2004. LNCS, vol. 3102, pp. 287–298. Springer, Heidelberg (2004)
25. Gong, M.G., Zhang, J., Ma, J., Jiao, L.: An efficient negative selection algorithm with further training for anomaly detection. Knowledge-Based Syst. **30**, 185–191 (2012)
26. Li, D., Liu, S.L., Zhang, H.: A negative selection algorithm with online adaptive learning under small samples for anomaly detection. Neurocomputing **149**, 515–525 (2015)

Tensorial Biometric Signal Recognition Based on Feed Forward Neural Networks with Random Weights

Fan Zhang[1](✉) and An Qin[2]

[1] School of Information Engineering, North China University of Water Resources
and Electric Power, Zhengzhou 450045, China
zfgh8221@163.com
[2] Banan District Bureau, Chongqing Public Security Bureau,
Chongqing 400055, China

Abstract. Most biometric signals are naturally multi-dimensional objects, which are formally known as tensors. How to classify this kind of data is an important topic for both pattern recognition and machine learning. Commonly, these biometric signals are often converted into vectors in the process of recognition. However, the vectorization usually leads to the distortion of the potential spatial structure of the original data and high computational burden. To solve this problem, in this paper, a novel classifier as a tensor extension of neural networks with random weights (NNRW) for tensorial data recognition is introduced. Due to the proposed solution can classify tensorial data directly without vectorizing them, the intrinsic structure information of the input data can be reserved. Moreover, compared with the traditional NNRW, much fewer parameters need to be calculated through the proposed tensor based classifier. Extensive experiments are carried out on different databases, and the experiment results are compared against state-of-the-art techniques. It is demonstrated that the new tensor based classifier can get better recognition performance with an extremely fast learning speed.

Keywords: Pattern recognition · Neural networks · Random weights · Classification · Tensor objects

1 Introduction

In many pattern recognition problems, most biometric signals have multi-dimensional representation and they are formally called tensors [1]. For example, gray-level images of fingerprint, palm print, ear, face, and multichannel electroencephalography signals in neuroscience belong to two-dimensional biometric signals. Color biometric images, Gabor faces, silhouette sequences in gait analysis, and gray video sequences in action recognition belong to three-dimensional data. A few multi-dimensional biometric signals can be also formed

© Springer-Verlag Berlin Heidelberg 2015
M. Gong et al. (Eds.): BIC-TA 2015, CCIS 562, pp. 609–620, 2015.
DOI: 10.1007/978-3-662-49014-3_54

in more than three orders, such as color video sequence surveillance [2]. Therefore, tensor data analysis, classification, has become one of the most popular topics for both pattern recognition and computer vision.

For most practical pattern recognition systems, traditional feature extraction and classification methods are vector based. Such as feature extraction algorithms: principal component analysis (PCA) [3], liner discriminative analysis (LDA) [4], maximum scatter difference (MSD) [5], and locality preserving projections (LPP) [6]; classification methods: feed-forward neural network (FNN) [7], support vector machine (SVM) [8], and so on. Although the performances of classical feature extraction and classification approaches are effective in many cases, they may be lack of efficiency in managing tensor data. For example, when we reformulate an image matrix 10×100 as a vector, the reformulated vector is 1000 dimensional, this vectorization of data leads to many issues. First, the underlying structural information of the original data is disregarded. Second, with the increase of dimensionality, this may create overcoming high computational complexity, and large memory requirements. Therefore, several algorithms that used tensor representations have been recently proposed for a number of applications. For example, multilinear principal component analysis (MPCA) [9], a tensor vision of PCA, performs dimensionality reduction in all tensor modes to capture most of the variation presented in the original tensors. By the same way, multilinear discriminant analysis (MDA) [10], general tensor discriminant analysis (GTDA) [11], tensor subspace analysis (TSA) [12], support tensor machine (STM) [13], tensorial extreme learning machine (TELM) [14], apply LDA, maximum scatter difference (MSD) [15], LPP, SVM, extreme learning machine (ELM) [16] to transform each mode of the tensors respectively [17]. Due to the distance between two data with form either tensor or vector is the same, NN classifier can be used to classify the feature matrices directly. Therefore, NN classifier is usually applied after many multilinear dimension reduction methods just as in [9]. However, the structure of NN classifier is too simple to obtain satisfying recognition rate. Consequently, it is desirable to propose a novel classifier which can classify tensorial data directly and to preserve the intrinsic structure effectively.

In order to construct the classifier, a kind of special feed forward networks be employed that introduced first in [18], named neural networks with random weights (NNRW). Because NNRW randomly assigns the input weights and the bias of neurons in the hidden layer, these networks have fast learning speed and perfect classification performance [19]. As a tensor extension of NNRW, we introduce a novel tensor based classification method named as tensorial neural networks with random weights (TNNRW) for tensor objects classification. Without converting tensor objects into vectors, TNNRW can classify them directly. TNNRW not only takes the advantage of NNRW, but also preserves the natural structure of the input data. Furthermore, with fewer parameters to be calculated, a faster computing speed can be achieved.

The remainder of the paper is organized as follows. Section 2 introduces some basic tensor algebra and a brief introduction of NNRW. In Sect. 3, the new classifier TNNRW is summarized in detail. Section 4 provides some promising comparing results on various kinds of data sets to evaluate the performance of the proposed method. Finally, the major findings and conclusions are drawn in Sect. 5.

2 Notations and Related Works

Tensor is a generalization of vectors and matrices but not limit to. Vectors are first-order tensors, and matrices are second-order tensors. The elements of a tensor are to be addressed by a number of indices that are used to define the order of the tensor object. Notably, each index defines a "mode" [20]. Following the notation in [21], we denote vectors by lowercase letters, e.g., x; matrices by uppercase boldface, e.g., U; and tensors by calligraphic letters, e.g., $\mathcal{A}$. Tensor is a generalization of vector and matrix, as vectors are first-order tensors, and matrices are second-order tensors. An Nth-order tensor is denoted as $\mathcal{A} \in \mathbb{R}^{I_1 \times I_2 \times \cdots \times I_N}$. It is addressed by N indices i_n, and each i_n addresses the n-mode of $\mathcal{A}$.

This section firstly introduces the notations and some basic tensor operations that are necessary in defining the TNNRW. Then, NNRW and 2D-NNRW algorithm is presented.

2.1 Tensor Fundamentals

An Mth-order tensor is denoted as $\mathcal{A} \in \mathbb{R}^{I_1 \times I_2 \times \cdots \times I_M}$. Their elements are addressed by M indices I_m, $m = 1, \cdots M$, and each I_m addresses the m-mode of $\mathcal{A}$. The m-mode unfolding of $\mathcal{A}$ is defined as the I_m dimensional vectors

$$\mathcal{A}_{(m)} \in \mathbb{R}^{I_m \times (I_1 \times \cdots \times I_{m-1} \times I_{m+1} \times \cdots \times I_M)} \tag{1}$$

The column vectors of $\mathcal{A}_{(m)}$ are the m-mode vectors of $\mathcal{A}$. The m-mode product of a tensor $\mathcal{A}$ by a matrix $U \in \mathbb{R}^{J_m \times I_m}$, denoted by $\mathcal{A} \times_m U$, is a tensor with entries:

$$(\mathcal{A} \times_m U)(i_1, \cdots, i_{m-1}, j_m, i_{m+1}, \cdots, i_M) = \sum_{i_m} \mathcal{A}(i_1, i_2, \cdots, i_M) \cdot U(j_m, i_m) \tag{2}$$

One of the most commonly used tensor decompositions is Tucker, which can be regarded as higher-order singular value decomposition (HOSVD). Let $\mathcal{X} \in \mathbb{R}^{I_1 \times I_2 \times \cdots \times I_M}$ denotes an Mth-order tensor, then the Tucker decomposition is defined as follows:

$$\mathcal{X} = \mathcal{Y} \times_1 U^{(1)} \times_2 U^{(2)} \cdots \times_M U^{(M)} \tag{3}$$

Where $\mathcal{Y} \in \mathbb{R}^{P_1 \times P_2 \times \cdots \times P_M}$ with $P_m < I_m$, denotes the core tensor and $\mathcal{Y} = \mathcal{X} \times_1 U^{(1)^T} \times_2 U^{(2)^T} \cdots \times_M U^{(M)^T}$, $U^{(m)} = \left[u_1^{(m)} u_2^{(m)} \cdots u_{P_m}^{(m)} \right]$ is an $I_m \times P_m$

matrix. When all $\left\{ U^{(m)} \right\}_{m=1}^{M}$ are orthonormal and the core tensor is all orthogonal. According to [13], with $y = Vec(\mathcal{Y})$, $x = Vec(\mathcal{X})$, where $Vec(\cdot)$ is the vectorization operator (by connecting each column of this tensor), there is:

$$y = Vec(\mathcal{Y}) = Vec(\mathcal{X} \times_1 U^{(1)^T} \times_2 U^{(2)^T} \cdots \times_M U^{(M)^T}) \tag{4}$$
$$= (U^{(1)} \otimes U^{(2)} \otimes \cdots \otimes U^{(M)})^T Vec(\mathcal{X})$$

where $\otimes$ denotes the Kronecker product. The Frobenius norm of $\mathcal{X}$ is defined as:

$$\|\mathcal{X}\| = \sqrt{<\mathcal{X}, \mathcal{X}>} = \|\mathcal{X}_{(m)}\|_F = \sqrt{\sum_{i_1=1}^{I_1} \sum_{i_2=1}^{I_2} \cdots \sum_{i_M=1}^{I_M} x_{i_1 i_2 \cdots i_M}^2}. \tag{5}$$

2.2   A Brief Review of NNRW

Feed-forward neural networks are ideal classifiers for approximating complex nonlinear mappings directly from the input data. Among them, SLFNN has very strong learning ability and has been applied in many fields. However, due to the hidden layer parameters and the output weights need to be trained and tuned properly based on the input samples, the learning speed of SLFNN is too slow to meet the demand in actual situations. As a kind of special learning method for SLFNN, NNRW can randomly set the input weights, hidden layer biases, and the whole process of NNRW does not need iteration and can obviously improve the neural network learning speed.

Suppose a set of N arbitrary distinct samples (x_j, t_j), where

$$x_j = [x_{j1}, x_{j2}, \cdots, x_{jn}]^T \in \mathbb{R}^n$$

and $t_j = [t_{j1}, t_{j2}, \cdots, t_{jm}]^T \in \mathbb{R}^m$. t_j is the class label of the input data, if x_j belongs to the class m, then $t_{jm} = 1$ while other parameters in t_j is 0. A typical FNN with single hidden layer can be commonly modeled as:

$$y_j = \sum_{i=1}^{L} \beta_i g_i(x_j) = \sum_{i=1}^{L} \beta_i g(w_i \cdot x_j + b_i), j = 1, \cdots, N \tag{6}$$

Where L is the number of hidden nodes, $g(\cdot)$ is the active function,

$$w_i = [w_{i1}, w_{i2}, \cdots, w_{in}]$$

is the weight vector connecting the i-th hidden node and the input nodes,

$$\beta_i = [\beta_{i1}, \beta_{i2}, \cdots, \beta_{im}]^T$$

is the weight vector connecting the i-th hidden node and the output nodes, and b_i is the bias of the i-th hidden node. Figure 1 shows the architecture of a complete NNRW process.

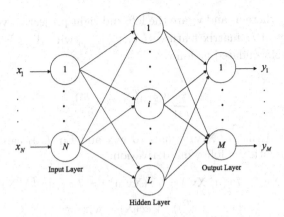

Fig. 1. Architecture of a complete NNRW classifier

Considering t_j is the corresponding observation value. The NNRW reliably approximates N samples with minimum error:

$$\sum_{i=1}^{L} \beta_i g(w_i \cdot x_j + b_i) = t_j, j = 1, 2, \cdots, N \tag{7}$$

According to NNRW proposed in [22], each element of the input weights and biases is selected randomly, then the output weights can be calculated by using Moore-Penrose generalized inverse.

$$\widehat{\beta} = \arg\min_{\beta} \sum_{j=1}^{N} \| \sum_{i=1}^{L} \beta_i g(w_i \cdot x_j + b_i) - t_j \| \tag{8}$$

$$= \arg\min_{\beta} \| H\beta - T \|$$

Where

$$H = \begin{bmatrix} G(w_1 \cdot x_1) + b_1 & \cdots & G(w_L \cdot x_1) + b_L \\ \vdots & \ddots & \vdots \\ G(w_1 \cdot x_N) + b_1 & \cdots & G(w_L \cdot x_N) + b_L \end{bmatrix} \tag{9}$$

is called the hidden layer output matrix of the neural network. Equation (8) can be reformulated as $\widehat{\beta} = H^\dagger T$, where $H^\dagger$ is the MP generalized inverse of H.

2.3 A Brief Review of 2D-NNRW

In [18], the 2D extension of NNRW is introduced for face recognition. It is noticed that one direct way to construct a two dimensional NNRW based classifier is to replace the traditional projection term $w_i x_j$ in Eq. (6) by its tensor counterpart, such as $u_i^T X_j v_i$, where u_i and v_i are the left and right projection vectors. Consequently, for a set of N matrix feature $\{(\mathcal{X}_j, t_j)\}_{j=1}^N$, with $\mathcal{X}_j \in \mathbb{R}^{m \times n}$, $t_j \in \mathbb{R}^C$, Eq. (6) can be reformulated as follows:

$$y_j = \sum_{i=1}^{L} \beta_i g(u_i^T X_j v_i + b_i) \tag{10}$$

It is demonstrated that $u_i^T X_j v_i$ equals to $w_i x$ and Eq. (10) can get the same result as Eq. (6) with the following derivation:

$$u_i^T X v_i = Tr(u_i^T X v_i) = Tr(X v_i u_i^T) = Tr\left((u_i v_i^T)^T X\right) \tag{11}$$
$$= \left(Vec(u_i v_i^T)\right)^T Vec(X) = w_i x$$

Although 2D-NNRW shows its effectiveness for face recognition, unfortunately, this classifier focus on dealing with two dimensional data rather than tensor objects with higher order. It is desirable to extend NNRW for tensor objects classification.

3   The Proposed Method

Inspired by the derivation in Eqs. (3) and (4), one direct way to construct a tensor classifier is to replace $w_i^T x_j$ by its tensor counterpart, such as $\mathcal{X}_j \times_1 u_i^{(1)^T} \times_2 u_i^{(2)^T} \cdots \times_M u_i^{(M)^T}$. Consequently, in order to deal with tensorial data directly, for a set of N tensor data $\{(\mathcal{X}_j, t_j)\}_{j=1}^N$, with $t_j \in \mathbb{R}^C$, Formula (6) can be reformulated as follows:

$$y_j = \sum_{i=1}^{L} \beta_i g\left(\mathcal{X}_j \times_1 u_i^{(1)^T} \times_2 u_i^{(2)^T} \cdots \times_M u_i^{(M)^T} + b_i\right) \tag{12}$$
$$= \sum_{i=1}^{L} \beta_i g\left(\mathcal{X}_j \prod_{m=1}^{M} \times_m u_i^{(m)^T} + b_i\right)$$

where $\mathcal{X}_j \in \mathbb{R}^{I_1 \times I_2 \times \cdots \times I_M}$ is a Mth-order tensor, $u_i^{(m)} \in \mathbb{R}^{I_m}$ are corresponding transformation vectors for $m = 1, \cdots, M$, $b_i \in \mathbb{R}$, and $\beta_i \in \mathbb{R}^C$, $i = 1, 2, \cdots, L$, and L is the number of hidden nodes.

In order to discuss the relationship between Eqs. (6) and (12), let

$$\mathcal{X} \in \mathbb{R}^{I_1 \times I_2 \times \cdots \times I_M},$$

and $x = Vec(\mathcal{X})$ as the input vector in Eq. (6), and the input weight vector w will be a column vector with $I_1 I_2 \cdots I_M$ elements. It is known that the Kronecker product of matrices $A \in \mathbb{R}^{I \times J}$ and $B \in \mathbb{R}^{K \times L}$ is denoted by $A \otimes B$ of size $(IK) \times (JL)$. By the same way, we can define w of size $I_1 I_2 \cdots I_M \times 1$ by:

$$w = u^{(1)} \otimes u^{(2)} \otimes \cdots \otimes u^{(M)} \tag{13}$$

where $u^{(m)} \in \mathbb{R}^{I_m}$. Because of the elements in w are randomly determined, the parameters in $u^{(m)}$ can be randomly generated too. Evoked by the above formulation, Eq. (4) can be reformulated as follows:

$$y = Vec(\mathcal{Y}) = Vec(\mathcal{X} \times_1 u^{(1)^T} \times_2 u^{(2)^T} \times \cdots \times_M u^{(M)^T}) \tag{14}$$
$$= (u^{(1)} \otimes u^{(2)} \otimes \cdots \otimes u^{(M)})^T Vec(\mathcal{X}) = w^T x$$

where $u^{(m)}$, $\mathcal{X}$, w, and x are defined as previous. As seen from above derivation, we notice that TNNRW can be regarded as a special case of NNRW, provided that the constraint is $w = u^{(1)} \otimes u^{(2)} \otimes \cdots \otimes u^{(M)}$. More concretely, the corresponding w is determined by only $(I_1 + I_2 + \cdots + I_M)$ variables through TNNRW while there is $(I_1 I_2 \cdots I_M)$ elements to be calculated for NNRW. In a word, utilizing the tensor based conversion in Eq. (12), the input tensor data sets can be calculated directly without vectoring them. Not only the inner structural information among the elements of the data can be preserved, but also fewer parameters need to be computed. All the weights and bias will be determined randomly. After confirming the projecting vectors and biases, the output weights β can be determined by solving Eq. (9) while the matrix H should be changed as follows:

$$\Phi = \begin{bmatrix} G\left(\mathcal{X}_1 \prod_{m=1}^{M} \times_m u_1^{(m)^T} + b_1\right) & \cdots & G\left(\mathcal{X}_1 \prod_{m=1}^{M} \times_m u_L^{(m)^T} + b_L\right) \\ \vdots & \ddots & \vdots \\ G\left(\mathcal{X}_N \prod_{m=1}^{M} \times_m u_1^{(m)^T} + b_1\right) & \cdots & G\left(\mathcal{X}_N \prod_{m=1}^{M} \times_m u_L^{(m)^T} + b_L\right) \end{bmatrix} \tag{15}$$

Φ is the hidden output matrix for TNNRW, then the output weights can be solved by the following optimal

$$\hat{\beta} = \arg\min_{\beta} \sum_{j=1}^{N} \left\| \sum_{i=1}^{L} \beta_i g\left(\mathcal{X}_j \prod_{m=1}^{M} \times_m u_i^{(m)^T} + b_i\right) - t_j \right\| \tag{16}$$
$$= \arg\min_{\beta} \|\Phi\beta - T\| = \Phi^{\dagger} T$$

where

$$\beta = \begin{pmatrix} \beta_1^T \\ \vdots \\ \beta_L^T \end{pmatrix}, \quad \text{and} \quad T = \begin{pmatrix} t_1^T \\ \vdots \\ t_N^T \end{pmatrix} \tag{17}$$

With the above description, this algorithm is called tensorial neural networks with random weights for tensorial data classification.

The detailed calculation process of the proposed TNNRW algorithm is listed in Algorithm 1.

Algorithm 1. The main procedure of TNNRW

INPUT: a set of Nth order tensors $\{\mathcal{X}_l \in \mathbb{R}^{I_1 \times I_2 \times \cdots \times I_N}, l = 1, \cdots, L\}$, their corresponding label targets $t_j \in \mathbb{R}^C$, the number of hidden notes L, and the active function $g(\cdot)$

OUTPUT: The determined network $y_j = \sum_{i=1}^{L} \beta_i g \left(\mathcal{X}_j \prod_{m=1}^{M} \times_m \mathbf{u}_i^{(m)^T} + b_i \right)$

Algorithm:
1. Initialize: Randomly set the hidden layer biases $b \in \mathbb{R}^L$, and input weights $\{\mathbf{u}_1^{(m)}, \mathbf{u}_2^{(m)}, \cdots, \mathbf{u}_L^{(m)}\}$
2. Calculate the hidden output matric Φ according to Eq. 15
3. Compute the output weights $\widehat{\beta} = \Phi^{\dagger} T$ as in Eq. 16.

---

4   Performance Evaluation

4.1   Databases

In this section, we will evaluate the proposed method in two different databases. The first one is a standard face database named FERET [23] which comprises 14126 gray-scale face images acquired from 1199 subjects. FERET is widely used for evaluating face recognition problem. In this experiment, a subset of 700 faces from 100 subjects is selected from the FERET database, seven face images per subject with a resolution of 80×80 pixels. The second database is one of the USF HumanID "gait challenge" data sets [24] which has used in [9]. The selected gait database contains 71 subjects and 731 human gait samples of size $32 \times 22 \times 10$ for preliminary evaluation. There is an average of roughly 10 samples for each subject.

4.2   Experiments on the Face Databass

The first experiment is conducted to compare the face recognition (FR) performance of TNNRW with NNRW on FERET database. As gray-level face images are natively second-order tensors, they are input directly for the TNNRW algorithms as 80×80 tensors, while for NNRW, they need to be vectorized to 6400×1 vectors first. Three images per person are randomly selected for training while the rest are used for testing. In order to fairly evaluate the effectiveness of the proposed algorithm, we report the recognition accuracies averaged by over ten such random repetitions. The corresponding transformation vectors $\mathbf{u}^{(m)}$ for TNNRW and the input weights $\mathbf{w}$ for NNRW are randomly distributed on $(-1, 1)$, while the bias b_i on $(0, 1)$. Figure 2 shows the FR results against different numbers of hidden nodes and different feature dimensionality on the face database. As shown in Fig. 2, with L (the number of hidden nodes) from 100 to 3000, except $L = 300, 400$ and 500, the proposed TNNRW obviously outperforms NNRW across all Ls and the FRs improve with the increasing number of L for both methods.

In the second test, MPCA is employed for feature extraction and then TNNRW or NNRW with $L = 1500$ is used for features classification. Figure 3 shows the FRs with P (the number of selected features) from 1 to 20. It is can be seen that the superiority of TNNRW still exists with the feature extraction tool

MPCA. Because of most redundancy information of the images is avoided after the feature extraction step, the gap between MPCA+TNNRW and MPCA+ NNRW is much smaller than that directly putting TNNRW and NNRW on the original face images. Moreover, the gap grows as the number of extracted features increases.

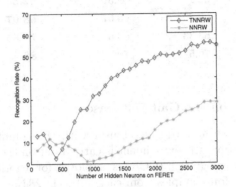

Fig. 2. Comparison recognition rate (%) versus different number of hidden nodes of the proposed TNNRW against NNRW on FERET

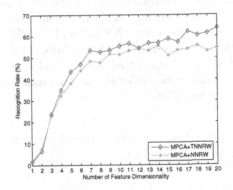

Fig. 3. Comparison the recognition rate (%) versus different number of feature dimensionality of MPCA+TNNRW against NNRW on FERET

The third test is carried out on the FRs comparison of different classifiers, such as NN and SVM with the same feature extraction tool MPCA on FERET database. With P samples are randomly selected per class for training and the rest are used for testing, the recognition results are listed in Table 1 for $P = 1, 2, 3, 4, 5, 6$, where the best recognition accuracy are shown in bold. From Table 1, MPCA+TNNRW algorithm provides the best recognition accuracy among all other algorithms except when $P = 1$, MPCA+NNRW is slightly higher than MPCA+TNNRW.

Table 1. Face recognition (%) on the FERET database for various Ps

P	MPCA+NN	MPCA+SVM	MPCA+NNRW	MPCA+TNNRW
1	39.33	42.83	**45.83**	45.67
2	46.88	48.76	47.4	**52.2**
3	50.96	52.1	58.5	**62.3**
4	56.88	60.8	60.67	**68.67**
5	68.83	63.33	63.5	**78.85**
6	76.83	70.5	70	**83**

4.3   Experiments on the Gait Database

Gait video is naturally a third-order tensor with the column, row, and time mode. In this subsection, the experiment is carried out on the gait base and the correct classification recognition (CCR) is employed for algorithms performance evaluation. The first four samples from each subject (284 in total) are used for training and the rest 447 samples are used for testing. With the same feature extraction method MPCA, Fig. 4 shows the CCRs comparison of three different classifiers. The three-order tensor features can be input directly for the proposed TNNRW and NN while for SVM, they need to be vectorized first. In this test, we use the first P numbers of extracted features from each mode of the training samples to calculate the performance of each classifier and the scale of P is from 1 to 10. Furthermore, both of TNNRW and NNRW set the number of hidden nodes with 1000. As seen from Fig. 4 that MPCA+TNNRW achieves the highest accuracies in all cases and the advantage is obvious. This is benefit by the reservation of the inner structure of the original data for TNNRW and the classification superiority for NNRW.

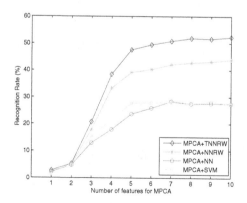

Fig. 4. Recognition rate comparison of the classifiers with MPCA as the feature extraction tool

5   Conclusions

Since most of biometric signals in the real world are naturally multi-dimensional data. In this paper, a novel TNNRW classification is designed to classify tensorial data directly for biometric data classification. For the proposed solution, instead of using the high dimensional input weight vector in the hidden layer of NNRW, a set of corresponding transformation vectors with random values are applied to preserve the natural structure information of the input high-order data. There are two advantages of using TNNRW for face image classification, one is higher recognition rate can be obtained by classifying tensorial data directly, the other is faster computing speed can be achieved benefits by much less parameters to be calculated with TNNRW than the traditional NNRW. In addition, MPCA is used to extract features to reduce the dimension of the original data. Experiments are carried out on the two-order face database and the three-order gait database, then the test results indicate that both of TNNRW and MPCA+TNNRW can achieve a much better accuracy with a faster computing speed.

References

1. Law, M.H.C., Jain, A.K.: Incremental nonlinear dimensionality reduction by manifold learning. IEEE Trans. Pattern Anal. Mach. Intell. **28**(3), 377–391 (2006)
2. Liu, C., Xu, W., Wu, Q.: TKPCA: tensorial kernel principal component analysis for action recognition. Math. Problems Eng. Article ID: 816836 (2013)
3. Turk, M., Pentland, A.: Eigenfaces for recognition. J. Cogn. Neurosci. **3**(1), 71–86 (1991)
4. Belhumeur, P.N., Hespanha, J.P., Krigman, D.J.: Eigenfaces vs. Fisherfaces: recognition using class specific linear projection. IEEE Trans. Pattern Anal. Mach. Intell. **19**(7), 711–720 (1997)
5. Tao, D., Li, X., Wu, X., Maybank, S.J.: General tensor discriminant analysis and gabor features for gait recognition. IEEE Trans. Pattern Anal. Mach. Intell. **29**(10), 1700–1715 (2007)
6. He, X., Cai, D., Niyogi, P.: Tensor subspace analysis. Adv. Neural Inf. Process. Syst. **4**(4), 499–506 (2005)
7. Er, M.J., Wu, S., Lu, J., Toh, H.L.: Face recognition with radial basis function (RBF) neural networks. IEEE Trans. Neural Netw. **13**(3), 697–710 (2002)
8. Qin, J., He, Z.S.: A SVM face recognition method based on gabor-featured key points. In: Proceedings 4th IEEE Conference on Machine Learning and Cybernetics, pp. 5144–5149 (2005)
9. Lu, H., Plataniotis, K.N., Venetsanopoulos, A.N.: MPCA: multilinear principal component analysis of tensor objects. IEEE Trans. Neural Netw. **19**(1), 18–39 (2008)
10. Yan, S., Xu, D., Yang, Q., Zhang, L., Tang, X., Zhang, H.J.: Multilinear discriminant analysis for face recognition. IEEE Trans. Image Process. **16**(1), 212–220 (2007)
11. Tao, D., Li, X., Wu, X., Maybank, S.: General tensor discriminant analysis and gabor features for gait recognition. IEEE Trans. Pattern Anal. Mach. Intell. **29**(10), 1700–1715 (2007)

12. He, X., Cai, D., Niyogi, P.: Tensor subspace analysis. In: Advances in Neural Information Processing Systems, pp. 499–506 (2005)
13. Tao, D., Li, X., Wu, X., Hu, W., Maybank, S.J.: Supervised tensor learning. Knowl. Inf. Syst. **13**(1), 1–42 (2007)
14. Zhang, F., Qi, L., Chen, E.: Extended extreme learning machine for biometric signal classification. J. Comput. Theor. Nanosci. **12**(7), 1247–1251 (2015)
15. Song, F., Zhang, D., Mei, D., Guo, Z.: A multiple maximum scatter difference discriminant criterion for facial feature extraction. IEEE Trans. Syst. Man Cybern. Part B: Cybern. **37**(6), 1599–1606 (2007)
16. Huang, G.B., Zhu, Q.Y., Siew, C.K.: Extreme learning machine: theory and applications. Neurocomputing **70**, 489–501 (2006)
17. Wang, S.J., Zhou, C.G., Fu, X.: Fusion tensor subspace transformation framework. PLoS One **8**(7), e66647 (2013)
18. Lu, J., Zhao, J., Cao, F.: Extended feed forward neural networks with random weights for face recognition. Neurocomputing **136**, 96–102 (2014)
19. Tyukin, I., Prokhorov, D.: Feasibility of random basis function approximators for modeling and control (2009). arXiv:0905.0677
20. De Lathauwer, L., De Moor, B., Vandewalle, J.: On the best rank-1 and rank-$(R_1, R_2, \cdots, R_N)$ approximation of higher-order tensors. SIAM J. Matrix Anal. Appl. **21**(4), 1324–1342 (2000)
21. Kolda, T.G., Bader, B.W.: Tensor decompositions and applications. SIAM Rev. **51**(3), 455–500 (2009)
22. Schmidt, W.F., Kraaijveld, M., Duin, R.P.W.: Feed forward neural networks with random weights. In: Proceedings 11th IAPR International Conference on Pattern Recognition, Conference B: Pattern Recognition Methodology and Systems, vol. II, pp. 1–4. IEEE (1992)
23. Phillips, P.J., Moon, H., Rizvi, S.A., Rauss, P.: The FERET evaluation method for face recognition algorithms. IEEE Trans. Pattern Anal. Mach. Intell. **22**, 1090–1104 (2000)
24. Sarkar, S., Phillips, P.J., Liu, Z., Vega, I.R., Grother, P., Bowyer, K.W.: The human ID gait challenge problem: data sets, performance, and analysis. IEEE Trans. Pattern Anal. Mach. Intell. **27**(2), 162–177 (2005)

Application of DNA Self-assembly for Maximum Matching Problem

Hui Zhang[1], Xiaoli Qiang[1(✉)], and Kai Zhang[2]

[1] College of Computer Science, South-Central University for Nationalities,
Wuhan 430074, Hubei, People's Republic of China
zhanghuigary@163.com, qiangxl@mail.scuec.edu.cn
[2] School of Computer Science, Wuhan University of Science and Technology,
Wuhan 430081, Hubei, People's Republic of China
zhangkai@wust.edu.cn

Abstract. DNA tile self-assembly have been demonstrated to be used to solve graph theory or combinatorial optimization problem because of its high-density storage and huge-scale parallel computing ability. In this paper, tile self-assembly have been shown to be used for solving the maximum matching problem by mainly constructing four sub-systems which are seed configuration system, nondeterministic guess system, verification system and output system. These systems can be used to probabilistically get the feasible solution of the problem. The model can successfully perform the maximum matching problem in polynomial time with distinct tile types, parallel and at very low cost.

Keywords: DNA tile · Self-assembly model · Maximum matching problem

1 Introduction

DNA computing is a new research field of computer science and molecular biology. It takes DNA as the computing tool, uses its powerful parallel computing power and large storage capacity to solve the problem which can not be solved by the electronic computer. Since Adleman [1] applied DNA molecules to solve a directed Hamiltonian path problem, lots of attentions from researchers has been attracted to the field of molecular computing.

In 1995, Winfree [2–5] proposed a method to simulate one-dimensional cellular automata by DX molecule self-assembly process according to the properties of DX double crossover molecules self-assembly constructed by Seeman [6], which is the ideological roots of DNA self-assembly calculation model. In 1999, Gehani [7] et al. realized the XOR operation of binary string in one-time pad system by DNA molecular self-assembly calculation model. In 2000, Mao et al. realized the logic operation [8,9] by using self-assembly process of TX molecule which is one of the DNA three cross molecule. In 2002, Seeman [10,11] proposed DNA tiles could be used in logical computation and viewed as a circuit that realized the parity of the input elements. Besides, other DNA self-assembly structures were also

© Springer-Verlag Berlin Heidelberg 2015
M. Gong et al. (Eds.): BIC-TA 2015, CCIS 562, pp. 621–630, 2015.
DOI: 10.1007/978-3-662-49014-3_55

exploited to carry out addition and logical computation. In 2005, Rothemund [12] et al. proposed a method to complete the XOR computation by constructing the Sierpinski triangle with DNA self-assembly calculation model. After that, Brun [13] presented a method of arithmetic operation by DNA self-assembly calculation model, completed the addition and multiplication of binary number and accomplished the operation of resolving large integer by the multiplication system. In 2009, Zhang [14] et al. used the DNA self-assemble computing model to complete the corresponding subtraction and division operations on the basis of Burn. Recently, Lin [15] and Xu [16,17] et al. solved the coloring problem of graph vertices using 3D DNA self-assembly model.

The maximum matching problem is a well-known combinatorial optimization problem in graph theory, which has important practical significance in economic production. In this paper, a theoretical model for the maximum matching problem [18] based on DNA self-assembly was proposed.

2   Definition of the Maximum Matching Problem

Given a graph with n nodes and m edges, a matching in G is defined as a subset in which there is no common vertices between any two edges. The Maximum Matching Problem (MMP) involves finding the biggest subset, which contains the largest numbers of edges. Here, a small paradigm (see Fig. 1) is used to verify the proposed algorithm.

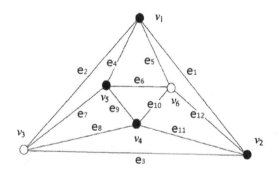

Fig. 1. A graph G with 6 nodes and 12 edges.

3   Models for Algorithmic Self-assembly

The abstract tile assembly model, which provides a rigorous framework for analyzing algorithmic self-assembly, was originally proposed by Rothemund and Winfree [19]. It extends the theoretical model of tiling proposed by Wang [20] to include a mechanism for growth based on the physics of molecular self-assembly. This model considers the assembly of rigid square objects or tiles.

Formally, a tile over a set of binding domains Σ is a 4-tuple $\{\sigma_N, \sigma_E, \sigma_S, \sigma_W\}$ $\in \Sigma^4$, indicating the binding domains on the north, east, south and west sides. A position (x, y) is an element of $\mathbb{Z}^2$. The set of directions $D = \{N, E, S, W\}$ is a set of four functions from positions to positions, i.e. $\mathbb{Z}^2$ to $\mathbb{Z}^2$, such that for all positions (x, y), $N(x, y) = (x, y+1)$, $E(x, y) = (x-1, y)$, $S(x, y) = (x, y-1)$ and $W(x, y) = (x + 1, y)$. The positions (x, y) and (x', y') are neighbors if $\exists d \in D$ such that $d(x, y) = (x', y')$. For a tile t and $d \in D$, $bd_d(t)$ means the binding domain of tile t on the direction d. A special tile $empty = (null, null, null, null)$ represents the absence of all other tiles.

The binding domains determine the interaction between tiles, that is a tile could be connected with some specific tiles according to the specific binding domain. A function g: Σ^2 to $\mathbb{R}$, where $null \in \Sigma$, is a strength function that denotes the strength of the binding domains, which may be 0, 1, or 2 (called null, weak, and strong bonds, respectively). If $\forall \sigma, \sigma' \in \Sigma$ then $g(\sigma, \sigma') = g(\sigma', \sigma)$ and $g(null, \sigma) = 0$.

Let T be a finite set of tile types containing the empty tile. A configuration of T is a map from $\mathbb{Z}^2$ to T. A tile system is a quadruple $\mathbb{S} = \langle T, S, g, \tau \rangle$, where T, g are the same as those mentioned above, S is a seed configuration and $\tau \geq 0$ is the parameter associated with thermodynamics.

If A is a configuration, then within system $\mathbb{S}$, a tile t can attach to A at position (x, y) and produce a new configuration A' if: 1. $(x, y) \notin A$; 2. $\Sigma_{d \in D} g(bd_d(t), bd_{d-1}(A(d(x, y)))) \geq \tau$ where d^{-1} denotes the opposite direction of d, for example, N and S are opposite directions, E and W are opposite directions; 3. $\forall (u, v) \in \mathbb{Z}^2$, $(u, v) \neq (x, y) \Rightarrow A'(u, v) = A(u, v)$; 4. $A'(x, y) = t$. That is, a tile can attach to a configuration only in empty positions and if the total strength of the appropriate binding domains on the tiles in neighboring positions meets or exceeds the τ.

Given a tile system $\mathbb{S} = \langle T, S, g, \tau \rangle$, if the above-mentioned conditions are satisfied, tiles of T can be attached to S. Configurations produced by repeated attachments of tiles from T are said to be produced by $\mathbb{S}$ on S. If this process terminates, then the configuration achieved when no more attachments are possible is called the final configuration. If for all sequences of tile attachments, all possible final configurations are identical, then $\mathbb{S}$ is said to produce a unique final configuration on S.

4   Solving the Maximum Matching Problem Based on DNA Tile Self-assembly

Here, the algorithm for solving the maximum matching problem have been introduced by mainly constructing four sub-systems which are seed configuration system, nondeterministic matching system, verification system and output system. Examples can be given to indicate how the tile assembly model performs this problem.

4.1 Seed Configuration System

The seed configuration system is used to construct the initial input frame (see Fig. 2). It consists of all the encoded vertex tiles and the boundary tiles. Here, two types of tiles have been used to encode the vertexes in this system. The set of these tiles are $\{(v_j, null, null, null), (null, null, null, v_i)\}$ $(1 \leq i, j \leq n)$. Two special tiles called boundary tiles encoding $(null, null, null, null)$ and $(|, null, null, null)$ are used to denote the start and the end of input vertexes, respectively. These set limits on the extent of the calculation or patterning, which will facilitate a modular approach to the process. All the encoded vertexes arrange in order between the S_0 and E_0.

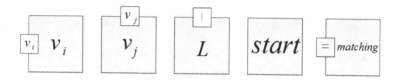

Fig. 2. The basic tile types of the seed configuration system.

4.2 Nondeterministic Matching System

The nondeterministic matching system uses the random allocation matching scheme, it can be defined as a tile system to produce a unique final seed configuration if for all sequences of tile attachments, and all possible final configurations are not necessarily the same. The nondeterministic matching system is a system that nondeterministically decides which edges should be chosen for the vertex v_j. $E(v_j)$ is an edge set which consist of all the edges connected with the vertex v_j. As is shown in the Fig. 1, $\{e_1, e_2, e_4, e_5\} \in E(v_1)$, $\{e_1, e_3, e_{11}, e_{12}\} \in E(v_2)$. Here, we will use two types of tiles to construct this system, and the set of these tiles are $\{E_j = (v_j E(v_j), =, v_j, =), L = (|, =, |, null)\}$. A graphical representation of the two types of tile is shown in Fig. 3. L is the boundary tile of the nondeterministic system.

4.3 Verification System

According to the description of the matching problem, if the matching scheme has a common vertex between two edges in a certain graph, then the matching scheme is not correct. Therefore, to ensure the matching scheme is correct, the verification system should be construct to get the correct computation result. This system verifies whether the connected edges of every vertex are conflict with other vertex from bottom to up in the self-assembly process.

For simplicity, in a given graph (see Fig. 1), the process have been described with the form of tables, as show in the following table. The following table

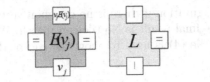

Fig. 3. The basic tile types of the nondeterministic matching system.

describes the verification of a matching scheme for $\{e_2, e_{11}, e_2, e_{11}, e_6, e_6\}$ (see Fig. 4). The first row (from the bottom to up) of the table is the nondeterministic matching scheme, the first column (from the right to left) of the table is the vertex. In this table, verification system in each row only to verify a vertex, and the vertex i starts to verify from the vertex behind it. Also the i-th vertex achieve its matching edge in the i-th row and the i-th column, and then check whether there is a conflict between the achieved matching edge and the matching edges of the vertex one by one from the $i+1$ column. Straight, this table will filling from bottom to up. Each cell is carried out according to the following rules:

$$C_j^i = \begin{cases} E(v_i), & i \geq j, \\ OK, & i < j \cap (v_i \notin E(v_j) \cap v_j \notin E(v_i)) \cup (v_i, v_j \in E(v_i)), \\ NO, & otherwise. \end{cases} \quad (1)$$

where, C_j^i indicates the unit information of the i-th row and the j-th column in the Fig. 4.

E_6	E_6	E_{11}	E_2	E_{11}	E_2	S
OK	E_6	E_{11}	E_2	E_{11}	E_2	v_5
OK	OK	E_{11}	E_2	E_{11}	E_2	v_4
OK	OK	OK	E_2	E_{11}	E_2	v_3
OK	OK	OK	OK	E_{11}	E_2	v_2
OK	OK	OK	OK	OK	E_2	v_1
v_6e_6	v_5e_6	v_4e_{11}	v_3e_2	v_2e_{11}	v_1e_2	START

Fig. 4. The verification operation.

Figure 5 depicts the concept behind the tiles and the 4 actual types of tiles with south and west sides as the input sides and the east side as the output side in the verification system. The set of these tiles are $\{(v_j E(v_j), v_i, v_j E(v_j), v_i),$ $(v_j E(v_j), v_i, v_j E(v_j), v_i E(v_i)), (v_j E(v_j), v_i E(v_i), v_j E(v_j), v_i E(v_i)), (|, v_i E(v_i), |,$ $null)\}$. When $i > j$, tile (1) plays the role of transmission, which transfer the input sides to the output sides. When $i = j$, the input side of tile (2) is a vertex v_i, and its output side is the matching edge of the vertex. When $i < j$, tile (3) assembles to the configuration if there is no common vertex between $E(v_i)$ and $E(v_j)$. Otherwise, the final result is No tile can match. When the self-assembly reach the boundary, tile (4) is used to show the end of the verification of that vertex.

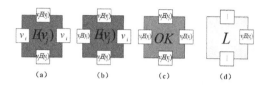

Fig. 5. The basic tile types of the verification system.

4.4   Output System

The top layer of the self-assembly is the solution of the problem with a matching scheme output, which gives a SUCCESS mark on the left top corner. The output system contains two types of tiles, $(null, -, v_j E(v_j), -)$ and $(null, -, |, null)$ respectively. A graphical representation of the two types of tile is shown in Fig. 6.

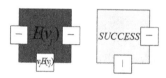

Fig. 6. The basic tile types of the output system.

4.5   Example

Here the graph shown in Fig. 1 is used to demonstrate this model and the steps are as follows.

Step 1: Encoding, and design all kind of tiles for the following self-assembly. And build the seed configuration system with the designed boundary tiles and the coded vertex tiles (Fig. 7).

Step 2: Establishing the initial solution space. Use the DNA tiles designed in the nondeterministic matching system to establish all the probable solutions for the next step. For this example, one of the initial solutions $\{e_2, e_{11}, e_2, e_{11}, e_6, e_6\}$ is given to illustrate the algorithm this paper proposed (Fig. 8).

Step 3: Picking up all valid solutions. Verification system have been used to verify whether the solution $\{e_2, e_{11}, e_2, e_{11}, e_6, e_6\}$ is valid or not. The rule (1)

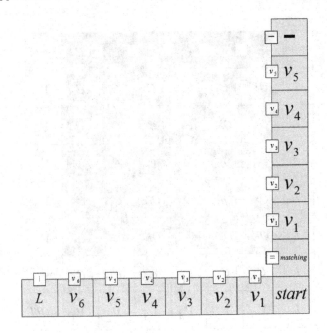

Fig. 7. The seed configuration system of the success example.

proposed above can detect the correct solution among the initial solution space. If a solution like $\{e_2, e_{11}, e_2, e_7, e_6, e_6\}$, it does not match the rule, will assemble fail (Fig. 9).

Step 4: Output all the matching scheme by DNA self-assembly. Due to the strong parallelism of DNA, the correct solution that satisfy the rule will be detected when all the initial solution space assembled with the seed configuration system. From them, searching for the schemes that contains the largest numbers of edges. They are the solutions of maximum matching problem (Fig. 10).

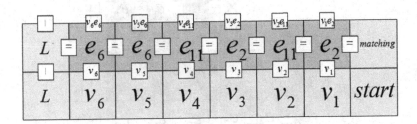

Fig. 8. The verification system of the success example.

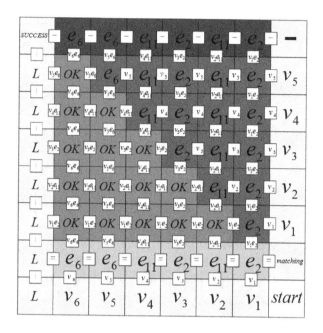

Fig. 9. The final stage of the successful example.

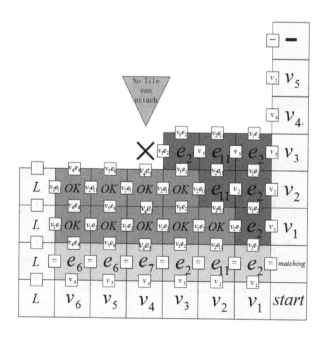

Fig. 10. The final stage of failure example.

4.6 Complexity Analysis

The complexity of the design is considered in terms of computation time, computation space and number of distinct tiles required. It is obvious from he given examples that the upper bound of the computation time T is $T = n + n = O(n)$.

The computation space S taken for each assembly is the area of the assemble complexes represented by, $S = (n + 2)[(n - 1) + 1] = O(n^2)$.

5 Conclusion

DNA tile self-assembly is looked forward to many applications in different fields. This paper mainly shows how the DNA self-assembly process can be used for solving the maximum matching problem of arbitrary graph by constructing four small systems. The advantage of this method is that once the graph is given, we can compute fast parallel through the process of DNA self-assembly without any participation of manpower, thus the algorithm is proposed which can be successfully solved the maximum matching problem in polynomial time within optimal distinct tile types, parallel and at very low cost. So we can see that the DNA tile self-assembly model has various applications in many fields and it also might open up a host of other applications in materials science, medicine, biology and other ways.

In [27], DNA strands displacement was used to simulate logic gates based on neural-like manner. Recently, some novel and powerful neural-like computing models, see, e.g. [21–26], have been used in solving computational hard problems. It is of interests to use DNA strands displacement to simulate the computation of neural-like computing models, thus achieving bio-molecular neural-like computing systems.

Acknowledgments. The authors thank the financial support for the work from Chinese National Natural Science Foundation (61379059, 61472293), the Fundamental Research Funds for the Central Universities (CZZ13003, CZQ12006).

References

1. Adleman, L.M.: Molecular computation of solutions to combinatorial problems. Science **266**, 1021–1024 (1994)
2. Winfree, E., Liu, F.R., Wenzler, L.A., Seeman, N.C.: Design and self-assembly of two-dimensional DNA crystals. Nature **394**, 539–544 (1998)
3. Winfree, E., Eng, T., Rozenberg, G.: String tile models for DNA computing by self-assembly. In: Condon, A., Rozenberg, G. (eds.) DNA 2000. LNCS, vol. 2054, pp. 63–88. Springer, Heidelberg (2001)
4. Winfree, E.: Algorithmic self-assembly of DNA. Ph.D. Dissertation, California Institute of Technology (1998)
5. Winfree, E., Liu, F., Wenzler, L.A.: Design and self-assembly of 2D DNA crystals. Nature **394**, 539–544 (1998)

6. Seeman, N.C.: DNA nanotechnology: novel DNA constructions. Annu. Rev. Biophys. Biomol. Struct. **27**, 225–248 (1998)
7. Gehani, A., LaBean, T.H., Reif, J.H.: DNA-based cryptography. In: 5th DIMACS Workshop on DNA Based Computers. MIT (1999)
8. Mao, C., Sun, W., Seeman, N.C.: Designed two-dimensional DNA Holliday junction arrays visualized by atomic force microscopy. J. Am. Chem. Soc. **121**, 5437–5443 (1999)
9. Mao, C., LaBean, T.H., Reif, J.H.: Logical computation using algorithmic self-assembly of DNA triple-crossover molecules. Nature **407**, 493–496 (2000)
10. Carbone, A., Seeman, N.C.: Circuits and programmable self-assembling DNA structures. PNAS **99**, 12577–12582 (2002)
11. Carbone, A., Seeman, N.C.: Molecular tiling and DNA self-assembly. In: Jonoska, N., Păun, G., Rozenberg, G. (eds.) Aspects of Molecular Computing. LNCS, vol. 2950, pp. 61–83. Springer, Heidelberg (2003)
12. Rothemund, P., Papadakis, N., Winfree, E.: Algorithmic self-assembly of DNA Sierpinski triangles. PLoS Biol. **2**(12), 2041–2053 (2004)
13. Brun, Y.: Arithmetic computation in the tile assembly model: addition and multiplication. Theor. Comput. Sci. **378**(1), 17–31 (2007)
14. Zhang, X.C., Wang, Y.F., Chen, Z.H.: Arithmetic computation using self-assembly of DNA tiles: subtraction and division. Prog. Nat. Sci. **19**(3), 377–388 (2009)
15. Lin, M.Q., Xu, J., Zhang, D.F.: 3D DNA self-assembly model for graph vertex coloring. J. Comput. Theor. Nanosci. **7**(1), 246–253 (2010)
16. Pan, L.Q., Xu, J., Liu, Y.C.: A surface-based DNA algorithm for the minimal vertex problem. Prog. Nat. Sci. **13**, 81–84 (2003)
17. Pan, L.Q., Liu, G.W., Xu, J.: Solid phase based DNA solution of the coloring problem. Prog. Nat. Sci. **14**, 104–107 (2004)
18. Liu, W.B., Gao, L., Wang, S.D.: A surface-based DNA algorithm for maximal matching problem. Acta Electronica Sin. **31**(10), 1496–1500 (2003)
19. Barish, R., Rothemund, P., Winfree, E.: Two computational primitives for algorithmic self-assembly: copying and counting. Nano Lett. **5**(12), 2586–2592 (2005)
20. Wang, H.: Proving theorems by pattern recognition I. Bell Syst. Tech. J. **40**, 1–42 (1961)
21. Song, T., Pan, L.: Spiking neural P systems with rules on synapses working in maximum spikes consumption strategy. IEEE Trans. Nanobiosci. **14**(1), 38–44 (2015)
22. Song, T., Pan, L.: Spiking neural P systems with rules on synapses working in maximum spiking strategy. IEEE Trans. NanoBiosci. **14**(4), 465–477 (2015)
23. Song, T., Pan, L., Jiang, K., et al.: Normal forms for some classes of sequential spiking neural P systems. IEEE Trans. NanoBiosci. **12**(3), 255–264 (2013)
24. Song, T., Pan, L., Păun, G.: Asynchronous spiking neural P systems with local synchronization. Inf. Sci. **219**, 197–207 (2013)
25. Song, T., Pan, L., Wang, J., et al.: Normal forms of spiking neural P systems with anti-spikes. IEEE Trans. NanoBiosci. **11**(4), 352–359 (2012)
26. Zhang, X., Pan, L., Paun, A.: On the universality of axon P systems. IEEE Trans. Neural Netw. Learn. Syst. (2015). doi:10.1109/TNNLS.2015.2396940
27. Shi, X., Wang, Z., Deng, C., Song, T., Pan, L., Chen, Z.: A novel bio-sensor based on DNA strand displacement. PLoS One **9**, e108856 (2014)

A Multiobjective Evolutionary Algorithm Based on Decomposition and Preselection

Jinyuan Zhang$^{(\boxtimes)}$, Aimin Zhou, and Guixu Zhang

Shanghai Key Laboratory of Multidimensional Information Processing,
Department of Computer Science and Technology, East China Normal University,
Shanghai 200235, China
jyzhang@ecnu.cn, {amzhou,gxzhang}@cs.ecnu.edu.cn

Abstract. The preselection aims to choose promising offspring solutions from a candidate set in evolutionary algorithms. Usually the preselection process is based on the real or estimated objective values, which might be expensive. It is arguable that the preselection is doing classification in nature, which requires to know a solution is good or not instead of knowing how good it is. In this paper we apply a *classification based preselection (CPS)* to a *multiobjective evolutionary algorithm based on decomposition (MOEA/D)*. In each generation, a set of candidate solutions are generated for each subproblem and only a good one is chosen as the offspring by the CPS. The modified MOEA/D, denoted as MOEA/D-CPS, is applied to a set of test instances, and the experimental results suggest that the CPS can successfully improve the performance of MOEA/D.

Keywords: Preselection · Classification · MOEA/D

1 Introduction

In scientific and engineering areas, many problems can be modeled as *multiobjective optimization problems (MOP)*. In this paper, we consider the following continuous MOP:

$$\min F(x) = (f_1(x), \cdots, f_m(x))^T$$
$$\text{s.t } x \in \Pi_{i=1}^{n}[a_i, b_i] \tag{1}$$

where $x = (x_1, \cdots, x_n)^T \in R^n$ is a decision variable vector, $\Pi_{i=1}^{n}[a_i, b_i] \subset R^n$ defines the feasible region of the search space, $f_i : R^n \to R, i = 1, \cdots, m$, is a continuous mapping, and $F(x)$ is an objective vector.

Since the objectives of (1) usually conflict with each other, there does not exit a solution that can minimize all the objects at the same time. Therefore, the tradeoff solutions, called *Pareto optimal solutions* [1], between the objectives are of interests. The set of all the Pareto optimal solutions is called the *Pareto set (PS)* in the decision space and the *Pareto front (PF)* in the objective space. Since evolutionary algorithms are able to approximate the PS (PF) in a single run, they have become the major method to deal with MOPs. A variety of

© Springer-Verlag Berlin Heidelberg 2015
M. Gong et al. (Eds.): BIC-TA 2015, CCIS 562, pp. 631–642, 2015.
DOI: 10.1007/978-3-662-49014-3_56

multiobjective evolutionary algorithms (MOEAs) [2] have been proposed in last decades. Most of these algorithms can be classified into three categories.

1. Domination based MOEAs: In these algorithms, the selection operators are based on the Pareto domination relationship [3–5].
2. Indicator based MOEAs: These algorithms use the performance metrics as the objective to optimize and thus do selection [6–8].
3. Decomposition based MOEAs: This kind of algorithms decompose an MOP into a set of scalar-objective subproblems (SOPs), and solve them simultaneously [9,10].

The *multiobjective evolutionary algorithm based on decomposition (MOEA/D)* is one of the most popular decomposition based MOEAs. The basic idea of MOEA/D is to decompose the MOP into a set of scalar-objective subproblems. The neighboring subproblems collaborate with each other to generate new offspring solutions, and a new one will update not only the solution of the corresponding subproblem but also that of the neighboring subproblems. By this way, all the subproblems are tackled simultaneously, and the final solutions of the subproblems form an approximation to the PS (PF) of the original MOP. In MOEA/D and its variants, either the crossover and/or mutation operators [10,11] or probabilistic model based reproduction operators [12–14] are used to generate new offspring solutions.

This paper focuses on the preselection in MOEA/D, which has not been studied to the best of our knowledge. Following our previous work in preselection [15,16], a *classification based preselection (CPS)* is applied to MOEA/D. In each generation, a classification model is built according to a set of recorded training data set with either positive or negative labels. After that, a set of candidate offspring solutions are generated, the classification model is applied to label the candidate offspring solutions, and only those with positive labels are kept as the offspring solutions. In the approach, the nondominated sorting scheme [4] is used to maintain the training data set.

The rest of the paper is organized as follows. Section 2 presents the MOEA/D framework with CPS. The algorithm implementation details, such as classifier training, and offspring reproduction are introduced as well. The proposed approach is systematically studied in Sect. 3. Finally Sect. 4 concludes this paper with some future work remarks.

2   MOEA/D with Classification Based Preselection

This section introduces the proposed modified MOEA/D with the CPS. For simplicity, we denote this approach as MOEA/D-CPS.

2.1   Basic Idea

There is no reason that only one offspring solution is generated for each subproblem in MOEA/D. As shown in Fig. 1, there is a high probability to generate a good solution if more offspring solutions are generated. However, it may need more function evaluations as well. To deal with this problem, we can use the preselection to filter bad ones and keep promising ones.

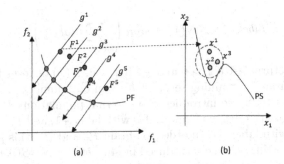

Fig. 1. An illustration of the advantage to generate more offspring solutions for each subproblem in MOEA/D

The purpose of preselection is to select some promising offspring solutions from a set of candidate offspring solutions. Usually, the preselection is based on the estimated objective values through surrogate models or meta models. However, the surrogate model building itself is an expensive procedure. Actually, the preselection only needs to know which solution is good and which one is bad instead of knowing how good or how bad it is. Thus the preselection can be naturally regarded as a classification process, i.e., to classify the candidate offspring solutions into two sets: the selected good ones and the unselected bad ones. Basically, a classification model needs to find a boundary between two classes of points while a surrogate model needs to find the function values of each point in the space. Therefore, the classification model building will be generally cheaper than the surrogate model building.

The key point here is to build a classifier to differentiate the candidate solutions. Fortunately, there are a variety of classification models in the community of statistical and machine learning that we can use directly [17–19]. Furthermore in the running process of MOEA/D, we can record some good and bad solutions found so far and use them as the classification model training samples.

2.2 Classifier Training

The classification model training problem can be formulated as follows. Let $\{< x, label >\}$ be a set of training data, where x is a feature vector of a data point, $label \in L$ is the label of the data point and L is a set of labels. The relationship between a feature vector and the corresponding label can be denoted as $label = Class(x)$. The target of a classifier training is to find a relationship $label = \hat{Class}(x)$ that can approximate the real relationship $label = Class(x)$ at most based on the training data set.

In our case, a solution x can be directly regarded as a feature vector, and $L = \{-1, +1\}$ in which $+1$ is the label of good solutions and -1 denotes bad solutions. Following our previous work [15,16], this paper will use k-*nearest neighbor (KNN)* [20] as the classification algorithm.

$$label = KNN(x) = sign\left(\sum_{y \in N(x)} label_y\right)$$

where $sign(x)$ returns $+1$ if $x > 0$ and -1 if $x < 0$, $N(x)$ denotes the K nearest neighbors of x from the training set, and K is an odd number.

To implement CPS, we introduce two external populations P_+ and P_-: P_+ contains some 'good' solutions found so far with label $+1$, and P_- contains some 'bad' solutions with label -1. In order to obtain P_+ and P_-, this paper uses the nondominated sorting scheme introduced in [4]. Let $q = NDS(p, n)$ denote this scheme, which selects the best n solutions from p and stores the selected ones in q. The details of this procedure are referred to [4]. Let P be the initial population and N be the size of P, P_+ and P_- are initialized as

$$P_+ = NDS\left(P, \left\lfloor \frac{N}{2} \right\rfloor\right)$$

and

$$P_- = P\backslash P_+.$$

Let Q be the set of newly generated solutions in each generation, Q_+ and Q_- contain the nondominated and dominated solutions in Q respectively. P_+ and P_- are updated as

$$P_+ = NDS\left(P_+ \cup Q_+, \left\lfloor \frac{N}{2} \right\rfloor\right)$$

and

$$P_- = NDS\left(P_- \cup Q_-, \left\lfloor \frac{N}{2} \right\rfloor\right).$$

2.3   Offspring Reproduction

Different reproduction operators can be used in MOEA/D. In this paper, we choose some operators based on *differential evolution (DE)* [11] and the polynomial mutation [10] to generate a set of candidate offspring solutions.

Multiple Operator Search. In [11], we proposed to use multiple DE operators to generate offspring solutions following the idea in [21]. Let x^i be the solution with the ith subproblem, $r1, r2, r3, r4, r5$ be five randomly selected neighboring subproblems, and F be randomly selected from $\{0.5, 0.7\}$. The three operators are defined as follows.

$$\begin{aligned}
\hat{y}^1 &= x^i + F(x^{r1} - x^{r2}). \\
\hat{y}^2 &= x^i + rand()(x^{r1} - x^{r2}) + F(x^{r3} - x^{r4}). \\
\hat{y}^3 &= x^{r1} + rand()(x^{r2} - x^{r3}) + F(x^{r4} - x^{r5}).
\end{aligned} \tag{2}$$

In [11], the best one according to real objective value is chosen as the offspring solution, while in our approach the best one according to the classifier is chosen.

Polynomial Mutation. It should be noted that after the above operation, each candidate solution $\hat{y}$ is repaired in (3) and then mutated by the polynomial mutation in (4) before the function evaluation or classification.

$$\bar{y}_j = \begin{cases} a_j + 0.5(x_j^i - a_j) & \text{if } \hat{y}_j < a_j \\ b_j - 0.5(b_j - x_j^i) & \text{if } \hat{y}_j > b_j \\ \hat{y}_j & \text{otherwise} \end{cases} \tag{3}$$

where $j = 1, \cdots, n$.

$$y_j = \begin{cases} \bar{y}_j + \sigma_j \times (b_i - a_i) & \text{if } rand() < p_m \\ \bar{y}_j & \text{otherwise.} \end{cases} \tag{4}$$

with

$$\sigma_j = \begin{cases} (2 \times rand)^{\frac{1}{\eta+1}} - 1 & \text{if } rand() < 0.5 \\ 1 - (2 - 2 \times rand)^{\frac{1}{\eta+1}} & \text{otherwise.} \end{cases}$$

where $j = 1, \cdots, n$, $rand$ is a uniform random number in $[0,1]$. η and p_m are two control parameters. a_j and b_j are the lower and upper bound of the ith decision variable.

2.4 MOEA/D-CPS Framework

An MOEA/D decomposes an MOP into a set of scalar-objective subproblems and solves them simultaneously. The optimal solution of each subproblem will hopefully be a Pareto optimal solution of the original MOP, and a set of well selected subproblems may produce a good approximation to the PS (PF). Therefore, a key issue with MOEA/D is the subproblem definition. In this paper, we use the Tchebycheff technique as follows.

$$\min g(x|\lambda, z^*) = \max_{1 \leq j \leq m} \lambda_j |f_j(x) - z_j^*| \tag{5}$$

where $\lambda = (\lambda_1, \cdots, \lambda_m)^T$ is a weight vector with the subproblem,

$$z^* = (z_1^*, \cdots, z_m^*)^T$$

is a reference point, i.e., z_j^* is the minimal value of f_j in the search space. For simplicity, we use $g^i(x)$ to denote the above subproblem with the ith subproblem. In most cases, two subproblems with close weight vectors will have similar optimal solutions. Based on the distances between the weight vectors, MOEA/D defines the neighborhood of a subproblem where the subproblems with the nearest weight vectors. In MOEA/D, the offspring reproduction and solution selection are based on the concept of neighborhood.

Algorithm 1. Main Framework of MOEA/D-CPS

---

1 Initialize a set of subproblems (x^i, F^i, B^i, g^i), $i = 1, \cdots, N$, initialize the reference point z^* as $z_j^* = \min\limits_{i=1,\cdots,N} f_j(x^i)$, $j = 1, \cdots, m$;

2 Set $P_+ = NDS\left(\{x^1, \cdots, x^N\}, \lfloor \frac{N}{2} \rfloor\right)$, and $P_- = \{x^1, \cdots, x^N\} \backslash P_+$;

3 **while** *not terminate* **do**

4   Set $Q = \emptyset$;

5   Train a classifier $label = \hat{Class}(x)$ with data set $P_+ \cup P_-$;

6   **foreach** $i \in \{1, \cdots, N\}$ **do**

7   Set the mating pool as

$$\pi = \begin{cases} B^i & \text{if } rand() < p_n \\ \{1, \cdots, N\} & \text{otherwise} \end{cases}$$

8   Generate M trial solutions $Y = \{y^1, \cdots, y^M\}$ by the mating pool π;

9   Set $V = \{y \in Y | \hat{Class}(y) = 1\}$, and reset $V = Y$ if $V = \emptyset$;

10   Randomly choose $y \in V$ as the offspring solution and evaluate it;

11   Update the reference point

$$z_j^* = \begin{cases} f_j(y) & \text{if } f_j(y) < z_j^* \\ z_j^* & \text{otherwise} \end{cases}$$

12   Set counter $c = 0$;

13   **foreach** $j \in \pi$ **do**

14   **if** $g^j(y) < g^j(x^j)$ *and* $c < C$ **then**

15   Replace x^j by y;

16   Set $c = c + 1$;

17   **end**

18   **end**

19   Set $Q = Q \cup \{y\}$;

20   **end**

21   Set Q_+ and Q_- be the nondominated and dominated solutions in Q respectively;

22   Update $P_+ = NDS\left(P_+ \cup Q_+, \lfloor \frac{N}{2} \rfloor\right)$;

23   Update $P_- = NDS\left(P_- \cup Q_-, \lfloor \frac{N}{2} \rfloor\right)$;

24 **end**

25 **return** *the population P.*

In MOEA/D, the ith $(i = 1, \cdots, N)$ subproblem will maintain following information:

- its weight vector λ^i and its objective function g^i,
- its current solution x^i and the objective vector of x^i, i.e. $F^i = F(x^i)$, and
- the index set of its neighboring subproblems, B^i.

The main framework of MOEA/D-CPS is shown in Algorithm 1. It is basically a general MOEA/D framework and only several steps with the classification model building and using are added. We would like to make the following comments.

- Some notations are as follows. N is the number of subproblems and it is also the population size. $K = |B^i|$ is the neighborhood size. p_n denotes the probability to generate trial solutions using the neighboring solutions. M is the number of generated candidate offspring solutions for each subproblem. C is the maximal number of old solutions that can be replaced by a new one. $rand()$ generates a random real number in $[0, 1]$.
- As in the original MOEA/D [10], the population is initialized in *Line 1*. The mating pool is set in *Line 7* and the candidate offspring solutions are generated in *Line 8* by the reproduction operators introduced in Sect. 2.3. The reference point is updated in *Line 11*. The population is updated by the offspring solutions in *Lines 12–18*.
- In the CPS, two external populations are maintained in *Line 2* and *Lines 21–23*. The two external populations are then used as a data set to train a classifier in *Line 5*, which is defined in Sect. 2.2. A promising offspring is chosen out according to the classifier in *Line 9*.

3 Experimental Study

3.1 Experimental Settings

In this section we apply MOEA/D-CPS to 9 test instances named as LZ1-LZ9, which are introduced in [10]. MOEA/D-MO [11], a modified MOEA/D that uses the reproduction operators introduced in Sect. 2.3 to generate new trial solutions, is chosen for the comparison study. For simplicity, we use MO to denote MOEA/D-MO that uses the multiple operator search strategy, and use CPS-MO to denote MOEA/D-CPS with the classification based search strategy.

The parameter settings are as follows.

- The number of decision variables are $n = 30$ for all the test instances.
- The algorithms are executed 50 times independently on each instance and stop after $150,000$ for bi-objective and $297,500$ for tri-objective problems respectively.
- The population size is $N = 300$ and $N = 595$ for bi-objective and tri-objective problems respectively, and the neighborhood size is $K = 15$ and $K = 30$ for bi-objective and tri-objective problems respectively.
- The other parameters are $T = 20$, $p_n = 0.9$, $C = 2$, $\eta = 20$ and $p_m = \frac{1}{n}$.
- In CPS, the number of nearest points used in KNN is $K = 3$.

All the algorithms are implemented in Matlab and executed in the same computer.

3.2 Performance Metrics

In this paper we use *Inverted Generational Distance (IGD)* metric [22] to assess the performance of the algorithms in our experimental.

Let P^* be a set of well-distributed Pareto optimal points from the PF, and P be the set of nondominated solutions found. The IGD metric is defined as follows.

$$IGD(P^*, P) = \frac{\sum_{x \in P^*} d(x, P)}{|P^*|}$$

where $d(x, P)$ is the minimum Euclidean distance between x and any point in P, and $|P^*|$ is the cardinality of P^*. The IGD value denotes some kind of distance from the given reference set P^* to the obtained set P. In our experiments, $10,000$ evenly distributed points in PF are generated as the P^*.

3.3 Experimental Results

Statistical Results. Table 1 shows the mean, std, min, max IGD value of CPS-MO and MO over 50 runs. In order to get statistically conclusions, the Wilcoxon's rank sum test at a 5 % significance level is employed to compare the IGD values obtained by different algorithms. In the table, $\sim$, $+$, and $-$ denote that the results obtained by the CPS version are similar to, better than, or worse than that obtained by the original version.

Table 1 clearly shows that with the Wilcoxon rank test on the obtained values, the CPS-MO beats the MO on 4 test instances: LZ2-LZ4, and LZ9. And on other 5 instance the two algorithms get similar results. According to the mean values, CPS-MO performs better than MO on LZ2-LZ9 and gets the same result on LZ1.

Runtime Performance. Figure 2 plots the run time performance in terms of the IGD values obtained by the two variants on the 9 test instances.

Figure 2 shows the run time performance of CPS-MO and MO. It is clear that the convergence speeds of the two algorithms are similar on LZ1, LZ3, LZ5, LZ6 while CPS-MO beats MO on LZ2, LZ4, LZ7-LZ9.

Visual Results. Figures 3 and 4 plot the final PF and PS approximations obtained by CPS-MO and MO over 50 runs respectively.

It is clear that the two algorithms perform similar. However there are also some differences. For example on LZ7, the convergence of the population obtained by CPS-MO is better than MO. Also the similar results can be found on LZ6 and LZ8.

Table 1. The statistical results obtained by CPS-MO and MO on LZ1-LZ9.

Instance	CPS-MO				MO			
	mean	std.	min	max	mean	std.	min	max
LZ1	**1.39e-03(∼)**	1.29e-05	1.36e-03	1.42e-03	**1.39e-03**	1.50e-05	1.36e-03	1.43e-03
LZ2	**3.92e-03(+)**	5.42e-04	3.14e-03	5.39e-03	4.51e-03	9.88e-04	3.25e-03	8.50e-03
LZ3	**3.39e-03(+)**	6.58e-04	2.67e-03	5.67e-03	3.71e-03	9.47e-04	2.76e-03	6.68e-03
LZ4	**4.03e-03(+)**	1.12e-03	2.82e-03	8.31e-03	4.87e-03	1.25e-03	3.12e-03	8.81e-03
LZ5	**7.66e-03(∼)**	1.44e-03	5.93e-03	1.49e-02	7.70e-03	9.80e-04	6.38e-03	1.01e-02
LZ6	**4.19e-02(∼)**	7.44e-03	3.02e-02	5.59e-02	4.22e-02	7.37e-03	2.91e-02	5.92e-02
LZ7	**1.20e-01(∼)**	1.02e-01	4.13e-03	3.66e-01	1.24e-01	1.07e-01	5.21e-03	3.40e-01
LZ8	**1.37e-02(∼)**	1.11e-02	2.66e-03	5.26e-02	1.48e-02	1.16e-02	3.08e-03	6.51e-02
LZ9	**4.99e-03(+)**	1.14e-03	3.19e-03	7.58e-03	5.96e-03	1.39e-03	3.84e-03	9.44e-03

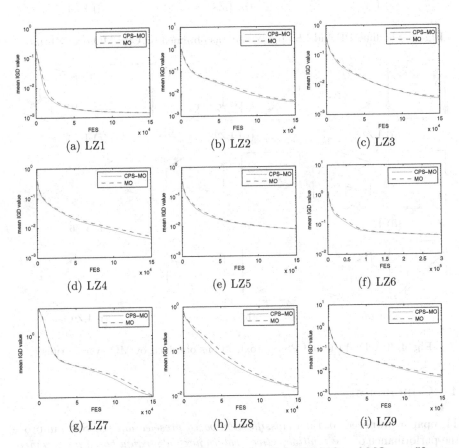

Fig. 2. The mean IGD values versus FES obtained by CPS-MO and MO over 50 runs.

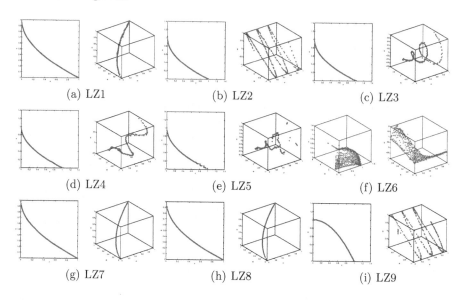

Fig. 3. The final PF and PS approximations obtained by CPS-MO over 50 runs.

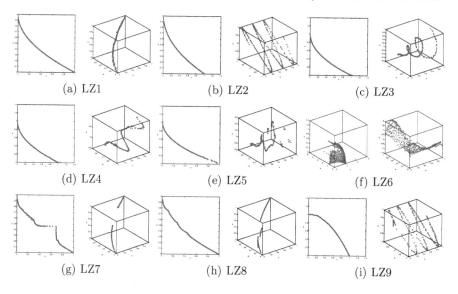

Fig. 4. The final PF and PS approximations obtained by MO over 50 runs.

4   Conclusion

This paper proposed to use a *classification based preselection (CPS)* to improve the performance of the *multiobjective evolutionary algorithm based on decomposition (MOEA/D)*. This algorithm, named as MOEA/D-CPS, utilizes the *non-domination sorting (NDS)* operator to choose some solutions to form a training set, and then builds a classifier based on the training set. In each generation, a set of candidate offspring solutions are generated for each subproblem and only a promising one according to the classifier is chosen as the offspring solution.

MOEA/D-CPS is applied to a test suite, and the experimental results suggest that the CPS can successfully improve the performance of an MOEA/D variant.

The work reported in this paper is preliminary and there are still some work that could be done in the future. For example, we could (a) improve the efficiency of the CPS, (b) try other classification models, and (c) apply this approach to other MOEAs.

Acknowledgment. This work is supported by China National Instrumentation Program under Grant No.2012YQ180132, the National Natural Science Foundation of China under Grant No.61273313, and the Science and Technology Commission of Shanghai Municipality under Grant No.14DZ2260800.

References

1. Deb, K.: Multi-Objective Optimization Using Evolutionary Algorithms. Wiley, Chichester (2001)
2. Zhou, A., Qu, B.Y., Li, H., Zhao, S.Z., Suganthanb, P.N., Zhang, Q.: Multiobjective evolutionary algorithms: a survey of the state of the art. Swarm Evol. Comput. **1**, 32–49 (2011)
3. Knowles, J., Corne, D.: Approximating the nondominated front using the pareto archived evolution strategy. Evol. Comput. **8**, 149–172 (2000)
4. Deb, K., Pratap, A., Agarwal, S., Meyarivan, T.: A fast and elitist multiobjective genetic algorithm: NSGA-II. IEEE Trans. Evol. Comput. **6**, 182–197 (2002)
5. Zitzler, E., Laumanns, M., Thiele, L.: SPEA2: improving the strength pareto evolutionary algorithm. In: Evolutionary Methods for Design Optimisation and Control, pp. 95–100 (2001)
6. Basseur, M., Zitzler, E.: Handling uncertainty in indicator-based multiobjective optimization. Int. J. Comput. Intell. Res. **2**, 255–272 (2006)
7. Zitzler, E., Künzli, S.: Indicator-based selection in multiobjective search. In: Yao, X., et al. (eds.) PPSN 2004. LNCS, vol. 3242, pp. 832–842. Springer, Heidelberg (2004)
8. Bader, J., Zitzler, E.: HypE: an algorithm for fast hypervolume-based manyobjective optimization. Technical report TIK 286, Computer Engineering and Networks Laboratory, ETH Zurich 19, pp. 45–76 (2010)
9. Zhang, Q., Li, H.: MOEA/D: a multiobjective evolutionary algorithm based on decomposition. IEEE Trans. Evol. Comput. **11**, 712–731 (2007)
10. Li, H., Zhang, Q.: Multiobjective optimization problems with complicated Pareto sets, MOEA/D and NSGA-II. IEEE Trans. Evol. Comput. **13**, 284–302 (2009)
11. Li, Y., Zhou, A., Zhang, G.: An MOEA/D with multiple differential evolution mutation operators. In: 2014 IEEE Congress on Evolutionary Computation (CEC), pp. 397–404 (2014)
12. Zhang, Q., Zhou, A., Jin, Y.: RM-MEDA: a regularity model-based multiobjective estimation of distribution algorithm. IEEE Trans. Evol. Comput. **12**, 41–63 (2008)
13. Zhou, A., Zhang, Q., Zhang, G.: A multiobjective evolutionary algorithm based on decomposition and probability model. In: 2012 IEEE Congress on Evolutionary Computation (CEC), pp. 1–8 (2012)

14. Zhou, A., Zhang, Y., Zhang, G., Gong, W.: On neighborhood exploration and subproblem exploitation in decomposition based multiobjective evolutionary algorithms. In: 2015 IEEE Congress on Evolutionary Computation (CEC) (2015)
15. Zhang, J., Zhou, A., Zhang, G.: A classification based preselection for evolutionary algorithms. Swarm and Evolutionary Computation (2015, under review)
16. Zhang, J., Zhou, A., Zhang, G.: A classification and pareto domination based multiobjective evolutionary algorithm. In: 2015 IEEE Congress on Evolutionary Computation (CEC) (2015)
17. Bishop, C.: Pattern Recognition and Machine Learning. Springer, New York (2006)
18. Weiss, S.M., Kapouleas, I.: An empirical comparison of pattern recognition, neural nets, and machine learning classification methods. In: Proceedings of the Eleventh International Joint Conference on Artificial Intelligence, pp. 781–787 (1989)
19. Michie, D., Spiegelhalter, D.J., Taylor, C.: Machine Learning, Neural and Statistical Classification. Ellis Horwood, Upper Saddle River (1994)
20. Coomans, D., Massart, D.: Alternative k-nearest neighbour rules in supervised pattern recognition: Part 1. k-Nearest neighbour classification by using alternative voting rules. Anal. Chim. Acta **136**, 15–27 (1982)
21. Wang, Y., Cai, Z., Qingfu, Z.: Differential evolution with composite trial vector generation strategies and control parameters. IEEE Trans. Evol. Comput. **15**, 55–66 (2011)
22. Zhou, A., Zhang, Q., Jin, Y.: Approximating the set of Pareto-optimal solutions in both the decision and objective spaces by an estimation of distribution algorithm. IEEE Trans. Evol. Comput. **13**, 1167–1189 (2009)

Discrete Particle Swarm Optimization Algorithm for Solving Graph Coloring Problem

Kai Zhang[1,2], Wanying Zhu[1], Jun Liu[1,2], and Juanjuan He[1,2(✉)]

[1] School of Computer Science, Wuhan University of Science and Technology,
Wuhan 430081, People's Republic of China
[2] Hubei Province Key Laboratory of Intelligent Information Processing
and Real-time Industrial System, Wuhan, China
hejuanjuan@wust.edu.cn

Abstract. Graph coloring problem is a well-known NP-complete problem in graph theory. Because GCP often finds its applications to various engineering fields, it is very important to find a feasible solution quickly. In this paper, we present a novel discrete particle swarm optimization algorithm to solve the GCP. In order to apply originally particle swarm optimization algorithm to discrete problem, we design and redefine the crucial position and velocity operators on discrete state space. Moreover, the performance of our algorithm is compared with other published method using 30 DIMACS benchmark graphs. The comparison result shows that our algorithm is more competitive with less chromatic numbers and less computational time.

Keywords: Graph coloring problem · Discrete particle swarm optimization algorithm · NP-complete problem

1 Introduction

The graph coloring problem (GCP) is an assignment of colors to each vertex such that any pair of adjacent points of edge have different colors. The challenge is to find the least number of colors, which is a NP-complete problem. In real life, the GCP has numerous practical applications including for instance, scheduling [1], register assignment in timetabling [2], register allocation in compilers [3], frequency assignment in mobile networks [4], and noise reduction in VLSI circuits [5]. So, it is necessary to design efficient algorithms that are reasonably fast and that can be used successfully in practice.

In recent years, a wide variety of algorithms have been proposed for Solving GCP, such as well-known RLF [6] and DSATUR [7] and heuristic algorithms including genetic algorithm [8,9] ant colony optimization algorithm [10,11], tabu search algorithm [12], neural network algorithm [13], etc. However, enormous amount of computation time still unsatisfactory for many applications, where a solution is required in a limited amount of time.

In this paper, a novel discrete particle swarm optimization algorithm for GCP is proposed. The particle swarm optimization (PSO) algorithm [14,15] is

© Springer-Verlag Berlin Heidelberg 2015
M. Gong et al. (Eds.): BIC-TA 2015, CCIS 562, pp. 643–652, 2015.
DOI: 10.1007/978-3-662-49014-3_57

a stochastic global optimization method [16,17] based on swarm intelligence. The PSO has obvious advantages in optimization problem of continuous-valued space because of its fast convergence rate, simple computation and easy realization. It is originally developed for continuous problem, so it does not effectively solve the discrete combination optimization problem such as GCP. In order to apply originally particle swarm optimization algorithm to discrete problem, we design and redefine the crucial arithmetic position and velocity operators on discrete state space, including addition, subtraction and multiplication. Moreover, the discrete PSO algorithm has been implemented on Visual Studio 2013 and tested using 30 benchmark graphs provided by the DIMACS computational symposium web site http://mat.gsia.cmu.edu/color/instances.html. In compare to other published method, the comparison result shows that our algorithm is more competitive with less chromatic numbers and less computation time.

2   Graph Coloring Problem

Given a graph $G = (V, E)$ with n vertices and m edges, a coloring of G is an assignment of colors to each vertex such that any pair of adjacent points of edge have different colors. The graph coloring problem is to determine the smallest number of colors $\chi(G)$ and to find a coloring of G that uses $\chi(G)$ colors.

In this algorithm, vertex numbers range from 1 through n. The algorithm try to color n vertices with given k colors, numbered $\{0, 1, ..., k-1\}$. If v_i is a vertex, x_i is a variable that means vertex v_i has color x_i, $x_i \in \{0, 1, ..., k-1\}$. The position vector X of each particle P is defined as following vertex color sequence.

$$X = (x_1, x_2, \cdots, x_i, \cdots, x_n), \quad x_i \in \{0, 1, \ldots, k-1\} \tag{1}$$

A proper coloring formula as sequence $X(x_1, x_2, ..., x_n)$, which should guarantee that each vertex v_i must receive exactly one color x_i. And each sequence must be checked with all edges constraints conditions $x_i \neq x_j$, if $e(v_i, v_j) \in E$. A simple example is shown in Fig. 1.

3   Discrete PSO for Graph Coloring Problem

3.1   Particles Positions and State Space

In this section, we present a discrete PSO algorithm for graph coloring problem. The algorithm try to color n vertices with given k colors. The search space is defined as follows: the finite set of all vertex color sequences k^n. For example, an undirected graph G with 3 vertices and 2 colors, the state space is 2^3. All of binary color sequences with length 3 constitutes a solution space. Figure 2 illustrates its associated state-space.

If the smallest number of colors $\chi(G)$ increase to 3, the search state space also increase to 3^3 candidate particle positions. As shown in Fig. 3.

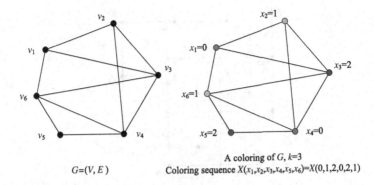

Fig. 1. The Graph G has 6 vertices and can be colored with 3 colors (Color figure online).

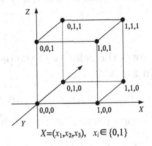

Fig. 2. Particles positions and state space for a graph G with 3 vertices and 2 colors.

3.2 Fitness Function

The algorithm define a fitness function $f(X)$ to evaluate candidate particle position X. Given a graph $G = (V, E)$ with n vertices and m edges, the fitness function $f(X)$ is the sum of conflicting vertices and conflicting edges. The mathematical description is as shown in Eq. 2.

$$f(X) = a \times \sum_{i=1}^{n} ConflictV(x_i) + \sum_{i=1}^{m} ConflictE(x_i, x_j)$$

$$ConflictV(x_i) = \begin{cases} 1, & \text{if } v_i \text{ have conflict edge} \\ 0, & \text{else} \end{cases} \qquad (2)$$

$$ConflictE(x_i, x_j) = \begin{cases} 1, & \text{if } e(v_i, v_j) \in E, \ x_i = x_j \\ 0, & \text{else} \end{cases}$$

where X is the position vector of particle P. $ConflictV(x_i)$ is the number of conflicting vertices. $ConflictE(x_i, x_j)$ is the number of conflicting edges. Sometimes the number of edges is far more than the number of vertices. To avoid the influence of the number of conflicting vertices being ignored, the number of conflicting vertices is multiplied by a positive coefficient a. It is obvious that $f(X) \geq 0$. The aim of the optimizing process is to minimize $f(X)$ until reaching $f(X) = 0$ for a fixed k colors, which corresponds to a valid k-coloring.

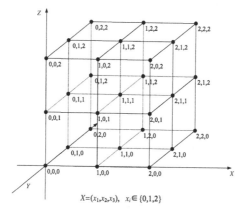

Fig. 3. Particles positions and state space for a graph G with 3 vertices and 3 colors.

3.3   Velocity Vectors

In our PSO algorithm, V denotes the velocity of the particle, and velocity is also defined a vector, as shown in Eq. 3.

$$V = (v_1, v_2, \cdots, v_i, \cdots, v_n), \quad v_i \in Z \tag{3}$$

In addition, the velocity V of a particle at timestep $t+1$ is updated as Eq. 4.

$$V_{t+1} = \omega \times V_t + c_1 \times r_1 \times (P_{pbest} - X_t) + c_2 \times r_2 \times (P_{gbest} - X_t) \tag{4}$$

where P_{pbest} is personal best position of the particle, and P_{gbest} is the best position of its neighborhood, respectively. ω is an inertia weight, c_1 and c_2 are two acceleration coefficients, and r_1 and r_2 are two random real numbers in $[0,1]$.

However, in this equation the value of V_{t+1} is not an integer vector, but a real vector. In order to guarantee that the V_{t+1} is an integer vector, the algorithm round off V_{t+1} to an integer, as shown in Eq. 5.

$$V_{t+1} = \text{INT}(\omega \times V_t) + \text{INT}(c_1 \times r_1 \times (P_{pbest} - X_t)) + \text{INT}(c_2 \times r_2 \times (P_{gbest} - X_t)). \tag{5}$$

3.4   Subtraction Between Position and Position

The subtraction of two positions is a vector of velocity. The $P_{pbest} - X_t$ is the difference between personal best position and current position of the particle. The $P_{gbest} - X_t$ is the difference between particle position X_t with the best position of its neighborhood, as shown in Fig. 4.

3.5   External Multiplication Between Real Number and Velocity

In Eq. 5, the velocity vector is multiplied by another real number, which is the product of acceleration coefficients and random number, as shown in Eq. 6.

$$\begin{aligned} c_1 \times r_1 \times (P_{pbest} - X_t) \\ c_2 \times r_2 \times (P_{gbest} - X_t) \end{aligned} \tag{6}$$

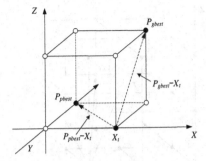

Fig. 4. Subtraction between position P_{best} and position X_i.

For the given coefficients $c(c_1$ or $c_2)$ and the random number $r(r_1$ or $r_2)$ can lead to the value change of velocity, meanwhile keep the direction same, as shown in Fig. 5.

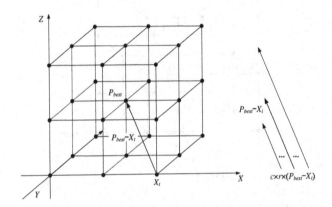

Fig. 5. External multiplication between real number and velocity.

3.6 Addition Between Velocity and Velocity

The velocities addition have meaningful geometric explanation, which is composed of three components, known as inertia current velocity, cognitive component personal best position and social component neighbor best position, respectively. The velocity addition operator is shown in Fig. 6.

3.7 Move by Position Plus Velocity

The sum of position X_t and velocity V_t of particle P_t is a new position X_{t+1}. However, sometimes the value of $X_t + V_t$ is bigger than the given color k. That means the new position would be out of the solution state, as shown in Fig. 7.

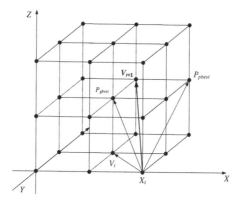

Fig. 6. Addition between velocity and velocity.

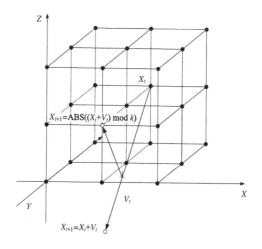

Fig. 7. Move by position X_t plus velocity V_t.

If the particle position X_t is out of given color k, we think that the particle collides with the boundary, then the particle returns to the interior of the solution state. So we take the modular operation of $X_t + V_t$ and get its absolute value. If the particle collides with the boundary, the components of the velocity vector reverse to the opposite direction, as shown in Eq. 7.

$$X_{t+1} = \text{Abs}((X_t + V_t) \mod k)$$
$$x_{(t+1)d} = \text{Abs}((x_{td} + v_{td}) \mod k) \tag{7}$$
$$v_{(t+1)d} = (-1) \times v_{(t+1)d}, \quad \text{if } (x_{td} + v_{td}) > k \text{ or } (x_{td} + v_{td}) < 0.$$

3.8 Algorithm Flowchart

The algorithm starts with an initialize q particles with random position and velocity vectors. For each position vector $X_t(x_1, x_2, ..., x_n)$, the component of

x_i is assigned from $[0,\chi(G)\text{-}1]$ randomly. Then every particles position X_t is optimized and evaluated by fitness function $f(X_t)$. If the fitness value of position is better than the particle personal best fitness value, the particle best position should be replaced by current position. If all the particles are evaluated, the best of particles P_{pbest} positions is chose and replaced the P_{gbest} position. If the value of fitness $f(X_{gbest})$ decrease to 0, the position X_{gbest} is the optimization solution. Otherwise, the algorithm should repeat updating the particles velocities and positions until reach the maximum iterate. The flowchart is shown in Fig. 8.

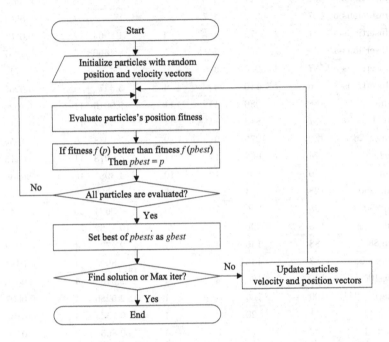

Fig. 8. The flowchart of discrete particle swarm optimization algorithm.

4   Results and Discussion

The algorithm has been implemented on C++ language of Visual Studio 2013. In this section, the compute results of our discrete particle swarm optimization algorithm are tested on 30 DIMACS benchmark graphs. The 'Best Known' column indicate the best known upper and lower bounds on the chromatic number. The HPGA is a hierarchical parallel genetic approach for GCP [8]. 'HPGA Time' column is the average running times in seconds.

In this algorithm, the initial particles number is 200. The inertia weight ω is set to be 0.5, acceleration coefficients c_1 and c_2 are set to be 0.6 and 0.7 respectively. The values of parameters are selected based on some preliminary trials. The comparison results are summarized in Table 1.

Table 1. Comparison results on DIMACS graph coloring challenge instances

Graph instances	Vertex numbers	Edge numbers	Best known	HPGA colors	HPGA time	DPSO colors	DPSO time
1-FullIns-5	282	3247	6			6	1.5571
2-FullIns-4	212	1621	6			6	0.7638
2-FullIns-5	852	12201	7			7	15.62
1-Insertions-4	67	232	5	5	2.4476	5	0.1038
1-Insertions-5	202	1227	4–5			6	0.3933
1-Insertions-6	607	6337	4–7			7	6.8907
2-Insertions-3	37	72	4	4	1.8964	4	0.0388
2-Insertions-4	149	541	4	5	6.4666	5	0.1387
2-Insertions-5	597	3936	3–6			6	11.171
3-Insertions-3	56	110	4	4	3.347	4	0.0265
anna	138	986	11	11	2.9016	11	1.7026
david	87	812	11	11	2.5522	11	0.101
games120	120	1276	9	9	5.0038	9	0.1055
huck	74	602	11	11	4.6278	11	0.0413
jean	80	508	10	10	4.398	10	0.0436
miles250	128	774	8	8	5.8828	8	0.1423
miles500	128	2340	20	20	6.0624	20	0.8848
miles1500	128	10396	73	73	10.1062	73	0.695
mug88-1	88	146	4	4	2.173	4	0.0492
mug88-25	88	146	4	4	1.8002	4	0.0488
mug100-1	100	166	4	4	2.016	4	0.06
mug100-25	100	166	4	4	2.5286	4	0.0607
myciel3	11	20	4	4	0.753	4	0.013
myciel4	23	71	5	5	0.865	5	0.075
myciel5	47	236	6	6	1.7608	6	0.0246
myciel6	95	755	7	7	1.479	7	0.347
myciel7	191	2360	8	8	5.3352	8	4.008
queen5-5	25	160	5	5	2.3717	5	0.0154
queen6-6	36	290	**7**	**8**	2.5062	**7**	2.039
queen7-7	49	476	**7**	**8**	2.8361	**7**	0.9938

For each instance in Table 1, 10 independent runs of algorithm are carried out. The comparison results show that our algorithm runs faster than HPGA, meanwhile the chromatic numbers are same. In addition, our algorithm can find less chromatic numbers for some graph instances such as queen6-6 and queen7-7 by using less computational time. Moreover, our algorithm can solve larger graph instance with more vertices and edges, such as 2-FullIns-5 and 1-Insertions-6. In the experiment, our algorithm adopted the same values of parameters for all benchmark graphs. It's possible and promising to improve the solution of coloring by fine-tuning values of parameters for each graph.

5 Conclusions

In this paper, we present a novel discrete particle swarm optimization algorithm to solve the GCP. We have improved originally continuous PSO algorithm to discrete problem. In order to apply originally particle swarm optimization algorithm to discrete problem, we design and redefine the crucial position and velocity operators on discrete state space. Therefore, the Discrete PSO algorithm is applied to discrete problem and maintains advantages in optimization problem because of its fast convergence rate, simple computation and easy realization. Moreover, the performance of our algorithm is compared with the other graph coloring method by using 30 DIMACS benchmark graphs. The comparison results show that our algorithm is more competitive with less computation time. Moreover, our algorithm can find less chromatic numbers and solve larger graph instances.

The human brain has rich computation intelligences obtained from millions of years evolution, which has provided plenty of ideas to construct powerful artificial intelligent computing models. Recently, neural-like computing models, see, e.g. [6,9,15,16,22,23], have been used in solving computational hard problems. It is of interests to use neural-like computing models to solve graph coloring problem.

Acknowledgments. This work was supported by the National Natural Science Foundation of China (Nos. 61402187, 61472293, 61273225, 61403287 and 31201121), and the Natural Science Foundation of Hubei Province (Grant No. 2015CFB335), and the Youth Foundation of Wuhan University of Science and Technology (Grant No. 2015xz017).

References

1. Bianco, L., Caramia, M., Olmo, P.D.: Solving a preemptive project scheduling problem with coloring technique. In: Weglarz, J. (ed.) Project Scheduling Recent Models, Algorithms and Applications, pp. 135–145. Kluwer Academic Publishers, US (1998)
2. Werra, D.D.: An introduction to timetabling. Eur. J. Oper. Res. **19**, 151–162 (1985)
3. Kannan, S., Proebsting, T.: Register allocation in structured programs. J. Algorithms **29**, 223–237 (1998)
4. Smith, K., Palaniswami, M.: Static and dynamic channel assignment using neural networks. IEEE J. Select. Areas Commun. **15**, 238–249 (1997)
5. Maitra, T., Pal, A.J.: Noise reduction in VLSI circuits using modied GA based graph coloring. Int. J. Control Autom. **3**(2), 37–44 (2010)
6. Song, T., Pan, L., Jiang, K., et al.: Normal forms for some classes of sequential spiking neural P systems. IEEE Trans. NanoBiosci. **12**(3), 255–264 (2013)
7. Leighton, F.T.: A graph coloring algorithm for large scheduling problems. J. Res. National Bureau Stan. **84**, 489–505 (1979)

8. Brlaz, D.: New methods to color vertices of a graph. Commun. ACM **22**, 251–256 (1979)
9. Song, T., Pan, L.: Spiking neural P systems with rules on synapses working in maximum spikes consumption strategy. IEEE Trans. NanoBiosci. **14**(1), 38–44 (2015)
10. Mouhoub, M.: A hierarchical parallel genetic approach for the graph coloring problem. Appl. Intell. **39**(3), 510–528 (2013)
11. Hong, B.: Generic algorithm of color planar graph. J. Guizhou Univ. (Nat Seil) **11**(16), 232–297 (1999)
12. Wang, X.H., Zhao, S.M.: Ant algorithms for solving graph coloring. J. Inner Mongolia Agric. Univ. **9**(26), 79–82 (2005)
13. Salari, E., Eshghi, K.: An ACO algorithm for graph coloring problem. IEEE Serv. Center **1**, 20–21 (2005)
14. Hertz, A., Werra, D.: Using tabu search techniques for graph coloring. Computing **39**, 345–351 (1987)
15. Song, T., Pan, L., Păun, G.: Asynchronous spiking neural P systems with local synchronization. Inf. Sci. **219**, 197–207 (2013)
16. Song, T., Pan, L., Wang, J., et al.: Normal forms of spiking neural P systems with anti-spikes. IEEE Trans. NanoBiosci. **11**(4), 352–359 (2012)
17. Wang, X.H., Wang, Z.O., Qiao, Q.L.: Artificial neural network with transient chaos for four-coloring map problems and k-colorability problems. Syst. Eng. Theory Pract. **5**, 92–96 (2002)
18. Kumar, P., Singh, A.K., Srivastava, A.K.: A novel optimal capacitor placement algorithm using Nelder-Mead PSO. Int. J. Bio-Inspired Comput. **6**(4), 290–302 (2014)
19. Ram, G., Mandal, D., Kar, R., Ghoshal, S.P.: Optimal design of non-uniform circular antenna arrays using PSO with wavelet mutation. Int. J. Bio-Inspired Comput. **6**(4), 424–433 (2014)
20. Zhang, X., Tian, Y., Jin, Y.: A knee point driven evolutionary algorithm for many-objective optimization. IEEE Trans. Evol. Comput. (2014). doi:10.1109/TEVC.2014.2378512
21. Zhang, X., Tian, Y., Cheng, R., Jin, Y.: An efficient approach to non-dominated sorting for evolutionary multi-objective optimization. IEEE Trans. Evol. Comput. **19**(2), 201–213 (2015)
22. Song, T., Pan, L.: Spiking neural P systems with rules on synapses working in maximum spiking strategy. IEEE Trans. NanoBiosci. **14**(4), 465–477 (2015)
23. Zhang, X., Pan, L., Paun, A.: On the universality of axon P systems. IEEE Trans. Neural Netw. Learn. Syst. (2015). doi:10.1109/TNNLS.2015.2396940

Parallel Hybrid Genetic Algorithm for Maximum Clique Problem on OpenCL

Li Li[1], Kai Zhang[1,2]($\boxtimes$), Siman Yang[1], and Juanjuan He[1,2]

[1] School of Computer Science, Wuhan University of Science and Technology,
Wuhan 430081, People's Republic of China
zhangkai@wust.edu.cn
[2] Hubei Province Key Laboratory of Intelligent Information Processing
and Real-time Industrial System, Wuhan, China

Abstract. The maximum clique problem is to find the maximum sized clique of pairwise adjacent vertices in a given graph, which is a NP-Complete problem. In this paper, an effective parallel hybrid genetic algorithm is proposed, which consists of genetic algorithm and a local optimization strategy for solving maximum clique problem. In this algorithm, selection, crossover, mutation, fitness evaluation and replacement operators are implemented parallel on OpenCL. In addition, we have tested our algorithm by using a set of benchmark instances from the DIMACS graphs. The comparison results shows that the implementation on GPU provide better performance that CPU, even when the benchmark graphs become more large and complicate.

Keywords: Maximum clique problem · Genetic algorithm · OpenCL

1 Introduction

The maximum clique problem (MCP) is an NP-Complete problem [1], there is no effective polynomial algorithm to solve it. Many practical problems can be formulated to it, such as cluster analysis, information retrieval, mobile networks, coding theory, fault diagnosis, printed circuit board testing and computer vision [2,3]. Therefore, to design an effective algorithm for solving MCP is full of significance both in theory and in practice.

In recent years, many algorithms have been proposed to solve MCP, and the benchmark graph instances are chose from the DIMACS challenge [4], which has great difficulty to find the maximum clique effectively. Exact algorithm [5] is effective for solving small instances, but when the scale of the graph becomes larger, it would cost much time to find MC, moreover it cannot find MC in reasonable time. Some approximation algorithms are also proposed for MCP, such as simulated annealing, artificial neural network and genetic algorithm [6–10]. However, these algorithms usually cannot find maximum clique quickly. In the past few years, compute unified device architecture (CUDA) and open computing language (OpenCL) [11] are developed in full use of the graphics processing

© Springer-Verlag Berlin Heidelberg 2015
M. Gong et al. (Eds.): BIC-TA 2015, CCIS 562, pp. 653–663, 2015.
DOI: 10.1007/978-3-662-49014-3_58

unit (GPU) [12]. The OpenCL architecture has the characteristics of heterogeneous computing platform with CPU/GPU. It has better platform independence and portability, which simplifies the programming for parallel computing under CPU/GPU heterogeneous platform.

In this paper, an efficient parallel hybrid genetic algorithm for MCP is proposed. The algorithm provides massively parallel selection, crossover, mutation, fitness evaluation and replacement operators on OpenCL. Moreover we have evaluated our implementation using a set of benchmark instances from the DIMACS library. The GPU performance is compared with the corresponding CPU implementation, and the results shows that the performance of our GPU algorithm is very encouraging.

2   Parallel Hybrid Genetic Algorithm for MCP

2.1   Maximum Clique Problem

Given an undirected graph $G = (V, E)$ with n vertices and m edges, let $G' = (V', E')$ is the subgraph of G. In our algorithm, let vector X be a 0-1 vector of size n representing G'. Assuming all the vertices in G are labeled with indices $1, 2, \ldots, |V|$. If vertex i is in subgraph G', let $X[i]$ be 1, otherwise let $X[i]$ be 0. This encoding method is really simple and straightforward. For example, graph $G = (V, E)$ have 8 vertices and 13 edges, as shown in Fig. 1. According to the definition, subgraph $\{v_1, v_2, v_7\}$ and $\{v_4, v_5, v_6, v_7\}$ are complete subgraphs, but they are not the maximum clique. There is a larger complete subgraph $G'\{v_1, v_2, v_4, v_6, v_7\}$, which is a maximum clique of G, corresponding vector X is (1, 1, 0, 1, 0, 1, 1, 0).

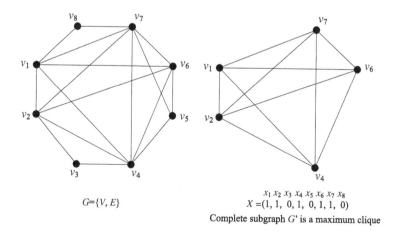

$G=\{V, E\}$

$x_1\ x_2\ x_3\ x_4\ x_5\ x_6\ x_7\ x_8$
$X =$(1, 1, 0, 1, 0, 1, 1, 0)

Complete subgraph G' is a maximum clique

Fig. 1. The subgraph vector X is the candidate chromosome.

2.2   Fitness Function

The adaptability of an individual is proportional to its fitness value. The most adaptive individuals are more likely to keep in evolution. In our algorithm, the fitness of a individual X is equal to the size of the subgraph which represents if the subgraph is a clique (i.e., the number of 1s occurring in the string), otherwise, it is equal to zero. This is very easy to compute and cost-saving, since computing fitness is needed to be down in each generation for all changed chromosomes.

2.3   Initialization

The initial population is generated randomly. A chromosome individual consists of a string of bits. Every bit in the chromosome have the same probability to be 0 or 1. As we know the chromosome needn't to represent a clique because we want to diversify the initial population. A local optimization technique will be proposed to produce maximal cliques.

2.4   Extraction and Extension

After initialization, a local optimization step is adapt in our algorithm which includes a greedy heuristic procedure. It attempts to find a clique contained in a chromosome as large as possible. The idea is to build a maximal clique by starting with a random subgraph of the given graph: extracting a clique and enlarging it. More precisely, the algorithm consists of two steps: extraction and extension. The process of local optimization is shown in Fig. 2.

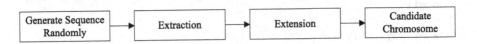

Fig. 2. The process of local extraction and extension optimization.

Clique Extraction. The clique extraction is based on the greedy strategy. For all the component $X[i]$ in X, the algorithm choose each $X[i]$ randomly, if the value of $X[i]$ is 1, the algorithm check whether vertex i is connected to all vertices in current clique obtained so far. If it is connected with all vertices, it can increase the clique, the algorithm should add i into current clique. Otherwise, the algorithm set the value of $X[i]$ to be 0. The pseudo code is shown as bellow.

```
Input: A subgraph G' represented by a chromosome X
Output: A Clique X of G'
begin
  A = nil
  B = nil
  for i = 1 to |V|:
```

```
    if X[i] = 1 then
        put i in vector A
    end if
  end for
  do
      Randomly choose one vertex j from A and set j visited
      if j is connected with all vertices in vector B then
            put j in B
      else
            X[j] = 0
      end if
  until (all vertices in A are visited)
  return X
end
```

Clique Extension. After extracting a clique form a chromosome, the clique extension algorithm attempts to increase the size of the clique. For all the component $X[i]$ in X, the algorithm choose each $X[i]$ randomly, if the value of $X[i]$ is 0, the algorithm check whether vertex i is connected to all vertices in current clique obtained so far. If it is connected with all vertices, it can increase the clique, the algorithm should add i into current clique and set the value of $X[i]$ to be 1. The pseudo code is shown as bellow.

```
Input: A clique C represented by a chromosome X
Output:A new clique C'
begin
  A = nil
  B = C
  for  i = 1 to |V|:
      if  X[i] = 0  then
          put i in A
      end if
  end for
  do
      Randomly choose one vertex j from A and set j visited
      if j is connected with all vertices in B then
            put j in B
            X[j] = 1
      end if
  until (all vertices in A are visited)
  return X
end
```

2.5   Selection

For each generation, two parents are selected from the current population using a roulette wheel scheme in Eq. 1. The probability of a chromosome being selected is proportional to its fitness. However, the good individuals have a very high probability of being selected at each generation, thus the population will become homogeneous too quickly. To avoid this, the algorithm scale the fitness before applying the selection algorithm to make sure that the best fitness and the worst fitness is in a certain range.

$$p_i = f_i / \sum_{i=1}^{popsize} f_i \tag{1}$$

In which, f_i is the fitness value of individual X_i, and p_i is the probability to be selected.

2.6   Crossover

The multiple points crossover operator is used in our algorithm. For each crossover operation, two selected parent individuals genetic material can be separated into several blocks. Thus, crossover can be describe rather natural, the child individual $child1$ copies from the odd blocks of the parent individual $parent1$ and the even blocks of the parent individual $parent2$. In our algorithm, we set the starting cut points number to 10 and reduce it to 2 eventually. Taking advantage of the problem encoding and the parallelism of the OpenCL architecture, the crossover operator is highly effective and straightforward (Fig. 3).

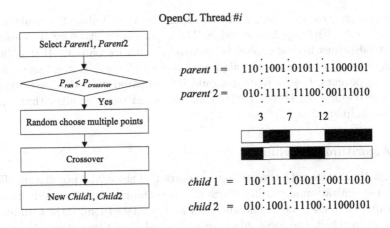

Fig. 3. Multiple points crossover operator on OpenCL.

2.7   Mutation

The algorithm allocate m work-items which map m individuals generated by crossover. Each individual is selected for mutation with a random probability P_{ran}. If P_{ran} is less than the $P_{mutation}$ which defined first, then two positions p and q are generated randomly and the genes between them are rotated (Fig. 4).

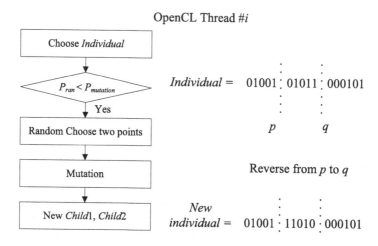

Fig. 4. Two points mutation operator on OpenCL.

2.8   Replacement

After selection, crossover and mutation operations are finished, the algorithm compute every offsprings fitness value. The replacement strategy is as follows: the best offsprings fitness should be compared with its parents. If it is better than any one of the parents, the algorithm replace the one. If it is less than any one of the parents, the individual should be compared with the least adaptive one of the population. If it is better than the worst one, the algorithm replace the worst individual.

2.9   Algorithm Flowchart

Our algorithm starts with the random generation of the initial population. Then, the local optimization algorithm which contains clique extraction and extension will be applied to each individual and then well evaluate them. If the termination criteria are reached, the most adaptive individual would be output. Otherwise, the evolution process selection, crossover, mutation and replacement operators are used to create new offspring individuals. Then the local optimization is used to make these new individuals more adaptive. The algorithm flow chart is depicted in Fig. 5.

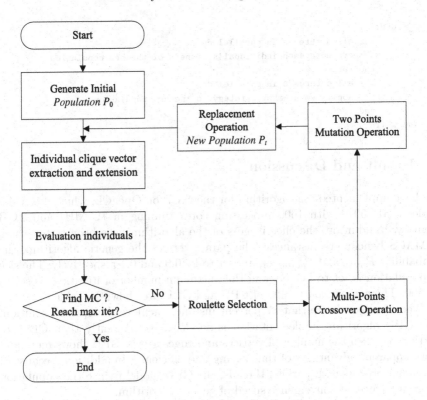

Fig. 5. The algorithm flowchart.

2.10   Parallel Algorithm on OpenCL

The pseudo-code of the algorithm implemented on OpenCL is as follows:

```
CPU:
    Produce the initial population of individuals
    Evaluate all individuals' fitness
    while(not termination condition)
        GPU:
            for all n threads in parallel do
                select two individuals for reproduction
            end for
            for all n/2 threads in parallel do
                do crossover to produce two offsprings
            end for
            for all n threads in parallel do
                do mutation for each new individual
            end for
        CPU:
            for all individuals in new population do
                apply extraction and extension algorithm to each individual
            end for
```

```
GPU:
    for all n threads in parallel do
        evaluate each individual's fitness of the new population
    end for
    for all n threads in parallel do
        apply replacement strategy to the new population
    end for
end while
```

3 Result and Discussion

We have implemented our algorithm for the MCP on Opencl, which use AMD Radeon HD 5970 with 1600 processing cores running in 725 MHz and 2 GB memory. In addition, the effectiveness of the algorithm have been tested using DIMACS benchmark instances. The parameters of the genetic algorithm, the probability P_{cross} and $P_{mutation}$, are set to be 0.9 and 0.1 respectively. The size of population is set to be 100, and the maximum number of iterations is set to be 500. The comparison results of CPU and GPU are shown in Table 1.

The results indicate that 87 percent instances achieve the optimal solution. The GPU algorithm implementation is accelerated apparently than CPU. In particular, when the number of vertices and edges grows, GPU shows more and more apparent advantages of time saving and efficiency. In addition, because of the massively OpenCL parallel threads, the GPU model reduce the population scales influence on convergence speed of genetic algorithm.

4 Conclusions

In this paper, we present a parallel hybrid genetic algorithm for maximum clique problem. All of the genetic operators which consist of selection, crossover, mutation, replacement and fitness function are implemented on OpenCL. Moreover, GPU performance is compared with the corresponding CPU implementation with DIMACS benchmark instances, and the results shows that GPU computations provide better performance than traditional CPU implementation. When the graph instances become more complicated, the speed-up radio shows that GPU acceleration is becoming more and more apparently. Recently, neural-like computing models, see, e.g. [4,5,9,12,13,17], have been used in solving computational hard problems. It is of interests to use neural-like computing models to solve graph coloring problem.

Acknowledgments. This work was supported by the National Natural Science Foundation of China (Grant Nos. 61472293, 61379059, 61273225, 61403287 and 31201121). Supported by the Natural Science Foundation of Hubei Province, China (No. 2015CFB335), and Youth Foundation of Wuhan University of Science and Technology (No. 2015xz017).

Table 1. Comparison results on DIMACS maximum clique problem challenge instances

Graph (Node)	Edge Number	CPU Time	GPU Time	Speedup	CPU Clique	GPU Clique	Best Clique
Brock200-1 (200)	14834	1.122	1.529	0	21	21	21
Brock200-2 (200)	9876	0.965	1.435	0	12	12	12
Brock200-3 (200)	12048	1.384	2.232	0	15	15	15
Brock200-4 (200)	13089	1.464	2.355	0	17	17	17
Brock400-1 (400)	59723	8.063	3.152	2.56	25	25	27
Brock400-2 (400)	59786	4.935	3.759	1.31	25	25	29
Brock400-3 (400)	59681	10.53	4.25	2.48	31	31	31
Brock400-4 (400)	59765	14.213	7.52	1.89	33	33	33
C125.9 (125)	6963	2.403	1.95	1.23	34	34	34
C250.9 (250)	27984	4.231	2.309	1.83	44	44	44
C500.9 (500)	112332	10.372	5.231	1.98	57	57	57
C1000.9 (1000)	450079	30.67	7.737	3.96	67	67	68
C2000.5 (2000)	999836	15.533	6.755	2.3	15	15	16
C2000.9 (2000)	1799532	50.404	36.386	1.39	74	74	75
C4000.5 (4000)	4000268	29.586	12.729	2.32	17	17	18
c-fat200-1 (200)	1534	1.562	1.872	0	12	12	12
c-fat200-2 (200)	3235	2.369	2.176	1.09	24	24	24
c-fat200-5 (200)	8473	6.109	2.749	2.22	58	58	58
c-fat500-1 (500)	4459	3.009	2.309	1.3	14	14	14
c-fat500-2 (500)	9139	3.807	2.558	1.49	26	26	26
c-fat500-5 (500)	23191	8.352	3.744	2.23	64	64	64
c-fat500-10 (500)	46627	3.471	1.31	2.67	126	126	126
DSJC500-5 (500)	125248	2.231	2.371	0	13	13	13
DSJC1000-5 (1000)	499652	6.595	3.603	1.83	15	15	15
gen200-p0.9-44 (200)	17910	5.586	2.558	2.18	44	44	44
gen200-p0.9-55 (200)	17910	6.875	2.59	2.65	55	55	55
gen400-p0.9-55 (400)	71820	17.528	5.476	3.2	55	55	55
gen400-p0.9-65 (400)	71820	19.316	5.522	3.49	65	65	65
gen400-p0.9-75 (400)	71820	13.252	4.258	3.11	75	75	75
hamming6-2 (64)	1824	2.443	2.169	1.12	32	32	32
hamming6-4 (64)	704	0.805	1.684	0	4	4	4
hamming8-2 (256)	31616	23.299	6.318	3.69	128	128	128
hamming8-4 (256)	20864	2.506	2.262	1.11	16	16	16
hamming10-2 (1024)	518656	10.551	4.524	2.33	512	512	512
hamming10-4 (1024)	434176	6.894	4.025	1.71	40	40	40
johnson8-2-4 (28)	210	0.227	1.428	0	4	4	4
johnson8-4-4 (70)	1855	1.379	1.576	0	14	14	14
johnson16-2-4 (120)	5420	1.558	1.576	0	14	14	14
johnson32-2-4 (496)	107880	7.56	2.418	3.13	16	16	16
keller4 (171)	9435	1.894	1.653	1.15	11	11	11
keller5 (776)	225990	10.351	2.886	3.59	27	27	27
keller6 (3361)	4619898	72.623	26.926	2.7	59	59	59

Table 1. *(Continued.)*

Graph (Node)	Edge Number	CPU Time	GPU Time	Speedup	CPU Clique	GPU Clique	Best Clique
MANN-a9 (45)	918	1.597	1.606	0	**16**	**16**	**16**
MANN-a27 (378)	70551	39.395	6.099	6.56	125	125	126
MANN-a45 (1035)	533115	110.831	34.336	3.23	342	342	345
MANN-a81 (3321)	5506380	104.689	35.303	2.97	1096	1096	1100
p-hat300-1 (300)	10933	1.976	1.669	1.18	**8**	**8**	**8**
p-hat300-2 (300)	21928	4.036	1.887	2.14	**25**	**25**	**25**
p-hat300-3 (300)	33390	5.882	2.059	2.86	**36**	**36**	**36**
p-hat500-1 (500)	31569	3.083	1.794	1.72	**9**	**9**	**9**
p-hat500-2 (500)	62946	7.304	2.246	3.25	**36**	**36**	**36**
p-hat500-3 (500)	93800	10.883	2.59	4.2	**50**	**50**	**50**
p-hat700-1 (700)	60999	3.771	2.106	1.79	**11**	**11**	**11**
p-hat700-2 (700)	121728	7.052	2.683	2.63	**44**	**44**	**44**
p-hat700-3 (700)	183010	10.696	4.088	2.62	**62**	**62**	**62**
p-hat1000-1 (1000)	122253	3.786	3.713	1.02	**10**	**10**	**10**
p-hat1000-2 (1000)	244799	10.128	4.415	2.29	**46**	**46**	**46**
p-hat1000-3 (1000)	371746	28.986	9.953	2.91	**68**	**68**	**68**
p-hat1500-1 (1500)	284923	8.679	5.553	1.56	11	11	12
p-hat1500-2 (1500)	568960	18.301	8.502	2.15	**65**	**65**	**65**
p-hat1500-3 (1500)	847244	35.951	12.35	2.91	**94**	**94**	**94**
san200-0.7-1 (200)	13930	3.352	2.278	1.47	**30**	**30**	**30**
san200-0.7-2 (200)	13930	2.675	2.246	1.19	**18**	**18**	**18**
san200-0.9-1 (200)	17910	8.66	3.307	2.62	**70**	**70**	**70**
san200-0.9-2 (200)	17910	7.598	3.105	2.45	**60**	**60**	**60**
san200-0.9-3 (200)	17910	9.222	2.793	3.3	**44**	**44**	**44**
san400-0.5-1 (400)	39900	2.994	2.48	1.21	**13**	**13**	**13**
san400-0.7-1 (400)	55860	5.825	3.057	1.91	**40**	**40**	**40**
san400-0.7-2 (400)	55860	5.02	3.011	1.67	**30**	**30**	**30**
san400-0.7-3 (400)	55860	4.326	2.886	1.5	**22**	**22**	**22**
san400-0.9-1 (400)	71820	17.677	4.821	3.67	**100**	**100**	**100**
san1000 (1000)	250500	8.196	4.509	1.81	**15**	**15**	**15**
sanr200-0.7 (200)	13868	2.582	2.247	1.15	**18**	**18**	**18**
sanr200-0.9 (200)	17863	5.585	2.855	1.96	**42**	**42**	**42**
sanr400-0.5 (400)	39984	3.064	2.449	1.25	**13**	**13**	**13**
sanr400-0.7 (400)	55869	4.572	2.808	1.63	**21**	**21**	**21**

References

1. Bomze, I., Budinich, M., Pardalos, P., Pelillo, M.: The maximum clique problem. In: Du, D.-Z., Pardalos, P.M. (eds.) Handbook of Combinatorial Optimization, pp. 1–74. Kluwer Academic Publishers, Dordrecht (1999)
2. Wang, X., Miao, Y.: GAEM: a hybrid algorithm incorporating GA with EM for planted edited motif finding problem. Curr. Bioinform. **9**(5), 463–469 (2014)

3. Ostergard, P.R.J.: A fast algorithm for the maximum clique problem. Discrete Appl. Math. Sixth Twente Workshop Graphs Comb. Optim. **3**, 197–207 (2002)
4. Song, T., Pan, L.: Spiking neural P systems with rules on synapses working in maximum spiking strategy. IEEE Trans. NanoBiosci. **14**(4), 465–477 (2015)
5. Song, T., Pan, L., Jiang, K., et al.: Normal forms for some classes of sequential spiking neural P systems. IEEE Trans. NanoBiosci. **12**(3), 255–264 (2013)
6. Resende, M., Feo, T.: A GRASP for satisfiability. In: Johnson, D.S., Trick, M.A. (eds.) Cliques, Coloring, and Satisfiability: The Second DIMACS Implementation Challenge, vol. 26, pp. 499–520. American Mathematical Society, Providence (1996)
7. Wang, X., Miao, Y., Cheng, M.: Finding motifs in DNA sequences using low-dispersion sequences. J. Comput. Biol. **21**(4), 320–329 (2014)
8. Battiti, R., Mascia, F.: Reactive and dynamic local search for max-clique: engineering effective building blocks. Comput. Oper. Res. **37**(3), 534–542 (2010)
9. Song, T., Pan, L., Păun, G.: Asynchronous spiking neural P systems with local synchronization. Inf. Sci. **219**, 197–207 (2013)
10. Bui, T.N., Eppley, P.H.: A hybrid genetic algorithm for the maximum clique problem. In: Proceedings of the 6th International Conference on Genetic Algorithms, Pittsburgh, pp. 478–484 (1995)
11. Marchiori, E.: A simple heuristic based genetic algorithm for the maximum clique problem. In: Proceedings of the ACM Symposium on Applied Computing, pp. 366–373 (1998)
12. Song, T., Pan, L.: Spiking neural P systems with rules on synapses working in maximum spikes consumption strategy. IEEE Trans. NanoBiosci. **14**(1), 38–44 (2015)
13. Zhang, X., Pan, L., Paun, A.: On the universality of axon P systems. IEEE Trans. Neural Netw. Learn. Syst. (2015). doi:10.1109/TNNLS.2015.2396940
14. Zhang, X., Tian, Y., Jin, Y.: A knee point driven evolutionary algorithm for many-objective optimization. IEEE Trans. Evol. Comput. (2014). doi:10.1109/TEVC.2014.2378512
15. Zhang, X., Tian, Y., Cheng, R., Jin, Y.: An efficient approach to non-dominated sorting for evolutionary multi-objective optimization. IEEE Trans. Evol. Comput. **19**(2), 201–213 (2015)
16. Du, P., Weber, R., Luszczek, P.: From CUDA to OpenCL: towards a performance-portable solution for multi-platform GPU programming. Parallel Comput. **38**(8), 391–407 (2011)
17. Song, T., Pan, L., Wang, J., et al.: Normal forms of spiking neural P systems with anti-spikes. IEEE Trans. NanoBiosci. **11**(4), 352–359 (2012)
18. Shimobaba, T., Ito, T., Masuda, N.: Fast calculation of computer-generated-hologram on AMD HD5000 series GPU and OpenCL. Opt. Express **18**(10), 9955–9960 (2010)

A Two-Phase External Archive Guided Multiobjective Evolutionary Algorithm for the Software Next Release Problem

Ning Zhang, Yuhua Huang, and Xinye Cai$^{(\boxtimes)}$

College of Computer Science and Technology,
Nanjing University of Aeronautics and Astronautics,
Nanjing 210016, Jiangsu, China
zhangning_0920@163.com, hyuhua2k@163.com, xinye@nuaa.edu.cn

Abstract. Decomposition based multiobjective evolutionary algorithms have been used widely in solving the multiobjective optimization problems, by decomposing a MOP into several single objective subproblems and optimizing them simultaneously. This paper proposes an adaptive mechanism to decide the evolutionary stages and dynamically allocate computational resource by using the information extracted from the external archive. Different from previous proposed EAG-MOEA/D [2], the information extracted from the external archive is explicitly divided into two categories - the convergence information and the diversity information. The proposed algorithm is compared with five well-known algorithms on the Software Next Release Problem. Experimental results show that our proposed algorithm performs better than other algorithms.

Keywords: Multiobjective optimization · Decomposition · Pareto optimality · Resource allocation

1 Introduction

Many real-world optimization problems are, by nature, multiobjective optimization problems (MOPs), where the objectives are usually conflicting with each other. Different from single objective optimization, MOPs aims to obtain a number of tradeoff solutions among objectives. These solutions are usually called Pareto-optimal solutions. The set of Pareto-optimal solutions is called the Pareto Set (PS), and the set of their corresponding objective vectors is called the Pareto Front (PF). The aim of the Multiobjective Evolutionary Algorithms is to find a good approximation of the PF (PS) [5].

For the past few years, multiobjective evolutionary algorithms (MOEAs) have been widely used in solving MOPs. Traditionally, MOEAs can be classified into the domination-based [5,6,23], the performance indicator-based [1,22] and the decomposition-based algorithms [8,9,15,16], based on different selection mechanisms of solutions during the optimization process. However, all the above MOEAs attempt to select the promising solutions in terms of both convergence

© Springer-Verlag Berlin Heidelberg 2015
M. Gong et al. (Eds.): BIC-TA 2015, CCIS 562, pp. 664–675, 2015.
DOI: 10.1007/978-3-662-49014-3_59

and diversity. Among all the MOEAs, MOEA/D [16] (MultiObjective Evolutionary Algorithm based on Decomposition) is a very popular decomposition-based algorithm. MOEA/D decomposes a MOP into a set of single objective subproblems, by aggregating all the objectives with different weight vectors and solves all the subproblems in parallel. In addition, MOEA/D conduct more effective search by using information from each subproblem's neighboring subproblems.

However, it is difficult to set appropriate weight vectors apriori to maintain the diversity of the population. Thus, a number of MOEA/D variants have been proposed [10,11,14], to address this issue. For example, the hybridization of the decomposition-based with the domination-based approach has been proposed in [2,3,13]. The working population represents the decomposition-based population, and the external archive is used to select promising solutions through the domination-based approach. In addition, some parts of the PF in an MOP can be more difficult to approximate than others [4,17]. Thus, it is necessary to provide different computational resources to different subproblems during the optimization process. Zhang et al. [17] proposed MOEA/D-DRA, where a dynamic resource allocation strategy based on the utility function (convergence information) for allocating different computational resources to different subproblems. Similar to MOEA/D-DRA, Zhou et al. [20] proposes a generalized resource allocation (GRA) strategy for dynamic resource allocation for MOEA/D. Each subproblem is selected to invest according to a probability of improvement vector, maintained and updated by an offline/online measurements of the subproblems' hardness. In [2], both of a decomposition-based working population and a domination-based external population are used. The proposed algorithm, called EAG-MOEA/D, allocates different computational resources to different subproblems based on the both the convergence and diversity information extracted from the external archive, to guide the search in the working population. The work of the paper is along this research direction.

In this paper, we propose a two-phase external archive guided multiobjective evolutionary algorithm (2EAG-MOEA/D). Different from EAG-MOEA/D, the evolutionary process is explicitly divided into two phases: convergence and diversity phase. 2EAG-MOEA/D utilizes either convergence or diversity information, depending on the evolutionary status. The experiments on the Software Next Release Problem [7,18] indicate that 2EAG-MOEA/D outperforms than others.

The rest of the paper is organized as follows. Section 2 explains the background knowledge and motivation of 2EAG-MOEA/D. Section 3 details 2EAG-MOEA/D. Experimental studies and discussions are presented in Sect. 4, where we compare our proposed algorithm with NSGA-II [6], MOEA/D [16], MOEA/D-DRA [17], EA-MOEA/D and EAG-MOEA/D [2]. Section 5 concludes the paper.

2   Backgrounds and Motivations

2.1   Multiobjective Optimization Problem

A *multiobjective optimization problem* (MOP) can be defined as follows:

$$\text{minimize } F(x) = (f_1(x), \ldots, f_m(x)), \tag{1}$$
$$\text{subject to} \qquad x \in \Omega.$$

where $x = (x_1, x_2, \ldots, x_n)$ is a n-dimensional decision variable, and Ω is the decision space; $F : \Omega \to R^m$ consists of m objective functions, mapping decision space Ω to objective space R^m.

Definition 1. *u is said to* dominate *v, denoted by $u \preceq v$, if and only if $u_i \leq v_i$ for every $i \in \{1, \ldots, m\}$ and $u_j < v_j$ for at least one index $j \in \{1, \ldots, m\}$.*

Definition 2. *A solution $x^* \in \Omega$ is* Pareto-optimal *if there is no other solution in Ω can dominate it.*

Definition 3. *The set of all the Pareto-optimal solutions is called the* Pareto set *(PS).*

Definition 4. *The set of all the Pareto-optimal objective vectors is the* Pareto front *(PF).*

2.2 Motivation

Although the original EAG-MOEA/D achieves better performance than NSGA-II and MOEA/D, its performance may be deteriorated by the following reasons.

- The number of solutions that successfully enter the external archive is used as the feedback information in the original EAG-MOEA/D. However, it may not work well, especially at the late stage of the evolutionary process, as similar solutions, which have not much contributions to increasing the diversity of the external archive, may frequently be added to and removed from the external archive. This phenomenon becomes increasing severe, which has also been observed in our experimental studies, as shown in Fig. 1, especially at the late stage of the evolutionary process.
- The feedback information implicitly contains both the convergence and diversity information for each subproblem. Intuitively, the convergence may be more important at the early stage of the evolutionary process and diversity may be more important at the late stage. The observations in our experimental studies, in Sect. 4, also support this idea.

Based on the above motivations, in this paper, we propose a Two-Phase External Archive Guided Multiobjective Evolutionary Algorithm (2EAG-MOEA/D), which explicitly divide the evolutionary process into convergence phase (Phase 0) and diversity phase (Phase 1). Intuitively, the corresponding feedback information should be extracted from the external archive, to guide the search in the working population, depending on the evolutionary status.

3   2EAG-MOEA/D

2EAG-MOEA/D is based on MOEA/D-DE. Weighted sum approach is used in 2EAG-MOEA/D for decomposition, as follows.

$$g^{ws}(x|\lambda^i) = \sum_{j=1}^{m} \lambda_j^i f_j(x), \tag{2}$$

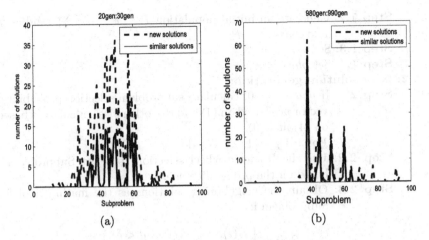

Fig. 1. The two figures represent different stages of the evolutionary process on a MNRP instance. (a) from generation 20 to 30, (b) from generation 980 to 990. The dotted line is the number of solutions that successfully enter the external archive, and the solid line represent the number of the similar solutions. Note that a solution is called a similar one when its distance with the removed solution in the external archive is less than $3 * 10^{-5}$.

where $\lambda^i = (\lambda_1^i, \ldots, \lambda_m^i)$ is the weight vector of the i-th subproblems, and $f(x) = (f_1^i(x), \ldots, f_m^i(x))$ is the objective vector of the solution x.

Similar to EAG-MOEA/D, one decomposition-based working population P and one domination-based external archive A are used in 2EGA-MOEA/D. The algorithm flow is given as follows:

Input:

(1) a combinatorial MOP;
(2) a stopping criterion;
(3) N: the number of subproblems; the population size of P and A;
(4) $\lambda^1, \ldots, \lambda^N$: a set of N weight vectors;
(5) T: the size of the neighborhood of each subproblem;
(6) n_r: the maximal number of solutions replaced by each child solution;
(7) δ: the probability that parent solutions are selected from the neighborhood;
(8) LG: learning generations;
(9) *phase*: Boolean value for marking the evolutionary status: 0 for convergence phase and 1 for diversity phase.

Output: A set of non-dominated solutions;

Step 1: Initialization:

   Step 1.1. Calculate the Euclidean distance between any two weight vectors. For each $i = 1, \ldots, N$, set $B(i) = \{i_1, \ldots, i_T\}$, where $\lambda^{i_1}, \ldots, \lambda^{i_T}$ are the T closest weight vectors to λ^i;

Step 1.2. Generate an initial population $P : \{x^1, \ldots, x^N\}$ randomly, and make $A = P$;

Step 1.3. Set $gen = 0$;

Step 1.4. Set $phase = 0$;

Step 2: New solution generation:

Step 2.1. If $phase == 0$, calculate subproblem-selection-probability-vector pro based on (4) and (5); otherwise, calculate it based on (4) and (6).

For all $j \in \{1, \ldots, N\}$ do

Step 2.2. Use the Roulette wheel selection to select Subproblem i based on the probability pro.

Step 2.3. Obtain the neighboring solutions as the mating pool for Subproblem i:

$$R(j) = \begin{cases} B(i), & if(rand < \delta), \\ \{1 \ldots, N\}, & otherwise. \end{cases} \quad (3)$$

Step 2.4. Select two indexes k and l from R randomly.

Step 2.5. Generate a new solution y_j for Subproblem i from x_k and x_l by the uniform crossover operator and bit-flip mutation operator.

End for

Step 3: Update of solutions:

Step 3.1. For $j \in \{1, \ldots, N\}$, randomly pick an index m from $R(j)$, set $x_m = y_j$ if $g^{ws}(y_j|\lambda^m) \leq g^{ws}(x_m|\lambda^m)$. Then delete this index from $R(j)$ and randomly choose other indexes until $R(j)$ is empty or the newly generated solution y_j has replaced n_r solutions.

Step 3.2. Merge the set of new solutions $\{y_1, \ldots, y_N\}$ with A; select N best solutions from the combined population by NSGA-II selection for A.

Step 4: Phase division:

Step 4.1. $gen = gen + 1$;

Step 4.2. If gen is a multiplication of 50, computer convergence utility Δ_m, defined in (7). If $\Delta_m < \vartheta$, set $phase = 1$.

Step 5: Termination:

Step 5.1. If the stopping criteria are satisfied, terminate the algorithm and output A. Otherwise, go to **Step 2**.

The subproblem-selection-probability-vector pro is defined as follows. In the convergence phase (phase $== 0$), if a new solution enters the external archive and dominates any old solution in the external archive, it has made one contribution to the convergence. We regard the number of such solutions generated by i-th subproblem at generation k as the feedback information, defined as $s_{i,k}$; and pro is updated as follows:

$$pro_{i,gen} = \frac{D_{i,gen}}{\sum_{i=1}^N D_{i,gen}}, (i = 1, 2, \ldots, N, gen \geq LG), \quad (4)$$

where

$$D_{i,gen} = \frac{\sum_{G=gen-LG}^{gen-1} s_{i,G}}{\sum_{i=1}^{N} \sum_{G=gen-LG}^{gen-1} s_{i,G}} + \epsilon, \qquad (5)$$

Here, $\epsilon = 0.002$ is used to avoid zero probability selection for any subproblems.

In the diversity phase (phase $== 1$), we consider the ranks of the crowding distance as feedback information $f_{i,k} = 1/r_{i,k}$. Here, $r_{i,k}$ is the average ranks of the solutions' crowding distance which belonged to the i-th subproblem at generation k. Note that some subproblems may contribute more than one solution to A, the average ranking is calculated in this case. pro is calculated by (4) and $D_{i,gen}$ is computed as follows.

$$D_{i,gen} = \frac{\sum_{G=gen-LG}^{gen-1} f_{i,G}}{\sum_{i=1}^{N} \sum_{G=gen-LG}^{gen-1} f_{i,G}}. \qquad (6)$$

When a subproblem contributes no solutions to the external archive, $r_{i,g}$ is set to $(length(A) + 1)$.

To determine the evolutionary status of the algorithm, a convergence utility Δ_m, which indicate the mean of the relative decrease of the objective for each subproblem during the last 50 generations, is adopted, as follows.

$$\Delta_m = \frac{1}{N} \sum_{i=1}^{N} \frac{g^{ws}(t_{i,old}|\lambda^i) - g^{ws}(t_{i,new}|\lambda^i)}{g^{ws}(t_{i,old}|\lambda^i)}, \qquad (7)$$

where $t_{i,old}$ is the best solution for subproblem i and $t_{i,new}$ is the current best solution for subproblem i.

The algorithm starts with the convergence phase (phase $== 0$) and is switched to the diversity phase (phase $== 1$), when $\Delta_m < \vartheta$. ϑ is a preset parameter.

4   Experimental Studies

4.1   Test Problems

We consider one of the NP-hard combinatorial problems–the multiobjective software next release problem (MNRP), which is a widely known problem in Search Based Software Engineering [12]. The Multiobjective Next Release Problem [3,19] is to determine which requirements from different customers should be implemented in the next release of the software. The MNRP has two objectives to optimize: One is to minimize the required cost:

$$C = \sum_{i=1}^{n} c_i \cdot x_i, \qquad (8)$$

and the other is to maximize the total satisfaction score:

$$S = \sum_{u=1}^{U} \sum_{i=1}^{n} s_{i,u} \cdot x_i, \qquad (9)$$

where c_i is the cost of implementing requirement i. $s_{i,u}$ is the satisfaction score of customer u in terms of requirement i. $x_i \in \{0, 1\}$. $x_i = 0$ means that requirement i is not implemented, and $x_i = 1$ means that it is implemented.

$Cu - U/R - n$ is used to denote a specific MNRP test instance, where U denotes the number of customers and n denotes the number of requirements. In our studies, eight randomly generated test instances, $Cu - 30/R - 300$, $Cu - 50/R - 200$, $Cu - 50/R - 500$, $Cu - 80/R - 800$, $Cu - 100/R - 1000$, $Cu - 120/R - 1200$, $Cu - 160/R - 1600$ and $Cu - 200/R - 2000$, are used.

4.2   Performance Metrics

Inverted Generational Distance (IGD) [21] and Hypervolume metric (HV) [24] are adopted as the performance indicators in this paper. IGD measures the average distance from the true Pareto front to the closest solutions in the obtained solution set, which reflects closeness of the obtained solution set to the true Pareto Front. On the other hand, HV calculates the volume of the region between the obtained solutions and a preset reference point. Both lower IGD and higher HV values indicate a better performance of the algorithm. Note that the true Pareto Front of the MNRP is unknown. Alternatively, we use the set of all the non-dominated solutions obtained by all algorithms as the reference Pareto Front to calculate IGD in this paper. The reference point is set to be the 1.1 times the upper bounds of the obtained solutions.

4.3   Experimental Setups

In this paper, five algorithms are used for comparison, including NSGA-II [6], MOEA/D [16], MOEA/D-DRA [17], EA-MOEA/D and EAG-MOEA/D [2]. It's worth to note that EA-MOEA/D can be considered as 2EAG-MOEA/D without the dynamic resource allocation strategy. All the algorithms were run 30 independent times on each test instance. The number of the weight vectors N is determined by H $(N = C_{H+m-1}^{m-1})$. Here H is set to be 99 for all the instance, and the population size of all test instances was 100. Each weight vector λ^i in $(\lambda^1, \ldots, \lambda^N)$ takes a value from

$$\{\frac{0}{H}, \frac{1}{H}, \ldots, \frac{H}{H}\}.$$

The crossover probability was set to $p_c = 1.0$ ($p_c = 0.8$ for NSGA-II) and the mutation probability was $p_m = 1/n$, where n denotes the number of decision variables. The uniform crossover operator and bit-flip mutation operator were adopted. We also set $LG = 10$ for all the test problems. The neighborhood size T was set to 10, and the parameter δ was set to 0.9. We set $n_r = 10$ and $\vartheta = 0.005$ for the 2EAG-MOEA/D. The number of function evaluation was set to 50,000 for $Cu - 30/R - 300$, $Cu - 50/R - 500$ and $Cu - 50/R - 200$; and 100,000 for all the remaining test instances for all the algorithms.

4.4 Experimental Results

Table 1 gives the comparative results of six algorithms on all test instances in terms of the hypervolume metrics. The significance test is performed between 2EAG-MOEA/D and each of other compared algorithms. The symbol $*$ indicates a significant difference between the results of 2EAG-MOEA/D and the corresponding algorithm. It can be observed form Table 1 that 2EAG-MOEA/D performs better than all five compared algorithms on all test instances. For $Cu - 50/R - 200$, the mean values of 2EAG-MOEA/D is larger than EA-MOEA/D and EAG-MOEA/D, but no significant differences can be observed.

Table 1. Performance comparison on MNRP in terms of the mean and standard deviation values of HV.

Instance		2EAG-MOEA/D	MOEA/D	NSGA-II	MOEA/D-DRA	EA-MOEA/D	EAG-MOEA/D
$Cu - 30/$ $R - 300$	mean	**0.7321**	0.7142*	0.5788*	0.7154*	0.7312*	0.7317*
	std	4.29E-04	0.0047	0.0067	0.0035	5.21E-04	2.91E-4
$Cu - 50/$ $R - 200$	mean	**0.7404**	0.7272*	0.6132*	0.7284*	0.7403	0.7403
	std	4.00E-04	0.0022	0.0132	0.0023	4.72E-04	1.84E-4
$Cu - 50/$ $R - 500$	mean	**0.7444**	0.7245*	0.5533*	0.7258*	0.7429*	0.7407*
	std	3.40E-04	0.0040	0.0095	0.0036	5.90E-04	3.40E-4
$Cu - 80/$ $R - 800$	mean	**0.7404**	0.7141*	0.5236*	0.7130*	0.7392*	0.7375*
	std	4.73E-04	0.0068	0.0057	0.0083	6.02E-04	2.73E-4
$Cu - 100/$ $R - 1000$	mean	**0.7467**	0.7108*	0.5140*	0.7084*	0.7452*	0.7399*
	std	6.05E-04	0.0139	0.0066	0.0137	7.90E-04	3.07e-4
$Cu - 120/$ $R - 1200$	mean	**0.7453**	0.7114*	0.5038*	0.6938*	0.7418*	0.7308*
	std	4.59E-04	0.01016	0.0054	0.0163	0.0010	4.20e-4
$Cu - 160/$ $R - 1600$	mean	**0.7359**	0.6975*	0.4801*	0.6847*	0.7309*	0.7089*
	std	9.97E-04	0.0125	0.0051	0.0171	0.0017	8.19e-4
$Cu - 200/$ $R - 2000$	mean	**0.7382**	0.6851*	0.4696*	0.6712*	0.7347*	0.7272*
	std	6.35E-04	0.0135	0.0046	0.0120	0.0013	8.19e-4

The similar results can be obtained in terms of IGD metric. Table 2 shows the mean and standard deviation of the IGD metric values, respectively. Clearly, 2EAG-MOEA/D outperforms all the other compared algorithms on all the test instances, except for $Cu - 200/R - 2000$. For $Cu - 200/R - 2000$, EA-MOEA/D achieves the best performance.

Table 2. Performance comparison on MNRP in terms of the mean and standard deviation values of *IGD*.

Instance		2EAG-MOEA/D	MOEA/D	NSGA-II	MOEA/D-DRA	EA-MOEA/D	EAG-MOEA/D
$Cu - 30/$ $R - 300$	mean	**0.0053**	0.0204*	0.1292*	0.0197*	0.0057*	0.0055
	std	2.44E-04	0.0035	0.0077	0.0026	2.88E-04	4.75e-4
$Cu - 50/$ $R - 200$	mean	**0.0053**	0.0181*	0.1021*	0.0171*	0.0053	0.0055*
	std	1.68E-04	0.0020	0.0145	0.0020	2.26E-04	5.45e-4
$Cu - 50/$ $R - 500$	mean	**0.0054**	0.0203*	0.1891*	0.0191*	0.0061*	0.0080*
	std	2.22E-04	0.0026	0.0121	0.0024	3.32E-04	1.26e-4
$Cu - 80/$ $R - 800$	mean	**0.0055**	0.0236*	0.2224*	0.0240*	0.0060*	0.0079*
	std	2.27E-04	0.0040	0.0080	0.0046	2.96E-04	4.48e-4
$Cu - 100/$ $R - 1000$	mean	**0.0055**	0.0261*	0.2506*	0.0270*	0.0061*	0.0132*
	std	2.71E-04	0.0057	0.0107	0.0055	3.27E-04	3.10e-4
$Cu - 120/$ $R - 1200$	mean	**0.0056**	0.0256*	0.2637*	0.0326*	0.0070*	0.0225*
	std	2.53E-04	0.0056	0.0087	0.0076	5.01E-04	2.63e-4
$Cu - 160/$ $R - 1600$	mean	**0.0069**	0.0291*	0.2962*	0.0365*	0.0096*	0.0421*
	std	5.10E-04	0.0071	0.0091	0.0091	5.01E-04	4.46e-4
$Cu - 200/$ $R - 2000$	mean	0.0077	0.0162*	0.3330*	0.0387*	**0.0068***	0.0217*
	std	0.0120	0.0013	8.19e-4	0.0043	4.42E-04	4.46e-4

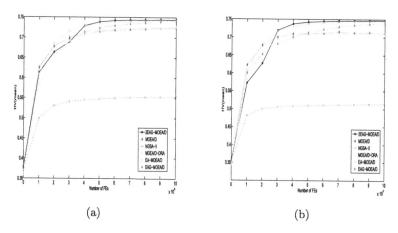

(a)   (b)

Fig. 2. The evolution of the mean HV metric values versus the number of function evaluations in each algorithm on $Cu - 50/R - 500$ and $Cu - 100/R - 1000$. (a) $Cu - 50/R - 500$, (b) $Cu - 100/R - 1000$.

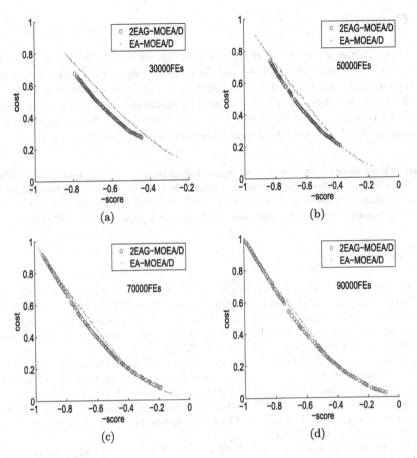

Fig. 3. The solutions obtained by 2EAG-MOEA/D and EA-MOEA/D on $Cu-200/R-2000$ instance at (a) $30000FEs$, (b) $50000FEs$, (c) $70000FEs$, (d) $90000FEs$.

To visualize the performance, the evolution of all algorithms on $Cu-50/R-500$ and $Cu-100/R-1000$, in terms of HV metric, is presented in Fig. 2. It can be observed that 2EAG-MOEA/D outperforms others in the final performance. Obviously, 2EAG-MOEA/D is not the best at early stage, but can outperforms at late stages. This observation is consistent with our motivations in Sect. 2.2.

In addition, the non-dominated solution set obtained by EA-MOEA/D and 2EAG-MOEA/D at 30000, 50000, 70000 and 90000 function evaluations are plotted in Fig. 3, to demonstrate the evolutionary process of these two algorithms. It can be seen that the solutions obtained by 2EAG-MOEA/D has better convergence in the convergence phase (phase 0), although the diversity of it is worse than that of EA-MOEA/D, as shown in Fig. 3a and b. However, its diversity is improved drastically and becomes as good as that of EA-MOEA/D in the diversity phase (phase 1), as shown in Fig. 3c and d.

5   Conclusion

The paper proposed 2EAG-MOEA/D, which explicitly divides the evolutionary process into the convergence phase and diversity phase; and the convergence and diversity information extracted from the external archive, are used to guide the search in the decomposition-based working population, depending on in which phase the evolution is. 2EAG-MOEA/D is compared with five algorithms and the experimental results show it outperforms other compared algorithms.

Acknowledgments. This work was supported in part by the National Natural Science Foundation of China (NSFC) under grant 61300159, by the Natural Science Foundation of Jiangsu Province under grant BK20130808, by the Research Fund for the Doctoral Program of Higher Education of China under grant 20123218120041.

References

1. Beume, N., Naujoks, B., Emmerich, M.: SMS-EMOA: multiobjective selection based on dominated hypervolume. Eur. J. Oper. Res. **181**(3), 1653–1669 (2007)
2. Cai, X., Li, Y., Fan, Z., Zhang, Q.: An external archive guided multiobjective evolutionary algorithm based on decomposition for combinatorial optimization. IEEE Trans. Evol. Comput. **19**, 508–523 (2014)
3. Cai, X., Wei, O.: A hybrid of decomposition and domination based evolutionary algorithm for multi-objective software next release problem. In: 10th IEEE International Conference on Control and Automation, pp. 412–417, June 2013
4. Chiang, T.C., Lai, Y.P.: MOEA/D-AMS: improving MOEA/D by an adaptive mating selection mechanism. In: Congress on Evolutionary Computation (CEC 2011), pp. 1473–1480 (2011)
5. Deb, K.: Multi-Objective Optimization Using Evolutionary Algorithms. Wiley, Chichester (2001)
6. Deb, K., Pratap, A., Agarwal, S., Meyarivan, T.: A fast and elitist multiobjective genetic algorithm: NSGA-II. IEEE Trans. Evol. Comput. **6**(2), 182–197 (2002)
7. Durillo, J.J., Zhang, Y., Alba, E., Nebro, A.J.: A study of the multi-objective next release problem. In: 2009 1st International Symposium on Search Based Software Engineering, pp. 49–58. IEEE (2009)
8. Hughes, E.: Msops-ii: a general-purpose many-objective optimiser. In: IEEE Congress on Evolutionary Computation, CEC 2007, pp. 3944–3951, September 2007
9. Hughes, E.J.: Multiple single objective pareto sampling. In: Proceedings of the 2003 Congress on Evolutionary Computation (CEC 2003), vol. 4, pp. 2678–2684. IEEE Press, Canberra, December 2003
10. Ke, L., Zhang, Q., Battiti, R.: MOEA/D-ACO: a multiobjective evolutionary algorithm using decomposition and antcolony. IEEE Trans. Cybern. **43**(6), 1845–1859 (2013)
11. Li, H., Landa-Silva, D.: An adaptive evolutionary multi-objective approach based on simulated annealing. Evol. Comput. **19**, 561–595 (2011)
12. Malhotra, R., Khari, M.: Heuristic search-based approach for automated test data generation: a survey. IJBIC **5**(1), 1–18 (2013)

13. Mei, Y., Tang, K., Yao, X.: Decomposition-based memetic algorithm for multiobjective capacitated arc routing problem. IEEE Trans. Evol. Comput. 15(2), 151–165 (2011)

14. Sato, H.: Inverted PBI in MOEA/D and its impact on the search performance on multi and many-objective optimization. In: Genetic and Evolutionary Computation Conference, GECCO 2014, pp. 645–652 (2014)

15. Schaffer, J.D., Grefenstette, J.J.: Multiobjective learning via genetic algorithms. In: Proceedings of the 9th International Joint Conference on Artificial Intelligence (IJCAI 1985), pp. 593–595. AAAI, Los Angeles (1985)

16. Zhang, Q., Li, H.: MOEA/D: a multiobjective evolutionary algorithm based on decomposition. IEEE Trans. Evol. Comput. 11(6), 712–731 (2007)

17. Zhang, Q., Liu, W., Li, H.: The performance of a new version of MOEA/D on CEC09 unconstrained mop test instances. Working Report CES-491, School of CS and EE, University of Essex, Feburary 2009

18. Zhang, Y., Harman, M., Mansouri, S.A.: The multi-objective next release problem. In: Genetic and Evolutionary Computation Conference, GECCO 2007, Proceedings, London, England, UK, 7–11 July 2007, pp. 1129–1137 (2007)

19. Zhang, Z.: Immune optimization algorithm for constrained nonlinear multiobjective optimization problems. Appl. Soft Comput. 7(3), 840–857 (2007)

20. Zhou, A., Zhang, Q.: Are all the subproblems equally important? resource allocation in decomposition based multiobjective evolutionary algorithms. IEEE Trans. Evol. Comput. PP(99), 1 (2015)

21. Zitzler, E., Thiele, L., Laumanns, M., Fonseca, C., da Fonseca, V.: Performance assessment of multiobjective optimizers: an analysis and review. IEEE Trans. Evol. Comput. 7(2), 117–132 (2003)

22. Zitzler, E., Künzli, S.: Indicator-based selection in multiobjective search. In: Yao, X., et al. (eds.) PPSN 2004. LNCS, vol. 3242, pp. 832–842. Springer, Heidelberg (2004)

23. Zitzler, E., Laumanns, M., Thiele, L.: SPEA2: improving the strength pareto evolutionary algorithm. In: Giannakoglou, K., Tsahalis, D., Periaux, J., Papailou, P., Fogarty, T. (eds.) EUROGEN 2001. Evolutionary Methods for Design, Optimization and Control with Applications to Industrial Problems, Athens, Greece, pp. 95–100 (2002)

24. Zitzler, E., Thiele, L.: Multiobjective evolutionary algorithms: a comparative case study and the strength pareto approach. IEEE Trans. Evol. Comput. 3(4), 257–271 (1999)

Controllable DNA Nano-Tweezer Technique Based on the Combinatorial Strand Displacement

Xuncai Zhang, Chaonan Shen, Guangzhao Cui, and Yanfeng Wang[⊠]

Henan Key Lab of Information-based Electrical Appliances,
College of Electrical and Electronic Engineering,
Zhengzhou University of Light Industry, Zhengzhou 450002, Henan, China
805629540@qq.com

Abstract. Toehold-mediated strand displacement has great advantage in DNA molecular computing. It is widely applied to build the large-scale and complex logic circuits. However, in general, the detection of molecular circuits is achieved by DNA double helices with nicked segment. So to some extent it limits the detection method of molecular circuits. Here, we report a strategy implemented by the combinatorial strand displacement technology to control the state of DNA nano-tweezer. The distance between the fluorescent dye and the quencher dye is drawn closer because of the closed DNA nano-tweezer, inducing the fluorescence signal disappeared in response to the logic gate function. Four logic circuits (AND gate, OR gate, Inhibit gate and XOR gate) are designed in this paper based on the combinatorial strand displacement.

Keywords: Combinatorial strand displacement · DNA nano-tweezer · Logic circuits

1 Introduction

The unique predictability and stability of Watson-Crick base pairing allows the hybridization of complementary sequences with highly programmable [1,2]. Bio-computing models are hot in natural computing, mainly including membrane computing models [10,11] (the well known class are neural-like membrane computing models, see e.g. [17,18,22,23]) and DNA computing [8,9]. With development of DNA computing, DNA nanotechnology has been made great achievements in the field of constructing nano-devices [3–5], molecular logic circuits [6–9,12–14], and material self-assemblies [15,16,19]. Since the Yurke group first introduced the toehold-mediated strand displacement technology [3], this technology played an important role in DNA dynamic nanotechnology, because this method could make the reaction process with dynamic and programmable pathways [20].

The design of DNA nano-devices was almost based on the toehold-mediated DNA strand displacement reaction. In [3], Yurke constructed a DNA nano-device

© Springer-Verlag Berlin Heidelberg 2015
M. Gong et al. (Eds.): BIC-TA 2015, CCIS 562, pp. 676–682, 2015.
DOI: 10.1007/978-3-662-49014-3_60

named DNA nano-tweezer. Its state could be controlled by addition of auxiliary strands. In [4], Shin demonstrated a bipedal DNA walker that could move along with the one-dimensional orbit in response to external DNA strand stimuli. In DNA molecular computing, Seelig constructed the logic AND, OR, and NOT gates [6], and made it possible to create the large-scale logic circuits. Ghadiriutilized a set of logic gates (AND, OR, and AND-NOT gates) to construct a three-level circuit [7], which could realize the logic XOR gate function. Significantly, Winfree utilized strand displacement strategy to realize a four-bit square-root logic circuit and the neural networks [8,9]. Turberfield designed a combinatorial DNA strand displacement, which the toehold and displacement domains were linked by hybridization of linking domains rather than directly connected in [12]. In 2013, Liu proposed a method implemented by strand displacement technology to build a three-input logic gate [13], which could convert into the five input logic circuit through the two layer cascades of the logic gate. After that, Shi designed intelligent DNA molecular systems that could perform logic computation, including logic AND, OR and XOR gates [14].

In this study, we utilize the combinatorial DNA strand displacement strategy to control the state of DNA nano-tweezer. The stem part of the DNA nano-tweezer is modified with the fluorescent dye and the quencher dye. When adding input strands, the distance between the fluorescent dye and the quencher dye is drawn closer because of the closed DNA nano-tweezer, inducing the fluorescence signal disappeared in response to the logic gate function. Four logic circuits (AND gate, OR gate, Inhibit gate and XOR gate) are designed in this paper.

2 Design and Modeling

Under normal circumstances, the toehold and displacement domains are directly linked in a DNA strand. Different from this method, the toehold and displacement domains are distributed on the different DNA strands in the combinatorial strand displacement strategy. The toehold and displacement domains are linked by hybridization of linking domains, as shown in Fig. 1. Once two input strands are introduced, leading to the formation of the functional displacing complex. Subsequently, the functional displacing complex hybridized with reporter complex, and an output strand is displaced. This mechanism realizes dynamically and combinatorially link between the toehold domain and the displacement domain to form the functional displacing complex. Obviously, through a combination of strands, 2n DNA strands can be programmed to form n^2 functional displacing complexes and to invade n^2 substrates. The number of strands we use is highly reduced by using this mechanism. Furthermore, each input strand contains the bulgy domain. Bulged thymidines can accelerate the strand displacement reactions [21].

The structure of the DNA nano-tweezer contains three DNA strands named 'a', 'b' and 'c', where domain a1 is the Watson-Crick complement of c2, and domain a2 is the Watson-Crick complement of b1. The fluorescent dye and the quencher dye are separately tethered to the 3' and 5' end of strand 'a' (see Fig. 2). The DNA nano-tweezer is initially in the open state in the absence of any inputs, the combinatorial domains b2 and c1 as the specific target recognition domains can hybridize with the target DNA strand, resulting in the closure of DNA nano-tweezer. When adding input strands s1 and s2 concurrently, the functional displacing complex as the specific target DNA complex hybridized with the combinatorial domains b2 and c1, inducing the state of DNA nano-tweezer from an open state to a closed state. The fluorescence signal disappears because of the near distance between the fluorescent dye and the quencher dye in response to the logic AND gate function.

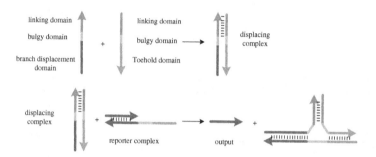

Fig. 1. Principle of the combinatorial strand displacement.

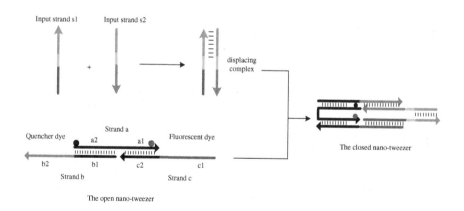

Fig. 2. Control process of state of DNA nano-tweezer using the combinatorial strand displacement.

3   Construction of the Logic Circuit

A simple AND gate circuit has been designed based on the combinatorial strand displacement strategy, as shown in Fig. 2. In a similar way, we also design the

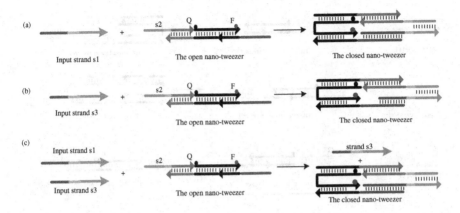

Fig. 3. The logic OR gate circuit using the combinatorial strand displacement. (a) The reaction process of adding input strand s1 alone. (b) The reaction process of adding input strand s3 alone. (c) The reaction process of adding input strand s1 and s3 concurrently.

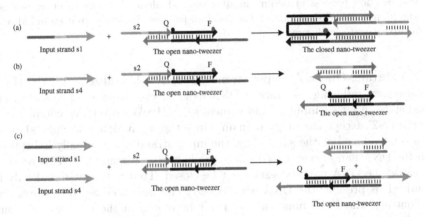

Fig. 4. The logic Inhibit gate circuit using the combinatorial strand displacement. (a) The reaction process of adding input strand s1 alone. (b) The reaction process of adding input strand s4 alone. (c) The reaction process of adding input strand s1 and s4 concurrently.

logic OR gate circuit. In the initial state, strand 's2' has been bound to the DNA nano-tweezer rather than as the input signal strand (see Fig. 3). The inputs of the circuit are DNA strands named 's1' and 's3', and strand 's3' is formed by only decreasing the specific target sequence length of strand 's1'. Therefore, in the presence of either or both input strands, the open DNA nano-tweezer will be closed. By comparison, the longer input strand 's1' may form a more stable, closed DNA nano-tweezer due to more complementary base pairings.

The same design method is used to construct the inhibit logic gate circuit (see Fig. 4). Similarly, strand 's2' has been bound to the DNA nano-tweezer in

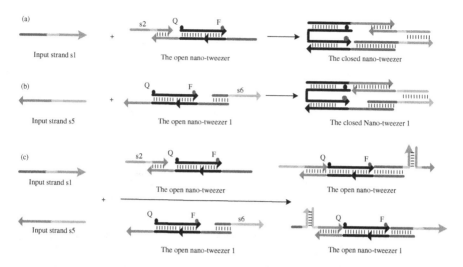

Fig. 5. The logic XOR gate circuit using the combinatorial strand displacement. (a) The reaction process of adding input strand s1 alone. (b) The reaction process of adding input strand s5 alone. (c) The reaction process of adding input strand s1 and s5 concurrently (Color figure online).

the initial state. Obviously, input strand 's1' can be hybridized with the DNA nano-tweezer, inducing the state of DNA nano-tweezer from an open state to a closed state. Another input strand named 's4' is the Watson-Crick complement of strand 's2' except the bulgy domain. Once the input signal strands 's1' and 's4' are introduced at the same time, the input strand 's4' gradually hybridizes with the DNA nano-tweezer to displace pre-hybridized strand 's2'. This process will cause the DNA nano-tweezer can't be closed. That is to say, if and only if strand 's1' is present, the DNA nano-tweezer can be closed as the output. On the contrary, the DNA nano-tweezer can't be closed in the presence of input strand 's4'.

To design a logic XOR gate circuit, two DNA nano-tweezers as substrate complexes are used in here, as shown in Fig. 5. Meanwhile, another pair of linking domains is also introduced. Two sets of linking domains are denoted respectively with green and pink colors. Analogously, strand 's2' and 's6' are bound to the DNA nano-tweezer in advance to form two DNA nano-tweezers. Strands 's2' and 's6' have a short sequence complementarity to one side of the DNA nano-tweezer respectively. When adding input strands 's1' or 's5' alone, the DNA nano-tweezer will be closed due to the hybridization of two sets of linking domains. Note that the formed, closed DNA nano-tweezer has nicked segment in the specific target domain. Therefore, if two input strands 's1' and 's5' are present concurrently, the long complementary domains of both inputs will base pair to the DNA nano-tweezer, inducing the state of DNA nano-tweezer from a closed state back to an open state.

4 Conclusion

In this paper, four logic circuits (AND gate, OR gate, Inhibit gate and XOR gate) are designed based on the combinatorial strand displacement. The change of the state of DNA nano-tweezer is regarded as the response to a certain logic gate circuit. Different from the conventional strand displacement method, the combinatorial strand displacement method realizes dynamically and combinatorially link between the toehold domain and the displacement domain to form a functional displacing complex. Obviously, through a combination of strands, 2n DNA strands can be programmed to form n^2 functional displacing complexes and to invade n^2 substrates. The number of strands used is highly reduced by using this mechanism. Moreover, we hope that these DNA logic gate circuits as the units is used more for constructing complicated biological information processing and can be used to detect and respond only to the specific target miRNA inside a living cell.

Acknowledgments. The work for this paper was supported by the National Natural Science Foundation of China (Grant Nos. 6147237161472372), Basic and Frontier Technology Research Program of Henan Province (Grant Nos. 142300413214), Program for Science and Technology Innovation Talents in Universities of Henan Province (Grant No. 15HASTIT019), and Young Backbone Teachers Project of Henan province (Grant No. 2013GGJS-106), Innovation Scientists and Technicians Troop Construction Projects of Henan Province (154200510012).

References

1. Watson, J.D., Crick, F.H.: Molecular structure of nucleic acids: a structure for deoxyribose nucleic acid. Nature **171**(4356), 737–738 (1953)
2. Klenerman, D., Zhou, D.J., Liu, D.S., et al.: A reversible pH-driven DNA nanoswitch array. J. Am. Chem. Soc. **128**(6), 2067–2071 (2006)
3. Yurke, B., Turberfield, A.J., Mills, A.P., et al.: A DNA-fuelled molecular machine made of DNA. Nature **406**(6796), 605–608 (2000)
4. Shin, J.S., Pierce, N.A.: A synthetic DNA walker for molecular transport. J. Am. Chem. Soc. **126**(35), 10834–10835 (2004)
5. Wang, X., Miao, Y., Cheng, M.: Finding motifs in DNA sequences using low-dispersion sequences. J. Comput. Biol. **21**(4), 320–329 (2014)
6. Seelig, G., Zhang, D.Y., Winfree, E., et al.: Enzyme-free nucleic acid logic circuits. Science **314**(5805), 1585–1588 (2006)
7. Frezza, B.M., Cockroft, S.L., Ghadiri, M.R.: Modular multi-level circuits from immobilized DNA-based logic gates. J. Am. Chem. Soc. **129**(48), 14875–14879 (2007)
8. Qian, L., Winfree, E.: Scaling up digital circuit computation with DNA strand displacement cascades. Science **332**(6034), 1196–1201 (2011)
9. Qian, L., Winfree, E., Bruck, J.: Neural network computation with DNA strand displace-ment cascades. Nature **475**(7356), 368–372 (2011)
10. Song, T., Pan, L.: Spiking neural P systems with rules on synapses working in maximum spikes consumption strategy. IEEE Trans. NanoBiosci. **14**(1), 38–44 (2015)

11. Song, T., Pan, L.: Spiking neural P systems with rules on synapses working in maximum spiking strategy. IEEE Trans. NanoBiosci. **14**(4), 465–477 (2015)
12. Genot, A.J., Bath, J., Turberfield, A.J.: Combinatorial displacement of DNA strands: application to matrix multiplication and weighted sums. Angew. Chem. **52**(4), 1189–1192 (2013)
13. Li, W., Yan, H., Liu, Y., et al.: Three-input majority logic gate and multiple input logic circuit based on DNA strand displacement. Nano Lett. **13**(6), 2980–2988 (2013)
14. Wang, X., Miao, Y.: GAEM: a hybrid algorithm incorporating GA with EM for planted edited motif finding problem. Curr. Bioinform. **9**(5), 463–469 (2014)
15. Rothemund, P.W.K.: Folding DNA to create nanoscale shapes and patterns. Nature **440**(7082), 297–302 (2006)
16. Wei, B., Dai, M., Yin, P.: Complex shapes self-assembled from single-stranded DNA tiles. Nature **485**(7400), 623–626 (2012)
17. Song, T., Pan, L., Jiang, K., et al.: Normal forms for some classes of sequential spiking neural P systems. IEEE Trans. NanoBiosci. **12**(3), 255–264 (2013)
18. Song, T., Pan, L., Păun, G.: Asynchronous spiking neural P systems with local synchronization. Inf. Sci. **219**, 197–207 (2013)
19. Sun, J.W., Shen, Y.: Quasi-ideal memory system. IEEE Trans. Cybern. **45**(7), 1353–1362 (2015)
20. Yin, P., Choi, H.M.T., Calvert, C.R., Pierce, N.A.: Programming biomolecular self-assembly pathways. Nature **451**(7176), 318–323 (2008)
21. Chen, X.: Expanding the rule set of DNA circuitry with associative toehold activation. J. Am. Chem. Soc. **134**(1), 263–271 (2011)
22. Song, T., Pan, L., Wang, J., et al.: Normal forms of spiking neural P systems with anti-spikes. IEEE Trans. NanoBiosci. **11**(4), 352–359 (2012)
23. Zhang, X., Pan, L., Paun, A.: On the universality of axon P systems. IEEE Trans. Neural Netw. Learn. Syst. (2015). doi:10.1109/TNNLS.2015.2396940

Chaos Multi-objective Particle Swarm Optimization Based on Efficient Non-dominated Sorting

Xuncai Zhang, Xiaoxiao Wang, Ying Niu, and Guangzhao Cui[✉]

College of Electrical and Information Engineering,
Zhengzhou University of Light Industry, No. 5 Dongfeng Road,
Zhengzhou 450002, China
cgzh@zzuli.edu.cn

Abstract. In order to reduce computational complexity of multiobjective particle swarm optimization algorithm in non-dominated sort, and make the global convergence of the algorithm more quickly in processing continuous problems, a chaos multi-objective particle swarm optimization using efficient non-dominated sort (CMOPSO-ENS) is proposed. In this algorithm, a solution to be assigned to a front needs to be compared only with those solutions that have already been assigned to a front, thereby avoiding many unnecessary comparisons. What's more, the chaotic map is used to optimize globe best solution in the algorithm. Based on the ergodicity, stochastic property and regularity of chaos, a new superior individual is reproduced by chaotic maps in the current global best individual, and a stochastic selected individual in the current population is replaced by the new superior individual. The algorithm embedded into chaotic maps quickens the evolution process, and improves the abilities of seeking the global excellent solutions. Several benchmark functions are used to test the search capability of the improved algorithm. The simulation results demonstrate that the convergence speed of the proposed CMOPSO-ENS algorithm is superior to original MOPSO algorithms, especially in solving problems with convex and piecewise Pareto front.

Keywords: Multi-objective · Particle swarm optimization · Non-dominated solutions · Chaotic maps · Convergence speed

1 Introduction

Evolution of Nature. The use of evolutionary algorithms for multi-objective optimization (an area called "multi-objective evolutionary algorithms", or MOEAs for short) has significantly grown in the last few years, giving rise to a wide variety of evolutionary algorithms [1]. A crucial challenge in MOEAs is the problem of local optima and the speed of convergence. MOEAs researchers have produced some clever techniques to maintain diversity (e.g., the adaptive grid by the Pareto

© Springer-Verlag Berlin Heidelberg 2015
M. Gong et al. (Eds.): BIC-TA 2015, CCIS 562, pp. 683–695, 2015.
DOI: 10.1007/978-3-662-49014-3_61

Archive Evolutionary Strategy (PAES)) [2] and these algorithms that use non-dominated sort (NSGA-II) [3]. In most existing literatures, the most well-known and efficient MOEAs have been suggested in a large number of fields The main application domains of the MOEAs include neural network training [5], data mining [6], web content organizing [7], computing equilibrium in strategic games [8], etc.

Particle swarm optimization (PSO) algorithm is firstly applied to solve multi-objective problems by Moore and Chapman (1999) [9]. After that, until 2002, Hu and Eberhart (2002) have proposed a kind of multi-objective optimization using dynamic neighborhood PSO. The algorithm optimizes only one goal value chosen the global optimal in the area for guiding the evolutionary species [10]. Coello (2004) has put forward an improved multi-objective particle swarm optimization (MOPSO) algorithm. The optimization has added a constraint-handing mechanism that reasonably improves the exploratory capacities of most original algorithms [11,12]. In order to prevent the MOPSO algorithm from jumping into local extreme points, Natsuki (2003) has given a PSO with Gaussion mutation, which made it more easily to jump out of local extreme point [13] Mahfouf Linkens (2004) came up with a MOPSO based on mixed strategy, in which they applied to adaptive goal weights and mutation operator to maintain the diversity of the population [14]. Cabrera proposes a micro-MOPSO algorithm which has a small population size. Its main goal is to serve as a good alternative for applications such as microcontroller, aeronautical engineering problems, and so on [15]. A competitive and cooperative co-evolutionary approach proposed by Goh (2010) is adapted for solving complex optimization problems of traditional MOPSO algorithms. The algorithm shows considerable potential which is explicitly modeling the co-evolution of competing and cooperating species. The model helps to produce decompositions of the reasonable problem by exploiting interdependency between components of the problem [16] Since search ways of MOPSO algorithm in the parameter space are still randomly direction, a directed search method (2015) is proposed to steer the searches toward the desired direction. A major highlight of the strategy is that it eliminates gradient computations of the Jacobian to produce good direction [17]. According to the feedback information detected from the evolutionary environment, a novel method (2015), named parallel cell coordinate system (PCCS) is proposed to dynamically adjust the balance in exploration and exploitation and assess the evolutionary environment Based on PCCS, a strategy, to meet a series of requirements which are selecting global best and personal best, maintaining archive and adjusting flight parameters, is integrated into a self-adaptive MOPSO [19].

Although various approaches have been adopted for MOEAs. Over the past years, the main shortages of the most MOPSO algorithms have been as follows: (1) High computational complexity of non-dominated sorting: the currently-used non-dominated sorting algorithms have a computational complexity of $O(N^2)$ (where N is the population size). (2) Easily plunged into local optimum: the solutions of most benchmark functions are easily trapped into local optima, such as ZDT2, ZDT4 etc. Based on above deficiencies, a novel MOPSO, called chaos multi-objective particle swarm optimization using efficient non-dominated sort (CMOPSO-ENS), is proposed in this paper. In this work, the two major highlights are chaos idea [20,21,24] which increases its convergence rate and resulting precision and non-dominated method which reduces runtime largely.

The rest of this paper is organized as follows. In Sect. 2, we briefly introduce existing MOPSO methods. In Sect. 3, we bring forth a novel CMOPSO-ENS algorithm in details. Simulation results are presented in Sect. 4 to empirically compare our algorithm with existing MOPSO algorithms. Finally, conclusions of this paper are given in Sect. 5.

2 Analysis of Existing Methods

2.1 Multiple Objective Particle Swarm Optimization

PSO by Kennedy and Eberbart (1995) is a relatively recent heuristic inspired by the choreography of a bird flock. It is basically a technique of parallel multi-agent research. It has been found to be successful in a wide variety of optimization tasks [25]. At any given time, each particle has a position and a velocity. The position vector of a particle relative to the origin of the search space is a test solution to the problem of search. These particles fly with a certain velocity then look for the best global position after some iterations In words, it can search for the global optimization position by simply adjusting the trajectory of each individual towards its own best location and the best particle swarm with each evolution generation according to Eqs. (1) and (2) [26–29].

$$v_{ij}(t+1) = w * v_{ij}(t) + c1 * r1(p_i(t) + x_{ij}(t)) + c2 * r2(p_g(t) - x_{ij}(t)) \quad (1)$$

$$x_{ij}(t+1) = x_{ij}(t) + v_{ij}(t+1)1 \leq i \leq K(2) \quad (2)$$

Where w is the inertia weight, $c1$ and $c2$ are learning factor $r1$ and $r2$ are random variables in the range $[0 \dots 1]$. $p_i(t)$ is the best local solution of the i_{th} particle until the i_{th} iterations. $p_g(t)$ is the best global solution of all particles. Velocity of a particle can be updated according to Eq. (1), and the particle is changed position using Eq. (2).

PSO seems to be fairly suitable for multi-objective optimization mainly because of the high convergence speed in single-objective optimization in [30]. However, as for dealing with multi-objective optimization problems, a few modifications must be set up. Firstly, the objective function is to seek not one "global best" solution, but a set of solutions. Then, a repository of non-dominated solutions is created and kept, where all non-dominated solutions found in the process of each iteration are stored in the repository.

2.2 Efficient Non-dominated Sort

Efficient non-dominated sort (ENS) proposed by Zhang [31,32] is different from most existing non-dominated sorting methods which a solution needs to be compared with all other solutions. In ENS, a solution to be assigned to a front needs to be compared only with those solutions that have already been assigned to fronts, thereby avoiding many unnecessary non-dominated comparisons.

The main idea of the ENS approach is show in Fig. 1. For solution P_k the algorithm checks firstly whether there exists a solution that has been assigned to the first front F_1. If P_k is dominated by any solutions in F_1, start comparing P_k with the solutions assigned to F_2. If no solution in front F_2 dominates P_k, assign P_k to the front F_2. If P_k is not assigned to any of the existing fronts, create a new front and assign P_k to this new front. There is a little trick in checking whether a front has a solution dominating P_k. Remember that solutions assigned to an existing front are also sorted according to the same order in the population. The major reason is that the comparisons between P_k and solutions assigned to the front should begin the last one in the front and end with the first one Therefore, unnecessary comparisons can be avoided and save a lot of time. The idea of this non-dominated strategy is quite direct.

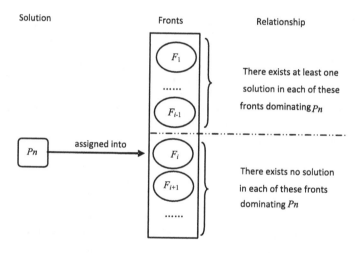

Fig. 1. The relationships between P_k and the solutions having been assigned to a front.

3   CMOPSO Using ENS Framework

Here, using chaotic search and a sequential search strategy of ENS instead of non-dominated sorting we present a novel CMOPSO-ENS algorithm which is conceptually different from existing MOPSO algorithms.

The improved algorithm is as follows. Firstly, we set up two empty collections, called C and X_c, reserving non-dominated solutions in C and positions of non-dominated solutions in X_c separately. Secondly, the individuals of the initial population P are sorted in ascending order according to fitness values of the first objective function, and a new species Q is produced. At the same time, location coordinates of solutions in set A corresponding solutions in set Q are left with the set R. Then, the first place in set R points to a solution P_1 in set A, in which P_1 is stored in the first front C_1, and the place is set up set X_{c1}. Taking a closer look, we can conclude that the result of the non-dominance comparison can be categorized into the following three cases

Case 1: The second place in set R points to a solution P_2 in set A. P_2 is dominated by P_1, create a new front C_2, and P_2 is assigned to this new front C_2, as well as the place coordinates of P_2 is set up in X_{c2}.

Case 2: P_1 is dominated by P_2, and P_2 is assigned to the fist front C_1, and then the place coordinate of P_2 is assigned to in X_{c1}.

Case 3: The two solutions are non-dominated, and P_2 is assigned to the first front C_1, and the place coordinate of P_2 is assigned to X_{c1}.

Algorithm 1. CMOPSO-ENS

Step 1: Initialize the population Pop:
  Step 1.1: For i=0 to max /*max=number of particles*/;
  Step 1.2: Initialize Pop[i];
Step 2: Initialize the speed of each particle;
  Step 2.1: For i=0 to max;
  Step 2.2: Vel[i]=0;
Step 3: Initialize the extreme value of each particle
Step 4: Evaluate each of the particles in Pop. And, store the positions of the particles that represent non-dominated vectors in the repository REP.
  Step 4.1: Sort the population in ascending order, x=size(F); {the number of fronts having been found}
  Step 4.2: k=1; {the front now checked}
  Step 4.3: While true do compare Pop[n] with the solutions in $F[k]$ starting from the last one and ending with the first one
  Step 4.4: If $F[k]$ contains no solution dominating Pop[n] then return k;{move Pop[n] to $F[k]$ and move position of Pop[n] to R}
        else if Pop[n] dominates any solution in $F[k]$,create a new front $F[k+1]$, {move Pop[n] to $F[k+1]$ and move position of Pop[n] to$R$}.
Step 5: While maximum number of cycles has not been reached do
  Step 5.1: Compute the speed of each particle using the following expression: $V[i] = W * R_1*$(Pbests[i]-Pop[i])+ R_2*(R[i]-Pop[i])
  Step 5.2: Compute the new positions of the particles adding the speed produced from the previous step: Pop[i]= Pop[i]+V[i].
Step 6: Update the particle's position and speed, calculation crowded distance, get the global optimal particle P_g
Step 7: The optimal particle P_g chaos optimization
  Step 7.1: $P_{g,i}$ (i=1,2,...,n) is mapped to the Logistic Eq. (1): $z_{n+1} = \mu z_n(1-z_n)$. Domain of the equation is [0, 1], and $z_i = (P_{g,i} - a_i)/(b_i - a_i)$, ($i$=1,2,...,$n$).
  Step 7.2: Iterate through the Eq. (1) and produce chaotic variables sequence $Z_i^{(m)}$ (m=1, 2, ...)

Step 7.3: Through the inverse mapping $P_{g,i}^{(m)} = a_i + (b_i - a_i)\ z_i^{(m)}$ $(m=1,2,\dots)$, $Z_i^{(m)}$ return to the original solution space, get $P_g^{(m)} = (P_{g,1}^{(m)}, P_{g,2}^{(m)}, \cdots, P_{g,n}^{(m)})(m=1,2,\dots)$

In the original solution space, adaptive value is calculated for every feasible solution $P_g^{(m)}$ $(m=1,2,\dots)$ that chaotic variables experience, and we keep the best feasible solution p^*. If best feasible solution p^* is local solution, then return to *Step 7.1.*

Step 8: From the current group, randomly select a particle and replacing it with p^*.

Step 9: If it reached the maximum number of iterations or get satisfied solution, optimization process is over. Otherwise, return to *step 5.*

Then, this procedure is continued until no more solutions can be accommodated. Finally, by calculating crowding distance, we get the global optimal value, and then add the chaotic maps into this algorithm. The basic idea of the algorithm is that we apply the chaos optimization to the global optimal particle, and the particles of the chaos optimization are randomly replaced the population. The idea is used to get rid of local extreme value point, improve the convergence speed and enhance precision of the algorithm. The details of our algorithm are given in Algorithm 1. The step-by-step procedure shows that our algorithm is simple and straightforward.

Table 1. Test problems

Problem	n	Variable bounds	Objective functions	Optimal solutions	Comments
ZDT1	30	[0,1]	$f_1(x) = x_1$ $f_2(x) = g(x)[1 - \sqrt{x_1/g(x)}]$ $g(x) = 1 + 9(\sum_{i=2}^{n} x_i)/(n-1)$	$x_1 \in [0,1]$ $x_i = 0, i = 2, \cdots, n$	convex
ZDT2	30	[0,1]	$f_1(x) = x_1$ $f_2(x) = g(x)[1 - (x_1/g(x))^2]$ $g(x) = 1 + 9(\sum_{i=2}^{n} x_i)/(n-1)$	$x_1 \in [0,1]$ $x_i = 0, i = 2, \cdots, n$	nonconvex
ZDT3	10	[0,1]	$f_1(x) = x_1$ $f_2(x) = g(x)[1 - \cdots$ $\sqrt{x_1/g(x)} - \frac{x_1}{g(x)} \sin(10\pi x_1)]$ $g(x) = 1 + 9(\sum_{i=2}^{n} x_i)/(n-1)$	$x_1 \in [0,1]$ $x_i = 0, i = 2, \cdots, n$	convex
ZDT4	10	$x_1 \in [0,1]$ $x_i \in [-5,5], i = 2, \cdots, n$ [0,1]	$f_1(x) = x_1$ $f_2(x) = g(x)[1 - \cdots \sqrt{x_1/g(x)} - \frac{x_1}{g(x)} \sin(10\pi x_1)]$ $g(x) = 1 + 9(\sum_{i=2}^{n} x_i)/(n-1)$	$x_1 \in [0,1]$ $x_i = 0, i = 2, \cdots, n$	nonconvex

4   Simulation Results

In this work, to test the performance of the proposed algorithm, four famous benchmark optimization problems are described in Table 1 [33]. The table shows the number of dimensions, the number of variables, their bounds of the Pareto-optimal solutions and the nature of the Pareto-optimal front for each problem.

Table 2. Parameters of MOPSO and CMOPSOENS

Parameters	value
Initial size of the population P	100
Learning factor $C1$	2
Learning factor $C2$	2
w_{max}	0.9
w_{min}	0.4
$iter_{max}$	300

Both cases are optimized by MOPSO and CMOPSOENS algorithms. The stopping criterion for the two algorithms is the maximum number of iterations. Because of the randomness nature, all experiments have been run 30 times with 300 iterations independently. The parameters taken in the two algorithms are given (Table 2).

Table 3. Runtime of MOPSO and CMOPSOENS

Runtime(s)	ZDT1	ZDT2	ZDT3	ZDT4
MOPSO	7.426618	9.763511	18.552819	28.653173
CMOPSO	3.130069	1.344712	2.204915	2.461840

The comparison results of MOPSO and CMOPSO-ENS in the test problems ZDT1, ZDT2, ZDT3 and ZDT4 are shown in Table 3 and Figs. 2, 3, 4 and 5. These problems have a Pareto-optimal front respectively. In Table 3 and Fig. 2, we can clearly see that ZDT1 problem, which is a convex function and has no local optima, is a relatively easy problem. So we easily prove that the proposed algorithm doesn't have bigger improvement on solving ZDT1 problem. ZDT2 problem is a nonconvex function and the solutions sometimes fall into the local optimum. Table 3 and Fig. 3 show the simulation effects of non-dominated solutions and runtime can be more excellent in the proposed algorithm, while comparing with ordinary MOPSO algorithms. The Pareto front of ZDT3 problem in Fig. 4 is segmented, in which our algorithm can not only find more non-dominated solutions but also have shorter runtime and better convergence speed.

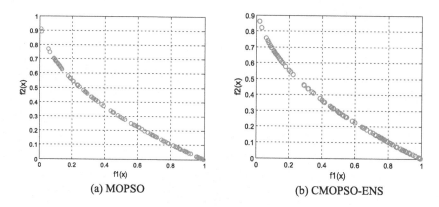

(a) MOPSO   (b) CMOPSO-ENS

Fig. 2. Non-dominated solutions with the two algorithms on ZDT1.

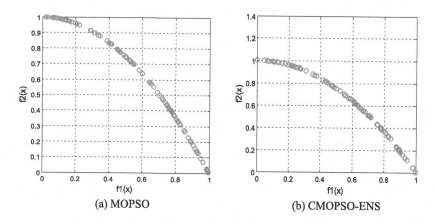

(a) MOPSO   (b) CMOPSO-ENS

Fig. 3. Non-dominated solutions with the two algorithms on ZDT2.

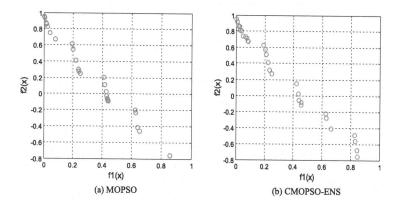

(a) MOPSO   (b) CMOPSO-ENS

Fig. 4. Non-dominated solutions with the two algorithms on ZDT3.

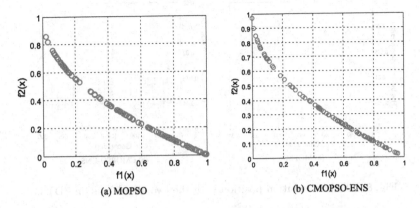

Fig. 5. Non-dominated solutions with the two algorithms on ZDT4.

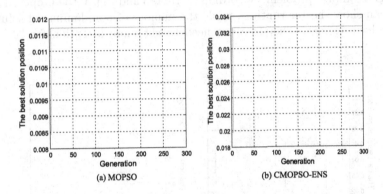

Fig. 6. The best solution position with the two algorithms on ZDT1.

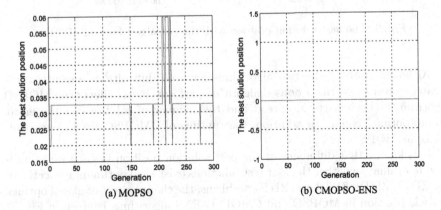

Fig. 7. The best solution position with the two algorithms on ZDT2.

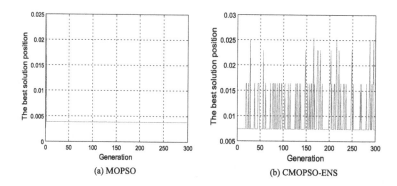

Fig. 8. The best solution position with the two algorithms on ZDT3.

ZDT4 problem, in which it has many local Pareto-optimal fronts in the search space, is a complex problem. According to Table 3 and Fig. 5, the proposed algorithm can show shorter runtime, while the number of non-dominated solutions doesn't have change. Therefore, we need to get more attention for ZDT4 in future.

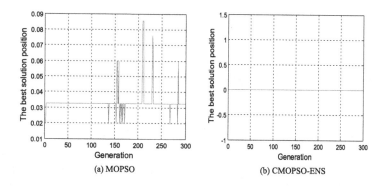

Fig. 9. The best solution position with the two algorithms on ZDT4.

Although both of the two algorithms have no difficulty to move towards greater convergence, the proposed algorithm performs better effect than MOPSO algorithm in both parts of spread and the number of solutions in the entire Pareto-optimal region. In addition, the runtime of CMOPSO-ENS clearly outperforms MOPSO [34].

It is known that difference of the best solution position in each iteration is used to evaluate whether the four test functions exist local optimum respectively. For ZDT1, ZDT2, ZDT3 and ZDT4 problems, the change curve of global optimal particle position in MOPSO and CMOPSO-ENS algorithms is given in Figs. 6, 7, 8 and 9. In Fig. 6, the graph shows that chaotic map has almost no effect on ZDT1 problem. Figure 7(a) shows that the solutions of ZDT2 problem sometimes fall into the local optimum. However, after adding the chaotic mind, it can be easy to jump out of local optimum and get better convergence speed (Fig. 7(b)). In Fig. 9(a), the solutions of ZDT4 problem are easily trapped into local optima, but chaotic maps can better improve the distribution of the solutions. On the contrary, in Fig. 8, we can see that chaos has an even worse result for ZDT3 problem. Therefore, the chaotic map isn't universal for MOEAs and cannot make all the test problems get an excellent result. We need further exploration and improvement for CMOPSO-ENS in the future.

5   Conclusion

A computationally fast CMOPSO-ENS approach is proposed. The algorithm is able to maintain a better spread of solutions, get more quickly runtime and improve convergence speed with comparing to existing MOPSO algorithms. This paper shows that highly epistatic problems may also cause many difficulties for most MOEAs. More importantly, researchers in the field should consider epistatic problems to test a newly developed algorithm for multi-objective optimization. With the properties of non-dominated sorting procedure, an elitist strategy, a paramaterless approach and a simple yet efficient method should get more attentions and applications in the near future.

In the history of constructing high-performance computing models and efficient algorithms, nature has provided rich source of ideas. One of the well-known candidates, neural-like computing models, such as artificial neural network [36] and spiking neural network [18,35]. Recently, some powerful variants of spiking neural models, see, e.g. [4,37,38], were proposed. It is worthy for further research to use neural-like models to do chaos multi-objective optimization.

Acknowledgments. The work for this paper was supported by the National Natural Science Foundation of China (Nos. 6147237161472372), Basic and Frontier Technology Research Program of Henan Province (Grant Nos. 142300413214), Program for Science and Technology Innovation Talents in Universities of Henan Province (No. 15HASTIT019), the Innovation Scientists and Technicians Troop Construction Projects of Henan Province (154200510012), and Young Backbone Teachers Project of Henan province (Grant No. 2013GGJS-106).

References

1. Coello, C.A.C., Van Veldhuizen, D.A., Lamont, G.B.: Evolutionary Algorithms for Solving Multi-objective Problems. Kluwer Academic Publishers, Norwell (2002)
2. Knowles, J.D., Corne, D.W.: Approximating the non-dominated front using the pareto archived evolution strategy. Evol. Comput. **8**(2), 149–172 (2000)
3. Deb, K., Pratap, A., Agarwal, S.: A fast and elitist multi-objective genetic algorithm: NSGA-II. IEEE Trans. Evol. Comput. **6**(2), 182–197 (2002)
4. Song, T., Pan, L.: Spiking neural P systems with rules on synapses working in maximum spikes consumption strategy. IEEE Trans. NanoBiosci. **14**(1), 38–44 (2015)

5. Lu, Y., Yan, D., Levy, D.: Friction coefficient estimation in servo systems using neural dynamic programming inspired particle swarm search. Appl. Intell. **43**(1), 1–14 (2015)
6. Yang, X., Liu, P.: Tailoring fuzzy C-means clustering algorithm for big data using random sampling and particle swarm optimization. Int. J. Database Theory Appl. **8**(3), 191–202 (2015)
7. Fan, X., Fang, X., Jiang, C.: Research on web service selection based on cooperative evolution. Expert Syst. Appl. **38**(8), 9736–9743 (2011)
8. Rachid, E., Francesco, D.P., Habib, B.A.S., Vijay, K.: Evolutionary forwarding games in delay tolerant networks: equilibria, mechanism design and stochastic approximation. Comput. Netw. **57**(4), 1003–1018 (2013)
9. Moore, J., Chapman, R.: Application of Particle Swarm to Multi-objective Optimization Department of Computer Science and Software Engineering (1999)
10. Hu, X., Eberhart, R.C.: Multi-objective optimization using dynamic neighborhood particle swarm optimization. In: Proceeding of Congress Evolutionary Computation, vol. 4(2), pp. 1617–1681 (2002)
11. Coello, C.A.C., Pulido, G.T., Lechuga, M.S.: Handing multiple objectives with particle swarm optimization. IEEE Trans. Evol. Comput. **8**(3), 256–279 (2004)
12. Liang, J.J., Suganthan, P.N.: Dynamic multiswarm particle swarm optimizer. In: Proceedings of the Swarm Intelligent Symposium, vol. 6(5), pp. 1–6 (2005)
13. Higasshi, N., Iba, H.: Particle swarm optimization with gaussian mutation. In: Proceedings of the Congress on Evolutionary Computation, 7279 (2003)
14. Mahfouf, M., Chen, M.-Y., Linkens, D.A.: Adaptive weighted particle swarm optimisation for multi-objective optimal design of alloy steels. In: Yao, X., Burke, E.K., Lozano, J.A., Smith, J., Merelo-Guervós, J.J., Bullinaria, J.A., Rowe, J.E., Tiňo, P., Kabán, A., Schwefel, H.-P. (eds.) PPSN 2004. LNCS, vol. 3242, pp. 762–771. Springer, Heidelberg (2004)
15. Wang, X., Miao, Y.: GAEM: a hybrid algorithm incorporating GA with EM for planted edited motif finding problem. Curr. Bioinform. **9**(5), 463–469 (2014)
16. Goh, C.K., Tan, K.C., Liu, D.S.: A competitive and cooperative co-evolutionary approach to multi-objective particle swarm optimization algorithm design. Eur. J. Oper. Res. **202**(1), 22–54 (2010)
17. Ho, S.L., Yang, J., Yang, S., Bai, Y.: Integration of directed searches in particle swarm optimization for multi-objective optimization. IEEE Trans. Magn. **51**(3), 1–4 (2015)
18. Song, T., Pan, L., Păun, G.: Asynchronous spiking neural P systems with local synchronization. Inf. Sci. **219**, 197–207 (2013)
19. Wang, H., Yen, G.G.: Adaptive multiobjective particle swarm optimization based on parallel cell coordinate system. IEEE Trans. Evol. Comput. **19**(1), 1–18 (2015)
20. Sun, J., Shen, Y.: Quasi-ideal memory system. IEEE Trans. Cybern. **45**(7), 1353–1362 (2015)
21. Sun, J., Yin, Q., Shen, Y.: Compound synchronization for four chaotic systems of integer order and fractional order. Europhys. Lett. **106**(4), 40005–40010 (2014)
22. Song, T., Pan, L.: Spiking neural P systems with rules on synapses working in maximum spiking strateg. IEEE Trans. NanoBiosci. **14**(4), 465–477 (2015)
23. Song, T., Pan, L., Jiang, K., et al.: Normal forms for some classes of sequential spiking neural P systems. IEEE Trans. NanoBiosci. **12**(3), 255–264 (2013)
24. Sun, J., Shen, Y., Zhang, G.: Transmission projective synchronization of multi-systems with non-delayed and delayed coupling via impulsive control. chaos: an interdisciplinary. J. NonlinearSci. **22**(4), 043107–043116 (2012)

25. Kennedy, J., Eberhart, R.C.: Swarm Intelligence. Morgan Kaufmann, San Mateo (2001)
26. Walid, E., Nesrine, B., Ajith, A., Adel, M.A.: The multi-objective hybridization of particle swarm optimization and fuzzy ant colony optimization. J. Intell. Fuzzy Syst. **27**(1), 515–525 (2014)
27. Aote, S.S., Raghuwanshi, M.M., Malik, L.: A brief review on particle swarm optimization: limitations & future directions. Int. J. Comput. Sci. Eng. **2**(5), 196–200 (2013)
28. Sedighizadeh, D., Masehian, E.: Particle swarm optimization methods, taxonomy and applications. Int. J. Comput. Theory Eng. **1**(5), 486–502 (2009)
29. Wang, X., Miao, Y., Cheng, M.: Finding motifs in DNA sequences using low-dispersion sequences. J. Comput. Biol. **21**(4), 320–329 (2014)
30. Reddy, M.J., Kumar, D.N.: An efficient multi-objective optimization algorithm based on swarm intelligence for engineering design. Eng. Optim. **39**(1), 4968 (2007)
31. Zhang, X., Tian, Y., Cheng, R., Jin, Y.: An efficient approach to non-dominated sorting for evolutionary multi-objective optimization. IEEE Trans. Evol. Comput. **19**(2), 201–213 (2015)
32. Zhang, X., Tian, Y., Jin, Y.: A knee point driven evolutionary algorithm for many-objective optimization. IEEE Trans. Evol. Comput., 1–18 (2014)
33. Deb, K.: Multi-objective genetic algorithms: problem difficulties and construction of test functions. Evol. Comput. **7**(3), 205–230 (1999)
34. Zitzler, E., Deb, K., Thiele, L.: Comparison of multi-objective evolutionary algorithms: empirical results. Evol. Comput. **8**(2), 173–195 (2000)
35. Song, T., Pan, L., Wang, J., et al.: Normal forms of spiking neural P systems with anti-spikes. IEEE Trans. NanoBiosci. **11**(4), 352–359 (2012)
36. Gerstner, W., Kistler, W.M.: Spiking Neuron Models: Single Neurons, Populations, Plasticity. Cambridge University Press, Cambridge (2002)
37. Zhang, X., Pan, L., Paun, A.: On the Universality of Axon P Systems. IEEE Trans. Neural Netw. Learn. Syst. (2015). doi:10.1109/TNNLS.2015.2396940
38. Shi, X., Wang, Z., Deng, C., Song, T., Pan, L., Chen, Z.: A novel bio-sensor based on DNA strand displacement. PLoS One, e108856 (2014)

Three-Class Change Detection in Synthetic Aperture Radar Images Based on Deep Belief Network

Qiunan Zhao, Maoguo Gong[⊠], Hao Li, Tao Zhan, and Qian Wang

Key Laboratory of Intelligent Perception and Image Understanding of Ministry of Education, International Research Center for Intelligent Perception and Computation, Xidian University, Xi'an 710071, China
gong@ieee.org

Abstract. In this paper, we propose a novel three-class change detection approach for synthetic aperture radar images (SAR) based on deep learning. In most literatures, change detection in images is a method that classifies the ratio images into two parts: the changed and unchanged classes. However, multitemporal SAR images have either increase or decrease in the backscattering values, so it is significative to further classify the changed areas into the positive and negative changed classes. We accomplish this novel three-class change detection method through Deep Learning. Given the multitemporal images, a difference image which shows difference degrees between corresponding pixels is generated by modified log-ratio operator. Then, we establish a deep belief network to analyze the difference image and recognize the positive changed pixels, negative changed pixels and unchanged pixels.

Keywords: Image change detection · Deep learning · Deep belief network · Synthetic aperture radar

1 Introduction

Image change detection is a process which analyzes the changed part between two images of the same place at different times [1,2]. In the last decades, this technology has extensively applied to both civil and military fields, such as disaster evaluation, medical diagnosis and video surveillance. With the development of remote sensing technology, change detection in multitemporal remote sensing images has roused extensive attention [3–7]. For the reason that the synthetic aperture radar (SAR) is independent of various weather conditions and sunlight conditions, it has become a valuable source of information in change detection [8–11].

In most literatures, change detection in SAR is a method that classifies the SAR ratio images into two parts, the changed and unchanged classes. However, multitemporal SAR images have either increase or decrease in the backscattering values for many cases. Its very meaningful that the changed areas can be

© Springer-Verlag Berlin Heidelberg 2015
M. Gong et al. (Eds.): BIC-TA 2015, CCIS 562, pp. 696–705, 2015.
DOI: 10.1007/978-3-662-49014-3_62

further classified into the positive and negative changed classes. For example, in river exploration, we need to identify the change of the riverway, including the disappearance of the old riverway and the appearance of new riverway. We have tried traditional methods to solve this problem but there are some disadvantages: (1) They have no ability to learn and cannot complete a knowledge accumulating process. The capability of classification is defined artificially; (2) The traditional algorithms classify the image by optimizing an objective function which may cause the results stuck in local optimum value. In machine learning, change detection can be formulated as an incremental learning problem. Neutral network is a suitable solution. So in this paper, we try to use a deep neural network to solve this problem.

In modern time, with the development of brain science and neurosciences, scientists have revealed the working principle of human brain. Inspired by the latest research and findings from neuroscience, deep learning became a novel kind of machine learning algorithm [12]. The main idea of deep learning is establishing deep hierarchical model to realize expression and analysis of data. Now deep learning has been used in many fields, such as handwriting recognition, medical diagnosis, image processing and nature language. In this paper, in order to realize the novel three-class SAR images change detection which we put forward, we tried deep learning method and got excellent results. The algorithm we proposed mainly includes two steps: (1) Use pre-classification and selection strategy to get some accurate labels of data. (2) Then construct a deep neural network to realize feature extraction of different images and three-class change detection.

The rest of this paper is organized as follows: Sect. 2 introduces the methodology. Section 3 describes the experiment in detail and shows the results of experiment. In last section, we conclude this algorithm.

2 Methodology

2.1 Introduction to Three-Class Change Detection

Consider two SAR images $I_1 = \{I_1(i,j), 1 \le i \le W, 1 \le j \le H\}$ and $I_2 = \{I_2(i,j), 1 \le i \le W, 1 \le j \le H\}$ which are taken from the same area at two different times t_1 and t_2. In the images, W and H represent the width and the height of the images, respectively. There are some noise points which have polluted the data of two original images. Because SAR images have either increase or decrease in the backscattering values, the three-class change detection method, which is shown in Fig. 1, further classifies the changed areas into positive and negative changed classes.

2.2 Pre-processing and Sample Selection

Given I_1 and I_2, the multitemporal SAR images, usually we generate the difference image by log-ratio operator. The formula is shown in Eq. (1).

$$I(i,j) = \left| log \left[\frac{I_1(i,j)}{I_2(i,j)} \right] \right| \tag{1}$$

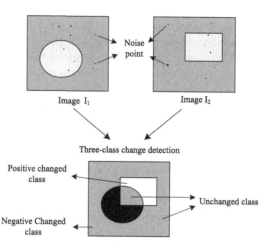

Fig. 1. The description of three-class change detection problem

Using this formula, the unchanged pixels will acquire small values, while the changed pixels perform oppositely. Since there is no information about the positive and negative changes, we modify the formula and get Eq. (2). Obviously, if I_1 is bigger than I_2, the pixels in this difference image exhibit positive values, otherwise represent negative changes.

$$I(i,j) = log\left[\frac{I_1(i,j)}{I_2(i,j)}\right] \qquad (2)$$

The training of deep neutral network needs sufficient correct classified data. Because of the influence of noise points, we need to select correct classified data after classing the difference images into three parts. Given a classed change detection result obtained by another method, we judge a pixel by the attribute of neighborhood pixels. A pixel will be considered as a noise point if the majority of the neighborhood pixels is much different, the degree of difference can be calculated by Eq. (3).

$$\frac{N(P_{xy} \in N_{ij} \cap P_{xy} = P_{ij})}{N(N_{ij})} > \lambda \qquad (3)$$

The P_{ij} is the pixel (i,j) which we want to predict, P_{xy} is the neighborhood of the pixel (i,j), in this paper the size of the neighborhood is 5×5. $N(x)$ is the number of pixels under the condition x. The parameter λ is very important, which decides whether the pixel is a noise point or not. It should be an appropriate value. If the parameter is too large, we will lose the correct point. If the parameter is too small, the formula which we put forward can distinguish the noise point. Here are some examples in selecting samples.

In Fig. 2 "2" represents the positive changed class, "1" represents the unchanged class and "0" represents the negative changed class. Because the

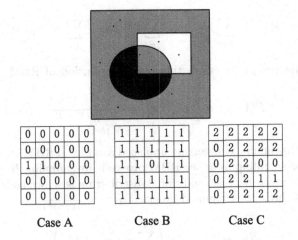

0	0	0	0	0
0	0	0	0	0
1	1	0	0	0
0	0	0	0	0
0	0	0	0	0

1	1	1	1	1
1	1	1	1	1
1	1	0	1	1
1	1	1	1	1
1	1	1	1	1

2	2	2	2	2
0	2	2	2	2
0	2	2	0	0
0	2	2	1	1
0	2	2	2	2

Case A   Case B   Case C

Fig. 2. Examples to illustrate sample selection

traditional methods are not robust to noise, there will be some spots in the final change detection images. In case A, almost all the neighborhood points have the same label with the central point, so the central point is a negative changed point. In case B, almost all of the points belong to unchanged class while the central point is from negative changed class, so the central point is a noise point. In case C, nearly half of the points have the same labels with the central point, according to the formula we consider that the central point belongs to the positive changed class.

2.3   A Deep Belief Network for Three-Class Change Detection

The establishment of deep belief network includes two main steps. Firstly, get a reliable representation of input data by layer-wise unsupervised learning per-training. Then, fine-tune the network by BP algorithm [13].

Traditional methods to establish a deep neutral network are faulty in optimizing the parameters. Because of the existence of multiple hidden layers, it is hard to find the satisfied result. If we start training the network with impertinent parameter values, the result will trap into local optimization. So the Restricted Boltzmann Machine (RBM) [14] was applied to solve this problem.

As a crucial component of our algorithm, we train RBM for layer-wise unsupervised learning. The RBM is a two-layer structure network. In this paper, we define the neighbor pixels around the center pixel which at position (i, j) as the input data. The RBM has two main parts, a visible layer $V = \{v_1, v_2, ..., v_k\}$ which has k units and a hidden layer $H = \{h_1, h_2, ..., h_s\}$ which has s units. $Vb = \{vb_1, vb_2, ..., vb_k\}$ is the bias of the visible layer and $Hb = \{hb_1, hb_2, ..., hb_s\}$ is the bias of the hidden layer. Every visible unit is connected with all of the hidden units and $W = \{W_{ij} | 1 \leq i \leq k, 1 \leq j \leq s\}$ is the weight matrix of the connection between two layers. But in the same layer, the units are independent. The energy of the state (V, H) of RBM is defined as follows.

$$E(V,H) = -\sum_{i=1}^{k} vb_i \cdot v_i - \sum_{j=1}^{l} hb_j \cdot h_j - \sum_{i,j} v_i \cdot h_j \cdot w_{ij} \tag{4}$$

Based on the energy function, the joint distribution of RBM is defined as follows:

$$P(V,H) = \frac{1}{Z}e^{-E(V,H)} = \frac{e^{-E(V,H)}}{\sum\limits_{V,H} e^{-E(V,H)}} \tag{5}$$

Because of the difficulty in getting unbiased sample, in RBM we adopt Gibbs sampling. Gibbs sampling from the RBM proceeds by sampling H given V, and then sampling V given H. The conditional distribution is shown as follows, where $S(x)$ represents the logistic sigmoid function $S(x) = \frac{1}{(1+e^{-x})}$.

$$P(h_j = 1|V) = S\left(\sum_{i=1}^{i} v_i \cdot w_{ij} + hb_j\right) \tag{6}$$

$$P(v_i = 1|H) = S\left(\sum_{j=1}^{j} h_j \cdot w_{ij} + vb_i\right) \tag{7}$$

Then, the states of hidden units are updated by the learning rule, which aimed at representing the features finally. The formula is defined as follows, $\langle V,H \rangle_{\text{data}}$ denotes the expectation of the data distribution and $\langle V,H \rangle_{\text{re}}$ denotes reconstructing the distribution of data after one step. θ is a learning rate.

$$\triangle w_{ij} = \theta\left(\langle V,H \rangle_{\text{data}}, \langle V,H \rangle_{\text{re}}\right) \tag{8}$$

The main steps of pre-training can summarize as follows. The first step, after giving a training vector x, we set the states of visible units, that is $V = x$. Then, compute the states of the hidden units using the formula in Eq. (6). After that, we compute the starting value the visible units by the formula in Eq. (7). The gradient is got using Eq. (8), then we update the parameters. The second step, after training a layer network, we train the next layer. The output data of one layer are the input data of the next layer. After the whole network is trained, it will form a representation of the local features. After that, using the samples we have selected, we fine-tune the parameters by the back-propagation algorithm. Finally we can get the final three-class change detection results though the network (Fig. 3).

3   Experimental Study

3.1   Data Sets and Evaluation Criteria

We test the method we proposed on two SAR images data sets. The first data set used in experiments acquired by Radarsat-2 is two large SAR images of the region of Yellow River Estuary in China, which was acquired in June 2008 and

(a)   (b)   (c)

Fig. 3. The Yellow River Estuary data set. (a) The image acquired in June 2008. (b) The image acquired in June 2009. (c) The ground truth image

June 2009 respectively. The original size of these two SAR images is 7666×7692 that is too huge to show in this paper, so we chose a part of the data sets which is 290×290 (Fig. 4).

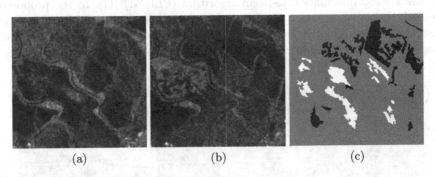

(a)   (b)   (c)

Fig. 4. San Francisco data set. (a) The image acquired in August 2003. (b) The image acquired in May 2004. (c) The ground truth image

The second data set is two SAR images, which is acquired by the ESAERS-2 satellite on the city of San Francisco, in August 2003 and May 2004, respectively. The original size is also too huge for showing, so we choose one area of the original image which is 390×370. In order to analyse the efficiency of the three-class change detection, a brief introduction to the evaluation criteria should be given firstly. In traditional SAR images change detection, the result of change detection is compared with reference image to acquire the index such as TP and TN, which represent the number of changed pixels and unchanged pixels that are correctly detected, respectively. While in this paper, we redefined the index. We compare the reference map with the results, and get the number of pixels that are correctly detected as positive changed classes, negative changed classes and unchanged classes. Therefore, PC (the correct positive changed pixels), UC (the correct unchanged pixels), NC (the correct negative changed pixels) are defined, which severally represent the number of correct positive changed pixels, correct unchanged pixels and correct negative changed pixels. Then, the overall error (OE) can be defined as:

$$OE = N - PC - UC - NC \qquad (9)$$

where N is the number of the pixels in the difference image.

In evaluation criteria of change detection we usually use percentage correct classification (PCC), which expresses the correct rate of the result and can be defined as:

$$PCC = \frac{PC + UC + NC}{N}. \qquad (10)$$

3.2   Experimental Results

In this part, the change detection results that obtained by three representative methods are given. Those methods includes the expectation maximization clustering algorithm (EM) [15], the fuzzy C-means algorithm (FCM) [16] and the fuzzy local information C-mean algorithm (FLICM) [17]. In the proposed method, the network, which has five hidden layers, is pre-trained by layer-wise unsupervised training, then we set $\lambda = 0.5$ and set the learning rate $\theta = 1$ in order to selecting the samples form the result of EM, FCM, and FLICM. We use

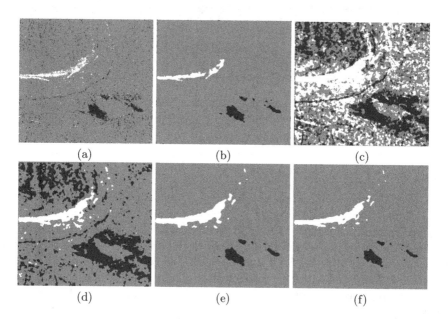

Fig. 5. Change detection maps of the Yellow River data set obtained by (a) EM, (b) proposed method using samples obtained by EM (DBN_EM), (c) FCM, (d) proposed method using samples obtained by FCM (DBN_FCM), (e) FLICM and (f) proposed method using samples obtained by FLICM (DBN_FLICM)

Table 1. Comparison of change detection results of Yellow River data set with five different methods

Method	PC	UC	NC	OE	$PCC(\%)$
EM	1099	69594	883	3824	94.93 %
DBN_EM	1134	71682	918	1666	97.79 %
FCM	1997	39536	1080	32787	56.52 %
DBN_FCM	2005	53775	1082	18538	75.41 %
FLICM	1851	70857	948	1744	97.69 %
DBN_FLICM	1697	71334	864	1505	98.00 %

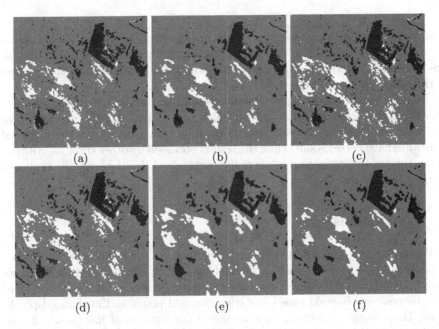

Fig. 6. Change detection maps of the San Francisco data set obtained by (a) EM, (b) proposed method using samples obtained by EM (DBN_EM), (c) FCM, (d) proposed method using samples obtained by FCM (DBN_FCM), (e) FLICM and (f) proposed method using samples obtained by FLICM (DBN_FLICM)

the samples to train the network, which aims at realizing the three-class change detection. The proposed algorithm based on the results obtained by the three methods are named as DBN_EM, DBN_FCM and DBN_FLICM respectively.

Figure 5 shows the change detection results of the Yellow River data sets, which were obtained by three different algorithms. As shown in Fig. 5, the change detection results obtained by EM, and FCM are influenced by speckle noise, several unchanged areas are incorrectly classified into changed classes. However, because of using local information and sample selection rule, FLICM and the

Table 2. Comparison of change detection results of San Francisco data set with five different methods

Method	PC	UC	NC	OE	PCC(%)
EM	6836	117309	11218	8937	93.81 %
DBN_EM	6868	118240	11388	7804	94.59 %
FCM	7515	113844	11525	11416	92.09 %
DBN_FCM	7634	114784	11748	10134	92.98 %
FLICM	7756	116407	12139	7998	94.46 %
DBN_FLICM	6540	119227	11465	7068	95.10 %

proposed algorithm which based on them have preferable results. Table 1 shows the evaluation index of five methods, according to evaluation indexes the proposed method is better than any other methods, which indicate the effectiveness of the proposed algorithm.

Figure 6 shows the change detection results of the Yellow River data sets which were obtained by three different algorithms. Just like the previous data set, using local information and sample selection rule, FLICM and the proposed algorithm have better results than the results obtained by other three algorithms. Table 2 shows the evaluation index of five methods of this data set, the proposed method still better.

4   Conclusions

In this paper, we establish a deep neural network to solve the novel three-class change detection problem. Firstly, we used log-ratio operations to generate three-class SAR difference images. Then, we establish a deep neutral network to identify the positive changed pixels, negative changed pixels and unchanged pixels. Using Deep learning method, we can extract the features of images which cannot be obtained by traditional method. What's more, the network extracts the local features of each pixel, so proposed method is robust to speckle noise. The experiments on two real SAR data sets have shown the advantage and practicability of the proposed method. In the future, we will research on the topic of three-class change detection of hyperspectral image using deep learning method without generating difference images.

References

1. Kuruoglu, E.E., Zerubia, J.: Modeling SAR images with a generalization of the Rayleigh distribution. IEEE Trans. Image Process. **13**, 527–533 (2004)
2. Yousif, O., Ban, Y.: Improving urban change detection from multitemporal SAR images using PCA-NLM. IEEE Trans. Geosci. Remote Sens. **51**, 2032–2041 (2013)

3. Gong, M., Su, L., Jia, M.: Fuzzy clustering with a modified MRF energy function for change detection in synthetic aperture radar images. IEEE Trans. Fuzzy Syst. **22**, 98–109 (2014)
4. Hao, M., Shi, W., Zhang, H., Li, C.: Unsupervised change detection with expectation-maximization-based level set. IEEE Geosci. Remote Sens. Lett. **11**, 210–214 (2014)
5. Hou, B., Wei, Q., Zheng, Y., Wang, S.: Unsupervised change detection in SAR image based on Gauss-log ratio image fusion and compressed projection. IEEE J. Sel. Topics Appl. Earth Observ. Remote Sens. **7**, 3297–3317 (2014)
6. Li, H., Gong, M., Liu, J.: A local statistical fuzzy active contour model for change detection. IEEE Geosci. Remote Sens. Lett. **12**, 582–586 (2015)
7. Wu, C., Du, B., Zhang, L.: Slow feature analysis for change detection in multispectral imagery. IEEE Trans. Geosci. Remote Sens. **52**, 2858–2874 (2014)
8. Gong, M., Zhou, Z., Ma, J.: Change detection in synthetic aperture radar images based on image fusion and fuzzy clustering. IEEE Trans. Image Process. **21**, 2141–2151 (2012)
9. Ban, Y., Yousif, O.: Multitemporal spaceborne SAR data for urban change detection in China. IEEE J. Sel. Topics Appl. Earth Observ. Remote Sens. **5**, 1087–1094 (2012)
10. Hu, H., Ban, Y.: Unsupervised change detection in multitemporal SAR images over large urban areas. IEEE J. Sel. Topics Appl. Earth Observ. Remote Sens. **7**, 3248–3261 (2014)
11. Huang, X., Zhang, L., Zhu, T.: Building change detection from multitemporal high-resolution remotely sensed images based on a morphological building index. IEEE J. Sel. Topics Appl. Earth Observ. Remote Sens. **7**, 105–115 (2014)
12. Hinton, G.E., Osindero, S., Teh, Y.: A fast learning algorithm for deep belief nets. Neural Comput. **18**, 1527–1554 (2006)
13. Zhong, Y., Liu, W., Zhao, J., Zhang, L.: Change detection based on pulse-coupled neural networks and the NMI feature for highspatial resolution remote sensing imagery. IEEE Geosci. Remote Sens. Lett. **12**, 537–541 (2015)
14. Hinton, G.E., Salakhutdinov, R.R.: Reducing the dimensionality of data with neural networks. Science **313**, 504–507 (2006)
15. Dempster, A.P., Laird, N.M., Rubin, D.B.: Maximum likelihood from incomplete data via the EM algorithm. J. R. Statist. Soc. **39**, 1–38 (1977)
16. Bezdek, J.C.: Pattern Recognition with Fuzzy Objective Function Algorithms. Plenum, New York (1981)
17. Krinidis, S., Chatzis, V.: A robust fuzzy local information c-means clustering algorithm. IEEE Trans. Image Process. **19**, 1328–1337 (2010)

An Agglomerate Chameleon Algorithm Based on the Tissue-Like P System

Yuzhen Zhao, Xiyu Liu$^{(\boxtimes)}$, and Wenping Wang

School of Management Science and Engineering, Shandong Normal University,
Jinan 250014, China
sdxyliu@163.com

Abstract. The Chameleon algorithm plays an important role in data mining and data analysis. Membrane computing, as a new kind of parallel biological computing model, can reduce the time complexity and improve the computational efficiency. In this study, an agglomerate Chameleon algorithm is proposed which generates the sub-clusters by the K-medoids algorithm method. Then, the agglomerate Chameleon algorithm based on the Tissue-like P system is constructed with all the rules being created. The time complexity of the proposed algorithm is decreased from $O(K * (n - K)^2 * C_n^K)$ to $O(n * C_n^K)$ through the parallelism of the P system. Experimental results show that the proposed algorithm has low error rate and is appropriate for big cluster analysis. The proposed algorithm in this study is a new attempt in applications of membrane system and it provides a novel perspective of cluster analysis.

Keywords: Clustering algorithm · Chameleon algorithm · Membrane computing · P system

1 Introduction

The implicit pattern or knowledge can be extracted from huge amounts of data by data mining techniques. Cluster analysis, as one of the important area of data mining, is an effective method to pack data and discover useful information from these data. It is a hot area of research in machine learning, statistics, biology and many other fields. Through the process of clustering, the whole dataset can be partitioned into different clusters. The intra-cluster data are similar and the inter-cluster data are dissimilar. Then, the data can be analysed and useful information can be obtained. For example, the dense and sparse areas can be recognized, the global distribution patterns and the interesting relationship between data attributes can be found [1]. With the emergence of big data, which shows several characteristics, such as volume, variety, velocity, and value, the data mining is paid a greater attention [2]. People need more efficient algorithms to deal with the big data. Membrane computing, as a new biological computing model, has maximal parallelism and can significantly improve the efficiency of computation.

© Springer-Verlag Berlin Heidelberg 2015
M. Gong et al. (Eds.): BIC-TA 2015, CCIS 562, pp. 706–723, 2015.
DOI: 10.1007/978-3-662-49014-3_63

The Chameleon algorithm is a typical hierarchical clustering algorithm which is proposed by George Karypis et al. in 1999. The generation of the Chameleon algorithm is based on the observation of the shortcomings of two hierarchical clustering algorithms (ROCK and CURE). Clusters will be merged if the inter-connectivities of them are very high and they are very closely. The methodology of dynamic modeling of clusters used in this algorithm makes Chameleon algorithm can be used to all types of datasets. The authors have searched for the Elsevier ScienceDirect, the IEEE and the Springer Link, but no papers which improved the algorithm was found.

P system, the computing model of the new biological calculation method membrane computing, is abstracted based on the structure and function of the cell. In general, P systems have 3 components, i.e. a membrane structure used to place multisets of objects in its compartments, multisets of objects evolving in a synchronous maximally parallel manner, and evolution rules. P system has the great parallelism so it can decrease the time complexity of computing [3]. The researchers have proposed three types of P systems: Cell-like P Systems, Tissue-like P Systems and Neural-like P Systems and have studied the computational ability and the computational efficiency [4-6]. Recently, the new variants of P systems (numerical P systems [7], enzymatic numerical P systems [8], spatial P systems [9] and so on) were proposed. For providing a concrete model of P systems, Verlan [10] proposed a formal framework for P systems in 2013. Gheorghe and Ipate [11] proposed the kernel P systems in 2013. Gazdag [12] used P Systems with Active Membranes to solve the Boolean Satisfiability Problem (SAT). Cienciala et al. [13] used 2D P colonies to model the surface runoff in 2013. Banu-Demergian and Stefanescu [14] used the geometric membrane structure to realize the finite interactive systems scenarios in 2013. Sun and Liu [15] used the P system with active membranes to solve the density-based clustering in 2014. There are many software packages to simulate the P system such as Transition P Systems Simulator provided by Baranda [16], A Membrane Systems Simulator provided by Ciobanu and Paraschiv [16], SubLP-Studio provided by Georgiou [16], SimCM provided by Chamorro [16] among others. These software packages provide an environment to enter the components of P system. They then provide not only the intermediate and final results but also the graphical displays of the P system.

Since the volume characteristic of big data, it is very difficult for the existing computing model to obtain the calculation results quickly. P system gains higher computing power through the parallelism, so it reduces the time complexity of data processing and satisfies the requirement of improving the processing speed of the big data [17,18]. Membrane computing has been widely applied to many fields such as biology [19,20], linguistics [21,22], network communication [23,24], and graphics [4,5]. But the application in data mining, especially in cluster analysis, is less [25,26]. Using the membrane computing to the clustering can reduce the time complexity of clustering, so it has a certain theoretical and practical significance.

An agglomerate Chameleon algorithm is proposed in this study first which generates the sub-clusters by the K-medoids algorithm method. Next the agglomerate Chameleon algorithm based on the Tissue-like P system is constructed with all the rules being created. Finally, an illustrative example is used to show how this proposed algorithm runs. Applied experiment databases are used to show the feasibility of the proposed algorithm.

This paper is organized as follows. The agglomerate Chameleon algorithm is proposed in Sect. 2. Section 3 proposes the agglomerate Chameleon algorithm based on the Tissue-like P system and lists all the rules. The computational process and the time complexity are analysed in Sect. 4. In Sect. 5, an illustrative experiment and iris database of UC Irvine Machine Learning Repository are described. Then the experimental results and the sensitivity analysis are presented. Finally, some conclusions are drawn in Sect. 6.

2   The Agglomerate Chameleon Algorithm

The Chameleon algorithm is a typical hierarchical clustering algorithm which is proposed by George Karypis et al. in 1999. The methodology of dynamic modeling of clusters used in this algorithm makes Chameleon algorithm can be used to all types of datasets.

2.1   Original Chameleon Algorithm

The generation of the Chameleon algorithm is based on the observation of the shortcomings of the two hierarchical clustering algorithms ROCK and CURE. ROCK and its related schemes emphasize the interconnectivity of clusters, while ignoring the information about the closeness of clusters. CURE and its related schemes emphasize the closeness of clusters, but they ignore the interconnectivity of clusters. The Chameleon algorithm evaluates the similarities among clusters based on both the closeness and the interconnectivity. That is to say, two clusters will be merged if the interconnectivities of them are very high and they are very closely.

Definition 2.1 Sparse Graph. The number of edges in the graph is much smaller than the possible number of edges.

In Chameleon algorithm, the vertex in sparse graph represents a data object in dataset and the weight of edge represents the similarity between the two vertices it connects. The sparse graph is built by the method of the k-nearest neighbor graph. If one object is one of the k most similar objects of another object, an edge is added between the two vertexes. These edges are weighted to show the similarities between the objects.

Definition 2.2 Absolute Interconnectivity. The weights sum of all edges that connect the clusters C_i and C_j is called the absolute interconnectivity between them. The absolute interconnectivity is often denoted by $EC_{\{C_i,C_j\}}$.

Definition 2.3 Internal Interconnectivity. The weights sum of all edges that should be got rid of when a minimum truncation of cluster C_i is done. The internal interconnectivity is often denoted by EC_{C_i}.

Definition 2.4 Relative Interconnectivity. The relative interconnectivity between clusters C_i and C_j is their absolute interconnectivity normalized with respect to their internal interconnectivities. The relative interconnectivity is often denoted by $RI(C_i, C_j)$. That is:

$$RI(C_i, C_j) = \frac{|EC_{\{C_i, C_j\}}|}{\frac{|EC_{C_i}| + |EC_{C_j}|}{2}}.$$

Definition 2.5 Absolute Closeness. The average weights of all edges that connect clusters C_i and C_j is called the absolute closeness between them. The absolute closeness is often denoted by $\overline{S}_{EC_{(C_i, C_j)}}$.

Definition 2.6 Internal Closeness. The average weights of all edges that should be got rid of when a minimum truncation of cluster C_i is done. We often denote it by $\overline{S}_{EC_{C_i}}$.

Definition 2.7 Relative Closeness. The relative closeness between clusters C_i and C_j is their absolute closeness normalized with respect to their internal closeness. The relative closeness is often denoted by $RC(C_i, C_j)$. That is:

$$RC(C_i, C_j) = \frac{\overline{S}_{EC_{\{C_i, C_j\}}}}{\frac{|C_i|}{|C_i| + |C_j|} \overline{S}_{EC_{C_i}} + \frac{|C_j|}{|C_i| + |C_j|} \overline{S}_{EC_{C_j}}}.$$

Definition 2.8 Similarity Function. The similarity function is the product of the relative interconnectivity and the relative closeness $RI(C_i, C_j) * RC(C_i, C_j)^\epsilon (0 \leqslant \epsilon \leqslant 1)$. ϵ is a argument between 0 and 1 which is set to show the different weight of the relative interconnectivity $RI(C_i, C_j)$ and the relative closeness $RC(C_i, C_j)$.

The original Chameleon algorithm works as follows.

1. The distance between each object and all the other objects are calculated to find the k nearest objects of each object. For this, all distances need to be sorted according to the ascending order. And the objects corresponding to the first k distances are the objects of k neighbor objects.
2. The k-nearest neighbor graph of the dataset is built by linking a line between each object and its k neighbors.
3. A graph partitioning algorithm is used to divide the k nearest neighbor graph into a large number of relatively small sub-clusters.
4. The agglomerative hierarchical clustering algorithm is used to repeatedly merge the sub-clusters based on their similarity function. This similarity function is based on the relative interconnectivity and the relative closeness [27].

2.2   The Agglomerate Chameleon Algorithm

The original Chameleon algorithm gains the sub-clusters by a partitioning algorithm. This study uses the opposite thought. A typical agglomerate algorithm,
K-medoids algorithm, is used to gain the sub-clusters. The agglomerate
Chameleon algorithm works as follows.

1. The distance between each object and all the other objects are calculated to
   find the k nearest objects of each object.
2. The distances between the objects and their k nearest neighbors are defined as
   the dissimilarities of them and the weights between other objects are defined
   as infinity. In this way, the dissimilarity matrix of the dataset is obtained.
3. The K-medoids algorithm is used to cluster the k sub-clusters. Value of K is
   set based on the formula $[\sqrt{n}]$.
4. The agglomerative hierarchical clustering algorithm is used to repeatedly
   merge the sub-clusters based on their similarity function. This similarity function is based on the absolute interconnectivity and the absolute closeness.

The parallelism of this agglomerate Chameleon algorithm is realized by using
P system. The detail of the P system will be introduced in Sect. 3.

2.3   An Example

A small example is taken to compare the original and the agglomerate Chameleon
algorithms:

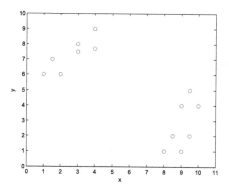

Fig. 1. The 14 data points that need to be clustered

Figure 1 shows the 14 objects need to be clustered. Firstly, these objects are
clustered according to the original algorithm. Let $k = 3$, $\epsilon = 0.5$. The similarity
of these points is obtained by taking the reciprocal of its distance. The 3-nearest
neighbor graph is constructed as Fig. 2. Next this graph is partitioned to four
sub-clusters. The 2 clusters are obtained as Fig. 3.

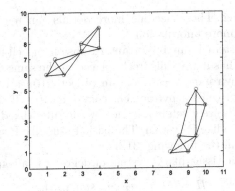

Fig. 2. The gained k-nearest neighbor graph (M = 3)

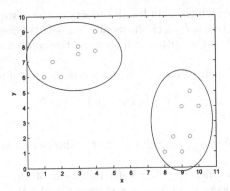

Fig. 3. The cluster result

Then, these objects are clustered according to the agglomerate algorithm. Let $K = 4$. The dissimilarity of these points is obtained by taking the value of the distance. The K-medoids algorithm is used to cluster. The sub-clusters obtained are the same with the original algorithm. Merge these sub-clusters according to the similarity function. The final result is the same with the above algorithm too.

Arbitrary n objects can be clustered by the agglomerate Chameleon algorithm mentioned above.

3   Rules

3.1   Tissue-Like P System

Since the concept of membrane computing was proposed, researchers have proposed different types of P systems to simulate the different biochemical response mechanisms of the cells or tissues. These P systems can be roughly divided into three categories, i.e. cell-like P systems, tissue-like P systems and neural-like P systems. They are abstracted from the cells, tissues, and nervous system [28, 29], respectively. It is assumed that readers have the basic knowledge about membrane computing. Those needing more details can refer to G. Paun and A. Salomaa [30] for more information.

Tissue-like P system is an important extension of cell-like P system. An tissue-like P system has many cells freely placed in the same environment. Both the cells and the environment can contain objects. Rules existed are used to regulate cell-to-cell or cell-to-environment communicates. If the communication channels between cells are given in advance by the rules (fixed), such a P system is called a basic tissue-like P system. The basic tissue-like P system used in this study is introduced in the following [31,32].

In general, a basic tissue-like P system of degree t is a construct

$$\Pi = (O, \sigma_1, \sigma_2...\sigma_t, syn, i_{out}),$$

where:

(1) O is the alphabet which includes all objects of the system;
(2) $syn \subseteq \{1, 2, ..., t\} * \{1, 2, ..., t\}$ shows all channels between cells;
(3) $i_{out} \in \{1, 2, ..., t\}$ is the output cell showing the computational result of the system;
(4) $\sigma_1, \sigma_2, ..., \sigma_t$ represent the t cells respectively. Each cell is in the form

$$\sigma_i = (w_{i,o}, R_i), 1 \leq i \leq t,$$

where:

(a) $w_{i,o}$ is the initial objects in cell i, object λ shows that there is no object in cell i;
(b) R_i is the set of rules in cell i with the form of $(u \rightarrow v)_z$, u is a string composed of objects in O and v is a string in the form of $v = v'$. v' is a string over $\{a_{here}, a_{out}, a_{in_j}, a_{go} | a \in O, 1 \leq j \leq t\}$. a_{here} means object a remains in membrane i. This $here$ can be omitted. a_{out} means object a goes in to the environment. a_{in_j} means object a goes into membrane j. If object a is copied and sent to all membranes that connect to membrane i, a_{go} is used. The parameter z is promoters or inhibitors and it is in the form of $z = z'$ or $z = \neg z'$. A rule can execute only when the promoters z' appear and stop only when the inhibitors appear. In this study, the concept of sub-rule is defined. Multi rules realizing the closely related functions are connected by U to be used as one rule. Each constituent rule in this type of rule is called a sub-rule. The precedence relation is shown by ρ_l which defines the partial order relation over. High priority rule is executed prior.

Rules are executed in the maximum parallel way and in the uncertain way in each membrane. That is to say, rules should be used in parallel to the maximum degree possible. If more than one rule can possibly be used but the objects in the membrane can only support some of them, the rules to be used are chosen arbitrarily. This is very helpful to solve the computationally hard problems. The P system will halt after some steps if no more rules can be executed or an end mark # appears. The objects in the output membrane are the final result. The P system will not halt if rules are always executed, then this calculation is invalid, and there is no result being output [33].

3.2 Rules of Agglomerate Chameleon Algorithm Based on the Tissue-Like P System

The dataset $X = \{x_1, x_2, ..., x_n\}$ of n objects which should be clustered is considered in this study. These n objects can be any types. The Euclidean distance is used to define their dissimilarity.

First of all, the distance matrix $D_{nn}{}'$ between any two objects is defined as follows.

$$D_{nn}{}' = \begin{pmatrix} f_{11}' & f_{12}' & .. & f_{1n}' \\ f_{21}' & f_{22}' & .. & f_{2n}' \\ & & ... & \\ f_{n1}' & f_{n2}' & .. & f_{nn}' \end{pmatrix} \tag{1}$$

Where, f_{ij}' is the distance between the x_i and x_j.

Next step, matrix elements f_{ij}' are changed into integer f_{ij} by expanding f_{ij}' to 100 times and then rounding it off because membrane computing can deal with integers up to now. The new matrix D_{nn} is as follows.

$$D_{nn} = \begin{pmatrix} f_{11} & f_{12} & .. & f_{1n} \\ f_{21} & f_{22} & .. & f_{2n} \\ & & ... & \\ f_{n1} & f_{n2} & .. & f_{nn} \end{pmatrix} \tag{2}$$

This matrix D_{nn} is defined as the dissimilarity matrix.

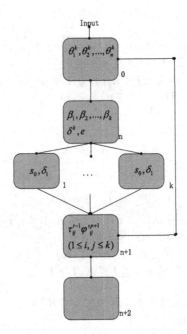

Fig. 4. The P system for the Chameleon clustering method

The structure of the P system for the agglomerate Chameleon algorithm is depicted in Fig. 4. The dataset needing to be dealt with is put into membrane 0 to activate the computing process. Rules in membrane 0 runs to generate the k-nearest neighbors of each object and the result are passed to membrane n and membrane $n+1$. Membrane n and membrane 1 to membrane K realize the K-medoids algorithm using the k-nearest neighbors information. So the objects are divided into sub-clusters. These sub-clusters information are put into membrane $n+1$. Membrane $n+1$ merges the sub-clusters and put the final result into membrane $n+2$. In the database, a_i represents the $i-th$ object x_i. The number of nearest neighbors being considered is k, and the number of medoids in K-medoids algorithm is K. So the P system for the algorithm is

$$\Pi = (O, \sigma_0, \sigma_1...\sigma_k, \sigma_n, \sigma_{n+1}, \sigma_{n+2}, syn, i_{out}),$$

where:

(1) $O = \{a_i, b_i, \theta_i, U_{ij}^t, d_{ij}, \beta_h, \delta, \sigma, e, A_{hj}, \psi, s_g, \eta, a_{hj}, \delta_1, \zeta_i, \alpha_h, b_{ij}, \alpha_{hh'}, \beta'_{hh'},$
    $\beta_{hh'}, \tau_{hh'} | 1 \le i, j \le n, 0 \le t \le max\{f_{ij}\}, |g| \le nAbs, 1 \le h,$
    $h' \le K$

(2) $syn = \{\{0,n\}\{0, n+1\}, \{n, 1\}, \{n, 2\}, ..., \{n, k\}, \{1, n+1\}, \{2, n+1\}, ...,$
    $\{k, n+1\}\{n+1, n+2\}\}$

(3) $i_{out} = n+2$

(4) $\sigma_0 = (w_{0,0}, R_0)$

where:

$w_{0,0} = \theta_1^k, \theta_2^k, ..., \theta_n^k$

R_0:

$r_1 = \{a_i \to b_i U_{i1}^{f_{i1}}, U_{i2}^{f_{i2}}, ..., U_{i(i-1)}^{f_{i(i-1)}}, U_{i(i+1)}^{f_{i(i+1)}}, ..., U_{in}^{f_{in}} | 1 \le i \le n\}$

$r_2 = \{U_{ij}^0 \theta_i{}^t \to d_{ij}\theta_i{}^{t-1} | 1 \le i, j \le n, 1 \le t \le k\}$

$r_3 = \{(U_{ij}^t)_{\theta^p} \to U_{ij}^{t-1} | 1 \le i, j \le n, t > 0, 1 \le p \le k\}$

$r_4 = \{d_{ij} \to d_{ij_{inn,(n+1)}} | 1 \le i, j \le n\}$

$r_5 = \{b_i \to a_{i_{inn}} | 1 \le i \le n\}$

$\sigma_n = (w_{n,0}, R_n)$

where:

$w_{n,0} = \beta_1, \beta_2, ..., \beta_K, \delta^K, e$

R_n:

$r_1 = \{a_i\beta_t \to A_{ti}A_{ti_{in_t}} | 1 \le i \le n, 1 \le t \le K\}$

$r_2 = \{(d_{ij})_{A_{tj}\delta^K a_i \cup \neg \sigma} \to d_{ij}U_{it}^{f_{ij}}\sigma | 1 \le t \le K, 1 \le i, j \le n\}$

$r_3 = \{U_{it}^0 a_i \to a_{i_{int}} | 1 \le i \le n, 1 \le t \le K\}$

$r_4 = \{(U_{ij})_{\neg a_i} \to \lambda | 1 \le i \le n \le, 1 \le j \le K\}$

$r_5 = \{U_{it}^j \to U_{it}^{j-1} | 1 \le i \le n, 1 \le t \le K, j \ge 1\}$

$r_6 = \{\sigma\delta^K \to \lambda\}$

$r_7 = \{e^i\psi^j \to \theta_{in1,2,...,K} | 1 \le i \le K, 0 \le j \le K\}$
    $\cup \{\psi^K \to \alpha_{1_{in1}}\alpha_{2_{in2}}...\alpha_{K_{inK}}\}$

$r_8 = \{A_{ij} \to \lambda | 1 \le i \le K, 1 \le j \le n\}$

$\sigma_i = (w_{i,0}, R_i)(1 \le i \le K)$

where:

$w_{i,0} = s_0, \delta_1$

R_i :

$r_1 = \{(a_j)_{\alpha_i} \rightarrow a_{ij_{in(n+1)}} | 1 \leq i \leq K, 1 \leq j \leq n\}$

$r_2 = \{\alpha_i \rightarrow \eta_{in(n+1)} | 1 \leq i \leq K\}$

$r_3 = \{(\theta A_{jh})_{\neg a_i} \rightarrow A_{jh}(\psi, A_{jh}, \delta)_{inn} \# | 1 \leq i, h \leq n, 1 \leq j \leq K\}$

$r_4 = \{\theta\delta_i a_i \rightarrow \theta\zeta_i O_i \,|\, 1 \leq i \leq n\} \cup \{(\theta\delta_i \rightarrow \theta\delta_{i+1})_{\neg a_i} | 1 \leq i \leq n\}$

$r_5 = \{s_t O_i a_j A_{hp} \rightarrow b_j O_i s_{t+w_{ij}-w_{pj}} A_{hp} |$
$\quad 1 \leq i, j, p \leq n, \ 1 \leq h \leq K, |t| \leq nAbs\}$

$r_6 = \{s_i A_{jp} O_h \rightarrow s_0 A_{jh} a_p \eta | -nAbs \leq i < 0, 1 \leq j \leq K, 1 \leq p, h \leq n\}$
$\quad \cup \{s_i A_{jp} O_h \rightarrow s_0 A_{jp} a_h \sigma\} | 0 \leq i \leq nAbs, 1 \leq j \leq K, 1 \leq p, h \leq n\}$

$r_7 = \{b_i \rightarrow a_i | 1 \leq i \leq n\}$

$r_8 = \{\zeta_i \rightarrow \delta_{i+1} | 1 \leq i \leq n\}$

$r_9 = \{\eta^i \sigma^j \rightarrow e_{inn} | 1 \leq i \leq n, 0 \leq j \leq n\} \cup \{(\sigma^i \rightarrow \psi_{inn})_{\neg \eta^j} | 1 \leq i, j \leq n\}$

$r_{10} = \{a_i \rightarrow a_{i_{inn}} | 1 \leq i \leq n\}$

$r_{11} = \{\delta_{n+1} A_{jp} \theta \rightarrow (\delta A_{jp})_{inn} \delta_1 A_{jp} \# | 1 \leq j \leq K, 1 \leq p \leq n\}$
$\quad \cup \{(A_{jp}\theta)_{\neg \delta_{n+1}} \rightarrow (\delta A_{jp})_{inn} \delta_1 A_{jp} \# | 1 \leq j \leq K, 1 \leq p \leq n\}$

$\sigma_{n+1} = (w_{n+1,0}, R_{n+1})$

where:

$w_{n+1,0} = \tau_{ij}^{t-1} (\varphi')_{ij}^{p+1} (1 \leq i, j \leq k)$

R_{n+1} :

$r_1 = \{\eta^k \rightarrow b_{11}, b_{21}, ..., b_{n1}\}$

$r_2 = \{b_{ij} d_{ij} a_{ti} a_{pj} \rightarrow b_{i(j+1)} d_{ij} a_{ti} a_{pj} \alpha_{tp}^{f_{ij}} \beta'_{tp} | 1 \leq i, j \leq n, 1 \leq t \neq p \leq K\}$
$\quad \cup \{(b_{ij})_{\neg d_{ij}} \rightarrow b_{i(j+1)} | 1 \leq i, j \leq n\}$

$r_3 = \{((\beta')_{ij})_{(\varphi')_{ij}^{p+1}} \rightarrow \beta_{ij} \varphi_{ij}^{p+1} | 1 \leq i, j \leq K\}$

$r_4 = \{\alpha_{ij} \varphi_{ij} \rightarrow \lambda | 1 \leq i, j \leq k\} \cup \{\beta_{ij} \tau_{ij} \rightarrow \lambda | 1 \leq i, j \leq K\}$

$r_5 = \{(a_{tp})_{\neg(\beta_{ij} \cup \varphi_{ij})} \rightarrow a_{tp_{in(n+2)}} 1 \leq i, j, t \leq K, 1 \leq p \leq n\}$

$r_6 = \{()_{\neg(\beta_{ij} \cup \varphi_{ij})} \rightarrow \# | 1 \leq i, j \leq K\}$

$r_7 = \{(a_{jt} \rightarrow a_{it})_{\beta_{ij} \varphi_{ij}} | 1 \leq i, j \leq K, 1 \leq t \leq n\}$

$r_8 = \{(\alpha_{ij}{}^t \beta_{ij}{}^p \tau_{ij}^q \varphi_{ij}^v)_{b_{1(n+1)} b_{2(n+1)} ... b_{n(n+1)}} \rightarrow \lambda | 1 \leq i, j \leq K, t, p, q, v > 0\}$

$r_9 = \{b_{1(n+1)} b_{2(n+1)} ... b_{n(n+1)} \rightarrow b_{11}, b_{21}, ..., b_{n1}, \tau_{ij}^{t-1}, \varphi_{ij}^{p+1} |$
$\quad 1 \leq i, j \leq K, t, p > 0\}$

$\sigma_{n+2} = (w_{n+2,0}, R_{n+2})$

where:

$w_{n+2,0} = \lambda$

$R_{n+2} : \Phi$

$\rho = \{r_i > r_j | i < j\}$.

Above these, a_i represents the $i - th$ object x_i of the dataset. U_{ij}^t is the auxiliary object which is used to compare the dissimilarity of different objects. θ_i is the auxiliary object which is used to compute the number of neighbors needing to be found. d_{ij} represents a_j is one of the k nearest neighbors of a_i. A_{ij} represents the medoid of the $j - th$ sub-cluster is a_i. α_{ij}^t represents the weight of edge that straddle the $i - th$ sub-cluster and the $j - th$ sub-cluster is t. β_{ij}^t represents the edges that straddle the $i - th$ sub-cluster and the $j - th$

sub-cluster is t. φ_{ij}^{p+1} represents the closeness threshold is p. τ_{ij}^{t-1} represents the interconnectivity threshold is t. The use of this P system is shown in Sect. 4.1.

4   Computations and Complexity

4.1   Computations

The Generation of the K-Nearest Neighbors. The computation starts when objects $a_1, a_2, ..., a_n$ are put into membrane 0. Rule r_1 runs to generate auxiliary object $U_{ij}^{f_{ij}}$ to show that the dissimilarity between a_i and a_j is f_{ij}. Another auxiliary object θ_i is used to compute the number of neighbors needing to be found. The original number of θ_i is k which means each a_i need to find k nearest neighbors. In the computing process, rule r_3 runs to let all superscripts of U_{ij}^t reduce at the same time. If there is a U_{ij}^0 appears and there exists the object θ_i, a_j is one of the k nearest neighbors of a_i and an object d_{ij} is generated to show that. At the same time, the number of θ_i decreases 1 to show 1 less neighbors of a_i is need to be found. When all k nearest neighbors of a_i are found, objects d_{ij} are put into membrane n and membrane $n+1$. And a_i are put into membrane n.

The Generation of the K Sub-clusters. When d_{ij} and a_i go into membrane n, membrane n begins to generate the K sub-clusters. K a_i are chose randomly as the medoids of the K sub-clusters and A_{ti} are used to show a_i is the medoid of the $t-th$ sub-cluster. Then the non-medoids a_i goes into the sub-cluster which has the smallest dissimilarity with it. This process is similar with the process of finding the k nearest neighbors. Because there is an object e in this membrane, objects θ are put into membrane 1 to k respectively. Old medoids objects A_{ij} disappear.

Each of membrane 1 to k gains the object θ. If one membrane has only its medoid in it, A_{jh} is put into membrane n and the computation in it is over. If there are also other objects a_i in it, the best medoid will be looked for. It starts with a_1. If a_1 does not exist, δ_1 adds 1 and goes into the next cycle directly. If a_1 exists, a_1 is set as the new medoid. Then the distance sum between the new medoid and the non-medoid are calculated to compare with the old sum. The value is stored by subscript of s_t. If the subscript of s_t is less than 0, a_1 can reduce the total consumption. So a_1 is set as the new medoid and an object η is produced to inform the new medoid has been generated. If the subscript of s_t is greater than or equal to 0, the new medoid cant reduce the total consumption. Therefore the original medoid does not change, and an object σ is produced to show that. Next it goes to the next cycle to compare the object a_2 and the medoid, and so on. Until all the objects are compared. If there is any η in this membrane, an object e is put into membrane n to inform that the data need to be reclassified out of the membrane and an object ψ is put into membrane n to inform that the medoid in this membrane is not changed. Then objects a_i return to membrane n. Finally the objects in this membrane are restored to initial state and the information of the medoid A_{ij} are put into membrane n. Object # is used to stop the computation step and an object δ is sent to membrane n to show it.

Membrane n gains the objects a_i, δ^K and A_{ij}. Then the process mentioned above is repeated to distribute a_i to the K membranes according to the new medoids. And so on, until no medoid is changed. Then membrane n put the object α_i to membrane 1 to K.

The object a_j in membrane $i(1 \le i \le K)$ is changed to a_{ij} and is put into membrane $n+1$ to show a_j is belonged to sub-cluster i. An object η is put into membrane $n+1$ too to show the computation in membrane 1 to K and membrane n is over.

The Mergence of the Sub-clusters. When k η enter into membrane $n+1$, all computations in membrane 1 to k all over. If a_{pj} is one of the k nearest neighbor of a_{ti}, $\alpha_{tp}^{f_{ij}}$ is generated to show that the weight of edge that straddle cluster t and cluster p adds f_{ij} and β'_{tp} is generated to show that the edges that straddle cluster t and cluster p add 1. When all $\alpha_{tp}^{f_{ij}}$ and β'_{tp} are generated, β'^{t}_{ij} are changed to $\beta_{ij}{}^{t}$ and φ_{ij}^{p+1} are generated. The number of α_{ij} and φ_{ij} and the number of β_{ij} and τ_{ij} are compared. If φ_{ij} and β_{ij} are more, it means that cluster i and cluster j have edges more than or equal to the threshold and the average weight between them are small or equal to the threshold. So cluster i and cluster j are merged. a_{jt} is changed to a_{it}. Finally objects in this membrane are restored to the initial state and the next circle begins. When no clusters meet the interconnectivity and the closeness, a_{tp} are put into membrane $n+2$ and the computation is over. The result of the cluster is shown in membrane $n+2$. The object a_{tp} shows that the $p-th$ object is belonging to the $t-th$ cluster.

4.2 Complexity Analysis

The worst condition of the improved Chameleon algorithm is considered. Membrane 0 is to find the k nearest neighbors of each object a_i. The steps are $1 + k + \max\{f_{ij}\} + 1 + 1 = \max\{f_{ij}\} + k + 3(1 \le i, j \le n)$. Membrane n is to distribute the object a_i to its nearest cluster. The steps are $1 + 1 + 1 + 1 + \max\{f_{ij}\} + 1 + 1 + 1 = \max\{f_{ij}\} + 7(1 \le i, j \le n)$. Membrane 1 to k are to find their best medoids. The steps are $1+1+(1+1+1+1+1)*n+1+1+1 = 5n+5$. The steps in membrane n and membrane 1 to k will be circled for at most C_n^K times for selecting the best K medoids for the K sub-clusters. So the steps are $(\max\{f_{ij}\} + 7 + 5n + 5) * C_n^K = (\max\{f_{ij}\} + 5n + 12) * C_n^K$. Membrane $n+1$ is to merge the K sub-clusters above to appropriate clusters. These steps will circle for at most $K-1$ times. So the steps are $(1 + n + 1 + 1 + 1 + 1 + 1 + 1 + 1) * (K-1) = (n+8) * (K-1)$. The total steps of the computation are $\max\{f_{ij}\} + k + 3 + (\max\{f_{ij}\} + 5n + 12) * C_n^K + (n+8) * (K-1)(1 \le i, j \le n) = O(n * C_n^K)$.

The original K medoids algorithm has the time complexity of $O(K * (n - K)^2 * C_n^K)$ [1]. Because n represents the number of the objects which should be clustered, this number is usually very big. The variable K is the number of sub-clusters so it is smaller compared to n. So the time complexity of $O(n * C_n^K)$ is lower than $O(K * (n - K)^2 * C_n^K)$. This improved algorithm reduces the time complexity.

5 Experiments and Analysis

5.1 Illustrative Experiment

The original algorithm is used to cluster the data points shown in Fig. 5. Three clusters are gained as Fig. 6.

Then, the agglomerate Chameleon algorithm is used to cluster the above data points. Let $k = 3$, $K = 5$ ($[\sqrt{32}] = 5.66$). The finally result is the same with the above algorithm.

5.2 Applied Numerical Experiment

The Iris database of UC Irvine Machine Learning Repository is used as an experiment [34]. This database contains 150 records. Each record contains four Iris property values and the corresponding Iris species. All data are divided into three species.

The 150 sets of data are numbered 1 to 150 following the order. The dissimilarity is defined as the quadratic sum of the four attributes difference. Let $k = 5$. Pretreat the dissimilarity matrix by expanding it to 100 times and then rounding it off. Then use the K medoids algorithm to cluster. In this example, K is set 12 because $\sqrt{150} = 12.25$. The 12 sub-clusters got through the K medoids algorithm are listed in Table 1 as follow:

Merge the clusters according to the absolute interconnectivity and the absolute closeness. Finally, all data points are clustered into three species:

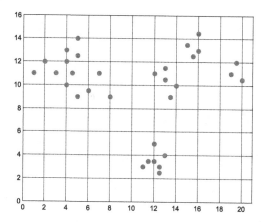

Fig. 5. The data points waiting for being clustered

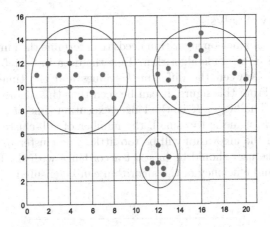

Fig. 6. The three clusters formed by the algorithm

Table 1. The 12 sub-clusters got through the K-medoids algorithm

Sub-clusters	Medoid	The serial number of data belonging to the corresponding sub-cluster
1	11	6,15,16,17,19,20,21,22,32,33,34,37,45,47,49
2	9	4,14,39,42,43
3	8	1,5,7,12,18,23,24,25,27,28,29,38,40,41,44,50
4	35	2,3,10,13,26,30,31,36,46,48
5	87	51,53,55,59,66,77,78
6	79	56,62,64,67,69,71,72,73,74,85,88,92,96,97,98,127,139
7	70	54,58,60,61,63,65,68,80,81,82,83,89,90,91,93,94,95,99,100,107
8	52	57,75,76,86
9	148	104,105,109,111,112,113,117,124,125,129,133,134,138,140,141,142,146
10	149	101,116,137,145
11	126	103,106,108,110,118,119,121,123,130,131,132,136,144
12	143	84,102,114,115,120,122,128,135,147,150

Species 1: 1–50.
Species 2: 51–83, 85–100, 127, 139.
Species 3: 84, 101–126, 128–138, 140–150.

Compared with the original species, its easily to know that the $84-th$, the $127-th$ and the $139-th$ data point are misclassified. Error rate is 2 per cent. The error rate gained by using the SOM algorithm to the Iris data set is 8 per cent and the error rate gained by using the K-means algorithm to the Iris data set is 7.13 per cent [35–44]. The error rate gained by this paper is lower compared to the above two algorithm. This experiment verifies the feasibility of the algorithm.

5.3   Sensitivity Analysis

The agglomerate Chameleon algorithm needs to determine the number of medoids when it uses the K medoids algorithm. Take the data in Sect. 5.1 for example. The relationship between the different K values and the time complexity is shown in Fig. 7. From this figure, it can be seen that this algorithm is sensitive to the K values. The bigger K is, the longer execution time of the algorithm is. However, if the K value is too small, the number of sub-clusters generated in the first phase of the algorithm will be too little. The cluster result will not be right. So, only the user should be in strict accordance with the formula ($[\sqrt{n}]$), the correctness and efficiency of the algorithm can be ensured.

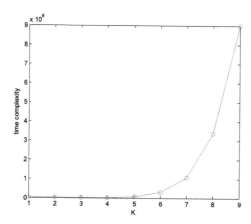

Fig. 7. The relationship between the different K values and the time complexity

6   Conclusions

With the advent of the era of big data, the traditional way of data processing becomes more and more difficult to meet the requirement for high efficiency. Due to the great parallelism, the P system can decrease the time complexity of computation and improve the computational efficiency. As a new biological computing method, the theory of membrane computing has been widely studied recently. It has been applied to many fields such as combinatorial problem, finite state problems, and graph theory. However, more studies can be done to improve the applications. An agglomerate Chameleon algorithm based on the Tissue-like P system is constructed in this study. This proposed algorithm is suitable for cluster analysis as shown through the example and experiments. This study applies membrane computing into the typical cluster algorithm Chameleon algorithm, which enlarges the research field of P system. Additionally, membrane computing can be applied to a variety of other data mining methods. And it can combine with many other methods to decrease the process time.

Acknowledgments. This study is supported by Natural Science Foundation of China (No. 61170038), Natural Science Foundation of Shandong Province, China (No. ZR2011FM001), Humanities and Social Sciences Project of Ministry of Education, China (No. 12YJA630152), Social Science Fund of Shandong Province (No. 11CGLJ22), Science-Technology Program of the Higher Education Institutions of Shandong Province, China (No. J12LN22), Science-Technology Program of the Higher Education Institutions of Shandong Province (No. J12LN65), Research Award Foundation for Outstanding Young Scientists of Shandong Province (No. BS2012DX041).

References

1. Han, J., Kambr, M.: Data Mining Concepts and Techniques. Elsevier Inc., USA (2012)
2. Che, D., Safran, M., Peng, Z.: From big data to big data mining: challenges, issues, and opportunities. In: Hong, B., Meng, X., Chen, L., Winiwarter, W., Song, W. (eds.) DASFAA Workshops 2013. LNCS, vol. 7827, pp. 1–15. Springer, Heidelberg (2013)
3. Paun, G.: A quick introduction to membrane computing. J. Logic Algebraic Program. **79**(1), 291–294 (2010)
4. Freund, R., Oswald, M., Paun, G.: Catalytic and purely catalytic P systems and P automata: control mechanisms for obtaining computational completeness. Fundamenta Informaticae **136**, 59–84 (2015)
5. Freund, R., Kari, L., Oswald, M., Sosik, P.: Computationally universal P systems without priorities: two catalysts are sufficient. Theoret. Comput. Sci. **330**(2), 251–266 (2005)
6. Gheorghe, M., Krasnogor, N., Camara, M.: P systems applications to systems biology. Biosystems **91**(3), 435–437 (2008)
7. Romero-Campero, F.J., Prez-Jimnez, M.J.: Modelling gene expression control using P systems: the lac operon, a case study. Biosystems **91**(3), 438–457 (2008)
8. Enguix, G.B.: Preliminaries about some possible applications of P systems in linguistics. In: Păun, G., Rozenberg, G., Salomaa, A., Zandron, C. (eds.) WMC 2002. LNCS, vol. 2597, pp. 74–89. Springer, Heidelberg (2003)
9. Enguix, G.B.: Unstable P systems: applications to linguistics. In: Mauri, G., Păun, G., Jesús Pérez-Jímenez, M., Rozenberg, G., Salomaa, A. (eds.) WMC 2004. LNCS, vol. 3365, pp. 190–209. Springer, Heidelberg (2005)
10. Andrei, O., Ciobanu, G., Lucanu, D.: A rewriting logic framework for operational semantics of membrane systems. Theoret. Comput. Sci. **373**(3), 163–181 (2007)
11. Idowu, R.K., Maroosi, A., Muniyandi, R.C., Othman, Z.A.: An application of membrane computing to anomaly-based intrusion detection system. In: International Conference on Electrical Engineering and Informatics, vol. 11(1), pp. 585–592 (2013)
12. Daz-Pernil, D., Berciano, A., Pena-Cantillana, F., GutiRrez-Naranjo, M.A.: Segmenting images with gradient-based edge detection using membrane computing. Pattern Recogn. Lett. **34**(8), 846–855 (2013)
13. Peng, H., Wang, J., Prez-Jimnez, M.J., Riscos-Núñez, A.: The framework of P systems applied to solve optimal watermarking problem. Sig. Process. **101**(4), 256–265 (2014)
14. Paun, G., Rozenberg, G., Salomaa, A.: The Oxford Handbook of Membrane Computing. Oxford University Press, New York (2010)

15. Paun, G., Paun, R.: Membrane computing and economics: numerical P systems. Fundamenta Informaticae (2006)
16. http://ppage.psystems.eu/index.php/Software
17. Pavel, A., Arsene, O., Buiu, C.: Enzymatic numerical P systems - a new class of membrane computing systems. In: 2010 IEEE Fifth International Conference on Bio-Inspired Computing: Theories and Applications (BIC-TA), pp. 1331–1336. IEEE (2010)
18. Barbuti, R., Maggiolo-Schettini, A., Milazzo, P., Pardini, G., Tesei, L.: Spatial P systems. Nat. Comput. **10**(1), 3–16 (2011)
19. Verlan, S.: Using the formal framework for P systems. In: Alhazov, A., Cojocaru, S., Gheorghe, M., Rogozhin, Y., Rozenberg, G., Salomaa, A. (eds.) CMC 2013. LNCS, vol. 8340, pp. 56–79. Springer, Heidelberg (2014)
20. Gheorghe, M., Ipate, F.: A kernel P systems survey. In: Alhazov, A., Cojocaru, S., Gheorghe, M., Rogozhin, Y., Rozenberg, G., Salomaa, A. (eds.) CMC 2013. LNCS, vol. 8340, pp. 1–9. Springer, Heidelberg (2014)
21. Gazdag, Z.: Solving SAT by P systems with active membranes in linear time in the number of variables. In: Alhazov, A., Cojocaru, S., Gheorghe, M., Rogozhin, Y., Rozenberg, G., Salomaa, A. (eds.) CMC 2013. LNCS, vol. 8340, pp. 189–205. Springer, Heidelberg (2014)
22. Cienciala, L., Ciencialová, L., Langer, M.: Modelling of surface runoff using 2D P colonies. In: Alhazov, A., Cojocaru, S., Gheorghe, M., Rogozhin, Y., Rozenberg, G., Salomaa, A. (eds.) CMC 2013. LNCS, vol. 8340, pp. 101–116. Springer, Heidelberg (2014)
23. Banu-Demergian, I.T., Stefanescu, G.: The geometric membrane structure of finite interactive systems scenarios. In: Membrane Computing, pp. 63–80. Springer, Heidelberg (2013)
24. Sun, J., Liu, X.Y.: Density-Based Clustering by P System with Active Membranes on Commodity Recommendation in E-commerce Websites. Wseas Org (2014)
25. Peng, H., Zhang, J., Jiang, Y., Huang, X., Wang, J.: DE-MC: a membrane clustering algorithm based on differential evolution mechanism. Rom. J. Inf. Sci. Technol. **17**(1), 76–88 (2014)
26. Peng, H., Jiang, Y., Wang, J., Prez-Jimnez, M.J.: Membrane clustering algorithm with hybrid evolutionary mechanisms. J. Softw. **26**(5), 1001–1012 (2015)
27. Karypis, G., Han, E., Kumar, V.C.: A hierarchical clustering algorithm using dynamic modeling. IEEE Comput. (1999)
28. Zhang, G.X., Pan, L.Q.: A survey of membrane computing as a new branch of natural computing. Chin. J. Comput. **33**(2), 208–214 (2010)
29. Paun, G.: A quick introduction to membrane computing. J. Logic Algebraic Program. **287**(1), 73–100 (1999)
30. Paun, G., Salomaa, A.: Membrane Computing. Oxford University Press, New York (2008)
31. Martn-Vide, C., Paun, G., Pazos, J., Rodrguez-Patn, A.: Tissue P systems. Theoret. Comput. Sci. **296**(2), 295–326 (2001)
32. Han, J., Kambr, M.: Data Mining Concepts and Techniques, Chap. 5, pp. 237–238. Elsevier Inc., USA (2012)
33. Paun, G., Rozenberg, G.: A guide to membrane computing. Theor. Comput. Sci. **287**(1), 73–100 (2002)
34. http://archive.ics.uci.edu/ml
35. Wei, Y., Xiangting, L.: Statistics and consultation, the empirical comparison between the SOM algorithm and the K-means algorithm, pp. 22–23, March 2009

36. Cottrell, M., Fort, J.-C., Pages, G.: Theoretical aspects of the SOM algorithm. Neurocomputing **21**(1), 119–138 (1998)
37. Tokunaga, K., Furukawa, T.: Modular network SOM. Neural Netw. **22**(1), 82–90 (2009)
38. Kohonen, T.: Self-Organizing Maps. Springer, Heidelberg (2001)
39. Kohonen, T.: The self-organizing map. Proc. IEEE **78**(9), 1464–1480 (1990)
40. Kangas, J.A., Kohonen, T.K., Laaksonen, J.T.: Variants of self-organizing maps. IEEE Trans. Neural Netw. **1**(1), 93–99 (1990)
41. MacQueen, J.: Some methods for classification and analysis of multivariate observations. In: Proceedings of the 5th Berkeley Symposium on Mathematical Statistics and Probability, pp. 281–297. University of California Press, Berkeley (1967)
42. Cox, D.R.: Note on grouping. J. Am. Stat. Assoc. **52**(280), 543–547 (1957)
43. Fisher, W.D.: On grouping for maximum homogeneity. J. Am. Stat. Assoc. **53**(284), 789–798 (1958)
44. Sebestyen, G.S.: Decision Making Process in Pattern Recognition. Macmillan, New York (1962)

Author Index

Printed in the United States
By Bookmasters

Printed in the United States
By Bookmasters